Frommer's®

Australia 2011

by Lee Mylne, Marc Llewellyn,
Ron Crittall & Lee Atkinson

WILEY
Wiley Publishing, Inc.

Published by:
WILEY PUBLISHING, INC.
111 River St.
Hoboken, NJ 07030-5774

ISBN 978-0-470-64013-5 (paper); ISBN 978-0-470-92258-3 (ebk); ISBN 978-0-470-42128-4 (ebk); ISBN 978-1-118-00398-5 (ebk)

Editor: Emil J. Ross
Production Editor: Jana M. Stefanciosa
Cartographer: Andrew Murphy
Photo Editor: Richard Fox
Production by Wiley Indianapolis Composition Services
Front cover photo: An eastern gray kangaroo (*Macropus giganteus*), Murramarang National Park, New South Wales ©Frans Lanting / DanitaDelimont.com
Back cover photo: The wind-eroded Remarkable Rocks of Flinders Chase National Park, Kangaroo Island, South Australia ©Paul Kingsley / Alamy Images

For information on our other products and services or to obtain technical support, please contact our Customer Care Department within the U.S. at 877/762-2974, outside the U.S. at 317/572-3993 or fax 317/572-4002.

Wiley also publishes its books in a variety of electronic formats. Some content that appears in print may not be available in electronic formats.

Manufactured in the United States of America

5 4 3

CONTENTS

LIST OF MAPS

ABOUT THE AUTHORS

Lee Mylne (chapters 1, 3, 4, 7, 8, 9, 10, 13, 14, 16, and 17) is Melbourne-based but writes for a range of consumer and travel trade publications around Australia. Born and raised in New Zealand, she has worked in newspapers, magazines, and radio and traveled widely before she started to make a living out of it. She has lived in Australia since 1986 and is a life member and past president of the Australian Society of Travel Writers. Her other books include *Frommer's Portable Australia's Great Barrier Reef* and *Australia For Dummies.*

Sydney resident **Marc Llewellyn** (chapters 1, 2, 4, 5, and 6) is one of Australia's premier travel writers and the winner of several writing awards. He is the president of the Australian Society of Travel Writers. He's written two travelogues, *Riders to the Midnight Sun,* which tells of his journey from the Ukrainian Black Sea to the Russian Arctic on a cheap bicycle, and *Finding Nino,* which recounts his year working as a peasant farmer and shrimp fisherman on an island off Sicily. He is also the co-author of *Australia For Dummies.*

Ron Crittall (chapters 1, 4, and 13) was on a long slow loop around the world when he arrived in Perth for a possible two-year stay. Thirty-five years on, he knows there's no place better to live. A travel writer for 15 years, he loves traveling round, and writing about, the vast expanse of Western Australia. He is the author of *Walking Perth.*

Author of *On the Road: 40 Great Driving Holidays in Australia* and *The Australian Adventure Atlas,* **Lee Atkinson** (chapters 1, 12, and 15) has been writing about her adventures on and off the road since 1991. Lee's latest book to hit the streets is *Caravanning Australia,* and her work appears in a wide range of newspapers and magazines across the country. When not traveling on assignment, Lee divides her time between Sydney and the New South Wales mid-north coast.

HOW TO CONTACT US

In researching this book, we discovered many wonderful places—hotels, restaurants, shops, and more. We're sure you'll find others. Please tell us about them, so we can share the information with your fellow travelers in upcoming editions. If you were disappointed with a recommendation, we'd love to know that, too. Please write to:

Frommer's Australia 2011
Wiley Publishing, Inc. • 111 River St. • Hoboken, NJ 07030-5774

AN ADDITIONAL NOTE

Please be advised that travel information is subject to change at any time—and this is especially true of prices. We therefore suggest that you write or call ahead for confirmation when making your travel plans. The authors, editors, and publisher cannot be held responsible for the experiences of readers while traveling. Your safety is important to us, however, so we encourage you to stay alert and be aware of your surroundings. Keep a close eye on cameras, purses, and wallets, all favorite targets of thieves and pickpockets.

FROMMER'S STAR RATINGS, ICONS & ABBREVIATIONS

Every hotel, restaurant, and attraction listing in this guide has been ranked for quality, value, service, amenities, and special features using a **star-rating system.** In country, state, and regional guides, we also rate towns and regions to help you narrow down your choices and budget your time accordingly. Hotels and restaurants are rated on a scale of zero (recommended) to three stars (exceptional). Attractions, shopping, nightlife, towns, and regions are rated according to the following scale: zero stars (recommended), one star (highly recommended), two stars (very highly recommended), and three stars (must-see).

In addition to the star-rating system, we also use **seven feature icons** that point you to the great deals, in-the-know advice, and unique experiences that separate travelers from tourists. Throughout the book, look for:

- **special finds**—those places only insiders know about
- **fun facts**—details that make travelers more informed and their trips more fun
- **kids**—best bets for kids and advice for the whole family
- **special moments**—those experiences that memories are made of
- **overrated**—places or experiences not worth your time or money
- **insider tips**—great ways to save time and money
- **great values**—where to get the best deals

The following abbreviations are used for credit cards:

AE	American Express	DISC	Discover	V	Visa
DC	Diners Club	MC	MasterCard		

TRAVEL RESOURCES AT FROMMERS.COM

Frommer's travel resources don't end with this guide. Frommer's website, **www.frommers.com**, has travel information on more than 4,000 destinations. We update features regularly, giving you access to the most current trip-planning information and the best airfare, lodging, and car-rental bargains. You can also listen to podcasts, connect with other Frommers.com members through our active-reader forums, share your travel photos, read blogs from guidebook editors and fellow travelers, and much more.

THE BEST OF AUSTRALIA

1

Maybe we're biased because we live here, but Australia has a lot of bests—world bests, that is. It has some of the best natural scenery, the weirdest wildlife, the most brilliant scuba diving and snorkeling, the best beaches, the oldest rainforest (110 million years and counting), the oldest human civilization (some archaeologists say 40,000 years, some say 120,000; whatever—it's old), the best wines, the best weather (give or take the odd Wet season in the north), the most innovative East-meets-West-meets-someplace-else cuisine—all bathed in sunlight that brings everything up in Technicolor.

"Best" means different things to different people, but scarcely a visitor lands on these shores without having the Great Barrier Reef at the top of the "Things to See" list. So they should, because it really is a glorious natural masterpiece. Also high on most folks' lists is Uluru. This monolith must have some kind of magnet inside it designed to attract planeloads of tourists. We're not saying the Rock isn't special, but we think the vast Australian desert all around it is even more so. The third attraction on most visitors' lists is Sydney, the Emerald City that glitters in the antipodean sunshine on—here we go with the "bests" again—the best harbor, spanned by the best bridge in the world.

But as planes zoom overhead delivering visitors to the big three attractions, Aussies in charming country towns, on far-flung beaches, on rustic sheep stations, in rainforest villages, and in mountain lodges shake their heads and say sadly, "They don't know what they're missin'." Well, that's the aim of this chapter—to show you what you're missin'. Read on, and consider taking the road less traveled.

THE top TRAVEL EXPERIENCES

- **Hitting the Rails on the Indian Pacific Train:** This 3-day journey across the Outback regularly makes it onto travel magazines' "Top Rail

Australia

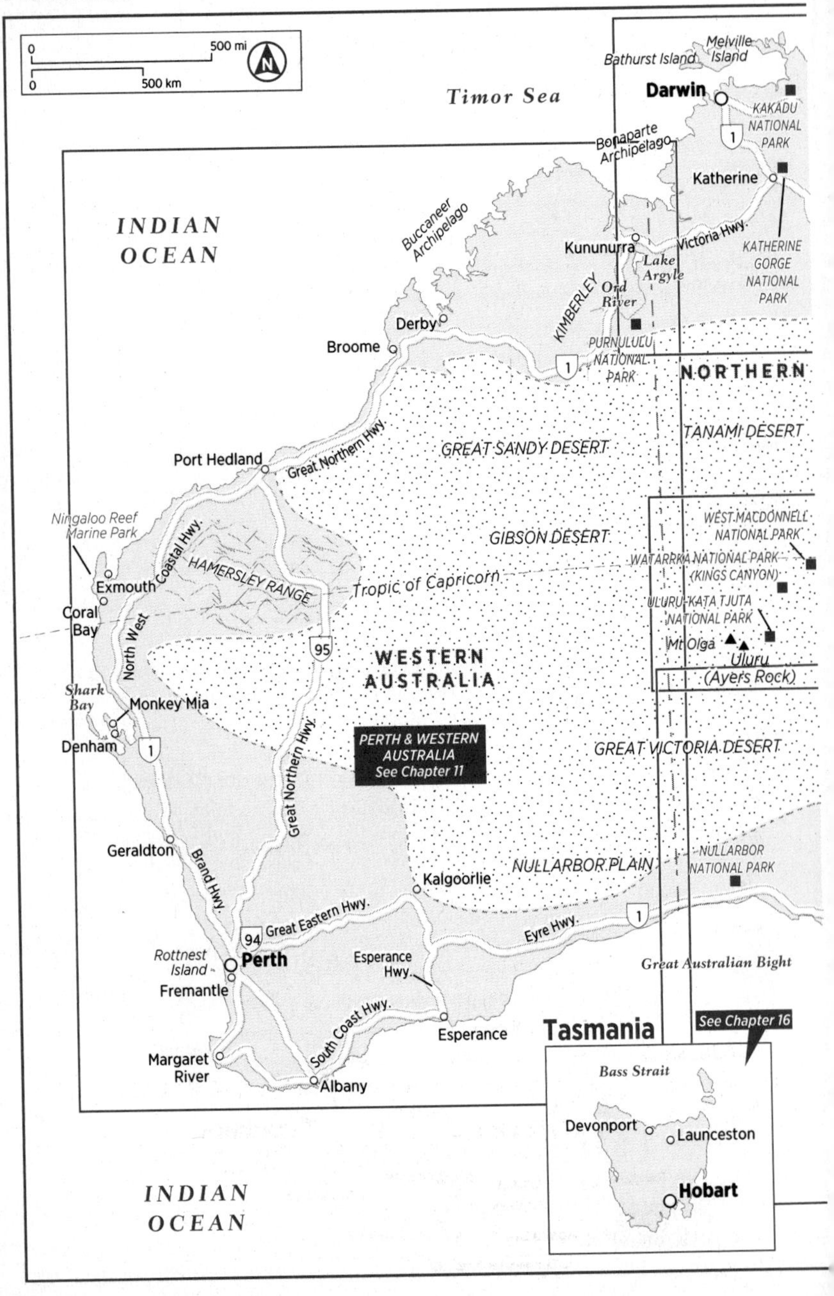
0
500 mi
0
500 km
N
Timor Sea
Bathurst Island
Melville Island
Darwin
KAKADU NATIONAL PARK
Bonaparte Archipelago
Katherine
KATHERINE GORGE NATIONAL PARK
Victoria Hwy.
Kununurra
Lake Argyle
Ord River
KIMBERLEY
PURNULULU NATIONAL PARK
INDIAN OCEAN
Buccaneer Archipelago
Derby
Broome
NORTHERN
TANAMI DESERT
GREAT SANDY DESERT
Port Hedland
Great Northern Hwy.
Ningaloo Reef Marine Park
Exmouth
Coastal Hwy.
HAMERSLEY RANGE
Tropic of Capricorn
GIBSON DESERT
WEST MACDONNELL NATIONAL PARK
WATARRKA NATIONAL PARK (KINGS CANYON)
ULURU-KATA TJUTA NATIONAL PARK
Mt Olga
Uluru (Ayers Rock)
Coral Bay
North West
95
WESTERN AUSTRALIA
Shark Bay
Monkey Mia
Denham
1
PERTH & WESTERN AUSTRALIA See Chapter 11
Great Northern Hwy.
GREAT VICTORIA DESERT
Geraldton
Brand Hwy.
Kalgoorlie
NULLARBOR PLAIN
NULLARBOR NATIONAL PARK
Great Eastern Hwy.
94
Eyre Hwy.
Rottnest Island
Perth
Fremantle
Esperance Hwy.
Great Australian Bight
South Coast Hwy.
Esperance
Margaret River
Albany
Tasmania
See Chapter 16
Bass Strait
Devonport
Launceston
Hobart
INDIAN OCEAN

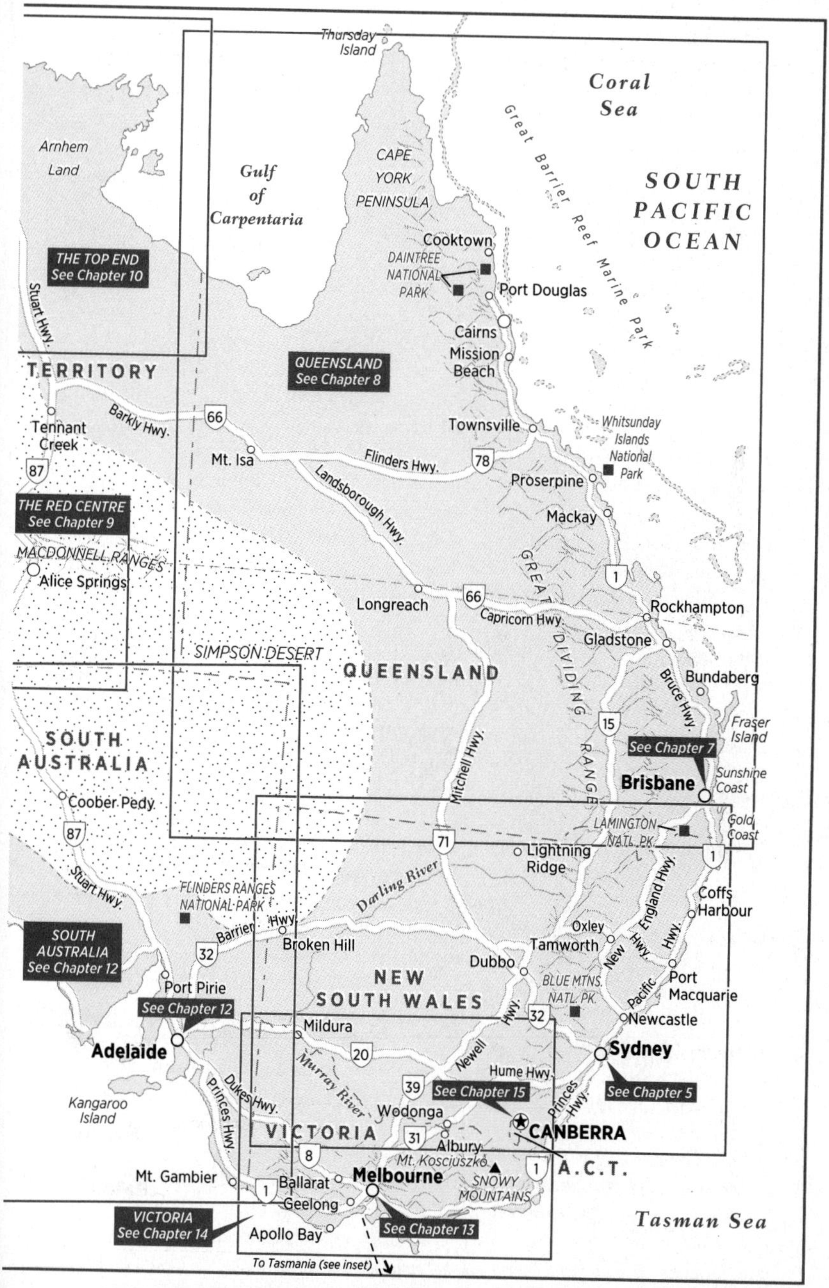
Thursday Island
Coral Sea
Great Barrier Reef Marine Park
SOUTH PACIFIC OCEAN
Arnhem Land
Gulf of Carpentaria
CAPE YORK PENINSULA
Cooktown
DAINTREE NATIONAL PARK
Port Douglas
THE TOP END See Chapter 10
Stuart Hwy.
Cairns
Mission Beach
TERRITORY
QUEENSLAND See Chapter 8
Tennant Creek
Barkly Hwy.
66
Townsville
Whitsunday Islands National Park
Mt. Isa
Flinders Hwy.
78
87
Proserpine
Landsborough Hwy.
THE RED CENTRE See Chapter 9
Mackay
MACDONNELL RANGES
Alice Springs
GREAT DIVIDING RANGE
1
Longreach
66
Capricorn Hwy.
Rockhampton
Gladstone
SIMPSON DESERT
QUEENSLAND
Bundaberg
Bruce Hwy.
Fraser Island
15
SOUTH AUSTRALIA
See Chapter 7
Mitchell Hwy.
Brisbane
Sunshine Coast
Coober Pedy
Gold Coast
LAMINGTON NATL. PK.
87
71
Lightning Ridge
1
Stuart Hwy.
Darling River
FLINDERS RANGES NATIONAL PARK
England Hwy.
Coffs Harbour
Barrier Hwy.
Oxley
SOUTH AUSTRALIA See Chapter 12
Broken Hill
Tamworth
New
Hwy.
32
Dubbo
NEW SOUTH WALES
Pacific
Port Macquarie
Port Pirie
BLUE MTNS. NATL. PK.
See Chapter 12
Hwy.
32
Newcastle
Mildura
Adelaide
20
Newell
Sydney
Hume Hwy.
Princes Hwy.
39
See Chapter 15
See Chapter 5
Dukes Hwy.
Murray River
Kangaroo Island
Princes Hwy.
Wodonga
CANBERRA
VICTORIA
31
Albury
8
Mt. Kosciuszko
A.C.T.
1
Mt. Gambier
Ballarat
Melbourne
SNOWY MOUNTAINS
1
Geelong
VICTORIA See Chapter 14
Apollo Bay
See Chapter 13
Tasman Sea
To Tasmania (see inset)

A Note on Abbreviations

In the listings below and throughout the book, NSW stands for New South Wales, QLD for Queensland, NT for the Northern Territory, WA for Western Australia, SA for South Australia, VIC for Victoria, TAS for Tasmania, and ACT for the Australian Capital Territory.

Journeys in the World" lists. The desert scenery ain't all that magnificent—it's the unspoiled, empty vastness that passengers appreciate. It includes the longest straight stretch of track in the world, 478km (296 miles) across the treeless Nullarbor Plain. Start in Sydney and end in Perth, or vice versa, or just do a section. See p. 53.

- **Experiencing Sydney** (NSW): Sydney is more than just the magnificent Harbour Bridge and Opera House. No other city has beaches in such abundance, and few have such a magnificently scenic harbor. Our advice is to board a ferry, walk from one side of the bridge to the other, and try to spend a week here, because you're going to need it. See p. 93.
- **Seeing the Great Barrier Reef** (QLD): It's a glorious 2,000km-long (1,240-mile) underwater coral fairyland with electric colors and bizarre fish life—and it comes complete with warm water and year-round sunshine. When you're not snorkeling over coral and giant clams almost as big as you, scuba diving, calling at tropical towns, or lying on deserted island beaches, you'll be trying out the sun lounges or enjoying the first-rate food. See p. 272.
- **Exploring the Wet Tropics Rainforest** (QLD): Folks who come from such skyscraper cities as New York and London can't get over the moisture-dripping ferns, the neon-blue butterflies, and the primeval peace of this World Heritage rainforest stretching north, south, and west from Cairns. Hike it, four-wheel-drive it, or glide over the treetops in the Skyrail gondola. See p. 289.
- **Bareboat Sailing** (QLD): "Bareboat" means unskippered—that's right, even if you think port is an after-dinner drink, you can charter a yacht, pay for a day's instruction from a skipper, and then take over the helm yourself and explore the 74 island gems of the Whitsundays. It's easy. Anchor in deserted bays, snorkel over dazzling reefs, fish for coral trout, and feel the wind in your sails. See p. 332.
- **Exploring Kata Tjuta (the Olgas) & Uluru** (NT): This sacred, mysterious, and utterly unforgettable landscape may well be the highlight of your time in Australia. Uluru and Kata Tjuta demand at least 3 days to see everything there is to offer. See p. 407.
- **Taking an Aboriginal Culture Tour in Alice Springs** (NT): Eating female wasps, contemplating a hill as a giant resting caterpillar, and imagining that the stars are your grandmother smiling down at you will give you a new perspective on Aboriginal culture. See what we mean on a half-day tour from the Aboriginal Art & Culture Centre. See p. 393.
- **Discovering the Kimberley** (WA): Australia's last frontier, the Kimberley is a sometimes romantic, sometimes rough and ready cocktail of South Sea pearls, red mountain ranges, aqua seas, deadly crocodiles, Aboriginal rock art, and million-acre ranches in a never-ending wilderness. Cross it by four-wheel-drive, swim

under waterfalls, ride a camel along the beach in Broome, be besotted by the awesome striped splendor of the Bungle Bungle, and more. See p. 531.

- **Rolling in Wildflowers** (WA): Imagine Texas three times over and covered in wildflowers. That's what much of Western Australia looks like every spring, from around August through October, when pink, mauve, red, white, yellow, and blue wildflowers bloom. Aussies flock here for this spectacle, so book ahead. See p. 452.
- **Drinking Some of Australia's Best Wines** (SA): Despite its larger-than-life reputation in the wine world, the Barossa Valley is a snug collection of country towns surrounded by vineyards that is very easy to explore on a day trip from Adelaide. See p. 570.
- **Getting Dusty in the Desert** (SA): Get a taste of what life is like in the Outback in the vast arid plains, salt lakes, and underground mining towns north of Adelaide; and see some of the world's oldest mountains in the dramatically beautiful Flinders Ranges. See p. 594.
- **Seeing the Sights Along the Great Ocean Road** (VIC): This 106km (66-mile) coastal road carries you past wild and stunning beaches, forests, and dramatic cliff-top scenery—including the Twelve Apostles, a scattering of pillars of red rock standing in isolation in the foaming Southern Ocean. See p. 664.

THE best OUTDOOR ADVENTURES

- **Horse Trekking in the Snowy Mountains** (NSW): Ride the ranges like the man from Snowy River, staying in bush lodges or camping beneath the stars. See p. 227.
- **Abseiling (Rappelling) in the Blue Mountains** (NSW): Careening backward down a cliff face with the smell of eucalyptus in your nostrils is not everyone's idea of fun, but you sure know you're alive. Several operators welcome novices and the more experienced. See p. 182.
- **White-Water Rafting on the Tully River** (QLD): The Class III to IV rapids of the Tully River swoosh between lush, rainforested banks. The guides are professional, and the rapids are just hairy enough to be fun. It's a good choice for first-time rafters. See p. 293.
- **Four-Wheel-Driving on Fraser Island** (QLD): All roads here are sand, and even spectacular 75-Mile Beach is a designated road. Getting around by 4×4 on the biggest sand island in the world is quite an experience. The island is ecologically important and popular with nature lovers. Hike its eucalyptus forests and rainforests, swim its clear lakes, and fish off the beach. See p. 350.
- **Sea Kayaking:** Kayaking is a great way to explore Queensland's Whitsunday Islands as well as Dunk Island off Mission Beach in Queensland. **Rivergods,** in Perth (✆ **08/9259 0749;** www.rivergods.com.au), even takes you on a sea-kayaking day trip to snorkel with wild sea lions and to watch penguins feeding. This Western Australian company also runs multiday expeditions past whales, dolphins, and sharks in Shark Bay, and over coral at Ningaloo Reef on the Northwest Cape. For details on the Whitsunday Islands and Dunk Island, see p. 327. For information about Perth and Western Australia, see p. 449.

- **Canoeing the Top End** (NT): Paddling between the sun-drenched ocher walls of Katherine Gorge sharpens the senses, especially when a (harmless) freshwater crocodile pops up! **Gecko Canoeing** (✆ **1800/634 319** in Australia, or 08/ 8972 2224; www.geckocanoeing.com.au) will take you downriver to the rarely explored Flora and Daly River systems to visit Aboriginal communities, shower under waterfalls, hike virgin bushland, and camp in swags on the banks. See p. 446.
- **Game Fishing:** Battle a black marlin off Cairns and you might snare the world record; that's how big they get down there. Marlin and other game catches run around much of the Australian coastline—Broome and Exmouth, in Western Australia (see p. 529), and Darwin in the Top End (see p. 426) are also hot spots.
- **Surfing:** No visit to Oz could really be considered complete without checking out one of the iconic Aussie activities—surfing. It's not just the rush of the waves that pulls people in, it's the ethos and everything that goes with surfing. Every state has its special spots where the surf can be especially challenging. Some of the best breaks are in Margaret River in Western Australia (see p. 501), and Bells Beach in Victoria (see p. 666), which both host tournaments where the world's best come to pit their skills against the waves and other surfers.
- **Skiing in the Victorian Alps** (VIC): When you've had enough coral and sand—and if it's winter—you can hit the slopes in Victoria. Where else can you swish down the mountain between gum trees? See p. 677.

THE best PLACES TO VIEW WILDLIFE

- **Pebbly Beach** (NSW): The eastern gray kangaroos that inhabit Murramarang National Park, 20 minutes south of Ulladulla on the south coast of New South Wales, tend to congregate along this beach and the adjoining dunes. See p. 222.
- **Montague Island** (NSW): This little island just offshore from the seaside town of Narooma, on the south coast, is a haven for nesting seabirds, but the water around it is home to the main attractions. Dolphins are common; fairy penguins, too. In whale-watching season, you're sure to spot southern right and humpback whales. See p. 224.
- **Jervis Bay** (NSW): This is probably the closest place to Sydney where you're certain to see kangaroos in the wild—and where you can pet them, too. The national park here is home to hundreds of bird species, including black cockatoos, as well as plenty of possums. See p. 220.
- **Lone Pine Koala Sanctuary** (QLD): Cuddle a koala (and have your photo taken doing it) at this park in Brisbane, the world's first and largest koala sanctuary. Apart from some 130 koalas, lots of other Aussie wildlife—including wombats, Tasmanian devils, 'roos (which you can hand-feed), and colorful parakeets—are on show. See p. 252.
- **Tangalooma** (QLD), **Bunbury and Rockingham** (WA), and **Monkey Mia** (WA): In several places, you can see, hand-feed, or swim with wild dolphins. At Bunbury and Rockingham, south of Perth, you can swim with them or join cruises to see them. (They come right up to the boat.) If you want an almost guaranteed dolphin sighting, head to Tangalooma Wild Dolphin Resort on Moreton Island,

off Brisbane (see p. 267), where you can hand-feed them, or to Monkey Mia on the lonely Outback coast (see p. 523), where they cruise past your legs. Even better is a cruise on the *Shotover* catamaran to see some of the area's 10,000 dugongs (manatees), plus turtles, sea snakes, sharks, and more (see p. 525).

- **Hervey Bay** (QLD): The warm waters off Hervey Bay—and in particular the lovely Platypus Bay—on the Queensland coast are where the humpback whales come each year between June and October in increasing numbers to give birth. The long journey from Antarctica brings them up the coast to frolic with their young for several months before making the return trip. Hervey Bay's many cruises can bring you closer to these gentle giants than you'll ever come elsewhere. See p. 349.
- **Australian Butterfly Sanctuary** (QLD): Walk through the biggest butterfly "aviary" in Australia, in Kuranda, near Cairns, and you'll spot some of the most gorgeous butterflies on the continent, including the electric-blue Ulysses. See many species of butterfly feed, lay eggs, and mate; and inspect caterpillars and pupae. Wearing pink, red, or white encourages the butterflies to land on you. See p. 292.
- **Wait-a-While Rainforest Tours** (QLD): Head into the World Heritage–listed Wet Tropics Rainforest behind Cairns or Port Douglas with this ecotour operator to spot possums, lizards, pythons, and even a platypus, so shy that most Aussies have never seen one in the wild. About once a month, a group will spot the rare, bizarre Lumholtz's tree kangaroo. See p. 289.
- **Currumbin Wildlife Sanctuary** (QLD): Tens of thousands of unbelievably pretty red, blue, green, and yellow rainbow lorikeets have been screeching into this park on the Gold Coast for generations to be hand-fed by delighted visitors every morning and afternoon. The sanctuary has 'roos and other Australian animals, too, but the birds steal the show. See p. 368.
- **Heron Island** (QLD): There's wonderful wildlife on this "jewel in the reef" off Gladstone any time of year, but the best time to visit is November to March, when the life cycle of giant green loggerhead and hawksbill turtles is in full swing. From November to January, the turtles come ashore to lay their eggs. From late January to March, the hatchlings emerge and head for the water. You can see it all by strolling down to the beach, or join a university researcher to get the full story. See p. 345. Mon Repos Turtle Rookery, near Bundaberg in Queensland (see p. 347) and the Northwest Cape in Western Australia (see p. 522) are two other good turtle-watching sites.
- **Kakadu National Park** (NT): A third of Australia's bird species live in Kakadu; so do lots of saltwater crocs. A cruise on the Yellow Water Billabong (a small lake), and aboard the Original Jumping Crocodile Cruise en route to the park, are some of the best ways to see them in the wild. See p. 435.
- **The Northwest Cape** (WA): For the thrill of a lifetime, go snorkeling with a whale shark. No one knows where they come from, but these mysterious monsters (up to 18m/60 ft. long) surface in the Outback waters off Western Australia every year from March to June. A mini-industry takes snorkelers out to swim alongside the sharks as they feed (on plankton, not snorkelers). See p. 522.
- **Kangaroo Island** (SA): You're sure to see more native animals here—including koalas, wallabies, birds, echidnas, reptiles, seals, and sea lions—than anywhere else in the country, apart from a wildlife park. Another plus: The distances

between major points of interest are not great, so you won't spend half the day just getting from place to place. See p. 579.

- **Eyre Peninsula** (SA): Swimming with wild sea lions in the waters off Baird Bay and Port Lincoln on the Eyre Peninsula is a truly amazing experience and one not to be missed. See p. 587.

THE best OF THE OUTBACK

- **Broken Hill** (NSW): There's no better place to experience real Outback life than in Broken Hill. There's the city itself, with its thriving art scene and the Royal Flying Doctor service; a historic ghost town on its outskirts; a national park with Aboriginal wall paintings; an opal mining town nearby; and plenty of kangaroos, emus, and giant wedge-tailed eagles. See p. 230.
- **Lightning Ridge** (NSW): This opal-mining town is as rough-and-ready as the stones the miners pull out of the ground. Meet amazing characters, share in the eccentricity of the place, and visit opal-rush areas with molehill scenery made by the old sun-bleached mine tailings. See p. 233.
- **Uluru-Kata Tjuta National Park** (NT): Uluru will enthrall you with its eerie beauty. Nearby Kata Tjuta is equally interesting, so make the time to wander through the Valley of the Winds. Hike around Uluru's base, burn around it on a Harley-Davidson, saunter up to it on a camel . . . but don't climb it. Don't go home until you've felt the powerful heartbeat of the desert. See p. 407.
- **The MacDonnell Ranges** (NT): The Aborigines say these red rocky hills were formed by the Aboriginal "Caterpillar Dreaming" that wriggled from the earth here. To the west of Alice Springs are dramatic gorges, idyllic (and bloody cold) water holes, and cute wallabies. To the east are Aboriginal rock carvings and the Ross River Homestead, where you can crack a cattle whip, throw a boomerang, feast on damper and billy tea, and ride a horse or camel in the bush. See p. 402.
- **Kings Canyon** (NT): Anyone who saw the cult flick *The Adventures of Priscilla, Queen of the Desert* will remember the scene in which the transvestites climb a soaring orange cliff and survey the desert floor. That was Kings Canyon, in Watarrka National Park, about 320km (198 miles) from Alice Springs in one direction, with Uluru in the other. Trek the dramatic rim or take the easier shady route along the bottom. See p. 405.
- **"Inside Australia"** (WA): "Inside Australia" provides a modern take on the Outback, with 51 metal figures scattered across Lake Ballard, a broad, dry salt lake set in rough desert country. About 55km (34 miles) west of Menzies along a gravel road, British sculptor Antony Gormley (of "Angel of the North" fame) created this unique installation based on computer scans of the Menzies residents. See p. 520.
- **The Gibb River Road** (WA): The Kimberley is remote, rough, and rugged, and this bone-shaker is its only road. Driving here takes you through dramatic red ranges and past gloriously cool and welcoming falls and waterholes. Facilities are few and far between, other than outlying Aboriginal communities and million-acre-plus cattle stations. See p. 546.
- **Coober Pedy** (SA): It may be hot and dusty, but you'll get a true taste of the Outback when you tag along with the local mail carrier as he makes his rounds to the area's remote cattle stations (ranches). It's a 12-hour, 600km (372-mile) journey along sun-baked dirt roads. See p. 598.

THE best BEACHES

- **Palm Beach** (NSW): At the end of a string of beaches stretching north from Sydney, Palm Beach is long and white, with good surfing and a golf course. See p. 158.
- **Hyams Beach** (NSW): This beach in off-the-beaten-path Jervis Bay is said to be the whitest in the world. You need to wear sun block if you decide to stroll along it, because the reflection from the sun, even on a cloudy day, can give you a nasty sunburn. The beach squeaks as you walk. See p. 220.
- **Four Mile Beach** (QLD): The sea is turquoise, the sun is warm, the palms sway, and the low-rise hotels starting to line this country beach in Port Douglas can't spoil the feeling that it is a million miles from anywhere. But isn't there always a serpent in paradise? In this case, the "serpents" are north Queensland's seasonal potentially deadly marine stingers. Come from June through September to avoid them, or confine your swimming to the stinger net the rest of the year. See p. 306.
- **Mission Beach** (QLD): Azure water, islands dotting the horizon, and white sand edged by vine forests make this beach a real winner. The bonus is that hardly anyone comes here. Cassowaries (giant emulike birds) hide in the rainforest, and the tiny town of Mission Beach makes itself invisible behind the leaves. Visit from June through September to avoid marine stingers. See p. 311.
- **Whitehaven Beach** (QLD): It's not a surf beach, but this 6km (3¾-mile) stretch of white silica sand on uninhabited Whitsunday Island is pristine and peaceful. Bring a book, curl up under the rainforest lining its edge, and fantasize that the cruise boat is going to leave without you. See p. 333.
- **Surfers Paradise Beach** (QLD): Actually, all 35 of the beaches on the 30km (19-mile) Gold Coast strip in south Queensland are worthy of inclusion here. Every one has sand so clean that it squeaks, great surf, and fresh breezes—turn your back on the tacky high-rises. Surfers will like Burleigh Heads. See p. 365.
- **Cable Beach** (WA): Is it the South Sea pearls pulled out of the Indian Ocean, the camels loping along the sand, the sunsets, the surf, or the red earth meeting the green sea that gives this Broome beach its exotic appeal? Maybe it's the 26km (16 miles) of white sand. The only recommended time to swim here is June through September, when deadly marine stingers are largely absent. See p. 542.
- **Cottesloe Beach** (WA): Perth has 19 great beaches, but this petite crescent is the prettiest. After you've checked out the scene, join the fashionable set for brunch in the Indiana Tea House, a mock-Edwardian bathhouse fronting the sea. Surfers head to Scarborough and Trigg. See p. 475.
- **Wineglass Bay** (TAS): This spectacular crescent of pristine beach in Freycinet National Park regularly makes lists of the world's top beaches. Find out why. See p. 723.

THE best DIVING & SNORKELING

- **Port Douglas** (QLD): Among the fabulous dive sites off Port Douglas, north of Cairns, are Split-Bommie, with its delicate fan corals and schools of fusiliers; Barracuda Pass, with its coral gardens and giant clams; and the swim-through coral spires of the Cathedrals. Snorkelers can glide over the coral and reef fish life of Agincourt Reef. See p. 300.

- **Lizard Island** (QLD): Snorkel over 150-year-old giant clams—as well as gorgeous underwater coral—in the Clam Garden, off this exclusive resort island northeast of Cairns. Nearby is the famous Cod Hole, where divers can hand-feed giant potato cod. See p. 298.
- **Cairns** (QLD): Moore, Norman, Hardy, Saxon, and Arlington reefs and Michaelmas and Upolu cays—all about 90 minutes off Cairns—offer great snorkeling and endless dive sites. Explore on a day trip from Cairns, or join a live-aboard adventure. See p. 281.
- **Coral Sea** (QLD): In this sea, east of the Great Barrier Reef off north Queensland, you'll see sharks feeding at Predator's Playground; 1,000m (3,280-ft.) drop-offs into the Abyss; reefs covering hundreds of square miles; and tropical species not found on the Great Barrier Reef. This is not a day-trip destination; many dive operators run multiday trips on live-aboard vessels. Visibility is excellent—up to 100m (328 ft.). See p. 276.
- **The Yongala Wreck** (QLD): Sunk by a cyclone in 1911, the 120m (394-ft.) SS *Yongala* lies in the Coral Sea off Townsville. Schools of trevally, kingfish, barracuda, and batfish surround the wreckage; giant Queensland grouper live under the bow, lionfish hide under the stern, turtles graze on the hull, and hard and soft corals make their home on everything. It's too far for a day trip; live-aboard trips run from Townsville and Cairns. See p. 278.
- **The Whitsunday Islands** (QLD): These 74 breathtaking islands offer countless dive sites both among the islands and on the Outer Great Barrier Reef, 90 minutes away. Bait Reef on the Outer Reef is popular for its drop-offs. Snorkelers can explore not just the Outer Reef but also patch reefs among the islands and rarely visited fringing reefs around many islands. See p. 327.
- **Heron Island** (QLD): Easily the number-one snorkel and dive site in Australia—if you stayed in the water for a week, you couldn't snorkel all the acres of coral stretching from shore. Take your pick of 22 dive sites: the Coral Cascades, with football trout and anemones; the Blue Pools, favored by octopus, turtles, and sharks; Heron Bommie, with its rays, eels, and Spanish dancers; and more. Absolute magic. See p. 345.
- **Lady Elliot Island** (QLD): Gorgeous coral lagoons, perfect for snorkeling, line this coral cay island off the town of Bundaberg. Boats take you farther out to snorkel above manta rays, plate coral, and big fish. Divers can swim through the blowhole, 16m (52 ft.) down, and see gorgonian fans, soft and hard corals, sharks, barracudas, and reef fish. See p. 348.
- **Rottnest Island** (WA): Just 19km (12 miles) off Perth, this former prison island has excellent snorkeling and more than 100 dive sites. Wrecks, limestone overhangs, and myriad fish will keep divers entertained. There are no cars, so snorkelers should rent a bike and snorkel gear, buy a visitor-center map of suggested snorkel trails, and head off to find their own private sea garden. The sunken grotto of Fishhook Bay is great for fish life. See p. 485.
- **Ningaloo Reef** (WA): A well-kept secret is how we'd describe Australia's second great coral reef, which stretches 260km (161 miles) along the Northwest Cape halfway up Western Australia. Coral starts right on shore, not 90 minutes out to sea as at the Great Barrier Reef. You can snorkel or dive with manta rays, and dive to see sharks, angelfish, turtles, eels, grouper, potato cod, and much more. Snorkel with whale sharks up to 18m (59 ft.) long from March to June. See p. 522.

THE best PLACES TO BUSHWALK

- **Blue Mountains** (NSW): Many bushwalks in the Blue Mountains National Park offer awesome views of valleys, waterfalls, cliffs, and forest. All are easy to reach from Sydney. See p. 185.
- **Whitsunday Islands** (QLD): Most people think of snorkeling and watersports when they come to these subtropical national-park islands clad in dense rainforest and bush, but every resort island in this chain that we recommend has hiking trails. Some are flat, some hilly. Wallabies and butterflies are common sights. South Molle has the best network of trails and 360-degree island views from its peak. The new Ngaro Sea Trail also allows active travelers to combine kayaking sea routes with walks on Hook, Whitsunday, and South Molle islands. See p. 327.
- **Lamington National Park** (QLD): Few other national parks in Australia have such a well-marked network of trails (160km/99 miles in all) as this one, just 90 minutes from the Gold Coast. Revel in dense subtropical rainforest, marvel at mossy 2,000-year-old Antarctic beech trees, delight in the prolific wallabies and birds, and soak up the cool mountain air. See p. 374.
- **Larapinta Trail** (NT): You can start from Alice Springs in the Red Centre and walk the entire 250km (155-mile) semidesert trail, which winds through the stark crimson McDonnell Ranges. You don't have to walk the entire length—plenty of day-length and multiday sections are possible. This one's for the cooler months only (Apr–Oct). See p. 396.
- **Kakadu National Park** (NT): Whether a wetlands stroll or an overnight hike in virgin bushland, you can find it in this World Heritage–listed park. You'll see red cliffs, cycads, waterfalls, lily-filled lagoons hiding man-eating crocodiles, what sometimes looks like Australia's entire bird population, and Aboriginal rock art. See p. 435.
- **The Bibbulmun Track** (WA): Australia's answer to the great Appalachian Trail, the Bibbulmun weaves its way through almost 1,000km (625 miles) of some of WA's finest scenery. It starts in the hills outside Perth and then swirls through granite mountains and jarrah forests, south to the great karri forests of the southwest, and then along the dramatic south coast before reaching WA's oldest town, Albany. The walk can be done in bits, connecting where it crosses major roads, or in much longer stretches, utilizing the many timber shelters built 1 day's walking apart. There are also "Walking Break" packages, based on the towns through which the track passes. See p. 505.
- **Cape-to-Cape** (WA): Rugged sea cliffs, a china-blue sea, eucalyptus forest, white beaches, and coastal heath are what you will find as you hike between Cape Naturaliste and Cape Leeuwin, in the southwest corner of Western Australia. In season, you'll see whales and wildflowers. See p. 493.
- **The Great Ocean Walk** (VIC): This 91km (56-mile) trail from Apollo Bay to Glenample Homestead (near the Twelve Apostles) on Victoria's Great Ocean Road is designed so walkers can step on and step off at a number of places, completing short walks of around 2 hours, or day or overnight hikes. And the views are to die for. See p. 667.

- **Freycinet National Park** (TAS): The trek to Wine Glass Bay passes pink-granite outcrops, with views over an ocean sliced by a crescent of icy sand. It's prehistorically beautiful. See p. 723.
- **Cradle Mountain & Lake St. Clair National Park** (TAS): The 80km (50-mile) Overland Track is the best hike in Australia. The trek, from Cradle Mountain to Lake St. Clair, takes 5 to 10 days, depending on your fitness level. Shorter walks, some lasting just half an hour, are also accessible. See p. 731.
- **Maria Island** (TAS): Whether you take a 4-day guided walk or a day trip by ferry, Maria Island National Park has it all: abundant wildlife, convict ruins, untouched sandy beaches, mountains, and fossil cliffs. The park covers 11,550 hectares (28,541 acres), including 1,878 hectares (4,641 acres) of marine reserve and the 7.4-hectare (18-acre) Ile des Phoques. See p. 720.

THE best PLACES FOR ABORIGINAL CULTURE

- **Umbarra Aboriginal Cultural Centre** (NSW): This center in Wallaga Lake, near Narooma, offers boomerang- and spear-throwing instruction, painting with natural ochers, discussions on Aboriginal culture, and guided walking tours of Aboriginal sacred sites. See p. 224.
- **Tjapukai Aboriginal Cultural Park** (QLD): This multimillion-dollar center near Cairns showcases the history of the Tjapukai people—with their Dreamtime creation history and their often-harrowing experiences since the white man arrived—using film, superb theatrical work, and dance performance. Its Aboriginal art-and-crafts gift shop is one of the country's best. See p. 286.
- **Anangu Tours** (NT): The Anangu are the owners of Uluru. Join them for walks around the Rock as you learn about the poisonous "snake men" who fought battles here, pick bush food off the trees, throw spears, visit rock paintings, and watch the sun set over the monolith. The Cultural Centre, near the base of the Rock, has displays about the Aboriginal Dreamtime. See p. 410.
- **Manyallaluk—The Dreaming Place** (NT): This Aboriginal community near Katherine welcomes visitors and teaches them to paint, weave, throw boomerangs, and perform other tasks of daily life—a low-key day and the chance to chat one-on-one with Aboriginal people in their bush home. See p. 447.
- **Mangarrayi People** (NT): Mike Keighley of **Far Out Adventures** (**© 0427/152 288;** www.farout.com.au) takes tours to beautiful Elsey Station (a ranch) near Katherine, where you visit with the children of the local Mangarrayi people. Sample bush tucker, learn a little bush medicine, and swim in a natural "spa-pool" in the Roper River. See p. 447.
- **Injalak Arts and Crafts Centre** (NT): This nonprofit community arts center at Gunbalanya (Oenpelli) in Arnhem Land draws its inspiration from Injalak Hill, a site rich in rock paintings. Watch the artists work; buy fine indigenous contemporary art, carvings, and weavings at their source; or take a guided tour and learn about the Dreaming stories of this amazing place. See p. 440.
- **Wardan Aboriginal Centre** (WA): The Wardandi people share their knowledge of the Margaret River region—and their culture—with visitors. Take a guided stroll

through the bush to discover the multiple applications of the local plants, then observe the use of traditional tools and fire-lighting. See p. 501.

THE best OF SMALL-TOWN AUSTRALIA

- **Central Tilba** (NSW): Just inland from Narooma on the south coast, this historic hamlet is one of the cutest you'll see, complete with blacksmiths and leatherwork outlets. The ABC Cheese Factory offers free tastings, and you can spend hours browsing antiques stalls or admiring the period buildings. See p. 224.
- **Broken Hill** (NSW): Known for its silver mines, the quirky town of Broken Hill has more pubs per capita than just about anywhere else. It's the home of the School of the Air—a "classroom" that transmits lessons by radio to communities spread over thousands of miles of Outback. Here you'll also find the Palace Hotel, made famous in *The Adventures of Priscilla, Queen of the Desert,* as well as plenty of colonial mansions and heritage homes. See p. 230.
- **Port Douglas** (QLD): What happens when Sydneysiders and Melbournians discover a one-street fishing village in tropical north Queensland? Come to Port Douglas and find out. A strip of groovy restaurants and a championship golf course have not diminished "Port's" old-fashioned air. Four Mile Beach is at the end of the street, and boats depart daily for the Great Barrier Reef. See p. 300.
- **Mission Beach** (QLD): You'd never know this tidy village existed (it's hidden in lush rainforest off the highway) if you weren't well-informed. Aussies know it's here, but few bother to patronize its dazzling beach, offshore islands, and rainforest trails, so you'll have the place to yourself. There's great white-water rafting on the nearby Tully River, too. See p. 311.
- **Broome** (WA): This romantic pearling port on the remote Kimberley coast on the Indian Ocean blends Aussie corrugated-iron architecture with the red pagoda roofs of Chinatown. The town fuses a sophisticated international ambience with Outback attitude. Play on Cable Beach (see p. 542) and stay at glamorous Cable Beach Club Resort. This is the place to add to your South Sea pearl collection. See p. 539.
- **Kalgoorlie** (WA): This is it, the iconic Australian country town. Vibrant Kalgoorlie sits on what used to be the richest square mile of gold-bearing earth ever. It still pumps around 2,000 ounces *a day* out of the ground. Have a beer in one of the gracious 19th-century pubs, peer into the world's biggest open-cut gold mine, and check out the operations of the Royal Flying Doctor Service. See p. 516.
- **Goolwa** (SA): At the mouth of the Murray, Australia's longest river, this historic port is full of beautiful sandstone buildings, many of them now art galleries and restaurants. Take a walk along the river's edge, past historic boatsheds and slipways, where paddle steamers once docked, or head out to the sand dune boardwalk for great coastal views. The wineries of McLaren Vale are a short drive away. See p. 575.
- **Coober Pedy** (SA): Because of the intense summer heat, and because the inhabitants who've spent their lives excavating opal mines are pretty handy when it comes to digging out underground passages, the townsfolk here have created a

subterranean town—the biggest in Australia. Even the churches are underground. See p. 598.

- **Launceston** (TAS): Tasmania's second city is not much larger than your average European or American small town, but it's packed with Victorian and Georgian architecture and remnants of Australia's convict past. Spend a few days and discover the scenery; splurge a little on a stay in a historic hotel. See p. 725.

THE best MUSEUMS

- **Australian National Maritime Museum** (NSW): The best things about this Sydney museum are the ships and submarines often docked in the harbor out front. You can climb aboard and experience what it's like to be a sailor. Inside are some fascinating displays relating to Australia's dependence on the oceans. See p. 152.
- **Alice Springs Telegraph Station Historical Reserve** (NT): It's not called a museum, but that's what this restored telegraph repeater station out in the picturesque hills by a spring—Alice Springs—really is. From the hot biscuits turned out of the wood-fired oven to the old telegraph equipment, this 1870s settlement is as real as history can get. See p. 393.
- **Australian Aviation Heritage Centre** (NT): The pride of this hangar in Darwin is a B-52 bomber on permanent loan from the U.S. But there's loads more, and not just planes, engines, and other aviation paraphernalia: There are stories, jokes, and anecdotes associated with the exhibits that will appeal even if you don't have avgas (aviation fuel) running in your veins. See p. 426.
- **Warradjan Aboriginal Cultural Centre** (NT): "Memorable and moving" were the words used by one reader to describe her visit to this small, stylish museum in Kakadu National Park. Learn about Dreamtime myths and daily life of Aboriginal people in Kakadu. See p. 440.
- **Western Australian Maritime Museum & Shipwreck Galleries** (WA): Housed in the historic port precinct of Fremantle, this museum (and its adjacent galleries) tells tales of the harsh Western Australian coastline since the Dutch first bumped into it and abandoned it as useless in the 1600s. Anyone who ever dreamed of finding a shipwreck laden with pieces of eight will relish the displays of treasure recovered from the deep. See p. 479.
- **New Norcia Museum and Art Gallery** (WA): This tiny museum in the Spanish Benedictine monastery town of New Norcia holds a mind-boggling collection of European Renaissance art. The museum has all kinds of memorabilia: the monks' manuscripts, clothing, instruments, and gifts from Queen Isabella of Spain. See p. 492.
- **The Migration Museum** (SA): Just like the U.S., Australia is a land of immigrants, and this Adelaide museum tells their stories. It's an innovative museum that doesn't pull any punches, letting firsthand stories (many written by visitors and posted on notice boards) tell the history without the gloss of hindsight or political agendas. See p. 563.
- **National Sports Museum** (VIC): This outstanding museum inside the Melbourne Cricket Ground (see p. 633) tells Australia's sporting story from its early beginnings to the present, celebrating Australian sporting heroes, memorable moments, and achievements. It includes the Australian Cricket Hall of Fame and the Sport Australia Hall of Fame, and has a large interactive area popular with all ages. See p. 628.

- **Old Melbourne Gaol** (VIC): This historic prison, with its tiny cells and spooky collection of death masks and artifacts of 19th-century prison life, was the scene of 135 hangings, including that of notorious bushranger (and Australian folk hero) Ned Kelly, in 1880. You can also visit the former City Watch House and the old Magistrate's Court. See p. 629.
- **National Museum of Australia** (ACT): Australia's national museum is housed in an innovative, purpose-built building and profiles 50,000 years of indigenous heritage, settlement since 1788, and key events including Federation and the 2000 Sydney Olympics. There are five permanent galleries and changing exhibitions. See p. 698.

THE best LUXURY ACCOMMODATIONS

- **Park Hyatt Sydney** (NSW; © **800/633-7313** in the U.S. and Canada, or 02/9256 1234 in Australia): You'll have to book well in advance to snag a room at Sydney's best-situated property, at the edge of the city's historic Rocks district. Many rooms have fabulous views across the harbor to the Sydney Opera House. See p. 115.
- **The Sebel Reef House & Spa Palm Cove** (Cairns, QLD; © **1800/079 052** in Australia, or 07/4055 3633): Everyone who stays here says the same thing: "It feels like home." Airy rooms look into tropical gardens, waterfalls cascade into the pools, mosquito nets drape over the beds, and you could swear pith-helmeted colonial officers will be back any minute to finish their gin-and-tonics in the Brigadier Bar. Idyllic Palm Cove Beach is just across the road. See p. 296.
- **Lizard Island** (off Cairns, QLD; © **1300/233 432** in Australia, or 03/9413 6288): Lizard Island has long been popular with Americans for its game fishing, wonderful coral and diving, smart food, and simple upscale lodge accommodations. See p. 298.
- **Bedarra Island** (off Mission Beach, QLD; © **1300/384 417** in Australia, or 07/4047 4747): Presidents and princesses in need of a little time out come to this small rainforest island ringed by beaches. The timber villas are cozy, and the discreet staff assures privacy. Best of all, though, is the extravagant 24-hour bar. See p. 317.
- **Hayman** (Whitsunday Islands, QLD; © **1800/075 175** in Australia: This is Australia's most glamorous resort. It has classy rooms, excellent restaurants, a staff that's keen to please, a superb hexagonal swimming pool, and a fleet of charter boats waiting to spirit you off to the Reef or your own deserted isle. See p. 338.
- **Longitude 131°** (Uluru, Red Centre, NT; © **08/8957 7888**): The luxury option at the Ayers Rock resort scene, Longitude 131° is an African-style safari camp set in the sand dunes, with great views of Uluru. It's very exclusive and very expensive, but you experience the Outback in style. See p. 414.
- **El Questro Homestead** (The Kimberley, WA; © **08/9169 1777**): Charming country decor spiced up with Indonesian antiques, great cuisine, strict privacy, and a dramatic gorge location make this glamorous homestead on a million-acre cattle station popular with jet-setters. Cruise wild gorges, heli-fish for barramundi, and hike to Aboriginal rock art while you're here. See p. 538.

- **Cable Beach Club Resort Broome** (WA; © **1800/199 099** in Australia, or 08/9192 0400): Chinatown meets the Outback at this elegant corrugated-iron-and-pagoda-studded resort lying low along glorious Cable Beach in the romantic pearling port of Broome. Three to-die-for suites are decorated with superb Asian antiques and paintings by luminaries of the Australian art world. See p. 544.
- **Southern Ocean Lodge** (Kangaroo Island, SA; © **02/9918 4355**): Australia's only super luxury wilderness lodge sits high on the cliff tops overlooking a wild and windswept bay. If you can drag yourself away from the view and resist the spa, the wilderness safaris offer some of the best wildlife viewing opportunities in Australia. See p. 586.
- **Arkaba Station** (Flinders Ranges, SA; © **1300/790 561**): Get a feel for how the squattocracy (Australia's version of landed gentry) once lived in this historic homestead on a sheep station at the edge of the outback. There's also opportunity to sleep out under the stars in a five-star swag on overnight walking safaris. See p. 596.
- **The Como Melbourne** (VIC; © **1800/033 400** in Australia, or 03/9825 2222): Great service, nice rooms, and free rubber ducks for the bathtub make this one of our favorite top-flight Australian hotels. See p. 616.
- **Hyatt Hotel Canberra** (ACT; © **800/633-7313** in the U.S. and Canada, or 02/6270 1234): Visiting heads of state and pop stars make this their residence when staying in Canberra. It's a 2-minute drive from the central shopping district and a stone's throw from Lake Burley Griffin and the Parliamentary Triangle. See p. 691.
- **The Islington** (Hobart, TAS; © **1800/703 006** in Australia, or 03/6220 2123): This Regency-style house, built in Hobart's "dress circle" in 1847, may well be the most beautiful, personal, and exclusive small hotel in Australia. A modern extension has a soaring ceiling and glass walls, with views of Mt. Wellington. See p. 714.

THE best MODERATELY PRICED ACCOMMODATIONS

- **Hotel George Williams** (Brisbane, QLD; © **1800/064 858** in Australia, or 07/3308 0700): It's hard to believe that this trendy, clean, and bright hotel is a Y. This is what an affordable hotel should be like, with helpful staff, a pleasant, inexpensive restaurant, and the kind of services you'd expect to be paying more for. See p. 247.
- **The Reef Retreat** (Cairns, QLD; © **07/4059 1744**): It's not often you find so much decorating taste—wooden blinds, teak furniture, and colorful upholstery—at a price you want to pay, but that's what you get at the apartments in trendy Palm Cove, one of Cairns's most desirable beachfront suburbs. There's a pool on the lovely landscaped grounds, but the beach is just a block away. See p. 297.
- **By the Sea** (Port Douglas, QLD; © **07/4099 5387**): They may be tiny, but these pretty apartments have a homey atmosphere and are seconds from Four Mile Beach. Some units have sea views. The solicitous proprietor is a font of advice on things to see and do. See p. 307.

- **Miss Maud Swedish Hotel** (Perth, WA; ✆ **1800/998 022** in Australia, or 08/9325 3900): Staying here is like staying at Grandma's—just as she's finished a major redecoration job. You're right in the heart of Perth, and the friendly staff and huge buffet breakfasts (included in the room rate) complete the picture. See p. 463.
- **North Adelaide Heritage Group** (Adelaide, SA; ✆ **08/8272 1355**): The very elegant Bishop's Garden, on Molesworth Street, is just one of 18 beautifully restored historic properties in the portfolio. Originally the house and gardens of Bishop Nutter Thomas, the fourth Anglican Bishop of Adelaide, it's full of gorgeous antiques and artwork collected by the current owners, Rodney and Regina Twiss. See p. 559.
- **York Mansions** (Launceston, TAS; ✆ **03/6334 2933**): If where you stay is as important to your visit as what you see, don't miss staying here for a night or two. This National Trust–classified building has five spacious apartments, each with a distinct character. It's like living the high life in the Victorian age. See p. 729.

THE best ALTERNATIVE ACCOMMODATIONS

- **Underground Motel** (White Cliffs, NSW; ✆ **08/8091 6677**): All but two of this motel's rooms are underground. Rooms are reached by a maze of spacious tunnels dug out of the rock beneath this opal-mining town. See p. 233.
- **Paradise Bay Eco Escape** (The Whitsunday Islands, QLD; ✆ **07/4946 9777**): You'll be one of only a maximum of 14 guests staying in the 10 comfy and recently refurbished beachfront cabins at this island ecoretreat (formerly South Long Island Nature Lodge). Sea kayak, snorkel, swim, hike rainforest trails, dine with other guests outside under the Milky Way, and take sailing trips on the lodge's own yacht. Considering you'll only shell out for wine and maybe a seaplane trip to the Reef, this is a great value for its exclusivity. See p. 338.
- **Kingfisher Bay Resort** (Fraser Island, QLD; ✆ **1800/072 555** in Australia, or 07/4120 3333): If it weren't for the ranger station and natural-history videos in the lobby, the wildlife walks, the guided four-wheel-drive safaris, and the other eco-activities, you'd hardly know that this comfortable, modern hotel is an ecoresort. See p. 352.
- **Binna Burra Mountain Lodge** (✆ **1300/246 622** in Australia, or 07/5533 3622) and **O'Reilly's Rainforest Guesthouse** (✆ **1800/688 722** in Australia, or 07/5502 4911), both in the Gold Coast Hinterland, QLD: Tucked almost 1,000m (3,280 ft.) up on rainforested ridges, these cozy retreats offer fresh mountain air, activities, and instant access to the hiking trails of Lamington National Park. At O'Reilly's you can hand-feed brilliantly colored rainforest birds every morning. See p. 376.
- **Bamurru Plains** (Kakadu, NT; ✆ **1300/790 561** in Australia, or 02/9571 6399): Set on a working buffalo station on the edge of the Mary River floodplains, just west of Kakadu National Park, this stylish luxury lodge offers a rich array of wildlife encounters and an ecofriendly environment. Accommodation is in luxury tents with one-way screens to ensure the stupendous views aren't obstructed. See p. 443.

- **Sal Salis** (Coral Coast, WA; © **02/9571 6677**): This tiny ecoretreat is hidden within the sand dunes, just meters from the Indian Ocean and the magical Ningaloo Reef. The large safari tents are set up on raised timber floors; kangaroos bound past your door and the sunsets from your room are superb. It's privacy and peace par excellence. See p. 530.
- **Emma Gorge Resort** (The Kimberley, WA; © **08/9169 1777**): At this spick-and-span little safari camp on the 400,000-hectare (1-million-acre) El Questro cattle station, guests stay in cute tents with wooden floors and electric lights, eat at a rustic gourmet restaurant, and join in the many hikes, bird-watching tours, river cruises, and other activities. See p. 538.
- **Prairie Hotel** (Flinders Ranges, SA; © **08/8648 4844**): From the outside, it looks like any other Outback pub, but the guest book is full of Hollywood's A-list. (The rooms in the historic hotel have become a favorite with visiting movie stars, as Flinders is often the backdrop for films.) The restaurant is best known for its feral food (camel, kangaroo, emu, and bush herbs and native spices); keep an eye out for the distinctive road signs advertising the menu on the way into the town. See p. 597.
- **Freycinet Lodge** (Freycinet National Park, Coles Bay, TAS; © **1800/420 155** or 03/6225 7000): These ecofriendly bush cabins are right next to one of the nation's best walking trails. The ocean views from the magnificent restaurant and the surrounding balconies are spectacular. See p. 724.
- **Cradle Mountain Lodge** (Cradle Mountain, TAS; © **1300/806 192** in Australia, or 03/6492 2103): Just minutes from your comfortable cabin are 1,500-year-old trees, moss forests, craggy mountain ridges, limpid pools and lakes, and hordes of scampering marsupials. See p. 732.

THE best BED & BREAKFASTS

- **The Russell** (The Rocks, Sydney; © **02/9241 3543**): This B&B, wonderfully positioned in the city's old quarter, is the coziest place to stay in Sydney. It has creaky floorboards, a ramshackle feel, brightly painted corridors, and rooms with immense character. See p. 117.
- **Echoes Boutique Hotel & Restaurant** (Katoomba, NSW; © **02/4782 1966**): Echoes is right on the edge of a dramatic drop into the Jamison Valley. The views from the balconies are breathtaking. See p. 188.
- **Casuarina Estate** (Pokolbin, Hunter Valley, NSW; © **02/4998 7888**): Each suite here has an unusual theme, like the Moulin Rouge, the Oriental, Casanova's Loft, the Mariners Suite, Out of Africa, Palais Royale, and Romeo's Retreat. The most popular is the Bordello, with a pedestal king-size bed, voluptuous pink curtains, and strategically placed mirrors. See p. 203.
- **Ulladulla Guest House** (Ulladulla, NSW; © **02/4455 1796**): Works of art on the walls, fabulous food, and a lagoonlike pool among the palm trees—all this and lovely rooms, with hosts who can't do enough for you. See p. 222.
- **Lilybank Bed & Breakfast** (Cairns, QLD; © **07/4055 1123**): This rambling 1890s homestead used to be the Cairns mayor's residence. Today, owners Pat and Mike Woolford welcome guests to its comfy rooms, wide verandas, and blooming gardens. You can also stay in the renovated gardener's cottage. See p. 296.

- **Marae** (near Port Douglas, QLD; ✆ **07/4098 4900**): Lush bushland full of butterflies and birds is the setting for this gorgeous contemporary Queenslander house with hip rooms. Owners John and Pam Burden promise a warm welcome and a wonderful breakfast. See p. 308.
- **Fothergills of Fremantle** (Perth, WA; ✆ **08/9335 6784**): Two lovely old terrace houses have been converted into a classy B&B, within walking distance of the delights of Fremantle. The balconies are great for sundowners, and the place is filled with owner David Cooke's wonderful art collection. See p. 465.
- **The Rocks Albany** (Albany, WA; ✆ **08/9842 5969**): The Rocks is a superbly sited and furnished heritage mansion. The double-story stone building, enclosed by broad timber balconies, is set within a .8-hectare (2-acre) garden with sweeping views across Albany's harbor. It was built in 1882 and later became the summer residence of WA's governors; it has since been restored to that level of luxury with facilities such as billiard and piano rooms. See p. 508.
- **Collingrove Homestead** (Angaston, the Barossa Valley, SA; ✆ **08/8564 2061**): This grand homestead was built for the original Angaston patriarch, John Howard Angas, in 1856. The house is full of original family furnishings and memorabilia. It's open as a museum during the day, but you can stay in one of two rooms within the historic homestead or several en-suite rooms in former maids' quarters. See p. 573.
- **Cotterville** (Melbourne, VIC; ✆ **03/9826 9105** or 0409/900 807 mobile): A beautifully and lovingly restored terrace house with elegant courtyard gardens, where you will be surrounded with art and music and entertained by gregarious hosts and their friendly dogs. A home away from home in every sense. See p. 617.

THE best RESTAURANTS

- **Guillaume at Bennelong** (Sydney, NSW; ✆ **02/9241 1999**): With amazing views of the Sydney Harbour Bridge, great food, and a position inside the Sydney Opera House, how could dinner at Guillaume go wrong? See p. 130.
- **Quay** (Sydney, NSW; ✆ **02/9251 5600**): Sydney's best seafood restaurant offers perhaps the loveliest view in town. Gaze through the large windows toward the Opera House, the city skyline, the North Shore suburbs, and the Harbour Bridge. See p. 132.
- **Tetsuya's** (Sydney, NSW; ✆ **02/9267 2900**): Chef Tetsuya Wakuda is arguably Sydney's most famous chef, and his nouveau Japanese creations are imaginative enough to guarantee that this hip eatery is a constant number one in Australia. In 2007, the restaurant ranked no. 5 in the world. See p. 136.
- **Icebergs Dining Room and Bar** (Sydney, NSW; ✆ **02/9365 9000**): Come here for exquisite food and one of the best ocean views in the Southern Hemisphere. Not surprisingly, seafood features highly on the menu. Probably the best place to have lunch in Sydney. See p. 142.
- **e'cco bistro** (Brisbane, QLD; ✆ **07/3831 8344**): Simple food elegantly done has won this small but stylish bistro a stack of awards, and you'll see why. Not least among its titles is Australia's top restaurant award, the Remy Martin Cognac/Gourmet Traveller Restaurant of the Year. Booking ahead is essential. See p. 249.

- **Star Anise** (Subiaco, Perth, WA; ✆ **08/9381 9811**): This small restaurant tucked away on a leafy suburban street serves up tasty, innovative, Asian-influenced food. The menu is kept simple, with just five courses in each section, but each dish is a gem. See p. 469.
- **Voyager Estate** (Margaret River, WA; ✆ **08/9757 6354**): Everything about this winery and restaurant reeks of class. Superb Cape Dutch architecture, impeccable gardens, and imaginative cuisine make this a top dining spot. Recommended wines available by the glass. See p. 504.
- **Prairie Hotel** (Flinders Ranges, SA; ✆ **08/8648 4844**): While you may be tempted to dismiss the hotel's signature dish, a "feral mixed grill" (camel sausage, goat chop, kangaroo filet, and wallaby kabob on mashed potatoes with gravy), as a tourist gimmick, the Prairie's food is definitely worth going out of your way for. Aside from a few other novelty dishes ('roo burger or wallaby stir-fry), the entrees are a blend of different tastes and textures combining native foods with more contemporary ingredients. See p. 597.
- **Flower Drum** (Melbourne, VIC; ✆ **03/9662 3655**): Praise pours in for this upscale eatery serving Cantonese food. The food is exquisite and the service impeccable. See p. 618.
- **Donovans** (Melbourne, VIC; ✆ **03/9534 8221**): A glass in hand while the sun goes down over St. Kilda beach, watched from the veranda at Donovans, is a perfect way to end the day. This 1920s bathing pavilion has been transformed into a welcoming beach-house-style restaurant, complete with views across the sand and a seafood-rich menu. See p. 624.

THE best MODERATELY PRICED RESTAURANTS

- **Phillip's Foote** (Sydney, NSW; ✆ **02/9241 1485**): In the heart of the historic neighborhood known as The Rocks, this barbecue restaurant serves fish, meat, and poultry. Pick your own protein and throw it on the "barbie" in the courtyard behind a historic pub. See p. 134.
- **Green Papaya** (East Brisbane, QLD; ✆ **07/3217 3599**): Flavorful North Vietnamese cuisine in a cheerful setting—a simple formula that draws enthusiastic crowds. If you need advice as you contemplate the menu, the helpful staff will offer as much guidance as you need. See p. 251.
- **Salsa Bar & Grill** (Port Douglas, QLD; ✆ **07/4099 4922**): The animated atmosphere and attractive surroundings set the scene for an excellent dining experience. Appetizers and main courses run the gamut from simple fare to sophisticated tropical creations; desserts are fantastic. See p. 310.
- **Spirit House** (Sunshine Coast, QLD; ✆ **07/5446 8994**): Winding jungle paths lead to tables set around a lagoon, illuminated at night by torches and discreet lighting. The flavors from the kitchen are mainly Thai but with other Asian influences; there's nowhere else quite like this in Queensland for atmosphere and terrific food. See p. 361.
- **Red Ochre Grill** (Alice Springs, NT; ✆ **08/8952 9614**): "Gourmet bush tucker" might sound like a contradiction, but this restaurant (part of an upscale chain)

pulls it off. The kitchen combines native ingredients and international techniques to exceptionally good effect. See p. 401.

- **Romany Restaurant** (Northbridge, Perth, WA; ✆ **08/9328 8042**): A full house on a Tuesday night speaks volumes. Good hearty Italian meals are served quickly, in a companionable atmosphere. Food and wine prices are eminently reasonable. See p. 468.
- **Star of Greece Café** (Port Willunga, SA; ✆ **08/8557 7420**): Don't let appearances fool you. This little 1950s kiosk perched high on the cliff top overlooking the coastline of Port Willunga, around an hour's drive from Adelaide, serves up some of the best seafood you'll find in the country. And the views are pretty spectacular, too. See p. 578.
- **MoVida** (Melbourne, VIC; ✆ **03/9663 3038**): This little corner of Spain is relaxed and fun, with seriously good food and good wine. Melbournians flock here for the tapas and *raciones*. See p. 622.

2

AUSTRALIA IN DEPTH

by Marc Llewellyn

When most people think of Australia, they conjure up romantic images of skipping kangaroos, dusty red deserts, and golden sand. They see the Sydney Opera House, perhaps, or maybe the Sydney Harbour Bridge. They imagine drawling accents and slouch hats, and people who wrestle crocodiles for the fun of it. Of course, it's all that—and more. This huge continent is truly remarkable. There are rolling green hills, thick ancient rainforests, historic towns, vast areas of sparsely inhabited Outback, thousands of beaches to choose from, unique animals and plants, cosmopolitan cities, and intriguing Aboriginal cultures to explore.

Most people visiting for the first time head to Sydney or Melbourne. They explore the Red Centre and the giant rock Uluru; or they take to the warm waters and dive or snorkel on the Great Barrier Reef. But it's also often the places that come to them by chance, or deeper research, that remain locked in their memory forever. Who could forget wandering around an opal field with its underground houses? Or riding a horse through the Snowy Mountains? Or skiing through the gum trees? Or snorkeling with whale sharks in Western Australia? Or marveling at the thousands of koalas on Kangaroo Island? Or traveling dusty tracks more suitable to emus in the company of an Outback postman? Of course, no experience is complete without a little background information, which is where this chapter comes in.

LOOKING BACK AT AUSTRALIA

The Beginning

In the beginning, there was the Dreamtime—at least according to the Aborigines of Australia. Between then and now (perhaps), the

THE ancient art OF AUSTRALIA

A history of the Aboriginal people lies partly in the **rock art** they have left behind all over Australia. In the tropical north, for example, a wide-ranging body of prehistoric art decorates sandstone gorges near the tiny township of Laura. Here, in rugged Cape York Peninsula, depictions on rock-shelter sites range from spirit figures of men and women to eels, fish, wide-winged brolga birds, crocodiles, kangaroos, snakes, and stenciled hands. One wall, the "Magnificent Gallery," stretches more than 40m (131 ft.) and is adorned with hundreds of Quinkan figures—Quinkans being the Aboriginal spirits associated with this region.

Much Aboriginal rock art is preserved in national parks. Examples readily accessible on day trips from major Australian cities include Ku-Ring-Gai Chase National Park and the Royal National Park near Sydney. Then there's Namadgi National Park near Canberra, the Grampians National Park west of Melbourne, and the fabulous hand stencils at Mutawintji National park near Broken Hill in New South Wales. Arnhem Land, encompassing Kakadu National Park, is a priceless wellspring of indigenous art. Rock paintings of the escarpments and plateaus in that area date to the early Holocene Period. One style, called "X-ray," depicts bones and internal organs inside animal bodies. There are also ancient dot paintings near Uluru in Australia's Red Centre.

In Queensland, Carnarvon National Park (about 400km/249 miles west of Brisbane) offers a breathtaking display of early indigenous paintings, while in Tasmania, Mount Cameron West is considered one of the world's foremost sites of hunter-gatherer art.

Perhaps most amazing are the mysterious "Bradshaw" paintings in Western Australia's wild Kimberley region, which continue to astound scholars. Explorer Joseph Bradshaw found the figures, likened to those in Egyptian temples, in 1891. Today there are an estimated 100,000 sites across 50,000 sq. km (31,069 sq. miles) of the Kimberley, dating from approximately 17,000 years ago.

supercontinent referred to as Pangaea split into two huge continents called Laurasia and Gondwanaland. Over millions of years, continental drift carried the landmasses apart. Laurasia broke up and formed North America, Europe, and most of Asia. Meanwhile, Gondwanaland divided into South America, Africa, India, Australia and New Guinea, and Antarctica. Meanwhile, giant marsupials evolved to roam the continent of Australia. Among them was a plant-eating animal that looked like a wombat the size of a rhinoceros, a marsupial "lion" that probably climbed trees, a giant squashed-face kangaroo standing 3m (10 ft.) tall, and a flightless bird the same size as an emu but four times heavier. The last of these giant creatures are believed to have died out some 20,000 years ago, possibly helped toward extinction by drought, or by Aborigines, who lived alongside them for around 40,000 years or more.

Early European Explorers

The existence of Australia had been on the minds of Europeans since the Greek astronomer Ptolemy drew a map of the world in A.D. 150 showing a large landmass in the south, which he believed had to exist to balance out the land in the Northern Hemisphere. He called it Terra Australia Incognita—the "Unknown Southland."

Portuguese ships reached Australia as early as 1536 and even charted part of its coastline. In 1606, William Jansz was sent by the Dutch East India Company to open up a new route to the Spice Islands, and to find New Guinea, which was supposedly rich in gold. He landed on the north coast of Queensland instead and fought with local Aborigines. Between 1616 and 1640, many more Dutch ships made contact with Australia as they hugged the west coast of what they called "New Holland," after sailing with the westerlies (west winds) from the Cape of Good Hope.

In 1642, the Dutch East India Company, through the governor general of the Indies, Anthony Van Diemen, sent Abel Tasman to search out and map the great southland. During two voyages, he charted the northern Australian coastline and discovered Tasmania, which he named Van Diemen's Land.

The Arrival of the British

In 1697, English pirate William Dampier published a book about his adventures. The text mentioned Shark Beach, on the northwest coast of Australia, as the place his pirate ship made its repairs after robbing ships on the Pacific Ocean. Sent to further explore by England's King William III, Dampier returned and found little to recommend.

In 1766, the Royal Society hired James Cook to travel to the Pacific Ocean to observe and record the transit of Venus across the Sun. He was promoted to lieutenant and later captain. In 1770 he charted the east coast of Australia in his ship the HMS *Endeavour.* He claimed the land for Britain and named it New South Wales, probably as a favor to Thomas Pennant, a Welsh patriot and botanist who was a friend of the *Endeavour*'s botanist, Joseph Banks. On April 29, Cook landed at Botany Bay, which he named after the discovery of scores of plants hitherto unknown to science. Turning northward, Cook passed an entrance to a possible harbor that appeared to offer safe anchorage and named it Port Jackson, after the secretary to the admiralty, George Jackson. Back in Britain, King George III viewed Australia as a potential colony and repository of Britain's overflowing prison population, which could no longer be transported to the United States of America following the War of Independence.

The First Fleet left England in May 1787, made up of 11 store and transport ships (none of them bigger than the passenger ferries that ply modern-day Sydney Harbour from Circular Quay to Manly) led by Arthur Phillip. Aboard were 1,480 people, including 759 convicts. Phillip's flagship, the *Supply,* reached Botany Bay in January 1788, but Phillip decided the soil was poor and the surroundings too swampy. On January 26, now celebrated as Australia Day, he settled for Port Jackson (Sydney Harbour) instead.

The convicts were immediately put to work clearing land, planting crops, and constructing buildings. The early food harvests were failures, and by early 1790, the fledgling colony was facing starvation.

Phillip decided to give some convicts pardons for good behavior and service, and even granted small land parcels to those who were really industrious. In 1795, coal was discovered; in 1810, Governor Macquarie began extensive city-building projects; and in 1813, the explorers Blaxland, Wentworth, and Lawson forged a passage over the Blue Mountains to the fertile plains beyond.

When gold was discovered in Victoria in 1852, and in Western Australia 12 years later, hundreds of thousands of immigrants from Europe, America, and China flooded the country in search of fortune. By 1860, more than a million non-Aboriginal people were living in Australia.

The last 10,000 convicts were transported to Western Australia between 1850 and 1868, bringing the total shipped to Australia to 168,000.

Some early colonial architecture, built and designed by those convicts, still remains in Sydney. Look out for the buildings designed by the colonial architect Francis Greenway. Between 1816 and 1818, while still a prisoner, Greenway was responsible for the Macquarie Lighthouse on South Head, at the entrance to Sydney Harbour, and also Hyde Park Barracks and St. James Church in the city center.

Another great place to look for early colonial architecture is in Tasmania. Many fascinating buildings still exist along the Heritage Highway linking Hobart and Launceston, and you can't miss Port Arthur, Tasmania's most infamous colonial prison complex.

By the way, in 1964, a group of 20 nomadic women and children became the last Aboriginal people to make "first contact" with Europeans. They were living in the Great Sandy Desert, south of Broome, in Western Australia. When they first saw two officers from the Weapons Research Establishment, who were checking land destined for a series of rocket tests, the Aborigines presumed the white-skinned creatures were ghosts.

Federation and the Great Wars

On January 1, 1901, the six states that made up Australia proclaimed themselves to be part of one nation, and the Commonwealth of Australia was formed. In the same ceremony, the first governor general was sworn in as the representative of the Queen, who remained head of state.

In 1914, Australia joined the mother country in World War I. In April of the following year, the Australian and New Zealand Army Corps (Anzac) formed a beachhead on the peninsula of Gallipoli in Turkey. The Turkish troops had been warned, and 8 months of fighting ended with 8,587 Australian dead and more than 19,000 wounded.

Australians fought in World War II in North Africa, Greece, and the Middle East. In March 1942, Japanese aircraft bombed Broome in Western Australia and Darwin in the Northern Territory. In May 1942, Japanese midget submarines entered Sydney Harbour and torpedoed a ferry before being destroyed. Later that year, Australian volunteers fought an incredibly brave retreat through the jungles of Papua New Guinea on the Kokoda Track against superior Japanese forces.

Recent Times

Following World War II, mass immigration to Australia, primarily from Europe, boosted the non-Aboriginal population. "White" Australia was always used to distinguish the Anglo-Saxon population from that of the indigenous people of Australia, and until 1974 there existed a "White Australia Policy"—a result of conflict between European settlers and Chinese immigrants in the gold fields in the 1850s. This policy severely restricted the immigration of people who lacked European ancestry. In 1974, the left-of-Center Whitlam government put an end to the White Australia policy that had largely restricted black and Asian immigration since 1901. In 1986, an act of both British and Australian Parliament severed any remaining ties to the United Kingdom. Australia had begun the march to complete independence.

Waves of immigration have brought in millions of people since the end of World War II. Results from the last census, conducted in 2006, show that 25% of the population was born overseas. Of those, 7% were born in Northern Europe (including

THE ABORIGINAL "stolen generations"

When Captain James Cook landed at Botany Bay in 1770 determined to claim the land for the British Empire, at least 300,000 **Aborigines** were already on the continent. Whether you believe a version of history that suggests the Aboriginal people were descendants of migrants from Indonesia to the north, or the Aboriginal belief that they have occupied Australia since the beginning of time, there is scientific evidence that people were walking the continent at least 60,000 years ago.

At the time of the white "invasion" of their lands, there were at least 600 different, largely nomadic tribal communities, each linked to their ancestral land by **"sacred sites"** (certain features of the land, such as hills or rock formations). They were hunter-gatherers, spending about 20 hours a week harvesting the resources of the land, the rivers, and the ocean. The rest of their time was taken up by complex social and belief systems, as well as by life's practicalities—making utensils, weapons, and musical instruments such as didgeridoos and clapsticks.

The basis of Aboriginal spirituality rests in the **Dreamtime** stories, which recount how ancient spirits created the universe—earth, stars, moon, sun, water, animals, and humans. Much Aboriginal art is related to their land and the sacred sites that are home to the Dreamtime spirits. Some Aboriginal groups believe these spirits came in giant human form, while others believed they were animals or huge snakes. According to Aboriginal custom, individuals can draw on the power of the Dreamtime spirits by reenacting various stories and practicing certain ceremonies.

Aboriginal groups had encountered people from other lands before the British arrived. Dutch records from 1451 show that the Macassans, from islands now belonging to Indonesia, had a long relationship trading smoking pipes, Dutch glass, and alcohol for edible sea slugs from Australia's northern coastal waters, which they sold to the Chinese in the Canton markets. Dutch, Portuguese, French, and Chinese vessels also encountered Australia—in fact, the Dutch fashion for pointy beards caught on through northern Australia long before the British First Fleet arrived in 1778.

When the British came, bringing their diseases with them, coastal communities were virtually wiped out by smallpox. Even as late as the 1950s, large numbers

the U.K.), 7% were born in Asia, and 4% were born in Southern Europe. In 2009 immigrant numbers from China topped those from the U.K. for the first time. New waves of immigration have recently come from countries such as Iraq and Somalia. So what's the typical Australian like? Well, he's hardly Crocodile Dundee.

Today, the "land Down Under" is a modern nation coming to terms with its identity. The umbilical cord with Mother England has been cut, and the nation is still trying to find its position within the Asian sphere of influence. One thing Australia realized early on was the importance of tourism to its economy. Millions visit every year. You'll find Australians helpful and friendly, and services, tours, and food and drink to rival any in the world. Factor in the landscape, the native Australian culture, the sunshine, the animals, and some of the world's best cities, and you've got a fascinating, accessible destination of amazing diversity and variety.

of Aborigines in remote regions of South Australia and the Northern Territory succumbed to deadly outbreaks of influenza and measles.

Although relationships between the settlers and Aborigines were initially peaceful, conflicts over land and food led to skirmishes in which Aborigines were massacred and settlers and convicts attacked. Governor Phillip was speared in the back by an Aborigine in 1790.

Within a few years, some 10,000 Aborigines and 1,000 Europeans had been killed in Queensland alone, while in Tasmania, a campaign to rid the island entirely of local Aborigines was ultimately successful, with the last full-blooded Tasmanian Aborigine dying in 1876. By the start of the 20th century, the Aboriginal people were considered a dying race. Most of those who remained lived in government-owned reserves or church-controlled missions.

Massacres of Aborigines continued to go largely or wholly unpunished into the 1920s, by which time it was official government policy to remove light-skinned Aboriginal children from their families and to sterilize young Aboriginal women. Many children of the "stolen generations" were brought up in white foster homes or church refuges and never reunited with their biological families—in fact, many children with living parents were told that their parents were dead. This process occurred even into the 1970s.

Today, there are some 517,000 people who claim Aboriginal and Torres Strait Islander descent living in Australia, or 2.5% of the population. Some 32% of these live in the major cities, while 25% live in remote or very remote areas. In general, a great divide still exists between them and the rest of the population. Aboriginal life expectancy is 20 years lower than that of other Australians, with overall death rates between two and four times higher. Aborigines make up the highest percentage of the country's prison population, and reports continue to emerge about Aborigines dying while incarcerated.

The first act to be carried on by the Labor Government following electoral victory in the general election held at the end of 2007 was to officially apologize to the "stolen generations" of Aborigines.

THE LAY OF THE LAND

People who have never visited Australia wonder why such a huge country has a population of just 21 million people. The truth is, Australia can barely support that many. About 90% of those 21 million people live on only 2.6% of the continent. Climatic and physical land conditions ensure that the only relatively decent rainfall occurs along a thin strip of land around Australia's coast. Compounding that is the fact that Australia is in the grip of the worst drought in a century (see "The Drought Continues," below). The vast majority of Australia is harsh Outback, characterized by saltbush plains, arid brown crags, shifting sand deserts, and salt-lake country. People survive where they can in this arid land because of one thing—the Great Artesian Basin. This saucer-shaped geological formation comprises about a fifth of

Australia's landmass, stretching over much of inland New South Wales, Queensland, South Australia, and the Northern Territory. Beneath it are massive underground water supplies stored during Jurassic and Cretaceous times (some 66–208 million years ago), when the area was much like the Amazon basin is today. Bore holes bring water to the surface and allow sheep, cattle, and humans a respite from the dryness.

As for the climate, as you might expect with a continent the size of Australia, it can differ immensely. The average rainfall in central Australia ranges from between just 200 to 250mm (8–10 in.) a year. Summer daytime temperatures range from between 90° and 104°F (32°–40°C). In winter, temperatures range from around 64° to 75°F (18°–24°C). Summer in the Southern Hemisphere roughly stretches from early November to the end of February, though it can be hot for a couple of months on either side of these dates, depending where you are.

Parts of the Northern Territory and far northern Queensland are classified as tropical, and as such suffer from very wet summers—often referred to simply as "the Wet." Flooding can be a real fact of life up here. The rest of the year is called "the Dry," for obvious reasons.

Most of Queensland, Western Australia, and New South Wales is classified as subtropical. This means warm summers and cool winters. Parts of southern South Australia and Western Australia are often described as "Mediterranean-like"—meaning hot summers and cold winters. Tasmania has mild summers and cold winters. The Tasmanian high country and parts of central Victoria can get snow in winter, while the Australian Alps, which run through southern central NSW and northeastern Victoria, have good snow cover in winter. Come here to ski.

The Queensland coast is blessed with one of the greatest natural attractions in the world. The Great Barrier Reef stretches 2,000km (1,240 miles) from off Gladstone in Queensland to the Gulf of Papua, near New Guinea. It's relatively new, not more than 8,000 years old, although many fear that rising seawater, caused by global warming, will cause its demise. As it is, the nonnative Crown of Thorns starfish and a bleaching process believed to be the result of excessive nutrients flowing into the sea from Australia's farming land are already causing significant damage. The Reef is covered in chapter 8.

Australia's other great natural formation is, of course, Ayers Rock—which is more commonly known these days by its Aboriginal name of Uluru (see p. 407).

Australia's Wildlife

Australia's isolation from the rest of the world over millions of years has led to the evolution of forms of life found nowhere else. Probably the strangest of all is the **platypus.** This monotreme, or egg-laying marsupial, has webbed feet, a ducklike bill, and a tail like a beaver's. It lays eggs, and the young suckle from their mother. When a specimen was first brought back to Europe, skeptical scientists insisted it was a fake—a concoction of several different animals sewn together. You will probably never see this shy, nocturnal creature in the wild, although there are a few at Sydney's Taronga Zoo.

Another strange one is the **koala.** This fluffy marsupial, whose nearest relative is the wombat, eats virtually indigestible gum (eucalyptus) leaves and sleeps about 20 hours a day. There's just one koala species, although those found in Victoria are much larger than their brethren in more northern climes.

THE drought CONTINUES

Australia has been experiencing a severe drought since 1992. Most state capitals have been trying to cope with severe water restrictions for years, as lakes dry up and the population grows due to increased immigration. Some major reservoirs are so depleted of water that emergency water procedures have been put in place. One of Australia's largest water supplies, Lake Eucumbene, in the Snowy Mountains of NSW, is so low that the remains of the town of Old Adaminaby have been exposed. The town had been submerged deep underwater since 1957, during the construction of Australia's biggest hydroelectric project.

Australians are seeing trees die and important wetlands for breeding birds dry up or become polluted by salt and other contaminants. Desalination plants designed to turn seawater into fresh are to be built in Sydney and Melbourne. Irrigators along the enormous Murray–Darling river system have had their water supplies cut off. Fruit and vegetable prices have risen, and some farmers have committed suicide. The threat of bushfires is ever present. On February 7, 2009, Australia suffered its highest ever loss of life from a bushfire. The so-called "Black Saturday" bushfires ravaged Victoria, killing 173 people and injuring over 400. Many towns were badly damaged or almost completely destroyed. And so it goes on . . . and on . . . despite floods in parts of Queensland and NSW in early 2010.

Australia is among the world's biggest per-capita energy consumers and produces more carbon dioxide emissions per person than anywhere else in the world. Australian environmentalists point to this fact as a potential cause of the drought—the increasing frequency and severity of drought-causing El Niño weather patterns can be blamed on global warming, which is affected in turn by CO_2 emissions.

Australia is also famous for **kangaroos.** There are 45 kinds of kangaroos and wallabies, ranging in scale from small rat-size kangaroos to the man-size red kangaroos.

The animal you're most likely to come across in your trip is the **possum,** named by Captain James Cook after the North American opossum, which he thought they resembled. (In fact, they are from entirely different families of the animal kingdom.) The brush-tailed possum is commonly found in suburban gardens, including those in Sydney.

Then there's the **wombat.** There are four species of this bulky burrower in Australia, but the common wombat is, well, most common. You might come across the smaller hairy-nosed wombat in South Australia and Western Australia.

The **dingo,** thought by many to be a native of Australia, was in fact introduced—probably by Aborigines or traders from the north. These wild dogs vary in color from yellow to a russet red and are heavily persecuted by farmers. Because dingoes can breed with escaped "pet" dogs, full-blooded dingoes are becoming increasingly rare.

The carnivorous marsupial **Tasmanian devil** can be found in (you guessed it) the island-state of Tasmania, though a virulent face cancer has swept through the animals and is quickly wiping out the wild population.

Commonly seen birds in Australia include the fairy penguin or **Little Penguin** along the coast, **black swans, parrots** and **cockatoos,** and **honeyeaters.**

DANGEROUS NATIVES

Snakes are common throughout Australia, but you will rarely see one. The most dangerous land snake is the taipan, which hides in the grasslands in northern Australia—one bite contains enough venom to kill up to 200 sheep. If by the remotest chance you are bitten, immediately demobilize the limb, wrapping it tightly (but not tight enough to restrict the blood flow) with a cloth or bandage, and call ✆ 000 for an ambulance. Antivenin should be available at the nearest hospital.

One creature that scares the living daylights out of anyone who visits coastal Australia is the **shark,** particularly the great white (though these marauders of the sea are uncommon, and mostly found in cooler waters, such as those off South Australia). Shark attacks are very rare, particularly when you consider how many people go swimming. A total of 194 people have been killed in shark attacks in Australia over the past 2 centuries. Some years there are none, other years there have been up to three in a year, but the average is around one per year. There has not been a single fatality on a Sydney beach since 1963, though in February 2009 there were three shark attacks in Sydney. The first involved a navy diver who was attacked by a bull shark in Sydney Harbour, not far from the Opera House. Doctors later amputated his arm and a leg. The second attack involved a 2.5m (8¼-ft.) great white shark, which savaged a surfer's hand off Bondi Beach. In the third attack, a shark bit a teenage surfer's leg to the bone off Avalon, one of Sydney's northern beaches. In February 2010 a surfer was bitten on the leg by a usually non-aggressive wobbegong shark.

Apart from the great white, the most dangerous sharks are the tiger shark and the bull shark. Bull sharks are particularly annoying as they tend to swim up rivers.

There are two types of **crocodile** in Australia: the relatively harmless freshwater croc, which grows to 3m (10 ft.), and the dangerous estuarine (or saltwater) crocodile, which reaches 5 to 7m (16–23 ft.). Freshwater crocs eat fish; estuarine crocs aren't so picky. Never swim in or stand on the bank of any river, swamp, or pool in northern Australia unless you know for certain it's croc-free.

Spiders are common all over Australia, with the funnel web spider and the red-back spider being the most aggressive. Funnel webs live in holes in the ground (they spin their webs around a hole's entrance) and stand on their back legs when they're about to attack. Red-backs have a habit of resting under toilet seats and in car trunks, generally outside the main cities. Caution is a good policy.

If you go bushwalking, check your body carefully. **Ticks** are common, especially in eastern Australia, and can cause severe itching and fever. If you find one on you, dab it with methylated spirits or another noxious chemical. Wait awhile and pull it out gently with tweezers, taking care not to leave the head behind.

Fish to avoid are **stingrays** (remember poor old Steve Irwin and his tragic death due to a stingray barb through the heart; see "Television," below), as well as **porcupine fish, stonefish, lionfish,** and **puffer fish.** Never touch an **octopus** if it has blue rings on it, or a **cone shell,** and be wary of the painful and sometimes deadly tentacles of the **box jellyfish** along the northern Queensland coast in summer. This jellyfish is responsible for more deaths in Australia than snakes, sharks, and saltwater crocodiles.

Closely related to the box jellyfish is the **Irukandji,** which also inhabits northern Australian waters. This deadly jellyfish is only 2.5 centimeters (1 in.) in diameter, which makes it very hard to spot in the water.

If you brush past a jellyfish, or think you have, pour vinegar over the affected site immediately—authorities leave bottles of vinegar on beaches for this purpose. Vinegar deactivates the stinging cells that haven't already affected you, but doesn't affect the ones that already have. If you are in the tropics and you believe you may have been stung by a box jellyfish or an Irukandji, seek medical attention immediately.

In Sydney, you might come across **"stingers,"** also called "blue bottles." These long-tentacled blue jellyfish can inflict a nasty stinging burn that can last for hours. Sometimes you'll see warning signs on patrolled beaches. The best remedy if you are severely stung is to wash the affected area with fresh water and have a very hot bath or shower (preferably with someone else, just for the sympathy).

Threats to the Landscape

Australia is suffering from climate change, water shortages, and serious threats to wildlife and ecosystems. Australia is one of the highest per capita polluters in the world, thanks largely to its reliance on mining and coal-fired power generation. Much of the country has been suffering from extreme drought for around 14 years. Most of the major cities are on water restrictions, farmers are doing it tough, grand schemes to pipe water from areas that have some to areas that don't are being considered, and there are desalination plants popping up in some of our major cities.

Meanwhile, the Great Barrier Reef is being damaged by coral bleaching, which occurs when water temperatures rise. Corals can recover, but if the heat persists, or if bleaching happens too frequently, they can die. Nutrient-rich sediment washed out to sea from farmland doesn't help matters much, as hard-hit corals become colonized by nutrient-loving algae. The runoff can also contain pesticides and herbicides, which damage the reef further and make it more vulnerable to the introduced crown-of-thorns starfish, which likes snacking on coral.

Elsewhere, mass-clearing of land for farming purposes continues largely unabated, particularly in Queensland. And, in Tasmania, wildlife and native forests are suffering from clear-felling of trees and the use of noxious chemicals—including napalm—aimed at killing "undesirable" species that might eat young saplings in forestry plantations. Tasmania's "old growth" forests—or original forests—are still being destroyed, and the environment is also under threat from a giant proposed paper mill.

The Introduction of the Species

Among the most destructive introduced animals to Australia are the **European rabbit**, the **European red fox**, and the **domestic cat**. Several other introduced animals are also causing major problems, including the **cane toad**, which was introduced into Australia in an attempt to control beetles in sugarcane plantations. The toads turned out to prefer to eat everything else but, and their prolific breeding capacity meant they soon began to swarm across the country in the millions. These animals are huge, measuring up to 24 centimeters (9.5 in.) and weighing up to 1.8 kilograms (4 lbs.). They also have poisonous glands in their skin, which means that anything that eats one will most likely die. There's enough poison in one toad to kill a large dog, so heaven help a lizard or a bird that fancies a meal of one.

As for Australia's native animals and birds—well, history hasn't been too kind to them. At least 23 species of birds, 4 frog species, and 27 mammal species have become extinct since European settlement in Australia. Habitat destruction and introduced species have been the main causes of extinctions.

Threatened with extinction today are 19 species of fish, 15 species of frogs, 14 species of reptiles, 46 species of birds, 36 species of mammals, and 513 species of plants. Many more are classified as vulnerable.

See p. 61 for more information on responsible and sustainable tourism, and for advice on minimizing your impact on the Australian landscape.

AUSTRALIA IN POPULAR CULTURE

Movies

Australia has produced its fair share of movies good and bad. Some of the better ones are listed here.

- ***Walkabout*** (1971): The hauntingly beautiful and disturbing movie set in the Australian desert stars Jenny Agutter and the Aboriginal actor David Gulpilul. A white girl and her brother get hopelessly lost and survive with help from a doomed Aboriginal hero.
- ***Picnic at Hanging Rock*** (1974): This Peter Weir movie is about a group of schoolgirls and a teacher who go missing at an eerie rock formation north of Melbourne. It's set at the beginning of the 20th century, when bonnets and teapots were the norm.
- ***Mad Max*** (1979): Mel Gibson fights to the death in the Outback, which presents the ideal setting for a post-apocalyptic world. The movie was so popular that it spawned two sequels: *The Road Warrior* (1981) and *Mad Max: Beyond Thunderdome* (1985).
- ***Gallipoli*** (1981): Peter Weir's brilliant movie tries to capture the reality of the World War I military disaster that saw Australian and New Zealand troops fighting against overwhelming odds on the Turkish coastline.
- ***The Man from Snowy River*** (1982): Kirk Douglas, Tom Burlinson, and Sigrid Thornton star in this startling Australian movie that showcases the mountainous wilderness of Australia, where wild horses roam.
- ***Crocodile Dundee*** (1986): Paul Hogan shot to worldwide fame as a "typical" crocodile-wrestling Outback hero. He wears the same hat and a few more wrinkles in *Crocodile Dundee II* (1988) and *Crocodile Dundee in L.A.* (2001).
- ***Shine*** (1991): This portrayal of the real-life classical pianist David Helfgott, who rose to international prominence in the 1950s and 1960s before having a nervous breakdown, is remarkable. Oscar-winner Geoffrey Rush gives a powerful performance as the adult Helfgott; Sir John Gielgud plays Helfgott's teacher.
- ***Romperstomper*** (1992): If you like Russell Crowe, you might prefer not to see him as a neo-Nazi skinhead attempting to fight Vietnamese immigrants in Melbourne. That said, despite the unsettling themes, the violence, and the baldness, it's a well-crafted movie with a good story line.

- ***Strictly Ballroom*** (1992): A boy, played by Paul Mercurio, becomes a champion ballroom dancer in this whimsical, playful movie with, thankfully, not too much dancing.
- ***Bad Boy Bubby*** (1993): This low-budget cult movie was filmed in and around Adelaide. It's about the adventures of "Bubby" (Nicholas Hope), a 35-year-old man encountering the outside world for the first time after suffocating his cat and both parents by wrapping them up in plastic wrap.
- ***Muriel's Wedding*** (1994): This classic Australian comedy tells the tale of Muriel Heslop (Toni Collette), a young woman who dreams of getting married and moving far away from her boring life in Porpoise Spit. Fabulous characters, great catchphrases, and Abba music abound.
- ***The Adventures of Priscilla, Queen of the Desert*** (1994): A transsexual takes to traveling through the desert in a big pink bus with two drag queens. They sing Abba classics and dress the part, kind of. Where else but Australia . . .
- ***Babe*** (1995): A story about a talking pig that learns to round up sheep. Filmed in New South Wales, it was a surprise hit and was nominated for six Academy Awards, including Best Picture, Director, and Screenplay. It won an Oscar for its visual effects.
- ***The Dish*** (2000): This comedy about Australia's role in the *Apollo 11* mission in 1969 was set around a group of characters operating the Parkes/Canberra radio telescope.
- ***Finding Nemo*** (2003): Well, it's not exactly Australian, but the little clown fish does swim through Sydney Harbour.
- ***Australia*** (2008): An English aristocrat in the 1930s, played by Nicole Kidman, arrives in northern Australia. After an epic journey across the country with a rough-hewn cattle drover played by Hugh Jackman, she is caught in the bombing of Darwin during World War II.
- ***Samson and Delilah*** (2009): This movie depicts two indigenous Australian 14 year olds living in a remote Aboriginal community who steal a car and escape their difficult lives by heading off to Alice Springs.

Television

Apart from *Skippy the Bush Kangaroo* and a few long-running soap operas, such as *Neighbours,* Australia basks largely in worldwide television anonymity. The one major exception was Steve Irwin's series *The Crocodile Hunter,* with its "Crikey" catchphrase.

With his colorful personality, broad Aussie accent, and khaki shirt and shorts, Steve Irwin—the "crocodile hunter"—shot to worldwide fame with his television show of the same name. Irwin was born in Melbourne in 1962 and moved north with his family to Queensland in 1970, where his parents opened the Queensland Reptile and Fauna Park near Beerwah on the Sunshine Coast.

The park was renamed Australia Zoo in 1992, a year after Irwin met American Terri Raines. The pair was soon married and took off on a honeymoon, which involved filming Irwin trapping crocodiles. The footage became the first episode of *The Crocodile Hunter.*

On September 4, 2006, Irwin was killed while snorkeling on the Great Barrier Reef off the coast of Port Douglas in Queensland. He had succumbed to a stingray spine to the heart while filming clips for a show.

Music

Aboriginal music has been around for tens of thousands of years, well before Kylie Minogue. The **didgeridoo,** made from a hollowed-out tree limb, is perhaps the oldest musical instrument in the world, if you don't count banging a couple of rocks or sticks together. Listen carefully and you might hear animal sounds, including the flapping of wings and the thumping of feet on the ground. You might hear the sounds of wind, or of thunder, or trees creaking, or water running. It just goes to show how connected the Aboriginal people were, and still are in many cases, to the landscape they lived in.

As far as Australian rock 'n' roll goes, you might know a few of the following names. The big star in the '50s was Johnny O'Keefe, but he soon gave way to the likes of the Eastbeats. Running into the 1970s, we find the Bee Gees, AC/DC, Sherbet, John-Paul Young, and the Little River Band. Others that made a name for themselves included the solo stars Helen Reddy, Olivia Newton-John, and Peter Allen. The 1980s saw Men at Work, Crowded House, The Go-Betweens, Hunters and Collectors, Kylie Minogue, and Midnight Oil. INXS took us into the 1990s, which Kylie managed to stitch up, too. Jet and the Vines were both Australian rock groups that saw considerable international success in the 21st century, along with, you guessed it, Kylie Minogue.

Australia's Literature

Australian literature has come a long way since the days when the bush poets A. B. "Banjo" Paterson and Henry Lawson penned their odes to a way of life now largely lost. The best known of these is Paterson's epic *The Man from Snowy River,* which first hit the bestseller list in 1895 and was made into a film. But the literary scene has always been lively, and Australia has a wealth of classics, many of them with the Outback at their heart.

Miles Franklin wrote *My Brilliant Career* (2001), the story of a young woman faced with the dilemma of choosing between marriage and a career, in 1901 (made into a film starring Judy Davis); Colleen McCullough's *Thorn Birds* (1996) is a romantic epic about forbidden love between a Catholic priest and a young woman (made into a famous television miniseries); *We of the Never Never* (1984), by Mrs. Aeneas Gunn, tells the story of a young woman who leaves the comfort of her Melbourne home to live on a cattle station in the Northern Territory; and *Walkabout* (1984), by James V. Marshall, explores the relationship between an Aborigine and two lost children in the bush. It was later made into a powerful film by Peter Weir.

If you can find it, *The Long Farewell* (1983), by Don Charlwood, presents first-hand diary accounts of long journeys from Europe to Australia in the last century. A good historical account of the early days is Geoffrey Blainey's *The Tyranny of Distance,* first published in 1966. Robert Hughes's *The Fatal Shore: The Epic of Australia's Founding* (1988) is a best-selling nonfiction study of the country's early days (and later adapted into the award-winning play *Our Country's Good*).

For a contemporary, if somewhat dark, take on the settlement and development of Sydney, delve into John Birmingham's *Leviathan* (1999). From an Aboriginal perspective, *Follow the Rabbit-Proof Fence* (1997), by Doris Pilkington, tells the true story of three young girls from the "stolen generation," who ran away from a mission school to return to their families. (A movie version was released in 2002.)

Modern novelists include David Malouf, Elizabeth Jolley, Helen Garner, Sue Woolfe, and Peter Carey, whose *True History of the Kelly Gang* (2001), a fictionalized autobiography of the outlaw Ned Kelly, won the Booker Prize in 2001. West Australian Tim Winton evokes his part of the continent in stunning prose; his latest novel, *Dirt Music* (2002), is no exception.

Outsiders who have tackled Australia include Jan Morris and Bill Bryson. Morris's *Sydney* was published in 1992, and Bryson's *In a Sunburned Country* (2001), while not always a favorite with Australians, may appeal to American readers.

EATING & DRINKING IN AUSTRALIA

It took a long time for the average Aussie to realize that there is more to food than English-style sausage and mashed potatoes, "meat and three veg," and a Sunday roast. Spaghetti was something foreigners ate, and zucchini and eggplant were considered exotic. Then came mass immigration and all sorts of food that people only read about in *National Geographic*.

The first big wave of Italian immigrants in the 1950s caused a national scandal. The great Aussie dream was to have a quarter-acre block of land with a hills hoist (a circular revolving clothesline) in the backyard. When Italians started hanging freshly made pasta out to dry on this Aussie icon, it caused uproar, and some clamored for the new arrivals to be shipped back. As Australia matured, southern European cuisine became increasingly popular until olive oil was sizzling in frying pans the way only lard had previously done.

In the 1980s, waves of Asian immigrants hit Australia's shores. Suddenly, everyone was cooking with woks. These days, a fusion of spices from the east and ingredients and styles from the Mediterranean make up what's become known as Modern Australian cuisine.

Still, some of the old ways remain. Everyone knows that Aussies like a barbecue, usually referred to as a "barbie." Most Aussies aren't really that adventurous when it comes to throwing things on the hot plate and are usually content with some cheap sausages and a steak washed down by beer.

The typical Aussie worker also likes a hot pie, usually about as large as your hand and filled with something that resembles meat. They tend to squirt ketchup on top of it.

Seafood is popular, as you would expect, and a typical Christmas Day meal will usually include prawns and/or fish.

Aussies eat out of course, but away from the main cities and some of the larger county towns you'll be hard- pressed to find much more than a Chinese restaurant, usually of dubious quality. Actually, I say that, but occasionally you do come across a gem or two specializing in regional produce. Popular restaurants in the big cities include those specializing in Thai, Vietnamese, Italian, Spanish, Middle Eastern, and Indian.

Melbournites are proud of their coffee culture. American readers should note that the bottomless cup of coffee is rare. Many restaurants allow you to bring your own wine (referred to simply as BYO), but some may charge a corkage fee of a few dollars (even when there's a screw-cap and no cork).

While you might see kangaroo, crocodile, and emu on the odd menu, Australians tend not to indulge in their local wildlife, preferring to stick to introduced species instead.

Beer & Wine

If you order a beer in a pub or bar, you should be aware that the standard glass size differs from state to state. Thus, in Sydney you can order a schooner or a smaller midi. In trendy places you might be offered an English pint or a half-pint. In Melbourne and Brisbane a midi is called a pot, while in Darwin it's called a handle, and in Hobart a ten. You can get smaller glasses, too, though thankfully they're becoming rare. These could either be called a pony, a seven, a butcher, a six, or a bobbie, depending on which city you're in. If in doubt, just mime a big one or a small one, and they'll get what you mean.

As far as wine goes, Australia has come a long way since the first grape vines arrived on the First Fleet in 1788. These days, more than 550 major companies and small winemakers produce wine commercially in Australia. There are dozens of recognized wine-growing regions, but the most well known include the Hunter Valley in New South Wales; the Barossa Valley, McClaren Vale, Coonawarra, Adelaide Hills, and the Clare Valley in South Australia; the Yarra Valley in Victoria; and Margaret River in Western Australia.

Aboriginal Foods

In the past couple of decades, many Australian chefs have woken to the variety and tastes of "bush tucker," as native Aussie food is tagged. Now it's all the rage in the most fashionable restaurants, where wattle seed, lemon myrtle, and other native tastes have a place in one or two dishes on the menu. Below is a list of some of those foods you may encounter.

- **Bunya nut:** Crunchy nut of the bunya pine, about the size of a macadamia.
- **Bush tomato:** Dry, small, darkish fruit; more like a raisin in look and taste.
- **Native cranberry:** Small berry that tastes a bit like an apple.
- **Illawarra plum:** Dark berry with strong, rich, tangy taste.
- **Kangaroo:** A strong meat with a gamey flavor. Tender when correctly prepared, tough when not. Excellent smoked.
- **Lemon aspen:** Citrusy, light-yellow fruit with a sharp tangy flavor.
- **Lemon myrtle:** Gum leaves with a fresh lemon tang; often used to flavor white meat.
- **Lillipilli:** Delicious juicy, sweet pink berry.
- **Quandong:** A tart, tangy native peach.
- **Rosella:** Spiky petals of a red flower with a rich berry flavor.
- **Wattle seed:** Roasted ground acacia seeds that taste a little like bitter coffee. Sometimes used in cakes.
- **Wild lime:** Smaller and sourer than regular lime.

One ingredient you will not see on menus is **witchetty grubs;** most people are too squeamish to eat these fat, juicy slimy white creatures. They live in the soil or in dead tree trunks and are a common source of protein for some Aborigines. You eat them alive, not cooked. If you are offered one in the Outback, you can either freak out (as most locals would do)—or enjoy its pleasantly nutty taste as a reward for your bravery.

PLANNING YOUR TRIP TO AUSTRALIA

3

Distance plays a big part in planning any trip to Australia. First, it's a very long way from almost anywhere (except New Zealand). And, once you arrive, the distances between the places you most want to see are likely to be huge—this is a vast continent, as big as western Europe and about the same size as the 48 contiguous U.S. states. Melbourne and Brisbane are a long day's drive from Sydney, and driving from Sydney to Perth takes the better part of a week.

About 90% of Australia's 21 million people huddle in cities around the coast covering a mere 2.6% of this vast continent. The reason is simple: Much of Australia is harsh Outback country, characterized by savanna land, spectacular rocky outcrops, shifting deserts, and dry salt lakes. This is spectacular and unforgettable country, but the soil is poor and the rainfall scarce, and some rivers don't even make it to the ocean. The roads that traverse the interior are sometimes barely distinguishable, and most people choose air travel or stick to the coastal fringe.

In contrast, on the coast—particularly in the east, where most people live—nature's bounty has almost overdone it with splendor and diversity. Here, Australia is blessed with one of the greatest natural attractions in the world: the Great Barrier Reef. There are rainforests in Queensland, alpine scenery in Tasmania, wildflowers in Western Australia, rolling wine country in South Australia, a great coastal drive in Victoria, bird-filled wetlands in the Northern Territory, and countless sand beaches more or less everywhere.

Australia consists of six states—New South Wales (NSW), Queensland (QLD), Victoria (VIC), South Australia (SA), Western Australia (WA), and Tasmania (TAS)—and two internal territories, the Australian Capital Territory (ACT) and the Northern Territory (NT). The national capital is Canberra, in the ACT. See the map on p. 687 or the map on the inside back cover to visualize the regions.

For additional help in planning your trip and for more on-the-ground resources in Australia, please turn to "Fast Facts," on p. 735.

WHEN TO GO

When it is winter in the Northern Hemisphere, Australia is basking in the Southern Hemisphere's summer, and vice versa. Midwinter in Australia is July and August, and the hottest months are November through March. Remember, unlike in the northern hemisphere, the farther south you go in Australia, the colder it gets.

The Travel Seasons

Airfares to Australia are lowest from mid-April to late August—the best time to visit the Red Centre, the Top End, and the Great Barrier Reef.

HIGH SEASON The peak travel season in the most popular parts of Australia is the Aussie winter. In much of the country—Queensland from around Townsville and northward, all of the Top End and the Red Centre, and the northern half of Western Australia—the most pleasant time to travel is April through September, when daytime temperatures are 66°F to 88°F (19°C–31°C) and it rarely rains. June, July, and August are the busiest months in these parts; you'll need to book accommodations and tours well in advance, and you will pay higher rates then, too.

On the other hand, Australia's summer is a nice time to visit the southern states—New South Wales, Victoria, South Australia, Western Australia from Perth to the south, and Tasmania. Even in winter, temperatures rarely dip below freezing, and snow falls only in parts of Tasmania, in the ski fields of Victoria, and in the Snowy Mountains of southern New South Wales.

Steer Clear of the Vacation Rush

Try to avoid Australia from Boxing Day (Dec 26) to the end of January, when Aussies take their summer vacations. In popular seaside holiday spots, hotel rooms and airline seats get scarce as hen's teeth, and it's a rare airline or hotel that will discount full rates by even a dollar.

Generally, the best months to visit Australia are September and October, when it's often still warm enough to hit the beach in the southern states, it's cool enough to tour Uluru, the humidity and rains have not come to Cairns and the Top End (although it will be very hot by Oct), and the wildflowers are in full bloom in Western Australia.

LOW SEASON October through March (summer) is just too hot, too humid, or too wet—or all three—to tour the Red Centre, the Top End, and anywhere in Western Australia except Perth and the southwest. The Top End, the Kimberley, and North Queensland, including Cairns, suffer an intensely hot, humid Wet season from November or December through March or April. In the Top End and Kimberley, this is preceded by an even stickier "buildup" in October and November. Some attractions and tour companies close, floodwaters render others off-limits, and hotels drop their rates, often dramatically. So if you decide to travel in these areas at this time—and lots of people do—be prepared to take the heat, the inconvenience of floods, and, in tropical coastal areas, the slight chance of encountering cyclones.

Australia Calendar of Events

For an exhaustive list of events beyond those listed here, check http://events.frommers.com, where you'll find a searchable, up-to-the-minute roster of what's happening in cities all over the world.

JANUARY

Sydney Festival: Highlights of Sydney's visual and performing arts festival are free jazz or classical music concerts held outdoors on 2 Saturday nights near the Royal Botanic Gardens. (Take a picnic and arrive by 4pm to get a spot on the grass.) The festival involves about 80 events featuring 500 artists. Call ✆ **02/8248 6500** or go to **www.sydneyfestival.org.au**. Three weeks from early January.

Hyundai Hopman Cup, Perth: Tennis greats from the world's nine top tennis nations battle it out in a 7-day mixed-doubles competition. For tickets, contact Ticketek (✆ **13 28 49** in Australia; www.ticketek.com.au), or check **www.hopmancup.com.au**. Early January.

Tamworth Country Music Festival, Tamworth (459km/285 miles northwest of Sydney), New South Wales: It may look like an akubra hat convention, but this gathering of rural folk and city folk who would like to be rural folk is Australia's biggest country music festival. Tourism Tamworth (✆ **02/6767 5300;** www.tcmf.com.au) takes bookings. January 14 to January 23.

Australia Day: Australia's answer to the Fourth of July marks the landing of the First Fleet of convicts at Sydney Cove in 1788. Every town puts on some kind of celebration; in Sydney, there are ferry races and tall ships on the harbor, food and wine stalls in Hyde Park, open days at museums and other attractions, and fireworks in the evening. January 26.

FEBRUARY

Sydney Gay & Lesbian Mardi Gras: A month of events, culminating in a spectacular parade of costumed dancers and decorated floats, watched by several hundred thousand onlookers, followed by a giant warehouse party (by invitation only). Contact Sydney Gay & Lesbian Mardi Gras (✆ **02/9383 0900;** www.mardigras.org.au).

Perth International Arts Festival: This annual 3-week-long festival covers everything from theater and music to film, visual arts, street arts, literature, and free community events, and attracts around 300,000 patrons. It also incorporates the **Perth Writers Festival.** For more details, contact the festival organizers (✆ **08/6488 2000;** www.perthfestival.com.au).

MARCH

Australian Formula One Grand Prix, Melbourne: The first Grand Prix of the year, on the international FIA Formula 1 World Championship circuit, is battled out on one of its fastest circuits, in Melbourne. For tickets, contact Ticketek (✆ **13 19 31** in Australia), or order online at **www.grandprix.com.au**. Four days in the first or second week of March.

Australian Surf Life Saving Championships, Kurrawa Beach, Gold Coast: Around 8,000 bronzed Aussie and international men and women swim, ski paddle, sprint relay, pilot rescue boats, parade past admiring crowds, and resuscitate "drowning" swimmers in front of about 10,000 spectators. Contact Surf Life Saving Australia (✆ **02/9300 4000;** www.slsa.com.au). Third week of March.

APRIL

Anzac Day, nationwide: April 25 is Australia's national day of mourning for servicemen and women who have died in wars and conflict. Commemorative services are held even in the smallest towns, some at dawn and some later, with major cities holding street parades for returned servicemen and women. Huge crowds turn out. Details of all services in Australia can be found at **www.dva.gov.au/anzac**.

JUNE

Sydney Film Festival: World and Australian premieres of Aussie and international movies take place in the State Theatre and other venues. Contact the Sydney Film Festival (✆ **02/9318 0999;** www.sydneyfilmfestival.org). Two weeks from first or second Friday in June.

AUGUST

***Sun-Herald* City to Surf,** Sydney: Fifty thousand Sydneysiders pound the pavement (or walk or wheelchair it) in this 14km (8¾-mile) "fun run" from the city to Bondi Beach. It's been going on for the past 35 years. For entry details, visit **http://city2surf.sunherald.com.au** (from May onward), or call ✆ **1800/555 514** in Australia. If slots are available, you can enter the day of the race. The fee is A$30. Second Sunday in August.

Henley-on-Todd Regatta, Alice Springs: Sounds sophisticated, doesn't it? It's actually a harum-scarum race down the dry bed of the Todd River in homemade "boats," made from anything you care to name—an old four-wheel-drive chassis, say, or beer cans lashed together. The only rule is the vessel has to look *vaguely* like a boat. The 50th annual regatta will be run this year. Contact the organizers at ✆ **0418/897 027** (mobile phone) or **www.henleyontodd.com.au**. Usually held late August.

SEPTEMBER

Floriade, Canberra: A million tulips, daffodils, hyacinths, and other blooms carpet the banks of Canberra's Lake Burley Griffin in stunning themed flower-bed designs at this celebration, which features performing arts and other entertainment. Contact Canberra & Region Visitors Centre (✆ **1300/554 114** in Australia; www.visitcanberra.com.au). For more detail on Floriade, check out the website **www.floriadeaustralia.com**. Four weeks from mid September.

OCTOBER

SuperGP, Surfers Paradise, Queensland: The world's best racing car drivers compete on a street circuit around Surfers Paradise on the glitzy Gold Coast as part of the A1GP World Cup of Motorsport Powered by Ferrari, alongside Australia's V8 Supercar Championship Series. Contact Ticketek (✆ **1300/303 103** in Australia; www.ticketek.com), or check the event's website (www.supergp.com). Four days in mid- or late October.

NOVEMBER

Melbourne Cup, Flemington: They say the entire nation stops to watch this horse race. That's about right. If you're not actually at the A$3.5-million race, you're glued to the TV—or, well, you're probably not an Australian. Women wear hats to the office, files on desks all over the country make way for a late chicken and champagne lunch, and don't even think about flagging a cab at the 3pm race time. For tickets, contact Ticketmaster (✆ **1300/136 122** in Australia; www.ticketmaster.com.au); for information, visit **www.vrc.net.au**. First Tuesday in November.

DECEMBER

Sydney-to-Hobart Yacht Race: Find a clifftop spot near the Heads to watch the glorious show of spinnakers, as 100 or so yachts leave Sydney Harbour for this grueling world-class event. The organizer is the Sydney-based Cruising Yacht Club of Australia (✆ **02/8292 7800;** www.cyca.com.au). Starts December 26.

New Year's Eve, Sydney: Watching the Sydney Harbour Bridge light up with fireworks is a treat. The main show is at 9pm, not midnight, so young kids don't miss out. Pack a picnic and snag a Harbourside spot by 4pm, or even earlier at the best vantage point—Mrs. Macquarie's Chair in the Royal Botanic Gardens. December 31.

ENTRY REQUIREMENTS

Passports

It is advised to always have at least one or two consecutive blank pages in your passport to allow space for visas and stamps that need to appear together. It is also important to note when your passport expires. Australia, like many countries, requires your passport to have at least 6 months left before its expiration when you apply for a visa.

Visas

Along with a current passport valid for the duration of your stay, the Australian government requires a visa from visitors of every nation, except New Zealand, to be issued before you arrive. If you are a short-term visitor or business traveler, the process is easy and can be done in a few minutes on the Internet using the Australian government's **Electronic Travel Authority (ETA).** This is an electronic visa that takes the place of a stamp in your passport.

Tourists should apply for a **Visitor ETA.** The visa itself is free—though there is a service charge for getting it via the Internet—and permits unlimited visits to Australia of up to 3 months each, within a 1-year period. Tourists may not work in Australia, so if you are visiting for business, you have two choices: Apply for a **Short Validity Business ETA,** which covers a single visit of 3 months within a 1-year period, or pay A$70 to apply for a **Long Validity Business visa,** which entitles you to as many 3-month stays in Australia as you like, for the life of your passport; but this cannot be done online. You can apply for an ETA yourself, or have your travel agent or airline do it when you book your plane ticket. (This service may incur an additional fee from the airline or travel agent.) To apply online, visit **www.eta.immi.gov.au**; the A$20 charge is payable by credit card (Amex, Diners Club, MasterCard, or Visa). European and U.K. passport holders should apply through **www.ecom.immi.gov.au**. Assuming you do not have a criminal conviction and are in good health, your ETA should be approved quickly. You can also apply for the visa at Australian embassies, high commissions, and consulates (see below for their locations). Children traveling on their parent's passport must have their own ETA.

If your travel agent or airline is not connected to the ETA system, you will need to apply for a visa the old-fashioned way—by taking or mailing your passport, a completed visa application form, and the appropriate payment to your nearest Australian embassy or consulate.

In the United States, Canada, the United Kingdom, Ireland, and many other countries, most agents and airlines are ETA-compatible. You will also need to go the old-fashioned route if you are someone other than a tourist or a business traveler—for example, a student studying in Australia; a businessperson staying longer than 3 months; a long-term resident; an athlete going for a competition; a member of the media on assignment; a performer; or a member of a social group or cultural exchange. If you fall into one of these categories, you will need to apply for a **Temporary Residence visa.** Non-ETA visa application fees for other kinds of travelers vary, from free to thousands of dollars. Contact the Australian embassy, consulate, or high commission to check the forms of payment they accept.

Apply for non-ETA visas at Australian embassies, consulates, and high commissions. In the **United States,** apply to the Australian Embassy, 1601 Massachusetts Ave. NW, Washington, D.C. 20036 (✆ **905/280-1437; www.usa.embassy.gov.au**).

In **Canada,** contact the Australian High Commission, Suite 710, 50 O'Connor St., Ottawa, ON K1P 6L2 (✆ **613/236-1437;** www.canada.embassy.gov.au).

In the **United Kingdom** and **Ireland,** contact the Australian High Commission, Australia House, The Strand, London WC2B 4LA (✆ **09065/508 900** for 24-hr. recorded information, or you can speak to an operator Mon–Fri 9am–4pm; www.uk.embassy.gov.au). There is counter service only from 9am to 11am Monday to Friday.

You should obtain an application form for a non-ETA visa by post or over the Internet at the **Australian Department of Immigration and Multicultural Affairs** website (www.immi.gov.au). This site also has a good explanation of the ETA system. Allow at least a month for processing of non-ETA visas.

U.S., Canadian, British, and Irish citizens ages 18 to 30 may qualify for a working holiday visa that allows them to stay and work in Australia for a year (with conditions).

Customs

WHAT YOU CAN BRING INTO AUSTRALIA

The duty-free allowance in Australia is A$900 or, for those under 18, A$450. Anyone over 18 can bring in up to 250 cigarettes or 250 grams of cigars or other tobacco products, 2.25 liters (41 fluid oz.) of alcohol, and "dutiable goods" to the value of A$900 or A$450 if you are under 18. "Dutiable goods" are luxury items such as perfume, watches, jewelry, furs, plus gifts of any kind. Keep this in mind if you intend to bring presents for family and friends in Australia; gifts given to you also count toward the dutiable limit. Personal goods that you're taking with you are usually exempt from duty, but if you are returning with valuable goods that you already own, file form B263. Customs officers do not collect duty—less than A$50—as long as you declared the goods in the first place.

A helpful brochure, available from Australian consulates or Customs offices, as well as online, is *Know Before You Go*. For more information, contact the **Customs Information and Support Centre** (✆ **1300/363 263** in Australia, or 02/6275 6666), or check out **www.customs.gov.au**.

You need not declare cash in any currency, and other currency instruments, such as traveler's checks, under a value of A$10,000.

Australia is a signatory to the **Convention on International Trade in Endangered Species** (CITES), which restricts or bans the import of products made from protected wildlife. Banned items include ivory, tortoise (marine turtle) shell, rhinoceros or tiger products, and sturgeon caviar. Bear this in mind if you stop in other countries en route to Australia, where souvenirs made from items like these may be sold. Australian authorities may seize these items.

Because Australia is an island, it is free of many agricultural and livestock diseases. To keep it that way, strict quarantine applies to importing plants, animals, and their products, including food. "Sniffer" dogs at airports detect these products (as well as drugs). Some items may be confiscated, and others may be held over for you to take with you when you leave the country. Amnesty trash bins are available before you reach the immigration counters in airport arrivals halls for items such as fruit.

Don't be alarmed if, just before landing, the flight attendants spray the aircraft cabin (with products approved by the World Health Organization) to kill potentially disease-bearing insects. For more information on what is and is not allowed, contact the nearest Australian embassy or consulate, or Australia's Department of Agriculture, Fisheries, and Forestry, which runs the **Australian Quarantine and Inspection Service** (✆ **02/6272 3933;** www.daff.gov.au/aqis). Its website has a list of restricted or banned foods, animal and plant products, and other items.

WHAT YOU CAN TAKE HOME FROM AUSTRALIA

For information on what you're allowed to bring home, contact one of the following agencies:

U.S. Citizens: U.S. Customs & Border Protection (CBP), 1300 Pennsylvania Ave., NW, Washington, DC 20229 (✆ **877/287-8667;** www.cbp.gov).

Canadian Citizens: Canada Border Services Agency, Ottawa, Ontario, K1A 0L8 (✆ **800/461-9999** in Canada, or 204/983-3500; www.cbsa-asfc.gc.ca).

U.K. Citizens: HM Customs & Excise, Crownhill Court, Tailyour Road, Plymouth, PL6 5BZ (✆ **0845/010-9000;** from outside the U.K., 020/8929-0152; www.hmce.gov.uk).

Australian Citizens: Australian Customs Service, Customs House, 5 Constitution Avenue, Canberra City, ACT 2601 (✆ **1300/363-263;** from outside Australia, 612/6275-6666; www.customs.gov.au).

New Zealand Citizens: New Zealand Customs, The Customhouse, 17–21 Whitmore St., Box 2218, Wellington, 6140 (✆ **04/473-6099** or 0800/428-786; www.customs.govt.nz).

Medical Requirements

You don't have to worry much about health issues on a trip to Australia. Hygiene standards are high, hospitals are modern, and doctors and dentists are well qualified. Because of the continent's size, you can sometimes be a long way from a hospital or a doctor, but help is never far away, thanks to the **Royal Flying Doctor Service.** However, standard medical travel insurance may be advisable (see p. 736). No vaccinations are needed to enter Australia unless you have been in a yellow fever danger zone—that is, South America or Africa—in the 6 days prior to your arrival.

GETTING THERE & GETTING AROUND

Getting to Australia

BY PLANE

Australia is a long, long haul from anywhere except New Zealand. Sydney is a nearly 15-hour nonstop flight from Los Angeles, longer if you come via Honolulu. From the East Coast of the U.S., add 5½ hours. If you're coming from the States via Auckland, add transit time in New Zealand plus another 3 hours for the Auckland–Sydney leg. If you are coming from the United Kingdom, brace yourself for a flight of 12 hours, more or less, from London to Asia; then possibly a long day in transit, because flights to Australia have a habit of arriving in Asia early in the morning and departing around midnight; and finally the 8- to 9-hour flight to Australia.

Sydney (SYD), Cairns (CNS), Melbourne (MEL), Brisbane (BNE), Adelaide (ADL), Darwin (DRW), and Perth (PER) are all international gateways. Sydney is the major entry point to Australia, but depending where you are coming from, you may also fly through another port first.

To find out which airlines travel to Australia, please see below.

BY BOAT

Sydney Harbour is Australia's main port for cruise ships and is the only port in Australia with two dedicated cruise-passenger terminals—the Overseas Passenger Terminal at Circular Quay and Wharf 8 Darling Harbour Passenger Terminal. Both are located in the heart of the city and close to major tourist attractions. Melbourne and Brisbane are also major ports, with Hobart, Darwin, and Adelaide on some itineraries.

Getting Around Australia

Possibly the biggest mistake tourists make Down Under (apart from getting horribly sunburned) is failing to comprehend the distances between popular locations. You won't be able to see Uluru from your Sydney hotel room window. It's 2,841km (1,761 miles) away. One of the urban legends that grew up around the 2000 Olympics was the tale of the tourist who asked where in Sydney Harbour he could catch the boat to the Great Barrier Reef. That's a mere 2,800km (1,736 miles) north. The best advice is to not try to cram too much into your trip.

Traveling overland may make sense in Europe or North America, but in Australia flying is often the best way between most points. People who go by train, bus, or car are often disappointed at Australia's flat vistas of desert, wheat fields, and gum trees—the same landscape can go on for days. A good compromise is to take to the air for long trips and save the land travel for short hops of a few hours. Try not to backtrack, which eats up valuable time and money.

BY PLANE

Australia is a big country with a small population to support its air routes, so airfares may be higher than you are used to paying. Australia's air network is not as well developed as that of North America or Europe, so don't assume there is a direct flight to your chosen destination, or that there is a flight every hour or even every day.

Most domestic air travel is operated by **Qantas** (✆ **800/227-4500** in the U.S. and Canada, 13 13 13 in Australia, 208/600 4300 in the U.K., 1/407 3278 in Ireland, 09/357 8900 in Auckland, 0800/808 767 in New Zealand; www.qantas.com.au), **Virgin Blue** (✆ **13 67 89** in Australia, or 07/3295 2296; www.virginblue.com.au), or Qantas-owned **Jetstar** (✆ **13 15 38** in Australia, or 03/8341 4901; 0800/800 995 in New Zealand; www.jetstar.com.au). **Regional Express** (✆ **13 17 13** in Australia; www.regionalexpress.com.au) serves regional New South Wales, South Australia, Victoria, and northern Tasmania.

Between them, Virgin Blue and Qantas and its subsidiaries, QantasLink and Jetstar, service every capital city, as well as most major regional towns on the east coast, Tasmania, and such places as Broome in Western Australia. Melbourne has two airports: the main international and domestic terminals at Tullamarine, and Avalon Airport, about 50km (31 miles) from the city, which is used by some Jetstar flights. Make sure you check which one your flight leaves from before you book. Competition is hot, so it's likely that all airlines will have added to their route networks by the time you read this.

Low-cost carrier **Tiger Airways** (© **03/9335 3033;** www.tigerairways.com) continues to challenge Virgin Blue and Jetstar. It has expanded its network out of Melbourne and added a second hub out of Adelaide. Tiger now flies the all-important route between Melbourne and Sydney, as well as linking Melbourne to Perth, Alice Springs, Canberra, Adelaide, Launceston, and Hobart in Tasmania; and the Queensland ports of Brisbane, Mackay, Rockhampton, Sunshine Coast, and Gold Coast. It also flies between Adelaide and Perth, Alice Springs, Hobart, Canberra, and the Gold Coast.

Note: All flights in Australia are nonsmoking.

FARES FOR INTERNATIONAL TRAVELERS Qantas typically offers international travelers a discount of around 30% off the full fares that Australians pay for domestic flights bought within Australia. To qualify, quote your passport number and international ticket number when reserving. Don't assume the fare for international travelers is the best deal, though—the latest deal in the market that day (or even better, perhaps, a package deal with accommodations thrown in) may be cheaper still.

AIR PASSES If you are visiting from the U.S. or Canada and plan on whipping around to more than one city, purchasing a Qantas **Aussie AirPass** is much cheaper than buying regular fares. The pass is good for travel on certain flights between Los Angeles, San Francisco, Honolulu, or Vancouver and Sydney, Melbourne, or Brisbane, and also gives you up to another three destinations within Australia (or more for an extra A$110 each).

The AirPass price starts from US$999, depending on the season, and is for economy-class travel only. Prices also vary according to which "zone" you are traveling to. Zone 1 covers travel to Sydney, Canberra, Melbourne, Brisbane, Adelaide, Hobart, and Launceston. Zone 2, which costs an extra A$100, will take you to Cairns, Townsville, Hamilton Island, the Gold Coast, the Sunshine Coast, and Newcastle in New South Wales. Zone 3, costing an extra A$200, will get you as far as Mackay, Rockhampton, Gladstone, Hervey Bay, Ballina, Coffs Harbour, Port Macquarie, Lord Howe Island, Alice Springs, and Ayers Rock. Zone 4, for an extra A$300, covers travel to more remote places such as Perth, Karratha, Kalgoorlie and Broome in Western Australia, Darwin and Gove in the Top End, and exclusive Hayman Island in Queensland's Whitsundays.

If you are starting your trip in the U.S. from somewhere other than Los Angeles, San Francisco, or Honolulu, special fares are available—but only from San Diego; Seattle; Portland; Las Vegas; Dallas; Denver; St. Louis; Chicago; New York (JFK and Newark); Washington, D.C.; Miami; Orlando; and Boston.

From Canada, special fares are available from Calgary, Edmonton, Ottawa, Montreal, Toronto, and Halifax. Check with Qantas (© **800/227 4500;** www.qantas.com) for details.

The AirPass is also only available on certain flights, but you can pay a surcharge to travel on other flights and still get an AirPass.

The Aussie AirPass has a minimum stay of 7 days and a maximum of 21 days from your first trans-Atlantic flight. The deals change regularly, so it pays to check the website for your travel dates.

You must buy the pass before you arrive in Australia. Residents of Europe, New Zealand, and Australia cannot purchase this pass.

AERIAL TOURS The great thing about aerial touring is that it allows you to whiz around the vast Australian continent to see many highlights, and you get to skip all the featureless countryside that typically separates Australia's most fascinating bits. Much of the landscape (such as the weird Bungle Bungles formations in the Kimberley) is best seen from the air, anyhow. **Aircruising Australia ★★** (✆ **1800/252 053** in Australia, or 02/9693 2233; 0800/445 700 in New Zealand; www.aircruising.com.au) operates upscale aerial tours of 9 to 12 days in a private aircraft, usually a 38-passenger Dash 8, which is nimble enough to "flight-see" as low as 300m (1,000 ft.). One factor you may regard as a plus is that the company mainly markets within Australia, so your fellow passengers are likely to be Aussies. Perhaps because the tours are expensive for Australians, most passengers are over 55. Those who have taken these tours recommend them, saying they are extremely well organized, with lots of time for the land-based sightseeing, some free time, and a maximum 2 hours in the air most days. Accommodations are usually the best available, and the itineraries include "fun extras." Fares in 2010 ranged from A$8,295 to A$12,845 per person sharing a double or twin room.

You may not think of Antarctica as part of your Australian vacation, but **Antarctica Sightseeing Flights** (✆ **1800/633 449** in Australia, or 03/8814 5701; www.antarcticaflights.com.au) offers once-in-a-lifetime visits to the icy continent. The 12-hour journey offers spectacular viewing over the frozen beauty of Antarctica—a truly memorable experience that comes at a high price for a day trip. Flights are seasonal (Nov–Feb) and include a New Year's Eve flight. Most leave from Sydney or Melbourne, with connections from Brisbane, Canberra, and Adelaide. The tours have been running since 1994, operated by Croydon Travel with chartered Qantas jumbo jets carrying 350 passengers. You reach the Antarctic coastline after about 4 hours flying and spend the next 4 hours above some of the world's most pristine and spectacular territory. Below are magnificent glaciers, mountain ranges, soaring coastal cliffs, and ice floes. There's no problem viewing all this, despite the fact that you might not have a window seat—everyone moves around and takes turns, and a rotating seating system works well. In 2010, fares ranged from A$999 in an economy center seat to A$7,299 in first class—but this is unlike any other flight you've been on.

BY CAR

Australia's roads sometimes leave a bit to be desired. The taxes of 21 million people get spread pretty thin when it comes to maintaining roads across a continent. Most highways are two-lane affairs with the occasional rut and pothole, often no outside line markings, and sometimes no shoulders to speak of.

When you are poring over the map of Australia, remember that what looks like a road may be an unsealed (unpaved) track suitable for four-wheel-drive vehicles only. Many roads in the Top End are passable only in the Dry season (about Apr–Nov). If you plan long-distance driving, get a road map (see "Maps" below for sources) that marks paved and unpaved roads.

You cannot drive across the middle of the country (except along the north–south Stuart Hwy. linking Adelaide and Darwin) because most of it is desert. In most places, you must travel around the edge on Highway 1. The map inside the back cover of this book marks the major highways.

You can use your current driver's license or an international driver's permit in every state of Australia. By law, you must carry your license with you when driving. The minimum driving age is 16 or 17, depending on which state you visit, but some car-rental companies require you to be 21, or sometimes 26, if you want to rent a four-wheel-drive vehicle.

Car Rentals

Think twice about renting a car in tourist hot spots such as Cairns. In these areas most tour operators pick you up and drop you back at your hotel door, so having a car may not be worth the expense.

The "big four" car-rental companies–Avis, Budget, Hertz, and Thrifty—all have networks across Australia. Other major car rental companies are Europcar, which has the third largest fleet in Australia, and Red Spot Car Rentals, which has depots in Sydney, Melbourne, Brisbane, Perth, Cairns, the Gold Coast, Hobart, and Launceston.

Sample Driving Distances & Times

ROUTE	DISTANCE	APPROX. DRIVING TIME
Cairns–Sydney	2,495km (1,547 miles)	29 hr. (allow 4–5 days)
Sydney–Melbourne	873km (541 miles)	15 hr. (allow 1–2 days)
Sydney–Perth	4,131km (2,561 miles)	51 hr. (allow 6–7 days)
Adelaide–Darwin	3,024km (1,875 miles)	31 hr. (allow 4–6 days)
Perth–Darwin	4,163km (2,581 miles)	49 hr. (allow 6–8 days)

A small sedan for zipping around a city or touring a wine region will cost about A$45 to A$80 a day. A feistier vehicle with enough grunt to get you from state to state will cost around A$70 to A$100 a day. Rentals of a week or longer usually reduce the price by A$5 a day or so.

A regular car will get you to most places in this book, but because the country has many unpaved roads, it can make sense to rent a four-wheel-drive vehicle. All the major car-rental companies rent them. They are more expensive than a regular car, but you can get them for as little as A$75 per day if you shop around (cheaper for rentals of a week or longer).

The rates quoted here are only a guide. Many smaller local companies—and the big guys, too—offer competitive specials, especially in tourist areas with distinct off seasons. Advance purchase rates, usually 7 to 21 days ahead, can offer significant savings.

If you are concerned about reducing your carbon emissions, consider hiring a **hybrid car.** In Australia, all the "big five" major car-hire companies have the hybrid Toyota Prius available. Ask when making your bookings.

INSURANCE Insurance for loss of or damage to the car and third-party property insurance are usually included, but read the agreement carefully because the fine print contains information the front-desk staff may not tell you. For example, damage to the car body may be covered, but not damage to the windshield or tires, or damage caused by water or driving too close to a bushfire.

Insurance Alert

Damage to a rental car caused by an animal (hitting a kangaroo, for instance) may not be covered by your car-rental company's insurance policies. Different car-rental companies have very different rules and restrictions, so make sure you check each one's coverage. For example, some will not cover animal damage incurred at night, while others don't have such limits. The same applies to the rules about driving on unpaved roads, of which Australia has many. Avis and Budget say you may only drive on roads "properly formed and constructed as a sealed, metalled, or gravel road," while the others limit you largely to sealed roads. Check the fine print.

The deductible, known as "excess" in Australia, on insurance may be as high as A$2,000 for regular cars and up to A$5,500 on four-wheel-drives and motor homes. You can reduce it, or avoid it altogether, by paying a premium of between about A$20 to A$50 per day on a car or four-wheel-drive, and around A$25 to A$50 per day on a motor home. The amount of the excess reduction premium depends on the vehicle type and the extent of reduction you choose. Your rental company may bundle personal accident insurance and baggage insurance into this premium. And again, check the conditions; some excess reduction payments do not reduce excesses on single-vehicle accidents, for example.

ONE-WAY RENTALS Australia's distances often make one-way rentals a necessity, for which car-rental companies can charge a hefty penalty amounting to hundreds of dollars. A one-way fee usually applies to motor-home renters, too—usually around A$250 to A$350. An extra A$450 remote-location fee can apply for Outback areas such as Broome and Alice Springs. And there are minimum rental periods of between 7 and 21 days.

MOTOR HOMES Motor homes (Aussies call them camper vans) are popular in Australia. Generally smaller than the RVs in the United States, they come in two-, three-, four-, or six-berth versions and usually have everything you need, such as a minifridge and/or freezer (icebox in the smaller versions), microwave, gas stove, cooking and cleaning utensils, linens, and touring information, including maps and campground guides. All have showers and toilets, except some two-berthers. Most have air-conditioned driver's cabins, but not all have air-conditioned living quarters, a necessity in most parts of the country from November through March. Four-wheel-drive campers are available, but they tend to be small, and some lack hot water, toilet, shower, and air-conditioning. Minimum driver age for motor homes is usually 21.

Australia's biggest national motor-home-rental companies are **Apollo Motorhome Holidays** (✆ **1800/777 779** in Australia, or 07/3265 9200; www.apollocamper.com), **Britz Campervan Rentals** (✆ **1800/331 454** in Australia or 1800/2008 0801 from outside Australia; www.britz.com), and **Maui** (✆ **800/2008 0801** from anywhere in the world including within Australia; www.maui.com.au).

For a two-berth motor home with shower and toilet, Britz's rates range from around A$100 to A$205 per day over a 5- to 20-day rental period. For a four-berth with shower and toilet over the same period, you are looking at A$130 to A$290 per day. Rates vary with the seasons. May and June are the slowest months; December and January are the busiest. It's sometimes possible to get better rates by booking in your home country before departure. Renting for longer than 3 weeks knocks a few dollars off the daily rate. Most companies will demand a minimum 4- or 5-day rental. Give the company your itinerary before booking, because some routes, such as the ferry across to Tasmania—or, in the case of a four-wheel-drive motor home, the Gibb River Road in the Kimberley—may need the company's permission.

Frustratingly, most local councils take a dim view of "free camping," the practice of pulling over by the roadside to camp for the night. Instead, you will likely have to stay in a campground.

On the Road

GAS The price of petrol (gasoline) will probably elicit a cry of dismay from Americans and a whoop of delight from Brits. Prices go up and down, but at press time you were looking at around A$1.27 a liter for unleaded petrol in Sydney, and A$1.40 a liter, or more, in the Outback. Most rental cars take unleaded gas, and motor homes run on diesel.

DRIVING RULES Australians drive on the left, which means you give way to the right. Left turns on a red light are not permitted unless a sign says so.

Roundabouts (traffic circles) are common at intersections; approach these slowly enough to stop if you have to, and give way to all traffic on the roundabout. Flash your indicator as you leave the roundabout (even if you're going straight, because technically that's a left turn).

The only strange driving rule is Melbourne's requirement that drivers turn right from the left lane at certain intersections in the city center and in South Melbourne. This allows the city's trams to carry on uninterrupted in the right lane. Pull into the left lane opposite the street you are turning into, and make the turn when the traffic light in the street you are turning into becomes green. These intersections are signposted.

The maximum permitted blood alcohol level when driving is .05%, which equals approximately two 200-milliliter (6.6-oz.) drinks in the first hour for men, one for women, and one drink per hour for both sexes after that. The police set up random breath-testing units (RBTs) in cunningly disguised and unlikely places all the time, so getting caught is easy. You will face a court appearance if you do.

The speed limit is 50kmph (31 mph) or 60kmph (37 mph) in urban areas, 100kmph (62 mph) in most country areas, and sometimes 110kmph (68 mph) on freeways. In the Northern Territory, the speed limit is set at 130kmph (81 mph) on the Stuart, Arnhem, Barkly, and Victoria highways, while rural roads are designated 110kmph (68 mph) unless otherwise signposted. But be warned: The Territory has a high death toll. Speed-limit signs show black numbers circled in red on a white background.

Drivers and passengers, including taxi passengers, must wear a seatbelt at all times when the vehicle is moving forward, if the car is equipped with a belt. Young children are required to sit in the rear seat in a child-safety seat or harness; car-rental companies will rent these to you, but be sure to book them. Tell the taxi company you have a child when you book a cab so that it can send a car with the right restraints.

MAPS The maps published by the state automobile clubs listed below in "Auto Clubs" will likely be free if you are a member of an affiliated auto club in your home country. None will mail them to you overseas; pick them up on arrival. Remember to bring your auto-club membership card to qualify for discounts or free maps.

Two of the biggest map publishers in Australia are **HEMA Maps** (✆ **07/3340 0075;** www.hemamaps.com.au) and **Universal Publishers** (✆ **1800/021 987** in Australia, or 02/9857 3700; www.universalpress-online.com). Both publish an extensive range of national (including road atlases), state, regional, and city maps. HEMA has a strong list of regional maps ("Gold Coast and Region" and "The Red Centre" are just a few), while Universal produces a complete range of street directories by city, region, or state under the "UBD" and "Gregory's" labels. HEMA produces four-wheel-drive and motorbike road atlases and many regional four-wheel-drive maps—good if you plan to go off the trails—an atlas of Australia's national parks, and maps to Kakadu and Lamington national parks.

TOLL ROADS Electronic "beeper" or e-tags are used on all major Australian toll roads, including Melbourne's City Link motorways, Brisbane's Logan and Gateway motorways, the Sydney Harbour Bridge and tunnel and all Sydney's major tunnels and motorways. The tag is a small device attached to the front windscreen of the vehicle which transmits signals to the toll points on the road. This deducts the toll amount from your toll account. The same e-tag can be used on all Australian toll roads. While some toll roads still have physical collection points at which you can pay the toll, others—such as Melbourne's freeways—don't. If you are likely to need an e-tag, your car rental company will organize it for you.

ROAD SIGNS Australians navigate by road name, not road number. The easiest way to get where you're going is to familiarize yourself with the major towns along your route and follow the signs toward them.

AUTO CLUBS Every state and territory in Australia has its own auto club. Your auto association back home probably has a reciprocal agreement with Australian clubs, which may entitle you to free maps, accommodations guides, and emergency roadside assistance. Don't forget to bring your membership card.

Even if you're not a member, the clubs are a good source of advice on local traffic regulations, touring advice, road conditions, traveling in remote areas, and any other motoring questions you may have. They sell maps, accommodations guides, and camping guides to nonmembers at reasonable prices. They share a website: **www.aaa.asn.au**, which lists numerous regional offices.

Road Conditions & Safety

Here are some common motoring dangers and ways to avoid them:

FATIGUE Fatigue is a killer on Australia's roads. The rule is to take a 20-minute break every 2 hours, even if you don't feel tired. In some states, "driver reviver" stations operate on major roads during holiday periods. They serve free tea, coffee, and cookies, and are often at roadside picnic areas that have restrooms.

KANGAROOS & OTHER WILDLIFE It's a sad fact, but kangaroos are a road hazard. Avoid driving in country areas between dusk and dawn, when 'roos are most active. If you hit one, always stop and check its pouch for live joeys (baby kangaroos), because females usually have one in the pouch. Wrap the joey tightly in a towel or old sweater, don't feed or overhandle it, and take it to a vet in the nearest town or call one of the following wildlife care groups: **Wildlife Information & Rescue Service (WIRES)** in New South Wales (✆ 1300/094 737); **Wildlife Victoria** (✆ 1300/094 535); **Wildcare Australia** in Queensland (✆ 07/5527 2444); **RSPCA Wildlife** in the ACT (✆ 02/6287 8100 or 0413/495 031); **Wildcare** in Western Australia (✆ 08/9474 9055); **Wildlife Rescue** in the Northern Territory (✆ 0409/090 840); **Fauna Rescue of S.A.** in South Australia (✆ 08/8289 0896); or **Wildlife Incidents** in Tasmania (✆ 03/6233 6556). Most vets will treat native wildlife for free.

Some highways run through unfenced stations (ranches), where sheep and cattle pose a threat. Cattle like to rest on the warm bitumen road at night, so put your lights on high to spot them. If an animal does loom up, slow down—but never swerve, or you may roll. If you have to, hit it. Tell farmers within 24 hours if you have hit their livestock.

Car-rental companies will not insure for animal damage to the car, which should give you an inkling of how common an occurrence this is.

ROAD TRAINS Road trains consist of as many as three big truck carriages linked together to make a "train" up to 54m (177 ft.) long. If you're in front of one, give the driver plenty of warning when you brake, because the trains need a lot of distance to slow down. Allow at least 1 clear kilometer (over a half mile) before you pass one, but don't expect the driver to make it easy—"truckies" are notorious for their lack of concern for motorists.

UNPAVED ROADS Many country roads are unsealed (unpaved). They are usually bone-dry, which makes them more slippery than they look, so travel at a moderate speed—35kmph (22 mph) is not too cautious, and anything over 60kmph (37 mph) is dangerous. That said, when you are on a heavily corrugated or rutted road (which many are), you may need to keep to a higher speed (60kmph/37 mph) just to keep on top of them. Don't overcorrect if you veer to one side. Keep well behind any vehicles, because the dust they throw up can block your vision.

FLOODS Floods are common in the Top End and north of Cairns from November or December through March or April (the Wet season). Never cross a flooded road unless you are sure of its depth. Crocodiles may be in the water, so do not wade in to test it! Fast-flowing water is dangerous, even if it's very shallow. When in doubt, stay where you are and wait for the water to drop; most flash floods subside in 24 hours. Check the road conditions ahead at least once a day in the Wet season.

RUNNING OUT OF GAS Gas stations (also called "roadhouses" in rural areas) can be few and far between in the Outback, so fill up at every opportunity.

What If Your Vehicle Breaks Down?

Warning: If you break down or get lost, never leave your vehicle. Many a motorist—often an Aussie who should have known better—has died wandering off on a crazy quest for help or water, knowing full well that neither is to be found for maybe hundreds of miles. Most people who get lost do so in Outback spots; if that happens to you, conserve your body moisture by doing as little as possible and staying in the shade of your car. Put out distress signals in patterns of three—three yells, three columns of smoke, and so on. The traditional Outback call for help is "Coo-*ee,*" with the accent on the "ee" and yodeled in a high pitch; the sound travels a surprisingly long way.

Emergency Assistance

The emergency breakdown assistance telephone number for every Australian auto club is © **13 11 11** from anywhere in Australia. It is billed as a local call. If you are not a member of an auto club at home that has a reciprocal agreement with the Australian clubs, you'll have to join the Australian club on the spot before the club will tow or repair your car. This usually costs only around A$80, not a big price to pay when you're stranded—although in the Outback, the charge may be considerably higher. Most car-rental companies also have emergency assistance numbers.

Tips for Four-Wheel Drivers

Always keep to the four-wheel-drive track. Going off-road causes soil erosion, a significant environmental problem in Australia. Leave gates as you found them. Obtain permission from the owners before venturing onto private station (ranch) roads. On an extended trip or in remote areas, carry 5 liters (1⅓ gallons) of drinking water per person per day (dehydration occurs fast in the Australian heat); enough food to last 3 or 4 days more than you think you will need; a first-aid kit; spare fuel; a jack and two spare tires; spare fan belts, radiator hoses, and air-conditioner hoses; a tow rope; and a good map that marks all gas stations. In seriously remote areas outside the scope of this book, carry a high-frequency and a CB radio. (A cellphone may not work in the Outback.) Advise a friend, your hotel manager, the local tourist bureau, or a police station of your route and your expected time of return or arrival at your destination.

BY TRAIN

Australia's trains are clean, comfortable, and safe, and for the most part service standards and facilities are perfectly adequate. The rail network in Australia links Perth to Adelaide and continues on to Melbourne and north to Canberra, Sydney, Brisbane, and right up the coast to Cairns. There's also a line from Adelaide to Alice Springs and Darwin. Some rural towns, such as Broken Hill, also have rail service. Trains generally cost more than buses but are still reasonably priced. Two trains that are more than a mere mode of transport—the *Indian Pacific* and the *Ghan* (described below)—are a bit more expensive, but worth it.

Most long-distance trains have sleepers with big windows, air-conditioning, electric outlets, wardrobes, sinks, and fresh sheets and blankets. First-class sleepers have en-suite (attached private) bathrooms, and fares often include meals. Second-class sleepers use shared shower facilities, and meals are not included. Some second-class sleepers are private cabins; on other trains you share with strangers. Single cabins are usually of broom-closet dimensions but surprisingly comfy, with their own toilet and basin. The food ranges from mediocre to pretty good. Smoking is banned on all Australian rail networks.

Different entities manage Australia's rail routes. They are the private enterprise **Great Southern Rail** (© **13 21 47** in Australia, or 08/8213 4592; www.gsr.com.au), which runs the *Indian Pacific*, the *Overland*, the *Ghan*, and the new *Southern Spirit*, and these government bodies: **Traveltrain Holidays,** the long-distance train division of Queensland Rail (© **1300/131 722** in Australia, or 07/3235 7322; www.traveltrain.com.au), which handles rail within that state; **Countrylink** (© **13 22 32** in Australia or 02/4907 7501; www.countrylink.info), which manages travel within New South Wales and from Sydney to Canberra, Melbourne, and Brisbane;

and **Transwa** (© **1300/662 205** in Western Australia, or 08/9326 2600; www.transwa.wa.gov.au), which operates trains in Western Australia.

Outside Australia, the umbrella organization **Rail Australia** (www.railaustralia.com.au) markets these rail journeys through major travel wholesalers and travel agents.

Great Southern Rail's ***Indian Pacific*** ★★ is a glamorous train linking Sydney, Broken Hill, Adelaide, Kalgoorlie, and Perth in a 3-day Outback run twice a week. Slightly less posh but still comfortable, the ***Ghan*** (named after Afghani camel trainers who traveled the Outback in the 19th century) travels between Adelaide and Darwin twice a week via Alice Springs, with connections from Sydney and Perth on the *Indian Pacific* and from Melbourne on the ***Overland.*** The *Overland* travels in daylight between Adelaide and Melbourne three times a week. All three trains offer a choice of economy seats and second- or first-class sleepers. The newest train, the ***Southern Spirit,*** links Adelaide, Melbourne and Brisbane but runs services seasonally, in January and February.

Countrylink runs daily trains from Sydney to Melbourne, Canberra, Brisbane, and a number of New South Wales country towns.

Queensland Rail's Traveltrain operates two trains on the Brisbane-Cairns route: The ***Sunlander*** runs twice a week from Brisbane to Cairns, offering a choice of the premium, all-inclusive Queenslander Class; single-, double-, or triple-berth sleepers; or economy seats. Two services also run as far as Townsville on this route without Queenslander Class. The high-speed **Tilt Train** operates three weekly trips on the same route in less time—by about 5 hours—with business-class-style seating. Tilt Trains also serve Rockhampton daily (except Sat) from Brisbane. Traveltrain also operates trains to Outback towns. All Traveltrain and most Countrylink long-distance trains stop at most towns en route, so they're useful for exploring the eastern states.

RAIL PASSES Rail passes are available from **Rail Australia** (see above) at its overseas agents. Passes are not valid for first-class travel, but upgrades are available. The national **Ausrail Pass** is good for economy seats on all long-distance trains (except Transwa services in Western Australia). It allows you unlimited travel within a 6-month period and costs A$890, or A$990 if bought after you arrive in Australia. You can upgrade to a sleeper at additional cost.

Countrylink's **Backtracker** pass gives you unlimited economy class trips in both directions between Melbourne and Brisbane for up to 6 months. If traveling within New South Wales, you also receive around A$40 worth of travel on Sydney's CityRail network—enough to get you to Bondi Beach or to Katoomba in the Blue Mountains. A 14-day pass costs A$232, a 1-month pass A$275, a 3-month pass A$298, and a 6-month pass A$420. The Ausrail and Backtracker passes are available only to holders of non-Australian passports.

Great Southern Rail also offers a pass for international visitors traveling in Red Service or Red Service Daynighter seats. The **Rail Explorer** Pass gives 6 months unlimited travel for A$690 on any of its trains.

The **East Coast Discovery** rail pass covers travel between Melbourne and Cairns. It provides 6 months of unlimited one-way travel in economy seating on coastal trains between Cairns, Brisbane, Sydney, and Melbourne. Fares range from A$130 for Sydney–Brisbane or Sydney–Melbourne services, to A$450 for Melbourne–Cairns.

The new **Queensland Explorer** pass offers unlimited economy seat travel for 3 or 6 months across the Traveltrain network, from Cairns in the north to Brisbane in the south, and in the Queensland outback that extends to Charleville, Longreach, and Mount Isa. It costs A$351 for 3 months or A$495 for 6 months if purchased outside Australia, or A$390 for 3 months and A$550 for 6 months if purchased in Australia.

BY BUS

Bus travel in Australia is a big step up from the low-rent affair it can be in the United States. Terminals are centrally located and well lit, the buses—called "coaches" Down Under—are clean and air-conditioned, you sit in adjustable seats, videos play onboard, and the drivers are polite and sometimes even point out places of interest along the way. Some buses have restrooms. Unlike Australia's train service, the extensive bus network will take you almost everywhere. However, there is no bus service across the Nullabor Plain, from South Australia to Western Australia; and the only bus service into Perth comes from Darwin. Buses are all nonsmoking.

Australia has one national coach operator: **Greyhound Australia** (✆ **1300/473 946** in Australia, or 07/3868 0937; www.greyhound.com.au; no relation to Greyhound in the U.S.). The company does not operate within Tasmania, which is serviced by **Redline Coaches** (✆ **1300/360 000** in Australia; www.redlinecoaches.com.au). In addition to point-to-point services, Greyhound Australia also offers a limited range of tours at popular locations on its networks, including Uluru, Kakadu, Monkey Mia in Western Australia, and the Great Ocean Road in Victoria.

Note: Fares and some passes are considerably cheaper for students, backpacker cardholders, and Hostelling International/YHA members.

BUS PASSES Bus passes are a great value. There are several kinds: day passes (3–30 days), hop-on-hop-off passes for 45 days or 6 months, minipasses, preset itinerary passes, and kilometer passes. Note that even with a pass, you may still need to book the next leg of your trip 12 or 24 hours ahead as a condition of the pass; during school vacation periods, which are always busy, booking as much as 7 days ahead may be smart.

If you know where you are going and are willing to obey a "no backtracking" rule, consider Greyhound Australia's **Aussie Explorer** predetermined itinerary pass. These passes allow unlimited stops in a generous time frame on a preset one-way route (you are permitted to travel the route in either direction). There is a huge range of itineraries to choose from. As an example, the **Aussie Highlights** pass allows you to travel from Darwin to Cairns to Brisbane to Sydney to Melbourne to Adelaide to Alice Springs, and costs A$1,772. You don't have to start in Sydney; you can start at any point along any of the pass routes, in which case the pass may be cheaper. The **All Australian Pass** costs A$2,934. Both are valid for a year.

The **Kilometre Pass,** valid for 12 months, allows unlimited stops in any direction within the mileage you buy. Passes are available for 500km (310 miles) at A$99, 750km (465 miles) for A$143, and 1,000km (620 miles) for A$187, and then in increments of 1,000km (620 miles). A 2,000km (1,240 miles) pass—enough to get you from Cairns to Brisbane—will cost A$363, and from there you can go up to A$2,129 for a whopping 20,000km (6,200 miles).

MONEY & COSTS

THE VALUE OF THE AUSTRALIAN DOLLAR VS. OTHER POPULAR CURRENCIES

Aus$	US$	Can$	UK£	Euro (€)	NZ$
1	$0.91	C$0.94	£0.58	€0.69	NZ$1.26

Frommer's lists exact prices in the local currency. The currency conversions quoted above were correct at press time. However, rates fluctuate, so before departing consult a currency exchange website such as **www.oanda.com/currency/converter** to check up-to-the-minute rates.

The Australian dollar is divided into A100¢. Coins are A5¢, A10¢, A20¢, and A50¢ pieces (silver) and A$1 and A$2 pieces (gold). Prices often end in a variant of A1¢ and A2¢ (for example, A78¢ or A$2.71), a relic from the days before 1-cent and 2-cent pieces were phased out. Prices are rounded to the nearest A5¢—so A77¢ rounds down to A75¢, and A78¢ rounds up to A80¢. Bank notes come in denominations of A$5, A$10, A$20, A$50, and A$100.

You should consider changing a small amount of money into Australian currency before you leave (though don't expect the exchange rate to be ideal), so you can avoid lines at airport ATMs (automated teller machines). You can exchange money at your local American Express or Thomas Cook office or your bank. If you're far away from a bank with currency-exchange services, **American Express** offers traveler's checks and foreign currency, though with a A$15 order fee and additional shipping costs, at **© 800/807-6233** or **www.americanexpress.com**.

ATMS

The easiest and best way to get cash away from home is from an ATM (automated teller machine), sometimes referred to as a "cash machine" or a "cashpoint." The **Cirrus** (**© 800/424-7787;** www.mastercard.com) and **PLUS** (**© 800/843-7587;** www.visa.com) networks span the globe. Go to your bank card's website to find ATM locations at your destination. Be sure you know your daily withdrawal limit before you depart. Australian ATMs use a four-digit code, so check with your bank and make sure you change yours before you leave. ***Note:*** Many banks impose a fee every time you use a card at another bank's ATM, and that fee can be higher for international transactions (A$5 or more) than for domestic ones (rarely more than A$2). In addition, the bank from which you withdraw cash may charge its own fee. For international withdrawal fees, ask your bank.

> **Going with the Gold**
>
> **It's common for attractions or charities to request "gold coin"—a A$1 or A$2 coin—donations as an entry fee. So keep some handy!**

CREDIT CARDS

Credit cards are another safe way to carry money. They also provide a convenient record of all your expenses, and they generally offer relatively good exchange rates. You can withdraw cash advances from your credit cards at banks or ATMs but high

WHAT THINGS COST IN SYDNEY	A$
Taxi from the airport to downtown Sydney	35.00
Double room, moderate	140.00–160.00
Double room, inexpensive	100.00
Three-course dinner for one without wine, moderate	45.00–50.00
Bottle of beer	4.50–6.50
Bottle of Coca-Cola	3.00
Cup of coffee	3.50–4.00
1 liter of premium gas	1.22
Admission to most museums	10.00
Admission to most national parks	11.00

fees make this a pricey way to get cash. Keep in mind that you'll pay interest from the moment of your withdrawal, even if you pay your monthly bills on time.

Visa and MasterCard are universally accepted in Australia; American Express and Diners Club are less common; and Discover is not used. Always carry a little cash, because many merchants will not take cards for purchases under A$15 or so.

Beware of hidden credit-card fees while traveling. Check with your credit or debit card issuer to see what fees, if any, will be charged for overseas transactions. Recent reform legislation in the U.S., for example, has curbed some exploitative lending practices. But many banks have responded by increasing fees in other areas, including fees for customers who use credit and debit cards while out of the country—even if those charges were made in U.S. dollars. Fees can amount to 3% or more of the purchase price. Check with your bank before departing to avoid any surprise charges on your statement.

TRAVELER'S CHECKS

You can buy traveler's checks at most banks. They are offered in denominations of A$20, A$50, A$100, A$500, and sometimes A$1,000. Generally, you'll pay a service charge ranging from 1% to 4%.

The most popular traveler's checks are offered by **American Express** (✆ **800/807-6233,** or 800/221-7282 for card holders—this number accepts collect calls, offers service in several foreign languages, and exempts Amex gold and platinum cardholders from the 1% fee); **Visa** (✆ **800/732-1322**) or Visa through AAA (members can obtain Visa checks for a A$9.95 fee for checks up to A$1,500 at most AAA offices or by calling ✆ **866/339-3378**); and **MasterCard** (✆ **800/223-9920**).

However, be warned that traveler's checks are not as widely accepted in Australia as in many other countries. If you do opt for them, get them in Australian dollars. Checks in U.S. dollars are accepted at banks, big hotels, currency exchanges, and some shops in major tourist regions, but smaller shops, restaurants, and other businesses will have no idea what the exchange rate is when you present a U.S. check. Another advantage of Australian-dollar checks is that the two largest Aussie banks,

ANZ and Westpac, cash them free; it will cost you around A$5 to A$11 to cash checks denominated in foreign currency.

Be sure to keep a record of the traveler's checks' serial numbers separate from your checks in the event that they are stolen or lost. You'll get a refund faster if you know the numbers.

American Express, Thomas Cook, Visa, and **MasterCard** offer **foreign currency traveler's checks,** useful if you're traveling to just one country; they're accepted at locations where dollar checks may not be.

STAYING HEALTHY

Before you go: No vaccinations are needed to enter Australia unless you have been in a yellow fever danger zone—that is, South America or Africa—in the 6 days prior to entering. For more information, see "Medical Requirements" on p. 43.

Australian pharmacists may only fill prescriptions written by Australian doctors, so carry enough medication with you for your trip. Doctors are listed under "M," for "Medical Practitioners," in the yellow pages, and most large towns and cities have 24-hour clinics. Failing that, go to the local emergency room.

Health Concerns

TROPICAL ILLNESSES Some parts of tropical far north Queensland have sporadic outbreaks of the mosquito-borne dengue fever. The areas affected include Cairns, Port Douglas, and Townsville. But as dengue fever mosquitoes breed in urban environments, tourist activities in north Queensland such as reef and rainforest trips carry a low risk. The risk can be further minimized by staying in screened or air-conditioned accommodations, using insect repellant at all times, and wearing long, loose, light-colored clothing that covers arms and legs.

BUGS, BITES & OTHER WILDLIFE CONCERNS Snake and spider bites may not be as common as the hair-raising stories you will hear would suggest, but it pays to be wary. Your other concerns should be marine life, including jellyfish, and saltwater crocodiles. For more information and background on the fauna of Australia, and how to avoid dangerous encounters with them, see p. 30.

SUN, ELEMENTS & EXTREME WEATHER EXPOSURE Australians have the world's highest death rate from skin cancer because of the country's intense sunlight. Limit your exposure to the sun, especially during the first few days of your trip, and from 11am to 3pm in summer and 10am to 2pm in winter. Remember that UV rays reflected off walls, water, and the ground can burn you even when you're not in direct sunlight. Use a broad-spectrum sunscreen with a high protection factor (SPF 30 or higher).

Wear a broad-brimmed hat that covers the back of your neck, ears, and face (a baseball cap won't do it), and a long-sleeved shirt. Remember that children need more protection than adults do. Don't even think about traveling without sunglasses, or you'll spend your entire vacation squinting against Australia's "diamond light."

Cyclones occasionally affect tropical areas, such as Darwin and Queensland's coastal regions, from about Gladstone north, during January and February; but serious damage is relatively rare.

If You Get Sick

Generally, you don't have to worry much about health issues on a trip to Australia. Hygiene standards are high, hospitals are modern, and doctors and dentists are well qualified. Because of the continent's size, you can sometimes be a long way from a hospital or a doctor. Remote areas are served by the Royal Flying Doctor Service. However, standard medical travel insurance may be advisable. We list additional **emergency numbers** in "Fast Facts," p. 735.

CRIME & SAFETY

Travelers to Australia should follow the same precautions against petty theft and potential identity theft as they would at home or in any other country. Violent crime is, of course, not uncommon but you are not likely to become a target of it in the normal course of your travels.

Driving probably poses one of the greatest risks to visitors to Australia. Australians drive on the left, something that North American and European visitors often have difficulty remembering. Drivers and passengers, including taxi passengers, must wear a seatbelt at all times, by law. Avoid driving between dusk and dawn in country areas, because this is when kangaroos are most active, and a collision with a 'roo is something to be avoided at all costs. Road trains—as many as three big truck carriages linked together, which can be up to 54m (177 ft.) long—are another danger, particularly in the Outback.

Warning: If you break down or get lost, *never* leave your vehicle. Most people who get lost do so in Outback spots, and those who wander off to look for help or water usually die in the attempt. If it happens to you, stay with your car. See "By Car" in the "Getting There & Getting Around" section, p. 46.

SPECIALIZED TRAVEL RESOURCES

In addition to the destination-specific resources listed below, please visit Frommers.com for other specialized travel resources.

Lesbian, Gay, Bisexual & Transgender Travelers

Sydney is one of the most gay-friendly cities in the world, and across most of Australia, the gay community has a high profile and lots of support services. There are plenty of gay and lesbian bars, and most Saturday nights see a privately operated gay dance party taking place in an inner-city warehouse somewhere. The cafes and pubs of Oxford Street in Darlinghurst, a short cab ride or long stroll from Sydney's downtown area, are the liveliest gay spots. The annual **Sydney Gay & Lesbian Mardi Gras,** culminating in a huge street parade and party in late February or early March, is a high point on the city's calendar.

In rural areas of Australia, you may still encounter a little conservative resistance to gays and lesbians, but Australians everywhere are generally tolerant. Noosa, on Queensland's Sunshine Coast, is a favored destination for revelers after Mardi Gras, and a couple of resorts in north Queensland cater to gay and lesbian travelers. One of the best known is **Turtle Cove Resort & Spa** (✆ **1300/727 979** in Australia, or 07/4059 1800; www.turtlecove.com), on a private beach between Cairns and Port Douglas.

Some services you may find useful are the **Gay & Lesbian Counselling and Community Service of NSW** (✆ **02/8594 9596**), which runs a national hotline (✆ **1800/184 527** in Australia) from 7:30 to 10pm daily. Its website, **www.glccs.org.au**, has contact information for each state. In Sydney, the **Albion Street Centre** (✆ **02/9332 9600** for administration; 1800/451 600 or 02/9332 9700 for the information line) is a HIV clinic and information service.

The International Gay and Lesbian Travel Association (IGLTA; ✆ **954/630-1637** in the U.S.; www.iglta.org) is the trade association for the gay and lesbian travel industry, and offers an online directory of gay- and lesbian-friendly travel businesses and tour operators. **Gay & Lesbian Tourism Australia** (www.galta.com.au) has listings of businesses in each state.

Many agencies offer tours and travel itineraries specifically for gay and lesbian travelers. **Above and Beyond Tours** (✆ **800/397-2681;** www.abovebeyondtours.com) are gay Australia tour specialists based in California.

Travelers with Disabilities

Most disabilities shouldn't stop anyone from traveling to Australia. There are more options and resources than ever before. Most hotels, major stores, attractions, and public restrooms in Australia have wheelchair access. Many smaller lodges and even B&Bs are starting to cater to guests with disabilities, and some diving companies cater to scuba divers with disabilities. National parks make an effort to include wheelchair-friendly pathways. Taxi companies in bigger cities can usually supply a cab equipped for wheelchairs.

TTY facilities are still limited largely to government services. For information on all kinds of facilities and services (not just travel-related organizations) for people with disabilities, contact **National Information Communication Awareness Network,** Unit 5, 48 Brookes St., Mitchell ACT 2911 (✆ **1800/806 769** voice and TTY in Australia, or 02/6241 1220; www.nican.com.au). This free service can put you in touch with accessible accommodations and attractions throughout Australia, as well as with travel agents and tour operators who understand your needs.

Family Travel

Australians travel widely with their own kids, so facilities for families, including family passes to attractions, are common.

A great accommodations option for families is Australia's huge stock of serviced or unserviced apartments (with or without daily maid service). Often less expensive than a hotel room, they offer a living room, a kitchen, a bathroom or two, and the privacy of a separate bedroom for adults. "Tips on Accommodations," later in this chapter, has details on the major apartment chains. Most Australian hotels will arrange babysitting when given a day's notice.

International airlines and domestic airlines in Australia charge 75% of the adult fare for kids under 12. Most charge 10% for infants under 2 not occupying a seat. Australian transport companies, attractions, and tour operators typically charge half price for kids under 12 or 14 years.

Many Australian resorts have "kids' clubs" with extensive programs designed for children under 12 and, in some cases, teenagers. The French-owned Accor chain of hotels and resorts, which is Australia's largest chain, has kids' clubs, kids' menus designed by a nutritionist (and not just the same boring fodder you get everywhere else), and other family-friendly facilities including family rooms. Other resorts, such as Hamilton Island in Queensland's Whitsunday region, have "kids stay, eat, and play free" offers, particularly during holiday periods. Many hotels will offer connecting units or "family rooms." Ask when booking.

Don't forget that children entering Australia on their parent's passport still need their own visa. See "Entry Requirements," earlier in this chapter.

Rascals in Paradise (✆ **415/273-2224;** www.rascalsinparadise.com) is a San Francisco-based company specializing in family vacation packages to Australia.

The Australian travel magazine ***Holidays with Kids*** has a comprehensive website listing great options for family travel in Australia (www.holidayswithkids.com.au).

To locate accommodations, restaurants, and attractions that are particularly kid-friendly, refer to the "Kids" icon throughout this guide.

Senior Travel

Seniors—often called "pensioners" in Australia—from other countries don't always qualify for the discounted entry prices to tours, attractions, and events that Australian seniors enjoy, but it is always worth asking. Inquire about discounts when booking hotels, flights, and train or bus tickets. The best ID to bring is something that shows your date of birth or that marks you as an "official" senior, such as a membership card from AARP.

Many reliable agencies and organizations target the 50-plus market. **Exploritas** (formerly **Elderhostel;** ✆ **800/454-5768** in the U.S.; www.exploritas.org) arranges worldwide study programs for those ages 55 and over.

In Australia, pick up a copy of Get Up & Go (www.getupandgo.com.au), the only national travel magazine for the over-50 crowd and the official Seniors Card travel magazine. It's a glossy quarterly, available at most newsstands and has an extensive section called "Destination Australia," which covers a region in each state/territory in every issue.

Student Travel

Under a new agreement between Australia and the U.S. in late 2007, students between 18 and 30 years old can apply for a "working holiday" visa to stay in Australia for up to 12 months. You must apply for your visa outside of Australia, show evidence of your student or recent graduate status, and hold a return ticket as well as sufficient funds for the first part of your stay. Canadian and U.K. students may qualify for similar visas. For more information, check the website **www.immi.gov.au/visitors**.

Check out the **International Student Travel Confederation** (**ISTC;** www.istc.org) website for comprehensive travel-services information and details on how to get an **International Student Identity Card (ISIC),** which qualifies students for substantial savings on rail passes, plane tickets, entrance fees, and more. It also provides students with basic health and life insurance and a 24-hour helpline. The card is valid for a maximum of 16 months. You can apply for the card online or in person at **STA Travel,** the biggest student travel agency in the world; check out the website (www.statravel.com) to locate STA Travel offices worldwide. If you're no longer a student but are still under 26, you can get an **International Youth Travel Card (IYTC)** from the same people, which entitles you to some discounts. **Travel CUTS** (✆ **800/592-2887;** www.travelcuts.com) offers similar services for Canadians and U.S. residents. Irish students may prefer to turn to **USIT** (✆ **01/602-1906;** www.usit.ie), an Ireland-based specialist in student, youth, and independent travel.

RESPONSIBLE TOURISM

Sustainable travel—and its close cousin, responsible travel—are important issues in Australia, and you'll find plenty of places that claim to be ecofriendly. So how do you find the places that will truly help you make as little impact as possible on our fragile environment, while still enjoying your holiday? When planning your holiday, look for Australian tourism operators who have their tour, attraction, or accommodations accredited under **Ecotourism Australia**'s Eco Certification Program (www.ecotourism.org.au). The **Eco Certification** logo is carried by those businesses that are recognized as being tours, attractions, cruises, or accommodations that are environmentally, socially, and economically sustainable. The program assures travelers that these products are backed by a strong, well-managed commitment to sustainable practices and provide high quality nature-based tourism experiences. The website allows you to search for companies that are accredited. Ecotourism Australia also publishes the free **Green Travel Guide** which carries a list of all accredited businesses. You can order it online (postage is A$20 in Australia or A$30 for international mailing of up to two copies). You should also look for nature and ecotour guides who have credentials through the EcoGuide Australia Certification Program, also accredited by Ecotourism Australia. **Eco Directory** (www.ecodirectory.com.au) also offers sustainable travel tips and directories of green businesses. Another good online guide is the **Green Directory** at **www.thegreendirectory.com.au**.

Savannah Guides (✆ **0408/772 513** mobile phone; www.savannah-guides.com.au) is a network of professional tour guides, mostly in north Queensland, the Northern Territory, and Western Australia's Kimberley region, who have in-depth knowledge of the natural and cultural assets of the tropical savannas of northern Australia. Savannah Guides sites and stations feature nature- and/or culture-based interpretive activities; all Savannah Guides promote ecologically sustainable tourism principles, encourage the protection and conservation of natural and cultural resources, and are committed to conservation values.

Ecotourism Australia has also developed a new arm, Climate Action Australia (www.sustainabletourismaustralia.com), and introduced the **Climate Action Certification Program,** developed in collaboration with the Great Barrier Reef Marine Park Authority and the South Australian Tourism Commission. This rates tourism products and businesses on their commitment to reducing emissions and becoming carbon neutral. As a new initiative it had, at press time for this book, only 22 accredited members, most of them in South Australia and Queensland.

Each time you take a flight, greenhouse gases release into the atmosphere. You can help neutralize this danger to the planet through "carbon offsetting"—paying someone to invest your money in programs that reduce your greenhouse-gas emissions by the same amount you've added. Before buying carbon offset credits, just make sure that you're using a reputable company, one with a proven program that invests in renewable energy. Most Australian domestic airlines offer the chance to carbon-offset your travel when you buy your ticket, and there are several other Australian-based carbon-offset companies worth checking out. These include **www.mycleansky.com.au** and **www.climatefriendly.com**. Some travel agents will offer you the chance to carbon-offset when you make your bookings. If they don't—ask!

You can also reduce your carbon emissions when driving by hiring a **hybrid car.** In Australia, all the "big five" major car-hire companies have the hybrid Toyota Prius available. Ask when making your bookings. There is very little difference to driving a conventional vehicle, except a somewhat strange silence when the engine is idling, and you soon get used to the way the car operates. And of course, best of all is to use public transport, walk, or hire a bicycle to get around.

Eat at locally owned and operated restaurants that use produce grown in the area. This contributes to the local economy and cuts down on greenhouse-gas emissions by supporting restaurants where the food is not flown or trucked in across long distances.

It's also possible to choose an environmentally friendly hotel—some go further than just asking you to reuse your towel. AAA Tourism's star rating system (see "Tips on Accommodations," p. 73) now also offers a **Green Star** rating that lists hotels that are committed to environmentally good practices. The Green Star is awarded to properties based on an assessment of their energy efficiency, waste minimization and management, water saving, and education of their guests on environmentally friendly practices. The standards used were developed in partnership with Green Globe. Check out the website (www.accommodationguide.com.au) to find out which hotels rate.

Conserving water is probably the most important issue for travelers in Australia, where many parts of the country are arid or have been seriously drought-stricken for years. You will become accustomed to seeing water-saving tips in your hotel bathroom—please adhere to them. The 4-minute (or less) shower is *de rigueur* for water-savvy Australians.

Indigenous Culture

One of the most memorable and significant parts of a trip to Australia for many people is the chance to meet indigenous Australians. When choosing a tour that covers Aboriginal culture, make sure it is one that is owned and run by Aborigines, such as Anangu Tours at Uluru (p. 410). These tours will teach you much about Australia's indigenous people, their lives, and their culture. Make sure you ask before taking anyone's photo, and respect requests not to photograph certain sites—for example, some parts of Uluru are considered sacred and should not be photographed. Be aware that some questions may be evaded or not answered to your satisfaction; this is often a matter of cultural tradition and the need for some things to not be shared with outsiders. Many Aboriginal people are very shy, and direct eye contact is often avoided; this is not rudeness, simply a cultural matter.

One of the ways in which many visitors meet Aboriginal people is through visiting art centers and buying indigenous art. It is important to buy Aboriginal art from an authentic source (preferably from the artist, or a reputable center where they work).

RESOURCES FOR responsible TRAVEL

In addition to the resources for Australia listed above, the following websites provide valuable wide-ranging information on sustainable travel.

- **Sustainable Travel International** (www.sustainabletravelinternational.org) promotes ethical tourism practices, and manages an extensive directory of sustainable properties and tour operators around the world.
- **Carbonfund** (www.carbonfund.org), **TerraPass** (www.terrapass.org), and **Cool Climate** (http://coolclimate.berkeley.edu) provide info on "carbon offsetting," or offsetting the greenhouse gas emitted during flights.
- **Greenhotels** (www.greenhotels.com) recommends green-rated member hotels around the world that fulfill the company's stringent environmental requirements.
- For general info on volunteer travel, visit **www.volunteerabroad.org** and **www.idealist.org**.

But if you choose to buy from a gallery or souvenir shop, there are some questions you should ask first. Fakes have been an issue since the popularity—and prices—of indigenous art soared a decade or so ago. So how do you know if the Aboriginal artwork you're buying is authentic? The city of Melbourne has introduced a code of practice for galleries and retailers with guidelines on the ethical sale of indigenous art—and these are good rules to apply whichever part of Australia you are in. If in Melbourne, check if the shop you're dealing with has adopted it. For a list of those who subscribe to the code of practice, check **www.melbourne.vic.gov.au/indigenousarts** or call ✆ **03/9658 9658.** Other questions to ask before buying artwork include who the artist is, where they come from, are they part of a cooperative, and have they signed the work? For crafts and souvenirs such as boomerangs and didgeridoos, ask what kind of wood it is made of (fakes are often bamboo or teak).

Animal-Rights Issues

Cuddling a koala might be top of your list of things to do in Australia, but a word of warning first: Koalas might look soft and cuddly, but the reality is a bit different. They are wild animals with sharp claws, and you should treat them with caution. Koalas in the wild are not safe to approach—even if you could reach them. Most of your encounters with them will be at a distance, looking on as they rest high in the branches of a tree, or in a wildlife park where "controlled cuddling" is allowed. Holding a koala is allowed only in Queensland, South Australia, and Western Australia. In Victoria, New South Wales, and Tasmania, it is banned, but in some places you can pose beside one and have your photo taken. There are no koalas in the Northern Territory.

For more on koalas and where to see them in their natural habitat, contact the **Australian Koala Foundation** (✆ 07/3229 7233; www.savethekoala.com) or drop into their office at 40 Charlotte St., Brisbane.

For information on animal-friendly issues throughout the world, visit **Tread Lightly** (www.treadlightly.org). For information about the ethics of swimming with dolphins, visit the **Whale and Dolphin Conservation Society** (www.wdcs.org).

Respecting the Reef

Snorkelling and diving on the Great Barrier Reef is at the top of the list for many visitors to Australia. But there's no doubt that the Reef is in decline due to human factors and climate change. So how to best reduce your impact on this imperiled natural wonder? The best advice is "look—don't touch." Watch out for careless movements that might destroy fragile coral or disturb sandy areas, and remember that if you have sunscreen on your hands that can also kill corals. Resist the temptation to souvenir corals or shells (that goes for the beach too). In fact, collecting anything—alive or dead—in the Great Barrier Reef Marine Park is illegal unless you have a Marine Parks permit, and you will be subject to a fine. Although some tour operators may do so, don't take part in fish-feeding—it can disturb their natural eating habits or encourage aggressive behavior.

SPECIAL INTEREST & ESCORTED TRIPS

Aboriginal Tours

Learning about Australia's pre-European history and the indigenous culture of this country may be one of the most rewarding experiences of your visit. Don't think that you have to go to the desert to find out about Aboriginal people and their traditions. While you will find the largest range of tours in the Northern Territory and Red Centre, there are Aboriginal-led tours in all states, even in city areas, where you can learn about how the land was before Europeans arrived, and about the beliefs, spirituality, and traditional way of life of Aboriginal people. A useful website is **www.aboriginaltouroperators.com.au**, which has links to many individual operators around the country. State tourism bodies including Tourism Queensland (www.queenslandholidays.com.au), the Northern Territory Tourist Commission (www.travelnt.com), Tourism Victoria (www.visitvictoria.com), and Tourism Western Australia (www.westernaustralia.com) also have listings of Aboriginal tours in their regions.

Food & Wine Trips

The beauty of doing an organized food-and-wine tour, of course, is that you have your own designated driver to avoid any potential tangles with Australia's tough drunk-driving laws. If your appetite is whetted for gourmet touring, South Australia and Tasmania are the places to head for (although you can manage it almost anywhere—Australia's best food is very good indeed). In South Australia, try **Adelaide's Top Food and Wine Tours** (✆ **08/8386 0888;** www.topfoodandwinetours.com.au), which offers a range of food-based tours, including the Central Market and full-day tours to the Barossa Valley and McLaren Vale wine regions. In Tasmania, Hobart-based **Apple Isle Wine Tours** (✆ **0414/430 033;** www.appleislewinetours.com) offers guided full- and half-day tours to wine regions, including the Coal Valley, Huon Valley and Tamar Valley. **Tourism Tasmania** (www.discovertasmania.com.au) publishes a **Farm Gate Guide** that shows you where to pick cherries or apples and sample world-class cheeses, beers, wines, and liqueurs, and lists annual food and wine events. In Victoria, **Grape Escape** Wine Tours (✆ **03/9735 1333** or 0409/846 908 mobile phone; www.grapeescapetours.com.au) offers full- and half-day tours, or customized tours, of the Yarra Valley wine region.

Volunteer & Working Trips

Many of the volunteer travel opportunities in Australia center on environmental issues and conservation projects, which gives you a chance to explore the great outdoors in a way you might otherwise miss. Volunteering doesn't usually require special skills, just a willingness to work hard and get on with others. Some programs provide free housing and food, but many require volunteers to pay for travel expenses, which can sometimes amount to thousands of dollars. In those cases, part of the cost of your trip usually goes toward materials for the project or into a community fund. For general info on volunteer travel, visit **www.volunteerabroad.org** and **www.idealist.org**.

World Expeditions ★ (✆ **613/241-2700** in Canada and the U.S., 020/8545 9030 in the U.K., 09/368 4161 in New Zealand, or 02/8270 8400 or 1300/720 000 in Australia; www.worldexpeditions.com) runs two Australian trips as part of its Community Project Travel scheme. In 2010, these included a marine rescue project in the Northern Territory's Arnhem Land and a river-care project on Tasmania's Franklin River (combined with a rafting holiday), which will be repeated in March 2011. **Earthwatch** (✆ **03/9682 6828;** www.earthwatch.org.au) has a range of Australian environmental projects, which change each year. Examples include monitoring the effects of climate change on various species living in Queensland's Wet Tropics World Heritage Area, collecting data on vanishing frogs in New South Wales, studying manta rays on Lady Elliot Island, or helping research the impact of marine pollution on threatened sea turtle species on Brisbane's North Stradbroke Island.Volunteers work alongside leading scientists, typically for between 8 and 15 days.

World Wildlife Fund (WWF) Australia (✆ **1800/032 551** in Australia or 02/9281 5515; www.wwf.org.au) has volunteer opportunities around Australia. You can choose from weekend options to 2-week trips. Watch the website for details of upcoming projects.

Youth Challenge Australia (✆ **02/9514 5512;** www.youthchallenge.org.au) offers the chance to work in a remote Central Australian Aboriginal community. You need to be 18 to 30 years old and be prepared to commit 10 to 12 weeks of your time to do this. Work is usually in schools or youth programs and sometimes with artists' centers. There is a participation fee of A$2,000, but for overseas participants, there will be greater costs once travel expenses are included.

Wellness Trips

Like elsewhere in the world, Australia's spa industry has grown tremendously over the last few years. If you like to be pampered, then head to a day spa in a luxury hotel or one of the many scattered throughout the major cities. Spa resorts are also growing in number, with several major ones opening recently. These include The **Spa at Château Élan** (www.chateauelan.com.au), in the Hunter Valley, NSW, and **Emirates' Wolgan Valley Resort & Spa** (www.wolganvalley.com), in the Blue Mountains, NSW. To find one near you, consult **Day Spa Guide** (www.dayspaguide.com.au), which claims to list every day spa and spa resort in Australia.

Escorted General Interest Tours

Escorted tours are structured group tours, with a group leader. The price usually includes everything from airfare to hotels, meals, tours, admission costs, and local transportation.

Topdeck (✆ 1300/886 332 in Australia or 02/8252 5300; 208/987 330 in the U.K.; www.topdeck.travel) specializes in escorted tours for 18- to 39-year-olds in Queensland, Tasmania and the Northern Territory. Another company serving this market is Contiki (✆ 1300/188 635 in Australia; www.contiki.com). These trips attract a lot of Australians, too, so they are a good way to meet locals.

For more information on Escorted General-Interest Tours, including questions to ask before booking your trip, see **www.frommers.com/planning**.

ACTIVE VACATIONS

Australia's wide-open spaces and great weather cry out to even the most dedicated lazybones. Most operators and outfitters listed below specialize in adventure vacations for small groups. Meals, accommodations, equipment rental, and guides are usually included in their packages, though international airfares are not. Where you end up spending the night varies depending on the package you select—on a sea-kayaking trip, you almost always camp on the beach; on a hiking expedition you may stay at a wilderness lodge; and on a biking trip you often stop over at B&B-style lodgings. More information on the outdoor activities discussed below appears in the relevant regional chapters.

Scuba Diving

Diving Down Under is one of the best travel experiences in the world. There are good dive sites all around the coastline, not just on the Great Barrier Reef. A second barrier reef in Ningaloo Reef Marine Park stretches 260km (161 miles) off the coast of Western Australia. (See p. 529 for a description of dive sites there.) Not all the good sites are on coral. In Tasmania, for instance, you can dive kelp beds popular with seals, and in South Australia you can cage-dive with great white sharks. For a rundown on the country's outstanding dive areas, see "The Best Diving & Snorkeling Sites," on p. 9.

Wherever you find coral in Australia, you'll find dive companies offering learn-to-dive courses, day trips, and, in some cases, extended journeys on live-aboard vessels. Most international dive certificates, including PADI, NAUI, SSI, and BSAC, are recognized. It's easy to rent gear and wet suits wherever you go, or you can bring your own.

Beginners' courses are known as "open-water certification" and usually require 2 days of theory in a pool at the dive company's premises, followed by 2 or 3 days on a live-aboard boat where you make between four and nine dives, including a night dive if you opt for the 5-day course. Open-water certification courses range from an intensive 3 to 5 days, for which you can expect to pay about A$350 to A$600. A 5-day course is seen as the best. When comparing the value offered by dive schools, keep in mind that if the practical section of your course does not take place on a live-aboard boat, you will have to budget for accommodations and meals. Most operators offer courses right up to instructor level. If you're pressed for time, a

"PADI referral" course might suit you. It allows you to do your theory work at home, do a few hours of pool work at a PADI dive center in your home country, and then spend 2 or 3 days in the Australian ocean doing your qualifying dives. Remember to allow time in your itinerary for a medical exam in Australia (see below), and expect the dive instructor to grill you on your theory again before you hit the water.

If you're already a certified diver, remember to bring your "C" card and log book. If you're going to do a dive course, you'll need a medical certificate from an Australian doctor that meets Australian standard AS4005.1, stating that you are fit for scuba diving. (An all-purpose physical is not enough.) Virtually all dive schools will arrange the medical exam for you; expect to pay around A$50 for it. Remember, you must complete your last dive 24 hours before you fly in an aircraft. This catches a lot of people off guard when they are preparing to fly to their next destination the day after a visit to the Reef. You won't be able to helicopter off the Reef back to the mainland, either. Check to see if your travel insurance covers diving. **The Divers Alert Network** (✆ **800/446-2671** in North America or 03/9886 9166 in Australia; www.diversalertnetwork.org) sells diving insurance and has diving and nondiving medical emergency hotlines and an information line for dive-related medical questions.

Peak Time on the Reef

April through October is peak visibility time on the Great Barrier Reef, but the marine life will amaze you any time of year.

If you've never been diving and don't plan to become qualified, you can see what all the fuss is about on an "introductory" dive that lets you dive in the company of an instructor, on a one-time basis, with a briefing beforehand. Most dive operators on the Great Barrier Reef and other dive locations offer introductory dives.

See "Exploring the Great Barrier Reef," p. 272, for more information.

For information on dive regions and operators, try the state tourism marketing boards' websites (see "Fast Facts," p. 735). **Tourism Queensland**'s website (www.queenslandholidays.com.au) has information on most dive operators working the Great Barrier Reef. If you know where you want to dive, you may obtain an even more detailed list of operators by bypassing the big tourism boards and contacting the local tourist office for a list of local dive operators. **Dive Queensland** (the Queensland Dive Tourism Association; ✆ **07/4051 1510;** fax 07/4051 1519; www.dive-queensland.com.au) requires its member operators to abide by a code of ethics. Its website has a list of members and the services they offer. It includes a few in other states, too. Another good source is **Diversion Dive Travel** (✆ **1800/607 913** in Australia, or 07/4039 0200; www.diversionoz.com), a Cairns-based travel agent that specializes in dive holidays on the Great Barrier Reef, as well as in other good dive spots in Australia. It books day trips and extended diving excursions on a choice of live-aboard vessels, as well as dive courses, island resorts with diving, accommodations, and nondiving tours. It also sells diving insurance. Its proprietors are both dive instructors, and one of them is trained as a handicapped diving instructor for divers with disabilities.

Bushwalking (Hiking)

With so much unique scenery and many rare animals and plants, it's not surprising that Australia is full of national parks crisscrossed with hiking trails. You're never far from a park with a bushwalk, whether it's an easy stroll or a 6-day odyssey on the Cape-to-Cape trail in Western Australia.

A good Australian bushwalking website is **www.bushwalking.org.au**. The best place to get information about bushwalking is the **National Parks & Wildlife Service** (www.environment.nsw.gov.au/nationalparks), or its equivalent in each state. Some parks charge an entry fee, often ranging from A$6 to A$18.

More Active Vacations From A to Z

ABSEILING Rappelling is another name for this sport that involves backing down vertical cliff faces on a rope and harness. The rugged, beautiful Blue Mountains near Sydney are Australia's abseiling capital. In the Margaret River region in Western Australia, you can do it as mighty breakers crash on the cliffs below. You can even do it in the heart of Brisbane on riverside cliffs.

BIKING Much of Australia's countryside is flat and ideal for cycling, but consider the heat and vast distances before setting out. There are plenty of biking trails. The rainforest hills behind Cairns hosted the world mountain-biking championships in 1996, and Sydney's Blue Mountains have good mountain-biking trails. On Rottnest Island off Perth, it's the only mode of transport from one coral-filled bay to the next. All major towns and most resort centers rent regular bikes and mountain bikes.

Remote Outback Cycle Tours (© **1800/157 830;** www.cycletours.com.au) takes novice and expert riders, young and old, on extended tours across the country. The distances are vast, but the trip combines cycling with four-wheel-drive travel. Itineraries include the Red Centre, the remote Gibb River Road, the Flinders Ranges, and from Adelaide to Perth across the Nullarbor Plain desert and through the Margaret River wine region in southern Western Australia.

BIRD-WATCHING Australia's unique geography as an island continent means it has birds you won't see anywhere else. It is probably best known for its brilliant parrots, but you will see species from the wetlands, savanna, mulga scrub, desert, oceans, dense bushland, rainforest, mangroves, rivers, and other habitats. More than half of the country's species have been spotted in the Daintree Rainforest area in north Queensland, and one-third live in wetlands-rich Kakadu National Park in the Top End. The Coorong in South Australia and Broome in Western Australia are home to marvelous waterfowl populations.

To get in touch with birding clubs all over Australia, contact **Birds Australia** (© **1300/730 075** in Australia, or 03/9347 0757; www.birdsaustralia.com.au).

Something Different: Camel Trekking

Camels Down Under? You bet. Australia has one of the world's largest camel populations and even exports racing camels to the Middle East. Camels were imported to negotiate waterless deserts in the 1900s but were later set free. They are now a popular way to trek the country. Short rambles of an hour or two in Alice Springs and at Uluru are a novel way to see the Outback; or you can join extended camel treks through Outback deserts offered by a number of operators. Several companies in Broome lead guided rides along beautiful Cable Beach.

Kirrama Wildlife Tours (© **07/4065 5181;** www.kirrama.com.au) operates birding expeditions to remote regions in northern Australia and Western Australia's southwest, from a base in north Queensland. Broome-based ornithologist George Swann, of **Kimberley Birdwatching, Wildlife & Natural History Tours** (© **08/9192 1246;** www.kimberleybirdwatching.com.au), leads extended birding trips throughout the Kimberley and the Northern Territory. **Fine Feather Tours** (© **07/4094 1199;** www.finefeathertours.com.au), based near Port Douglas, near the Daintree Rainforest, operates bird-watching day trips and afternoon river cruises.

CANOEING & SEA KAYAKING Katherine Gorge in the Northern Territory offers some spectacular flat canoeing. You'll find delightful canoeing on the bird-rich Ord River in the Top End. Katherine Gorge and the Ord are full of generally harmless freshwater crocodiles, but *never* canoe in saltwater-crocodile territory. White-water canoeing can be found in Barrington Tops National Park north of Sydney.

A growing number of operators all around the coastline rent kayaks and lead guided expeditions. Popular spots are the Whitsunday Islands in north Queensland, the cold southern seas around Tasmania, and Byron Bay, where you can take a 3-hour "dolphin kayaking" trip to see wild dolphins (and whales June–Oct) and "kayak-surf" the waves.

Rivergods (© **08/9259 0749;** www.rivergods.com.au) conducts multiday sea-kayaking, canoeing, and white-water-rafting adventures throughout Western Australia's pristine ocean and rivers, in which whales, sharks, dugongs (manatees), sea snakes, turtles, and dolphins abound. The company also runs a "sea kayak with wild seals" day outing from Perth. **Gecko Canoeing** (© **1800/634 319** in Australia, or 08/8972 2224; www.geckocanoeing.com.au) leads canoeing trips of 1 to 6 days from Katherine along remote Top End rivers between April and October.

CAVING Australia doesn't have a lot of caves, but the ones it has are spectacular. The best spots are in the Blue Mountains west of Sydney and the Margaret River region in southwest Western Australia. For tourists who want to see caves and stay clean and safe (as opposed to spelunkers), the best caves are the spectacular Jenolan Caves in the Blue Mountains, a honeycomb of caverns bursting with intricate stalactites and stalagmites, and the 350 limestone caves in Margaret River, five of which are open to the public. Two are "adventure caves," which any novice caver (as opposed to an experienced spelunker) can explore on a 2- or 3-hour tour. You can also go caving at Olssen's Capricorn Caverns, near Rockhampton, in Central Queensland.

FISHING Reef, game, deep sea, beach, estuary, and river fishing—Australia's massive coastline lets you do it all. Drop a line for coral trout on the Great Barrier Reef; go for the world-record black marlin off Cairns; hook a fighting "barra" (barramundi) in the Northern Territory or the Kimberley; or cast for trout in Tasmania's highland lakes. Charter boats will take you out for the day from most towns all around the coast.

GOLFING Australians are almost as passionate about golf as they are about football and cricket—after all, Greg Norman started life as an Aussie! Queensland has the lion's share of the stunning resort courses, such as the Sheraton Mirage in Port Douglas, Laguna Quays Resort near the Whitsundays, and the Hyatt Regency Sanctuary

Cove Resort on the Gold Coast. The Gold Coast has more than 40 courses. One of the world's best desert courses is at Alice Springs.

Most courses rent clubs for around A$30. Greens fees start at around A$20 for 18 holes but average A$65 or more on a championship course. **Australian Golf Tours** (© **02/9746 6606;** www.australiangolftours.com.au) offers escorted day trips and package tours to excellent golf courses in major cities and holiday areas around Australia.

The **Nullarbor Links** (© **0407/990 049** mobile phone; www.nullarborlinks.com) is one of the world's most unusual golf courses, with its 18 holes spread over 1,365km (853 miles) between Kalgoorlie in Western Australia and Ceduna in South Australia, with one at each of the remote roadhouses along the long, lonely Eyre Highway, which crosses the Nullarbor Plain. See p. 520 for more details.

HORSEBACK RIDING Horseback-riding operators are everywhere in Australia. A particularly pleasant vacation is a multiday riding and camping trek in *The Man from Snowy River* country, the Snowy Mountains in New South Wales.

SAILING The 74 islands of the Whitsundays in Queensland are an out-of-this-world backdrop for sailing. And you don't have be an expert—the Whitsunday region is Australia's "bareboating" capital. Bareboating means you can charter an unskippered yacht and sail yourself. Even those without a scrap of experience can do it, although it's best to have someone on board who knows aft from fore. Perth and Sydney are mad about sailing; experienced sailors can head to the nearest yacht club to offer themselves as crew, especially during summer twilight races. The clubs are often short of sailors, and most will welcome out-of-towners.

SURFING You'll have no trouble finding a good surf beach along the Australian coast. Perth and Sydney are blessed with loads right in the city. Other popular spots include the Gold and Sunshine coasts in Queensland, the legendary Southern Ocean swells along Victoria's southern coast, and magnificent sets off Margaret River in Western Australia. Don't take your board much north of the Sunshine Coast—the Great Barrier Reef puts a stop to the swell from there all the way to the northern tip of Queensland. Loads of companies rent surf gear. Beginner lessons are offered at many surf beaches. Remember, surf only at patrolled beaches, and never surf alone.

WHITE-WATER RAFTING The best rapids are the Class V torrents on the Nymboida and Gwydir rivers behind Coffs Harbour in New South Wales. More Class V rapids await you on the Johnstone River in north Queensland, where access is by helicopter. Loads of tourists who have never held a paddle hurtle down the Class III to IV Tully River or the gentler Class II to III Barron River on a day trip from Cairns. The Snowy River National Park in Victoria and the Franklin River in the wilds of Tasmania are other popular spots. See also "Canoeing & Sea Kayaking," above.

Outfitters & Operators

Auswalk (© **03/5356 4971;** www.auswalk.com.au) offers self-guided or escorted/accommodated walking tours through picturesque parts of Australia such as the Great Ocean Road in Victoria, Lamington National Park Island in Queensland, the Red Centre, and the Blue Mountains in New South Wales, among many others.

Tasmanian Expeditions (✆ **1300 666 856** in Australia or 03/6339 3999; www.tas-ex.com) conducts day trips and extended expeditions featuring hiking, cycling, rafting, abseiling, canoeing, sea kayaking, and rock-climbing throughout Tasmania's national parks and unspoiled rural areas.

World Expeditions (✆ **613/241-2700** in Canada and the U.S., 020/8545 9030 in the U.K., 09/368 4161 in New Zealand, or 02/8270 8400 or 1300/720 000 in Australia; www.worldexpeditions.com) runs expeditions in many parts of Australia. Destinations include places less traveled, such as the long-distance Bibbulmun Track in Western Australia's southwest, the Red Centre's Larapinta Trail, and the Flinders and Gammon Ranges in South Australia. Some trips incorporate other pursuits, such as rafting, sailing, or biking.

The **World Outdoors** (✆ **800/488-8483** or 303/413-0938; www.theworldoutdoors.com) offers a multisport diving, hiking, mountain-biking, sailing and rafting packages to the Great Barrier Reef and Daintree rainforest.

STAYING CONNECTED

Mobile Phones

The three letters that define much of the world's wireless capabilities are **GSM** (Global System for Mobile Communications), a big, seamless network that makes for easy cross-border cellphone use throughout Europe and dozens of other countries worldwide. In the U.S., T-Mobile and AT&T Wireless use this quasi-universal system; in Canada, Microcell and some Rogers customers are GSM; and all Europeans and most Australians use GSM. GSM phones function with a removable plastic SIM card, encoded with your phone number and account information. If your cellphone is on a GSM system, and you have a world-capable multiband phone such as many Sony Ericsson, Motorola, or Samsung models, you can make and receive calls across civilized areas around much of the globe. Just call your wireless operator and ask for "international roaming" to be activated on your account.

For many, **renting** a phone is a good idea. While you can rent a phone from any number of overseas sites, including kiosks at airports and at car-rental agencies, we suggest renting the phone before you leave home. North Americans can rent one before leaving home from **InTouch U.S.A.** (✆ **800/872-7626;** www.intouchglobal.com) or **RoadPost** (✆ **888/290-1606** or 905/272-5665; www.roadpost.com). InTouch will also, for free, advise you on whether your existing phone will work overseas; simply call ✆ **703/222-7161** between 9am and 4pm EST, or go to **http://intouchglobal.com/travel.htm**.

In Australia, mobile phone company **Vodafone** (✆ **1300/300 404** in Australia; www.vodarent.com.au) has outlets at Brisbane, Sydney, Perth and Melbourne international airports, and at Sydney and Perth domestic airports. Vodaphone mobiles cost around A$8 a day, plus call charges and insurance, depending on the kind of phone and coverage you want. You can rent a SIM card for A$1 a day or A$15 a month.

In Australia—reputed to have one of the world's highest per-capita rates of ownership of "mobile" telephones, as they are known here—the cell network is digital, not analog. Calls to or from a mobile telephone are generally more expensive than calls to or from a fixed telephone. The price varies depending on the telephone company, the time of day, the distance between caller and recipient, and the telephone's pricing plan.

Buying a prepaid phone can be economically attractive. Once you arrive in Australia, stop by a local cellphone shop and get the cheapest package; you'll probably pay less than A$100 for a phone and a starter calling card with a significant amount of free credit.

Internet & E-mail

More and more hotels, resorts, airports, cafes, and retailers are going **Wi-Fi** (wireless fidelity), becoming "hot spots" that offer free high-speed Wi-Fi access or charge a small fee for usage. To find public Wi-Fi hot spots at your destination, go to **www.jiwire.com**; its hot spot finder holds the world's largest directory of public wireless hot spots.

For dial-up access, most business-class hotels throughout Australia offer dataports for laptop modems, and some of them offer free high-speed Internet access. Wherever you go, bring a **connection kit** of the right power and phone adapters, a spare phone cord, and a spare Ethernet network cable—or find out whether your hotel supplies them to guests.

Australia's electricity supply is 240 volts, 50 Hz. North Americans and Europeans will need to buy a converter before they leave home, because Australian stores usually only stock converters for Aussie appliances to fit American and European outlets.

Aside from formal cybercafes, most **youth hostels** and **public libraries** have Internet access. Avoid **hotel business centers** unless you're willing to pay exorbitant rates. Cybercafes (called Internet cafes in Australia) can be found almost everywhere. In major tourist cities, such as Cairns and Darwin, there are entire streets full of them. Most major airports have **Internet kiosks** that provide basic Web access for a per-minute fee that's usually higher than cybercafe prices. To find cybercafes in your destination, check **www.cybercaptive.com** and **www.cybercafe.com**. For help locating cybercafes and other establishments where you can go for Internet access, please see the "Fast Facts" sections of each city and state chapter in this book, as well as chapter 17.

Newspapers & Magazines

The national daily newspaper is ***The Australian,*** which publishes an expanded edition with a color magazine on Saturday. Most capital cities have their own daily papers, either tabloid or broadsheet, and sometimes both. There is an Australian edition of *Time.* Newspapers and magazines can be bought at a wide range of places including newsagents, supermarkets, gas stations and convenience stores.

Telephones

TO CALL AUSTRALIA FROM ABROAD: First dial the international access code: 011 from the U.S.; 00 from the U.K., Ireland, or New Zealand. Next dial Australia's country code, 61. Then dial the city code (drop the 0 from any area code given in this book) and then the number.

TO MAKE INTERNATIONAL CALLS FROM AUSTRALIA: First dial 0011 and then the country code (U.S. or Canada: 1; U.K.: 44; Ireland: 353; New Zealand: 64). Next you dial the area code and number. For example, if you wanted to call the British Embassy in Washington, D.C., you would dial 0011-1-202-588-7800. You may want to invest in an international online telephone card such as **ekit** (www.ekit.com), which will allow you to call overseas at much cheaper rates. For example, calling from Sydney to the United States will cost around US5¢ per minute plus a US60¢ service fee. Cards are rechargeable online.

FOR DIRECTORY ASSISTANCE: Dial ✆ **12455** if you're looking for a number inside Australia, and dial ✆ **1225** for numbers to all other countries.

FOR OPERATOR ASSISTANCE: If you need operator assistance in making a call, dial ✆ **12550** if you're trying to make an international call and ✆ **1234** if you want to call a number in Australia.

CALLING WITHIN AUSTRALIA: Each Australian state has a different area code: 02 for New South Wales and the ACT; 07 for Queensland; 03 for Victoria and Tasmania; 08 for South Australia, the Northern Territory, and Western Australia. You must dial the appropriate code if calling outside the state you are in; however, you also need to use the code if you are calling outside the city you are in. For example if you are in Sydney, where the code is 02, and you want to call another New South Wales town, you still dial 02 before the number.

TOLL-FREE NUMBERS: Numbers beginning with 1800 within Australia are toll-free, but calling a 1-800 number in the United States from Australia is not toll-free. In fact, it costs the same as an overseas call.

OTHER NUMBERS: Numbers starting with 13 or 1300 in Australia are charged at the local fee of A30¢ anywhere in Australia. Numbers beginning with 1900 (or 1901 or 1902 and so on) are pay-for-service lines, and you will be charged as much as A$5 a minute.

PAY PHONES: The primary telecommunications network in Australia is **Telstra** (www.telstra.com). Telstra pay phones are found in most city streets, shopping centers, transport terminals, post offices, and along highways—even in some of the most remote areas of Australia. To find the nearest one to you, call ✆ **1800/011 433** or look online at **www.telstra.com.au/payphoneservices/index.htm**. The cost of a local call from a pay phone is A50¢, either in coins or by using a phone card. Some phones only take prepaid phone cards, which can be purchased from newsstands and other retailers in denominations of A$5, A$10, and A$20 and are good for local, national, and international calls. There are no access numbers—you just insert the card and dial. Credit phones take most major credit cards. Some phones also allow you to send SMS messages. Pay phones can be found in the usual booths, but you may also find some inside convenience stores and the like, called "blue phones" or "gold phones."

TIPS ON ACCOMMODATIONS

Accommodations properties in Australia carry star ratings given by AAA Tourism, which has been awarding ratings since the 1950s. This independent assessment is based on facilities, amenities, maintenance, and cleanliness. Ratings run from one to five stars. Stars are featured in AAA Tourism guides, and recent research shows 70% of travelers use the star ratings when choosing their accommodations (these star ratings are noted using asterisks). The rating scheme covers over 18,000 accommodations throughout every state and territory.

HOTELS It's a rare hotel room that does not have air-conditioning for heating and cooling, a telephone, a color TV, a clock radio, a minifridge (if not a minibar), an iron and ironing board, and self-serve coffee and tea. Private bathrooms are standard, although they often have only a shower, not a tub.

The largest hotel group in Australia is the French chain **Accor,** which has more than 100 properties (that's about 15,000 rooms) under its Sofitel, Novotel, Mercure, All Seasons, Ibis, and Formule 1 brands. Many other international chains, such as Marriott, Sheraton, and Hilton, have properties in Australia.

SERVICED APARTMENTS Serviced apartments are favored by many Aussie families and business travelers. You get a fully furnished apartment with one, two, or three bedrooms, a living room, a kitchen or kitchenette, a laundry, and often two bathrooms—in other words, all the facilities of a hotel suite and more, often for less than the cost of a four-star hotel room. (Not every apartment kitchen has a dishwasher, so check if that's important to you.) A nice two-bedroom apartment can cost anywhere from around A$170 to A$720 a night, depending on your location and the season. Australia's apartment inventory is enormous and ranges from clean and comfortable, if a little dated, to luxurious. Most apartments can be rented for 1 night, especially in cities, but in popular vacation spots, some proprietors will insist on a minimum 3-night stay, or even a week in high season.

Medina Serviced Apartments (✆ **1300/633 462** in Australia, or 02/9356 5061; www.medina.com.au) has a chain of 23 midrange to upscale properties in Sydney, Melbourne, Brisbane, Canberra, Adelaide, Perth, and Darwin. Australia's biggest apartment chain, with more than 110 properties, is **Quest Serviced Apartments** (✆ **1800/334 033** in Australia, or 03/9645 8357 or 0800/944 400 in New Zealand; www.questapartments.com.au). It has apartments in every state and territory.

MOTELS & MOTOR INNS Australia's plentiful motels are neat and clean, if often a little dated. You can count on them to provide air-conditioning, a telephone, a color TV, a clock radio, a minifridge or minibar, and self-serve tea and coffee. Most have only showers, not bathtubs. Some have restaurants attached, and many have swimming pools. Motor inns offer a greater range of facilities and a generally higher standard of rooms than motels. Rates average A$80 to A$120 double.

BED & BREAKFASTS B&Bs are cheap and plentiful in Australia. It is easy to find charming rooms for under A$100 for a double. Bathroom facilities are often shared, although more properties now offer private, if not always en-suite (attached), bathrooms.

B&Bs can be hard to find because most travel agents don't list them (the establishments are not big enough to pay a commission). A good source is the ***Australian Bed & Breakfast Book*** (✆ **02/8208 5959;** www.bbbook.com.au), which lists more than 400 B&Bs across Australia. The individual entries are supplied by the B&B operators themselves. The entire book is posted on the website. In Australia you can buy the latest edition in bookshops and at newsdealers, or you can order it online for A$20 plus A$10 for overseas airmail postage.

What Next? Productions (✆ **0438/600 696** mobile phone; www.beautifulaccommodation.com) publishes a series of ***Beautiful Accommodation*** color guides, listing around 500 exquisite properties in every state and territory, many in charming country areas. Each has been checked out by the editorial team before

House-Swapping

House-swapping is becoming a more popular and viable means of travel; you stay in their place, they stay in yours, and you both get an authentic and personal view of the area, the opposite of the escapist retreat that many hotels offer. Try **HomeLink International** (www.homelink.org), the largest and oldest home-swapping organization, founded in 1952, with over 11,000 listings worldwide. There is a branch of HomeLink in Australia. Swap at your own risk.

being included in the book. The properties listed are more upscale than most, roughly in the range of A$150 to A$300. Each book sells for A$30 in bookstores or can be ordered online once you are in Australia.

Another good website is that of **Bed & Breakfast and Farmstay Australia** (www.australianbedandbreakfast.com.au), which has links to all state B&B organizations.

PUBS Aussie pubs are really made for drinking, not spending the night, but many offer rooms upstairs, usually with shared bathroom facilities. Because most pubs are decades old, the rooms may be either old-fashioned or just plain old. Pub accommodations are dying out in the cities but still common in the country. Australians are rowdy drinkers, so sleeping over the bar can be hellishly noisy, but the pub's saving grace is incredibly low rates. Most charge per person, not per room, and you will rarely pay more than A$50 per person a night.

FARMSTAYS The Aussie answer to the dude ranch is a farmstay. Australian farmstays are rarely as well set up for tourists as the dude ranch Billy Crystal's character visited in *City Slickers*. Most are farms first, tourist operations second, so you may have to find your own fun and know how to take care of yourself, at least to a degree.

Accommodations on farms can be anything from a basic bunkhouse (ask if it's air-conditioned, because most farms are in very hot areas) to rustically luxurious digs. Do some research on your farm—a lot of activities are seasonal, some farmers will not allow you to get involved in dangerous work, not all will offer horseback riding, and "farm" means different things in different parts of Australia. If you like green fields and dairy cows, Victoria may be the place for you. If checking fences on a dusty 500,000-hectare (1.2-million-acre) Outback station (ranch) sounds wildly romantic, head to Western Australia, Queensland, or the Northern Territory.

The website of **Bed & Breakfast and Farmstay Australia** (www.australianbedandbreakfast.com.au) has links to all state farmstay organizations. Rates vary, but you will find many properties charging under A$200 for a double, which sometimes includes breakfast. Meals are often available as an optional extra.

For tips on surfing for lodging deals online, visit **Frommers.com**.

SUGGESTED ITINERARIES

4

Australia's size and its distance from Northern Hemisphere destinations are the two most daunting things about planning a visit. It's a long way to come for just a week, but if that's all you can spare, you still want to see as much as possible. While our inclination is to immerse ourselves in one spot, we're aware that not everyone wants to do that. Seeing as much as you can is often a priority.

Australia is a complex and fascinating place, merging ancient Aboriginal culture with modern life. You'll learn a lot in a week or two but will have just scraped the surface of this vast nation.

If you're a first-time visitor, with only 1 or 2 weeks, you may find these two itineraries most helpful: **"Australia in 1 Week"** or **"Australia in 2 Weeks."** These itineraries can be shifted around to suit your needs; you could substitute the Cairns section of "Australia in 1 Week" for the Uluru/Red Centre suggestions in "Australia in 2 Weeks," flying from Sydney to Uluru.

If you've been to Australia before, or have already visited our major icons—Sydney, the Great Barrier Reef, or Uluru—you might want to focus on another aspect of the country. You may even want to head out west to see the lesser-known, but still very rewarding, parts of the country. If you're bringing your family with you, our **"Australia for Families"** itinerary may give you some ideas to keep the young ones occupied (while entertaining any parents at the same time).

You might also review our "Best of" chapter (p. 1) to see what experiences or sights have special appeal to you, and adjust the itineraries to suit your own interests.

Getting around this vast continent, where the major attractions are thousands of miles apart, is daunting and time-consuming. Flying is the only way to cover long distances efficiently, but unfortunately it can also be expensive. Remember to allow flying time in your itineraries and don't try to pack too much in on the days you fly—even domestic flights can be around 3 hours and can be draining. See "Getting There & Getting Around," in chapter 3 (p. 43), for information about air passes and getting the best rate on Australia's domestic carriers.

Our best advice is to take a tip from Australians: If the pace gets too hectic, just chill out and reorder your sightseeing priorities. Take time to meet the locals and ask their advice on what you should see as well.

AUSTRALIA IN 1 WEEK

Impossible! Australia is so vast that in 1 week, you'll only be able to get in a small corner of it—perhaps one city or a few of the natural wonders. It will be memorable, nevertheless, and careful planning will maximize your time and allow you to see some of the major sights.

Use the following itinerary to make the most out of a week in Australia, but make sure you don't exhaust yourself trying to cram everything in. Australians are a laid-back lot, generally, and in some places the pace is relaxed. And that's just the way to enjoy it. One week provides barely enough time to see the best of Sydney, which for most people is the entry point to Australia. (Luckily, you'll have a spectacular introduction to this great city: You may well get a view of the **Sydney Harbour Bridge** and the **Opera House** from the air as your plane comes in.)

If you have only a week and want to head farther afield, there are two main choices, depending on your interests. The **Great Barrier Reef** is a "must" for divers, but don't forget that you must allow time on either side of your reef trip for flying. There are no such problems with Australia's other icon, **Uluru,** in the heart of the **Red Centre.** This triangle, of course, is something of a cliché, but it still gives you a complete Australian experience. Realistically, you will have to choose between the Reef and the Rock, or choose not to scuba dive while you are in Queensland.

Days 1 & 2: Arrive in Sydney ★★★

Check into your hotel and spend whatever time you have after arrival recovering from the almost-guaranteed jet lag. If you arrive in the morning and have a full day ahead of you, try to stay up and hit the nearest cafe for a shot of caffeine to keep you going. Head to **Circular Quay,** and from there get a fantastic view of **Sydney Harbour Bridge** (p. 148) before strolling to the **Sydney Opera House** (p. 149) and soaking up some history at **The Rocks.** If you have time, you can take the ferry from Circular Quay to Manly beach and round off a fairly easy day with fish and chips. Then head to bed for some much-needed sleep.

Start Day 2 with a ride to the top of the Sydney Tower to experience Sydney's newest and highest open-air attraction, **Skywalk** (p. 154), a breathtaking 260m (853 ft.) above Sydney. Harnessed onto a moving, glass-floored viewing platform that extends out over the edge of the tower, you can view all of Sydney's landmarks, including the Sydney Harbour Bridge, Sydney Opera House, Sydney Harbour, and even the Blue Mountains beyond. Don't worry, it's not actually as scary as it sounds. Sydney Tower has several attractions, including **OzTrek** (p. 154)—a simulator ride that takes you across Australia's vast geography (virtually) that the kids will love. For an introduction to Australia's wildlife, head to **Taronga Zoo** (p. 156) or the **Sydney Aquarium** (p. 153). **Featherdale Wildlife Park** (p. 155) is about an hour and a half from the city center, but if you have time to spare, it's a great choice. If you enjoy museums, put the **Australian Museum** (p. 159), the **Australian National Maritime Museum at Darling Harbour** (p. 152), and the interactive **Powerhouse Museum**

Australia in 1 or 2 Weeks

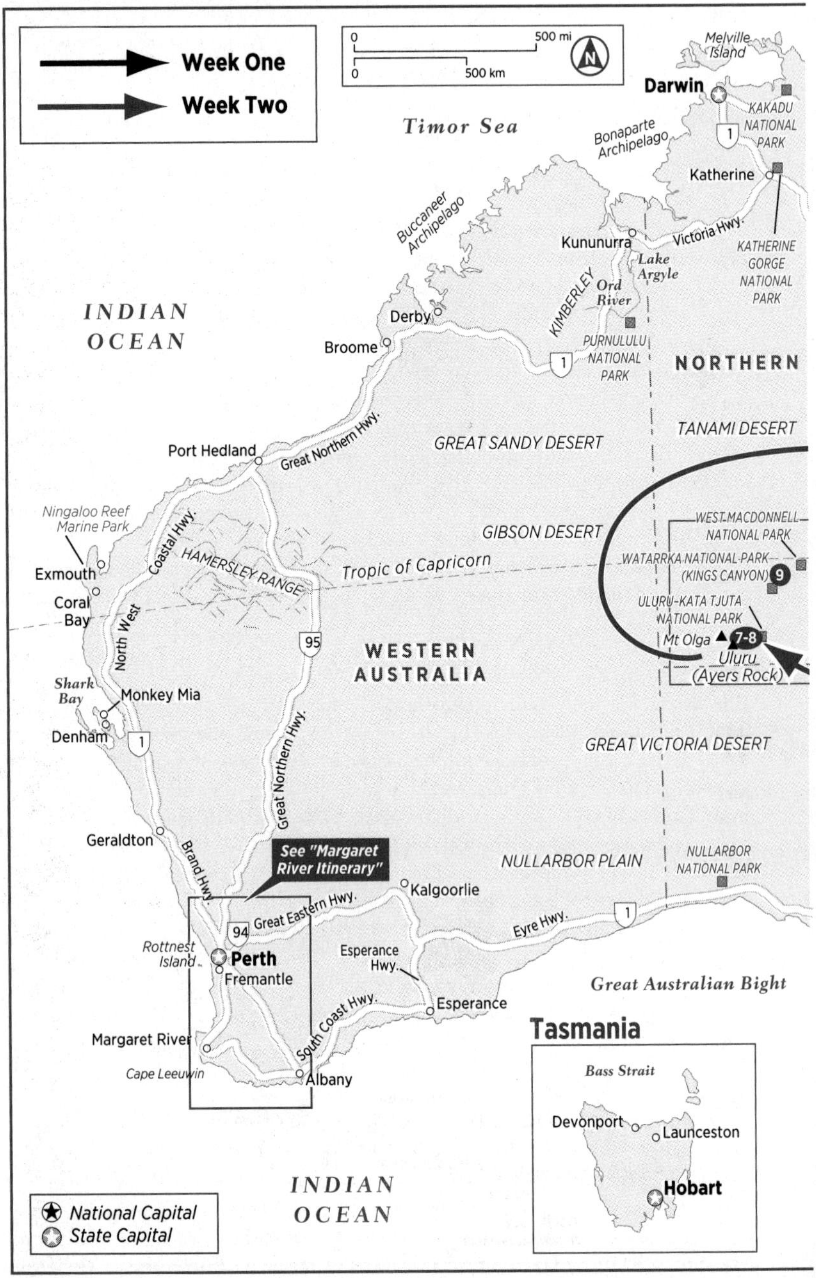

Great Barrier Reef Area
Coral Sea
Daintree
Newell
DAINTREE NATIONAL PARK
Port Douglas
Yorkeys Knob
Cairns
Thursday Island
Coral Sea
Arnhem Land
Gulf of Carpentaria
CAPE YORK PENINSULA
Cooktown
DAINTREE NATIONAL PARK
Port Douglas
Cairns
Mission Beach
Great Barrier Reef Marine Park
Stuart Hwy.
TERRITORY
Barkly Hwy.
Tennant Creek
Mt. Isa
Townsville
Whitsunday Islands National Park
PACIFIC OCEAN
Flinders Hwy.
Landsborough Hwy.
Proserpine
Mackay
MACDONNELL RANGES
Alice Springs
Longreach
GREAT DIVIDING RANGE
Rockhampton
Capricorn Hwy.
Gladstone
SIMPSON DESERT
QUEENSLAND
Bundaberg
Bruce Hwy.
Fraser Island
SOUTH AUSTRALIA
Mitchell Hwy.
See "Outback Itinerary"
Brisbane
Sunshine Coast
Gold Coast
LAMINGTON NATL. PK.
Coober Pedy
Lightning Ridge
New England Hwy.
Stuart Hwy.
FLINDERS RANGES NATIONAL PARK
Darling River
Coffs Harbour
Barrier Hwy.
Broken Hill
Oxley Hwy.
Tamworth
Dubbo
Pacific Hwy.
Port Macquarie
Port Pirie
NEW SOUTH WALES
BLUE MTNS. NATL. PK.
Newcastle
Mildura
Adelaide
Sydney
Newell Hwy.
Hume Hwy.
Murray River
Kangaroo Island
Dukes Hwy.
Princes Hwy.
Wodonga
Princes Hwy.
CANBERRA
VICTORIA
Albury
Mt. Kosciuszko
A.C.T.
Mt. Gambier
Ballarat
Melbourne
SNOWY MOUNTAINS
Geelong
Apollo Bay
To Tasmania (see inset)
Tasman Sea

4 SUGGESTED ITINERARIES | Australia in 1 Week

(p. 153) on your list for the day. For an insight into Sydney's beginnings as a convict settlement, visit the **Hyde Park Barracks Museum** (p. 153), a convict-built prison. Finish off your day with a twilight (or later on weekends) **BridgeClimb ★** (p. 149) up the Sydney Harbour Bridge, or take the kids to **Luna Park** (p. 148), a small and fairly traditional amusement park that's at its best at night.

Day 3: The Blue Mountains ★★★

Take the train from Central Station to **Katoomba** (p. 186) for a day, exploring the beauty of the Blue Mountains—only 2 hours from Sydney. Once there, jump on the Blue Mountains Explorer Bus, which allows you to hop on and off wherever you please. There are also many day-tour operators running to the Blue Mountains from Sydney. Whichever mode of transport you use, don't miss the spectacular **Three Sisters** (p. 187) rock formations, best viewed from Echo Point Road at Katoomba.

The adventurous might prefer to take a tour from Katoomba to the **Jenolan Caves** (p. 193), about a 90-minute drive southwest. Nine caves are open for exploration, and you can take canyoning tours of between 3 hours and a full day. Head back to Sydney and have dinner somewhere with a view of the harbor.

Day 4: Cairns, Gateway to the Great Barrier Reef

On Day 4, take the earliest flight you can from Sydney to Cairns—flight time is 3 hours—and check into a hotel in the city, which on such a tight schedule will make getting to the major attractions quicker and easier than staying on the northern beaches, out of town. Explore the city a little, and see some wildlife—including a massive saltwater crocodile—in the bizarre setting of the **Cairns Wildlife Dome** (p. 287), atop the Hotel Sofitel Reef Casino. You will have the rest of the day to head out to visit the **Tjapukai Aboriginal Cultural Park ★** (p. 286). If you are not going to the Red Centre, this is a great place to learn about Aboriginal culture and life, albeit in a theme-park kind of way. You could spend several hours here, or save the visit for the evening, when **Tjapukai by Night** tours give a different look at traditional ceremonies, including dinner and a fire-and-water outdoor show.

Day 5: A Day Trip to the Reef ★★★

Day trips to the Great Barrier Reef leave from the **Reef Fleet Terminal.** The trip to the outer reef takes about 2 hours, and once there, you will spend your day on a pontoon with about 300 people. Experienced divers may prefer to take a day trip with one of the dive charter companies who take smaller groups and visit two or three reefs. The pontoons of the big operators also offer the chance to take a scenic flight—a truly spectacular experience. Divers must spend another 24 hours in Cairns before flying. If you are content to snorkel, ride the glass-bottom boats, and soak up the sun, you will be able to fly the next day. After returning to Cairns, take a stroll along the **Esplanade** and eat at one of the busy cafes and restaurants that line the strip.

Day 6: Kuranda or the Daintree ★★

Waiting out the day after diving (you can't fly for 24 hr. after you've been on a dive) can be spent discovering another aspect to Australia—its rainforests. Take a trip to the mountain village of **Kuranda** aboard the steam train along the **Kuranda Scenic Railway** (p. 290), past waterfalls and gorges. In Kuranda, explore the markets and the nature parks, and maybe take a **Kuranda Riverboat Tour** (p. 292), which runs about 45 minutes. Return on the **Skyrail** cableway (p. 290), which carries you over the rainforest (you can get to ground level at a couple of stations on the way) to the edge of Cairns. The views are sensational.

Another option is to head to the World Heritage–listed **Daintree Rainforest ★**, a 2-hour drive north of Cairns. Many tour operators, including Port Douglas–based **Heritage & Interpretive Tours** (p. 304), run day tours into the Daintree and Cape Tribulation National Parks. If you are exploring on your own, make time for a 1-hour cruise on the **Daintree River** with **Dan Irby's Mangrove Adventures** (p. 304), where you will travel in a small open boat and see lots of fascinating wildlife. Both day and night tours are highly recommended.

If you choose the Daintree option, overnight in the lovely resort town of **Port Douglas** and head to one of its great restaurants—try **Salsa Bar & Grill** (p. 310) for a relaxed and lively atmosphere.

Day 7: Cairns to Sydney

Drive back to Cairns in the morning, and head to the airport for your flight to Sydney. Unless you have a flight directly out of Cairns, you will spend most of your last day in Australia returning to Sydney. With the time you have left in Sydney, treat yourself to dinner at a restaurant overlooking the harbor, with its bridge and Opera House illuminated. It's a sight you'll carry home with you.

AUSTRALIA IN 2 WEEKS

With 2 weeks, your visit to Australia will be much more relaxed and you'll get a greater sense of the diversity of Australia landscape, wildlife, and people. You will get to see all three icons—Sydney, the Great Barrier Reef, and Uluru—in more depth, and maybe even have time to go outside those areas, especially if you limit your icons to two instead of three.

Days 1–6: Sydney to Cairns

Follow the itinerary as outlined in "Australia in 1 Week," above.

Day 7: Cairns to Uluru

On Day 7, leave Cairns as early as you can (this will probably mean spending the night in Cairns rather than Port Douglas). Your flight to Ayers Rock Airport will take around 3 hours, or possibly more, depending on the type of aircraft you are on. Make sure you book a direct flight, and not one that goes via Sydney! Try to get a window seat for the spectacular views as you fly over the Outback.

If you take the early flight, you can be in **Uluru** by around 9am, which gives you the entire day to take in the enormity of this fabulous monolith. Take the shuttle from **Ayers Rock Resort** (which is the only place to stay, but offers many accommodations choices; p. 413) to the Rock. Join **Anangu Tours** (p. 410) for a guided walk at Uluru; one of the best is the late-afternoon Kuniya walk, which concludes with watching sunset over Uluru—an unforgettable sight. Spend some time in the impressive and interesting **Uluru–Kata Tjuta Cultural Centre** (p. 409), near the base of Uluru. And after doing all that in a day, you'll be ready for a quiet dinner at whatever hotel you've chosen.

If you decide to **climb Uluru** (remembering that the Aboriginal traditional owners would prefer you didn't), make sure you don't do it at the hottest time of day. A climb will take you between 2 and 4 hours, depending on your fitness.

Day 8: Exploring Uluru ★★★

Sunrise is one of those magic times at Uluru, so make the effort to get up early on Day 8. This is also a great time to do the 9.6km (6-mile) **Base Walk** circumnavigating Uluru (p. 410), which takes 2 to 3 hours. There are a range of other ways to experience Uluru, including camel rides, Harley-Davidson tours, and helicopter joy flights, but walking up close to the Rock beats them all.

You will also have time today to head to **Kata Tjuta** (also called "The Olgas"; p. 412), where you'll see there's much more to the Red Centre than just one rock. Kata Tjuta is about 48km (30 miles) west of Uluru, but plenty of tours go there if you don't have your own wheels.

End your day in the desert with the **Sounds of Silence** dinner (p. 413), run by Ayers Rock Resort. Sip champagne as the sun sets over Uluru to the eerie music of the didgeridoo, and then tuck into kangaroo, barramundi, and other native foods. But it's not the food you're here for—it's the silence and the stars. A short stargazing session with an astronomer ends a memorable evening.

Day 9: Uluru to Kings Canyon

Hire a four-wheel-drive vehicle and tackle the long Outback drive from Uluru to Alice Springs, stopping for a night at **Kings Canyon** (p. 405). It is 306km (190 miles) from Uluru to Kings Canyon (also known as **Watarrka National Park**), which offers another unbeatable look at Outback Australia. You can spend the afternoon walking up the side of the canyon and around the rim. It is very steep and will take you around 4 hours. A gentler walk is the short and shady canyon floor walk. Stay overnight at Kings Canyon Resort.

Day 10: Kings Canyon to Alice Springs

Get an early start for Alice Springs, and take the unpaved but interesting **Mereenie Loop Road,** which will take you through the **Glen Helen Gorge** or the historic **Hermannsburg** mission settlement (p. 404). Whichever road you take, the scenery is like nowhere else in Australia. You will probably spend most of the day driving to Alice, making a few stops along the way.

On arrival, check into a hotel and head out to one of the local restaurants, several of which offer sophisticated versions of "bush tucker," including kangaroo, emu, and crocodile dishes.

Day 11: Alice Springs

If you can stand another early start, take a **dawn balloon flight** over the desert (p. 200), followed by a champagne breakfast. If you don't head back to bed immediately for a few hours catch-up sleep, there are plenty of attractions to discover, including the **Alice Springs Desert Park** (p. 393), for a look at some unusual Australian creatures; the **School of the Air** (p. 394); and the **Royal Flying Doctor Service** base (p. 394). In the afternoon, take a half-day tour with an Aboriginal guide at the **Aboriginal Art & Culture Centre** (p. 393). Alternatively, visit the **Alice Springs Telegraph Station Historical Reserve** (p. 393), set in an oasis just outside town, for a look at early settler life. Finish the day with a **sunset camel ride** (p. 396) down the dry Todd River bed and have dinner at the camel farm.

Day 12: Alice Springs to Sydney

Direct flights from Alice Springs to Sydney leave in the early afternoon, so you have all morning to explore more of the town and perhaps buy some Aboriginal art. (This is one of the best places to get it.)

On arrival in Sydney, after an almost 3-hour flight, check into your hotel and spend the night discovering some of the city's nightlife.

Day 13: A Day at Bondi Beach

For sands of a different hue from those you've experienced in recent days, take the bus to Sydney's most famous beach, **Bondi** (p. 157), and spend it lazing on the sand or—in summer, at least—taking a dip in the surf. Take the Bondi Explorer bus from Circular Quay, which gives you a choice of harborside bays and coastal beaches, or take the train to Bondi Junction and then a bus to the beach. The scenic cliff-top walk to **Bronte Beach** (p. 157) is worth doing, or you can continue farther to **Coogee** (p. 158).

Day 14: Sydney

Your final day in Australia can be spent on last-minute shopping and seeing those Sydney sights that you haven't yet had time for. Cap it all off with a slap-up seafood dinner somewhere with a fantastic view of the Harbour Bridge.

AUSTRALIA FOR FAMILIES

Australia is an unbelievable destination for kids—and not just because of the kangaroos and koalas. Our suggestion is to explore Sydney for 2 days with family in tow; then head up to the beautiful Blue Mountains on a day trip to ride the cable car and the world's steepest railway. The climax comes with a few days exploring the Barrier Reef and the rainforest around Port Douglas.

Days 1 & 2: Sydney

First off, head to Circular Quay to see the **Sydney Opera House.** A tour inside might be a bit much for younger kids, but you can walk around a fair bit of it and take the obligatory photos of Australia's most famous landmark. To stretch your legs, head from here into the **Royal Botanic Gardens** (p. 161) to spot long-beaked ibises wandering around the grass and hundreds of fruit bats squabbling among the treetops in the jungle section. Walk back past the Opera House and the ferries to **The Rocks,** where you can take a quick stroll through the historic streets, stopping off for a look at some of the trendy shops or the Market on Saturdays.

There are plenty of places to eat lunch, but a filling prospect is pasta at **Rossini** (p. 131), opposite the ferry terminals, where you can sit outside and watch the world go by. Portions are large, so you might want to split a meal between younger kids.

After lunch, take a ferry to **Taronga Zoo,** where a cable car takes you up the hill to the main entrance. All the kids' favorites are here, from kangaroos and koalas to platypuses, located in a nocturnal house. A farmyard section edges onto a playground of sorts, with lots of water features to give your kids a sprinkle on a hot day.

On Day 2, head to the city center for an elevator ride up to the top of **Sydney Tower** (p. 154), where you can look right across Sydney as far as the Blue Mountains in the distance. Entry to the Tower includes admission to Skytour, which features a darkened storytelling room where the kids can learn a little about Australian legends and Aborigines, as well as a thrilling simulator ride that takes you on adventures throughout Australia.

It's a short walk from here to Darling Harbour, where you can cap off the morning with a visit to **Sydney Aquarium.** The sharks are huge here, and they swim right above your head, but the real attraction is the Barrier Reef section, where tens of thousands of colorful fish swim by in huge tanks to the sound of classical music.

Eat lunch at one of the many cheap eateries on the other side of the bridge before taking the monorail back to Town Hall or taking another ferry from near the Aquarium back to Circular Quay.

If it's a hot day, or you just want to go to the beach, you have two main choices: From Circular Quay, you can take a half-hour ferry ride, or you can take a 15-minute high-speed JetCat trip to **Manly** (p. 158). Here you can laze the afternoon away, and you can even rent a surfboard, body board, or in-line skates. Or take a CityRail train from Town Hall to Bondi, and then a bus to **Bondi Beach,** where you can reward your efforts with ice cream or a late-afternoon pizza from **Pompei's** (p. 143), on the main drag.

Day 3: The Blue Mountains

You could easily spend a couple more days with the kids having fun in Sydney, but you shouldn't miss a trip to the mountains. Several companies run tour buses to the area, stopping off at an animal park along the way. The best one to visit is **Featherdale Wildlife Park** (p. 155), where you can get up close to more kangaroos, koalas, and Tasmanian devils. The tour will also stop at **Scenic World** (p. 187), where you can take the short ride on the Scenic Railway. It's very steep, so hold on tight. At the bottom you'll find yourselves among an ancient tree fern forest—it's truly remarkable. A short walk takes you to the **Skyway,** a cable car that travels 300m (984 ft.) above the Jamison Valley.

Elsewhere in the mountains there are fabulous views across craggy bluffs and deep bowls of gum trees. It's a long day, so pack plenty of snacks and a few favorite toys.

Days 4, 5 & 6: The Reef & the Rainforest

Now it's time to head north, up the Tropics. You'll need to fly, of course, otherwise it would take you several days to drive up the coast. Most people base themselves in **Port Douglas** rather than Cairns, because the beach is huge and uncrowded and some of the best trips originate from here.

After the flight, relax on the beach, but remember to swim inside the nets off the sand; the "stingers" (box jellyfish) around here can cause life-threatening stings, especially where kids are concerned.

The next day, it's time to visit the **Reef.** Thankfully, once on the Reef itself, the dangerous jellyfish are very uncommon. Cruise boats take around 90 minutes to get from Port Douglas to the outer Reef; but once there, you are in for some amazing snorkeling. Expect to see numerous species of corals and fish, and even an occasional turtle. A good seafood lunch is generally served on board, so you won't go hungry!

Day 6 will be a real jungle experience. Tours leave Port Douglas daily for the **Daintree National Park and the Cape Tribulation Rainforests.** Usually included in the tour is a boat trip among the local crocodiles, a stroll along an isolated beach, and, of course, walks in the rainforest, where you emerge into a dripping world of palms, strangler figs, staghorns, pythons, frogs, and electric-blue butterflies.

Day 7: Fly Back to Sydney

If you have time, take the kids by ferry to **Luna Park,** just across from Circular Quay, or walk there across the Harbour Bridge. The fun park is small, with a few rides suitable for younger kids, but it does boast a magnificent view across to the Harbour Bridge and Opera House, which look glorious after the sun's gone down.

SPLURGING IN SYDNEY

It's unfair, but some people are simply rolling in cash. If you have a pay-as-you-please budget, or you have a nice business account to play with, then this 2-day itinerary to Sydney will help relieve your itch to spend. But even if you don't have a bankroll, some of the options in this itinerary can be done for free, or on the cheap.

Day 1: Sydney & Bondi

Firstly, you need to make sure you're staying in the best possible hotel. I'd probably try to get a room with a view of the Sydney Opera House at the **Park Hyatt Sydney** (p. 115), or opt for a nice colonial-style room at the **Observatory Hotel** (p. 115). If you feel like something a bit more modern, then why not try out one of the Star Suites at **Star City** in Darling Harbour (p. 121). These split-level suites are amazing, and as they are a couple of rungs below the hotel's most expensive suites, you can sleep safe in the knowledge that you're getting to spend up big without quite breaking the bank.

You've settled in, but you need breakfast. You could always be boring and eat in your hotel, or you could jump in a cab and head to **Bill's** (p. 141) in the inner-city suburb of Darlinghurst. The scrambled eggs, eaten around a communal table, have become a Sydney institution of sorts.

Now it's time to do some serious sightseeing. For those with a head for heights you can't have a better experience than climbing across the Sydney Harbour Bridge with **Bridgeclimb** (p. 149). The views of the city and its wonderful harbor are awe-inspiring. If that doesn't get your attention, how about discovering the city on the back of a Harley-Davidson motorcycle with **Blue Thunder Motorcycle Tours** (p. 166)?

You should have worked up an appetite by now. Time for lunch, and a taxi with a difference. Hop aboard a **Sydney by Seaplane** (p. 166) and zip across Sydney Harbour and all its wonderful attractions before heading north along the glorious coastline.

Of all the lunch options, I'd opt for the **Berowra Waters Inn,** set in bushland on the beautiful Hawkesbury River (© **02/9456 1027;** www.berowrawatersinn.com).

This is one of Australia's greatest dining rooms, positioned right on the water's edge and nestled among the gum trees. Chef Dietmar Sawyere serves up internationally acclaimed cuisine, and there's a stunning wine collection.

By the time you arrive back in Sydney you might feel like a bit of a rest back at your hotel, or you could keep pressing on with a late afternoon visit to Bondi. The **cliff-top walk from Bondi Beach to Bronte** via trendy Tamarama is free, but that shouldn't stop you spending time on it. The views out across the pounding surf and far out to sea are just perfect.

It will be time for a cocktail by the time you get to Bondi. The panoramic views at the **Icebergs Dining Room & Bar** (p. 142) will take your breath away. If you still have an appetite after that huge lunch, this is the place for dinner, too.

After a bite to eat (and maybe a wickedly addictive gelato from **Pompei's**) head back to town for a nightcap. You could try the **Ivy** (p. 178) for some sophisticated cocktails with the in crowd, or flop into a plush lounge with a glass of Dom Perignon at Hemmesphere in the **Establishment Hotel** (p. 118).

Day 2: Manly

Go for breakfast somewhere different today, where the usual tourists don't frequent. Take a taxi across the Sydney Harbour Bridge to exclusive Mosman, and drop in to one of the cafes along Balmoral Beach. The smartest joint here is the **Bathers' Pavilion Restaurant** (p. 159), which does a nice line in French toast with rhubarb, fresh fig, and mascarpone cheese, as well as eggs Benedict and slap-up bacon-and-egg meals. Make sure you bring your swimsuit! The water's calm and there's quite a social scene.

Call a cab (or catch a local bus up the hill to Mosman shops—buses leave from opposite the beach—and then take a cab) and head onwards to Manly. It will take about 20 minutes. Spend the morning in **Manly,** either just lazing on the beach, diving with sharks at **Oceanworld Manly** (p. 156), or taking a private surfing lesson for the fun of it from **Manly Surf School** (p. 167). Have a quick lunch in one of the beachfront restaurants—you can't go wrong with any of them—before catching the fast ferry back to Circular Quay.

If you don't fancy a quick zap around on one of **Harbour Jet**'s jet boats (p. 151), you could opt for a stroll through the **Royal Botanic Gardens,** stopping off to see the fruit bats hanging from the trees. Options from here include a look at the paintings in the **Art Gallery of New South Wales** (p. 159), or a short walk up **Macquarie Street** to look at some of the historic colonial buildings, such as Hyde Park Barracks.

Break up a little afternoon shopping with a coffee at the **Old Coffee Shop** in the Strand Arcade (p. 141).

Freshen up back at the hotel and then head out for a cocktail or two. A great bar with a view is the **Opera Bar** (**© 02/9247 1666;** www.operabar.com.au), nestled beside the Sydney Opera House. It's truly magical.

Then the culinary highlight of your 2-day tour awaits—an evening at one of the world's best restaurants, **Tetsuya's** (p. 136). Expect an inspirational gourmet journey the likes of which you may have never experienced before, with matching wines. Just make sure you book well in advance!

INLAND ODYSSEY: SYDNEY TO MELBOURNE

When Sydneysiders get tired of the city, they often dream of "going bush." If they could, they'd head west into the setting sun and out into the Outback. Not many local city slickers ever get to realize their dream, but you can do it for them on this 7-day inland odyssey from Sydney to Melbourne.

Day 1: The Blue Mountains

Armed with your road map, leave Sydney via Parramatta Road, by the M4 motorway and the Great Western Highway. Two hours should see you safely in the cool of the Blue Mountains. Drive into the little town of **Katoomba,** where you could stop for a quick coffee break or early lunch at the historic **Paragon Café** (p. 190) before taking a short spin to see the incredible views across to the **Three Sisters** rock formation from Echo Point. From here, follow the signs to **Scenic World,** where you can take the world's steepest railway into an enchanting world of tree ferns—it will take just a couple of minutes to get down. Take the cable car up and continue on your journey.

Keep following the Great Western Highway as it heads west for 39km (24 miles), through Blackheath, Mount Victoria, and Hartley, and then downhill toward the old mining town of Lithgow. The most famous attraction around here is the **Zig Zag Railway ★★** (p. 191), a former coal route that crosses the valleys on impressive viaducts and winds around the eucalyptus-covered hills. A steam train runs the 18km (11-mile) back-and-forth route on Wednesdays, Saturdays, Sundays, and school holidays, and a diesel train does the route on other days. It costs A$20 for adults round-trip and A$10 for kids, and takes 1½ hours.

The highway leads from here down onto the plains and into **Bathurst ★** (p. 194), approximately 200km (124 miles) west of Sydney, and 5km (3 miles) west of Lithgow. Bathurst, which was proclaimed a city in 1815, is the oldest inland settlement in Australia. Its 19th-century architecture is beautifully preserved, and it makes for pleasant wandering. Stay here for the night.

Day 2: Canowindra to Dubbo

It's a 56km (34-mile) drive along the Mitchell Highway from Bathurst to Orange. Highly recommended is a 58km (36-mile) sidetrack down through a landscape of spare trees and orange soil to **Canowindra,** to visit the **Age of Fishes Museum** (p. 195). A chance discovery in 1955 near here revealed an extensive fossil bed dating back 360 million years and containing over 3,500 fish, some with armored shells, lungs, and huge jaws like crocodiles. The fish are well displayed, many still in their muddy-looking rock shelves.

Make your way back to the Mitchell Highway for the 150km (93-mile) trek northwest to Dubbo, which has that beginning-of-the-Outback feel, with plenty of Akubra hats around. South of town is the **Western Plains Zoo,** set in over 300 hectares (741 acres) of bushland and home to more than 1,000 animals, which roam large outdoor enclosures. The zoo has paths for walking, cycling, and vehicles, and is worth visiting if you have the time.

Inland Odyssey: Sydney to Melbourne

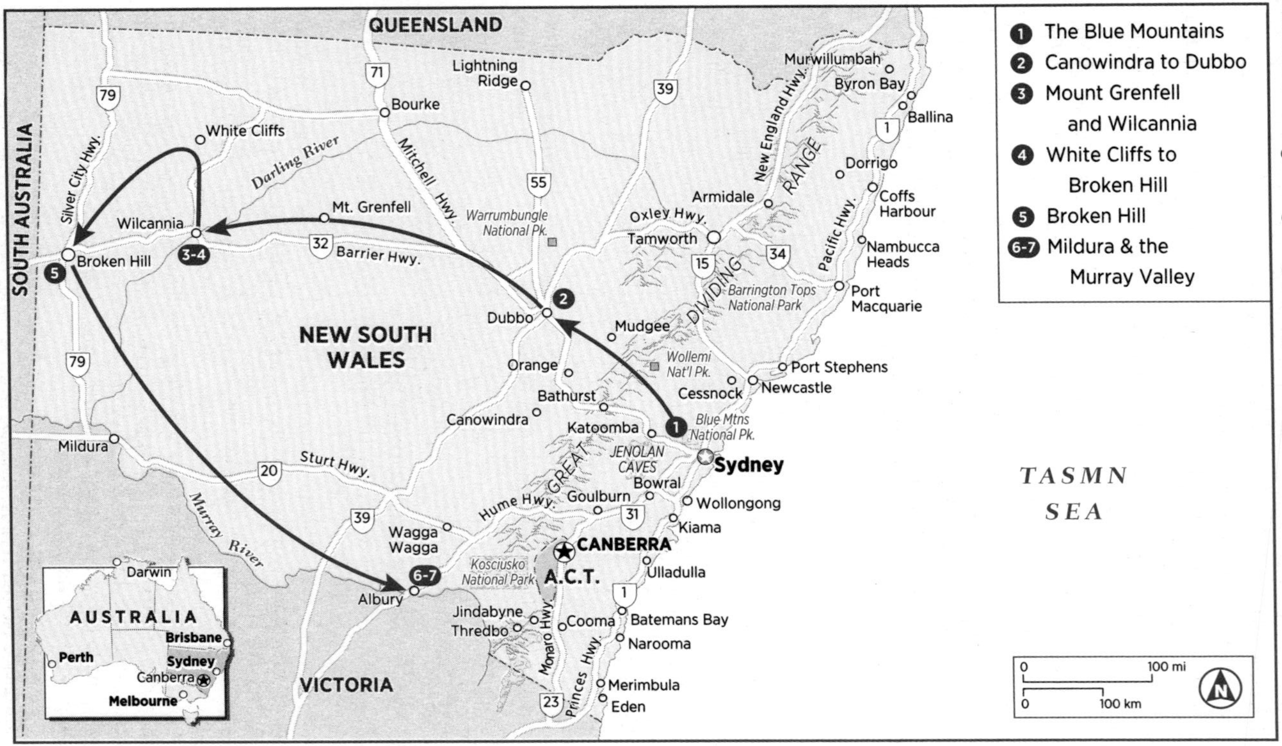

Day 3: Mount Grenfell & Wilcannia

From Dubbo, continue along the highway to **Nyngan,** a small township on the edge of the true Outback, where you can while away a short time in the local museum or spot birds among the rivergums at Rotary Park.

From here, the Barrier Highway scoots across dusty arid red plains for 597km (370 miles) to Broken Hill. The best place to stop for the night is **Cobar,** 133km (83 miles) from Nyngan. There's an excellent rural museum here, and some fascinating local pubs and historic buildings.

You'll find some of the best Aboriginal art in NSW at **Mount Grenfell,** 40km (25 miles) farther along the Barrier Highway from Cobar—a signpost directs you off the main road, and it's another 32km (19 miles) to three rock overhangs where 1,300 richly colored stencils and drawings cover the surfaces.

It's a 265km (164-mile) drive from here to **Wilcannia,** across a landscape scuttling with giant lizards and emus. (The 'roos usually come out at dusk.)

From Wilcannia, you can veer north along a bitumen road for 97km (60 miles) to the opal-mining town of **White Cliffs** (p. 232), where most people live underground.

Day 4: The White Cliffs

It's worth spending most of the day discovering the sights of **White Cliffs** before making your way back to the highway and completing the 197km (122-mile) journey to Broken Hill.

Day 5: Opal Mining in Broken Hill

Rest up in **Broken Hill ★** (p. 230) for the day, and make sure you take a tour of the town with a local tour company; you won't regret it. Sights to see include the **School of the Air** (p. 394) and the **Royal Flying Doctor Service** base (p. 519), as well as popping out to **Silverton** (p. 232).

Days 6 & 7: Down to Mildura and the Murray Valley

A long, 295km (183-mile) drive takes you south along the Silver City Highway to **Mildura** (p. 670), where you can stop for lunch. It's another 544km (337 miles) from here to Melbourne, but there are good highways much of the way. A good stopover for the night is **Echuca** (p. 671), 210km (130 miles) north of Melbourne, reached by the Murray Valley Highway, where you can spend the morning on a paddle steamer on the Murray River.

A FEW DAYS IN MARGARET RIVER

Getting to see more of Australia than its most famous icons and the east-coast beaches is not always easy. But if you have the time, there are many wonderful places to discover off the beaten track, which will give another dimension to your image and memories of Down Under. We suggest a few days in the **Margaret River ★★★** region, just a few hours' drive south of the Western Australia capital, Perth. You can add it on to the end of a week or so in the east, or change it with the latter part of the 1- or 2-week itineraries earlier.

Note that each year, from August to mid-November, the southern half of Western Australia is blessed with an amazing range of white, yellow, mauve, pink, red, and blue **wildflowers ★★**. The Margaret River region has its displays, especially among the forests and coastal heath land, with September and October the peak months.

Starting from the pleasant, sunny city of Perth, you can tailor your trek to take in some great beaches and surfing, winery tours, excellent food and wine, and the chance to see kangaroos, whales, and dolphins.

Fly to Perth from any of the other destinations above; for specific information on getting to Perth from the other capitals or overseas (if you choose to start in the west and head east), see chapter 11, "Perth & Western Australia."

Day 1: Welcome to Perth

The capital of Western Australia, **Perth ★★** (p. 453), has a superb climate, a great setting on the Swan River, a fabulous outdoor life of biking and beaches, excellent restaurants, and a beautiful historic port, Fremantle. If you'd like to spend a day or so recovering from jet lag as well as getting to know the city, you can overnight here before taking off on your exploration of the southwest. A relaxing way to spend the day is at the port of **Fremantle ★** (p. 476), at the mouth of the Swan River.

"Freo" is a bustling district of 150 National Trust buildings, alfresco cafes, museums (including the wonderful **Maritime Museum,** p. 479), galleries, pubs, weekend markets, and shops in a masterfully preserved historical atmosphere. It's still a working port, so you will see container ships and fishing boats unloading, the occasional U.S. Navy fleet on R&R, and yachts gliding in and out of the harbors. It's a favorite destination every weekend, resulting in an exciting hubbub of shoppers, merchants, cappuccino drinkers, tourists, and fishermen. You can enjoy the passing parade as you knock back a beer or two on the veranda of a gorgeous old pub.

Day 2: Perth to Margaret River

A leisurely 4-hour drive southwest from Perth will put you among the vineyards of Margaret River, one of Australia's finest and most scenic wine regions. En route, stop off at **Rockingham** or **Bunbury** (p. 494), where you may be lucky enough to see **wild dolphins ★**, which regularly come in to "play" with visitors. The Margaret River area is really compact, so you can make your base at any one of the numerous boutique lodges or B&Bs. You can then readily visit any of around 100 wineries, as well as numerous art and craft galleries and the many gourmet produce outlets. Eat out at one of the excellent local restaurants—try one of the local specialties, marron (a freshwater crustacean) or venison, with a bottle of Margaret River wine.

Day 3: South to Cape Leeuwin

Spend the day traveling the winding country roads of the southern part of the region. **Prevelly,** west of Margaret River, has some of Australia's best surfing. Follow Caves Road south from here to Augusta and the historic lighthouse at **Cape Leeuwin,** where the Indian and Southern Oceans meet. Augusta is one of the top spots to see migrating whales in season—with tours available. Both humpback and southern right whales cruise offshore June through August. Your trip will take you through stands of massive karri and jarrah trees. Don't miss **Boranup Drive** (p. 499), a scenic detour that cuts through a magnificent karri forest, and nearby **Boranup Gallery** (p. 500) for superb furniture. For the adventurous, there is a maze of caves, some of which are open to the public. Have lunch at one of the winery restaurants

A Few Days in Margaret River

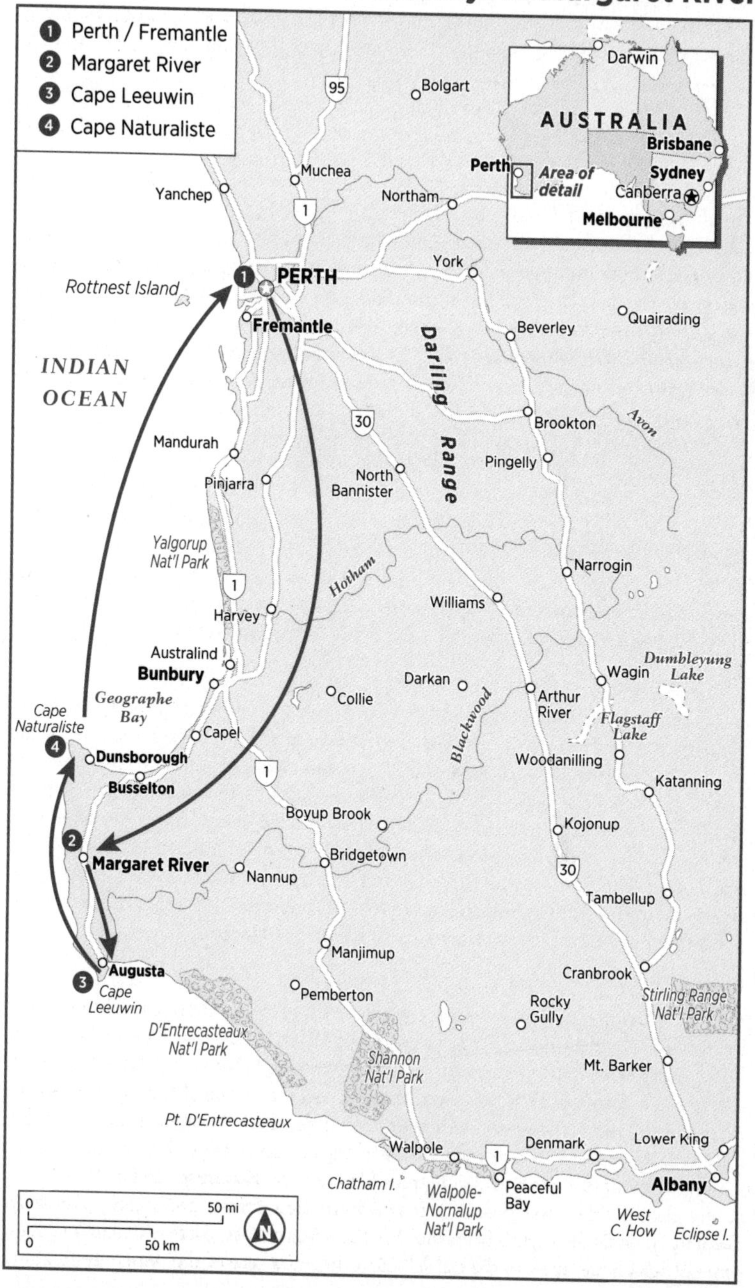

4 SUGGESTED ITINERARIES | A Few Days in Margaret River

or picnic in their lovely gardens. Wind your way back to your accommodation, with the car stocked with some newly favorite wines to drink or take home, but remember to designate a driver before setting out; Australia's drunk-driving laws are strictly enforced and carry heavy penalties.

Day 4: North to Cape Naturaliste and Dunsborough

The area north of Margaret River town has the biggest concentration of wineries, including some of Australia's big names. But you should make time to visit the **Wardan Aboriginal Centre** and some of the gourmet outlets for chocolate, olive oil, cheese, ice cream, or venison. Don't hurry along the winding tree-lined roads; take time to explore the local galleries for pottery, jewelry, woodwork, and artworks, and enjoy the scenery. Cliffs and exquisite bays alternate along the coast, while **Cape Naturaliste** has several walking trails, including the start of the **Cape-to-Cape Walk. Dunsborough** offers whale-watching between September and November.

Day 5: Dunsborough to Perth

You have time to visit another gallery or stroll the Dunsborough beaches before heading off. Make a stop on the way at the seaside town of **Busselton,** where a visit to the underwater observatory at the end of the longest timber jetty in the Southern Hemisphere is well worthwhile.

SYDNEY

by Marc Llewellyn

Sunny, sexy, and sophisticated, Sydney (pop. 4.3 million) basks in its worldwide recognition as the shining star of the Southern Hemisphere. Some people compare it to San Francisco—it certainly has that relaxed feel—but the gateway to Australia is very much its own unique metropolis.

5

Fortunately most of the interesting things in this huge city are concentrated in a relatively compact area around one of the finest urban harbors in the world. First, of course, there's the Sydney Opera House, one of the most recognized buildings in the world. This white-sailed construction on Sydney Cove, designed by Jørn Utzon, is the pride of the city. Then there's that other great icon, the Sydney Harbour Bridge. Those with a daredevil spirit can join a BridgeClimb Sydney tour across catwalks and ladders to the top of the main arch for 360-degree views across the Opera House and the ferries and boats far below.

There are also over 20 beaches strung along the city's oceanfront and dozens more around the harbor; you'll be spoiled for choice. The most famous is Bondi, a strip of golden sand legendary for its Speedo-clad Lifesavers and surfboard riders. From here, a "must do" is the 3.2km (2-mile) coastal path that leads off across the cliff tops, via Tamarama Beach (dubbed "Glamourama" for its chic sun worshipers), to Bronte Beach, where you can cool down in the crashing waves.

Another beach favorite is Manly, a 30-minute ferry trip from Circular Quay. Pick up some fish and chips and head for the main beach, flanked by a row of giant pines that chatter with hundreds of colorful lorikeets at dusk.

Back on the mainland, modern Sydney comes alive in the more recent developments around Darling Harbour and the nearby restaurant and entertainment areas in Cockle Bay and on King Street Wharf. You'll find the world-class Sydney Aquarium there, or you can start your gourmet tour of Sydney's Contemporary cooking style, which encompasses the best of freshness with spices from Asia and flavors from the Mediterranean.

The frugal traveler will find that, compared to many other major international cities, Sydney offers good value. Food and public transport are cheap, and attractions are generally not prohibitively expensive. (Senior and student prices are almost always available with ID.) The price of a hotel room is far cheaper than in other major population centers such as New York and London.

Whichever way you look at it, there's so much to do in Sydney that you could easily spend a week here and still find yourself crashing into bed each night, exhausted from trying to see it all.

ORIENTATION

Arriving

BY PLANE Sydney International Airport is 8km (5 miles) from the city center. Shuttle buses link the international and domestic terminals. Single tickets cost A$5. The journey takes up to 10 minutes and operates frequently in the morning peak period, and then every half-hour until 8pm. The bus stops are on arrivals levels, at T1 Bus Bay 21 near the McDonald's, and at T2 Bus Bay 3 near baggage carousel 6. In both terminals, you'll find luggage carts, wheelchairs, a post office (Mon–Fri 9am–5pm), mailboxes, currency exchange, duty-free shops (including one before you go through Customs on arrival, selling alcohol and perfume), restaurants, bars, stores, showers, luggage lockers, a baggage-held service for larger items, ATMs, and tourist-information desks. You can rent mobile phones in the international terminal. There is also a **Sydney Visitors Centre bookings desk** (© **02/9667 6050**) offering cheap deals on hotels (see p. 111), as well as car rentals, phone cards, and maps and brochures. Here you can also buy the SydneyPass (see p. 101). The airport is efficient, has extremely strict quarantine procedures—you must declare all food—and is completely nonsmoking. On arrival, pick up a copy of "Sydney: The Official Guide," from the rack just before passport control, which contains tear-out discount tickets for some of Sydney's major attractions. Luggage trolleys are free to use in the international arrival terminal but cost A$4 outside departure terminals (you'll need coins). ***Tip:*** Duty-free alcohol and perfumes are available on arrival in Sydney from an international flight. You can take two bottles of standard alcohol through Customs without declaring them.

Airport Link trains connect the international and domestic airports to the city stations of Central, Museum, St. James, Circular Quay, Wynyard, and Town Hall. You'll need to change trains for other Sydney stations. Unfortunately, the line has no dedicated luggage areas and, because it's on a scheduled route into the city from the suburbs, it gets very crowded during rush hours (approximately 7–9am and 4–6:30pm). If you have lots of luggage and you're traveling into the city at these times, it's probably best to take a taxi. Otherwise walk to the end of the platform, and there should be more room onboard. There are elevators at the Airport Link stations and some at the city train stations (but the crowds and lack of staff and signs mean you'll probably end up lugging it all up loads of steps anyway). The train takes 10 minutes to reach the Central Railway Station and continues to Circular Quay. Trains leave every 15 minutes or so and cost around A$15 one-way for adults and A$10 for children. Round-trip tickets are only available if you really hate Sydney and want to return to the airport on the same day. Ask at the ticket office about group tickets and family-fare tickets that allow a second child, or more, to travel for free with an adult. (The first child pays the standard child fare.)

Greater Sydney

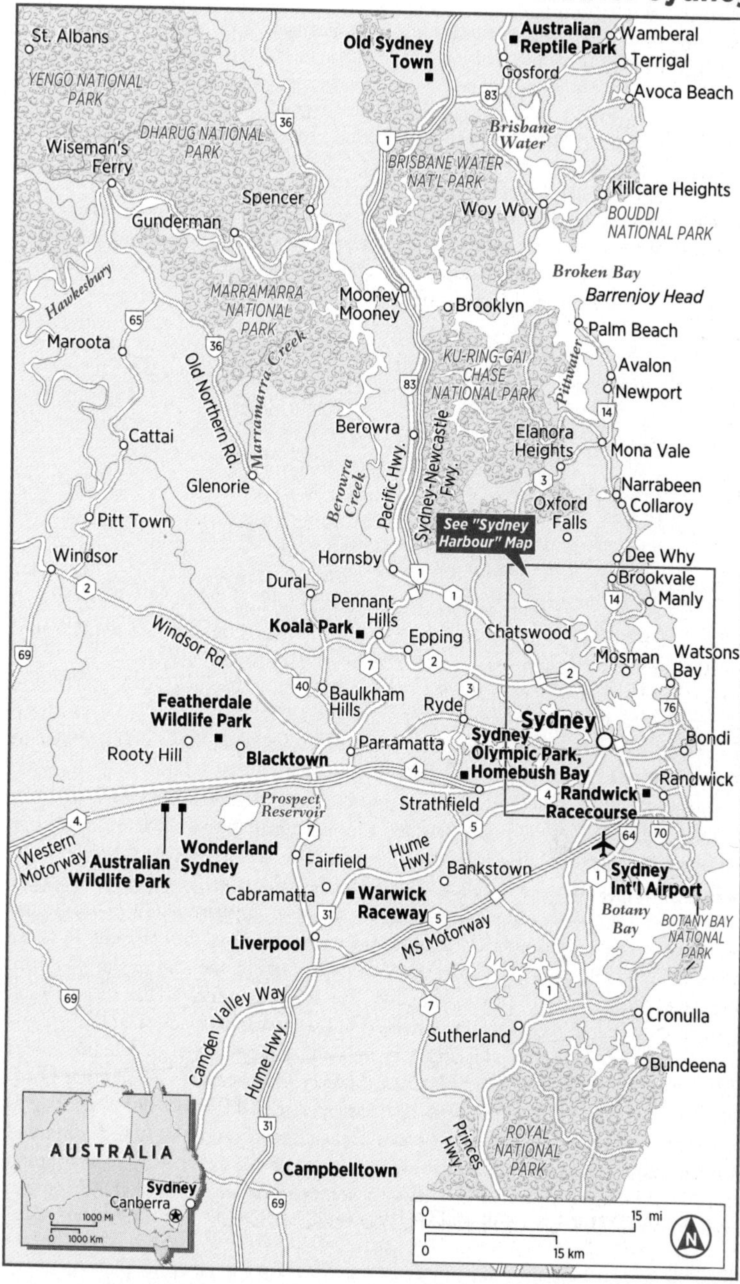

St. Albans
YENGO NATIONAL PARK
Old Sydney Town
Australian Reptile Park
Wamberal
Terrigal
Gosford
Avoca Beach
DHARUG NATIONAL PARK
Wiseman's Ferry
Brisbane Water
BRISBANE WATER NAT'L PARK
Spencer
Gunderman
Woy Woy
Killcare Heights
BOUDDI NATIONAL PARK
Broken Bay
Hawkesbury
MARRAMARRA NATIONAL PARK
Mooney Mooney
Brooklyn
Barrenjoy Head
Palm Beach
Maroota
Marramarra Creek
Old Northern Rd.
KU-RING-GAI CHASE NATIONAL PARK
Pittwater
Avalon
Newport
Berowra
Elanora Heights
Mona Vale
Cattai
Berowra Creek
Pacific Hwy.
Sydney-Newcastle Fwy.
Glenorie
Narrabeen
Collaroy
Oxford Falls
Pitt Town
See "Sydney Harbour" Map
Windsor
Hornsby
Dee Why
Brookvale
Dural
Pennant Hills
Manly
Windsor Rd.
Koala Park
Epping
Chatswood
Mosman
Watsons Bay
Baulkham Hills
Ryde
Featherdale Wildlife Park
Sydney
Rooty Hill
Blacktown
Parramatta
Sydney Olympic Park, Homebush Bay
Bondi
Randwick
Randwick Racecourse
Prospect Reservoir
Strathfield
Western Motorway
Wonderland Sydney
Australian Wildlife Park
Fairfield
Hume Hwy.
Bankstown
Sydney Int'l Airport
Cabramatta
Warwick Raceway
Botany Bay
BOTANY BAY NATIONAL PARK
Liverpool
M5 Motorway
Camden Valley Way
Hume Hwy.
Cronulla
Sutherland
Bundeena
AUSTRALIA
Sydney
Canberra
0 1000 Mi
0 1000 Km
Princes Hwy.
ROYAL NATIONAL PARK
Campbelltown
0 15 mi
0 15 km
N

Taxi Savvy

Taxi queues can be long, and drivers may try to cash in by insisting you share a cab with other passengers in line at the airport. Here's the scam: After dropping off the other passengers, the cabdriver will attempt to charge you the full price of the journey, despite the fact that the other passengers paid for their sections. You certainly won't save any money sharing a cab if this happens, and your journey will be a long one. If you are first in line in the taxi stand, the law states that you can refuse to share the cab. Taxi drivers obviously like a tip, but there is no requirement to do so. If you've had good service, then 10% extra on top of the fare is enough.

Sydney Airporter coaches (✆ **02/9666 9988;** www.kst.com.au) operate to the city center from bus stops outside the terminals every 15 minutes. This service will drop you off (and pick you up) at hotels in the city, Kings Cross, and Darling Harbour. Pickups from hotels require at least 3 hours advance notice, and you can book online. Tickets cost A$14 one-way and A$23 round-trip (slightly cheaper if booked over the web) from both the international and domestic terminals. The return portion can be used any time in the future.

Both short-term and long-term parking are available at both terminals. An example is a 4-day stay at the domestic terminal, which costs around A$80.

A **taxi** from the airport to the city center costs about A$45 to A$50 total. An expressway, the Eastern Distributor, is the fastest way to reach the city from the airport. There's a A$5 toll from the airport to the city (the taxi driver pays the toll and adds the cost to your fare), but there is no toll to the airport. A 10% credit-card charge applies. The flag-fall rate is A$3 and there's an airport booking fee of A$1.60.

BY TRAIN **Central Station** (✆ **13 15 00** for CityRail, or 13 22 32 for Countrylink interstate trains) is the main city and interstate train station. It's at the top of George Street in downtown Sydney. All interstate trains depart from here, and it's a major CityRail hub. Many city buses leave from neighboring Railway Square for such places as Town Hall and Circular Quay.

BY BUS **Greyhound** coaches operate from the **Sydney Coach Terminal** (✆ **02/9212 1500**), on the corner of Eddy Avenue and Pitt Street, bordering Central Station.

BY CRUISE SHIP Cruise ships dock at the **Overseas Passenger Terminal** in The Rocks, opposite the Sydney Opera House, or in Darling Harbour if The Rocks facility is already occupied.

BY CAR Drivers enter Sydney from the north on the Pacific Highway, from the south on the M5 and Princes Highway, and from the west on the Great Western Highway.

Visitor Information

The Sydney Visitor Centre at The Rocks, First Floor, The Rocks Centre, Corner of Argyle and Playfair streets, The Rocks (✆ **1800/067 676** in Australia, or 02/9240 8788; www.sydneyvisitorcentre.com), is a good place to pick up maps, brochures, Youth Hostel Association (YHA) cards, and general tourist information about Sydney as well as towns in New South Wales. It also sells books, T-shirts, DVDs, postcards, and the like. The office is open daily from 9am to 5pm. There's also the **Sydney Visitors Centre Darling Harbour,** 33 Wheat Rd., Darling Harbour, near the IMAX Theatre. It's open from 9:30am to 5:30pm daily. You can ask questions by e-mailing them (visitorinformation@shfa.nsw.gov.au). In Manly, find the **Manly Visitors Information Centre** (✆ **02/9976 1430**) at Manly Wharf (where the ferries come in). It's open Monday to Friday from 9am to 5pm, and on weekends between 10am and 4pm.

Also in The Rocks is the **National Parks & Wildlife Centre,** in Cadmans Cottage (a little sandstone building, built in 1816, which is set back from the water in front of The Rocks), 110 George St. (✆ **02/9247 5033**). This place has lots of national park information and runs boat tours to some of the islands in Sydney Harbour. It's open Monday to Friday 9:30am to 4:30pm, Saturday and Sunday 10am to 4:30pm.

Elsewhere, there are **City Host information kiosks,** at Martin Place (btw. Elizabeth and Castlereagh sts.), on George Street (adjacent to Sydney Town Hall), and at Circular Quay (corner of Pitt and Alfred sts.). They provide maps, brochures, and advice and are open daily from 9am to 5pm. There's also a Visitor Centre at the international terminal of the airport. If you want to inquire about destinations and holidays in Sydney or the rest of New South Wales, call **Tourism New South Wales**'s help line (✆ **13 20 77** in Australia).

A good website is **CitySearch Sydney** (www.sydney.citysearch.com.au), for events, entertainment, dining, and shopping. Another is www.sydney.com.

City Layout

Sydney is one of the largest cities in the world by area, covering more than 1,730 sq. km (675 sq. miles) from the sea to the foothills of the Blue Mountains. Thankfully, the city center, or Central Business District (CBD), is compact. The jewel in Sydney's crown is its harbor, which empties into the South Pacific Ocean through headlands known as North Head and South Head. On the southern side of the harbor are the high-rises of the city center; the Sydney Opera House; a string of beaches, including Bondi; and the inner suburbs. The Sydney Harbour Bridge and a tunnel connect the city center to the high-rises of the North Sydney business district and the affluent northern suburbs and ocean beaches beyond.

MAIN ARTERIES & STREETS The city's main thoroughfare, **George Street,** runs up from **Circular Quay,** past Wynyard CityRail station and Town Hall, to Central Station. A host of streets run parallel to George, including Pitt, Elizabeth, and Macquarie streets. **Macquarie Street** runs up from the Sydney Opera House, past the Royal Botanic Gardens and Hyde Park. **Martin Place** is a pedestrian thoroughfare that stretches from Macquarie to George streets. It's about halfway between Circular Quay and Town Hall—in the heart of the city center. The easy-to-spot Sydney Tower (also known as Centrepoint Tower), facing onto pedestrian-only **Pitt Street Mall** on Pitt Street, is the main city-center landmark. Next to Circular Quay and across from the Opera House is **The Rocks,** a cluster of small streets that was once part of a larger slum and is now a tourist attraction. Roads meet at **Town Hall** from Kings Cross in one direction and Darling Harbour in the other. From

Circular Quay to The Rocks, it's a 5- to 10-minute stroll, to Wynyard about 10 minutes, and to Town Hall about 20 minutes. From Town Hall to the near side of Darling Harbour it's about a 10-minute walk.

Neighborhoods in Brief

SOUTH OF SYDNEY HARBOUR

Circular Quay This transport hub for ferries, buses, and CityRail trains is tucked between the Harbour Bridge and the Sydney Opera House. The Quay, as it's called, is a good spot for a stroll, and its outdoor restaurants and street performers are popular. The Rocks, the Royal Botanic Gardens, the Contemporary Art Museum, and the start of the main shopping area (centered on Pitt and George sts.) are a short walk away. To get there by public transit, take a CityRail train, ferry, or city bus to Circular Quay.

The Rocks This small historic area, a short stroll west of Circular Quay, is packed with colonial stone buildings, intriguing back streets, boutiques, pubs, tourist stores, and top-notch restaurants and hotels. It's the most exclusive place to stay in the city because of its beauty and its proximity to the Opera House and harbor. Shops are geared toward Sydney's yuppies and wealthy tourists—don't expect bargains. On weekends, a portion of George Street is blocked off for The Rocks Market, with stalls selling souvenirs and crafts. A smaller farmers' market (www.therocks.com) operates on Fridays and Saturdays. To reach the area on public transport, take any bus for Circular Quay or The Rocks (on George St.) or a CityRail train or ferry to Circular Quay.

Town Hall In the heart of the city, this area is home to the main department stores and two Sydney landmarks, the Town Hall and a historic shopping mall called the Queen Victoria Building (QVB). In this area are Sydney Tower and the boutique-style chain stores of Pitt Street Mall. Farther up George Street are movie houses, the entrance to Sydney's Spanish district (around Liverpool St.), and the city's Chinatown. To reach the area by public transit, take any bus from Circular Quay on George Street or a CityRail train to the Town Hall stop.

Darling Harbour Designed as a tourist precinct, Darling Harbour features Sydney's main convention, exhibition, and entertainment centers; a waterfront promenade; the Sydney Aquarium; the Panasonic IMAX Theatre; the Australian Maritime Museum; the Powerhouse Museum; Star City (Sydney's casino); a food court; and plenty of shops. Nearby are the funky restaurants of Cockle Bay and King Street Wharf. To reach Darling Harbour by public transport, take a ferry from Circular Quay (Wharf 5), the monorail from Town Hall, or the light rail (tram) from Central Station. It's a short walk from Town Hall.

Kings Cross & the Suburbs Beyond "The Cross," as it's known, is the city's red-light district—though it's also home to some of Sydney's best-known nightclubs and restaurants. The area has plenty of backpacker hostels, a few bars, and some upscale hotels. The main drag, Darlinghurst Road, is short but crammed with strip joints, prostitutes, drunks, and such. It's certainly colorful. Also here are cheap e-mail centers that offer discount overseas phone rates. There's a heavy police presence, and usually plenty of "nice" people around, but do take care. Beyond the strip clubs and glitter, the neighborhoods of Elizabeth Bay, Double Bay, and Rose Bay hug the waterfront. To reach the area on public transport, take a CityRail train to Kings Cross. From the next stop, Edgecliff, it's a short walk to Double Bay and a longer one to Rose Bay along the coast.

Paddington/Oxford Street This central-city neighborhood, centered on trendy Oxford Street, is known for its expensive terrace houses, off-the-wall boutiques and bookshops, and restaurants, pubs, and nightclubs. It's also the heart of Sydney's

Sydney Harbour

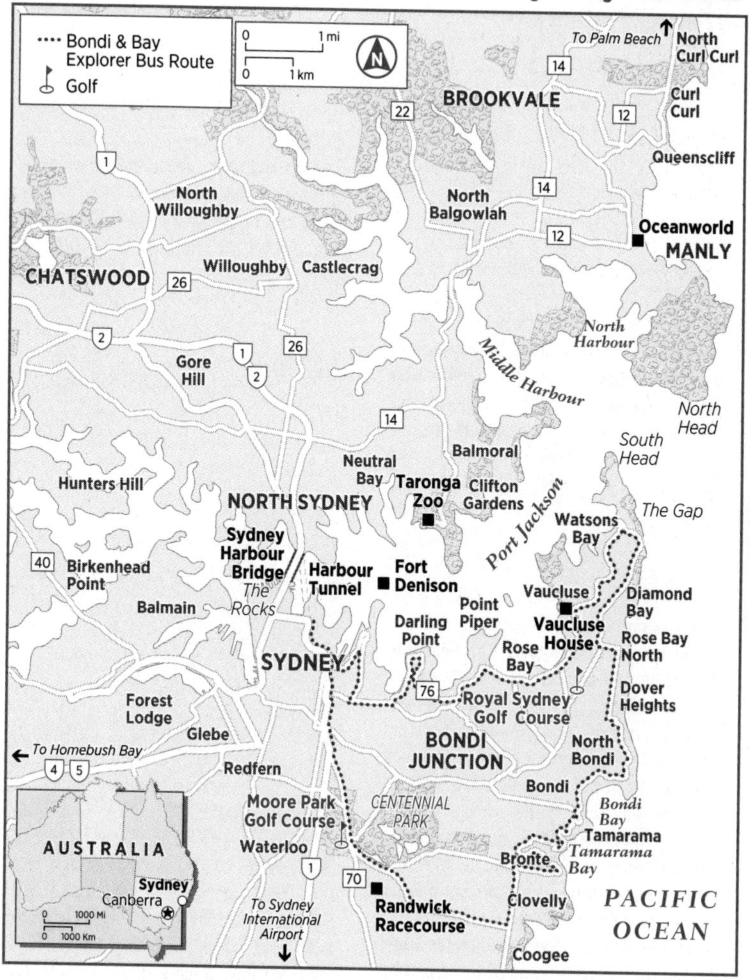

large gay community and has a liberal scattering of gay bars and dance spots. To reach the area by public transport, take bus no. 380 or 382 from Circular Quay (on Elizabeth St.); no. 378 from Railway Square, Central Station; or no. 380 or 382 from Bondi Junction. The lower end of Oxford Street is a short walk from Museum CityRail Station (take the Liverpool St. exit).

Darlinghurst Between grungy Kings Cross and upscale Oxford Street, this extroverted, grimy, terraced area is home to some of Sydney's best cafes—though it's probably not wise to wander around here at night alone. Take the CityRail train to Kings Cross and head right from the exit.

Central The congested, polluted crossroads around Central Station, the city's main train station, has little to recommend it. Buses run from here to Circular Quay, and it's a 20-minute walk to Town Hall. The Sydney Central YHA (youth hostel) is here.

Newtown This popular student area centers on car-clogged King Street, which is lined with alternative shops, bookstores, and ethnic restaurants. People-watching is the thing to do—see how many belly-button rings, violently colored hairdos, and Celtic arm tattoos you can spot. To reach the area on public transport, take a CityRail train to Newtown Station.

Glebe Young professionals and students come to this central-city neighborhood for the cafes, restaurants, pubs, and shops along the main thoroughfare, Glebe Point Road. All this, plus a location 15 minutes from the city and 30 minutes from Circular Quay, makes it a good place for budget-conscious travelers. To reach Glebe, take bus no. 370, 431, 432, 433, or 434 from Millers Point, The Rocks, and at bus stops on George Street.

Bondi & the Southern Beaches Some of Sydney's most glamorous surf beaches—Bondi, Bronte, and Coogee—lie along the South Pacific coast, southeast of the city center. Bondi has a wide sweep of beach (crowded in summer), some interesting restaurants and bars, plenty of attitude, and beautiful bodies—and no CityRail station. To reach Bondi by public transport, ride bus no. 380 to Bondi Beach from Circular Quay—it takes up to an hour—or (a quicker alternative) take a CityRail train to Bondi Junction to connect with the same buses. The new bus no. 333 takes around 40 minutes from Circular Quay to Bondi Beach. It has limited stops, but you can catch it from Elizabeth Street near Martin Place, along Oxford Street, and from the bus terminal at Bondi Junction. You need to buy a ticket at a newsdealer or 7-Eleven store beforehand. A Travelten bus ticket (See "Getting Around," below) is a good option if you are staying in Bondi. Bus no. 378 from Railway Square, Central Station, goes to Bronte, and bus no. 373 or 374 travels to Coogee from Circular Quay.

Watsons Bay Watsons Bay is known for The Gap—a section of dramatic sea cliffs—as well as several good restaurants, and a good beer garden. It's a terrific spot to spend a sunny afternoon. To reach it on public transportation, take bus no. 324 or 325 from Circular Quay. There's limited ferry service daily from Circular Quay (Wharf 2), starting at 10:15am on weekdays, 9:15am on weekends and holidays.

NORTH OF SYDNEY HARBOUR

North Sydney Across the Harbour Bridge, the skyscrapers of North Sydney attest to its prominence as a business area. There's little for tourists here. Chatswood (take a CityRail train from Central or Wynyard station) has some good suburban-type shopping; and Milsons Point has a decent pub, the Kirribilli Hotel, and Luna Park, an amusement park that continues to do battle with wealthy locals who complain it's too noisy. You can see the giant smiling clown face from Circular Quay.

The North Shore Ferries and buses provide access to these wealthy neighborhoods across the Harbour Bridge. Gorgeous Balmoral Beach, Taronga Zoo, and upscale boutiques are the attractions in Mosman. Take a ferry from Circular Quay (Wharf 2) to Taronga Zoo (10 min.) and a bus to Balmoral Beach (another 10 min.).

Manly & the Northern Beaches Half an hour away by ferry, Manly is famous for its ocean beach—it gives Bondi a run for its money—and scores of cheap food outlets. Farther north are more beaches popular with surfers. CityRail train lines do not go to the northern beaches. The farthest beach from the city, Palm Beach, has magnificent surf and lagoon beaches, walking paths, and a golf course. To reach the area by public transport, take the ferry from Circular Quay to Manly. A privately operated fast-ferry service also runs from Circular Quay to Manly. Change at Manly interchange (transfer point) for bus nos. 148 and 154 through 159 to the northern beaches. You can also take bus no. L90 from Wynyard station.

WEST OF THE CITY CENTER/CENTRAL BUSINESS DISTRICT (CBD)

Balmain West of the city center, a short ferry ride from Circular Quay, Balmain was once Sydney's main shipbuilding area. In the last few decades, the area has become trendy and expensive. The neighborhood has a village feel to it, abounds with restaurants and pubs, and stages a popular Saturday market at the local church. Take bus no. 441, 442, or 432 from Town Hall or George Street, or a ferry from Circular Quay (Wharf 5), and then a short bus ride up the hill to the main shopping area.

Homebush Bay Sydney Olympic Park was the main site of the 2000 Olympic games. You'll find the ANZ Stadium (previously the Telstra Stadium and before that the Stadium Australia—the name changes are the result of sponsorship naming rights), the Aquatic Center, and Homebush Bay Information Centre, parklands, and a water-bird reserve. To reach the area by public transport, take a CityRail train from Circular Quay to the Olympic Park station.

GETTING AROUND

By Public Transportation

State Transit operates the city's buses and the ferry network, CityRail runs the urban and suburban trains, and Sydney Ferries runs the public passenger ferries. Some private bus lines operate buses in the outer suburbs. In addition, a monorail connects the city center to Darling Harbour, and a light rail line runs between Central Station and Wentworth Park in Pyrmont. Public transit fares seem to change a couple of times a year, depending on the results of the latest review or budgeting disaster, so the prices below can only act as a guide. Interestingly, when fares changed in mid-2010, some actually went down (though most went up). There is no proper underground metro system, no trams (the last one was scrapped in 1961), a shortage of taxis, and worsening congestion—but it doesn't feel *that* bad, honest, unless you live here of course. By the way, **Infoline** (✆ **13 15 00;** www.131500.info) is a one-stop search engine for bus, train, and ferry timetables.

MONEY-SAVING TRANSIT PASSES Several passes are available for visitors who will be using public transportation frequently. All work out to be much cheaper than buying individual tickets. Child fares exist for kids between 4 and 15 years old.

The **SydneyPass** includes unlimited travel on Sydney buses, Sydney Ferries, and CityRail trains within the city center, as well as to Bondi Junction. It also allows a one-way trip on the train from the airport or back. The SydneyPass costs A$116 for adults and A$58 for children for 3 days of travel over a 7-day period; A$152 for adults and A$76 for children for 5 days over a 7-day period; and A$172 for adults and A$86 for children for 7 consecutive days. Family fares are also available. Buy tickets at the information desk at the airport, at the TransitShop at Circular Quay (near the McDonald's), from the Sydney Ferries ticket offices at Circular Quay, and from Explorer bus drivers. Do your research beforehand though, as these prices seem high for the amount of public transport you might actually use.

A **MyMulti** ticket allows unlimited travel on buses, trains, and ferries. There are three different passes depending on the distance you need to travel. The passes visitors most commonly use range in price from A$41 to A$48. You can buy either pass at newsdealers or bus, train, and ferry ticket outlets.

Sydney Public Transit Systems

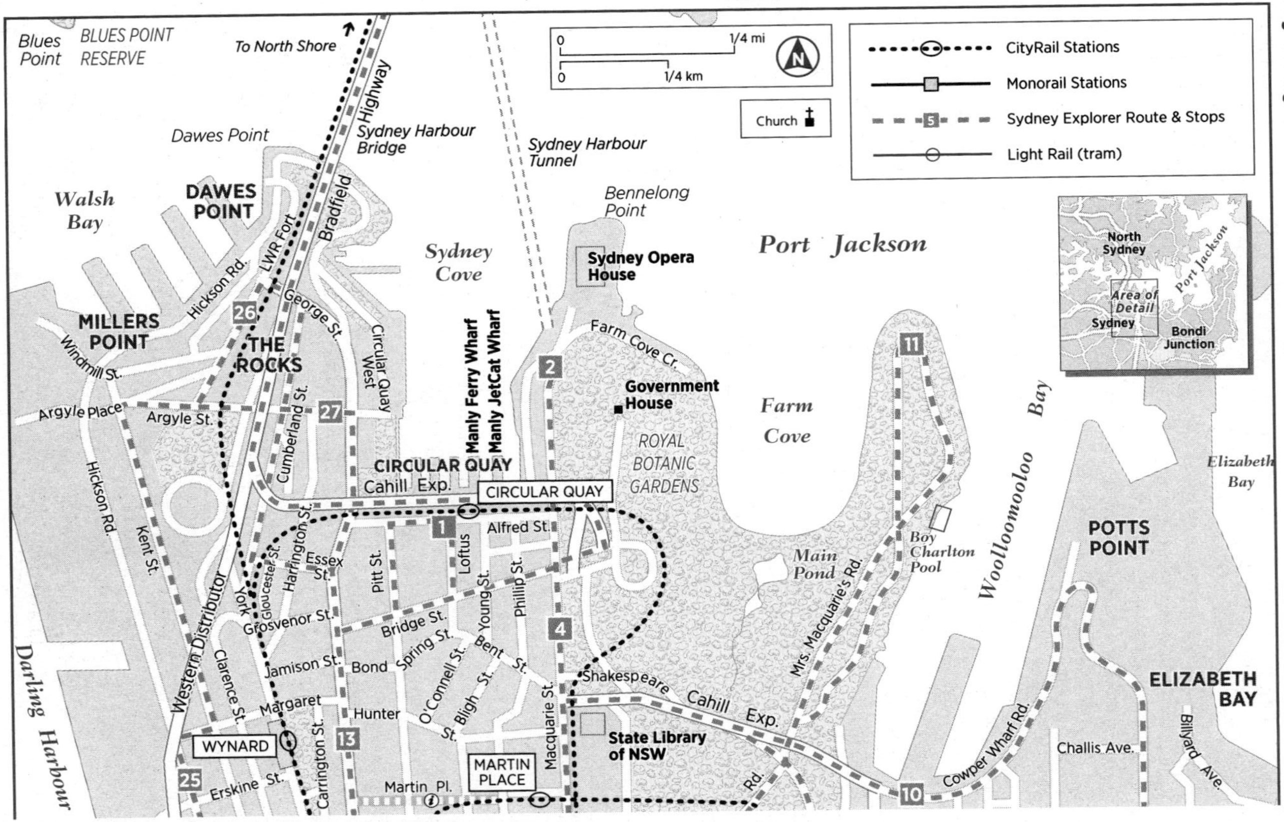

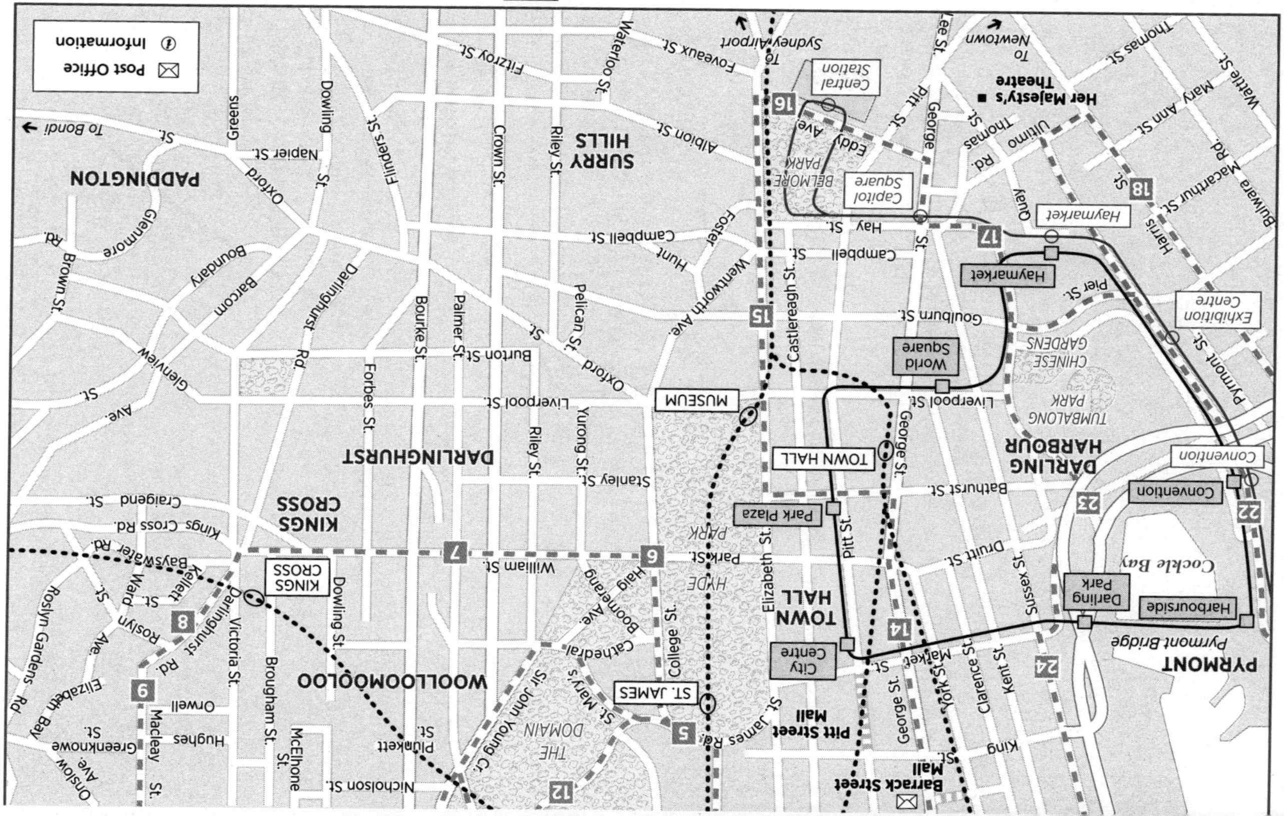
Post Office
Information
PADDINGTON
To Bondi
SURRY HILLS
DARLINGHURST
KINGS CROSS
WOOLLOOMOOLOO
TOWN HALL
DARLING HARBOUR
PYRMONT
Pyrmont Bridge
Cockle Bay
THE DOMAIN
HYDE PARK
TUMBALONG PARK
CHINESE GARDENS
BELMORE PARK
KINGS CROSS
ST. JAMES
MUSEUM
TOWN HALL
City Centre
Park Plaza
World Square
Haymarket
Darling Park
Harbourside
Convention
Capitol Square
Central Station
Exhibition Centre
Haymarket
Convention
Her Majesty's Theatre
Pitt Street Mall
Barrack Street Mall
To Sydney Airport
To Newtown
Oxford St.
Flinders St.
Crown St.
Riley St.
Bourke St.
Palmer St.
Burton St.
Liverpool St.
William St.
Park St.
College St.
Elizabeth St.
Castlereagh St.
Pitt St.
George St.
York St.
Clarence St.
Kent St.
Sussex St.
King St.
Market St.
Druitt St.
Bathurst St.
Goulburn St.
Campbell St.
Hay St.
Pier St.
Harris St.
Pyrmont St.
Ultimo Rd.
Thomas St.
Wattle St.
Mary Ann St.
Macarthur St.
Bulwara Rd.
Quay St.
Lee St.
Eddy Ave.
Foveaux St.
Albion St.
Waterloo St.
Fitzroy St.
Foster St.
Hunt St.
Wentworth Ave.
Pelican St.
Yurong St.
Stanley St.
Darlinghurst Rd.
Victoria St.
Brougham St.
Dowling St.
Nicholson St.
Plunkett St.
McElhone St.
Hughes St.
Orwell St.
Macleay St.
Greenknowe St.
Onslow Ave.
Elizabeth Bay Rd.
Roslyn Gardens Rd.
Roslyn St.
Ward Ave.
Kellett St.
Bayswater Rd.
Kings Cross Rd.
Craigend St.
Glenview St.
Ave.
Barcom Ave.
Boundary St.
Glenmore Rd.
Brown St.
Greens Rd.
Napier St.
Forbes St.
Sir John Young Cr.
St. Mary's Rd.
Cathedral St.
Boomerang St.
Haig Ave.
St. James Rd.
5
6
7
8
9
12
14
15
16
17
18
22
23
24

The **City Hopper** allows unlimited all day CityRail travel around 11 stations within the city area. The stations include Central, Martin Place, Museum, Town Hall, St. James, Circular Quay, Kings Cross, Wynyard, Redfern, Milsons Point, and North Sydney. Tickets cost A$8.40 for adults and A$4.20 for kids if bought before 9am, and A$5.80 for adults and A$3 for kids after 9am.

Your family can enjoy a fun day out with unlimited travel on Sydney's buses, trains, and ferries every Sunday with the **Family Funday Sunday** pass (A$2.50 per person). The ticket can only be purchased on Sundays. A minimum of one adult and one child related by family must travel together. Buy your ticket from bus drivers (excluding PrePay services), CityRail stations, ferry ticket offices, and 7-Eleven convenience stores.

BY PUBLIC BUS Buses are frequent and reliable and cover a wide area of metropolitan Sydney—though you might find the system a little difficult to navigate if you're visiting some of the outer suburbs. The minimum fare (which covers most short hops in the city) is A$2 for a 4km (2½-mile) "section." The farther you go, the cheaper each section is. For example, the 44km (27-mile) trip to Palm Beach, way past Manly, costs A$4.20. Sections are marked on bus-stand signs, but most Sydneysiders are as confused about the system as you will be—when in doubt, ask the bus driver.

A **Mybus ticket** offers 10 bus rides for a discounted price. Tickets cost A$16 for trips within the city center, and A$26 for trips farther out. Most buses bound for the northern suburbs, including night buses to Manly and the bus to Taronga Zoo, leave from Wynyard Park on Carrington Street, behind the Wynyard CityRail station on George Street. Buses to the southern beaches, such as Bondi and Bronte, and the western and eastern suburbs leave from Circular Quay. Buses to Balmain leave from behind the QVB.

Buses run from 4am to around midnight during the week, less frequently on weekends and holidays. Some night buses to outer suburbs run after midnight and throughout the night. You can purchase single tickets onboard; exact change is not required.

BY SYDNEY EXPLORER & BONDI EXPLORER BUSES Bright red Sydney Explorer buses operate every day, traveling a 28km (18-mile) circuit and stopping at 27 places of interest. These include the Sydney Opera House, the Royal Botanic Gardens, the State Library, Mrs. Macquarie's Chair, the Art Gallery of New South Wales, Kings Cross, Elizabeth Bay House, Wynyard CityRail station, the QVB, Sydney Tower, the Australian Museum, Central Station, Chinatown, Darling Harbour, and The Rocks. Sydney Explorer bus stops are identified by a distinctive red Explorer sign. The interval between services is approximately 20 minutes and you can board the bus at any stop along the route. The first departure from Circular Quay is at 8:40am and the last is at 5:20pm. The last service will return you to Circular Quay at 7:20pm. If you prefer to stay on the bus, the full circuit will take around 2 hours to complete. When planning your itinerary for the day, remember that some attractions, such as museums, close at 5pm.

The Bondi Explorer operates every day, traveling a 30km (19-mile) circuit around the eastern harborside bays and coastal beaches. There are 19 stops along the way, which include Kings Cross, Double Bay, Watsons Bay, Bondi Beach, Bronte Beach, Coogee Beach, Paddington, Oxford Street, and Martin Place. Bondi Explorer bus

Sydney Ferries

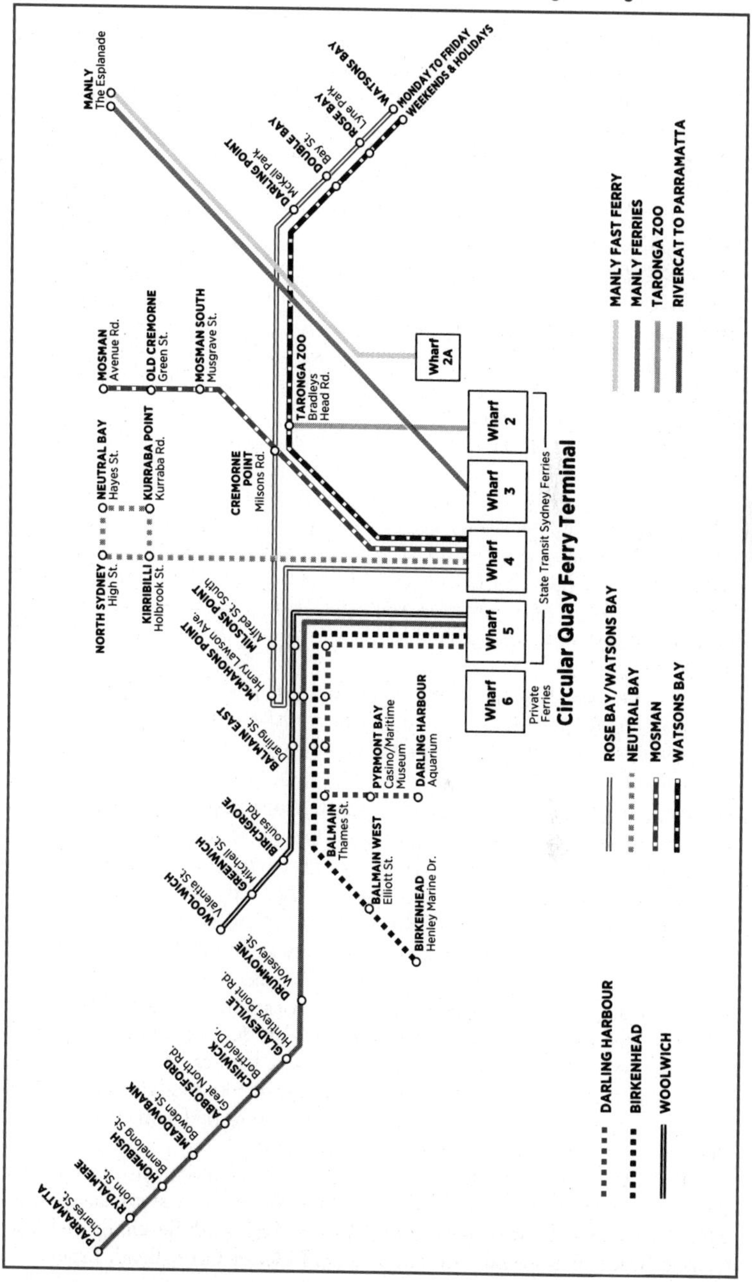

stops are identified by a distinctive blue Explorer sign. The interval between services is approximately 30 minutes and you can board the bus at any stop along the route. The first departure from Circular Quay is at 8:45am and the last is at 4:15pm. The last service will return you to Circular Quay at 6:15pm. If you prefer to stay on the bus, the full circuit takes around 2 hours. Tickets entitle you to free travel on regular "blue and white" Sydney Buses within the same zones covered by your Explorer tickets until midnight. You also get discounts on some attractions, such as a 15% discount on tickets to Sydney Aquarium.

Combined 1-day tickets for both buses cost A$40 for adults, A$20 for children 4 to 16, and A$100 for a family. Buy tickets onboard the bus.

BY FERRY The best way to get a taste of a city that revolves around its harbor is to jump aboard a ferry. The main ferry terminal is at Circular Quay. Machines at each wharf dispense tickets. (There are also change machines.) For ferry information, call © **13 15 00** or visit the ferry information office opposite Wharf 4. Timetables are available for all routes. One-way journeys within the inner harbor (virtually everywhere except Manly and Parramatta) cost A$5.30 for adults and A$2.70 for children ages 4 to 15. Kids under 4 travel free.

The **MyFerry ticket** costs A$42 for adults and is good for 10 trips within the inner harbor (this excludes Manly). Kids tickets are half price. Buy Travelten tickets at newsdealers, bus depots, or the Circular Quay ferry terminal. Tickets are transferable, so if two or more people travel together, you can use the same ticket.

The ferry to Manly takes 30 minutes and costs A$6.60 for adults and A$3.30 for children. It leaves from Wharf 3. A Manly Ferry Ten ticket (allowing 10 journeys) costs A$53 for adults and A$26 for kids. Ferries run from 6am to midnight. There is also a fast ferry that runs to Manly from Circular Quay, which takes 18 minutes. This is a privately run service by Bass and Flinders Cruises that came into operation in February 2009, replacing the state-government-run JetCat. The **Manly Fast Ferry** uses its own ticketing system and turnstiles, and departs from Wharf 2a, a small pontoon wharf beside the walkway to the Opera House, close to the main ferry terminals. Tickets cost A$8.50 one way, or you can buy a weekly ticket costing A$70. Kids are defined by this company as being under 14 (presumably because they can possibly deliver newspapers house to house at this age and thus can pay their own way). The first craft leaves Circular Quay at 6:40am and the last at 7:25pm; the last fast ferry departs Manly at 7:50pm. They operate every 25 minutes or so. Call © **02/9583 1199** or visit http://manlyfastferry.com.au for details. Buy tickets at the Manly Fast Ferry booth at Manly Wharf and at the private ticket booth at Circular Quay, or onboard.

BY CITYRAIL Sydney's publicly owned train system is a good news/bad news way to get around. The good news is that it can be a cheap and relatively efficient way to see the city; the bad news is that the system is limited. Many tourist areas—including Manly, Bondi Beach, and Darling Harbour—are not connected to the network. Though trains tend to run regularly, the timetable is unreliable. Oh, and many carriages aren't air-conditioned, so it can be really hot in summer.

Single tickets within the city center cost A$3.20 for adults and A$1.70 for children for travel starting before 9am on weekdays. Return (two-way) tickets cost twice as much. After 9am on weekdays, and on weekends, it costs A$4.40 for adults and A$2.20 for children for a return ticket. The **Family Fare** deal means when at least one fare-paying adult travels with their children or grandchildren, the first child travels for a child fare and the other children travel free. Weekly tickets are also available. It costs more to travel to Bondi Junction. Prices also regularly increase. Information is available from **Infoline** (✆ **13 15 00** in Australia).

BY COUNTRYLINK Comfortable and efficient **Countrylink** trains out of Central Station link the city with the far suburbs and beyond. For reservations, call ✆ **13 22 32** in Australia between 6:30am and 10pm, or visit the **Countrylink Travel Center,** Station Concourse, Wynyard CityRail station (✆ **02/9224 2742;** www.countrylink.info), for brochures and bookings.

BY METRO MONORAIL The metro monorail, with its single overhead line, is seen by many as a blight and by others as a futuristic addition to the city. Either way, it looks like it is going to be scrapped. The monorail connects the central business district to Darling Harbour—though it's only a 15-minute walk from Town Hall. However, if you are going to the Powerhouse Museum, it's probably your best option. The system operates Monday through Thursday from 7am to 10pm, Friday and Saturday from 7am to midnight, and Sunday from 8am to 10pm. Tickets are A$4.90, free for children under 5. An all-day monorail pass costs A$9.50. The trip from the city center to Darling Harbour takes around 12 minutes. Look for the gray overhead line and the plastic tubelike structures that are the stations. Call **Metro Monorail** (✆ **02/8584 5288;** www.metrotransport.com.au) for more information.

BY METRO LIGHT RAIL A system of trams runs on a route that traverses a 3.6km (2¼-mile) track between Central Station and Wentworth Park in Pyrmont. It provides good access to Chinatown, Paddy's Markets, Darling Harbour, the Star City casino, and the Sydney Fish Markets. The trams run every 10 minutes. The one-way fare is A$3.40 to A$4.40 for adults and A$2.20 to A$3.40 for children 4 to 15, depending on distance. Two-way tickets are also available. A day pass costs A$9 for adults, A$6.50 for children, and A$20 for a family of five. Contact **Metro Light Rail** (✆ **02/8584 5288;** www.metrotransport.com.au) for details.

By Taxi

Taxis are a relatively economical way to get around. Several companies serve the city center and suburbs. All journeys are metered. If you cross either way on the Harbour Bridge or through the Harbour Tunnel, it will cost an extra A$2.50 to A$3 (depending on the time of day)—a rip-off considering there's only an official toll on the way into the city. If you take the Eastern Distributor from the airport, it's A$5. An extra 10% will be added to your fare if you pay by credit card.

Taxis line up at stands in the city, such as those opposite Circular Quay and Central Station. They are also frequently found in front of hotels. A yellow light on top of the cab means it's vacant. Cabs can be hard to get on Friday and Saturday nights and between 2 and 3pm every day, when cabbies are changing shifts after 12 hours on the road. Some people prefer to sit up front, but it's certainly not considered rude if you don't. Passengers must wear seatbelts in the front and back seats. The **Taxi Complaints Hotline** (✆ **1800/648 478** in Australia) deals with problem taxi drivers. Taxis are licensed to carry four people. The main taxi companies are: **Taxis Combined Services** (✆ **13 33 00;** www.taxiscombined.com.au); **Silver Service Fleet** (✆ **13 31 00;** www.silverservice.com.au); **RSL Cabs** (✆ **02/9581 1111**);

Legion Cabs (✆ **13 14 51;** www.legioncabs.com.au); **Premier Cabs** (✆ **13 10 17;** www.premiercabs.com.au); and **St. George Cabs** (✆ **13 21 66;** www.stgeorge cabs.com.au).

By Water Taxi

Water Taxis operate 24 hours a day and are a quick, convenient way to get to waterfront restaurants, harbor attractions, and some suburbs. They can also be chartered for private cruises. Fares for a direct transfer are based on an initial flag-fall for the hire of the vessel, and then a charge per person traveling. On most transfers, the more people that are traveling, the lower the fare per person. The typical fare for a group of six people would be A$10 to A$15 per person for an inner harbor jaunt. Sometimes you can combine with other people if you ring up well in advance. The main operators are **Water Taxis Combined** (✆ **02/9555 8888;** www.watertaxis.com.au) and **Beach Hopper** (✆ **1300/306 676** in Australia; www.watertaxi.net.au).

By Car

Traffic restrictions, parking, and congestion can make getting around by car frustrating, but if you plan to visit some of the outer suburbs or take excursions elsewhere in New South Wales, then renting a car will give you more flexibility. The **National Roads and Motorists' Association (NRMA)** is the New South Wales auto club; for emergency breakdown service, call ✆ **13 11 11.**

Tolls also apply for some roads, including the Cross City Tunnel (customer service: ✆ **02/9033 3999**); increasingly you must go through automatic toll booths using a prepaid electronic tag called an **E-Tag.** If you are a tourist or irregular user of these roads, you have to contact the motorway operator and arrange payment within 2 days. Call the **Roads and Traffic Authority** at ✆ **13 18 65** within 2 days and they'll inform you of your payment options. The Sydney Harbour Bridge was the latest to get cashless tolls (in 2009), meaning you need a tag or have to mess around paying beforehand or afterward. Other toll routes look likely to go the same way. If you are hiring a car, make sure you get the latest information about how and when you have to pay, and/or if your car has an E-Tag.

Car-rental agencies in Sydney include **Avis,** 214 William St., Kings Cross (✆ **1800/225 553**); **Budget,** 93 William St., Kings Cross (✆ **13 27 27** in Australia, or 02/9339 8888); **Hertz,** corner of William and Riley streets, Kings Cross (✆ **13 30 39** in Australia); and **Thrifty,** 75 William St., Kings Cross (✆ **02/9380 5399**). Avis, Budget, Hertz, and Thrifty also have desks at the airport. Rates average about A$60 per day for a small car. One of the best-value operations is **Bayswater Car Rentals,** 180 William St., Kings Cross (✆ **02/9360 3622;** www.bayswater carrental.com.au), which has small cars for around A$40 a day with everything included. A good option is to compare prices and book discounted vehicles through **Vroom, Vroom, Vroom** (www.vroomvroomvroom.com.au).

You can rent a motor home or "camper van" from **Britz Campervans,** 653 Gardeners Rd., Mascot, NSW 2020 (✆ **1800/331 454** in Australia, or 02/9667 0402; www.britz.com). Plan to pay about A$140 a day for a two-person van in winter and around A$180 in summer. You can drop off your van at most state capitals and in Cairns, a convenience that costs extra.

[FastFACTS] SYDNEY

American Express The main Amex office is at Level 3, 130 Pitt St., near Martin Place (✆ **02/9236 4200**). It cashes traveler's checks and acts as a travel-booking service. It's open Monday through Friday from 8:30am to 5pm and Saturday from 9am to noon. Another foreign exchange office is on the walkway leading up to the Sydney Opera House (✆ **02/9251 1970**). To report lost or stolen traveler's checks, call ✆ **1800/251 902.**

Business Hours General office and banking hours are Monday through Friday from 9am to 5pm. Many banks, especially in the city center, are open from around 9:30am to 12:30pm on Saturday. Shopping hours are usually from 8:30am to 5:30pm daily (9am–5pm Sat), and most stores stay open until 9pm on Thursday. Most city-center stores are open from around 10am to 4pm on Sunday.

Currency Exchange Most major bank branches offer currency exchange services. Small foreign-currency exchange offices are clustered at the airport and around Circular Quay and Kings Cross.

Dentists A well-respected office in the city is **City Dental Practice,** Shop 1A, Lower Ground Floor, Hunter Arcade, 5 Hunter St., near Wynyard CityRail station (✆ **02/9235 2251**). For dental problems after hours, call **Dental Emergency Information** (✆ **02/9369 7050**).

Doctors The **Park Medical Centre,** Shop 4, 27 Park St. (✆ **02/9264 4488**), in the city center near Town Hall, is open Monday through Friday from 8am to 6pm; consultations cost A$60 for 15 minutes. The **Kings Cross Travellers' Clinic,** Suite 1, 13 Springfield Ave., Kings Cross, just off Darlinghurst Road (✆ **1300/369 359** in Australia, or 02/9358 3066), is great for travel medicines and emergency contraception pills, among other things. Hotel visits in the Kings Cross area cost A$80; consultations cost A$40. The **Travellers' Medical & Vaccination Centre,** Level 7, the Dymocks Building, 428 George St., in the city center (✆ **02/9221 7133**), stocks and administers travel-related vaccinations and medications.

Embassies & Consulates All foreign embassies are based in Canberra. You'll find the following consulates in Sydney: **Canada,** Level 5, 111 Harrington St., The Rocks (✆ **02/9364 3000**); **New Zealand,** 55 Hunter St. (✆ **02/9223 0144**); **United Kingdom,** Level 16, Gateway Building, 1 Macquarie Place, Circular Quay (✆ **02/9247 7521**); and **United States,** Level 59, MLC Centre, 19–29 Martin Place (✆ **02/9373 9200**).

Emergencies Dial ✆ **000** to call the police, the fire service, or an ambulance. Call the **Emergency Prescription Service** (✆ **02/9235 0333**) for emergency drug prescriptions, and the **NRMA** for car breakdowns (✆ **13 11 11**).

Eyeglass Repair **Perfect Vision,** Shop C22A, in the Sydney Tower, 100 Market St. (✆ **02/9221 1010**), is open Monday through Friday from 9am to 6pm (until 9pm Thurs) and Saturday from 9am to 5pm. It's the best place to replace lost contact lenses; bring your prescription.

Holidays See "Holidays" in the "Fast Facts" chapter, p. 736. New South Wales also observes Labour Day on the first Monday in October.

Hospitals Make your way to **Sydney Hospital,** Macquarie Street, at the top end of Martin Place (✆ **02/9382 7111** for emergencies). **St. Vincent's Hospital** is at Victoria and Burton streets in Darlinghurst, near Kings Cross (✆ **02/9339 1111**).

Hot Lines Call the **Poisons Information Center** (✆ **13 11 26**); the **Rape Crisis Center** (✆ **02/9819 6565**); or the **Crisis Center** (✆ **02/9358 6577**).

Internet Access Several Internet and e-mail centers are scattered around Kings Cross, Bondi, and Manly.

Lost Property There is no general lost property bureau in Sydney. Contact the nearest police station if you think you've lost something. For items lost on trains, contact the **Lost Property Office,** 494 Pitt St., near Central Railway Station (✆ **02/9379 3000**). The office is open Monday through Friday from 8:30am to 4:30pm. For items left behind on planes or at the airport, go to the **Federal Airport Corporation**'s administration office on the top floor of the International Terminal at Sydney International Airport (✆ **02/9667 9583**). For stuff left behind on buses or ferries, call ✆ **02/9245 5777.** Each taxi company has its own lost property office.

Luggage Storage You can leave your bags at the International Terminal at the airport. The storage room charges around A$8 per bag for up to 6 hours and A$11 for up to 24 hours. The room is open from 4:30am to the last flight of the day. Call ✆ **02/9667 0926** for information. Otherwise, leave luggage at the cloakroom at Central Station, near the front of the main building (✆ **02/9219 4395**). Storage at the rail station costs A$5 per article per day. The **Travelers Contact Point,** seventh floor, 428 George St., above the Dymocks bookstore (✆ **02/9221 8744**), stores luggage for A$15 per piece per month. It also operates a general delivery service; has Internet access, a travel agency, and a jobs board; and ships items to the U.K. and Ireland.

Newspapers The ***Sydney Morning Herald*** is considered one of the world's best newspapers—by its management, at least—and is available throughout metropolitan Sydney. The equally prestigious ***Australian*** is available nationwide. The metropolitan ***Daily Telegraph*** is a more casual read and publishes a couple of editions a day. The *International Herald Tribune, USA Today,* the British *Guardian Weekly,* and other U.S. and U.K. newspapers can be found at Circular Quay newspaper stands and most newsdealers.

Pharmacies (Chemist Shops) Most suburbs have pharmacies that are open late. For after-hours referral, contact the **Emergency Prescription Service** (✆ **02/9235 0333**).

Police In an emergency, dial ✆ **000.** Make nonemergency police inquiries through the **Sydney Police Centre** (✆ **02/9281 0000**).

Post Office The **General Post Office (GPO)** is at 130 Pitt St., not far from Martin Place (✆ **13 13 18** in Australia). It's open Monday through Friday from 8:30am to 5:30pm and Saturday from 10am to 2pm. General-delivery letters can be sent c/o Poste Restante, G.P.O., Sydney, NSW 2000, Australia (✆ **02/9244 3733**), and collected at 310 George St., on the third floor of the Hunter Connection shopping center. It's open Monday through Friday from 8:15am to 5:30pm. For directions to the nearest post office, call ✆ **1800/043 300.**

Restrooms These can be found in the QVB (second floor), at most department stores, at Central Station and Circular Quay, near the escalators by the Sydney Aquarium, and in the Harbourside Festival Marketplace in Darling Harbour.

Safety Sydney is an extremely safe city, but as anywhere else, it's good to keep your wits about you and your wallet hidden. If you wear a money belt, keep it under your shirt. Be wary in Kings Cross and Redfern at all hours and around Central Station and the cinema strip on George Street near Town Hall station in the evening—the latter is a hangout for local gangs, though they're usually busy holding each other up. Other places of concern are the back lanes of Darlinghurst, around the naval base at Woolloomooloo, and along the Bondi restaurant strip when beet-root-red, drunken British tourists spill out after midnight. Several people have reported thieves at the airport on occasion. If traveling by train at night, travel in the carriages next to the guard's van, marked with a blue light on the outside.

Taxes Australia imposes a 10% **Goods and Services Tax (GST)** on most goods sold in Australia and most services. The GST applies to most travel-related goods and services, including transport, hotels, tours, and restaurants. By law, the tax has to be included in the advertised price of the product, though it doesn't have to be displayed independently of the pretax price. Visitors to Australia are entitled to claim a GST refund on purchases over A$300 per store. Do this at the refund booth located past Customs. After doing the paperwork—you need to have the goods and receipt with you, not in your checked luggage—you will receive your refund by check on the spot. Claims are only available up to 30 minutes prior to the scheduled departure of your flight.

Taxis See "Getting Around," earlier in this chapter.

Telephones Sydney's public phone boxes take coins, and many also accept credit cards and A$10 phone cards, available from newsdealers. Local calls cost A40¢.

Transit Information Call the **Infoline** (✆ **13 15 00** in Australia) daily from 6am to 10pm.

Useful Telephone Numbers For **news,** dial ✆ **1199;** for the **time,** ✆ **1194;** for Sydney **entertainment,** ✆ **11 688;** for **directory assistance,** ✆ **12 455;** for **Travelers Aid Society,** ✆ **02/9211 2469.**

Weather For the local forecast, call ✆ **1196.**

WHERE TO STAY

Although it's unlikely you'll find the city's hotels completely booked if you turn up looking for a bed for the night, it's probably wise to reserve rooms in advance.

DECIDING WHERE TO STAY The best location for lodging in Sydney is in The Rocks and around Circular Quay—a short stroll from the Sydney Opera House, the Harbour Bridge, the Royal Botanic Gardens, and the ferry terminals.

Hotels around Darling Harbour offer good access to the local facilities, including museums, the Sydney Aquarium, and the Star City casino. Most Darling Harbour hotels are a 10- to 15-minute walk, or a short monorail or light rail trip, from Town Hall and the central shopping district in and around Sydney Tower and Pitt Street Mall.

Another way to hunt for discounted hotel rooms is through an independent hotel search site. The two most popular are **www.lastminute.com.au** and **www.wotif.com**. Lastminute allows you to check prices of various room categories at least a month in advance. Wotif allows you to search for a room up to 14 days in the future. Hotels also provide both sites with special deals for rooms for the next couple of days.

More hotels are grouped around Kings Cross, Sydney's red-light district. Some of the hotels here are among the city's best, and you'll also find a range of cheaper lodgings, including several backpacker hostels. Kings Cross can be unnerving at any time, but especially on Friday and Saturday nights when the area's strip joints and nightclubs are jumping. Staying here does have its advantages: You get a real inner-city feel, and it's close to excellent restaurants and cafes around the Kings Cross, Darlinghurst, and Oxford Street areas.

Glebe, with its ethnic restaurants, is another inner-city suburb popular with tourists. It's well served by local buses.

Where to Stay in Central Sydney

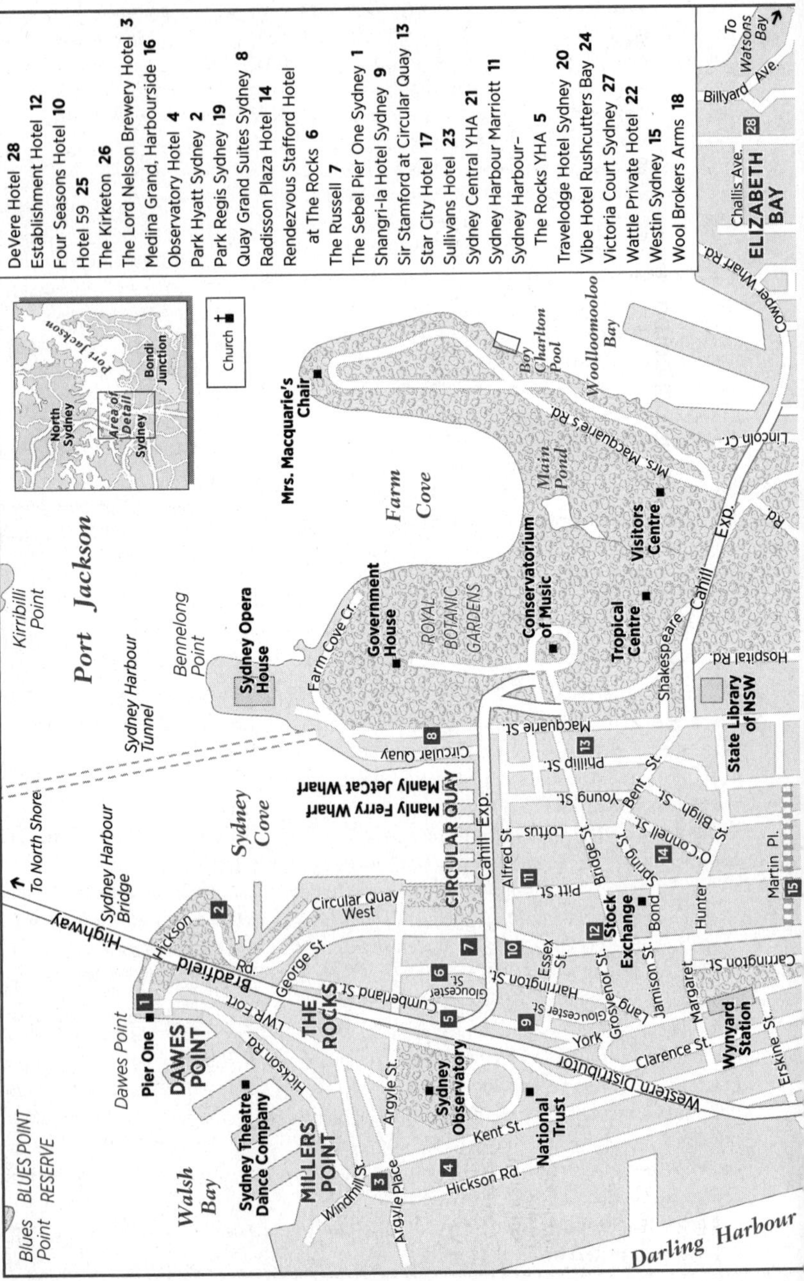
DeVere Hotel 28
Establishment Hotel 12
Four Seasons Hotel 10
Hotel 59 25
The Kirketon 26
The Lord Nelson Brewery Hotel 3
Medina Grand, Harbourside 16
Observatory Hotel 4
Park Hyatt Sydney 2
Park Regis Sydney 19
Quay Grand Suites Sydney 8
Radisson Plaza Hotel 14
Rendezvous Stafford Hotel at The Rocks 6
The Russell 7
The Sebel Pier One Sydney 1
Shangri-la Hotel Sydney 9
Sir Stamford at Circular Quay 13
Star City Hotel 17
Sullivans Hotel 23
Sydney Central YHA 21
Sydney Harbour Marriott 11
Sydney Harbour–The Rocks YHA 5
Travelodge Hotel Sydney 20
Vibe Hotel Rushcutters Bay 24
Victoria Court Sydney 27
Wattle Private Hotel 22
Westin Sydney 15
Wool Brokers Arms 18
Church
Port Jackson
North Sydney
Area of Detail
Sydney
Bondi Junction
Kirribilli Point
Sydney Harbour Tunnel
Bennelong Point
Sydney Opera House
To North Shore
Sydney Harbour Bridge
Sydney Cove
Farm Cove
Mrs. Macquarie's Chair
Government House
ROYAL BOTANIC GARDENS
Conservatorium of Music
Tropical Centre
Visitors Centre
Main Pond
Boy Charlton Pool
Woolloomooloo Bay
ELIZABETH BAY
To Watsons Bay
Manly JetCat Wharf
Manly Ferry Wharf
CIRCULAR QUAY
Circular Quay West
State Library of NSW
Stock Exchange
Wynyard Station
THE ROCKS
DAWES POINT
MILLERS POINT
Pier One
Dawes Point
Sydney Observatory
National Trust
Sydney Theatre Dance Company
Walsh Bay
BLUES POINT RESERVE
Blues Point
Darling Harbour

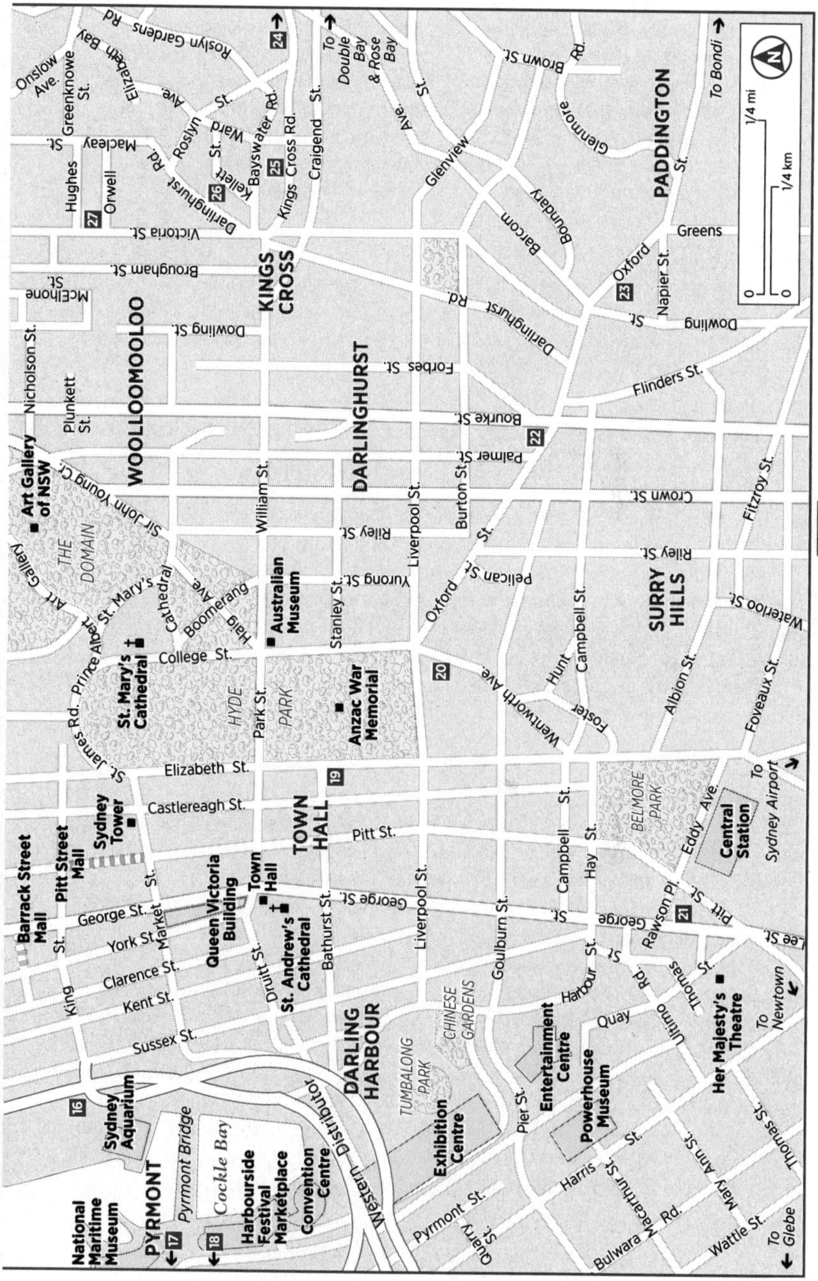

WOOLLOOMOOLOO
KINGS CROSS
DARLINGHURST
PADDINGTON
SURRY HILLS
TOWN HALL
DARLING HARBOUR
PYRMONT
THE DOMAIN
HYDE PARK
BELMORE PARK
TUMBALONG PARK
CHINESE GARDENS
Cockle Bay
Art Gallery of NSW
St. Mary's Cathedral
Australian Museum
Anzac War Memorial
Sydney Tower
Pitt Street Mall
Barrack Street Mall
Queen Victoria Building
Town Hall
St. Andrew's Cathedral
Central Station
Her Majesty's Theatre
Powerhouse Museum
Entertainment Centre
Exhibition Centre
Convention Centre
Harbourside Festival Marketplace
Sydney Aquarium
National Maritime Museum
Pyrmont Bridge
Western Distributor
To Double Bay & Rose Bay
To Bondi
To Sydney Airport
To Newtown
To Glebe
0 1/4 mi
0 1/4 km
N
16
17
18
19
20
21
22
23
24
25
26
27
William St.
Oxford St.
Liverpool St.
George St.
Pitt St.
Castlereagh St.
Elizabeth St.
College St.
Park St.
Macleay St.
Victoria St.
Darlinghurst Rd.
Bayswater Rd.
Kings Cross Rd.
Craigend St.
Bourke St.
Crown St.
Riley St.
Flinders St.
Cleveland St.

Last-Minute Room Deals

If you turn up in town without a reservation, you should definitely use the Sydney Visitors Centre bookings desk (© 02/9667 6050), in the arrivals hall of the airport's international terminal. It negotiates deals with many of Sydney's hotels (but not hostels) and offers exceptional discounts on rooms that haven't been filled that day. You can save up to 50%. The desk is open from 6am to the last flight of the day. It also offers discounts on tours (to the Blue Mountains, for example) and cheap tickets for flights within Australia.

If you want to stay near the beach, check out the options in Manly and Bondi, though you should consider their distance from the city center and the lack of CityRail trains to these areas. A taxi to Manly from the city will cost around A$55 and to Bondi around A$35.

MAKING A DEAL The prices given below for very expensive and expensive hotels are mostly the **rack rates,** the recommended retail price, which guests can pay at the busiest periods if they book at short notice or walk in off the street. Always ask about discounts, package deals, and any other special offerings when booking a hotel, especially if you are traveling in winter when hotels are less likely to be full. Ask about weekend discounts, corporate rates, and family plans.

Booking direct through a hotel's website can also yield savings. For instance, a search of the website for Accor, a company that manages 31 quality hotels in and around Sydney, shows that you could save up to 50% off the rack rate. On the Accor website (www.accorhotels.com.au), you can check rates months in advance.

Serviced apartments are also well worth considering because you can save a bundle by cooking your own meals; many also have free laundry facilities. We list a couple of choices below. Almost all hotels offer nonsmoking rooms; inquire when you make a reservation if it's important to you. Most moderately priced to very expensive rooms will have tea- and coffee-making facilities and an iron. Like hotels elsewhere, some of Sydney's lodgings are in on the increasing trend to rip off guests with pay-per-view movie channels (around A$16 per movie), rather than to provide full access to a range of free cable TV channels.

If you're looking for a hotel with spa facilities, then check into either the Observatory Hotel, the Grace Hotel, the Sheraton on the Park, Swissotel Sydney, Star City Hotel, the Four Seasons Hotel Sydney, or the Shangri-la Hotel Sydney. Every day spa in Sydney (and Australia for that matter) is listed on **www.dayspaguide.com.au**.

By the way, coffeemakers as such are rare in Australian hotels, but most hotels have tea- and coffee-making facilities (such as tea bags, instant coffee, small plastic milk cartons, and a kettle). In-room irons and ironing boards are also common, apart from in the cheapest hotels.

The price categories used are as follows: Very Expensive, A$300 and up; Expensive, A$200 to A$300; Moderate, A$100 to A$200; Inexpensive, below A$100. Prices are for a double. In Australia, a "double" room means you get one double, queen-size, or king-size bed in a room.

Around The Rocks & Circular Quay

VERY EXPENSIVE

Four Seasons Hotel Sydney ★★★ The Four Seasons features impressive views of Sydney Harbour and the Opera House and is perfectly positioned close to the historic Rocks district and the Sydney Opera House. The rooms are elegantly decorated, with marble bathrooms and plenty of mahogany, and though neither a modern nor a historic hotel—there's a bit of a 1970s feel from the outside—it still has a nice charm about it. The staff is helpful and efficient, the outdoor pool is the largest in any hotel in Sydney, the spa is one of the city's best, and the restaurant, **Kable's** (✆ **02/9250 3306** for reservations), is a high-standard eatery, too. Kable's signature dishes include soft-cured ocean trout with smoked sour cream, baby radish, and fennel salad; Black Angus beef, chateau potatoes, king brown mushrooms, béarnaise, and red wine sauce; and West Australian lobster thermidor with cherry tomato and watercress salad. If you are traveling with kids, then little touches, such as a gingerbread man with your child's name iced across its chest left in your room, make it all the more welcoming.

199 George St., The Rocks, Sydney, NSW 2000. ✆ **02/9238 0000.** Fax 02/9251 2851. www.fourseasons.com/sydney. 531 units. A$350 city-view double; A$395 Opera House–view double; A$470 full-harbor-view double; A$530–A$1,050 suite. Children 13 and under stay free in parent's room. AE, MC, V. Parking A$27. Bus, train, ferry: Circular Quay. **Amenities:** Restaurant; bar; babysitting; concierge; health club; outdoor pool; room service; sauna; spa. *In room:* A/C, TV w/pay movies, hair dryer, minibar, free Wi-Fi.

Observatory Hotel ★★★ If I were to stay in any hotel in Sydney, then this would be at the top of my list. This exclusive colonial-style hotel, a 10-minute walk uphill from The Rocks and 15 minutes from Circular Quay, or a stroll down to Wynyard CityRail station, is a turn-of-the-20th-century beauty competing for top-hotel-in-Sydney honors. It's fitted with antiques, objets d'art, and the finest carpets, wallpapers, and draperies. Plus, it's renowned for its personalized service. Rooms are plush and quiet, with huge bathrooms. Some rooms have city views; others look out over the harbor. The pool here is one of the best in Sydney. (Note the Southern Hemisphere constellations on the roof.) The day spa is also one of the most exclusive in the city, as is the hotel's restaurant, **Galileo,** where superb Japanese-French fusion is served in luxurious surroundings with a clubby feel. Everyone loves this hotel.

89–113 Kent St., Sydney, NSW 2000. ✆ **1800/806 245** in Australia, or 02/9256 2222. Fax 02/9256 2233. www.observatoryhotel.com.au. 100 units. A$415–A$450 double; from A$510 suite. Extra person A$66. Children 13 and under stay free in parent's room. AE, MC, V. Parking A$30. Bus: 339, 431, or 433 to Millers Point. **Amenities:** Restaurant; bar; concierge; health club w/flotation tank; chemical-free heated indoor pool; 24-hr. room service; sauna; floodlit tennis court; free Wi-Fi in lobby. *In room:* A/C, TV/DVD w/pay movies, CD player, hair dryer, minibar.

Park Hyatt Sydney ★★★ This artistically curving property on The Rocks foreshore is the best-positioned hotel in Sydney. It's right on the water, and some rooms have fantastic views across the harbor to the Sydney Opera House. Its location and general appeal mean it's usually full. The building itself is a pleasure to look at, and from a ferry on the harbor, it looks like a wonderful addition to the toy-town landscape of The Rocks. The good-size rooms incorporate every possible luxury. Room rates here depend on views; the least expensive units have only glimpses of the harbor. (The most expensive rooms look over the Opera House.) Each of the 33 executive suites has two balconies with a telescope. Either way, this is the most expensive hotel in Sydney by a long shot. The **harbourkitchen&bar** offers good Mediterranean-inspired meals on the edge of the harbor, and it's worth a visit even if you don't stay here. Visit the **Little Kitchen** for high tea (2:30–5pm; A$35 per person); the **Club Bar** for cognac; and the **Harbour Bar** for a good martini.

7 Hickson Rd., The Rocks, Sydney, NSW 2000. ✆ **800/633-7313** in the U.S. and Canada, or 02/9256 1234. Fax 02/9256 1555. www.sydney.hyatt.com. 158 units. A$650–A$700 double; A$820–A$920 executive studio; from A$1,000 suite. Extra person A$55. Children 17 and under stay free in parent's room. Ask about weekend discounts and packages. AE, DC, MC, V. Parking A$40. CityRail, bus, or ferry: Circular Quay. **Amenities:** 2 restaurants; bar; lounge; babysitting; concierge; health club and spa; heated outdoor pool; room service. *In room:* A/C, TV, hair dryer, minibar.

Quay Grand Suites Sydney ★★ The best serviced-apartment complexes, like this one, can outdo superior AAA-rated five-star hotels—even in price. This building, on the pedestrian concourse leading up to the Sydney Opera House, also houses private apartments costing upwards of A$850,000—so you know you are in exclusive territory. The spacious, ultramodern apartments either face the Botanic Gardens or have fantastic views across the ferry terminals and the Sydney Harbour Bridge. The fully equipped units have balconies so you can admire the views. The noises from the CityRail station (including train announcements) and the ferry horns are captivating but can easily be shut out. Bathrooms are large and feature good-size Jacuzzis. You might want to eat at the hotel's **Quadrant** restaurant, which serves Contemporary food and has spectacular views to Circular Quay and the harbor. The bar is the trendy **ECQ.** The Dendy cinema, in the same strip, has good art-house movies.

61 Macquarie St., E. Circular Quay, Sydney, NSW 2000. ✆ **1800/091 954** in Australia, or 02/9256 4000. Fax 02/9256 4040. www.mirvachotels.com.au. 68 units. A$360 1-bedroom apt. Extra person A$35. Ask about weekend packages and long-term discounts. AE, DC, MC, V. Valet parking A$25. CityRail, bus, or ferry: Circular Quay. **Amenities:** Restaurant; bar; babysitting; concierge; small health club; room service. *In room:* A/C, TV w/pay movies, hair dryer, kitchen, minibar, free Wi-Fi.

Shangri-La Hotel Sydney ★★ For a room with a view, you're not going to do better than this ultramodern landmark hotel with a touch of Asian flair. It's just a 5-minute walk from Circular Quay. Try to book a room on the 20th floor or above: From here, Sydney and its harbor are laid out at your feet, with ferries buzzing around below you like bath toys. All rooms are contemporarily furnished and rely on the views perhaps more than the decor to impress. The top five room floors, from level 29 to level 34, have use of the Horizon Club lounge, which supplies breakfast and evening canapés. The trendy **Café Mix,** on level 1, serves breakfasts and has a good lunch and dinner buffet with Contemporary and Asian-style meals (including Japanese). Also here is the **Rocks Teppanyaki** restaurant, which serves good Japanese cuisine. The stylish **Altitude** restaurant and **Blue Horizon Bar** (both on the 36th floor) have panoramic harbor views. The associated historic **Harts Pub,** at street level, offers a lunchtime Aussie barbecue in the beer garden Tuesdays to Fridays.

176 Cumberland St., The Rocks, Sydney, NSW 2000. ✆ **1800/801 088** in Australia, or 02/9250 6000. Fax 02/9250 6250. www.shangri-la.com. 563 units. A$295 double; A$400–A$500 corner room; suites from A$550. Extra person A$60. Children stay free in parent's room. Ask about packages. AE, DC, MC, V. Parking A$42. CityRail or ferry: Circular Quay. **Amenities:** 2 restaurants; 2 bars; lounge; babysitting; concierge; exercise room; Jacuzzi; heated indoor pool; room service; sauna. *In room:* A/C, TV w/pay movies, hair dryer, minibar, free Wi-Fi.

Sir Stamford at Circular Quay ★★ From the moment the doorman doffs his top hat to you, you've entered the world of aristocracy, complete with the slight scent of aged brandy. This boutique luxury hotel has a European flavor reminiscent of a private club. It's in a prime location, just a short walk from Circular Quay and the Opera House, and just across the road from the Royal Botanic Gardens. Rooms are exceptionally large and luxurious, with good-size marble bathrooms. Most rooms have a small balcony. The rooms on the east side of the hotel have the best views across the Botanic Gardens. Most rooms are accessible to wheelchairs.

93 Macquarie St., Sydney, NSW 2000. ✆ **1300/301 391** in Australia, or 02/9252 4600. Fax 02/9252 4286. www.stamford.com.au. 105 units. A$270 double; A$320 deluxe harbor-view double; suites from A$420. AE, DC, MC, V. Parking A$40. CityRail, bus, or ferry: Circular Quay. **Amenities:** Restaurant; bar; babysitting; concierge; exercise room; solar-heated outdoor pool; room service; sauna. *In room:* A/C, TV w/pay movies, fax, hair dryer, minibar.

EXPENSIVE

Rendezvous Hotel The Rocks The Rendezvous offers some of the best-positioned serviced apartments in Sydney, right in the heart of The Rocks, very close to the harbor and Circular Quay, and a short stroll from the central business district. The property consists of spacious modern apartments with varying kitchen facilities in one six-story building (the best units, with harbor and Opera House views, are on the top three floors) and seven two-story terrace houses dating from 1870 to 1895. Studio rooms are the least expensive and come with a choice of a queen-size bed or two single beds, a shower over a tub, a microwave, a toaster, and a refrigerator.

75 Harrington St., The Rocks, Sydney, NSW 2000. ✆ **02/9251 6711.** Fax 02/9251 3458. www.rendezvoushotels.com. 61 units. A$235–A$275 studio double; A$280 1-bedroom apt; A$320 executive 1-bedroom apt; A$295 terrace house; A$370 1-bedroom penthouse. Extra person A$15. Children 11 and under stay free in parent's room. Ask about weekly discounts. AE, DC, MC, V. Parking A$15. CityRail or ferry: Circular Quay. **Amenities:** Babysitting; exercise room; Jacuzzi; small outdoor pool; room service; sauna; free Wi-Fi in lobby lounge. *In room:* A/C, TV, hair dryer, kitchen, minibar.

The Russell ★★ This is the coziest place to stay in The Rocks, and perhaps in all of Sydney. It's more than 100 years old, and it shows its age wonderfully in the creaks of the floorboards and the ramshackle feel of the brightly painted corridors. Every room is different in style, size, and shape, though all rooms have immense character, including a series of rooms added on in 1990 above the Fortune of War Hotel next door. There are no harbor views, but from some rooms you can see the tops of the ferry terminals at Circular Quay; they all come with queen-size beds as well. Guests have the use of a sitting room, a living room with magazines and books, and a rooftop garden. The apartment is a large, open-plan unit with a king-size bed and small kitchen; it's suitable for three people (there's a double sofa bed). It overlooks Circular Quay. At press time, the hotel was undergoing renovations, which will hopefully be concluded by fall 2010.

143A George St., The Rocks, Sydney, NSW 2000. ✆ **02/9241 3543.** Fax 02/9252 1652. www.therussell.com.au. 29 units, 19 with bathroom. A$150–A$199 double without bathroom; A$245–A$265 double with bathroom; A$290 suite or apt. Extra person A$30. Rates include continental breakfast. AE, DC, MC, V. No parking available. CityRail or ferry: Circular Quay. **Amenities:** Restaurant; lounge. *In room:* TV.

The Sebel Pier One Sydney ★ A premier waterfront hotel, the Sebel is in the historic Woolloomooloo Wharf complex and has been painstakingly renovated, leaving as much of the original early-20th-century Pier One structure intact as possible. It's a wonderfully intoxicating blend of old wooden beams and tasteful modern art. The only drawback to staying in one of the tastefully appointed waterfront rooms is that the harbor views—through windows that run all the way to the polished wooden floorboards—could make you want to stay in for the rest of the day. Or perhaps the cocktail bar, one of the trendiest in town, is more your scene.

11 Hickson Rd., Walsh Bay, Sydney, NSW 2000. ✆ **1800/780 485** in Australia, or 02/8298 9999. Fax 02/8298 9777. www.mirvachotels.com.au. 160 units. A$235 double; A$290 waterfront room. Rates include breakfast. AE, DC, MC, V. CityRail or ferry: Circular Quay. Bus: George St. **Amenities:** Restaurant; bar; gym; Jacuzzi. *In room:* A/C, TV, hair dryer.

MODERATE

The Lord Nelson Brewery Hotel Sydney's oldest pub was established in 1841 after serving as a private residence since its construction in 1836. It's an attractive, three-story sandstone building with a busy pub on the ground floor, a good brasserie on the second, and hotel accommodations on the third. The rooms are compact and simple, but spacious enough to swing your bags around without hitting the walls. From its creaky floorboards and bedroom walls made from convict-hewn sandstone blocks to the narrow corridors, the wood fire, and the homemade beer in the bar, the Lord Nelson positively wallows in colonial atmosphere.

At the corner of Kent and Argyle sts., The Rocks, Sydney, NSW 2000. ✆ **02/9251 4044.** Fax 02/9251 1532. www.lordnelsonbrewery.com. 9 units, 8 with bathroom. A$130 double without bathroom; A$190 double with bathroom. Extra person A$30. Rates include continental breakfast. AE, DC, MC, V. No parking available. **Amenities:** 2 restaurants; bar. *In room:* TV, hair dryer.

Sydney Harbour–The Rocks YHA ☺ Supplying budget-ish accommodations in the heart of The Rocks historic district, the new Sydney Harbour YHA opened with much fanfare in early 2010. The hostel is modern (though it sits within a historic footprint) and rooms are basic but clean. Some have harbor views if you stand on tiptoes. All are air-conditioned, and even the dorms have private bathrooms. There are also some nice small touches, including an electric socket inside each of the dorm-room lockers, so you can charge your iPod/laptop/camera and not worry about it. In some ways, it may remind you more of a hotel than a hostel. The kitchen is stocked, there's a very large common area, and the roof terrace is an excellent place to hang out, particularly as it has fabulous views of the Opera House, the Sydney Harbour Bridge, and the harbor itself. For the fabulous position you pay a premium, of course. You do have to lug your luggage up a lot of steps to get to the building.

110 Cumberland St., The Rocks, Sydney, NSW 2000. ✆ **02/8272 0900.** Fax 02/8272 0950. www.yha.com.au. A$38–A$44 dorm; A$128–A$143 double; A$160–A$178 family room (4 people). MC, V. CityRail or ferry: Circular Quay. **Amenities:** Self-catering kitchen and dining area; Internet cafe; coffee bar; lounge; laundry facilities; convenience store. *In room:* A/C.

In the City Center

VERY EXPENSIVE

Establishment Hotel ★★★ Sydney's coolest hotel offers sleek modernist rooms in two styles: one with beautifully restored warehouse ceilings, Japan black floorboards, and flashes of strong color, and the other more tranquil in color and softer in feel. All rooms come with generous-size marble or bluestone bathrooms. If you were a superstar with a taste for cutting-edge fashion, this is where you'd choose to stay. In the same building, you'll find one of Sydney's best restaurants, **est.,** and the small but gorgeous **Sushi E.** Also here are a couple of trendy bars, as well as the popular **Tank** nightclub. The building is a historic Sydney landmark, but the feel is "now" rather than then.

5 Bridge Lane (off George St., near Wynyard CityRail Station), Sydney, NSW 2000. ✆ **02/9240 3110.** Fax 02/9240 3101. www.merivale.com. A$350 Junior Room; A$415 Establishment Room; A$970–A$1,150 penthouse. AE, DC, MC, V. Parking A$35. CityRail: Wynyard. **Amenities:** 2 restaurants; 2 bars; nightclub; concierge; gym; room service. *In room:* A/C, TV, CD/DVD, hair dryer.

Radisson Plaza Hotel Sydney ★★ Right in the heart of the city in a gorgeous heritage building, the Radisson Plaza Hotel Sydney has a nice feel, with chic rooms in muted chocolate tones and sensual fabrics. Each modern-style guest room features an en-suite bathroom with marble vanity, separate shower, and extra-deep European-style bathtub. Premier rooms feature king-size, queen-size, or two double beds; Atrium rooms overlook the light well, which is open to the sky. Deluxe rooms are located on the 11th and 12th floors of the hotel and feature full-length glass doors which open onto a Juliet-style balcony. Studio Spa Suites are larger and open, while one-bedroom Spa Suites have a separate living area and a balcony.

27 O'Connell St., Sydney, NSW 2000. ✆ **800/333-3333** in the U.S., 1800/333 333 in Australia, or 02/8214 0000. Fax 02/8214 1000. www.radisson.com/sydneyau_plaza. 362 units. A$235 premier and Atrium rooms; A$270 deluxe room; A$330 studio Spa Suite; A$365 1-bedroom Spa Suite. AE, DC, MC, V. Parking A$35. CityRail: Wynyard. **Amenities:** Restaurant; bar; babysitting; concierge; gym; heated indoor lap pool; room service; sauna. *In room:* A/C, TV, free Wi-Fi.

Sydney Harbour Marriott ★ One of two Marriotts in town, this property is a quick stroll to Circular Quay and The Rocks. A third of the rooms have views over the harbor, with deluxe bridge-view rooms and deluxe opera-view rooms having the pick of the vantage points. The indoor/outdoor pool is a nice touch, the contemporary rooms are a fair size and always nice and bright, and each room features a large work desk and a safe for your laptop. The historic **Customs House Bar** down below has a pretty courtyard for an outside drink.

30 Pitt St. (corner of Alfred St.), Sydney, NSW 2000. ✆ **1800/251 259** in Australia, 02/9259 7000. Fax 02/9251 1122. www.marriott.com.au. 550 units. A$550–A$850 double (but always check for online specials/packages, which can reduce rates considerably). AE, DC, MC, V. Parking A$35. CityRail: Circular Quay. **Amenities:** Restaurant; bar; concierge; gym; pool; room service. *In room:* A/C, TV, hair dryer.

Westin Sydney ★ One of Sydney's most celebrated AAA-rated five-star hotels, the Westin is in the center of the city, in the Martin Place pedestrian mall. Integrated into a 19th-century post office, the Westin's charm is modern and classic all at once. The large rooms have comfortable beds and floor-to-ceiling windows. The hotel is home to several bars, restaurants, and clothing shops. Just steps from the central shopping streets and the QVB, and a 10- to 15-minute walk from both the Sydney Opera House and Darling Harbour, the hotel features an impressive seven-story atrium, a wonderful two-level health club, and an exclusive day spa.

1 Martin Place, Sydney, NSW 2000. ✆ **800/WESTIN-1 [937-8461]** in the U.S., or 02/8223 1111. Fax 02/8223 1222. www.westin.com.au. 416 units. A$286 double. AE, DC, MC, V. Parking A$25. CityRail: Martin Place. **Amenities:** Cafe; bar; babysitting; day spa. *In room:* A/C, TV, hair dryer.

EXPENSIVE

Park Regis Sydney This corporate hotel occupies the top 15 floors of a 45-story building and is well placed in the central business district, 2 blocks from Hyde Park and Town Hall. The rooms are light, modern, and practical, though there's nothing spectacular about them or the hotel. However, the suites are much nicer, having been refurbished in 2009. These come with free cable TV in the lounge, a separate bedroom with a king bed, a second LCD TV, and a work desk. The hotel is relatively good value considering the location. Rooms at the front have views over the city and park. All guests have access to the roof terrace, which has a pool and great views.

27 Park St. (at Castlereagh St.), Sydney, NSW 2000. ✆ **1800/060 954** in Australia, or 02/9267 6511. Fax 02/9264 2252. www.leisureinnhotels.com.au. 120 units, all with shower only. A$175 double; A$198 suite. Extra person A$22. Children 13 and under stay free in parent's room. Aussie auto club discounts available. AE, DC, MC, V. Parking A$20. CityRail: Town Hall. Monorail: Park Plaza. **Amenities:** Babysitting; concierge; small heated outdoor pool; room service. *In room:* A/C, TV, fridge, hair dryer, free Wi-Fi.

MODERATE

Travelodge Hotel Sydney ★ This business-oriented hotel is cheap for Sydney, comfortable, and reasonably well located—making it a good option for travelers who just want to unpack and explore. The rooms are Ikea-like in appearance, with a queen-size bed or twin beds. All include a kitchenette with a microwave. From here it's a short walk to Oxford Street, Town Hall, Hyde Park, and the monorail to Darling Harbour. The more upmarket **Travelodge Wynyard,** 7–9 York St. (✆ **02/9274 1222**), is more in the heart of the action and is surrounded by cafes and restaurants. It underwent renovation in 2007. Rooms there are nice and plush and cost A$174 for a standard room, A$195 for an executive room (with better views), and A$277 for larger rooms and studio apartments.

27–33 Wentworth Ave., Sydney, NSW 2000. ✆ **1300/886 886** in Australia, or 02/8267 1700. Fax 02/8267 1800. www.travelodge.com.au. 406 units. A$119 double or twin. Extra person A$16. AE, DC, MC, V. Parking around corner A$17. CityRail: Museum. **Amenities:** Restaurant; babysitting. *In room:* A/C, TV, hair dryer, kitchenette.

INEXPENSIVE

Sydney Central YHA ★★ This multiple-award-winning hostel is one of the biggest and busiest in the world. With a 98% year-round occupancy rate, you'll have to book early. It's in a historic nine-story building and offers far more than standard basic accommodations. In the basement is the **Scu Bar,** a popular drinking hole with pool tables and occasional entertainment. There's also an entertainment room with more pool tables and e-mail facilities, TV rooms on every floor, and an audiovisual room that shows movies. Rooms are clean and basic. Three dorm rooms hold eight people each; 24 sleep up to six; and 70 accommodate four. The YHA is accessible to travelers with disabilities.

Another hostel, the **Railway Square YHA,** 8–10 Lee St., at the corner of Upper Carriage Lane and Lee St., or enter via the Henry Dean Plaza (✆ **02/9281 9666;** fax 02/9281 9688), opened in 2004. The historic 1904 building adjoining "Platform Zero" at Central Railway Station offers 64 beds in four- to eight-bed dorm rooms and 10 double rooms. Some dorm rooms are even located in railway carriages. There's a sauna, pool, Internet cafe, tour desk, indoor and outdoor communal areas, and a self-catering kitchen. Dorm rooms are A$32 to A$35 a night, doubles with shared bathroom are A$91 to A$102, and doubles with bathroom are A$100 to A$112.

There are more than 140 YHA hostels in Australia. Check **www.yha.com.au** for the full list, which includes other hostels in Sydney, such as the **Glebe Point YHA,** the **Sydney Beachhouse YHA** in the beachside suburb of Collaroy, **Bondi Beachhouse YHA,** and **Pittwater YHA** in Ku-ring-gai Chase National Park (accessible only by boat, and a fabulous way to experience the "bush" around Sydney).

11 Rawson Place (at Pitt St., outside Central Station), Sydney, NSW 2000. ✆ **02/9281 9000.** Fax 02/9281 9099. www.yha.com.au. 97 dorm units with 448 beds; 54 twin units, 43 with bathroom. A$36–A$43 dorm bed; A$106–A$120 double. MC, V. Parking A$20. CityRail: Central. **Amenities:** Restaurant; bar; small heated outdoor pool; sauna. *In room:* No phone.

In Darling Harbour

Medina Grand, Harbourside ★★ This impressive hotel offers modern, very comfortable rooms (which are essentially furnished apartments with maid service) at competitive prices. It's a little oddly placed—reached by an offshoot road and a short, unattractive walk from the Sydney Aquarium in Darling Harbour—but it's still close to all of the Darling Harbour, Cockle Bay, and Town Hall attractions and shops. You can choose between studio and one-bedroom apartments, which all come with Italian designer furniture, large windows, and balconies (some with good harbor views). Studio units have a kitchenette, and one-bedrooms have a fully equipped kitchen and a second TV. All have dataports. Medina offers very good package and weekend rates, which means this place can work out to be a real bargain. Higher prices listed are for water-view units.

Medin also operates several other serviced-apartment complexes in Sydney, including the **Medina Executive Sydney Central,** in a historic building near Central Station (✆ **02/8396 9800**); the pleasant **Medina Classic** in Martin Place (✆ **02/9224 6400**); and the luxury **Medina Grand,** between Town Hall and Darling Harbour (✆ **02/9274 0000**).

Corner of Shelley and King sts., King St. Wharf, Sydney, NSW 2000. ✆ **1300/300 232** in Australia, or 02/9249 7000. Fax 02/9249 6900. www.medinaapartments.com.au. 114 units. A$238–A$254 studio; A$265–A$330 1-bedroom apt. AE, DC, MC, V. CityRail: Town Hall. **Amenities:** Concierge; exercise room; small heated indoor pool; Wi-Fi ($6 for 30 min.). *In room:* A/C, TV, hair dryer.

Star City Hotel ★★ This gambling and entertainment complex has rooms overlooking Darling Harbour and the architecturally interesting Pyrmont Bridge. The four split-level Star Suites are spectacular—each with three TVs, a giant Jacuzzi, a full kitchen, two bathrooms, its own sauna, and the services of the former butler to the governor of Queensland. These suites were revamped in 2009 and now sport a much more modern decor of tasteful grays and blacks. Royal suites had a much more dated feel to them at the time of writing, but these too, along with the standard rooms, are due to be updated throughout 2010. Standard rooms are somewhat small. If you break the casino, use your winnings to pay for a room with views over Darling Harbour. The excellent **Astral** restaurant is at the summit of the hotel tower on level 17.

80 Pyrmont St., Pyrmont, Sydney, NSW 2009. ✆ **1800/700 700** in Australia, or 02/9777 9000. Fax 02/9657 8344. www.starcity.com.au. 491 units. A$350–A$370 double; from A$510 and way up suite. Extra person A$40. Ask about special packages. AE, DC, MC, V. Parking A$20. Ferry: Pyrmont Bay. Monorail: Harbourside. Light Rail: Star City. **Amenities:** 4 restaurants, casino; concierge; Jacuzzi; large heated outdoor pool; room service; sauna. *In room:* A/C, TV, hair dryer, free Wi-Fi.

Wool Brokers Arms You'll find this friendly 1886 heritage building on the far side of Darling Harbour, next to the prominent Novotel hotel and hidden behind a monstrous aboveground parking garage. It's on a noisy road, so unless you're used to traffic, avoid the rooms at the front. Rooms are simply furnished, with a double bed and a sink. Room no. 3 is one of the nicer ones. Family rooms have a king-size bed, a set of bunks, and two singles through an open doorway. There are 19 shared bathrooms. It's adequate for a few nights. The website allows you to book up to 2 weeks in advance and offers a range of discounts.

22 Allen St., Pyrmont, Sydney, NSW 2009. ✆ **02/9552 4773.** Fax 02/9552 4771. www.woolbrokershotel.com.au. 26 units, none with bathroom. A$89 double; A$110 triple; A$130 family room for 4. Rates include continental breakfast. Extra person A$20. AE, MC, V. Parking A$11 nearby. Bus: 501 from central business district or Central Station. Light Rail: Convention Centre. *In room:* TV.

In Kings Cross & the Suburbs Beyond

DeVere Hotel The DeVere has been recommended by several readers who commented on the friendly staff and the bargain-basement prices when they booked at the Tourism New South Wales Travel Centre at the Sydney airport. Although the rooms are very modern, they are a little too motel-like for the price (unless you get a special deal). Superior rooms are a bit larger than standard rooms, and the executive room is larger still and comes with nicer furniture. The suites have views of Elizabeth Bay, a Jacuzzi, and a king-size bed rather than a queen-size. Some suites have a kitchenette with no cooking facilities. Some standard rooms have an extra single bed. Breakfast is available.

44–46 Macleay St., Potts Point, NSW 2011. ✆ **1800/818 790** in Australia, 0800/441 779 in New Zealand, or 02/9358 1211. Fax 02/9358 4685. www.devere.com.au. 100 units. A$180 double; A$230 superior room; A$265 executive room or studio; A$320 suite. Extra person A$45. Check website for packages. Children 11 and under stay free in parent's room. AE, DC, MC, V. Parking at nearby Landmark Hotel A$15 per exit. CityRail: Kings Cross. Bus: 311 from Circular Quay. *In room:* A/C, TV, fridge, hair dryer.

Hotel 59 ☺ This popular and friendly B&B is well worth considering if you want to be near the Kings Cross action but far enough away to get a decent night's sleep. Deluxe rooms have queen- or king-size beds and tub/shower combos, while the smaller standard rooms come with double beds and showers. The two large family rooms come with separate living rooms, two single beds, and two more that can be locked together to form a king-size. One comes with a small kitchen with a microwave and hot plates. All rooms are well kept and comfortable, with private bathrooms. The cafe below serves breakfast. ***Warning:*** A flight of stairs and the lack of an elevator might make this a bad choice for travelers with disabilities.

59 Bayswater Rd., Kings Cross, NSW 2011. ✆ **02/9360 5900.** Fax 02/9360 1828. www.hotel59.com.au. 8 units, some with shower only. A$110 standard double; A$121 deluxe double; A$132 family room. Extra person A$15; extra child 2–12 A$10. Rates include breakfast. MC, V. No parking. CityRail: Kings Cross. **Amenities:** Cafe; TV lounge. *In room:* A/C, TV, hair dryer, kitchen.

The Kirketon ★ If you want to stay somewhere a bit offbeat and class yourself as a hip, fashionable type, then this boutique hotel in Darlinghurst is a fascinating option. Rooms come with king-size, queen-size, double, or twin beds, and are lightly stocked with modernist furniture and custom-made fittings, including mirrored headboards, sleek bathrooms hidden away behind mirrored doors, and interestingly textured bedspreads and areas of wallpaper. Standard rooms are quite compact, and come with a double bed. Some come with a tub as well as shower. Premium rooms have a queen-size bed. Executive rooms are quite large, have a king-size bed, and some have a small balcony overlooking the main road (the road can be noisy at night). The inside scoop is that the best standard unit is no. 330, the best premium no. 340, and the best executive no. 323. Definitely ask for a room away from the main road. The same company operates another stylish boutique hotel, **Medusa,** 267 Darlinghurst Rd. (✆ **02/9331 1000;** www.medusa.com.au). Rooms start at A$310 a night there, and the overall size and quality of the rooms reflect the price jump.

229 Darlinghurst Rd., Darlinghurst, NSW 2010. ✆ **02/9332 2011.** Fax 02/9332 2499. www.kirketon.com.au. 40 rooms. A$155 junior room; A$185 premium double; A$225 executive double (book these rates over the Internet). Maximum 2 people per room. AE, DC, MC, V. Parking A$25. **Amenities:** Restaurant; bar. *In room:* A/C, TV, hair dryer, minibar.

Vibe Hotel Rushcutters Bay ★ Vibe Hotels have been making quite an impact over the last couple of years, with new properties opening up in Sydney, Melbourne, and the Gold Coast. This one, on the far side of Kings Cross, is the flagship. Compared to other hotels in this price bracket, this really is a bargain, especially when you book online. The large hotel has a good cafe, called **Curve,** brightly colored rooms with all you need, a heated rooftop swimming pool, and a good gym. Sister hotels **Vibe Hotel Sydney,** 111 Goulburn St. (✆ **02/8372 3300;** rooms A$140–A$170), and **Vibe North Sydney,** 88 Alfred St., Milsons Point (✆ **02/9955 1111;** rooms A$340–A$495), are a little less glamorous, but considering their positions and the price of real estate in Sydney these days, they too pull off great deals. Vibe North Sydney is very close to North Sydney Olympic Pool, which almost laps up to the far edge of the Sydney Harbour Bridge. From here, one stop of the CityRail network brings you to Wynyard in the center of the city.

100 Bayswater Rd., Rushcutters Bay, NSW 2011. ✆ **02/8353 8988.** Fax 02/8353 8999. www.vibehotels.com.au. 259 units. A$160 standard room. AE, DC, MC, V. Parking A$30. CityRail: Kings Cross. **Amenities:** Restaurant; bar; concierge; gym; small heated outdoor pool; Wi-Fi in restaurant only. *In room:* A/C, TV, hair dryer.

Victoria Court Sydney ★ This cute, well-priced place is made up of two 1881 terrace houses joined together. It's near a string of backpacker hostels and popular cafes on a leafy street running parallel to sleazy Darlinghurst Road. The glass-roofed breakfast room on the ground floor is a work of art, decked out with hanging ferns, giant bamboo, wrought-iron tables and chairs, and a trickling fountain. Just off this space is a peaceful guest lounge stacked with books and newspapers. The very plush rooms come with king- or queen-size beds but lack a tub in the bathroom. There's a coin-op laundry just down the road.

122 Victoria St., Potts Point, NSW 2011. ✆ **1800/630 505** in Australia, or 02/9357 3200. Fax 02/9357 7606. www.victoriacourt.com.au. 22 units. A$125 double; A$175 deluxe double with sun deck; A$265 honeymoon suite with balcony. Extra person A$20. Rates include buffet breakfast. AE, DC, MC, V. Free secure parking. CityRail: Kings Cross. **Amenities:** Guest lounge. *In room:* A/C, TV.

Around Oxford Street & Darlinghurst

Sullivans Hotel Sullivans is right in the heart of the action in one of Sydney's most popular shopping, entertainment, restaurant, and gay pub and club areas. About half of this hotel's guests come from overseas, mainly from the United Kingdom, Europe, and the United States. It's particularly popular with Americans during Gay and Lesbian Mardi Gras. All rooms are simple, very motel-like, and compact but are fine for a few nights. They come with an attached shower. Standard rooms have two single beds, and the garden rooms have queen-size beds and pleasant garden views.

21 Oxford St., Paddington, NSW 2021. ✆ **02/9361 0211.** Fax 02/9360 3735. www.sullivans.com.au. 64 units. A$165 standard double; A$180 garden room double and triple; A$180 family room; A$225 2 connecting rooms. AE, DC, MC, V. Limited free parking. Bus: 378 from Central Station or 380 from Circular Quay. **Amenities:** Breakfast cafe; free use of bikes; small heated outdoor pool; free Wi-Fi. *In room:* A/C, TV w/free movies, fridge, hair dryer.

Wattle Private Hotel This attractive Edwardian-style house built between 1900 and 1910 offers basic to very pleasant accommodations in the increasingly fashionable suburb of Darlinghurst, known for its great cafes, nightlife, and restaurants. Double rooms are rather basic and quite small, but the large windows give the rooms an airy feel. Nicer and larger queen rooms have a queen-size bed, king rooms have a king-size bed (some have harbor views), while a deluxe twin room has two king-size beds or a spa. There's also a family room that sleeps up to six people. Expect period features, nice furniture, high ceilings, and ornate moldings. Rooms are on four stories, but there's no elevator, so if you don't fancy too many stairs, try to get a room on a lower floor. There's a rooftop garden with harbor and city views.

108 Oxford St. (at corner of Palmer St.), Darlinghurst, NSW 2010. ✆ **02/9332 4118.** Fax 02/9331 2074. www.thewattle.com. 11 units. A$110–A$130 double; A$110–A$130 queen; A$120–A$145 king; A$130–A$150 king with harbor views; A$165–A$175 deluxe king with spa or with 2 king-size beds; A$185–A$195 family unit. More expensive rates are for Fri–Sat nights. Extra person A$30. Rates include continental breakfast. MC, V. No parking. Bus: Any to Taylor Sq. from Circular Quay. *In room:* A/C, TV.

In Newtown

Billabong Gardens For that inner-city feel, you can't beat Newtown, with its busy street happenings, cheap restaurants, and grunge look. It's also easy to get to by bus or CityRail. Billabong Gardens is just off the main drag, King Street, and earned a five-star backpackers' rating from the National Roads and Motorists' Association. Rooms are simply furnished in pine and have exposed brickwork. Besides the dormitory accommodations, you might consider the double or twin rooms, which offer pretty good value. The more expensive rooms have their own bathrooms. It's a friendly place with lots of native plants scattered around, and a pool in a pleasant courtyard. On the property are a comfortable TV lounge, a large kitchen, and a barbecue. It's very secure and offers 24-hour access. There are discount rates for weekly stays.

5–11 Egan St., Newtown, NSW 2042. ✆ **02/9550 3236.** Fax 02/9550 4352. www.billabonggardens.com.au. 37 units. A$25–A$27 dorm bed; A$90 double or twin. Family rooms available. MC, V. Parking A$5. CityRail: Newtown. Bus: 422, 423, 426, or 428. **Amenities:** Free Internet access; Jacuzzi; small heated outdoor pool. *In room:* TV, free Wi-Fi.

In Glebe

Alishan International Guest House The Alishan is a quiet place with a real Aussie feel. It's at the city end of Glebe Point Road, just 10 minutes by bus from the shops around Town Hall. It's a mixture of upmarket youth hostel and typical guesthouse. Standard dorm rooms are spotless, light, and bright, and come with two sets of bunks. Doubles have a double bed, a sofa and armchair, and a shower. Grab room no. 9 if you fancy sleeping on one of two single mattresses on the tatami mat floor, Japanese-style.

100 Glebe Point Rd., Glebe, NSW 2037. ✆ **02/9566 4048.** Fax 02/9525 4686. www.alishan.com.au. 19 units. A$27–A$35 dorm bed; A$99–A$145 double; A$165 family room. Extra person A$16. AE, MC, V. Secured parking for 6 cars; metered street parking. Bus: 431 or 433 from George St., or Kingsford Smith Shuttle from airport. **Amenities:** Internet access. *In room:* TV, fridge.

Tricketts Luxury Bed & Breakfast ★★ As soon as I walked into this atmospheric old place, I wanted to ditch my modern Sydney apartment and move in. Your first impression as you enter the tessellated, tiled corridor of the 1880s Victorian mansion is the jumble of plants and ornaments, the high ceilings, the Oriental rugs, and the leaded windows. Guests relax over a decanter of port or with a magazine on wicker furniture on the veranda overlooking fairly busy Glebe Point Road. The guest rooms are quiet and homey. Favorites are no. 2, with its wooden floorboards and king-size bed, and the Honey Room Suite—with an 1820s king-size four-poster bed.

There's a nice courtyard out back. The owner, Liz Tricketts, is a delight, and a rich source of Sydney's history.

270 Glebe Point Rd., Glebe (the water end), NSW 2037. ✆ **02/9552 1141.** Fax 02/9692 9462. www.tricketts.com.au. 7 units, all with shower only. A$198 double; A$245 honeymoon suite. Rates include continental breakfast. MC, V. Free parking. Bus: 431 from George St. *In room:* A/C, TV, hair dryer.

In Bondi

Bondi Beach is a good place to stay if you want to be close to the surf and sand; though if you're getting around by public transport, you'll need to catch a bus to Bondi Junction and then a train to the city center. (You can stay on the bus all the way, but it takes forever.)

In addition to the properties recommended below, there are two good backpacker hostels. **Surfside Backpackers,** 35a Hall St. (✆ **02/9365 4900;** www.surfsidebackpackers.com.au), offers four- to eight-person dorm rooms from A$23 in winter and A$36 in summer, and double rooms in a separate building opposite North Bondi Surf Club for the same price per person. **Noah's,** 2 Campbell Parade (✆ **02/9365 7100;** www.noahsbondibeach.com), has a great ambience and offers modern four- to eight-person dorm rooms for A$24 to A$27, as well as doubles for A$55 and beach doubles for A$65. Weekly rates range from A$144 to A$330.

Ravesi's on Bondi Beach ★★ Right on Australia's most famous golden sands, this boutique property offers modern minimalist rooms with white marble bathrooms—all very chic, with African tribal wall hangings. Side View double rooms are spacious, modern, and come with all the gadgets, including free cable TV. The Beach Front King rooms have the best views of the ocean. All rooms have Juliet balconies. The four split-level suites each have a white marble bathroom downstairs, and a bedroom, lounge area, and private outdoor terrace on the second level. An attractive glass-sided ground-floor bar is the "in" place on the Bondi scene, with lounge, house, and "chill" music every evening. The bar is a great place to watch the outside street scene.

Corner of Hall St. and Campbell Parade, Bondi Beach, NSW 2026. ✆ **02/9365 4422.** Fax 02/9365 1481. www.ravesis.com.au. 16 units. A$249–A$299 Side View room; A$329 Beach Front King; A$299–A$399 split-level suite with terrace. Extra person A$30. 1 child 11 or under stays free in parent's room. AE, DC, MC, V. Parking at the Swiss-Grand Hotel nearby A$8. CityRail: Bondi Junction; then bus no. 380. Bus: 380 or 333 from Circular Quay. **Amenities:** Restaurant; bar; room service. *In room:* A/C, TV, hair dryer, minibar.

Swiss-Grand Hotel ★★ Right on Bondi Beach, overlooking the Pacific, the Swiss-Grand is the best hotel in Bondi. It occupies a unique position overlooking the waves and sand of one of Australia's most famous cultural icons. The lobby is grand indeed, with high ceilings and stylish furniture. Each room is a suite, with separate bedroom and living room. All are spacious, and each comes with a rather luxurious bathroom and two TVs; some have Jacuzzis. All oceanfront units have balconies. The general sumptuousness of the accommodations and a terrific day spa help make this a fine place to stay. It's popular with American and European travelers with a bit of money to spend.

Corner of Campbell Parade and Beach Rd. (P.O. Box 219), Bondi Beach, NSW 2026. ✆ **800/344-1212** in the U.S.; 1800/655 252 in Australia; 0800/951 000 in the U.K.; 0800/056 666 in New Zealand; or 02/9365 5666. Fax 02/9365 9710. www.swissgrand.com.au. 230 units. A$308 standard double; A$352 ocean-view double; from A$396 suite. Packages are available on their website. Extra person A$44. AE, DC, MC, V. Free parking. Bus: 380 or 333 from Circular Quay. **Amenities:** 2 restaurants; fitness center; Jacuzzi; rooftop and indoor heated pools. *In room:* A/C, TV, hair dryer; free Wi-Fi.

In Manly

If you decide to stay in my favorite beachside suburb, be aware that ferries from the city stop running at midnight. If you get stranded, you'll be facing an expensive taxi ride (around A$50), or you'll need to make your way to the bus stand behind Wynyard CityRail station to catch a night bus. Consider buying a multiple-ride ticket, which will save you a bit of money if you're staying in Manly for a few days.

Manly has several backpacker places that are worth checking out. The best is **Manly Backpackers Beachside,** 28 Ragland St. (✆ **02/9977 3411;** fax 02/9977 4379; www.manlybackpackers.com.au), which offers dorm beds from A$26 to A$50, doubles from A$75 to A$120. The more expensive prices are for the peak Christmas period. The hostel charges a A$30 key deposit.

Manly Paradise Motel and Beach Plaza Apartments ★ I walked into this place and immediately felt more at home here, compared to the modern Manly Waterfront Apartment Hotel next door. The motel and apartment complex are separate but share a reception area. The irregularly shaped rooms are big yet cozy and come with a shower and a springy double bed. Though there is no restaurant, you can get breakfast in bed. The traffic can make it a little noisy in your room during the day (but you'll probably be on the beach then, anyway). Some rooms have glimpses of the sea. Residents of the apartment complex share the swimming pool (with views) on the roof.

The apartments are magnificent—very roomy, with thick carpets. They're stocked with everything you need, including a washing machine and dryer, a full kitchen with dishwasher, and two bathrooms (one with a tub). The sea views from the main front balcony are heart-stopping.

54 N. Steyne, Manly, NSW 2095. ✆ **1800/815 789** in Australia, or 02/9977 5799. Fax 02/9977 6848. www.manlyparadise.com.au. 40 units, some with shower only. A$185–A$220 double motel unit; A$210–A$330 1-bedroom unit; A$325–A$450 2-bedroom apt. Higher prices in summer (btw. around Dec 10 and Jan 31). Extra person A$25. Ask about long-term discounts. AE, DC, MC, V. Free secured parking. Ferry: Manly. **Amenities:** Indoor heated pool. *In room:* A/C, TV, hair dryer.

Novotel Sydney Manly Pacific Hotel ★★ If you could bottle the views from this top-class hotel—across the sand and through the Norfolk Island Pines to the Pacific Ocean—you'd make a fortune. Standing on your private balcony in the evening with the sea breeze in your nostrils and the chirping of hundreds of lorikeets is nothing short of heaven. The Manly Pacific, with its broad expanse of glittering foyer to its wide corridors and spacious accommodations, is the only hotel of its class in this wonderful beachside suburb. Each standard room is light and modern, with two double beds, a balcony, limited cable TV, and all the necessities. Views over the ocean are really worth the extra money. The ocean view rooms were renovated in 2009 and are suitable for families. The hotel is a 10-minute stroll or a A$5 taxi ride from the Manly ferry.

55 North Steyne, Manly, NSW 2095. ✆ **02/9977 7666.** Fax 02/9977 7822. www.accorhotels.com.au. 213 units. A$283–A$327 double; A$512 suite. Extra person A$32. AE, DC, MC, V. Parking A$18. Ferry: Manly. **Amenities:** 2 restaurants; 2 bars; concierge; exercise room; Jacuzzi; heated rooftop pool; room service; sauna. *In room:* A/C, TV, hair dryer, Wi-Fi.

Periwinkle–Manly Cove Guesthouse Nicely positioned across the road from one of Manly's two harbor beaches, the Periwinkle is a short walk from the ferry, the shops along the Corso, and the main ocean beach. Rooms are small and come with a double bed. Some have a shower and toilet (these go for the higher prices, noted below), but otherwise you'll have to make do with one of four separate bathrooms (one has a tub). A full kitchen next to a pleasant-enough communal lounge means you could save money by not eating out. Room nos. 5 and 10 are the nicest and have screened balconies overlooking the harbor (but no bathrooms). For atmosphere, go to the Manly Paradise Motel (see above) instead. There's no smoking inside.

18–19 E. Esplanade, Manly, NSW 2095. ✆ **02/9977 4668.** Fax 02/9977 6308. www.periwinkle.citysearch.com.au. 18 units, 12 with bathroom. A$139 double without bathroom; A$170–A$199 double with bathroom. Units with harbor views A$10 extra. Extra person A$25. Rates include continental breakfast. MC, V. Free parking. Ferry: Manly. *In room:* TV, fridge.

At the Airport

Stamford Sydney Airport ★★ This is the best airport hotel (just 7 min. from the terminals, and pickup service is free). It has the largest rooms, each with a king-size bed or two doubles, access to airport information, and a good-size bathroom with tub. You can reach the airport via the Airport Shuttle, which costs A$6 one way.

Corner of O'Riordan and Robey sts. (P.O. Box 353), Mascot, Sydney, NSW 2020. ✆ **1300/301 391** in Australia, or 02/9317 2200. Fax 02/9317 3855. www.stamford.com.au. 314 units. A$170–A$199 double; from A$370 suite. Extra person A$25. Children 16 and under stay free in parent's room. Ask about discount packages and weekend rates. AE, DC, MC, V. Parking A$15 per day. **Amenities:** 2 restaurants; bar; babysitting; concierge; executive rooms; fitness center; Jacuzzi; good-size outdoor pool; room service; sauna; free Wi-Fi. *In room:* A/C, TV, hair dryer.

WHERE TO DINE

Sydney is a gourmet paradise, with an abundance of fresh seafood, a vast range of vegetables and fruit always in season, prime meats at inexpensive prices, and top-quality chefs making international names for themselves. Asian and Mediterranean cooking have had a major influence on Australian cuisine, with spices and herbs finding their way into most dishes. Immigration has brought with it almost every type of cuisine, from African to Tibetan, Russian to Vietnamese. Some areas of the city are dedicated to one type of food, while other areas are melting pots of styles.

Sydney is a great place to try Contemporary, or "Mod Oz," cuisine, which has been applauded by chefs and food critics around the world. Contemporary cuisine emphasizes fresh ingredients and a creative blend of European styles with Asian influences. (Some foodies complain that some restaurants use the label "Contemporary" as an excuse to serve skimpy portions—like one lamb chop atop a tiny mound of mashed potatoes sprinkled with curry sauce.) At its best, Contemporary food is world class, but you'll probably have to go to the best of Sydney's restaurants to see what the scene is all about.

Australians think American-style coffee tastes like ditch water and favor a range of Italian-style coffee creations. Ask for a latte if you just want coffee with milk. "Bottomless" cups of coffee are rare in Australia. By the way, in Australia, the first course is called the entree and the second course the main.

The websites of some of the top-class restaurants are included in the listings below, as you would be advised to reserve well in advance if you want a table.

Near Circular Quay

VERY EXPENSIVE

Forty One ★★ MODERN FRENCH Powerful people, international celebrities, and average Sydneysiders out for a special celebration all come here to feel

Where to Dine in Central Sydney

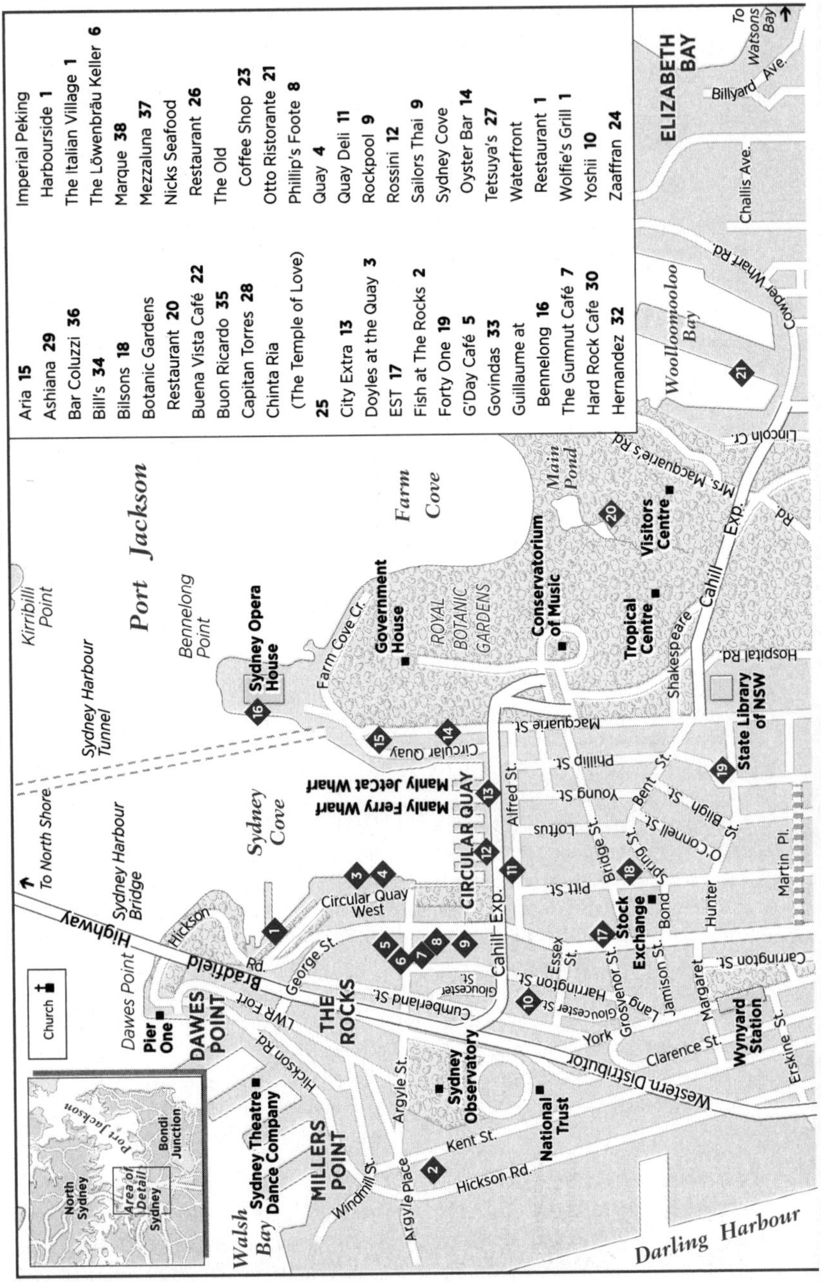

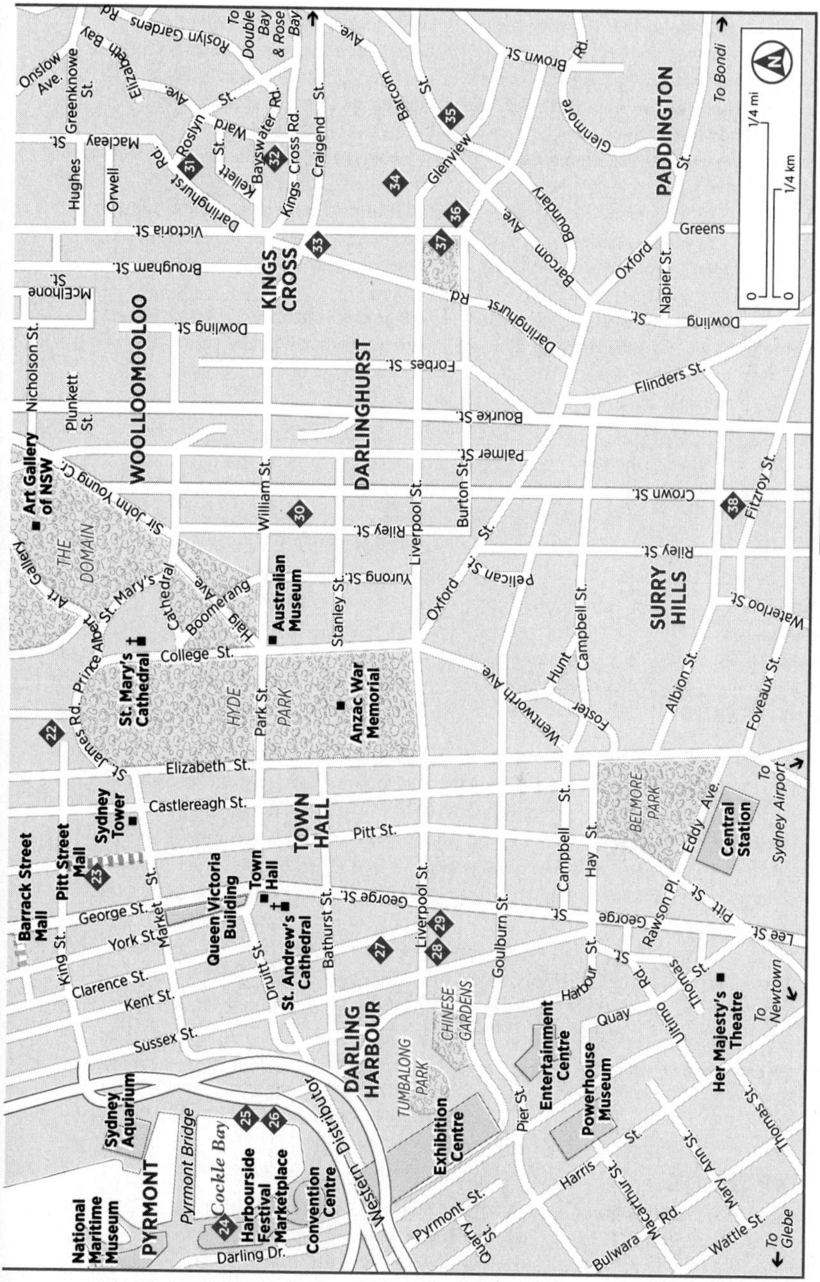
WOOLLOOMOOLOO
KINGS CROSS
DARLINGHURST
PADDINGTON
SURRY HILLS
TOWN HALL
DARLING HARBOUR
PYRMONT
Art Gallery of NSW
THE DOMAIN
Australian Museum
St. Mary's Cathedral
HYDE PARK
Anzac War Memorial
Sydney Tower
Barrack Street Mall
Pitt Street Mall
Queen Victoria Building
Town Hall
St. Andrew's Cathedral
CHINESE GARDENS
TUMBALONG PARK
Exhibition Centre
Entertainment Centre
Powerhouse Museum
Her Majesty's Theatre
BELMORE PARK
Central Station
Sydney Aquarium
National Maritime Museum
Cockle Bay
Pyrmont Bridge
Harbourside Festival Marketplace
Convention Centre
Western Distributor
To Double Bay & Rose Bay
To Bondi
To Sydney Airport
To Newtown
To Glebe
1/4 mi
1/4 km
William St.
Liverpool St.
Oxford St.
George St.
Pitt St.
Castlereagh St.
Elizabeth St.
College St.
Park St.
Darlinghurst Rd.
Victoria St.
Macleay St.
Bourke St.
Crown St.
Riley St.
Flinders St.
Campbell St.
Hay St.
Harbour St.
Sussex St.
Kent St.
Clarence St.
York St.
King St.
Market St.
Bathurst St.
Goulburn St.
Wentworth Ave.
Foveaux St.
Albion St.
Fitzroy St.
Cathedral St.
Sir John Young Cr.
Art Gallery Rd.
Prince Albert St.
St. James Rd.
Harris St.
Pier St.
Ultimo Rd.
Thomas St.
Mary Ann St.
Bulwara Rd.
Macarthur St.
Wattle St.
Pyrmont St.
Quarry St.
Darling Dr.
Eddy Ave.
Rawson Pl.
Lee St.
Greens Rd.
Napier St.
Dowling St.
Glenview St.
Glenmore Rd.
Brown St.
Barcom Ave.
Boundary St.
Craigend St.
Kings Cross Rd.
Bayswater Rd.
Ward Ave.
Roslyn St.
Kellett St.
Elizabeth Bay Rd.
Roslyn Gardens Rd.
Onslow Ave.
Greenknowe St.
Hughes St.
Orwell St.
Brougham St.
McElhone St.
Nicholson St.
Plunkett St.
Dowling St.
Forbes St.
Palmer St.
Burton St.
Yurong St.
Stanley St.
Pelican St.
Hunt St.
Foster St.
Waterloo St.
Boomerang St.
Haig Ave.
Druitt St.
Quay St.
22
23
24
25
26
27
28
29
30
31
32
33
34
35
36
37
38

What to Know About Dining Down Under

Most moderate and inexpensive restaurants in Sydney are BYO, as in "bring your own" bottle, though some places also have extensive wine and beer lists. More moderately priced restaurants are also introducing corkage fees, which mean you pay anywhere from A$2 to A$8 per person for the privilege of the waiter opening your bottle of wine. Very expensive restaurants discourage BYO.

Sydney's cheap eats congregate in center-city areas such as along King Street in Newtown, Crown Street in Darlinghurst, and Glebe Point Road in Glebe. There are also inexpensive joints scattered among the more upscale restaurants in Kings Cross and along trendy Oxford Street.

Avoid the takeout booths along the ferry wharves at Circular Quay. The fish-and-chip shop opposite the "bottle shop" (liquor store) is an exception—it serves some of the best french fries in Sydney.

Smoking is banned in all Sydney restaurants, except if you're eating at a sidewalk table or in a courtyard.

exclusive. It's won plenty of awards. Actually on the 42nd floor, Forty One offers an amazing vista over the Sydney Harbour Bridge. The service is fun, the cutlery is the world's best, and Swiss chef and owner Dietmar Sawyere has given the modern French cuisine a masterly touch. In all, it's a glamorous place to experience some of the best of Australian cuisine. Oh, and did I mention the restrooms? Wow, what amazing city views! The menu changes every 2 weeks to keep up with seasonal produce.

Level 42, Chifley Tower, 2 Chifley Sq. ✆ **02/9221 2500.** www.forty-one.com.au. Reservations required. Lunch: 2 courses A$65, 3 courses A$80. Dinner: Multicourse degustation menu A$150, A$255 with matching wines. AE, DC, MC, V. Tues–Fri noon–4pm; Mon–Sat 6–10pm. CityRail: Wynyard.

Guillaume at Bennelong ★★★ FRENCH If you go to Bondi, you have to swim in the Pacific; if you see the Harbour Bridge, you have to walk across it; if you visit the Opera House, you must eat at Guillaume at Bennelong. The restaurant is as uniquely designed as the building itself, with tall glass windows that furrow around in an arch and grab the harbor and Circular Quay by the throat. Renowned French chef Guillaume Brahimi's offerings could include sealed veal sweetbreads, or chicken breast with duck foie gras ravioli, or confit of Atlantic salmon on braised endive with red-wine sauce. Many would rather miss the first half of the opera they've paid a fortune to see than leave before dessert. The best bar in town is upstairs, where you can see over the water to the bridge and up to the other "sails." Good bar food is available until 11:30pm.

In the Sydney Opera House, Bennelong Point. ✆ **02/9241 1999.** www.guillaumeatbennelong.com.au. Reservations recommended. Main courses A$35–A$50. Multicourse degustation meal A$180 (with matching wines A$250). AE, DC, MC, V. Thurs–Fri noon–3pm; pretheater menu Mon–Sat 5:30–7:45pm; dinner Mon–Sat 8–10:30pm. CityRail, bus, or ferry: Circular Quay.

EXPENSIVE

Botanic Gardens Restaurant CONTEMPORARY You couldn't ask for a better walk to a restaurant than through the Royal Botanic Gardens, next to the Sydney Opera House. Enjoying lunch on the wisteria-covered balcony in the middle of

Sydney's most beautiful park is a treat every visitor should enjoy. Main courses often mix a bit of Mediterranean, French, and Asian. They include the popular *boudin blanc* (white sausage) with lentils and braised fennel. Try a perfect crème brûlée with underlying plum purée for dessert (A$12).

In the Royal Botanic Gardens. ✆ **02/9241 2419.** Reservations recommended. Main courses A$23–A$30. AE, DC, MC, V. Daily 8am–4:30pm. Bus or ferry: Circular Quay.

Sydney Cove Oyster Bar SEAFOOD Just before you reach the Sydney Opera House, you'll notice a couple of small shedlike buildings with tables and chairs set up to take in the stunning views of the harbor and the Harbour Bridge. The first is a Sydney institution, serving some of the best oysters in town. A half dozen oysters will cost A$22 and A$39 for a dozen. Main meals, such as barbecued swordfish steak or aged sirloin steak, are also on the menu.

No. 1 Eastern Esplanade, Circular Quay East. ✆ **02/9247 2937.** www.sydneycoveoysterbar.com. Main courses A$40. 10% surcharge Sat–Sun and public holidays. AE, DC, MC, V. Mon–Sat 11am–11pm; Sun 11am–8pm. CityRail, bus, or ferry: Circular Quay.

MODERATE

City Extra ITALIAN/AUSTRALIAN Because this place stays open 24 hours, it's convenient if you get the munchies at a ridiculous hour. It's also nicely placed, right next to the ferry terminals. Over several visits here I've found the food to be pretty variable in quality. The burgers are fine, but some of the pastas are disappointing. Friends of mine complain that it's overpriced for what you get, and the high turnover can tend to lead to a perception of poor service. However, the plastic chairs and outdoor tables make it a pleasant enough spot for a quick bite at any time of the day or night. A range of salads, pies, steaks, ribs, fish, and Asian-influenced dishes are also available. There's also a fat selection of desserts. In my opinion, the food is much nicer and a better value next door at Rossini (see below).

Shop E4, Circular Quay. ✆ **02/9241 1422.** Reservations not accepted. Main courses A$13–A$26. 10% surcharge midnight–6am, Sun, public holidays. AE, DC, MC, V. Daily 24 hr. CityRail, bus, or ferry: Circular Quay.

Rossini ☺ ITALIAN This cafeteria-style Italian restaurant opposite Ferry Wharf 5 at Circular Quay is wonderfully positioned for people-watching—especially if you sit around one of the outside tables next to the walkway. The place is perfect for breakfast or a quick bite before a show at the Opera House. Wait to be seated for

A Great Place for Picnic Grub

If you're looking for something to take with you on a harbor cruise or on a stroll through the Royal Botanic Gardens, you can't go wrong with Quay Deli, E5 Alfred St., next to the pharmacy under the Circular Quay CityRail station, facing the road (✆ 02/9241 3571). You'll find all sorts of goodies, including gourmet sandwiches and takeout foods such as olives, Greek dishes, pastas, salads, meat pies, and the best English-style custard tarts around. Everything is fresh and tasty. Lunch items go for A$1.80 to A$4.50. It's open Monday through Friday from 5am to 6:45pm, Saturday from 9am to 4pm. No credit cards.

What's the Restaurant Surcharge?

Some Australian restaurants charge surcharges on public holidays and Sundays. Typically this can amount to an extra A$2 to A$6 or more per person. Restaurants argue that it's difficult to get staff to work on these days, so they need to provide a cash incentive not to call in with a hangover from the previous night. In Australia, waiters rely on their wages rather than tips.

lunch or dinner, make your choice, pay at the counter, take a ticket, and then pick up your food. Meals, including veal parmigiana, cannelloni, ravioli, chicken crepes, and octopus salad, are often huge. Last time I went I was disappointed with my chicken meal (costing A$28), and wished I'd chosen a pasta dish (at A$16). My partner felt her *caponatina* (sweet and sour Mediterranean vegetables) was "umm, quite nice, alright." Summing up, while it's not the best Italian you'll ever eat, it is tasty.

Shop W5, Circular Quay. ✆ **02/9247 8026.** Main courses A$16–A$28. No credit cards. Daily 7am–10pm. CityRail, bus, or ferry: Circular Quay.

In the Rocks

VERY EXPENSIVE

Aria ★★★ MODERN AUSTRALIAN With front-row views of the Harbour Bridge and the Sydney Opera House, Aria stands in one of the most enviable spots in the city. The windows overlooking the water are huge, the atmosphere is elegant and buzzy, and many of the tables have an intimate relationship with the stunning view. The food, created by Matthew Moran, one of Australia's great chefs, is imaginative and mouthwatering. Standout dishes at the time of writing included the sweet pork belly with pork croquettes; and the *ballotine* of rabbit, foie gras, and *capocollo* with ginger bread, pumpkin, and a pomegranate dressing.

1 Macquarie St., East Circular Quay. ✆ **02/9252 2555.** www.ariarestaurant.com.au. Reservations essential. Main courses lunchtime A$42 for 1 course, A$68 for 2 courses, A$85 for 3 courses. 7-course tasting dinner A$160 for food only, A$250 including matching wines. 10% surcharge on Sun and public holidays. AE, DC, MC, V. Mon–Fri noon–2:30pm; pretheater daily 5:30–7pm; Mon–Sat 7–11:30pm; Sun 6–11:30pm. CityRail, bus, or ferry: Circular Quay.

Quay ★★★ CONTEMPORARY With its enviable location on top of the cruise-ship terminal, Quay offers another of the loveliest views in the city, and the *Sydney Morning Herald* named Quay the 2009 and 2010 Best Restaurant of the Year (though I prefer Tetsuya's; see below). In good weather, the sun sparkles off the water and through the large windows; the Opera House, city skyline, North Shore suburbs, and Harbour Bridge all look magnificent. At night, when the city lights wash over the harbor and bridge and the Opera House's sails are lit up, the view is even better. Chef Peter Gilmore's menu is a revelation of French, Italian, and Australian ideas. Selections from the four-course dinner meal might include a confit of shaved South Australian squid, octopus, garlic custard, baby radishes, native violets, roasted squid consommé, followed by roasted loin of South Australian Suffolk lamb, heirloom baby carrots, Arbequina olives, nasturtiums, capers, calendula, and sheep's milk cheese.

On the upper level of the Overseas Passenger Terminal, Circular Quay West, The Rocks. ✆ **02/9251 5600.** www.quay.com.au. Reservations recommended well in advance. Lunch: 2 courses A$75, 3 courses A$95. Dinner: 4 courses A$145. AE, DC, MC, V. Mon–Fri noon–2:30pm; daily 6–10pm. CityRail, bus, or ferry: Circular Quay.

Rockpool ★★★ CONTEMPORARY The Rockpool is an institution in Sydney and is known for its inventive food. It's approached by a steep ramp and opens up into two stories of ocean-green carpet, designer chairs, and stainless steel. Along with the bar, the kitchen—with its busy chefs and copper pots and pans—is very much at the center of things. Rather than serving individual courses, the restaurant favors many smaller offerings. On the chef's tasting menu, expect the freshest fish, oysters, quail eggs, abalone, clams, oysters, and all sorts of delicacies, which are expertly parceled out and served. It's really worth checking out the website and booking well in advance; it's a true Sydney dining experience—if you can afford it.

Making waves in Sydney for its fish dishes, rotisserie meats, prime steaks, and pastas is the new **Rockpool Bar and Grill,** 66 Hunter St. (✆ **02/8078 1900**).

109 George St., The Rocks. ✆ **02/9252 1888.** www.rockpool.com. Reservations essential. Chef's tasting menu A$195 per person; 4-course set-price menu with selections A$145 per person; main courses A$30–A$45. Matching wines cost A$65 extra. AE, DC, MC, V. Tues–Sat 6–11pm. CityRail, bus, or ferry: Circular Quay.

Yoshii ★★★ JAPANESE Yoshii is about as far away from the increasingly popular conveyor-belt sushi service as you can imagine. Sit at the sushi counter and watch the chef slice and dice, or in the more muted tones of the very small main restaurant. At lunchtime there are seven set menus to choose from; and at dinner, there are two 13-course options: the Yoshii Menu and the Saqura Menu. Tastes from the latter could include smoked salmon mousse wrapped in marinated dried apricot, a Tasmania oyster with plum-wine jelly, and a grilled persimmon and scallop with saffron *sumiso* sauce. This is a fabulous lunch option too, with several set meal choices, including a sashimi sushi set that comes with tempura and miso soup. There are some memorable moments here and the sushi is some of the best I have ever tasted.

115 Harrington St., The Rocks. ✆ **02/9247 2566.** www.yoshii.com.au. Reservations essential. Lunch: A$45–A$50. Dinner: Yoshii Menu A$130 per person; Saqura Menu A$120 per person. AE, DC, MC, V. Tues–Fri noon–3pm; Mon–Sat 6–9:30pm. CityRail, bus, or ferry: Circular Quay.

EXPENSIVE

Doyles at the Quay ✋ SEAFOOD Just below Quay (see above) is Doyles, a name synonymous with seafood in Sydney. Most customers sit outside to enjoy the fabulous views across the harbor, though green guard railings do somewhat interrupt the view of the Opera House. Businesspeople and tourists come here if they don't want to lay out the cash for Quay or if they fancy a more relaxed style. The most popular dish is basically pricey fish and chips, which costs A$35. You can also get a dozen oysters for A$30 or half a lobster for A$65. One word of advice though: Australian lobsters (crayfish in reality) aren't nearly as tasty as lobsters in other parts of the world in my experience. Still, if you want the views and it's a pretty day, then it's a nice place to sit.

Overseas Passenger Terminal, Circular Quay. ✆ **02/9252 3400.** Main courses A$30–A$60. DC, MC, V. Daily 11:30am–3pm; Mon–Sat 5:30–10:30pm; Sun 5:30–9:30pm. CityRail, bus, or ferry: Circular Quay.

Fish at the Rocks ★★ SEAFOOD This midsize eatery opposite the Lord Nelson Hotel, a 10-minute stroll up the main hill leading from The Rocks, serves delicious food with a focus on fresh seafood. There are a few little tables outside, as well as plenty inside below the photographs of sailing boats. The staff is very friendly and the service very professional. Portions are not huge, so don't expect to fill up on a single main course if you're starving. The dishes are well crafted, though: Try the Queensland scallops on polenta and braised peas, and the beer-battered whiting filets (a common Indo-Pacific fish). Don't pass on the chocolate mud cake, either—it's stunning.

29 Kent St., The Rocks. ✆ **02/9252 4614.** www.fishattherocks.com.au. Reservations recommended. Main courses A$30–A$35. AE, MC, V. Daily noon–2:30pm and 6–10:30pm. CityRail, bus, or ferry: Circular Quay.

Phillip's Foote ★★ BARBECUE Venture behind this historic pub and you'll find a courtyard strung with tables, benches, and large barbecues. Choose your own steak, lemon sole, trout, chicken, or pork, and throw it on the "barbie." It's fun, it's filling, and you might even make some new friends while your meal's sizzling. Some Sydneysiders think it's a bit pricey (especially the salads), but then again you are eating in prime-real-estate land. You may experience an off night, when the salads don't look all that fresh and the service is barely existent, but there's no excuse if you burn your own steak.

101 George St., The Rocks. ✆ **02/9241 1485.** www.phillipsfoote.com.au. Main courses A$29 weekdays, A$30 weekends. AE, DC, MC, V. Mon–Sat noon–midnight; Sun noon–10pm. CityRail, bus, or ferry: Circular Quay.

Sailors Thai ★ THAI With a reputation as hot as the chilies in its jungle curry, Sailors Thai canteen attracts casual lunchtime crowds who come to eat great-tasting noodles, pork and prawn wonton soup, red curry with litchis, and Thai salads at its one stainless steel table with some 40 chairs. Four other tables overlook the cruise-ship terminal and the quay. Downstairs, the a la carte restaurant serves inventive food that's a far cry from the fare at your average Thai restaurant, such as stir-fried pineapple curry with chilies and cashew nuts, and wonderfully glutinous coconut ash pudding, made from the ash of burned coconuts cooked with licorice root, coconut water, rice flour, and sugar.

106 George St., The Rocks. ✆ **02/9251 2466.** www.sailorsthai.citysearch.com.au. Reservations required well in advance in restaurant, not accepted in canteen. Main courses A$26–A$35 in restaurant, A$15–A$23 in canteen. AE, DC, MC, V. Restaurant Mon–Fri noon–2pm; Mon–Sat 6–10pm. Canteen daily noon–9pm. CityRail, bus, or ferry: Circular Quay.

Waterfront Restaurant ★ CONTEMPORARY You can't help but notice the mast, rigging, and sails that mark this restaurant in a converted stone warehouse. It's one of four in a row next to the water below the main spread of The Rocks. It's popular at lunchtime, when businesspeople snap up the best seats outside in the sunshine. At night, with the colors of the city washing over the harbor, it can be magical. You get a choice of such things as steaks, mud crab, fish filets, or prawns. The seafood platter, at A$150 for two, includes lobsters, Balmain bugs (small, odd-looking crayfish), prawns, scallops, baby squid, fish pieces, and octopus. The food is simple and fresh, at prices that reflect the glorious position and views. Come here instead of Doyles.

In the same building you'll find sister restaurants **Wolfie's Grill** (**✆ 02/9241 5577**), which serves good chargrilled beef and seafood dishes for A$24 to A$34, the **Italian Village** (**✆ 02/9247 6111**), which serves regional Italian cuisine for A$24 to A$34, and the **Imperial Peking Harbourside,** which has Pekingese food, such as five-spices crispy duckling and salt-and-pepper crab, for between A$23 and A$38. All four restaurants offer fantastic water views and indoor and outdoor dining.

In Campbell's Storehouse, 27 Circular Quay West, The Rocks. ✆ **02/9247 3666.** www.waterfront restaurant.com.au. Reservations recommended. Main courses A$35–A$39. Surcharge Sat–Sun and public holidays. AE, DC, MC, V. Daily noon–10:30pm. CityRail, bus, or ferry: Circular Quay.

MODERATE

The Gumnut Teagardens ☺ CONTEMPORARY A hearty lunch in a courtyard shaded from the sun by giant umbrellas—ah, it could be heaven. With a great location in the heart of The Rocks, this 1890 sandstone cottage restaurant also has an extensive indoor seating area, so it's a perfect place to take a break from all that sightseeing. On weekends, live jazz sets the mood. The breakfast specials are popular with guests from surrounding hotels, and at lunchtime the cafe bustles with tourists. More regular fare includes the disappointing Ploughman's Lunch (why spoil a traditional English meal of bread, cheese, and pickles by limiting the bread and adding unappealing vegetables and salad?), the better chicken and leek pies, and good pasta and noodle dishes. The courtyard is heated in winter, making it cozy. The service can really have its off days though, so you might need a thick skin. It's BYO (no corkage fee).

28 Harrington St., The Rocks. ✆ **02/9247 9591.** Main courses A$8.50–A$14. AE, DC, MC, V. Sun–Wed 8am–5pm; Thurs–Sat 8am–10:30pm. CityRail, bus, or ferry: Circular Quay.

The Löwenbräu Keller ★ BAVARIAN Renowned for celebrating Oktoberfest every day for getting on 30 years now, this is the place to watch Aussies let their hair down. Come for lunch, and munch a club sandwich or focaccia in the glassed-off atrium while watching the daytime action of The Rocks. For a livelier scene, head here on Friday or Saturday night, when mass beer-sculling (chugging) and yodeling are accompanied by a brass band and costumed waitresses ferrying foaming beer steins about the atmospheric, cellarlike space. Options include hearty southern German and Austrian fare and several varieties of German beers in bottles or on draft (tap). There's a good wine list, and, surprisingly, vegetarians have a few choices, too. Expect the likes of goulash with mashed potato, pork knuckle with potato salad, and Bavarian sausages. Filling and fun if not entirely gourmet. Try a good Bavarian beer during the daily happy hour, between 4 and 6pm.

18 Argyle St. (at Playfair St.), The Rocks. ✆ **02/9247 7785.** www.lowenbrau.com.au. Reservations recommended. Main courses A$17–A$23. AE, DC, MC, V. Daily 9:30am–2am (kitchen closes at 11pm Sun–Thurs, 2am Fri–Sat). CityRail, bus, or ferry: Circular Quay.

INEXPENSIVE

G'Day Café CAFE According to the manager, about half the tourists who visit Sydney eat at this little place in the heart of The Rocks. That's not surprising, considering it offers simple, satisfying food at around half the price you'd expect to pay in such a tourist precinct. The interior is uninspiring, but in back there's a leafy courtyard. Among the offerings are focaccia sandwiches, hearty soups, salads, burgers, lasagna, chili con carne, and beef curry.

83 George St., The Rocks. ✆ **02/9241 3644.** Main courses A$3–A$7. AE. Sun–Thurs 5am–midnight; Fri–Sat 5am–3am. CityRail, bus, or ferry: Circular Quay.

Zia Pina PIZZA/PASTA With 10 tables crammed downstairs and another 24 upstairs, there's not much room to breathe in this cramped traditional pizzeria and spaghetti house. But squeeze in between the bare-brick walls and wallow in the clashes and clangs coming from the hardworking chefs in the kitchen. Pizzas come in two sizes; the larger feeds two people. They cost between A$17 and A$20. There are several chicken dishes, seafood dishes, and salads, too.

93 George St., The Rocks. ✆ **02/9247 2255.** www.ziapina.com.au. Reservations recommended. Main courses A$9–A$20. AE, DC, MC, V. Mon–Fri noon–3pm; Mon–Sat 5–11pm; Sun 5–10pm. CityRail, bus, or ferry: Circular Quay.

Near Town Hall

VERY EXPENSIVE

Bilsons ★★★ FRENCH/CONTEMPORARY Tucked away at the back of the Radisson Plaza Hotel is one of those great restaurants that could easily compete with some of the Michelin-starred classics in Europe. The chef, Tony Bilson, is a well-known Sydney personality, and the quality of his French-influenced food is a testament to some 30 years in the business. The restaurant is modern in its look but comfortable too, and the service is impeccable. Expect something in the same vein as a *petite salade* of braised oxtail and rock oysters, or a *boudin* of red mullet, squid ink jelly, and bouillabaisse sauce.

The Foyer, Radisson Plaza Hotel, 27 O'Connell St., Sydney. ✆ **02/8214 0496.** www.bilsons.com.au. Reservations essential. 9-course degustation menu without wine A$165 per person; 6-courses A$135. Wines A$65 extra. AE, DC, MC, V. Mon–Fri noon–2:30pm; Mon–Sat 6–10pm. CityRail or bus: Town Hall or Wynyard.

est. at Establishment Hotel ★★★ MODERN AUSTRALIAN Upstairs in the trendy Establishment Hotel complex you'll find est., a restaurant that culinary luminary Peter Doyle has melded into a Sydney icon. The decor is a sensual masterpiece, with white columns and rich felt-brown carpets adding to an ambience already sexed up by the coolest lounge music. To its credit, est. won the ultimate score of three "hats" in the *Sydney Morning Herald's Good Food Guide* for the seventh year in a row in 2010. (Only six restaurants in Sydney received this score in 2010, including Bilson's, Marque, Pier, Quay, and Tetsuya's.) Dishes that make an appearance on the menu include grilled rock lobster with herbs and lemon butter, and juniper-crusted saddle of venison, with beetroot purée, potato, and semolina gnocchi. It's more laid-back on the top floor, where you'll find the city's best sushi bar—a trendy raw-fish and rice place with one long table bathed in natural light called **Sushi E.** This is partitioned off from **Hemisphere**—a moody drinking place strung out with leather armchairs and comfy sofas.

Level 1, 252 George St., Sydney. ✆ **02/9240 3010.** www.merivale.com. Reservations essential. Main courses A$43–A$57. AE, DC, MC, V. Mon–Fri noon–3pm; Mon–Sat 6–10pm. CityRail or bus: Wynyard.

Tetsuya's ★★★ JAPANESE/FRENCH FUSION So what makes Tetsuya's so good—and my favorite restaurant in Sydney? Well, you'll have to find out for yourself. Secure a table right next to the floor-to-ceiling windows with intimate views across a Japanese-inspired courtyard of maples and waterfalls. Choose the wine-matching option to go with your 11 courses, in my opinion the best thing to do here. (Corkage costs A$25 if you bring your own wine, and the tasting option means you get to try wines to complement Tetsuya's dishes.) The service is impeccable, and the food truly inspired. Small delicate morsels appear: perhaps an incredible shot of pea soup with bitter chocolate sorbet, followed by a roulette of chopped smoked ocean trout capped with caviar, and then a leek and spanner crab custard. Then comes the signature dish: a confit of Tasmanian ocean trout with a crust of konbu seaweed, on a bed of daikon radish and fennel. From this taste of air and sea, the culinary journey goes on, to thick dark forests heady with mushrooms, veal, and red wine. It may be a once-in-a-lifetime experience. Everybody who is anybody wants to come here—so getting a table is difficult. To have a chance, you need to book when reservations become available, 4 weeks in advance, and reconfirm a few days before.

529 Kent St., Sydney. ✆ **02/9267 2900.** www.tetsuyas.com. Reservations essential; accepted 4 weeks ahead. 13-course degustation menu A$200 per person. Drinks extra. AE, DC, MC, V. Sat noon–3pm; Tues–Sat 6–10pm. CityRail: Town Hall.

EXPENSIVE

Capitan Torres SPANISH Sydney's Spanish quarter, around Liverpool Street (a 10-min. walk from Town Hall station on your right just past Sydney's main cinema strip), offers some good restaurants, of which Capitan Torres is my favorite. It's not fine dining, and certainly not up there with the best Madrid-style Spanish restaurants found in the Spanish-speaking world, but it's a good choice for something casual. Downstairs is a tapas bar with traditional stools, Spanish staff, and lots of authentic dark oak. Upstairs on two floors is a fabulous restaurant with heavy wooden tables and an atmosphere thick with sangria and regional food. The garlic prawns are good, and the whole snapper is a memorable experience. The tapas are better at **Asturiana** (✆ **02/9264 1010**), another Spanish restaurant a couple of doors down—but make sure you insist on eating at the bar for that authentic experience. ***Warning:*** Spanish serving staff in Sydney can be a bit gruff, so come armed with your sense of humor.

73 Liverpool St. (just past the cinema strip on George St., near Town Hall). ✆ **02/9264 5574.** Fax 02/9283 2292. Main courses A$23–A$27; tapas A$12–A$19. AE, DC, MC, V. Daily noon–3pm; Mon–Sat 6–11pm; Sun 6–10pm. CityRail: Town Hall.

INEXPENSIVE

Buena Vista Cafe ★ 🎁 CAFE If you happen to be in the city center, this fabulous, largely undiscovered restaurant and cafe is a must for the great value and the absolutely fantastic views reaching over Hyde Park and even to the harbor. It's very large inside, has panoramic windows, and serves meals from the counter. Hearty breakfasts include bacon and eggs, omelets, and cereals. All-day dishes run to sandwiches, Caesar salad, homemade pies, pastas, and lasagna. Even if you're not hungry, it's well worth popping in for a coffee.

Level 14, Law Courts Building, 184 Phillip St. (Queens Sq.). ✆ **02/9230 8221.** www.buenavistacafe.com.au. Breakfast A$10–A$15; sandwiches A$6.50–A$9; main courses A$16–A$25. Mon–Fri 7am–5pm. CityRail or bus: Museum.

Near Central Station

Marque ★★ FRENCH Seriously sophisticated, Marque offers a small menu featuring classic French dishes with pizzazz in an eggplant-colored room. Politicians, actors, and food critics all rave about the place. One such scribe, writing for the *New York Times,* wrote lyrically about the beet tart on flaky pastry and suggested that the "sardine fillet, baked inside a thin, crisp, translucent crust until it looks like a fossil, and then served with mackerel jelly" could only have been created by a "culinary wizard." Expect some real highlights here.

4–5/355 Crown St., Surry Hills. ✆ **02/9332 2225.** www.marquerestaurant.com.au. Reservations essential. Main courses A$48. 8-course degustation meal A$145, plus A$75 matching wines. AE, DC, MC, V. Mon–Sat 6:30–10:30pm. Taxi: Surry Hills (5 min. drive from Central Station).

In Darling Harbour

EXPENSIVE

Nick's Seafood Restaurant ★ 🎁 ☺ SEAFOOD This nice indoor and alfresco eatery overlooking the water on the same side as Darling Harbour (to the left of Sydney Aquarium if you're looking at the boats) offers good cocktails and plenty of seafood. The best seats are outside in the sunshine, where you can watch the world go by over a bottle of wine. My choice of dish is the seafood platter for two, which has enough crab, prawns, fish, oysters, and lobster to satisfy. It costs A$145. Otherwise there are various fish, prawn, and octopus dishes to choose from. A kids' menu offers either chicken, calamari, or fish, with french fries and a soft drink, followed by ice cream. It costs A$14. Nick's has another equally nice eatery on the other side of the Aquarium called **Nick's Bar & Grill** (✆ **02/9279 0122**) and one in the Bondi Pavillion (across the grass and opposite the beach) called **Nick's Bar & Grill Bondi Beach** (✆ **02/9365 4122**). The food and prices at all three places are similar. A sister establishment, **I'm Angus Steakhouse** (✆ **02/9264 5822**), caters to meat-eaters. It's on Cockle Bay Wharf, too.

The Promenade, Cockle Bay Wharf (on the city side of Darling Harbour). ✆ **02/9264 1212.** www.nicks-seafood.com.au. Reservations recommended. Main courses A$29–A$42. A$5 per person surcharge on Sat–Sun and public holidays. AE, MC, V. Daily noon–3pm and 6–11pm. Ferry or monorail: Darling Harbour.

Zaaffran ★★ CONTEMPORARY INDIAN Sydney certainly hasn't seen an Indian restaurant quite like this one before. Forget dark interiors and Indian murals; here you find white surfaces, a glass-fronted wine cellar, and magnificent views of the water and the Sydney skyline from the far side of Darling Harbour. (An outdoor terrace provides the best views.) The restaurant started when two brothers from Bombay joined forces with Chef Vikrant Kapoor, formerly the chef de cuisine at Raffles in Singapore. Together, they've revolutionized classic Indian cuisine. Expect such delights as the famed chicken *biryani,* baked in a pastry case and served with mint yogurt, or the tiger prawns in coconut cream and a tomato broth. Even fans of traditional Indian food are impressed by the creations here. There are plenty of vegetarian options.

Level 2, 345 Harbourside Shopping Centre, Darling Harbour. ✆ **02/9211 8900.** www.zaaffran.com.au. Reservations recommended. Main courses A$23–A$29. AE, DC, MC, V. Daily noon–2:30pm and 6–11pm. Ferry or monorail: Darling Harbour.

MODERATE

Chinta Ria ★ MODERN MALAYSIAN Cockle Bay's star attraction for those who appreciate good food and fun ambience without paying a fortune, Chinta Ria is on the roof of the three-story development. In a round building dominated by a giant golden Buddha in the center, it serves fairly good "hawker-style" (read: cheap and delicious) Malaysian food. While the food is good, the atmosphere is even more memorable. The service can be slow, but who cares in such an interesting space, with plenty of nooks, crannies, and society folk to look at. There are seats outside (some within range of the noise of the highway, though it's pleasant on a sunny day), but the best views unfold inside. I recommend the chicken laksa, or the sambal chicken (chicken filets in a light chili-and-shrimp paste with onion and tomato).

Cockle Bay Wharf Complex. ✆ **02/9264 3211.** www.chintaria.com. Main courses A$13–A$26. AE, DC, MC, V. Daily noon–2:30pm and 6–11pm. Ferry or monorail: Darling Harbour.

On Woolloomooloo Wharf

Otto Ristorante ★★ MODERN ITALIAN Recognized as one of Sydney's premier restaurants, Otto boasts lush designer appointments and dim lighting that make it popular with local celebrities and socialites. Outside it's all light and breezy, with nice views of a boardwalk and some harbor water. Menu possibilities include beef carpaccio with truffle dressing, aioli, capers, Parmesan, and baby rocket leaves; or porcini mushrooms with seared scallops, and puréed celeriac.

Area 8, Woolloomooloo Wharf, 6 Cowper Wharf Rd., Woolloomooloo 2011. ✆ **02/9368 7488.** www.ottoristorante.com.au. Reservations required. Main courses A$24–A$39. AE, DC, MC, V. Tues–Sun noon–3:30pm; Mon 6–10:30pm; Tues–Sat 6pm–midnight; Sun 6–9pm. Limited street parking. Bus: 311 from Circular Quay. Water taxi: Berth 53.

In Kings Cross & Darlinghurst

VERY EXPENSIVE

Mezzaluna ★★ NORTHERN ITALIAN Exquisite food, flawless service, and an almost unbeatable view across the city's western skyline have all helped Mezzaluna position itself firmly among Sydney's top waterside eateries. An open, candlelit place with white walls and polished wooden floorboards, the main dining room opens onto a huge all-weather terrace kept warm in winter by giant overhead fan heaters. The restaurant's owner, Sydney culinary icon Beppi Polesi, provides an exceptional wine list to complement a menu that changes daily. There's always a fabulous risotto on the menu. Other delights may include spatchcock oven roasted with prosciutto, Asiago cheese, and sage, served with a black-truffle potato purée and braised leek; or oven-roasted lamb rump served with black olive Parmesan gratin, braised tomatoes, and basil oil. Whatever you choose, you really can't go wrong.

123 Victoria St., Potts Point. ✆ **02/9357 1988.** Fax 02/9357 2615. www.mezzaluna.com.au. Reservations recommended. Main courses A$36–A$45. AE, DC, MC, V. Fri noon–3pm; Mon–Sat 6–11pm. CityRail: Kings Cross.

MODERATE

Hard Rock Cafe AMERICAN The obligatory half-Cadillac through the wall beckons you into this shrine to rock 'n' roll. Among the items on display are costumes worn by Elvis, John Lennon, and Elton John, as well as guitars from Sting and the Bee Gees, drums from Phil Collins and the Beatles, and one of Madonna's bras. The mainstays here are the burgers, with ribs, chicken, fish, salads, and T-bone steaks on the menu, too. Most meals come with french fries or baked potatoes and a salad. It's really busy on Friday and Saturday evenings from around 7:30 to 10:30pm, when you might have to line up to get a seat.

121–129 Crown St., Darlinghurst. ✆ **02/9331 1116.** Reservations not accepted. Main courses A$9.95–A$22. 10% surcharge Sat–Sun and public holidays. AE, DC, MC, V. Daily noon–midnight. Shop daily 10am–midnight. Closed Dec 25. CityRail: Museum, and then walk across Hyde Park, head down the hill past the Australian Museum on William St., and turn right onto Crown St. Sydney Explorer bus.

INEXPENSIVE

Govindas VEGETARIAN When I think of Govindas, I can't help smiling. Perhaps it's because I'm recalling the happy vibe from the Hare Krishna center it's based in, or maybe it's because the food is so cheap! Or maybe it's because they even throw in a decent movie with the meal. (The movie theater is on a different floor.) The food is simple vegetarian, served buffet-style and eaten in a basic room off black-lacquer tables. The menu changes nightly, but it always includes a delicious Indian dahl soup, vegetable curry, penne pasta, lentil pie or potato au gratin, cauliflower pakoras, potato wedges, rice, poppadums, and salads. It's BYO and doctrine-free. Movies start at 7pm and you watch them prostrate on large cushions. Very bohemian.

112 Darlinghurst Rd., Darlinghurst. ✆ **02/9380 5155.** www.govindas.com.au. Dinner A$20. Movie A$8.80. AE, MC, V. Daily 6–11pm. CityRail: Kings Cross.

In Glebe

The Boathouse on Blackwattle Bay ★ SEAFOOD Above Sydney University's rowing club and overlooking a working area of Sydney Harbour, this converted boat shed offers water views across to the city and the Anzac Bridge. It serves terrific French-inspired seafood in an elegant yet informal atmosphere of white tablecloths and natural lighting. Oh, and you can see the chefs at work in the open kitchen. You can't go wrong with the signature dish, the fabulous snapper fish pie with roasted tomatoes and mashed potatoes. Plus, there are usually nine varieties of oysters on the menu. A good wine list and delicious desserts cap off the meal. Unfortunately, the service is variable (but hopefully improving after a few recent not-so-hot reviews). You may also want to try the Boathouse for a lunchtime treat. Catch a taxi—it's a little hard to find.

End of Ferry Rd., Glebe. ✆ **02/9518 9011.** www.boathouse.net.au. Main courses A$37–A$43. AE, DC, MC, V. Tues–Sun noon–2:30pm and 6:30–10pm. Bus: 431, 433, or 434 from Millers Point or The Rocks (on George St.); 459 from behind Town Hall.

In Paddington

The top end of Oxford Street, which runs from Hyde Park in central Sydney toward Bondi, has a profusion of trendy and glamorous bars and cafes and a scattering of cheaper eateries, in addition to the recommended listing below.

Buon Ricordo ★★ ITALIAN With yellow walls pinned with antique plates and artwork and padded-wooden chairs and archways, Buon Ricordo oozes trattoria-style charm. The food is rich and the prices for main courses are high, but the food is just perfection. Dishes might include such seasonal specialties as crispy fried harbor prawns, or a delicious winter salad of raw fennel and artichoke hearts. A favorite is the polenta cake with grilled radicchio flavored with sweet vincotto. The house signature dish is *fettuccine al tartufovo*—fettuccine served in a cream sauce with lightly fried, truffle-infused eggs.

108 Boundary St., Paddington. ✆ **02/9360 6729.** www.buonricordo.com.au. Reservations essential. Pastas A$33–A$35; main courses A$45–A$60. 6-course *degustazione* menu A$125 per person, plus an extra A$80 for matching wines. AE, DC, MC, V. Fri–Sat noon–3pm; Tues–Sat 6:30–11pm. Bus: 360 or 361.

In Newtown

Newtown is three stops from Central Station on CityRail, and 10 minutes by bus from central Sydney. On Newtown's main drag, **King Street,** many inexpensive ethnic restaurants offer food from all over the world.

Le Kilimanjaro AFRICAN With so many excellent restaurants in Newtown—they close down or improve quickly enough if they're bad—Kilimanjaro is one of the most unusual. It's a tiny place, with limited seating on two floors. Basically, you enter, you choose a dish off the blackboard menu (while standing), and a waiter escorts you to your seat. On a recent visit I had couscous, African bread (similar to

cafe CULTURE

Debate rages over which cafe serves the best coffee in Sydney, which has the best atmosphere, and which has the tastiest snacks. The main cafe scenes center on **Victoria Street** in Darlinghurst, **Stanley Street** in East Sydney, and **King Street** in Newtown. Other places, including Balmoral Beach on the North Shore, Bondi Beach, and Paddington all have their own favored hangouts.

Note: Americans will be sorry to learn that, unlike in the States, free refills of coffee are rare in Australian restaurants and cafes. Sip slowly. Expect a cup of coffee to cost around A$3 to A$3.50; main courses run A$8 to A$15.

The following are the best cafes around town.

- **Bar Coluzzi,** 322 Victoria St., Darlinghurst. (✆ **02/9380 5420**), may no longer offer the best coffee in Sydney, but this cafe's claim to fame is that long ago it served real espresso when the rest of the city was drinking Nescafé. People-watching is a favorite hobby at this fashionably worn-around-the-edges spot in the heart of Sydney's cafe district. MC, V. Daily 5am–8pm. CityRail: Kings Cross.
- **Bill's,** 433 Liverpool St., Darlinghurst (✆ **02/9360 9631**), a bright and airy place strewn with flowers and magazines, serves nouveau cafe-style food. It's so popular you might have trouble finding a seat. The signature breakfast dishes—including ricotta hotcakes with honeycomb butter and banana, and sweet corn fritters with roast tomatoes and bacon—are the stuff of legend. AE, MC, V. Mon–Sat 7:30am–3pm. CityRail: Kings Cross.
- The walls of the tiny, cluttered **Café Hernandez** ★ 60 Kings Cross Rd., Potts Point (✆ **02/9331 2343;** www.cafehernandez.com.au), are crammed with eccentric fake masterpieces, and the aroma of 20 types of coffee roasted and ground on the premises permeates the air. It's almost a religious experience for discerning central-city coffee addicts. The Spanish espresso is a treat. AE, MC, V. Daily 24 hr. CityRail: Kings Cross.
- Sydney's oldest coffee shop, the aptly named **Old Coffee Shop** ★ (✆ **02/9231 3002**) opened on the ground floor of the Victorian Strand Arcade in 1891. The shop may or may not serve Sydney's best java, but the old-world feel of the place and the sugary snacks, cakes, and pastries make up for it. It's a good spot to take a break from shopping and sightseeing. MC, V. Mon–Fri 7:30am–5pm; Sat 8:30am–5pm; Sun 10:30am–4pm. CityRail: Town Hall.

Indian chapati), and *saussou-gor di guan* (tuna in a rich sauce). Another favorite dish is *yassa* (chicken in a rich sauce). All meals are served on traditional wooden plates. The servings are rather small though, so order more than you think your stomach can manage. The service can feel a little rude (such as slapping you with a bill before you've finished eating), but bear in mind they have to churn through customers to make profits at these prices.

280 King St., Newtown. ✆ **02/9557 4565.** Reservations not accepted. Main courses A$10–A$13. No credit cards. CityRail: Newtown.

Old Saigon ★ 🎁 VIETNAMESE I highly recommend this place for a cheap night out. Bursting with atmosphere, Old Saigon was owned, until 1998, by a former American Vietnam War correspondent who loved Vietnam so much he ended up living there and marrying a local before coming to Australia. Just to make sure you knew his history, he put up his photos on the walls and scattered homemade tin helicopters around the place. His Vietnamese brother-in-law has taken over, but the food is still glorious; the spicy squid dishes are among my favorites. A popular pastime is grilling your own strips of venison, beef, wild boar, kangaroo, or crocodile over a burner at your table, then wrapping the meat in rice paper with lettuce and mint, and dipping it in chili sauce. The salt-and-pepper squid is the best in town. It's certainly not a classy joint, and diners come for the food rather than great service. It's BYO.

107 King St., Newtown. ✆ **02/9519 5931.** Reservations recommended. Main courses A$16–A$22; most dishes around A$18. AE, DC, MC, V. Wed–Fri noon–3pm; Tues–Sun 6–11pm. CityRail: Newtown.

In Bondi Beach

EXPENSIVE

Icebergs Dining Room & Bar ★★★ SEAFOOD/MEDITERRANEAN The restaurant at the Bondi Icebergs Club, a revamped old swimming club complex, overlooks Bondi Beach and is a truly fabulous place to hang out. From its corner position on the cliffs, the Icebergs Bar looks directly across the beach and water, and its floor-to-roof windows make sure you get to experience what's probably the best view in Sydney. The bar features lots of cushions and even hammocks, and the views stretch on across the balcony and into the restaurant. Inside this highly recommended eating place, it's all frosted glass dividers (to match the color of the ocean) and crisp white tablecloths and napkins (to resemble the surf). Not surprisingly, seafood features highly on the menu. You may well find wild scallops; risotto with coral trout and oregano; a fish stew from Livorno; and spaghetti with clams.

Here too is the **Sundeck Café,** which boasts a variety of light snacks and meals ranging from focaccia, salads, and burgers to fresh local seafood and pasta, all served out on a terrace with fantastic views.

1 Notts Ave., Bondi Beach. ✆ **02/9365 9000.** www.idrb.com. Reservations essential. Main courses A$38–A$48. AE, DC, MC, V. Tues–Sat noon–3pm and 6:30–10:30pm; Sun noon–3pm and 6:30–9pm. CityRail to Bondi Junction and bus no. 380 or 333 to Bondi Beach; or bus no. 380 or 333 from the city.

Ravesi's ★ CONTEMPORARY Set on a corner beside a run of surf shops, Ravesi's is a kind of fish tank—with the water on the outside. Downstairs, it's all glass windows and bar stools, the perfect place to watch the street life go by. On weekend nights, the place is packed. Upstairs is a fine casual restaurant with seating both inside and out on the balcony overlooking the beach. On a recent visit, I had the smoked chicken salad with avocado, chili, mango, and peanuts, and it easily outclassed any salad I've had for a long while. The seafood, meat, and varied vegetarian options also make a big impression. Weekend breakfast up here is a wonderful experience, and they do excellent Bloody Marys, comforting after a night on the town.

Corner of Campbell Parade and Hall Street, Bondi Beach. ✆ **02/9365 4422.** Reservations recommended. Main courses A$35; pastas A$25. Breakfasts A$10–A$22. AE, MC, V. Mon–Sat noon–3pm and 6–10pm; Sun noon–4pm; Sat–Sun 9am–noon. CityRail to Bondi Junction and bus no. 380 or 333 to Bondi Beach; or bus no. 380 or 333 from the city.

MODERATE

Thai Terrific THAI Thai Terrific by name, terrific Thai by nature. This simple but great place is around the corner from the Bondi Hotel. Sometimes it falls a little short on service or the food doesn't quite hit the right note, but when it's spot on, it's fabulous. The back room can be noisy, so if you prefer less din with your dinner, sit at one of the sidewalk tables. The servings are enormous—three people could fill up on just two main courses. The *tom yum* (hot-and-sour) soups and spicy prawn or seafood laksa noodle soups (made with coconut milk) are the best I've tasted in Australia and very filling. I also highly recommend the red curries.

Equally nice (and quieter) is the Bangkok-style **Nina's Ploy Thai Restaurant ★**, 132 Wairoa Ave. (✆ **02/9365 1118**), at the corner of Warners Avenue at the end of the main Campbell Parade strip. Main courses here cost A$10 to A$15; cash only.

147 Curlewis St., Bondi Beach. ✆ **02/9365 7794.** www.thaiterrific.com.au. Reservations recommended Fri–Sat night. Main courses A$14–A$20. AE, DC, MC, V. Daily noon–11pm. CityRail to Bondi Junction and bus no. 380 or 333 to Bondi Beach; or bus no. 380 or 333 from the city.

INEXPENSIVE

Pompei's ★ 🎁 PIZZA/PASTA/ICE CREAM The recipe is simple: Use good ingredients and you'll get good pizzas—regulars swear they are the best in Sydney. Toppings include figs, prosciutto, fresh goat cheese, and pumpkin. Pompei's also has a selection of pizzas without cheese. And leave some room for the homemade gelato, the best in Sydney by far—in fact, the last time I had anything so good was in Pompeii, Italy, itself, and I swore then it was the best I'd ever eaten. Try dense raspberry, thick chocolate, tiramisu, or limoncello. The water views and outside tables are another plus.

126–130 Roscoe St. at Gould St., Bondi Beach. ✆ **02/9365 1233.** Reservations recommended. Pizza A$13–A$17. AE, DC, MC, V. Tues–Sun 11am–11pm. CityRail to Bondi Junction and bus no. 380 or 333 to Bondi Beach; or bus no. 380 or 333 from the city.

In Manly

Manly is 30 minutes from Circular Quay by ferry. The takeout shops that line **the Corso,** as well as the **pedestrian mall** that runs between the ferry terminal and the main Manly Beach, offer everything from Turkish kabobs to Japanese noodles. There are better restaurants along the seafront (though there's a road btw. them and the beach). Everything is pretty good, so just take a lunchtime walk, check out their blackboard menus, and take a seat if something takes your fancy. Or follow the recommendations below.

Ashiana ★ INDIAN You'll be hard-pressed to find a better moderately priced Indian restaurant in the Sydney area. Tucked away up a staircase next to the Steyne Hotel (just off the Corso near the main beach), Ashiana has won prizes for its traditional spicy cooking. I've eaten there for years. Portions are large and filling, though creamy in that kind of pampering-to-Western-tastes style. The service is friendly. The butter chicken is magnificent, while *malai kofta* (cheese and potato dumplings in mild, creamy sauce) is the best this side of Bombay. Work off the excellent meal with a beachside stroll afterward.

Corner of Sydney Rd. and the Corso, Manly. ✆ **02/9977 3466.** Reservations recommended. Main courses A$10–A$19. AE, MC, V. Daily 5:30–11pm. Ferry: Manly.

Out of Africa ★ 🎁 MOROCCAN Low lighting and authentic Moroccan decor add an interesting touch to the fabulous food served here. One of my favorites is the chicken tajine—a taste sensation of marinated chicken pieces with olives, preserved lemon, and Moroccan spicy dressing. The signature dish is the Moroccan meatballs, featuring spicy minced balls of beef simmered in a tomato, onion, and garlic sauce. Couscous dishes are great too, and there are plenty of tasty dips to start with. Find the restaurant beside the ferry terminal.

43-45 East Esplanande, Manly. ✆ **02/9977 0055.** www.outofafrica.com.au. Reservations recommended. Main courses A$25–A$35. AE, MC, V. Thurs–Sun noon–3pm; daily 6–10:30pm.

WHAT TO SEE & DO IN SYDNEY

The only problem with visiting Sydney is fitting in everything you want to do and see. Of course, you won't want to miss the iconic attractions: the **Opera House** and the **Harbour Bridge.** Everyone seems to be climbing over the arch of the bridge these days on the BridgeClimb Sydney Tour, so look up for the tiny dots of people waving to the ferry passengers below.

You should also check out the native wildlife in **Taronga Zoo** and the **Sydney Aquarium,** stroll around the tourist precinct of **Darling Harbour,** and get a dose of Down Under culture at the not-too-large **Australian Museum.** Also try to take time out to visit one of the nearby national parks for a taste of the Australian bush. If it's hot, take your "cozzie" (swimsuit) and towel to **Bondi Beach** or **Manly.**

I also recommend a quick trip out of town. Go bushwalking in the **Blue Mountains,** wine tasting in the **Hunter Valley,** or dolphin spotting at **Port Stephens** (see chapter 6 for details on all three).

Whatever you decide to do, you won't have enough time. Don't be surprised if you start planning your next visit before your first is even finished.

Attraction Passes are shared by Sydney Tower/OzTrek, Sydney Aquarium, and Wildlife World, and you can buy them online at their websites or at the attractions themselves. The **Aqua + Tower Pass** includes entry to Sydney Aquarium and Sydney Tower/OzTrek. It costs A$50 for an adult and A$28 for a child. The **Wildlife + Tower Pass** includes entry to Sydney Wildlife World and Sydney Tower/OzTrek. This costs the same as above. The **Sydney Attractions Pass** includes entry to Sydney Aquarium, Sydney Wildlife World, and Sydney Tower/OzTrek. It costs A$70 for an adult and A$40 for a child, Family passes are available.

Deals on Sightseeing?

The **See Sydney & Beyond card** (✆ 1300/661 711; www.seesydneycard.com), a cashless smart card packaging more than 40 of the city's main attractions and tours, may save you money, although you'll have to plan well to get the most out of it. I've had a good look through their website and done the figures and I feel that unless you intend to pack a huge amount of things into a day, you should really do your homework on the figures. The card can be purchased for a 2-, 3-, or 7-day period, and there are options that also include public transport; the basic 2-day pass costs A$149 for adults and A$109 for children; a 3-day pass costs A$179 for adults and A$129 for kids, and a 7-day pass costs A$259 for adults and A$180 for kids. Buy through the website.

Sydney Harbour & The Rocks

Officially called Port Jackson, **Sydney Harbour** is the focal point of Sydney and one of the features—along with the beaches and easy access to surrounding national parks—that makes this city so special. It's entered through **the Heads,** two bush-topped outcrops (you'll see them if you take a ferry to Manly), beyond which the harbor laps at some 240km (149 miles) of shoreline before stretching out into the Parramatta River. Visitors are often awestruck by the harbor's beauty, especially at night, when the sails of the Opera House and the girders of the Harbour Bridge are lit up, and the waters are swirling with the reflection of lights from the abutting high-rises—reds, greens, blues, yellows, and oranges. During the day, it buzzes with green-and-yellow ferries pulling in and out of busy Circular Quay, sleek tourist craft, fully rigged tall ships, giant container vessels making their way to and from the wharves of Darling Harbour, and hundreds of white-sailed yachts.

The greenery along the harbor's edges is a surprising feature, thanks to the **Sydney Harbour National Park,** a haven for native trees and plants, and a feeding and breeding ground for lorikeets and other nectar-eating bird life. In the center of the harbor is a series of islands; the most impressive is the tiny isle supporting **Fort Denison,** which once housed convicts and acted as part of the city's defense.

The Rocks neighborhood is compact and close to the ferry terminals at Circular Quay. Sydney's historic district is hilly and crosscut with alleyways. Some of Australia's oldest pubs are here, as well as boutique restaurants, stores, and hotels. Pick up a walking map from the visitor center and make sure to get off the main streets and see the original working-class houses that survived the bulldozers.

The Eora Aboriginal people originally inhabited the rocky headland, now known as The Rocks, and the surrounding shoreline for thousands of years. Then in 1788, British convicts and their guards arrived. A jail was built where the Four Seasons Hotel now stands, on George Street, and public hangings were common. Later, the area evolved into a vibrant port community, though its history is colored with outbreaks of plague, shanghaied sailors, and cutthroat gangs.

By the turn of the 20th century, the harbor was polluted and the wharves were not much better. The Sydney Harbour Trust was formed in 1902 to clean things up. That year, a report outlined what they retrieved from the water off The Rocks: "2,524 rats, 1,068 cats, 283 bags of meat, 305 bags of fish, 1,467 fowls, 25 parrots, 23 sheep, 14 pigs, 1 bullock, 9 calves, 9 goats, 5 hares, 3 kangaroos, 162 rabbits, 18 bags of chaff, 8 bales of straw, 3 flying foxes [large bats], and 2 sharks." In subsequent years, much of The Rocks was torn down to make way for roads, the Harbour Bridge, and newer housing developments. Ah, progress.

In 1973, bulldozers and protesters clashed with police over plans to tear down many of the buildings that remain today. This resulted in the Green Bans, led by unionist Jack Mundey, which halted any further demolition work. In 1975, a compromise was reached and the bans were lifted, in return for heritage protection and community consultation on future projects.

Today, there are 96 heritage buildings in The Rocks. The oldest house is Cadmans Cottage, built in 1815, while the Dawes Point Battery, built in 1791, is the oldest remaining European structure. On Observatory Hill you'll find the three remaining walls of Fort Phillip, built in 1804.

Central Sydney Attractions

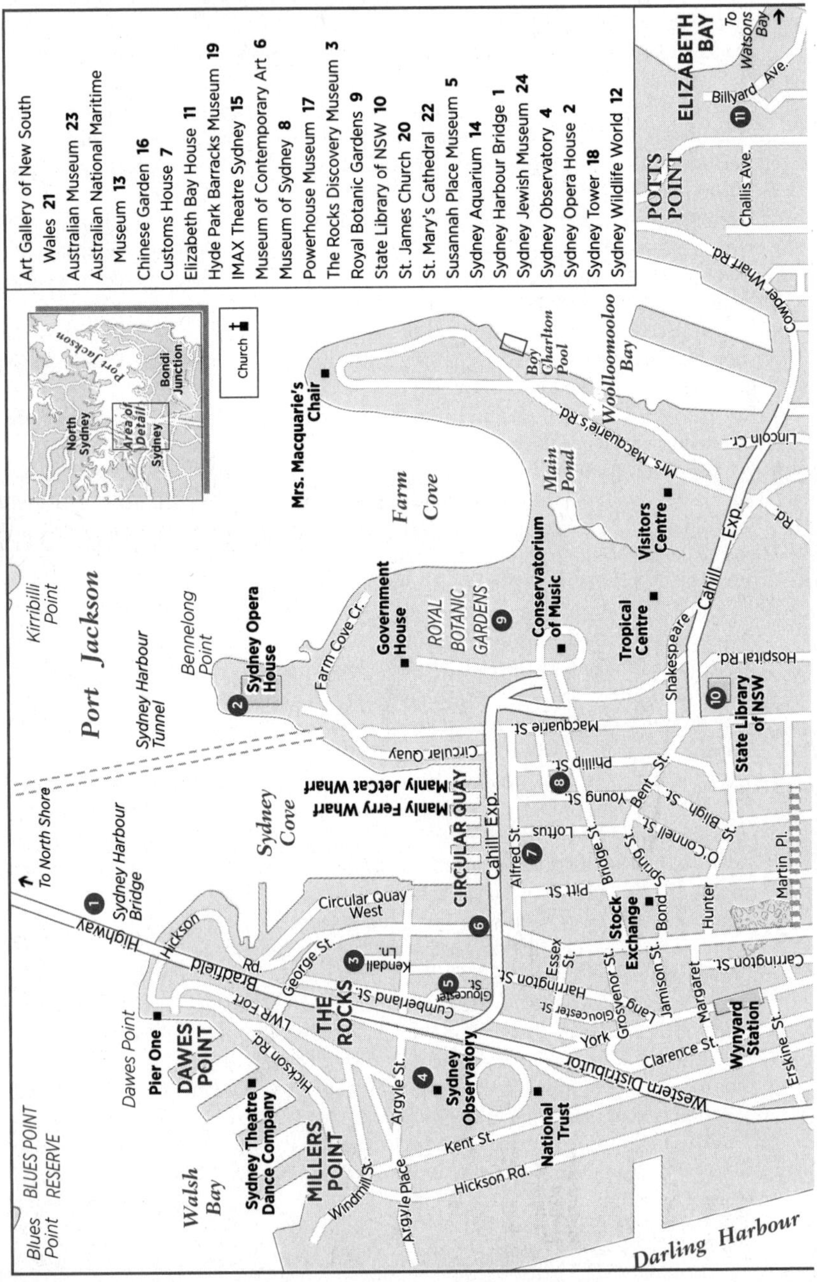

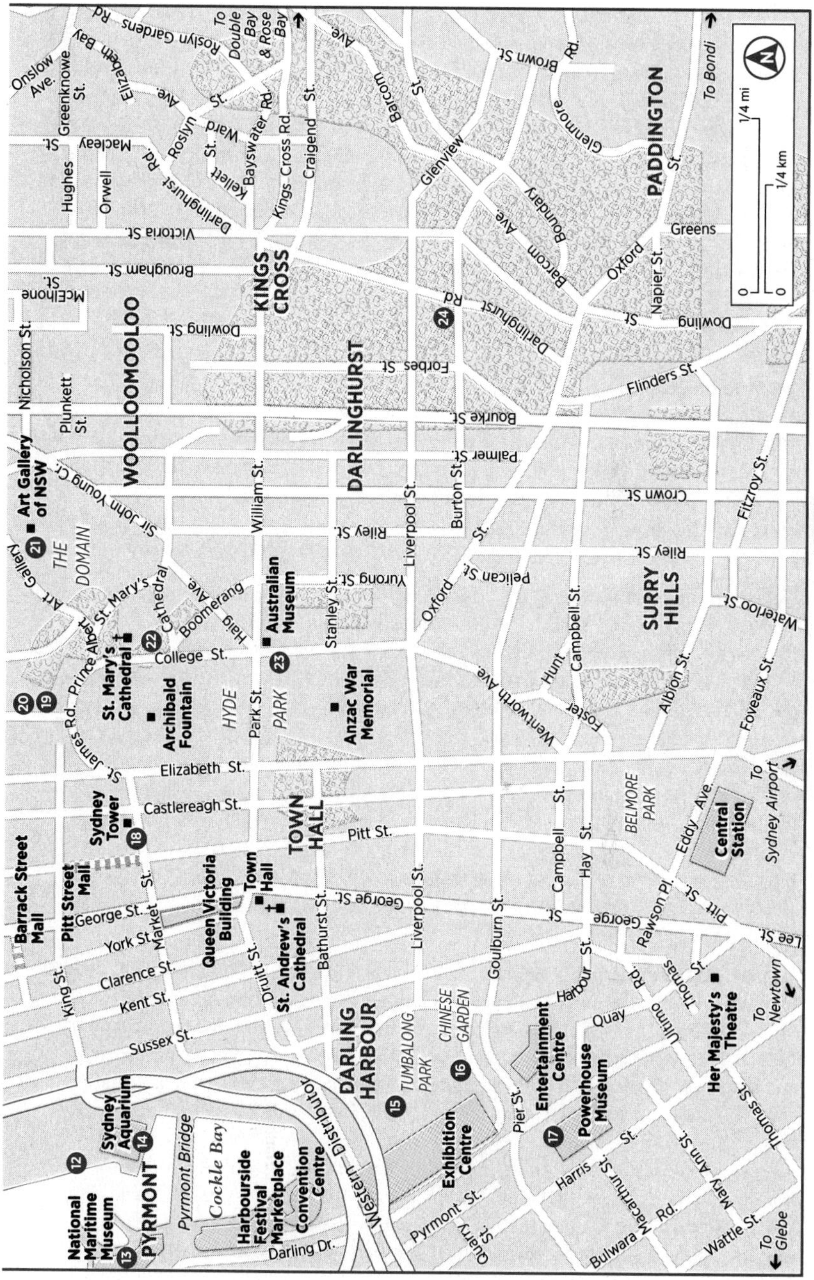
National Maritime Museum
PYRMONT
Sydney Aquarium
Pyrmont Bridge
Cockle Bay
Harbourside Festival Marketplace
Convention Centre
Darling Dr.
Western Distributor
Exhibition Centre
DARLING HARBOUR
TUMBALONG PARK
CHINESE GARDEN
Entertainment Centre
Powerhouse Museum
Her Majesty's Theatre
Barrack Street Mall
Pitt Street Mall
Sydney Tower
Queen Victoria Building
Town Hall
TOWN HALL
St. Andrew's Cathedral
St. Mary's Cathedral
Archibald Fountain
HYDE PARK
Anzac War Memorial
Australian Museum
Art Gallery of NSW
THE DOMAIN
WOOLLOOMOOLOO
KINGS CROSS
DARLINGHURST
SURRY HILLS
BELMORE PARK
Central Station
PADDINGTON
To Double Bay & Rose Bay
To Bondi
To Sydney Airport
To Newtown
To Glebe
Pyrmont St.
Harris St.
Pier St.
Quay St.
Ultimo Rd.
Thomas St.
Mary Ann St.
Macarthur St.
Bulwara Rd.
Wattle St.
Quarry St.
Sussex St.
Kent St.
Clarence St.
York St.
King St.
Market St.
George St.
Pitt St.
Castlereagh St.
Elizabeth St.
Park St.
Druitt St.
Bathurst St.
Liverpool St.
Goulburn St.
Campbell St.
Hay St.
Harbour St.
Rawson Pl.
Eddy Ave.
Lee St.
College St.
St. James Rd.
Prince Albert Rd.
St. Mary's Rd.
Art Gallery Rd.
Cathedral St.
Boomerang St.
Haig Ave.
Sir John Young Cr.
William St.
Stanley St.
Yurong St.
Riley St.
Palmer St.
Bourke St.
Forbes St.
Burton St.
Oxford St.
Pelican St.
Wentworth Ave.
Hunt St.
Foster St.
Albion St.
Foveaux St.
Waterloo St.
Crown St.
Fitzroy St.
Flinders St.
Dowling St.
Napier St.
Greens Rd.
Barcom Ave.
Boundary St.
Glenmore Rd.
Glenview St.
Brown St.
Darlinghurst Rd.
Victoria St.
Kings Cross Rd.
Craigend St.
Bayswater Rd.
Kellett St.
Ward Ave.
Roslyn St.
Roslyn Gardens Rd.
Elizabeth Bay Rd.
Greenknowe St.
Onslow Ave.
Macleay St.
Hughes St.
Orwell St.
Broughams St.
McElhone St.
Nicholson St.
Plunkett St.
0
1/4 mi
0
1/4 km
N

Luna Park ☺ The huge smiling clown face and the fairground attractions, which are visible from Circular Quay, make up one of Australia's most iconic attractions. Opened in 1935 and closed for many years, it reopened in 2004. It's small but fun, with traditional theme-park amusements rather than high-tech rides. It has a carousel, dodge-'em cars, a Ferris wheel, and the like. Several rides are suitable for small children, too. You buy tickets at booths inside the park. The best way to get here is either to walk over the Sydney Harbour Bridge from The Rocks (you might have to ask for directions to the entrance stairs), or you can catch a CityRail train from the city centre to Milsons Point. Leave some time to take a walk along the foreshore of Sydney Harbour (you get to walk right beneath the Harbour Bridge, and I highly recommend it).

1 Olympic Dr., Milsons Point (across the harbor from the Sydney Opera House). ✆ **02/9922 6644,** or 02/9033 7676 for information. www.lunaparksydney.com. Free admission. Day pass with unlimited rides A$20–A$25 small child; A$40–A$45 big kids and adults. More expensive prices during school holidays. Mon and Thurs 11am–6pm; Fri 11am–11pm; Sat 10am–11pm; closed Tues–Wed. In school holidays: Sun–Thurs 10am–10pm; Fri–Sat 10am–midnight. Ferry or CityRail: Milsons Point.

The Rocks Discovery Museum ★ This small but interesting museum is in a restored 1850s sandstone warehouse. It tells the story of The Rocks from pre-European days to the present. Learn about the area's traditional landowners; the establishment of the English colony; the sailors, whalers, and traders who made the area their home; and the 1970s union-led protests that preserved this unique part of Sydney.

Kendall Lane, The Rocks. ✆ **1800/067 676.** www.rocksdiscoverymuseum.com.au. Free admission. Daily 10am–5pm. Bus: 308, 339, 343, 431, 432, 433, or 434. CityRail: Circular Quay or Wynyard.

Susannah Place Museum ★ This small but interesting museum, set around a terrace of four houses built in 1844, is a real highlight of The Rocks area. It provides visitors with the opportunity to explore domestic working-class life from 1844 to 1990. The modest interiors and rear yards illustrate the restrictions of 19th-century inner-city life. The many layers of the paint finishes, wallpapers, and floor coverings that have survived provide a valuable insight into the tastes of the working class. The original brick privies and open laundries are some of the earliest surviving washing and sanitary amenities remaining in the city. There's also a delightful little shop selling cordials, postcards, old-fashioned candies, and knickknacks. Allow 45 minutes.

58–64 Gloucester St., The Rocks. ✆ **02/9241 1893.** www.hht.net.au. Admission A$8 adults, A$4 kids, A$17 family (entry to shop free). Entry includes a guided tour. Mon–Fri 2–6pm; Sat–Sun and NSW school holidays 10am–6pm. Bus, Ferry, or CityRail: Circular Quay.

Sydney Harbour Bridge ★★★ One thing few tourists do, although it only takes an hour or so, is to walk across the Harbour Bridge. The bridge, completed in 1932, is 1,150m (3,772 ft.) long and spans 503m (1,650 ft.) from the south shore to the north. It accommodates pedestrian walkways, two railway lines, and an eight-lane road. The 30-minute stroll from one end to the other offers excellent harbor views. From the other side, you can take a CityRail train from Milsons Point back to the city (to Wynyard—change there for Circular Quay, Town Hall, or Central).

As you walk across, stop off at the **Pylon Lookout** (✆ **02/9247 3408**; www.pylonlookout.com.au) at the southeastern pylon. Admission is A$9.50 for adults, A$4 for children over 7. From the top of this bridge support, 89m (292 ft.) above the water, you get panoramic views of Sydney Harbour, the ferry terminals of Circular

Walk on the Wild Side: Climb the Harbour Bridge

At one time, only bridge workers had the opportunity to view Sydney from the top of the main bridge arch. But since October 1998, Sydneysiders and tourists have been able to experience the spectacular view and the exhilarating achievement of climbing to the top of one of Australia's icons. **BridgeClimb,** 3 Cumberland St., The Rocks (✆ **02/ 8274 7777;** fax 02/9240 1122; www.bridgeclimb.com), offers three climbs. The **Bridge Climb** takes you along the outer arch of the bridge on catwalks and ladders all the way to the summit. The **Discovery Climb** takes climbers into the heart of the bridge. You traverse the suspension arch and then wind your way through a tangle of hatchways and girders suspended above the traffic. You also climb between the arches to the summit. Both experiences take 3½ hours from check-in to completion. An **Express Climb** is basically the same as the standard Bridge Climb but there are fewer people and a quicker preparation, which allows you to discover the wonders of the bridge in just 2 hours and 15 minutes. In October 2009, BridgeClimb opened the **Sydney Harbour Bridge Visitor Centre** to complement its office. There are good displays featuring Sydney's famous icon. It's open daily from 8am to 6pm. Climbers leave in small groups every 10 minutes or so. Climbers wear "Bridge Suits" and are harnessed to a line. Participants are also breath-tested for alcohol and are banned from carrying anything, including cameras. All climbs cost A$198 for adults and A$128 for children 10 to 15 every day during the day. Daily twilight climbs cost A$258 for adults and A$188 for kids. Daily night climbs cost A$188 for adults and A$118 for kids. Children under 10 are not allowed to climb. A dawn climb, on the first Saturday of each month, costs A$295 for adults and A$195 for kids.

Quay, and beyond. An interesting museum charts the building of the bridge. The Pylon Lookout is open daily from 10am to 5pm (closed Dec 25). Reach the pylon by walking to the far end of George Street in The Rocks toward the Harbour Bridge. Just past the Mercantile pub, you'll see some stone steps that take you onto Cumberland Street. From there, it's a 2-minute walk to the steps underneath the bridge on your right. Climb four flights to reach the bridge's Western Footway, and then walk along to the first pylon. ***Note:*** Climbing up inside the pylon involves 200 steps.

Sydney Opera House ★★★ Only a handful of buildings around the world are as architecturally and culturally significant as the Sydney Opera House. But what sets it apart from, say, the Taj Mahal and the great pyramids of Egypt is that this white-sailed construction caught midbillow over the waters of Sydney Cove is a working building. Most visitors are surprised to learn it's not just an opera house but a full-scale performing-arts complex with five major performance spaces. The biggest and grandest is the 2,690-seat **Concert Hall,** which has the best acoustics of any building of its type in the world. Come here to experience opera, chamber music, symphonies, dance, choral performances, and even rock 'n' roll. The **Opera Theatre** is smaller, seating 1,547, and books operas, ballets, and dance. The **Drama Theatre,** seating 544, and the **Playhouse,** seating 398, specialize in plays and smaller-scale performances. The **Boardwalk,** seating 300, is used for dance and experimental music.

The history of the building is as intriguing as the design. The New South Wales Government raised the construction money with a lottery. Danish architect Jørn Utzon won an international competition to design it. From the start, the project was controversial, with many Sydneysiders believing it was a monstrosity. Following a disagreement, Utzon returned home without ever seeing his finished project. The interior fell victim to a compromise in design, which, among other things, left too little space to perform full-scale operas. And the cost? Initially the project was budgeted at a cool A$7 million, but by the time it was finished in 1973 it had cost a staggering A$102 million, most raised through a series of lotteries. Since then, continual refurbishment and the major task of replacing the asbestos-laden grouting between the hundreds of thousands of white tiles that make up its shell has cost many millions more.

A long-overdue reconstruction is being completed, aimed at putting into practice what Jørn Utzon had long visualized. The tatty old reception hall has already been transformed into an impressive welcome room. Its centerpiece is Utzon's first foray into visual art: a glorious floor-to-ceiling tapestry inspired by Bach's Hamburg Symphonies and Raphael's painting *Procession to Calvary.*

Also finished is work on the Western Loggia, or colonnade, which opens up the foyers of the Playhouse, the Drama Theatre, and the Studio to harbor views and creates spaces for cafes and functions. Investigations are also going ahead into refurbishing the Opera Theatre and improving the acoustics in the Concert Hall.

Utzon died in 2008. He never returned to Australia after leaving Sydney in 1966, nearly 7 years before the building was finished.

Guided tours of the Opera House last about an hour and are conducted daily from 9am to 5pm, except on Good Friday and December 25. Though guides try to take groups into the main theaters and around the foyers, if you don't get to see everything you want, it's because the Opera House is a working venue. There's almost always some performance, practice, or setting up to be done. Reservations are essential. Tour sizes are limited, so be prepared to wait. Tours include about 200 stairs. (Tours for people with disabilities can be arranged.) Specialized tours, focusing on the building's architecture and engineering, for example, can also be arranged.

The Tourism Services Department at the Sydney Opera House can book **combination packages,** including dinner and a show; a tour, dinner, and a show; or a champagne-interval performance. Prices vary depending on shows and dining venues. Visitors from overseas can buy tickets by credit card and pick them up at the box office on arrival, or contact a local tour company specializing in Australia. Advance ticket purchases are a good idea, because performances are very popular. The views from the back rows are hardly worth the effort and expense if you turn up on the day of performance. Tickets for performances vary from as little as A$15 for children's shows to A$180 for good seats at the opera. Plays average A$40 to A$60.

Free performances take place outside on the Opera House boardwalks on Sunday afternoons and during festival times. The artists range from musicians and performance artists to school groups.

Bennelong Point. ✆ **02/9250 7250** for guided tours and information, or 02/9250 7777 box office. Fax 02/9251 3943. www.sydneyoperahouse.com. Box office Mon–Sat 9am–8:30pm; Sun 2 hr. before performance. Tours A$35 for adults, A$25 for kids, and A$74 for a family. Book online for discounts. Tours daily 9am–5pm (every 30 min.), subject to theater availability. Backstage Tour A$150 starts daily at 7am, for 2 hr., with breakfast. CityRail, bus, or ferry: Circular Quay. Sydney Explorer bus. Parking: Mon–Fri daytime A$9 per hour; weekend daytime flat rate A$15 (leave before 5pm); evening A$32 flat rate.

SEEING SYDNEY HARBOUR THROUGH aboriginal EYES

The *Deerubbun,* a former Australian navy torpedo recovery vessel, makes quite an impression as it pulls up to the dock near the Opera House concourse with speakers blaring out a recording of clapsticks and didgeridoos. The boat, which is owned by the Tribal Warrior Association (an Aboriginal-operated nonprofit organization that aims to provide maritime training programs for Aboriginal youths) revolutionized the multimillion-dollar Sydney cruise industry in late 2006 by offering an Aboriginal perspective of the famous waterway. Tourists learn that Circular Quay was once occupied by the Cadigal people; they also learn about Bennelong, the captured Aborigine who once lived on the point where the Opera House now stands, and his wife Barangaroo, who opposed her husband's conciliatory efforts with the Europeans. The boat putters past the Royal Botanic Gardens, and the guide tells stories of the early Europeans and their hopeless farms, and the smallpox epidemic of 1789, which the local Aborigines thought was caused by evil spirits. Mixed in with the observations of the landscape are tales of the first Aboriginal tour guides, who took early settlers inland from the harbor, as well as mentions of soldiers, statesmen, and farmers who came into contact with the Aborigines, and much more. Tourists disembark at Clark Island to see cave shelters with roofs stained black from ancient fireplaces, convict engravings, and a natural fish trap. Two Aboriginal guides, their bodies plastered in ghostly white ocher, beat a rhythm with hardwood sticks and growl through a didgeridoo as they beckon the tourists to the Welcoming Ceremony. Then comes a repertoire of haunting songs, music, and dance. Every visitor to Sydney should do this trip. **Aboriginal Cultural Cruises ★** depart at 12:45pm, Tuesday to Saturday, from the Eastern Pontoon (near the Sydney Opera House). The cost is A$60 adults, A$45 children 5 to 14. Tickets are available from Sydney Visitor Centres. For more information, call **© 02/9699 3491** or visit **www.tribalwarrior.org**.

SYDNEY HARBOUR ON THE CHEAP

The best way to see Sydney Harbour is from the water. Several companies operate tourist craft (see "Harbor Cruises & Organized Tours," later in this chapter), but it's easy enough just to hop on a regular passenger ferry (see "Getting Around," earlier in this chapter). The best ferry excursions are over to the beachside suburb of **Manly** (come back after dusk to see the lights ablaze around The Rocks and Circular Quay); to **Watsons Bay,** where you can have lunch and wander along the cliffs; to **Darling Harbour,** for all the area's entertainment and the fact that you travel right under the Harbour Bridge; and to **Mosman Bay,** just for the ride and to see the grand houses that overlook exclusive harbor inlets.

FAST ACTION ON SYDNEY HARBOUR

For a thrill ride, you can board a 420-horsepower jet boat, which zooms about on three high-speed waterway tours at speeds of up to 40 knots (about 80kmph/50 mph), with huge 240-degree turns and instant stops. **Harbour Jet** (**© 1300/887 373** in

Australia, or 02/9212 3555; www.harbourjet.com) offers a 35-minute Jet Blast Adventure costing A$65 for adults, A$45 for kids under 15, and A$190 for a family. It leaves at noon, 2:30pm, and 4:30pm daily. A 50-minute Sydney Harbour Adventure costs A$80 for adults, A$55 for kids, and A$243 for a family. It leaves at 10:30am, 1:30pm, and 3:30pm daily. An 80-minute Middle Harbour Adventure cruise costs A$95 for adults, A$70 for kids, and A$297 for a family. It leaves at 9am on Fridays, Saturdays, and Sundays. Rides are fast and furious and pump with rock music. The boat leaves from the Convention Jetty, between the Convention Centre and the Harbourside Shopping complex on the far side of Darling Harbour. These trips don't operate every day, so check beforehand.

Another option is **Oz Jet Boat** (✆ **02/9808 3700;** www.ozjetboating.com), which departs every hour from the Eastern Pontoon at Circular Quay (on the walkway to the Opera House). These large red boats are a bit more powerful than the blue Harbour Jet ones, but you might not notice the difference. This company offers a 30-minute Thrill Ride for A$60 for adults, A$40 for kids, and A$170 for a family. It leaves every hour from 11am to sunset.

Attractions at Darling Harbour

Many tourists head to Darling Harbour for the Harbourside Festival Marketplace, a huge structure beside the Pyrmont pedestrian and monorail bridge that's crammed full of cheap eateries and a few interesting shops. However, Sydney's tourist precinct has a lot more to offer. See **www.darlingharbour.com** for what's on while you're in town.

Australian National Maritime Museum ★ ☺ Modern Australia owes almost everything to the sea, so it's not surprising that there's a museum dedicated to ships, from Aboriginal vessels to submarines. You'll find ships' logs and things to pull and tug at. Docked in the harbor are several ships and launches, including an Australian navy destroyer, the *Vampire,* an Oberon Class submarine, and a replica of the *Endeavour,* the ship Captain James Cook commanded when he laid claim to Australia. You can clamber over many of them. Allow 2 hours.

Darling Harbour. ✆ **02/9298 3777.** www.anmm.gov.au. Free admission to main exhibition. Admission to all ships A$32 adults, A$17 children 5–15, A$70 families. Navy Package (includes museum and 2 ships) A$20 adults, A$10 children, A$42 families. Admission to single vessels available A$10–A$18 for adults and A$7–A$10 for kids. Daily 9:30am–5pm (until 6:30pm in Jan). Ferry: Darling Harbour. Monorail: Harbourside. Sydney Explorer bus.

Chinese Garden The largest Chinese garden of its type outside China offers a pleasant escape from the city concrete. Expert gardeners from China's Guangdong Province planned the garden according to principles of design dating to the 5th century. Allow 30 minutes.

Darling Harbour (adjacent to the Entertainment Centre). ✆ **02/9281 6863.** www.chinesegarden.com.au. Admission A$6 adults, A$3 children, A$15 families. Daily 9:30am–5pm. Ferry: Darling Harbour. Monorail: Convention. Sydney Explorer bus.

IMAX Theatre Sydney Four different IMAX films are usually showing on the gigantic eight-story-high screen. Each flick lasts about 50 minutes or so. If you've ever been to an IMAX theater before, you know what to expect. As you watch, your mind is tricked into feeling that it's right in the heart of the action. Also shown are 3-D movies, which cost A$1 extra.

Southern Promenade, Darling Harbour. ✆ **02/9281 3300.** www.imax.com.au. Admission A$18 adults, A$13 children 3–15, A$50 families. Sun–Thurs 10am–10pm; Fri–Sat 10am–11:30pm. Ferry: Darling Harbour. Monorail: Convention. Sydney Explorer bus.

Powerhouse Museum ★ ☺ Sydney's most interactive museum is also one of the largest in the Southern Hemisphere. In the postmodern industrial interior, you'll find all sorts of displays, sound effects, and gadgets relating to the sciences, transportation, human achievement, decorative art, and social history. Much of it has connections to Sydney and Australian exploration. It's really great for kids, and interesting for adults too. It's worthy of 2 or 3 hours of your time. There's a good kids' playground and an unadventurous cafe.

500 Harris St., Ultimo (near Darling Harbour). ✆ **02/9217 0111.** www.powerhousemuseum.com. Admission A$10 adults, A$5 students and children 5–15, A$24 families. Free admission 1st Sat of every month. Daily 9:30am–5pm. Ferry: Darling Harbour. Monorail: Harbourside. Sydney Explorer bus.

Sydney Aquarium ★★ ☺ This is one of the world's best aquariums and should be near the top of your itinerary. The main attractions are the underwater walkways through two enormous tanks—one full of giant rays and gray nurse sharks and the other where you can see the seals. The sharks get fed at 2pm daily. Other exhibits include a magnificent section on the Great Barrier Reef, where thousands of colorful fish school around coral outcrops. Sit on the steps beside the huge, main Barrier Reef tank, listening to the classical music, and you might never want to leave. Also on display are two saltwater crocodiles and some fairy penguins. A touch pool allows you to stroke baby sharks. New in 2009 was a Mermaid Lagoon, featuring two dugongs (or sea cows). Try to visit during the week, when it's less crowded. Allow around 2 hours. Tickets are a little cheaper if bought through the website.

Aquarium Pier, Darling Harbour. ✆ **02/8251 7800.** http://sydneyaquarium.myfun.com.au. Admission A$35 adults, A$18 children 3–15, A$85 families. Tickets cheaper prebooked over the Internet. Daily 9am–10pm. Seal Sanctuary closes at 7pm in summer. CityRail: Town Hall. Ferry: Darling Harbour. Sydney Explorer bus.

Other Top Attractions

Hyde Park Barracks Museum ★ These Georgian-style barracks were designed in 1819 by the convict and architect Francis Greenway. They were built by convicts and inhabited by prisoners. These days they house relics from those early days in modern displays, including log books, early settlement artifacts, and a room full of ships' hammocks in which visitors can lie and listen to fragments of prisoner conversation. If you are interested in Sydney's early beginnings, I highly recommend a visit. The displays are far more straightforward that those at the Museum of Sydney (see listing later in this chapter). The courtyard cafe is excellent. Allow 1 hour or more.

Queens Sq., Macquarie St. ✆ **02/8239 2311.** www.hht.nsw.gov.au. Admission A$10 adults, A$5 children, A$20 families. Daily 9:30am–5pm. CityRail: St. James or Martin Place. Sydney Explorer bus.

Museum of Contemporary Art (MCA) This imposing sandstone museum, set back from the water on The Rocks side of Circular Quay, offers wacky, entertaining, inspiring, and befuddling displays of what's new (and dated) in modern art. It houses the J. W. Power Collection of more than 4,000 pieces, including works by Andy Warhol, Christo, Marcel Duchamp, and Robert Rauschenberg, as well as temporary exhibits. A fourth floor opened up in 2005, and part of its permanent collection is displayed there. This museum isn't as impressive as major modern art museums in, say, London or New York; still, it's worth at least 1 hour. Free guided tours are conducted midweek at 11am and 1pm, and on weekends at noon and 1:30pm. The **MCA cafe** (✆ **02/9241 4253**) is a nice spot, with good views of the harbor and Opera House. It's serves up contemporary food from 10am to 5pm daily.

140 George St., Circular Quay. ✆ **02/9245 2400.** www.mca.com.au. Free admission. Daily 10am–6pm (5pm in winter). CityRail, bus, or ferry: Circular Quay. Sydney Explorer bus.

Sydney Olympic Park The site of the 2000 Olympic games is still a tourist attraction as well as a major sporting venue. Start at the **Homebush Bay Information Centre,** which has displays, walking maps, and tour tips. It's open daily from 9am to 5pm.

Nearby is **ANZ Stadium** (formally the Telstra Stadium; ✆ **02/8765 2926;** www.anzstadium.com.au), the site of the opening and closing ceremonies, the track and field events, and some Olympic soccer games. It was called Stadium Australia back then. Today it schedules Australian Rules games and rugby league, rugby union, and soccer matches. A 60-minute tour of the stadium costs A$29 for adults, A$19 for children, and A$70 for a family. Tours leave at 11am, 12:30pm, 2pm, and 3:30pm.

Also at the Olympic Park is the **Sydney International Aquatic Centre** (✆ **02/9752 3666;** www.sydneyaquaticcentre.com.au), which comprises the Olympic pool, diving pool, and training facilities. A swim here costs A$5.80 adults, A$4.60 kids, A$19 families.

There are wonderful views of the Sydney Olympic Park and the city from level 17 of the **Novotel** hotel (✆ **02/8762 1111**), located in the park. Entry to the observation area costs A$4 for adults and A$2 for children over 7. One of the best ways to get to the Olympic site is on the Sydney Explorer bus.

Sydney Olympic Site, Olympic Park, Homebush Bay. ✆ **02/9714 7888.** www.sydneyolympicpark.nsw.gov.au. Visitor Centre daily 9am–5pm. CityRail: Olympic Park. Sydney Explorer bus.

Sydney Tower (aka Centrepoint Tower) ★ ☺ The tallest building in the Southern Hemisphere is not hard to miss—it resembles a giant steel pole skewering a golden marshmallow. Standing more than 300m (984 ft.) tall, the tower offers stupendous 360-degree views across Sydney and as far as the Blue Mountains. Fortunately, an elevator takes you to the indoor viewing platform on the top floor; if you were to walk up, you'd have to climb 1,504 steps. The general ticket price includes admission to **OzTrek,** where visitors are strapped into moving chairs in front of a 180-degree screen. On this simulator ride, you white-water raft in Queensland, climb Uluru (Ayers Rock), and have a close encounter with a saltwater crocodile. It's fun, and kids love it. Don't be too concerned if you feel the building tremble slightly, especially in a stiff breeze—I'm told it's perfectly natural. Below the tower are stores and restaurants (though at the time of writing the area was boarded up and undergoing major redevelopment). Right up at the top, too, is a revolving restaurant and bar if you're keen to stick around. See also Sydney Tower Skywalk (see below). Allow 2 hours.

100 Market St. (another entrance on Pitt St. Mall). ✆ **02/9333 9222.** http://sydneytower.myfun.com.au. Admission A$25 adults, A$15 children 4–15, A$55 families. Sun–Fri 9am–10:30pm; Sat 9am–11:30pm. CityRail: St. James or Town Hall. Sydney Explorer bus.

Sydney Tower Skywalk ★★ This addition to the Sydney thrill scene is a heart-stopping experience that is definitely not for people who are scared of heights. The deal is, you don a special suit, walk out onto a glass-floored platform 260m (853 ft.)

above the city floor and walk around the building. The views are breathtaking (even between your feet!). You are harnessed to a safety rail with a sliding harness, so there's no chance of falling off, and funny, well-informed guides offer a helping hand to the nervous. Each Skywalk lasts approximately 1 hour and 30 minutes and operates daily from 9am to 10pm, with the last Skywalk departing at 8:15pm. Cameras aren't allowed for safety reasons, but group or individual shots help clean-out your wallet. Children under 10 aren't allowed on the Skywalk.

Centrepoint Podium Level, 100 Market St. (entrance also through Pitt St. Mall). ✆ **02/9333 9222.** http://sydneytower.myfun.com.au. Day Skywalk A$65 for adults, A$45 for kids. Daily 9am–10pm (last Skywalk departs 8:45pm). CityRail: St. James or Town Hall. Sydney Explorer bus.

'Roos, Koalas & Other Aussie Wildlife

The Sydney Aquarium is discussed on p. 153.

Australian Reptile Park What started as a one-man operation supplying snake antivenin in the early 1950s has become a nature park teeming with the slippery-looking creatures. But it's not all snakes and lizards; you'll also find saltwater crocodiles and American alligators, as well as plenty of somewhat cuddlier creatures, such as koalas, platypuses, wallabies, dingoes, and flying foxes. The park is on beautiful bushland crossed by nature trails. A devastating fire burned down the entire park in mid-2000, killing all of the animals. The staff has worked valiantly to start up a new collection. It's a short detour off the route heading up to the Hunter Valley, Barrington Tops, and Port Stephens. Somersby is near Gosford, 84km (52 miles) north of Sydney. Several tour operators to the Hunter Valley stop off here.

Pacific Hwy., Somersby. ✆ **02/4340 1022.** www.reptilepark.com.au. Admission A$23 adults, A$12 children 3–15, A$60 families. Daily 9am–5pm. Closed Dec 25. CityRail: Gosford (trains leave Central Station every 30 min.); then by taxi. By car: Take the Pacific Hwy. and the Sydney–Newcastle Fwy. (F3); the trip takes about 1 hr.

Featherdale Wildlife Park ★★ ☺ If you have time to visit only one wildlife park in Sydney, make it this one. The selection of Australian animals is excellent, and, most important, the animals are very well cared for. You could easily spend a couple of hours here, despite the park's compact size. You'll have the chance to hand-feed friendly kangaroos and wallabies and get a photo taken next to a koala. (There are many here, both the New South Wales variety and the larger Victorian type.) The park's newest addition is the **Reptilian Pavilion.** It houses 30 different native species of reptiles in 26 realistic exhibits. If you are heading to the Blue Mountains on a bus tour, you are well advised to choose one that stops off here. Give yourself 1½ hours to get here by public transport from the city center.

217 Kildare Rd., Doonside. ✆ **02/9622 1644.** www.featherdale.com.au. Admission A$20 adults, A$10 children 3–15, A$58 families. Daily 9am–5pm. CityRail: Blacktown station; then bus no. 725 (ask driver to tell you when to get off). By car: Take the M4 motorway to Reservoir Rd., turn off, travel 4km (2½ miles); then turn left at Kildare Rd.

Koala Park Sanctuary ★ This is probably the only place in the country (unless you travel all the way to Kangaroo Island in South Australia) where you'll be able to spot this many koalas in one place. In all, around 55 koalas roam within the park's leafy boundaries (it's set in 4 hectares/10 acres of rainforest). Free koala cuddling sessions take place at 10:20 and 11:45am, and 2 and 3pm daily. There are wombats, dingoes, kangaroos, wallabies, emus, and native birds here, too. Hitch onto one of the free "hostess" guides who wander around the park like Pied Pipers. Give yourself 1½ hours each way by public transport from the city center.

84 Castle Hill Rd., West Pennant Hills. ✆ **02/9484 3141.** www.koalaparksanctuary.com.au. Admission A$19 adults, A$9 children. Daily 9am–5pm. Closed Dec 25. CityRail: Pennant Hills station via North Strathfield (45 min.). Cross over railway line and join Glenorie Bus routes 651 to 655. The bus takes about 10 min. to Koala Park.

Oceanworld Manly ☺ Though not as impressive as the Sydney Aquarium, Oceanworld can be combined with a visit to Manly Beach (see "North of Sydney Harbour," below) for a nice day's outing. There's a decent display of Barrier Reef fish, as well as giant sharks. Also here are the five most venomous snakes in the world. Shark feeding is at 11am on Monday, Wednesday, and Friday. There is also a **"dive with the sharks" ★★★** program, where you can dive in the tanks with giant gray nurse sharks. It costs A$185 for qualified divers, A$220 for qualified divers who have logged less than 15 dives or haven't dived in the last 6 months, or A$250 for non-qualified divers (includes an introduction to scuba diving course). You must download an application form from the website.

West Esplanade, Manly. ✆ **02/8251 7878.** http://oceanworld.myfun.com.au. Admission A$19 adults, A$9.95 children, A$46 families (15% off admission prices after 3:30pm). Daily 10am–5:30pm. Ferry: Manly.

Sydney Wildlife World Opened in late 2006, Sydney Wildlife World shook the tourism world when it announced it would house several thousand animals—a veritable Noah's Ark? Well, no, unless you count all the insects that is, and leave elephants and most of the other large creatures to be stranded over at Taronga Zoo. Still, this place has a few highlights. You get to see a cassowary up close (a flightless bird about the size of an emu, but armed with a dangerous spiked toe) and some endangered yellow-footed rock wallabies. Throw in a few snakes and lizards, some smaller birds, a few nocturnal marsupials and, of course, the inevitable koala, and you have a collection that almost becomes worth the entry money to see them.

Aquarium Pier, Darling Harbour. ✆ **02/9333 9288.** http://sydneywildlifeworld.myfun.com.au. Admission A$35 adults, A$18 kids 3–15, A$85 family. Discount tickets are available if you book over the Net, and you can buy a special Attractions Pass which allows discounted entry to here, Sydney Aquarium, and Sydney Tower. Daily 9am–10pm. Ferry/Monorail: Darling Harbour.

Taronga Zoo ★ ☺ Taronga has the best view of any zoo in the world. Set on a hill, it looks out over Sydney Harbour, the Opera House, and the Harbour Bridge. It's easiest on the legs to explore the zoo from the top down. The main attractions are the fabulous chimpanzee exhibit, the gorilla enclosure, and the Nocturnal Houses, where you can see some of Australia's many nighttime marsupials, including the platypus and the cuter-than-cute bilby (the official Australian Easter bunny), out and about. There's an interesting reptile display, a couple of impressive Komodo dragons, a scattering of indigenous beasties—including a few koalas, echidnas, kangaroos, dingoes, and wombats—and lots more. The kangaroo and wallaby exhibit is unimaginative; you'd be better off going to Featherdale Wildlife Park (see above). Animals are fed at various times during the day. The zoo can get crowded on weekends (though the entry price probably puts a lot of people off), so I strongly advise visiting during the week or early in the morning on weekends. Allow around 3 hours.

Bradley's Head Rd., Mosman. ✆ **02/9969 2777.** www.taronga.org.au. Admission A$43 adults, A$21 children 4–15, A$109 family. Admission includes a trip on the Aerial Safari cable car. Daily 9am–5pm (until 9pm Jan). Ferry: Taronga Zoo. Lower zoo entrance is at ferry terminal.

Hitting the Beach

One of the big bonuses of visiting Sydney in the summer (Dec–Feb) is that you get to experience the beaches in their full glory.

Most major city beaches, such as Manly and Bondi, have lifeguards on patrol, especially during the summer. They check the water conditions and are on the lookout for **"rips"**—strong currents that can pull a swimmer far out. Safe places to swim are marked by red and yellow flags. You must always swim between these flags. If you are using a foam or plastic body board or "boogie board," it's advisable to use it between the flags. Fiberglass surfboards must be used outside the flags. (Expect a warning from the beach loudspeakers and a A$100 fine if you fail to take notice.)

WHAT ABOUT SHARKS & OTHER NASTIES? One of the first things visitors wonder when they hit the water in Australia is: *Are there sharks?* The answer is yes, but fortunately they are rarely spotted inshore—you are far more likely to spy a migrating whale. In reality, sharks have more reason to be scared of us than we of them; most of them end up as the fish in your average packet of fish and chips. (Shark filets are often sold as "flake.") Though some beaches—such as the small beach next to the Manly ferry wharf—have permanent shark nets, most rely on portable nets that are moved from beach to beach. Shark attacks do happen though, mostly at dawn and dusk—so don't swim at these times!

Another common problem off Sydney's beaches are **"blue bottles"**—small blue jellyfish, often called "stingers" in Australia and Portuguese man-o'-war elsewhere. You'll often find these creatures (which are not the same as the stingers around the Great Barrier Reef) washed up along the beach; they become a hazard for swimmers when there's a strong breeze coming off the ocean and they're blown in to shore (watch out for warning signs erected on the shoreline). Minute individual stinging cells often break off the main body of the creature, and they can cause minor itching or stinging. Or you might be hit by the full force of a blue bottle, which will often stick to your skin and wrap its tentacles around you. Blue bottles deliver a hefty punch from their many stinging cells, causing a severe burning sensation almost immediately. Wearing a T-shirt in the water reduces the risk somewhat (though a pair of waterlogged jeans isn't a good idea). If you are stung, rinse the area liberally with seawater or fresh water to remove any tentacles stuck in the skin. For intense pain, apply heat or cold, whichever feels better. If you experience breathing difficulties or disorientation, seek medical attention immediately.

SOUTH OF SYDNEY HARBOUR

Sydney's most famous beach is **Bondi ★★**. In many ways, it's a raffish version of a California beach, with plenty of tanned skin and in-line skaters. Though the beach is nice, it's cut off from the cafe and restaurant strip that caters to beachgoers by a road that pedestrians have to funnel across in order to reach the sand. On summer weekend evenings, it's popular with souped-up cars and groups of disaffected youths from the suburbs. To reach Bondi Beach, take the CityRail train to Bondi Junction, and then transfer to bus no. 380 or 333 (a 15-min. bus journey). You can also catch bus no. 380 directly from Circular Quay (but it can take an hour or so at peak times) or, better still, bus no. 333 (a long, bendy bus). This takes about 40 minutes. You will need to buy a ticket for this bus at newsdealers or 7-Eleven stores.

If you follow the water along to your right at Bondi, you'll come across a scenic cliff-top trail that takes you to **Bronte Beach** (a 20-min. walk) via gorgeous little

Tamarama, nicknamed "Glamourama" for its trendy sun-worshipers. This boutique beach is known for its dangerous rips and is often closed to swimming. Bronte has better swimming. To go straight to Bronte, catch bus no. 378 from Circular Quay, or pick up the bus at the Bondi Junction CityRail station.

Clovelly Beach, farther along the coast, is blessed with a large rock pool carved into a rock platform and sheltered from the force of the Tasman Sea. This beach is accessible for visitors in wheelchairs on a series of ramps. To reach Clovelly, take bus no. 339 from Circular Quay.

The cliff walk from Bondi will eventually bring you to **Coogee,** which has a pleasant strip of sand with a couple of hostels and hotels nearby. To reach Coogee, take bus no. 373 or 374 from Circular Quay (on Pitt, George, and Castlereagh sts., and Taylor Sq. on Oxford St.), or bus no. 314 or 315 from Bondi Junction.

NORTH OF SYDNEY HARBOUR

On the North Shore you'll find **Manly ★★**, a long curve of golden sand edged with Norfolk Island pines. Follow the crowds shuffling through the pedestrian Corso to the main ocean beach. (Don't be fooled by the two small beaches on either side of the ferry terminal, as some people have—including the novelist Arthur Conan Doyle, who traveled to Manly by ferry and, presuming the small beach near the ferry station was the best the suburb had to offer, did not bother to disembark.)

You'll find one of Sydney's nicest walks here, too. Looking at the ocean, head to your right along the beachfront and follow the coastal path to small and sheltered **Shelly Beach ★**, a nice area for snorkeling and swimming. (A small takeout outlet that sells drinks and snacks sits next to the good, but pricey, Le Kiosk beachfront restaurant.) Follow the bitumen path up the hill to the car park. Here, a track cuts up into the bush and leads toward a firewall, which marks the entrance to the Sydney Harbour National Park. Around here you'll have spectacular ocean views across to Manly and the northern beaches. (The headland farther in the distance is Palm Beach.) The best way to reach Manly is on a ferry from Circular Quay.

Farther north along the coast are a string of ocean beaches. (See the "Greater Sydney" map earlier in this chapter for a map of this area.) They include the surf spots of **Curl Curl, Dee Why, Narrabeen, Mona Vale, Newport, Avalon,** and finally **Palm Beach ★**, a long and beautiful strip of sand separated from the calmer waters of **Pittwater** by sand dunes and a golf course. Here you'll find the Barrenjoey Lighthouse, which offers fine views along the coast. Take bus no. 136 or 139 from

Grin & Bare It

If getting an all-over tan is your scene, you have a couple of options in Sydney. The nudist beach at Lady Jane Bay is a short walk from Camp Cove Beach. You get there from Cliff Street in Watsons Bay, reached by walking along the strip of sand—to the right as you look at the sea—at the back of the Watsons Bay Hotel. Or you can try Cobblers Beach, off the short, but steep, bush track that leads from the far side of the playing field oval next to the main HMAS *Penguin* naval base at the end of Bradley's Head Road in Mosman. (Follow the procession of men in shorts.) Be prepared for a largely male-oriented scene—as well as the odd boatload of beer-swigging peeping toms.

Manly to Curl Curl. Bus no. 190 runs from Wynyard to Newport and then via the other northern beaches as far as Palm Beach.

The best harbor beach is at **Balmoral ★**, a wealthy North Shore hangout with some good cafes (the **Sandbar** is the best for food) and two good, upmarket beach-view restaurants—the **Bathers' Pavilion** (✆ **02/9969 5050**) and the **Watermark** (✆ **02/9968 3433**). The beach itself is split into three parts: As you look toward the sea, the middle section is the most popular with sunbathers, and the wide expanse to your left and the sweep of surreally beautiful sand to your right have a mere scattering. Reach Balmoral on the ferry to Taronga Zoo and then a 10-minute ride on a connecting bus from the ferry wharf, or catch the bus from the stop outside the zoo's top entrance.

Museums, Galleries, Historic Houses & More

Art Gallery of New South Wales The galleries here present some of the best of Australian art and many fine examples by international artists, including good displays of Aboriginal and Asian art. You enter from the Domain parklands (across the road from the Royal Botanic Gardens) on the third floor of the museum. On the fourth floor you will find an expensive restaurant and a gallery that often mounts free photography displays. On the second floor is a wonderful cafe overlooking the wharves of Woolloomooloo. Every January and February there is a display of the best work created by school students throughout the state. Allow at least 1 hour.

Art Gallery Rd., The Domain. ✆ **02/9225 1744.** www.artgallery.nsw.gov.au. Free admission to most galleries. Special exhibitions vary; usually around A$15 adults, A$8 children. Thurs–Tues 10am–5pm; Wed 10am–9pm. Tours of general exhibits Sat–Sun 11am, 1 and 2pm; Mon 1 and 2pm; Tues–Fri 11am, noon, 1 and 2pm. Tours of Aboriginal galleries Tues–Sun 11am. Free Aboriginal performance Tues–Sat noon. CityRail: St. James. Sydney Explorer bus.

Australian Museum Though nowhere near as impressive as, say, the Natural History Museum in London, Sydney's premier natural history museum is still worth a look. Displays are presented thematically, the best being the Aboriginal section with its traditional clothing, weapons, and everyday implements. There are some sorry examples of stuffed Australian mammals, as well as stuffed birds, an insect display, and a mineral collection. Allow 1 to 2 hours.

6 College St. ✆ **02/9320 6000.** www.austmus.gov.au. Admission A$12 adults, A$6 children, A$30 families. Special exhibits extra. Daily 9:30am–5pm. Closed Dec 25. CityRail: Museum, St. James, or Town Hall. Sydney Explorer bus.

Elizabeth Bay House A good example of colonial architecture, this house was built in 1835 and was described at the time as the "finest house in the colony." Visitors can tour the entire house and get a real feeling of the history of the fledgling settlement. The house is on a headland and has some of the best harbor views in Sydney. Allow 1 hour.

7 Onslow Ave., Elizabeth Bay. ✆ **02/9356 3022.** www.hht.net.au. Admission A$8 adults, A$4 children, A$17 families. Fri–Sun 9:30am–4pm. Closed Good Friday and Dec 25. Bus: 311 from Circular Quay. Sydney Explorer bus.

Museum of Sydney You'll need to have your brain in full working order to make the most of the contents of this three-story postmodern building near Circular Quay, which encompasses the remnants of Sydney's first Government House. The place is far from a conventional showcase of history; instead, it houses a rather minimalist collection of first-settler and Aboriginal objects and multimedia displays that "invite" the museumgoer to discover Sydney's past for him- or herself. Some Frommer's readers have criticized the place—saying it's not just minimalist, it's simply unfathomable—but if you have the time and inclination, give it a go. By the way, that forest of poles filled with hair, oyster shells, and crab claws in the courtyard adjacent to the industrial-design cafe tables is called *Edge of Trees*. It's a metaphor for the first contact between Aborigines and the British. There's a reasonable cafe out front. Allow anywhere from an hour to a lifetime to understand.

37 Phillip St. ✆ **02/9251 5988.** www.hht.net.au. Admission A$10 adults, A$5 children 14 and under, A$20 families. Daily 9:30am–5pm. CityRail, bus, or ferry: Circular Quay. Sydney Explorer bus.

St. James Church Sydney's oldest surviving colonial church, begun in 1822, was designed by the government architect and former convict Francis Greenway. At one time, the church's spire served as a landmark for ships coming up the harbor, but today it looks lost amid the skyscrapers. It's worth seeking out, especially for the plaques on the wall, which pay testament to the early days of the colony when people were lost at sea, were "speared by blacks," and died while serving the British Empire overseas.

Queens Sq., Macquarie St. ✆ **02/9232 3022.** www.sjks.org.au. Free admission. Daily 8am–5pm. CityRail: St. James.

St. Mary's Cathedral Sydney's most impressive place of worship, built for its large population of Irish convicts, is a giant sandstone construction between the Domain and Hyde Park. The foundation stone was laid in 1821, but the Roman Catholic chapel was destroyed by fire in 1865. Work on the present cathedral began in 1868; but due to lack of funds, it remained unfinished until 2000, when the two spires were completed in extra-quick time for the Olympics. The stained-glass windows are impressive.

College and Cathedral sts. ✆ **02/9220 0400.** www.sydney.catholic.org.au/Cathedral/index.shtml. Free admission. Mon–Fri 6:30am–6:30pm; Sat 8am–7:30pm; Sun 6:30am–7:30pm.

State Library of New South Wales The state's main library consists of two side-by-side sections, the Mitchell and Dixon libraries. A newer reference-library complex nearby has two floors of reference materials, local newspapers, and microfiche viewers. Leave your bags in the free lockers downstairs. (You'll need a A$2 coin, which is refundable.) I highly recommend the library's leafy **Glasshouse Café,** in my opinion one of the best walk-in lunch spots in Sydney. The older building contains many older books on the ground floor, and often mounts free art and photography displays in the upstairs galleries.

Macquarie St. ✆ **02/9273 1770.** Free admission. Mon–Thurs 9am–9pm; Fri 9am–6pm; Sat–Sun and selected holidays 11am–5pm. Closed Jan 1, Good Friday, and Dec 25–26. CityRail: Martin Place. Sydney Explorer bus.

Sydney Jewish Museum Harrowing exhibits here include documents and objects relating to the Holocaust and the Jewish culture, mixed with soundscapes, audiovisual displays, and interactive media. There's also a museum shop, a resource center, a small theater, and a traditional kosher cafe. It's considered one of the best museums of its type in the world. Allow 1 to 2 hours.

148 Darlinghurst Rd., Darlinghurst. ✆ **02/9360 7999.** www.sydneyjewishmuseum.com.au. Admission A$10 adults, A$6 children, A$22 families. Mon–Thurs 10am–4pm; Fri 10am–2pm. Closed Sat–Sun, Jewish holidays, Good Friday, and Dec 25. CityRail: Kings Cross.

Sydney Observatory ★ The city's only major museum of astronomy offers visitors a chance to see the southern skies through modern and historic telescopes. The best time to visit is during the night on a guided tour, when you can take a close-up look at some of the planets. (During the day you can still see the fascinating telescopes, but no stars.) A **Space Theatre 3D ride,** which takes you zooming through the stars, is worth trying, too. The Space Theatre starts at 2:30 and 3:30pm Mondays to Fridays, and 11am, noon, and 2 and 3:30pm on weekends and daily during school holidays. Night tours go from 6:15 to 8pm and 8:15 to 10pm April to September; 8:15 to 10pm October and November; 8:30 to 10:15pm December and January; and 8:15 to 10pm February and March. Schedules are subject to change, so be sure to check the times when you book your tour. The planetarium and hands-on exhibits are also interesting.

Observatory Hill, Watson Rd., Millers Point. ✆ **02/9921 3485.** www.sydneyobservatory.com.au. Daytime A$7 adults, A$5 children, A$20 family. Guided night tours (reservations required) A$15 adults, A$10 children, A$40 families. Daily 10am–5pm. CityRail, bus, or ferry: Circular Quay.

Vaucluse House Overlooking Sydney Harbour, this house has lavish entertainment rooms and impressive stables and outbuildings. It was constructed in 1803 and was the home of Charles Wentworth, the architect of the Australian Constitution. It's set in 11 hectares (27 acres) of gardens, bushland, and beach frontage—perfect for picnics. Allow 1 hour.

Wentworth Rd., Vaucluse. ✆ **02/9388 7922.** www.hht.nsw.gov.au. Admission A$8 adults, A$4 children, A$17 family. House Tues–Sun 10am–4:30pm; grounds daily 7am–5pm. Free guided tours. Closed Good Friday and Dec 25. Bus: 325 from Circular Quay. Bondi & Bay Explorer buses.

Parks & Gardens

IN SYDNEY

ROYAL BOTANIC GARDENS If you are going to spend time in one of Sydney's green spaces, make it the **Royal Botanic Gardens** ★ (✆ **02/9231 8111**), next to the Sydney Opera House. I love the occasional signs on the lawns: PLEASE WALK ON THE GRASS! WE ALSO INVITE YOU TO SMELL THE ROSES, HUG THE TREES, TALK TO THE BIRDS, AND PICNIC ON THE LAWNS. The gardens were laid out in 1816 on the site of a farm that supplied food for the colony. They're informal in appearance, with a scattering of duck ponds and open spaces, though several areas are dedicated to particular plant species. These include the rose garden, the cacti and succulent display, and the central palm and rainforest groves. (Watch out for the thousands of large fruit bats, which chatter and argue among the rainforest trees.) **Mrs. Macquarie's Chair,** along the coast path, offers superb views of the Opera House and the Harbour Bridge. The "chair" is a step cut out of sandstone with a huge stone plaque on top. It bears the name of Elizabeth Macquarie (1788–1835), the wife of Governor Lachlan Macquarie. (It's a favorite stop for tour buses.) The sandstone building dominating the gardens nearest to the Opera House is the **Government House,** once the official residence of the governor of New South Wales. (He moved out in 1996, in the spirit of republicanism.) The gardens are open to the public daily from 10am to 4pm, and the house is open Friday through Sunday from 10am to 3pm. Entrance to both is free.

A popular walk takes you through the Royal Botanic Gardens to the **Art Gallery of New South Wales** (see above). The gardens are open daily from 7am to dusk. Admission is free.

HYDE PARK In the center of the city is Hyde Park, a favorite with lunching businesspeople. Of note here are the **Anzac Memorial** to Australian and New Zealand troops killed in action and the **Archibald Fountain,** complete with spitting turtles and sculptures of Diana and Apollo. At night, twinkling lights illuminate avenues of trees, giving the place a magical appearance.

MORE CITY PARKS Another Sydney favorite is giant **Centennial Park** (✆ **02/9339 6699**), usually entered from the top of Oxford Street. It opened in 1888 to celebrate the centenary of European settlement and today encompasses huge areas of lawn, several lakes, picnic areas with outdoor grills, cycling and running paths, and a cafe. It's open from sunrise to sunset. To get there, take bus no. 373, 374, 378, 380, or 3333 from the city, or the Bondi & Bay Explorer.

A hundred years later, **Bicentennial Park,** at Australia Avenue, in Homebush Bay, came along. Forty percent of the park's total 100 hectares (247 acres) is general parkland reclaimed from a city dump; the rest is the largest existing remnant of wetlands on the Parramatta River, home to many species of local and migratory wading birds, cormorants, and pelicans. Follow park signs. To reach the park, take a CityRail train to Homebush Bay station.

BEYOND SYDNEY

SYDNEY HARBOUR NATIONAL PARK You don't need to go far to experience Sydney's nearest national park. The Sydney Harbour National Park stretches around parts of the inner harbor and includes several small islands. (Many first-time visitors are surprised at the amount of bushland remaining in prime-real-estate territory.) The best walk through the Sydney Harbour National Park is the **Manly to Spit Bridge Scenic Walkway** (✆ **02/9977 6522**). This 10km (6-mile) track winds its way from Manly (it starts near the Oceanarium) via Dobroyd Head to Spit Bridge, where you can catch a bus back to the city. The walk takes around 3 hours at a casual pace, and the views across busy Sydney Harbour are fabulous. There are a few Aboriginal stone carvings, which are signposted along the route. Maps are available from the **Manly Visitors Information Centre** in the ferry terminal building.

Also part of the national park is the restored **Fort Denison,** that tiny island fort you can see in the middle of the harbor between Circular Quay and Manly. The fort was built during the Crimean War, in response to fears of a Russian invasion, and was later used as a penal colony. **Heritage Tours** of the island leave from Cadmans Cottage, 110 George St., The Rocks (✆ **02/9247 5033**). Tours operate at 10:15am, 12:15pm, and 2:30pm Wednesday to Sunday; and 12:15pm and 2:30pm Monday and Tuesday. They cost A$27 for adults, A$17 for students and children. The return ferry trip, tour, and time spent on the island means you should plan on 3 hours or so. Pick up maps of the Sydney Harbour National Park at Cadmans Cottage.

Another great walk in Sydney can be combined with lunch or a drink at Watsons Bay. A 15-minute bush stroll to **South Head** starts from the small beach outside the Watsons Bay Hotel. Walk to the end of the beach (to your right as you look at the water), up the flight of steps to Short Street, and then left along Cliff Street to the end of Camp Cove Beach. Continue along the coast past the nudist Lady Bay Beach to the lighthouse at South Head, where there are some great views (of the coastline, not the nudists). Across the road in front of the Watsons Bay Hotel is another section of the national park, known for its cliff-top views. Here you'll find The Gap, a sheer cliff popular for suicides, sadly. Ferries from Circular Quay and the Bondi & Bay Explorer go to Watsons Bay.

MORE NATIONAL PARKS The largest national parks in the Sydney area form a semicircle around the city: To the west is the **Blue Mountains National Park** (see chapter 6); to the northeast is **Ku-ring-gai Chase National Park;** and to the south is the magnificent **Royal National Park.** All three parks are home to marsupials such as echidnas and wallabies, numerous bird and reptile species, and a broad range of native plant life. Walking tracks, which take as little as half an hour to as long as a few days to cover, make each park accessible to visitors.

Ku-ring-gai Chase National Park (✆ **02/9457 9322** or 9457 9310) is a great place to take a bushwalk through gum trees and rainforest; look out for wildflowers, sandstone rock formations, and Aboriginal art. There are plenty of tracks through the park; one of my favorites is a relatively easy 2.5km (1½-mile) tramp to the **Basin** (Track 12). The well-graded dirt path takes you down to a popular estuary with a beach and passes some significant Aboriginal engravings. There are also wonderful water views over Pittwater from the picnic areas at **West Head.** Pick up a free walking guide at the park entrance, or gather maps and information in Sydney at the National Parks & Wildlife Service's center at **Cadmans Cottage,** 110 George St., The Rocks (✆ **02/9247 8861**).

The park is open from sunrise to sunset, and admission is A$11 per car. You can either drive to the park or catch a ferry from Palm Beach to the Basin (from there, you can walk up Track 12 and back). Ferries run on the hour (except at 1pm) from 9am to 5pm daily and cost A$4.50 one-way; call ✆ **02/9918 2747** for details. Shorelink bus no. 577 runs from the Turramurra CityRail station to the nearby park entrance every hour Monday to Friday and every 2 hours Saturday and Sunday; call ✆ **02/9457 8888** for details. There is no train service to the park. Camping is allowed only at the Basin (✆ **02/9457 9853**) and costs A$14 per adult and A$7 per child.

If you have a car, you can visit the **Ku-ring-gai Wildflower Garden,** 420 Mona Vale Rd., St. Ives (✆ **02/9440 8609**), which is essentially a huge area of natural bushland and a center for urban bushland education. There are plenty of bushwalking tracks, self-guided walks, and a number of nature-based activities. It's open daily from 8am to 4pm. Admission is free.

South of Sydney is the remarkable **Royal National Park,** Farrell Avenue, Sutherland (✆ **02/9542 0648**). It's the world's oldest national park, declared in 1879. (The main competitor to the title is Yellowstone in the United States, which was set aside for conservation in 1872 but not designated a national park until 1883.) There's a visitor center at Audley Weir (past the main park entrance). You'll have to pay a A$11 per-car entry fee to enter the park, but not if you only intend to go to Bundeena or are driving through to the south coast. Be careful on this road: Cars and motorbikes tend to speed, and a lack of a bicycle path (on a popular bicycle route) can make things even more tricky.

There are several ways to reach the park, but my favorites are the little-known access points from Bundeena and Otford. To get to **Bundeena,** take a CityRail train from Central Station to the seaside suburb of Cronulla (around 1 hr.). Just below the train station, through an underpass, you'll find Cronulla Wharf. From there, hop on the delightful little ferry run by **National Park Ferries** (✆ **02/9523 2990**) to Bundeena, which I highly recommend you visit. There are three main beaches here, two of them edged by national park. All of them are beautiful. Shops and cafes are also here. Ferries run on the half-hour from Cronulla (except 12:30pm on weekdays). The last one back from Bundeena is at 7pm (6pm in winter). After you get off the ferry, the first turn on your left just up the hill will take you through part of the village to wonderful Jibbon Beach. Walk along the beach to the end, hop up some rocks, and follow the track (about 20 min.) through the park to Jibbon Head for some stunning ocean views. Look out for the Aboriginal rock carvings off to your right before you reach it. (A sign points toward the headland, but the carvings are to your right.) It's around a 3-hour round-trip walk to Marley Beach (which has strong surf and dangerous rips) and a 6-hour round-trip to beautiful Wattamolla, where there's safe swimming for children in the salty lagoon. The ferry returns to Cronulla from Bundeena hourly on the hour (except 1pm). The fare is A$5.70 for adults, A$2.70 for children aged 4 to 15, and A$17 for a family, each way. Look up **www.visitbundeena.com** for more details.

A good way to see the park from Bundeena is to hire a canoe from **Bundeena Kayaks** (**© 02/9544 5294;** www.bundeenakayaks.com.au) at the gorgeous Bonnievale Beach. Single kayaks cost A$20 per hour, A$50 for a half-day, and A$70 for a full day. Kayaks built for two people cost A$30 per hour, A$80 for a half-day, and A$100 for a full day. There are guided options too.

If you fancy exploring the water from Cronulla, including the edge of the Royal National Park, make your way to the ferry terminal for an exploration of Port Hacking. **Cronulla Ferries** (**© 02/9523 2990;** www.cronullaferries.com.au) runs daily cruises onboard the historic *Tom Thumb III* daily from September to May, and on Sundays, Mondays, Wednesdays, and Fridays from June to August. Three-hour cruises depart at 10:30am and cost A$20 for adults, A$15 for kids, and A$55 for a family. Another operator, **Cronulla Cruises** (**© 02/9544 1400;** www.cronullacruises.com.au), runs ecocruises on a flat-bottomed pontoon boat, which allows for better views and more maneuverability. Cruises run from 9am every Wednesday, Saturday, and Sunday and cost A$33 for adults and A$22 for kids under 12. The cruise takes 3½ hours, and you have the option of stopping off at Audley Weir for 4 hours, which is a bit of a waste of time if you have a packed day ahead of you. One of their newer cruises takes in Aboriginal culture. This 4½-hour boat ride leaves Cronulla Wharf at 9am and includes informative talks on the native plants and wildlife, visits to Aboriginal shell middens, local rock art created thousands of years before European settlement, and meeting a couple of Aboriginal dancers. The cost of the cruise is A$125.

An alternative way to reach the park is to take the train from Central Station to **Otford,** and then climb the hill up to the sea cliffs. If you're driving, you might want to follow the scenic cliff-edge road down into Wollongong. The entrance to the national park is a little tricky to find, so you might have to ask directions—but roughly, it's just to the left of a cliff top popular for hang gliding, radio-controlled airplanes, and kites. A 2-hour walk from the sea cliffs through beautiful and varying bushland and a palm forest will take you to Burning Palms Beach. There is no water along the route. ***Warning:*** The walk back up is steep, so attempt this trek only if you're reasonably fit. Trains to the area are irregular, and the last one departs around 4pm, so give yourself at least 2½ hours for the return trip to the train station to make sure you don't get stranded. It's possible to walk the memorable 26km (16 miles) from Otford to Bundeena, or vice versa, in 2 days. (Take all your food, water, and camping gear.) The track sticks to the coast, crosses several beaches, and is relatively easy to follow. If you have A$850 per person to spend you could opt for a guided 2-day tour with tent accommodation and gourmet food. Look up **www.thecoasttrack.com.au** for details. If you are contemplating doing it alone then this website has some nice pictures.

HARBOR CRUISES & ORGANIZED TOURS

For details on the **Sydney Explorer** bus, see "Getting Around," p. 101.

Harbor Cruises

The best thing about Sydney is the harbor, and you shouldn't leave without taking a harbor cruise. **Captain Cook Cruises,** departing Jetty 6, Circular Quay (✆ **02/9206 1111;** www.captaincook.com.au), also offers several harbor excursions on its sleek vessels, with commentary along the way. Examples include a three-course **Top Deck Lunch,** departing at 12:30pm daily, and costing A$82 for adults and A$50 for children. Its **Sydney Harbour Explorer cruise** is popular and stops off at The Rocks, Watson's Bay, Taronga Zoo, and Darling Harbour. You get on and off when you want. It costs A$35 for adults, A$19 for kids aged 5 to 14. It leaves from Wharf 6, Circular Quay at 9:45am, and every 45 minutes until 5:15pm. Another favorite is the 1-hour 15-minute **Harbour Highlights Cruise,** which costs A$29 for adults, A$15 for kids, and A$59 for families. It leaves Circular Quay at 9:30am, 11am, 12:45pm, 2:30pm, and 4:30pm. The company also offers a range of other cruises, including dinner cruises, coffee cruises, and a Sunday morning breakfast cruise.

Captain Cook cruises have ticket booths at Jetty 6, Circular Quay (open 8:30am–7pm daily), and at 1 King Street Wharf, Darling Harbour (near the Sydney Aquarium). It has limited opening hours of 11am to 4pm daily.

Matilda Cruises (✆ **02/9264 7377;** www.matilda.com.au) offers a whole range of sightseeing, lunch, and dinner cruises. Its 1-hour **Rocket Harbour Express** narrated sightseeing tour leaves the pontoon at the far end of Sydney Aquarium at Darling Harbour eight times daily beginning at 9:30am (six times daily in winter, Apr–Sept, beginning at 10:30am). You can stay on for the full hour, or get off and on again at Circular Quay, Darling Harbour, Watsons Bay, Luna Park, and Taronga Zoo. The last boat leaves Taronga Zoo at 5:10pm in summer (4:10pm in winter). The cruise costs A$38 for adults and A$22 for children 5 to 14.

The company also offers a **Zoo Express,** including zoo entry, from both Darling Harbour and Circular Quay. It costs A$45 for adults and A$39 for kids.

Matilda Cruises have a ticket booth at Jetty 6 at Circular Quay, and a ticket office next to the Sydney Aquarium at Darling Harbour. Other cruise operators also have booths and information available at Circular Quay and Darling Harbour.

Yellow Water Taxis (✆ **02/9299 0199;** www.yellowwatertaxis.com) offers a 15-minute Mini Tour by small water taxi operating from their harbor bases at King Street Wharf in Darling Harbour and Circular Quay Jetty 1. This tour is good for a quick look at Sydney's famous harbor and a great way to travel to or from Darling Harbour and Circular Quay. The tours depart every 20 minutes from 10am until sunset and cost A$15 for adults, A$10 children (4–12 years of age), and A$80 for a family. A 45-minute Harbour Highlights Tour includes "Hop on–Hop off" options at Darling Harbour, Luna Park, Taronga Zoo, and the Sydney Opera House. This tour costs A$40 for adults, A$20 for kids, and A$100 for a family.

HARBOR CRUISE TICKETS & INFO It's a good idea to check websites before you come to Australia, or pop into a ticket office at Darling Harbour or Circular Quay, because cruise options, departure times, and prices change frequently. You can book on the Net, too.

Sydney by Air

If you have the cash, then a scenic tour of Sydney Harbour and beyond by plane or helicopter might be a nice investment in time. Sydney Helicopters, 25 Wentworth St., Granville (✆ 02/9637 4455; www.sydney helicopters.com.au), offers short flights from A$195 per person including lunch; longer flights—including a fabulous 7-hour country pub crawl for A$895—are on offer as well.

Sydney by Seaplane, Rose Bay Seaplane Base, Lyne Park, Rose Bay (✆ 02/9974 1455; www.sydneyby seaplane.com), flies over Sydney Harbour, Bondi Beach, the Northern Beaches, and beyond, and has several flight and dining packages. A 15-minute scenic flight costs A$160. A 30-minute flight costs A$240. Sydney Harbour Seaplanes, same address as above (✆ 02/9388 1978; www.seaplanes.com.au), offers similar packages but doesn't have a discount rate for children.

Yachting

Sydney by Sail (✆ **02/9280 1110;** www.sydneybysail.com.au) offers sailing courses on Sydney Harbour. It's based at Darling Harbour. A skippered, 3-hour afternoon sail leaving at 1pm costs A$150 for adults and A$75 for kids under 12.

Walking Tours

The center of Sydney is compact, and you can see a lot in a day on foot. If you want to learn more about Sydney's early history, you can book an excellent guided tour with **The Rocks Walking Tours ★★**, based at 23 Playfair St., Rocks Square, The Rocks (✆ **02/9247 6678;** www.rockswalkingtours.com.au). They leave Monday through Friday at 10:30am, 12:30pm, and 2:30pm (in Jan 10:30am and 2:30pm), and Saturday and Sunday at 11:30am and 2pm. The 1½-hour tour costs A$30 for adults, A$15 for children ages 10 to 16, A$75 for families, free for accompanied children under 10.

Another interesting experience is **The Rocks Pub Tour** (✆ **1300/797 010;** www.therockspubtour.com), a journey aimed at illuminating the lives of the sailors and whalers who once lived around here. You get to meet some of the locals, visit three historic pubs, take a wander around the alleyways, try a brew or two, and enjoy special offers for pub meals. The 1½-hour tour departs from Cadmans Cottage at 5pm daily (except public holidays, New Year's Eve, and St. Patrick's Day). It costs A$36. You must be over 18.

Motorcycle Tours

Blue Thunder Motorcycle Tours (✆ **1300 258 384** in Australia; www.blue thunderdownunder.com.au) runs Harley-Davidson tours of Sydney, the Blue Mountains, and places around New South Wales. A 1-hour ride (you sit on the back of the bike) around the city costs A$110. A 1½-hour ride through the city and out to Bondi costs A$155. A 3-hour trip to the northern beaches or down the south coast through the Royal National Park costs A$240. Full-day trips including lunch and snacks cover the Hunter Valley, the south coast, Bathurst, or the Blue Mountains.

If you love motorbikes and want to take one out on your own for a self-guided or guided tour, contact **Bikescape** (✆ **02/9356 2453;** www.bikescape.com.au). It will rent you a bike to go around Sydney, or as far afield as Byron Bay or the Great Ocean Road in Victoria.

STAYING ACTIVE

BIKING The best place to cycle in Sydney is Centennial Park. Rent bikes from **Centennial Park Cycles,** 50 Clovelly Rd., Randwick (✆ **02/9398 5027;** www.cyclehire.com.au), which is 200m (656 ft.) from the Musgrave Avenue entrance. (The park has five main entrances.) Mountain bikes cost A$15 for the first hour, A$20 for 2 hours, A$40 for 4 hours, and A$50 for a full day. Extra days cost just A$10 each.

Bonza Bike Tours (✆ **02/9247 8800;** www.bonzabiketours.com) runs regular bike tours of the city, and also hires out bikes. A half-day city tour costs A$89 for adults and A$69 for kids, including a bike and helmet. They also offer a tour of Manly, and another that takes you across Sydney Harbour Bridge. Bike hire alone costs A$50 a day and A$35 a half-day, plus a A$20 delivery fee to your hotel. Visit, and meet at, their shop at 55 Harrington St., The Rocks.

GOLF Sydney has over 90 golf courses and plenty of fine weather. The 18-hole championship course at **Moore Park Golf Club,** Cleveland Street and Anzac Parade, Waterloo (✆ **02/9663 1064**), is the nearest to the city. Greens fees are A$45 Monday through Friday, and A$55 Saturday and Sunday. For general information on courses, call the **New South Wales Golf Association** (✆ **02/9264 8433**).

IN-LINE SKATING The best places to skate are along the beachside promenades at Bondi and Manly beaches and in Centennial Park. **Skater HQ Manly,** 49 N. Steyne (✆ **02/9976 3833**), rents skates for A$20 for 1 hour, A$25 for 2 hours, A$30 overnight, and A$35 for 24 hours. Kids skates are A$5 cheaper. It also hires skateboards. Lessons are A$30, including 1-hour skate rental and a half-hour lesson.

JOGGING The **Royal Botanic Gardens, Centennial Park,** and any **beach** are the best places to kick-start your body. You can also run across the Harbour Bridge, though you'll have to put up with the car fumes. Another popular spot is along the sea cliffs from Bondi Beach to Bronte Beach.

SCUBA DIVING Plenty of people learn to dive in Sydney before taking off for the Barrier Reef. Don't expect coral reefs, though. **Pro Dive,** 27 Alfreda St., Coogee (✆ **1800/820 820;** www.prodive.com), offers a 4-day learn-to-dive program (Tues–Thurs, or over 2 weekends), which costs A$387 and includes six ocean dives.

SURFING **Bondi Beach** and **Tamarama** are the best surf beaches on the south side of Sydney Harbour. **Manly, Narrabeen, Bilgola, Collaroy, Long Reef,** and **Palm** beaches are the most popular on the north side. Most beach suburbs have surf shops where you can rent a board. At Bondi Beach, **Lets Go Surfing,** 128 Ramsgate Ave. (✆ **02/9365 1800;** www.letsgosurfing.com.au), rents surfboards for A$25 for 2 hours or A$40 all day. There are discounts for all-week hire, and you can also hire wet suits. The company also offers a range of surfing lessons, both in a group and individually. A 2-hour session in a small group costs between A$89 and A$99. One-hour private lessons cost A$140. In Manly, **Aloha Surf,** 44 Pittwater Rd. (✆ **02/9976 3732**), rents surfboards. **Manly Surf School** (✆ **02/9977 6977,**

A Surf Adventure

If you've always fancied learning to surf, then head for **Waves Surf School** (✆ **1800/851 101** in Australia, or 02/9369 3010; www.wavessurfschool.com.au). It takes budding surfers on 1-day trips from Sydney to the Royal National Park. Trips cost A$79, including equipment and lunch. You might consider a 2-day surfing trip to Seal Rocks, north of Sydney, for A$199. The company also takes adventurous travelers on a 4-day surfing trip from Sydney to Byron Bay for A$439. There are options to get back to Sydney too.

or 0418/717 313 mobile; www.manlysurfschool.com) offers 2-hour small-group surf classes for A$60. The more lessons you take, the cheaper each one turns out. For A$99 you get a full day outing including pick up from the city, lessons, and surfing at various places on the northern beaches.

SWIMMING If you don't mind the trek to get there, the best place to swim indoors in Sydney is the **Sydney Aquatic Centre,** at Olympic Park, Homebush Bay (✆ **02/9752 3666**). It's open Monday through Friday from 5am to 9:45pm and Saturday, Sunday, and public holidays from 6am to 7:45pm (6:45pm May–Oct). The charge is A$6.60 adults, A$5.20 children 4 to 15, and A$21 families.

The most central of Sydney's pools is **Cook and Phillip Park,** 4 College St., at William Street (✆ **02/9326 0444**). The center has three pools: one for serious swimmers, another with a wave machine, and a hydrotherapy pool with easy ramp access and bubble jets. Entry is A$6.20 for adults and A$4.70 for kids. To find it, walk to the cathedral across Hyde Park and continue for a couple of minutes along the dark paved area outside the cathedral's front entrance (keeping Hyde Park on your right). Look for signs directing you down some stairs to the entrance. It's open daily from 6am to 10pm.

Another good pool is the **Andrew (Boy) Charlton Swimming Pool,** the Domain, Mrs. Macquaries Road, near the Royal Botanical Gardens (✆ **02/9358 6686**). From this heated outdoor pool there are fabulous views across Sydney Harbour. There's also a learner's pool and a toddler's pool. Entry is A$6.20 for adults and A$4.70 for kids. It's open from 6am to 7pm daily.

Across the Harbour Bridge, near Luna Park, is the **North Sydney Olympic Pool,** Alfred South Street, Milsons Point (✆ **02/9955 2309**). You can refresh yourself in this outdoor pool after a walk over the bridge. Entry costs A$5.80 for adults and A$2.90 for children. There's a separate indoor pool, too. It's open from 5:30am to 9pm Monday to Friday, and 7am to 7pm on weekends.

The **Bondi Icebergs Club,** 1 Notts Ave. (✆ **02/9130 4804**), at Bondi Beach, on the rocks to the right of the beach as you look at the sea, has an Olympic-size pool and a children's pool. Entrance costs A$5 for adults and A$3 for kids, and includes a sauna. It's open from 6am to 7pm Monday to Friday and 6:30am to 6:30pm on weekends.

TENNIS There are hundreds of places around the city to play one of Australia's most popular sports. A nice spot is the **Miller's Point Tennis Court,** Kent Street, The Rocks (✆ **02/9256 2222**). It's run by the Observatory Hotel and is open daily from 7:30am to 10pm. The court costs A$20 per hour. Racket hire is A$5 per hour. The **North Sydney Tennis Centre,** 1A Little Alfred St., North Sydney (✆ **02/9371 9952**), has three courts available daily from 6am to 10pm. They cost A$18 until 5pm on weekdays and A$22 at other times.

SPECTATOR SPORTS

CRICKET The **Sydney Cricket Ground,** at the corner of Moore Park and Driver Avenue, is famous for its 1-day and test matches, played October through March. Tickets cost from A$44. Over the winter months, Aussie Rules games featuring the Sydney Swans are also played here. Look up **www.sydneycricketground.com.au** for match details. Tours of the stadium start at 10am and 1pm Monday to Friday and at 10am on Saturday. They cost A$25 for adults, A$17 for kids, and A$65 for a family. Call ✆ **1300/724 737** to book.

FOOTBALL In this city, "football" means rugby league. If you want to see burly chaps pound into one another while chasing an oval ball, then be here between May and September. The biggest venue is the **Sydney Football Stadium,** Moore Park Road, Paddington (✆ **02/9360 6601,** or 1900/963 133 for match information). Buy tickets through **Ticketek** (✆ **02/9266 4800**).

HORSE RACING Sydney has four horse-racing tracks: Randwick, Canterbury, Rosehill, and Warwick Farm. The most central and best known is **Randwick Racecourse,** Alison Street, Randwick (✆ **02/9663 8400**). The biggest race day of the week is Saturday. Entry costs from A$25. Call the **Sydney Turf Club** (✆ **02/9930 4000**) with questions about Rosehill and Canterbury, and the Randwick number for Warwick Farm information.

SURFING CARNIVALS Every summer, these uniquely Australian competitions bring crowds to Sydney's beaches to watch surf clubs compete in various watersports. Contact the **Surf Lifesaving Association** (✆ **02/9597 5588**) for times and locations. Other beach events include Iron Man and Iron Woman competitions, during which Australia's fittest struggle it out in combined swimming, running, and surfing events.

YACHT RACING Sailing competitions take place on the harbor most summer weekends, but the start of the **Sydney to Hobart Yacht Race,** on Boxing Day (Dec 26), is a must-see. The race starts from the harbor near the Royal Botanic Gardens.

SHOPPING

You'll find plenty of places to keep your credit cards in action in Sydney. Most shops of interest to the visitor are in **The Rocks** and along **George and Pitt streets** (including the shops below the Sydney Tower and along Pitt Street Mall, although at press time, there was a massive redevelopment effort going on here). Other precincts worth checking out are **Mosman,** on the North Shore; **Double Bay,** in the eastern suburbs, for boutique shopping; **Chatswood,** for its shopping centers; the **Sydney Fishmarket,** for the sake of it; and various **weekend markets** (listed later).

Don't miss the **Queen Victoria Building (QVB),** on the corner of Market and George streets. This Victorian shopping arcade is one of the prettiest in the world and has some 200 boutiques—mostly men's and women's fashion—on four levels.

The arcade is open 24 hours, but the shops do business Monday through Saturday from 9am to 6pm (Thurs to 9pm) and Sunday from 11am to 5pm.

The **Strand Arcade** (btw. Pitt St. Mall and George St.) was built in 1892 and is interesting for its architecture and small boutiques, food stores, and cafes, and the Downtown Duty Free store on the basement level.

On **Pitt Street Mall** you'll find a few shops—but lots of building work that will continue through much of 2011. **Oxford Street** runs from the city to Bondi Junction through Paddington and Darlinghurst and is home to countless clothing stores for the style conscious. You could easily spend anywhere from 2 hours to an entire day making your way from one end to the other. Detour down William Street, once you get to Paddington, to visit the headquarters of celebrated international Australian designer Collette Dinnigan. On the same street are the trendy boutiques Belinda and Corner Store (cutting-edge designs), and Pelle and Di Nuovo (luxury recycled goods).

Tip: American Express cards seem to be unpopular with many shop owners.

SHOPPING HOURS Regular shopping hours are generally Monday through Wednesday and Friday from 8:30 or 9am to 6pm, Thursday from 8:30 or 9am to 9pm, Saturday from 9am to 5 or 5:30pm, and Sunday from 10 or 10:30am to 5pm. Exceptions are noted in the store listings below.

Sydney Shopping from A to Z

ABORIGINAL ARTIFACTS & CRAFTS

Gavala Aboriginal Art & Cultural Education Centre I'd head here first if I were in the market for a decent boomerang or didgeridoo. Gavala is owned and operated by Aborigines, and it stocks plenty of authentic Aboriginal crafts, including carved emu eggs, grass baskets, cards, and books. A first-rate painted didgeridoo will cost anywhere from A$100 to A$450. Gavala also sponsors cultural talks, didgeridoo-making lessons, and storytelling sessions. Open daily from 10am to 9pm. Shop 131, Harbourside, Darling Harbour. ✆ **02/9212 7232.**

Original & Authentic Aboriginal Art Quality Aboriginal art from some of Australia's best-known painters is on sale here. Artists include Paddy Fordham Wainburranga, whose paintings hang in the White House in Washington, D.C., and Janet Forrester Nangala, whose work has been exhibited in the Australian National Gallery in Canberra. Expect to pay in the range of A$1,000 to A$4,000 for the larger paintings. There are some nice painted pots here, too, costing A$30 to A$80. Open daily from 10am to 6pm. 79 George St., The Rocks. ✆ **02/9251 4222.**

ANTIQUES

Bottom of the Harbour Antiques This Rocks institution has recently moved to a new home farther toward the Harbour Bridge. It sells a wide range of maritime-related antiques, including clocks, shells, books, brass items, statues, compasses, and other things. A real treasure chest. Open daily 10am to 6pm. 31 George St., The Rocks. ✆ **02/9247 8107.**

ART PRINTS & ORIGINALS

Billich Charles Billich has a fine-arts gallery's worth of paintings here, all done by himself. Sydney scenes intermingle with Asian-influenced works of grand scale. Open daily from 9am to 8pm. 104 George St., The Rocks. ✆ **02/9252 1481.**

131 Harbourside Darling Harb

Done Art and Design Ken Done is well known for having designed his own Australian flag, which he hopes to raise over Australia should it abandon its present one following the formation of a republic. The art here is his. The clothing designs—which feature printed sea- and beachscapes, the odd colorful bird, and lots of pastels—are by his wife, Judy. Open daily from 10am to 5:30pm. 1 Hickson Rd., off George St., The Rocks. ✆ **02/9247 2740.**

Ken Duncan Gallery This photographer-turned-salesman is making a killing from his exquisitely produced large-scale photographs of Australian scenery. Open daily from 9am to 8pm (to 9pm Thurs) in summer, 9am to 7pm in winter. 1 Hickson Rd., The Rocks. ✆ **02/9247 2740.**

BOOKS

You'll find a good selection of books on Sydney and Australia for sale at the Art Gallery of New South Wales; the Garden Shop, in the Royal Botanic Gardens; the Museum of Contemporary Art; the Museum of Sydney; the Australian Museum; and the State Library of New South Wales (see listings earlier in this chapter).

Abbey's Bookshop This interesting, centrally located shop specializes in literature, history, and mystery, and has an entire floor dedicated to language and education. 131 York St., behind the QVB. ✆ **02/9264 3111.**

Gleebooks Bookshop Specializing in art, general literature, psychology, sociology, and women's studies, Gleebooks also has a secondhand store (with a large children's department) down the road at 191 Glebe Point Rd. Open daily 8am to 9pm. 49 and 191 Glebe Point Rd., Glebe. ✆ **02/9660 2333.**

Goulds Book Arcade Come here to search for unusual dusty volumes. About a 10-minute walk from the Newtown CityRail station, the place is bursting with thousands of secondhand and new books, all in rough order. You can browse for hours here. Open daily from 8am to midnight. 32 King St., Newtown. ✆ **02/9519 8947.**

CRAFTS

Collect Some of Australia's most respected craft artists and designers are represented here. There are some wonderful glass, textile, ceramic, jewelry, metal, and wood-turned items for sale. Open daily from 9:30am to 5:30pm. 88 George St., The Rocks. ✆ **02/9247 7984.**

DEPARTMENT STORES

The two big names in Sydney shopping are David Jones and Myer. Both stores are open Monday through Wednesday and Friday through Saturday from 9am to 6pm, Thursday from 9am to 9pm, and Sunday from 11am to 5pm.

David Jones (✆ **02/9266 5544**) is the city's largest department store, selling everything from fashion to designer furniture. You'll find the women's section on the corner of Elizabeth and Market streets, and the men's section on the corner of Castlereagh and Market streets. The food section here offers expensive delicacies and eateries, and is worth a look.

Myer (✆ **02/9238 9111**), formally Grace Brothers, is similar to David Jones, but the building is newer and flashier. It's on the corner of George and Market streets.

FASHION

One of the best places to shop for fashion is the **QVB.** Fashion-statement stores featuring the best of Australian design at the QVB include Oroton, Country Road, and the fabulous woman's clothing designer Lisa Ho. In the **Strand Arcade,** off Pitt Street Mall, find Third Millennium, Allanah Hill, and Wayne Cooper.

Farther down toward Circular Quay is **Chifley Plaza,** home to a selection of the world's most famous and stylish international brands. For really trendy clothing, walk up Oxford Street to **Paddington,** and for alternative clothes, go to **Newtown.**

If you are looking for trendy surf- and swim-wear, the main drags at Bondi Beach and Manly Beach offer plenty of choices.

Australian Outback Clothing

R. M. Williams Moleskin trousers may not be the height of fashion at the moment, but you never know. R. M. Williams boots are famous for being both tough and fashionable. You'll find Akubra hats, Driza-bone coats, and kangaroo-skin belts here, too. 389 George St. (btw. Town Hall and Central CityRail stations). ✆ **02/9262 2228.**

Thomas Cook Boot & Clothing Company Located between Town Hall and Central CityRail stations, this place specializes in Australian boots, Driza-bone coats, and Akubra hats. There's another shop at 129 Pitt St., near Martin Place (✆ **02/9232 3334**). 790 George St., Haymarket. ✆ **02/9212 6616.** www.thomascookclothing.com.au.

Men's Fashion

Outdoor Heritage Quality clothing with a yachting influence is what you'll find at this good-looking store specializing in casual, colorful gear. Shop 13G, Sydney Central Plaza, 450 George St. ✆ **02/9235 1560.**

Unisex Fashion

Robby Ingham The collection here is made up of men's and women's brand names such as Hugo Boss and Chloe. There's a second location at 424–428 Oxford St., Paddington (✆ **02/9332 2124**). The MLC building, 19 Martin Place. ✆ **02/9232 6466.**

Women's Fashion

In addition to the places listed below, head to **Oxford Street** (particularly Paddington) for more avant-garde designers.

Akira Isagawa Internationally lauded and locally adored, few have left such an indelible watermark on the Australian fashion pages. 12a Queen St., Woollahra. ✆ **02/9361 5221.**

Belinda For those who love shoes, you can't go past this cute little shop just off Oxford Street. 39 William St., Paddington. ✆ **02/9380 8728.**

Collette Dinnigan Cinema sirens, pop royalty, and the world's most glamorous women all appreciate her seriously sexy designs; Collette's exquisite choice of fabrics has helped bring her prominence as a renowned ready-to-wear and couture designer. 33 William St., Paddington. ✆ **02/9360 6691.**

Zimmerman Zimmerman is a real Saturday-afternoon fix for lots of Sydney girls. Looking for an outfit for a big night out, or some funky swimwear? Zimmerman is the place to go. 24 Oxford St., Woollahra. ✆ **02/9360 5769.**

FOOD

The goodies you'll find downstairs in the food section of **David Jones** department store on Castlereagh Street (the men's section) are enough to tempt anyone. The store sells the best local and imported products to the rich and famous (and the rest of us).

Coles One of the few supermarkets in the city center, this place is a good bet if you want to cook for yourself or are after ready-made food (including tasty sandwiches) and cheap soft drinks. There's another Coles beneath the giant Coca-Cola sign on Darlinghurst Road, Kings Cross. Open daily from 6am to midnight. Wynyard Station, Castlereagh St., Wynyard (opposite the Menzies Hotel and the public bus stands). ✆ **02/9299 4769.**

Darrell Lea Chocolates This is the oldest location of Australia's most famous chocolate shop. Pick up some wonderful handmade chocolates as well as other unusual candies, including the best licorice this side of the Casbah. At the corner of King and George sts. ✆ **02/9232 2899.**

Sydney Fishmarket Finding out what people eat can be a good introduction to a new country, and, in my opinion, nowhere is this more fascinating than at the local fish market. Here you'll find seven major fish retailers selling everything from shark to Balmain bugs (small crayfish), with hundreds of species in between. Watch out for the local pelicans being fed the fishy leftovers. There's also a Doyles restaurant and a sushi bar, a couple of cheap seafood eateries, a fruit market, and a good deli. The retail sections are open daily from 7am to 4pm. At the corner of Bank St. and Pyrmont Bridge Rd., Pyrmont. ✆ **02/9004 1100.**

GIFTS & SOUVENIRS

The shops at **Taronga Zoo,** the **Oceanarium** in Manly, the **Sydney Aquarium,** and the **Australian Museum** are all good sources for gifts and souvenirs. Many shops around **The Rocks** are worth browsing, too.

Australian Geographic A spinoff of the Australian version of *National Geographic* magazine, this store sells good-quality crafts and Australiana. On hand are camping gadgets, telescopes, binoculars, garden utensils, scientific oddities, books, calendars, videos, music, toys, and lots more. Shop 34, Lower Ground Floor, 455 George Street, Sydney ✆ **02 9257 0086.**

National Trust Gift and Bookshop You can pick up some nice souvenirs, including books, Australiana crafts, and indigenous foodstuffs here. An art gallery on the premises presents changing exhibits of paintings and sculpture by Australians. There's also a cafe. Closed Monday. Observatory Hill, The Rocks. ✆ **02/9258 0154.**

MARKETS

Balmain Market Active from 8:30am to 4pm every Saturday, this market has some 140 vendors selling crafts, jewelry, and knickknacks. Take the ferry to Balmain (Darling St.); the market is a 10-minute walk up Darling Street. On the grounds of St. Andrew's Church, Darling St., Balmain ✆ **02/9555 1791.**

Bondi Markets A nice place to stroll around on Sunday after your brunch on Campbell Parade and discover the upcoming young Australian designers. This market specializes in clothing and jewelry, new, secondhand, and retro. It's open Sunday from 9am to 5pm. Bondi Beach School, Campbell Parade. ✆ **02/9398 5486.**

Paddington Bazaar At this Saturday-only market you'll find everything from essential oils and designer clothes to New Age jewelry and Mexican hammocks. Expect things to be busy from 10am to 4pm. Take bus no. 380 or 389 from Circular Quay and follow the crowds. On the grounds of St. John's Church, Oxford St., on the corner of Newcome St. ✆ **02/9331 2646.**

Paddy's Markets A Sydney institution, Paddy's Markets has hundreds of stalls selling everything from cheap clothes and plants to chickens. It's open Thursday through Sunday from 9am to 5pm. Above Paddy's Markets is **Market City** (✆ **02/9212 1388**), which has three floors of fashion stalls, food courts, and specialty shops. Of particular interest is the largest Asian-European supermarket in Australia, on level 1. At the corner of Thomas and Hay sts., Haymarket, near Chinatown. ✆ **1300/361 589** in Australia, or 02/9325 6924.

The Rocks Market Held every Saturday and Sunday, this touristy market has more than 100 vendors selling everything from crafts, housewares, and posters to jewelry and curios. The main street is closed to traffic from 10am to 4pm to make it easier to stroll around. George St., The Rocks. ✆ **02/9240 8717.**

OPALS

There are plenty of opal shops around in Sydney, but don't expect to walk away with any bargains. Better just to choose one you like than to haggle.

Altman & Cherny A good selection of opals—black, white, and boulder varieties—as well as jewelry is on sale here. Ask to see the "Aurora Australis," the world-famous black opal valued at A$1 million. 18 Pitt St. (near Circular Quay). ✆ **02/9251 9477.**

Australian Opal Cutters Learn more about opals before you buy at this shop. The staff will give you lessons about opals to help you compare pieces. Suite 10, Level 4, National Building, 295 Pitt St. ✆ **02/9261 2442.**

SUN GEAR & SUNGLASSES

The Cancer Council Australians are generally very aware of how damaging the sun can be. And you can get burned very quickly on a Sydney beach! The Cancer Council runs several shops throughout Sydney, with this one being in the large Westfield shopping center in the heart of Bondi Junction. You can buy great sun glasses (for around A$40), sun hats, and protective clothes, as well as discounted sun cream. Shop 5042, Westfield Bondi Junction, Oxford Street, Bondi Junction. ✆ **02/9369 4199.**

SYDNEY AFTER DARK

Australians are party animals when they're in the mood. Whether it's a few beers around the barbecue with friends or an all-night rave at a trendy dance club, they're always on the lookout for the next event. You'll find that alcohol plays a big part in the Aussie culture. The best way to find out what's going on is to get hold of the "Metro" section of the Friday *Sydney Morning Herald* or the "Seven Days" pullout from the Thursday *Daily Telegraph.*

The Performing Arts

If you have an opportunity to see a performance in the **Sydney Opera House,** jump at it. The "House" is actually not that impressive inside, but the walk back after the show toward the ferry terminals at Circular Quay, with the Sydney Harbour Bridge lit up and the crowd all around you debating the best part of this play or who dropped a beat in that performance—well, it's like hearing Gershwin on the streets of New York. You'll want the moment to stay with you forever. For details on Sydney's most famous performing-arts venue, see "What to See & Do in Sydney," earlier in this chapter.

THE OPERA, SYMPHONY & BALLET

Australian Ballet Based in Melbourne, the Australian Ballet tours the country with its performances. The Sydney season, at the Opera House, is from mid-March until the end of April. A second Sydney season runs November through December. Level 15, 115 Pitt St. ✆ **02/9223 9522.** www.australianballet.com.au.

Australian Chamber Orchestra Based in Sydney, this well-known company performs at various venues around the city, from nightclubs to specialized music venues, including the Concert Hall in the Sydney Opera House. Opera Quays, 2 East Circular Quay. ✆ **02/9357 4111,** or 02/8274 3888 box office. www.aco.com.au.

Opera Australia Opera Australia performs at the Sydney Opera House's Opera Theatre. The opera runs January through March and June through November. 480 Elizabeth St., Surry Hills. ✆ **02/9699 1099,** or 02/9319 1088 bookings. www.opera-australia.org.au.

Sydney Symphony Orchestra Sydney's finest symphony orchestra is conducted by Vladimir Ashkenazy, who succeeded Gianluigi Gelmetti as chief conductor and artistic director in January 2009. It performs throughout the year in the Opera House's Concert Hall. The main symphony season runs March through November, and there's a summer season in February. Level 5, 52 William St., East Sydney. ✆ **02/9334 4644** or 02/9334 4600 box office.

THEATER

Sydney's blessed with plenty of theaters, many more than I have space for here—check the *Sydney Morning Herald,* especially the Friday edition, for information on what's currently in production.

Belvoir Street Theatre The hallowed boards of the Belvoir are home to Company B, which pumps out powerful local and international plays upstairs in a wonderfully moody main theater, formerly part of a tomato-sauce factory. Downstairs, a smaller venue generally shows more experimental productions, such as Aboriginal performances and dance. 25 Belvoir St., Surry Hills. ✆ **02/9699 3444.** Tickets around A$34.

Capital Theatre Sydney's grandest theater plays host to major international and local productions. It's also been the Sydney home of musicals such as *Miss Saigon*

It's a Festival!

If you happen to be in Australia in January, plan to attend one of the many events that are part of the annual Sydney Festival. The festival kicks off just after New Year's and continues through the month, with recitals, plays, films, and performances at venues throughout the city, including Town Hall, the Royal Botanic Gardens, the Sydney Opera House, and Darling Harbour. Some events are free. "Jazz in the Domain" and "Symphony in the Domain" are two free outdoor performances held in the Royal Botanic Gardens, generally on the third and fourth weekends in January; each event attracts thousands of Sydneysiders. For more information, contact Festival Ticketek (✆ 02/9266 4111; fax 02/9267 4460). Buy tickets and find out about performances on the Web at www.sydneyfestival.org.au.

and *My Fair Lady.* 13–17 Campbell St., Haymarket, near Town Hall. ✆ **02/9320 5000.** Ticket prices vary.

Her Majesty's Theatre A quarter of a century old, this large theater is still trawling in the big musicals. Huge productions that have run here include *Evita* and *The Phantom of the Opera.* 107 Quay St., Haymarket, near Central Station. ✆ **02/9212 3411.** Ticket prices average A$55–A$75.

Wharf Theatre This wonderful theater is on a refurbished wharf on the edge of Sydney Harbour, just beyond the Harbour Bridge. The long walk from the entrance of the pier to the theater along old creaky wooden floorboards builds up excitement for the show. Based here is the Sydney Theatre Company, a group well worth seeing, whatever the production. Dinner before the show at the Wharf's restaurant offers special views of the harbor. Pier 4, Hickson Rd., The Rocks. ✆ **02/9250 1777.** www.sydneytheatre.com.au. Ticket prices vary.

The Club & Music Scene

DANCE CLUBS

Clubs come and go, so check the latest with a phone call. Nightclub entrance charges also change regularly, but generally are A$15 to A$20.

Home This club for the serious partier is cavelike in shape and feel, with a balcony to look down upon the throng. There's a padded "silver room" for ravers. Friday nights are big for trance and hip-hop, and Saturdays for house music. Open Friday and Saturday 11pm until dawn. Cockle Bay Wharf, Darling Harbour. ✆ **02/9267 0654.**

Lady Lux Sophisticated and intimate, Lady Lux throbs to the latest party sounds. Getting in might be tricky unless you dress and act the part. It's open Thursday to Sunday from 10pm until late. 2 Roslyn St., Potts Point (near Kings Cross). ✆ **02/9361 5000.**

Q Bar If you are in town any night of the week, then the Q Bar will be open for you. It attracts a varied crowd from youngsters to wrinklies and has everything from a serious dance spot to pool tables. Expect house music every night, with some funk on Sunday and classic hits and disco on Thursdays. Open 9pm until 7am. 44 Oxford St. ✆ **02/9360 1375.**

Tank House music, of course, is the name of the game at this belowground offshoot of the Establishment Hotel, the city's trendiest historic hot spot. The surrounds, which include three bars on two levels, attract models and film stars when they are in town. Dress casual but designer. Open Friday and Saturday from 10pm until 6am. 3 Bridge Lane, Sydney. ✆ **02/9240 3094.**

GAY & LESBIAN CLUBS

Sydney has a huge gay community, so there's a very happening scene. The center of it all is Oxford Street, though Newtown has established itself as a gay hangout, too. For information on events, pick up a copy of the *Sydney Star Observer* or *Lesbians on the Loose,* available at art-house cinemas, cafes, and stores around Oxford Street. Nightclub covers generally range from A$10 to A$15.

Arq This 24-hour club has an amazing light show and some of the best DJs in town. A very big place specializing in the latest dance tunes. Dress in drag or get buffed up. Open Thursday to Sunday 9pm to 9am. 16 Flinders St., Taylors Square, Darlinghurst. ✆ **02/9380 8700.**

Sydney Gay & Lesbian Mardi Gras

Each March, some 450,000 people pack into the city center, concentrated on Oxford Street, to watch as members of Sydney's GLBT communities pack a punch with colorful floats and frocks. The crowd is diverse, from kids to grannies, and those in the know bring a stepladder or milk crate to get a better view. Sydney's hotels are at their busiest during Mardi Gras, particularly anything with a view of the route. The postparade party is an affair not for the fainthearted! Sequins, tight pants, and anything outrageously glamorous goes. Some 19,000 revelers attend. For more information check out the official Mardi Gras website, www.mardigras.org.au.

Civic This original Art Deco hotel has been tastefully spruced up to accommodate three levels of entertainment. There's a theater on the lower first floor (basement), a saloon bar on the ground floor, and an Australian restaurant with live jazz upstairs and an outdoor cocktail terrace. Great bands. Corner of Pitt and Goulburn sts., Sydney. ✆ **02/8267 3181.**

Columbian Hotel An enormous heritage building plays host to a thriving gay scene with heterosexual undercurrents. There's a bar with music videos downstairs and a nightclub on top with a sparkling ruby chandelier. It's tasteful in its attention to detail, and both throbbing and intimate when it counts. It's open to at least 4am daily. 117–123 Oxford St., Darlinghurst. ✆ **02/9360 2152.**

Gilligan's & Ginger's A cocktail bar on the first floor of the Oxford Hotel, Gilligan's & Ginger's is home to a thriving social scene and great views of Oxford Street and the city skyline. DJs spin the latest handbag hits for the drag queens. 134 Oxford St., Darlinghurst, corner of Taylor Sq. ✆ **02/9331 3467.**

The Stonewall Hotel An institution with three levels of entertainment and many special nights. Don't miss Sydney's diva, Ricca Paris, on Wednesday nights at the Malebox party, where lustful notes are passed between guests. Daily noon to 5am. 175 Oxford St., Darlinghurst. ✆ **02/9360 1963.** Free entry most nights.

Taxi Club "Tacky Club," as it's affectionately known, is a Sydney institution good for "handbag music"—or old pop and new pop. 40 Flinders St., Darlinghurst (near Taylor Sq., Oxford St.). ✆ **02/9331 4256.**

JAZZ, FOLK & BLUES

The Basement ★ Australia's hottest jazz club also manages to squeeze in plenty of blues, folk, and funk. Acts appear every night, and it's best to book ahead. Call for the schedule, pick up one at the club, or visit the website. 29 Reiby Place, Circular Quay. ✆ **02/9251 2797.** www.thebasement.com.au Cover A$15–A$20 for local acts, A$20–A$40 for international performers.

side-on café Known by locals as one of the few live venues in Sydney to showcase diverse jazz nearly every night, this surprisingly decent restaurant is part of an arts complex and serves a two-course meal for A$27. Patrons are a blend of artists, musicians, and jazz lovers. The side-on endeavors to promote upcoming local talent as well as established acts and is also home to an art gallery upstairs. Located just over 5km (3 miles) from the center of town, it's not all that central but is easily reached by public transport and well worth the detour. Daily 7pm until late. 83 Parramatta Rd., Anandale, near Anandale Hotel. ✆ **02/9516 3077.** Cover A$13.

The Bar Scene

Most of Australia's drinking holes are known as "hotels," after the tradition of providing room and board alongside a good drink in the old days. Occasionally you might hear them referred to as pubs. The term "bar" tends to apply in upscale hotels and trendy establishments. Bars close at various times, generally from midnight to around 3am. Unless the listing says otherwise, these bars do not charge a cover.

Bondi Hotel This huge conglomerate across the road from Bondi Beach offers pool upstairs, a casual beer garden outside, and a resident DJ Thursday through Sunday from 8pm to 4am. There's also a free nightclub on Friday nights. Watch yourself; too much drink and sun turns some people nasty here. 178 Campbell Parade, Bondi Beach. ✆ **02/9130 3271.**

Cargo Bar & Lounge This split-level waterfront bar on the city side of Darling Harbour (past the Sydney Aquarium) has a large ground-floor bar with access to an outdoor beer garden. The lounge upstairs features trendy leather and red footstools (apparently you sit on them). Cocktails and cigars are upstairs and more casual beers downstairs. Some nice pizzas here, too—if you like them topped with emu, crocodile, or kangaroo. 52–60 The Promenade, King St. Wharf. ✆ **02/9262 1777.**

The Establishment If you want to see Sydney at its sexiest and most sophisticated, head to this four-level venue, where style is everything. Swing through the ground floor entrance on George Street near Wynyard CityRail station and you enter a huge cream-washed space with a long white marble bar and phallic columns. It's a seriously sexy place—and it doesn't end here. Upstairs there are the famous eateries est. and Sushi E, as well as Hemmesphere, a moody drinking place strung out with leather armchairs and ottomans. 252 George St., City. ✆ **02/9240 3040.**

The Friend in Hand The Friend in Hand offers cheap drinks, poetry readings on Tuesdays at 8:30pm, a comedy night on Thursdays from 7:30pm, and the distinctly unusual Crab Racing Party every Wednesday at around 8pm. Crab fanciers buy a crustacean for around A$5, give it a name, and send it off to do battle in a race against about 30 others. There are heats and finals, and victorious crustaceans win their owners prizes. 58 Cowper St., Glebe. ✆ **02/9660 2326.**

Hero of Waterloo Hotel ★ This sandstone landmark, built in 1845, was once reputedly the stalking ground of press gangs, who'd whack unsuspecting landlubbers on the head, push them down a trapdoor, and cart them out to sea. Today, the strangely shaped drinking hole is popular with the locals. It schedules piano music from 7 to 11:30pm on Wednesday and Thursday; folk music on Friday and Saturday from 8 to 11:30pm; Old Time Jazz on Saturday and Sunday from 2 to 6:30pm; and an Irish jam session on Sunday from 7 to 10pm. 81 Lower Fort St., The Rocks. ✆ **02/9252 4553.**

The Ivy ★★ The Ivy complex is the new star on the block, owned and operated by bar tsar Justin Hemmes, who also owns the Establishment. If you're part of the fashionable crowd, this is the place to be seen. There are eight zones in all, spread out over several levels. At the front of the building is the Royal George, a British "alehouse." Upstairs is a crowded courtyard with tea-light candles hanging from a Japanese maple tree; you can buy cocktails and bar food here. Also on this level is a New York–style grill called Mad Cow, which features big booths and ornate birdcages. Upstairs are other bars, including the Den, with turquoise divans and a DJ; the Ivy Lounge, with armchairs, marble-topped tables, and ceramic elephants; and also a dimly lit Japanese-influenced restaurant area called Teppanyaki. 320–330 George St., City. ✆ **02/9240 3000.**

Lord Dudley Hotel This great English-style pub has the best atmosphere of just about any drinking hole in Sydney, with log fires in winter, couches to relax on, three bars, and a restaurant. The best way to get here is from the Edgecliff CityRail station (btw. Kings Cross and Bondi Junction, which makes it a bit out of the way if you're staying in the city). From there, bear right along the edge of the bus station, walk up the hill for 5 minutes, and then take a right onto Jersey Road. Ask the railway staff for the correct exit if you can find anyone working. 236 Jersey Rd., Woollahra. ✆ **02/9327 5399.**

Lord Nelson Hotel ★ A sandstone landmark, the Lord Nelson rivals the Hero of Waterloo (see above) for the title of Sydney's oldest pub. The drinks are sold English-style, in pints and half pints, and the landlord makes his own prizewinning beers. Of those, Three Sheets is the most popular—but if you can't handle falling over on your way home, you might want to try a drop of Quail (a pale beer), Victory (based on an English bitter), or a dark beer called Admiral. You can get some reasonable pub grub here in the style of hot meat pies and mashed potatoes. Upstairs there's a more formal brasserie. Kent and Argyle sts., The Rocks. ✆ **02/9251 4044.**

Marble Bar Inside the Hilton Hotel complex, the Marble Bar is unique: the only grand cafe–style drinking hole in Australia. With oil paintings, marble columns, and brass everywhere, the Marble Bar is the picture of 15th-century Italian Renaissance architecture—despite being crafted in 1893. It's a tourist attraction in itself. Live music, generally jazz or soul, plays here Tuesday through Saturday at 8:30pm. Dress smart on Friday and Saturday evenings. In the Sydney Hilton, 259 Pitt St. ✆ **02/9266 2000.**

The Mercantile Sydney's original Irish bar is scruffy and loud when the Irish music's playing in the evening, but it's an essential stop on any pub-crawl in The Rocks. The Guinness is some of the best you'll taste in Sydney. Irish bands kick off every night around 8pm. 25 George St., The Rocks. ✆ **02/9247 3570.**

Slip Inn This multifunction bar and nightclub setup is a popular place to drink and meet. There's a garden bar downstairs in a courtyard, and a Thai bistro, too. Dug out below is a serious nightclub, the Chinese Laundry, which features house, hip-hop, and electro on Fridays and Saturdays. On Sundays, from noon until dusk, the garden bar attracts university students and 30-somethings who like to boogie. 111 Sussex St., Darling Harbour (a 2-min. walk toward the city from the Town Hall/Cockle Bay side of the pedestrian bridge across to Darling Harbour). ✆ **02/8295 9911.**

Watson's Bay Hotel ★★ If it's a sunny afternoon, get over to Watsons Bay for its glorious beer garden serving good seafood and barbecue meat dishes. The views of the harbor make this one of Sydney's best sunny-day options. It can get quite crowded on a sunny weekend.1 Military Rd., Watsons Bay. ✆ **02/9337 5644.**

Movies

The city's major movie houses, **Hoyts** (✆ **13 27 00** in Australia), **Greater Union** (✆ **02/9267 8666**), and **Village** (✆ **02/9264 6701**), are right next to one another on George Street, just past Town Hall. They tend to show big-budget movie releases. Other options are the **Dendy Cinemas,** at 19 Martin Place (✆ **02/9233 8166**); 261–263 King St., Newtown (✆ **02/9550 5699**); and 2 East Circular Quay, just before you reach the Opera House (✆ **02/9247 3800**). All show art-house movies; the Dendy Quay allows wine and beer bought on the premises to be consumed in the cinema. In Paddington, the **Palace Verona,** 17 Oxford St. (✆ **02/9360 6099**), and the **Academy Twin,** 2 Oxford St. (✆ **02/9361 4455**), conveniently located next to each other, always screen the best local and foreign films in Sydney.

Another exceptional art-house and recent-blockbuster cinema is the **Hayden Orpheum Picture Palace,** 380 Military Rd., Cremorne (✆ **02/9908 4344;** www.orpheum.com.au). This eight-screen Art Deco gem is an experience in itself, especially on Saturday and Sunday evenings, when a Wurlitzer pops up from the center of the Cinema 2 stage and a musician in a tux gives a stirring rendition of times gone by. Eat "Jaffas," round candy-coated chocolates, if you want to fit in.

Movie prices hover around A$18 for adults and A$12 for kids.

The Casino

Star City This huge entertainment complex has eight bars, several restaurants, two theaters—the Showroom, which presents Las Vegas–style revues, and the Lyric, Sydney's largest theater—as well as a huge complex of retail shops. The all-you-can-eat Garden Buffet offers lots of hot and cold dishes, including unlimited prawns, for around A$30 for lunch and A$35 for dinner. All the usual gambling tables are here, in four main gambling areas. In all, there are 2,500 slot machines to gobble your change. You must be over 18 to gamble. Open 24 hours. 80 Pyrmont St., Pyrmont (adjacent to Darling Harbour). ✆ **02/9777 9000.** Ferry: Pyrmont (Darling Harbour). Monorail: Casino.

NEW SOUTH WALES

6

by Marc Llewellyn

With so much to experience in a state as big as New South Wales, you're not going to see all the major attractions in one hit, so you must prioritize. If you have a couple of days to spare, you should certainly head out to the Blue Mountains, part of the Great Dividing Range that separates the lush eastern coastal strip from the more arid interior. Or spend a day in the vineyards of the the Hunter Valley. If you have a few more days, I recommend heading to Barrington Tops National Park, north of the Hunter, for the rainforest and native animals, or down to the pristine beaches of Jervis Bay for gorgeous scenery and great bushwalks.

For longer trips, you can head north toward the Queensland border on the 964km (598-mile) route to Brisbane. You'll pass pretty seaside towns, deserted beaches, and tropical hinterland. Another option is to travel along the south coast 1,032km (640 miles) to Melbourne. Along the way are some of the country's most spectacular beaches, quaint hamlets, opportunities to spot dolphins and whales, and extensive national parks. If you want to experience the Outback, then head west across the Blue Mountains. The main Outback destinations are the extraordinary opal-mining town of Lightning Ridge, where you can meet some of the most eccentric "fair-dinkum" (authentic or genuine) Aussies you'll come across anywhere, and the fascinating inland town of Broken Hill.

Exploring the State

VISITOR INFORMATION The **Sydney Visitor Centre at The Rocks,** First Floor, The Rocks Centre, Corner of Argyle and Playfair streets, will give you general information on what to do and where to stay throughout the state. There's another **Sydney Visitor Centre at Darling Harbour,** near the Sydney Aquarium. They share the same contact details: ✆ **1800/067 676** in Australia, or 02/9240 8788; **www.sydneyvisitorcentre.com**. Both are open daily from 9:30am to 5:30pm.

GETTING AROUND **By Car** From Sydney, the **Pacific Highway** heads along the north coast into Queensland, and the **Princes Highway** hugs the south coast and runs into Victoria. The **Sydney–Newcastle Freeway** connects Sydney with its industrial neighbor and the vineyards of the Hunter Valley. The **Great Western Highway** and the **M4 motorway** head west to the Blue Mountains. The **M5 motorway, Hume Highway,** is the quickest way to get to Melbourne.

The state's automobile association, the **National Roads and Motorists' Association (NRMA),** has a pretty good online distance calculator and route planner at **www.drivethere.com.au**.

BY TRAIN **Countrylink** (© **13 22 32** in Australia; www.countrylink.info) trains travel to most places of interest in the state and as far south as Melbourne in Victoria and across the border into southern Queensland. Countrylink also has special rates for car rentals.

BY PLANE **Qantas** (© **13 13 13** in Australia; www.qantas.com.au) flies to most major cities and towns in the state; **Virgin Blue** (© **13 67 89** in Australia; www.virginblue.com.au) also flies to most major Australian destinations, as well as from Sydney to Newcastle, Ballina (near Byron Bay), Port Macquarie, Coffs Harbour, and Albury. Virgin Blue's main rival, the Qantas offshoot **Jetstar** (© **13 15 38** in Australia; www.jetstar.com) also flies around Australia. Meanwhile, **Regional Express** (© **13 17 13** in Australia; www.rex.com.au) flies to several destinations in NSW, including to the north and south coasts and to Broken Hill.

THE BLUE MOUNTAINS ★★

The **Blue Mountains** offer breathtaking views, rugged tablelands, sheer cliffs, deep inaccessible valleys, enormous chasms, colorful parrots, cascading waterfalls, historic villages, and stupendous walking trails. In 2000, UNESCO classified it as a World Heritage Site. Although the Blue Mountains are where Sydneysiders go now to escape the humidity and crowds of the city, in the early days of the colony, the mountains kept at bay those who wanted to explore the interior. In 1813, three explorers—Gregory Blaxland, William Charles Wentworth, and William Lawson—managed to conquer the cliffs, valleys, and dense forest, and cross the mountains (which are hardly mountains but rather a series of hills covered in eucalyptus and ancient fern trees) to the plains beyond. There they found land the colony urgently needed for grazing and farming. The **Great Western Highway** and **Bells Line of Road** are the access roads through the region today—winding and steep in places, they are surrounded by the Blue Mountains and Wollemi national parks.

Color Me Blue

The Blue Mountains derive their name from the ever-present blue haze that is caused by light striking the droplets of eucalyptus oil that evaporate from the leaves of the dense surrounding forest.

The entire area is known for its spectacular scenery, particularly the cliff-top views into the valleys of gum trees and across to craggy outcrops that tower from the valley floor. It's colder up here than down on the plains, and clouds can sweep in and fill the canyons with mist in minutes, while waterfalls

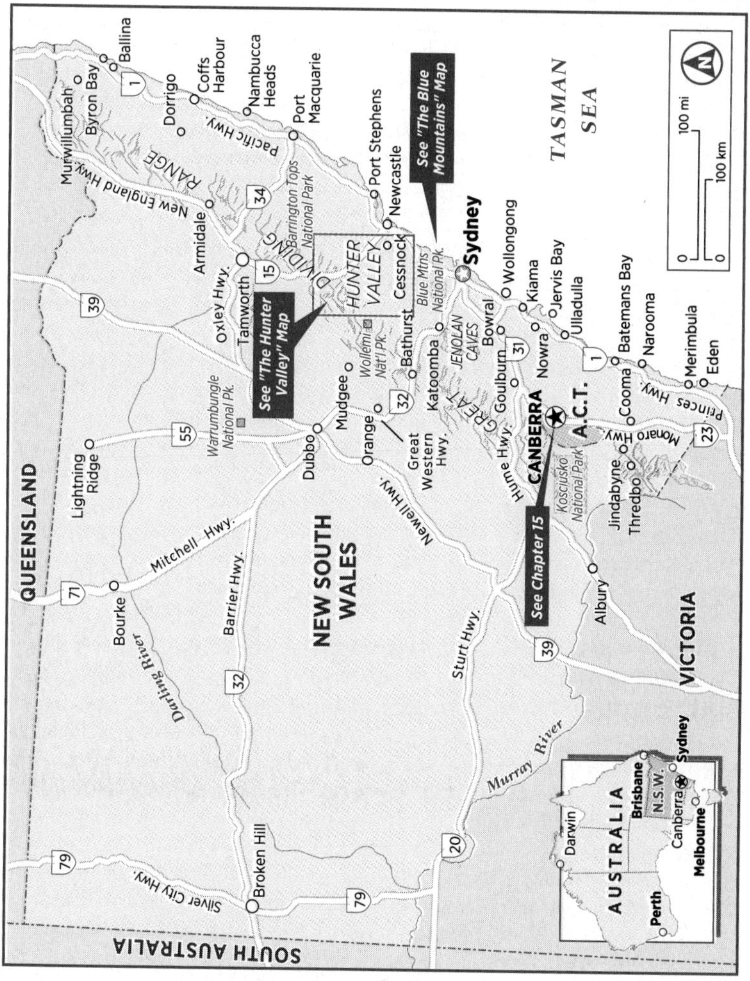

cascade down sheer drops, spraying the dripping fern trees that cling to the gullies. You'll need at least a couple of days up here to get the best out of it—a single-day tour, with all the traveling involved, can only just scratch the surface.

The Blue Mountains are also one of Australia's best-known adventure playgrounds. Rock climbing, caving, abseiling (rappelling), bushwalking, mountain biking, horseback riding, and canoeing are practiced here year-round.

Blue Mountain Essentials

VISITOR INFORMATION You can pick up maps, walking guides, and other information and book accommodations at **Blue Mountains Tourism,** Echo Point

Timing Is Everything: When to Visit

If you can, try to visit the Blue Mountains on weekdays, when most Sydneysiders are at work and prices are lower. Note that the colder winter months (June–Aug) are the busiest season. This period is known as Yuletide—the locals' version of the Christmas period, when most places offer traditional Christmas dinners and roaring log fires. It's kind of, almost, just nearly, authentic. But it's fun if a year between Christmases is just a little too long.

Road, Katoomba, NSW 2780 (© **1300/653 408** in Australia; www.visitbluemountains.com.au). The information center is an attraction itself, with glass windows overlooking a gum forest, and cockatoos and lorikeets feeding on seed dispensers. It's open from 9am to 5pm daily.

The **National Park Shop,** Heritage Centre, end of Govetts Leap Road, Blackheath (© **02/4787 8877;** www.npws.nsw.gov.au), is run by the National Parks and Wildlife Service and offers detailed information about the Blue Mountains National Park. The staff can also arrange personalized guided tours of the mountains. It's open daily from 9am to 4:30pm (closed Dec 25).

The Blue Mountains is one of Australia's most popular spa regions, along with the likes of the Hunter Valley, the Gold Coast and Cairns in Queensland, and Daylesford and Hepburn Springs in Victoria. Many properties offer massages and treatments for visitors and guests. See **www.dayspaguide.com.au** for every day spa and spa resort in Australia.

Check the great website **www.bluemts.com.au** for more information on the area, including bushwalks.

GUIDED TOURS FROM SYDNEY Many private bus operators offer day trips from Sydney, but it's important to shop around. Some offer a guided coach tour, during which, you just stretch your legs occasionally; while others let you get your circulation going with a couple of longish bushwalks. One highly recommended operator is **Oz Trek Adventure Tours** (© **1300/661 234** in Australia, or 02/9666 4262; www.oztrek.com.au). Its trips include a tour of the Sydney Olympic site, tours of all the major Blue Mountain sites, and a 1½-hour bushwalk. It costs A$55 for adults and A$44 for kids. You can add overnight packages, horseback riding, and abseiling.

Sydney Tours-R-Us (© **02/8004 0500;** www.sydneytoursrus.com) runs minicoaches to the Blue Mountains, stopping off at the Telstra Stadium (where the Sydney Olympics were held) and Featherdale Wildlife Park. Then you see all the major sights in the mountains and come home via ferry from Parramatta to Circular Quay. The trip costs A$98 for adults and A$68 for kids. It's a big 10-hour day. The company also operates tours to the Hunter Valley, Port Stephens, and Jenolan Caves.

Wonderbus (© **02/9666 8433;** www.wonderbus.com.au) offers an exceptional tour to the Blue Mountains, with stop offs at Featherdale Wildlife Park for A$105 for adults and A$95 for kids under 12, including all entry fees. You also come back by ferry.

Grayline (© **1300/858 687** in Australia; www.grayline.com) offers several Blue Mountains trips in large coaches from around A$80. A combined Blue Mountains/Jenolan Caves trip costs A$110. Kids are charged roughly half-price. If you hate big-group travel, choose another option.

The Blue Mountains

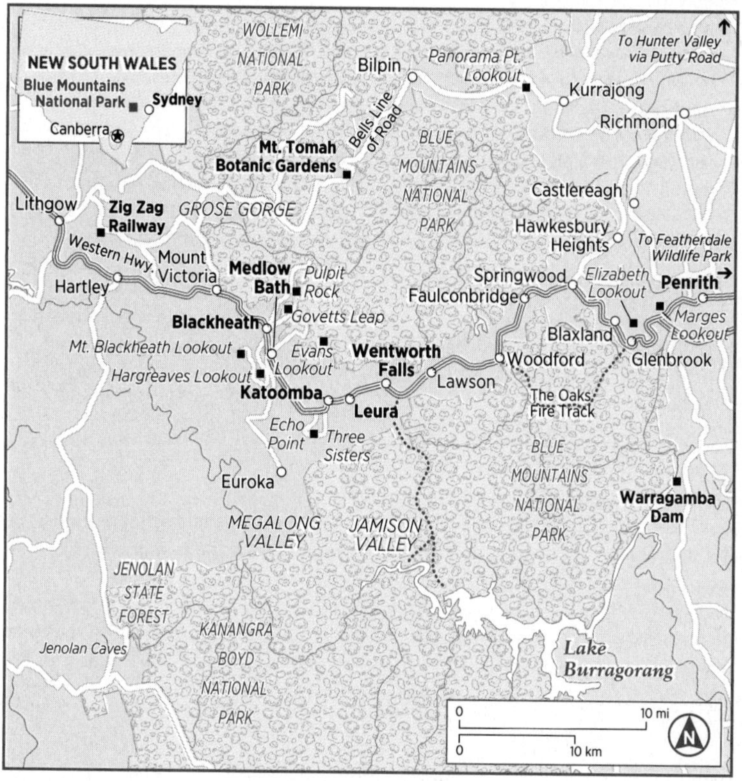

Bushwalking & Other Active Endeavors

Almost every other activity costs money, but bushwalking (hiking) is the exception to the rule that nothing in life is free. There are some 50 walking trails in the Blue Mountains, ranging from routes you can cover in 15 minutes to the 3-day **Six Foot Track ★** that starts outside Katoomba and finishes at Jenolan Caves. The staff at the tourist offices and national park office will be happy to point you in the right direction, whether it be for an hour's stroll or a full day's hike.

One of the best adventure operators in the area, **High 'n' Wild,** 3–5 Katoomba St., Katoomba, NSW 2780 (✆ **02/4782 6224;** www.high-n-wild.com.au), offers a series of canyoning expeditions, taking in scenic rainforest gullies and caverns made up of dramatic rock formations and fern-lined walls. There's a bit of swimming and plenty of walking, wading, and squeezing through tight spaces involved—and sometimes rappelling (called "abseiling" in Australia)—but fortunately, being double-jointed is not a prerequisite.

If you really want to test your head for heights, try High 'n' Wild's 150m (492-ft.) "Mega Jump"—the highest continuous rappel in the Southern Hemisphere. This

See the Mountains Through Aboriginal Eyes

Blue Mountains Walkabout (✆ **0408/443 822** mobile; www.bluemountainswalkabout.com) is an Aboriginal-owned and -guided walk that follows a traditional walkabout song line. This 8km (5-mile) challenging off-track walk explores secluded Blue Mountains wilderness for 8 hours in the bush (including 4 hr. walking and 4 hr. of relaxation and activities). Along the way, you'll see ancient art, ceremonial sites, and artifacts, and hear Dreamtime stories. Also included is ochre-bark and body painting, bush-tucker tasting, wildlife viewing, sandstone cave exploring, and bathing in a crystal-clear billabong (pond) below a waterfall. The tour leaves every day in rain, hail, or shine. You should be reasonably fit. Bring wet-weather gear, good boots or walking shoes, and lunch. The walk begins in the Blue Mountains on Faulconbridge Railway Station platform at 10am. From Central Station in Sydney, purchase a fare for A$13; take the Lithgow train departing 9:09am Monday to Friday (arrive 10:34am), or 9:18am on weekends and public holidays (arrive 10:44am). Get off at Faulconbridge Station. The trek itself costs A$95; a new half-day tour leaving at 10am costs A$75.

heart-pumping descent down a sheer cliff is suitable for the fearless beginner, but the staff assures me that you soon settle in by learning the ropes on the 10-story-high junior slopes beforehand.

If that's too much to handle, you could always try a day on an inflatable raft between huge towering rock walls on the Wollangambe River. There are a few minor rapids to navigate, and the bushwalk down to the river and back up again can be a little testing, but it's certainly suitable for a family outing. Prices start at A$99 for abseiling and A$179 for canyoning.

Other excellent adventure operators are the **Blue Mountains Adventure Company,** 84a Bathurst Rd. (P.O. Box 242), Katoomba, NSW 2780 (✆ **02/4782 1271;** www.bmac.com.au), located above the Summit Gear Shop; and the **Australian School of Mountaineering,** 166 Katoomba St., Katoomba, NSW 2780 (✆ **02/4782 2014**). Both offer rock climbing, rappelling, and canyoning trips. The Adventure Company also offers caving and mountain biking, and the School of Mountaineering offers bushcraft and survival training.

Katoomba: Gateway To The Blue Mountains

114km (71 miles) W of Sydney

Katoomba (pop. 11,200) is the largest town in the Blue Mountains and the focal point of the Blue Mountains National Park. It's an easy 1½- to 2-hour trip from Sydney by train, bus, or car. However, it's also a low socioeconomic pocket in a very affluent region, with one of the highest unemployment rates in the state.

GETTING THERE By car from central Sydney, travel along Parramatta Road and turn off onto the M4 motorway (around 2 hr. to Katoomba). Another route is via the Harbour Bridge to North Sydney, along the Warringah Freeway (following signs to the M2). Then take the M2 to the end and follow signs to the M4 and the Blue Mountains. This takes around 1½ hours.

Frequent rail service connects Sydney to Katoomba from Central Station; contact **CityRail** (© **13 15 00**) or **Countrylink** (© **13 22 32;** www.countrylink.info) for details. The train trip takes 2 hours. Trains leave almost hourly from platform nos. 12 and 13, stopping at Katoomba, and then at Mount Victoria and Lithgow. An adult same-day round-trip ticket costs around A$15 off-peak and A$22 during commuter hours. A child's ticket costs around A$4.

GETTING AROUND The best way to get around the Blue Mountains without your own transport is the **Blue Mountains Explorer Bus** (© **02/4782 4807;** www.explorerbus.com.au). The double-decker bus leaves from outside the Katoomba train station regularly from 9:45am until 4:05pm and stops at 29 attractions, resorts, galleries, and tearooms in and around Katoomba and Leura. You can get on and off as often as you want. Tickets cost A$36 for adults, A$18 for children, and A$90 for a family; other passes include rides on the Scenic Railway and the Skyway (see "Exploring the Area," below).

Another option is **Trolley Tours** (© **1800/801 577** in Australia; www.trolley tours.com.au), which is a kind of tram on wheels with commentary. An all-day pass costs A$20 and includes stops at 29 various attractions around Katoomba and Leura, too. The trolley leaves from outside the Carrington Hotel on Katoomba Street once an hour from 9:45am until 4:45pm.

EXPLORING THE AREA

The most visited and photographed attractions in the Blue Mountains are the rock formations known as the **Three Sisters ★★**. For the best vantage point, head to **Echo Point Road,** across from the Blue Mountains Tourism office. Or try Evans Lookout, Govetts Leap, and Hargreaves Lookout, all at Blackheath (see "Blackheath," p. 192)—none of which are on the Blue Mountains Explorer Bus or Trolley Tours route.

One thing you have to do in the Blue Mountains is ride the **Scenic Railway,** the world's steepest; follow the road signs to **Scenic World.** It consists of a carriage on rails that is lowered 415m (1,361 ft.) into the Jamison Valley at a maximum incline of 52 degrees. It's *very* steep and quite a thrill. Originally the rail line was used to transport coal and shale from the mines below in the 1880s. The trip takes only a

The Legend of the Three Sisters

The Aboriginal Dreamtime legend has it that three sisters, Meehni, Wimlah, and Gunnedoo, lived in the Jamison Valley as members of the Katoomba tribe. These beautiful young ladies had fallen in love with three brothers from the Nepean tribe, yet tribal law forbade them to marry. The brothers were not happy to accept this law and so decided to use force to capture the three sisters, which caused a major tribal battle. As the lives of the three sisters were seriously in danger, a witch doctor from the Katoomba tribe took it upon himself to turn the three sisters into stone to protect them from any harm. While he had intended to reverse the spell when the battle was over, the witch doctor himself was killed. As only he could reverse the spell to return the ladies to their former beauty, the sisters remain in their magnificent rock formation as a reminder of this battle for generations to come.

few minutes; at the bottom are some excellent walks through forests of ancient tree ferns. A boardwalk makes it suitable for those who like their bushwalking easy. Another popular attraction is the **Skyway,** a cable car that travels 300m (984 ft.) above the Jamison Valley. The round trip takes 6 minutes. The Scenic Railway and the Skyway combination (✆ **02/4780 0200;** www.scenicworld.com.au) costs A$21 round trip for adults, A$10 for children, and A$52 for families. They operate from 9am to 5pm daily (last trip at 4:50pm) and depart from the ticket office at 1 Violet St., Katoomba (follow the signs). I'd advise taking the Scenic Railway down, going for a walk, and taking the cable car back up.

Canyons, waterfalls, underground rivers—the Blue Mountains have them all, and before you experience them in person you can catch them on the (giant) screen at **The Edge Cinema,** 225–237 Great Western Hwy., Katoomba (✆ **02/4782 8900**). The special effects shown on this 18m- (59-ft.) high, 24m- (79-ft.) wide screen make you feel like you're part of the action. At the time of writing, the 38-minute film *The Edge* was being shown every day at 10:20, 11:05am, 12:10, 1:30, 2:15, and 5:30pm. Tickets cost A$15 for adults and A$10 for children. The cinema is a 5- to 10-minute walk from the train station. Recently released movies play on part of the giant screen in the evening. A restaurant and a snack bar are on the premises.

> **Seeing the Blue Mountains from the Back of a Harley**
>
> **A thrilling way to see the Blue Mountains is on the back of a chauffeur-driven Harley-Davidson motorcycle. Wild Ride Australia (✆ 1300/783 338, or 0410/418 740 mobile; www.wildride.com.au) will pick you up from your hotel in the Blue Mountains and take you on a 1-hour exhilarating ride to see some of the sights around Katoomba. Rides cost A$130.**

To get back to Sydney, I highly recommend taking the Bells Line of Road through Bilpin. This route takes up to 3 hours, but you can stop off at the wonderful **Mount Tomah Botanic Gardens ★**. (You can't miss the large sign on your right about 10 min. before you get to Bilpin.) An adjunct of the Royal Botanic Gardens in Sydney, Mount Tomah is dedicated to cold-climate plants. It's compact and has a very good cafe serving lunch daily. Allow around 2 hours for a stop here.

WHERE TO STAY

Very Expensive

Echoes Boutique Hotel & Restaurant, Blue Mountains ★★ Echoes is a small and cozy spruced-up hotel that sits on the edge of a cliff overlooking the Jamison Valley. Large windows, balconies, a pretty garden, and a sizable deck allow guests to soak up the fantastic scenery. Its 14 rooms are average size, but they do boast individual personalities—and all offer stunning mountain and rainforest panoramas. The restaurant is good and you can pamper yourself in the day spa. Bottom line: Echoes is nice but pricey, and relies strongly on the views.

3 Lilianfels Ave., Katoomba, NSW 2780. ✆ **02/4782 1966.** Fax 02/4782 3707. www.echoeshotel.com.au. 14 units. Sat–Sun A$650 per night, A$695 suite; weekday A$495 double, A$550 suite. You can get A$150–A$200 off a room night if you book last minute. AE, DC, MC, V. Free parking. **Amenities:** Restaurant; bar; Jacuzzi; sauna, day spa. *In room:* A/C, TV, hair dryer, minibar.

Lilianfels Blue Mountains ★★ Set just over a road from Echo Point, this Victorian country-house hotel is a full-service yet cozy establishment. Rooms are spacious, expensive, and furnished with antiques. Most have king-size beds. Those with views are more expensive. The living areas are just as grand, with roaring log fires and more antiques. Views are impressive, especially from the lounge, which overlooks the Jamison Valley. The hotel has old-world charm, with a tea lounge, a reading room, a billiard room, and a great outdoor swimming pool overlooking the valley. If you want a spa treatment make sure you book well in advance. The restaurant here, **Darley's,** is a much awarded regional eatery and serves highly regarded contemporary food. A three-course set meal costs A$105, and a degustation menu costs A$130 (plus A$70 with matching wines). The room rates below are what you might usually find when booking through the website, but these are some A$200 or so lower than the so-called "rack rate" (when you just walk up to the front door and ask for a room).

Lilianfels Ave., Katoomba, NSW 2780. ✆ **1800/024 452** in Australia, or 02/4780 1200. Fax 02/4780 1300. www.lilianfels.com.au. 85 units. Doubles A$410–A$560; suites A$650. Extra person A$60. Check the website for packages. AE, DC, MC, V. Free parking. **Amenities:** 2 restaurants; bike rental; health club w/flotation tank; exercise room; Jacuzzi; small indoor pool; 24-hr. room service; sauna; smoke-free rooms. *In room:* A/C, TV, hair dryer, minibar.

Moderate

The Carrington Hotel ★★ Construction started on this grand Victorian hotel in 1880, and it reopened in 2000 after a major renovation. A ramshackle structure, the Carrington is a must-stay if you're into buildings of the British Raj/colonial style. Downstairs is a restaurant and breakfast room (once a ballroom), a couple of lounges with antiques, and a gorgeous wood-paneled billiard room. Chandeliers and 1930s-style lamps reflecting off silver trophies won by the local Rifle Club give everything a warm glow. Unfortunately, heavy Plexiglas doors greet you as you enter each of the many corridors—a necessary fire precaution. All the rooms are delightful, with royal gold and blue carpets and drapes that would probably be gaudy if they didn't fit in with the overall style. Traditional rooms share bathrooms; Colonial rooms come with a deep tub in the bathroom (with a noisy fan) and no view to speak of; Deluxe Colonial rooms have a balcony and mountain views; Premier rooms have Jacuzzis and great views; and the suites are fit for a duke and duchess. Dinner here costs A$48 for two courses and A$65 for three courses (with extra for side dishes). The breakfast is one of the best I've encountered.

15–47 Katoomba St. (P.O. Box 28), Katoomba, NSW 2780. ✆ **02/4782 1111.** Fax 02/4782 7033. www.thecarrington.com.au. 63 units. Traditional double A$129 Sun–Thurs, A$149 Fri–Sat; Colonial double A$205 Sun–Thurs, A$250 Fri–Sat; Premier double A$235–A$275 Sun–Thurs, A$285–A$315 Fri–Sat. Ask about weekend packages. Rates include full breakfast. AE, DC, MC, V. **Amenities:** Restaurant; bar. *In room:* TV.

Echo Point Holiday Villas ★ These are the closest self-contained accommodations to the Three Sisters Lookout. The two front-facing villas are the best because of their partial mountain views. All villas are clean and spacious and have two bedrooms, a full kitchen, and a laundry. They have either a king or queen bed in the master bedroom, while the second bedroom either has a double bed or two singles. There are barbecue facilities in the backyard.

36 Echo Point Rd., Katoomba, NSW 2780. ✆ **02/4782 3275.** Fax 02/4782 7030. www.echopointvillas.com.au. 5 villas, all with shower only. A$150 Fri–Sat and public holidays; A$120 Sun–Thurs. Extra person A$15. AE, DC, MC, V. *In room:* TV, fridge, hair dryer, kitchen.

Inexpensive

Katoomba YHA Hostel ★ This wonderful YHA hostel has won several major tourism awards. It's set in a former 1930s cabaret club and still retains some of the fun atmosphere. It's very roomy and friendly, and also well located in the heart of Katoomba. There's a fireplace in the living room (usually with log fire), a communal kitchen, a dining room, a game room with billiards table, and a television. Also here is a nice balcony and barbecue area. Some double rooms include a set of bunks for kids. Dorm rooms accommodate four to eight people. People from all walks of life, and of all ages, stay here and rave about the place.

207 Katoomba St., Katoomba. ✆ **02/4782 1416.** Fax 02/4782 6203. www.yha.com.au. 57 rooms, 29 doubles/twin/family rooms. A$79–A$88 double with shared bathroom; A$88–A$98 double with private bathroom; A$28–A$31 dorm. MC, V. **Amenities:** Bike rental. *In room:* No phone.

WHERE TO DINE

Katoomba Street has many ethnic dining choices, whether you're hungry for Greek, Chinese, or Thai. Restaurants in the Blue Mountains are generally more expensive than equivalent places in Sydney. As well as the ones below, try the **Elephant Bean,** at 159 Katoomba Rd. (✆ **02/4782 4620**), for hearty soups, burgers, muffins, and good coffee. You may want to eat breakfast, or brekkies as they often call it in Australia, at a cafe rather than in your hotel. It can work out cheaper, and you often get more of a choice. The **Stockmarket Café,** 179 Leura Mall, Leura (✆ **02/4784 3121**), is small and casual with good coffee ordered at the counter. They have good eggs (and great soups, pies, and stews at lunchtime, by the way). The **Fresh Espresso and Food Bar,** 181 Katoomba St., Katoomba (✆ **02/4782 3602**), has a large range of coffees to choose from and does good scrambled eggs. The signature breakfast dishes here are basins of porridge, either with fresh ricotta, strawberries, honey, and cinnamon, or yogurt and rhubarb compote, for around A$10.

Expensive

TrisElies GREEK Perhaps it's the belly dancers, the plate smashing, or the smell of moussaka, but as soon as you walk through the door of this lively eatery you feel as if you've been transported to an authentic Athenian *taverna*. The restaurant folds out onto three tiers of tables, all with a good view of the stage, where Greek or international performances take place every night. The food is solid Greek fare—souvlakia, traditional dips, fried halloumi cheese, Greek salads, casseroles like Mother could have made, whitebait (tiny fried fish), and sausages in red wine—with a few Italian and Spanish extras. In winter, warm up beside one of two log fires.

287 Bathurst Rd., Katoomba. ✆ **02/4782 4026.** www.triselies.com.au. Reservations recommended. Main courses A$26–A$30. AE, DC, MC, V. Sun–Thurs 5pm–midnight; Fri–Sat 5pm–3am.

Inexpensive

Chork Dee Thai Restaurant THAI Loved by the locals, Chork Dee offers good Thai food in a pleasant but modest setting. It serves the usual Thai fare, including satay, spring rolls, and fish cakes to start, followed by lots of curries, noodles, and sweet-and-sour dishes. While vegetarians won't find any starters without meat or fish, plenty of veggie and tofu dishes are available as main courses. It's BYO.

216 Katoomba St., Katoomba. ✆ **02/4782 1913.** Main courses A$9–A$17. AE, MC, V. Sun–Thurs 5:30–9pm; Fri–Sat 5:30–10pm.

Paragon Café CAFE The Paragon has been a Blue Mountains institution since it opened for business in 1916. Inside, it's decked out with dark-wood paneling,

The Zig Zag Railway

The Zig Zag Railway (✆ 02/6355 2955; www.zigzagrailway.com.au), an impressive narrow-gauge tourist railway, is located at Clarence, 10km (6 miles) east of Lithgow in the Blue Mountains. The line was built in the 1860s to transport people and produce from the western plains of NSW to Sydney. Today, the steam trains, track, and rolling stock are maintained and operated by a voluntary cooperative of train buffs.

The return journey takes around 1½ hours, and there's nothing like a face full of grit from a steam-train funnel. Oh, those were the days. The scenery is both beautiful and dramatic, with steep gradients, tunnels, and sandstone viaducts.

Steam trains run every Saturday, Sunday, Wednesday, public holiday, and almost every day during NSW school holidays. Diesel trains run Mondays, Tuesdays, Thursdays, and Fridays, outside of NSW public school holidays. Trains run daily (except Christmas Day) at 11am, 1pm, and 3pm from Clarence Station. Additional trains run on Sundays and some public holidays. Check the timetable on the website for further details. Two-way trips cost A$28 for adults, A$14 for kids, and A$70 for a family.

bas-relief figures guarding the booths, and chandeliers. The homemade soups are delicious. The cafe also serves breakfasts, pies, pastas, grills, seafood, waffles, cakes, and a Devonshire tea of scones and cream.

65 Katoomba St., Katoomba. ✆ **02/4782 2928.** Menu items A$3–A$10. AE, MC, V. Tues–Fri 10am–3:30pm; Sat–Sun 10am–4pm.

Leura

107km (66 miles) W of Sydney; 3km (2 miles) E of Katoomba

The fashionable capital of the Blue Mountains, Leura is known for its gardens, its attractive old buildings (many holiday homes for Sydneysiders), and its cafes and restaurants. The National Trust has classified Leura's main street as an urban conservation area. Just outside Leura is the **Sublime Point Lookout,** which has spectacular views of the Three Sisters in Katoomba. From the southern end of **Leura Mall,** a cliff drive takes you all the way back to Echo Point in Katoomba; along the way you'll enjoy spectacular views across the Jamison Valley.

There are a couple of high-class dining options here, the best being **Solitary,** at 90 Cliff Dr., Leura Falls (✆ **02/4782 1164;** www.solitary.com.au). It's open for lunch daily from noon to 4:30pm and dinner on Saturday and Sunday from 6 to 10:30pm. It serves excellent Contemporary food such as ocean trout fillet with soft polenta, parsnip chips, and roast garlic; or chicken and mushroom roulade with barley risotto and wilted spinach. Lunch costs from A$17 to A$31, and at dinner, two courses cost A$59 and three courses cost A$69.

Wentworth Falls ★★

103km (64 miles) W of Sydney; 7km (4½ miles) E of Katoomba

This pretty town has numerous crafts and antiques shops, but the area is principally known for its 281m (922-ft.) waterfall, situated in **Falls Reserve.** On the far side of the falls is the **National Pass Walk**—one of the best in the Blue Mountains. It's cut into a cliff face with overhanging rock faces on one side and sheer drops on the other. The views over the Jamison Valley are spectacular. The track takes you down to the base of the falls to the **Valley of the Waters.** Climbing up out of the valley is quite a bit more difficult, but just as rewarding.

A NICE SPOT FOR LUNCH

Conservation Hut Café ★ CAFE This pleasant cafe is in the national park on top of a cliff overlooking the Jamison Valley. It's a good place for a bit of lunch on the balcony after the Valley of the Waters walk, which leaves from outside. Dishes may include the likes of pan-roasted chicken with bacon, mustard-braised leeks, and an onion reduction; or oven-roasted lamb rump with a potato and rosemary hash, peas, minted pistou, and a madeira jus. There are vegetarian and great breakfast options, too. There's a nice log fire inside in winter. Children are welcome.

At the end of Fletcher St., Wentworth Falls. ✆ **02/4757 3827.** Lunch items A$21–A$28; dinner entrees A$30. AE, MC, V. Daily 9am–5pm.

Blackheath

114km (71 miles) W of Sydney; 14km (8¾ miles) NW of Katoomba

Blackheath is the highest town in the Blue Mountains at 1,049m (3,441 ft.). The **Three Brothers** at Blackheath are not as big or as famous as the Three Sisters in Katoomba, but you can climb two of them for fabulous views. Or you could try the **Cliff Walk** from **Evans Lookout** to **Govetts Leap** (named after a surveyor who mapped the region in the 1830s), where there are magnificent views over the **Grose Valley** and **Bridal Veil Falls.** The 1½-hour tramp passes through banksia, gum, and wattle forests, with spectacular views of peaks and valleys. Blackheath also has some tearooms and antiques shops. The local pub does reasonable food.

GETTING THERE The Great Western Highway takes motorists from Katoomba to Blackheath. CityRail trains also stop at Blackheath.

VISITOR INFORMATION The **Heritage Centre** (✆ **02/4787 8877;** www.npws.nsw.gov.au), operated by the National Parks and Wildlife Service, is close to Govetts Leap Lookout on Govetts Leap Road. It has information on guided walks, camping, and hiking, as well as information on local European and Aboriginal historic sites. It's open daily from 9am to 4:30pm.

EXPLORING THE AREA ON HORSEBACK

One of the nicest ways to get around is on horseback. **Werriberri Trail Rides** (✆ **02/4787 9171;** fax 02/4787 6680), at the base of the Blue Mountains, 10km (6 miles) from Blackheath on Megalong Road in the Megalong Valley, offers guided multiday rides through the Megalong Valley and beyond. These are suitable for beginners to advanced riders.

WHERE TO STAY

Jemby-Rinjah Lodge ★ ☺ The Blue Mountains National Park is just a short walk away from this interesting alternative accommodations option, which is close to both Katoomba and Blackheath. There are nine standard cabins (seven two-bedroom cabins, and two one-bedroom loft cabins), one deluxe cabin called Treetops Retreat, and three pole-frame lodges good for groups. The well-spaced cabins are right in the bush and can sleep up to six people. Each has a slow-combustion heater, carpets, a bathroom, a fully equipped kitchen, and a lounge and dining area, though the "roto-loo" pit toilet might be a new experience and there's no phone coverage here. But there are laundry and barbecue areas nearby, and kids will like this place. Free pickup can be arranged from Blackheath train station. The nearby walking trails take you to the spectacular Grand Canyon; the Grose Valley Blue Gum forests; and Walls Cave, a resting place for local Aborigines 10,000 years ago. There's a pretty good restaurant here, which is also open to people not staying at the lodge. Two-course meals cost A$39 and three-course meals A$49.

336 Evans Lookout Rd., Blackheath, NSW 2785. ✆ **02/4787 7622.** Fax 02/4787 6230. www.jembyrinjahlodge.com.au. 10 cabins. Standard 1- and 2-bedroom cabins A$170 Mon–Thurs, A$219 Fri–Sun; deluxe cabins A$219 Mon–Thurs, A$265 Fri–Sun. Extra adult A$30, extra child A$20. AE, DC, MC, V. **Amenities:** Restaurant w/lounge area. *In room:* TV, fridge, kitchenette.

Jenolan Caves ★

182km (113 miles) W of Sydney; 70km (43 miles) SW of Katoomba

The winding road from Katoomba eventually takes you to a spur of the Great Dividing Range and a series of underground limestone caves considered some of the world's best. Known to the local Aborigines as Binoomea, meaning "dark place," the caves are an impressive amalgamation of stalactites, stalagmites, and underground rivers and pools. They have been open to the public since 1866.

GETTING THERE From Sydney, take the M4 Motorway traveling west through the Blue Mountains, Katoomba, and Mt. Victoria. Find the Jenolan Caves turnoff just past the village of Hartley. There is no fuel available at Jenolan. When traveling from Sydney the last service station is at Mount Victoria or Lithgow. It's a 1½-hour drive from Katoomba to the caves. CityRail trains run to Katoomba and link up with daily Jenolan Caves excursions run by **Fantastic Aussie Tours** (✆ **02/4782 1866,** or 1300/300 915 in Sydney; www.fantastic-aussie-tours.com.au). The day tour departs Katoomba at 10:30am and returns at 5:15pm. It costs A$75 for adults, A$38 for children, and A$200 for a family. The company also runs transfers to Jenolan from Katoomba, departing at 10:30am and leaving Jenolan at 3:45pm daily. They cost A$85 for adults and A$43 for kids. The company can transfer you to Jenolan Caves for A$50 for adults and A$25 for kids. Ask about family fares.

EXPLORING THE CAVES

Nine caves are open for exploration, with guided tours operated by **Jenolan Caves Reserves Trust** (✆ **02/6359 3311;** www.jenolancaves.org.au). The first cave tour starts at 10am weekdays and 9:30am weekends and holidays. The final tour departs at 4:30pm (5pm in warmer months). Tours last 1 to 2 hours, and each costs A$28 to A$35 for adults, A$19 to A$25 for children under 15. Family rates and multiple cave packages are available. The best all-around cave is **Lucas Cave; Imperial Cave** is best for seniors. Adventure Cave Tours, which include canyoning, last 3 hours to a full day and cost A$75 to A$200 per person.

WHERE TO STAY

A relatively inexpensive option is to stay at **Jenolan Cabins** (✆ **02/6335 6239;** www.jenolancabins.com.au). These cozy wood cabins, set up high on a ridge, accommodate six people, with one queen-size bed and two sets of bunks. There's a kitchenette (bring your own food) and a TV. Cabins cost A$98 per night midweek, and A$125 on Friday and Saturday nights.

Jenolan Caves House ★ This heritage-listed hotel built between 1888 and 1906 is one of the most outstanding structures in New South Wales. The main part of the enormous three-story building is made of sandstone and fashioned in Tudor-style black and white. Around it are several cottages and former servants' quarters. Accommodations within the main house vary, from simple Traditional rooms with shared bathrooms to Classic rooms with private bathrooms. The Traditional and Classic rooms are old world and cozy, with heavy furniture and views over red-tile rooftops or steep slopes. Classic rooms have views of Jenolan Caves Valley and gardens; Grand Classic rooms have spectacular views across the hills and countryside. Mountain Lodge rooms, in a building behind the main house, are more motel-like. The 2-night weekend rates show why you should avoid this place on weekends. Check the website for specials.

Jenolan Caves Village, NSW 2790. ✆ **02/6359 3322.** Fax 02/6359 3227. www.jenolancaves.org.au. 101 units, 87 with bathroom. A$100–A$125 Traditional double; A$165–A$195 Classic double; A$220–A$275 Grand Classic double; A$270–A$325 Classic family suite; A$295–A$350 Classic two-room suite; A$125–A$280 Mountain Lodge double. Rates include dinner. Higher rates Fri–Sun, public holidays, and NSW school holidays. 2-night minimum on Sat–Sun. Extra person A$60. AE, DC, MC, V. **Amenities:** 2 restaurants; bar. *In room:* TV, hair dryer.

Beyond the Blue Mountains

The first few decades of European settlement saw the rapid colonization of the coastal land around Sydney and beyond. The Blue Mountains, however, acted as a barrier that needed to be overcome, not least because increasing immigration was putting pressure on the available farming country. Many an escaped convict tried to make their way past the mountains, thinking that China or New Guinea lay beyond. Official attempts to break through the mountains, by following rivers and streams, invariably ended in sheer cliff faces or impassable gorges.

Then, in May 1813, three land-owning settlers—Gregory Blaxland, William Lawson, and William Wentworth—set off with four packhorses, five dogs, and four servants. Instead of following the rivers and streams, the explorers cut their way along ridge tops. They reached a hilltop (Mount Blaxland) 21 days later, from which they could see a great expanse of lightly treed open country to the west. It looked perfect for grazing sheep.

Six months later, George Evans led a team that followed the same route. This time he continued on, over the Great Dividing Range, to where Bathurst now stands. In doing so, he became the first European to have reached the rich pasture land of the Western Slopes and Plains. (Keep in mind, though, that history is written by the victorious, and not usually by forgotten escaped convicts.)

Governor Macquarie commissioned George Cox to build a road along the route, and personally made the trip to Bathurst soon after it was completed. Bathurst, named after Lord Bathurst, Secretary of State for War and Colonies, was to become Australia's first inland city.

BATHURST

207km (129 miles) W of Sydney, 98km (61 miles) W of Katoomba

If you're a tourist from abroad, you probably wouldn't make a special trip to see Bathurst (pop. 37,500). But if you're passing through, some of the old buildings, like Abercrombie House or the heritage courthouse, might appeal to you, and its parks and streetscapes make a pleasant place for a stroll. Bathurst's most famous attraction (to Australian "rev-heads" at least), is the car-racing track on Mount Panorama. For most of the year it's a public road though. The biggest race is the Bathurst 1000, a V-8 supercar challenge held in October. Bathurst's fortunes once relied on gold discoveries, and there are several small, historic gold-rush settlements within easy driving distance, such as Hill End, Sofala, and Ophir.

GETTING THERE **By Car** Follow the Great Western Highway from Katoomba in the Blue Mountains downhill to Lithgow (around a 45 min. drive), and then keep going across the plains for another 50 minutes or so to reach Bathurst.

VISITOR INFORMATION The **Bathurst Visitor Information Centre** is at 1 Kendall Ave. (✆ **1800/681 000** in Australia, or 02/6332 1444; www.visitbathurst.com.au). It's open daily 9am to 5pm.

Exploring the Region

One of the area's best attractions is **Abercrombie Caves,** located 70km (43 miles) south of Bathurst, via Trunkey Creek (✆ **02/6368 8603;** www.nationalparks.nsw.gov.au). Here you'll find the **Archway**—the largest natural arch in the Southern Hemisphere—and a number of other richly decorated caves that rival those at Jenolan. One of the most interesting caves from a historical perspective is **Bushrangers Cave,** which once acted as a hideout for the Ribbon Gang, led by the ill-fated Ralph Entwistle. Ralph began his life on the run after being caught swimming nude in the Macquarie River at Bathurst. (Funny enough, he had been transported to Australia for stealing clothes.) In 1829, Ralph was flogged for his nude bathing, ran away with several other convicts, and started a rebellion. (He wore green ribbons in his hair as a symbol of the Irish anticolonial struggle.) Ralph and his comrades were eventually captured and ended up swinging from the gallows. The caves today are surrounded by native bushland protected by a nature reserve; there are swimming holes in the creek, a camping area, and an impressive waterfall. The caves are open daily from 9am to 4pm. Guided tours start at 2pm on weekends only.

A remarkable place to visit is the **Age of Fishes Museum,** at the corner of Gaskill and Ferguson streets, Canowindra (✆ **02/6344 1008;** www.ageoffishes.org.au). The museum is dedicated to an amazing find of strange-looking armored fish that lived about 360 million years ago in the Devonian period. Thousands of these creatures perished when a billabong (or pond) dried up during a drought. The whole lot, including huge adults and smaller juveniles, died crowded together, and were soon covered in sediment. Over time the sediment turned to rock. Part of the fossil bed was discovered in 1955, by a road worker. It's importance was not identified until some time later, when experts from the Australian Museum in Sydney realized they were looking at one of the most remarkable discoveries of its kind in the world. In all, there are around 3,000 prehistoric fish on display in the rock slabs. Canowindra is a 1½-hour drive west of Bathurst, via the town of Orange.

Where to Stay & Dine

The Kelso Hotel You want a motel, you've got one! Ten simple rooms have double beds plus single beds; one room has a double bed plus a set of bunk beds; and one room has a double bed, a single bed, and a set of bunks. The Kelso is attached to a lively pub, though, where you might get a chance to mingle with the locals. The bistro serves up country favorites like steak, fish and chips, pastas, and chicken schnitzel.

37 Sydney Rd., Kelso, NSW 2795. ✆ **02/6331 6675.** Fax 02/6331 6812. www.thekelsohotel.com. 12 rooms. A$80 double. Extra person A$15. DC, MC, V. **Amenities:** Bistro; bar. *In room:* A/C, TV, fridge.

MUDGEE

128km (80 miles) N of Bathurst, 261km (162 miles) W of Sydney

Mudgee, a pretty country town surrounded by vineyards, has grown rapidly over the last few years into a major wine and food region. Today you can pop in and sample wines from more than 35 individual cellar-door outlets. The wineries are mostly clustered together, so the area is great for cycling. You can add Mudgee onto an interesting round-trip tour from Sydney, taking in the Blue Mountains, Bathurst and surrounds, Mudgee, and then the Hunter Valley, before heading back to the "Big Smoke."

GETTING THERE **By Car** Take the Great Western Highway through the Blue Mountains, or alternatively the Bells Line of Road through Richmond and Windsor to Lithgow. Follow the directions to Bathurst, and then turn left for Mudgee. The trip takes around 3½ hours.

By Train **Countrylink** (✆ **13 22 32** in Australia; www.countrylink.info) operates daily trains (with a bus connection from Lithgow) between Sydney and Mudgee. The trip takes around 4 hours and 40 minutes and costs A$75 return.

VISITOR INFORMATION The **Mudgee Visitor Information Centre** is at 84 Market St., Mudgee (✆ **1800/816 304** in Australia, or 02/6372 1020; www.visitmudgeeregion.com.au). It's open daily 9am to 5pm.

BICYCLE HIRE **Country Fit Bicycle Hire,** 36–42 Short St., Mudgee (✆ **02/6372 3955;** www.countryfitbicyclehire.com.au), hires bikes (and tandems!) for A$30 a day.

Where to Stay

The Cobb & Co Court Boutique Hotel This upscale sleepover is located right in the heart of Mudgee. It offers luxury bed-and-breakfast accommodation, as well as the acclaimed **Wineglass Bar & Grill** restaurant. The chocolate-and-cream-colored rooms are a good size and luxurious, with exceptionally comfortable beds. Deluxe queen rooms are remarkably large. The duck confit with a warm salad of crispy bacon, kipfler potatoes, and a balsamic glaze is a standout at the restaurant downstairs, where main courses come in at around A$33.

97 Market St., Mudgee, NSW 2850. ✆ **02/6372 7245.** Fax 02/6372 7525. www.cobbandcocourt.com.au. 13 rooms. A$145–A$250 double; A$160–A$290 Queen room; A$220–A$320 Deluxe Queen room. Higher rates are for weekends. Rates include cooked breakfast. AE, MC, V. **Amenities:** Restaurant. *In room:* A/C, TV, fridge, hair dryer.

Where to Wine & Dine

Blue Wren Wines, 433 Cassilis Rd., Mudgee (✆ **02/6372 6205;** www.bluewrenwines.com.au), serves nice wines from its cellar door, but it's also home to one of Mudgee's best restaurants. The **Blue Wren Restaurant** has won plenty of awards for its innovative modern Australian food. Lunch is from noon to 2:30pm Wednesday to Sunday, dinner from 6:30 to 10:30pm Wednesday to Saturday.

Craigmoor, Craigmoor Road, Mudgee (✆ **02/6372 2208**), was established in 1858. It's situated just 5 minutes from the center of town. The property features picnic grounds around the Craigmoor Cricket Oval, a cellar door, and a wine museum. The cellar door is open daily from 10am to 4pm.

THE HUNTER VALLEY ★

Cessnock: 190km (118 miles) N of Sydney

The Hunter Valley (or "the Hunter," as it's also called) is the oldest commercial wine-producing area in Australia, as well as a major site for coal mining. Internationally acclaimed wines have poured out of the Hunter since the early 1800s. Though the region falls behind the major wine-producing areas of Victoria in terms of volume, it has the advantage of being just 2 hours from Sydney.

The **Lower Hunter,** centered on the towns of Cessnock and Pokolbin, has around 110 wineries and cellar doors. Many varieties of wine are produced here, including Semillon, Shiraz, chardonnay, cabernet sauvignon, and pinot noir.

Farther north, the **Upper Hunter** represents the very essence of Australian rural life, with its sheep and cattle farms, historic homesteads, more wineries, and rugged bushland. The vineyards here tend to be larger than those in the south, and they produce more aromatic varieties, such as traminers and Rieslings. February through March is harvest time.

The Upper Hunter gives way to the forested heights of the World Heritage–listed Barrington Tops National Park. The ruggedly beautiful park is home to some of the highest Antarctic beech trees in the country. It abounds with animals, including several marsupial species and a profusion of birds.

Hunter Valley Essentials

GETTING THERE To get to the wine-producing regions of the Hunter, leave Sydney by the Harbour Bridge or Harbour Tunnel and follow the signs for Newcastle. Just before Hornsby, turn off the highway and head up the National 1/F3 freeway. After around an hour, take the Cessnock exit and follow signs to the vineyards. The trip will take about 2½ hours. Barrington Tops National Park is reached via the Upper Hunter town of Dungog.

A rental car should cost at least A$45 a day from Sydney, and you might put in around A$40 worth of gas for a couple of days of touring (the price hovers around A$1.20 a liter). In the Hunter, contact **Hertz,** 1A Aberdare Rd., Cessnock (✆ **13 30 39** in Australia, or 02/4991 2500).

ORGANIZED TRIPS FROM SYDNEY Several companies offer **day trips** to the Hunter Valley from Sydney. **Boutique Wine Tours** (✆ **02/9499 5444;** www.boutiquewinetours.com.au), takes small groups to the Hunter to visit up to six wineries, as well as cheese and fudge producers. The trip costs A$110, A$125 with a cafe lunch, or A$165 with a restaurant lunch. **Grayline** (✆ **1300/858 687;** www.grayline.com.au) offers unadventurous big-coach trips to the vineyards every Tuesday, Wednesday, Friday, and Sunday costing A$169 for adults and A$85 for kids. It visits three wineries and includes lunch.

VISITOR INFORMATION **Wine Country Visitors Information Centre,** Main Road, Pokolbin, NSW 2325 (✆ **02/4990 4477;** fax 02/4991 4518; www.winecountry.com.au), is open Monday through Friday from 9am to 5pm, Saturday from 9:30am to 5pm, and Sunday from 9:30am to 3:30pm. The staff can make accommodations bookings and answer any questions. The **Dungog Visitors Information Centre,** Dowling Street, Dungog (✆ **02/4992 2212**), has plenty of information on the Barrington Tops area. A good general website is **www.winecountry.com.au**.

Pick up a copy of the free Hunter Valley Wine Country Visitors Guide in any visitor center in Sydney or the Hunter Valley.

Visiting the Wineries

Many people start their journey through the Hunter by popping into the **Hunter Valley Wine Society,** 455 Wine Country Dr., Pokolbin (© **1300/303 307** in Australia, or 02/4941 3000). The club basically acts as a Hunter Valley wine clearinghouse, sending bottles and cases to members all over Australia and some overseas. It's also a good place to talk to experts about the area's wines and to taste a few of them. It's open daily from 9am to 5pm.

You might also like to visit the **Small Winemakers Centre,** 426 McDonalds Rd., Pokolbin (© **02/4998 7668**). At any one time it represents around six of the region's smaller producers.

Most of the wineries in the region are open for cellar-door tastings, and it's perfectly acceptable just to turn up, taste a couple of wines or more, and then say your goodbyes without buying anything. Though you will come across some unusual vintages, especially at the boutique wineries, don't expect to find any bargains—city bottle shops buy in bulk and at trade price, which means you can probably get the same bottle of wine for less in Sydney than at the cellar door in the Hunter.

Remember a Designated Driver!

Australia's drunk-driving laws are strict and rigidly enforced. Both easily identifiable and unmarked police cars patrol the vineyard regions. If you are interested in tasting some grapes in the Hunter Valley, choose a designated driver or take a guided tour.

A nice way to get around is by bicycle—maybe even on a bicycle made for two! You can hire them from **Grapemobile Bicycle Hire,** Pokolbin Brothers Wines, 307 Palmers Lane, Pokolbin (© **02/4998 7660;** www.grapemobile.com.au). Tandem and mountain bikes cost A$20 for a half-day, A$25 for a full day, and A$35 for 2 days. Special family rates are available. Meanwhile, **Hunter Valley Cycling** (© **0418/281 480** mobile; www.huntervalleycycling.com.au) delivers bicycles to your hotel. Prices are similar, and there are tours, too. ***Note:*** Riding without a helmet is illegal in Australia.

Just as fun is an all-day horse and carriage ride around the wine region with **Pokolbin Horse Coaches** (© **0408/161 133** mobile; http://pokolbinhorsecoaches.com.au). Half-day tours cost A$45 for adults and A$25 for kids, and day tours cost A$60 and A$30.

Cheese with Your Wine?

The **Hunter Valley Cheese Company,** McGuigan's Complex, 447 McDonalds Rd., Pokolbin (© **02/4998 7744;** www.huntervalleycheese.com.au), is worth visiting for its range of local cheeses.

Another interesting store for local and imported cheeses is the **Hunter Valley Smelly Cheese Shop,** 3/2188 Broke Rd., Pokolbin (© **02/4998 6960;** www.huntervalleysmellycheeseshop.com.au).

The Hunter Valley

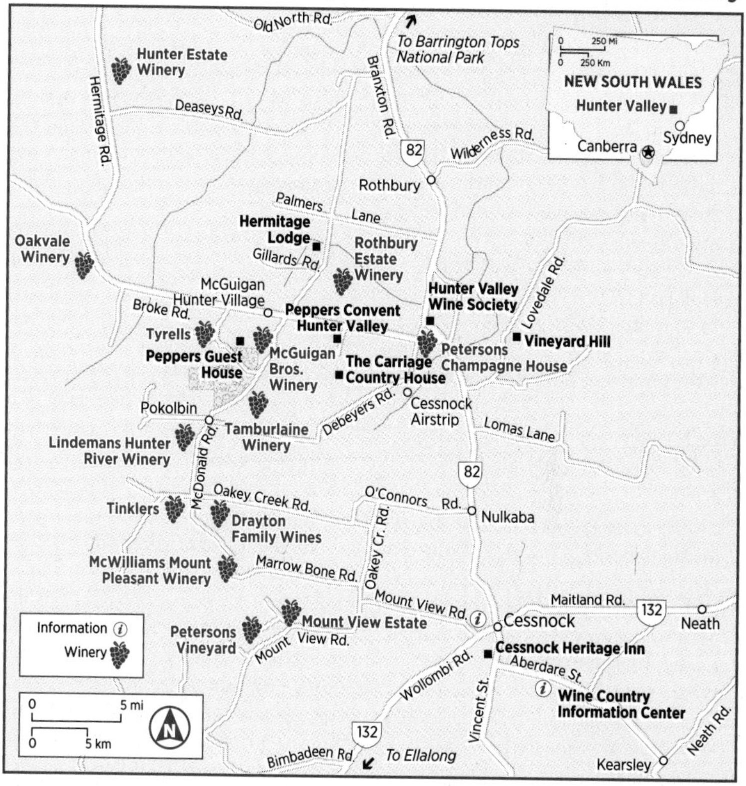

Drayton Family Wines Drayton's produces some spectacular Shiraz. Open Monday to Friday 9am to 5pm; Saturday and Sunday 10am to 5pm. Tours Monday to Friday 11am. 555 Oakey Creek Rd., Pokolbin. ✆ **02/4998 7513.**

Lindemans Hunter River Winery This famous winery offers an interesting sparkling red Shiraz. Open Monday to Friday 9am to 4:30pm; Saturday and Sunday 10am to 4:30pm. McDonald Rd., Pokolbin. ✆ **02/4998 7684.**

McGuigan Brothers Cellars A winery worth visiting, McGuigan also has a cheese factory and bakery on the site. Open daily 9:30am to 5pm with tours at noon. Corner of Broke and McDonalds roads, Pokolbin. ✆ **02/4998 7402.**

McWilliams Mount Pleasant Winery Famous for its Elizabeth Semillon, which has won 39 trophies and 214 gold medals since 1981, and its Lovedale Semillon, which has won 39 trophies and 74 gold medals since 1984. Open daily 10am to 4:30pm with tours at 11am. Marrowbone Rd., Pokolbin. ✆ **02/4998 7505.**

Peterson's Champagne House This is the only specialist champagne winery in the Hunter. Open daily 9am to 5pm. At the corner of Broke and Branxton roads, Pokolbin. ✆ **02/4998 7881.**

Peterson's Vineyard Peterson's produces fine chardonnay, Semillon, and Shiraz. Open Monday to Saturday 9am to 5pm, Sunday 10am to 5pm. Mount View Rd., Mount View. ✆ **02/4990 1704.**

Wine-Tasting the Finest

Some wineries routinely offer some of their inferior wines for tastings. Make a habit of asking for a list of their premium wines available for tasting. Most wineries usually have a bottle or two of their better wines uncorked for those with a serious interest.

Rothbury Estate ★ This very friendly winery produces the magnificent Brokenback Shiraz and the nice Mudgee Shiraz. Open daily 9:30am to 4:30pm. Broke Rd., Pokolbin. ✆ **02/4998 7555.**

Tamburlaine Winery Don't miss this boutique winery, the winner of many wine and tourism awards. Open daily 9:30am to 5pm. 358 McDonald Rd., Pokolbin. ✆ **02/4998 7570.**

Tinklers If you want to taste grapes in season, head to Tinklers. It sells some 30 different varieties of eating grapes between December and March, and nectarines, plums, peaches, and vegetables at other times of the year. It also offers wine tasting and free vineyard walks at 11am Saturday and Sunday. Open daily 10am to 4pm. Pokolbin Mountains Rd., Pokolbin. ✆ **02/4998 7435.**

Tyrell's Tyrell's has produced some famous wines and exports all over the world. Tours Monday to Saturday 1:30pm. Broke Rd., Pokolbin. ✆ **02/4993 7000.**

Day & Hot-Air Balloon Tours

If you don't have a car, you'll have to get around as part of a tour, because no public transport runs between the wineries.

Trekabout Tours (✆ **02/4990 8277;** www.hunterweb.com.au/trekabout) offers half-day and full-day winery tours for a maximum of six people. Half-day tours cost A$50, with visits to five or six wineries; full-day tours cost A$60 and take in up to nine wineries, mostly boutique ones. The company can pick you up from your hotel in Cessnock or Pokolbin.

Also offering local pickup is **Hunter Vineyard Tours** (✆ **02/4991 1659;** www.huntervineyardtours.com.au), which has a full-day tour on a 12- or 21-seat bus, taking in five wineries. It costs A$65, or A$95 with lunch.

A tranquil way to see the wineries is from above. **Balloon Aloft,** in Cessnock (✆ **1800/028 568** in Australia, or 02/4938 1955; www.balloonaloft.com.au), offers year-round dawn balloon flights that include postflight champagne and optional breakfast costing A$18. Flights last about an hour and cost A$299 for adults midweek (A$335 weekends) and A$235 for kids ages 8 to 12.

Where to Stay

The Hunter Valley is far more expensive on weekends and during public holidays than on weekdays. Room prices jump significantly, and some properties insist on a 2-night stay. It's worth checking out the information board in the Wine Country Visitors Information Centre (see "Visitor Information," above) for special deals, including self-contained accommodations, cottages, resorts, and guesthouses.

IN CESSNOCK

Staying in Cessnock is a good idea if you don't have a car and are relying on local tour companies to pick you up and show you around the area.

Cessnock Heritage Inn This 1920s building, built as a pub, is right in the center of Cessnock, so there's easy access to pubs and restaurants. All the rooms are simple and done in country style, with dried grasses, floral bedspreads, and the like. All are quite large, with high ceilings, but differ greatly—the smallest room has a double bed, others have queen-size beds and singles, and there are two family rooms (sleeping five).

Vincent St. (P.O. Box 714), Cessnock, NSW 2325. ✆ **02/4991 2744.** Fax 02/4991 2720. www.cessnockheritageinn.com.au. 13 units. Fri–Sat A$150 double, Sun–Thurs A$80 double. A$160–A$240 family. Some rates include breakfast. AE, MC, V. *In room:* A/C, TV w/free videos, minibar.

IN POKOLBIN

Very Expensive

Peppers Convent Hunter Valley ★★ Originally a convent for Brigidine nuns in the early part of the 20th century, this building was transported some 600km (372 miles) from Coonamble in central New South Wales to its present location in 1990. A year later, it opened as a hotel. Rooms are elegant and spacious, with baroque decor, including plaster frieze ceilings and thick, rich drapes. French doors open onto private verandas overlooking patches of bushland. King rooms are larger and have wicker lounge areas. There is an elegant sitting area where drinks are served, and a light and airy breakfast room serving the best breakfasts in the Hunter. The Pepper Tree Complex includes Pepper Tree Wines and the excellent **Robert's Restaurant** (see "Where to Dine," below). Check the website for ever-changing packages.

In the Pepper Tree Complex, Halls Rd., Pokolbin, NSW 2320. ✆ **02/4998 7764.** Fax 02/4998 7323. www.peppers.com.au. 17 units. Sat–Sun A$323–A$387 double; weekday A$291–A$332 double. Extra adult A$44. Extra child 5–15 A$22. Children 4 and under stay free in parent's room. 2-night minimum on Sat–Sun. Ask about packages and check website the week before for specials. AE, DC, MC, V. **Amenities:** Restaurant; babysitting; free use of bikes; concierge; Jacuzzi; medium-size heated outdoor pool; outdoor lit tennis court. *In room:* A/C, TV, hair dryer, minibar.

Peppers Guest House This tranquil escape is set in beautiful bush gardens. The spot is so peaceful that kangaroos hop up to the veranda in the evenings looking for treats. The "classic" rooms downstairs have French doors that you can fling open;

Bunking Down in a Caravan

If you happen to be touring the country in a caravan (otherwise known as a camper or recreational vehicle), the Valley Vineyard Tourist Park, on Mount View Road on the way to the vineyards (✆/fax 02/4990 2573; www.valleyvineyard.com.au), offers reasonably comfortable accommodations with space for your caravan. It has a range of cabins costing from A$70 to A$130 for two people. Prices are noticeably more expensive on weekends, and during NSW school holidays. Powered sites for your RV cost A$30 to A$60 per night and camping costs A$30 to A$45 a night. There is a restaurant, a campers' kitchen, and a swimming pool on site.

upstairs rooms have just a tad more old-fashioned charm and come with air-conditioning. All rooms are compact, have king-size beds and are furnished with colonial antiques. (The hotel is starting to look a bit tired, though, and given the choice, I'd go for Peppers Convent instead.) A spa offers massages and facials, and a gentle 30-minute trail winds through the bush. The restaurant, **Chez Pok,** is an upscale establishment that tends to have mixed reviews.

Ekerts Rd., Pokolbin, NSW 2321. © **02/4998 7596.** Fax 02/4998 7739. www.peppers.com.au. 47 units, 1 cottage. Sat–Sun A$277 Colonial double, A$303 Classic double, A$315 Vintage double, A$347 Heritage Suite; weekday A$273 Colonial double, A$283 Classic double, A$292 Vintage double, A$327 Heritage Suite. 2-night minimum on Sat–Sun. Weekday rates include buffet breakfast. AE, DC, MC, V. **Amenities:** Restaurant; bike rental; small heated indoor pool; outdoor lit tennis court. *In room:* A/C, TV, hair dryer, minibar.

Tower Lodge ★★★ This lodge's rather plain exterior and heavy doors hide something very special. The check-in area looks through a wall of glass to a tantalizing, terra-cotta-floored Tuscan-style courtyard. In the middle, an impressive fountain splashes, and soft shadows fall across white columns, darkening sections of the mulberry-colored walls of surrounding rooms and buildings. Radiating out from the courtyard along portico passageways are ten Lodge Rooms, each decorated in a style of its own. Some have fireplaces, others small private courtyards. Expect something large and welcoming, with a sofa and chairs set out in front of a huge mantle perhaps, a king-size bed, and a deep double spa bath. More expensive is the Oriental Room, featuring polished timber floors and paneling and a private veranda with romantic wooden hot tub. Top of the range is the Chairman's Suite, which is in a freestanding building with its own tower. There is a separate sitting room with an open fire for cold winter nights. The main lodge area includes a bar, a baronial dining room, and a cozy library.

Halls Rd., Pokolbin, NSW 2320. © **02/4998 7022.** Fax 02/4998 7164. www.towerlodge.com.au. 12 rooms. A$655–A$745 Lodge Room; A$730 Oriental Room; A$850 Chairman's Suite. Rates include breakfast, afternoon tea, predinner drink. 2-night minimum stay is required Fri and Sat nights. **Amenities:** Restaurant; bar; 18-hole pitch and putt golf course; gym; medium-size outdoor heated pool; room service; sauna. *In room:* A/C, TV, hair dryer.

Expensive

The Carriages Country House ★★ Tucked away on 15 hectares (37 acres), a kilometer (⅔ mile) off the main road, the Carriages is a secluded retreat in the heart of Pokolbin. A two-suite cottage, the Gatehouse, is on a separate part of the grounds. In the main two-story house, a veranda circles downstairs rooms, which are furnished in antique country pine. Upstairs, the two lofty gable suites center on huge fireplaces. The Gatehouse suites offer incredible luxury; although relatively new, the stained-glass windows and rescued timber give them a rustic feel (these two Jacuzzi rooms share a lounge with a full kitchen and an open fire). There are open fires in six of the rooms. (The two standard doubles don't have them.) Breakfast is served in your room, and **Robert's Restaurant** is next door. The friendly owner, Ben Dawson, assures me he'll take Frommer's readers up to the top of a nearby hill where they can see plenty of wild kangaroos.

Halls Rd., Pokolbin, NSW 2321. © **02/4998 7591.** Fax 02/4998 7839. www.thecarriages.com.au. 10 units. A$175–A$225 double; A$225–A$280 suite; A$265–A$325 Jacuzzi suite. Rates include breakfast. 2-night minimum on Sat–Sun. AE, MC, V. **Amenities:** Babysitting; Jacuzzi; large heated outdoor pool; outdoor lit tennis court. *In room:* A/C, TV, fridge, hair dryer, kitchenette.

Casuarina Estate ★★ Now, this place is really an oddity. Each of its very different suites has an unusual theme. Just naming them will give you an idea: the Moulin Rouge, the Oriental, the Bordello, Casanova's Loft, the Mariners Suite, British Empire, Out of Africa, Edwardian, Palais Royale, and Romeo's Retreat. The most popular is the Bordello, with a pedestaled king-size bed, voluptuous pink curtains, and strategically placed mirrors. To get the full picture, it's well worth roaming around the website before you book. The award-winning **Casuarina Restaurant** serves Mediterranean-style food.

Hermitage Rd., Pokolbin, NSW 2321. ✆ **02/4998 7888.** Fax 02/4998 7692. www.casuarinainn.com.au. 10 units. A$190 weekday; A$240–A$270 Sat–Sun. 2-night minimum on Sat–Sun. AE, DC, MC, V. **Amenities:** Restaurant; large heated outdoor pool; smoke-free rooms. *In room:* A/C, TV, hair dryer.

Try a B&B

The Hunter Valley has plenty of moderately priced bed and breakfast options. Among them is the Hunter Valley Bed & Breakfast, 1443 Wine Country Dr., North Rothbury (✆ 02/4938 2193; www.huntervalleybedandbreakfast.com.au). Rooms cost A$135 Sunday to Thursday and A$195 on Friday and Saturday nights. Rates include a cooked breakfast.

Hermitage Lodge ★ If you want to be in the heart of vineyard country, stay at this friendly property, which is surrounded by vineyards. Standard rooms are large, sunny, and nicely decorated; they come with a queen-size bed and a double sofa bed. The spa suites are larger, with queen-size beds (two also come with double sofa beds), cathedral ceilings, Jacuzzis, and separate showers. Two of the newer rooms are two-story suites, each with a nice living area, king-size bed, and a big deck with a spa tub overlooking the vineyard. Five of them have fireplaces. Continental breakfast is served in all rooms, and a cooked one is available on request. For lunch or dinner, **Il Cacciatore** is one of the best restaurants in the region.

At Gillards and McDonalds roads, Pokolbin, NSW 2320. ✆ **02/4998 7639.** Fax 02/4998 7818. www.hermitagelodge.com.au. 20 units. Sat–Sun A$250 standard double, A$270 spa suite; weekday A$175 standard double, A$195 spa suite. Extra person A$20. Kids 4 and under stay free in parent's room. 2-night minimum on Sat–Sun. Rates include continental breakfast. Ask about packages. AE, DC, MC, V. **Amenities:** Restaurant; bar; babysitting; golf course nearby; medium-size outdoor pool; room service. *In room:* A/C, TV, fridge, hair dryer.

Where to Dine

IN POKOLBIN

The three restaurants in the Hunter with the biggest reputations are **Robert's Restaurant,** in the Peppers Convent Hunter Valley guesthouse; **Chez Pok,** in Peppers Guest House; and **Casuarina Restaurant.** (Robert's is reviewed below; for the others, see "Where to Stay," above.) For good coffee, don't go past **Bliss Coffee Roasters,** shop 2, Hunter Valley Gardens Shopping Centre, Broke Road, Pokolbin (✆ **02/4998 6700**).

Café Enzo ITALIAN This charming little cafe offers a nice ambience and good cuisine—though the prices are high. Full breakfasts are excellent and hearty but come in at around A$25. The house-made pasta with prawns, chorizo, and parmesan is a standout dish; I also like the unique smoked trout tart, and the baby spinach salad with pumpkin and panchetta. There's a sun-drenched courtyard beside the winery and a fountain, and a fire inside in winter. The cafe also serves afternoon teas.

At the corner of Broke and Ekerts roads (adjacent to Peppers Creek Antiques, near Peppers Guest House), Pokolbin. ✆ **02/4998 7233.** Main courses A$18–A$26; AE, DC, MC, V. Wed–Fri and Sun 10am–5pm; Sat 10am–10pm.

Robert's Restaurant ★★ EUROPEAN Within easy walking distance to Tower Lodge (its latest owners; see p. 202), Robert's is located among the vineyards in a National Trust slab cottage dating from around 1876. It's candlelight-moody inside, with elegant white tablecloths, rustic antiques, wide wooden floorboards, and a high wood-beamed ceiling. While the menu changes frequently, Robert's prides itself on sourcing the freshest local seasonal ingredients. An example is a first course of local partridge with sweet baby root vegetables, parsnip purée, and orange and caraway jus. A main course might be the peppered local venison served with pressed swede and baby Brussels sprouts, this time with a jus of vanilla and chestnut. There is a strong emphasis on wine, and Robert's has arguably the best cellar in the area.

Halls Rd., Pokolbin. ✆ **02/4998 7330.** www.robertsrestaurant.com. Main courses A$36–A$44. A$5 per-person surcharge Sat–Sun and public holidays. AE, DC, MC, V. Daily noon–5pm and 7pm–midnight.

PORT STEPHENS ★★

209km (130 miles) N of Sydney

Port Stephens, just 2½ hours north of Sydney, should be at the top of any New South Wales itinerary. It's a perfect add-on to a trip to the Hunter Valley (p. 197). Though you can come up from Sydney for the day, I recommend staying in the general area for at least 1 night. The sheltered Port Stephens bay is more than twice the size of Sydney Harbour and is as clean as a newly poured bath. The sea literally jumps with fish, and the creamy islands and surrounding Tomaree National Park boast more species of birds than even Kakadu National Park in the Northern Territory. Two pods of bottlenose dolphins, around 70 individuals in all, call the bay home, and you are almost certain to see some on a dolphin-watching cruise. Port Stephens is also a fabulous place to watch whales during their migration to the breeding grounds farther north (roughly from June to mid-Nov—though they are less frequently seen in Aug). There is also a large breeding colony of koalas in Lemon Tree Passage on the south side of the Tomaree Peninsula, which makes up the southern shoreline of the bay.

The main town, **Nelson Bay** (pop. 7,000), is on the northern side of the peninsula. The township of Shoal Bay, farther along the peninsula, has a spectacular beach edged with wildflowers. Another small resort town, **Anna Bay,** is the largest development on the southern side of the peninsula and has excellent surf beaches. The Stockton Bight stretches some 32km (20 miles) from Anna Bay south to the large industrial town of Newcastle. The Stockton Sand Dunes, which run behind the beach, are the longest in the Southern Hemisphere.

Opposite the Tomaree Peninsula, across the bay, are the small tourist townships of Tea Gardens and Hawks Nest, both at the mouth of the Myall River.

Essentials

GETTING THERE To get to Port Stephens, take the Sydney–Newcastle Freeway (F3) to its end, and then follow the Pacific Highway signs to Hexham and Port Stephens. **Port Stephens Coaches** (✆ **1800/045 949** in Sydney, or 02/4982 2940; www.pscoaches.com.au) travels between Port Stephens and Newcastle, and to

Nelson Bay from Sydney daily at 2pm. Buses from Sydney leave from Eddy Avenue, near Central Station; the journey takes 3½ hours. Round-trip tickets cost around A$57 for adults and A$44 for children. There's no train service to Port Stephens. You must book ahead.

VISITOR INFORMATION The **Port Stephens Visitor Information Centre,** Victoria Parade, Nelson Bay (✆ **02/4980 6900;** www.portstephens.org.au), is open Monday through Friday from 9am to 5pm and Saturday and Sunday from 9am to 4pm.

Seeing the Area

Several operators offer **dolphin- and whale-watching cruises.** Some of the best are aboard the ***Imagine*** (✆ **02/4984 9000;** www.imaginecruises.com.au), a 15m (49-ft.) catamaran operated by Frank Future and Yves Papin, two real characters. They offer a daily Island Discovery trip that includes dolphin-watching and a trip around the offshore islands. The 4-hour cruise departs from D'Albora Marina in Nelson Bay from Thursday to Sunday at 12:30pm from mid-December to March only. It costs A$60 for adults, A$30 for children 1 to 14, and A$150 for families, including lunch. Four-hour whale-watching tours cost the same and leave at 11am from June 1 to November 15. You are most likely to spot humpback whales, but there's also a chance to see minke and southern right whales. A 2-hour dolphin-watching cruise starts at 10:30am daily between mid-November and the end of March (with extra sailings at 1:30pm and 3:30pm on Tues and Wed). It costs A$30 for adults, A$15 for children ages 1 to 14, and A$75 for families. If you happen to be around on the weekend nearest a full moon, ask about overnight Full Moon Tours. It's really worthwhile checking the website or calling by phone in advance of your visit as tour times seem to change frequently.

The **Port Stephens Ferry Service** (✆ **02/4984 1262**) operates a 2½-hour Early Bird Dolphin Watch, with a stop at Tea Gardens township, daily at 8:30am. A similar 3½-hour cruise departs at noon (you can eat lunch in Tea Gardens), and a 2-hour dolphin-watching cruise departs at 3:30pm. All cruises cost A$20 for adults, A$10 for children 4 to 17, and A$50 for families.

For more information on cruises, and to book cruises, it's worth looking through the website: **www.cruiseportstephens.com.au**.

Where To Stay

Port Stephens is very popular with Sydneysiders, especially during the Christmas holidays, January, and Easter, so you'll need to book well in advance then.

Peppers Anchorage Port Stephens ★★ This low-rise resort, split into a main guesthouse and four separate lodges, is built onto a headland and runs almost directly into the bay—it's stopped from sliding in by a boardwalk and a picturesque marina. Rooms are light and luxurious; the suites each have a good-size Jacuzzi, perfect for two. Rooms on the top floor have a large balcony, from which uninterrupted views take in the bay and the islands; those below have private verandas. Two rooms are designed for wheelchairs. A nearby beach is the perfect spot for a sunset stroll. **Merretts** restaurant is romantic and the food is standard but tasty.

Corlette Point Rd., Corlette, NSW 2315. ✆ **1800/809 142** in Australia, or 02/4984 2555. Fax 02/4984 0300. www.peppers.com.au. 80 units. Sat–Sun, 2-night stay, A$377 double, A$449–A$764 suite; weekday, 1-night stay, A$148 double, A$181–A$306 suite. Ask about packages. AE, DC, MC, V. **Amenities:** Restaurant; bar; babysitting; children's program (public holidays only); exercise room; Jacuzzi; good-size heated outdoor pool; room service; sauna. *In room:* A/C, TV, fax, hair dryer, minibar.

Port Stephens Motor Lodge Surrounded by tall trees and gardens, this motor lodge a short stroll from the main township is a peaceful place to stay. The standard rooms are quite plain, with raw-brick walls, a comfy double bed (and an extra single bed in most rooms), a private balcony, and an attached shower with half-tub. Adjacent to the lodge is a self-contained family unit for four; it has two bedrooms, a laundry, and water views. There's a barbecue area on the grounds. Rates peak during the Christmas holiday period. The lodge offers plenty of packages including dolphin cruises and the like.

44 Mangus St., Nelson Bay, NSW 2315. ✆ **02/4981 3366.** Fax 02/4984 1655. www.portstephensmotorlodge.com.au. 17 units. A$115–A$220 standard double. AE, DC, MC, V. **Amenities:** Heated outdoor pool. *In room:* A/C, TV, hair dryer.

Salamander Shores ★ Salamander Shores looks like a beached, ramshackle paddle steamer—it's all white-painted bricks and rails and stairs, fixed to the bay by a jetty. Set in a well-tended, sloping garden, this five-story hotel retains a certain 1960s charm, despite undergoing selective modernization. Garden-view rooms are similar to most motel rooms, but you really should throw caution to the wind and get a sea-view room—you won't regret it. These rooms have Jacuzzis and large balconies with extensive views of the bay. When the sun rises over the water and the garden is full of lorikeets and corellas, it couldn't be more picture-perfect. Bedding consists of a queen bed, two single beds, and a sofa and separate en-suite bathroom. Two-bedroom family rooms look out over the gardens or the sea. Down below is a pub and shop selling alcohol.

147 Soldiers Point Rd., Soldiers Point, NSW 2317. ✆ **1800/655 029** in Australia, or 02/4982 7210. Fax 02/4982 7890. www.salamander-shores.com. 90 units. A$119–A$134 garden-view double; A$139 sea-view double; A$200 family rooms. Extra person A$20. Ask about packages. AE, DC, MC, V. **Amenities:** 2 restaurants; bar; babysitting; small heated outdoor pool; sauna. *In room:* A/C, TV, hair dryer, minibar.

Where to Dine

Most people head to **Nelson Bay** for their meals because of the great views. You'll find a host of cheap takeout joints and a few pleasant sit-down eateries.

Rock Lobster Restaurant ★ SEAFOOD Seafood is heavily dominant in this popular restaurant (though there is beef, pork belly, duck confit, and chicken, too), which has an outdoor area overlooking the water. Lobster, prawns, crab, and oysters are the big sellers—coupled with the fresh produce here, you can't really go wrong.

Level 1, d'Albora Marinas, 6 Teramby Rd., Nelson Bay. ✆ **02/4981 1813.** www.rocklobsterrestaurant.com.au. Reservations recommended. Main courses A$19–A$33. MC, V. Daily noon–3pm and 6–10pm.

NORTH ALONG THE PACIFIC HIGHWAY

The Pacific Highway leads over the Sydney Harbour Bridge and merges into the Sydney–Newcastle Freeway. It continues to the industrial coast town of Newcastle, bypassing Tuggerah Lake and Lake Macquarie (neither of real interest compared to what follows). From here, the Pacific Highway stays close to the coast until it reaches Brisbane, some 1,000km (620 miles) from Sydney.

Though the road is gradually being upgraded, conditions vary, and distances are long. Travelers should be aware that the route is renowned for its accidents. Though you could make it to Brisbane in a couple of days, you could also easily spend more than a week stopping off at the attractions along the way. The farther north you travel, the more tropical the landscape gets. By the time visitors reach the coastal resort town of Coffs Harbour, temperatures have noticeably increased, and banana palms and sugar-cane plantations start to appear.

Along the coast, you'll find excellent fishing and some superb beaches, most of them virtually deserted. Inland, the Great Dividing Range, which separates the wetter eastern plains from the dry interior, throws up rainforests, extinct volcanoes, and hobby farms growing tropical fruit as you head farther north toward Queensland. Along the way is a series of national parks—to visit most of them requires a detour of several kilometers. Those you shouldn't miss include the **Dorrigo** and **Mount Warning** national parks, both of which encompass some of the country's best and most accessible rainforests.

Port Macquarie

423km (262 miles) N of Sydney

Port Macquarie (pop. 40,000), about halfway between Sydney and the Queensland border, boasts some fabulous beaches; Flynn's Beach in particular is a haven for surfers. Boating and fishing are other popular pastimes. It used to be a penal colony for convicts who found life in Sydney Cove a touch too easy.

ESSENTIALS

GETTING THERE From Sydney, motorists follow the Pacific Highway and then the Sydney-Newcastle Freeway (F3). The coach trip from Sydney takes about 7 hours.

VISITOR INFORMATION The **Port Macquarie Visitor Information Centre,** at the corner of Clarence and Hay streets, under the Civic Centre (✆ **1800/025 935** in Australia, or 02/6581 8000; www.portmacquarieinfo.com.au), is open Monday through Friday from 8:30am to 5pm and Saturday and Sunday from 9am to 4pm.

EXPLORING THE AREA

The Billabong Koala and Wildlife Park, 61 Billabong Dr., Port Macquarie (✆ **02/6585 1060;** www.billabongkoala.com.au), is a family-owned nature park where you can get up close to hand-raised koalas, kangaroos, emus, wombats, many types of birds, and fish. You can pat (but not hold) the koalas at 10:30am, 1:30pm, and 3:30pm. There are also barbecue facilities, picnic grounds, and a restaurant. Allow 2 hours to fully experience this recommended wildlife park. It's open daily from 9am to 5pm; admission is A$18 for adults and A$11 for children.

The 257-passenger vessel ***Port Venture*** (✆ **02/6583 3058;** www.portventure.com.au) offers scenic cruises on the Hastings River. It leaves from the wharf at the end of Clarence Street. Daily barbecue-lunch cruises leave at 10am and cost A$40 for adults, A$20 for children 6 to 14, and A$112 for families. Reservations are essential. It docks at a private bush park along the way, and passengers can tuck into a traditional Aussie barbecue of steaks, fish, and salad. You can then fish, take a bushwalk, or swim. A 2-hour Devonshire Tea cruise costs A$22 for adults, A$10 for children, and A$60 for families. A half-hour sunset cruise costs A$13 for adults and A$10 for children.

WHERE TO STAY

El Paso Motor Inn Right on the waterfront, the El Paso offers a bit-better-than-standard motel-type rooms; the more expensive deluxe doubles are a little larger and have newer furniture. Two rooms have Jacuzzis, and some come with kitchenettes. The third-floor three-room suite has good ocean views and a kitchenette.

29 Clarence St., Port Macquarie, NSW 2444. ✆ **02/6583 1944.** www.elpasomotorinn.com.au. 53 units. A$125 standard double; A$139 deluxe double; A$195 Jacuzzi room; A$185–A$210 suite. Extra person A$20. A$35 surcharge per room per night NSW school holidays, Easter, Christmas, and some long weekends. DC, MC, V. **Amenities:** Restaurant; bar; babysitting; Jacuzzi; good-size heated outdoor pool; sauna. *In room:* A/C, TV, hair dryer, minibar.

Coffs Harbour ★

554km (344 miles) N of Sydney; 427km (265 miles) S of Brisbane

Rainforests, beaches, and sand surround the relaxed capital of Australia's Holiday Coast. The area used to produce more bananas than any other in Australia—but these days you have to go farther north to Queensland for the huge plantations. Inland, the rolling hills plateau into Dorrigo National Park, one of the best examples of accessible rainforests anywhere. Also inland is the Nymboida River, known for its excellent white-water rafting.

Coffs Harbour is a rather disjointed place, with an old town-center retail area; the Jetty Strip (with restaurants and fishing boats) near the best swimming spot, Park Beach; and a retail area called the Plaza. Wide sweeps of suburbia separate the three areas.

ESSENTIALS

GETTING THERE It takes around 7 hours to drive from Sydney to Coffs Harbour without stops; from Brisbane it takes around 5 hours. The Pacific Highway in this region is notoriously dangerous; many serious accidents have involved drivers enduring long hours behind the wheel. Ongoing road-widening projects should improve things. **Qantas** (✆ **13 13 13** in Australia) flies nonstop to Coffs Harbour from Sydney. Several coach companies, including **Greyhound Australia** (✆ **13 14 99** in Australia, or 07/4690 9950; www.greyhound.com.au), make the trip from Sydney in about 9 hours. A **Countrylink** (✆ **13 22 32** in Australia) train from Sydney costs around A$80.

VISITOR INFORMATION The **Coffs Harbour Visitors Information Centre** is just off the Pacific Highway, at the corner of Grafton and McLean streets (✆ **1300/369 070** in Australia, or 02/6652 1522; www.coffscoast.com.au). It's open daily from 9am to 5pm. A good general website is **www.holidaycoast.com.au**.

GETTING AROUND If you don't have a car, you can get around on **Coffs Harbour Coaches** (✆ **02/6652 2877**), which runs day trips around the local area on weekdays.

VISITING THE BIG BANANA

You can't miss the 10m (33-ft.) reinforced-concrete banana alongside the highway at the **Big Banana Theme Park** (✆ **02/6652 4355;** www.bigbanana.com), 3km (2 miles) north of town. The adjoining park offers ice-skating and other attractions. It's open daily from 9am to 4:30pm (3pm in winter). Admission to the Big Banana is free. I had my doubts about this place before I visited, but I ended up charmed—even if it was simply by the wackiness of the place.

canoeing THE VALLEY OF THE MIST ★★★

People tend to make a lot of claims that don't stand up, but when Dennis Ryan, proprietor of **Valley of the Mist** tours, tells you he has the "best backyard in Australia" you can easily believe him. Not only does he have a thriving organic vegetable patch, a highly-productive citrus grove, hundreds of macadamia trees, and dozens of other bush-tucker plants, his 44-hectare (110-acre) property backs onto one of the most important wetlands in Australia. This once remote area of tidal marshland and estuary connects up to the Nambucca River, just west of Macksville, on the New South Wales mid-north coast.

"My grandfather spent most of his life trying to drain it, to make this area more European," Dennis said on one of his signature canoe trips, as his paddle dipped into the shallow, tannin-stained water. "He used a shovel and an axe to make floodgates and miles of drains, but luckily for me and the wildlife he failed."

Today, the 73-hectare (180-acre) waterway—known traditionally as the **Hundred Acre Swamp**—is home to some 117 species of birds, including jabirus, egrets, flycatchers, and azure kingfishers. More than 400 black swans nest here, ospreys keep watch from a giant ironbark tree, and the water teems with prawns and native fish.

"An Aboriginal friend of mine talked me into doing canoe tours," Dennis said. "He reckoned I had to show people if I wanted to save the place.

"There are just seven canoe trips a week," he continued. "I don't want it to turn into simply tourism. I want it to remain special. We use the wildlife and the wetlands as much as they use us."

On our journey, we paddled past tiny islands of reeds and she oaks. Some islands were so small that they could only support a single stunted sapling. The wetland was so shallow that the canoe's hull cut through the pondweed. Slipping between two mounds of paperbarks, we moved into a slightly deeper and wider channel marked by mangroves and a half-flooded fence, put up by his grandfather around 1928. Birds were calling from all directions, and we watched as dozens of ducks took off in a noisy flurry of beating wings. At one point, 80 black swans glided by. Later, hundreds of flycatchers darted across the surface, picking insects out of the air. Back on dry land, Dennis showed us around the wetland's swampy edge, pointing out various trees and shrubs and stopping occasionally to crush a leaf or inspect a dry seed head.

"My mum spoke the local Aboriginal dialect," Denis said. "She learned it as a kid. Years ago, the Aboriginal women would come when the paperbark trees were in flower. It was the time of the mullet run. My grandmother traded with them for bush medicine. We've been using it ever since."

Wetland canoe tours cost A$60 per person. Valley of the Mist is north of Port Macquarie and south of Coffs Harbour, at 88 Congarinni North Rd., Talarm (✆ **02/6568 3268;** 0428/683 268 mobile; www.valleyofthemist.com.au).

A free natural attraction is **Mutton Bird Island,** which you can get to from the Coffs Harbour jetty. A steep path leads up the side of the island, but views from the top are worth it. Between September and April, the island is home to thousands of shearwaters (mutton birds), which make their nests in burrows in the ground.

If you prefer fish, try diving with gray nurse sharks, manta rays, and moray eels with **Jetty Dive Centre,** 398 Harbour Dr., Coffs Harbour (✆ **02/6651 1611**).

Two dives cost A$175. If you'd rather catch them than swim with them, the ***Pamela Star*** (✆ **02/6658 4379**) offers good-value deep-sea-fishing trips.

For a taste of gold fever, head to **George's Gold Mine,** 40km (25 miles) west of Coffs Harbour on Bushman's Range Road (✆ **02/6654 5355** or 6654 5273). You get to go into an old-time gold mine, see the "stamper battery" crushing the ore, and pan for gold yourself. The mine is open Wednesday through Sunday (daily during school and public holidays) from 10:30am to 5pm. Admission is A$10 for adults, A$5 for children, and A$28 for families.

EXPLORING THE RAINFORESTS & OTHER OUTDOOR ADVENTURES

Coffs Harbour's main advantage is its position as a good base for exploring the surrounding countryside. You must see the World Heritage–listed **Dorrigo National Park ★★**, 68km (42 miles) west of Coffs Harbour, via Bellingen. Perched on the Great Dividing Range that separates the lush eastern seaboard from the arid interior, the rainforest here is one of the best I've seen in Australia. (It's a pity that so much fell to the axes of early settlers.) Entry is free.

The **Dorrigo Rainforest Centre** (✆ **02/6657 2309**) is the gateway to the park and has extensive information on the rainforest. (I also highly recommend the **Canopy Café** inside.) Just outside is the 21m-high (69-ft.) **Skywalk,** which offers a bird's-eye view of the forest canopy. Several walks leave from the Rainforest Centre, the Glade Picnic Area (about 1km/½ mile away), and the Never-Never Picnic Area (a 10km/6¼-mile drive along Dome Rd.). Most tracks are suitable for wheelchairs. Bring a raincoat or an umbrella; it is a rainforest, after all! For more information, the **Dorrigo Tourist Information** office (✆ **02/6657 2486**) is in the center of Dorrigo township.

By the way, an interesting way to get to Dorrigo is by helicopter—if you have the money. **Precision Helicopters** (✆ **02/6652 9988;** www.precisionhelicopters.com.au) offers scenic flights around the area. For a bit more personal action, try horseback riding through the rainforest 23km (14 miles) southwest of Coffs Harbour with **Valery Trails** (✆ **02/6653 4301;** www.valerytrails.com.au). Two-hour rides leave at 10am and 2pm daily and cost A$50 for adults and A$45 for kids. Reservations are essential.

Looking for an adrenaline rush? Then head to the **Raleigh International Raceway** (✆ **02/6655 4017**), where you can zip around the track behind the wheel of your very own go-kart. It's 23km (14 miles) south of Coffs Harbour and 3km (2 miles) along Valery Road, off the Pacific Highway, north of Nambucca Heads. Eleven high-speed laps cost A$35, and sixteen cost A$47, and 24 costs A$60. It's open daily from 9am to 5pm (to 6pm in summer).

If you have your own wheels, I'd recommend a visit to the little town of Sawtell, 10km (6 miles) south of Coffs Harbour. Despite its size, it has plenty of designer stores, chic cafes, and gourmet restaurants. The beach is nice too, with hypnotic views up and down the coast. If you want to stay the night here, the **Creekside Inn B&B,** 59 Boronia St., Sawtell (✆ **02/6658 9099;** www.creeksideinn.com.au), is your best option. Rooms cost from A$140 per couple, including gourmet breakfast and afternoon tea. Some of the town's best restaurants are in the main street; these include **Barrels Global Bistro** (✆ **02/6658 8255;** www.barrelsbistro.com.au) and **Taste Restaurant** (✆ **02/6658 3583**).

WHERE TO STAY

Coffs Harbour is a popular beachside holiday spot, with plenty of motels along the Pacific Highway offering standard roadside rooms. Vacancy signs are common outside Australian school holiday periods and the Christmas and Easter periods (when Coffs really fills up). A few nicer ones to try are the **Caribbean Motel,** 353 High St., Coffs Harbour, NSW 2450 (✆ **02/6652 1500;** fax 02/6651 4158; www.caribbeanmotel.com.au), with doubles ranging from A$95 to A$199, depending on the season and the view; and the **Quality Inn City Centre,** 22 Elizabeth St., Coffs Harbour, NSW 2450 (✆ **02/6652 6388;** fax 02/6652 6493; www.citycentre.com.au), with doubles from A$158.

Sanctuary Motor Inn Resort If you love animals, you'll like this animal sanctuary and guesthouse complex 2km (1¼ miles) south of town. Wandering around the grounds are wallabies, kangaroos, peacocks, and several species of native birds. Standard doubles are comfortable though simple, while superior rooms have an extra single bed. Family rooms come with a queen bed and either two or three single beds, plus a kitchen.

Pacific Hwy., Coffs Harbour, NSW 2450. ✆ **02/6652 2111.** Fax 02/6652 4725. www.sanctuaryresort.net.au. 38 units. A$75 standard double; A$95 deluxe double. Extra person A$20. Holiday surcharge A$25 per room per night. Ask about Aussie auto club discounts. AE, DC, MC, V. **Amenities:** Restaurant; bar; minigolf; Jacuzzi; large heated outdoor pool; room service (7–9am and 6–8pm); sauna; lit tennis and squash courts. *In room:* A/C, TV w/free satellite channels, fridge, hair dryer.

WHERE TO DINE

The Jetty on Harbour Drive is where you'll find most of the main eateries. Some good ones include the **Foreshore's Café,** 394 Harbour Dr. (✆ **02/6652 3127**), which serves huge breakfasts and lunches on an ocean-view terrace, and **Crying Tiger,** 386 Harbour Dr. (✆ **02/6650 0195**), which has good Thai food at dinnertime.

Wild Harvest Seafood Restaurant and Cafe This bi-level restaurant offers superb views out to sea and serves up great seafood—which is perhaps not surprising since it's owned by a fishermen's co-operative. The downstairs cafe, called **At the Courtyard,** is cheaper and has tables inside and outside. It's open daily for breakfast and lunch. **With the Waves** is the name of the upper level, which is open for breakfast on weekends from 8am, lunch from Tuesday to Sunday, and dinner from Tuesday to Saturday. Try and book an outdoor table on nice days.

9 Marina Drive, Coffs Harbour. ✆ **02/6652 2811.** Reservations recommended. Main courses A$20–A$30. AE, MC, V. Daily 8am–early evening.

Byron Bay: A Beach Bohemia ★

790km (490 miles) N of Sydney; 200km (124 miles) S of Brisbane; 78km (48 miles) SE of Murwillumbah

At the easternmost point on the Australian mainland, the sun's rays hit Byron before anywhere else. This geographical position is good for two things: It's attractive to the town's "alternative" community, and you can spot migrating whales. The humpback migration begins in May and June, when they head north to warmer waters to breed; and they return south around September and October, when they often come into the Bay and breach and frolic with their calves. Painters, craftspeople, glass blowers, and poets are so plentiful that they almost fall from the macadamia trees. The place

NATIONAL parks IN NSW

New South Wales has more than 780 national parks and reserves, which protect everything from rainforests and rugged bush to alpine woodland and Outback deserts. We mention a few in parts of this chapter, but here is a taste of what you can expect from a handful of others:

- **Botany Bay National Park** straddles two headlands at the entrance to Botany Bay in Sydney. It commemorates the site of first contact between the crew of James Cook's *Endeavour* and the Aboriginal people of Australia in 1770. Here you'll find remnants of the heathland vegetation that Joseph Banks, Cook's botanist, studied in 1770. One of Australia's most iconic plants, the banksia, was named after him. Enjoy the Cape Baily Coast Walk, with its windswept heaths and spectacular coastal views.
- North of the Hunter Valley is **Barrington Tops National Park,** a huge area of World Heritage–listed subtropical rainforest, chock full of staghorns, vines, and birds, as well as an area of subalpine woodland on the high plateau. The woodland is regularly snowbound in winter. There are a series of well-defined walking tracks, and the park is a good add-on to any multiday visit to the Hunter Valley region.
- Just north of Port Stephens you can find **Myall Lakes National Park,** one of the state's largest coastal lake systems—a Ramsar Wetland of International Significance. As well as a myriad of bird species, there are plenty of beaches and sand dunes. A sliver of land separates the lakes from the beach. This is a very popular holiday destination for people who love fishing, swimming, canoeing, sailboarding, surfing, and bushwalking.
- If you want space and solitude, rolling red-sand dunes, wide open blue skies, giant eagles, and kangaroos and emus, then the remote, arid **Sturt National Park** is for you. Situated in the far western corner of New South Wales, Sturt is a land of rocky tabletop hills, saltbush, remnant dry woodland, and occasional creeks lined with river red gums.
- Lovers of true wilderness will be happy that **Wollemi National Park** exists. Though it starts just west of the popular wine district of the Hunter Valley, this largest wilderness area in NSW is no tame forest. In 1994, a bushwalker stumbled across what became known as the Wollemi Pine. It caused a worldwide sensation—it was supposed to have become extinct 200 million years earlier! There are also remarkable Aboriginal cave paintings seen by few modern humans, hidden within this maze of canyons and cliffs. The Glow Worm Tunnel, another favorite attraction, is part of the old railway that serviced Wollemi; access is from Clarence on the Bells Line of Road, heading toward the Blue Mountains. Dunns Swamp also has easy walks.

is loaded with float tanks, "pure body products," beauty therapists, and massage centers. Though it attracts squadrons of backpackers to its party scene and discos each summer, many of the locals simply stay at home, sipping their herbal tea and preparing for the healing light of the coming dawn. Families love Byron Bay for the beautiful beaches, and surfers flock here for some of the best waves in the world.

ESSENTIALS

GETTING THERE If you're driving up the north coast, leave the Pacific Highway at Ballina and take the scenic coast road via Lennox Head. It's around 10 hours by car from Sydney, and 2 hours from Brisbane.

Regional Express (✆ **13 17 13** in Australia; www.regionalexpress.com.au) flies from Sydney to Ballina, south of Byron Bay. The round-trip fare is around A$300. **Virgin Blue** (www.virginblue.com.au) also flies to Ballina. **Byron Bus Transfers** (✆ **02/6681 3354**) meets all flights and transfers to Byron Bay for A$20 single and A$35 round-trip. **Coolangatta Airport** is 1 hour north of Byron Bay (112km/69 miles). **Countrylink** (✆ **13 22 32** in Australia) runs daily trains from Sydney to Byron Bay; the one-way fare is around A$98 for adults and A$47 for children, and the trip takes 12 hours. **Greyhound Australia** (✆ **13 14 99** in Australia, or 07/4690 9950; www.greyhound.com.au) buses from Sydney take around 14 hours; the one-way coach fare costs from A$85.

ORGANIZED TOURS FROM SYDNEY An unusual way to get to Byron is on a 5-day surf safari from Sydney with **Surfaris** (✆ **1800/634 941** in Australia; www.surfaris.com). You can learn to surf along the way, as you stop off at several beaches, staying in dorm accommodations overnight (you can upgrade to double rooms). Trips leave Sydney on Monday morning and Byron Bay on Sunday morning. The safari is an all-inclusive A$599. A 3-day surf safari leaves either on Sunday or Monday and costs A$399.

Another great trip is with **Ando's Outback Tours** (✆ **1800/228 828** in Australia; www.outbacktours.com.au), which operates from Sydney every Sunday. It heads inland deep into the Outback on a 5-day trip and returns to Byron Bay. Among the highlights are visits to Lightning Ridge and the wild Glengarry opal fields (see "Outback New South Wales," later in this chapter). The trip costs A$500.

VISITOR INFORMATION The **Byron Visitors Centre,** 80 Jonson St., Byron Bay, NSW 2481 (✆ **02/6680 9271;** www.visitbyronbay.com), is open daily from 9am to 5pm. A half-hour farther south is the **Ballina Tourist Information Centre,** on the corner of Las Balsas Plaza and River Street, Ballina (✆ **02/6686 3484**), open daily from 9am to 5pm.

SPECIAL EVENTS Byron really goes to town during 4 days over the Easter weekend with the **East Coast Blues & Roots Festival** (www.bluesfest.com.au). Up to 30,000 people camp out to listen to up to 80 acts, including the likes of Ben Harper, Midnight Oil, and Joan Armatrading. Book tickets on the Web. On the first Sunday of every month, the extraordinary local **crafts market** brings hippies and funky performers out from the hinterland. Byron Bay is very popular over the Christmas period, so book well in advance.

HITTING THE SURF & SAND

Many accommodations in Byron Bay offer free surfboards for guests. If yours doesn't, head to the **Byron Surf Shop,** Lawson Street at the corner of Fletcher

Street (© **02/6685 7536**), which rents boards. The shop can also arrange surf lessons for around A$25 per hour. The **Byron Bay Surf School,** 127 Jonson St. (© **1800/707 274**), offers surfing classes from A$60.

Wategos Beach and an area off the tip of Cape Byron called **"The Pass"** are two particularly good surf spots; and since each of the beaches faces a different direction, you are bound to find the surf is up on at least one. **Main Beach,** which stretches along the front of the town (it's actually some 50km/31 miles long), is good for swimming. West of Main Beach is **Belongil Beach,** the unofficial nudist beach (when authorities aren't cracking down on covering up). **Clarke's Beach** curves away to the east of Main Beach toward Cape Byron.

The **Cape Byron Lighthouse** on Cape Byron is one of Australia's most powerful. It's eerie to come up here at night to watch the stars and see the light reach some 40km (25 miles) out to sea. A nice walk just south of town goes through the rainforest of the **Broken Heads Nature Reserve.**

The best place to dive around Byron Bay is at **Julian Rocks,** about 3km (2 miles) offshore. Cold currents from the south meet warmer ones from the north here, which makes it a good spot to find a large variety of marine sea life. **Byron Bay Dive Centre,** 111 Jonson St. (© **1800/243 483** in Australia, or 02/6685 8333; www.byronbaydivecentre.com.au), offers a range of diving and snorkeling tours and runs dive courses, too.

EXPLORING THE HILLS & RAINFORESTS

Behind Byron you'll find hills that could make the Irish weep, as well as rainforests, waterfalls, and small farms burgeoning with tropical fruits. A good operator taking trips inland is **Byron Bay Eco Tours** (© **0429/770 686** mobile; www.byronbaywildlifetours.com). Tours cost A$63 for adults and A$27 for kids. On a typical tour you will see plenty of birdlife, as well red-necked pademelons, whiptail wallabies, red-necked wallabies, a flying fox colony, kangaroos, and koalas.

The **Nimbin Shuttle** (© **02/6680 9189;** www.nimbinaustralia.com/nimbinshuttle) operates a shuttle bus service to Nimbin from Byron Bay Monday to Saturday for A$15 one-way. The Nimbin Market is on every third Sunday of the month. If you like that sort of thing, you could also visit the Hemp Embassy (© **02/6689 1842;** www.hempembassy.net) for all things marijuana-related. There are some interesting art galleries in Nimbin, too.

WHERE TO STAY

The **Byron Bay Accommodation Booking Office** (© **02/6680 8666;** www.byronbayaccom.net) is very helpful for booking places to stay before you arrive.

Arts Factory Lodge This is a wacky kind of place. Once famous as a music club popular with American draft-dodgers during the Vietnam War, it's now big with young travelers seeking an alternative place to stay and older folk who cut their hair short years ago. Accommodations include tepees, tents, rooms made from bark strips, and funky indoor "cubes." The so-called Love Shack is more standard and quite tropical in appearance. Workshops include didgeridoo making, massage, yoga, and even boxing! The entertainment lineup includes live music, fire shows, Aboriginal culture, and sports. A cafe serves vegetarian meals, and the property has a great outdoor pool and lush gardens.

Skinners Shoot Rd., Byron Bay, NSW 2481. © **02/6685 7709.** Fax 02/6685 8534. www.artsfactory.com.au. A$25 dorm; A$63 cube; A$70 Love Shack. 3-night minimum. Discounts for 5 nights. AE, DC, MC, V. **Amenities:** Cafe; free use of bikes; outdoor pool.

The Byron at Byron Resort & Spa ★★★ The number-one place to stay at Byron Bay, the relatively new Byron at Byron is set within a stunning 18-hectare (45-acre) lush rainforest, just a short distance out of town. Each one-bedroom suite has a king-size bed, kitchen, separate lounge and dining area, and plasma TV, as well as two enclosed balconies. Luxurious bathrooms have deep free-standing bathtubs and separate showers. The main building opens onto large verandas that overlook the rainforest canopy. There are six luxurious treatment rooms, offering hot stone massages, body wraps, facials, hydrotherapy treatments, and specialized spa therapies. The large infinity pool is very inviting. You can hire bikes here, too. It's a harmonious, gorgeous place, and well worth the money.

77–79 Broken Head Rd., Suffolk Park, Byron Bay, NSW 2481. ✆ **1300/554 362.** www.byronatbyron.com.au. 92 units. Superior suites A$385 per night, spa suites A$425. 2-night minimum. AE, DC, MC, V. **Amenities:** Restaurant; bar; bike hire; gym; Jacuzzi; 25m (82-ft.) outdoor heated pool; spa; tennis court. *In room:* A/C, TV, hair dryer, minibar.

The Byron Bay Waves Motel (The Waves) ★ This exceptional motel is only 60m (197 ft.) from Main Beach and just around the corner from the town center. Each of the standard suites comes with a queen-size bed, a marble bathroom with shower, and a king-size tub. They also have a pullout sofa bed. Toasters, in-house massage, and beauty treatments are also available. There are two State suites: The Bay Suite has stunning beach and ocean views, and a large private terrace, while the Lawson Suite has views of the hinterland and its own private terrace, too. Each of these has a king-size bed. The penthouse is a very plush, fully self-contained one-bedroom apartment. A new beachfront terrace studio sleeps four, has great ocean views, a large plasma TV with a DVD/CD player, a king-size bed, and an enclosed courtyard with barbecue. The first room rate below is based on low season (essentially winter), and the second rate on high season (Christmas and New Year). Mid-season rates are somewhere in between.

Corner of Lawson and Middleton sts. (P.O. Box 647), Byron Bay, NSW 2481. ✆ **02/6685 5966.** Fax 02/6685 5977. www.wavesbyronbay.com.au. 20 units. A$250–A$390 standard suite; A$300–A$470 state suites; A$375–A$475 beachfront terrace; A$400–A$650 penthouse. Extra person A$50. AE, DC, MC, V. **Amenities:** Babysitting. *In room:* A/C, TV, fax, hair dryer, minibar.

Byron Central Apartments If you don't want to eat out all the time, then this is the place for you. The self-contained apartments come with a queen-size bed and free in-house movies. First-floor units have balconies. There are also a few loft-style apartments with separate dining, lounge, and sleeping areas. Units for people with disabilities are available. The landscaped garden has a barbecue. The apartments are a 2-minute walk from the beach and town. Rates are at their highest in the Christmas and New Year period; low season is April through September. The website has a booking engine with varying rates.

Byron St., Byron Bay, NSW 2481. ✆ **02/6685 8800.** Fax 02/6685 8802. www.byroncentral.com. 26 units. A$112–A$200 standard apt. Ask about long-term discounts. AE, DC, MC, V. **Amenities:** Medium-size saltwater pool. *In room:* TV, hair dryer, kitchen.

WHERE TO DINE

Byron Bay's **Jonson Street** is crammed with eateries, so you certainly won't starve.

Dish ★ MEDITERRANEAN This down-to-earth restaurant with its classical white-cloth tables and long opening onto the street scene is a Byron institution, which keeps getting better. The menu is small but enticing, and though it changes regularly, you can get an idea from the likes of pork belly confit with slow-poached pork fillet with potato and carrot gratin and braised cabbage; and seared venison with caramelized butternut pumpkin, pearl onions, and blueberry jus. A seven-course "tasting menu" costs A$95, or A$150 with matching wines.

Corner Jonson and Marvel sts. ✆ **02/6685 7320.** www.dishbyronbay.com.au. Reservations recommended. Main courses A$34–A$40. AE, MC, V. Daily 6pm–midnight.

Fins ★★ SEAFOOD The best seafood place in Byron Bay is located in the popular Beach Hotel. The food is inspired by the chef's travels, and she uses locally caught seafood and fresh ingredients, including herbs from her own garden. The signature dish is the "Cataplana of Seafood" (for two people). It's a southern-Portuguese bouillabaisse-style dish of local seafood and potatoes poached in a saffron and star anise–flavored broth.

In the Beach Hotel, at Bay and Jonson sts. ✆ **02/6674 4833.** www.fins.com.au. Main courses A$30–A$38. AE, MC, V. Daily noon–3pm and 6–10pm.

Olivo ★ CONTEMPORARY Warm service, a laid-back atmosphere, a wafer-thin room, bare-brick walls, an open kitchen, chic mirrors, and beige leather seating all add up to make Olivo one of Byron's "in" places to eat. Expect the likes of pork belly layered with roasted figs, and Spanish mackerel sashimi.

34 Jonson St. ✆ **02/6685 7950.** Reservations recommended. Main courses A$24–A$28. AE, MC, V. Daily 6:30–9pm.

Rae's on Watego's ★ MODERN AUSTRALIAN/SEAFOOD You can't beat Rae's for its location or its food. It's right on the beach, about a 2-minute drive from the town center, and has a secluded, privileged air about it—in the nicest of ways. Inside it's all Mediterranean blue and white, perfectly complementing the waves hitting the sand. The menu changes daily, but you may find the likes of grilled Atlantic salmon, red curry of roast beef filet, braised lamb shanks, and yellowfin tuna. If you have any special dietary requirements, tell the chef, and he will go out of his way to please you. Next door to the restaurant, but part of the same establishment, is **Rae's on Watego's,** an exclusive AAA-rated five-star guesthouse offering luxury accommodations. There are seven units; prices run from around A$400 for a double suite to A$990 for the penthouse suite.

Watago's Beach, Byron Bay. ✆ **02/6685 5366.** Fax 02/6685 5695. www.raes.com.au. Reservations recommended. Main courses A$35–A$40 lunch, A$38–A$50 dinner. AE, DC, MC, V. Daily 7–10pm; Sat-Sun noon–3pm.

Murwillumbah

321km (199 miles) N of Coffs Harbour; 893km (554 miles) N of Sydney; 30km (19 miles) S of Queensland border

The main town of the Tweed Valley, Murwillumbah is a good base for touring the surrounding area, which includes **Mount Warning,** picturesque towns, and countryside dominated by sugar cane and banana.

ESSENTIALS

GETTING THERE Murwillumbah is inland from the Pacific Highway. The nearest airport is at **Coolangatta,** 34km (21 miles) away, over the Queensland border. **Countrylink** trains (✆ **13 22 42** in Australia) link Murwillumbah with Sydney, taking around 13 hours. The one-way fare is around A$110 in standard class, A$149 in first class. **Greyhound Australia** (✆ **13 14 99** in Australia, or 07/4690 9950; www.greyhound.com.au) runs from Sydney to Murwillumbah; the trip takes 15 hours.

VISITOR INFORMATION The **Murwillumbah Visitors Centre,** at the corner of the Pacific Highway and Alma Street, Murwillumbah, NSW 2484 (✆ **02/6672 1340;** www.tweedtourism.com.au), is worth visiting before heading out to see more of the Tweed Valley or the beaches to the east. Another option is the **Tweed Heads Visitors Centre,** at the corner of Bay and Wharf streets, Tweed Heads, NSW 2485 (✆ **07/5536 4244**). Both are open Monday through Friday from 9am to 5pm, and Saturday from 9am to 1pm.

SEEING THE AREA

If you're looking for a Big Avocado to go with your Coffs Harbour Big Banana, head for **Tropical Fruit World,** on the Pacific Highway (✆ **02/6677 7222;** www.tropicalfruitworld.com.au), 15km (9½ miles) north of Murwillumbah and 15km (9½ miles) south of Coolangatta. The Tweed Valley's top attraction grows some 400 varieties of tropical fruit, which you can discover on an interesting 1½-hour tractor-train tour of the 81-hectare (200-acre) plantation, as well as on four-wheel-drive rainforest drives and riverboat rides. It's open daily from 10am to 4pm. Also on the property are a kiosk, fruit market, and gift shop. Admission to food and shopping areas is free.

The 1,154m (3,785-ft.) **Mount Warning** is part of the rim of an extinct volcano formed some 20 to 23 million years ago. You can hike around the mountain and to the top on trails in the Mount Warning World Heritage Park.

WHERE TO STAY & DINE

Crystal Creek Rainforest Retreat ★★ Pricey but nice Crystal Creek is tucked away in a little valley of rainforest just 25 minutes by car from the Pacific Highway. Self-contained cabins skirt the edge of the rainforest that borders the Border Ranges National Park, a World Heritage Site. There are plenty of native birds, possums, echidnas, wallabies, and bandicoots around and about. Guests can swim in the cold natural pools and laze around on hammocks strung up in the bush. Cabins have two comfortable rooms, a balcony, a kitchen, a barbecue, and plenty of privacy. Two glass-terrace cabins overlook the rainforest and mountain. All rooms have king-size beds and double Jacuzzis—with no curtains in the bathroom, because the rainforest gives enough privacy. Several tours are offered, including four-wheel-drive rainforest tours and visits to local country markets and arts-and-crafts galleries, as well as walking tours around the property. Guests cook their own food (bring it with you) or eat at the casual restaurant.

Brookers Rd., Upper Crystal Creek, Murwillumbah, NSW 2484. ✆ **02/6679 1591.** Fax 02/6679 1596. www.crystalcreekrainforestretreat.com.au. 7 cabins. A$345–A$525 double. There's generally a 2-night minimum. Ask about weekday specials. AE, DC, MC, V. Pickup service from the airport, bus, and train stations available. Children not accepted. **Amenities:** Restaurant; Jacuzzi; room service. *In room:* TV, CD player, hair dryer, kitchen.

THE TWEED VALLEY AFTER DARK

The clubs up here on the border of Queensland are huge and offer cheap bistro meals as well as pricier ones in more upscale restaurants, inexpensive drinks at the bar, entertainment, and hundreds of poker machines. The biggest in New South Wales is the **Twin Towns Services Club,** Wharf Street, Tweed Heads (✆ **07/5536 2277**). Another worth checking out is **Seagulls Rugby League Club,** Gollan

Drive, Tweed Heads (© **07/5536 3433**). Major entertainers, such as Tom Jones and Joe Cocker, have played here over the last few years. It's open 24 hours. To gain admittance to these "private" clubs, you must sign the registration book just inside the door. Tweed Heads is 40km (25 miles), or about a 30-minute drive, from Murwillumbah.

SOUTH ALONG THE PRINCES HIGHWAY

Two main roads lead south out of Sydney: the M5, which turns into the Hume Highway, and the Princes Highway. Both routes connect Sydney to Melbourne, but the M5/Hume Highway route is quicker. A favorite with truckers and anyone in a hurry, the M5/Hume Highway will get you to Melbourne in about 11 hours. The Princes Highway is a scenic coastal route that can get you to Melbourne in 2 days, though the many attractions along the route make it well worth taking longer.

The best start to your southern odyssey is a trip along the Grand Pacific Drive. This twisting touring route through the Royal National Park (south of Sydney) to the coastal town of Wollongong is being touted as New South Wales's answer to Victoria's Great Ocean Road (p. 664). The scenic climax to the 169km-long (105-mile) route is the Sea Cliff Bridge, an engineering marvel that swerves out from the cliffs and soars above the pounding waves.

From Sydney, follow the Princes Highway south toward the city of Wollongong. Between the southern Sydney suburbs of Sutherland and Engadine, turn off at the sign pointing to the entrance to the Royal National Park. You will only need to pay the A$11 national park entrance fee if you intend to stop inside the park. Just driving through, or visiting the village of Bundeena, is free. There are three main turnoffs within the national park. The first takes you to the villages of Bundeena (p. 163) and Maianbar, with their wonderful beaches. The second takes you to Wattamolla, which has a beautiful shallow lagoon. (It takes around 3 hr. to walk from here along the cliff tops back to Bundeena.) The third turnoff takes you to Garie Beach—a wild-looking and stunning stretch of sand with a large surf club building and great on-shore fishing. The road through the national park splits after the Garie Beach turn—continue straight ahead. (Turn right and you'll head back to the main highway due south.)

Grand Pacific Drive then leads uphill through some magnificent stands of eucalyptus trees, before it breaks out of the forest and arrives at Bald Hill, an awe-inspiring lookout offering panoramic coastal views. It's worth a quick stop.

The road slowly winds its way downhill to the Sea Cliff Bridge. The bridge, which is 665m (2,182 ft.) long, was opened in December 2005 at a total cost of A$52 million. It's well worth stopping at the northern side of the bridge (park in the village of Coal Cliff) and walking across it. The ocean views are inspiring.

Grand Pacific next heads through the coastal towns of Thirroul and Austinmer, which both have nice beaches. There is a swimming pool on Austinmer beach carved out of a rock shelf and topped up by incoming tides.

The road finally winds on to Wollongong, which has a pretty harbor with fishing boats and seagulls and the like, before darting south again to Kiama.

Sydney to Melbourne by the Inland Route

If you were to drive from central Sydney to the center of Melbourne in one go, it would take around 11 hours to cover the 860km (534 miles)—much of it driving through pretty boring landscape. Given the distance, it's probably best to do it in 2 days—though you could do a couple of side trips, too.

This is how I'd do it: I'd set off from Sydney, head down the Hume Highway, and take my first break in **Goulburn** (famous for its tough "supermax" prison—you can't visit!). The journey takes about 2 hours. Depending on what time I left Sydney, I would have lunch or a coffee break here. I'd then continue southwest past **Gundagai,** another almost-2-hour stretch. (At a pinch, you can stay in a cabin park here.) Then on to **Holbrook** (another hour), where I'd have a good rest. There's a huge **submarine** next to the highway that you can't miss, as well as a submarine museum (odd in the middle of the country, I know). The **cafe** next to the submarine, in the park, has excellent snacks and good inexpensive meals; don't bother eating in any of the local pubs (called "hotels"). It's about another hour to **Albury** in Victoria. From here, I might make a detour to explore **Ned Kelly country** and the **Alpine region.** (Stay in the pretty town of **Bright**—less than 1 hr. from Albury.) Otherwise I'd be very tempted to stay the night in **Wangaratta** (visitor center: ✆ **1800/801 065;** www.visitwangaratta.com.au). Wangaratta is about an hour from Albury. Continue on to Melbourne the next day. It's about another 3 hours.

Kiama

119km (74 miles) S of Sydney

Kiama (pop. 10,300) is famous for its **blowhole.** In fact, there are two, a large one and a smaller one; both spurt seawater several meters into the air. The larger of the two can jet water up to 60m (197 ft.), but you need a large swell and strong southeasterly winds to force the sea through the rock fissure with enough force to achieve that height. The smaller of the two is more consistent and fares better with a good northeasterly wind.

Pick up a map from the **Kiama Visitors Centre** (see below) to guide you on a Heritage Walk through the historic district of this quaint village, where you can tour a row of National Trust workers' cottages built in 1896. There's little reason to stay the night—plenty of more scenic places await farther south.

ESSENTIALS

GETTING THERE From Sydney, travel south on the Princes Highway via the steelworks city of Wollongong. There's also regular train service from Sydney, and **Greyhound Australia** (✆ **13 14 99** in Australia, or 07/4690 9950; www.greyhound.com.au) coach service. The trip by coach takes about 2 hours, the train trip a little less.

VISITOR INFORMATION The **Kiama Visitors Centre,** Blowhole Point, Kiama (✆ **02/4232 3322;** or 1300 654 262 in Australia; www.kiama.com.au), is open daily from 9am to 5pm.

Jervis Bay: An Off-the-Beaten-Track Gem ★★

182km (113 miles) S of Sydney

Booderee National Park, at Jervis Bay, is nothing short of spectacular. How does this grab you: miles of deserted beaches, the whitest sand imaginable, kangaroos you can stroke, lorikeets that mob you for food during the day and possums that do the same at night, pods of dolphins, great walks through gorgeous bushland, and a real Aboriginal spirituality of place? A word of warning, though: Don't turn up and just expect to see wildlife everywhere, and don't come if you don't like walking. (Most marsupials come out in the evening, and you'll only get the best from the place if you bring your walking shoes and spend a couple of days.) A car will get you from beach to beach and to various walking tracks.

ESSENTIALS

GETTING THERE It's best to reach Jervis Bay via Huskisson, 24km (15 miles) southeast of Nowra on the Princes Highway. Approximately 16km (10 miles) south of Nowra, turn left onto the Jervis Bay Road to Huskisson. The entrance to Booderee National Park—formally named Jervis Bay National Park—is just after Huskisson. It's about a 3-hour drive from Sydney. You'll probably need at least 2 days to get to know the area. Watch out for the black cockatoos.

> **Safeguarding Your Valuables**
>
> **Jervis Bay is notorious for its car break-ins, a situation the local police force has been unable to control. If you park your car anywhere in the national park, remove all valuables, including things in the trunk.**

Australian Pacific Tours (✆ **02/9247 7222;** fax 02/9247 2052; www.aptours.com.au) runs a dolphin-watching cruise to Jervis Bay from Sydney every day between early October and mid-April, and Monday and Thursday in winter. The 12-hour trip—7 hours of which are on the coach—includes a visit to the Kiama blowhole, a 3-hour luncheon cruise looking for bottle-nose dolphins, and a stop on the way back at Fitzroy Falls in the Southern Highlands. The trip costs A$117 for adults and A$109 for children.

VISITOR INFORMATION For information on the area, contact the **Shoalhaven Visitors Centre,** at the corner of Princes Highway and Pleasant Way, Nowra (✆ **1800/024 261** in Australia, or 02/4421 0778; www.shoalhaven.nsw.gov.au). Pick up maps and book camping sites at the **Booderee National Park** office (✆ **02/4443 0977**), located just beyond Huskisson; it's open daily from 9am to 4pm. **Hyams Beach Store** (✆ **02/4443 0242**) has an accommodations guide listing 34 rental properties for A$100 and up for a weekend.

SEEING THE AREA

If you want to see the best spots, you'll need to pay the park-entrance fee of A$11 per day; a standard NSW National Parks Pass doesn't work here. Places to visit include **Hyams Beach ★**, reputed to have the whitest sand in the world. Notice how it squeaks when you walk on it. Wear sunscreen! The reflection off the beach can burn your skin in minutes, even on a cloudy day. **Hole in the Wall Beach** has interesting rock formations and a lingering smell of natural sulfur. Secluded **Summer Cloud Bay** offers excellent fishing.

Dolphin Watch Cruises, 74 Owen St., Huskisson (✆ **1800/246 010** in Australia, or 02/4441 6311; www.dolphinwatch.com.au), runs a hardy vessel out of Huskisson on the lookout for the resident pod of bottlenose dolphins—you have "more than a 95% chance of seeing them," the company claims. A 2-hour coffee cruise runs daily and costs A$30 for adults and A$16 for children. A 2½-hour dolphin watch and bay cruise leaves at 1pm and costs A$35 for adults and A$20 for children. It's possible to see humpback and southern right whales in June and July and from mid-September to mid-November. A 3-hour whale-watch cruise costs A$65 for adults and A$35 for children.

WHERE TO STAY & DINE

If you have a tent and camping gear, all the better. **Caves Beach** is a quiet spot (except when the birds chorus at dawn); it's home to eastern gray kangaroos. It's about a 250m (820 ft.) walk from the car park to the campground. **Greenpatch** is more dirt than grass, but you get your own area, and it's suitable for motor homes. If you're lucky you might get your own campfire area. It's infested with overfriendly possums around dusk. Campsites cost between A$10 and A$20 per tent. Large tents cost extra. At some times of the year there is also a per-person fee, ranging from A$5 to A$10. The campsites fill up on summer weekends in particular and are almost impossible to secure around Christmas. Book in advance by calling ✆ **02/4443 0977** or e-mailing **booderee.mail@environment.gov.au**.

For supplies, head to the area's main towns, **Huskisson** (pop. 930) and **Vincentia** (pop. 2,350). The **Huskisson RSL Club,** overlooking the wharf area on Owen Street (✆ **02/4441 5282**), has a good bistro and a bar. You'll have to sign in inside the main entrance. The Huskisson Hotel (also called the "Huskie Pub") is down the road and has a nice beer garden and cheapish meals at lunchtime.

Huskisson Beach Tourist Resort This resort is the very pinnacle of cabin accommodations on this part of the east coast. Cabins vary in price depending on size, but even the smallest has room enough for a double bed, triple bunks, and a small kitchen with microwave. Larger cabins have two separate bedrooms. There's a game room and barbecue facilities. Weekend prices are huge, so it's best to stay weekdays. Rates also rise significantly over Christmas and Easter.

Beach St., Huskisson, Jervis Bay, NSW 2540. ✆/fax **02/4441 5142.** www.huskissonbeachtouristresort.com.au. 38 cabins. Weekdays A$90–A$175. DC, MC, V. **Amenities:** Small heated outdoor pool; lit tennis court. *In room:* TV, hair dryer, kitchen.

Jervis Bay Guest House ★ This relatively new guesthouse has four distinctly different rooms (different color schemes, beds, and so on), each with a private bathroom. One room has a Jacuzzi, and two rooms face the water and have coffeemakers. Breakfast is a hearty affair that could include emu sausages and thick slabs of bacon followed by a tropical fruit platter.

1 Beach St., Huskisson, NSW 2540. ✆ **02/4441 7658.** Fax 02/4441 7659. www.jervisbayguesthouse.com.au. 4 units. A$195–A$265 double. Rates include breakfast. AE, DC, MC, V. After the Jervis Bay Hotel, take the 2nd road to the left (Nowra St.) and follow it to the end. Children 15 and under not accepted. **Amenities:** Lounge. *In room:* A/C, hair dryer.

Ulladulla

220km (136 miles) S of Sydney

Very much a supply town as well as a fishing center, especially for tuna, Ulladulla is a pleasant stopover on your journey south. This is also a good place to stock up on supplies from local supermarkets. On the outskirts of town (just to the south) are a series of saltwater lakes with good fishing, though you'll have competition from the pelicans. Inland is the giant Morton National Park, marked by the peak of Pigeonhouse Mountain. The 3- to 4-hour walk to the top and back starts at a parking lot a 30-minute drive from Ulladulla. The going is steep at first, but the trail levels out as it crosses a sandstone plateau. Another upward climb and you're rewarded with a magnificent view of peaks and ocean.

Several side roads worth exploring spur off between Ulladulla and Batemans Bay (see below). These lead to the tiny villages of Bawley Point and Kioloa, where holiday cottages nestle between isolated beaches, gum forests, and green patches studded with gray kangaroos.

There are more kangaroos at pristine **Pebbly Beach ★** in Murramarang National Park, a short hop—20 minutes south—of Ulladulla. The furry creatures actually wander around the beach and adjacent campsite, or gather on the grassy dunes to graze. It's a good area for birding, too.

ESSENTIALS

GETTING THERE Ulladulla is about a 3-hour drive down the Pacific Highway from Sydney Central Business District.

VISITOR INFORMATION **Ulladulla Visitors Centre,** Civic Center, Princes Highway (✆ **02/4455 1269;** www.shoalhaven.nsw.gov.au), is open Monday through Friday from 10am to 5pm, Saturday and Sunday from 9am to 5pm.

WHERE TO STAY & DINE

Ulladulla is well known for its food (particularly seafood and beef) and wine (there are a few boutique wineries in the area). For some of the best fish in Australia, head to one of the fish-and-chips shops on Wason Street, close to the harbor; the best is **Tiger Fish and Chips** (no phone).

Supreeya's Thai Restaurant, 391 Princes Hwy., Ulladulla (✆ **02/4455 4579**), is a good and reasonably priced dinner option. The best food in town though is at the **Ulladulla Guest House** (below). The restaurant here is open from 6 to 10pm daily (except Wednesday). Mains cost between A$25 and A$34.

Ulladulla Guest House ★★★ This fabulous, award-winning property is one of the best places to stay in Australia. Run by the friendly Andrew and Elizabeth Nowosad—try and guess his accent—the Ulladulla Guest House is an impressive AAA-rated five-star establishment. It's surrounded by small but lovely tropical gardens—Andrew insists his coconut palms are the only ones this far south—and overlooks the harbor. Unusually, the house is also a registered art gallery, and the walls are festooned with paintings for sale. Past the cozy lounge are three types of rooms. Two self-contained units with private entrances to the garden are the lowest in price. The one-bedroom unit has a queen-size bed and a fold-out sofa bed, and the two-bedroom unit has a double bed in one room, two singles in another, and a double foldout sofa bed in the lounge. Luxury rooms have a queen-size bed, custom-made furniture, and original artwork. Executive rooms come with a marble bathroom and a Jacuzzi. There are three masseurs on standby. In the rates listed below, peak periods are weekends, public holidays, Easter, and Christmas school holidays. The hotel prides itself on its food, too. The rates below are the "rack rates," but it's well worth checking the website's booking engine for discounted rates (up to A$100 a night).

39 Burrill St., Ulladulla, NSW 2539. ✆ **02/4455 1796.** Fax 02/4454 4660. www.guesthouse.com.au. 10 units. Luxury room A$248; Executive room A$298; 2-bedroom family room A$278; 1-bedroom garden suite A$208. 2-night minimum on Sat–Sun. 3-course dinner A$50. AE, DC, MC, V. **Amenities:** Restaurant; babysitting; bike rental; golf course nearby; exercise room; Jacuzzi; lagoon-style heated outdoor pool; room service; watersports equipment rental. *In room:* A/C, TV, fax, fridge, hair dryer.

Batemans Bay

275km (171 miles) S of Sydney

This laid-back holiday town offers good surfing beaches, arts-and-crafts galleries, boat trips up the Clyde River, good game fishing, and bushwalks in the Morton and Deua national parks.

ESSENTIALS

GETTING THERE Batemans Bay is a 3- to 4-hour drive from Sydney, depending on the traffic. (Avoid leaving Sydney at rush hour, and prepare for long delays on holidays.) **Premier Motor Service** (✆ **1300/368 100** in Australia, or 02/4423 5233) runs coaches to Batemans Bay from Sydney's Central Station.

VISITOR INFORMATION **Batemans Bay Visitor Information Centre,** at the corner of Princes Highway and Beach Road (✆ **1800/802 528** in Australia, or 02/4472 6800), is open daily from 9am to 5pm.

GAME FISHING & RIVER CRUISES

If you fancy some serious fishing, contact **OB1 Charters,** Marina, Beach Road, Batemans Bay (✆ **02/4471 2738,** or 0416/241 586 mobile; www.southcoast.com.au/ob1). The company runs full-day game-fishing trips and morning snapper-fishing trips (afternoon snapper trips in summer, too). Expect to encounter black marlin, blue marlin, giant kingfish, mako sharks, albacore tuna, yellowfin tuna, and blue tuna from November through June. The trip includes all tackle, bait, and afternoon and morning tea, but you must provide your own lunch. It costs A$900 to hire the six-person boat for the day; if there are just a couple of you, the charter company may be able to fill the rest of the boat if you make reservations far enough in advance.

A river cruise on the **MV *Merinda,*** Innes Boatshed, Orient Street, Batemans Bay (✆ **02/4472 4052;** fax 02/4472 4754), is a pleasant experience. The 3-hour cruise leaves at 11:30am daily and travels inland past townships, forests, and farmland. It costs A$22 for adults, A$11 for children, and A$50 for families; a fish-and-chips lunch is A$6 extra, and a seafood basket for two is A$12.

A NICE PLACE TO STAY

The Esplanade Motor Inn ★ ☺ This AAA-rated four-star motel right on the Batemans Bay river estuary has fabulous views and is close to the town center. Rooms are light and well furnished, and all have balconies (some with water views). Some doubles and suites have Jacuzzis; they cost the same as non-Jacuzzi rooms, so specify if you want one when booking. Eat at the associated **Batemans Bay Soldiers' Club** (✆ **02/4472 4117;** www.baysoldiers.com.au) just opposite, which has a restaurant, a bistro, and cheap drinks.

23 Beach Rd. (P.O. Box 202), Batemans Bay, NSW 2536. ✆ **1800/659 884** in Australia, or 02/4472 0200. Fax 02/4472 0277. www.esplanade.com.au. 23 units. A$125–A$160 double (the 2nd rate is for a room with water views); A$180–A$250 suite. Extra person A$15. Children 17 and under stay free in parent's room. AE, DC, MC, V. **Amenities:** Restaurant. *In room:* A/C, TV, hair dryer, kitchenette.

Narooma ★

345km (214 miles) SW of Sydney

Narooma is a seaside town with beautiful deserted beaches, a golf course right on a headland, a natural rock formation in the shape of Australia (popular with camera-wielding tourists), and excellent fishing. However, its major attraction is **Montague Island ★★**, the breeding colony for thousands of shearwaters (or mutton birds, as they're also called) and a hangout for juvenile seals.

Just 18km (11 miles) farther south is **Central Tilba ★**, one of the prettiest towns in Australia and the headquarters of the boutique ABC Cheese Factory (see box below). You'll kick yourself if you miss this charming historic township (pop. 35; 1 million visitors annually).

ESSENTIALS

GETTING THERE Narooma is a 7-hour drive from Sydney down the Princes Highway. **Premier Motor Service** (✆ **1300/368 100** in Australia, or 02/4423 5233) runs coaches to Narooma from Sydney's Central Station.

VISITOR INFORMATION The **Narooma Visitors Centre,** Princes Highway, Narooma (✆ **1800/240 003** in Australia, or 02/4476 2881; fax 02/4476 1690; www.naturecoast-tourism.com.au), is open daily from 9am to 5pm.

WHAT TO SEE & DO: WHALES, GOLF & MORE

A must if you're visiting the area is a boat tour with **Narooma Charters** (✆ **02/4476 2240;** 0407/909 111 mobile; www.naroomacharters.com.au). It offers spectacular tours of the coast on the lookout for dolphins, seal colonies, and little penguins, and also includes a tour of Montague Island. Morning and afternoon tours take 3½ hours and cost A$130 for adults, A$99 for children. A 4½-hour tour includes some of the world's best whale-watching (btw. mid-Sept and early Dec) and costs the same. The last time I went on this trip, we saw no fewer than eight humpback whales, some of them mothers with calves. The company also offers game fishing, from February to the end of June, and standard fishing trips of 4 hours for A$120 for adults and A$99 for kids. A full-day's fishing costs A$200 for adults and A$175 for kids. You may also see giant fish-eating gray nurse sharks, dolphins, and even orcas. Dives cost A$99 for a double dive. Ask about family prices.

Narooma Golf Club, Narooma (✆ **02/4476 2522;** www.naroomagolf.com.au), has one of the most interesting and challenging coastal courses in Australia. A round of golf will cost you A$25.

While you're in the area, I recommend stopping off at the **Umbarra Aboriginal Cultural Centre ★**, Wallaga Lake, off the Princes Highway on Bermagui Road (✆ **02/4473 7232;** www.umbarra.com.au). It's 20km (12 miles) south of Narooma. The center offers activities such as boomerang throwing, spear throwing, and painting with natural ochers. There are also discussions, Aboriginal archival displays, and a retail store. It's open Monday through Friday from 9am to 5pm, Saturday and Sunday from 9am to 4pm (closed Sun in winter). The center's guides also offer 2- to 4-hour four-wheel-drive or walking trips of nearby **Mount Dromedary ★** and **Mumbulla Mountain,** taking in sacred sites. The tours cost A$50 per person. Reservations are essential.

If you want to attempt Mount Dromedary without a guide, ask for directions in Narooma. The hike to the top takes around 3 hours.

WHERE TO STAY

Whale Motor Inn ★ This nice, quiet motor inn has the best panoramic ocean views on the south coast and the largest rooms in town. Standard rooms have a queen-size bed and a single-person sofa bed. Standard suites have a separate bedroom, two sofa beds, and a kitchenette. Spacious executive and Jacuzzi suites are better furnished and have a kitchenette and a balcony or patio.

Princes Hwy., Narooma, NSW 2546. ✆ **02/4476 2411.** Fax 02/4476 1995. www.whalemotorinn.com.au. 17 units. A$120–A$150. Family rooms available. Extra person A$20. AE, DC, MC, V. **Amenities:** Restaurant; small unheated outdoor pool. *In room:* A/C, TV, fridge, hair dryer.

Merimbula

480km (298 miles) S of Sydney; 580km (360 miles) NE of Melbourne

This seaside resort (pop. approximately 7,000) is the last place of interest before the Princes Highway crosses the border into Victoria. Merimbula is a good center from which to discover the surrounding **Ben Boyd National Park** and **Mimosa Rocks National Park;** both offer bushwalking. Another park, **Bournda National Park,** surrounds a lake and has good walking trails and a surf beach.

Golf is the game of choice in Merimbula, and the area's most popular venue is the **Pambula-Merimbula Golf Club** (✆ **02/6495 6154;** www.merimbulagolf.com.au). You can spot kangaroos grazing on the fairways of the 27-hole course. Green fees cost around A$35. Another favorite is **Tura Beach Country Club** (✆ **02/6495 9002;** www.turaclub.com.au), which is known for its excellent coastal views.

Eden, 20km (13 miles) south of Merimbula, was once a major whaling port. The rather gruesome **Eden Killer Whale Museum ★**, on Imlay Street in Eden (✆ **02/6496 2094;** www.killerwhalemuseum.com.au), is the only reason to stop here. It has a fascinating array of relics, including boats, axes, and remnants of the last of the area's killer whales, called Old Tom. I highly recommend it.

Whaling in Twofold Bay

In the early 20th century, whaling in Twofold Bay, which laps up to the shores of the south-coast town of Eden, was far from normal. The killer whales there learned to work with humans in a hunt to the death. The orcas (which are, of course, large dolphins) would locate a whale, and then breach or thrash their tails on the water surface until they got the whalers' attention. Then, as the whalers rowed out to meet them, they would herd the giant creature into shallower water. The whalers would harpoon the hapless creature and the killer whales would move in for the kill. They got the lips and the huge meaty tongue for their efforts. The relationship became so close that the whalers would attempt to rescue their partners in crime if they became entangled in ropes or netting, and the killer whales would protect the humans from sharks if ever their flimsy whaleboats were destroyed by big waves or a thrashing whale tail. The pod of killer whales eventually became victims themselves though: A vagrant knifed one to death as it came close to a beach, and Norwegian whalers working from Jervis Bay shot most of the rest. The last of the pod, "Old Tom," died in 1930.

waltzing THE TILBAS

The south coast of New South Wales hides two little gems between hills the color of emeralds. The first is the tiny gold rush town of **Tilba Tilba.** Its rolling hills are studded with contented cows and frogs croaking from the verges in the valleys. Long-neck turtles often stumble toward the creek across from the wide veranda belonging to the charming 1879 bed-and-breakfast stopover **Green Gables,** 269 Corkhill Dr., Tilba Tilba (© **02/4473 7435;** www.greengables.com.au; A$150–A$180 per night, extra person A$20–A$40). They do dinners too for between A$30 and A$40 a person. It's hard to believe this is Australia; the countryside is just so remarkably green.

Across the road from Green Gables, at the historic Pam's Store, you'll find the Tilba Tilba Track, which leads to the top of Gulaga (or **Mount Dromedary**). This ancient extinct volcano is heavily wooded and topped with rainforest. It's a moderate walk, with some relatively steep sections toward the top. Allow 5 hours return. The mountain is the spiritual heart of the local Yuin Aboriginal people.

Back in town, the highlight of Tilba Tilba is **Foxglove Spires** (open to the public daily; admission A$7.50), a complex of businesses that include antiques and gift shops, a fabulous cafe, a gorgeous nursery specializing in rare herbs and perennials, and one of the best **open gardens** in Australia. The gardens are set around a 100-year-old cottage and run to nearly 1.6 hectares (4 acres) of flower beds, oak trees, rambling roses, and half-wild fruit trees. Areas of note include a secluded woodland that tumbles downhill to a large swampy frog pond and a long shady arbor of trained Manchurian pears. The colors are amazing in autumn. Plan your entire day around lunch at the associated **Love at First Bite Café** (© **02/4473 7055**). This is a seriously good eatery, with a wood-dominated interior, groovy jazz, and a huge range of meals including gourmet sandwiches and fresh vegetable and fruit juices. Standout dishes include the Thai chicken laksa and a legendary lentil burger.

A short drive away is **Central Tilba;** like its smaller twin, it's classified as a heritage village under the National Trust. The quaint wooden buildings here make it perhaps the most attractive of all the historic settlements in Australia. You'll develop a soft spot for the village's **Old Time Lolly Shop** and love the warm feeling of the **Tilba Teapot Café.** There are also antiques stores and art galleries and shops selling crystals and jewelry. My favorite was the **Tilba Woodturning Gallery,** which specializes in carved bowls, wind chimes, rocking horses, and so much more. I left with fine-spun jumpers from the **Tilba Alpaca Shop** (shipped in from Nepal), Tilba Famous Fudge from the **general store,** and some Applebox Smoke and Summer Herb cheeses from the award-winning **ABC Cheese Factory,** the first cheese co-op in NSW. With a bottle or two from **Tilba Valley Wines** and a loaf of granary bread from the local bakery, you're well set up for the next day's lunch. Follow it all up with a snooze to the tune of mooing cows.

For more information, visit **www.tilba.com.au**.

ESSENTIALS

GETTING THERE The drive from either Sydney or Melbourne takes about 7 hours. The **Greyhound Australia** (© **13 14 99** in Australia, or 07/4690 9950; www.greyhound.com.au) bus trip from Sydney takes more than 8 hours.

VISITOR INFORMATION The **Merimbula Tourist Information Centre,** Beach Street, Merimbula (✆ **1800/150 457** in Australia, or 02/6495 1129; www.merimbulatourism.com.au), is open daily from 9am to 5pm (10am–4pm in winter).

SPECIAL EVENTS Jazz fans should head for the **Merimbula Jazz Festival** held over the long Queens Birthday weekend, the second weekend in June. A country-music festival takes place the last weekend in October.

WHERE TO STAY

Ocean View Motor Inn This pleasant motel has good water views from 12 of its rooms (the best are nos. 9, 10, and 11). The rooms are spacious and modern, with plain brick walls, patterned carpets, and one long balcony serving the top six rooms. Fourteen units have kitchenettes, and all have showers. This is just a friendly place.

Merimbula Dr. and View St., Merimbula, NSW 2548. ✆ **02/6495 2300.** Fax 02/6495 3443. www.oceanviewmotorinn.com.au. 20 units. A$85–A$125 double; family rooms available. Higher rate at Christmas and Easter. Extra person A$15. MC, V. **Amenities:** Babysitting; medium-size solar-heated outdoor pool; room service; free Wi-Fi. *In room:* A/C, TV, kitchenette.

THE SNOWY MOUNTAINS ★

Thredbo: 519km (322 miles) SW of Sydney; 208km (129 miles) SW of Canberra; 543km (337 miles) NE of Melbourne

Made famous by Banjo Paterson's 1890 poem "The Man from Snowy River," the Snowy Mountains are most commonly used for what you'd least expect in Australia: skiing. It starts to snow around June and carries on until September. During this time hundreds of thousands of people flock here to ski at the major ski resorts: Thredbo and Perisher Blue, and, to a lesser extent, Charlotte Pass and Mount Selwyn. It's certainly different skiing here, with ghostly white gum trees as the obstacles instead of pine trees.

The entire region is part of the **Kosciuszko** (pronounced Ko-zi-*os*-co) **National Park,** the largest alpine area in Australia. During the summer months the park is a beautiful place for walking, and in spring the profusion of wildflowers is exquisite. A series of lakes in the area, including the one in the resort town of Jindabyne, are favorites with trout fishermen.

Visitors stay in **Jindabyne,** 62km (38 miles) south of Cooma, or **Thredbo Village,** 36km (22 miles) southwest of Jindabyne. Jindabyne is a bleak-looking resort town on the banks of the man-made Lake Jindabyne, which came into existence when the Snowy River was dammed to provide hydroelectric power.

Thredbo Village is set in a valley of Mount Crackenback and resembles European-style resorts. From here, the Crackenback Chairlift provides access to an easy-grade pathway that leads to the top of Mount Kosciuszko, which at 2,228m (7,308 ft.) is Australia's highest peak. The mountain has stunning views of the alpine region and some good walks.

Snowy Mountain Essentials

GETTING THERE From Sydney, take the Eastern Distributor road toward Sydney Airport and turn right just before the planes, following the signs to Wollongong, and then Canberra, on the M5 motorway and the Hume Highway. Follow the Hume Highway south to Goulburn, where you turn onto the Federal Highway toward Canberra. From there take the Monaro Highway to Cooma, and then follow the Alpine Way through Jindabyne and on to Thredbo. Tire chains may be necessary on the slopes in winter and can be rented from local service stations. The trip takes around 6 hours from Sydney with short breaks. From Melbourne, travel the Hume Highway to Albury-Wodonga. Head east through Khancoban, and take the Alpine Way through Thredbo to Jindabyne.

Qantas (✆ **13 13 13** in Australia) has daily flights from Sydney to Cooma. A connecting bus to the ski fields takes about 1 hour and operates from June through October. It's run by **Snowy Mountain Hire Cars** (✆ **02/6456 2957**) and costs around A$52 one-way. **Alpine Charters** (✆ **02/6456 7340**) also runs coaches.

In winter only (around June 19–Oct 5), **Greyhound Australia** (✆ **13 14 99** in Australia, or 07/4690 9950; www.greyhound.com.au) operates daily buses between Sydney and Cooma, via Canberra. The journey takes around 7 hours from Sydney and 3 hours from Canberra. A one-way ticket costs around A$55.

VISITOR INFORMATION Pick up information about the ski fields and accommodations options at the **Cooma Visitors Centre,** 119 Sharp St., Cooma, NSW 2630 (✆ **02/6450 1740;** fax 02/6450 1798); or at the **Snowy Region Visitor Centre,** Kosciuszko Road, Jindabyne, NSW 2627 (✆ **02/6450 5600;** fax 02/6456 1249; srvc@npws.nsw.gov.au). Perisher Blue has its own website, **www.perisher blue.com.au**, as does Thredbo, **www.thredbo.com.au**. Another good website is **www.snowymountains.com.au**.

Hitting the Slopes & Other Adventures

Obviously, skiing is the most popular activity here. More than 50 ski lifts serve the fields of Perisher Valley, Mount Blue Cow, Smiggins Holes, and Guthega. Perisher Valley offers the best overall slopes; Mount Blue Cow is generally very crowded; Smiggins Holes offers good slopes for beginners; and Guthega has nice light, powdery snow and is less crowded. Thredbo has some very challenging runs and the longest downhill runs, but I prefer Perisher for atmosphere. A day's ski pass at Thredbo and Perisher Blue costs a huge A$103 for adults, A$57 for children 6 to 14.

You can drive directly to the Perisher Blue resort, or you can take the ski-tube train (starts btw. Jindabyne and Thredbo on the Alpine Way). This travels through the mountains to Perisher Blue and then to Blue Cow. (A "ski-tube train" is a train that goes through a mountain tunnel.) It costs A$47 return for adult skiers, A$26 for kids, and A$112 for a family of four. Ski gear can be rented at numerous places in Jindabyne and Thredbo.

In summer, the region is popular for hiking, canoeing, fishing, and golf. Thredbo Village has tennis courts, a 9-hole golf course, and mountain-bike trails.

Where to Stay

You'll have to book months ahead to find a place during the ski season (especially on weekends). And don't expect to find a lot of bargains. It's well worth checking out the Jindabyne and Snowy Mountain Accommodation website, **www.snowaccommodation.com.au**, because lots of private apartments are listed here, as well as rooms in resorts. The website for Thredbo, **www.thredbo.com.au**, is another option.

Ski Condition Updates

For up-to-date ski field information, call the Snowy Region Visitor Centre (✆ 02/6450 5600).

In the Footsteps of the Man from Snowy River

Horseback riding is a popular activity for those who fancy themselves "Men from Snowy River" (see p. 70). **Reynella Alpine Horseback Safaris,** in Adaminaby, 44km (27 miles) northwest of Cooma (✆ **1800/029 909** in Australia, or 02/6454 2386; fax 02/6454 2530; www.reynellarides.com.au), offers multinight rides through the Kosciuszko National Park from October to the end of April. Three-day, four-night rides cost around A$1,133. Five-day, six-night rides are A$1,778. The trips are all-inclusive and include camping and homestead accommodations. This is about as close as you can get to living out Banjo Paterson's epic poem.

IN THREDBO

Riverside Cabins These self-contained studio and one-bedroom cabins sit above the Thredbo River and overlook the Crackenback Range. They're also a short walk from the Thredbo Alpine Hotel and local shops. Most rooms have balconies. Rates vary wildly from weekday to weekend and season to season.

Thredbo, NSW 2625. ✆ **02/6459 4196** in Australia, or 02/6459 4299. Fax 02/6459 4195. 36 units. Winter A$160–A$516 double; summer A$117–A$164 double. Ask about weekly rates. AE, DC, MC, V. *In room:* TV, hair dryer, kitchen.

Thredbo Alpine Apartments These apartments are very similar to the Riverside Cabins (see above) and are managed by the same people. All have balconies with mountain views. Some have queen-size beds. There's limited daily maid service and free in-room movies. Winter rates apply from July 30 through September 2.

Thredbo, NSW 2628. ✆ **1800/026 333** in Australia, or 02/6459 4299. Fax 02/6459 4195. 35 units. Winter Sat–Sun A$210–A$441 1-bedroom apt, A$289–A$628 2-bedroom apt, A$394–A$770 3-bedroom apt, weekday rates about 20% cheaper; summer A$127–A$164 1-bedroom apt, A$159–A$190 2-bedroom apt, A$180–A$210 3-bedroom apt. Ask about weekly rates. AE, DC, MC, V. Covered parking. *In room:* TV, hair dryer, kitchen.

Thredbo Alpine Hotel After the skiing is finished for the day, the center of activity in Thredbo is this large resort-style lodge. Rooms vary; those on the top floor of the three-story hotel have king-size beds instead of standard queen-size ones. The rooms are all wood-paneled and have free in-house movies. Thredbo's only nightclub is here.

P.O. Box 80, Thredbo, NSW 2625. ✆ **02/6459 4200.** Fax 02/6459 4201. www.thredbo.com.au. 65 units. Winter A$198–A$498 double; summer A$129–A$189 double. Rates include breakfast. Ask about weekly rates and packages. AE, DC, MC, V. **Amenities:** 2 restaurants; bistro, 4 bars; golf course nearby; Jacuzzi; heated outdoor pool; room service (winter only); sauna; 3 lit tennis courts. *In room:* TV/VCR, hair dryer, minibar.

OUTBACK NEW SOUTH WALES

The Outback is a powerful Australian image. Hot, dusty, and prone to flies, it can also be a romantic place where wedge-tailed eagles float in the shimmering heat, tracing the unbroken horizon. If you drive out here, you have to be constantly on the lookout for emus, large flightless birds that dart across roads open-beaked and wide-eyed. When you turn off the car engine, it's so quiet you can hear the scales of a sleepy lizard, as long as your forearm, scraping the rumpled track as it turns to taste the air with its long, blue tongue.

The scenery is a huge canvas with a restricted palette: blood red for the dirt, straw yellow for the blotches of Mitchell grass, searing blue for the surreally large sky. There is room to be yourself in the Outback, and you'll soon find that personalities tilt toward the eccentric. It's a hardworking place, too, where miners and sheep and cattle farmers try to eke out a living in Australia's hard center.

Broken Hill ★★

1,157km (717 miles) W of Sydney; 508km (315 miles) NE of Adelaide

At its heart, Broken Hill—or "Silver City," as it's been nicknamed—is still very much a hardworking mining town. Its beginnings date to 1883, when the trained eye of a boundary rider named Charles Rasp noticed something odd about the craggy rock outcrops at a place called the Broken Hill. He thought he saw deposits of tin, but they turned out to be silver and lead. Today, the city's main drag, Argent Street, bristles with finely crafted colonial mansions, heritage homes, hotels, and public buildings. Look deeper and you see the town's quirkiness. Around one corner you'll find the radio station, built to resemble a giant wireless set with round knobs for windows, and around another the headquarters of the Housewives Association, which ruled the town with an iron apron for generations. Then there's the Palace Hotel—made famous in the movie *The Adventures of Priscilla, Queen of the Desert*—with its high painted walls and a mural of Botticelli's *Birth of Venus* on the ceiling two flights up.

> **What Time Is It, Anyway?**
>
> **Broken Hill runs its clocks on Central Standard Time, to correspond with South Australia. The surrounding country, however, runs a half-hour faster at Eastern Standard Time.**

Traditionally a hard-drinking but religious town, Broken Hill has 23 pubs (down from 73 in its heyday) and plenty of churches, as well as a Catholic cathedral, a synagogue, and a mosque to serve its 21,000 inhabitants.

ESSENTIALS

GETTING THERE By car, take the Great Western Highway from Sydney to Dubbo, and then the Mitchell Highway to the Barrier Highway, which will take you to Broken Hill. **Southern Australian Airlines** (book through Qantas, ✆ **13 13 13** in Australia) also connects Broken Hill to Adelaide, Melbourne, and Mildura.

The ***Indian Pacific*** train stops here on its way from Sydney to Perth, via Adelaide, twice a week. It takes nearly 16 hours from Sydney to Broken Hill, leaving Sydney at 2:55pm on Saturday and Wednesday and arriving in Broken Hill at 6:40am the next day. You only get to stay a very short time in Broken Hill though. A 1-hour whistle stop tour is available. The fare from Sydney to Adelaide is around A$694 for adults and A$527 for children in a first-class sleeper, A$501 for adults and A$365 for children in an economy sleeper, and A$308 for adults and A$138 for children in an economy seat. These prices regularly go up though. Contact **Great Southern Railways** (✆ **08/8213 4530;** www.gsr.com.au) for timetables, latest fares, bookings, and more information.

Greyhound Australia (✆ **13 14 99** in Australia, or 07/4690 9950; www.greyhound.com.au) runs buses from Adelaide for around A$60; the trip takes 7 hours. The 16-hour trip from Sydney costs from A$96.

VISITOR INFORMATION The **Broken Hill Visitors Information Centre,** Blende and Bromide streets, Broken Hill, NSW 2880 (✆ **08/8080 3560;** www.visitbrokenhill.com.au), is open daily from 8:30am to 5pm. The **National Parks & Wildlife Service (NPWS)** office is at 183 Argent St. (✆ **08/8088 5933**); and the **Royal Automobile Association of South Australia,** which offers reciprocal services to other national and international auto-club members, is at 261 Argent St. (✆ **08/8088 4999**).

Note: The area code in Broken Hill is **08,** the same as the South Australia code, not 02, the New South Wales code.

GETTING AROUND Free, volunteer-led tours lead off from the Visitors Information Centre at 10am on Mondays, Wednesdays, and Fridays from March to October. **Silver City Tours,** 380 Argent St. (✆ **08/8087 6956;** www.silvercitytours.com.au), conducts tours of the city and surroundings every day apart from Monday. Half-day city tours take around 4 hours and cost A$67 for adults and A$37 for children. The company also offers other tours, including a Saturday tour to White Cliffs costing A$172 for adults and A$100 for kids.

Other good operators are **Tri State Safaris** (✆ **08/8088 2389;** www.tristate.com.au), which runs many multiday tours into the Outback, including 1-day tours to Mutawintji National Park for A$165 and White Cliffs for A$168. It's well worth doing some solid research before you leave home.

Hertz (✆ **08/8087 2719**) rents four-wheel-drive vehicles suitable for exploring the area.

EXPLORING THE TOWN: GALLERIES, MINE TOURS & THE WORLD'S LARGEST SCHOOLROOM

With the largest regional public gallery in New South Wales and 27 private **galleries,** Broken Hill has more places per capita to see art than anywhere else in Australia. The **Broken Hill Regional Art Gallery,** Chloride Street, between Blende and Beryl streets (✆ **08/8080 3440;** www.brokenhill.net.au/bhart/main.html), houses an extensive collection of Australian colonial and Impressionist works. Look for the *Silver Tree,* a sculpture created out of the pure silver mined beneath Broken Hill. This is also a good place to see works by the "Brushmen of the Bush," a well-known group of artists including Pro Hart, Jack Absalom, Eric Minchin, and Hugh Schultz who spend many days sitting around campfires in the bush trying to capture its essence in paint. The gallery is open daily from 10am to 5pm. Admission is A$3 for adults, A$2 for children, and A$6 for families.

Be sure not to miss the School of the Air and the Royal Flying Doctor Service base, both of which help show the enormity of the Australian interior. The **School of the Air**—the largest schoolroom in the world, with students scattered over 800,000 sq. km (312,000 sq. miles)—conducts lessons via two-way radios. Visitors can listen in on part of the day's first teaching session Monday through Friday at 8:30am (except school and public holidays). Bookings are essential and must be made the day before through the **Broken Hill Visitors Information Centre** (see "Visitor Information," above). Tours costs A$3.50 for adults and A$2.50 for kids. The **Royal Flying Doctor Service** base is at the Broken Hill Airport (✆ **08/8080 1777**). The service maintains communication with more than 400 Outback stations, ready to fly at once in case of an emergency. The base at Broken Hill covers 25% of New South Wales, as well as parts of Queensland and South Australia. Explanations of the role of the flying doctor service run continuously at the base Monday through Friday from 9am to 5pm. Admission is A$6 for adults and A$3 for children.

Join the **Bush Mail Run** (✆ **02/8087 2164,** or 0411/102 339 mobile), an Outback mail delivery service by four-wheel-drive that operates every Wednesday and Saturday. The day starts at 7am, and you cover roughly 500km (310 miles). You stop at various homesteads. The run costs A$142.

OTHER THINGS TO SEE & DO NEARBY

VISITING A GHOST TOWN At least 44 movies have been filmed in the Wild West town of **Silverton ★** (pop. 50), 23km (14 miles) northwest of Broken Hill. It's the Wild West Australian-style, though, with camels instead of horses sometimes placed in front of the **Silverton Pub,** which is well worth a visit for its kitschy Australian appeal. Silverton once had a population of 3,000 following the discovery of silver here in 1882, but within 7 years almost everyone had left. There are some good art galleries here, as well as a restored jail and hotel.

DISCOVERING ABORIGINAL HANDPRINTS **Mutawintji National Park ★** (also known and pronounced by its old name, Mootwingee), 130km (81 miles) northeast of Broken Hill, was one of the most important spiritual meeting places for Aborigines on the continent. Groups came from all over to peck out abstract engravings on the rocks with sharpened quartz tools and to sign their handprints to show they belonged to the place. The ancient, weathered fireplaces are still here, laid out like a giant map to show where each visiting group came from. Hundreds of ocher outlines of hands and animal paws, some up to 30,000 years old, are stenciled on rock overhangs. The fabulous 2-hour Outback trip from Broken Hill to Mootwingee is along red-dirt tracks not really suitable for two-wheel-drives. It should not be attempted after a heavy rain.

The **National Park office** (✆ **1300/361 967** in Australia, or 08/8080 3200) has details on walks. You can camp at the **Homestead Creek** campground for A$5 per person per night. It has its own water supply, but no firewood is available. Book through the National Park office.

EXPLORING WHITE CLIFFS ★★ White Cliffs, 290km (180 miles) east of Broken Hill, is an opal-mining town that's bigger than it looks. To escape the summer heat, most houses are built underground in mine shafts, where the temperature is a constant 72°F (22°C). Unlike Lightning Ridge (see below), which produces mainly black opals, White Cliffs is known for its less valuable white opals—as is Coober Pedy in South Australia (see chapter 12). Prospecting started in 1889, when kangaroo shooters found the colorful stones on the ground. A year later, the rush was on, and by the turn of the 20th century, about 4,000 people were digging and sifting in a lawless, waterless hell of a place. White Cliffs is smaller than Coober Pedy and less touristy—which is its charm. You also have more freedom to wander around the opal tailings here, which is discouraged in Coober Pedy. Given the choice between White Cliffs and Lightning Ridge, I'd opt for the latter—though if you have time, you should see both.

The countryside here looks like an inverted moonscape, pimpled with bone-white heaps of gritty clay dug from the 50,000 mine shafts that surround the town. These days, White Cliffs is renowned for its eccentricity. Take **Jock's Place,** for instance, an underground museum full to the beams with junk pulled from old mine shafts.

A Fabulous Place to Enjoy the Sunset

Just outside Broken Hill, in the Living Desert Nature Park, is the best collection of sculptures this side of Stonehenge. Twelve sandstone obelisks, up to 3m (10 ft.) high and carved totemlike by artists from as far away as Georgia, Syria, Mexico, and the Tiwi Islands, make up the Sculpture Symposium. Surrounding them on all sides is brooding mulga scrub. It's fantastic at sunset.

Then there's a house made of beer flagons, and a 9-hole **dirt golf course** where locals play at night with fluorescent green balls.

WHERE TO STAY: ABOVEGROUND & BELOW

One option is to rent a local cottage from **Emaroo Cottages** (✆ **08/8595 7217;** www.emaroocottages.com.au) from A$80 a night.

Best Western Broken Hill Oasis Motor Inn This is my favorite place to stay in Broken Hill, although admittedly that's not really saying much in this Outback town. It's set way back from the road, has nice green areas and barbecue facilities, and is very quiet. The more expensive AAA-rated four-star rooms are much nicer than the cheaper options and considerably larger. Two family rooms sleep up to six in a combination of single and queen-size beds. You can order off several menus supplied by local restaurants; the hotel supplies plates and cutlery.

142 Iodide St., Broken Hill, NSW 2880. ✆ **08/8088 2255.** Fax 08/8088 2255. http://brokenhilloasis.bestwestern.com.au. 15 units. A$120 double; A$145 2-bed unit. Extra person A$10. AE, DC, MC, V. **Amenities:** Heated outdoor pool; sauna; smoke-free rooms. *In room:* A/C, TV, hair dryer.

Underground Motel ★★ I love this place; it's worth making the scenic trip out to White Cliffs just to stay here for the night. All but two of the rooms are underground; they're reached by a maze of spacious tunnels dug out of the rock and sealed with epoxy resin to keep out the damp and the dust. The temperature below ground is a constant 72°F (22°C), which is decidedly cooler than a summer day outside. Rooms are comfortable though basic, with shared toilets and showers. Turn the light off and it's dark as a cave. Every night, guests sit around large tables and dig into the roast of the day. (Vegetarians have options, too.) The three-course meal costs A$35.

Smiths Hill, White Cliffs (P.O. Box 427), NSW 2836. ✆ **08/8091 6677.** Fax 08/8091 6654. www.undergroundmotel.com.au. 30 units, none with bathroom. A$125 double. Extra person A$35. MC, V. **Amenities:** Restaurant; bar; small heated outdoor pool.

WHERE TO DINE

The best place for a meal Aussie-style is a local club. You'll find one of the best bistros at the **Barrier Social & Democratic Club,** 218 Argent St. (✆ **08/8088 4477**). It serves breakfast, lunch, and dinner. Another good one is at the **Southern Cross Hotel,** at 357 Cobalt St. (✆ **02/8088 4122**). Interestingly, the fresh fish is a standout. Locals go for steaks at the **Sturt Club,** at 321 Blende St. (✆ **02/8087 4541**).

Lightning Ridge: Opals Galore ★★

793km (492 miles) NW of Sydney; 737km (457 miles) SW of Brisbane

Lightning Ridge, or "The Ridge" as the locals call it, is perhaps the most fascinating place to visit in New South Wales. Essentially, it's a hardworking opal-mining town in the arid northern reaches of New South Wales—where summer temperatures hover at the 113°F (45°C) mark. Lightning Ridge thrives off the largest deposit of black opals in the world. Quality opals can fetch a miner around A$8,000 per carat, and stones worth more than A$500,000 each are not unheard of. Tourists come to get a taste of Australia's "Wild West." A popular activity in the opal fields is to pick over the old heaps of mine tailings. Stories (perhaps tall tales) abound of tourists finding overlooked opals worth thousands.

I strongly recommend you visit the **Grawin** and **Glengarry opal fields ★★**, both about an hour or so from Lightning Ridge on a dirt track suitable for two-wheel-drive cars in dry weather only. (Check with the Tourist Information Centre before you go.) Bristling with drills and hoists pulling out bucket-loads of dirt, these frontier townships buzz with news of the latest opal rush. If you can convince a local to take you there, all the better—the tracks can be misleading. **Ando's Outback Tours** (see "Byron Bay: A Beach Bohemia," earlier in this chapter) takes in Glengarry and Lightning Ridge on its 5-day trip.

ESSENTIALS

GETTING THERE From Sydney, it takes about 9 hours to drive to Lightning Ridge, via Bathurst, Dubbo, and the fascinating town of Walgett. **Airlink** (✆ **02/6884 2435**) flies to Lightning Ridge from Sydney via Dubbo. **Countrylink** (✆ **13 22 32**) runs trains from Sydney to Dubbo, and then it's a bus from there. The trip from Dubbo takes around 4½ hours and costs A$60.

VISITOR INFORMATION The **Lightning Ridge Tourist Information Centre,** Morilla Street (P.O. Box 1380), Lightning Ridge, NSW 2834 (✆ **02/6829 1670**), is open daily from 9am to 5pm. The most useful website for Lightning Ridge is **www.lightningridgeinfo.com.au**.

SPECIAL EVENTS If you're in Australia around Easter, make sure you come to Lightning Ridge for the **Great Goat Race** and the rodeo. For more information, check **www.lightningridgeinfo.com.au**.

SEEING THE TOWN

Any visit to Lightning Ridge should start with an orientation trip with **Black Opal Tours** (✆ **02/6829 0368;** www.blackopaltours.com.au). The company offers 3-hour tours starting at 8:30am, 9:30am, and 1:30pm (Mar–Oct only). Tours cost A$25 for adults and A$10 for kids.

The 15m-tall (49-ft.) **Amigo's Castle,** dominates the worked-out opal fields surrounding the modern township of Lightning Ridge. Complete with turrets, battlements, dungeons, and a wishing well, the castle has been rising out of these arid lands for the past 18 years, with every rock scavenged from the surrounding area and lugged in a wheelbarrow or in a rucksack on Amigo's back. The wonderful Amigo hasn't taken out insurance on the property, so there are no official tours—though if he feels like a bit of company, he'll show you around.

The **Artesian Bore Baths,** 2km (1¼ miles) from the post office on Pandora Street, are free, open 24 hours a day, and said to have therapeutic value. The water temperature hovers between 104°F and 122°F (40°C–50°C). A visit at night, when the stars are out, is amazing.

Bevan's Black Opal & Cactus Nursery (✆ **02/6829 0429**) contains more than 2,000 species of cactus and succulent plants, including rare specimens. Betty

Bevan cuts opals from the family's mine, and many are on display. Admission is A$5 to the cactus nursery, free to see the opals.

Lightning Ridge has plenty of opal shops, galleries, walk-in opal mines, and other unique things to see. You might want to take a look at **Gemopal Pottery** (✆ **02/6829 0375**), on the road to the Bore Baths. The resident potter makes some nice pots out of clay mine tailings and lives in one of his five old Sydney railway carriages.

Another unusual one is the **Black Queen** (✆ **02/6829 0980;** www.blackqueen.com.au), Australia's foremost antique lamp museum. There are some 200 magnificent lamps here, and it hosts an interactive light show daily at 9am and 1 and 3pm. Admission is A$25. Family tickets and tours are available.

The **Bottle House,** 60 Opal St. (✆ **02/6829 0618**), is worth seeing too. Originally a miner's camp, the Bottle House now houses an astonishing collection of artifacts and other items of curious interest. It's open from 9am to 5pm daily, and entry costs A$5 for adults (free for kids).

WHERE TO STAY & DINE

An interesting addition to the Lightning Ridge lodging scene is the **Lightning Ridge Hotel/Motel** (✆ **02/6829 0304;** www.ridgehotelmotel.com.au), set on 4 hectares (10 acres) of bush, complete with a birdbath to attract the native parrots. There are 40 log cabins, as well as a trailer park and camping sites. Cabins cost A$65 without a bathroom or A$75 with a bathroom; motel rooms go for A$90 double, A$100 triple, and A$170 family room.

A nice B&B in the opal fields is **Sonja's Bed and Breakfast,** 60 Butterfly Ave. (✆ **02/6829 2010;** www.sonjasbedandbreakfast.com). Rooms cost A$130 for a double and A$180 for a family. Another option is **Black Opal Holiday Units,** Morilla Street (✆ **02/6829 0222;** www.blackopalholidayunits.com.au). The self-contained apartments are basic but comfortable, and cost A$95 a double. If you want to stay at the Glengarry opal fields, your only option is the **Glengarry Hilton** (✆ **02/6829 3808**), a rustic Outback pub (not associated with the major hotel chain). Here you stay in mobile units sleeping 24. A night costs A$16.

You can get a reasonable bistro meal at **Nobbies Restaurant,** in the Lightning Ridge Hotel (✆ **02/6829 4226**). It's open for breakfast from 7 to 9am, with lunch from noon to 2pm and dinner from 6 to 9pm. The **Lightning Ridge Bowling Club,** on Morilla Street (✆ **02/6829 0408**), also offers inexpensive bistro meals costing between A$12 and A$16. It's open for lunch between noon and 2pm and dinner from 6 to 9pm.

The Wallangulla Motel My choice of the motels in town, the Wallangulla offers two standards of rooms, the cheaper ones being in an older section of the property. Newer rooms are better furnished and generally nicer; they're worth the extra money. Two large family rooms each have two bedrooms and a living room; one has a Jacuzzi. Guests can use the barbecue facilities. The **Lightning Ridge Bowling Club** across the road has a restaurant with pretty good food and a very cheap bistro; motel guests can charge meals to their room bills.

Morilla St. (at Agate St.), Lightning Ridge, NSW 2834. ✆ **02/6829 0542.** Fax 02/6829 0070. www.lrbc.com.au/wallangulla. 42 units. A$70–A$100 double; A$90–A$115 triple; A$130–A$135 family room with Jacuzzi. AE, DC, MC, V. *In room:* A/C, TV.

BRISBANE

by Lee Mylne

Brisbane is one of those cities that seems always to be changing, without ever losing its essential character. The city skyline has been bristling with construction cranes—a sure sign that the laid-back capital of Queensland is once again booming. This subtropical city, set along the banks of the wide, brown Brisbane River, saw overzealous development in the '70s demolish some of its elegant colonial buildings, but the city has kept enough of them—including the wonderfully imposing City Hall, currently closed to visitors for a A$215 million 3-year restoration project—to provide a nice sense of history among the glass towers favored by modern architects.

Brisbane (pronounced *Briz*-bun), or just "Brizzie," is one of those places that people don't always appreciate until they spend some time in it. But you'll usually find a welcome as warm as the weather. Friendly locals will start chatting with just about anyone, and they'll urge you to discover the city, rich in history and character.

Brisbane is in the southeast corner of Queensland, flanked by the Sunshine Coast, about 2 hours to the north, and the Gold Coast, 1 hour to the south. The city is green and leafy: Moreton Bay fig trees give shade and, in summer, the purple haze of jacarandas competes with the scarlet blaze of poinciana trees. A mango tree in the backyard is practically de rigueur.

Brisbane is known for its timber "Queenslanders," cottages and houses set high on stumps to catch the breeze with wide verandas to keep out the midday sun. In some suburbs, Queenslander houses have been converted to trendy cafes, restaurants, and shops selling antiques, clothes, and housewares.

Wander in the botanic gardens, in-line skate or bike along the riverfront pathways, have a drink in a pub beer garden, or get out on the river on a CityCat ferry. The Brisbane River flows into Moreton Bay, dotted with beautiful islands to explore, and is crossed by several bridges. The most famous and attractive among these is the Story Bridge, on the Town Reach of the river. All in all, getting around here is cheap and easy, good food—including fantastic seafood—is abundant, and accommodations are affordable, especially in some of the city's comfortable, elegant B&Bs.

ORIENTATION

Arriving

BY PLANE About 30 international airlines serve Brisbane from Europe, North America, Asia, and New Zealand, including Qantas, Air New Zealand, Pacific Blue, Singapore Airlines, Thai International, Malaysia Airlines, British Airways, United, American Airlines, and Cathay Pacific. From North America, you can fly direct from Los Angeles to Brisbane on Qantas, but from other places you will likely fly to Sydney and connect on Qantas, or fly direct from Auckland, New Zealand.

Qantas (✆ **13 13 13** in Australia; www.qantas.com.au) and its subsidiary **QantasLink** (book through Qantas) operate daily flights from all state capitals (except Hobart), Cairns, Townsville, and several other towns. No-frills **Jetstar** (✆ **13 15 38** in Australia; www.jetstar.com.au) has daily service from the Queensland centers of Cairns, Rockhampton, Mackay, Townsville, Proserpine and Hamilton Island, Melbourne's Avalon airport, Adelaide, Darwin, Sydney, Newcastle, and Launceston in Tasmania. **Virgin Blue** (✆ **13 67 89** in Australia; www.virginblue.com.au) offers direct services from all capital cities as well as Cairns, Townsville, Hamilton Island and Proserpine in the Whitsundays, Mackay and Rockhampton in Queensland, Launceston in Tasmania, and Newcastle in New South Wales. **Tiger Airways** (✆ **03/9335 3033;** www.tigerairways.com.au) flies from Melbourne, Adelaide, and Rockhampton.

Brisbane International Airport is 16km (10 miles) from the city, and the domestic terminal is 2km (1¼ miles) farther away. The arrivals floor of the international terminal, on Level 2, has a check-in counter for passengers transferring to domestic flights and an information desk to meet all flights, help with flight inquiries, dispense tourist information, and make hotel bookings. **Travelex** currency-exchange bureaus are on the departures and arrivals floors. **Avis** (✆ 07/3860 4200), **Budget** (✆ 07/3860 4466), **Europcar** (✆ 07/3874 8150), **Hertz** (✆ 07/3860 4522), **Thrifty** (✆ 1300/367 227), and local company **Red Spot Rentals** (✆ 07/3860 5766) have desks on Level 2. On levels 2, 3, and 4 you will find ATMs, free showers, and baby-changing rooms. The domestic terminal has a Travelex currency-exchange bureau, ATMs, showers, and the big four car-rental desks. For security reasons, luggage lockers are not available at either terminal.

Coachtrans (✆ **07/3238 4700;** www.coachtrans.com.au) runs a shuttle between the airport and city hotels and the Roma Street Transit Centre every 30 minutes from 5am to 11pm. The one-way cost is A$14 adults and A$8 children ages 4 to 13. The round-trip fare is A$18 adults and A$16 children. Tickets for a family of four cost A$72 or A$36 one-way. The trip takes about 40 minutes, and reservations are not needed. No public buses serve the airport. A **taxi** to the city costs around A$28 from the international terminal and A$33 from the domestic terminal, plus A$3 for departing taxis.

Airtrain (✆ **07/3216 3308;** www.airtrain.com.au), a rail link between the city and Brisbane's domestic and international airport terminals, runs every 15 minutes from around 6am to 8pm daily. Fares from the airport to city stations are A$15 per adult one-way, A$27 round-trip; kids aged 14 and under travel free. The trip takes about 20 minutes. The Airtrain fare between the international and domestic terminals is A$5, unless you are traveling on Virgin or Pacific Blue flights, when it is free upon showing your boarding pass. A taxi between terminals costs about A$10.

BY TRAIN **Queensland Rail** (✆ **1300/131 722** in Queensland; www.traveltrain.com.au) operates several long-distance trains to Brisbane from Cairns. The high-speed Tilt Train takes about 25 hours and costs A$310 for business class. The slower *Sunlander* takes 32 hours and costs A$212 for a sitting berth, A$271 for an economy-class sleeper, A$417 for a first-class sleeper, or A$761 for the all-inclusive Queenslander class. **Countrylink** (✆ **13 22 32** in Australia; www.countrylink.info) runs two daily train services to Brisbane from Sydney. The 7:15am departure arrives in the town of Casino, south of the border, at 6:34pm, where passengers transfer to a bus for the rest of the trip to Brisbane, arriving at 10:20pm. The trip costs A$130 for an adult economy seat or A$174 for a first-class seat. The overnight train, which leaves Sydney at 4:20pm and arrives in Brisbane at 6:30am the next day, costs A$175 for a seat or an extra A$88 for a sleeper. Ask about off-peak discounts, depending on the time of year.

All intercity and interstate trains pull into the city center's **Brisbane Transit Centre at Roma Street,** often called the Roma Street Transit Centre. From here, most city and Spring Hill hotels are a few blocks' walk or a quick cab ride away. The station has food outlets, showers, tourist information, and lockers.

Queensland Rail CityTrain (✆ **13 12 30** in Queensland) provides daily train service from the Sunshine Coast and plentiful service from the Gold Coast.

BY BUS All intercity and interstate coaches pull into the Brisbane Transit Centre (see "By Train," above). **Greyhound Australia** (✆ **1300/473 946** in Australia, or 07/3236 3035 for the Brisbane terminal; www.greyhound.com.au) serves the city several times daily. A one-way Cairns-Brisbane ticket costs A$253; the trip takes nearly 30 hours. The Sydney-Brisbane trip takes nearly 17 hours and costs A$126 one-way. Coachtrans provides daily service from the Gold Coast. Call **Transinfo** (✆ **13 12 30**) for details.

BY CAR The Bruce Highway from Cairns enters the city from the north. The Pacific Highway enters Brisbane from the south.

Visitor Information

The **Brisbane Visitor Information Centre** (✆ **07/3006 6290;** www.visitbrisbane.com.au) is in the Queen Street Mall, between Edward and Albert streets. It's open Monday through Thursday from 9am to 5:30pm, Friday 9am to 7pm or later, Saturday 9am to 5pm, Sunday and public holidays 9:30am to 4:30pm, and from 1:30pm on Anzac Day (Apr 25). It's closed Christmas Day and Good Friday. The Brisbane City Council website, **www.ourbrisbane.com**, and the Brisbane Transit Centre (✆ **07/3236 2020**) are other good sources of information.

City Layout

The city center's office towers shimmer in the sun on the north bank of a curve of the Brisbane River. At the tip of the curve are the lush Brisbane City Gardens (sometimes called the City Botanic Gardens). The 30m (98-ft.) sandstone cliffs of Kangaroo Point rise on the eastern side of the south bank; to the west are the South Bank Parklands and the Queensland Cultural Centre, known as South Bank. The **Goodwill Bridge,** for pedestrians and bikes only, links South Bank with the City Gardens, while further along the river a new pedestrian bridge was under construction at press time and will likely be completed before your visit. The **Kurilpa Bridge**

Greater Brisbane

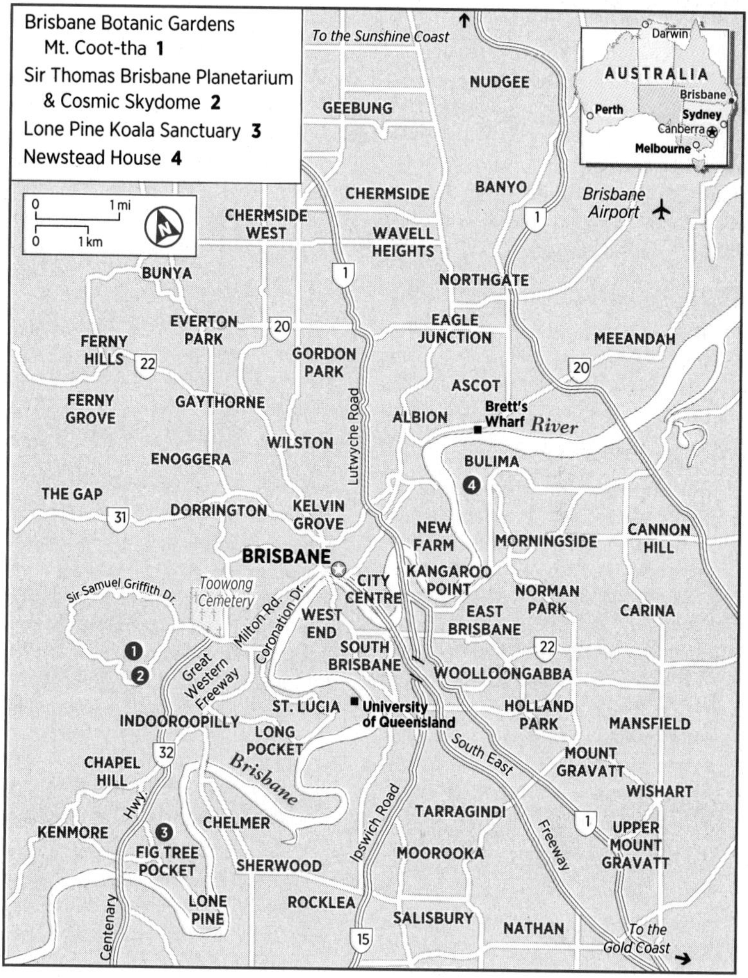

links Tank Street, in the city center, with the Gallery of Modern Art at South Bank. To the west 5km (3 miles), Mount Coot-tha (pronounced *Coo*-tha) looms out of the flat plain.

MAIN ARTERIES & STREETS It's easy to find your way around central Brisbane once you know that the east-west streets are named after female British royalty, and the north-south streets are named after their male counterparts. The northernmost is Ann, followed by Adelaide, Queen, Elizabeth, Charlotte, Mary, Margaret, and Alice. From east to west, the streets are Edward, Albert, George, and William, which becomes North Quay, flanking the river's northeast bank.

Queen Street, the main thoroughfare, becomes a pedestrian mall between Edward and George streets. Roma Street exits the city diagonally to the northwest. Ann Street leads all the way east into Fortitude Valley. The main street in Fortitude Valley is Brunswick Street, which runs into New Farm.

STREET MAPS The **Brisbane Map,** free from the Brisbane Visitor Information Centre (see "Visitor Information," above) or your hotel concierge, is a lightweight map that shows the river and suburbs as well as the city. It's great for drivers because it shows parking lots and one-way streets on the city grid. It can also be downloaded from **www.ourbrisbane.com**. Rental cars usually come with street directories. Newsdealers and some bookstores sell this map; the state auto club, the **RACQ,** in the General Post Office, 261 Queen St. (© **13 19 05**), is also a good source.

Neighborhoods in Brief

City Center The vibrant city center is where residents eat, shop, and socialize. Queen Street Mall, in the heart of town, is popular with shoppers and moviegoers, especially on weekends and Friday night (when stores stay open until 9pm). The Eagle Street financial and legal precinct has great restaurants with river views and, on Sunday, markets by the Riverside Centre tower and the Pier. Much of Brisbane's colonial architecture is in the city center, too. Strollers, bike riders, and in-line skaters shake the summer heat in the green haven of the Brisbane City Gardens at the business district's southern end.

Fortitude Valley "The Valley," as locals call it, was once one of the sleazier parts of town. Today, it is a stamping ground for street-smart young folk who meet in restored pubs and eat in cool cafes. The lanterns, food stores, and shopping mall of Chinatown are here, too. Take Turbot Street to the Valley's Brunswick Street, or venture a little farther to trendy James Street.

New Farm Always an appealing suburb, New Farm is an in-spot for cafe-hopping. Merthyr Street is where the action is, especially on Friday and Saturday night. From the intersection of Wickham and Brunswick streets, follow Brunswick southeast for 13 blocks to Merthyr.

Paddington This hilltop suburb, a couple of miles northwest of the city, is one of Brisbane's most attractive. Brightly painted Queenslander cottages line the main street, Latrobe Terrace, as it winds west along a ridge top. Many of the houses have been turned into shops and cafes, where you can browse, enjoy coffee and cake, or just admire the charming architecture.

Milton & Rosalie Park Road, in Milton, is not quite a little bit of Europe, but it tries hard—right down to a replica Eiffel Tower above the cafes and shops. Italian restaurants line the street, buzzing with office workers who down cappuccinos at alfresco restaurants, scout interior design stores for a new objet d'art to grace the living room, and stock up on European designer rags. A few minutes' drive away, Baroona Road and Nash Street, in Rosalie, are catching up.

West End This small inner-city enclave is alive with ethnic restaurants, cafes, and the odd, interesting housewares or fashion store. Most action centers on the intersection of Vulture and Boundary streets, where Asian grocers and delis abound.

Bulimba One of the emerging fashionable suburbs, Bulimba has a long connection with the river through the boat-building industry. One of the nicest ways to get there is by CityCat. Oxford Street is the main drag, lined with trendy cafes and shops.

GETTING AROUND

By Public Transportation

TransLink operates a single network of buses, trains, and ferries. For timetables and route inquiries, call **TransInfo** (✆ **13 12 30;** www.translink.com.au). It uses an integrated ticket system, and the easiest place to buy your tickets is on the buses and ferries or at the train stations. You can also buy tickets and pick up maps and timetables at the Queen Street bus station information center (in the Myer Centre, off Queen St. Mall) and the Brisbane Visitor Information Centre in the Queen Street Mall. Tickets and electronic go-cards are also sold at some inner-city newsdealers and 7-Eleven convenience stores.

A trip in a single sector or zone on the bus, train, or ferry costs A$3.40. A single ticket is good for up to 2 hours on a one-way journey on any combination of bus, train, or ferry. When traveling with a parent, kids under 5 travel free and kids 5 to 14 and students pay half fare. If you plan on using public transport a lot, it is worth investing in a go-card, which gives discounted rates (you can also buy online and you just top up the card balance as you need it). This would reduce the price of a one-zone one-way trip to A$2.65.

You will probably not need to travel farther than four zones on the transport system. This will cost you the princely sum of A$5.30 each way. A 1-day ticket for four zones will cost A$8.

On weekends and public holidays, it's cheaper to buy an **off-peak ticket,** which lets you travel all day for A$5.10 in the city center (one zone) for adults. The off-peak ticket is also available on weekdays, but you must plan your sightseeing around the fact that it cannot be used before 9am or between 3:30 and 7pm.

The **Brisbane Mobility Map,** produced by the Brisbane City Council, outlines wheelchair access to buildings in the city center and includes a detailed guide to the Queen Street Mall and a map of the Brisbane Botanic Gardens at Mount Coot-tha. The council's disability-services unit also has a range of publications, including a Braille Trail and an access guide to parks, available from council customer service centers (✆ **07/3403 8888**).

BY BUS Buses operate from around 5am to 11pm weekdays, with less service on weekends. On Sunday, many routes stop around 5pm. Most buses depart from City Hall at King George Square, Adelaide, or Ann Street. The Downtown Loop is a free bus service that circles the city center. The Loop's distinctive red buses run on two routes, stopping at convenient places including Central Station, Queen Street Mall, City Botanic Gardens, Riverside Centre, and King George Square. Look for the red bus stops. They run every 10 minutes from 7am to 5:50pm Monday through Friday. You can also pick up the free Spring Hill Loop bus, which runs every 10 minutes from 8:10am to 6:05pm weekdays, and takes in 12 city-fringe locations including Roma Street Parklands and the convict-built Old Observatory.

BY FERRY The fast **CityCat** ferries run to many places of interest, including South Bank and the Queensland Cultural Centre; the restaurants and Sunday markets at the Riverside Centre; and New Farm Park, not far from the cafes of Merthyr Street. They run every half-hour between Queensland University, about 9km (5½ miles) to the south, and Brett's Wharf, about 9km (5½ miles) to the north. Slower but more frequent CityFerry service (the **Inner City** and **Cross River** ferries) stops at a few more points, including the south end of South Bank Parklands, Kangaroo Point, and Edward Street right outside the Brisbane City Gardens. Ferries run from around 6am to 10:30pm daily. Two hours on the CityCat takes you the entire length of the run.

BY TRAIN Brisbane's suburban rail network is fast, quiet, safe, and clean. Trains run from around 5am to midnight (until about 11pm on Sun). All trains leave Central Station, between Turbot and Ann streets at Edward Street.

By Car or Taxi

Brisbane's grid of one-way streets can be confusing, so plan your route before you leave. Brisbane's biggest parking lot is at the Myer Centre (off Elizabeth St.), open 24 hours (✆ **07/3229 1699**). Most hotels and motels have free parking for guests.

Avis (✆ **13 63 33** or 07/3221 2900), **Budget** (✆ **1300/362 848** in Australia, or 07/3220 0699), **Europcar** (✆ **13 13 90** in Australia, or 07/3006 7440), and **Hertz** (✆ **13 30 39** or 07/3221 6166) all have outlets in the city center. **Thrifty** (✆ **1300/367 227** in Australia) is on the edge of the city center at 49 Barry Parade, Fortitude Valley.

For a taxi, call **Yellow Cabs** (✆ **13 19 24** in Australia) or **Black and White Taxis** (✆ **13 10 08** in Australia). There are taxi stands at each end of Queen Street Mall, on Edward Street and on George Street (outside the Treasury Casino).

[Fast FACTS] BRISBANE

American Express The office at 156 Adelaide St. (✆ **1300/139 060**) cashes traveler's checks, exchanges foreign currency, and replaces lost traveler's checks. It's open 9am to 5pm Monday to Friday and 9am to noon Saturday.

Business Hours Banks are open Monday through Thursday from 9:30am to 4pm, until 5pm on Friday. See "The Shopping Scene," later in this chapter, for store hours. Some restaurants close Monday night, Tuesday night, or both; bars are generally open from 10 or 11am until midnight.

Currency Exchange **Travelex,** in the Myer Centre, Queen Street Mall (✆ **07/3210 6325;** www.travelex.com.au), is open Monday through Thursday from 9am to 5:30pm, Friday 9am to 8pm, Saturday from 9am to 5pm, and Sunday from 10am to 4pm. Locations at the airport are open whenever flights are arriving, usually between 5am and 12:30am.

Dentists The **Dental Centre,** 171 Moray St., New Farm (✆ **07/3358 1333**), is open 8am to 8pm weekdays and 9am to 3pm weekends and public holidays. For after-hours emergencies, call for recorded info on who to contact.

Doctors The **Travel Doctor** (✆ **07/3221 9066;** www.thetraveldoctor.com.au) is on Level 5 of the Qantas building, 247 Adelaide St., between Creek and Edward streets. It is open Monday and Friday from 8am to 5pm, Tuesday and Wednesday 8am to 7pm, Thursday 8am to 4:30pm, and Saturday 8:30am to 2pm. For after-hours emergencies, call ✆ **0408/199 166.**

Embassies & Consulates The United States, Canada, and New Zealand have no representation in Brisbane; see chapter 5, "Sydney," for those countries' nearest offices. The **British Consulate** is at Level 26, Waterfront Place,

1 Eagle St. (✆ **07/3223 3200**). It is open weekdays from 10am to 3pm.

Emergencies Dial ✆ **000** for fire, ambulance, or police help in an emergency. This is a free call from a private or public telephone.

Hospitals The nearest one is **Royal Brisbane Hospital,** about a 15-minute drive from the city at Herston Road, Herston (✆ **07/3636 8111**).

Hot Lines **Lifeline** (✆ **13 11 14**) is a 24-hour emotional crisis counseling service.

Internet Access The **South Bank Visitor Information Centre,** Stanley Street Plaza, South Bank Parklands (✆ **07/3867 2051**), offers Internet access daily from 9am to 5pm and charges A$1 per 10 minutes. There are several Internet cafes on Adelaide Street, including the **Cyber Room,** Level 1, 25 Adelaide St. (✆ **07/3012 9331**).

Luggage Storage & Lockers The **Brisbane Transit Centre** on Roma Street (✆ **1800/632 640**) has baggage lockers. Medium-size lockers are also available to hire at **South Bank Parklands,** in the Stanley Street Plaza near Streets Beach. The cost is A$4 for 3 hours or A$8 for 6 hours storage.

Newspapers & Magazines The ***Courier-Mail*** (Mon–Sat) and the ***Sunday Mail*** are Brisbane's daily newspapers. Another good news source is the online newspaper ***Brisbane Times*** (www.brisbanetimes.com.au). The free weekly ***Brisbane News*** magazine is a good guide to dining, entertainment, and shopping.

Pharmacies (Chemist Shops) The **Pharmacy on the Mall,** 141 Queen St. (✆ **07/3221 4585**), is open Monday through Thursday from 7am to 9pm, Friday from 7am to 9:30pm, Saturday from 8am to 9pm, Sunday from 8:30am to 6pm, and public holidays from 9am to 7:30pm.

Police Dial ✆ **000** in an emergency, or ✆ **07/3364 6464** for police headquarters. Police are stationed 24 hours a day at 67 Adelaide St. (✆ **07/3224 4444**).

Safety Brisbane is relatively crime free, but as in any large city, be aware of your personal safety, especially when you're out at night. Stick to well-lit streets and busy precincts.

Time Zone The time in Brisbane is Greenwich Mean Time plus 10 hours. Brisbane does not observe daylight saving time, which means it's on the same time as Sydney and Melbourne in winter, and 1 hour behind those cities October through March. For the exact local time, call ✆ **1194.**

Weather Call ✆ **1196** for the southeast Queensland weather forecast.

WHERE TO STAY

In the City Center

VERY EXPENSIVE

Emporium Hotel ★★★ With its zebra-skin chairs, frangipani motifs, rich fabrics and colors, huge antique chandelier, and French stained glass window in the cocktail bar, this is Brisbane's grooviest and most eclectic hotel. Opened in 2007, it has luxury touches such as bathrobes and slippers, a pillow menu, and a pampering menu. The whole place oozes modern elegance. Kitchens—cunningly hidden from view—are standard in all rooms and have a small dishwasher as well as a microwave. There is one suite designed for guests with disabilities, at standard room rates.

1000 Ann St. Brisbane, QLD 4006. ✆ **1300/883 611** in Australia, or 07/3253 6999. Fax 07/3253 6966. www.emporiumhotel.com.au. 102 units, 42 with spa baths. A$230 double standard room; A$250 double King suite; A$270 double King Spa suite; A$420 double Emporium suite; A$445 double Deluxe

Brisbane Accommodations, Dining & Attractions

ACCOMMODATIONS ■

Emporium Hotel **2**
Eton **11**
Hotel George Williams (YMCA) **14**
Hotel Ibis Brisbane **13**
The Limes **1**
Novotel Brisbane **9**
One Thornbury **5**
Portal Hotel **10**
Quay West Suites **23**
Stamford Plaza Brisbane **21**

DINING ◆

e'cco bistro **6**
Gianni's **22**
Govinda's **24**
Jo Jo's **16**
Plough Inn **29**
Story Bridge Hotel **19**
Tognini's BistroCafeDeli **7**
Walt Moden Dining **4**

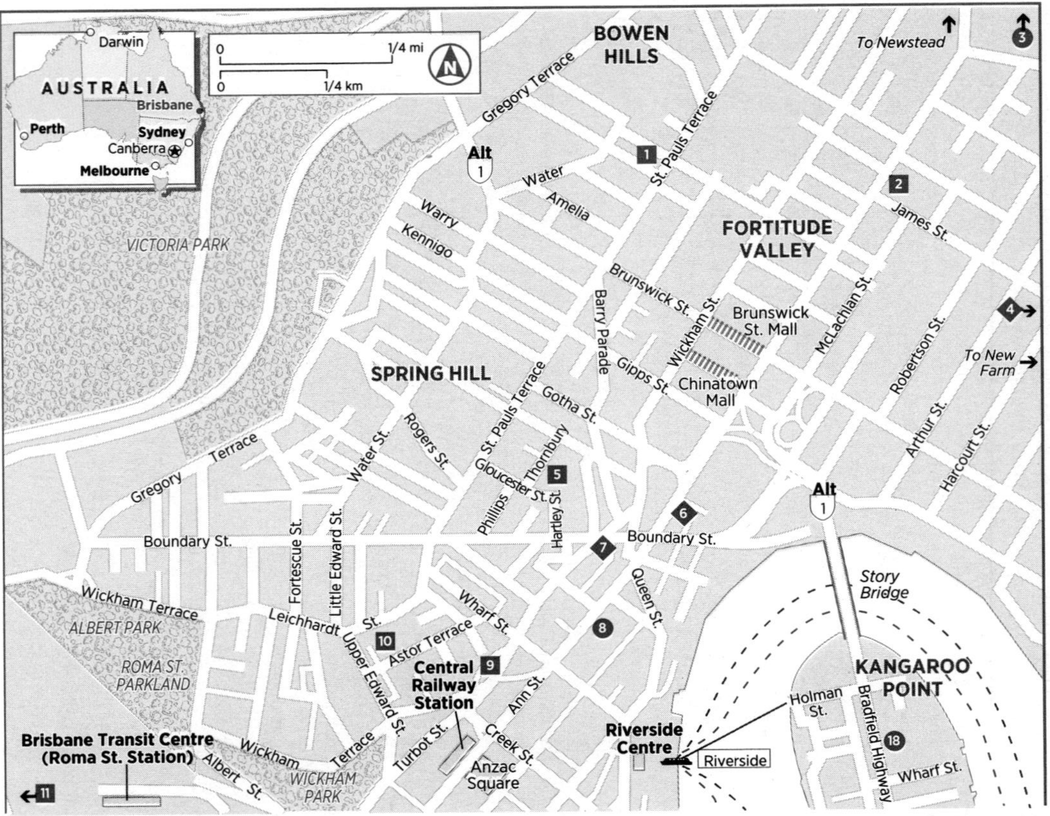

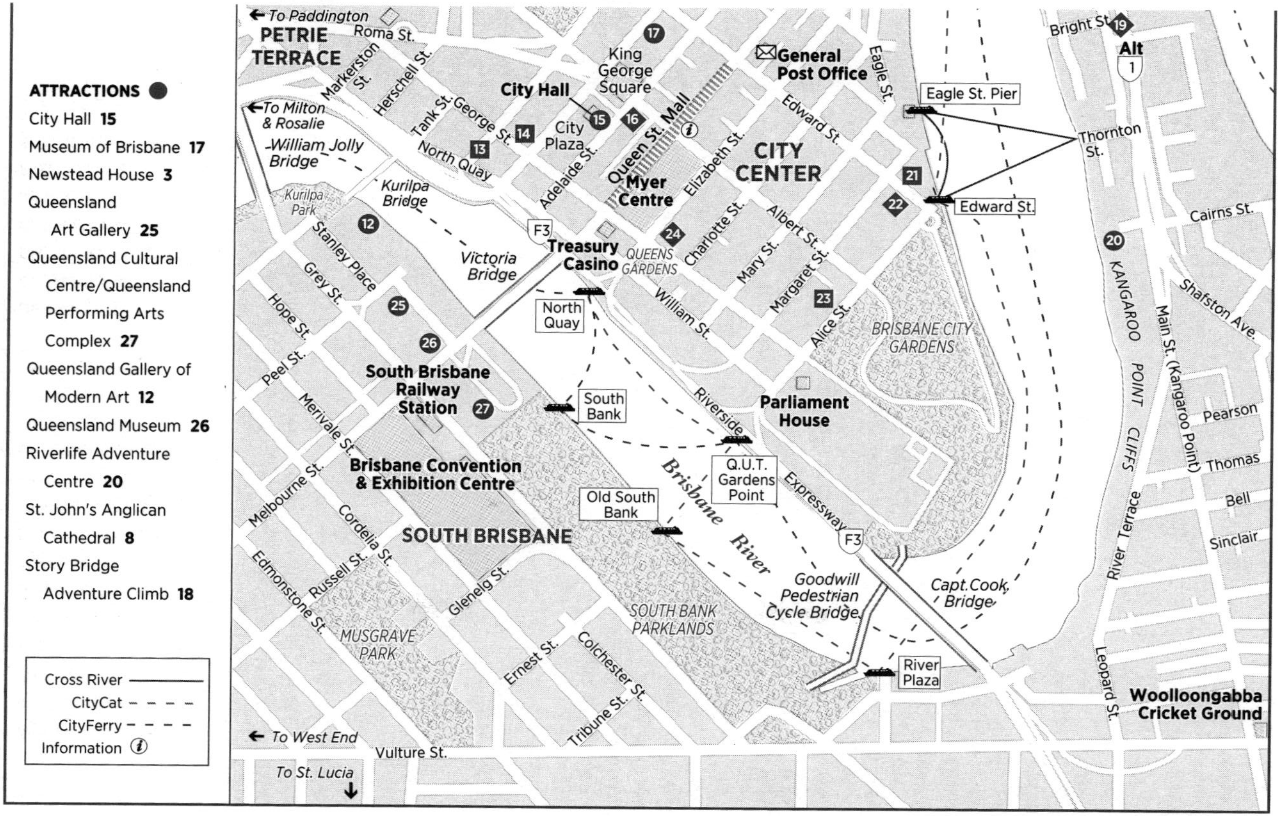
ATTRACTIONS
City Hall 15
Museum of Brisbane 17
Newstead House 3
Queensland Art Gallery 25
Queensland Cultural Centre/Queensland Performing Arts Complex 27
Queensland Gallery of Modern Art 12
Queensland Museum 26
Riverlife Adventure Centre 20
St. John's Anglican Cathedral 8
Story Bridge Adventure Climb 18
Cross River
CityCat
CityFerry
Information
To Paddington
PETRIE TERRACE
Roma St.
Markerston St.
Herschell St.
To Milton & Rosalie
William Jolly Bridge
Tank St.
George St.
North Quay
City Hall
King George Square
City Plaza
Adelaide St.
Queen St. Mall
Myer Centre
Elizabeth St.
General Post Office
Eagle St.
Edward St.
CITY CENTER
Eagle St. Pier
Edward St.
Thornton St.
Bright St.
Alt 1
Kurilpa Park
Kurilpa Bridge
Victoria Bridge
F3
Treasury Casino
QUEENS GARDENS
Charlotte St.
Albert St.
Mary St.
Margaret St.
Alice St.
William St.
North Quay
BRISBANE CITY GARDENS
Parliament House
Riverside
Expressway
Stanley Place
Grey St.
Hope St.
Peel St.
South Brisbane Railway Station
South Bank
Q.U.T. Gardens Point
Brisbane River
Merivale St.
Brisbane Convention & Exhibition Centre
Melbourne St.
Cordelia St.
SOUTH BRISBANE
Old South Bank
Edmonstone St.
Russell St.
Glenelg St.
MUSGRAVE PARK
SOUTH BANK PARKLANDS
Goodwill Pedestrian Cycle Bridge
Capt.Cook Bridge
Ernest St.
Colchester St.
Tribune St.
River Plaza
To West End
Vulture St.
To St. Lucia
Cairns St.
KANGAROO POINT CLIFFS
Main St. (Kangaroo Point)
Shafston Ave.
Pearson
Thomas
Bell
Sinclair
River Terrace
Leopard St.
Woolloongabba Cricket Ground

corner suite. Ask about packages. AE, DC, MC, V. Valet parking A$25 per day. **Amenities:** Restaurant; bar; concierge; exercise room; outdoor heated lap pool; room service; sauna. *In room:* A/C, TV/VCR w/pay movies, hair dryer, kitchenette, minibar, Wi-Fi (A$10 for 1 hr., A$20 for 24 hr., A$45 for 3 days).

Quay West Suites Brisbane ★★ When the business folk go home on Fridays, they leave available this glamorous apartment hotel, just 4 blocks from Queen Street Mall; you'll find excellent packages here. The apartments have all the amenities of a five-star hotel—daily servicing, concierge, 24-hour room service, bar and restaurant with a lovely outdoor terrace—and their own laundry facilities, dining areas, separate bedrooms, and fully equipped kitchens. Pamper yourself in the pool or Jacuzzi, relax in the sauna, then head back to your apartment, get into your bathrobe, gaze over the Botanic Gardens, read the free newspaper, and turn up the CD player or watch one of the two TVs.

132 Alice St. (btw. Albert and George sts.), Brisbane, QLD 4000. ✆ **1800/672 726** in Australia, or 07/3853 6000. Fax 07/3853 6060. www.mirvachotels.com/quay-west-suites-brisbane. 70 apts. A$515 1-bedroom apt; A$630 2-bedroom apt. Extra person A$50. Ask about special packages. AE, DC, MC, V. Covered secure valet parking A$20. Bus: Downtown Loop. Ferry: Edward St. (Inner City and Cross River Ferry); or Riverside (CityCat); then a 10-min. stroll. **Amenities:** Restaurant; bar; concierge; gymnasium; Jacuzzi; outdoor pool; room service; sauna. *In room:* A/C, TV w/in-house movies, CD player, hair dryer, Internet (A$10 per hr., A$20 for 24 hr., A$45 for 3 days, A$60 for 7 days), kitchen, minibar.

Stamford Plaza Brisbane ★★★ The Stamford is one of Brisbane's most beautiful hotels: comfy oversize chairs and sofas, enormous still-life oils, gilt mirrors, and palms dot the marble lobby. It prides itself on being the only city hotel with river views from every room—especially stunning from the southern rooms at night, when the Story Bridge lights up. The plush rooms were refurbished in mid-2009 and are also the largest in Brisbane, all with a king-size or twin beds. What must be the biggest bathrooms in town sport small TVs. A riverside boardwalk leads from the hotel to the Eagle Street Pier restaurants, and the Brisbane City Botanical Gardens abut the hotel.

Edward and Margaret sts. (adjacent to the Brisbane City Botanical Gardens), Brisbane, QLD 4000. ✆ **1800/773 700** in Australia, or 07/3221 1999. Fax 07/3221 6895. www.stamford.com.au. 252 units. A$245–A$650 double; A$690–A$3,500 suite. Extra person A$40. Children 11 and under stay free in parent's room. Ask about packages. AE, DC, MC, V. Covered parking. Train: Central; then taxi or walk 6 blocks. Bus: Downtown Loop. Ferry: Riverside Centre, Eagle St. **Amenities:** 3 restaurants; 3 bars; babysitting; bikes; concierge; health club; Jacuzzi; small outdoor heated lap pool; room service; sauna. *In room:* A/C, TV w/pay movies, DVD, hair dryer, minibar, MP3 docking station, Wi-Fi (A60¢ per min. for 40 min.; A$25 per day).

EXPENSIVE

The Limes Hotel ★ The first Australian hotel to be part of Design Hotels, the Limes considers itself "backstreet boutique." There are no frills or frippery, but that doesn't mean it's not stylish, interesting, and functional, designed with an eye to what travelers want. Three rooms on the ground floor have courtyards with hammocks and a table and chairs; all are practical in design, with a kitchen area that doubles as a work station. The hotel bar is also home to a popular 30-seat rooftop cinema (and an area for smokers on the mezzanine), and a guest swipe card for lift access assures security.

142 Constance St., Fortitude Valley, Brisbane, QLD 4006. ✆ **07/3852 9000.** Fax 07/3852 9099. www.limeshotel.com.au. 21 units, all with shower only. A$440 double; A$550 double courtyard rooms. AE, DC, MC, V. Train: Brunswick St. Parking A$10 per day (nearby). **Amenities:** Bar; free access to nearby health club. *In room:* A/C, TV w/pay movies, hair dryer, kitchenette, MP3 docking station, free Wi-Fi.

Novotel Brisbane ★ This well-appointed contemporary hotel, a short walk from Brisbane's main shopping areas, is popular with families and business travelers. The modern, stylish rooms and suites are spacious and have superb views over the city. The lap pool is very inviting and has terrific city views. There's live music in the **Spring Bar,** and you can choose between the upmarket **Cilantro** restaurant or the more casual **eat@astor** cafe. All rooms are nonsmoking.

200 Creek St., Brisbane, QLD 4000. ✆ **1300/656 565** in Australia, 800/221-4542 in the U.S. and Canada, 0870/609 0961 in the U.K., 0800/44 4422 in New Zealand, or 07/3309 3309. Fax 07/3309 3308. www.novotelbrisbane.com.au. 296 units. A$199–A$349 double. Children 15 and under stay free in parent's room with existing bedding. Free crib. Ask about packages. AE, DC, MC, V. Free covered parking. Train: Central. **Amenities:** 2 restaurants; bar; babysitting; concierge; gymnasium; outdoor pool; room service; sauna. *In room:* A/C, TV w/pay movies, hair dryer, minibar, Wi-Fi (some floors only; 55¢ per min. or A$28 for 24 hr.).

MODERATE

Eton ★ This heritage-listed colonial cottage, not far from the Brisbane Transit Centre, has five rooms and an attic suite that sleeps three, all with en-suite bathrooms. The attic suite is a self-contained apartment with its own entrance and kitchen. Room no. 1, at the front of the house, is my pick—it has a claw-foot tub and king-size bed. Out in the back is a garden courtyard, where you can have breakfast among the palms, ferns, and frangipani trees. There's a guest laundry and kitchen. There's no smoking indoors and children under 4 are not allowed.

436 Upper Roma St., Brisbane, QLD 4000. ✆ **07/3236 0115.** www.babs.com.au/eton. 6 units, 5 with shower only. A$125–A$145 double; A$595 apt weekly. Extra person A$25. Rates include breakfast (except apt). AE, MC, V. Limited free parking. Train: Roma St. *In room:* A/C, TV, hair dryer, Wi-Fi (A$5 per day).

Hotel George Williams ★ This smart, great value YMCA hotel is a good budget choice for inner-city stays. Rooms are small but some can sleep up to four adults. Queen terrace rooms have a small sheltered balcony with table and chairs. Among the useful facilities are a 24-hour front desk and business center, and safe-deposit boxes. Hair dryers are available on request. Guests have access to the YMCA Wellness Studio, the largest hotel gym in Australia, which offers aerobics classes, personal trainers, and massage (for an extra fee). Several rooms are designed for guests with disabilities, and there is also easy access to the gym.

317–325 George St. (btw. Turbot and Ann sts.), Brisbane, QLD 4000. ✆ **1800/064 858** in Australia, or 07/3308 0700. Fax 07/3308 0733. www.hgw.com.au. 106 units, most with shower only. A$195–A$280 double. Extra person A$30. Children 3 and under stay free in parent's room. Ask about packages. AE, DC, MC, V. Limited parking, A$20 per night. Train: Roma St. Bus: Downtown Loop. Ferry: North Quay (CityCat or CityFerry). **Amenities:** Restaurant; bar; health club. *In room:* A/C, TV, Wi-Fi (A$4.40 for 30 min. to A$22 for 24 hr.).

Hotel Ibis Brisbane You get what you pay for at this AAA three-and-a-half-star sister property to the Novotel Brisbane (see above). In this case, it is basically a comfortable room, with few amenities you might expect in a large hotel. But if you don't mind doing without river views, porters, a pool, or other small luxuries, this could be the place for you. The hotel has rooms—renovated in 2008 to the tune of A$1.5 million and much larger than those in most hotels of this standard—furnished in contemporary style, with sizable work desks and small but smart bathrooms. Facilities include 24-hour reception and storage lockers, and guests can also use the restaurant and bar at the adjoining **Mercure Hotel.**

27–35 Turbot St. (btw. North Quay and George St.), Brisbane, QLD 4000. ✆ **1300/656 565** in Australia, 800/221-4542 in the U.S. and Canada, 020/8283 4500 in the U.K., 0800/44 4422 in New Zealand, or 07/3237 2333. Fax 07/3237 2444. www.accorhotels.com.au. 218 units. From A$149 double. Extra person A$36. One child 11 or under stays free in parent's room with existing bedding. Ask about packages. AE, DC, MC, V. Parking (at the Mercure Hotel) A$14. Train: Roma St. Bus: Downtown Loop. Ferry: North Quay (CityCat or CityFerry). **Amenities:** Restaurant; bar; babysitting. *In room:* A/C, TV w/pay movies, hair dryer, Wi-Fi (A$28 for 24 hr.).

One Thornbury ★ A 15-minute walk to Spring Hill from the city center brings you to this 1886 Queenslander cottage on a quiet street. The heritage-listed exterior belies a chic modern interior, where everything was refurbished and renewed in 2008, right down to the mattresses and new bathrooms for each room. The attic suite sleeps three and has two bedrooms, a dining and sitting room, and a bathroom. Fresh flowers, bathrobes, extra large fluffy towels, and handmade soap are among the thoughtful extras. Breakfast is served in the cool, restful courtyard, where you can help yourself to tea, coffee, cookies, and the newspaper any time of day. The airport bus stops at the front door. This establishment is not suitable for children.

1 Thornbury St., Spring Hill, Brisbane, QLD 4000. ✆ **07/3839 5334.** www.onethornbury.com. 6 units, 5 with shower only. A$140–A$190 double. Rates include breakfast. AE, MC, V. Limited free parking. Train: Central. **Amenities:** Access to nearby pools, golf club, and health club; free Internet. *In room:* A/C, TV, hair dryer, no phone.

Portal Hotel ★ The standard rooms are just big enough to swing a cat, but the location is terrific and there's a nice modern edge to this new (2009) hotel just on the city fringe. Executive rooms are bigger, and a suite has a self-contained kitchen, a lounge chair with a 42-inch TV, and a bathtub to soak in. Parking—even just while you check in—can be a problem on the street outside, and there's only one dropping-off space at the hotel, which can be tricky.

52 Astor Terrace, Spring Hill, QLD 4000. ✆ **1300/767 825** in Australia or 07/3009 3400. Fax 07/3009 3410. www.portalhotel.com.au. 84 units. A$249–A$299 double. AE, DC, MC, V. Valet parking. Train: Central. **Amenities:** Restaurant; bar; room service. *In room:* A/C, TV, CD player, hair dryer, MP3 docking station, Wi-Fi.

In Paddington

Aynsley B&B ★ In a quiet street just off the main shopping and restaurant strip in Paddington, this restored 1905 Queenslander house retains most of its original features, such as leadlight windows, tongue-and-groove walls, high ceilings, and polished timber floors. The two air-conditioned guest bedrooms are nicely furnished and have good quality, comfy mattresses. Each has its own en-suite bathroom. Your hosts, Gena and Garth Evans, have been in the B&B business for many years and know how to look after their guests. A rear deck on both levels overlooks mango trees, busy with birdlife, and it's hard to believe you are only 3km (2 miles) from the city center. There's also a large swimming pool and a guest laundry. No smoking indoors.

14 Glanmire St., Paddington, Brisbane, QLD 4064. ✆ **07/3368 2250** or 0417/482 021 mobile. Fax 07/3368 2250. www.aynsley.com.au. 2 units, both with shower only. A$155–A$195 double. Weekly rates available. Rates include full breakfast. AE, DC, MC, V. Free off-street parking. Bus: 375 or 377; stop 200m (656 ft.) away. **Amenities:** Outdoor pool. *In room:* A/C, TV, hair dryer, free Internet.

WHERE TO DINE

Brisbane has a fairly sophisticated dining scene: Stylish bistros and cafes line Merthyr Street and James Street in New Farm; cute cafes are plentiful in Paddington; Asian eateries are a good choice around the intersection of Vulture Street and Boundary Street in West End; and in Fortitude Valley, you'll find Chinatown. A street full of upscale but laid-back restaurants, many with a Mediterranean flavor, sits under the kitsch replica Eiffel Tower on Park Road in Milton, and in the city center you can find slick riverfront restaurants at Eagle Street Pier and Riverside. The intersection of Albert and Charlotte streets buzzes with inexpensive, good-quality cafes.

In the City Center

EXPENSIVE

e'cco bistro ★★★ CONTEMPORARY *E'cco* means "here it is" in Italian, and that's the philosophy behind the food at this award-winning bistro. It serves simple food, done exceptionally well and with passion. In a former tea warehouse on the city fringe, it's one of Australia's best. Dishes include such delights as roast spatchcock with sweet corn risotto, tomato pickle, chile, and spring onion; or seared ocean trout with shaved fennel, zucchini flowers, pickled red onion, and a soft herb beurre blanc. The bistro is enormously popular, and bookings are essential. Large windows, bold colors, and modern furniture make it a pleasant setting. There's an extensive wine list—many by the glass. A simple pricing structure has all items for each course at the same price.

100 Boundary St. (at Adelaide St.). ✆ **07/3831 8344.** Fax 07/3831 8460. www.eccobistro.com. Reservations required. Main courses A$43. AE, DC, MC, V. Tues–Fri noon–2:30pm; Tues–Sat 6–10pm. Metered street parking or nearby parking buildings.

Gianni's ★★★ MEDITERRANEAN Whether you choose the more formal and private mezzanine floor, or the relaxed courtyard dining area, you're sure to enjoy this contemporary European-flavored restaurant. Gianni's has garnered a sheaf of awards and is acknowledged as one of Brisbane's best. The mezzanine has a climate-controlled wine cellar, presided over by co-owner Gianni Greghini, where you can select your wine. The food is a blend of European and Californian styles, and is always delicious and interesting. It changes fortnightly, but dishes might include something like lobster bisque infused with coconut and lemongrass and Mooloolaba prawns; or free-range chicken deglace with sherry, polenta, and borlotti beans.

12 Edward St. ✆ **07/3221 7655.** www.giannisrestaurant.com. Reservations recommended. Main courses A$35–A$42; 4-course degustation menu A$85 (A$135 with wine); 6-course degustation menu A$110 (A$185 with wine). AE, DC, MC, V. Tues–Fri noon–2:30pm; Tues–Sat 6:30–10:30pm. Metered street parking or nearby parking buildings.

Watt Modern Dining ★★ MODERN AUSTRALIAN With a menu of modern fare with Asian, Middle Eastern, and European influences and a terrific wine list, Watt is one of my favorite places to eat out in Brisbane—partly because of the riverside setting in New Farm Park, and partly because of the great food. Whether it's for a leisurely weekend breakfast, lunch, or dinner before a show at the Brisbane Powerhouse, dishes are always interesting, such as lamb rump with spiced yoghurt, smoky eggplant, and sumac; or snapper with wild rice, braised cuttlefish, and preserved lemon aioli. Dine at 6pm and you can get two courses (from a limited menu) for A$45.

Brisbane Powerhouse, 119 Lamington St. (near the river), New Farm. ✆ **07/3358 5464.** www.aihgroup.com.au. Reservations recommended. Main courses A$31–A$49. AE, DC, MC, V. Lunch Tues–Sun from noon; dinner Tues–Sat from 6pm; Sat–Sun breakfast 8–10:30am. Ample free parking.

MODERATE

Jo Jo's INTERNATIONAL/CAFE FARE A spectacular timber, limestone, and glass bar dominates the center of this casual cafe-style eating spot, housing more than 1,000 bottles of wine. Three menus—chargrill, Oriental, and Mediterranean—are available, and the locals have dropped in here for years for a shopping pit stop or a postcinema meal. The food is well priced and good. You order at the bar and meals are delivered to the table (try to get one on the balcony overlooking the Queen St. Mall). Among your options are steaks and seafood from the grill; curries and stir-fries from the Oriental menu; and Mediterranean pastas, antipasto, and wood-fired-oven pizzas.

1st floor, Queen St. Mall, at Albert St. ✆ **07/3221 2113.** www.jojos.com.au. Main courses A$17–A$38. AE, DC, MC, V. Mon–Fri 10am–midnight; Sat–Sun 11am–midnight. Train or bus: Central.

INEXPENSIVE

Govinda's VEGETARIAN If you're on a budget, or a committed vegetarian, seek out the Hare Krishnas' chain of Govinda restaurants. This one serves vegetable curry, dal soup, samosas, and other tasty stuff with a north-Indian influence. The atmosphere is pretty spartan, but the food is very satisfying. This is a stimulant-free zone, so don't come expecting alcohol, tea, or coffee—you're likely to get something like homemade ginger and mint lemonade instead. On the first Sunday of every month, there is a "feast" at 5pm for A$5—along with lectures, chanting, and meditation.

99 Elizabeth St. (opposite Myer Centre), 2nd floor. ✆ **07/3210 0255.** www.brisbanegovindas.com.au. A$10 all-you-can-eat; A$9 students and seniors, A$6 students 2–3pm only. No credit cards. Mon–Thurs 11am–3pm and 5–7:30pm; Fri 11am–8:30pm; Saturday 11am–2:30pm. Bus: Downtown Loop.

In Spring Hill

Tognini's BistroCafeDeli MODERN AUSTRALIAN Owners Mark and Narelle Tognini run this relaxed modern bistro, incorporating an extensive deli and walk-in cheese room. Popular with inner-city dwellers and business folk, it serves gourmet delights to eat in or take out. Sit at one of the communal tables and try the spaghetti with chile prawns or perhaps a corned beef sandwich with caramelized cabbage, Swiss cheese, and cornichons. They also offer a breakfast menu and a brunch menu on Saturdays. There's another Tognini's CafeDeli at Baroona Road, Milton, and Tognini's CafeWineBar at the State Library at South Bank.

Turbot and Boundary sts., Spring Hill. ✆ **07/3831 5300.** Fax 07/3831 5311. www.togninis.com. Reservations not accepted. Main courses A$15–A$23. AE, DC, MC, V. Mon–Fri 7am–5pm; Sat 8am–2:30pm.

In Mount Coot-tha

The Summit ★★ MODERN AUSTRALIAN It would be hard to find a better view of Brisbane than from this spot. A teahouse of some kind has been on this mountaintop for more than a century. Part 19th-century Queenslander house and part modern extension, the restaurant has wraparound covered decks with a view of the city and Moreton Bay. A changing menu features local produce and wines. Try saltwater barramundi filet, or grilled Queensland Hereford tenderloin beef with a

Moreton Bay bug. The early bird offer—A$34 for three courses if you finish by 7pm—is available starting at 5pm. There's also a kids' menu of two courses for A$17 (for those under 12). When you've finished dining, spend some time on the observation deck—the city lights provide a glittering panorama.

Sir Samuel Griffith Dr., Mt. Coot-tha. ✆ **07/3369 9922.** Fax 07/3369 8937. www.brisbanelookout.com. Reservations recommended Fri-Sat night. Main courses A$28–A$38. AE, DC, MC, V. Daily 11:30am–midnight; Sun brunch 8–10:30am. Closed for lunch Jan 1, Good Friday, Dec 26; closed for dinner Dec 25. Free parking. Bus: 471. From Roma St. Transit Centre, take Upper Roma St. and Milton Rd. 3.5km (2¼ miles) west to the Western Fwy. roundabout at Toowong Cemetery, veer right into Sir Samuel Griffith Dr., and go approximately 3km (2 miles).

In East Brisbane

Green Papaya ★ NORTH VIETNAMESE Clean, fresh, and simple dishes have been the hallmark of this popular restaurant since it opened 13 years ago. Chef Thang Nguyen has been at the helm in the kitchen for the past 10 years, and the menu changes very little. There are two chic, cheerful rooms, usually crowded with a faithful clientele. If you don't know your *bo xao cay ngot* (spicy beef) from your *nom du du* (green papaya salad), the helpful staff willingly gives advice. The restaurant is licensed, but you can bring your own bottled wine (no beer or spirits) for a corkage charge of A$6 per bottle. The restaurant also does takeout.

898 Stanley St. E (at Potts St., 1 block from Woolloongabba Cricket Ground), East Brisbane. ✆ **07/3217 3599.** www.greenpapaya.com.au. Reservations recommended. Main courses A$21–A$38; banquet menus (for minimum of 4 people) A$55–A$65. AE, DC, MC, V. Tues–Sat 6–9:30pm. Closed Good Friday and Dec 25 to early Jan. Parking at rear of restaurant and on street. Train: Woolloongabba.

In Albion

Breakfast Creek Hotel ★ STEAK A A$4.5-million renovation and restoration in 2002 gave fresh life to this Brisbane treasure. Built in 1889 and listed by the National Trust, the Renaissance-style pub is fondly known as the Brekky Creek—or simply the Creek. The quintessentially Queensland establishment is famed for its gigantic steaks (choose your own), served with baked potato, bacon sauce, coleslaw, and salad, and for serving beer "off the wood" (from the keg). Also on the premises, the **Spanish Garden Steakhouse** and the **Staghorn beer garden** are always popular, and an outdoor dining area overlooks Breakfast Creek. The **Substation No. 41** bar, created in the shell of a derelict electricity substation next to the hotel, makes the most of its exposed brick walls and soaring ceilings. The 4.5m-long (15-ft.) wooden bar is just the place to sip the latest cocktail.

2 Kingsford Smith Dr. (at Breakfast Creek Rd.), Albion. ✆ **07/3262 5988.** www.breakfastcreekhotel.com. Main courses A$19–A$46. AE, DC, MC, V. Daily 10am–late. Substation 141 daily noon–late. Bus: 300 or 322. Wickham St. becomes Breakfast Creek Rd.; the hotel is just off the route to the airport.

EXPLORING BRISBANE

Cuddling a Koala & Other Top Attractions

Brisbane Botanic Gardens at Mount Coot-tha These 52-hectare (128-acre) gardens at the base of Mount Coot-tha feature Aussie natives and exotic plants you probably won't see at home. There's an arid zone, a Tropical Dome conservatory housing rainforest plants, a cactus house, a bonsai house, fragrant plants, a Japanese garden, African and American plants, wetlands, and a bamboo grove. There are lakes and trails, usually a horticultural show or arts-and-crafts display in the auditorium on weekends, and a cafe. Free 1-hour guided tours leave the kiosk at 11am and 1pm Monday through Saturday (except public holidays). The Sir Thomas Brisbane Planetarium & Cosmic Skydome (see below) is also in the botanic gardens.

Mt. Coot-tha Rd., Toowong (7km/4⅓ miles from the city). ✆ **07/3403 2535.** www.brisbane.qld.gov.au. Free admission to Botanic Gardens. Sept–Mar daily 8am–5:30pm; Apr–Aug daily 8am–5pm. Free parking. Bus: 471.

Lone Pine Koala Sanctuary ★★ ☺ This is the best place in Australia to cuddle a koala—and one of the few places where koala cuddling is actually still allowed. Banned in New South Wales and Victoria, holding a koala is legal in Queensland under strict conditions that ensure that each animal is handled for less than 30 minutes a day—and gets every third day off! When it opened in 1927, Lone Pine had only two koalas, Jack and Jill; it is now home to more than 130. You can cuddle them anytime and have a photo taken holding one for A$16; once you've purchased a photograph, you can have some photos taken using your own camera, too. Lone Pine isn't just koalas—you can also hand-feed kangaroos and wallabies and get up close with emus, snakes, baby crocs, parrots, wombats, Tasmanian devils, skinks, lace monitors, frogs, bats, turtles, possums, and other native wildlife. There is a currency exchange, a gift shop, and a restaurant and cafe. You can also take advantage of the picnic and barbecue facilities.

The nicest way to get to Lone Pine is a cruise down the Brisbane River aboard the MV ***Mirimar*** (✆ **1300/729 742** in Australia), which leaves the Cultural Centre at South Bank Parklands at 10am. The 19km (12-mile) trip to Lone Pine takes 90 minutes and includes commentary. You have 2 hours to explore before returning, arriving in the city at 2:45pm. The round-trip fare is A$55 for adults, A$33 for children ages 3 to 13, and A$160 for families of five, including entry to Lone Pine. Cruises run daily except April 25 (Anzac Day) and December 25.

Jesmond Rd., Fig Tree Pocket. ✆ **07/3378 1366.** Fax 07/3878 1770. www.koala.net. Admission A$28 adults, A$19 children 3–13, A$65 families of 5. Daily 8:30am–5pm; Apr 25 (Anzac Day) 1:30–5pm; Dec 25 8:30am–4:30pm. By car (20 min. from the city center), take Milton Rd. to the roundabout at Toowong Cemetery, and then Western Fwy. toward Ipswich. Signs point to Fig Tree Pocket and Lone Pine. Ample free parking. Bus: 430 from the city center hourly 8:45am–3:40pm weekdays, 8:30am–3:30pm Sat–Sun and public holidays; 445 at 8:45am and 3:45pm, and hourly from 9:10am–2:10pm weekdays, 7:55am–2:55pm Sat. Bus fare A$3.40 adults, A$1.70 children. Taxi from the city center about A$40.

Museum of Brisbane This smallish museum has been temporarily relocated while its usual home, the historic City Hall, undergoes a 3-year multimillion-dollar restoration. Now on the ground floor of a city office building, the museum nevertheless gives a good insight into the history and essence of Brisbane. Changing exhibitions relate the stories, events, and ideas that have shaped the city, as well as giving practical information for visitors. It is a good starting point for your visit.

157 Ann St. ✆ **07/3403 8888.** www.museumofbrisbane.com.au. Free admission. Daily 10am–5pm. Closed Jan 1, Good Friday, Dec 25 and 26, and until 1pm Apr 25 (Anzac Day). Train: Roma St. Bus: City Circle.

Newstead House ★ Brisbane's oldest surviving home has been restored to its late Victorian splendor in a peaceful park overlooking the Brisbane River. Wander the rooms, admire the gracious exterior dating from 1846, and on some Sunday afternoons enjoy a free band concert. The U.S. Army occupied the house during

Brisbane on the Cheap

Visitors to Brisbane can now purchase a new "Five in One" discount card to save more than 30 percent on entry to five of the city's top attractions. You can choose from a list of attractions that includes Lone Pine Koala Sanctuary, the Story Bridge Adventure Climb, Kookaburra River Queen Cruises, Riverlife Adventure Centre, Brisbane Ghost Tours, the XXXX Brewery Tour, walking tours, wine tasting, and kayaking. The card costs A$145 for adults and A$109 for children aged 4 to 15, and can be purchased from the Queen Street Mall Visitor Information Centre, major hotels, or online at www.brisbanefiveinone.com.

World War II, and the first American war memorial built in Australia stands on Newstead Point.

Newstead Park, Breakfast Creek Rd., Newstead. ✆ **1800/061 846** or 07/3216 1846. www.newsteadhouse.com.au. A$6 adults, A$5 seniors and students, A$4 children 6–16, A$15 families. Mon–Thurs 10am–4pm; Sun 2–5pm. Last admittance 30 min. before closing. Closed Fri, Sat, Anzac Day (Apr 25), and for 10 days btw. Christmas and New Year's Day. Limited parking. Bus: 300 or 302.

Queensland Cultural Centre ☺ This modern complex stretching along the south bank of the Brisbane River houses many of the city's performing arts venues as well as the state art galleries, museum, and library. With plenty of open plazas and fountains, it is a pleasing place to wander or just sit and watch the river and the city skyline. It's a 7-minute walk from town.

The **Queensland Performing Arts Centre** (✆ **07/3840 7444** administration Mon–Fri 9am–5pm, or 13 62 46 for bookings Mon–Sat 9am–8:30pm; www.qpac.com.au) houses the 2,000-seat Lyric Theatre for musicals, ballet, and opera; the 1,800-seat Concert Hall for orchestral performances; the 850-seat Playhouse theater for plays; and the 315-seat Cremorne Theatre for theater-in-the-round, cabaret, and experimental works. The complex has a restaurant and a cafe.

The **Queensland Art Gallery ★★** (✆ **07/3840 7303;** www.qag.qld.gov.au) is one of Australia's most attractive galleries, with vast light-filled spaces and interesting water features inside and out. It is a major player in the Australian art world, attracting blockbuster exhibitions of works by the likes of Renoir, Picasso, and van Gogh, and showcasing diverse modern Australian painters, sculptors, and other artists. It also has an impressive collection of Aboriginal art. The adjacent **Queensland Gallery of Modern Art ★★** houses collections of modern and contemporary Australian, indigenous Australian, Asian, and Pacific art, and also gives a stunning sense of light and space. The **Australian Cinémathèque,** located at the Gallery of Modern Art, has two cinemas in which it presents retrospective and thematic film programs, as well as a gallery dedicated to screen-related exhibitions. Admission is free to both galleries. They are open Monday through Friday 10am to 5pm and weekends 9am to 5pm; closed Good Friday, December 25, and until noon on April 25 (Anzac Day).

The **Queensland Museum** (✆ **07/3840 7555;** www.qm.qld.gov.au), on the corner of Grey and Melbourne streets, houses an eclectic collection ranging from natural history specimens and fossils to a World War I German tank. Children will like the blue whale model; the dinosaurs, which include Queensland's own

Muttaburrasaurus; and the interactive Sciencentre on Level 1. The museum has a cafe and gift shop. Admission is free, except to the Sciencentre and traveling exhibitions. It's open daily 9:30am to 5pm; closed Good Friday, December 25, and until 1:30pm on April 25 (Anzac Day).

Adjacent to South Bank Parklands, across Victoria Bridge at western end of Queen St. ✆ **07/3840 7100.** Admission to Sciencentre A$12 adults, A$9 children 3–15, A$40 family of 6. Plentiful underground parking. Ferry: South Bank (CityCat) or Old South Bank (Inner City Ferry). Bus: Numerous routes from Adelaide St. (near Albert St.), including 100, 111, 115, and 120, stop outside. Train: South Brisbane.

Roma Street Parkland Thousands of plants, including natives and some of the world's most endangered, have been used to create lush subtropical gardens in an unused railway yard. The effect is stunning. Free 1-hour guided walks leave from the Hub, near the Spectacle Garden entrance at 10am and 2pm daily (excluding Good Friday and Christmas Day), and there are also self-guided walks for each themed area of the gardens. The "art walk" helps visitors discover the interesting public art on display. The park also has barbecues, picnic areas, a playground, and cafe. From King George Square, it is about a 500m (1,640-ft.) walk along Albert Street.

Roma St.; information booths at Spectacle Garden and Activity Centre. ✆ **07/3006 4545.** www.romastreetparkland.com. Free admission. Daily 24 hr.; Spectacle Garden daily dawn–dusk. Train: Roma St. By car, enter from Roma St. or the Wickham Terrace/College Rd./Gregory Terrace intersection.

St. John's Anglican Cathedral ★★ Brisbane's stunning neo-Gothic Anglican cathedral took more than a century to complete, but the result has been worth the wait. Plagued by lack of funding throughout its history, the final scaffolding was removed from the building in 2009. As the last Gothic-style cathedral to be completed anywhere in the world, the cathedral has seen stonemasons toiling for years using traditional medieval building techniques to complete this wonderful building. It is well worth a visit. Friendly, knowledgeable volunteer guides run tours and will point out some of the details that make this cathedral uniquely Queensland—such as the carved possums on the organ screen and the hand-stitched cushions.

373 Ann St. (btw. Wharf and Queen sts.). ✆ **07/3835 2231.** www.stjohnscathedral.com.au. Daily 9:30am–4:30pm; free tours Mon–Sat 10am and 2pm and most Sun at 2pm. Closed to visitors, except for services, Apr 25 (Anzac Day), Dec 25, and some other public holidays. Train: Central Station.

Sir Thomas Brisbane Planetarium & Cosmic Skydome ☺ Digital multimedia systems that present real-time digital star shows and computer-generated images in the Cosmic Skydome theater are a popular feature of a visit here for all ages. The fascinating 40-minute astronomical show includes a re-creation of the Brisbane night sky using a Ziess star projector. There are special shows designed for kids between 5 and 8 at 11:30am and 12:30pm on weekends; the planetarium is not recommended for younger children. Kids shows cost A$6.70 adults and children.

Brisbane Botanic Gardens, Mt. Coot-tha Rd., Toowong. ✆ **07/3403 2578.** www.brisbane.qld.gov.au/planetarium. A$13 adults, A$11 seniors and students, A$7.80 children 14 and under, A$34 families of 4. Tues–Fri 10am–4pm; Sat 11am–8:15pm (last entry at 7:30pm); Sun 11am–4pm. Shows Tues–Fri 3pm; Sat 11:30am, 12:30, 2, 3, 6, and 7:30pm; Sun 11:30am, 12:30, 2, and 3pm. Extended hours during school holidays. Closed public holidays. Reservations recommended. Bus: 471, 598, or 599.

South Bank Parklands ☺ Follow the locals' lead and spend some time at this delightful 16-hectare (40-acre) complex of parks, restaurants, cafes, shops, playgrounds, street theater, and weekend markets. There's a man-made beach lined with palm trees, with waves and sand, where you can swim, stroll, and cycle the meandering pathways. From the parklands it's an easy stroll to the museum, art gallery, and other parts of the adjacent **Queensland Cultural Centre** (see above). The South Bank Parklands are a 7-minute walk from town.

South Bank. ✆ **07/3867 2051** for Visitor Information Centre. www.visitsouthbank.com. Free admission. Park daily 24 hr.; Visitor Information Centre daily 9am–5pm. From the Queen St. Mall, cross the Victoria Bridge to South Bank or walk across Goodwill Bridge from Gardens Point Rd. entrance to Brisbane City Gardens. Plentiful underground parking in Queensland Cultural Centre. Train: South Brisbane. Ferry: South Bank (CityCat or Cross River Ferry). Bus: Numerous routes from Adelaide St. (near Albert St.), including 100, 111, 115, and 120, stop at the Queensland Cultural Centre; walk through the Centre to South Bank Parklands.

Wheel of Brisbane ☺ Take a 13-minute ride in an enclosed gondola on this giant observation wheel for a 360-degree bird's-eye view of Brisbane from 60m (197 ft.) up. The city's newest attraction, at South Bank Parklands, lets you see the surrounds from a comfortable air-conditioned bubble.

Russell St., South Bank. ✆ **07/3844 3464.** www.worldtouristattractions.co.uk. Mon–Thurs 10am–10pm; Fri–Sat 9am–midnight; Sun 9am–10pm. A$15 adults, A$10 children 4–12, A$2 children 1–3, A$42 family of 4, A$95 private gondola.

Taking a City Stroll

Because Brisbane is leafy, warm, and full of colonial-era Queenslander architecture, it is a great city for strolling. A self-guided walking tour, the **Brisbane City Walk,** takes you to 30 attractions, from shopping precincts to historic buildings, and links through three inner-city parks—Southbank Parklands, Roma Street Parkland, and the City Botanic Gardens. The route is marked on a map distributed by the Brisbane Visitor Information Centre in the Queen Street Mall Information Centre, or you can download it at **www.ourbrisbane.com/see-and-do/brisbanecitywalk**.

A "floating" **River Walk** connects more than 20km (13 miles) of pathways, roads, bridges, and parks along the Brisbane River. You can stroll along River Walk on the north bank of the river between the University of Queensland at St. Lucia and Teneriffe, and on the south bank from the West End ferry terminal at Orleigh Park to Dockside at Kangaroo Point.

For information on organized walking tours, see below.

RIVER CRUISES & ORGANIZED TOURS

RIVER CRUISES The best way to cruise the river, in my view, is aboard the fast **CityCat ferries ★★**. Board at Riverside and head downstream under the Story Bridge to New Farm Park, past Newstead House to the restaurant row at Brett's Wharf; or cruise upriver past the city and South Bank to the University of Queensland's lovely campus. (Take a look at its impressive Great Court while you're there.) This trip in either direction will set you back a whopping A$3.40. Or you can stay on for the full trip, which takes about 2 hours. For more information, see "Getting Around," earlier in this chapter.

For those who'd like a meal as they cruise, the **Kookaburra River Queen** paddle-wheelers (✆ **07/3221 1300;** www.kookaburrariverqueens.com) are a good option. Dinner cruises, offering both a seafood and roast carvery buffet, run daily except Monday and Wednesday and cost A$75 or A$85 on Friday and Saturday nights. The boat departs from the Eagle Street Pier (parking is available under the City Rowers tavern on Eagle St.) at 7:30pm. On the first Sunday of each month, a cruise with live jazz runs from 12:15 to 2pm. It costs A$20.

BUS TOURS For a good introduction to Brisbane, look no farther than a **City Sights** bus tour run by the Brisbane City Council (✆ **07/3403 8888;** www.citysights.com.au). City Sights buses stop at 19 points of interest in a continuous loop around the city center, Spring Hill, Milton, South Bank, and Fortitude Valley, including Chinatown. They take in various historic buildings and places of interest. The driver of the blue-and-yellow bus narrates, and you can hop on and off at any stop you like. The tour is a good value—your ticket also gives unlimited access to CityCat ferries for the day. The bus departs every 45 minutes from 9am to 3:45pm daily except Good Friday, April 25 (Anzac Day), and December 25. The entire trip, without stopping, takes about 80 minutes. Tickets cost A$35 for adults, A$20 for children 5 to 14 or A$80 for a family of 5. Buy your ticket on board. You can join anywhere along the route, but the most central stop is City Hall, stop 2, on Adelaide Street at Albert Street.

WALKING TOURS The Brisbane City Council has a wonderful program called **Gonewalking** (✆ **07/3403 8888**). About 80 free guided walks are run each week from somewhere in the city or suburbs, exploring all kinds of territory, from bushland to heritage buildings to riverscapes to cemeteries. The walks are aimed at locals, not tourists, so you get to explore Brisbane side by side with the townsfolk. Every walk has a flexible distance option and usually lasts about an hour. Most are easy, but some are more demanding. Most start and finish near public transport and end near a food outlet.

Free guided walks of the **City Botanic Gardens** at Alice Street leave from the rotunda at the Albert Street entrance Monday through Saturday at 11am and 1pm (except public holidays). They take about 1 hour. Bookings are not necessary.

Prepare for shivers up your spine if you take one of Jack Sim's **Ghost Tours ★** (✆ **07/3344 7265;** www.ghost-tours.com.au), which relive Brisbane's gruesome past. You can take a 90-minute walking tour of the city leaving from the Queen Street Mall at 7:30pm Sunday through Friday, for A$25 per person. Choose between the Bloody Brisbane crime and murder tour or Haunted Brisbane. On Saturday nights, you can take a tour of the historic and haunted Toowong cemetery for A$35 per person. Reservations are essential; not suitable for children under 12.

ENJOYING THE GREAT OUTDOORS

ABSEILING The Kangaroo Point cliffs just south of the Story Bridge are a breeze for first-time abseilers (rappellers)—or so they say. The **Riverlife Adventure Centre** (✆ **07/3891 5766;** www.riverlife.com.au), in the old naval stores building at the base of the cliffs, runs daily abseiling and rock-climbing classes. Abseiling costs A$39 per person and a 2-hour rock-climbing lesson is A$45 per person.

BIKING Bike tracks, often shared with pedestrians and in-line skaters, stretch for 400km (248 miles) around Brisbane. One great scenic route, about 9km (5½ miles) long, starts just west of the Story Bridge, sweeps through the Brisbane City Gardens,

Brisbane's Bridge Climb

Brisbane seems to have a fascination with building bridges across its wide river. There are 14 (at last count), but the most interesting is the Story Bridge, built in 1940. If you are over 12 years old and at least 130 centimeters (just over 4 ft., 3 in.) tall, you can "climb" this overgrown Meccano set. The Story Bridge Adventure Climb (✆ 1300/254 627 in Australia, or 07/3514 6900; www.storybridgeadventureclimb.com.au) peaks at a viewing platform on top of the bridge, 44m (143 ft.) above the roadway and 80m (262 ft.) above the Brisbane River. This is only the third "bridge climb" in the world (after Sydney's and Auckland's), so make the most of the chance. You'll be rewarded with magnificent 360-degree views of the city, river, and Moreton Bay and its islands. Climbs operate daily and start from the base headquarters at 170 Main St. (at Wharf St.), Kangaroo Point. Day climbs cost A$89 adults and A$76 children ages 10 to 16. Twilight climbs on Monday through Thursday cost A$99 adults and A$84 children, and A$130 adults or A$111 children Friday to Sunday. Night climbs are A$89 adults and A$76 children weekdays and A$99 or A$84 on weekends. Dawn climbs, only on Saturday and Sunday, cost A$99 adults and A$84 children. Children must be accompanied by an adult.

and follows the river all the way to the University of Queensland campus at St. Lucia. **Gardens Cycle Hire** (✆ **0408/003 198** mobile; www.gardens-cycle-hire.com) operates from the bicycle station in the City Botanic Gardens, near the Alice Street gate, from 9:30am until dark. The cost is A$18 for 1 hour or A$42 for a day. Kids' bikes and tandems are also available. You can also have your bike "valet" delivered to all city area accommodations at extra cost. All rentals include helmets, which are compulsory in Australia. The Brisbane City Council at City Hall (✆ **07/3403 8888**) and Brisbane Visitor Information Centre (see "Visitor Information," earlier in this chapter) also give out bike maps.

BUSHWALKING **D'Aguilar National Park ★★** (formerly known as Brisbane Forest Park), a 28,500-hectare (70,395-acre) expanse of bushland, waterfalls, and rainforest a 20-minute drive north of the city, has hiking trails ranging from just a few hundred meters up to 8km (5 miles). Some tracks have themes—one highlights the native mammals that live in the park, for example, and another, the 1.8km (just over 1-mile) **Mount Coot-tha Aboriginal Art Trail,** showcases Aboriginal art, with tree carvings, rock paintings, etchings, and a dance pit. Because the park is so big, most walks depart from one of the seven regional centers, which are up to a 20-minute drive from headquarters. (You will need a car.) Make a day of it and pack a picnic. At **Walkabout Creek Visitor Centre,** 60 Mount Nebo Rd., The Gap (✆ **1300/723 684;** www.derm.qld.gov.au/parks/daguilar), you will also find the **South East Queensland Wildlife Centre,** a showcase of the region's wildlife that is home to a platypus, lungfish, nocturnal wildlife (in a night-house), birds in a walk-through aviary, wallabies, reptiles, and frogs. It is open daily 9am to 4:30pm. Admission is A$5.85 adults, A$2.85 school children, or A$15 for a family of 4. There's a café on-site.

IN-LINE SKATING In-line skaters can use the network of bike and pedestrian paths. See "Biking," above, for locations that distribute maps, or head down to the Brisbane City Gardens at Alice Street and find your way along the river. **SkateBiz,** 101 Albert St. (✆ **07/3220 0157**), rents blades for A$13 for 2 hours, or A$25 for up to 24 hours. Protective gear is included. Take a photo ID. The store is open from 9am to 5:30pm Monday through Thursday, 9am to 9pm Friday, 9am to 4pm Saturday, and 10am to 4pm Sunday. They also run social skating sessions around Brisbane.

KAYAKING To get out on the Brisbane River, you can rent a kayak from **Riverlife Adventure Centre** (✆ **07/3891 5766;** www.riverlife.com.au), at the base of the Kangaroo Point cliffs, for A$25 per person for 90 minutes. Classes, in which you will learn how to launch the kayak, paddle, turn, stay out of the path of the CityCats, and much more, are run daily and cost A$35 per person. Night kayaking lessons are also run after 6pm and cost A$55 per person. The center is open 9am to 6pm daily.

THE SHOPPING SCENE

Brisbane's inner-city shopping centers on **Queen Street Mall** (www.queenstreetmall.com.au), which has around 500 stores. Fronting the mall at 171–209 Queen St., under the Hilton, is the three-level **Wintergarden** shopping complex (✆ **07/3229 9755;** www.wgarden.com.au), housing upscale jewelers and Aussie fashion designers. Farther up the mall at 91 Queen St. (at Albert St.) is the **Myer Centre** (✆ **07/3223 6900;** www.myercentreshopping.com.au), which has Brisbane's biggest department store and five levels of moderately priced stores, mostly fashion. The **Brisbane Arcade,** 160 Queen St. Mall (✆ **07/3831 2711;** www.brisbanearcade.com.au), abounds with the boutiques of local Queensland designers. Just down the mall from it is the **Broadway on the Mall** arcade (✆ **07/3229 5233;** www.broadwayonthemall.com.au), which stocks affordable fashion, gifts, and accessories on two levels. Across from the Edward Street end of the mall is a smart fashion and lifestyle shopping precinct, **MacArthur Central** (✆ **07/3007 2300;** www.macarthurcentral.com), right next door to the GPO on the block between Queen and Elizabeth streets. This is where you'll find top-name designer labels, Swiss watches, galleries, and accessory shops.

In Fortitude Valley, on the city center fringe, you'll find the **Emporium** precinct (www.emporium.com.au) at the bottom of Ann St., the place for designer labels (including shoes), gourmet food and wine, a couple of good bookshops, and other

Fireworks for Your Wall

If the Aboriginal art you see in the usual tourist outlets doesn't do it for you, what you'll see at Brisbane's FireWorks Gallery, 52a Doggett St., Newstead (✆ 07/3216 1250; www.fireworksgallery.com.au), might. This renowned gallery shows art by established and emerging artists from all over Australia. You may pale at some of the prices, but the range is wide and you may find something you can't live without—it's that kind of place. The staff will get your new acquisition shipped home for you. Open Tuesday to Friday 10am to 6pm, Saturday 10am to 4pm, or by appointment.

luxuries. James Street is home to some of the top Australian designers, including Scanlan & Theodore and Sass & Bide.

The trendy suburb of **Paddington,** just a couple of miles from the city by cab (or take the no. 144 bus to Bardon), is the place for antiques, books, art, crafts, one-of-a-kind clothing designs, and unusual gifts. The shops—housed in colorfully painted Queenslander cottages—line the main street, Given Terrace, which becomes Latrobe Terrace. Don't miss the second wave of shops around the bend.

SHOPPING HOURS Brisbane shops are open Monday through Thursday from 9am to 6pm, Friday 9am to 9pm, Saturday 9am to 5:30pm, and Sunday 10am to 6pm. On Friday evening in the city, the Queen Street Mall is abuzz with cinemagoers and revelers; the late (until 9pm) shopping night in Paddington is Thursday.

MARKETS Authentic retro '50s and '60s fashion, offbeat stuff such as old LPs, secondhand crafts, fashion by up-and-coming young designers, and all kinds of junk and treasure, are for sale at Brisbane's only alternative market, **Valley Markets,** Brunswick Street and Chinatown malls, Fortitude Valley. Hang around in one of the many coffee shops and listen to live music. It's open Saturday and Sunday from 9am to 4pm.

The buzzing outdoor **South Bank Lifestyle Market,** Stanley Street Plaza, South Bank Parklands, is illuminated by fairy lights at night. The market is open Friday from 5 to 10pm, Saturday 10am to 5pm, and Sunday 9am to 5pm. On the first Sunday of the month, you'll find the Young Designers section of the market, showcasing Brisbane's next hot young things.

Brisbane folk like trawling the **Riverside Markets ★** at the Riverside Centre, 123 Eagle St., and the adjacent **Eagle Street Pier Art & Craft Markets** for housewares, hand-crafted furniture, glassware, leather work, jewelry, fashion, alternative therapies, stained glass, food, art, handmade toys, sculpture, and more. They are both open on Sunday from around 7am to 4pm.

For an authentic taste of Queensland's best produce, the **Powerhouse Farmers Markets ★★** (www.janpowersfarmersmarkets.com.au) operate on the second and fourth Saturday of each month, from 6am to noon, in the grounds of the Brisbane Powerhouse, Lamington Street, New Farm. Here you'll find much to tempt your palate in about 100 stalls, selling everything from fresh fruit and vegetables to home-made chutneys, quail, fresh seafood, free-range eggs, and pâtés. There are even cooking classes. Foodies will be in heaven.

BRISBANE AFTER DARK

You can find out about festivals, concerts, and events, and book tickets through **Ticketek** (**© 13 28 49** in Queensland; www.ticketek.com.au). You can also book in person at Ticketek agencies, the most convenient of which are on Elizabeth Street, outside the Myer Centre, and in the Visitor Information Centre at South Bank Parklands. Or try **Ticketmaster** (**© 13 61 00;** www.ticketmaster.com.au).

QTIX (**© 13 62 46** in Australia; www.qtix.com.au) is a booking agent for the performing arts and classical music, including all events at the Queensland Performing Arts Complex (QPAC). There is a A$3 booking fee per ticket. You can also book in person at the box office at QPAC between 8:30am and 9pm Monday to Saturday, and at the South Bank Parklands Visitor Information Centre.

The free weekly magazine *Brisbane News* lists performing arts, jazz, and classical music performances, art exhibitions, rock concerts, and public events. The free weekly *TimeOff*, published on Wednesday and available in bars and cafes, is a good guide to live music, as is Thursday's *Courier-Mail* newspaper.

The Performing Arts

Many of Brisbane's performing arts events are at the **Queensland Performing Arts Centre (QPAC)** in the Queensland Cultural Centre (see "Exploring Brisbane," earlier in this chapter). The city also has a lively independent theater scene, with smaller companies making an increasing impact. To find out what's playing and to book tickets, contact QTIX (see above).

Queensland Theatre Company (✆ **07/3010 7600** for information; www.qldtheatreco.com.au), the state theater company, offers eight or nine productions a year, from the classics to new Australian works. It attracts some of the country's best actors and directors. The company performs at three venues: the Playhouse and Cremorne Theatre at the Queensland Performing Arts Centre (QPAC), South Bank; and its home venue, the new 228-seat Bille Brown Studio, 78 Montague Rd., South Brisbane. Tickets cost from A$30, if you are under 30, to between A$36 and A$63.

La Boite Theatre ★ (✆ **07/3007 8600** administration; www.laboite.com.au) is a well-established innovative company that performs contemporary Australian plays in the round. La Boite performs in the 400-seat Roundhouse Theater, 6 Musk Ave., Kelvin Grove. Take bus no. 390 from the city to Kelvin Grove Road, and get off at stop 7. Tickets cost A$46 to A$63 (opening nights); previews are A$25. If you are 30 or under, tickets cost A$26.

Brisbane Powerhouse Arts, 119 Lamington St., New Farm (✆ **07/3358 8600;** www.brisbanepowerhouse.org), is a venue for innovative (some might say fringe) contemporary works. A former electricity powerhouse, the massive brick factory is now a dynamic art space for exhibitions, contemporary performance, and live art. The building retains its character, an industrial mix of metal, glass, and stark surfaces etched with 20 years of graffiti. It's a short walk from the New Farm ferry terminal along the riverfront through New Farm Park.

The state opera company, **Opera Queensland** (✆ **07/3735 3030** administration; www.operaqueensland.com.au), performs a lively repertoire of traditional as well as modern works, musicals, and choral concerts. Free talks on the opera you are about to see start 45 minutes before every performance. Book tickets through QTIX (✆ **13 62 46;** www.qtix.com.au). Most performances take place at the Queensland Performing Arts Centre (QPAC). Tickets range from A$40 to A$150 or A$45 to A$55 at some performances if you're age 30 or younger.

The **Queensland Symphony Orchestra** (✆ **07/3833 5000** for administration; www.thequeenslandorchestra.com.au) provides classical music lovers with a diverse mix of orchestral and chamber music, with the odd foray into fun material, such as movie themes, pop, and gospel music. It schedules about 30 concerts a year. Free talks in the foyer begin 1 hour before major performances. The orchestra plays at the Concert Hall in the Queensland Performing Arts Centre (QPAC) and occasional other venues; more intimate works sometimes play at the Conservatorium Theatre, South Bank. Tickets for the Maestro concert series cost A$45 to A$75.

BRISBANE'S HISTORIC pubs

Brisbane's attractive historic pubs, many of them recently revitalized, have wide, shady verandas and beer gardens just perfect for whiling away a sunny afternoon or catching a quick meal at night.

The best known is the **Breakfast Creek Hotel,** 2 Kingsford Smith Dr., Breakfast Creek (✆ **07/3262 5988;** see "Where to Dine," earlier in this chapter). Built in 1889, the hotel is a Brisbane institution. For many people, a visit to the city isn't complete without a steak and beer "off the wood" at the Brekky Creek.

Another landmark is the **Regatta Hotel,** 543 Coronation Dr., Toowong (✆ **07/3871 9595;** www.regattahotel.com.au). This heritage hotel with three stories of iron-lace balconies is the perfect spot for a cool drink overlooking the Brisbane River and usually bursts at the seams on weekends. Its **Boatshed restaurant** (✆ **07/3871 9533**) is popular but not inexpensive—tables around the hotel verandas are a better choice.

Not far from the Regatta is the **Royal Exchange Hotel,** 10 High St., Toowong (✆ **07/3371 2555;** www.rehotel.com.au). Known simply as "the RE," it's popular with students, probably because of its proximity to the University of Queensland. It has a great garden bar at the back.

The **Story Bridge Hotel,** 200 Main St., Kangaroo Point (✆ **07/3391 2266;** www.storybridgehotel.com.au), is well known as the venue for some of Brisbane's most unusual events, such as the annual Australia Day (Jan 26) cockroach races. Built in 1886, the pub is also a great place to find live music, and has a wonderful beer garden under the bridge.

In Red Hill, on the city fringe, is the **Normanby Hotel,** 1 Musgrave Rd. (✆ **07/3831 3353;** www.thenormanby.com.au), built in 1872 and recently stylishly revamped. Features are the giant Moreton Bay fig tree in the beer garden and the biggest outdoor TV screen in town.

Another of the city's oldest pubs is the **Plough Inn** (✆ **07/3844 7777;** www.ploughinn.com.au), at South Bank Parklands, which has stood its ground through major changes in the neighborhood since 1885. There's even a ghost, they say . . .

Nightclubs & Bars

Friday's This indoor/outdoor bar, restaurant, and nightclub complex overlooking the Brisbane River is a haunt for 18- to 40-year-olds. Gather on the large outdoor terrace with its huge island bar, or head for the restaurant, supper club, or dance floor. Music spans acid jazz, urban groove, and dance anthems from resident DJs, with the latest R&B, soul, and funk by live bands. Wednesday through Saturday nights see some kind of happy-hour deal, cocktail club, or drinks special; the dance action starts pumping around 9pm on Friday and Saturday. Upstairs in Riverside Centre, 123 Eagle St. ✆ **07/3832 2122.** www.fridays.com.au. Cover varies. Ferry: CityCat to Riverside.

Treasury Casino This lovely heritage building—built in 1886 as, ironically enough, the state's Treasury offices—houses a modern casino. Three levels of 100 gaming tables offer roulette, blackjack, baccarat, craps, sic-bo, and traditional Aussie two-up. There are more than 1,300 gaming machines, six restaurants, and five bars.

It's open 24 hours. Live bands appear nightly in the **Livewire Bar** and on Thursday nights you can hear Brisbane's up-and-coming singer-songwriters in the **Premier's Bar.** Queen St. btw. George and William sts. ✆ **07/3306 8888.** www.conradtreasury.com.au. Must be 18 years old to enter; neat casual attire required (no beachwear or thongs). Closed Good Friday, Dec 25, and until 1pm Apr 25 (Anzac Day). Train: Central or South Brisbane, and then walk across the Victoria Bridge.

Zenbar Minimalist Manhattan-style interiors with an 8m-high (26-ft.) glass wall overlooking a bamboo garden make this one of the hippest joints in town. It's a restaurant as well, but the bar is packed on Friday and Saturday night with office workers and beautiful people. There are about 40 wines by the glass, but in this kind of place you should be drinking a mojito or martini. Park level, Post Office Sq., 215 Adelaide St. ✆ **07/3211 2333.** www.zenbar.com.au. Train: Central.

Cool Spots for Jazz & Blues

The Bowery ★★ Exposed brick walls, wooden booths, and a comfortable courtyard set the scene for one of Brisbane's (indeed, Australia's) most intimate and sophisticated jazz venues. This atmospheric cocktail bar, modeled on Prohibition-era speakeasies, has live jazz during the week and on Sundays—usually from around 8 or 8:30pm—and DJs on Friday and Saturday from 9pm. Open Tuesday to Sunday 5pm to 3am. 676 Ann St., Fortitude Valley. ✆ **07/3252 0202.** www.thebowery.com.au. Train: Brunswick St.

Brisbane Jazz Club ★ On the riverfront, under the Story Bridge, this is the only Australian jazz club still featuring big band dance music (every Sun night). Watch out for the slightly sloping dance floor—it was once a boat ramp! Traditional and mainstream jazz is featured on Saturday nights. It's open Fridays and Saturdays 6:30 to 11:30pm and Sundays 5:30 to 10pm. On the first and third Tuesday of the month from 7 to 10pm there's a jazz singers' jam session (A$10), and on the last Sunday of the month a breakfast session from 8:15am to noon. Phone and check what's on before heading over; bookings are necessary for some events. 1 Annie St., Kangaroo Point. ✆ **07/3391 2006.** www.brisbanejazzclub.com.au. Cover usually A$20, higher for some guest acts. Free parking lot. Ferry: CityCat to Holman St.

BRISBANE'S MORETON BAY & ISLANDS

The Brisbane River runs into Moreton Bay, which is studded with hundreds of small islands—and a few large ones. Some of them can be reached only by private vessel. Others are national parks and are accessible by tour boat or public ferry.

North Stradbroke Island ★★

Affectionately called "Straddie" by the locals, the island was once home to a large Aboriginal population and still retains much of their history. The town of Dunwich was used as a convict outstation, Catholic mission, quarantine station, and benevolent institution. The **North Stradbroke Island Historical Museum,** 15-17 Welsby St., Dunwich (✆ **07/3409 9699**), has a display of historical photographs, items salvaged from shipwrecks, and information about the Aboriginal history and

Moreton Bay & Islands

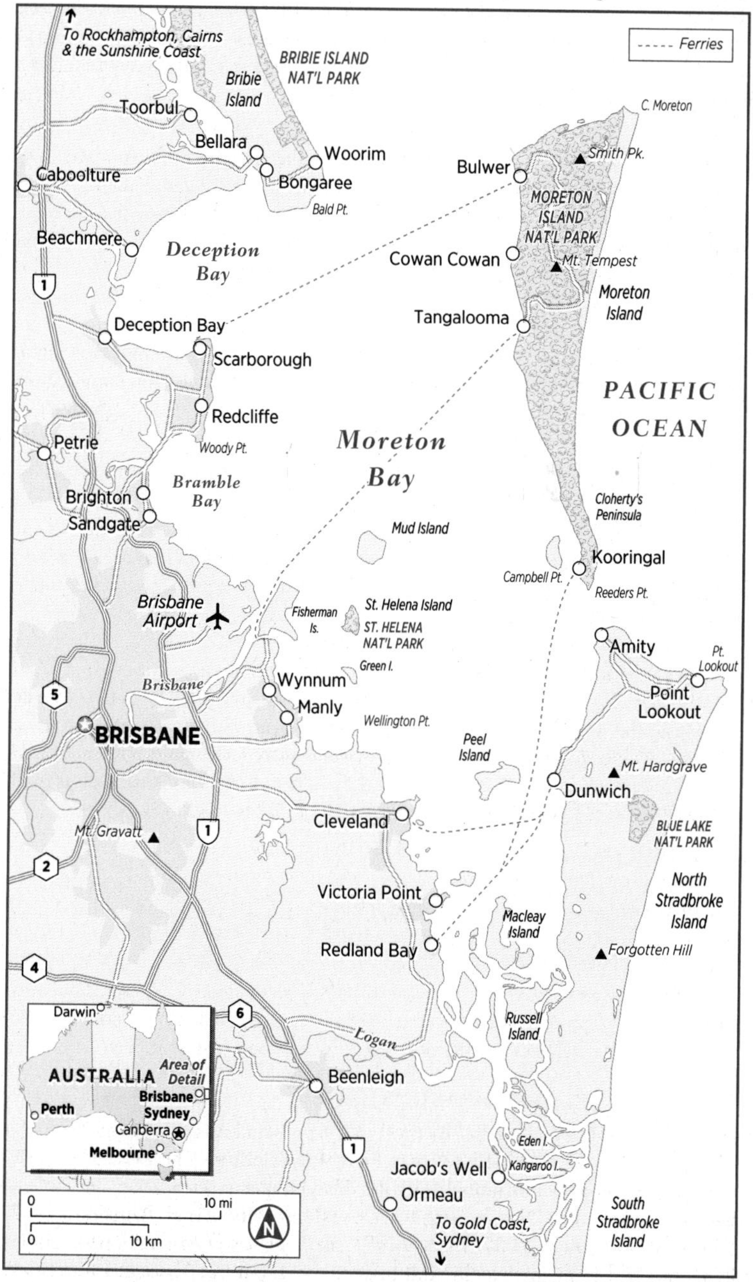

7

BRISBANE | Brisbane's Moreton Bay & Islands

early settlement of the island; it's open from 10am to 2pm Tuesday to Saturday. Entry costs A$3.30 adults and A$1.10 children. Pick up a guide to the heritage trail that features 30 points of interest at Dunwich, Amity, and Lookout Point, with details the history of the Dunwich Cemetery. The booklet is available at visitor centers on the mainland and at Dunwich, at the museum, and at tourist attractions on the island. Another "must" for visitors is the North Gorge Headlands Walk, for breathtaking views and for spotting turtles, dolphins, and whales.

GETTING THERE & GETTING AROUND **Stradbroke Ferries** (✆ **07/3488 5300;** www.stradbrokeferries.com.au) operates water-taxi service from Toondah Harbour, Middle Street, Cleveland, to Dunwich (about 30 min.); the round-trip adult fare is A$17, A$10 for children 5 to 14. The vehicle barge takes walk-on passengers for A$11 adults and A$5.50 children round-trip; the trip takes about 45 minutes. A bus meets almost every water taxi or ferry at Dunwich and connects it with the other two main settlements, Amity and Point Lookout. The trip to either place takes about 30 minutes and costs A$4.10 adults, A$2.10 for children 5 to 14.

To get to Cleveland by public transport from Brisbane, take the train from Central Station to Cleveland Station (A$6.70), and then walk about 300m (a quarter mile) to Middle Street.

VISITOR INFORMATION The **Stradbroke Island Tourism** information center (✆ **07/3415 3044;** www.stradbroketourism.com) is at 21 Cumming Parade, Point Lookout. It is open weekdays from 8:30am to 5pm and weekends 9am to 4pm. Another good source is the **Redlands on Moreton Bay Visitor Centre,** 152 Shore St., Cleveland (✆ **1300/667 386** in Australia; www.more2redlands.com.au). It's open 9am to 5pm weekdays and 9am to 3pm weekends.

South Stradbroke Island ★★

A turn-of-the-20th-century shipwreck (with a cargo of whiskey and explosives) weakened the link between this lovely island and North Stradbroke, and nature did the rest. South Stradbroke is less well known than its sister island, but that's changing. The island has four campgrounds and three resorts. South Stradbroke Island is accessible from Hope Harbour, about a 45-minute drive south of Brisbane.

GETTING THERE & GETTING AROUND From Brisbane, take the Pacific Highway exit after Dreamworld (exit 57), and follow signs to Hope Harbour and to the departure terminal for the island. The resorts run boats for guests only; the only other way to get there is by water taxi. **Gold Coast Water Taxi** (✆ **0418 759 789**) takes groups to the island for A$150 per transfer (10 people with no luggage, or six people plus camping gear).

Moreton Island ★★

At more than 200 sq. km (78 sq. miles), Moreton is the second-largest sand mass in the world (after Queensland's Fraser Island) and has the world's largest sand hill, Mount Tempest. It's home to three settlements and the Tangalooma Wild Dolphin Resort, where you can take part in hand-feeding a pod of wild dolphins. Moreton has other attractions: You can visit the 42-hectare (104-acre) "desert" and toboggan down the sand dunes, snorkel around the 12 wrecks just north of the resort, and visit historical points of interest, including the sandstone lighthouse at Cape Moreton, built in 1857. A four-wheel-drive vehicle is essential for getting around, but the

Whale-Watching in Moreton Bay

Gasps of delight and wonder are the norm aboard Captain Kerry Lopez's whale-watching boat, and Australia's only female whale-watching captain never tires of them. Lopez's purpose-built vessel, the MV *Eye-Spy,* was launched in 2002, and it now carries 320 passengers out into Moreton Bay between June and November for one of the most awesome sights you may ever see. When I traveled with them, we witnessed the antics of 17 humpback whales as they breached and displayed in the waters around the boat. It was an amazing, unforgettable experience. Brisbane Whale Watching ★★ (✆ 07/3880 0477; www.brisbanewhalewatching.com.au) will organize your 30-minute transfers from city hotels to the departure point in the northern suburb of Redcliffe. If you choose to drive yourself, there's free all-day parking near the jetty. Tours depart daily at 10am, returning at around 2:30 to 3pm. The trip onto the bay features excellent educational commentary about the whales while Kerry and her crew keep a lookout for these gentle giants of the deep. Prices are A$135 adults, A$125 seniors and students, A$95 children 4 to 14, or A$365 for a family of four, including lunch and morning and afternoon tea. Transfers from Brisbane hotels are an extra A$30 per person. And there's a guarantee you'll see a whale—or you can take another cruise for free.

resort runs tours. Permits for access (A$38 per vehicle) and camping (A$5 per person, or A$20 for a family) are available from national park rangers and ferry operators, or online at www.derm.qld.gov.au.

GETTING THERE & GETTING AROUND High-speed **catamarans** (✆ **1300/652 250** in Australia, or 07/3637 2000) leave Brisbane's Holt Street wharf at Pinkenba for Tangalooma Island Resort on Moreton Island (see "Where to Stay on the Islands," below) three times daily, at 7:30 and 10am, and 5pm (12:30pm on Mon and Sat–Sun). The trip takes 75 minutes. Return transfers leave Tangalooma at 9am and 4pm and after the evening dolphin feeding session at 7pm every day. On weekends and Mondays, they also leave at 2pm. The fare is A$70 adults, A$36 children 3 to 14. For A$14 per adult and A$8 per child, each way, coaches pick up passengers at the Roma Street Transit Centre, the Brisbane airport, and city hotels to connect with the 10am and 4pm launches. There is a range of day-trip options, starting from A$40 for adults, A$25 for children 3 to 14, and A$120 for a family of four (extra children A$15 each). Moreton Island Ferries' **MiCat** vehicular and passenger ferry (✆ **07/3909 3333;** www.moretonventure.com) departs from the Port of Brisbane (14 Howard Smith Dr.) for Tangalooma Monday to Saturday at 8:30am and 1pm, returning at 10:30am and 3:30pm, and on Sundays at 8:30am and 2:30pm, returning at 1 and 4:30pm. The trip takes about 2 hours; round-trip fares for walk-on passengers are A$50 adults, A$35 children 4 to 14, or A$140 for a family of five. The cost for a four-wheel-drive and two passengers is A$190 to A$220. The company also runs day tours to the island, which include some of the beauty spots, snorkeling and sandboarding (all equipment provided), and lunch. Prices range from A$99 to A$155 adults and A$65 to A$95 children depending on the tour inclusions. Timetables tend to change seasonally, so check the website.

St. Helena Island ★★

For 65 years, from 1867 to 1932, St. Helena was a prison island, known as the "hellhole of the Pacific" to the nearly 4,000 souls incarcerated there. Today, the prison ruins are a tourist attraction, with a small museum in the restored and reconstructed Deputy Superintendent's Cottage.

GETTING THERE & GETTING AROUND Entry to the island is by guided tour only. Excellent tours, most involving a reenactment of life on the island jail, are run by **AB Sea Cruises** (✆ **1300/438 787** in Australia or 07/3893 1240, 8:30am–4:30pm Mon–Sat; www.abseacruises.com.au) on the launch *Cat-o-Nine-Tails,* leaving from Manly Boat Harbour. The cost is A$69 adults, A$64 seniors and students, A$39 children ages 17 and under, or A$169 for a family of four. Tours operate on Wednesdays, leaving at 9:15am and returning at 2:15pm, and on Sundays leaving at 10am and returning at 3pm. The price includes a box lunch. **St. Helena Ghost Tours** run from Manly Boat Harbour on Saturday nights. They include dinner, a dramatized version of life in the prison, and a few spooky surprises. Night tours leave at 7pm and return at 11pm (A$90 adults, A$85 seniors and students, A$50 children, and A$230 for a family). Reservations are essential. To reach Manly Boat Harbour from Brisbane, take the train from Central Station to Manly (A$5.30) and walk 100m (328 ft.). The trip takes 50 minutes.

Where to Stay on the Islands

Moreton and South Stradbroke islands have resorts, and North Stradbroke has plenty of low-key accommodations. The smaller islands offer a variety of motels, cabins, motor-home parks, and camping grounds.

Couran Cove Island Resort ★★★ 🎁 You'll be lucky if you're able to find a more peaceful resort than this one. South Stradbroke Island has no cars—everyone gets around on foot, bicycle, or silent electric shuttle. You can hang around the pools or lagoon, head to the spectacular surf beach about 2km (1¼ miles) from the main resort, or stroll through remnants of primeval rainforest. The resort is committed to environmentally friendly practices and is unique for its huge range of recreational and sporting activities, including a three-lane sprint track, baseball and softball pitching cage, and high ropes challenge course. There's also beach volleyball, lawn bowling, shuffleboard, a golf driving range, surfing, fishing, stargazing tours, many watersports, and an extensive day spa. Accommodations offer a choice of hotel-style rooms or self-contained units. I like the colorful waterfront units, which have water views and are close to the restaurants and spa. All have kitchenettes or kitchens, and there's a general store and limited room service as well. Smoking is allowed only in designated outdoor areas and on balconies; no tobacco products are sold at the resort.

South Stradbroke Island, Moreton Bay (P.O. Box 224, Runaway Bay), QLD 4216. ✆ **1800/268 726** or 07/5509 3000. Fax 07/5509 3001. www.couran.com. 223 units. A$265 marine deluxe rooms; A$295 marine suite; A$495 2-bedroom lodge; A$805–A$905 4-bedroom villa. Children 13 and under stay free in parent's room using existing bedding. Extra person A$40 per night. Free crib. AE, DC, MC, V. Round-trip ferry transfers A$49 adults, A$27 children 3–14, A$125 family. **Amenities:** 3 restaurants; babysitting; bikes; children's programs; 2 fully equipped exercise rooms; golf driving range and putting green; free transfers to mainland golf courses; 10-lane heated pool and children's pool; room service; spa; 2 tennis courts. *In room:* A/C, TV/VCR w/pay movies, hair dryer, Internet, kitchen, minibar (on request).

Tangalooma Wild Dolphin Resort ★ ☺ Once the Southern Hemisphere's largest whaling station, Tangalooma is the only resort on Moreton Island. Its big attraction is the pod of wild dolphins that visits the jetty each evening. Guests are guaranteed one chance during their visit to hand-feed the dolphins, but don't get too excited—you can't swim with or touch them. The feeding is regulated, and your turn is over in a few seconds. Day-trippers can also take part in dolphin feeding for A$90 adults and A$50 children 3 to 14, as part of a day cruise.

Tangalooma is a good base for exploring the island, and a variety of tours are available, among them are seasonal (late June–Oct) whale-watching cruises for a rate of A$98 adults, A$60 children, and a Dugong Eco Cruise for A$58 adults and A$44 children. A dolphin research center is also based here.

There are lots of different accommodation options at Tangalooma. Deep Blue is a complex of two- and three-bedroom luxury beachfront apartments with views across Moreton Bay. The apartments have access to a private pool and barbecue areas, and have an optional lock-up garage. The resort also has 96 hotel rooms (built in 2002), 56 two-story family villas a year or so older, and older units which sleep four to five people. Villas are pricier than regular rooms, and a little farther from the resort facilities. Each has a full kitchen. A general store is on-site.

Moreton Island, off Brisbane (P.O. Box 1102, Eagle Farm), QLD 4009. ✆ **1300/652 250** or 07/3268 6333. Fax 07/3268 6299. www.tangalooma.com. 298 units, all with shower only. A$290–A$450 double; A$340–A$400 double for 1-bedroom apt (sleeps 5); A$380–A$480 double villa (sleeps 8). Extra adult A$30. Children 3–14 sharing with adults A$30. Rates include dolphin feeding. Rates for Deep Blue apts start at around A$600 double in low season and vary depending on the individual apt, number of guests, and level of servicing. AE, DC, MC, V. **Amenities:** 4 restaurants; 2 cafes; 3 bars; babysitting; children's' programs; driving range; putting green; Jacuzzi; 2 outdoor pools; limited room service (6–9pm daily); tennis and squash courts; watersports equipment rental. *In room:* A/C, TV, fridge, minibar.

QUEENSLAND & THE GREAT BARRIER REEF

by Lee Mylne

8

With a population that clings to the coast but embraces the Outback for its icons, Queensland is a vast and sprawling amalgam of stunning scenery, fantastic yarns, and eccentric personalities. Its most famous attraction is the Great Barrier Reef—but that is by no means the only thing worth seeing in an area that's two and a half times the size of Texas.

White sandy beaches grace almost the entire coastline, and a string of islands and coral reefs dangles just offshore. At the southern end, Gold Coast beaches and theme parks keep tourists happy. In the north, from Townsville to Cape York, the rainforest teems with flora and fauna.

Brisbane is the state capital, a former penal colony that today brims with style. While Brisbane boasts world-class theater, shopping, markets, art galleries, and restaurants, it retains the relaxed warmth of a country town. For more on this city, see chapter 7, p. 236.

Less than an hour's drive south of Brisbane is the **Gold Coast** "glitter strip," with its 35km (22 miles) of surf and sandy beaches. North of Brisbane lies the aptly named **Sunshine Coast**—more sandy beaches, crystal-clear waters, and rolling mountains dotted with villages.

Don't miss the wild beauty of the largest sand island in the world, **Fraser Island.** Each year, from August to October, humpback whales frolic in the waters between Fraser Island and Hervey Bay. If you're in the area at this time, you won't want to miss the opportunity to experience the whales firsthand.

As you travel north, you enter a land where islands, rainforest, mountains, and rivers unite. Green sugar cane fields are everywhere—**Mackay** is the largest sugar-producing region in Australia. This attractive city has its own beach, and the harbor and Airlie Beach to the north are departure points for cruises to the Great Barrier Reef and the Whitsunday Islands. Along this coast, you'll be tempted by one tropical island after another until you hit the cluster of 74 that makes up the **Whitsunday** and **Cumberland** groups.

The Whitsundays are on the same latitude as Tahiti, and for my money are equally lovely. The idyllic island group is laced with coral reefs rising out of calm, blue waters teeming with colorful fish—warm enough for swimming year-round.

North of the Whitsundays are **Dunk Island** and the rainforest settlement of **Mission Beach**—a perfect illustration of the contrasts in Tropical North Queensland. **Townsville** boasts 320 days of sunshine a year and marks the start of the Great Green Way—an area of lush natural beauty on the way to Cairns.

Then you come to **Cairns,** with rainforest hills and villages to explore and a harbor full of boats waiting to take you to the Reef. Cairns is a good base, but savvy travelers head an hour north to the village of **Port Douglas.**

A visit to Queensland would not be complete without at least one trip into the Outback. You can head west from Rockhampton, to discover the heart of Queensland at Longreach, Barcaldine, and Winton, or from Townsville to the mining town of Mount Isa. From Cairns, the Gulf Savannah region is rich in welcoming small towns.

Exploring the Queensland Coast

VISITOR INFORMATION The **Queensland Travel Centre** is a great resource on traveling and touring the state, including the Great Barrier Reef. Visit the Queensland Holidays website at www.queenslandholidays.com.au, or call ✆ **13 88 33** in Australia to speak to a Queensland travel specialist. Tourism Queensland, which runs the Queensland Travel Centre and Destination Queensland, has offices in the United States and the United Kingdom—see "Visitor Information" in chapter 17.

Travel Online (✆ **07/3512 8100;** fax 07/3876 4645; www.travelonline.com) is a Queensland-based private company offering itinerary planning and booking services for a wide range of accommodations and tours throughout the state.

For information on B&Bs and farmstays in Cairns, Port Douglas, Mission Beach, and Townsville, contact the **Bed & Breakfast and Farmstay Association of Far North Queensland,** P.O. Box 595, Ravenshoe, QLD 4888 (✆ **07/4097 7022;** www.bnbnq.com.au).

WHEN TO GO Winter (June–Aug) is high season in Queensland; the water can be chilly—at least to Australians—but its temperature rarely drops below 72°F (22°C). April through October is peak visibility time for divers. Summer is hot and sticky across the state. In North Queensland (Mission Beach, Cairns, and Port Douglas), the monsoonal Wet season is from November or December through March or April. It brings heavy rains, high temperatures, extreme humidity, and cyclones. But it's no problem to visit then, and the Wet season allows an unusual opportunity to explore this region during a time when it deserves its alternative name: the "Green" season.

GETTING AROUND **By Car** The Bruce Highway travels along the coast from Brisbane to Cairns. It is mostly a narrow two-lane highway, and the scenery most of the way is eucalyptus bushland, but from Mackay north, you pass through sugar cane fields, adding some variety to the trip.

Tourism Queensland (see "Visitor Information," above) publishes regional motoring guides. All you are likely to need, however, is a state map from the **Royal Automobile Club of Queensland** (**RACQ;** ✆ **13 19 05** in Australia). In Brisbane, you can get maps and advice from the centrally located RACQ office in the General Post Office (GPO) building, 261 Queen St. (✆ **07/3872 8465**). For recorded road

Queensland

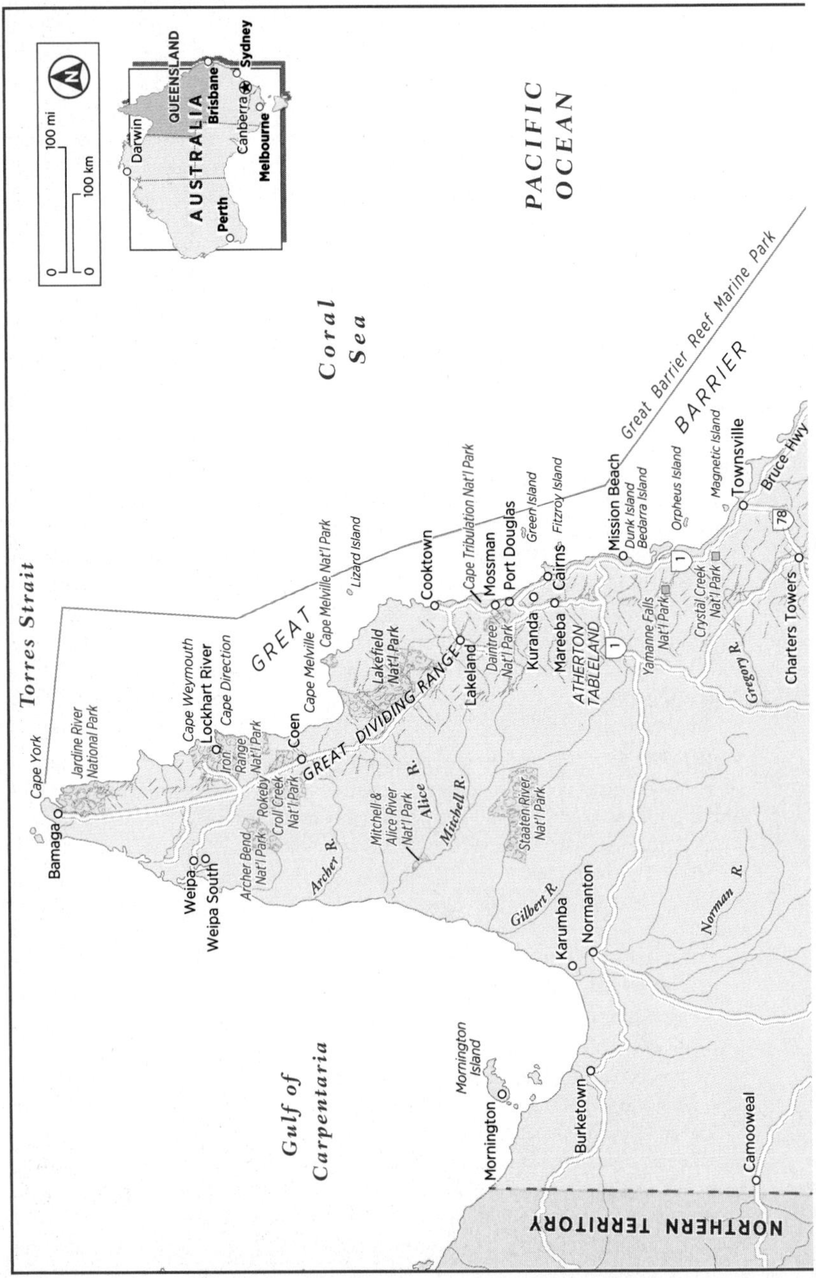
Torres Strait
Cape York
Bamaga
Jardine River National Park
Cape Weymouth
Lockhart River
Cape Direction
Iron Range Nat'l Park
Weipa
Weipa South
Archer Bend Nat'l Park
Rokeby Croll Creek Nat'l Park
Coen
Cape Melville
Cape Melville Nat'l Park
Lizard Island
GREAT
GREAT DIVIDING RANGE
Lakefield Nat'l Park
Archer R.
Mitchell & Alice River Nat'l Park
Alice R.
Mitchell R.
Cooktown
Lakeland
Cape Tribulation Nat'l Park
Mossman
Port Douglas
Daintree Nat'l Park
Kuranda
Green Island
Cairns
Fitzroy Island
Mareeba
ATHERTON TABLELAND
Staaten River Nat'l Park
Mission Beach
Dunk Island
Bedarra Island
Yamanne Falls Nat'l Park
Orpheus Island
Crystal Creek Nat'l Park
Magnetic Island
Townsville
Bruce Hwy
Charters Towers
Gregory R.
Gilbert R.
Karumba
Normanton
Norman R.
Mornington Island
Mornington
Burketown
Camooweal
NORTHERN TERRITORY
Gulf of Carpentaria
Coral Sea
PACIFIC OCEAN
Great Barrier Reef Marine Park
BARRIER
1
78
0
100 mi
0
100 km
N
AUSTRALIA
QUEENSLAND
Darwin
Perth
Brisbane
Canberra
Sydney
Melbourne

QUEENSLAND
NEW SOUTH WALES
SOUTH AUSTRALIA
REEF
Whitsunday Islands
Hook Is.
Daydream Is.
Whitsunday Is.
Brampton Island
Great Keppel Island
Heron Island
Lady Elliot Island
Fraser Island Nat'l Park
Fraser Is.
SUNSHINE COAST
GOLD COAST
Brisbane
See Chapter 7
Surfers Paradise
Coolangatta
Lamington Nat'l Park
Pacific Hwy
Grafton
Warwick
Ipswich
DARLING DOWNS
Toowoomba
Nambour
Noosa Heads
Cooloola Nat'l Park
Tamborine Nat'l Park
Maryborough
Childers
Hervey Bay
Gin Gin
Bundaberg
Gladstone
Rockhampton
Marlborough
Bruce Hwy
Mackay
Prosperine
Airlie Beach
Moranban
Clermont
Emerald
GREAT DIVIDING RANGE
Carnarvon Gorge Nat'l Park
Balonne R.
Macintyre R.
54
Charleville
Warrego R.
Cunnamulla
71
Bourke
Pentland
Hugenden
Richmond
Julia Creek
78
Cloncurry
66
Mt. Isa
Muttaburra
Winton
Middleton
Boulia
Longreach
Tropic of Capricorn
Barcoo R.
Thompson R.
Bedourie
Birdsville

When to Visit the Reef

April through November is the best time to visit the Great Barrier Reef, although southeast trade winds can sometimes make it a tad choppy at sea. December through March can be uncomfortably hot and humid, particularly as far north as the Whitsundays, Cairns, and Port Douglas. In the winter months (June–Aug), the water can be a touch chilly (Aussies think so, anyway), but it rarely drops below 72°F (22°C).

condition reports, call © **1300/130 595.** Specialist map shop **World Wide Maps & Guides,** in the Anzac Square Arcade, 267 Edward St., Brisbane (© **07/3221 4330;** www.worldwidemaps.com.au) is open Monday to Thursday 8:30am to 5pm and until 7pm on Fridays, and 10am to 3pm on Saturdays. They stock a wide range of Australia maps, atlases, street directories—indeed, almost anything map-related you can think of—or you can browse and buy online.

BY TRAIN Queensland Rail's **Traveltrain** (© **1300/131 722** in Australia or 07/3235 7322 www.traveltrain.com.au) operates two long-distance trains along the Brisbane-Cairns route, a 32-hour trip aboard the ***Sunlander*** or about 8 hours less on the high-speed **Tilt Train.** See the "Getting There & Getting Around" section in chapter 3, p. 43, for more details. Traveltrain also operates trains to Outback towns. See "Making Tracks through Queensland's Outback," p. 382.

BY PLANE This is the fastest way to see a lot in such a big state. **Qantas** (© **13 13 13** in Australia; www.qantas.com.au) and its subsidiaries **QantasLink** and the no-frills **Jetstar** (© **13 15 38** in Australia; www.jetstar.com.au) serve most coastal towns from Brisbane, and a few from Cairns. **Virgin Blue** (© **13 67 89** in Australia; www.virginblue.com.au) services Brisbane, Cairns, Townsville, Mackay, Proserpine and Hamilton Island in the Whitsundays, Rockhampton, Hervey Bay (the Fraser Coast), the Gold Coast, and Maroochydore on the Sunshine Coast.

EXPLORING THE GREAT BARRIER REEF

It's the only living thing on earth visible from the moon; at 348,700 sq. km (135,993 sq. miles), it's bigger than the United Kingdom and more than 2,000km (1,240 miles) long, stretching from Lady Elliot Island off Bundaberg to Papua New Guinea; it's home to 1,500 kinds of fish, 400 species of corals, 4,000 kinds of clams and snails, and who knows how many sponges, starfish, and sea urchins; the Great Barrier Reef region is listed as a World Heritage Site and contains the biggest marine park in the world.

There are three kinds of reef on the Great Barrier Reef—fringing, ribbon, and platform. **Fringing reef** is the stuff you see just off the shore of islands and along the mainland. **Ribbon reefs** create "streamers" of long, thin reef along the outer edge of the continental shelf and are only found north of Cairns. **Platform** or **patch reefs** can be up to 16 sq. km (10 sq. miles) of coral emerging off the continental shelf all the way along the Reef's length. Platform reefs, the most common kind, are what most people think of when they refer to the Great Barrier Reef. Island resorts in the Great Barrier Reef Marine Park are either "continental," meaning part of the Australian landmass, or "cays," crushed dead coral and sand amassed on the reef tops over time by water action. Dazzling coral and marine life surround the cays. On continental islands and coast, the coral is higher in diversity; but the visibility, due to soil runoff from the land, can be of varying quality.

Apart from the impressive fish life around the corals, the Reef is home to large numbers of green and loggerhead turtles, one of the biggest dugong (a relative of the manatee) populations in the world, sharks, giant manta rays, and sea snakes. In winter (June–Aug), humpback whales gather in the warm waters south of the Reef around Hervey Bay, in the Whitsundays, and as far north as Cairns to give birth to calves.

To see the Reef, you can snorkel, dive, ride a semisubmersible, walk on it, or fly over it. For most people, the Great Barrier Reef means the Outer Reef, the network of reefs that lie an average of 65km (40 miles) off the coast (about 60–90 min. by boat from the mainland). You should get out and see that, but there is plenty of fringing reef to explore around islands closer to the mainland.

Learning about the Reef before you get there will enhance your visit. **Reef Teach ★★** (✆ **07/4031 7794;** http://reefteach.wordpress.com) is an evening multimedia presentation by a team of experienced marine biologists, conservationists, and researchers. You will learn everything you need to know about the Reef, from how it was formed and how coral grows to what dangerous creatures to avoid and how to take successful underwater photos. The presentation takes place throughout the year upstairs in the Mainstreet Arcade, 85 Lake St., Cairns, Tuesday through Saturday from 6:30 to 8:30pm, and costs A$15 adults and A$8 children under 14. Bookings are not necessary; just turn up and pay at the door.

> **The Reef Tax**
>
> **Every passenger over 4 years old must pay a A$4.50 daily Environmental Management Charge (EMC), commonly called the "reef tax," every time they visit the Great Barrier Reef. This money goes toward the management and conservation of the Reef. Your tour operator will collect it from you when you pay for your trip.**

Townsville is the headquarters of the Great Barrier Reef Marine Park Authority, and a visit to its showcase, **Reef HQ** (p. 320), is a superb introduction. The star attraction at the aquarium is a re-created living-reef ecosystem in a massive viewing tank. Find out more about the Reef from the **Great Barrier Reef Marine Park Authority** (✆ **07/4750 0700;** fax 07/4772 6093; www.gbrmpa.gov.au or www.reefhq.com.au).

Discovering the Reef

The rich colors of the coral can be seen best with lots of light, so the nearer the surface, the brighter and richer the marine life. That means snorkelers are in a prime position to see it at its best. Snorkeling the Reef can be a wondrous experience. Green and purple clams, pink sponges, red starfish, purple sea urchins, and fish from electric blue to neon yellow to lime are truly magical sights.

If your Reef cruise offers a guided snorkel tour or "snorkel safari," take it. Some include it as part of the price, but even if you pay an extra A$30 or so, it is worth it.

Reef Health & Safety Warnings

Coral is very sharp, and coral cuts get infected quickly and badly. If you cut yourself, ask the staff on your cruise boat for immediate first aid as soon as you come out of the water.

The sun and reflected sunlight off the water can burn you fast. Remember to put sunscreen on your back and the back of your legs, especially around your knees and the back of your neck, and even behind your ears—all places that rarely get exposed to the sun but will be exposed as you swim facedown. Apply more when you leave the water.

Most safaris are suitable for beginners and advanced snorkelers, and are led by guides trained by marine biologists who tell you about the sea creatures you are seeing. Snorkeling is easy to master, and crews on cruise boats are always happy to tutor you.

A day trip to the Reef also offers a great opportunity to go scuba diving—even if you have never dived before. Every major cruise boat listed in "Day Trips to the Reef" (see below) and many dedicated dive boats listed in "Diving the Reef" (later in this chapter) offer introductory dives that allow you to dive without certification to a depth of 6m (20 ft.) in the company of an instructor. You will need to complete a medical questionnaire and undergo a 30-minute briefing on the boat. (Intro dives are also called "resort dives" because many resorts offer something similar, giving you 1 or 2 hr. of instruction before taking you to a nearby reef to dive.)

Choosing a Gateway to the Reef

Cairns and **Port Douglas** are good places from which to visit the Reef—but the quality of the coral is just as good off any town along the coast between **Bundaberg** and Cairns. The Reef is pretty much equidistant from any point on the coast north of Mission Beach—about 90 minutes away by high-speed catamaran. From **Townsville,** the Reef is about 2½ hours away.

Think carefully about where to base yourself. The main gateways, north to south, are **Port Douglas, Cairns, Mission Beach, Townsville, the Whitsunday Islands, Gladstone** (for Heron Island), and **Bundaberg.** The Whitsundays have the added attractions of dazzling islands to sail among; beautiful island resorts offering a wealth of watersports and other activities; and a large array of diving, fishing, and day cruises. Most important, you can snorkel every day off your island or join a sailing or cruise day trip to a number of magnificent fringing or inner shelf reefs much nearer than the main Outer Reef. Many people stay in Cairns simply because of its easy international airport access.

If you are a nonswimmer, choose a Reef cruise that visits a coral cay, because a cay slopes gradually into shallow water and the surrounding coral. The **Low Isles** at Port Douglas; **Green Island, Michaelmas Cay,** or **Upolu Cay** off Cairns; **Beaver Cay** off Mission Beach; and **Heron Island** are all good locations. Remember that staff will supply you with swimmer supports, allowing nonswimmers snorkel opportunities, too.

Day Trips to the Reef

The most common way to get to the Reef is on one of the motorized catamarans that carry up to 300 passengers each from Cairns, Port Douglas, Townsville, Mission Beach, the Whitsunday mainland and islands, and Yeppoon, near Rockhampton.

The boats are air-conditioned and have a bar, videos, and educational material, as well as a marine biologist who gives a talk on the Reef's ecology en route. The boats tie up at their own private permanent pontoons anchored to a platform reef. The pontoons have glass-bottom boats for passengers who don't want to get wet, dry underwater viewing chambers, usually a bar, sun decks, shaded seats, and often showers.

An alternative to traveling on a big tour boat is to go on one of the many smaller boats. These typically visit two or three Reef sites rather than just one. There are usually no more than 20 passengers, so you get more personal attention, and you get to know the other passengers. Another advantage is that you will have the coral pretty much all to yourself. The drawbacks of a small boat are that you have only the cramped deck to sit on when you get out of the water, and your traveling time to the Reef may be longer. If you're a nervous snorkeler, you may feel safer on a boat where you will be swimming with 300 other people.

Most day-trip fares include snorkel gear—fins, mask, and snorkel (plus wet suits in winter, although you rarely need them)—free use of the underwater viewing chambers and glass-bottom-boat rides, a plentiful buffet or barbecue lunch, and morning and afternoon refreshments. Diving is an optional activity for which you pay extra. The big boats post snorkeling scouts to keep a lookout for anyone in trouble and to count heads periodically. If you wear glasses, ask whether your boat offers prescription masks—this could make a big difference to the quality of your experience! Don't forget, you can travel as a snorkel-only passenger on most dive boats, too.

The major launching points for day trips to the Reef are Port Douglas, Cairns, Mission Beach, Townsville, and the Whitsundays (see individual sections on these regions later in this chapter).

Major Reef Sites

FROM CAIRNS Approximately 20 reefs lie within a 1½- to 2-hour boat ride from Cairns. These are the reefs most commonly visited by snorkelers and divers on day trips, because they are so close and so pretty. Some reefs are small coral "bommies," or outcrops, that you can swim completely around in a matter of minutes, whereas others are miles wide. Some reefs have more than one good dive site; Norman Reef, for example, has at least four. Three of the most popular reefs with snorkelers and divers are **Hastings, Saxon,** and **Norman ★**, which are all within a short boat ride of one another. Each has a wonderful array of coral, big colorful reef fish, schools of pretty rainbow-hued small reef fish, and the odd giant clam. Green sea turtles and white-tip reef sharks are common, especially at Saxon, though you will not necessarily spot one every day. Divers may see a moray eel and a grouper or two, barracuda, reef sharks, eagle and blue-spotted rays, and octopus. Norman is an especially lovely reef with several nice sites. South Norman has lovely sloping coral shelves. If you are an experienced diver and like swim-throughs, the Caves at Norman is a good spot; all have boulder and plate corals.

Some of the best diving anywhere on the Great Barrier Reef is on the **Ribbon Reefs ★** on the outer Reef edge, which fringes the continental shelf northward off Cairns and Port Douglas. Glorious coral walls, abundant fish, and pinnacles make these a rich, colorful dive area with lots of variety. The currents can be strong here, because the reefs force the tidal water flow into narrow channels into the open sea, so drift dives on a rising tide are a possibility. The Ribbon Reefs are beyond the reach

Overnighting on the Reef

Spirit of Freedom (✆ 07/4047 9150; fax 07/4047 9110; www.spiritoffreedom.com.au) in Cairns offers a chance to "sleep on the Reef" aboard the 36m (120-ft.) *Spirit of Freedom,* a sleek, modern motor yacht with electronic stabilizers, a widescreen TV with DVD player, comfortable lounge areas, sun decks, and 11 luxury double or quad shared cabins, each with an en-suite bathroom. There are 3-, 4-, and 7-day cruises to choose from. You will visit the popular Cod Hole and Ribbon Reef and, on the 4- and 7-day trips, venture into the Coral Sea. A 3-day, 3-night trip will cost A$1,350 to A$2,125 depending on your choice of cabin and ends with a 193km (120-mile) one-way low-level flight from Lizard Island back to Cairns. The 4-day, 4-night cruise begins with the flight and then cruises from Lizard Island back to Cairns. It costs between A$1,675 and A$2,425 and includes up to 16 dives. A 7-day cruise, priced from A$2,775 to A$4,300 is a combination of both shorter trips. On a 3-day trip you will fit in up to 11 dives, and up to 27 on the 7-day trip. Prices include meals and pickup from your Cairns accommodations. Allow A$120 to A$245 extra for equipment rental.

of day boats, but are commonly visited by live-aboard boats (see "Overnighting on the Reef," above). For divers, experts recommend **Steve's Bommie** and **Dynamite Pass.** Steve's Bommie is a coral outcrop in 30m (98 ft.) of water, often topped with barracudas, and covered in colorful coral and small marine life. You can swim through a tunnel here amid crowds of fish. Dynamite Pass is a channel where barracuda, trevally, grouper, mackerel, and tuna often gather to feed in the current. Black coral trees and sea whips grow on the walls, patrolled by eagle rays and reef sharks.

Cairns's most famous dive site is **Cod Hole ★**, where your guide may hand-feed giant potato cod as big as you are. The site also has Maori wrasse, moray eels, and coral trout. Cod Hole is about 20km (13 miles) off Lizard Island and 240km (149 miles) north of Cairns, so it is not a day trip unless you are staying at exclusive Lizard Island (see "Where to Stay," later in this chapter). However, it is a popular stop with just about every live-aboard vessel, often combined in a trip to the Ribbon Reefs, lasting about 4 days, or in a trip to the Coral Sea (see below), lasting between 4 and 7 days. Either itinerary makes an excellent dive vacation.

Keen divers looking for adventure in far-flung latitudes can visit the **Far Northern** region of the Great Barrier Reef, much farther north than most dive boats venture. Up in this region you will find a wide choice of good sites, little explored by the average diver. Visibility is always clear. **Silvertip City** on Mantis Reef has sharks, pelagics, potato cod, and lionfish that patrol a wall up to 46m (150 ft.) deep. Another goodie is the **Magic Cave** swim-through adorned with lots of colorful fans, soft corals, and small reef fish. Sleeping turtles are often spotted in caves on the reefs off **Raine Island,** the world's biggest green turtle rookery. Visibility averages 24m (80 ft.) at Rainbow Wall, a colorful wall that makes a nice gentle drift dive with the incoming tide.

More than 100 to 200km (63–126 miles) east of the coast, out in the **Coral Sea,** isolated mountains covered in reefs rise more than a kilometer (half-mile) from the ocean floor to make excellent diving. Although not within the Great Barrier Reef Marine Park, the Coral Sea is often combined into an extended live-aboard trip that also takes in Cod Hole and the Ribbon Reefs. The entire trip usually takes 4 to 7 days. In addition to showing you huge schools of pelagic and reef fish big and small, a wide range of corals, and gorgonian fans, the area is a prime place to spot sharks. The most popular site is **Osprey Reef,** a 100-sq.-km (39-sq.-mile) reef with 1,000m (3,300-ft.) drop-offs, renowned for its year-round visibility of up to 70m (230 ft.). White-tip reef sharks are common, but the area is also home to gray reef sharks, silvertips, and hammerheads. Green turtles, tuna, barracuda, potato cod, mantas, and grouper are also common.

Closer to shore, Cairns has several coral cays and reef-fringed islands within the **Great Barrier Reef Marine Park.** Less than an hour from the city wharf, **Green Island** is a 15-hectare (37-acre) coral cay with snorkeling equal to that of most other places on the Great Barrier Reef. It is also a popular diving spot. You can visit it in half a day if time is short. **Fitzroy Island** is a rainforest-covered national park, just 45 minutes by launch from Cairns, with a coral beach and great snorkeling right off the shore.

The **Frankland Islands** are a pristine group of uninhabited rainforest isles, edged with sandy beaches, reefs, and fish, 45km (28 miles) south of Cairns. The islands are a rookery for **green sea turtles,** which snorkelers and divers often spot in the water. In February and March, you may even be lucky enough to see dozens of baby turtles hatching in the sand. **Michaelmas Cay** and **Upolu Cay** are two pretty coral sand blips in the ocean, 30km (19 miles) and 25km (16 miles) off Cairns, surrounded by reefs. Michaelmas is vegetated and is home to 27,000 seabirds; you may spot dugongs (cousins of manatees) off Upolu. Michaelmas and Upolu are great for snorkelers and introductory divers, but experienced divers are probably better off visiting the excellent sites at such reefs as Norman, Hastings, or Saxon.

FROM PORT DOUGLAS The waters off Port Douglas boast just as many wonderful reefs and marine life forms as the waters around Cairns; the reefs are equally close to shore and equally colorful and varied. Some of the most visited reefs are **Tongue, Opal,** and **St. Crispin reefs.** The **Agincourt** complex of reefs also has many excellent dive sites; experts recommend the double-figure-eight swim-through at the **Three Sisters,** where baby gray whaler sharks gather, and the wonderful coral walls of **Castle Rock,** where stingrays often hide in the sand. **Nursery Bommie** is a 24m (79-ft.) pinnacle that is a popular haunt with such big fish as barracuda, rays, sharks, and moray eels; under the big plate corals of **Light Reef,** giant grouper hide out. Other popular sites are the staghorn coral garden (so named because the coral looks like a stag's antlers) at the **Playground;** one of the region's biggest swim-throughs at the **Maze,** where parrot fish and an enormous Maori wrasse hang out; the **Stepping Stones,** home of the exquisitely pretty clownfish (like Nemo!); **Turtle Bommie,** where hawksbill turtles are frequently sighted; and **Harry's Bommie,** where divers see the occasional manta ray. Among the 15-plus dive sites visited by *Poseidon* (see below) are **Turtle Bay,** where you may meet a friendly Maori wrasse; the **Cathedrals,** a collection of coral pinnacles and swim-throughs; and **Barracuda Pass,** home to coral gardens, giant clams, and schooling barracuda.

The closest Reef site off Port Douglas, the **Low Isles,** lies only 15km (9 miles) northeast. Coral sand and 22 hectares (55 acres) of coral surround these two coral cays; the smaller is a sand cay covered in rich vegetation and the larger is a shingle/rubble cay covered in mangroves and home to thousands of nesting Torresian Imperial pigeons. The coral is not quite as dazzling as the outer Reef's—head to the outer Reef if you have only 1 day to spend on the Great Barrier Reef—but the fish life here is rich, and you may spot sea turtles. Because you can wade out to the coral right from the beach, the Low Isles are a good choice for nervous snorkelers. A half-day or day trip to the Low Isles makes for a more relaxing day than a visit to outer Reef sites, because in addition to exploring the coral, you can walk or sunbathe on the sand or laze under palm-thatched beach umbrellas. ***Note:*** If you visit the Low Isles, wear old shoes, because the coral sand can be rough underfoot.

FROM MISSION BEACH Mission Beach is the closest point on the mainland to the Reef, 1 hour by boat. The main site visited is **Beaver Cay,** a sandy coral cay surrounded by marine life. The waters are shallow, making the cay ideal for snorkelers eager to see the coral's vibrant colors and novice divers still getting a feel for the sport. It's a perfect spot for an introductory dive.

FROM TOWNSVILLE Townsville's waters boast hundreds of large patch reefs, some miles long, and many rarely visited by humans. Here you can find excellent coral and fish life, including mantas, rays, turtles, and sharks, and sometimes canyons and swim-throughs in generally good visibility. One of the best reef complexes is **Flinders Reef,** which is actually located in the Coral Sea, beyond the Great Barrier Reef Marine Park boundaries. At 240km (149 miles) offshore, it has 30m (100-ft.) visibility, plenty of coral, and big walls and pinnacles with big fish to match, such as whaler shark and barracuda.

What draws most divers to Townsville, though, is one of Australia's best wreck dives, the **SS *Yongala* ★★**. Still largely intact, the sunken remains of this steamer lie 90km (56 miles) from Townsville, 16km (10 miles) off the coast, in 15 to 30m (50–98 ft.) of water, with visibility of 9 to 18m (approximately 30–60 ft.). A cyclone sent the *Yongala* and its 49 passengers and 72-member crew to the bottom of the sea in 1911. Today it's surrounded by a mass of coral and marine life, including barracuda, enormous grouper, rays, sea snakes, turtles, moray eels, shark, cod, and reef fish. You cannot enter the ship, but swimming along its length allows you to see an amazing array of marine life.

The *Yongala* is not for beginners—the boat is deep, and there is often a strong current. Most dive companies require their customers to have advanced certification or to have logged a minimum of 15 dives with open-water certification. The boat is usually visited on a live-aboard trip of at least 2 days, but some companies run day trips. There are also open-water certification dive courses that finish with a dive on the *Yongala,* but freshly certified scuba hounds might be wise to skip this advanced dive.

FROM THE WHITSUNDAYS Visitors to the Whitsundays get to have their cake and eat it too; they can visit the outer Reef and enjoy some good dive and snorkel sites in and around the islands. Many islands have rarely visited fringing reefs, which you can explore in a rented dinghy. The reef here is just as good as off Cairns, with many drop-offs and drift dives, a dazzling range of corals, and a rich array of marine life, including whales, mantas, shark, reef fish, morays, turtles, and pelagics. Visibility is usually around 15 to 23m (49–75 ft.).

The Stepping Stones, on 800-hectare (1,976-acre) **Bait Reef,** is one of the most popular sites on the outer Reef. It is made up of a series of pinnacles that abound with fish life and offer caverns, swim-throughs, and channels. A family of grouper often greets divers at Groupers Grotto on **Net Reef,** and a pod of dolphins hang around Net Reef's southeast wall. **Oublier Reef** has plate corals over 2m (7 ft.) wide in its coral gardens.

Among the island sites, most folks' favorite is **Blue Pearl Bay ★** off Hayman Island, whether they're snorkeling or diving. It has loads of corals and some gorgonian fans in its gullies, and heaps of reef fish, including Maori wrasse and sometimes even manta rays. It's a good place to make an introductory dive, walking right in off the beach. **Mantaray Bay** on Hook Island is renowned for its range of marine life, from small reef fish and nudibranchs to bigger pelagics farther out. Mantas hang around here in November. Other good snorkel and dive spots are on **Black and Knuckle Reefs ★**. A little island commonly called **Bali Hai Island,** between Hayman and Hook islands, is a great place to be left to your own devices. You'll see soft-shelf and wall coral, tame Maori wrasse, octopus, turtles, reef shark, various kinds of rays including mantas, eagles and cow-tails, plus loads of fish.

FROM BUNDABERG The southern reefs of the Great Barrier Reef are just as prolific, varied, and colorful as the reefs farther north off Cairns. However, because this part of the coast is less accessible by visitors and the reefs farther offshore, fewer snorkel and dive boats visit them. Many are the virgin reefs in these parts that have never seen a diver.

The only reef visited by snorkelers and divers on a daily basis from Bundaberg is pretty **Lady Musgrave Island,** a vegetated 14-hectare (35-acre) national-park coral cay, 52 nautical miles off the coast. It is surrounded by a lagoon 8km (5 miles) in circumference, filled with hundreds of corals and some 1,200 of the 1,500 species of fish and other marine creatures found on the Great Barrier Reef.

Lady Musgrave Island is one of the **Bunker Group** of islands and reefs, which lie approximately 80km (50 miles) due north of Bundaberg. They are due east of Gladstone and closer to that town, but only live-aboard boats visit them from there. Farther south of Bunker Group is **Lady Elliot Island,** which is accessed by air. Bundaberg's **Woongarra Marine Park** lies outside the borders of the Great Barrier Reef Marine Park and is a popular destination for divers visiting the Reef. This small park hugs the town's coastline in an area known as Bargara and has loads of soft and hard corals, nudibranchs, wobbegongs, epaulette sharks, sea snakes, some 60 fish species, and frequent sightings of green and loggerhead turtles. Most of this is in water less than 9m (30 ft.) deep, and you can walk right into it off the beach.

Beyond Woongarra, 2.5 nautical miles (4.6km) offshore, is **Cochrane artificial reef,** where a few Mohawk and Beechcraft aircraft have been dumped to make a home for fish. Other sites off Bunbaberg, in about 23m (75 ft.) of water, include the **manta "cleaning station"** at Evan's Patch, a **World War II Beaufort bomber** with lots of marine life.

Diving the Reef

Divers have a big choice: dive boats that make 1-day runs to the Outer Reef, overnight stays on some boats, live-aboard dive boats making excursions that last up to a week, or staying on an island. As a general rule, on a typical 5-hour day trip to the

Reef, you will fit in about two dives. The companies listed below give you an idea of the kinds of trips available and how much they cost. This is by no means an exhaustive list—there are far too many to include here. "Active Vacations," in chapter 3, has more tips for finding a dive operator. Prices quoted include full gear rental; knock off about A$20 if you have your own gear. It is recommended that you only dive with members of Dive Queensland, who follow a code of ethics and standards. Dive Queensland's website, **www.dive-queensland.com.au**, has a full list of member companies and their contact details. All dive operators listed in this book are members of Dive Queensland.

FROM CAIRNS **Tusa Dive Charters** (© **07/4047 9100;** www.tusadive.com) runs a custom-built 24m (72-ft.) dive boat daily to two dive sites from a choice of 15 locations on the Outer Reef. The day costs A$210 for divers and A$155 adult or A$95 child ages 4 to 14 for snorkelers, with wet suits, guided snorkel tours, lunch, and transfers from your Cairns or northern beaches hotel. If you want to be shown the best spots, you can take a guided dive for an extra A$10. Day trips for introductory divers cost A$220 for one dive or A$255 for two. The boat takes a maximum of 60 people, with a staff-to-passenger ratio of one to six, so you get a good level of personal attention.

FROM PORT DOUGLAS The waters off Port Douglas are home to dramatic coral spires and swim-throughs at the Cathedrals; giant clams at Barracuda Pass; a village of parrot fish, anemone fish, unicorn fish, and two moray eels at the pinnacle of Nursery Bommie; fan corals at Split-Bommie; and many other wonderful sites.

The ***Poseidon*** (© **1800/085 674** in Australia, or 07/4099 4772; www.poseidon-cruises.com.au) is a fast 24m (79-ft.) vessel that visits three Outer Reef sites. The day-trip price of A$185 for adults, A$130 for kids 4 to 14, or A$569 for families of four includes snorkel gear, a marine-biology talk, snorkel safaris, lunch, and pickups from Port Douglas hotels. Certified divers pay A$220 for two dives or A$235 for three, plus A$20 gear rental. Guides will accompany you, free of charge, to show you great locations. Introductory divers pay A$55 extra for one dive, and A$40 each for the second and third. The vessel gets you to the Reef in just over an hour, giving you 5 hours on the coral. The boat departs Marina Mirage daily at 8:30am. Transfers from Cairns and the Northern Beaches cost an extra A$20 per adult and A$15 per child.

FROM TOWNSVILLE Off Townsville, you can dive not only the Reef but also a wreck, the ***Yongala*** ★, which lies off the coast in 30m (98 ft.) of water with good visibility. **Adrenalin Dive** (© **07/4724 0600;** www.adrenalindive.com.au) runs day trips in which you will do two dives on the *Yongala*. The cost is A$220, plus A$40 for gear hire and A$30 per dive for a guide, if you have logged fewer than 15 dives.

FROM THE WHITSUNDAYS In and around the Whitsunday Islands, you can visit the Outer Reef and explore the many excellent dive sites close to shore. **H20 Sportz** (© **07/4946 9888;** www.h2osportz.com.au), based at Hamilton Island marina, runs day tours to **Bait Reef,** one of the best known locations on the Great Barrier Reef. Tours are limited to 30 passengers and leave at 9:30am, returning at 5pm. That gives you 3½ hours at the Reef, allowing plenty of time for lots of snorkeling or two dives. The cost is A$169 adults, A$89 kids ages 4 to 14. One child 13 years or under travels free when accompanied by two adults. The cost includes lunch, snacks, all snorkel equipment, and wet suit. Full gear hire is A$100 for certified divers.

DIVE COURSES

Many dive companies in Queensland offer instruction, from initial open-water certification all the way to dive-master, rescue-diver, and instructor level. To take a course, you will need to have a medical exam done by a Queensland doctor. (Your dive school will arrange it; it usually costs btw. A$45 and A$70). You can find out more about dive medicals on **www.divemedicals.com.au**. You will also need two passport photos for your certificate, and you must be able to swim! Courses usually begin every day or every week. Some courses take as little as 3 days, but 5 days is regarded as the best. Open-water certification usually requires 2 days of theory in a pool, followed by 2 or 3 days on the Reef, where you make four to nine dives. Prices vary, but are generally around A$600 for a 5-day open-water certification course, or A$500 for the same course over 4 nights.

> **Diving Reminders**
>
> **Don't forget your "C" certification card. Bringing along your dive log is also a good idea. Remember not to fly for 24 hours after diving.**

Deep Sea Divers Den (✆ **07/4046 7333;** www.diversden.com.au) has been in operation since 1974 and claims to have certified about 55,000 divers. Courses range from a 4-day open-water course with 2 days of theory in the pool in Cairns, and 2-day trips to the Reef for A$540 per person, to 5- and 6-day courses with 3 nights on a live-aboard boat. The 6-day course costs A$1,110 per person, including all meals on the boat, 13 dives (two are guided night dives), all your gear, a wet suit, and transfers from your city hotel. All courses also incur a A$15 per day charge for Reef tax, port and administration charges, and fuel levy. New courses begin every day of the week.

Virtually every Great Barrier Reef dive operator offers dive courses. Most island resorts offer them, too. You will find dive schools in Cairns, Port Douglas, Mission Beach, Townsville, and the Whitsunday Islands. Dive Queensland provides a list of its members who follow a code of ethics and standards on its website, **www.divequeensland.com.au**. We recommend that you only dive with members of Dive Queensland. Companies offering dive courses appear under the relevant regional sections throughout this chapter.

CAIRNS

346km (215 miles) N of Townsville; 1,807km (1,120 miles) N of Brisbane

This part of Queensland is the only place in the world where two World Heritage–listed sites—the Great Barrier Reef and the Wet Tropics Rainforest—lie side by side. In parts of the far north, the rainforest touches the Reef, reaching right down to sandy beaches from which you can snorkel the Reef. Cairns is the gateway to these natural attractions, as well as man-made tourist destinations such as the Skyrail Rainforest Cableway. It's also a stepping stone to islands of the Great Barrier Reef and the grasslands of the Gulf Savannah.

When international tourism to the Great Barrier Reef boomed a decade or two ago, the small sugar-farming town of Cairns boomed along with it. The town now boasts outstanding hotels, offshore island resorts, big Reef-cruise catamarans in the harbor, and too many souvenir shops. The only beach right in town is a man-made 4,000-sq.-m (43,000-sq.-ft.) saltwater lagoon and artificial beach on the Esplanade, which opened in early 2003 as part of a multimillion-dollar redevelopment of the city and port.

The 110-million-year-old rainforest, the Daintree, where plants that are fossils elsewhere in the world exist in living color, is just a couple of hours north of Cairns. The Daintree is part of the Wet Tropics, a World Heritage–listed area that stretches from north of Townsville to south of Cooktown, beyond Cairns, and houses half of Australia's animal and plant species.

If you are spending more than a day or two in the area, consider basing yourself on the city's pretty northern beaches, in Kuranda, or in Port Douglas (see "Port Douglas," later in this chapter). Although prices will be higher in the peak season (Australian winter and early spring, July–Oct), affordable accommodations are available year-round.

Essentials

GETTING THERE **By Plane** **Qantas** (✆ **13 13 13** in Australia) has direct flights throughout the day to Cairns from Sydney and Brisbane, and at least one flight a day from Darwin, Uluru, and Perth. From Melbourne you can sometimes fly direct, but most flights connect through Sydney or Brisbane. **QantasLink** also flies from Townsville, Hamilton Island in the Whitsundays, and Alice Springs. **Virgin Blue** (✆ **13 67 89** in Australia) flies to Cairns direct from Townsville, Brisbane, Sydney, Melbourne and Perth. **Jetstar** (✆ **13 15 38** in Australia) flies from Brisbane, Sydney, Adelaide, Melbourne (Tullamarine), Perth, Darwin, and the Gold Coast. Several international carriers serve Cairns from various Asian cities and New Zealand.

Cairns Airport (✆ **1800/177 748;** www.cairnsairport.com.au) is 8km (5 miles) north of downtown. A 5-minute walk along a covered walkway connects the international terminal with the domestic terminal, which has just completed a A$200-million redevelopment. **Baggage storage** at the terminal can be arranged through Smart Carte Australia (✆ **0407/359 678** mobile), and costs between A$7 and A$15 depending on the size of your bag and how long you want to leave it for. **Airport Connections** (✆ **07/4099 5950;** www.tnqshuttle.com) will meet all flights at both terminals. Transfers to the city cost A$11 adults and A$5.50 children 4 to 14, and they also run transfers to as far as Cape Tribulation, Mission Beach, and Dunk Island. **Sun Palm Australia Coach** (✆ **07/4087 2900;** www.sunpalm transport.com) provides transfers from the airport to the city and northern beaches. The one-way fare is A$10 adults and A$5 children 2 to 12 to the city, and A$18 adults and A$8 children to Palm Cove.

A taxi from the airport costs around A$20 to the city, A$50 to Trinity Beach, and A$60 to Palm Cove. There is a set fee of A$168 to Port Douglas. Call **Black & White Taxis** (✆ **13 10 08** in Australia).

Avis, Budget, Europcar, Hertz, Redspot, and **Thrifty** all have car-rental offices at the domestic and international terminals (see "Getting Around," below).

BY TRAIN Long-distance trains operated by Queensland Rail's **Traveltrain** (✆ **13 17 22** in Queensland; www.traveltrain.com.au) run from Brisbane several times a week. The 160kmph (100-mph) **Tilt Train** takes about 24 hours and costs A$310 for business class. Northbound trains leave Brisbane at 6:25pm on Monday

Cairns

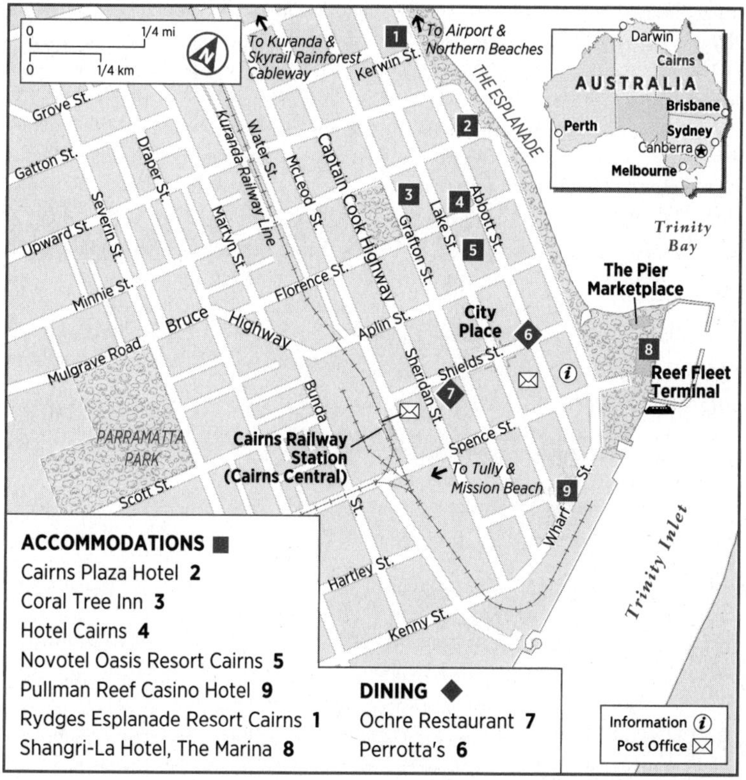

and Friday; southbound runs depart Cairns at 9:15am on Wednesday and Sunday. The train features luxury business-class seating, with an entertainment system for each seat, including multiple movie and audio channels.

The ***Sunlander,*** which runs four times a week between Brisbane and Cairns, takes 32 hours and costs A$212 for a sitting berth, A$271 for an economy-class sleeper, A$417 for a first-class sleeper, or A$761 for all-inclusive Queenslander class (only available twice a week). Trains pull into the Cairns Central terminal (**✆ 07/4036 9250**) on Bunda Street in the center of town. The station has no showers, lockers, or currency exchange booths, but you will find 24-hour ATMs outside the Cairns Central shopping mall, right above the terminal.

BY BUS **Greyhound Australia** (**✆ 1300/473 946** in Australia, or 07/4051 5899 in Cairns; www.greyhound.com.au) buses pull into Trinity Wharf Centre, on Wharf Street, in the center of town. Buses travel from the south via all towns and cities on the Bruce Highway; they also run from the west, from Alice Springs and Darwin, via Tennant Creek on the Stuart Highway, and the Outback mining town of Mount Isa to Townsville, where they join the Bruce Highway and head north. The 48-hour Sydney–Cairns trip costs A$458; the 30-hour trip from Brisbane is A$291.

BY CAR From Brisbane and all major towns in the south, you'll enter Cairns on the Bruce Highway. To reach the northern beaches or Port Douglas from Cairns, take Sheridan Street in the city center, which becomes the Captain Cook Highway.

VISITOR INFORMATION Tourism Tropical North Queensland's **Cairns & Tropical North Information Centre,** 51 The Esplanade, Cairns, QLD 4870 (✆ **07/4051 3588;** fax 07/4051 2509; www.cairnsgreatbarrierreef.org.au), has information on Cairns and its environs, Mission Beach, Port Douglas, the Daintree Rainforest, Cape York, and Outback Queensland. It's open daily from 8:30am to 6:30pm and 10am to 6pm on public holidays; it's closed December 25, New Year's Day, and Good Friday.

CITY LAYOUT The focal point of the city is the **Esplanade,** which has a 4,000-sq.-m (43,000-sq.-ft.) man-made saltwater swimming lagoon, with a wide sandy beach, and surrounding parkland, with public artworks and picnic areas. Suspended over the mud flats and providing a platform for birding, a timber boardwalk runs 600m (1,968 ft.) along the waterfront and is lit at night. A walkway links the Esplanade to the Reef Fleet Terminal, the departure point for Great Barrier Reef boats.

Downtown Cairns is on a grid 5 blocks deep, bounded in the east by the Esplanade on the water and in the west by McLeod Street, where the train station and the Cairns Central shopping mall are. In between are shops, offices, and restaurants.

Heading 15 minutes north from the city along the Captain Cook Highway, you come to the **northern beaches:** Holloway's Beach, Yorkey's Knob, Trinity Beach, Kewarra Beach, Clifton Beach, Palm Cove, and Ellis Beach.

> **Croc Alert!**
>
> **Dangerous crocodiles inhabit Cairns's waterways. Do not swim in or stand on the bank of any river or stream.**

GETTING AROUND **By Bus** **Sunbus** (✆ **07/4057 7411**) buses depart City Place Mall at the intersection of Lake and Shields streets. Buy all tickets and passes on board, and try to have correct change. You can hail buses anywhere it's convenient for the driver to stop. Bus nos. 1N, 1X, 2, and 2A travel to Trinity Beach and Palm Cove. The N route is an express bus that runs between the city and Palm Cove on Friday and Saturday nights only. Routes and timetables change, so check with the driver. Most buses run from early morning until almost midnight.

BY CAR **Avis** (✆ 07/4051 5911), **Budget** (✆ 07/4051 9222), **Europcar** (✆ 13 13 90 in Australia or 07/4034 9088), **Hertz** (✆ 07/4051 6399), and **Thrifty** (✆ 1300/367 227 in Australia or 07/4051 8099) have offices in Cairns city and at the airport. **Redspot Car Rentals** (✆ 07/4034 9052) has an airport office. One long-established local outfit, **Sugarland Car Rentals** (✆ 07/4052 1300), has reasonable rates. **Britz Campervan Rentals** (✆ 1800/331 454 in Australia, or 07/4032 2611) and **Maui Rentals** (✆ 1300/363 800 in Australia) rent motor homes. Britz and most major rental-car companies rent four-wheel-drive vehicles.

BY TAXI Call **Black & White Taxis** (✆ **13 10 08**).

Day Trips to the Reef

Large-scale operator **Great Adventures** (✆ **1800/079 080** in Australia, or 07/4044 9944; www.greatadventures.com.au) does daily cruises from Cairns, in fast, air-conditioned catamarans, to a three-level pontoon on the Outer Reef. The pontoon has a children's swimming area, a semisubmersible, and an underwater observatory. You get at least 3 hours on the Reef. The cost for the day is A$186 for adults, A$93 for children 4 to 14, and A$465 for families. Hotel transfers are available from Cairns, the northern beaches, and Port Douglas for an extra cost. The boat departs the Great Adventures terminal at the Reef Fleet Terminal at 10:30am.

You can also depart Cairns with Great Adventures at 8:30am and spend 2 hours on Green Island en route. This gives you time to walk nature trails, rent snorkel gear and watersports equipment, or laze on the beach before continuing to the Outer Reef. This cruise costs an extra A$20 per adult and A$10 per child, or A$50 per family.

Sunlover Cruises (**© 1800/810 512** in Australia, or 07/4050 1333; www.sunlover.com.au) motors large, fast catamarans to Moore Reef on the Outer Reef. The day costs A$198 for adults, A$83 for children 4 to 14, and A$497 for families of four, including transfers from city hotels. This trip includes a glass-bottom-boat ride and semisubmersible viewing. You spend about 4 hours on the Reef. Introductory dives cost A$120 for one dive or A$190 for two. Certified divers pay A$80 for one dive or A$125 for two, including all gear. The cruise includes lunch and leaves from the Reef Fleet Terminal in Cairns at 10am daily.

For a day cruise from Cairns, **Ocean Free** (**© 07/4052 1111;** www.oceanfree.com.au) gives you the option of a motor cruise or a sailing tour—in both cases with limited numbers to ensure you don't feel crowded. *Ocean Freedom* is a high-speed launch which gives you 5 hours on the reef with less than 65 passengers and takes you to two Reef sites including Upolu Cay. The day starts at 7:30am at the Reef Fleet Terminal, returning at about 4:30pm. The cost is A$169 adults, A$90 children, and A$466 for a family and includes pickup from your hotel, glass-bottom-boat rides, all snorkeling gear, and lunch. You can do an introductory dive for A$105 or if you are certified, dive for A$70. On the sailing trip aboard *Ocean Free,* introductory dives at Green Island cost A$75 and certified dives A$55. The friendly crew give you all the help you need. *Ocean Free* sails at 7:30am, bound for Pinnacle Reef, an exclusive mooring on the eastern lee of Green Island. The cruise costs A$119 adults, A$75 children, and A$349 for a family of four.

You can also take a coach transfer from Cairns or Palm Cove to join the **Quicksilver Wavepiercer** (**© 07/4087 2100;** www.quicksilver-cruises.com), based in Port Douglas, for a day trip to the Outer Reef (p. 302). Transfers cost A$18 per adult or A$10 per child, A$46 for families of four.

Great Adventures, Quicksilver, and Sunlover also all offer helicopter flights over the Reef from their pontoons—a spectacular experience! There are fly-and-cruise trips as well.

An alternative to motoring to the Reef is to sail to it. **Ocean Spirit Cruises** (**© 1800/644 227** in Australia, or 07/4031 2920; www.oceanspirit.com.au) operates two sailing cats that take no more than 150 passengers to Michaelmas Cay or Upolu Cay, lovely white-sand cays on the Outer Reef surrounded by rich reefs. This trip is a good value; it includes a pleasant 2-hour sail to either cay, a guided snorkeling safari, a guided beach walk, and a glass of bubbly and live music on the way home—in addition to the usual reef ecology talks, semisubmersible rides, lunch, and transfers from your Cairns or northern beaches hotel. Another plus is that you spend your out-of-water time on a beautiful beach, not on a pontoon or boat deck. You get about 4 hours on the Reef.

> **Diving Made Easy**
>
> Can't swim? Don't want to get your hair wet? Don't worry—you can still get underwater and see the wonders of the Reef. Several companies offer travelers the chance to don a dive helmet and "walk" underwater. Similar to old-style diving helmets, which allow you to breathe underwater, the helmet has air pumped into it by a hose. You walk into the water to a depth of about 4m (13 ft.), accompanied by instructors, and the Reef is right before you. **Quicksilver Cruises** calls it "Ocean Walker"; with **Sunlover Cruises** and at Green Island Resort it's called "Sea Walker." You must be at least 10 years old (at Green Island Resort) or 12 years old (with Quicksilver and Sunlover cruises). The cost is about A$140 for 20 minutes.

The day trip to Michaelmas Cay is A$189 for adults, A$95 for children 4 to 14, or A$488 for families of four. At Michaelmas Cay, introductory dives cost A$100 for one or A$160 for two; certified divers pay A$65 for one or A$110 for two, all gear included. The day trip to Upolu Cay and Oyster Reef costs A$125 for adults including one introductory dive. Snorkelers pay A$99 for adults, A$60 for kids, and A$258 for a family. At Upolu, a second dive costs A$45; for certified divers, the cost is A$55 for one and A$35 for the second dive. The boats depart Reef Fleet Terminal at 8:30am daily. Transfers from Cairns and the northern beaches are free, but from Port Douglas they cost an extra A$60 per person.

What to See & Do Around Cairns

If you're staying in Cairns, also check out activities in and around Port Douglas (see p. 300) and Mission Beach (see p. 311). Many tour operators in Port Douglas, and a few in Mission Beach, offer transfers from Cairns.

LEARNING ABOUT ABORIGINAL CULTURE

Tjapukai Aboriginal Cultural Park ★ Whether you choose the day or night experience, the Tjapukai (pronounced Jab-*oo*-guy) Aboriginal Cultural Park is one of the best chances you'll have to discover the history and culture of the Aborigines without going to Central Australia. However, it is a much different experience from that which you would have in the Red Centre. From humble beginnings in 1987, Tjapukai has become a slick, sophisticated production, which has won multiple international awards and is worth a look.

Housed in a striking modern building that incorporates Aboriginal themes and colors, the Tjapukai experience needs at least 2 to 3 hours. Start in the Creation Theatre, where performers use the latest in illusion, theatrics, and technology to tell the story of the creation of the world according to the spiritual beliefs of Tjapukai people. Actors work with special effects and holographic images to illustrate the legends. The production is performed in the Tjapukai language, translated through headsets.

Move on through the Magic Space museum and gallery section of the complex to the History Theatre, where a 20-minute film relates the history of the Tjapukai people since the arrival of white settlers 120 years ago.

Outside, there's a cultural village where you can attempt boomerang and spear throwing, fire-making, and didgeridoo playing, and learn about bush foods and medicines. Shows and demonstrations are planned so visitors can move from one to another easily, without missing anything. The complex also includes a restaurant and coffee shop. An arts-and-crafts gallery and shop stocks the work of Aboriginal artists and crafts workers.

Tjapukai by Night tours run daily from 7:30 to 10pm. They include interactive time in the Magic Space museum, a Creation Show performance, and an outdoor Serpent Circle—an interactive show featuring tap sticks for each guest to use, a join-in corroboree (an Aboriginal nighttime dance), and a ceremony involving fire and water. Following are a buffet dinner and dance show, and the chance to meet the dancers. The cost is A$112 adults or A$59 children, including transfers to and from Cairns.

Captain Cook Hwy. (beside the Skyrail terminal), Smithfield. ✆ **07/4042 9900.** www.tjapukai.com.au. Admission A$33 adults, A$17 children 5–14, A$83 families. Ask about packages that include entry to other Cairns attractions, including Cairns Tropical Zoo, Skyrail, and/or Kuranda Scenic Rail. Daily 9am–5pm. Closed Dec 25. Free parking. Bus: 1C or 1E. Round-trip shuttle transfers to and through the park from Cairns hotels A$22 adults and A$12 children. Park is 15 min. north of Cairns and 15 min. south of Palm Cove.

MORE ATTRACTIONS

In Cairns

Cairns Tropical Zoo ☺ Get a dose of your favorite Aussie wildlife here—some kind of talk or show takes place about every 15 or 30 minutes throughout the day, including koala cuddling and snake handling (have your photo taken for an extra A$15), and saltwater crocodile and lorikeet feedings. Lots of other animals are on show, too, such as kangaroos (which you can hand-feed for A$1 a bag), emus, cassowaries, dingoes, and native birds in a walk-through aviary. The park also runs a nocturnal tour, during which you can see many of the more elusive creatures on show. To take the park's 3-hour **Cairns Night Zoo** tour (www.cairnsnightzoo.com), book by 4pm on the same day (Mon–Thurs and Sat), earlier if you want transfers. The evening starts at 7pm and includes a wildlife spotlighting walk, during which you can pat a koala and a possum and feed kangaroos; a stargazing interlude; a barbecue dinner with beer and wine, billy tea, and damper; and dancing to an Aussie bush band.

Captain Cook Hwy. (22km/14 miles north of the city center), Palm Cove. ✆ **07/4055 3669.** www.cairnstropicalzoo.com. Admission A$32 adults, A$16 children 4–15 (valid for 3 days). Combination tickets with Hartley's Crocodile Adventures (see below) are A$58 adults, A$29 children. Cairns Night Zoo experience A$95 adults, A$48 children 4–15 (more if you want transfers from Cairns or Port Douglas). Daily 8:30am–4pm. Closed Dec 25. Free parking. Bus: 1B. Transfers from Cairns through Down Under Tours (✆ **07/4035 5566**) or from Port Douglas with Wildlife Discovery Tours (✆ **07/4099 6612**).

Cairns Wildlife Dome For some visitors to Cairns, exploring the rainforest and its wildlife doesn't even involve leaving the hotel, thanks to the city's newest attraction. Here, 200 animals—including a huge saltwater crocodile named Goliath—are housed in a 20m-high (66-ft.) glass dome on the rooftop of the Pullman Reef Hotel Casino (see "Where to Stay," later in this chapter). You can get up close with koalas, lizards, kookaburras, frogs, pademelons, turtles, and snakes. There are wildlife presentations and free guided tours throughout the day. Koala photos are A$20, or A$13 if you pay when you buy your entry ticket.

In the Hotel Sofitel Reef Casino, 35–41 Wharf St., Cairns. ✆ **07/4031 7250.** www.cairnsdome.com.au. Admission A$22 adults, A$11 children 4–14. Tickets are valid for reentry for up to 5 days. Daily 9am–6pm (5:30pm on public holidays). Closed Dec 25.

Hartley's Crocodile Adventures ★★ ☺ Hartley's is the original Australian croc show, and quite possibly the best. What makes it different from others is the fantastic natural setting—a 2-hectare (5-acre) lagoon surrounded by melaluca (Paperbark) and bloodwood trees that are home to 23 estuarine crocs. The best time to visit is for the 3pm "croc attack" show, when you can witness the saltwater crocodile "death roll" during the 45-minute performance. At 11am you can see these monsters get hand-fed or hear an eye-opening talk on the less aggressive freshwater crocodiles. There are tours of the croc farm at 10am and 1:30pm; at 2pm there is a snake show; 4:30pm is koala-feeding time. Cassowaries are fed at 9:30am and 4:15pm. There are also croc- and snake-handling opportunities. This attraction makes a good stop en route to Port Douglas if you are driving yourself, though many tours and transfer services will also get you here.

Capt. Cook Hwy. (40km/24 miles north of Cairns; 25km/16 miles south of Port Douglas). ✆ **07/4055 3576.** www.crocodileadventures.com. Admission (good for 3 days) A$32 adults, A$16 children 4–15, A$80 families of 4. Daily 8:30am–5pm. Closed Dec 25. Free parking.

Exploring the Islands

You don't have to go all the way to the Outer Reef to see coral. Less than an hour from the city wharf, Fitzroy Island has rainforest walks, coral accessible by dive and snorkel boat trips from the island, and watersports. Green Island also offers snorkeling and other activities. See "Where to Stay," later in this section, for details about the resorts on both islands.

GREEN ISLAND This 15-hectare (37-acre) coral cay is just 27km (17 miles) east of Cairns. You can rent snorkel gear, windsurfers, and paddle skis; take glass-bottom-boat trips; go parasailing; take an introductory or certified dive; walk vine-forest trails; or laze on the beach. The beach is coral sand, so it's a little rough underfoot. Day visitors have access to one of Green Island Resort's pools, its main bar, the casual or upscale restaurants there, and lockers and showers. Ask the beach staff to recommend the best snorkeling spots. If you don't snorkel, it's worth the admission charge to see the display of clownfish, potato cod, and anemones at the little underwater observatory, despite its cloudy, old viewing windows. The island has a small attraction called **Marineland Melanesia** (✆ **07/4051 4032;** www.marinelandgreenisland.com), where you can see old nautical artifacts, primitive art,

Wildife Passes

Wildlife enthusiasts who plan to visit several of the attractions in the Cairns region can save a few dollars by buying a Four Park Pass, which gives entry to Cairns Wildlife Dome, the Rainforestation Nature Park, the Australian Butterfly Sanctuary, and Rainforest Habitat. The discounted price of A$80 adults, A$40 children or A$200 for a family of four is a saving of A$29 per adult or A$73 per family. The pass is valid for 6 months and doesn't have to be used on consecutive days, giving a lot of freedom to visit whenever you wish. Buy it at any of the participating parks. A Kuranda Wildlife Experience pass offers discounted admission to Birdworld, the Kuranda Koala Gardens, and the Australian Butterfly Sanctuary (see p. 292). It can be bought on arrival at any of the three sanctuaries for A$42 adults, half-price for children.

a turtle and reef aquarium, and live crocodiles, including Cassius, reputed to be the largest croc in captivity in the world. Admission is A$17 adults, A$8 kids 5 to 14; croc shows are at 10:30am and 1:45pm.

Great Adventures (**© 07/4044 9944;** www.greatadventures.com.au) and **Big Cat Green Island Reef Cruises** (**© 07/4051 0444;** www.greenisland.com.au) run to Green Island from Cairns. Both offer a range of half-day and full-day trips with lots of options. Half-day trips with snorkel gear or a glass-bottom-boat cruise with Great Adventures costs from A$73 adults, A$37 children 4 to 14, or A$183 family of four. Big Cat makes a half-day trip for A$73 adults, A$40 children, or A$192 family. Both companies pick up from hotels in Cairns, the northern beaches, and Port Douglas for an extra cost.

FITZROY ISLAND Scenic Fitzroy Island, a national rainforest 45 minutes from Cairns, offers good diving and snorkeling. The island's only resort closed in late 2008 and at press time had not re-opened. But you can still take a day trip to the island for snorkeling and diving, glass-bottom-boat rides, watersports, or just to take a hike to the lighthouse at the top of the hill or do one of the other rainforest walks. A day trip can cost as little as the round-trip ferry fare, A$58 adults or A$32 for kids 4 to 14. Departure from Cairns is at 8:30am, returning at 4:30pm daily. Make reservations through **Raging Thunder Adventures** (**© 07/4030 7990;** www.ragingthunder.com.au). Raging Thunder also runs daily guided sea-kayak expeditions around Fitzroy Island. These include 3 hours of kayaking, snorkeling gear, a snack, and stinger suits (Nov–May), and then you can stay on the island for the rest of the day. Tours cost A$124 adults, A$90 children (including the ferry from Cairns). Kids must be over 8 years old and accompanied by an adult.

Exploring the Wet Tropics Rainforest

The 110-million-year-old World Heritage–listed Daintree Rainforest, 2 hours north of Cairns, gets most of the attention (see "Port Douglas," later in this chapter), but tracts of rainforest closer to Cairns are just as pristine. These rainforests and the Daintree are part of the Wet Tropics, a World Heritage area that stretches from Cape Tribulation to Townsville. This dense, lush environment has remained unchanged by ice ages and other geological events, and the plants and animals retain primitive characteristics. In the tract's mangroves, eucalyptus woodlands, and tropical rainforest are 65% of Australia's bird species, 60% of its butterfly species, and many of its frogs, reptiles, bats, marsupials, and orchids.

Because so much rainforest wildlife is nocturnal and often difficult to spot, consider joining **Wait-a-While Rainforest Tours** (**© 07/4093 8414** or 0429/083 338 mobile; www.waitawhile.com.au) on a day-into-night tour to the Atherton Tablelands, designed to maximize your encounters with the wild things. This tour costs A$190 adults and A$165 children, including afternoon tea, dinner at a country restaurant, and a light supper at the end. The tour begins from Cairns at 2pm and finishes at about 11:30pm. Pickups from Port Douglas can also be arranged.

A Side Trip to Kuranda, a Rainforest Village ★

Few travelers visit Cairns without making at least a day trip to the mountain village of **Kuranda,** 34km (21 miles) northwest of Cairns near the Barron Gorge National Park. Although it's undeniably touristy, the cool mountain air and mist-wrapped rainforest refuse to be spoiled, no matter how many tourists clutter the streets. The shopping in Kuranda—for leather goods, Australian-wool sweaters, opals, crafts, and more—is more unusual than in Cairns, and the handful of cafes and restaurants are much more atmospheric. The town is easy to negotiate on foot; pick up a visitors' guide and map at the Skyrail gondola station or train station (see below) when you arrive.

GETTING THERE

Getting to Kuranda is part of the fun. Some people drive up the winding 25km (16-mile) mountain road, but the most popular approaches are to chuff up the mountainside in a scenic train, or to glide silently over the rainforest canopy in the world's longest gondola cableway, the Skyrail Rainforest Cableway.

The most popular round-trip is one-way on the Skyrail (mornings are best for photography) and the other way on the train.

BY SKYRAIL The **Skyrail Rainforest Cableway ★★★** (**© 07/4038 1555;** www.skyrail.com.au) is a magnificent feat of engineering and one of Australia's top tourism attractions. There are about 114 six-person gondolas, which leave every few seconds from the terminal in the northern Cairns suburb of Smithfield for the 7.5km (4½-mile) journey. The view of the coast as you ascend is so breathtaking that even those afraid of heights will find it worthwhile. As you rise over the foothills of the coastal range, watch the lush green of the rainforest take over beneath you. Looking back, you have spectacular views over Cairns and north toward Trinity Bay. On a clear day, you can see Green Island. There are two stops during the 90-minute trip, at Red Peak and Barron Falls. After about 10 minutes, you reach Red Peak. You are now 545m (1,788 ft.) above sea level, and massive kauri pines dominate the view. You must change gondolas at each station, so take the time to stroll around the boardwalks for the ground view of the rainforest. Guided walks start every 20 minutes.

You'll continue on to Barron Falls station, built on the cleared site of an old construction camp for workers on the first hydroelectric power station on the Barron River in the 1930s. A rainforest information center has been established here, and there are boardwalks to the lookouts for wonderful views of the Barron Gorge and Falls. From Barron Falls station, the gondola travels over the thick rainforest of the range. It's easy to spot ferns and orchids and the brilliant blue butterflies of the region. As you reach the end of the trip, the gondola passes over the Barron River and across the Kuranda railway line into the station. Don't worry if it rains on the day you go—one of the best trips I've made on Skyrail was in a misty rain, which added a new dimension to the rainforest.

A one-way ticket is A$41 for adults, half-price for children 4 to 14, or A$103 for families of four; a round-trip ticket, including transfers from your Cairns or northern beaches hotel, is A$78 for adults, A$39 for children, or A$195 for families; from Port Douglas, it's A$99 for adults, A$50 for children, or A$248 for families. The cableway operates daily, except December 25, from 9am to 5:15pm. You must make a reservation to travel within a 15-minute time frame. The last boardings are at 2:45pm for a return trip, or 3:30pm for a one-way journey. The Skyrail terminal is on the Captain Cook Highway at Kamerunga Road, Caravonica Lakes, 15km (9½ miles) north of Cairns's city center.

BY SCENIC RAILWAY The 34km (21-mile) **Kuranda Scenic Railway** (**© 07/4036 9333;** www.ksr.com.au) is one of the most scenic rail journeys in the world. The train snakes through the magnificent vistas of the Barron Gorge National Park, past gorges and waterfalls on the 90-minute trip from Cairns to Kuranda. It rises 328m (1,076 ft.) and goes through 15 tunnels before emerging at the pretty Kuranda station, which is smothered in ferns. Built by hand over 5 years in the late 1880s, the railway track is today a monument to the 1,500 men who toiled to link the two towns, and the ride on the steam train adds to the atmosphere. The train departs Cairns Central at 8:30 and 9:30am daily (except Dec 25) and leaves Kuranda at 2 and 3:30pm. The one-way fare is A$41 for adults, A$21 for children 4 to 14, and A$103 for families of four.

SKYRAIL/TRAIN COMBINATION TICKETS In most cases, these packages represent convenience rather than savings. A package combining one-way travel on the Skyrail and a trip back on the Scenic Railway is A$90 for adults, half-price for children, or A$224 for families of four; A$101 for adults, half-price for kids, or A$253 for families, with round-trip transfers from Cairns or the northern beaches. Skyrail runs a shuttle bus from most Cairns hotels. A package including the Skyrail, the Scenic Railway, and entry to the Tjapukai Aboriginal Cultural Park (see above) is A$134 for adults, half-price for kids, and A$336 for families of four, including transfers from Cairns and the northern beaches. An option including the Skyrail, Scenic Railway, and Rainforestation (see below) is A$150 for adults, half-price for kids, and A$376 for families of four, including transfers from Cairns. All packages can upgrade to Gold Class service on the train for an extra A$45 per person. Book packages through Skyrail, Queensland Rail, or Tjapukai.

BY BUS **Trans North Bus & Coach Service** (**© 07/4061 7944;** www.transnorthbus.com) operates a bus to Kuranda from Cairns five times a day. The fare is A$4 one-way. ***A tip:*** Buying a return ticket will give you priority if the bus gets full at the end of the day. Catch it at 46 Spence St., Cairns, or at the railway station, or hail it at bus stops anywhere along Sheridan Street.

VISITOR INFORMATION The **Kuranda Visitor Information Centre** (**© 07/4093 9311;** www.kuranda.org) is in Centenary Park, at the top end of Coondoo Street. It is open 10am to 4pm daily, except Christmas Day.

EXPLORING KURANDA

A free shuttle bus operates between the Skyrail station and Kuranda's main attractions, leaving every 15 minutes between 10am and 3pm daily, but it is easy enough to walk around everything.

Kuranda is known for its markets that sell locally made arts and crafts, fresh produce, boomerangs, T-shirts, jewelry, and lots more. The **Kuranda Original Rainforest Markets,** which started in 1978, are at 7 Therwine St., entry through the Kuranda Market Mall (**© 07/4093 9440;** daily 9am–3pm), and are devoted exclusively to local artisans and craftspeople. You will find locally designed and produced fashion, jewelry, leather work, and indigenous art, as well as local produce including honey, coffee, fruit, sugar cane juice, coconuts, and macadamias. The 90-stall **Heritage Market** (**© 07/4093 8060;** www.kurandamarkets.com.au) is open daily from 9:30am to 3:30pm on Rob Veivers Drive, selling a range of souvenirs, food, produce, and crafts. The **New Kuranda Markets,** in an undercover complex on Coondoo Street, houses a range of stalls and shops including an Aboriginal art gallery. A group of about 50 local artisans sell their work in the **Kuranda Arts Co-Operative ★**, Shop 6, 12 Rob Veivers Dr. (**© 07/4093 9026;** www.artskuranda.asn.au), near the Butterfly Sanctuary. It's open from 10am to 4pm daily. You will find quality furniture crafted from recycled Australian hardwoods, jewelry, photography, glasswork, handicrafts, and other items.

You can explore the rainforest, the river esplanade, or Barron Falls along a number of easy walking trails. If you want to learn about the rainforest, explore it with Brian Clarke of **Kuranda Riverboat Tours** (✆ **07/4093 7476;** www.kurandariverboat.com), who runs informative 45-minute river cruises. The cruises depart hourly, from 10:30am to 2:30pm, from the riverside landing across the footbridge, near the train station. Brian is a former crocodile hunter and has lived in the rainforest for more than 30 years. The cruise costs A$15 for adults, A$7 for children 5 to 15, and A$37 for families of four. Buy your tickets on board.

KURANDA'S NATURE PARKS

Australian Butterfly Sanctuary ★ ☺ A rainbow-hued array of 1,500 tropical butterflies—including the electric-blue Ulysses and Australia's largest species, the Cairns bird wing—occupies a lush walk-through enclosure here. Take the free 30-minute guided tour and learn about the butterfly's fascinating life cycle. The butterflies will land on you if you wear pink, red, and other bright colors, and don't be put off if it's raining—this attraction is good in any weather.

8 Rob Veivers Dr. ✆ **07/4093 7575.** www.australianbutterflies.com. Admission A$17 adults, A$8.50 children 4–15, A$43 families of 4. Daily 10am–4pm. Closed Dec 25. Street parking.

Birdworld Behind the markets off Rob Veivers Drive, Birdworld has eye-catching macaws, a pair of cassowaries, and Australia's largest collection of free-flying birds—about 500 of them, representing 75 species from around the world. Two lakes are home to waterbirds including stilts, herons, and Australia's Black Swan.

Rob Veivers Dr. ✆ **07/4093 9188.** www.birdworldkuranda.com. Admission A$16 adults, A$8 children 4–15, A$40 families of 4. Daily 9am–4pm. Closed Dec 25. Street parking.

Kuranda Koala Gardens You can cuddle a koala and have your photo taken at this small wildlife park at the Heritage Markets. Or check out other animals, including freshwater crocodiles, wombats, lizards, and wallabies, or take a stroll through the walk-through snake enclosure while they slither at your feet—not for the fainthearted.

Rob Veivers Dr. ✆ **07/4093 9953.** www.koalagardens.com. Admission A$16 adults, A$8 children 4–15. Daily 9am–4pm. Closed Dec 25. Street parking.

Rainforestation Nature Park At this 40-hectare (99-acre) nature and cultural complex, you can take a 45-minute ride into the rainforest in a World War II amphibious Army Duck. You'll hear commentary on orchids and other rainforest wildlife along the way. You can also see a performance by Aboriginal dancers; learn about Aboriginal legends and throw a boomerang on the Dreamtime Walk; or have your photo taken cuddling a koala in the wildlife park (photos extra). The Army Duck runs on the hour, beginning at 10am; the Aboriginal dancers perform at 10:30am, noon, and 2pm; and the 30-minute Dreamtime Walk leaves at 10, 11, and 11:30am, and 12:30, 1:30, and 2:30pm.

Kennedy Hwy., a 5-min. drive from the center of Kuranda. ✆ **07/4085 5008.** www.rainforest.com.au. A$40 for adults, A$20 for kids 4–14, A$100 for families of 4 (or you can buy tickets to each attraction separately). Daily 9am–4pm. Closed Dec 25. Free parking. Shuttle from the Butterfly Sanctuary, Rob Veivers Dr., every 30 min. 10:45am–2:45pm for A$8 adults, A$4 children, A$20 families, round-trip.

White-Water Rafting & Other Thrills

RnR Rafting ★ (✆ **07/4041 9444;** www.raft.com.au) and **Raging Thunder Adventures** (✆ **07/4030 7990;** www.ragingthunder.com.au) serve as one-stop booking shops for action pursuits in and around Cairns, including hot-air ballooning, sky diving, jet-boating, horseback riding, ATV (all-terrain vehicle) safaris, parasailing, and rafting. Ask about multipursuit packages.

BUNGEE JUMPING Contact **A. J. Hackett Bungy** (✆ **1800/622 888** in Australia, or 07/4057 7188; www.ajhackett.com.au). The cost is A$130 per person, including transport to the site, which is 20 minutes north of town on McGregor Road.

FISHING Cairns is the world's giant black marlin capital. Catches of more than 1,000 pounds hardly raise an eyebrow in this neck of the woods. The game-fishing season is September through December, with November the busiest. Book early—game boats are reserved months in advance. Game fishers can also battle Pacific sailfish, dogtooth and yellowfin tuna, Spanish mackerel, wahoo, dolphin fish, barracuda, and tiger shark. Reef anglers can expect to land coral trout, red emperor (sea perch), and sweetlip. Mangrove jack, barramundi, and tarpon lurk in the estuaries. Contact **Fishing Cairns** (✆ **07/4041 1169;** www.fishingcairns.com.au) to book a charter. Expect to pay around A$1,980 per day for a sole charter for heavy-tackle game fishing for two people, plus A$40 for each extra angler, A$395 per person for light-tackle fishing, at least A$200 for reef fishing, and from A$85 for a half-day in Cairns's Trinity Inlet estuary.

WHITE-WATER RAFTING Several companies offer exciting white-water-rafting trips from Cairns on the Class III to IV **Tully River** ★★, 90 minutes south of Cairns near Mission Beach; the Class III Barron River in the hills behind the city; and the Class IV to V rapids of the inland Johnstone River. You must be 13 years or older to raft.

One-day trips on the Tully are the most popular (see "Mission Beach: The Cassowary Coast," later in this chapter). A trip with **RnR Rafting** (✆ **07/4041 9444**) costs A$160 from Cairns or the northern beaches, including transfers.

Closer to Cairns, the gentler **Barron River** is a good choice for the timid. A half-day trip with RnR Rafting costs A$98 from Cairns, including pickup and about 1½ hours of rafting. Prices do not include a A$30 levy for national park and other fees.

Where to Stay

High season in Cairns includes 2 weeks at Easter, the period from early July to early October, and the Christmas holiday through January. Book ahead in those periods. In low season (Nov–Jun), many hotels offer discounts or are willing to negotiate.

Cairns has a good supply of affordable accommodations, both in the heart of the city and along the northern beaches. You can also stay in the peaceful village of Kuranda, or get away from it all at an island resort.

Don't think you have to stay in Cairns city if you don't have a car. Most tour and cruise operators will pick you up and drop you off in Cairns, on the northern beaches, or even in Port Douglas (see p. 300).

IN CAIRNS

Unless noted otherwise, all accommodations below are within walking distance of shops, restaurants, cinemas, the casino, the tourist office, bus terminals, the train station, and the departure terminals for Great Barrier Reef cruises.

Very Expensive

Pullman Reef Hotel Casino ★ This stylish six-story hotel is a block from the water, with partial water views from some rooms, and city/hinterland outlooks from others. All the rooms have lots of light, high-quality amenities, bathrobes, and small balconies with smart timber furniture. The **Reef Casino** is attached to the hotel (see "Cairns After Dark," later in this chapter).

35-41 Wharf St., Cairns, QLD 4870. ✆ **1800/808 883** in Australia, 800/221-4542 in the U.S. and Canada, 020/8283 4500 in the U.K., 0800/44 4422 in New Zealand, or 07/4030 8888. Fax 07/4030 8777. www.accorhotels.com. 128 units. A$300–A$450 double. Extra person A$75. AE, DC, MC, V. Free valet and self-parking. **Amenities:** 4 restaurants, 3 bars; airport shuttle; babysitting; concierge; health club; Jacuzzi; small rooftop pool; room service; sauna. *In room:* A/C, TV/VCR, hair dryer, Internet (A15¢ per min.; A$28 for 24 hr.), minibar, Wi-Fi (level 2 rooms only; A$26 for 2 hr.).

Shangri-La Hotel, The Marina ★ This is a modern, sophisticated hotel, renovated in 2004, with swish, spacious rooms, all with balconies either overlooking the marina or the mountains. The exclusive Horizon Club has 36 rooms. These rooms are contemporary in style and exceptionally spacious—more than 56 sq. m (603 sq. ft.), with 3.3m (11-ft.) ceilings. Bathrooms have ocean views, and the rooms have large terraces. Even the standard rooms are larger than usual, at 32.5 sq. m (350 sq. ft.). The AAA-rated five-star hotel adjoins the Pier Shopping Centre and the new Esplanade lagoon, and it's not far from the Reef Fleet Terminal.

Pierpoint Rd., Cairns, QLD 4870. ✆ **1800/222 448** in Australia, 0800/442 179 in New Zealand, 1866/344 5050 in the U.S. and Canada, 0800/028 3337 in the U.K., or 07/4031 1411. Fax 07/4031 3226. www.shangri-la.com. 256 units. A$304–A$445 double; A$398–A$758 suite. Children 17 and under stay free in parent's room with existing bedding. AE, DC, MC, V. Free outdoor and covered self-parking. **Amenities:** Restaurant; 2 bars; airport shuttle (on request); babysitting; concierge; executive-level rooms; nearby golf course; health club; Jacuzzi; large outdoor pool and children's pool; room service; sauna; spa. *In room:* A/C, TV, VCR w/pay movies, hair dryer, minibar, free Wi-Fi.

Expensive

Novotel Cairns Oasis Resort The large pool, complete with swim-up bar and a little sandy beach, is the focus of this attractive six-story resort built in 1997 and completely refurbished and rebranded in 2008. All the contemporary-style rooms have balconies with views over the tropical gardens, the mountains, or the pool. The suites, with a TV in the bedroom and a large Jacuzzi bathtub, could well be the best-value suites in town.

122 Lake St., Cairns, QLD 4870. ✆ **1300/656 565** in Australia or 07/4080 1888. Fax 07/4080 1889. www.novotelcairnsresort.com.au. 314 units. A$169–A$199 double; A$319 suite. Extra person A$60. Children 15 and under stay free in parent's room with existing bedding. Free crib. Ask about packages. AE, DC, MC, V. Free valet and self-parking. **Amenities:** Restaurant; 2 bars; airport shuttle; babysitting; concierge; health club; outdoor pool; room service. *In room:* A/C, TV w/pay movies, hair dryer, Internet (A$12 per hr.; A$25 for 24 hr.), minibar.

Rydges Esplanade Resort Cairns Despite its lack of glitz, this 14-story hotel has been the choice of a number of movie stars while on location in Cairns. A 20-minute waterfront walk from downtown, the hotel offers a range of accommodations, from hotel rooms to penthouse apartments. The one- and two-bedroom apartments look out to the sea; hotel rooms have sea or mountain views. Kitchenettes are in studios and apartments only. The rooms are spacious, but the bathrooms are not. Out back are cheaper studios and apartments, with upgraded furnishings; in front is a pool and sun deck. They offer a shuttle service around the city.

The Esplanade (at Kerwin St.), Cairns, QLD 4870. ✆ **1800/079 105** in Australia, or 07/4031 2211. Fax 07/4031 2704. www.rydges.com. 342 units. A$149–A$219 double; A$159–A$199 double 1-bedroom studio; A$189–A$284 double 2-bedroom studio or 1-bedroom tower apt; A$259–A$350 double 2-bedroom apt. Ask about packages. AE, DC, MC, V. Free covered parking. Bus stop about 100m (328 ft.) from the hotel. **Amenities:** 2 restaurants; 3 bars; airport transfers; babysitting; bikes; concierge; golf course about 20 min. away; health club; Jacuzzi; 3 outdoor pools; room service; sauna; 2 lit tennis courts. *In room:* A/C, TV w/pay movies, hair dryer, Internet (hotel rooms only; A$29 for 24 hr.).

Moderate

Cairns Plaza Hotel The harbor views at this seven-story complex are better than those at most of the more luxurious hotels in Cairns. Two blocks from town, the accommodations are a good size, with fresh, appealing furnishings and modern bathrooms. Suites and studios have kitchenettes. If your balcony does not have a water vista, you overlook a nice aspect of the city or mountains instead. Families can book a connecting suite and standard room to create more space and privacy.

145 The Esplanade (at Minnie St.), Cairns, QLD 4870. ✆ **1800/117 787** in Australia, or 07/4051 4688. Fax 07/4051 8129. www.cairnsplaza.com.au. 60 units. A$180 double; A$210 suite. Extra person A$25. AE, DC, MC, V. Limited free parking. **Amenities:** Restaurant; bar; babysitting; golf course nearby; access to nearby health club; Jacuzzi; small outdoor pool; room service; 4 lit tennis courts nearby. *In room:* A/C, TV w/free movies, hair dryer, Internet (A$15 for 12 hr.), minibar, Wi-Fi (suites only; A$10 for 4 hr.).

The Hotel Cairns Stay at this hotel, and you get a free car to drive around in! In an Australian first, all guests at the Hotel Cairns have free access to drive five Mercedes Smart Cars—or one Cabriolet Smart Car for those who like the wind in their hair. The cars are available on a first-come, first-served basis, include unlimited mileage and a full tank of petrol. This plantation-style hotel, with its white shutters, verandas, and lattice work screens, is very Queensland. Family owned and operated, the hotel is set in tropical gardens and is just 5 minutes' walk from the city center. Rooms are modern, with bright splashes of color, marble floors, and large bathrooms, and some have balconies. Even the Plantation Rooms, on the lower two levels, are spacious, but for more luxury, the Tower Rooms have 33 sq. m (355 sq. ft.) of living area, as well as a generous balcony. There are three Tower Suites, which are even bigger.

Abbott and Florence sts., Cairns, QLD 4870. ✆ **07/4051 6188.** Fax 07/4031 1806. www.thehotelcairns.com. 92 units. A$195 double; A$225 double Tower Room; A$265 double suite. Extra person A$30. Crib A$10. Ask about packages. AE, DC, MC, V. Free covered parking. **Amenities:** Restaurant; bar; bikes; exercise room; Jacuzzi; outdoor pool; room service. *In room:* A/C, TV w/pay movies, DVD player, CD player, hair dryer, free Wi-Fi.

Inexpensive

Coral Tree Inn The focal point of this airy, modern resort-style motel a 5-minute walk from the city center is the friendly communal kitchen that overlooks the palm-lined saltwater pool and paved sun deck. It's a great spot to cook a steak or reef fish filet on the free barbecue and join other guests at the big shared tables. The smallish, basic-but-neat motel rooms have painted brick walls, terra-cotta tile or carpeted floors, and new bathrooms with marble-look laminate countertops. In contrast, the eight suites, which have kitchenettes, are huge and stylish enough for any corporate traveler. They are some of the best-value accommodations in town. All rooms have a balcony or patio; some look out onto the commercial buildings next door but most face the pool. Ask about packages that include cruises and other tours.

166–172 Grafton St., Cairns, QLD 4870. ✆ **07/4031 3744.** Fax 07/4031 3064. www.coraltreeinn.com.au. 58 units. A$125 double; A$153 suite. Extra person A$10. AE, DC, MC, V. Limited free parking; ample street parking. **Amenities:** Bar; airport shuttle; babysitting; bike rental; access to nearby health club; outdoor saltwater pool. *In room:* A/C, TV, hair dryer.

Lilybank Bed & Breakfast ★ This 1870s Queenslander homestead, originally a mayor's residence, is in a leafy suburb 6km (3¾ miles) from the airport and a 10-minute drive from the city. The large, attractive guest rooms, individually decorated with such features as wrought-iron beds and patchwork quilts, have good-size bathrooms. The largest room has French doors opening onto a "sleep-out" (an enclosed veranda with two extra beds). You can also stay in the gardener's cottage, with slate floors, stained-glass windows, a king-size bed, and a bar. The house is set in gardens with an attractive rock-lined saltwater pool. Breakfast is served in the garden room by the fishpond. Gregarious hosts Mike and Pat Woolford share their house with two poodles, a galah called Chook, and a giant green tree frog. There's a guest TV lounge and kitchen, and phone, fax, and e-mail access. Many tours pick up at the door, and several good restaurants are a stroll away, so you don't need a car to stay here. A taxi from the airport costs approximately A$16. No smoking indoors.
75 Kamerunga Rd., Stratford, Cairns, QLD 4870. ✆ **07/4055 1123.** Fax 07/4058 1990. www.lilybank.com.au. 6 units, 4 with shower only. A$110–A$132 double. Extra person A$33. Rates include full breakfast. AE, MC, V. Free parking. Bus: 1E or 1G. Bus stop 120m (394 ft.) away. Children not accepted. **Amenities:** Internet (A$2.20 for 15 min.; A$5.50 for 1 hr.); outdoor pool. *In room:* A/C, hair dryer, no phone.

ON THE NORTHERN BEACHES

A string of white sandy beaches starts 15 minutes north of the city center. Trinity Beach, 15 minutes from the airport, is secluded, elegant, and scenic. The most upscale is Palm Cove, 20 minutes from the airport. Here, rainbow-hued shops and tasteful apartment blocks nestle among giant Paperbarks and palms fronting a postcard-perfect beach. It has several advantages over other beach suburbs: A 9-hole resort golf course and a gym are within walking distance, the Quicksilver Wavepiercer Great Barrier Reef cruise boat picks up passengers here daily, and it has the greatest choice of places to eat. Add 5 to 10 minutes to the traveling times above to reach the city.

> **Safe Swimming**
>
> **All of the northern beaches have small, netted enclosures for safe swimming from October through May, when deadly stingers (box jellyfish) render all mainland beaches in north Queensland off-limits.**

Very Expensive

The Sebel Reef House & Spa ★★★ Picture yourself in a Somerset Maugham novel—substituting the Queensland tropics for Singapore—and you've almost got it. This is one of the most romantic hotels in Queensland, or all of Australia. The Reef House's guest list reads like an excerpt from *Who's Who.* But no matter who you are, you will not want to leave. The white walls are swathed in bougainvillea, and the beds with mosquito netting. Airy interiors feature handmade artifacts and white wicker furniture. The Verandah Spa rooms, which have a Jacuzzi on the balcony, overlook the pool, waterfalls, and lush gardens. They have extra touches, such as bathrobes, as well as balconies within earshot of the ocean. The beachfront **restaurant,** on a covered wooden deck beneath towering Paperbarks, is a favorite with locals and tourists alike for its unsurpassed ocean views, gentle breezes, and unpretentious food.

99 Williams Esplanade, Palm Cove, Cairns, QLD 4879. ✆ **1800/079 052** in Australia, or 07/4055 3633. Fax 07/4055 3305. www.reefhouse.com.au. 69 units, 14 with shower only. A$490–A$640 double; A$690–A$840 suite; A$590 family room (sleeps 4). AE, DC, MC, V. Free limited covered parking; ample street parking. Bus: 1, 1B, 1X, 2X, or N. **Amenities:** 2 restaurants; bar; airport shuttle; babysitting; concierge; nearby golf course; access to nearby health club; 3 small heated outdoor pools; room service; spa. *In room:* A/C, TV, VCR, CD player, hair dryer, Internet (A$6 for 30 min.; A$30 for 24 hr.), kitchenette, minibar.

Expensive

Peppers Beach Club & Spa ★ Set behind a grove of melaluca trees across the street from the beach, the main hotel in this resort, which opened in late 2002, has rooms and apartments with touches of Queensland colonial style. Hotel rooms are small but have Jacuzzis and timber outdoor furniture on the decks. Eight penthouses (three floors up) have private rooftop terraces and pools, but there's no elevator. A further 25 penthouses have Jacuzzis. The large lagoon-style pool has a sandy beach and swim-up bar. Coconut palms with white-painted trunks surround the lagoon, which is lit by flaming torches at night. The suites are secluded, with kitchens, gas barbecues, washers and dryers, and state-of-the-art entertainment units. Pampering awaits you at the **Sanctum Spa,** which has seven wet and dry treatment rooms and offers yoga classes, as well as beauty and massage treatments, for both men and women.

123 Williams Esplanade, Palm Cove, Cairns, QLD 4879. ✆ **1800/134 444** in Australia, 800/688-7444 in the U.S., or 07/4059 9200. Fax 07/4059 9222. www.peppers.com.au. 220 units. A$335 double; A$437 double 1-bedroom suite; A$627 2-bedroom suite; A$574–A$831 penthouse suite. Extra person A$45. 2-night minimum Sat–Sun. AE, DC, MC, V. Secure parking. **Amenities:** 4 restaurants; concierge; golf course nearby; health club; 3 outdoor pools; spa; tennis court. *In room:* A/C, TV w/pay movies, DVD player, CD player, hair dryer, minibar, Wi-Fi (A$6 for 30 min.).

Moderate

Ellis Beach Oceanfront Bungalows ★ On arguably the loveliest of the northern beaches, about 30 minutes from Cairns, these bungalows and cabins sit under palm trees between the Coral Sea and a backdrop of mountainous rainforest. Lifeguards patrol the beach, and there are stinger nets in season as well as a shady pool and toddlers' wading pool. There's plenty of privacy, and the accommodations are basic but pleasant. You can sit on the veranda and gaze at the ocean. Keep an eye out for dolphins. Each bungalow and cabin sleeps four and has full kitchen facilities (with microwave, fridge, and freezer), but cabins have no en-suite bathrooms (they use the communal facilities at the campground in the same complex). The property has a laundry, coin-operated barbecues, and phone and fax facilities.

Captain Cook Hwy., Ellis Beach, QLD 4879. ✆ **1800/637 036** in Australia, or 07/4055 3538. Fax 07/4055 3077. www.ellisbeach.com. 15 units, all with shower only. A$73–A$85 double cabin; A$130–A$185 double bungalow. Extra person A$15 cabin, A$25 bungalow. 2-night minimum stay; 3-night minimum June–Sept. AE, MC, V. **Amenities:** Restaurant; golf course nearby; 2 outdoor pools. *In room:* A/C, ceiling fans, TV, kitchen, no phone.

The Reef Retreat ★★ Tucked back one row of buildings from the beach is this little gem—a low-rise collection of contemporary studios and suites built around a swimming pool in a grove of palms and silver Paperbarks. All the rooms have cool tile floors and smart teak and cane furniture. The studios are a terrific value and much larger than the average hotel room. Some suites have two rooms; others have a Jacuzzi and a kitchenette outside on the balcony. There are also two-bedroom villas, which sleep up to six people. There's a barbecue and a Jacuzzi on the grounds.

There's no elevator. Units are serviced once for every 5-day stay. Extra cleanings are A$40 to A$58 or daily cleaning, on request, is A$25 to A$40 per day.

10–14 Harpa St., Palm Cove, Cairns, QLD 4879. ✆ **07/4059 1744.** Fax 07/4059 1745. www.reefretreat.com.au. 36 units, all with shower only. A$180 studio double; A$195 suite; A$310 2-bedroom suite or villa for up to 4; A$285 townhouse (sleeps up to 7). Extra person A$28. Children 2 and under stay free in parent's room with existing bedding. Crib A$10. AE, MC, V. Free parking. Bus: 1, 1B 1X, 2X, or N. **Amenities:** Nearby golf course; Jacuzzi; outdoor saltwater pool; nearby tennis courts. *In room:* A/C, TV, DVD, hair dryer, kitchenette, Wi-Fi (A$3 for 1 hr.; A$10 for 8 hr.).

ISLAND RESORTS

Several island resorts are within the Great Barrier Reef Marine Park off Cairns. They afford safe swimming year-round, because the infestations of deadly marine stingers that plague this area from October through May don't make it to the islands. They also offer snorkeling and diving opportunities every day.

Green Island Resort ★ Step off the beach at this Great Barrier Reef national park island and you are surrounded by acres of coral. The resort is a cluster of rooms tucked away in a dense vine forest. Each room is private and roomy, with wooden floors and a balcony looking into the forest. Windsurfing, surf-skiing, canoeing, diving and snorkeling (both on the island and on day trips to the outer Reef), glass-bottom-boat trips, self-guided rainforest walks, parasailing, and beach volleyball are among the activities available, or you can simply laze on the white-coral sand or by the guests-only pool. Helicopter and seaplane flights and cruises are available. Room rates include many activities and equipment, such as nonmotorized sports, snorkel gear, and glass-bottom-boat trips; there's a charge for scuba diving and other activities using fuel. Both the resort and the island are small (you can walk around it in 45 min.), and it is a popular day-tripper destination. But after they leave at 4:30pm, the place is blissfully peaceful.

Green Island, 27km (17 miles) east of Cairns (P.O. Box 898), Cairns, QLD 4870. ✆ **1800/673 366** in Australia, or 07/4031 3300. Fax 07/4052 1511. www.greenislandresort.com.au. 46 units. A$550–A$650 double. Extra person A$99. Children 13 and under stay free in parent's room using existing bedding. Rates include launch transfers. Ask about packages. AE, DC, MC, V. Helicopter and seaplane transfers available. **Amenities:** 2 restaurants; 2 bars; concierge; free Internet; 2 outdoor saltwater pools; spa. *In room:* A/C, TV, hair dryer, minibar.

Lizard Island ★★★ Luxury lodges, huge potato cod so tame divers can pet them, snorkeling off the beach, and isolation—that's what lures the well-heeled to this small, exclusive resort. Lizard is a rugged 1,000-hectare (2,470-acre) national park island on the Great Barrier Reef, sparsely vegetated but stunningly beautiful, ringed by 24 white sandy beaches, with fringing reefs that support a multitude of marine life including giant clams. No day-trippers are allowed. Room rates include many activities: snorkeling and glass-bottom-boat trips, catamarans, paddle-skis, fishing tackle, tennis, and hiking trails, such as the muscle-straining 545m (half-mile) climb to Cook's Look, where Captain Cook spied his way out of the treacherous reefs in 1770. You pay for fishing and diving trips to nearby Reef sites, including Cod Hole. Introductory dive lessons and night dives are available.

The 40 elegant free-standing villas are tucked under palms along the beach or perched on cliff tops overlooking the bay. They are built of timber and stone, in a casual tropical style, with earth and sea tone finishes. A guest lounge has Internet facilities, TV and video, bar facilities, and a book and games library. The **Azure Spa** offers a Vichy shower, double-massage room and steam room, and a range of therapies.

The most exclusive accommodations option, the **Pavilion,** is a villa offering complete privacy, sheer luxury, and spectacular panoramic views. It has private decks leading down to its own plunge pool, and comes with extras such as a laptop, binoculars, and Bollinger on arrival.

Lizard Island, 240km (149 miles) north of Cairns; 27km (17 miles) offshore. ✆ **1300/233 432** in Australia, or 03/9413 6288 (reservations office). Fax 03/9429 3992 (reservations office); 07/4043 1999 (resort). www.lizardisland.com.au. 40 units, all with shower only. A$3,400 double; A$3,996 villa double; A$4,560 suite double; A$7,500 Pavilion double. Extra person A$1,260. Rates are for 2-night minimum and include all meals and many activities. AE, DC, MC, V. Air transfers twice daily from Cairns take 1 hr. and cost A$510 per person round-trip. Aircraft luggage limit 15kg (33 lb.) per person. Air-charter transfers available. Children 11 and under not accepted. **Amenities:** Restaurant; health club; freshwater pool; spa; lit tennis court. *In room:* A/C, CD player, hair dryer, free Internet, minibar, MP3 docking station.

Where to Dine

IN CAIRNS

For cheap eats, head to the Esplanade along the seafront; it's lined with cafes, pizzerias, fish-and-chips places, food courts, and ice-cream parlors.

Ochre Restaurant ★ GOURMET BUSH TUCKER You could accuse this restaurant/bar of using weird and wonderful Aussie ingredients as a gimmick to pull in crowds, but the diners who have flocked here for the past decade or so know good food when they taste it. Daily specials are big on fresh local seafood, and the regular menu—which changes often—lets you devour the Aussie coat of arms in several different ways. Try salt-and-native-pepper crocodile and prawns with Vietnamese pickles and lemon aspen sambal, chargrilled kangaroo sirloin with a quandong chili glaze, sweet potato fritter, and bok choy, or maybe a slow-roasted emu filet. It can be very busy, and you may have to wait for a table, but the food is very good.

43 Shields St. ✆ **07/4051 0100.** www.ochrerestaurant.com.au. Reservations recommended. Main courses A$32–A$36. Australian game platter A$48 per person; seafood platter A$66 per person. Taste of Australia 4-course set menu A$66 per person (minimum 2 people). AE, DC, MC, V. Mon–Fri noon–3pm; daily 6pm–midnight. Closed Dec 25.

Perrotta's at the Gallery MODERN AUSTRALIAN The locals flock here for brunch and lunch, particularly on weekends, and you can team it with a visit to the Cairns Regional Art Gallery (the cafe is just outside). Breakfast differs from the usual bacon and eggs or pancakes, offering delights such as smoked salmon, sweet-potato hash browns with sour cream, and avocado. Those with a sweet tooth may go for French toast with cinnamon, caramelized apples, and honey mascarpone. For lunch, there's a choice of bruschettas, focaccia, panini, and pasta dishes, or more individual dishes such as barbecued Cajun Spanish mackerel with tomato and basil salad. At dinner, try wild barramundi, braised duck leg, or lamb shanks. Remember to check out the specials board.

Abbott and Shields sts. ✆ **07/4031 5899.** Reservations recommended. Breakfast A$3–A$8; lunch A$7–A$12; main courses at dinner A$15–A$25. AE, DC, MC, V. Daily 8:30am–11pm.

ON THE NORTHERN BEACHES

Colonies MODERN AUSTRALIAN It may not have the ocean frontage of the grander restaurants along Williams Esplanade, but the veranda of this cheery little aerie, upstairs behind a seafront building, is still within earshot of the waves. The atmosphere is simple, and the menu includes loads of inexpensive choices, such as pastas, soups, green chicken curry, and seafood. It's licensed and BYO, and there's often live music as well.

Upstairs in Paradise Village shopping center, Williams Esplanade, Palm Cove. ✆ **07/4055 3058.** Reservations recommended. Main courses A$24–A$41. MC, V. Daily 5–10pm. Bus: 1, 1B, 1X, 2X, or N.

Far Horizons MODERN AUSTRALIAN You can't quite sink your toes into the sand, but you are just yards from the beach at this pleasant restaurant in the Angsana Resort. The laid-back fine-dining fare includes plenty of fresh seafood—try offerings such as red emperor with roasted fennel and tomato salad, kipfler potato, and truffle cream dressing; or Hinchinbrook bluewater barramundi with brandade mash and saffron beurre blanc. The restaurant sometimes sets up tables on the lawn, among the palm trees beside the beach. The service is relaxed and friendly, and the crowd is a mix of guests from this and other nearby resorts.

In the Angsana Resort, 1 Veivers Rd. (southern end of Williams Esplanade), Palm Cove. ✆ **07/4055 3000.** Reservations recommended. Main courses A$25–A$30. AE, DC, MC, V. Daily 6:30–11am, noon–3pm, and 6:30–10pm. Bus: 1, 1B, 1X, 2X, or N.

Cairns After Dark

Young people and backpackers flock to **Gilligan's,** 57–89 Grafton St. (✆ **07/4041 6566;** www.gilligansbackpackers.com.au), where there are three bars to choose from. The **Beer Deck** has live entertainment Tuesday to Sunday, and you can watch all the big sporting events on the biggest outdoor screen in Cairns. The 1,000-person **Beer Hall** doubles as a nightclub with a dance floor, DJs, and live bands; and **The Attic** is a lounge and cocktail bar. For something more sophisticated, try **Ba8** (✆ **03/4052 7670;** www.ba8.com.au), at the Shangri-La hotel on the marina. It's open daily from noon to midnight. The **Reef Casino,** 35–41 Wharf St. (✆ **07/4030 8888**), has two levels of blackjack, baccarat, reef routine, roulette, sic-bo, money wheel, paradise pontoon, keno, and slot machines. It's open Sunday through Thursday 9am to 3am, and from 9am Friday and Saturday until 5am the next day. It's closed Good Friday, Christmas Day, and until 1pm on April 25 (Anzac Day). No entry for children under 18.

PORT DOUGLAS ★★

Port Douglas: 67km (42 miles) N of Cairns; Mossman: 19km (12 miles) N of Port Douglas; Daintree: 49km (30 miles) N of Port Douglas; Cape Tribulation: 34km (21 miles) N of Daintree

The fishing village of Port Douglas is where the rainforest meets the Reef. Just over an hour's drive from Cairns, through rainforest and along the sea, Port Douglas may be small, but stylish shops and seriously trendy restaurants line the main street, and beautiful Four Mile Beach is not to be missed. This is a favorite spot with celebrities big and small—you may find yourself dining next to anyone from Bill Clinton to Kylie Minogue, Sean Penn to rock bands or minor Aussie soap stars.

Travelers often base themselves in "Port," as the locals call it, rather than in Cairns, because they like the rural surroundings, the uncrowded beach, and the absence of tacky development (so far, anyway). Don't think you will be isolated—many Reef and rainforest tours originate in Port Douglas, and many of the tours discussed in the Cairns section earlier pick up from Port Douglas.

Port Douglas, Daintree & Cape Tribulation

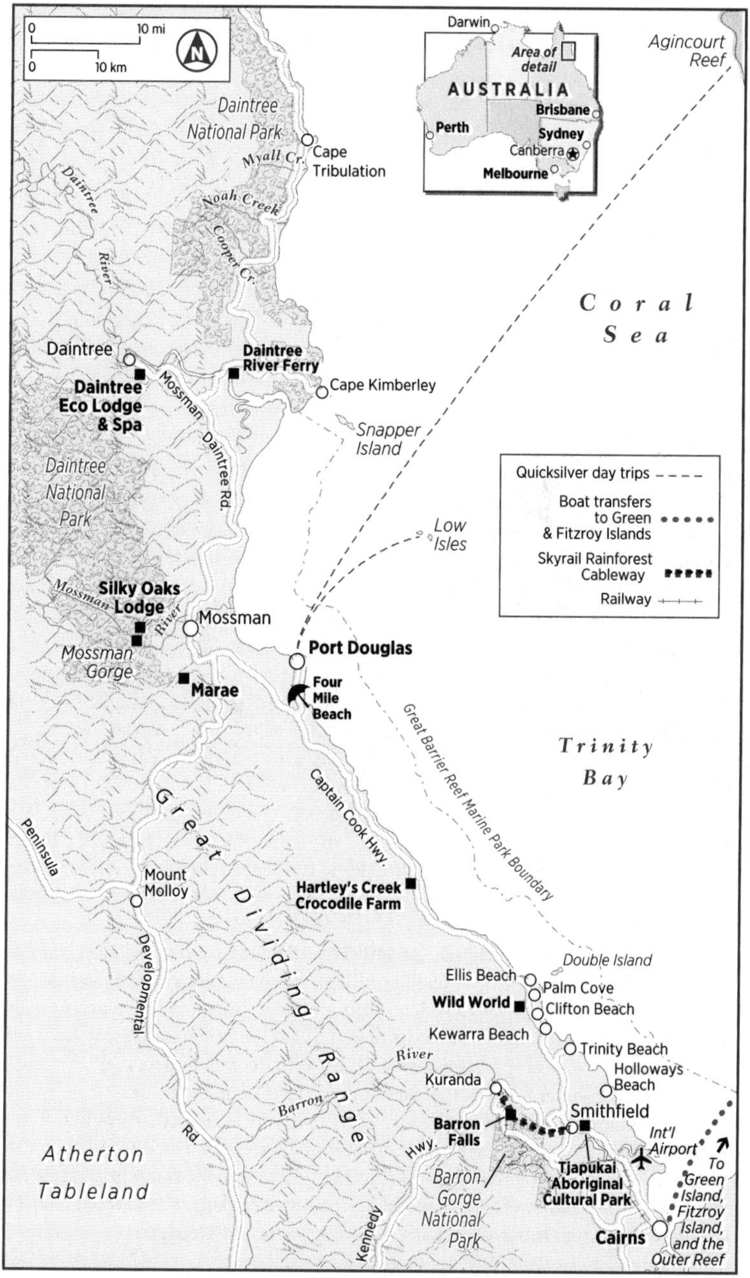

0
10 mi
0
10 km
N
Darwin
Area of detail
AUSTRALIA
Brisbane
Perth
Sydney
Canberra
Melbourne
Agincourt Reef
Daintree National Park
Cape Tribulation
Myall Cr.
Noah Creek
Cooper Cr.
Daintree River
Daintree
Daintree River Ferry
Cape Kimberley
Daintree Eco Lodge & Spa
Mossman Daintree Rd.
Snapper Island
Coral Sea
Quicksilver day trips
Boat transfers to Green & Fitzroy Islands
Skyrail Rainforest Cableway
Railway
Daintree National Park
Low Isles
Silky Oaks Lodge
Mossman River
Mossman
Port Douglas
Mossman Gorge
Marae
Four Mile Beach
Great Barrier Reef Marine Park Boundary
Trinity Bay
Captain Cook Hwy.
Great Dividing Range
Peninsula Developmental Rd.
Mount Molloy
Hartley's Creek Crocodile Farm
Double Island
Ellis Beach
Palm Cove
Wild World
Clifton Beach
Kewarra Beach
Trinity Beach
Barron River
Holloways Beach
Kuranda
Smithfield
Barron Falls
Int'l Airport
Kennedy Hwy.
Tjapukai Aboriginal Cultural Park
To Green Island, Fitzroy Island, and the Outer Reef
Atherton Tableland
Barron Gorge National Park
Cairns

Daintree National Park lies just north of Port Douglas; that is just north of Cape Tribulation National Park, another wild tract of rainforest and hilly headlands sweeping down to the sea. Exploring these two national parks is easy on a four-wheel-drive day safari from Port Douglas.

Essentials

GETTING THERE Port Douglas is a scenic 65-minute drive from Cairns, in part along a narrow winding road that skirts the coast. Take Sheridan Street north out of the city as it becomes the Captain Cook Highway; follow the signs to Mossman and Mareeba until you reach the Port Douglas turnoff on your right.

A one-way ticket with **Sun Palm Australia Coach** (✆ **07/4087 2900;** www.sunpalmtransport.com) to Port Douglas hotels from Cairns airport is A$35 adults, A$15 children 2 to 12. If you are staying in Cairns but taking a **Quicksilver ★** (✆ **07/4087 2100**) cruise to the Great Barrier Reef for the day, you can take a bus transfer to Port Douglas for A$18 adults, A$10 for kids, or A$46 for a family of four.

A **taxi** fare from Cairns to Port Douglas is a set price of A$168; call **Black & White Taxis** (✆ **13 10 08** in Cairns).

There is no train to Port Douglas, and no scheduled air service. A small airport handles light aircraft and helicopter charters.

VISITOR INFORMATION There is no official visitor information office in Port Douglas. Instead, visitors should stop into a private tour information and booking center in town. One of the biggest and most centrally located is the **Port Douglas Tourist Information Centre,** 23 Macrossan St. (✆ **07/4099 5599;** www.tourismportdouglas.com.au), open from 7:30am to 6pm daily. Another good source of information is **Tourism Port Douglas and Daintree** (✆ **07/4099 4588;** www.pddt.com.au).

GETTING AROUND Of the major rental companies, **Avis** (✆ **07/4099 4331**), **Budget** (✆ **07/4099 5702**), and **Thrifty** (✆ **07/4069 9977**) have offices in Port Douglas. All rent regular vehicles as well as four-wheel-drives, which you need if you plan to drive to Cape Tribulation. For a taxi, call **Port Douglas Taxis** (✆ **13 10 08**).

A good way to get around the town's flat streets is by bike. **Holiday Bike Hire,** 46 Macrossan St. (✆ **07/4099 6144**), or **Port Douglas Bike Hire,** 28 Wharf St. (✆ **07/4099 5799**), rent bikes for around A$10 for a half-day, A$15 for a full day.

Exploring the Reef & the Rainforest

DISCOVERING THE GREAT BARRIER REEF Without a doubt, the most glamorous large vessels visiting the Outer Reef are the **Quicksilver Wavepiercers** (✆ **07/4087 2100;** www.quicksilver-cruises.com) based out of Port Douglas. These ultrasleek, high-speed, air-conditioned 37m (121-ft.) and 46m (151-ft.) catamarans carry 300 or 440 passengers to Agincourt Reef, a ribbon reef 39 nautical miles (72km/45 miles) from shore on the outer edge of the Reef. After the 90-minute trip to the Reef, you tie up at a two-story pontoon, where you spend 3½ hours.

Quicksilver departs Marina Mirage at 10am daily except on December 25. The cost for the day is A$197 for adults, A$99 for kids 4 to 14, or A$493 for families of four. Guided snorkel safaris cost A$45 per adult, half-price for kids, and introductory dives cost A$139 per person. Qualified divers take a dive-tender boat to make one dive for A$97 or two dives for A$139 per person, all gear included. Because Quicksilver carries so many passengers, booking snorkel safaris and dives in advance is a good idea.

The dive boat ***Poseidon*** (see "Diving the Reef," earlier in this chapter) welcomes snorkelers. It presents a Reef ecology talk and takes you on a guided snorkel safari. The price of A$180 for adults, A$125 for children 4 to 14, or A$549 for a family of four includes lunch and transfers from Port Douglas hotels.

The snorkeling specialist boat ***Wavelength*** (**© 07/4099 5031;** www.wavelength.com.au) does a full-day trip to the Outer Reef for A$190 for adults, A$140 for children 14 and under, and A$600 for families of four. The trip visits three different snorkel sites each day and incorporates a guided snorkel tour and a reef presentation by a marine biologist. It carries only 30 passengers and includes snorkel gear, sunsuits, lunch, and transfers from your hotel. Both beginners and experienced snorkelers will like this trip. It departs daily at 8:15am from the Wavelength jetty on Wharf Street.

Another way to spend a pleasant day—closer to shore—on the Great Barrier Reef is to visit the **Low Isles,** 15km (9½ miles) northeast of Port Douglas. The isles are 1.5-hectare (3¾-acre) coral-cay specks of lush vegetation surrounded by white sand and 22 hectares (54 acres) of coral—which is what makes them so appealing. The coral is not quite as good as the outer Reef's, but the fish life is rich, and the proximity makes for a relaxing day.

The trip aboard the 30m (98-ft.) luxury sailing catamaran ***Wavedancer*** (**© 07/4087 2100**), operated by Quicksilver, is A$138 for adults, A$69 for kids 4 to 14, and A$345 for families. Once there, you can snorkel, take a glass-bottom-boat ride or do a guided beach walk with a marine biologist. Coach transfers are available through Quicksilver from your Port Douglas accommodations for A$6 adults, A$4 kids or A$16 for a family, or from Cairns and Palm Cove for A$18 adults, A$10 children or A$46 for a family of four.

EXPLORING DAINTREE NATIONAL PARK & CAPE TRIBULATION The World Heritage–listed Daintree Rainforest has remained largely unchanged over the past 110 million years. It is now home to rare plants that provide key links in the evolution story. In the 56,000-hectare (138,320-acre) **Daintree National Park,** you will find cycads, dinosaur trees, fan palms, giant strangler figs, and epiphytes such as the basket fern, staghorn, and elkhorn. Nighttime croc-spotting tours on the Daintree River vie for popularity with early morning cruises to see the rich bird life. Pythons, lizards, frogs, and electric-blue Ulysses butterflies attract photographers, and sport fishermen come here to do battle with big barramundi.

The **Daintree Discovery Centre** (**© 07/4098 9171;** www.daintree-rec.com.au) is a multi-award-winning attraction accredited by the Wet Tropics Management Authority. The center's aerial walkway links the entrance to the 23m (76-ft.) high Canopy Tower and the display center, which provides easy-to-understand information about the surrounding rainforest. The display center has the latest touch-screen technology, an audio-visual theater, and sweeping all-weather verandas. It is 10km (6 miles) north of the Daintree River ferry crossing. Entry costs A$28 adults, A$14 children 5 to 17, and A$68 for a family of four. The center is open daily 8:30am to 5pm (except Christmas Day).

Just about everyone who visits Port Douglas takes a guided four-wheel-drive day trip into the beautiful Daintree and Cape Tribulation rainforests. Although they are two separate national parks, the forests merge into one.

You can rent a four-wheel-drive and explore on your own, but you won't understand much about what you are seeing unless you have a guide. Most companies basically cover the same territory and sights; they include a 1-hour Daintree River cruise to spot crocs, a visit to the Marrdja Botanical Walk, a stroll along an isolated beach, lunch at a pretty spot somewhere in the forest, and a visit to Mossman Gorge. Some tours also go to the picturesque Bloomfield Falls in Cape Tribulation National Park. Expect to pay about A$150 per adult and about A$100 per child. Trips that include Bloomfield Falls cost more. A company that provides an excellent, gently adventurous alternative is Pete Baxendell's **Heritage & Interpretive Tours ★** (**© 07/4098 7897;** www.nqhit.com.au). On a daylong bushwalk into a tract of privately owned rainforest with Pete, a naturalist and professional tour guide, you taste green ants (be brave—it's quite an experience) and other native "bush tucker," discover how to rustle up a toothbrush from a shrub if you forgot to pack yours, learn about bush medicine and the wildlife around you, and clamber up a stream to a waterfall. He takes a maximum of six people at a time. Lunch and Port Douglas pickups are included in the price of A$140 per person. Pickups from Cairns and the northern beaches can be organized through BTS Tours (see below) for an extra cost. Walks run Tuesday and Saturday, leaving Port at 8:30am. On other days, the bushwalks run for A$185 per person (minimum of two). A "Rainforest Experience" tour costs A$200 per person for up to three people, or A$700 for a group of six.

You can also **charter** Pete and his four-wheel-drive for longer "go anywhere" adventures. The cost of this is A$700 per day for a group of up to six. The charter prices compare favorably to a regular Daintree four-wheel-drive tour—if there are three or more of you—and you get a tailored itinerary, Pete's knowledge, and the vehicle all to yourself. He often takes charter customers inland to Outback gold mining ghost towns, or north to tiny Cooktown, which boasts an excellent museum devoted to Australia's "discoverer," Capt. James Cook. If you have 2 days, he can take you farther west to see Aboriginal rock art, or to the amazing Undara Lava Tubes.

Other established operators are **Trek North Safaris** (**© 07/4033 2600;** www.treknorth.com.au) and **BTS Tours** (**© 07/4099 5665;** www.btstours.com.au). As is the case in most tourist hot spots, some tour operators battle fiercely to pay tour desks the highest commission to recommend their tours, even though those tours may not necessarily be the best for your needs. Take tour desks' recommendations with a grain of salt, and ask other travelers for their recommendations. You may not see too much wildlife—rainforest animals are shy, camouflaged, nocturnal, or all three! Most four-wheel-drive tours will pick you up in Port Douglas at no charge; there is usually a fee from Cairns and the northern beaches. Floods and swollen creeks can quash your plans to explore the Daintree in the Wet season (Dec–Mar or Apr), so keep your plans flexible.

If your chosen safari does not visit **Mossman Gorge,** 21km (13 miles) northwest of Port Douglas near the sugar town of Mossman, try to get there under your own steam. The gushing river tumbling over boulders and the short forest walks are magical. (Don't climb on the rocks or enter the river, because strong currents are extremely dangerous and have claimed at least one life in recent years.)

Most four-wheel-drive Daintree tours include a 1-hour cruise on the **Daintree River ★**, but if yours does not, or you want to spend more time on the river, cruises are available on a variety of boats, ranging from open-sided "river trains" to small fishing boats. One of the best is with **Dan Irby's Mangrove Adventures ★** (**© 07/4090 7017;** www.mangroveadventures.com.au), whose small open boat can get up side creeks the bigger boats can't. Originally from Tonkawa, Oklahoma, Dan has been in Australia for 36 years and is extremely knowledgeable about the wildlife and habitat. He takes no more than 10 people at a time on 2- to 4-hour cruises. It is very important to make advance reservations with Dan (at least 24 hr. ahead, if possible) to determine which days he is operating, departure times, and seat availability. Daytime tours (the first at 8am) leave from the public jetty next to the Daintree River ferry crossing. Take the Captain Cook Highway north to Mossman, where it becomes the Mossman Daintree Road, and follow it for 24km (15 miles) to the signposted turnoff for the ferry on your right. The ferry is 5km (3 miles) from the turnoff. You'll need a car to get there, as Dan does not do transfers from hotels. Chances are you will spot lots of fascinating wildlife and birds on his 2-hour night cruise, but even if you don't, it's worth it just to see the stars! Night tours leave from Daintree Eco Lodge, 20 Mossman Daintree Rd., 4km (2½ miles) south of Daintree village; you can combine an afternoon tour, followed by an hour's break, with the night tour. A 2-hour trip costs A$50.

Birders love the Wet Tropics rainforests, which include the Daintree and Cape Tribulation national parks. More than half of Australia's bird species have been recorded within 200km (120 miles) of this area. **Fine Feather Tours** (© **07/4094 1199;** www.finefeathertours.com.au) has a full-day bird-watching safari through the Wet Tropics to the edge of the Outback for A$235, an afternoon cruise on the Daintree River for A$175, and other tours.

Rainforest Habitat wildlife sanctuary (© **07/4099 3235;** www.rainforesthabitat.com.au) is a great place to see the animals that are too shy to be spotted in the wild. Here, 180 animal species from the Wet Tropics are in one place for you to see up close. You can see saltwater and freshwater crocodiles, hand-feed kangaroos, and have your photo taken with a koala. The highlight is the walk-through aviary, which houses more than 100 Wet Tropics bird species, including cassowaries. You'll get the most out of your visit if you take one of the excellent free guided tours that run regularly throughout the day from 9:30am to 3:15pm. Rainforest Habitat is on Port Douglas Road at the turnoff from the Captain Cook Highway. It's open daily (except Dec 25) from 8am to 5pm. Admission is A$30 for adults, A$15 for kids 4 to 14, or A$75 for families of four. Tickets allow entry for 3 consecutive days. Between 8 and 10:30am, the park serves "breakfast with the birds" for A$44 for adults, A$22 for kids, or A$110 families, including admission. Between noon and 2pm you can "lunch with the lorikeets" for the same price. Allow at least 2 hours here.

DISCOVERING ABORIGINAL CULTURE Members of the native KuKu-Yalanji tribe will teach you about bush medicines and food, Dreamtime legends, and the sacred sites their families have called home for thousands of years. **KuKu-Yalanji Dreamtime ★** (© **07/4098 2595;** www.yalanji.com.au) offers a guided walk through the rainforest to see cave paintings and visit special sites. The tour is followed by a Dreamtime story and didgeridoo performance over billy tea and damper in a bark *warun* (shelter). You can buy artifacts from the information center, gift shop, and art gallery (8:30am–5pm Mon–Sat; closed Christmas Day to New Year's Day, Easter, Mossman Show day—usually third Mon of July—and sometimes for cultural reasons). Walks last 90 minutes and leave daily (except Sun) at 9 and 11am, and 1 and 3pm from the KuKu-Yalanji community, on the road to Mossman Gorge (1km/half-mile before you reach the Gorge parking lot). Tours cost A$32 for adults, A$19 children under 12, A$80 for families of four. Pickups from Port Douglas can be arranged at an extra cost.

More to See & Do

Some companies in Cairns that offer outdoor activities will pick up from Port Douglas hotels. See "White-Water Rafting & Other Thrills," in the Cairns section earlier in this chapter for details.

The best outdoor activity in Port Douglas, however, is to do absolutely nothing on spectacular **Four Mile Beach ★★**. From May through September, the water is stinger-free. From October through April, swim in the stinger safety net.

Visitor greens fees at the championship **Sheraton Mirage** golf course on Port Douglas Road are A$150 for 18 holes or A$95 for 9 holes, including a cart. Club rental costs A$40 to A$60. Whacking a ball on the hotel's aquatic driving range costs A$6.50 for a bucket of 25, A$13 for 50 balls, plus A$2.15 for club rental. Contact the **pro shop** (✆ **07/4099 5537**).

Wonga Beach Equestrian Centre (✆ **07/4099 1117;** www.beachhorserides.com.au) does 3-hour horseback rides through the rainforest and along Wonga Beach, 35 minutes north of Port Douglas, for A$115 per person, plus A$10 per person for insurance. Transfers from Port Douglas are included. Rides start at 8:30am and 2:30pm. Riders must be age 7 or older. If you want a shorter ride, private 90-minute or 2½-hour rides (minimum two riders) can be arranged for A$180 or A$220 per person.

> **The Secret of the Seasons**
>
> **High season in Port Douglas is roughly June 1 through October 31. Low-season holiday periods run from approximately November to May (excluding Christmas and New Year's).**

Every Sunday from 7:30am to 1pm, a colorful handicrafts and fresh food market sets up on the lawn under the mango trees beside Dickson Inlet, at the end of Macrossan Street. Stalls offer everything from foot massages to fresh coconut milk. While you're here, take a peek or attend a nondenominational service inside the pretty timber St. Mary's by the Sea church.

Where to Stay

Port Douglas Accommodation Holiday Rentals (✆ **1800/645 566** in Australia, or 07/4099 4488; www.portdouglasaccom.com.au) has a wide range of apartments and homes for rent.

VERY EXPENSIVE

Sheraton Mirage Port Douglas ★★★ One of Australia's most luxurious properties, this low-rise Sheraton has 2 hectares (5 acres) of saltwater pools and a championship Peter Thomson–designed 18-hole golf course. It is a bit too far from Port's main street by foot, but a free shuttle runs from 9am to 6pm to the golf course's country club and health center, to Marina Mirage shopping center, and into town. All the rooms are large and light-filled, and the resort underwent extensive refurbishment in 2008, with new color schemes, furniture, and artwork, and such extras as mini–stereo systems. All rooms have minibars, PlayStations, and Internet access. You might upgrade to a Mirage room with a Jacuzzi and king-size bed, but I thought the standard rooms were just fine. The Sheraton also handles rentals of 101 privately owned two-, three-, and four-bedroom luxury villas with golf course, garden, or sea views; the decor varies, but each has a kitchenette, a Jacuzzi, and two bathrooms.

Davidson St. (off Port Douglas Rd.), Port Douglas, QLD 4877. ✆ **1800/073 535** in Australia; 800/325-3535 in the U.S. and Canada; 00800/325 353535 in the U.K., Ireland, and New Zealand; or 07/4099 5888. Fax 07/4099 4424, or Starwood Hotels reservation fax 07/4099 5398. www.sheraton.com. 394 units, including 101 villas. A$619–A$830 double; A$2,500 suite; A$990–A$1,190 2-, 3-, or 4-bedroom villa. Extra person A$69. Children 17 and under stay free in parent's room with existing bedding. Discounts available. AE, DC, MC, V. Free valet and self-parking. Helicopter transfers available. **Amenities:** 3 restaurants; 2 bars; babysitting; bikes; daily day care for kids 4 and under and kids' club for children 5–15 during school vacations (fee); concierge; 18-hole championship golf course w/country club and pro shop, aquatic driving range (w/targets in a lake), putting green, and golf clinics; health club; Jacuzzi; 25m (82-ft.) outdoor lap pool; room service; sauna; spa; 9 lit tennis courts. *In room:* A/C, TV, hair dryer, Internet (A$15 for 1 hr.; A$25 for 24 hr.).

EXPENSIVE

Port Douglas Peninsula Boutique Hotel ★★ This intimate studio apartment hotel fronting Four Mile Beach is one of the nicest places to stay in town. Every apartment features an open-plan living room/bedroom, a contemporary kitchenette (with microwave and dishwasher), and a groovy bathroom boasting a giant double tub (or Jacuzzi, in some units). Corner apartments are a little bigger. The decor is a stylish mélange of terra-cotta, mosaic tiles, granite, and wicker, with classy extra touches such as a CD player and boxed Twining's teas. Most units have great beach views from the roomy balcony or patio; a few look onto a green and mauve complex of petite Art Deco–ish pools, waterfalls, hot and cold Jacuzzis, and sun decks rising and falling on several levels. The Peninsula Suite has a private Jacuzzi and wrap-around veranda. A 2-minute walk brings you to the main street.

9–13 The Esplanade, Port Douglas, QLD 4877. ✆ **1800/676 674** in Australia, or 07/4099 9100. Fax 07/4099 5440. www.peninsulahotel.com.au. 34 units. A$290–A$420 double; A$470 double Peninsula Suite (3-night minimum). Rates include breakfast. Ask about packages and seasonal specials. AE, DC, MC, V. Free covered parking. Children 16 and under not accepted. **Amenities:** Restaurant; bar; free airport transfers; bikes; Jacuzzi; large outdoor pool. *In room:* A/C, TV, VCR, hair dryer, Internet (A$15 for 24 hr.; A$45 for whole stay), kitchenette.

MODERATE

By the Sea ★ You won't find a friendlier or more convenient place to stay in Port Douglas than these apartments, 10 seconds from the beach and less than 10 minutes' walk from town. New owners have completely refurbished the apartments, including new kitchens and televisions, without raising the rates. There are also heaps of new "extras" such as bikes and laptops on loan. The apartments are on the small side (most suit only three people), but all are well cared for. You can opt for a tiny Garden apartment with a patio; Balcony and Seaview apartments are a bit larger and have private balconies. Seaview apartments are quite roomy and have side views of Four Mile Beach. Towels are changed daily and linen weekly, and rooms are serviced every 5 days (or you can pay A$25 per day extra for daily service). There's no elevator and no porter, so be prepared to carry your luggage upstairs.

72 Macrossan St., Port Douglas, QLD 4877. ✆ **07/4099 5387.** Fax 07/4099 4847. www.bytheseaportdouglas.com.au. 21 units, all with shower only. High season (June–Oct) A$133–A$235 double; low season A$75–A$175 double. Additional person A$25. AE, MC, V. Free covered parking. **Amenities:** Bikes; nearby golf course; access to nearby health club; Jacuzzi; outdoor heated pool; 6 nearby lit tennis courts. *In room:* A/C, TV, hair dryer, Internet (A$5 for 1 hr. to A$25 for 20 hr.), kitchenette.

Port Douglas Retreat This well-kept two-story studio apartment complex on a quiet street, featuring the white-battened balconies of the Queenslander architectural style, is a good value. Even some of the ritzier places in town can't boast its lagoonlike saltwater pool, surrounded by dense jungle and wrapped by an ample shady sun deck that cries out to be lounged on with a good book and a cool drink. The apartments are not enormous, but they're fashionably furnished with terra-cotta tile floors, wrought-iron beds, cane seating, and colorful bedcovers. All have large furnished balconies or patios looking into tropical gardens; some on the ground floor open onto the common-area boardwalk, so you might want to ask for a first-floor (second-story) unit. The town and beach are a 5-minute walk away.

31–33 Mowbray St. (at Mudlo St.), Port Douglas, QLD 4877. ✆ **07/4099 5053.** Fax 07/4099 5033. www.portdouglasretreat.com.au. 36 units, all with shower only. A$145–A$179 double. Extra person A$50. Crib A$10 per night. Minimum 2-night stay. Ask about longer stay deals. AE, MC, V. Secure covered parking. **Amenities:** Free airport transfers; outdoor saltwater pool. *In room:* A/C, TV w/free movies, hair dryer, kitchenette, Wi-Fi.

INEXPENSIVE

Port O'Call Eco Lodge This modest lodge on a suburban street a 10-minute walk from town has gone "green." With 100% of its hot water provided by solar power, Port O'Call has become the first Queensland accommodations to gain a four-green-star rating for ecological sustainability from Australia's AAA Tourism rating system. It also operates with wind energy for public and outside lighting and water and waste minimization programs. Backpackers, families, and travelers on a budget seem to treat it like a second home, swapping stories as they cook a meal in the communal kitchen and dining room. The rooms are light, cool, and fresh with tile floors, loads of luggage and bench space, and small patios. New double and quad rooms were added in 2004, and half the double rooms have king-size beds. The hostel rooms have private bathrooms. There are six-share bunk rooms and backpacker double rooms, renovated in 2008. At night, the lively poolside **Port O'Call Bistro** is the place to be. Other features include free board games, a pay phone, and a kiosk selling refreshments.

Port St. at Craven Close, Port Douglas, QLD 4877. ✆ **1800/892 800** in Australia, or 07/4099 5422. Fax 07/4099 5495. www.portocall.com.au. 28 units, all with shower only. A$109–A$139 double for budget and deluxe motel rooms. Extra person A$20. Backpacker double rooms A$75 YHA members, or A$84 nonmembers; hostel quad rooms A$32 YHA members, or A$35 nonmembers; bunkhouse A$26 YHA members, A$29 nonmembers. Children 2 and under stay free in parent's room. MC, V. Free parking. Bus: 1X (stop at front door). **Amenities:** Restaurant (see review, p. 310); free airport transfers; bikes; 3 golf courses nearby; access to nearby health club; outdoor pool. *In room:* A/C, TV, DVD player and CD player (deluxe rooms only), hair dryer, Wi-Fi.

A LUXURY B&B IN THE COUNTRY

Marae ★★ John and Pam Burden's architecturally stunning timber home, on a hillside 15km (9½ miles) north of Port Douglas, is a glamorous and restful retreat. The rustic-meets-sleek contemporary bedrooms have white mosquito nets and smart linens on king-size beds, and elegant bathrooms. The garden room overlooks the valley and the cool plunge pool. Wallabies and bandicoots (small marsupials) feed in the garden, kingfishers and honeyeaters use the two busy birdbaths, and butterflies are everywhere. A delicious tropical breakfast is served on the west deck in the company of a flock of red-browed finches and peaceful doves. Afterward you can wander the rainforest trails of Mossman Gorge, just a few minutes away.

Lot 1, Chook's Ridge, Shannonvale (P.O. Box 133), Port Douglas, QLD 4877. ✆ **07/4098 4900.** www.marae.com.au. 2 units, 1 with shower only. A$145 single; A$195 double. 2-night minimum. Rates include full breakfast. MC, V. Covered parking. Children 12 and under not accepted. **Amenities:** Nearby golf courses. *In room:* A/C, TV, hair dryer, Wi-Fi (A$10 per stay).

RAINFOREST HIDEAWAYS

Daintree Eco Lodge & Spa ★ Check in and head straight for the Daintree Spa. Here you can relax and soak up all kinds of pampering treatments, including the 2-hour, A$295 Walbul-Walbul body treatment, in which you are wrapped in mud as you recline on a magnificent carved timber "wet bed," and the Wawa Jirakul waterfall treatment. It's bliss.

A multiple award winner for "green tourism," this lodge in the primeval forest books only a small number of guests. Don't think "eco" means sacrificing creature comforts: The large rooms boast marble floors, timber and bamboo furniture, and tiled bathrooms with robes. Five have Jacuzzis on their screened balconies.

You can join a yoga, meditation, or Pilates session, laze by the small solar-heated pool, walk rainforest trails, or join members of the local Aboriginal KuKu-Yalanji tribe on a bush tucker and native medicine stroll. The **Julaymba Restaurant** overlooks a lily pond and serves food with a gourmet bush-tucker slant. The lodge is 98km (61 miles) north of Cairns and 40km (25 miles) north of Port Douglas.

20 Daintree Rd. (4km/2½ miles south of Daintree village), Daintree, QLD 4873. ✆ **1800/808 010** in Australia, or 07/4098 6100. Fax 07/4098 6200. www.daintree-ecolodge.com.au. 15 units, 10 with shower only. A$550–A$598 double. Extra adult A$90, children A$60. Ask about packages. AE, DC, MC, V. Take Captain Cook Hwy. north to Mossman, where it becomes the Mossman-Daintree Rd.; follow to lodge. The road is paved all the way. No children 6 and under. **Amenities:** Restaurant; pool; spa. *In room:* A/C, TV w/free movies, CD player, hair dryer, minibar, Wi-Fi.

Silky Oaks Lodge & Healing Waters Spa ★★ Relax in the hammock on your veranda and listen to the waters of the Mossman River gushing through the rainforest. Stroll down for a swim—no crocs here. Despite its popularity, this luxury resort tucked away at the edge of cane fields exudes a restful feeling. There are Treehouses scattered through the rainforest and gardens; the five Riverhouses overlook the river frontage, and all have Jacuzzis. Each unit has timber floors, attractive furnishings, a king-size bed, bathrobes, a CD player—but no TV—and a double hammock. Rates include guided nature walks, tennis, mountain bikes, and kayaking or snorkeling in the Mossman River, and there is a daily activities program. For a spot of pampering, head to Healing Waters Spa. To reach Mossman Gorge's lovely walking trails, across the river, you'll need a car.

Finlayvale Rd., Mossman, 7km (4½ miles) west of Mossman township; 27km (17 miles) from Port Douglas. ✆ **07/4098 1666.** Fax 07/4098 1983. www.silkyoakslodge.com.au. 50 units. A$598–A$798 double. Extra person A$62. Rates include full breakfast, some activities, and a morning and afternoon shuttle from Port Douglas. Ask about packages. AE, DC, MC, V. Take Captain Cook Hwy. to Mossman, where it becomes the Mossman-Daintree Rd.; follow approximately 3.5km (2¼ miles) past Mossman and turn left onto Finlayvale Rd. at the small white-on-blue SILKY OAKS sign. Children 14 and under not accepted. **Amenities:** Restaurant; bar; exercise room; free Internet; outdoor pool; spa; lit tennis court. *In room:* A/C, ceiling fans, CD player, hair dryer, minibar.

Thala Beach Lodge ★★ "Where are the walls?" may be your first question on arriving at this Balinese-style luxury hideaway in the rainforest outside Port Douglas. The reception area and lobby are open, to stunning effect. From the elevated restaurant, the impact is even greater, with sweeping views from the Daintree to Cape Grafton, south of Cairns. Thala (pronounced *Ta*-la) Beach is on a 59-hectare (146-acre) private peninsula, bordered on three sides by private beaches and coves. Owners Rob and Oonagh Prettejohn opened the lodge in 1998, taking their inspiration from the flora and fauna of the World Heritage area that surrounds it. The secluded bungalows are spacious and comfortable, with timber-paneled walls and your choice of king-size or twin beds. All are built on high poles in the trees, where dazzling lorikeets and small red-faced flying foxes feed on blossoms and hang contentedly from the branches. The 16 Coral Sea bungalows overlook the ocean; the rest have forest and mountain views. Some of the bungalows are a bit of a hike from the public areas, but it's a small price to pay for the privacy and the rainforest setting.

Private Rd., Oak Beach, 16km (10 miles) south of Port Douglas. ✆ **07/4098 5700.** Fax 07/4098 5837. www.thalabeach.com.au. 85 units. A$249–A$698 double. AE, DC, MC, V. Free valet parking. **Amenities:** 2 restaurants; 2 bars; free airport transfers with some packages, A$26 for room-only rates; nearby golf course; 2 outdoor pools; room service; Wi-Fi (free). *In room:* A/C, ceiling fans, TV, DVD player, CD player, hair dryer, minibar.

Where to Dine

Nautilus ★ TROPICAL/SEAFOOD This restaurant has a fascinating history spanning more than 55 years and is a Port Douglas institution. But word from the locals is that service can be patchy, and that this is one restaurant that needs to sharpen its game against increasing competition down the street. The setting, however, makes up for some of the criticism: Tables are set under towering palm trees and the open sky, with a clever seating plan and unusual high-backed chairs that create a wonderfully intimate atmosphere. Local produce and seafood are the mainstays of the menu, and the signature dish is a whole coral trout dusted in spices and crisp-fried, with a palm sugar dressing and pickled green papaya salad. For true indulgence, order the six-course degustation menu for your table, at A$110 per person, with five matched wines for an extra A$50.

17 Murphy St. (entry also from Macrossan St.), Port Douglas. ✆ **07/4099 5330.** www.nautilus-restaurant.com.au. Reservations recommended. Main courses A$34–A$52. AE, DC, MC, V. Daily 5:30–10:30pm or until the last diners leave. Children 7 and under not accepted.

Port O'Call Bistro ☺ CAFE/BISTRO Locals patronize this poolside bistro and bar at the Port O'Call Lodge (p. 308) almost as often as guests do, because it offers good, honest food, such as lamb shanks and steaks, in hearty portions at painless prices. The atmosphere is fun and friendly. There are pasta and curry dishes, and every night you can try one of the chef's blackboard surprises, including local seafood. There are kids' meals for A$8, as well as burgers, chicken, and Asian stir-fries to appeal to everyone.

In the Port O'Call Lodge, Port St. at Craven Close. ✆ **07/4099 5422.** Main courses A$15–A$25. MC, V. Daily 6pm–midnight.

Salsa Bar & Grill ★★ ☺ MODERN/TROPICAL This trendy restaurant, in a timber Queenslander with wraparound verandas, has terrific food, great prices, and lively, fun service. Here you can choose simple fare such as gnocchi or Caesar salad, or such mouthwatering delights as a jambalaya with tiger prawns, squid, yabbie, smoked chicken, and crocodile sausages; or a rare seared yellowfin tuna steak with a kipfler potato and fennel salad; or macadamia and herb-crusted wild barramundi.

26 Wharf St. (at Warner St.). ✆ **07/4099 4922.** www.salsaportdouglas.com.au. Reservations essential. Main courses A$16–A$34. AE, DC, MC, V. Mon–Sat 10am–midnight; Sun 8am–midnight.

THE NORTH COAST

For years, the village of **Mission Beach** was a well-kept secret. Farmers retired here; then those who liked to chill out discovered it; today, it's a small, prosperous (and growing) rainforest town that hasn't lost its simple charm. The beach is one of the most beautiful in Australia, a long white strip fringed with dense tangled vine forests, the only surviving lowlands rainforest in the Australian tropics. It is also one of the least crowded and least spoiled, so clever has Mission Beach been at staying out of sight, out of mind, and off the tourist trail.

The nearby **Tully River** is white-water-rafting heaven for thrill-seekers. You can also bungee jump and tandem sky dive when you're not rushing down the rapids, flanked by lush rainforest.

From Mission Beach, it's a short ferry ride to **Dunk Island,** a large resort island that welcomes day-trippers. You can even sea kayak here from the mainland. Mission Beach is closer to the Great Barrier Reef than any other point along the coast—just an hour—and cruise boats depart daily from the jetty, stopping en route at Dunk Island.

A few hours' drive south brings you to the city of **Townsville,** a gateway to the Great Barrier Reef and to Magnetic Island, a picturesque, laid-back haven for hikers and watersports enthusiasts.

Mission Beach: The Cassowary Coast

140km (87 miles) S of Cairns; 240km (149 miles) N of Townsville

Tucked away off the Bruce Highway, the township of Mission Beach has managed to duck the tourist hordes. It's actually a conglomeration of four beachfront towns: South Mission Beach, Wongaling Beach, Mission Beach proper, and Bingil Bay. Most commercial activity centers on the small nucleus of shops and businesses at Mission Beach proper, but there are bigger shopping center developments springing up. One of the great attractions—apart from the beach—is the chance you might spot a cassowary emerging from the rainforest to cross the road. Signs on the way into town warn you to watch out for them. Rainforest hides the town from view until you round the corner to Mission Beach proper and discover appealing hotels and cabins, small shops, and smart little restaurants. Just through the trees is the fabulous beach. A mile or so north of the main settlement is Clump Point Jetty.

> **Mission Beach Money Matters**
>
> **There's no bank in Mission Beach and only two ATMs. Many small shops and cafes don't accept credit cards, so make sure that you take enough cash and traveler's checks to cover your expenses while you are there—just in case!**

ESSENTIALS

GETTING THERE From Cairns, follow the Bruce Highway south. The Mission Beach turnoff is at the tiny town of El Arish, about 15km (9½ miles) north of Tully. Mission Beach is 25km (16 miles) off the highway. It's a 90-minute trip from Cairns. If you're coming from Townsville, a turnoff just north of Tully leads 18km (11 miles) to South Mission Beach.

Mission Beach Connections (✆ **07/4059 2709**) provides door-to-door shuttles three times a day from Cairns and Cairns Airport for A$47 adults and A$24 kids.

Greyhound Australia (✆ **1300/473 946** in Australia) coaches stop at Wongaling Beach several times daily on Cairns-Brisbane-Cairns runs. The fare is A$34 from Cairns, A$280 for the 27-hour-plus trip from Brisbane.

Six **trains** a week on the Cairns-Brisbane-Cairns route serve the nearest station, Tully, about 20km (13 miles) away. One-way travel from Cairns on the Tilt Train costs A$47 for the 2-hour, 50-minute journey. From Brisbane, fares range from A$206 in an economy seat to A$408 for a first-class sleeper on the *Sunlander,* or A$748 for Queenslander Class. For more information, call Queensland Rail's long-distance division, **Traveltrain** (✆ **1800/872 467** in Australia, or 07/3235 1122; www.traveltrain.com.au). A taxi from Tully to Mission Beach with Supreme **Taxis** (✆ **07/4068 1427**) is about A$55. The **Beach Bus** (see below) also travels between Tully and Mission Beach for A$10 one-way or A$18 round-trip.

VISITOR INFORMATION The **Mission Beach Visitor Information Centre,** Porters Promenade, Mission Beach, QLD 4852 (✆ **07/4068 7099;** www.missionbeachtourism.com), is at the northern end of town. It's open Monday to Saturday from 9am to 4:45pm and Sunday 10am to 4pm. Closed December 25 and 26.

GETTING AROUND The **Beach Bus** (✆ **07/4068 7400**) provides a regular link between the beach communities from Bingal Bay to South Mission Beach. Just flag the bus down outside your accommodations or wherever you see it. The bus runs every day from 9am to 6pm. Fares are A$3 to A$8 for adults, depending where you want to go, or you can buy an A$8 all-day pass or a 3-day pass for A$14. Kids under 12 pay A$2 to travel anywhere. To hire a car, go to **Sugarland Car Rentals** (✆ **07/4068 8272**). For Mission Beach taxi service, call ✆ **0429/689366.**

WHAT TO SEE & DO

EXPLORING THE REEF Mission Beach is the closest point on the mainland to the Reef, just 1 hour by the high-speed **Quick Cat Cruises** catamaran (✆ **07/4068 7289;** www.quickcatcruises.com.au). The trip starts with an hour at Dunk Island, 20 minutes offshore, where you can walk rainforest trails, play on the beach, or parasail or jet-ski for an extra fee. Then it's a 1-hour trip to Beaver Cay on the Outer Reef, where you have 3 hours to snorkel or to check out the coral from a glass-bottom boat. There's no shade on the cay, so bring a hat and sunscreen. The trip departs daily from Clump Point Jetty at 9:30am. It costs A$138 for adults, half-price for children 4 to 14. An introductory scuba dive costs A$90 for the first dive and half-price for the second. You should prebook your introductory scuba dive to ensure a place. Qualified divers pay A$60 for the first dive, A$45 for the second, all gear included. Free pickups from Mission Beach are included. You can also join this trip from Cairns; coach connections from your Cairns or northern beaches hotel will cost extra.

WHITE-WATER RAFTING ON THE TULLY A day's rafting through the rainforest on the Class III to IV Tully River is an adventure you won't soon forget. In raft-speak, Class IV means "exciting rafting on moderate rapids with a continuous need to maneuver rafts." On the Tully, that translates to regular hair-raising but manageable rapids punctuated by calming stretches that let you float downstream.

The North Coast

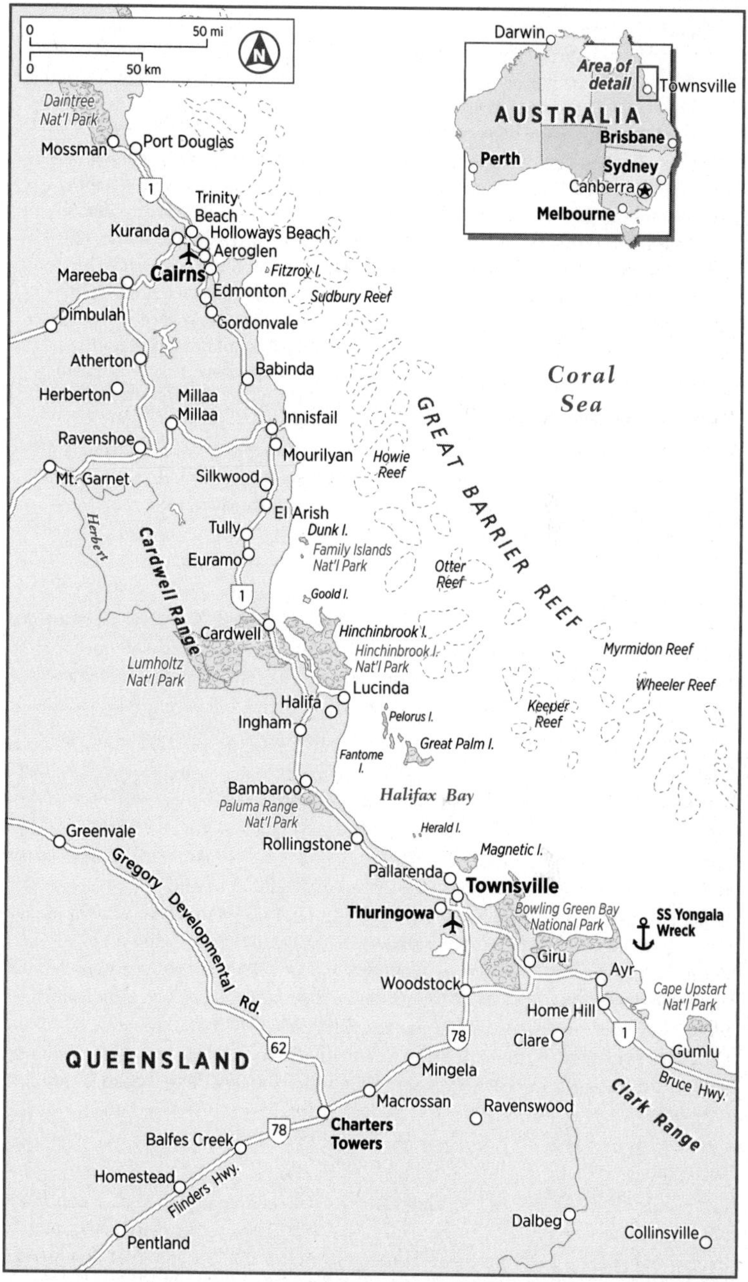

The Mamu Rainforest Canopy Walk

High in the canopy of the rainforest in Wooronooran National Park, the **Mamu Rainforest Canopy Walkway** (✆ 07/4064 5294; www.derm.qld.gov.au/parks/mamu) traces the path of a cyclone. Cyclone Larry tore through the region in March 2006, opening the canopy in several places; the route of the walkway, which opened in late 2008, was planned to take advantage of those natural openings to reduce the need for clearing parts of the forest. The walkway, 15m (50 ft.) off the ground, runs for 350m (1,150 ft.) through the lush forest, with spectacular views of the North Johnstone river gorge and the mountain peaks of the Wet Tropics World Heritage area. If you are like me, it will surprise and delight you. Along the way—both at ground level and higher—there are signs explaining the area's history and alerting you to the plants, insects, and birds to look out for. The best views are from a 10m (33 ft.) cantilever and a 37m-high (121-ft.) tower with two viewing decks. The whole walk is about 2.5km (1½ miles) and takes about an hour at an easy pace. To find it, take the Palmerston Highway about 116km (72 miles) south from Cairns, or from Mission Beach, travel north about 25km (15½ miles) to Innisfail, turn northwest, and continue about 30km (19 miles). The walkway is open daily 9:30am to 5:30pm (last entry at 4:30pm) and closed Christmas Day. Admission is A$20 adults, A$10 children 4 to 14, or A$50 for a family of four.

You don't need experience, just a decent level of agility and an enthusiastic attitude. **RnR Rafting** (✆ **07/4041 9444**) runs a daily trip that includes 5 hours on the river with fun, expert guides, a barbecue lunch in the rainforest, and a DVD screening of your adventure. With transfers, the day costs A$150 from Mission Beach; A$160 from Cairns and the northern beaches, plus A$30 for national park and other fees. You must be age 13 or over.

EXPLORING THE RAINFOREST & COAST Walking, wildlife spotting, canoeing in the forest, and kayaking along the pristine coast are all worth doing. Hiking trails abound through national parks, in rainforests, through fan palm groves, and along the beach. The 8km (5-mile) **Licuala Fan Palm** track starts at the parking lot on the Mission Beach–Tully Road about 1.5km (1 mile) west of the turnoff to South Mission Beach. The track leads through dense forest and over creeks and comes out on the El Arish–Mission Beach Road about 7km (4½ miles) north of the post office. When you come out, you can cross the road and keep going on the 1km (less than a mile) Lacey Creek loop in the Tam O'Shanter State Forest. A shorter Rainforest Circuit leads from the parking lot at the start of the Licuala Fan Palm track and makes a 1km (less than a mile) loop incorporating a fan palm boardwalk. There's also a 10-minute "follow the cassowary footprints to the nest" children's walk.

If you would rather see the sea, take the 7km (4½-mile) Edmund Kennedy track, which starts below the Horizon resort at the southern end of the Kennedy Esplanade in South Mission Beach. You get views of the ocean and the rainforest on this trail. The Mission Beach Visitor Centre has free trail maps.

Coral Sea Kayaking (✆ **07/4068 9154,** or 0419/782 453 mobile; www.coralseakayaking.com) offers a range of sea-kayaking expeditions that interpret the rich environment around you. Groups are usually between five and eight people, so you get personal attention and time to ask questions. The half-day sea-kayak trip (A$77 per person) follows the coast near South Mission Beach. Between mid-May and early November, owners David Tofler and Atalanta Willy also run a 3-day sea kayak camping trip to the nearby Family Islands. This costs A$570 including pickup from your accommodations, all meals, and equipment, including snorkeling gear. Extended 5- and 7-day paddles are also available.

HITTING THE BEACH Relaxing on the uncrowded beach is why everyone comes to Mission Beach. From June through September, you can swim anywhere, and the water is warm; October through May, stick to areas with stinger nets at Mission Beach proper (behind Castaways resort) and South Mission Beach.

A DAY TRIP TO DUNK ISLAND If you're a beachcomber at heart, Dunk will fulfill your dreams. Just 5km (3 miles) offshore from Mission Beach, Dunk was the inspiration for writer E. J. Banfield's book *Confessions of a Beachcomber.* The nervous Banfield moved to Dunk at the turn of the 20th century to live out what he thought would be a short life. He lived another 23 years, which must say something about the restorative powers of a piece of paradise. Ed and Bertha Banfield's graves are alongside the track to Mount Kootaloo.

Thick bushland and rainforest cover much of the island's 12 sq. km (4¾ sq. miles), most of which is a national park. The island is renowned for its myriad birds and electric-blue Ulysses butterflies.

You can stay at the upscale Dunk Island resort (see below) or pop over for the day to snorkel, hike in the forest, or do all sorts of watersports. **Quick Cat Cruises** (**© 07/4068 7289**) runs transfers for A$56 adults round-trip, half-price for kids 4 to 14, free for kids under 4. Daily departures are from Clump Point Jetty at 8:30 and 10am, and 2pm, returning at 1:30, 3:30, and 4:30pm. You can also get to Dunk by **water taxi** (**© 07/4068 8310**), which runs six times a day from Wongaling Beach, takes 10 minutes, and costs A$35 adults round-trip, half-price for children. Ask at your hotel about transfers between Clump Point and South Mission Beach.

Once on Dunk, you pay as you go for activities and equipment rental. Everything from water-skiing to catamaran sailing is available, and Dunk has lovely beaches and half a dozen rainforest walking trails, ranging in duration from 15 minutes to 4 hours.

Coral Sea Kayaking (**© 07/4068 9154,** or 0419/782 453 mobile; www.coralseakayaking.com) runs full-day guided paddles to Dunk Island. It takes about 90

Wildlife Safety Tips

The endangered **cassowary** (a spectacular ostrichlike bird with a blue bony crown on its head) can kill with its enormous claws, so never approach one. If you disturb one, back off slowly and hide behind a tree.

Dangerous **crocodiles** inhabit the local waterways. Do not swim in, or stand on, the bank of any river or stream.

You will spend plenty of time lazing and strolling the area's 14km (8¾ miles) of beaches, but be careful about where you swim. Deadly **marine stingers** inhabit the sea from October through May; during these months, swim only in the stinger nets erected at Mission Beach and South Mission Beach.

minutes to reach the small islands near Dunk and you may see dolphins and turtles. There's a stop at a nearby island for a midmorning snack; and while on Dunk Island, you can walk in the rainforest and swim or snorkel in a secluded bay. The trip costs A$136 per person, including park fees, lunch, and snacks. You must be over 13.

WHERE TO STAY

In Mission Beach

The Elandra ★ The downside of sleeping in at this comfortable resort is that you may miss a regular visitor at breakfast time—a male cassowary, sometimes with his chicks, who frequents the gardens here to the delight of guests who get up early. On the hill behind South Mission Beach, with beguiling views and a rainforest setting, this intimate resort was revamped in 2008 and now styles itself as "safari meets the sea." This simply means that it now has a semi-African theme with furniture, fabrics, and carvings to give it an exotic air. Guest rooms are painted white and all have balconies and bean bag chairs. The pavilion-style cabanas around the pool are inviting, with their day beds and views of the Coral Sea. It's a bit of a hike to the Mission Beach shops and restaurants so a good choice only if you have a car, or don't care about going outside the resort too much.

Explorer Drive, South Mission Beach, QLD 4852. ✆ **1800/079 090** in Australia, or 07/4068 8154. Fax 07/4068 8596. www.elandraresorts.com. 55 units, all with shower only. A$220–A$270 double; A$320–A$370 double Queen Suite; A$470–A$520 double King Suite. Ask about packages. AE, DC, MC, V. Free outdoor parking. **Amenities:** Restaurant; bar; bikes; outdoor saltwater pool; room service; lit tennis court; free Wi-Fi. *In room:* A/C, TV w/free in-house movies, hair dryer, minibar.

Mackays This delightfully well-kept motel is one of the best deals in town. It's just 80m (262 ft.) from the beach and 400m (a quarter mile) from the heart of Mission Beach. The friendly Mackay family repaints the rooms annually, so the place always looks brand new. All the rooms are pleasant and spacious, with white-tiled floors, cane sofas, queen-size beds with colorful bedcovers, and very clean bathrooms. Some have views of the attractive granite-lined pool and gardens. Rooms in the older painted-brick wing have garden views from a communal patio. Ask about special packages; they can offer extremely good deals on such extras as rafting on the Tully River and day trips to Dunk Island.

7 Porter Promenade, Mission Beach, QLD 4852. ✆ **07/4068 7212.** Fax 07/4068 7095. www.mackaysmissionbeach.com.au 18 units, 10 with shower only. A$105–A$135 double. Extra person A$20. Crib A$10. Ask about packages. AE, DC, MC, V. Free covered parking. **Amenities:** Babysitting; outdoor pool; room service; access to nearby tennis courts. *In room:* A/C, TV, hair dryer (deluxe rooms only).

On Dunk Island

Dunk Island ★ ☺ Aboriginal People called Dunk Island "Coonanglebah," or "the island of peace and plenty," and you may well agree. Families love Dunk Island because there's so much to do, but it's just as appealing for honeymooners or retired couples. For those who are more inclined to relaxation, Dunk has beautiful beaches and relaxing pastimes, such as sunset cruises. Just 5km (3 miles) offshore from Mission Beach, Dunk is a rainforested 12-sq.-km (7½-sq.-mile) island that attracts everyone. It's renowned for bird life and neon-blue Ulysses butterflies, which you will see everywhere.

Among the free activities are catamaran sailing, paddle skiing, pedal boats, tennis and squash courts, fitness classes, badminton, bocce, and croquet. You pay for a range of other activities, including guided jet-ski tours, waterskiing, tube rides, tandem sky diving, sunset wine-and-cheese cruises, horse riding, and a round on the 9-hole golf course. There are also loads of activities for children, and a kids' club.

All three kinds of low-rise (two-story) accommodations have been refurbished and restyled. The top-of-the-range units are the bright, spacious Beachfront Suites, which have virtually uninterrupted views over Brammo Bay and direct access to the beach. Set in small groups of four units (two units upstairs, two downstairs), suites have king-size beds, luxurious bathrooms, good-size balconies with day beds, and extras such as CD players, bathrobes, and minibars. Beachfront Rooms are just that, with views over Brammo Bay from most. Upstairs rooms have balconies, downstairs rooms have patios and open onto the gardens and the beach, and some have two queen-size beds. Connecting rooms are available. A short stroll from the central complex, resort facilities, and beach are the Garden Rooms, which are great for families. To truly relax, visit the **Spa of Peace and Plenty,** two tropical-style buildings connected by a floating boardwalk on a man-made lake, for a facial, massage, body wrap, or other pampering.

Off Mission Beach (c/o Hideaway Resorts, P.O. Box 1087, Cairns QLD 4870). ✆ **1300/384 403** in Australia, or 07/4047 4740 (Cairns reservations office) or 07/4068 8199 (resort). Fax 07/4047 4799 (Cairns reservations office). www.dunk-island.com. 160 units. A$348–A$654 double. Rates include full breakfast. Extra adult A$64. Children 12 and under stay free in parent's room using existing bedding. Ask about packages. AE, DC, MC, V. Hinterland Aviation operates daily 45-min. flights from Cairns to Dunk Island (book through reservations, ✆ 1300/384 403 in Australia). Aircraft luggage limit 23kg (50 lb.) per person. Quick Cat Cruises (✆ 07/4068 7289) makes round-trip ferry transfers from Mission Beach for A$56 adults, half-price kids. Mission Beach Dunk Island Water Taxi (✆ 07/4068 8310) also make regular ferry transfers from Mission Beach for A$20 adults and half-price kids. Sun Palm Transport (✆ 07/4087 2900) operate daily door-to-door coach connections from Port Douglas for A$95 and Cairns for A$75. Fares for children 4–14 are half-price. Disembarkation from the water taxi is into the shallows—be prepared to get at least your feet (and sometimes more!) wet. Airport pickups must be booked. Transfers also available by air charter. **Amenities:** 4 restaurants; bar; babysitting; bikes; daily kids' club for ages 3–12 (fee); exercise room; 9-hole golf course; Internet; 2 large outdoor pools; spa; 3 lit tennis courts (1 indoor); extensive watersports equipment rental. *In room:* A/C, ceiling fans, TV, hair dryer, minibar.

On Bedarra Island: The Ultimate Luxury Getaway

Only a mile long, Bedarra is home to an exclusive 15-room resort favored by the rich, famous, and anyone who desires privacy. The staff is discreet, and day-trippers are banned. Rainforested and fringed by beaches, Bedarra is a few miles south of Dunk Island.

Bedarra Island ★★★ Bedarra is one of those rare and fabulous places that throws not just meals but vintage French champagne, fine cognac and wine, and other potable treats into the price, shocking though that price may be. The private villas have large verandas, and there's a sense of light and space in the public areas. The lobby, restaurant, and 24-hour bar are open, with ironbark and recycled timber beams and feature panels of volcanic stone. Each villa, tucked into the rainforest, has a balcony and sea views. All come with generous living areas, king-size beds and bathrobes, and the important things in life, such as double bathtubs and aromatherapy oil-burners. Bathrooms offer divine pampering treats including signature Bedarra aromatherapy oils.

Four exclusive villas sit away from the main resort, perched on cliff tops overlooking Wedgerock Bay. The Pavilions and Point Villas offer superior facilities, including separate living and sleeping areas, large decks, and an outdoor area with a private plunge pool.

The emphasis here is on relaxation. Walk along rainforest trails, fish off the beach, snorkel. Take a catamaran, paddle-ski, kayak, or motorized dinghy out on the water. These activities are free; chartering a yacht or game-fishing boat costs extra. To visit the Great Barrier Reef, you have the choice of a 45-ft. catamaran for a spectacular sail around the local waters, a private charter on a purpose-built 50-ft. twin hull sports cruiser, or a scheduled Outer Reef trip departing from nearby Dunk Island (see "Exploring the Reef," above). The resort has a gym and massage therapy room as well as a lounge area with Internet access. Many guests do nothing more strenuous than have the chef pack a gourmet picnic with a bottle of bubbly and set off in search of a deserted beach. Dress at night is smart casual.

Off Mission Beach (c/o Hideaway Resorts, P.O. Box 1087, Cairns QLD 4870). ✆ **1300/384 417** in Australia, or 07/4047 4747 (Cairns reservations office). Fax 07/4047 4799 (Cairns reservations office). www.bedarra.com.au. 16 villas. A$1,700–A$2,070 double villas; A$3,300 double Point and Pavilions. 2-night minimum stay. Rates include all meals, 24-hr. open bar, return launch transfers from Dunk Island. Ask about packages. Air or coach/ferry transfer to Dunk Island from Cairns (see earlier), and then 15-min. boat transfer. Water transfers from Mission Beach available. Children 12 and under not accepted. **Amenities:** Restaurant; bar; exercise room; secluded outdoor pool w/private Jacuzzi area; lit tennis court; watersports. *In room:* A/C, ceiling fan, TV/VCR, CD player, hair dryer, minibar.

WHERE TO DINE

Friends Restaurant MEDITERRANEAN/SEAFOOD The beach-bar style interior and a menu favoring local seafood make this place a long-standing favorite with locals. Appetizers include smoked crocodile with gingered pumpkin and paw paw salad with sweet garlic and palm sugar dressing, while main courses feature smoked kangaroo filet, locally caught Asian-style barramundi (fish), steaks, and other hearty fare. There are touches of Asian and Mediterranean flavors here and there. Finish off with dessert or a platter of local Atherton Tableland cheeses.

Porters Promenade (opposite Campbell St.), Mission Beach. ✆ **07/4068 7107.** Reservations recommended. Main courses A$19–A$35. AE, MC, V. Fri–Tues 5–10:30pm or until the last diners leave and for lunch on Sat & Sun.

Townsville & Magnetic Island

346km (215 miles) S of Cairns; 1,371km (850 miles) N of Brisbane

With a population of 140,000, Townsville claims to be Australia's largest tropical city. Because of its size, and an economy based on mining, manufacturing, education, and tourism, it is sometimes overlooked as a holiday destination. Unjustly so. The people are friendly, the city is pleasant, and there's plenty to do. The town nestles by the sea below the pink face of Castle Rock, which looms 300m (about 1,000 ft.) directly above. The focus is the Strand park, which had a A$29-million revamp a couple of years ago.

Cruises depart from the harbor for the Great Barrier Reef, about 2½ hours away. Just 8km (5 miles) offshore is Magnetic Island—"Maggie" to the locals—a popular place for watersports, hiking, and spotting koalas in the wild.

Although Townsville can be hot and humid in the summer—and sometimes in the path of cyclones—it is generally spared the worst of the Wet-season rains and boasts 300 days of sunshine a year.

ESSENTIALS

GETTING THERE Townsville is on the Bruce Highway, a 3-hour drive north of Airlie Beach and 4½ hours south of Cairns. The Bruce Highway breaks temporarily in the city. From the south, take Bruce Highway Alt. 1 route into the city. From the north, the highway leads into the city. The drive from Cairns to Townsville through sugar-cane fields, cloud-topped hills, and lush bushland is a pretty one—one of the most picturesque stretches in Queensland.

Qantas (✆ **13 13 13** in Australia; www.qantas.com.au) flies direct from Brisbane. **QantasLink** flies from Cairns, Brisbane, and Mackay. **Jetstar** (✆ **13 15 38** in Australia) flies direct from Brisbane, Sydney, and Melbourne's Tullamarine airport; and **Virgin Blue** (✆ **13 67 89** in Australia) flies direct to Townsville from Brisbane, Cairns, Rockhampton, the Gold Coast, Canberra, and Sydney daily.

Abacus Charters & Tours (✆ **1300/554 378** in Australia or 07/4775 5544) runs a door-to-door airport shuttle. It meets all flights from Brisbane, and from Cairns or elsewhere if you book in advance. A trip into town is A$10 one-way. A **taxi** from the airport to most central hotels costs about A$18.

Seven **Queensland Rail** (✆ **1300 131 722** in Queensland, or 07/3235 1122; www.traveltrain.com.au) long-distance trains stop at Townsville each week. The 19-hour Tilt Train journey from Brisbane costs A$284. The 24-hour *Sunlander* journey costs A$189 for an economy seat, A$249 to A$386 for a sleeper, and A$715 in the luxury Queenslander Class.

Greyhound Australia (✆ **1300/473 946** in Australia or 07/4772 5100 in Townsville) coaches stop at Townsville many times a day on their Cairns-Brisbane-Cairns routes. The fare from Cairns is A$75; trip time is around 6 hours. The fare from Brisbane is A$257; trip time is 23 hours.

VISITOR INFORMATION **Townsville Enterprise Limited** (✆ **07/4726 2728;** www.townsvilleonline.com.au) has three information centers. One is in the heart of town on Flinders Mall (✆ **1800/801 902** in Australia or 07/4721 3660; www.townsvilleholidays.info); it's open Monday through Friday from 9am to 5pm, and weekends from 9am to 1pm. The other is on the Bruce Highway 10km (6¼ miles) south of the city (✆ **07/4778 3555**); it's open daily from 9am to 5pm. There's also an information center in the Museum of Tropical Queensland (see "The Top Attractions," p. 320). For information on Magnetic Island, also check **www.magneticinformer.com.au**, **www.magnetic-island.com.au**, or **www.magneticisland.info**.

GETTING AROUND Local **Sunbus** (✆ 07/4725 8482) buses depart Flinders Mall. Car-rental chains include **Avis** (✆ 07/4721 2688), **Budget** (✆ 07/4725 2344), **Europcar** (✆ 07/4762 7050), **Hertz** (✆ 07/4775 4821), and **Thrifty** (✆ 07/4725 4600).

Detour Coaches (✆ **07/4728 5311**) runs tours to most attractions in and around Townsville. For a taxi, call ✆ **13 10 08.**

DAY TRIPS TO THE REEF

Most boats visiting the Reef from Townsville are live-aboard vessels that make trips of 2 or more days, designed for serious divers. **Barrier Reef Dive, Cruise & Travel** (✆ **1800/636 778** in Australia, or 07/4772 5800; www.divecruisetravel.com) sells day trips to Wheeler Reef, where you can make introductory dives for A$80 for the first one and A$120 for two; certified divers can make two dives for A$80, all gear included. The cruise costs A$180 for adults and A$130 for children 6 to 12. The price includes lunch and morning and afternoon tea, and snorkel gear. Cruises depart Townsville at 6:30am, with a pickup at Magnetic Island en route at

7:25am, and return by 5 or 5:30pm. Several operators, including **Adrenalin Dive** (✆ **1300/664 600** in Australia or 07/4724 0600; www.adrenalindive.com.au), have trips to the *Yongala,* the Coral Sea, and the Reef.

THE TOP ATTRACTIONS

Museum of Tropical Queensland ★★ This fascinating museum, with its curved roof reminiscent of a ship in full sail, holds the relics salvaged from the wreck of HMS *Pandora,* which lies 33m (108 ft.) underwater on the edge of the Great Barrier Reef, 120km (74 miles) east of Cape York. The *Pandora* exhibit includes a full-scale replica of a section of the ship's bow and its 17m-high (56-ft.) foremast. Standing three stories high, the replica and its copper-clad keel were crafted by local shipwrights for the museum. The *Pandora* sank in 1791, and the wreck was discovered in 1977. The exhibition traces the ship's voyage and the retrieval of the sunken treasure. The museum has six galleries, including a hands-on science center and a natural history display that looks at life in tropical Queensland—above and below the water. Another is dedicated to north Queensland's indigenous heritage, with items from Torres Strait and the South Sea Islands, as well as stories from people of different cultures about the settlement and labor of north Queensland. Touring exhibitions change every 3 months. Allow 2 to 3 hours, and take time to watch the interesting film about the salvage.

70–102 Flinders St. (next to Reef HQ). ✆ **07/4726 0600** or 4726 0606 info line. www.mtq.qm.qld.gov.au. Admission A$14 adults, A$10 seniors and students, A$8 children 4–16, A$33 families of 5. Daily 9:30am–5pm. Closed Good Friday, Dec 25, and until 1pm Apr 25 (Anzac Day).

Reef HQ ★ ☺ Reef HQ is the education center for the Great Barrier Reef Marine Park Authority's headquarters and is the largest living coral reef aquarium in the world. The highlight is walking through a 20m-long (66-ft.) transparent acrylic tunnel, gazing into a giant predator tank where sharks cruise silently. A replica of the wreck of the SS *Yongala* provides an eerie backdrop for blacktip and whitetip reef sharks, leopard sharks, and nurse sharks, sharing their 750,000-liter (195,000-gal.) home with stingrays, giant trevally, and a green turtle. Watching them feed is quite a spectacle. The tunnel also reveals the 2.5-million-liter (650,000-gal.) coral-reef exhibit, with its hard and soft corals providing a home for thousands of fish, giant clams, sea cucumbers, sea stars, and other creatures. During the scuba show, the divers speak to you over an intercom while they swim with the sharks and feed the fish. Other highlights include a touch tank and a wild sea-turtle rehabilitation center, plus interactive activities for children. Reef HQ is an easy walk from the city center.

2–68 Flinders St. ✆ **07/4750 0800.** www.reefhq.com.au. Admission A$25 adults, A$19 seniors and students, A$12 children 5–16, A$37–A$62 families. Daily 9:30am–5pm. Closed Dec 25. Public parking lot opposite Reef HQ. Bus: 1, 1A, or 1B (stop 3-min. walk away).

MORE THINGS TO SEE & DO

The Strand is a 2.5km (1½-mile) strip with safe swimming beaches, a fitness circuit, a great water park for the kids, and plenty of covered picnic areas and free gas barbecues. Stroll along the promenade or relax at one of the many cafes, restaurants, and bars while you gaze across the Coral Sea to Magnetic Island. For the more active, there are areas to in-line skate, cycle, walk, or fish, and a basketball half-court. Four rocky headlands and a picturesque jetty adjacent to Strand Park provide good fishing spots, and there are two surf lifesaving clubs to service the three swimming areas along the Strand. Cool off in the Olympic-size Tobruk Pool, the seawater

Sail Away

While the Whitsundays is better known as the bareboating capital of Queensland, the waters off Townsville offer a less crowded alternative. Local charter company **Tropic Sail** (**✆ 07/4772 4773;** www.tropicsail.com.au) has a small fleet of yachts, catamarans, and motor cruisers and offers bareboat and skippered sailing holidays around Magnetic Island and to the 13 other unspoiled and secluded islands in the Palms group. Owners Shaun Watson and Wendy Keller are experienced sailors who will set you on the right course. Whether you choose a 3-day sail around Magnetic Island, or a week-long cruise that takes you to Great Palm, Curacoa, Fantome, and Orpheus islands, you can almost always count on ultimate seclusion at more than 42 potential anchorages. These are virtually untouched cruising grounds. As you sail, you may see dolphins, sea turtles, dugong, manta rays, and—at the right time of year—migratory whales. There are private moorings at Magnetic Island, so you can get off and enjoy a meal or drink in one of the many restaurants or bars. Charter rates start at A$440 to A$575 per boat per night for a six-berth yacht, plus marine park fees and fuel. You can hire a skipper for a half or full day, from A$300, and Tropic Sail can also organize provisions for you and suggest sailing itineraries. Ask about seasonal discounts and standby rates. A minimum charter of 3 nights (5 nights in peak season) applies.

Rockpool, or at the beach itself. During summer (Nov–Mar), three swimming enclosures operate to keep swimmers safe from marine stingers. If watersports are on your agenda, try a jet ski, hire a canoe, or take to the latest in pedal skis. A state-of-the-art water park has waterfalls, hydrants, water slides, and water cannons, plus a huge bucket of water that continually fills until it overturns and drenches laughing children.

Don't miss the views of Cleveland Bay and Magnetic Island from **Castle Hill;** it's a 2.5km (1½-mile) drive or a shorter, steep walk up from town. To drive to the top, follow Stanley Street west from Flinders Mall to Castle Hill Drive; the walking trails up are posted en route.

At the **Billabong Sanctuary** (**✆ 07/4778 8344;** www.billabongsanctuary.com.au), on the Bruce Highway 17km (11 miles) south of town, you can see Aussie wildlife in a natural setting and hand-feed kangaroos. You can also be photographed (starting at A$15) holding a koala, a (baby) crocodile, a python, a wombat, and other creatures. Interesting interactive talks and shows run continuously starting at 10:30am; one of the most popular is the saltwater-crocodile feeding at 12:15 and 2:45pm. There are also gas barbecues, a food kiosk, and a pool. Admission is A$29 for adults, A$26 for students, A$18 for kids 4 to 16, and A$88 for families of five. The sanctuary is open every day except December 25 from 8am to 5pm. Allow 2 to 3 hours.

WHERE TO STAY

Holiday Inn Townsville Right on Flinders Mall, and just a stroll from all the city's major attractions and the Magnetic Island ferries, this hotel is fairly standard but is a good choice for its location. The locals call it the "Sugar Shaker." (You'll know why when you see it.) The 20-story building is circular, so every room has a view of

Charlie's Trousers

If you hear the locals refer to "Charlie's Trousers," don't be startled. They are talking about Charters Towers, one of two small towns within an easy day trip that is well worth visiting. You'll find many remnants of bygone times in Charters Towers, which retains splendid examples of colonial architecture, historic pubs, museums, and displays of old gold-mining machinery and cottages. The town's One Square Mile has changed little since the 1800s gold rush days when it was the richest gold producing field in Australia. Heritage Walking Maps are available at the Visitor Information Centre, 74 Mosman St. (© 07/4752 0314; www.charterstowers.qld.gov.au), which is open daily 9am to 5pm, closed December 25 and 26, New Year's Day, and Good Friday. There you can follow the Ghosts of Gold Heritage Trail and listen to some tales of ghostly gold rush characters.

About 89km (55 miles) south is the heritage-listed town of Ravenswood, another good day trip. This tiny hamlet was once home to over 4,000 people and boasted more than 50 pubs—today there are just two, but they are worth stopping for. The Imperial Hotel is a flamboyant reminder of the town's boom times, with its multicolored brickwork, wide verandas, and Edwardian interior.

the city, the bay, or Castle Hill. Suites have kitchenettes. The star attractions are the rooftop pool and sun deck with barbecues.

334 Flinders Mall, Townsville, QLD 4810. © **1800/007 697** in Australia and in the U.S. and Canada, 0345/581 666 in the U.K. or 020/8335 1304 in London, 0800/154 181 in New Zealand, or 07/4729 2000. Fax 07/4721 1263. www.ichotelsgroup.com. 230 units. A$125–A$145 double; A$165 double suite. Ask about weekend rates, advance-purchase rates, and packages. AE, DC, MC, V. Parking A$12 per day. **Amenities:** Restaurant; 2 bars; airport transfers (A$12); babysitting; bikes; concierge; free access to nearby health club; rooftop pool; room service. *In room:* A/C, TV w/pay movies, hair dryer, Internet (A55¢ per min.; A$28 for 24 hr.), minibar.

Seagulls Resort This popular, low-key resort, a 5-minute drive from the city, is built around an inviting free-form saltwater pool in 1.2 hectares (3 acres) of dense tropical gardens. Despite the Esplanade location, the motel-style rooms do not boast waterfront views, but they are comfortable and a good size. The larger deluxe rooms have painted brick walls, sofas, dining furniture, and kitchen sinks. Studios and family rooms have kitchenettes; executive suites have Jacuzzis. Apartments have a main bedroom and a bunk bedroom (sleeps three), a kitchenette, dining furniture, and a roomy balcony. The entire resort is wheelchair friendly, with bathroom facilities for people with disabilities. The accommodations wings surround the pool and its pretty open-sided restaurant, which is popular with locals. It's a 10-minute walk to the Strand, and most tour companies pick up at the door.

74 The Esplanade, Belgian Gardens, QLD 4810. © **1800/079 929** in Australia, or 07/4721 3111. Fax 07/4721 3133. www.seagulls.com.au. 70 units, all with shower only. A$127–A$154 double; A$160 family rooms; A$176 2-bedroom apt; A$160–A$187 executive suite. Extra person A$15. AE, DC, MC, V. Free parking. Bus: 7. **Amenities:** Restaurant; bar; airport shuttle (A$3 one-way or A$5 round-trip); children's playground; access to nearby golf course; access to nearby health club; 2 large outdoor saltwater pools and children's wading pool; room service; small tennis court. *In room:* A/C, TV w/free movies, hair dryer, Wi-Fi (A$4 for 1 hr.; A$14 for 6 hr.).

WHERE TO DINE

There are many restaurants and cafes on **Palmer Street,** an easy stroll across the river from Flinders Mall, on Flinders Street East, and on the Strand.

C Bar MODERN AUSTRALIAN Right on the waterfront, this is a great place for casual seaside dining any time of day. It offers healthy choices for breakfast, tasty burgers for lunch and is a lovely spot for sundowners or dinner. For lunch, sink your teeth into a barramundi burger, garnished with salad, brie, and citrus aioli; at dinner try pan-fried honey prawns with roasted almond pilaf or maybe an Indian-style chicken curry. There's also a "grazing" menu from 3pm till late, if you just need something light with your drinks.

Gregory Street Headland, The Strand. ✆ **07/4724 0333.** www.cbar.com.au. Main courses A$24–A$35. AE, DC, MC, V. Daily 7am–9:30pm.

Michel's Cafe and Bar MODERN AUSTRALIAN This big contemporary space is popular with Townsville's "in" crowd. Choose a table on the sidewalk, or opt for air-conditioning inside. Owner-chef Michel Flores works in the open kitchen where he can keep an eye on the excellent servers. You might choose braised lamb shank with duck sausage, butter bean cassoulet, and caramelized vegetables; or North African spiced white king salmon with citrus butter sauce; or something more casual, such as a classic bouillabaisse, the stylish pastas, seafood, or warm salads.

7 Palmer St. ✆ **07/4724 1460.** www.michelsrestaurant.com. Reservations recommended. Main courses A$29–A$38. AE, DC, MC, V. Tues–Fri 11:30am–2:30pm; Tues–Sat 5:30pm–late.

Osman's MEDITERRANEAN/TURKISH One of Townsville's newest restaurants, Osman's is a family-run business serving up the flavors of owner Osman Gurkan's homeland. Turkish cuisine predominates with dishes such as *sucuk*—spiced beef sausage and warm hummus (chickpea dip)—and the signature kebab, lamb eye fillet rolled with eggplant and capsicum paste served with rice pilaf. You'll also be drawn by the warmth of the wood-fired oven, which produces *pide* (pizza). The decor is Middle Eastern too, with laid-back Turkish cushions giving a casual, comfortable feel to the place.

241–245 Flinders St. E. ✆ **07/4721 4772.** www.osmans.com.au. Main courses A$29–A$38. AE, DC, MC, V. Wed–Sun noon–3pm; Tues–Sun 6pm–late.

A SIDE TRIP TO MAGNETIC ISLAND

8km (5 miles) E of Townsville

"Maggie" is a delightful 51-sq.-km (20-sq.-mile) national park island 20 minutes from Townsville by ferry. About 2,500 people live here, and it's popular with Aussies, who love its holiday atmosphere. Don't be put off by the rather stark look of the brand-new resort developments flanking the ferry landing. Head farther into the island and you'll find a busy little place with plenty of unspoiled (for now at least) places to restore your soul. Small settlements dot the coastline and there's a good range of restaurants and laid-back cafes. Most people come for the 20 or so pristine and uncrowded bays and white beaches, but hikers, botanists, and birders may want to explore the eucalyptus woods, patches of gully rainforest, and granite tors. The island got its name when Captain Cook thought the "magnetic" rocks were interfering with his compass readings. It is famous for koalas, easily spotted in roadside gum trees; ask a local to point you to the nearest colony. Rock wallabies are often seen in the early morning. Maggie, by and large off the tourist trail, is definitely a flip-flops kind of place.

VISITOR INFORMATION There is no information center on Magnetic Island. Stop off at the **Flinders Mall Visitor Information Centre** (✆ **1800/801 902** in Australia, or 07/4721 3660) in Townsville before you cross to the island. It's open Monday through Friday from 9am to 5pm, and weekends from 9am to 1pm.

GETTING THERE & GETTING AROUND **Sunferries** (✆ **07/4726 0800**) runs 15 round-trips a day from the Breakwater terminal on Sir Leslie Thiess Drive. Round-trip tickets are A$29 for adults, A$15 for children 5 to 14, and A$66 for families of five. The trip takes about 25 minutes.

You can take your car on the ferry, but most people get around by renting an open-sided minimoke (similar to a golf cart) from the many rental outfits on the island. Minimokes are unlikely to go much over 60kmph (36 mph). **Moke Magnetic** (✆ **07/4778 5377;** www.mokemagnetic.com) rents them for around A$73 a day, including fuel. **Sun Bus** (✆ **07/4778 5130;** www.sunbus.com.au) runs a 3-hour guided tour of the island for A$40 for adults, half-price for kids 5 to 15, or A$120 for families of five. Tours leave at 9:15am and 1:15pm daily from Nelly Bay Harbour.

Out & About on the Island

There is no end to the things you can do on Maggie—snorkeling, swimming in one of a dozen or more bays, catamaran sailing, waterskiing, paraflying, horseback riding on the beach, biking, tennis or golf, scuba diving, sea kayaking, sailing or cruising around the island, taking a Harley-Davidson tour, fishing, and more. Equipment for all these activities is for rent on the island. Most activities spread out around Nelly Bay (where the ferry pulls in); the island's other two settlements, Arcadia and Horseshoe Bay; and Picnic Bay.

The island is not on the Great Barrier Reef, but surrounding waters are part of the Great Barrier Reef Marine Park. There is good reef snorkeling at Florence Bay on the southern edge, Arthur Bay on the northern edge, and Geoffrey Bay, where you can even reef-walk at low tide. (Wear sturdy shoes and do not walk directly on coral to avoid damaging it.) First-time snorkelers will have an easy time of it in Maggie's weak currents and softly sloping beaches. Outside stinger season, there is good swimming at any number of bays all around the island. Reef-free Alma Bay, with its shady lawns and playground, is a good choice for families; Rocky Bay is a small, secluded cove.

One of the best, and therefore most popular, of the island's 20km (13 miles) of hiking trails is the **Nelly Bay–Arcadia trail,** a one-way journey of 5km (3 miles) that takes 2½ hours. The first 45 minutes, starting in rainforest and climbing to a saddle between Nelly Bay and Horseshoe, are the most interesting. Another excellent walk is the 2km (1¼-mile) trail to the **Forts,** remnants of World War II defenses, which, not surprisingly, have great 360-degree sea views. The best koala spotting is on the track up to the Forts off Horseshoe Bay Road. Carry water when walking—some bays and hiking trails are not near shops.

If you feel like splurging, consider a jet-ski circumnavigation of the island with **Adrenalin Jet Ski Tours & Hire** (✆ **07/4778 5533**). The 3-hour tour on a two-seat jet ski costs A$370 per ski, which includes your wet suits, life jackets, and tinted goggles. Tours depart from Horseshoe Bay morning and afternoon. Keep your eyes peeled for dolphins, dugongs (manatees), sea turtles, and humpback whales in season. A 75-minute tour of the northern side of the island costs A$160 per ski and runs three times a day.

The World's Most Expensive Beverage

If strong coffee is on your mind, head to **Herveys Range Heritage Tea Rooms** (✆ **07/4778 0199; www.heritagetearooms.com.au**), about a 40-minute drive west from Townsville. There you'll find what Jack Nicholson's billionaire character in the film *The Bucket List* dubbed "the world's most expensive beverage"—and probably the world's most unique beverage, too. At A$50 a cup, you may only have one cup—but this is one of only a few places in the world you can buy *kopi luwak,* or what the locals call "cat-poo coffee." To explain: The catlike *luwak,* or Asian Palm Civet, which lives in the coffee-growing regions of Indonesia, likes eating ripe coffee cherries, but does not digest the inner bean, which can later be retrieved from its droppings. The beans are washed, dried, and roasted lightly so their complex flavors are not destroyed. This interesting—trust me, it's perfectly palatable—drop is sold alongside exotic teas and Australian fare such as scones, cakes, meat pies, and other home-style dishes. If you want to walk off your lunch or explore further, there's a 1.4km (1 mile) walking track around the property. Herveys Range Heritage Tea Rooms is on Thornton's Gap Road, Herveys Range, about 45km (28 miles) west of Townsville. It's open daily from 9am to 4pm, except Christmas Day.

Where to Stay on Magnetic Island

Bungalow Bay Koala Village Here's your chance to stay almost inside a wildlife sanctuary. Bungalow Bay is a collection of cabins (with and without en-suite bathrooms) and dormitories set on 6.5 hectares (16 acres) of bushland, home to rock wallabies, curlews, lorikeets, and koalas. Bungalow Bay is run by friendly hands-on owners Brett and Janelle Fielding, who ensure there's plenty of night-time entertainment, including movie and trivia nights and coconut bowling. Two-hour tours of the koala park are run at 10am, noon, and 2:30pm, starting at reception (the park is only open at these times). The first hour is within the wildlife park, where you can wrap yourself in a python, pet a lizard, hold a small saltwater crocodile, and get up close with a koala. The second hour is a guided bush walk to explore nearby habitats of eucalyptus forest, wetlands, mangroves, or coastal dunes, and to learn about the history of the traditional owners, the Wulgurukaba people. Entry to the park costs A$19 adults, A$17 backpackers or students, A$10 children 4 to 16, or A$55 for families of five. Koala holding costs A$14 including two souvenir photos, with proceeds supporting Magnetic Island wildlife care groups. Facilities include a camper's kitchen (all gear free of charge, with a refundable deposit), snorkeling gear for hire, and the island's best Internet cafe, with Skype, CD burners, five computers, and printing facilities. Bungalow Bay is also home to Maggie's only campground (tent sites A$13 per person; A$30 per couple for a powered site).

40 Horseshoe Bay Rd., Horseshoe Bay, Magnetic Island, QLD 4819. ✆ **1800/285 577** in Australia or 07/4778 5577. Fax 07/4778 5781. www.bungalowbay.com.au. 30 units. A$74–A$90 double; A$28 per person dorms. Ask about packages. MC, V. Free parking. **Amenities:** Restaurant; bar; bikes; Internet; pool. *In room:* A/C.

Peppers Blue on Blue This rather stark-looking resort is one of two brand-new developments flanking the Magnetic Island ferry terminal; it will be one of the first things you see when you arrive. But it is still somewhat soulless and is not representative of what you will discover when you venture farther in to some of the island's more preserved areas. The resort features well-appointed, comfortable, and contemporary guest rooms, including suites and two- and three-bedroom apartments with bright touches and views of the waterfront, marina, and mountains. There's a large saltwater-lagoon-style pool, some units have private plunge pools, and there's also a day spa if you want to indulge. The resort is near the island's new supermarket.

123 Sooning St., Nelly Bay, Magnetic Island, QLD 4819. ✆ **07/4758 2400.** Fax 07/4758 2499. www.peppers.com.au. A$179–A$295 double; A$299–A$365 2-bedroom apt; A$399–A$465 3-bedroom apt. Extra person (13 years and older) A$66. Crib A$10. Ask about packages. AE, DC, MC, V. Free undercover parking. **Amenities:** Restaurant; bar; concierge; 3 pools; room service; spa. *In room:* A/C, TV/DVD w/ pay movies, CD player, hair dryer, kitchen (except standard rooms), minibar, Wi-Fi (A$5 for 30 min.).

Orpheus Island

80km (50 miles) N of Townsville; 190km (118 miles) S of Cairns

From the moment the small white seaplane bringing you to Orpheus lands—either within stepping distance of the beach, or at the floating pontoon offshore—you'll know you're somewhere special. The waters surrounding Orpehus Island are home to 340 of the 350 or so coral species found in the Great Barrier Reef, 1,100 species of fish, green and loggerhead turtles, dolphins, manta rays, and, from June through September, humpback whales. With a maximum of 42 guests and no day-trippers, the only other people you will see are the attentive but unobtrusive resort staff and the occasional scientist from the James Cook University marine research station in the next bay. It's no wonder that since the 1930s, those seeking seclusion have headed to this beautiful island—among them actress Vivien Leigh, novelist Zane Grey, and rock star Elton John. One of the Great Barrier Reef's most exclusive retreats, Orpheus Island Resort is also a popular getaway for executives, politicians, honeymooners, and any savvy traveler eager for peace and beauty.

Transfers are by eight-seat Cessna seaplane from Townsville and Cairns daily. Return fares are A$450 from Townsville, A$850 from Cairns, or A$650 originating in one place and returning to the other, per person round-trip. Book through the resort. Luggage limit is 15 kilograms (55 lb.) per person.

Orpheus Island Resort ★ If seclusion and tranquillity are what you are looking for, this is the place to find them. The resort is a cluster of rooms lining one of the prettiest turquoise bays you'll find anywhere. Most guests spend their time snorkeling over coral reefs, chilling with a good book or magazine in the Quiet Lounge, or lazing in a hammock. Free activities include tennis, snorkeling, catamaran sailing, canoeing, paddle-skiing, fishing, and taking a motorized dinghy around the shore to explore some of the island's 1,300 hectares (3,211 acres) of national park. You can pay to go game fishing, charter a boat or seaplane to the outer Reef, or do a dive course. A seven-course degustation-style menu is served nightly in the restaurant.

All the rooms and suites on Orpheus are beachfront. Most of the 17 Orpheus retreats are in blocks of three, and each has a personal patio and a Jacuzzi. Four Nautilus suites are more spacious, with separate lounge and bedroom areas, large private patios, and large Jacuzzis. Two have enclosed garden courtyards.

Orpheus Island, Great Barrier Reef (P.M.B. 15), Townsville, QLD 4810. ✆ **07/4777 7377.** Fax 07/4777 7533. www.orpheus.com.au. 21 units. A$1,600 Orpheus Retreat double; A$2,000 Nautilus Suite double. Rates include all meals but not drinks. Ask about packages. AE, DC, MC, V. Children 14 and under not accepted. **Amenities:** Restaurant; 2 bars; concierge; exercise room; free Internet; Jacuzzi; 2 small outdoor pools, 1 w/swim-up bar; lit tennis court; watersports rentals. *In room:* A/C, CD player, hair dryer, minibar, no phone.

THE WHITSUNDAY COAST & ISLANDS

A day's drive or a 1-hour flight south of Cairns brings you to the dazzling collection of 74 islands known as the Whitsundays. No more than 3 nautical miles (3.4km/2 miles) separate most of the islands, and altogether they represent countless bays, beaches, dazzling coral reefs, and fishing spots that make up one fabulous Great Barrier Reef playground. Sharing the same latitude as Rio de Janeiro and Hawaii, the water is at least 72°F (22°C) year-round, the sun shines most of the year, and in winter you'll require only a light jacket at night.

All the islands consist of densely rainforested national park land, mostly uninhabited. The surrounding waters belong to the Great Barrier Reef Marine Park. But don't expect palm trees and coconuts—these islands are covered with dry-looking pine and eucalyptus forests full of dense undergrowth, and rocky coral coves far outnumber the few sandy beaches. More than half a dozen islands have resorts that offer just about all the activities you could ever want—snorkeling, scuba diving, sailing, reef fishing, water-skiing, jet-skiing, parasailing, sea kayaking, hiking, rides over the coral in semisubmersibles, fish feeding, putt-putting around in dinghies to secluded beaches, playing tennis or squash, and aqua-aerobics classes. Accommodations range from small, low-key wilderness retreats to midrange family havens to Australia's most luxurious resort, Hayman.

The village of Airlie Beach is the center of the action on the mainland. But the islands themselves are just as good a stepping stone to the outer Great Barrier Reef as Cairns, and some people consider them better, because you don't have to make the 90-minute trip to the Reef before you hit coral. Just about any Whitsunday island has fringing reef around its shores, and there are good snorkeling reefs between the islands, a quick boat ride away from your island or mainland accommodations.

Essentials

GETTING THERE **By Car** The Bruce Highway leads south from Cairns or north from Brisbane to Proserpine, 26km (16 miles) inland from Airlie Beach. Take the Whitsunday turnoff to reach Airlie Beach and Shute Harbour. Allow a good 8 hours to drive from Cairns. There are several car-storage facilities at Shute Harbour. **Whitsunday Car Security** (✆ **07/4946 9955**) will collect your car anywhere in the Whitsunday area and store it in locked covered parking for A$10 per day or A$15 overnight.

BY PLANE There are two air routes into the Whitsundays: Hamilton Island Airport and Whitsunday Coast Airport at Proserpine on the mainland. **QantasLink** (✆ **13 13 13** in Australia) flies direct to Hamilton Island from Cairns. **Virgin Blue** (✆ **13 67 89** in Australia) flies to Proserpine direct from Brisbane, with connections from other capitals, and direct from Brisbane and Sydney to Hamilton Island. **Jetstar** (✆ **13 15 38** in Australia) flies from Brisbane to Proserpine and from Brisbane, Melbourne, and Sydney to Hamilton Island. If you stay on an island, the resort may book your launch transfers automatically. These may appear on your airline ticket, in which case your luggage will be checked through to the island.

BY TRAIN Several **Queensland Rail** (© **1300 131 722** in Australia; www.traveltrain.com.au) long-distance trains stop at Proserpine every week. The one-way fare from Cairns on the Tilt Train is A$147. There is a bus link to Airlie Beach. Brisbane fares range from A$239 on the Tilt Train to A$343 for a first-class sleeper on the *Sunlander* or A$637 for the all-inclusive Queenslander Class service.

BY BUS **Greyhound Australia** (© **1300/473 946** in Australia; www.greyhound.com.au) operates plentiful daily services to Airlie Beach from Brisbane (trip time: around 19 hr.) and Cairns (trip time: 11 hr.). The fare is A$214 from Brisbane and A$131 from Cairns.

VISITOR INFORMATION The **Whitsundays Information Centre** (© **1300/717 407** in Australia, or 07/4945 3711; www.whitsundaytourism.com) is at 192 Main St., Proserpine (on the Bruce Highway in the town's south). It's run by Tourism Whitsundays and is open Monday to Friday from 9am to 5pm and weekends and public holidays (except Good Friday and Dec 25) from 10am to 4pm.

If you're staying in Airlie Beach, it's easy to pick up information from the private booking agents lining the main street. All stock a vast range of cruise, tour, and hotel information, and make bookings free of charge. They all have pretty much the same stuff, but because some represent certain boats exclusively, and because prices can vary a little from one to the next, shop around.

GETTING AROUND Island ferries and Great Barrier Reef cruises leave from Shute Harbour, a 10-minute drive south of Airlie Beach on Shute Harbour Road. Most other tour-boat operators and bareboat charters anchor at Abel Point Marina, a 15-minute walk west from Airlie Beach. Most tour-boat operators pick up guests free from Airlie Beach hotels and pick up at some or all island resorts.

Whitsunday Transit (© **07/4946 1800;** www.whitsundaytransit.com.au) meets all flights and trains at Proserpine and provides door-to-door transfers to Airlie Beach hotels or to Shute Harbour. The fare from the airport is A$15 adults and A$9 children to Airlie Beach or Shute Harbour. From the train station, it is A$8.20 adults and A$4.20 children to Airlie Beach or A$11 adults and A$5.50 children to Shute Harbour. Bookings are essential, and should be made 48 hours in advance if possible. They also run buses every half-hour between Airlie Beach and Shute Harbour to meet all ferries. The fare is A$4.65. A **10-trip ticket,** valid for 1 month and able to be used by more than one person, allows travel between Shute Harbour, Airlie Beach, Cannonvale, and Proserpine. It costs A$23 adults and A$12 children, which means A$2.25 per trip. An **Explorer Pass,** good for unlimited travel between Shute Harbour, Airlie Beach, Cannonvale, and Proserpine

Safety in the Water

Although they have not been sighted at Airlie Beach for several years, deadly marine stingers may frequent the shorelines from October through April. The best place to swim is in the beachfront Airlie Beach lagoon.

The rivers in these parts are home to dangerous saltwater crocodiles (which mostly live in fresh water, contrary to their name), so don't swim in streams, rivers, and water holes.

The Whitsunday Region

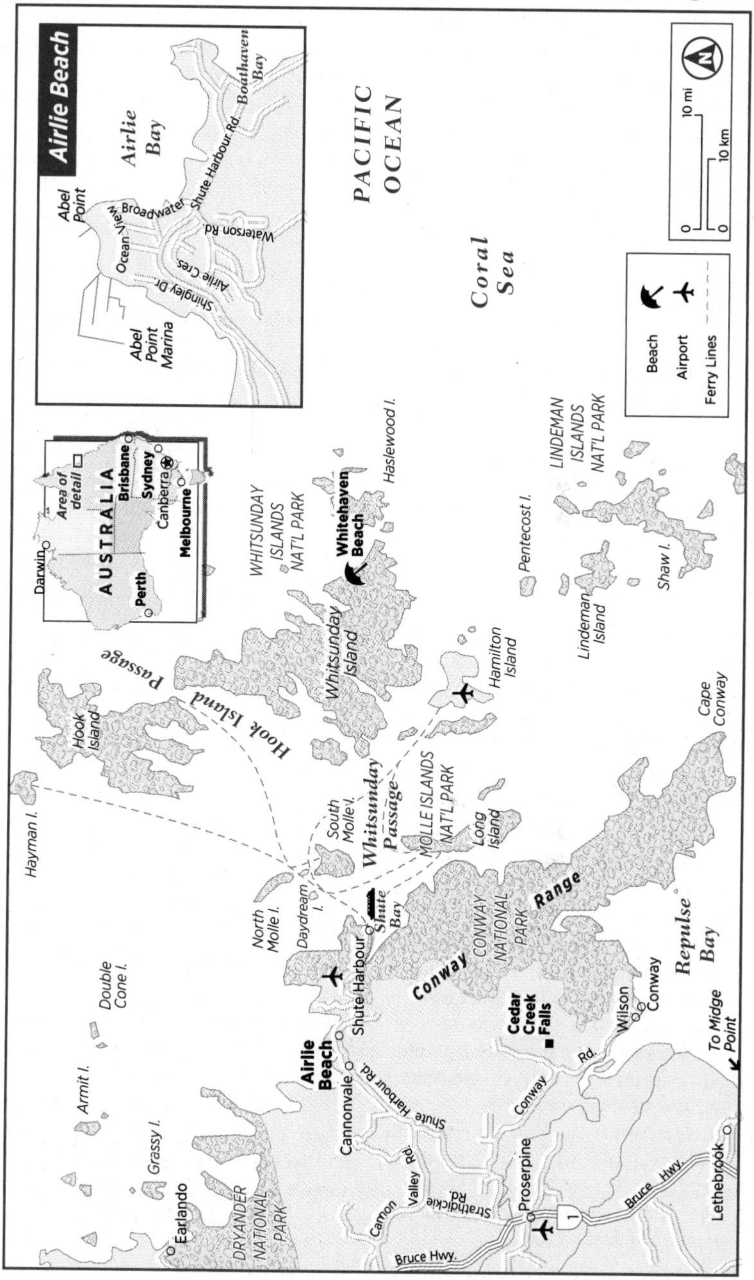
Airlie Beach
Airlie Bay
Boathaven Bay
Abel Point
Broadwater
Shute Harbour Rd.
Ocean View
Waterson Rd.
Airlie Cres.
Shingley Dr.
Abel Point Marina
PACIFIC OCEAN
Coral Sea
0
10 mi
10 km
Beach
Airport
Ferry Lines
AUSTRALIA
Darwin
Area of detail
Brisbane
Sydney
Canberra
Melbourne
Perth
WHITSUNDAY ISLANDS NAT'L PARK
Whitehaven Beach
Haslewood I.
LINDEMAN ISLANDS NAT'L PARK
Pentecost I.
Shaw I.
Lindeman Island
Hamilton Island
Whitsunday Island
Hook Island Passage
Hook Island
Hayman I.
Cape Conway
MOLLE ISLANDS NAT'L PARK
South Molle I.
Whitsunday Passage
Long Island
North Molle I.
Daydream I.
Shute Bay
Shute Harbour
Conway Range
CONWAY NATIONAL PARK
Repulse Bay
Double Cone I.
Airlie Beach
Cedar Creek Falls
Wilson
Conway
To Midge Point
Armit I.
Cannonvale
Shute Harbour Rd.
Conway Rd.
Grassy I.
Earlando
DRYANDER NATIONAL PARK
Valley Rd.
Strathdickie Rd.
Proserpine
Cannon
Bruce Hwy.
Lethebrook
1

COME Sail WITH ME

If "bareboating" is a mystery to you, take heart—you're not alone. It simply means you are sailing the boat yourself. And if that seems daunting, rest assured that thousands of people do it safely every year. Most of the many yacht-charter companies in the islands will want one person on the boat to have a little experience at the helm of a vessel, but don't worry if you're a total novice. You do not need a license, and sailing is surprisingly easy in these uncrowded waters, where the channels are deep and hazard-free and the seas are protected from big swells by the Great Barrier Reef. The 74 islands are so close to each other that one is always in sight, and safe anchorages are everywhere.

If you have no boating experience, or if you think you know what you're doing but just want extra reassurance, the company may require you to take a skipper along at an extra cost of around A$35 per hour or A$320 overnight. Most companies mail you a preparation kit before you leave home. Before departure, they give you a thorough 2- to 3-hour briefing and easy-to-read maps marking channels, anchorage points, and the very few dangerous reefs. Your charter company will radio in once or twice a day to check that you're still afloat, and you can contact the staff anytime for advice.

Most yachts are fitted for two to eight passengers. Try to get a boat with two berths more than you need if your budget will bear it, because space is always tight. The boats usually have a galley kitchen, a barbecue mounted to the stern, hot showers, a toilet, linens, a radio or stereo (or both), a motorized dinghy, and snorkeling equipment. Sleeping quarters usually include a mix of single galley berths and one or two very compact private cabins. You can buy your own provisions or have the charter company stock the boat at an extra cost of about A$45 per person per day. Most operators will load a windsurfer, fishing

from 6am to 10:30pm on the date of issue, costs A$8.50 for adults and half-price for children.

Fantasea Cruises (✆ **1800/650 851** in Australia, or 07/4946 5111; www.fantasea.com.au) connects Hamilton Island Airport, Hamilton Island Marina, and the Whitsunday mainland at Abel Point Marina (Airlie Beach) and Shute Harbour. Timetables coordinate with all arriving and departing flights into Hamilton Island Airport. Ferry services also connect with Whitsunday Transit for coach services to and from Whitsunday Coast Airport.

The Fantasea Express service operates between Hamilton Island Airport and Abel Point Marina. The fare includes coach transfers from Airlie Beach accommodations to the marina for the ferry transfer to Hamilton Island. The cost is A$45 adults and A$25 children 4 to 14 one-way.

Cruise Whitsundays (✆ **07/4946 4662;** www.cruisewhitsundays.com.au) operates Resort Connections, providing transfer services between Hamilton Island Airport and Whitsunday Coast Airport at Proserpine and Daydream Island and Long Island, as well as all Airlie Beach properties.

tackle, and scuba-diving equipment on request, for an extra fee if they are not standard.

In peak season, you may have to charter the boat for a week. At other times, most companies impose a minimum of 5 days, but many will rent for 3 nights if you ask, rather than let a vessel sit idle. Five nights is a good length; it allows you to get familiar enough with the boat to relax and enjoy yourself.

In peak season, expect to pay A$530 to A$700 per night for a standard four- to six-berth yacht, more if you want something luxurious. Rates in the off season, and even in the Whitsundays' busiest time, June through August, will be anywhere from A$100 to A$200 less. If you are prepared to book within 14 days of when you want to sail, the deals can be even better; you should be able to find a boat that late in the off season. You may be asked to post a credit card bond of around A$2,000. Fuel and park fees are extra, and mooring fees apply if you want to stop at one of the island resorts overnight. A number of bareboat-charter companies offer "sail-'n'-stay" packages that combine a few days of sailing with a few days at an island resort.

Most bareboat charter companies will make complete holiday arrangements for you in the islands, including accommodations, transfers, tours, and sporting activities. Most companies operate out of Airlie Beach, Hamilton Island, or both. Well-known operators include **Whitsunday Rent-A-Yacht** (© **1800/075 000** in Australia, or 07/4946 9232; www.rentayacht.com.au); **Queensland Yacht Charters** (© **1800/075 013** in Australia, or 07/4946 7400; www.yachtcharters.com.au); and **Sunsail** (© **1800/803 988** in Australia or 07/4948 9509; www.sunsail.com.au). Tourism Whitsundays (see "Visitor Information," above) can furnish you with a complete list of operators.

If you don't want to sail yourself, countless skippered sailing trips go through the islands (see "Sailing & Snorkeling Trips," below).

Avis (© **07/4946 6318**), **Europcar** (© **07/4946 4133**), and **Hertz** (© **07/4946 4687**) have outlets in Airlie Beach and Proserpine Airport (telephone numbers serve both locations).

Choosing a Whitsunday Base

The advantages of staying on the mainland are cheaper accommodations, a choice of restaurants, and the freedom to visit a different island each day. The mainland has jet-skiing, kayaking, parasailing, catamaran rental, and windsurfing.

The main advantage of staying on an island is that swimming, snorkeling, bushwalking, and a huge range of watersports, many of them free, are right outside your door. The deadly stingers that can infest Airlie's shores do not make it to the islands, so swimming in the islands is safe year-round. You won't be isolated if you stay on an island, because most Great Barrier Reef cruise boats, sail-and-snorkel yacht excursions, Whitehaven Beach cruises, dive boats, fishing tour vessels, and so on stop at the island resorts every day or on a frequent basis. Be warned, however, that once you're "captive" on an island, you may be slugged with high food and drink prices. Bear in mind, too, that although most island resorts offer nonmotorized watersports, such as windsurfing and catamaran sailing, free of charge, you will pay for activities that use fuel, such as parasailing, water-skiing, and dinghy rental.

In some places in the Whitsundays, extreme low tides may reveal rocky mud flats below the sand line. Watersports can be limited then because of the low water level.

Exploring the Islands & the Reef

REEF CRUISES **Fantasea Cruises** (© **07/4946 5111;** www.fantasea.com.au) makes daily trips to Hardy Reef from Shute Harbour, near Airlie Beach, in a high-speed, air-conditioned catamaran. The boat has a bar, and a biologist gives a marine ecology talk en route. You anchor at the massive Fantasea Reefworld pontoon, which holds up to 600 people, and spend up to 3½ hours on the Reef. The day trip costs A$225 for adults, A$102 for children 5 to 15, or A$589 for families of four. Guided snorkel safaris cost A$40 extra for adults and A$20 for children. You can book dives on board for A$115 for first-time divers and A$100 for certified dives. Cruises depart at 8am and pick up passengers at Daydream and Hamilton island resorts. Passengers from Long Island can connect by water taxi.

A fun alternative is Fantasea's 2-day, 1-night **ReefSleep,** during which you spend the night on the pontoon. This gives you a fabulous chance to snorkel at night when the coral is luminescent in the moonlight and nocturnal sea creatures get busy. The trip includes two scuba dives, plenty of night snorkeling, two buffet lunches, dinner under the stars with wine, and breakfast and more snorkeling on the second day. You can stay in a clean, comfortable bunkroom for four for A$460 per person, or in the double cabin, which has a king-size bed, for A$630 per person. With so few guests per night, you have the Reef all to yourself.

SAILING & SNORKELING TRIPS ★ A cheaper alternative to skippering your own yacht—also called "bareboating"—around the Whitsundays (see "Come Sail with Me," above) is a journey on one of the many yachts offering 3-day, 2-night sailing adventures around the islands. You can learn to sail or get involved with sailing the boat as much or as little as you want, snorkel to your heart's content over one dazzling reef after another, beach comb, explore national park trails, stop at secluded bays, swim, sunbathe, and generally have a laid-back good time. A few companies offer introductory and qualified scuba diving for an extra cost per dive. Most boats carry a maximum of 12 passengers, so the atmosphere is always friendly and fun. The food is generally good, the showers are usually hot, and you sleep in comfortable but small berths off the galley. Some have small private twin or double cabins.

The Secret of the Seasons

High season in the Whitsundays coincides with school vacations, which occur in January, in mid-April, from late June to early July, from late September to early October, and in late December. The Aussie winter, June through August, is popular, too. You have to book months ahead to get high-season accommodations, but any other time you can indeed find some good deals: Specials on accommodations, sailing trips, day cruises, and diving excursions fairly leap off the blackboards outside the tour-booking agents in Airlie Beach.

Hitting the Sand at Whitehaven Beach

The 6km (3¾-mile) stretch of pure-white silica sand on Whitehaven Beach ★★ will leave you in rapture. The beach, on uninhabited Whitsunday Island, does not boast a lot of coral, but the swimming is good and the forested shore is beautiful. Take a book and chill out. Some sailboat day trips visit it, as do some motorized vessels. A day trip with Fantasea Cruises (© 07/4946 5111; www.fantasea.com.au) costs A$110 per adult, A$50 for children ages 5 to 15, or A$295 for a family of four from Hamilton Island; or A$140 adults, A$55 children, or A$365 from Shute Harbour. Lunch is included.

Prices usually include all meals, Marine Park entrance fees, snorkel gear, and transfers to the departure point (Abel Point Marina or Shute Harbour). In the off season, the boats compete fiercely for passengers; you'll see signboards on the main street in Airlie Beach advertising standby deals.

Among the better known boats are the ***Ragamuffin*** (© **1800/454 777** in Australia or 07/4946 7777; www.maxiaction.com.au), a 17m (56-ft.) oceangoing yacht which runs two 2-hour sailing trips, to Blue Pearl Bay and Whitehaven Beach. Each costs A$156 adults, A$60 kids 5 to 15, or A$365 for a family of four. **Prosail** (© **07/4946 7533;** www.prosail.com.au) runs sailing trips through the Great Barrier Reef Marine Park. All trips include sailing, snorkeling, scuba diving, and bushwalking, and you can sail on megayachts such as the *Condor, Broomstick,* and *Hammer.* A 2-day, 2-night trip costs A$399 per person. Contact Tourism Whitsundays (see "Visitor Information," above) for details on other charters.

ISLAND HOPPING Day-trippers to Hamilton, Daydream, South Molle, Club Crocodile Long Island, and Hook Island resorts can rent the hotels' watersports equipment, laze by the beaches and pools, scuba dive, join the resorts' activities programs, hike their trails, and eat at some or all of their restaurants. See "The Whitsunday Island Resorts," below, for details on where to stay. Club Crocodile's Long Island Resort is rather noisy but unpretentious, with plentiful watersports, picturesque hiking trails, wild wallabies, and a large beach-cum-tidal-flat where you can relax on sun lounges.

SCENIC FLIGHTS Expect to pay around A$99 for a 10-minute flight (or A$300 for an hour) over the Whitsundays—a spectacular sight from the air. **Aviation Tourism Australia** (© **07/4946 8249;** www.avta.com.au) and **Air Whitsunday** (© **07/4946 9111;** www.airwhitsunday.com.au) offer a large range of tours, including seaplane flights to a Reef pontoon to snorkel for a couple of hours, or a helicopter trip to a private island with a picnic lunch and snorkel gear.

FISHING Reef fishing is superb throughout the islands; red emperor, coral trout, sweetlip, and snapper are common catches. One of the most popular charter vessels is the 16m (52-ft.) timber cruiser ***Moruya*** (© **07/4948 1029** or 0400/450 111 mobile phone; www.fishingwhitsunday.com.au). Day trips depart Shute Harbour daily at around 8am. They include lunch, bait, and fishing rods. The crew will even clean your catch for you. Adults pay A$150, students and children 4 to 14 pay A$90, and families of four pay A$380.

Great Whitsunday Walking

The Whitsundays Great Walk—one of six **Great Walks of Queensland**—covers 36km (22 miles) in Conway State Forest and Conway National Park, behind Airlie Beach. The trail starts at the end of Brandy Creek Road, a short drive from Cannonvale, and winds in three stages from Brandy Creek to Airlie Beach, with two campsites at 12km (7½-mile) intervals. The hills here are rich in giant strangler figs, ferns, and palms, and if you're lucky, you'll spot a giant blue Ulysses butterfly. Walkers should carry drinking water, because the water in natural systems is not good for drinking.

A permit is required for overnight walks and must be booked in advance (✆ **13 13 04** in Australia; www.qld.gov.au/camping). The cost is A$5 per person or A$20 for a family of two adults and up to six children ages 5 to 17. More information on this and other walks, including the new **Ngaro Sea Trail,** which links sea routes with walks on Hook, Whitsunday, and South Molle islands, can be obtained from the Queensland Parks and Wildlife Service information center, Shute Harbour Road at Mandalay Road (✆ **07/4967 7355**) 2.5km (1½ miles) northeast of Airlie Beach. It's open Monday through Friday from 9am to 4:30pm.

For more details on all Great Walks, log onto **www.derm.qld.gov.au/parks_and_forests/great_walks.**

If you want to undertake your own fishing expedition, **Harbourside Boat Hire,** in Shute Harbour (✆ **07/4946 9330**), rents motorized dinghies for A$60 for a half-day or A$90 for a full day. Half-cabin cruisers cost A$90 for a half-day, A$150 for a full day. They also rent fishing rods and sell tackle, bait, ice, and anything else you might need for angling.

ECOTOURS Visitors to the Whitsundays can get up close and personal with crocodiles in their natural habitat with **Proserpine River Eco Tours** (✆ **07/4948 3310;** www.crocodilesafari.com.au), which combines an open-air wagon ride through the pristine Goorganga wetlands and a boat trip on the river to learn more about one of Queensland's major crocodile-breeding grounds. This is the only place to see crocs in safety in the wild south of the Daintree. Bus pickups operate from Airlie Beach, Cannonvale, and Proserpine for the tours, which run about 4 hours, depending on tides, and cost A$110 for adults, A$55 for kids 1 to 14. Back on land, you'll enjoy billy tea, the best damper I've ever tasted (and they'll even give you the recipe), and a talk on native wildlife over a barbecue lunch.

GOLFING Queensland's **Hamilton Island Golf Club** (✆ **02/9433 0444;** www.hamiltonislandgolfclub.com.au) has opened as Australia's only 18-hole championship golf course on its own island. The 6,120m (6,690 yard), par-71 course sits on Dent Island, just a 5-minute ferry ride from Hamilton Island in the Whitsundays.

SEA KAYAKING ★ If you have strong arms, sea kayaking is a wonderful way to enjoy the islands. Daydream Island and the beaches and bays of the North, Mid, and South Molle group of islands are all within paddling distance of the mainland. It's common to see dolphins, turtles, and sharks along the way. One long-established operator is **Salty Dog Sea Kayaking** (✆ **07/4946 1388;** www.saltydog.com.au), which takes escorted trips through the islands. Half-day trips run on Tuesday, Wednesday, and Saturday, and full-day trips on Monday, Thursday, and Friday, departing Airlie Beach at 8:30am. A half-day trip is A$70 per person and a day trip is A$125 per person. Two- and 6-day trips, during which you camp out, are A$365 and A$1,490. All rates include snorkel gear, meals, pickup, and, on overnight trips, camping gear. The company also delivers sea kayaks anywhere in the Whitsundays. Rental prices start at A$50 for a single kayak, A$80 for a double for a half-day, including delivery, pickup, and safety equipment. A deposit of A$200 is required for rentals.

Airlie Beach

640km (397 miles) S of Cairns; 1,146km (711 miles) N of Brisbane

The little town of Airlie Beach is the focal point of activity on the Whitsunday mainland. The town is only a few blocks long, but you will find an adequate choice of decent accommodations, a small selection of good restaurants and bars, a nice boutique or two, and facilities such as banks and a supermarket. Cruises and yachts depart from Shute Harbour, a 10-minute drive south on Shute Harbour Road, and Abel Point Marina, a 10-minute walk west along the foreshore or a quick drive over the hill on Shute Harbour Road.

Airlie Beach has a massive beachfront artificial lagoon, with sandy beaches and landscaped parkland, which solves the problem of where to swim in stinger season. The lagoon is the size of about six full-size Olympic swimming pools, set in 4 hectares (10 acres) of botanic gardens, with a children's pool, plenty of shade, barbecues, picnic shelters, toilets, showers, and parking.

Perched on the edge of the Coral Sea, with views across Pioneer Bay and the Whitsunday Passage, Airlie Beach has a village atmosphere; life revolves around the beach and marina by day, and the bars and restaurants by night.

The spit of land between Airlie Bay and Boathaven Bay is home to the Airlie Beach Sailing Club. Shute Harbour, 11km (7¾ miles) from Airlie Beach, is one of Queensland's busiest ports, filled with yachts, cruisers, water taxis, ferries, and fishermen. For a bird's-eye view, head to the Lions Lookout.

WHERE TO STAY

Airlie Beach Hotel In the heart of Airlie Beach, this large hotel complex offers fairly standard accommodations but is ideal if you like to be in the thick of things. The hotel straddles an entire block, giving it frontage on both the Esplanade and the main street. Rooms are spacious and well appointed, with views over the inlet. There are standard motel rooms, or newer hotel rooms and executive-style suites with kitchens. My pick would be any of the rooms at the front, overlooking the Esplanade and the inlet, which have small balconies.

16 The Esplanade (at Coconut Grove), Airlie Beach, QLD 4802. ✆ **1800/466 233** in Australia, or 07/4964 1999. Fax 07/4964 1988. www.airliebeachhotel.com.au. 80 units. A$139 double standard motel room; A$189–A$209 double hotel room; A$289 double suite. Extra person A$49 (children 14 and under free using existing bedding). Crib free. AE, DC, MC, V. Free covered parking. **Amenities:** 3 restaurants; 3 bars; heated outdoor saltwater pool. *In room:* A/C, ceiling fans, TV, hair dryer, minibar, Wi-Fi (A$5 for 30 min.).

Coral Sea Resort ★ In Airlie Beach's best location, on the edge of Paradise Point, with 280-degree views of the ocean, this 7-year-old resort is one of the best places to stay on the Whitsunday mainland. The wide range of great accommodations styles suits everyone from honeymooners to families, and although it's relatively sprawling, the design is such that you can easily feel you're alone. All the rooms have a nautical feel. The Coral Sea suites are divine, complete with a Jacuzzi and double hammock on the balcony. There are four styles of suites, apartments, and family units. Bayview suites have a Jacuzzi inside. It's a 3-minute walk along the waterfront to Airlie Beach village.

25 Oceanview Ave., Airlie Beach, QLD 4802. ✆ **1800/075 061** in Australia, or 07/4964 1300. Fax 07/4946 6516. www.coralsearesort.com.au. 78 units. A$240–A$380 double; A$330 double 1-bedroom apt; A$350–A$400 2-bedroom apt; A$500 3-bedroom apt; A$400 1-bedroom penthouse; A$550 double 2-bedroom penthouse; A$700 double 3-bedroom penthouse. Extra person A$50. Crib A$15. Ask about packages. AE, DC, MC, V. Free parking. **Amenities:** Restaurant; bar; babysitting; bikes; exercise room; 25m (82-ft.) outdoor pool; room service; spa; watersports rental. *In room:* A/C, TV w/free movies, hair dryer, Internet (A55¢ per min., max A$10 for 2 hr.; A$28 for 24 hr.), kitchenette, minibar.

Martinique Whitsunday Resort ★ Apartments in this French Caribbean–style complex high on the hill above Airlie Beach have views that make the short but very steep walk from the town well worthwhile. The one-, two-, and three-bedroom apartments are roomy and light, and each has a big balcony. The infinity lap pool also overlooks the Coral Sea and is surrounded by tropical gardens and waterfalls. There's a barbecue area, and you can also order kitchen supplies to be ready when you arrive. Apartments are serviced weekly, and each has a washing machine and dryer.

18 Golden Orchid Dr. (off Shute Harbour Rd.), Airlie Beach, QLD 4802. ✆ **1800/251 166** in Australia or 07/4948 0401. Fax 07/4948 0402. www.martiniquewhitsunday.com.au. 20 units. A$210 double 1-bedroom apt; A$300 2-bedroom apt for 4 people; A$375 3-bedroom apt for up to 6. Minimum 2-night stay. Extra person A$30. Crib A$10. AE, DC, MC, V. Free covered parking. **Amenities:** Exercise room; 2 Jacuzzis; outdoor lap pool. *In room:* A/C, ceiling fans, TV, hair dryer, kitchen, minibar.

WHERE TO DINE

Mangrove Jack's Café Bar PIZZA/CAFE FARE Bareboat sailors, local sugar farmers, Sydney yuppies, and European backpackers all flock to this big, open-fronted sports bar and restaurant. The mood is upbeat and pleasantly casual, the surroundings are spick-and-span, and the food passes muster. Wood-fired pizzas with trendy toppings are the specialty. There is no table service; place your order at the bar and collect your food when your number is called. There are kids' meals, and more than 35 wines come by the glass.

In the Airlie Beach Hotel, 16 The Esplanade (enter from Shute Harbour Rd.). ✆ **07/4964 1888.** Reservations recommended. Main courses A$22–A$28. AE, DC, MC, V. Mon–Fri 11:30am–2:30pm and 5:30–9:30pm (10pm on Fri); Sat 11:30am–9:30pm.

The Whitsunday Island Resorts

There are about 10 resorts of varying degrees of splendor; accommodations range from positively plush to comfortably midrange to downright old-fashioned.

VERY EXPENSIVE

Daydream Island Resort ★★ ☺ One of the Whitsundays' oldest resorts is now one of Australia's most extensive and modern spa resorts. Daydream Island has a mixed clientele consisting of families and those seeking pampering and luxury. Features such as the outdoor cinema and kids' club have always made it popular with families, but the 16 therapy rooms at the Rejuvenation Spa appeal to those who are seeking one of the most sophisticated and well-equipped health resorts in Australia. The state-of-the-art spa has an in-house naturopath and a range of computerized health analyses using equipment and tests usually found only in clinics in Europe and the United States, such as iridology and measurement of vitamin and mineral imbalances and antioxidant levels. Rooms are large, smart, and comfortable, with uninterrupted ocean views. The "village" at the southern end of the island, a short stroll along the boardwalk from the resort, has shops, cafes, a pool and bar, and a tavern serving bistro-style meals. A rainforest walk stretches almost the entire length of the kilometer-long (just over half a mile) island; other activities include snorkeling, sailboarding, jet-skiing, parasailing, coral viewing, reef fishing, diving and dive school, tennis, volleyball, and minigolf.

Daydream Island (40km/25 miles northeast of Shute Harbour), Whitsunday Islands (P.M.B. 22), Mackay, QLD 4741. ✆ **1800/075 040** in Australia or 07/4948 8488. www.daydreamisland.com. 296 units. A$278–A$464 double; A$734–A$834 suite. Children 14 and under stay free in parent's room with existing bedding. Ask about packages. Minimum 3-night stay. AE, MC, V. Cruise Whitsundays (✆ 07/4946 4662) provides launch transfers from Abel Point Marina and Hamilton Island Airport to Daydream for A$59 adults and A$37 children. **Amenities:** 3 restaurants, 3 bars; 3 Jacuzzis; 3 freshwater outdoor pools (1 heated); 2 lit tennis courts; watersports. *In room:* A/C, TV w/pay movies, hair dryer, minibar, Wi-Fi.

Hamilton Island ★★ ☺ More a vacation village than a single resort, Hamilton has the widest range of activities, accommodations styles, and restaurants of any Great Barrier Reef island resort. The poshest part of the resort is the ultraluxe **qualia,** an exclusive, adults-only retreat area on the northern part of the island, away from the mere mortals at the other end. Here you will stay in one of 60 one-bedroom pavilions, with hand-crafted furniture and high thread-counts on your sheets. Each has a private swimming pool and a guest pavilion. There's a spa and two restaurants, and none of these facilities are available to other Hamilton Island guests.

If qualia is out of your league, the other accommodations choices are extra large rooms and suites in the high-rise hotel; high-rise one-bedroom apartments; Polynesian-style bungalows in tropical gardens (ask for one away from the road for real privacy); and still glamorous rooms in the two-story, adults-only **Beach Club** (with minimalist decor, a personal "host" to cater to every whim, and private restaurant, lounge, and pool for exclusive use of Beach Club guests); as well as one-, two-, three-, and four-bedroom apartments and villas. The best sea views are from the second-floor Beach Club rooms, from floors 5 to 18 of the **Reef View Hotel,** and from most apartments and villas. The hotel and Beach Club have concierge service. In-room amenities vary depending on your accommodations choice (for example, apartments have kitchens), so check when booking.

On one side of the island is a marina village with cafes, restaurants, shops, and a yacht club. On the other are the accommodations, a large free-form pool and swim-up bar, and the curve of Catseye Beach. Hamilton offers a huge range of watersports, fishing trips, cruises, speedboat rides, go-karts, a "wire flyer" flying-fox hang glider, a shooting range, where you can practice target or clay-pigeon shooting, minigolf, an aquatic driving range, beach barbecue safaris, hiking trails, a wildlife sanctuary, where you can cuddle a koala or hold a baby crocodile, and an extensive daily activities program. Because a steep hill splits the resort, the best way to get around is on the free bus service, which operates on three loops around the island from 7am to 11pm, or by rented golf buggy. To get away from the main resort area, hit the beach or the hiking trails—most of the 750-hectare (1,853-acre) island is virgin bushland. The biggest drawback is that just about every activity costs extra (and it's usually not cheap), so you are constantly adding to your bill.

Hamilton Island (16km/10 miles southeast of Shute Harbour), Whitsunday Islands, QLD 4803. ✆ **13 73 33** in Australia, 02/9433 3333 (Sydney reservations office), or 07/4946 9999 (the island). Fax 02/9433 0488 (Sydney reservations office), or 07/4946 8888 (the island). www.hamiltonisland.com.au or www.qualiaresort.com.au. 880 units, some with shower only. A$324 Palm Bungalow; A$350–A$422 hotel double; A$642–A$1,168 hotel suite; A$595 Beach Club double; A$360–A$443 Whitsunday Holiday Apartments; A$1,450–A$2,125 qualia; A$3,500–A$3,995 qualia house. Rates at qualia include all meals. Ask about packages and special deals. AE, DC, MC, V. **Amenities:** 12 restaurants, 7 bars; babysitting; child-care center for kids from 6 weeks to 14 years (in 3 groups); minigolf and driving range; health club; 7 outdoor pools; room service; lit tennis courts. *In room:* A/C, TV, hair dryer, Internet (hotel rooms only; A$5 for 30 min., A$15 for 24 hr.), minibar.

Hayman ★★★ This is the most luxurious, glitzy, and glamorous resort in Australia. Check-in is done over a glass of bubbly aboard the resort's sleek launch, which meets you at Hamilton Island Airport. On arrival, you won't take long to find your way through the open-air sandstone lanais, cascading ponds, and tropical foliage to the fabulous hexagonal complex of swimming pools by the sea. Despite the luxury, Hayman is relaxed. Dress is beachwear by day, smart casual at night (pack something elegant for dinner, if you wish). An impressive lineup of activities is available, and it's probably fair to say the staff at Hayman can organize almost anything you desire.

While Hayman is renowned for the antiques, artworks, and fine objets d'art gracing its public areas, the accommodations are welcoming. Every room, suite, villa, and penthouse has a balcony or terrace, bathrobes, and valet service (and butler service in the penthouses). Retreat rooms each have a private veranda, open patios, and outdoor rinse showers. For even greater privacy, the **Beach Villa** has a private Balinese-style courtyard, walled gardens, a private infinity plunge pool, and personalized concierge service. **Spa Chakra Hayman** has 13 treatment rooms, a meditation suite, a hydrotherapy area, saunas, and steam rooms.

Hayman Island (33km/20 miles from Shute Harbour), Great Barrier Reef, QLD 4801. ✆ **1800/075 175** in Australia, or 07/4940 1234 (the island). Fax 07/4940 1858 (reservations) or 07/4940 1567 (the island). www.hayman.com.au. 212 units. A$595–A$1,500 double; A$2,140–A$2,550 suite; A$2,800–A$5,100 penthouse; A$3,700–A$4,100 Beach Villa. Extra person A$182. 2-night minimum and 10% surcharge over Christmas/New Year. Ask about packages. AE, DC, MC, V. Resort launch meets all flights at Hamilton Island Airport for the 55-min. transfer, which costs A$155 adults, half price for children. Helicopter and seaplane transfers available. **Amenities:** 4 restaurants, 2 bars; babysitting; daily kids' club (ages 5–14), day care for younger kids; concierge; beachside 9-hole golf putting green; extensive health club; outdoor Jacuzzi; 3 pools (1 saltwater, 2 heated freshwater); spa; 5 lit tennis courts (w/ball machine and coaching); watersports and dive room service. *In room:* A/C, TV w/free and pay movies, DVD player (on request), CD player, hair dryer, minibar, free Wi-Fi.

Paradise Bay Eco Escape ★★★ No glass in your windows, no locks on your doors, no telephone in your room. And you don't need any of them. This environmentally sensitive lodge was designed to show off the Whitsundays' natural beauty with minimal impact on it. Tucked in a cove under towering hoop pines and palms, it appeals to people who want to explore the wilderness in comfort, without the crowds, noisy watersports, or artificial atmosphere of a resort. Wildlife abounds, including wallabies and abundant birdlife. No ferries or cruise boats stop here and the lodge is inaccessible to day-trippers. A maximum of 16 guests stay in eight smart cabins—refurbished in August 2007—each with a modern bathroom and private deck facing the sea. On your walls hang Aboriginal art from owner Peter Spann's private collection, including some of Australia's top indigenous painters. Solar power rules, so there are no TVs, hair dryers, irons, air-conditioning, or mobile phone reception (there is one public phone). Social life centers on an open-sided gazebo and deck by the beach, equipped with a natural-history library and CDs, where everyone dines together. Access is only by a short but stunning helicopter flight from Hamilton Island.

Excursions include sailing on the lodge's gleaming 10m (33-ft.) catamaran, sea kayaking the mangroves to spot giant green sea turtles (which are common around the lodge), snorkeling the fringing reef on uninhabited islands, or bushwalking to a magical milkwood grove. Or you may prefer to just laze in a hammock or head off with a sea kayak and snorkel gear. A half-day helicopter tour to the Outer Reef is available for an extra A$698 per person. This tour is exclusively for lodge guests; you will be flown to Fantasea's Reefworld pontoon in the early morning before the boat loads of tourists arrive. This is an exclusive experience not available to the general public. Guests can spend 1½ hours snorkeling the spectacular coral and fish surrounding the pontoon, or can dive for an extra A$80.

Paradise Bay, Long Island (16km/10 miles southeast of Shute Harbour), Whitsunday Islands (P.O. Box 842), Airlie Beach, QLD 4802. ✆ **07/4946 9777.** Fax 07/4946 9777. www.paradisebay.com.au. 8 units, all with shower only. A$1,798–A$2,390 per person for a minimum 3-night stay, depending on the season. A$498–A$698 per person extra nights. No single supplement. Rates include all meals, helicopter transfers from Hamilton Island Airport, daily excursions, and equipment. MC, V. Children 14 and under not accepted. **Amenities:** Restaurant; bar. *In room:* No phone.

Peppers Palm Bay ★ This is a private and romantic hideaway, with no phone, radio or television in the rooms . . . but there is a hammock on every veranda. The beachfront *bures* (a kind of hut common in Polynesia) have a glamorous Balinese style, and the dining and bar area overlooks the gorgeous pool area, which is surrounded by timber decking. The luxury Platinum House, with two bedrooms, is on the hill behind the *bures*. Each bedroom has its own private entry and bathroom, and features a separate lounge with large plasma TVs and stereo. A wide wraparound deck has views of the Whitsunday Passage. For those who want to be active, there are nonmotorized watersports, such as kayaking, available, or you can just head to the spa. No children under 14.

Palm Bay, Long Island (16km/10 miles southeast of Shute Harbour), Whitsunday Islands (P.M.B. 28), Mackay, QLD 4741. ✆ **1800/095 025** in Australia, or 07/4946 9233. Fax 07/4946 9309. www.peppers.com.au. 25 units. A$460 double cabin; A$660 double *bure;* A$780 1-bedroom bungalow; A$1,125 double Platinum House. Rates include breakfast. Ask about packages. AE, DC, MC, V. Cruise Whitsundays (✆ 07/4946 4662) provides launch transfers from Hamilton Island Airport and Airlie Beach. No children under 14. **Amenities:** Restaurant; bar; Jacuzzi; outdoor pool; spa; lit tennis court; watersports. *In room:* A/C, DVD and CD players (suites only), hair dryer, minibar, no phone.

MODERATE

Hook Island Wilderness Resort This humble collection of cabins and campsites on a white sandy beach is one of the few really affordable island resorts on the Great Barrier Reef. That makes it popular with backpackers and anybody who just wants to kayak, play beach volleyball, visit the underwater observatory, hike, fish, laze in the pool and Jacuzzi, or chill out. Good snorkeling is footsteps from shore (gear available from reception). Hook is a national park and the second-largest Whitsunday island. The cabins are very basic, with beds or bunks sleeping six or eight.

All come with fresh bed linens; bring your own bath towels. A store sells essentials for campers, who can use the camp kitchen for A$10 per day (not available to guests staying in cabins or bunkhouses). There is a beach bar and bistro open for breakfast, lunch, and dinner.

Hook Island (40km/25 miles northeast of Shute Harbour), Whitsunday Islands (P.M.B. 23), Mackay, QLD 4741. ✆ **1800 812 626** in Australia or 07/4946 9380. Fax 07/4946 9470. www.hookislandresort.com. 20 tent sites, 6 10-bed dormitories, 8 cabins (4 with bathroom, shower only). A$120 cabin without bathroom double; extra adult A$60, extra child 4-16 A$25. A$150 cabin with bathroom double; extra adult A$75, extra child A$25. Dorm bed A$35 per person. Tent site A$20 per adult, A$10 per child. MC, V. Transfers from mainland A$40 adults, A$30 children 4-16 one-way. **Amenities:** Restaurant; bar; Jacuzzi; outdoor pool; watersports equipment. *In room:* A/C.

THE CAPRICORN COAST

South of the Whitsundays, the Bruce Highway travels through rural country until it hits the beaches of the Sunshine Coast north of Brisbane. It may not be the tourism heartland of the state, but there's plenty to discover. The most spectacular of the Great Barrier Reef islands, Heron Island, is off the coast from Gladstone. Heron's reefs are a source of enchantment for divers and snorkelers; its waters boast 21 dive sites. In summer, giant turtles nest on its beaches, and in winter humpback whales cruise by.

North of Gladstone are Rockhampton and the Capricorn Coast, named after the tropic of Capricorn that runs through it. Rockhampton is also a stepping stone to the resort island of Great Keppel. The reefs and islands off Rockhampton are not a commonly visited part of the Great Barrier Reef, yet they offer some good dive sites, most of them not far out to sea. To the south, off the small town of Bundaberg, lies another tiny coral cay, Lady Elliot Island, which is a nesting site for tens of thousands of seabirds and has a first-rate fringing reef. Two little-known attractions in Bundaberg are its good shore scuba diving and a loggerhead turtle rookery that operates in summer on the beach. Farther south lies the world's largest sand island, the World Heritage–listed Fraser Island, which can be negotiated only on foot or by four-wheel-drive (see p. 349).

Rockhampton: The Beef Capital

1,055km (654 miles) S of Cairns; 638km (396 miles) N of Brisbane

You may hear Queenslanders talk dryly about "Rockvegas." Don't be fooled. "Rocky" is the unofficial capital of the sprawling beef-cattle country that lies inland and the gateway to Great Keppel Island, which boasts some of the few inexpensive island retreats in Queensland—but it bears no resemblance to Las Vegas. Heritage buildings line the Fitzroy River, where barramundi await keen fishermen. Turn up on Friday nights at 7pm at the **Great Western Hotel,** Stanley and Denison streets (✆ **07/4922 3888;** www.greatwesternhotel.com.au), to see local cowboys practice their bull-riding skills in the rodeo ring. It's free.

ESSENTIALS

GETTING THERE Rockhampton is on the Bruce Highway, a 3½-hour drive south of Mackay, and about 90 minutes north of Gladstone.

QantasLink (✆ **13 13 13** in Australia) has flights from Brisbane and Gladstone. **Virgin Blue** (✆ **13 67 89** in Australia) flies direct from Brisbane, Townsville, and

Sydney. **Jetstar** (✆ **13 15 38** in Australia) flies from Mackay, and new budget carrier **Tiger Airways** (✆ **03/9335 3033;** www.tigerairways.com) flies from Melbourne.

Queensland Rail (✆ **1300 131 722** in Queensland; www.traveltrain.com.au) trains stop at Rockhampton daily. The trip from Brisbane takes just 7 hours on the high-speed Tilt Train; the fare is A$105 in economy class and A$154 in business class.

Greyhound Australia (✆ **1300/473 946** in Australia or 07/4920 3900 in Rockhampton) serves Rockhampton on its many daily runs between Brisbane and Cairns. The fare is A$131 from Brisbane (trip time: 12 hr.) and A$202 from Cairns (trip time: 18 hr.).

VISITOR INFORMATION Drop by the **Capricorn Tourism** information center, at the city's southern entrance on Gladstone Road (Bruce Highway) at the Capricorn Spire (✆ **1800/676 701** in Australia, or 07/4927 2055; www.capricorn tourism.com.au). It's open daily from 9am to 5pm. In the city center, you'll find the **Rockhampton Customs House Tourist Information Centre** at 208 Quay St. (✆ **07/4922 5625;** www.capricornholidays.com.au). It's open weekdays 8:30am to 4:30pm, weekends and public holidays 9am to 4pm.

GETTING AROUND **Avis** (✆ 07/4927 3344), **Budget** (✆ 07/4922 8064), **Europcar** (✆ 07/4922 0044), **Hertz** (✆ 07/4922 2721), and **Thrifty** (✆ 07/4927 8755) have offices in Rockhampton. The local bus is **Sunbus** (✆ 07/4936 2133).

EXPLORING: CAVERNS, ABORIGINAL CULTURE & MORE

The **Capricorn Caves** ★ (✆ **07/4934 2883;** wwwcapricorncaves.com.au), 23km (14 miles) north of Rockhampton at Olsen's Caves Road, off the Bruce Highway, have been a popular attraction in this part of the world ever since Norwegian pioneer John Olsen stumbled upon them in 1882. The limestone caves originated in an ancient (380-million-year-old) coral reef and today are a maze of small tunnels and larger chambers. The 1-hour tour, which winds through large caverns with stalactite and stalagmite formations before entering the 20m-high (66-ft.) Cathedral Cave, is A$22 for adults, A$11 for children 5 to 15. It departs daily (except Christmas and New Year's Day) on the hour from 9am to 4pm (closing time is 5pm). Spelunkers over age 16 can squeeze through tunnels and chimneys and rock climb on a 2-hour adventure tour that costs A$60; minimum of two required. Book 24 hours ahead for this. In December and early January, the only time of year when the sun is directly over the tropic of Capricorn, a ray of pure light pours through a hole in the limestone caves. This is known as the Summer Solstice phenomenon and tours departing every morning at 11am highlight it. The caves are also home to thousands of small insectivorous bats, which leave the cave at sunset to feed. Plan enough time here to walk the 30-minute dry rainforest trail, watch the video on bats in the interpretive center, and feed the wild kangaroos. If you want to stay, there are cabins, a motor-home park, and a campground.

The **Dreamtime Cultural Centre** (✆ **07/4936 1655;** www.dreamtimecentre.com.au), on the Bruce Highway opposite the Yeppoon turnoff, 6km (3¾ miles) north of town, showcases Aboriginal culture. There's a sandstone cave replica, a display on the dugong (manatee) culture of the Torres Strait Islanders, and an Aboriginal crafts shop. The center is open Monday to Friday from 10am to 3:30pm. Admission, including a tour, is A$14 for adults, A$6.50 for children, and A$11 for students and backpackers. Tours of burial sites and rock art, with didgeridoo demonstrations and boomerang-throwing, start at 10:30am.

Rockhampton has two free public botanic gardens, both nice for a stroll and a picnic. The **Kershaw Gardens,** which display Aussie rainforest, wetland, and fragrant plants from north of the 30th parallel, also have a monorail and a pioneer-style slab hut where Devonshire teas are served. Enter off Charles Street. The **Rockhampton Botanic Gardens** (✆ **07/4922 1654**), established in 1869, are quite lovely. They have an impressive collection of large palm trees, cycads, heliconias, and giant banyan fig trees. Admission is free to the small zoo inside the grounds, which features 'roos, koalas, lorikeets, cassowaries, and a range of other creatures, including—rather bizarrely—some rather sad-looking chimpanzees. The gardens are open 6am to 6pm daily, the zoo daily from 8am to 5pm. Enter off Ann Street or Spencer Street.

WHERE TO STAY

Rydges Capricorn Resort ★ The 20km (13 miles) of unbroken beach that fronts this resort—and the fact that it is the only resort of any size or style in this region—are reasons enough to visit. The resort is about 9km (5½ miles) from the pretty seaside town of Yeppoon, about 45km (28 miles) north of Rockhampton Airport. Open since 1986, and now showing its age a little, the resort is nevertheless cheerful and pleasant, and the rooms are spacious. The best of the three accommodations blocks is the Palms, with views over the beach and out to Great Keppel Island. The main resort block is dominated by one of the largest freshwater swimming pools in the Southern Hemisphere, popular with visiting local families, especially on weekends. Accommodations vary: Some suites and all apartments have kitchenettes, hotel rooms have minibars, and two-bedroom apartments and Capricorn suites with kitchens have a washing machine and dryer. Set in 8,910 hectares (22,000 acres) of bushland, the resort also has extensive wetlands teeming with bird life. Wetlands tours are available for a fee, as are horseback riding, land yachting, fishing, canoeing, clay-pigeon shooting, WaveRunners, and rifle shooting. This is not the place for a quiet getaway—it is popular with large and sometimes noisy conference groups—but there are lots of activities, and it may be just the place to break up your coastal trek.

Farnborough Rd. (P.O. Box 350), Yeppoon, QLD 4703. ✆ **1800/075 902** in Australia, or 07/4925 2525. www.rydges.com/capricorn. 281 units. A$320 double; A$370 junior suite; A$395 junior suite with kitchenette; A$445 Capricorn Suite; A$470 Capricorn Suite with kitchenette; A$440 1-bedroom apt; A$490 2-bedroom apt. Extra person A$40. Free crib. Packages, including golf packages, available year-round. Rates include watersports and some other activities. AE, DC, MC, V. Free covered parking. **Amenities:** 4 restaurants; 2 bars; airport and train station transfers (A$20 adults, A$10 child 2–12); babysitting; bikes; free daytime kids' club (fee for evening sessions); concierge; 2 18-hole golf courses; exercise room; outdoor Jacuzzi; outdoor freshwater pool w/adjoining heated beach-style pool; room service; sauna; 4 lit tennis courts; extensive watersports. *In room:* A/C, TV w/pay movies, hair dryer, Internet (A$11 for 1 hr.; A$22 for 24 hr.).

Great Keppel Island

15km (9½ miles) E of Rockhampton

This 1,454-hectare (3,591-acre) island is home to 17 beaches, all accessible by walking trails or dinghy (which you can rent). The shallow waters and fringing reef make the island a good choice for beginner divers; experienced divers will see corals, sea snakes, turtles, and rays. If you stay overnight, you will most likely be rewarded with one of the spectacular sunsets for which the island is famous.

GETTING THERE **Freedom Fast Cats** (✆ **07/4933 6888;** www.freedomfastcats.com) operates launches that make the 30-minute crossing from Rosslyn Bay Harbour, about 55km (34 miles) east of Rockhampton. The round-trip costs A$49 for adults, A$41 seniors and students, A$29 for children 4 to 14, and A$127 for families of four. A water taxi will cost around A$60.

From Rockhampton, take the Capricorn Coast scenic drive Route 10 to Emu Park and follow the signs to Rosslyn Bay Harbour. If you're coming to Rockhampton from the north, the scenic drive turnoff is just north of the city, and from there it's 46km (29 miles) to the harbor. You can leave your car in covered storage at **Great Keppel Island Security Car Park,** 422 Scenic Hwy., near the harbor (✆ **07/4933 6670**), for around A$10 per day.

The most flexible option for getting to Rosslyn Bay Harbour by bus is with **Little Johnny's Tours Shuttle Service** (✆ **0414 793 637** mobile; littlejohnnystours@bigpond.com), which provides pickups to and from Rockhampton Airport and accommodations in Rockhampton and Yeppoon and will transfer you direct to the ferry terminal. It costs A$75 for up to four people, and A$20 for each extra person, and for an extra A$30 will stop for up to an hour so you can pick up supplies for the island.

Peace Aviation (✆ **07/4927 4355;** www.peaceaviation.com) connects with incoming flights to Rockhampton Airport to transfer to the island. It is a 20-minute flight daily except Sundays and costs A$275 one-way for up to three passengers, or A$385 for four or five.

VISITOR INFORMATION Pick up information about accommodations and activities on Great Keppel at the **Capricorn Tourism** information center (at the Capricorn Spire), on Gladstone Road, Rockhampton (✆ **1800/676 701** in Australia, or 07/4927 2055; www.capricornholidays.com.au). It's open daily from 9am to 5pm. You will also find some information at the ferry terminal at Rosslyn Bay Harbour.

WHERE TO STAY

Great Keppel Island Resort, the island's major resort for more than 30 years, closed its doors in early 2008 for a complete rebuild, and at press time for this book was still grappling with the Australian government's decision that the proposed project was unacceptable because of the environmental impact it would have on the Great Barrier Reef. Some locals believe it may never happen and the resort sits abandoned. Meanwhile, visitors can stay at a couple of smaller, family-oriented budget resorts on what has become a less-populated and more peaceful island.

Great Keppel Island Holiday Village Great Keppel Island Holiday Village is located in a garden setting less than a minute's walk to two great swimming beaches. Accommodations include twin or double rooms with shared bathrooms, twin or double canvas tents erected on timber decks, and en-suite cabins, sleeping four. Also available are two self-contained houses suitable for families of up to six people. The private two-bedroom Dolphin House has a queen-size bed in one room and a double bed and bunks in the other. The two-story, solar powered Keppel House is set among large shade trees on the southern end of Fisherman's Beach, and sleeps up to six. Verandas off the spacious lounge room offer plenty of shade, and there is a barbecue outside. All linen is provided (but bring your towel), as is snorkeling gear to use during your stay. There is a fully equipped communal kitchen for those in the tents and cabins, with gas stoves, refrigerators, and microwave available, as well as a barbecue. Basic grocery items, such as milk, bread, soft drinks, and some food items, are available to buy. Kayaking and snorkeling tours are offered. There is no smoking in the village area.

Great Keppel Island, off Rockhampton, QLD 4700. ✆ **1800/180 235** in Australia, or 07/4939 8655. www.gkiholidayvillage.com.au. 19 units. A$85 tent or room per person twin/double, A$65 single; A$140 cabin (all with bathroom, shower only) double; A$180–A$240 houses for 5 to 6 people. A$20 extra person. 2 night min. stay; 5 night min. for houses. MC, V. **Amenities:** Watersports rentals. *In room:* Ceiling fan, TV (houses only).

Gladstone: Gateway to Heron Island

550km (341 miles) N of Brisbane; 1,162km (720 miles) S of Cairns

The industrial port town of Gladstone is the departure point for beautiful Heron Island. About 25km (16 miles) south of the town (but off the Bruce Hwy.) are the twin beach towns of Boyne Island and Tannum Sands, which are worth the detour.

ESSENTIALS

GETTING THERE & GETTING AROUND Gladstone is on the coast 21km (13 miles) off the Bruce Highway. **QantasLink** (book through Qantas) has daily flights from Brisbane, Rockhampton, and Bundaberg.

Queensland Rail (✆ **1300/131 722** in Queensland; www.traveltrain.com.au) operates trains to Gladstone from Brisbane and Cairns most days. The economy fare on the high-speed Tilt Train from Brisbane (trip time: 6 hr.) is A$97; from Cairns (trip time: 18 hr.) it is A$265. Fares from Cairns on the *Sunlander* (trip time: 20 hr.) range from A$177 for a seat to A$700 for a sleeper in the luxury Queenslander Class.

Greyhound Australia (✆ **1300/473 946** in Australia; www.greyhound.com.au) operates daily coaches to Gladstone on the Brisbane-Cairns run. The fare is A$123 from Brisbane (trip time: 10 hr.), A$220 from Cairns (trip time: 20 hr.).

Avis (✆ **07/4978 2633**), **Budget** (✆ **07/4972 8488**), **Hertz** (✆ **07/4978 6899**), and **Thrifty** (✆ **07/4972 5999**) have offices in Gladstone.

VISITOR INFORMATION The **Gladstone Visitor Information Centre** is in the ferry terminal at Gladstone Marina, Bryan Jordan Drive, Gladstone, QLD 4680 (✆ **07/4972 9000;** www.gladstoneholidays.info). It's open from 8:30am to 5pm Monday through Friday, and from 9am to 5pm Saturday and Sunday. Closed Christmas Day.

WHERE TO STAY

Rydges Gladstone This four-level hotel in the center of town is Gladstone's largest and best hotel. It has a large business clientele, so there are ample facilities—spacious rooms with balconies, modern bathrooms, an upscale restaurant, and a pool and sun deck. Most rooms have views over the port or the city, and all harbor view rooms were refurbished (including brand new beds) in 2009. Executive rooms have a kitchenette.

100 Goondoon St., Gladstone, QLD 4680. ✆ **1300/857 922** in Australia or 07/4970 0000. Fax 07/4972 4921. www.rydges.com/gladstone. 95 units. A$200–A$240 double. AE, DC, MC, V. Free covered parking. **Amenities:** Restaurant; bar; outdoor pool; room service. *In room:* A/C, TV w/free movies, hair dryer, free Internet, minibar.

Heron Island: Jewel of the Reef ★★★

72km (45 miles) NE of Gladstone

The difference between Heron and other islands is that once there, you have no need to travel farther to the Reef. Step off the beach and you enter magnificent fields of coral that seem to stretch for miles. And the myriad life forms that abound here are accessible to everyone through diving, snorkeling, or reef walks at low tide, or aboard a semisubmersible vessel that allows you to view the ocean floor without getting wet.

There has been a resort on Heron since 1932, and in 1943 the island became a national park. It is a haven for wildlife and people, and an experience of a lifetime is almost guaranteed at any time of year, particularly if you love turtles—Heron is a rookery for giant green and loggerhead turtles. (When geologist Joseph Bette Jukes named this piece of paradise in 1843, he overlooked the turtles for which it is now famous in favor of the reef herons that abounded.) Resort guests gather on the beach from late November to February to watch the female turtles lay eggs, and from February to mid-April to see the hatched babies scuttle down the sand to the water. Humpback whales also pass through from June through September.

Three days on Heron will give you plenty of time to see everything. The island is so small that you can walk around it at a leisurely pace in about half an hour. One of the first things to do is to take advantage of the organized activities that operate several times a day and are designed so guests can plan their own days. Snorkeling and reef walking are major occupations for visitors—if they're not diving, that is. The island is home to 21 of the world's most stunning dive sites.

Guided walks provide another way to explore the island. Walks include a visit to the island's research station. As for the reef walk, just borrow a pair of sand shoes, a balance pole, and a viewing bucket, and head off with a guide at low tide. The walk can take up to 90 minutes, but there's no compulsion to stay; if it gets too hot, you can head to the sanctuary of your room or the shady bar area.

A fishing trip should also be on the agenda, even for the most inexperienced. The reef fish seem to just jump onto the hook, and the resort chef is happy to cook them for you for dinner!

GETTING THERE A courtesy coach meets flights from Brisbane (with connections from other cities) at Gladstone airport at 10am to take guests to Gladstone Marina for the launch transfer to the island; it departs 11am daily (except Dec 25). Transfers aboard a sleek 130-seater catamaran cost A$120 each way for adults, half-price for kids 3 to 14. Trip time is around 2 hours. Helicopter transfers can be arranged for A$275 per person each way.

WHERE TO STAY ON HERON ISLAND

Heron Island Resort ★★★ ☺ This lovely, low-key resort has been transformed over the past few years. The newest rooms are the chic Wistari suites, each with a private garden and veranda. But the focus here is still very much on the outdoors. The brilliant colors of the island's surrounding water and Reef are reflected in the interiors, and everything is light-filled and breezy. Heron's central complex is equal parts grand Queenslander home and sophisticated beach house, with smart bar and lounge areas open to ocean views and sunsets. Duplex-style Turtle rooms are designed for couples or families, with a casual living area and a veranda, or you can go for greater luxury in the suites or the private beach house.

The property has a lounge with a TV, public phones (only the four Point suites and the Beach House have private phones). Dial-up Internet access is available at reception. The **Aqua Soul Spa** offers double treatment rooms, therapies designed for two, and the usual spa treatments and pampering. The spa complex is in a secluded spot on the edge of the island's Pisonia forests, removed from the main resort.

Heron Island, off Gladstone, QLD 4680. © **1300/233 432** in Australia, or 03/9413 6288 (reservations office), or 07/4972 9055 (resort). www.heronisland.com. 109 units, some with shower only. A$398–A$438 Turtle Room double; A$472–A$518 Reef Room double; A$632–A$696 Beachside Suite double; A$882–A$970 Point Suite or Wistari Suite; A$920–A$998 Beach House double. Extra adult A$64. Children 11 and under stay free in parent's room. Free crib. Rates include breakfast and some activities. Meal packages are available for A$69 per person per night. Ask about special packages. AE, DC, MC, V. No children allowed in Point and Wistari suites or Beach House. **Amenities:** Restaurant; bar; babysitting; children's program (ages 7–12) during Australian school vacations; Internet; Jacuzzi; outdoor pool; spa; 2 lit tennis courts; limited watersports equipment rental. *In room:* A/C (beach house only and Wistari suite only), ceiling fan, CD player (beach house and suites only), hair dryer, minibar (beach house and suites only).

Bundaberg: Gateway to Lady Elliot Island

384km (238 miles) N of Brisbane; 1,439km (892 miles) S of Cairns

The small sugar town of Bundaberg is the closest to the southernmost point of the Great Barrier Reef. If you visit the area between November and March, allow an evening to visit the Mon Repos Turtle Rookery. Divers may want to take in some of Australia's best shore diving right off Bundaberg's beaches.

GETTING THERE & GETTING AROUND Bundaberg is on the Isis Highway, about 50km (31 miles) off the Bruce Highway from Gin Gin in the north and 53km (33 miles) off the Bruce Highway from just north of Childers in the south.

QantasLink (© **13 13 13** in Australia) flies from Brisbane daily and from Gladstone three times a week.

Queensland Rail (© **1300 131 722** in Queensland; www.traveltrain.com.au) trains stop in Bundaberg every day en route between Brisbane and Cairns. The fare is A$66 from Brisbane in economy class or A$98 business class on the Tilt Train; fares range from A$124 for a seat to A$190 for a sleeping berth on the *Sunlander* from Cairns. The trip takes 4½ hours from Brisbane and 8¼ hours from Cairns on the Tilt Train; the *Sunlander* takes 6¾ hours from Brisbane and 25 hours from Cairns.

Greyhound Australia (© **1300/473 946** in Australia) stops here many times a day on runs between Brisbane and Cairns. The 7-hour trip from Brisbane costs A$90. From Cairns it is a 22-hour trip, and the fare is A$246.

Avis (© 07/4152 1877), **Budget** (© 07/4151 1355), **Europcar** (© 07/4155 0333), **Hertz** (© 07/4155 0884), and **Thrifty** (© 07/4151 6222) all have offices in Bundaberg.

VISITOR INFORMATION The **Bundaberg Tourism Visitor Information Centre,** at 271 Bourbong St., Bundaberg West, QLD 4670 (© **1300/722 099** in Australia, or 07/4153 8888; www.bundabergregion.org) is open daily 9am to 5pm, public holidays (except Good Friday and Christmas Day) 10am to 3pm.

WHAT TO SEE & DO

The best shore diving in Queensland is in Bundaberg's **Woongarra Marine Park.** It has soft and hard corals, urchins, rays, sea snakes, and 60 fish species, plus a World War II Beaufort bomber wreck. There are several scuba operators. **Dive Musgrave** (© **1800/552 614** in Australia or 07/4154 3900; www.divemusgrave.com.au) runs

UP CLOSE & PERSONAL WITH A turtle

The egg in my hand is warm, soft, and about the size of a Ping-Pong ball. At my feet, a giant green turtle sighs deeply as she lays a clutch of about 120 eggs in a pear-shaped chamber dug from the sand. A large tear rolls from her eye. In the distance, the wedge-tailed shearwaters call eerily to each other, backed by the sound of the ocean.

The egg-laying ritual of the turtles is central to a trip to **Heron Island** in the summer months. At night and in the early morning, small groups of people gather on the beaches to witness the turtles lumber up the beach, dig holes in the sand, and lay their eggs. (The turtles are not easily disturbed, and you can get very close.) Every night during the season, volunteer guides from the University of Queensland research station on the island are on hand; you can watch and ask questions as the researchers tag and measure the turtles before they return to the water. The laying season runs December through February, and only one in 5,000 hatchlings will live to return in about 50 years to lay their own eggs.

Another good place to watch the turtles nesting is Mon Repos Beach, outside Bundaberg. **Mon Repos Conservation Park** is one of the two largest loggerhead-turtle rookeries in the South Pacific. The visitor center by the beach has a great display on the turtle life cycle and shows films at approximately 7:30pm daily in summer. There is a strict booking system for turtle-watching tours, to help cope with the crowds. Access to the beach is by ticket only, and you must book your visit to Mon Repos during the turtle season. Tickets are sold through the **Bundaberg Visitor Information Centre** at 271 Bourbong St., Bundaberg (✆ **1300/722 099** in Australia or 07/4153 8888), or you can book online at www.bookbundabergregion.com.au from September 1. The website has a lot of very useful information on how to get to the rookery and what to expect from your turtle-watching experience. Tours start at 7pm, but you may have to wait up to 2 hours or more, depending on when the turtles appear. Nesting happens around high tide; hatching usually occurs between 8pm and midnight. Take a sweater, as it can get quite cool.

The **Mon Repos Turtle Rookery** ★ (✆ **07/4159 1652** or 07/4131 1600) is 14km (8¾ miles) east of Bundaberg's town center. Follow Bourbong Street out of town toward Burnett Heads as it becomes Bundaberg-Bargara Road. Take the Port Road to the left and look for the Mon Repos signs to the right. During turtle-nesting season (Nov to late Mar), the park and information center are open 24 hours a day. Public access to the beach is closed from 6pm to 6am. Turtle viewing tours run from 7pm until 1am daily (except for Dec 24, 25, and 31). From April to early November (when there are no turtles around), the information center is open Monday to Friday from 8am to 3:30pm. The park is open 24 hours. Admission to the visitor center is free from April through November; but when the turtles start nesting, you pay A$9.60 for adults, A$5.10 for children ages 5 to 17 and seniors, or A$23 for families, including your tour.

3-day, 3-night dive cruises to Lady Musgrave Island twice a week. The cruise costs A$678, including all meals and 8 to 10 dives. Equipment rental, including a dive computer, is A$80 per person.

WHERE TO STAY

Sun City Motel This basic but neat and tidy motel is a short stroll across the river from the town center. The rooms are clean and well kept, and have a ceiling fan, toaster, and tea- and coffeemaking facilities. Two family rooms have a double bed and twin bunks. Home-cooked meals can be delivered to your room or you can use the guest barbecue and outdoor dining area.

11a Hinkler Ave., North Bundaberg, QLD 4670. ✆ **07/4152 1099.** Fax 07/4153 1510. www.suncitymotel.com.au. 12 units, all with shower only. A$80 double; A$130 family room (sleeps 4). Extra person A$10. AE, DC, MC, V. Free covered parking. **Amenities:** Free airport, train, or bus station transfers; nearby golf course; access to nearby health club; outdoor saltwater pool; room service. *In room:* A/C, TV, hair dryer, Wi-Fi.

Lady Elliot Island ★

80km (50 miles) NE of Bundaberg

The southernmost Great Barrier Reef island, Lady Elliot, is a 42-hectare (104-acre) coral cay ringed by a wide, shallow lagoon filled with dazzling coral life. Reef walking, snorkeling, and diving are the main reasons people come to this coral cay, which is so small you can walk across it in 15 minutes. You may snorkel and reef walk during only the 2 to 3 hours before and after high tide, so plan your schedule accordingly. You will see dazzling corals and brilliantly colored fish, clams, sponges, urchins, and anemones. Divers will see a good range of marine life, including green and loggerhead turtles (which nest on the beach Nov–Mar). Whales pass by from June through September.

Lady Elliot is a sparse, grassy island rookery, not a lush tropical paradise, so don't expect white sand and palm trees. Some people will find it too spartan; others will relish chilling out in a beautiful, peaceful location with reef all around. Just be prepared for the smell and constant noise of those birds.

GETTING THERE You reach the island by a 30-minute flight from Bundaberg or Hervey Bay that runs three times a day. Book your air travel with your accommodations. **Seair** (✆ **07/5599 4509;** www.seairpacific.com.au) offers a day-trip package from both departure points for A$298 for adults and A$161 for children 3 to 12 including flights, snorkel gear, glass-bottom-boat ride, lunch, and guided activities. Day-trip flights also operate from Brisbane and the Gold Coast for A$699 adults and A$349 children, and the Sunshine Coast for A$599 adults and A$330 children round-trip. There is a 10-kilogram (22-lb.) luggage limit.

WHERE TO STAY

Lady Elliot Island Eco Resort ★ Accommodations here are fairly basic, but visitors come for the Reef, not the room. Still, all suites and rooms have been refurbished over the past couple of years, with fresh paint and new queen-size beds and furniture in the suites and reef rooms. Top of the range are air-conditioned Island suites, which have one or two separate bedrooms and great sea views from the deck. Most Reef rooms sleep four and have decks with views through the trees to the sea. Shearwater bunk rooms sleep up to six. All rooms have modern private bathrooms. The cool, spacious safari-tent "eco-huts" have four bunks, electric lighting, and timber floors, but share the public toilets and showers used by day guests. The limited facilities include a boutique, an education center, and a dive shop, which runs shore and boat dives, introductory dives, and rents equipment. The resort has no air-conditioning, no keys (secure storage is at the front desk), no TVs, no radio, no mobile phone reception, and one public telephone. The food is basic. A low-key program of mostly free activities includes glass-bottom-boat rides, badminton, guided walks, and beach volleyball—but the true beauty of this place is that because of the relatively low number of guests, you pretty much get the Reef to yourself.

Great Barrier Reef, off Bundaberg (P.O. Box 348), Runaway Bay, QLD 4216. ✆ **1800/072 200** in Australia, or 07/4156 4444. Fax 07/4156 4400. www.ladyelliot.com.au. 40 units, 20 with bathroom with shower only. A$316–A$352 eco-hut double; A$374–A$402 bunk room double; A$432–A$446 double garden unit; A$472–A$630 double reef unit; A$584–A$622 suite double. A$96–A$101 children 3–12 years. 3-night minimum Christmas/New Year; 2-night minimum for suites. Ask about packages. Rates include breakfast, dinner, and some guided tours. AE, DC, MC, V. **Amenities:** Restaurant; bar; children's program (ages 3–12) during Queensland school holidays; saltwater pool. *In room:* A/C (suites only), ceiling or wall fans, hair dryer (suites only), no phone.

ECO-ADVENTURES ON FRASER ISLAND

1,547km (959 miles) S of Cairns; 260km (161 miles) N of Brisbane; 15km (9½ miles) E of Hervey Bay

The biggest sand island in the world, this 162,000-hectare (400,140-acre) World Heritage–listed island off the central Queensland coast attracts a mix of ecotourists and Aussie fishermen. Fraser is a pristine vista of eucalyptus woodlands, dunes, clear creeks, ancient rainforest, blue lakes, ocher-colored sand cliffs, and a stunning 121km-long (75-mile) beach. For four-wheel-drive fans, Fraser's beauty lies in its absence of paved roads. On weekends when the fish are running, it's nothing to see 100 four-wheel-drives lining 75-Mile Beach, which is an authorized road. Pedestrians, beware!

You'll need more than a day here to see everything and to truly appreciate how stunning this place is. Allow at least 3 days to soak it all up, and to allow for the slow pace dictated by the sandy trails that pass for roads.

Essentials

GETTING THERE Hervey (pronounced *Har*-vey) Bay is the main gateway to the island. Take the Bruce Highway to Maryborough, then the 34km (21-mile) road to Hervey Bay. From the north, turn off the highway at Torbanlea, north of Maryborough, and cut across to Hervey Bay. Allow 3 hours from the Sunshine Coast, a good 5 hours from Brisbane.

QantasLink (✆ **13 13 13** in Australia) flies from Brisbane to Hervey Bay. **Virgin Blue** (✆ **13 67 89** in Australia) and **Jetstar** (✆ **13 15 38** in Australia) both fly direct from Sydney.

Greyhound Australia (✆ **1300/473 946** in Australia) coaches stop in Hervey Bay on the Brisbane-Cairns-Brisbane routes. The 5½-hour trip from Brisbane costs A$67. From Cairns, the fare is A$264 and the trip is around 24 hours. Kingfisher Bay Resort runs a shuttle from Brisbane for A$85 per person.

The nearest **train** station is in **Maryborough West,** 34km (20 miles) from Hervey Bay. Passengers on the high-speed **Tilt Train** (Sun–Fri) can book connecting bus service to Pialba (a suburb of Hervey Bay) through **Queensland Rail** (✆ **1300/131 722** in Queensland; www.traveltrain.com.au). The fare from Brisbane for the 3½-hour Tilt Train trip is A$68 in economy class and A$98 in business class, including the bus fare. Fares are A$197 in a seat and A$712 in a Queenslander-class sleeper from Cairns (trip time: just under 27 hr.). Train passengers from the north must take a courtesy shuttle from Maryborough West to Maryborough Central; then take the next available local bus to Pialba.

Guests at Kingfisher Bay Resort (p. 352) can get to the resort aboard the **Kingfisher Ferry,** which makes the trip from the mainland six times a day. Round-trip fare for the 50-minute crossing is A$50 adults and A$25 kids 4 to 14. The resort runs a shuttle from Hervey Bay's airport and coach terminal to the harbor; the cost is A$7 adults, half-price for kids. You can park free at the Fastcat terminal. Drive to the terminal first to unload your luggage at the Kingfisher Bay reception desk, and then return to the parking lot and walk back (only 100m/328 ft.). Helicopter transfers are also available.

GETTING THERE & GETTING AROUND BY FOUR-WHEEL DRIVE ★ Four-wheel-drives are the only vehicle transportation on the island. Many four-wheel-drive rentals are based in Hervey Bay, but you must be 21 or over to rent one. You'll pay around A$200 a day, plus around A$20 to A$35 per day to reduce the deductible (usually A$4,000), plus a bond (typically A$500). You must also buy a government Vehicle Access Permit, which costs A$38 from your rental-car company, Urangan Boat Harbour, or the River Heads boat ramp.

Fraser Magic 4WD Hire (✆ **07/4125 6612;** www.fraser4wdhire.com.au) rents four-wheel-drives and camping gear, offers four-wheel-drive packages that include camping or accommodations, organizes Vehicle Access Permits, barge bookings, camping permits, and secure storage for your car and will pick you up from the airport, the coach terminal, or your hotel. **Aussie Trax 4×4 Rentals** (✆ **1800/062 275** in Australia, or 07/4124 4433; www.fraserisland4wd.com.au), has offices in Hervey Bay and at Kingfisher Bay Resort on Fraser Island (see below), and allows 1-day rentals. A four-wheel-drive will cost you between about A$150 and A$300 a day, plus a A$500 security deposit (by credit card), held until return of the vehicle in the original condition. Rates are cheaper if you book for a week. Book well in advance.

Four-wheel-drives reach the island on the **Fraser Venture** barge (✆ **1800/227 437** in Australia or 07/4194 9300; www.fraserislandbarges.com.au), which runs three times a day from River Heads, 17km (11 miles) south of Urangan Boat Harbour. Kingfisher Bay Resort (see below) also runs a barge from River Heads. The round-trip fare for a vehicle with up to four occupants is A$150. It's a good idea to book a place for the 45-minute crossing. Barges also provide access to Rainbow Beach and operate continuously between Inskip Point and Hook Point between 6am and 5:30pm daily. The cost is A$90 return for a vehicle and four passengers.

Fraser Island Taxi Service (✆ **07/4127 9188,** or 0429/379 188 mobile) is another option for getting around. There is only one taxi on the island (a four-wheel-drive, of course), so it's important to book ahead. They will pick you up anywhere on the island and will give you a quote on price before you set off. The taxi seats five, and there's also room for your luggage and fishing rods.

Fraser Explorer Tours (✆ **07/4194 9222;** www.fraserexplorertours.com.au), which runs day tours of the island from Hervey Bay and from Rainbow Beach, costs A$159 to A$199 adults and A$99 to A$145 children 4 to 14.

VISITOR INFORMATION The **Hervey Bay Visitor Information Centre** is at 227 Maryborough–Hervey Bay Rd. (at Urraween Rd.), Pialba (✆ **1800/811 728** in Australia, or 07/4215 9855; www.visitherveybay.info). It is open daily 9am to 5pm,

Fraser Island

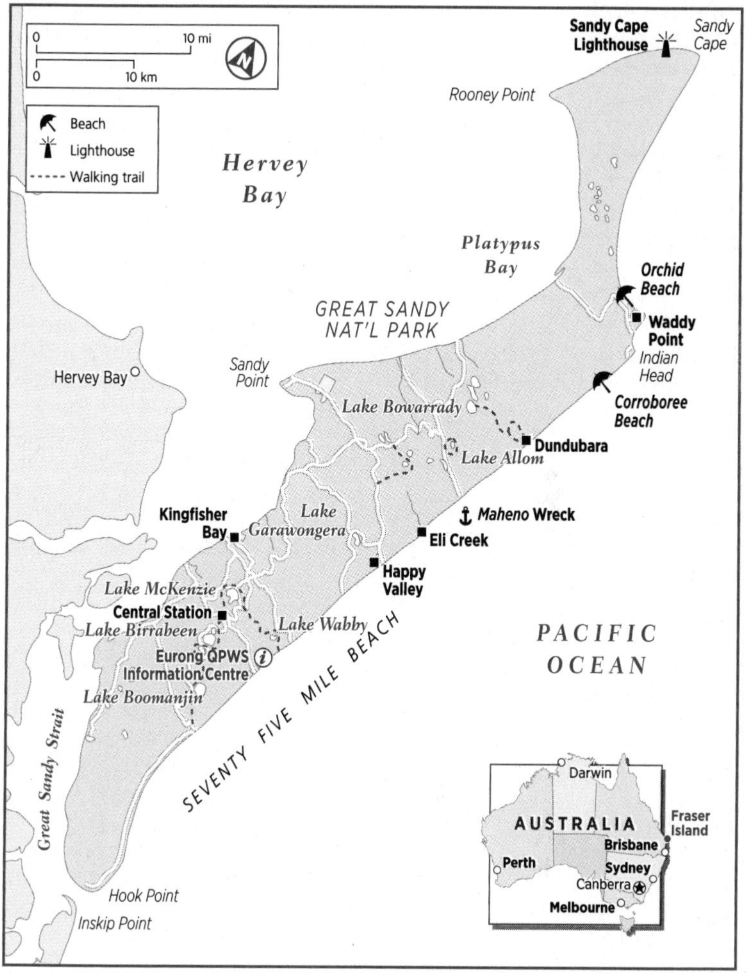

except Good Friday and Christmas Day. Another online source of information is **www.hervey.com.au**. The **Marina Kiosk** (**© 07/4128 9800**) at Urangan Boat Harbour is a one-stop booking and information agency for all Fraser-related travel. Several Queensland Parks and Wildlife Service information offices are on the island.

There are no towns and very few facilities, food stores, or services on the island, so if you're camping, take all supplies with you.

Exploring the Island

Fraser's turquoise lakes and tea-colored "perched" lakes in the dunes are among the island's biggest attractions. Brilliant blue **Lake McKenzie** is absolutely beautiful; a swim here may be the highlight of your visit. Lake Birrabeen is another popular swimming spot. Don't miss a refreshing swim in the fast-flowing clear shallows of **Eli Creek.** Wade up the creek for a mile or two and let the current carry you back down. You should also take the boardwalk through a verdant forest of palms and ferns along the banks of Wanggoolba Creek.

Don't swim at **75-Mile Beach,** which hugs the eastern edge of the island—it has dangerously strong currents and a healthy shark population. Instead, swim in the **Champagne Pools** (also called the Aquarium)—pockets of soft sand protected from the worst of the waves by rocks. The bubbling seawater turns the pools into miniature spas. The pools are just north of **Indian Head,** a 60m (197-ft.) rocky outcrop at the northern end of the beach.

View the island's famous colored sand in its natural setting—from the 70m (230-ft.) **Cathedrals,** cliffs that stretch for miles north of the settlement of Happy Valley on the eastern side of the island.

Some of Queensland's best fishing is on Fraser Island. Anglers can throw a line in the surf gutters off the beach. (Freshwater fishing is not allowed.) Bream, whiting, flathead, and swallowtail are the beach catches. Indian Head is good for rock species and tailor; the waters east off **Waddy Point** yield northern and southern reef fish. **Kingfisher Bay Resort** (see below) offers free fish clinics, rents tackle, and organizes half-day fishing jaunts.

From August through October, tour boats crowd the straits to see humpback whales returning to Antarctica with calves in tow. Kingfisher Bay Resort runs a whale-watching cruise from Urangan Harbour.

Where to Stay

Kingfisher Bay Resort ★★ ☺ This sleek, environment-friendly ecoresort lies low along Fraser's west coast. Hotel rooms are smart and contemporary, with air-conditioning and Japanese-style screens opening onto balconies that look into the bush, but my pick are the two- and three-bedroom villas just a short walk from the main resort area and pools. The hillside villas, which have Jacuzzis on their balconies, are fairly luxurious, but guests must contend with that long haul up the hill. Each villa has a kitchen, washing machine, and dryer. Houses are available to rent for those who want extra privacy away from the resort area. The only drawback is that you must have your own vehicle, as transport is not provided to get to them. An impressive lineup of ecoeducational activities includes daily four-wheel-drive tours with a ranger to points of interest around the island, free guided walks daily, and an

Don't Feed the Dingoes

The dingoes that roam the island are emboldened by visitors who have—sometimes deliberately, sometimes unwittingly—fed them over the years. These dangerous wild animals have been responsible for one death and several serious attacks in recent years. Do not feed them, and keep your distance. If you don't, rangers can impose on-the-spot fines of A$225. And be warned: The laws are strictly enforced by the rangers, and the maximum penalty is A$3,000.

Another Great Walk

The stunning Fraser Island World Heritage Area is the location for one of Queensland's six Great Walks (p. 334). The **Fraser Island Great Walk** (✆ 13 13 04 in Australia; www.derm.qld.gov.au) follows a winding track from Dilli Village to Lake Garawongera. The main trail is 85km (53 miles) long and takes 6 to 8 days to complete, but offshoots provide short, full-day, overnight, and 2- to 3-day walks. Overnight walkers must book huts and need a permit, which costs A$5 per person or A$20 for families of up to six with children ages 17 or under. The walk takes you to many of the island's popular landmarks, such as Lake McKenzie, Central Station, Wangoolba Creek, Valley of the Giants, and Lake Wabby.

excellent free Junior Eco-Ranger program on weekends and during school vacations. You can also join bird-watching tours, guided canoe trips, sunset champagne sails, and dolphin and dugong (manatee) spotting cruises. Wildlife videos play continuously in the lobby, and the on-site ranger office lists the animals and plants you are most likely to spot.

Fraser Island (P.M.B. 1), Urangan, QLD 4655. ✆ **1800/072 555** in Australia, or 07/4120 3333. Fax 07/4120 3326. www.kingfisherbay.com. 262 units. A$213–A$347 hotel double; A$285–A$427 2-bedroom villa; A$356–A$522 3-bedroom villa; A$421–A$537 executive villa; A$600–A$2,000 houses. 2- and 3-night minimums apply for villas and houses. Free crib. Ask about packages. AE, DC, MC, V. **Amenities:** 3 restaurants; 4 bars; babysitting; children's program; Jacuzzi; 4 outdoor saltwater pools (1 w/water slide); spa; lit tennis courts; watersports equipment rental and fishing tackle rental. *In room:* A/C, TV, hair dryer.

THE SUNSHINE COAST

Warm weather, miles of pleasant beaches, trendy restaurants, and a relaxed lifestyle attract Aussies to the Sunshine Coast in droves. Despite some rather unsightly commercial development in recent years, the Sunshine Coast is still a great spot if you like lazing on sandy beaches and enjoying a good meal.

The Sunshine Coast starts at **Caloundra,** 83km (51 miles) north of Brisbane, and runs all the way to **Rainbow Beach,** 40km (25 miles) north of **Noosa Heads ★**, where the fashionable crowd goes. There's a wide range of accommodations, from inexpensive motels and holiday apartments to AAA-rated five-star hotels and resorts.

Most of Noosa's sunbathing, dining, shopping, and socializing takes place on trendy Hastings Street, in Noosa Heads, and on adjacent Main Beach. The commercial strip of Noosa Junction is a 1-minute drive away; a 3-minute drive west along the river takes you to the low-key town of Noosaville, where Australian families rent holiday apartments. Giving Noosa a run for its money in recent years is newly spruced-up Mooloolaba, about 30km (19 miles) south, which has a better beach and about 90 great restaurants. For a quieter pace, but with equally lovely (and less crowded) beaches, head to Peregian or Coolum.

A short drive away, in the hinterland, mountain towns such as **Maleny, Montville,** and **Mapleton** lead to the stunning beauty of the **Glass House Mountains,** a dramatic series of 16 volcanic plugs.

Sunshine Coast Essentials

GETTING THERE If you're **driving** from Brisbane, take the Bruce Highway north, and exit onto the Sunshine Motorway to Mooloolaba, Maroochydore, or Noosa Heads. The road and various exits are well signposted. The trip takes about 2 hours, depending on which part of the coast you are heading to.

Virgin Blue (✆ **13 67 89** in Australia) flies direct from Melbourne and Sydney. **Jetstar** (✆ **13 15 38** in Australia) flies direct from Sydney and Melbourne (Tullamarine) airports to Maroochydore Airport. **Tiger Airways** (✆ **03/9335 3033;** www.tigerairways.com) flies direct from Melbourne. **Henry's Airport Bus Service** (✆ **07/5474 0199;** www.henrys.com.au) meets all flights; door-to-door transfers to Noosa Heads are A$22 for adults, half-price for kids 4 to 14, or A$60 for families of four, one-way. Bookings are essential and should be made 24 hours ahead if possible. A taxi from the airport will cost around A$32 to Maroochydore or A$65 to Noosa.

The nearest **train** station to Noosa Heads is in **Cooroy,** 25km (16 miles) away. **Queensland Rail** (✆ **13 16 17** in Queensland; www.qr.com.au) serves Cooroy once daily from Brisbane on its **CityTrain** (✆ **07/3606 5555;** www.citytrain.com.au) network. The trip takes about 2½ hours, and the fare is A$20. Other trains will take you there via Nambour or Caboolture. You will have to then get a bus connection to get to Noosa Heads. Queensland Rail's long-distance trains from Brisbane pick up but do not drop off passengers in Cooroy, with the exception of the high-speed **Tilt Train** (which runs Sun–Fri). The fare is A$34. The *Sunlander* makes several trips from Cairns each week; the fare to Nambour is A$212 for a seat, A$420 for a sleeper. **Sunbus** (✆ **13 12 30** in Australia, or 07/5450 7888) meets most trains at Cooroy station and travels to Noosa Heads.

Several **coach** companies have service to Noosa Heads from Brisbane, including **Sunair** (✆ **1800/804 340** in Australia or 07/5477 0888; www.sunair.com.au). **Greyhound Australia** (✆ **1300/473 946** in Australia) has many daily services from all major towns along the Bruce Highway between Brisbane and Cairns. Trip time to Noosa Heads is 2½ hours from Brisbane and 28 hours from Cairns. The fare is A$30 from Brisbane and A$281 from Cairns. The new A$11-million Noosa Transit Centre, opening early 2011, is the main public transport hub for the region. Located at the southern end of Noosa Junction, at Cooyar Street and Sunshine Beach Road, it is serviced by TransLink local bus services (operated by Sunbus), intercity coaches, and tourist service minibuses.

VISITOR INFORMATION **Tourism Sunshine Coast** (✆ **07/5458 8888;** www.tourismsunshinecoast.com.au) runs 15 visitor information centers around the region. In Noosa Heads, drop into the swish new **Noosa Visitor Information Centre** on Hastings Street (✆ **1800/002 624** in Australia or 07/5430 5000; www.tourismnoosa.com.au). It's open daily from 9am to 5pm. In **Maroochydore,** there are two main tourist information centers, at Sunshine Coast Airport (✆ **07/5459 9050;** www.discoverymaroochy.com.au) and at Sixth Avenue (at Melrose Parade), Maroochydore (which shares the same telephone number). The **Caloundra Visitor Information Centre** is at 7 Caloundra Rd., Caloundra (✆ **1800/644 969** in Australia or 07/5420 6240; www.caloundratourism.com.au).

GETTING AROUND Major car-rental companies on the Sunshine Coast are **Avis** (✆ **07/5443 5055** Sunshine Coast Airport, or 07/5447 4933 Noosa Heads),

The Sunshine Coast

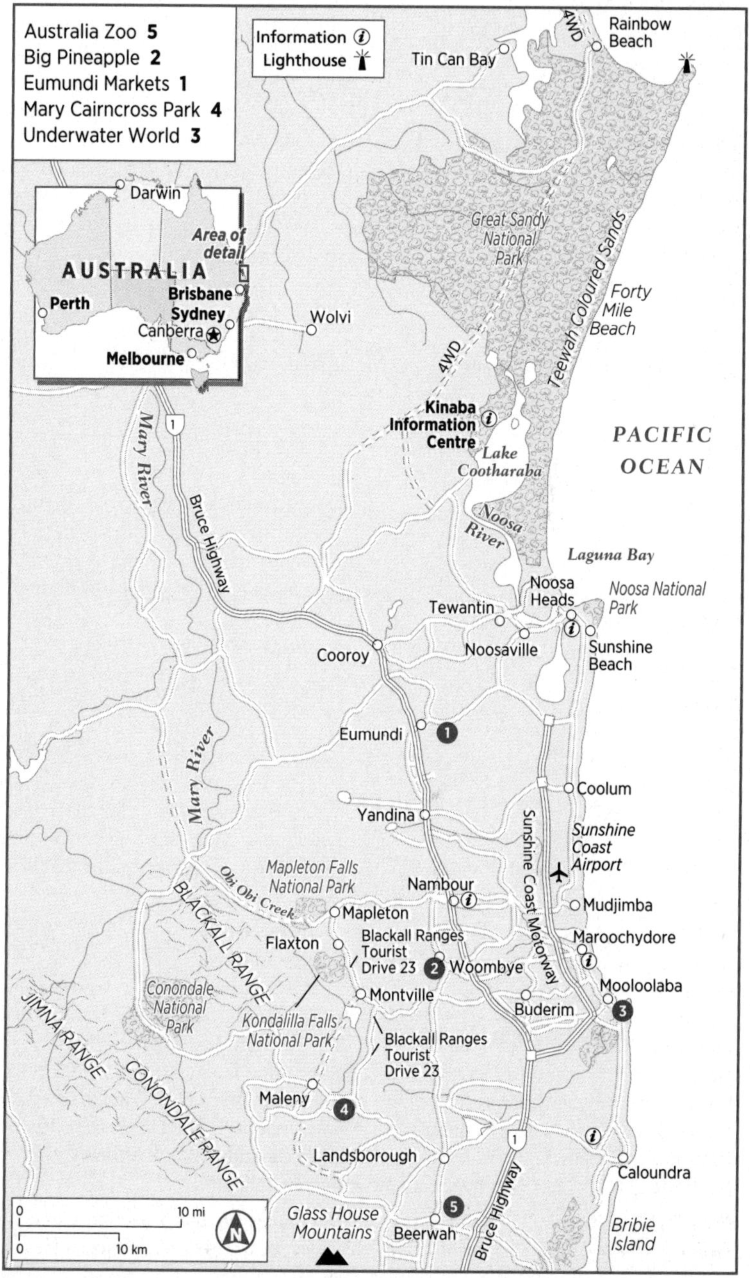

Australia Zoo 5
Big Pineapple 2
Eumundi Markets 1
Mary Cairncross Park 4
Underwater World 3
Information
Lighthouse
Rainbow Beach
Tin Can Bay
4WD
Darwin
Area of detail
AUSTRALIA
Perth
Brisbane
Sydney
Canberra
Melbourne
Wolvi
Great Sandy National Park
Teewah Coloured Sands
Forty Mile Beach
Kinaba Information Centre
Lake Cootharaba
PACIFIC OCEAN
Mary River
Bruce Highway
Noosa River
Laguna Bay
Noosa Heads
Noosa National Park
Tewantin
Noosaville
Sunshine Beach
Cooroy
Eumundi
Coolum
Yandina
Sunshine Coast Airport
Sunshine Coast Motorway
Mapleton Falls National Park
Obi Obi Creek
Nambour
Mapleton
Mudjimba
Maroochydore
BLACKALL RANGE
Flaxton
Blackall Ranges Tourist Drive 23
Woombye
Mooloolaba
Montville
Buderim
Conondale National Park
Kondalilla Falls National Park
JIMNA RANGE
CONONDALE RANGE
Maleny
Landsborough
Caloundra
Glass House Mountains
Beerwah
Bribie Island
10 mi
10 km
N

Budget (✆ **07/5448 7455** airport, or 07/5474 2820 Noosa Heads), **Europcar** (✆ **07/5448 9955** airport, or 07/5447 3777 Noosa Heads), **Hertz** (✆ **07/5448 9731** airport), and **Thrifty** (✆ **1300/367 227**). Many local companies rent cars and four-wheel-drives, including **Trusty** (✆ **07/5491 2444**).

The local bus company is **Sunbus** (✆ **07/5450 7888,** or 13 12 30 in Australia). For a taxi, call **Suncoast Cabs** (✆ **13 10 08** in Australia or 07/5451 7501).

Exploring the Area

HITTING THE BEACH & OTHER OUTDOOR FUN Main Beach, Noosa Heads, is the place to swim, surf, and sunbathe. If the bikini-clad supermodel look-alikes are too much for you, head to Sunshine Beach, just behind Noosa Junction off the David Low Way, about 2km (1¼ miles) from Noosa Heads, or to Peregian, slightly farther south. Both are just as beautiful, and all three are patrolled.

Learn to surf with two-time Australian and World Pro-Am champion **Merrick Davis** (✆ **0418/787 577** mobile; www.learntosurf.com.au), who's been teaching here since 1992. Merrick and his team run 2-hour lessons on Main Beach daily for A$60, 3-day certificate courses for A$165, and 5-day courses for A$240. They will pick you up and drop you off at your accommodations. They also rent surfboards, body boards, and sea kayaks.

If you want to rent a Windsurfer, canoe, kayak, surf ski, catamaran, jet ski, or fishing boat that you can play with on the Noosa River or take upriver into Great Sandy National Park (see below), check out the many outlets along Gympie Terrace between James Street and Robert Street in Noosaville.

The **Aussie Sea Kayak Company** (✆ **0407/049 747** mobile phone; www.aussea kayak.com.au), at the Wharf, Mooloolaba, runs a 2-hour sunset paddle on the Maroochy River every day for A$45—including a glass of champagne on your return as a reward for all the hard work! Half-day tours run every day for 3 to 4 hours at Mooloolaba (A$65). Day tours of the Noosa Everglades run for 7 hours on Tuesdays, Fridays, and Saturdays at Noosa (A$135), or there's an overnight tour leaving on Wednesdays and Saturdays, for A$295 per person.

EXPLORING NOOSA NATIONAL PARK A 10-minute stroll northeast from Hastings Street brings you to the 432-hectare (1,067-acre) **Noosa National Park.** Anywhere you see a crowd looking upward, you're sure to spot a koala. They're often seen in the unlikely setting of the parking lot at the entrance to the park. A network of well-signposted walking trails leads through the bush. The most scenic is the 2.7km (1½-mile) coastal trail. The shortest trail is the 1km (half-mile) Palm Grove circuit; the longest is the 4.8km (3-mile) Tanglewood trail inland to Hell's Gates—definitely worth the effort.

GREAT SANDY NATIONAL PARK Stretching north of Noosa along the coast is the 56,000-hectare (138,320-acre) Great Sandy National Park (often called **Cooloola National Park**). It's home to forests, beach, and freshwater lakes, including the state's largest, Lake Cootharaba. A popular activity is to cruise the Everglades formed by the Noosa River and tributary creeks. The Southern Cooloola section of the park starts just north of Noosa Heads and Tewantin, on the northern side of the Noosa River, and extends along the coast to Rainbow Beach. Conventional vehicles can drive to Elanda Point, just north of Boreen Point, or if you have a four-wheel-drive you can access the park from Cooloola Way and Harry's Hut

Road. The park's information office, the **Kinaba Information Centre** (✆ **07/5449 7364;** www.derm.qld.gov.au/parks/cooloola-southern; daily 9am–3pm;), is on the western shore of Lake Cootharaba, about 30km (19 miles) from Noosaville. It has a display on the area's geography and a mangrove boardwalk to explore; it's accessible only by boat, which you can rent from the numerous outfits in Noosaville or by walking from Elanda via the Kinaba track (6.6km/4 miles round-trip).There are half-day cruises into the Everglades, and guided kayak tours that explore the park's lower reaches.

Another option is to take a four-wheel-drive along Forty-Mile Beach, a designated highway with traffic laws, for a close-up view of the Teewah colored sand cliffs. This is a great place to get away from the crowds and enjoy nature's wonders. Lifeguards do not patrol the beach, so do not swim alone and take care. Tours are available, or you can rent a four-wheel-drive and explore on your own. To reach the beach, cross the Noosa River on the ferry at Tewantin; then take Maximilian Drive for 4km (2½ miles) to the beach. Stock up on water, food, and gas in Tewantin. The ferry (✆ **07/5447 1321;** www.noosacarferries.com) costs A$12 per vehicle round-trip; it operates from 5:30am to 10pm Sunday through Thursday, and 5:30am to midnight Friday and Saturday.

WILDLIFE PARKS & THEME PARKS Small theme parks seem to thrive on the Sunshine Coast. Don't expect thrill rides, but you might find some of them a pleasant way to spend a few hours.

A transparent tunnel with an 80m (262-ft.) moving walkway that takes you through a tank filled with sharks, stingrays, groupers, eels, and coral is the highlight at **Underwater World** (✆ **07/5458 6222;** www.underwaterworld.com.au) at the Wharf, Parkyn Parade, Mooloolaba. Kids can pick up starfish and sea cucumbers in the touch pool, and there are displays on whales and sharks, shark breeding, freshwater crocodile talks, an otter enclosure, and a 30-minute seal show. You can swim with the seals (A$90) or dive with the sharks (A$195 for certified divers, including gear, or A$225 for nondivers). Age restrictions apply. It's open daily (except Christmas Day) from 9am to 4:30pm and on April 25 from 1:30pm to 5:30pm (last entry 1 hour before closing). Admission is A$32 for adults, A$26 for seniors and students, A$22 for children 3 to 14, and A$90 for families of four. Allow 2 hours to see everything, more if you want to attend all the talks.

At the **Big Pineapple** (✆ **07/5442 1333**), 6km (3¾ miles) south of Nambour, on the Nambour Connection Road in Woombye—don't worry, you can't miss the 16m-tall (52-ft.) monument—you can take a train ride through a pineapple plantation, ride through a rainforest and a macadamia farm in a macadamia nut–shaped carriage, and visit a baby-animal farm. It's open daily, except Christmas Day, from 9am to 5pm (rides start at 10am); it opens later on April 25 (Anzac Day). Entry is free, but you pay for tours. The train ride costs A$16 adults and A$11 children 4 to 14 (including entry to the animal farm); the macadamia tour costs A$11 adults and A$8.50 children; the animal farm (without train ride) costs A$13 adults, A$8.50 children. A combination ticket that covers all attractions costs A$25 adults and A$18 children. The best option is a family pass, A$80 for two adults and up to four children, which covers everything.

Fans of crocodile hunter, TV star, and conservationist Steve Irwin will definitely want to visit the wildlife park founded by his family. The amazing **Australia Zoo** ★, on Glass House Mountains Tourist Drive, at Beerwah, off the Bruce Highway (✆ **07/5436 2000;** www.australiazoo.com.au) has been run by Irwin's wife Terri since his untimely death in 2006. The zoo continues with the expansion that has made it a world-class attraction covering 100 hectares (251 acres). The highlight is the "crocoseum," a 5,000-seat stadium in which the daily croc feedings are held at 3:30pm. Other demonstrations and feedings are held throughout the day, and you can also hand-feed 'roos, pat a koala, check out foxes and camels, and watch (even hold!) venomous snakes and pythons. For an extra fee (A$35 adults, A$20 kids, or A$95 families), you can tour the Koala and Wildlife Hospital next door to see how sick and injured animals are cared for. There are also lots of exotic animals: tigers, elephants, cheetahs, and more. Admission to the zoo is A$57 for adults, A$46 for seniors and students, A$34 for kids 3 to 14, and A$170 to A$187 for families. The park is open daily from 9am to 5pm and closed December 25. Courtesy buses operate daily from 8am, with pickups at Noosa and other spots around the Sunshine Coast, arriving at the zoo at 10:25am. The return bus leaves for Noosa at 4pm. The courtesy bus will also pick up train passengers at Beerwah railway station. **Sunbus** (✆ **07/5450 7888,** or 13 12 30 in Australia) services run to Australia Zoo from Maroochydore's Sunshine Plaza shopping center, Chancellor Park at Mooloolaba, and Landsborough railway station. Take bus no. 615.

A Mountaintop Drive Through the Sunshine Coast Hinterland

A leisurely drive along the lush green ridge top of the **Blackall Ranges ★** behind Noosa is a popular half- or full-day excursion. Mountain villages, full of crafts shops and cafes, and terrific views of the coast, are the main attractions. Macadamia nuts, peaches, and other local produce are often for sale by the road at dirt-cheap prices.

On Wednesdays and Saturdays from 8am to 1:30pm, head to the colorful outdoor **Eumundi Markets ★★** in the historic village of Eumundi, 13km (8 miles) west of Noosa along the Eumundi Road. Locals and visitors wander under the huge shady trees among dozens of stalls selling locally grown organic lemonade, fruit, groovy hats, teddy bears, antique linen, homemade soaps, handcrafted hardwood furniture and one-off fashions. Get your face painted, your palm read, or your feet massaged. Listen to local musicians—even some didgeridoo players. The markets are hugely popular but parking isn't usually a problem—it's worth paying a few dollars for the parking lots rather than cruising the streets looking for a spot. Saturdays are a quieter day than Wednesdays to visit, usually. And when your shopping's done, pop into one of the cafes on Eumundi's main street.

The Seasons of the Sunshine Coast

Room rates on the Sunshine Coast are mostly moderate, but they jump sharply in the Christmas period from December 26 to January 26, during school holidays, and in the week following Easter. Book well ahead at these times. Weekends are often busy, too.

From Eumundi, take the Bruce Highway to Nambour and turn right onto the **Nambour–Mapleton Road.** (The turnoff is just before you enter Nambour; if you hit the town, you've gone too far.) A winding 12km (7½-mile) climb up the range between rolling farmland and forest brings you to Mapleton. Stop at the century-old pub for some spectacular views from the veranda. From here, detour almost 4km (2½ miles) to see the 120m (394-ft.) Mapleton Falls. A 200m (656-ft.) bushwalk departs from the picnic grounds and ends with great views over the Obi Obi Valley. There is also a 1.3km (.8-mile) circuit. During drought conditions, the Falls are sometimes dry, but you can see that from the lookout before you start the walk—which is worth it for its own sake, through shady bush with some massive trees and vines.

Back on the main **Mapleton–Maleny Road,** head south 3.5km (2 miles) through lush forest and farms to Flaxton Gardens. Perched on the cliff with breathtaking coast views is a wine cellar offering tastings and sales, plus a pottery store, cafe, and gift shop. A bit farther south, you can detour right and walk the 4.6km (3-mile) round-trip trail to the base of 80m (262-ft.) Kondalilla Falls. You can swim here, too. It's a slippery downhill walk, and the climb back up can be tough.

Take the main road south for 5.5km (3½ miles) to **Montville.** This English-style village has become such a popular stop that it has lost some of its character, and lots of people decry its touristy facade. But everyone still ends up strolling the tree-lined streets and browsing the gift shops and galleries.

About 13km (8 miles) down the road is **Maleny,** more laid-back and less commercialized than Montville. Be sure to follow the signs to **Mary Cairncross Park** for spectacular views of the **Glass House Mountains ★★**, 16 volcanic plugs protruding out of the plains. The park has a food kiosk, a playground, free wood barbecues, and a rainforest information center; a 1.7km (1-mile) walking trail loops through the rainforest past some giant strangler figs, and you are likely to see pademelons and brush turkeys along the way.

You can either return to Noosa the way you came or, if you're in a hurry, drive down to Landsborough and rejoin the Bruce Highway.

Where to Stay

EXPENSIVE

Hyatt Regency Coolum ★★ A couple of hours under the expert care of the therapists at the **Sun Spa** and you'll feel years younger! This is one of the reasons the well-heeled flock to this sprawling bushland resort. The other is its 18-hole Robert Trent Jones, Jr.–designed golf course. The Spa does everything from aromatherapy baths to triglyceride checks—130 treatments in all—and has massage rooms, aqua-aerobics, yoga, a 25m (82-ft.) lap pool, and much more. The **golf course** has been rated as one of the top five resort courses in Australia. Golf widows and widowers can play tennis, do decoupage in the Creative Arts Centre, take the twice-daily free shuttle into Noosa to shop, and surf at the resort's private beach.

So spread out are the low-rise accommodations that guests rent a bike to get around, wait 15 minutes for the two free resort shuttles (frustrating sometimes), or get into the healthy swing of things and walk. Accommodations all have contemporary decor and come as "suites" (one room divided into living and sleeping quarters); two-bedroom President's Villas with a kitchenette; villas in the Ambassador Club, which has its own concierge, pool, tennis court, and lounge; and two-story, three-bedroom Ambassador Club residences boasting rooftop terraces with Jacuzzis.

The Village Square is just that: an attractive cluster of shops, restaurants, bars, and takeout joints that makes up the heart of the resort. Rates include breakfast, free golf and tennis clinics daily, and entry to the Spa.

Warran Rd., off David Low Way (approximately 2km/1¼ miles south of town), Coolum Beach, QLD 4573. ✆ **1800/266 586** in Australia, 800/633-7313 in the U.S. and Canada, 0845/758 1666 in the U.K. or 020/8335 1220 in London, 0800/44 1234 in New Zealand, or 07/5446 1234. Fax 07/5446 2957. www.coolum.regency.hyatt.com. 324 units. A$240–A$300 double; A$400–A$555 villa; A$705–A$1,350 Ambassador Residence. Extra person A$60–A$90. Children 12 and under stay free in parent's room with existing bedding. Rates include breakfast. Ask about golf, spa, and other packages. AE, MC, V. Valet parking A$10 per night. Free self-parking. **Amenities:** 3 restaurants; 3 bars; free airport transfers (bookings required); babysitting; bikes; children's programs daily for kids ages 6 weeks to 12 years (fee); concierge; executive rooms; health club and spa; golf course; 9 outdoor pools (2 heated); room service; 7 night/day tennis courts; watersports equipment rental. *In room:* A/C, TV w/pay movies, DVD player, CD player (villas only), hair dryer, Internet (A$13 for 1 hr.; A$25 for 24 hr.), kitchenette, minibar, Wi-Fi (villas only; A$16 for 1 hr.; A$25 for 24 hr.).

Sheraton Noosa Resort & Spa ★★★ A great place to enjoy a day spa by the sea is Noosa's first AAA-rated five-star resort. Right in the heart of Hastings Street, the Sheraton has a prime spot. There are several styles of rooms, but in my book the best are those with views away from the beach looking down the Noosa River to the mountains. Sit on the balcony at sunset and drink it in. All the rooms are extra-large, and all have Jacuzzis. You'll pay more for two-level poolside villas, which have private access to the pool area but no view. Some rooms have ocean (but not beach) views. The **Aqua Day Spa** has a Roman-bathhouse feel and offers a wide range of treatments. The restaurant, **Cato's**—named for the late Australian novelist Nancy Cato, who lived in Noosa—fronts Hastings Street and is a great place to people-watch.

Hastings St., Noosa Heads, QLD 4567. ✆ **1800/073 535** in Australia, 888/625-5144 in the U.S., or 07/5449 4888. Fax 07/5449 2230. www.sheraton.com. 175 units. A$580–A$830 double; A$850 spa studios; A$850–A$1,110 suites; A$900–A$990 villas; A$1,140 apts. Extra adult A$75. AE, DC, MC, V. Free covered parking, valet parking. **Amenities:** Restaurant; 3 bars; babysitting; bikes; concierge; health club and spa; Jacuzzi; outdoor heated pool; room service. *In room:* A/C, TV w/free and pay movies, hair dryer, Internet (A$15 for 1 hr.; A$25 for 24 hr.), kitchenette, minibar.

MODERATE

Noosa Village Motel All the letters from satisfied guests pinned up on the wall here are a testament to owners John and Mary Skelton's hard work in continually sprucing up this bright little motel in the heart of Hastings Street. The pleasant rooms are clean, comfortable, spacious, and freshly painted, with a cheerful atmosphere. All have ceiling fans and most have small balconies or an outdoor sitting area downstairs. And at these rates, it's one of Hastings Street's best values.

10 Hastings St., Noosa Heads, QLD 4567. ✆ **07/5447 5800.** Fax 07/5474 9282. www.noosavillage.com.au. 11 units, all with shower only. A$135–A$145 double; A$195–A$205 suite (sleeps 4); A$270–A$275 2-bedroom family unit (sleeps 6). Extra person A$10–A$15. Rates may be higher in peak season. Ask about specials. MC, V. Free parking. **Amenities:** Babysitting; bikes. *In room:* A/C, TV, hair dryer, kitchenette.

IN THE HINTERLAND

Avocado Grove Bed & Breakfast Joy Barron's modern, red-cedar Queenslander home is in a peaceful rural setting in the middle of an avocado grove just off the ridge-top road. The cozy, comfortable rooms have country-style furniture, full-length windows opening onto private verandas, and oil heaters for cool mountain nights. The big suite downstairs has a TV and kitchen facilities, and a private entrance. Parrots and other birds are a common sight. Guests are welcome to picnic on the sloping lawns, which have wonderful views west to Obi Obi Gorge in the Connondale Ranges.

10 Carramar Court, Flaxton via Montville, QLD 4560. ✆ /fax **07/5445 7585.** www.avocadogrove.com.au. 3 units. A$140 double; A$170 suite. Rates include full breakfast; dinner available on request. Ask about weekend and midweek packages. MC, V. Turn right off ridge-top road onto Ensbey Rd.; Carramar Court is the 1st left. **Amenities:** A/C in guest lounge. *In room:* Ceiling fan, hair dryer.

Where to Dine

Noosa's **Hastings Street** comes alive at night with vacationers wining and dining at restaurants as sophisticated as those in Sydney and Melbourne. Just stroll along and see what appeals to you—but make a reservation in high season. **Café Le Monde** at the southern end of Hastings Street (opposite the back of the Surf Club) is a Noosa institution and you'll always find a crowd there. **Noosa Junction** is a less attractive place to eat, but the prices are cheaper. There are about 90 restaurants at Mooloolaba.

Bistro C ★ CONTEMPORARY Walk through from Hastings Street to the beachfront, whether it's for the best breakfast in town, a casual lunch, a sunset cocktail, or dinner to the sound of the lapping surf. It's hard to know what is Bistro C's greatest asset—the location, the great food, or the terrific attentive staff. The food is interesting and the decor stylish, with interesting statues and artwork. I recommend the duck and pineapple curry, which comes with mango-lime chutney, flat bread, and jasmine rice, but everything on the menu is just as tantalising. Some nights, there's a fireplace lit on the sand across the boardwalk . . . and if the sun is setting or the moon is full, it's even more magical. A snack menu is available from 3 to 5pm if you want something light with your drinks, and later there's a throng at the cocktail bar.

49 Hastings St., Noosa Heads. ✆ **07/5447 2855.** www.bistroc.com.au. Reservations recommended. Main courses A$25–A$32. AE, DC, MC, V. Daily 7:30am–late.

Season ★ CONTEMPORARY With one of the few beachfront restaurant locations, this is another of Noosa's most popular restaurants, deservedly so, for the food is superb. Breakfast dishes can be as simple as muffins, or you can indulge yourself with buttermilk-and-banana pancakes (with palm sugar butter and maple syrup). For dinner? How about crispy-skin spitchcock with roast pumpkin, dates, green beans, merguez sausage, almonds, and labna? Or even simpler: crisp fried fish and chips with tartar sauce and fresh lemon? The restaurant is fully licensed.

25 Hastings St., Noosa Heads. ✆ **07/5447 3747.** www.seasonrestaurant.com.au. Reservations essential for dinner; accepted same day only. Main courses A$25–A$37; breakfast items A$5–A$21. MC, V. Daily 7:30am–10pm.

Spirit House ★★ ASIAN It's worth making the effort to get to this amazing restaurant—you will be thinking and talking about it long after you've left. Walk along the jungle paths to the hidden building and you'll start to get an idea of what's in store. Tables are set around a lagoon and among the trees, with massive statues and other artworks scattered throughout. At night, the effect is enhanced by torches and lighting. But it won't prepare you for the flavors that come out of this kitchen, mainly Thai but with other Asian influences—dishes such as whole crispy fish with tamarind and chili sauce; or barbecued prawns with golden shallot, ginger, and mint salad. I defy you to leave without buying the cookbook or signing up for the cooking classes.

20 Ninderry Rd., Yandina. ✆ **07/5446 8994.** www.spirithouse.com.au. Reservations essential. Main courses A$18–A$36. AE, DC, MC, V. Daily for lunch from noon; Wed–Sat from 6pm.

THE GOLD COAST

Love it or hate it, the Gold Coast is one of Australia's icons. Bronzed lifeguards, bikini-clad meter maids, tanned tourists draped with gold jewelry, high-rise apartment towers that cast long shadows over parts of the beach . . . but the glitz, the glitter, and the overdevelopment pale as soon as you hit the sand. The white shoreline stretches uninterrupted for 70km (43 miles), making up for the long strips of neon-lit motels and souvenir shops. Since the '50s, Australians have flocked to this strip of coastline, and that hasn't changed. Today, they're lining up with tourists from around the world to get into the theme parks, but everyone can still find a quiet spot on the beach.

The Gold Coast's theme parks are not as large or as sophisticated as Disney World, but they're exciting. Apart from the three major parks—Dreamworld, Warner Bros. Movie World, and Sea World—there are of plenty of smaller ones. There are also 40 golf courses, dinner cruises, and loads of adrenaline-fueled outdoor activities, from bungee jumping to jet-skiing. The best activity on the Gold Coast, though, is the natural kind, and it doesn't cost a cent—hitting the surf and lazing on the beach.

Gold Coast Essentials

GETTING THERE **By Car** Access to the Gold Coast Highway, which runs the length of the Coast, is off the Pacific Highway from Sydney or Brisbane. The drive takes about 80 minutes from Brisbane. From Sydney it's an 11-hour trip, sometimes longer, on the crowded, run-down Pacific Highway.

BY PLANE Domestic flights land at Gold Coast Airport, Coolangatta, 25km (16 miles) south of Surfers Paradise. **Qantas** (© **13 13 13**) offers direct flights from Sydney. **Virgin Blue** (© **13 67 89**) flies from Melbourne, Sydney, Canberra, Newcastle, and Adelaide, and **Jetstar** (© **13 15 38** in Australia) flies from Cairns, Melbourne, Sydney, Newcastle, and Adelaide. **Tiger Airways** (© **03/9335 3033;** www.tigerairways.com) flies direct from Melbourne and Adelaide. **Pacific Blue** (© **13 16 45** in Australia or 07/3295 2284; 0800/670 000 in New Zealand; www.flypacificblue.com) flies to Gold Coast Airport from Auckland, New Zealand. The **Gold Coast Tourist Shuttle** (© **1300/655 655** in Australia, or 07/5574 5111; www.gcshuttle.com.au) meets every flight and will take you to your accommodations; the fare is A$21 one-way and A$38 round-trip for adults, A$11 one-way or A$19 round-trip for kids ages 4 to 13, A$53 one-way or A$95 round-trip for families of four. A better deal, if you're going to use buses a lot, is to buy a Freedom Pass (see "Getting Around," p. 365), which includes your airport transfers. A **taxi** from the airport to Surfers Paradise is about A$55 but may be higher if traffic is heavy.

The nearest international gateway is **Brisbane International Airport** (see chapter 7, p. 237). The **Coachtrans** (© **1300/664 700** in Queensland, or 07/3358 9700; www.coachtrans.com.au) airport bus meets most flights and makes about 20 trips a day from the domestic and international terminals at Brisbane Airport to Gold Coast accommodations for A$40 adults, A$18 children 4 to 13, or A$98 for families of four. The trip takes about 90 minutes to Surfers Paradise. You do not need to book in advance unless you are on an evening flight.

The Gold Coast

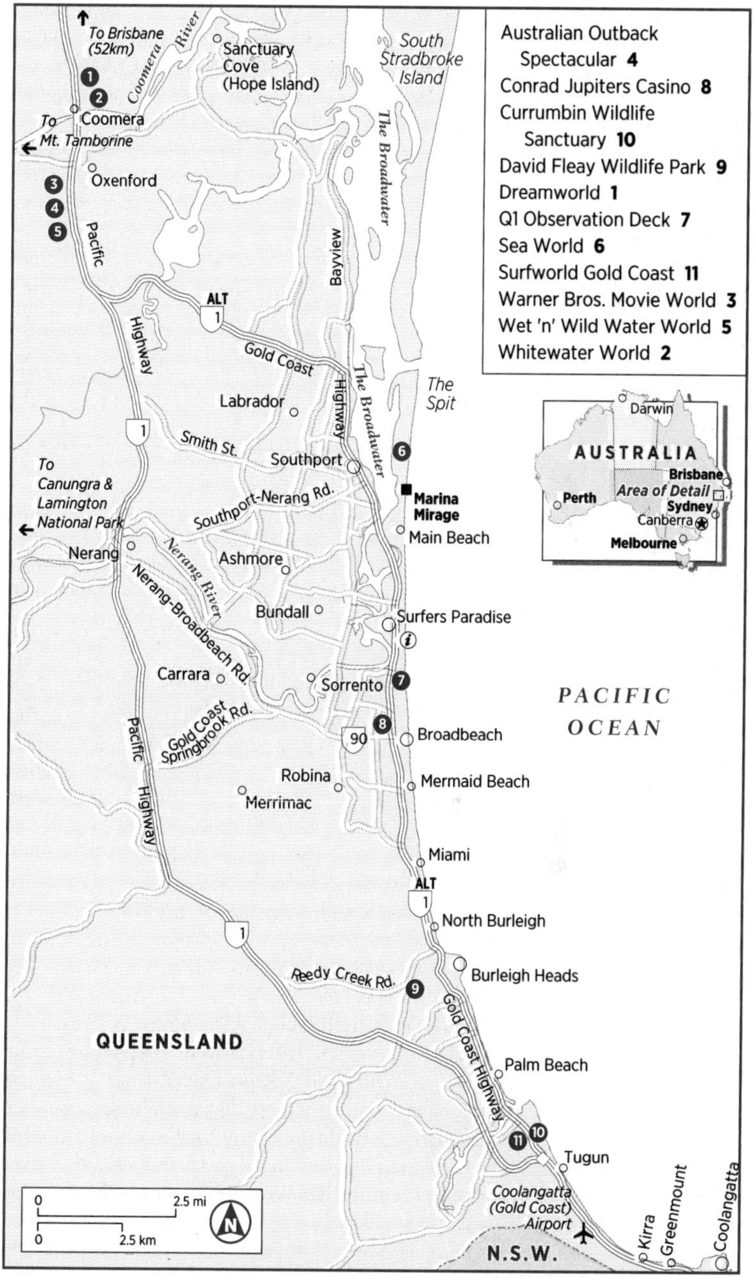

AirtrainConnect links Brisbane Airport and the Gold Coast by train and bus for A$45 adults, A$22 children 5 to 14, or A$90 for a family of four. Take Airtrain to the Gold Coast, and then an air-conditioned coach shuttle to any accommodations between Southport Spit at the northern end of the Gold Coast and Burleigh Heads to the south. Airtrain's SmartPass, for A$133 per adult, A$67 per child, or A$333 for families of four for 3 days, covers AirtrainConnect transfers, as well as unlimited door-to-door theme park transfers on the Gold Coast Tourist Shuttle and use of the local Surfside bus network, 24 hours a day. Passes are also available for 5, 7, and 10 days.

BY BUS **Coachtrans** (✆ **1300/664 700** in Queensland, or 07/3358 9700) runs between Brisbane and Gold Coast hotels. The fare is A$32 adults one-way, A$20 for kids 4 to 13; A$84 for families of four.

Greyhound Australia (✆ **1300/473 946**) makes daily stops at Surfers Paradise from Sydney and Brisbane. The trip from Sydney takes 15 to 16 hours, and the fare is A$139. Trip time from Brisbane is 90 minutes, and the fare is A$29.

BY TRAIN Suburban trains (call **Queensland Rail CityTrain;** ✆ **07/3235 5555**) depart Brisbane Central and Roma Street stations every 30 minutes for the 70-minute trip to the Gold Coast suburb of Nerang. The fare is A$11 adults, A$5.60 children 5 to 14. Numerous local buses meet the trains to take passengers to Surfers Paradise.

If you come by train to Surfers Paradise from Sydney or other southern cities, service is on **Countrylink** (✆ **13 22 32** in Australia; www.countrylink.info), and you will need to transfer to a connecting coach in Casino or Murwillumbah, just south of the Queensland border. The trip from Sydney takes 14 to 15 hours and the fare is A$118 for a first-class seat.

VISITOR INFORMATION **Gold Coast Tourism** (✆ **1300/309 440** in Australia, or 07/5538 4419; www.verygoldcoast.com) has an information kiosk on Cavill Avenue in Surfers Paradise. It is stacked with brochures on things to see and do, and the staff will book tours and arrange accommodations. The kiosk is open Monday through Saturday from 8:30am to 5pm, and Sunday and public holidays from 9am to 4pm. A second information booth (✆ **07/5569 3380**) is at the corner of Griffith and Warner streets in Coolangatta. It is open from 8:30am to 5pm weekdays and from 9am to 3pm Saturdays; closed Sundays and public holidays.

ORIENTATION The heart of the Gold Coast is **Surfers Paradise**—"Surfers" to the locals—a high-rise forest of apartment towers, shops, cheap eateries, taverns, and amusement parlors. The pedestrian-only Cavill Mall, in the center of town, connects the Gold Coast Highway to the Esplanade, which runs along the beach.

The Gold Coast Highway is the main artery that connects the endless beachside suburbs lining the coast. Just north of Surfers is **Main Beach ★★**, where Tedder Avenue abounds with shops, restaurants, and cafes. Heading south from Surfers, the main beach centers are **Broadbeach,** where retail complexes and restaurants are mushrooming; family-oriented **Burleigh Heads;** and the twin towns of **Coolangatta** in Queensland and **Tweed Heads** just over the border in New South Wales. Gold Coast Airport is on the other side of the highway from Coolangatta township.

West of Surfers Paradise and Broadbeach are the affluent suburbs of **Ashmore** and **Nerang,** where luxury residential estates and many of the region's championship golf courses have sprung up.

GETTING AROUND It's not necessary to have a car. The hotels listed below are within walking distance of the beach, shops, and restaurants, and many tour companies pick up at hotels. You can reach the theme parks by bus. A car is handy for a day trip to the hinterland, and to get around to restaurants and golf courses. Parking is cheap and plentiful in numerous lots and on the side streets between the Gold Coast Highway and the Esplanade.

> **The Secret of the Gold Coast Seasons**
>
> **School holidays, especially the Christmas vacation from mid-December to the end of January, are peak season on the Gold Coast. Accommodations are booked months in advance at these times. The rest of the year, occupancy levels plummet—and so do rates! Packages and deals abound in the off season, so make sure you ask.**

Avis (✆ **07/5539 9388**), **Budget** (✆ **07/5538 1344**), **Europcar** (✆ **13 13 90** in Australia or 07/5569 3370), **Hertz** (✆ **07/5538 5366**), and **Thrifty** (✆ **07/5570 9999**) have outlets in Surfers Paradise and at Gold Coast Airport. Endless local outfits rent cars at cheap rates.

Surfside Buslines (✆ **13 12 30** in Australia, or 07/5571 6555) is the local bus company. Its best deal is the **Freedom Pass,** which allows you to hop on and off the buses anytime you like. The 3-day pass costs A$67 adults and A$34 children 4 to 13, or A$168 for a family of four; 5-, 7-, and 10-day passes are also available. The pass gives you door-to-door return Gold Coast Airport transfers, unlimited door-to-door transfers to Dreamworld, Warner Bros. MovieWorld, Sea World, Wet 'n' Wild Water World, and Currumbin Wildlife Sanctuary, as well as unlimited use of the Surfside bus network, 24 hours a day.

For a taxi, call **Gold Coast Cabs** (✆ **13 10 08;** www.gccabs.com.au).

What to See & Do on the Coast

HITTING THE BEACHES

The white sandy beaches are the number-one attraction on the Gold Coast. No fewer than 35 patrolled beaches stretch almost uninterrupted from the Spit north of Surfers Paradise to Rainbow Bay, south of Coolangatta. In fact, the Gold Coast is just one long fabulous beach—all you need do is step onto it at any point, and you will spot the nearest set of red and yellow flags that signal safe swimming. The most popular beaches are **Main Beach ★★**, **Surfers North, Elkhorn Avenue, Surfers Paradise, Mermaid Beach, Burleigh Heads, Coolangatta,** and **Greenmount.** All are patrolled 365 days a year.

THE THEME PARKS

First, there are the "big three"—Dreamworld, Sea World, and Warner Bros. Movie World. You might also like to check out the **Australian Outback Spectacular,** also owned by Warner Bros., located between Movie World and Wet 'n' Wild Water World.

Sea World is the only major theme park in the center of town. The others are in northern bushland on the Pacific Highway, about 15 to 20 minutes away from Surfers Paradise. You can ride to the theme parks on the Gold Coast Tourist Shuttle (see p. 362) or on **Surfside Buslines** (✆ **13 12 30** in Queensland) buses. Take bus no. TX1, TX2, or TX5 to Dreamworld, Movie World, and Wet 'n' Wild, and bus no. 750 from Surfers Paradise or no. 715 from Southport to get to Sea World.

Money-Saving Theme Park Passes

Sea World, Warner Bros. Movie World, and **Wet 'n' Wild** sell a **Fun Pass** that gives you 1 day's entry to each park over a 5-day period. It costs A$150 for adults and A$96 for kids 4 to 13. A **Super Pass** gives unlimited entry to all three for 14 days and costs A$190 adults and A$130 for kids. You can buy passes at the parks, online, from a travel agency, or at most Gold Coast hotels, apartments, and tour desks. Sea World and Warner Bros. Movie World sell a return pass for A$35 extra adult or A$23 children, but you must use the second day within 14 days of your first visit. Wet 'n' Wild's second-day pass is A$25 adults and A$17 children.

Dreamworld and **WhiteWater World** have 2-day passes to both for A$109 adults or A$79 kids ages 3 to 13.

If you are driving, take the M1 Pacific Motorway for about 15 to 20 minutes north of the Gold Coast or 40 minutes south of Brisbane for Wet 'n' Wild, Warner Bros. Movie World, and Dreamworld. Exits are all well signposted. All the theme parks have huge free parking lots.

Trains (✆ **13 12 30**) run to Coomera and Helensvale on the Brisbane–Gold Coast line. Queensland Rail CityTrain sells tickets to the theme parks at Brisbane Central, Roma Street, Fortitude Valley, and South Bank stations.

Australian Outback Spectacular Aimed at introducing a largely international audience to the spirit of the Outback, this extravagantly staged show—part theme-park, part dinner show—features an unforgettable display of horsemanship. "Heroes of the Light Horse" celebrates the link between Australia's stockmen and the legendary mounted infantrymen of the Australian Light Horse Brigade, famed for its service in World War I. With seating for 1,000, the evening begins with preshow entertainment and a three-course Aussie-barbecue-style meal. The 90-minute show is staged during dinner.

Pacific Hwy. (21km/13 miles north of Surfers Paradise), Oxenford. ✆ **13 33 86** in Australia, or 07/5519 6200. www.outbackspectacular.com.au. Admission A$100 adults, A$70 children 4–13. Bookings essential. Tues–Sun doors open 6:15pm, entertainment starts 6:45pm. Lunchtime matinee shows are available on selected Sundays. Closed Dec 25. Ample free parking. Coach transfers (✆ 13 33 86) from Gold Coast accommodations cost A$15 per person round-trip.

Dreamworld ★ ☺ Adrenaline-crazed thrill-seekers will love the action rides, such as the aptly named Giant Drop, in which you free-fall 39 stories in 5 seconds, and the Tower of Terror, which propels you forward and upward at 4.5Gs before you fall backward 38 stories in 7 seconds. They'll also get a kick out of the hair-raising Cyclone roller coaster, with its 360-degree loop, and the Wipeout, which spins, twists, and tumbles you upside down in a random sequence (but only exerts a sissy 2.5Gs of pressure). These high-octane offerings make the park's other attractions look tame. Dreamworld is a family fun park, Disney-style—except that here giant koalas called Kenny and Belinda roam the streets instead of Mickey Mouse. Kids will love Nickelodeon Central, the only Nickelodeon cartoon attraction outside the U.S.

Other activities include an IMAX theater, a wildlife park where you can cuddle a koala and hand-feed kangaroos, river cruises livened up by a bushranger shootout, and a carousel and other rides for young kids. A big highlight is to watch trainers swim, wrestle, and play with Bengal tigers on Tiger Island. Souvenir stores, restaurants, cafes, and ice-cream shops abound.

Pacific Hwy. (25km/16 miles north of Surfers Paradise), Coomera. ✆ **1800/073 300** in Australia, 07/5588 1111, or 07/5588 1122 (24-hr. info line). www.dreamworld.com.au. Admission (all-inclusive except skill games, souvenir photos, and helicopter rides) A$75 adults, A$49 children 3-13. Daily 10am-5pm; Main St., Plaza Restaurant, and Koala Country open at 9am. Closed Dec 25 and until 1:30pm Apr 25 (Anzac Day). Extended hours during Easter and Dec-Jan. Free parking for 1,600 cars.

Sea World ★★ ☺ Canadian polar bear orphan cubs Hudson and Nelson—along with their bigger friend Lia—are the star attractions at this marine park, and crowds flock to see them frolic, dive, and hunt for fish in a large pool. Sea World may not be as sophisticated as similar parks in the United States, but it has its own charm, plus all the things you'd expect to see—performing dolphins and sea lions, ski shows, an aquarium, shark feeding, and an array of rides. The newest attraction is a state of the art Fairy Penguin exhibit, home to 11 of the cute little birds. At Shark Bay, you can see some of the larger and more dangerous species, such as tiger sharks. You can also snorkel with the sharks for A$60 per person (if you are 10 or over) or dive with them if you are a certified diver for A$90. Adults (14 and over) can snorkel with seals or dolphins for A$165 or A$225, including a souvenir photo. There are lots of other interactive options and behind-the-scenes tours. A monorail gets you around the park, and there's a free water-slide playground. Watersports are available for an extra fee.

Sea World Dr. (3km/1¾ miles north of Surfers Paradise), The Spit, Main Beach. ✆ **07/5588 2222,** or 07/5588 2205 (24-hr. info line). Fax 07/5591 1056. www.seaworld.com.au. Admission (all-inclusive except animal experiences, helicopter rides, and powered watersports) A$70 adults, A$46 children 3-13. Daily 10am-5pm; Apr 25 (Anzac Day) 1:30-6:30pm. Closed Dec 25. Free parking.

Getting Wet ('n' Wild!)

Long-established water park **Wet 'n' Wild Water World** (✆ **07/5556 1610** or 07/5573 2255 for 24-hr. recorded info; www.wetnwild.com.au) has got competition across the street. **WhiteWater World by Dreamworld** (✆ **1800/073 300** in Australia, or 07/5588 1111; www.whitewaterworld.com.au), which opened in late 2006, also has some terrifying turns and waves, and is themed around Australian surf culture. The Super Tubes HydroCoaster is a "roller coaster on water" and is one of only two in the world; there's also Nickelodeon's Pipeline Plunge, a playground for kids ages 5 to 12.

The water at both parks is heated May to September, there are lifeguards on duty, you can rent towels and lockers, and you can use showers. Both parks are open every day, except Christmas Day (Dec 25) and the morning of Anzac Day (Apr 25). WhiteWater World's hours are 10am to 5pm every day of the year (but may be extended during summer). Wet 'n' Wild opens at 10am daily but closes at 4pm May to August, 5pm September 1 to December 26 and January 26 to April 30, and stays open until 9pm December 27 to January 25 and on Dive-In Movie nights. Entry to the parks costs roughly the same: around A$50 adults and A$34 kids ages 4 to 13. Wet 'n' Wild offers an "afternoon rate" of A$25 adults and A$17 children after 2 or 3pm for the final 2 hours of operation each day, or after 5pm on Dive-In Movie nights.

Warner Bros. Movie World ★ ☺ Australia's answer to Universal Studios just about matches its U.S. counterpart for thrills and spills, and is also based around working studios. If you already know how Superman flies over skyscrapers, and you've heard a Foley sound studio in action, the train ride around the sets might not interest you, but it's a great introduction to cinema tricks for first-timers. Popular attractions are the hair-raising, stomach-turning rides such as the Superman Escape roller coaster, the indoor Scooby-Doo Spooky Coaster roller coaster, the Lethal Weapon roller coaster, and the simulated high-speed chase of Batman: The Ride. Young kids can take rides and see stage shows by Yosemite Sam and Porky Pig in the Looney Tunes Village, and there's a Looney Tunes Parade through the streets each day. Most parades and shows take place between 11am and 4pm.

Pacific Hwy. (21km/13 miles north of Surfers Paradise), Oxenford. ✆ **07/5573 3999** or 5573 8485 (recorded info). www.movieworld.com.au. Admission (all-inclusive) A$70 adults, A$46 children 3–13. Daily 9:30am–5:30pm; rides and attractions operate 10am–5pm. Closed Dec 25 and until 1:30pm Apr 25 (Anzac Day). Free parking.

EXPLORING THE WILDLIFE PARKS & OTHER ATTRACTIONS

Currumbin Wildlife Sanctuary ★ ☺ Currumbin began life as a bird sanctuary, and it is almost synonymous with the wild rainbow lorikeets that flock here by the hundreds twice a day for feeding. It's quite an experience—flocks of chattering birds descend onto visitors holding trays of food for them. Photographers go crazy, and tourists love it. The amazingly beautiful birds have vivid green backs, blue heads, and red-and-yellow chests. Lorikeet feeding is at 8am and 4pm, and lasts for about 90 minutes. Don't miss it.

The park's 27 hectares (67 acres) are home to 1,400 native birds and animals, including two saltwater crocodiles, and the wetlands on the grounds attract lots of native birds. You can also have your photo taken cuddling a koala, hand-feed kangaroos, take a free miniature steam-train ride through the park, attend animal talks and feeding demonstrations, and visit the new A$1.5-million animal hospital. An Aboriginal song-and-dance show takes place daily at 3:30pm. Allow several hours to see everything. A highlight is the free-flight birds show at 11:30am and 2pm. "Wildnight" tours are run daily and include dinner, a guided night tour, and an Aboriginal dance performance. Dinner is at 5:30pm, with the tour starting at 6:45pm. The cost is A$79 adults and A$49 children 4 to 13, but you must book at least by 3pm on the day of your tour.

28 Tomewin St., Currumbin (18km/11 miles south of Surfers Paradise). ✆ **1300/886 511** in Australia or 07/5534 1266. www.cws.org.au. Admission A$44 adults, A$26 children 4–13. Book online for discounts. Daily 8am–5pm. Closed Dec 25 and until 1pm Apr 25 (Anzac Day). Ample free parking. Bus: 700, 760, or 765 (stop 15m/49 ft. from entrance).

David Fleay Wildlife Park ★ Established in 1952 by Australian naturalist David Fleay, this is one of Australia's premier wildlife parks. You'll see a platypus, saltwater and freshwater crocodiles, wallabies, kangaroos, glider possums, dingoes, wombats, the rare Lumholtz's tree kangaroo, and a big range of Australian birds, including emus, cassowaries, wedge-tailed eagles, black swans, and lorikeets. You walk on a series of raised boardwalks through picturesque mangrove, rainforest, and eucalyptus habitats, where most of the animals roam free. The nocturnal house, open from 11am to 5pm daily, is where you'll see many of the most elusive animals, including a platypus and Australia's answer to the Easter bunny, the bilby.

On Top of the World

The Gold Coast's newest, tallest building is Q1, a gleaming steel-and-glass tower inspired by the Sydney 2000 Olympic torch. It's a stunner. Entry is on Surfers Paradise Boulevard, where you take the superfast elevator for just 43 seconds to reach the Q1 Observation Deck (✆ 07/5582 2700; www.qdeck.com.au), 230m (754 ft.) above the ground on levels 77 and 78 of the building. From there, you can gaze down on all the Gold Coast has to offer, with 360-degree views. A small theater in the Skyline Room shows a short film on the history of the Gold Coast, or you can stop in at the cafe for a piece of Q1-shaped cake and a coffee. Better still, head up there before sunset for a cocktail in the Skybar. The Observation Deck is open 9am to 9pm Sunday to Thursday, and until midnight Friday and Saturday. Entry costs A$19 adults, A$14 seniors and students, A$11 children ages 5 to 14, and A$49 families of four. A day/night ticket, which allows you to visit during the day and return after 6pm, costs A$29 adults, A$20 seniors and students, and A$17 children. Last tickets are sold 45 minutes prior to closing time.

Talks and demonstrations include saltwater-croc feeding—at 1pm daily, usually only October through April, when the crocs are hungry. Aboriginal rangers give talks about weaponry, bush medicine, and their links with this region. Volunteers also give free guided tours throughout the day. The Queensland National Parks and Wildlife Service (QNPWS) has run the park since 1983; David Fleay continued to live here until his death in 1993. Because the QNPWS frowns on handling animals, you can't cuddle a koala or hand-feed kangaroos here. However, there is a koala "contact zone" where you can enter a koala enclosure and take your own photos standing beside one. This costs an extra A$8.70 adults or A$12 for a family.

Kabool Rd. (17km/11 miles south of Surfers Paradise), West Burleigh. ✆ **07/5576 2411.** Admission A$17 adults, A$11 seniors and students, A$7.75 children 4–17, A$43 families of 6. Daily 9am–5pm. Closed Dec 25 and until 1pm on Apr 25 (Anzac Day). Ample free parking.

Surfworld Gold Coast Queensland's first surfing museum opened its doors at Currumbin in 2009 to celebrate the history and contribution of surfing and beach culture to this part of Australia. About 100 surfboards show the evolution of design and technology from 1915 through to today, alongside photographs of early surf scenes, videos, artwork, clothing, and current work by world-renowned surf photographers.

Level 1, 35 Tomewin St., Currumbin (18km/11 miles south of Surfers Paradise, opposite Currumbin Sanctuary). ✆ **07/5525 6380.** www.surfworldgoldcoast.com. Admission A$9 adults; A$5 seniors, students, and children; A$25 families of 4. Daily 10am–5pm. Ample free parking.

Where to Stay

VERY EXPENSIVE

Palazzo Versace You almost have to see this to believe it. In the unlikely location of the Australian Gold Coast, fashion designer Donatella Versace has created a tribute to her late brother, Gianni, in the form of an extravagantly opulent resort, furnished exclusively with Versace gear. You'll either love it or hate it—there's no in between. Everything was imported from Italy, from the river stones that pave the porte-cochere to the massive antique chandelier that dominates the vast, marbled lobby. Vaulted ceilings are hand-detailed in gold, and huge marble columns dominate. The rooms are decorated in four colors (red, blue, gold, and orange) and are less confronting than the public areas. Everything in them—furniture, cutlery, crockery, toiletries, the lot—is Versace (either from the housewares collection or specially created for the hotel). Many of the rooms overlook the huge pool, the Broadwater (a stretch of ocean), and the marina. As you'd expect, everything is beautifully appointed, and you'll enjoy strolling the corridors lined with Gianni's artwork and designs. There's an extensive spa and health club in the basement. You can choose from eight room types (Donatella stays in the A$4,000 Imperial Suite) or from a pool of two- and three-bedroom condominiums. All rooms and suites have Jacuzzis; condos have kitchens. And of course, should you get the urge to shop, there's a Versace boutique.

94 Sea World Dr., Main Beach, QLD 4217. ✆ **1800/098 000** in Australia, or 07/5509 8000. Fax 07/5509 8888. www.palazzoversace.com. 205 units, 72 condos. A$435–A$855 double; A$640–A$1,135 double suite; A$3,000–A$4,000 Imperial suite. AE, DC, MC, V. **Amenities:** 3 restaurants; 2 bars; concierge; health club and spa; saltwater heated lagoon pool and 27 other pools (some exclusive to condos); room service; wet and dry sauna. *In room:* A/C, TV w/pay movies, hair dryer, Internet (A$10 for 1 hr.; A$25 for 24 hr.), minibar, Wi-Fi (condominiums only; A$10 for 1 hr., A$25 for 24 hr.).

MODERATE

Paradise Resort Gold Coast ★ ☺ Parents, if your idea of a holiday is to not see your kids for most of the day, this place is for you. The resort has a licensed child-care center for little ones as young as 6 weeks and up to 5 years old. For 5- to 12-year-olds, there's the Zone 4 Kids, complete with pedal minicars, the Leonardo painting room, and an underwater-themed pirate adventure world. You can laze around the leafy pool area and watch the kids play on the water slide. The child-care center charges moderate fees, and the Zone 4 Kids is free; both operate daily year-round. The low-rise building is comfortable, and rooms have views of the pool or the gardens. Family quarters sleep up to five in two separate rooms, and some (the family studios) have kitchenettes. Junior Bunkhouse rooms have queen-size beds in the main room and brightly painted bunks in a separate kids' area, complete with their own TVs with Nickelodeon kids' channel, PlayStation, chalkboard, and play desk.

The resort rents a wide range of kiddy stuff, such as prams (strollers), bottle warmers, car seats, and PlayStations, and it has a minimarket and takeout meal service. The big range of activities makes this a great value for families, and the

Getting the Best Value out of Vacation Apartments

Apartments make good sense for families and for any traveler who wants to self-cater to save money. Because the Gold Coast has a dramatic oversupply of apartments that stand empty except during school vacations, you can get a spacious modern unit with ocean views for the cost of a midrange hotel. Apartment-block developers got in quick to snag the best beachfront spots when the Gold Coast boomed in the 1970s, so apartment buildings, not hotels, have the best ocean views. The Gold Coast Booking Centre (✆ 1300/553 800; www.gcbc.com.au) is a centralized booking service that offers great deals on more than 1,200 apartments.

Avoid Holiday Madness: Book Ahead

Most accommodations require a 1-week minimum stay during school holiday periods and a 4-day minimum stay at Easter. When the Gold Coast SuperGP car race takes over the town for 4 days in October, hotel rates skyrocket and most hostelries demand a minimum stay of 3 or 4 nights. Don't leave accommodations to the last minute! Contact the Gold Coast Tourism Bureau (✆ 07/5538 4419; www.verygc.com.au) to find out the exact dates.

center of Surfers Paradise and the patrolled beach are a few blocks across the highway. Some rooms are near the highway, so ask for a quiet spot.

122 Ferny Ave., Surfers Paradise, QLD 4217. ✆ **1800/074 111** in Australia, or 07/5579 4444. Fax 07/5579 4492. www.paradiseresort.com.au. 405 units. A$110–A$130 resort room for up to 4; A$170 King room (sleeps 3); A$190 Junior Bunkhouse rooms (sleeps 4); A$210 resort family room for up to 5; A$220 interconnecting room (sleeps 6). Ask about special packages. AE, DC, MC, V. Free covered secure parking. Bus: 1 or 1A (stop outside the resort). **Amenities:** 2 restaurants; cafe/sandwich bar; bar; babysitting; child-care center and kids' club; concierge; exercise room; Jacuzzi; 4 outdoor pools; sauna; spa; 2 tennis courts. *In room:* A/C, TV/VCR w/free and pay-per-view movies, hair dryer, kitchenette, Wi-Fi A$5 for 30 min.).

Q1 Resort & Spa This is the best view in town, and that's really saying something. Q1 opened in late 2005 as the world's tallest residential tower—it reaches 323m (1,058 ft.). From your aerie, you can truly look down on everyone else on the Gold Coast, especially if you are staying at level 46 or higher, which dwarfs all other Gold Coast buildings. From inside, or on your glass-enclosed balcony, you can see much of the wide expanse of the coast or hinterland—and for the complete 360-degree experience, head to the 77th floor for the **Observation Deck** (p. 369). Each apartment has a luxury kitchen, dining, and lounge area, and is given a daily miniservice. It's all glass, granite, and stainless steel, but there are nice personal touches. Each apartment has laundry facilities, and two- and three-bedroom apartments have two bathrooms.

Hamilton Ave. (at Northcliffe Terrace), Surfers Paradise, QLD 4217. ✆ **1300/792 008** in Australia, or 07/5630 4500. Fax 07/5630 4555. www.Q1.com.au. 527 units. A$265 double 1-bedroom apt; A$360 double 2-bedroom apt; A$545–A$895 double 3-bedroom apt. Extra person A$40. 3-night minimum stay (5 nights in high season, mid-Dec to mid-Jan). AE, DC, MC, V. **Amenities:** Restaurant; bar; concierge; health club and spa; 2 lagoon pools and indoor heated lap pool; sauna. *In room:* A/C, TV w/pay movies, hair dryer, Internet (A$4 for 30 min.; A$15 for 24 hr.), kitchenette, minibar.

Where to Dine

The Gold Coast is full to the rafters with good restaurants. Many stylish new restaurants and cafes, most reasonably priced, are springing up around **Surf Parade** and **Victoria Avenue** in Broadbeach, as well as in the nearby **Oasis shopping mall.** Other trendy spots are the stylish **Marina Mirage** shopping center, opposite the Sheraton on Sea World Drive in Main Beach, and the hip **Tedder Avenue** cafes in Main Beach.

Elephant Rock Cafe ★ MODERN AUSTRALIAN Take your seat under the pavilion overlooking Currumbin Beach and be mesmerized by the waves. The food's good too, but the view is something else. Elephant Rock Cafe is a chic, modern restaurant that's one of the best on the Gold Coast. Whether you go for breakfast, lunch, or dinner you won't be disappointed with the food, which includes vegetarian and gluten-free choices. Dinner might include duck risotto, a Mauritius-style fish curry, or a char-grilled black Angus scotch fillet, and the wines are usually from small boutique wineries. The cakes and biscuits are made at the cafe, and for lunch there are burgers, wraps, gourmet sandwiches, and more. Menus change seasonally and there's also a kids' menu.

776 Pacific Parade, Currumbin. ✆ **07/5598 2133.** www.elephantrock.com.au. Main courses A$20–A$33. AE, DC, MC, V. Daily 7am–10pm.

Ristorante Fellini ★ ITALIAN Locals and visitors flock here for the flavors of Italy—mainly from Naples and Tuscany—as well as the fantastic views of the marina and Broadwater. When the temperature is right, the huge windows are opened to let in the sea breeze, and the split-level design means every table gets the same view. For so stylish a place, you'd expect the prices to be sky high, but they're not. Family owned, the restaurant is friendly and welcoming, but the service is snappy. The menu includes pasta dishes such as ravioli filled with roasted duck and vegetables cooked in a light sauce of butter, fresh sage, and grated Parmesan topped with poppy seeds; and a range of chicken, beef, and seafood dishes, including fresh snapper filets pan-fried with zucchini, oven roasted tomato, shallots, thyme, white wine, and olive oil, baked in a paper envelope.

Level 1, Marina Mirage, Sea World Dr., Main Beach. ✆ **07/5531 0300.** www.fellini.com.au. Reservations recommended. Main courses A$30–A$39. AE, DC, MC, V. Daily noon–10:30pm.

The Gold Coast After Dark

It's not as big as some Vegas casinos, but **Conrad Jupiters Casino,** Gold Coast Highway, Broadbeach (✆ **07/5592 8282**), has plenty to keep the gambler amused—70 gaming tables and 1,300-plus slot machines with roulette, blackjack, Caribbean stud poker, baccarat and minibaccarat, craps, Pai Gow, and sic-bo. The 1,100-seat Jupiter's Theatre stages international musical theater productions, big-name bands, and solo artists, usually for a 3-month run. Then there are the three bars, including an English-style pub. Of the five restaurants, the good-value **Food Fantasy** buffet is outrageously popular, so be prepared to wait. The casino is open 24 hours. You must be 18 to enter, and smart, casual dress is required.

If you're not a gambler, head to **Saks,** Marina Mirage, Sea World Drive, Main Beach (✆ **07/5591 2755**), where on Friday and Saturday nights at about 9pm, the elegant cafe and wine bar turns into a dance floor for fashionable 20- and 30-somethings. There's also a live band on Sunday afternoons but no cover. There's a plethora of nightclubs in Surfers Paradise.

THE GOLD COAST HINTERLAND: BACK TO NATURE

The cool, green Gold Coast hinterland is only a half-hour drive from the coast, but it's a world away from the neon lights, theme parks, and crowds. Up here, at an altitude of 500 to 1,000m (1,640–3,280 ft.), the tree ferns drip moisture, the air is crisp, and the pace is slow.

Mount Tamborine shelters several villages known for their crafts shops, galleries, cafes, and B&Bs. Easy walking trails wander from the streets through rainforest and eucalyptus woodland, and as you drive you will discover magnificent views.

The impressive 20,200-hectare (49,895-acre) **Lamington National Park** lies south of Mount Tamborine. The park, at around 1,000m (3,328 ft.) above sea level, is a eucalyptus and rainforest wilderness crisscrossed with walking trails. It's famous for its colorful bird life, wallabies, possums, and other wildlife. The road to the park is full of twists and turns, and as you wind higher and higher, tangled vines and dense eucalyptus and ferns make a canopy across the road—it's so dark you need headlights. The park is about 90 minutes from the coast, but once you're ensconced in your mountain retreat, the world will seem remote.

The hinterland is close enough to the Gold Coast and Brisbane to make a pleasant day trip, but you will almost certainly want to stay overnight, or longer, once you breathe that restorative mountain air.

Mount Tamborine

40km (25 miles) NW of Surfers Paradise; 70km (43 miles) S of Brisbane

Crafts shops, teahouses, and idyllic vistas are Mount Tamborine's attractions. The mountaintop is more a plateau than a peak, and it's home to a string of villages, all a mile or two apart—Eagle Heights, North Tamborine, and Mount Tamborine proper. Many shops and cafes are open only Thursday through Sunday.

ESSENTIALS

GETTING THERE & GETTING AROUND From the Gold Coast, head to Nerang and follow signs to Beaudesert. The Mount Tamborine turnoff is off this road. Alternatively, take the Pacific Highway north to Oxenford and take the Mount Tamborine turnoff, the first exit after Warner Bros. Movie World. Many tour operators run minibus and four-wheel-drive day trips from the Gold Coast, and some run tours from Brisbane. A fun thing to do is take a tour with the **Tamborine Trolley Co.** buses (✆ **07/5545 4321;** www.tamborinetrolley.com.au), modeled on early-20th-century trams, which have a variety of tours to wineries and other attractions. A 3-hour winery tour costs A$45 per person, while a full-day food and wine tour costs A$95. Pickups from your coastal accommodations is another A$30. On Wednesdays, the company runs a hop-on-hop-off tour of about 20 attractions. The price of A$77 includes pick-up from Gold Coast accommodations or the Coomera railway station.

VISITOR INFORMATION Head to **Gold Coast Tourism**'s Visitor Information centers (see under "The Gold Coast," earlier in this chapter) to stock up on information and tourist maps before you set off. Brisbane Visitor Information Centre (see "Visitor Information," in chapter 7) also has information. The **Tamborine Mountain Information Centre** is in Doughty Park, where Geissmann Drive joins Main Western Road in North Tamborine (✆ **07/5545 3200;** www.tamborinemtncc.org.au). It's open Monday to Friday from 10am to 3:30pm, Saturdays from 9:30am to 3:30pm and Sundays from 10am to 3:30pm. Closed Christmas Day and Good Friday.

EXPLORING THE MOUNTAIN

With a map at hand, you are well equipped to drive around Mount Tamborine's roads, admire the views over the valleys, and poke around the shops. New Age candles, homemade soaps, maple-pecan fudge, tropical watercolors, German cuckoo clocks, and Aussie antiques are some of the things you can buy in the many stores. The best place to shop is the quaint strip of galleries, cafes, and shops known as **Gallery Walk** on Long Road, between North Tamborine and Eagle Heights. Eagle Heights has few shops but great views back toward the coast. North Tamborine is mainly a commercial center with the odd nice gallery or two. Mount Tamborine itself is mainly residential.

One of the area's latest attractions is the **Tamborine Rainforest Skywalk** (**© 07/5545 2222;** www.rainforestskywalk.com.au), set in 11 hectares (27 acres) of privately owned rainforest. The 1.5km (1-mile) rainforest walk includes about 300m (984 ft.) of steel bridges through the rainforest canopy, combined with a 40m-long (131-ft.) cantilever soaring 30m (98 ft.) over the creek below. It is accessed from 333 Geissmann Drive, North Tamborine, and is open daily (except Christmas Day) from 9am to 4pm. The walk takes about 50 minutes.

Allow time to walk some of the trails that wind through forest throughout the villages. Most are reasonably short and easy. The Mount Tamborine Information Centre has maps marking them.

WHERE TO STAY

Tamborine Mountain Bed & Breakfast ★ Ideally situated close to rainforest walks, arts and craft shops, wineries, and restaurants, Tony and Pam Lambert's restful timber home has stunning 180-degree views to the ocean from the breakfast balcony. Laze by the open fire in the timber-lined living room, or on the lovely veranda where rainbow lorikeets, kookaburras, and crimson rosellas flit about over the bird feeders. The ferny gardens have four purpose-built rustic timber suites, each individually decorated in style, named for the birdlife, and linked to the house by covered walkways. Rooms are heated in winter. There's no smoking indoors.

19–23 Witherby Crescent, Eagle Heights, QLD 4721. **© 07/5545 3595.** Fax 07/5545 3322. www.tmbb.com.au. 4 units, all with shower only. A$160 double midweek; A$210 double Sat–Sun. Rates include continental breakfast Mon–Fri, full breakfast Sat–Sun. MC, V. Free parking. Children 11 and under not accepted. *In room:* A/C, TV/VCR, hair dryer.

Lamington National Park ★★

70km (43 miles) W of Gold Coast; 115km (71 miles) S of Brisbane

Subtropical rainforest, 2,000-year-old moss-covered Antarctic beech trees, giant strangler figs, and misty mountain air characterize Lamington's high, narrow ridges and plunging valleys. Its stretches of dense rainforest make it one of the most important subtropical parks in southeast Queensland, and one of the loveliest. The park has 160km (99 miles) of walking trails that track through thick forest, past ferny waterfalls, and along mountain ridges with soaring views across green valleys. The trails vary in difficulty and length, from 1km (.5-mile) strolls to 23km (14-mile) treks.

The park is a haven for bird lovers, who come to see and photograph the rosellas, bowerbirds, rare lyrebirds, and other species that live here, but that's not the only wildlife you will see. Groups of small wallabies, called pademelons, graze outside your room. In summer, you may see giant carpet pythons curled up in a tree or large goannas sunning themselves on rock ledges. You may be stopped near streams by a hissing Lamington spiny crayfish, an aggressive little monster 6 inches long, patterned in royal blue and white. The park comes alive with owls, possums, and sugar-gliders at night.

Most visitors are fascinated by the park's Antarctic beech trees, which begin to appear above the 1,000m (3,280-ft.) line. Like something from a medieval fairy tale, these mossy monarchs of the forest stand 20m (66 ft.) tall and measure up to 8m (26 ft.) in girth. They are survivors of a time when Australia and Antarctica belonged to the supercontinent Gondwana, when it was covered by wet, tropical rainforest. The species survived the last Ice Age, and the trees at Lamington are about 2,000 years old, suckered off root systems about 8,000 years old. The trees are a 2½-hour walk from O'Reilly's Rainforest Retreat (see below).

EXPLORING LAMINGTON NATIONAL PARK

The easiest way to explore the park is to base yourself at **O'Reilly's Rainforest Retreat** in the Green Mountains section of the park, or at **Binna Burra Mountain Lodge** in the Binna Burra section (see "Where to Stay & Dine," below). Most of the trails lead from one or the other of these resorts, and a 23km (14-mile) **Border Trail** connects them; it follows the New South Wales–Queensland border for much of the way, and most reasonably fit folk can walk it in a day. Guided walks and activities at both resorts are for guests only; however, both properties welcome day visitors who want to walk the trails (which is free). Both have inexpensive cafes for day-trippers.

It is a good idea to bring a flashlight and maybe binoculars for wildlife spotting. The temperature is often significantly cooler than on the Gold Coast, so bring a sweater in summer and bundle up in winter when nights get close to freezing. September through October is orchid season, and the frogs come out in noisy abundance in February and March.

GETTING THERE **By Car** O'Reilly's is 37km (23 miles) from the town of Canungra. The road is twisty and winding, so take it slow. Allow an hour from Canungra to reach O'Reilly's, and plan to arrive before dark. Binna Burra is 35km (22 miles) from Nerang via Beechmont, or 26km (16 miles) from Canungra, on a winding mountain road. From the Gold Coast go west to Nerang, where you can turn off to Binna Burra via Beechmont, or go on to Canungra, where you will see the O'Reilly's and Binna Burra turnoffs. From Brisbane, follow the Pacific Highway south and take the Beenleigh/Mount Tamborine exit to Mount Tamborine. From there, follow signs to Canungra. Allow a good 2½ hours to get to either resort from Brisbane, and 90 minutes from the Gold Coast. Binna Burra sells unleaded fuel; O'Reilly's has emergency supplies only.

BY COACH The **Mountain Coach Company** (✆ **07/5524 4249;** www.mountaincoach.com.au) does daily transfers to O'Reilly's and Binna Burra from the Gold Coast, leaving the airport at 8am, picking up at hotels along the way, and arriving at O'Reilly's at around noon. The return trip leaves O'Reilly's at 2:30pm, arriving at the airport by 6pm. **Australian Day Tours** (✆ **07/3489 6455;** www.daytours.com.au) makes a daily coach run from outside the Roma Street Transit Centre in Brisbane at 8:45am, arriving at O'Reilly's at 12:45pm. The return trip leaves O'Reilly's at 2:15pm and gets to Brisbane at 6pm. The cost is A$84 adults and A$52 children.

The Binna Burra lodge runs limousine transfers from the Gold Coast and Brisbane. Bookings are essential and must be made at least 24 hours in advance. It costs A$88 per car (for one to four passengers) from Nerang railway station, A$138 from Gold Coast Airport, and A$253 from Brisbane Airport.

VISITOR INFORMATION The best sources of information on hiking are O'Reilly's Rainforest Retreat and Binna Burra Mountain Lodge (see "Where to Stay & Dine," below); ask them to send you copies of their walking maps. There are national parks information offices at both properties, but they are not always open. For detailed information on hiking and camping in the park, go to the website **www.derm.qld.gov.au/parks/lamington**.

WHERE TO STAY & DINE

Both of these mountaintop retreats have long and interesting histories. Both offer walking trails of a similar type and distance; guided walks, including nighttime wildlife-spotting trips; hearty food; and a restful, enjoyable experience. They offer similar experiences; the differences are perhaps in style, with O'Reilly's having become a more sophisticated and modern operation in recent years. Look into the special-interest workshops both properties run throughout the year, which can be anything from gourmet weekends to mountain-jogging programs.

Binna Burra Mountain Lodge ★★ ☺ Binna Burra is a postcard-perfect mountain lodge. The original cabins, built in 1935, are still in use; they've been outfitted with modern comforts but not with contemporary "inconveniences," such as telephones, televisions, radios, and clocks. All the accommodations have pine-paneled walls, floral bedcovers, heaters, and electric blankets. The popular Euphrasia Bella rooms have balconies with wonderful views of the Numinbah Valley and private bathrooms; they are furnished with queen or double twin beds. The spacious mudbrick and weatherboard Acacia cabins also have private bathrooms, unlike the Casurarina cabins, which are the least expensive option but have shared bathroom facilities.

Meals are served in the stone-and-timber dining room, where you can sit at a communal table with other guests or at a table for two. Free tea and coffee are on the boil all day. Also here are a crafts shop, a natural history library, and a large program of activities. **Rejoove Health Spa** is open daily from 10am to 8pm.

Beechmont via Canungra, QLD 4211. ✆ **1300/246 622** in Australia, or 07/5533 3622. Fax 07/5533 3747. www.binnaburralodge.com.au. 41 cabins, 22 with bathroom with shower only. A$180–A$280 double. Extra person A$70. Extra child 5–12 A$40. Crib A$10 per night. Rates include breakfast; packages with dinner included also available. MC, V. **Amenities:** Restaurant; bar; babysitting; free children's programs (ages 5–12) during school vacations; spa. *In room:* Minibar, no phone.

O'Reilly's Rainforest Retreat ★★ ☺ A third generation of the O'Reilly family is now involved in this historic guesthouse, which has been welcoming visitors since 1926. You will likely meet at least some of this extended clan during your visit, possibly presiding over the toaster at breakfast. Highlights of your stay will be the chance to hand-feed brilliantly colored rainforest birds every morning and the fact that the staff will remember you by name. Nestled high on a cleared plateau, the buildings are closed in on three sides by dense tangled rainforest and open to picturesque mountain views to the west. The timber resort complex is inviting, with upmarket new suites. The comfortable guest lounge has an open fire, old-fashioned sofas and chairs, and an upright piano. The six rooms in the Toolona block, built in the 1930s, have communal bathrooms and basic furniture. The six motel-style Garden View rooms have handcrafted maple furniture. The seven Bithongabel rooms are singles. Mountain View rooms look out to the McPherson Ranges and have balconies; the six family rooms in this block have bunks for kids, and two rooms have wheelchair access. Three large Canopy suites have king-size four-poster beds, fireplaces, Jacuzzis, libraries, stereo/CD players, minibars, and bars. One of the former O'Reilly family homes has been transformed into two suites, called "Vince" and "Lona," after the second-generation couple who raised their 10 children in the house. Each unit has two bedrooms (one with a king-size four-poster bed), two bathrooms, a separate living room, and a two-way fireplace. The large decks have a Jacuzzi, from which you can look out to magical sunsets. The latest accommodation choice is a range of 48 new one-, two-, and three-bedroom villas a short distance from the guesthouse complex.

At mealtime, the maitre d' assigns you to a table, so you get to meet other guests. Head to the hexagonal Rainforest Bar, perched up high for great sunset views, for half-price cocktails from 5 to 6:30pm or a light meal. Among other facilities are a cafe and gift shop, a basketball court, and free tea, coffee, and cookies all day. The **Lost World Spa** has eight treatment rooms and offers the full array of pampering treatments.

Via Canungra, Lamington National Park Rd., Lamington National Park, QLD 4275. ✆ **1800/688 722** in Australia, or 07/5502 4911. www.oreillys.com.au. 72 units. A$165–A$268 single rooms; A$325 double; A$410 Canopy Suite; A$520 2-bedroom suite; A$400–A$480 1-bedroom villa; A$435–A$510 2-bedroom villa; A$610–A$660 3-bedroom villa. 4-night minimum New Year's, Easter, Christmas. Ask about 2-night and longer packages. Meal plan A$99 adults, A$50 children 12–15, A$30 children 4–11; 2-meal packages available. AE, DC, MC, V. **Amenities:** Restaurant; bar; babysitting; children's programs (age 6 and up) on Sat–Sun and school vacations; Jacuzzi; heated outdoor plunge pool; sauna; spa; lit tennis court. *In room:* Wi-Fi (villas only; A$10 for 30 min.; A$35 for 24 hr.).

OUTBACK QUEENSLAND

Spread over 3,000km (1,875 miles), the Outback is a heart-stopping land of clear blue skies, burnished sunsets, rolling plains, rugged ranges, and endless vistas. Populated with colorful characters that could have walked off a movie set, the Outback is the heart and soul of Queensland. This is where the Aussie tradition of mateship was born, as pioneering cattlemen and their families battled the elements to make a go of it. The Queensland Outback is the birthplace of Australian legends like Waltzing Matilda. History comes alive when you get to places like the Burke River at Boulia, where explorers Burke and Wills filled their water bags and modern-day travelers are invited to do the same, or at Lark Quarry, where dinosaurs once roamed.

The main centers of Queensland Outback life are the towns of Charleville, Barcaldine, Longreach, and Winton, and the mining town of Mount Isa. They may be small, but they offer a completely different view of this vast state than you will get on the coast, and they are definitely worth the effort it takes to get to them.

Longreach

700km (437 miles) W of Rockhampton; 1,286km (804 miles) NW of Brisbane

With a population of about 4,500, Longreach is the largest town in Queensland's Central West. One of the biggest surprises for first-time visitors to Longreach is that the town is set on the banks of a wide brown river, the Thomson. And after a hard day's traveling or sightseeing around Longreach, there's nothing more relaxing than a sunset cruise on the river or a campfire on its banks. This is bushranger country, and wherever you go in this area, you'll hear the story of Captain Starlight, the cattle rustler who's become part of local folklore—it's one of those stories which gets better with each telling, and which has been immortalized in the classic Australian novel *Robbery Under Arms* by Rolf Boldrewood. There's plenty to do in Longreach, and tour operators are on hand to take the difficulty out of the distances involved.

GETTING THERE **By Car** From Brisbane, Longreach is 1,286km (804 miles) northwest. Take the Warrego Highway west through Toowoomba and Roma, heading toward Charleville. About 90km (56 miles) before Charleville, head north to Augathella and join the Matilda Highway. From there it is about 320km (200 miles) to Barcaldine, and from there another 108km (67 miles) west to Longreach. From Rockhampton, the Capricorn Highway heads almost directly west through Emerald and Alpha for about 590km (369 miles) before joining the Matilda Highway.

BY PLANE **Qantaslink** (✆ **13 13 13** in Australia; www.qantas.com.au) flies into Longreach Airport from Brisbane daily.

BY TRAIN **Queensland Rail Traveltrain** (✆ **1300/131 722**) runs the train *Spirit of the Outback* from Brisbane to Longreach via Rockhampton every Tuesday at 6:25pm and Saturday at 1:10pm, returning on Thursday and Monday. It's A$184 for a seat from Brisbane or A$242 to A$374 for a sleeper. Alternatively, you can join the train at Rockhampton on Wednesday or Sunday. The trip takes about 25 hours from Brisbane, or 14 hours from Rockhampton.

BY BUS **Greyhound Australia** (✆ **1300/473 946**) runs between Brisbane and Longreach daily. The trip takes nearly 18 hours and costs A$143.

VISITOR INFORMATION **The Longreach Visitor Information Centre** is at Qantas Park, Eagle Street, Longreach, QLD 4730 (✆ **07/4658 4150;** www.longreach.qld.gov.au). It is open Monday to Friday 8:30am to 5pm and weekends 9am to noon. Another good source of information is the **Outback Queensland Tourism Association** (✆ **1800/247 966;** www.outbackholidays.info).

GETTING AROUND Rental-car companies **Avis** (✆ **13 63 33** in Australia, or 07/4658 3541) and **Budget** (✆ **07/4982 1767**) both have outlets at Longreach Airport.

Several tour companies offer tours in and around Longreach and to other Central West Outback towns. One of the best is Alan and Sue Smith's **Outback Aussie Tours ★★** (✆ **07/4658 3000;** www.oat.net.au), which runs trips taking in Longreach, Ilfracombe, Winton, and Barcaldine, as well as the Lark Quarry dinosaur site. **Longreach Outback Travel Centre** (✆ **07/4658 1776;** www.lotc.com.au) at 115a Eagle St., has information on a variety of tours.

THE TOP ATTRACTIONS

Australian Stockman's Hall of Fame & Outback Heritage Centre ★★★

This should be the first stop on any visit to Longreach. I could spend all day at the Hall of Fame, but try to allow at least 4 hours. (If you run out of time they will give you a re-entry pass for the next day.) A tribute to the pioneers who developed the Outback, the center honors explorers, stockmen, poets, and artists. Part museum, part memorial, part interactive display, this world-class attraction is educational, entertaining, and quite amazing. Exhibits are updated regularly and give a fascinating insight into the Aboriginal and European history of Australia, blending modern technology with artifacts and relics of a bygone age. The Outback Stockman's Show, held Monday to Saturday at 11am and 2pm (May–Oct only), showcases the skills of a stockman and depicts working life in the bush. It costs an extra A$5 adults, A$2 children.

Ilfracombe Rd., Longreach. ✆ **07/4658 2166.** Fax 07/4658 2495. www.outbackheritage.com.au. A$23 adults, A$12 children 8–17, A$50 family. Daily 9am–5pm except Christmas.

Longreach School of Distance Education Tours of this unique school system—also known as the School of the Air—will give you insight into the isolation of Outback families. You can watch a teacher conducting on-air lessons via two-way radio to students on far-flung stations. Hundreds of children in western Queensland take advantage of this form of education. Tours even run during some school holidays, but it's much better to visit when there's action!

Sir James Walker Dr., Longreach. ✆ **07/4658 4222.** www.longreacsde.eq.edu.au. A$6 adults, A$3 children. Guided tours at 9 and 10:30am Mon–Fri (except public holidays and Dec–Jan school holidays).

Qantas Founders Museum Anyone who's ever flown on Australia's first airline will be interested in this tribute to pioneer aviators. Longreach is the original home of Qantas, as the airline's operational base from 1922 to 1934, when Australia's first six aircraft were built here. The acronym Q.A.N.T.A.S. stands for Queensland and Northern Territory Air Service. During World War II, Longreach was used as a base by U.S. Flying Fortress bombers for their Pacific operations. The original hangar is now complemented by a A$9-million world-class museum, with the main exhibit a full-size replica of an AVRO 504K, a 747 Jumbo, the first type of aircraft operated by Qantas. You can tour the 747, including walking out onto the wing, clambering down into the computer bay and cargo bays, and sitting in the pilot's seat. Tours of the 747 must be booked and cost A$19 adults, A$10 children, and A$45 for a family. They take between 1 and 2 hours, depending on whether you take the wing walk (this costs A$85 adults, A$55 children, and A$170 for a family). You can also take a 30-minute guided tour of the recently arrived, fully restored Boeing 707, VH-XBA, the first passenger jet registered in Australia and Qantas's first jet aircraft. Located at the airport, opposite the Australian Stockman's Hall of Fame, this sleek building, which resembles an aircraft hangar, contrasts perfectly with the original hangar.

Qantas hangar, Longreach Airport, Sir Hudson Fysh Drive, Longreach. ✆ **07/4658 3737.** www.qfom.com.au. A$19 adults, A$10 children 7–16, A$45 family. Ask about entry and tour packages. Daily 9am–5pm except Christmas Day.

OTHER THINGS TO SEE & DO

Thomson River cruises—usually at sunset—are run by two local companies, **Billabong Boat Cruises** and **Yellowbelly Express River Cruises.** Billabong operates the *Thomson Belle,* the only paddle wheeler in Western Queensland. The dinner cruise costs A$55 adults, A$40 children 3 to 14, and A$10 children under 3. At the end of the night, you'll be entertained by some of the local talent, which could be bush poetry or a singalong. A sunset cruise with Yellowbelly Express includes transfers from your accommodations, an informative and entertaining commentary on the river, and a few nibbles. It costs A$38 adults and A$15 children, A$10 for kids under 3. All drinks (not just alcohol) are BYO for both cruises. Both can be booked through the Longreach Outback Travel Centre (✆ **07/4658 1776;** www.lotc.com.au).

A 30-minute drive from Longreach is the small town of **Ilfracombe.** Attractions include the folk museum, with its large collection of old vehicles, including a horse-drawn wool wagon, sulkies, cart, and farm machinery. The museum also has a turn-of-the-20th-century police cell and a collection of Aboriginal artifacts, historic photographs, and early pioneering silver and china.

Stop at the historic **Wellshot Hotel** in Ilfracombe for a cool drink. Named for the largest sheep station in the world in its heyday, the pub is a popular local watering hole.

WHERE TO STAY

Albert Park Motor Inn This is a fairly standard motel, but is among the best in town, and location is everything. The Albert Park is close to all the major attractions—just 200m (660 ft.) from the airport and Qantas Founders Museum, and 500m (1,600 ft.) from the Australian Stockman's Hall of Fame. It's about 1.5km (just under a mile) to the center of town. The Oasis restaurant serves large meals at reasonable prices, and there's a nice lagoon-style pool to cool off in. You're also likely to spot some of the local wildlife including goannas, kangaroos, and wallabies.

Sir Hudson Fysh Dr., Longreach, QLD 4730. ✆ **1800/821 811** in Australia, or 07/4658 2411. Fax 07/4658 3181. 56 units (with shower only). A$128 double. Extra adult A$16, extra child 14 and under A$11. AE, DC, MC, V. Free parking. **Amenities:** Restaurant; bar; Internet (A$3 for 15 min.; A$5 for 30 min.); Jacuzzi; shaded heated saltwater pool and children's wading pool; room service. *In room:* A/C, TV w/free movies, hair dryer, minibar.

Winton

175km (109 miles) NW of Longreach; 1,500km (94 miles) NW of Brisbane; 470km (294 miles) E of Mount Isa

Winton is best known as the place where Banjo Paterson wrote "Waltzing Matilda" in 1885, for which the nearby Combo Waterhole was the inspiration. The town has a population of 1,200 and most of its major attractions are linked to the song.

GETTING THERE & GETTING AROUND The nearest car hire is in Longreach. Roads are all sealed between Winton, Longreach, and Mount Isa. **Greyhound Australia** (✆ **1300/473 946**) has daily coach services between Longreach and Winton. The trip takes about 2 hours and costs A$37. Coach connections from Longreach to Winton are also available to passengers on the *Spirit of the Outback* train, run by **Queensland Rail Traveltrain** (✆ **1300/131 722;** www.traveltrain.com.au). The fare from Brisbane is A$205 for a seat or A$264 to A$396 for a sleeper.

VISITOR INFORMATION The **Winton Visitor Information Centre** (✆ **1300/665 115** in Australia or 07/4657 1466; www.experiencewinton.com.au) is located in the Waltzing Matilda Centre, 50 Elderslie St., Winton. It's open daily from 9am to 5pm, with restricted hours on public holidays and weekends from October through March. It's closed Christmas Day, Boxing Day, and New Year's Day. If you're planning to spend a few days here, buy a "Shin Plaster" pass to Winton's attractions for A$23 adult or A$50 family. For A$32 adult or A$70 family, it also covers entry to the Lark Quarry dinosaur tracks.

OTHER TOP ATTRACTIONS

Combo Waterhole Conservation Park Believed to be the inspiration for the song "Waltzing Matilda," the waterhole is a short drive off the Matilda Highway, about 150km (94 miles) north of Winton. It is then an easy 40-minute walk from the parking lot to the waterhole. Combo Waterhole's story is told on interpretive signs along the way, which will take you across the Diamantina River channels on

ON THE dinosaur TRAIL

The stampeding footprints of 150 terrified coelurosaurs and ornithopods—reputedly Steven Speilberg's inspiration for a scene for the blockbuster *Jurassic Park*—can be found in Outback Queensland, where dinosaurs once roamed and have left their calling cards. **Lark Quarry** (www.dinosaurtrackways.com.au) is one of the most amazing fossil sites in the world, recording a dramatic moment in time 95 million years ago, when the hot, dusty area outside the town of Winton was once a small prehistoric lake. A large flesh-eating carnosaur trapped around 150 smaller coelurosaurs and ornithopods at the lake edge, causing them to flee in panic.

It is the only surviving record of a dinosaur stampede on Earth. The tracks were undiscovered until 1962 and are now protected by conservation works that include a building that helps conserve the footprints by controlling the temperature, humidity, and moisture levels, and an elevated walkway for best viewing and photography of the tracks. A lookout offers panoramic views over the vast Lark Quarry environmental park. There are also interpretive displays, picnic tables, and toilets.

Lark Quarry is 110km (69 miles) southwest of Winton, on the mostly unsealed Jundah Road, about a 2-hour drive. Before setting out, check road conditions and directions with the Waltzing Matilda Centre (✆ **07/4657 1466**). Several companies operate tours from Winton and Longreach, including **Carisbrooke Tours** ✆ **07/4657 0084;** www.carisbrooketours.com.au) and **Outback Aussie Tours** (✆ **1300 787 890** in Australia; www.oat.net.au). Lark Quarry is open daily from 9am to 4pm. Admission is A$10 adults, A$6 school-age children, and A$25 per family. Entry is by guided tour only, daily at 10am, noon, and 2pm. For more information call the **Winton Visitor Information Centre** (✆ **1300/665 115** in Australia, or 07/4657 1466).

Outback Queensland's other major dinosaur sites can be found in the towns of Richmond and Hughenden. If you're a real enthusiast and intend to take the **"Dinosaur Triangle"**—you'll need about a week to do it—it's worth buying a Dino Pass for A$20 adults or A$50 per family. Your drive will be a loop starting and ending in Mount Isa via various interesting spots covered in this chapter. Stop in Richmond to visit the **Kronosaurus Korner Marine Fossil Museum** (✆ **07/4741 3429;** www.kronosauruskorner.com.au) to discover an ancient time when this area was a great inland sea. You can go fossicking to find your own fossils which can be identified by the local palaeontologist.

Finally on to Hughenden, the start of the great ancient inland sea. (Take a side trip to Porcupine Gorge National Park, a spectacular sandstone gorge about 63km/33 miles outside the town.) The **Flinders Discovery Centre** (✆ **07/4741 1021**) in Hughenden includes a 7m (23-ft.) replica of the Muttaburrasaurus langdoni (named after the town of Muttaburra, where the remains were found close to the Thomson River in 1963).

century-old stone-pitched overshots. The waterhole might inspire you to break into a chorus of "Waltzing Matilda." This is a great place for bird-watching too.

150km (94 miles) north of Winton off Matilda Hwy. ✆ **07/4652 7333** for the Queensland Parks & Wildlife Service in Longreach. Free admission. Information center: Mon–Fri 8:30am–5pm; closed public holidays and Christmas to New Year.

MAKING tracks THROUGH QUEENSLAND'S OUTBACK

Queensland has long known the benefits of covering vast distances by train, and its iconic Outback trains are a fantastic way of seeing the countryside as you travel through it—in comfort. The most luxurious is ***Spirit of the Outback,*** which runs the 1,300km (808 miles) from Brisbane to Longreach via Rockhampton every Tuesday and Saturday, returning on Thursday and Monday. Alternatively, you can join the train at Rockhampton on Wednesday or Sunday. The trip takes about 25 hours from Brisbane, or 14 hours from Rockhampton.

The ***Inlander*** runs from Townsville to Mount Isa every Sunday and Thursday, returning on Monday and Friday. The 977km (610-mile) journey takes 22 hours.

The ***Westlander*** takes you from Brisbane across the Great Dividing Range through the lush green countryside of the Darling Downs, and on to the Outback town of Charleville, famed for its stargazing (make sure you visit the Cosmos Centre and Observatory). The 777km (483-mile) journey takes about 17 hours, leaving Brisbane on Tuesday and Thursday at 7:15pm. A one-way adult fare is A$102 for a seat, A$160 to A$244 for a sleeper.

The ***Savannahlander*** (© **1800/793 848** in Australia or 07/4053 6848; www.savannahlander.com.au) is a classic 1960s rail motor that takes 4 days to travel through the remote heart of Queensland's far northern Gulf country between Cairns and Forsayth. You can also do shorter day trips, joining the train at various points along the way. For the full journey, you first travel up the Kuranda range, before the "Silver Bullet" heads west for the tiny settlements of Almaden, Einsleigh, Mount Surprise, and Forsayth. Don't be in a hurry; the pace is leisurely and the driver will even stop the train here and there to point out things along the way, including wildlife alongside the track. The train stops overnight in Almaden so passengers can take a tour to the old

Waltzing Matilda Centre Dedicated to Australia's most famous song, written by Banjo Paterson in 1898 at Dagworth Station, near Winton, the center uses modern technology and interactive displays to celebrate the writer's life and times and the role his song has played in Australia's psyche. The complex also includes the Outback Regional Gallery, the Qantilda local history museum, a restaurant, and gift shop.

50 Elderslie St., Winton. © **07/4657 1466.** Fax 07/4567 1886. www.matildacentre.com.au. A$19 adults, A$8 children, A$42 family of 6. Apr–Oct daily 9am–5pm; Nov–Mar Mon–Fri 9am–5pm, Sat–Sun 9am–3pm; public holidays 9am–3pm. Closed Christmas Day and Boxing Day.

WHERE TO STAY

Boulder Opal Motor Inn This family-owned business is one of Winton's best motels. All rooms have a queen size and a single bed, and two rooms are specially designed for people with disabilities. The licensed restaurant has an Outback theme, but that doesn't extend to the cuisine, which is more Mediterranean-inspired. It is open daily for breakfast and Monday to Saturday for dinner. The reception area has a great display of handcrafted opal jewelry (the owners are also active in local opal mining). The motel is only 500m (1,600 ft.) from the Waltzing Matilda Centre.

mining village of Chillagoe where ruins of the Chillagoe Smelters, built around 1900 and operated until 1943, still dominate the skyline. Other attractions along the way include the therapeutic Tullaroo Hot Springs, the massive underground caves of the Undara Lava Tubes, and the stunning Cobbold Gorge. The train usually runs between early March and mid-December, depending on weather and track conditions. There are various touring options available, but if you want to do the whole trip over 4 days, with all tours and overnight accommodation in Chillagoe, Cobbold Gorge, and in the restored railway carriages at Undara Lava Lodge, it will cost A$1,040 adults and A$702 children.

An equally interesting journey is the half-day trip on the ***Gulflander*** (✆ **07/4036 9222;** www.gulflander.com.au). This train travels the 152km (95 miles) from Normanton to Croydon, through some of Queensland's most remote, inaccessible, and diverse countryside—from wetlands and grasslands to arid savannah country. Opened in 1891 to connect Normanton to the rich Croydon goldfields, the line has never been linked to the main Queensland Rail network. Affectionately known as the "Tin Hare," it leaves Normanton on Wednesdays at 8:30am and arrives in Croydon 4 or 5 hours later. It turns around for the return journey on Thursday at the same time. The fare is A$61 adults or A$31 children 4 to 14 one-way, or A$105 adults and A$53 children round-trip. Normanton is around 700km (435 miles) from Cairns, but if you don't want to drive, there are a number of *Gulflander* packages that include getting there. There are also packages which combine the *Savannahlander* and *Gulflander.*

For more information about all of Queensland's Outback, scenic, and long-distance trains, contact **Queensland Rail Traveltrain** (✆ **1300/131 722;** www.traveltrain.com.au).

16 Elderslie St., Winton. ✆ **07/4657 1211.** Fax 07/4657 1331. www.boulderopalmotorinn.com.au. 26 units, all with shower only. A$115–A$120 double; A$165 2-bedroom unit. A$12 extra person. Free crib. AE, DC, MC, V. Free undercover parking. **Amenities:** Restaurant; bar; free airport transfers; outdoor pool; room service. *In room:* A/C, TV, hair dryer, dial-up Internet.

Mount Isa

893km (558 miles) W of Townsville; 633km (395 miles) NW of Longreach

Mount Isa is Queensland's largest provincial city west of the Great Dividing Range. The town was built around mining, and the population of 22,000 reflects that in the 50 different nationalities represented. The huge Mount Isa Mine dominates the town. It is the world's largest single producer of copper, silver, lead, and zinc. A social highlight of the year is the annual **Mount Isa Rodeo** (✆ **07/4743 2706;** www.isarodeo.com.au), held every August (in 2011, it's Aug 10–12). It's the biggest rodeo in the southern hemisphere.

GETTING THERE **By Car** Mount Isa is 893km (558 miles) west of Townsville on the Flinders Highway. From Longreach, take the Landsborough Highway northwest through Winton and on to Cloncurry. Mount Isa is about 120km (75 miles)

west of Cloncurry on the Barkly Highway. The total trip from Longreach is 633km (395 miles). Motorists should check all road conditions with local authorities before setting out.

BY TRAIN **Queensland Rail Traveltrain** (✆ **1300/131 722**) operates the *Inlander* train from Townsville to Mount Isa every Sunday and Thursday, returning on Monday and Friday. The 977km (610-mile) journey takes 22 hours and costs A$123 per adult for a seat or A$182 to A$280 for a sleeper.

BY BUS **Greyhound Australia** (✆ **1300/473 946** in Australia) services Mount Isa from Townsville. The trip takes about 12 hours and costs A$143 one-way.

BY PLANE **Qantas** (✆ **13 13 13** in Australia; www.qantas.com.au) serves Mount Isa from Brisbane and Townsville.

VISITOR INFORMATION The **Outback@Isa Visitor Information Centre** is at 19 Marian St., Mount Isa, QLD 4825 (✆ **1300/659 660** in Australia, or 07/4749 1555; www.outbackatisa.com.au). It is open daily from 8:30am to 5pm.

GETTING AROUND Car hire companies **Avis** (✆ **07/4743 3733**), **Budget** (✆ **13 27 27** or 07/4749 1828), and **Hertz** (✆ **07/4743 4142**) have offices in Mount Isa.

THE TOP ATTRACTIONS

Boodjamulla (Lawn Hill) National Park Sheer red cliff walls, deep flowing green water, walking tracks, and Aboriginal sites are the features of this spectacular Outback oasis. World Heritage–listed Riversleigh is part of Lawn Hill's fossil section. This is a very remote area, and you really need a four-wheel drive to access it, as the last 280km (174 miles) is unsealed road. A better option is to take a 3-day, 2-night safari tour from Mount Isa with **Yididi Aboriginal Guided Tours** (book through Outback @ Isa, ✆ **07/4749 1555**). The tour costs A$990 adults, A$475 children 5 to 15, and A$238 children 2 to 4. Owner/operator Harry Burgen is a member of the Waanyi Aboriginal tribe, the traditional owners of these lands. The tour includes 2 nights' accommodation at the area's only permanent accommodation, Adel's Grove (www.adelsgrove.com.au; 10km/6 miles outside the park); all meals; canoe hire; and transfers. The guided tour takes you to Riversleigh's fossil fields, walking in the national park, to Aboriginal rock painting sites, canoeing on Lawn Hill Creek, and swimming in the natural spa. It only operates April to September.

About 500km (312 miles) northwest of Mount Isa. ✆ **07/4743 2055** for Queensland Parks & Wildlife Service in Mount Isa, or 07/4748 5572 for the ranger (3–4pm only).

Outback@Isa You may get better insight into this mining town with a **Hard Times Mine Tour.** The fully guided tours, run out of the Outback@Isa Visitor Information Centre, descend to the 1.2km (¾ miles) of tunnels in an Alimak cage at 10am and 2pm daily. Wearing protective clothing, including a miner's cap and lamp, you are led by former miners who really know what they are talking about. Tours take about 2½ hours and are not suitable for children under 7. The Outback@Isa complex also includes several other attractions. The **Outback Park** is a cool oasis with a lagoon, lush vegetation, and waterfalls. The **Deluxe Pass** includes the underground tour, and gives 2 days' entry to Riversleigh Fossil Centre (see below), the Isa Experience Gallery, and the Outback Park for A$55 adults, A$33 children, and A$150 for a family of four.

Outback @ Isa: 19 Marian St., Mount Isa. ✆ **1300/659 660** in Australia, or 07/4749 1555. www.outbackatisa.com.au. Undergound tour A$45 adult, A$26 child 7–17, A$120 family of 4. Bookings essential. Daily 8:30am–5pm. Closed Dec 25 and Good Friday.

Riversleigh Fossil Centre This interpretive center gives insight into life in the Riversleigh region some 25 million years ago when dinosaurs roamed. The fossil fields have given up some of their secrets, and dioramas re-create some of the ancient animal life, such as Obdurodon, an ancestral platypus, and the wonderfully named Thingodonta. In the fossil treatment laboratory, you can watch as fossils come to light for the first time in millions of years as a laboratory technician and paleontologist carry out preparatory work on the fossils gathered from the Riversleigh site. Tours to this section are held Monday to Friday at 10am and 2pm, and include a step-by-step explanation. It's a "must-see" for visitors to the center.

19 Marian St., Mount Isa. ✆ **07/4749 1555.** www.outbackatisa.com.au. A$10 adults, A$6.50 children ages 5–17, A$30 family of 4. Daily 8:30am–5pm. Closed Christmas Day and Good Friday.

Royal Flying Doctor Base A 15-minute movie shows "a day in the life" of a flying doctor who covers 1.3 sq. km (500,000 sq. miles) of northwest Queensland. There's also a small museum and display area and a souvenir shop, and picnic and barbecue facilities are available in the shady gardens.

11 Barkly Hwy., Mount Isa. ✆ **07/4743 2800.** www.flyingdoctor.org.au. Entry by donation. Mon–Fri 9:30am–4:30pm. Closed weekends, public holidays, and Queensland school holidays.

WHERE TO STAY & DINE

Mount Isa has plenty of accommodations, from backpacker hostels and caravan parks to host farms and four-star hotels. Make sure your lodgings are air-conditioned because you'll need it.

All Seasons Mount Isa Verona Hotel In this heat, you don't want to be far from anything, especially if you're walking, so this hotel's location, right in the heart of town, is a bonus. The hotel's restaurant is among the best in town, and the adjoining cocktail bar is a pleasant place for a predinner drink. There's also a small library to browse in. Executive rooms have a small desk area.

Rodeo Drive and Camooweal St., Mount Isa, QLD 4825. ✆ **1800/679 178** in Australia, or 07/4743 3024. Fax 07/4743 8715. www.accorhotels.com.au. 57 units. A$179 double; A$199 executive room. AE, DC, MC, V. Free parking. **Amenities:** Restaurant; bar; exercise room; outdoor pool. *In room:* A/C, TV w/free movies, hair dryer, minibar, Wi-Fi (A$28 for 24 hr.).

THE RED CENTRE

by Lee Mylne

The Red Centre is the landscape most closely associated with Australia's Outback—endless horizons, vast deserts of red sand, mysterious monoliths, and cloudless blue skies. If there is a soundtrack, it is the rhythmic haunting tones of the didgeridoo.

9

The Centre is home to sprawling cattle ranches, ancient mountain ranges, "living fossil" palm trees that survived the Ice Age, cockatoos and kangaroos, ochre gorges, lush water holes—and, of course, to Uluru, the massive rock monolith.

Aboriginal people have lived here for tens of thousands of years, but the Centre is still largely unexplored by non-Aboriginal Australians. One highway cuts from Adelaide in the south to Darwin in the north, and a few roads and four-wheel-drive tracks make a lonely spider web across it; in many other areas, non-Aborigines have never set foot.

Alice Springs is the only big town in Central Australia, which together with the Top End makes up the Northern Territory. And let's get one thing straight from the start: Alice Springs and Uluru are *not* side by side. Uluru is 462km (286 miles) away. You can get there and see it in a day from Alice Springs, but it's an effort, and in doing so you will miss much of what is on offer, for visiting Uluru is much more than just a quick photo opportunity. It may well be the most meaningful and memorable part of your trip to Australia.

Give yourself a few days to experience all there is in the Centre—visiting the magnificent domes of Kata Tjuta ("the Olgas") near Uluru, walking the rim of Kings Canyon, riding a camel down a dry riverbed, exploring the intricacies of Aboriginal paintings (either on rock or canvas), swimming in waterholes, or staying at an Outback homestead. Alice Springs gives you a better flavor for the Outback than Uluru. If you base yourself in Alice, it's easy to radiate out to less crowded but still beautiful attractions such as Palm Valley, Ormiston Gorge, and Trephina Gorge Nature Park, each an easy day trip. Too many visitors jet in, snap a photo of the Rock, and head home, only to miss the essence of the desert.

The Red Centre

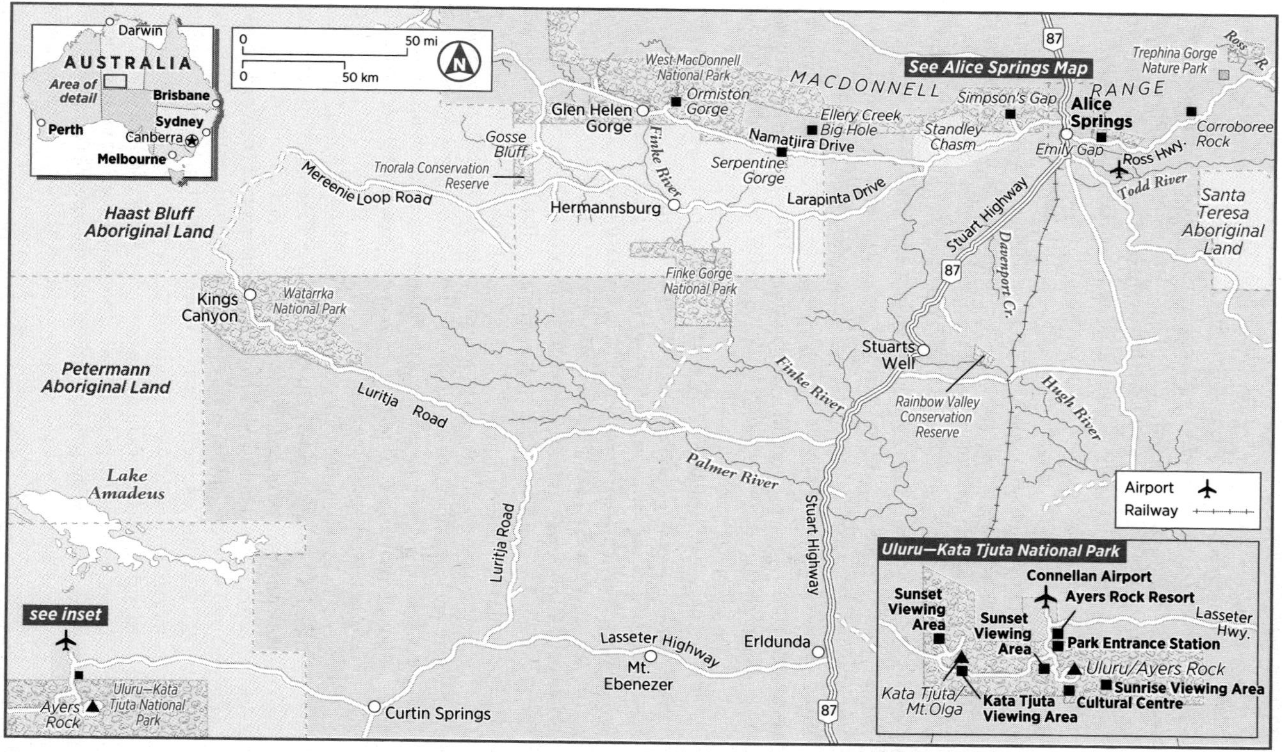
AUSTRALIA
Darwin
Area of detail
Brisbane
Perth
Sydney
Canberra
Melbourne
0
50 mi
0
50 km
N
See Alice Springs Map
87
MACDONNELL RANGE
West MacDonnell National Park
Trephina Gorge Nature Park
Ross R.
Glen Helen Gorge
Ormiston Gorge
Ellery Creek Big Hole
Simpson's Gap
Alice Springs
Corroboree Rock
Standley Chasm
Emily Gap
Ross Hwy.
Todd River
Namatjira Drive
Serpentine Gorge
Gosse Bluff
Tnorala Conservation Reserve
Mereenie Loop Road
Finke River
Hermannsburg
Larapinta Drive
Stuart Highway
Davenport Cr.
Santa Teresa Aboriginal Land
Haast Bluff Aboriginal Land
Finke Gorge National Park
Kings Canyon
Watarrka National Park
Stuarts Well
Rainbow Valley Conservation Reserve
Hugh River
Petermann Aboriginal Land
Luritja Road
Palmer River
Lake Amadeus
Airport
Railway
see inset
Lasseter Highway
Mt. Ebenezer
Erldunda
Curtin Springs
Uluru—Kata Tjuta National Park
Ayers Rock
Uluru—Kata Tjuta National Park
Connellan Airport
Ayers Rock Resort
Sunset Viewing Area
Sunset Viewing Area
Lasseter Hwy.
Park Entrance Station
Uluru/Ayers Rock
Sunrise Viewing Area
Kata Tjuta/Mt.Olga
Kata Tjuta Viewing Area
Cultural Centre

EXPLORING THE RED CENTRE

VISITOR INFORMATION The **Central Australian Tourism Industry Association** (see "Visitor Information" under "Alice Springs," p. 392) can send you a brochure pack. It is your best one-stop source of information.

Most of the Red Centre lies within the Northern Territory. The **Northern Territory Tourist Commission,** Tourism House, 43 Mitchell St., Darwin, NT 0800 (✆ **13 67 68** in Australia, or 08/8951 8471; www.travelnt.com), can supply information on traveling in this region. The website has special sections tailored for international travelers (choose your country) and for the self-drive market. It can help you find a travel agent who specializes in the Northern Territory and details many hotels, tour operators, rental-car companies, and attractions, as well as lots of information on local Aboriginal culture and Aboriginal tours. The Commission's Territory Discoveries division (www.holidaysnt.com) offers package deals.

WHEN TO GO April, May, September, and October have sunny days (coolish in May, hot in Oct). Winter (June–Aug) means mild temperatures with cold nights. Summer (Nov–Mar) is ferociously hot and best avoided. In summer, limit exertions to early morning and late afternoon, and choose air-conditioned accommodations. Rain is rare but can come at any time of year.

DRIVING TIPS The **Automobile Association of the Northern Territory,** 79–81 Smith St., Darwin, NT 0800 (✆ **08/8925 5901**), offers emergency breakdown service to members of affiliated overseas automobile associations and dispenses maps and advice. It has no office in the Red Centre. For a recorded report of **road conditions,** call ✆ **1800/246 199** in Australia.

Only a handful of highways and arterial roads in the Northern Territory are sealed (paved) roads. A conventional two-wheel-drive car will get you to most of what you want to see, but consider renting a four-wheel-drive for complete freedom. All the big car-rental chains have them. Some attractions are on unpaved roads good enough for a two-wheel-drive car, but your car-rental company will not insure a two-wheel-drive for driving on them.

Normal restricted speed limits apply in all urban areas, but speed limits on Northern Territory highways (introduced only in 2006) are considerably higher than in other states. The speed limit is set at 130kmph (81 mph) on the Stuart, Arnhem, Barkly, and Victoria highways, while rural roads are designated 110kmph (68 mph) speed limits unless otherwise signposted. However, drivers should be careful to keep to a reasonable speed and leave enough distance to stop safely. The road fatality toll in the Northern Territory is high: 27 fatalities per 100,000 people each year, compared with the Australian average of 8 per 100,000.

Another considerable risk while driving is that of hitting wildlife: camels, kangaroos, and other protected native species. Avoid driving at night, early morning, and late afternoon, when 'roos are more active; beware of cattle lying down on the warm bitumen at night.

Road trains (trucks hauling more than one container) and fatigue caused by driving long distances are two other major threats. For details on safe driving, review the tips in the "By Car" section of "Getting There & Getting Around" in chapter 3.

If you plan to "go bush" in remote regions not covered by this guide, you may need a permit from the relevant Aboriginal lands council to cross Aboriginal land. This can

Buzz Off!

Uluru is notorious for plagues of flies in summer. Don't be embarrassed to cover your head with the fly nets sold in souvenir stores—there will be "no flies on you, mate," an Aussie way of saying you are clever.

be a drawn-out bureaucratic affair that takes weeks, so plan ahead. The Northern Territory Tourist Commission (see "Visitor Information," above) can put you in touch with the appropriate council. All good road maps mark Aboriginal lands clearly.

OTHER TRAVEL TIPS **Always carry drinking water.** When hiking, carry 4 liters (about a gallon) per person per day in winter, and a liter (¼ gal.) per person per hour in summer. Wear a broad-brimmed hat, high-factor sunscreen, and insect repellent.

Bring warm clothing for chilly evenings in winter. Make sure you have a full tank of gas before setting out and check distances between places you can fill up.

TOUR OPERATORS Numerous coach, minicoach, and four-wheel-drive tour operators run tours that take in Alice Springs, Kings Canyon, and Uluru. They depart from Alice Springs or Uluru, offering accommodations ranging from spiffy resorts, comfortable motels, and basic cabins to shared bunkhouses, tents, or swags (sleeping bags) under the stars. Most pack the highlights into a 2- or 3-day trip, though leisurely trips of 6 days or more are available. Many offer one-way itineraries between Alice and the Rock (via Kings Canyon if you like), or vice versa, which will allow you to avoid backtracking.

Among the reputable companies are **AAT Kings** (**© 1300/556 100** in Australia, or 08/8952 1700 for the Alice Springs office; www.aatkings.com), which specializes in coach tours but also has four-wheel-drive camping itineraries; **Alice Springs Holidays** (**© 1800/801 401** in Australia or 08/8953 1411; www.alicesprings holidays.com.au), which does upscale soft-adventure tours for groups; **Connections Safaris** (**© 1300/886 332** in Australia, or 02/8252 5300 for the Sydney booking office; www.connections.travel), which conducts camping safaris in small groups for all ages; and **Discovery Ecotours** (**© 08/8953 7800;** www.ecotours.com.au), which specializes in ecotours for groups. **Tailormade Tours** (**© 1800/806 641** in Australia or 08/8952 1731; www.tailormadetours.com.au) offers public tours as well as customized luxury charters.

ALICE SPRINGS

462km (286 miles) NE of Uluru; 1,491km (924 miles) S of Darwin; 1,544km (957 miles) N of Adelaide; 2,954km (1,831 miles) NW of Sydney

"The Alice," as Australians fondly call it, is the unofficial capital of the Red Centre. In the early 1870s, a handful of telegraph-station workers struggled nearly 1,600km (992 miles) north from Adelaide through the desert to settle by a small spring in what must have seemed like the ends of the earth. Alice Springs, as the place was called, was just a few huts around a repeater station on the ambitious telegraph line that was to link Adelaide with Darwin and the rest of the world.

Today Alice Springs is home to 27,000 people, with supermarkets, banks, and the odd nightclub. It's a friendly, rambling, unsophisticated place. No matter what direction you come from, you will fly for hours over a vast, flat landscape to get here. On arrival, you will see that in fact it is close to a low, dramatic range of rippling red mountains, the **MacDonnell Ranges.** Many visitors excitedly expect to see Uluru, but that marvel is about 462km (286 miles) down the road.

Many tourists visit Alice only to get to Uluru, but Alice has charms of its own, albeit of a small-town kind. The red folds of the MacDonnell Ranges hide lovely gorges with shady picnic grounds. The area has an old gold-rush town to poke around in, quirky little museums, wildlife parks, a couple of cattle stations (ranches) that welcome visitors, hiking trails to put red dust on your boots, and one of the world's top 10 desert golf courses. You could easily spend 2 or 3 days here.

This is the heart of the Aboriginal Arrernte people's country, and Alice is a rich source of tours, shops, and galleries for those interested in Aboriginal culture, art, or souvenirs. However, parts of this region are also evidence that ancient Aboriginal civilization has not always meshed well with the 21st century, which has resulted in fractured riverbed communities plagued by alcohol and other social problems.

Essentials

GETTING THERE **By Plane** **Qantas** (✆ **13 13 13** in Australia) flies direct from Sydney, Adelaide, Darwin, Perth, Melbourne, Brisbane, Cairns, and Uluru. Flights from most other cities connect via Sydney or Adelaide. Low-cost newcomer **Tiger Airways** (✆ **03/9335 3033;** www.tigerairways.com.au) has direct flights from Melbourne and Adelaide.

The **Alice Springs Airport Shuttle** (✆ **08/8953 0310;** www.buslink.com.au) meets all flights and transfers you to your Alice hotel door for A$18 one-way or A$28 round-trip. A taxi from the airport to town, a distance of 15km (9⅓ miles), is around A$32.

BY TRAIN The ***Ghan*** train, named after Afghan camel-train drivers who carried supplies in the Red Centre during the 19th century, makes the trip from Adelaide to Alice every week, continuing to Darwin. The twice-weekly Adelaide-Alice service (leaving Adelaide on Sun and Wed at 12:20pm and Alice Springs on Thurs and Sun afternoons) takes roughly 24 hours. The *Ghan* departs Alice Springs for Darwin on Monday and Thursday at 6pm, arriving in Katherine on Tuesday and Friday mornings, and Darwin in the late afternoon. The service from Darwin departs on Wednesday and Saturday. Stopovers in Katherine last around 4 hours. The train has sleeper berths, but don't worry about missing much by overnighting on the train; much of the scenery is the same for hours, and you will see plenty of it during daylight hours. For information, contact **Great Southern Railway** (✆ **13 21 47** in Australia, or 08/8213 4592; www.gsr.com.au) or see "Getting There & Getting Around," in chapter 3, for its booking agencies abroad.

The **Airport Shuttle** (✆ **08/8953 0310**) runs between the station and the town center for A$9 one-way and A$14 round-trip. A taxi costs about A$10 for the trip.

BY BUS **Greyhound** (✆ **1300/473 946** in Australia; www.greyhound.com.au) runs from Adelaide and Darwin. It's a 21-hour trip from Adelaide, and the fare is around A$280. The 22-hour trip from Darwin costs about A$336.

BY CAR Alice Springs is on the Stuart Highway linking Adelaide and Darwin. Allow a very long 2 days or a more comfortable 3 days to drive from Adelaide, the same from Darwin. From Sydney, connect to the Stuart Highway via Broken Hill and Port Augusta north of Adelaide; from Cairns, head south to Townsville, then west via

Alice Springs

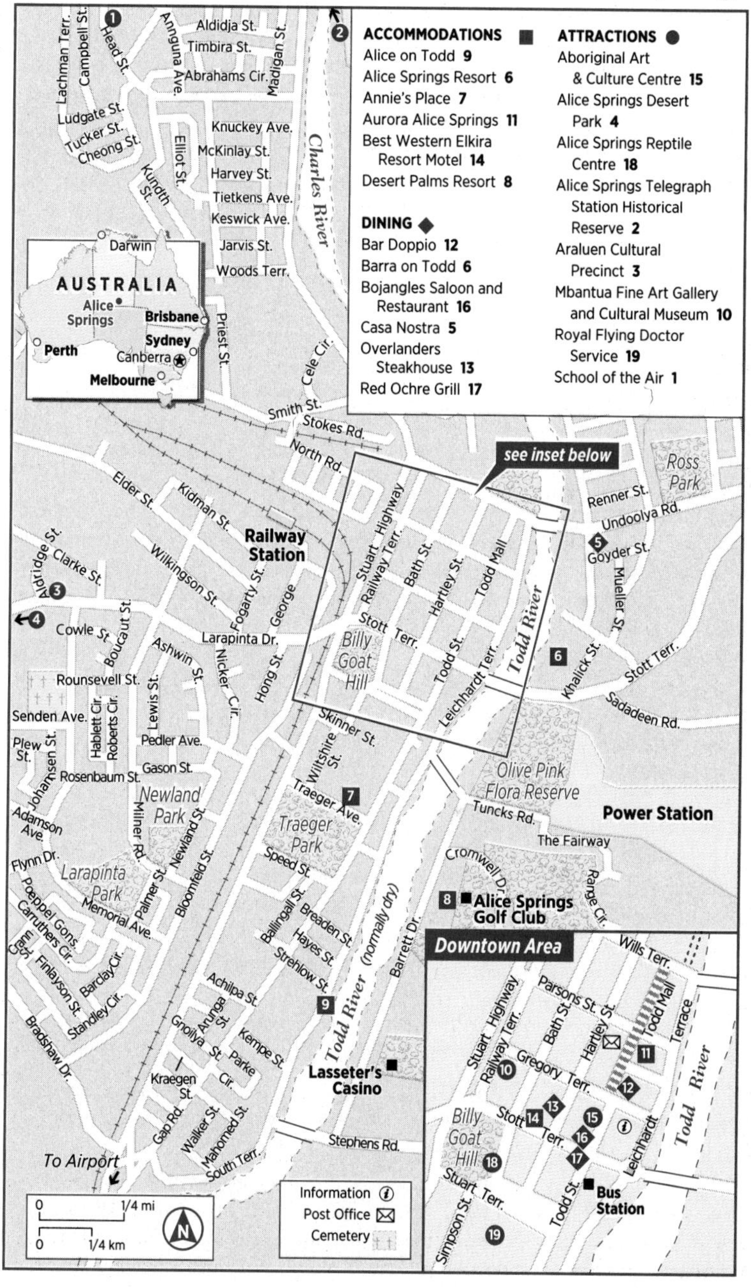

ACCOMMODATIONS
Alice on Todd 9
Alice Springs Resort 6
Annie's Place 7
Aurora Alice Springs 11
Best Western Elkira Resort Motel 14
Desert Palms Resort 8
DINING
Bar Doppio 12
Barra on Todd 6
Bojangles Saloon and Restaurant 16
Casa Nostra 5
Overlanders Steakhouse 13
Red Ochre Grill 17
ATTRACTIONS
Aboriginal Art & Culture Centre 15
Alice Springs Desert Park 4
Alice Springs Reptile Centre 18
Alice Springs Telegraph Station Historical Reserve 2
Araluen Cultural Precinct 3
Mbantua Fine Art Gallery and Cultural Museum 10
Royal Flying Doctor Service 19
School of the Air 1
AUSTRALIA
Darwin
Alice Springs
Brisbane
Sydney
Perth
Canberra
Melbourne
Charles River
Railway Station
see inset below
Ross Park
Billy Goat Hill
Todd River
Olive Pink Flora Reserve
Power Station
Newland Park
Traeger Park
Larapinta Park
Alice Springs Golf Club
Todd River (normally dry)
Lasseter's Casino
To Airport
Downtown Area
Bus Station
Information
Post Office
Cemetery
0 1/4 mi
0 1/4 km
N

the town of Mount Isa to join the Stuart Highway at Tennant Creek. Both routes are long and dull. From Perth, it is even longer; drive across the Nullarbor Plain to connect with the Stuart Highway at Port Augusta. If you fancy a driving holiday of the area, check out **www.travelnt.com** for specific advice on routes, accommodations, and everything else you'll need to know, including things like locations of fuel stops.

VISITOR INFORMATION The **Tourism Central Australia Visitor Information Centre,** 60 Gregory Terrace (✆ **1800/645 199** in Australia or 08/8952 5800; www.centralaustraliantourism.com), is the official one-stop shop for bookings and touring information for the Red Centre, including Alice Springs, Kings Canyon, and Uluru–Kata Tjuta National Park. It also acts as the visitor center for the Parks & Wildlife Commission of the Northern Territory. It's open Monday through Friday from 8am to 5pm and weekends and public holidays from 9:30am to 4pm. It also has desks at the airport and train station.

SPECIAL EVENTS Alice Springs hosts a couple of bizarre events. The **Camel Cup** camel race takes place on the second Saturday in July. In late August, folks from hundreds of miles around come out to cheer the **Henley-on-Todd Regatta ★**, during which gaudily decorated, homemade bottomless "boats" race down the dry Todd River bed. Well, what else do you do on a river that flows only 3 days a year? See "Australia Calendar of Events" in chapter 3 for more details.

GETTING AROUND Virtually all tours pick you up at your hotel. If your itinerary traverses unpaved roads, as it may in outlying areas, you will need to rent a four-wheel-drive vehicle, because regular cars will not be insured on an unpaved surface. However, a regular car will get you to most attractions. **Avis,** Gregory Terrace (at Bath St.; ✆ **08/8953 5533**); **Budget,** Shop 3, 79 Todd Mall (✆ **08/8952 8899**); **Europcar,** at the airport (✆ **08/8953 3799**); **Hertz,** 76 Hartley St. (✆ **08/8952 2644**); and **Thrifty,** corner of Stott Terrace and Hartley St. (✆ **08/8952 9999**), all rent conventional and four-wheel-drive vehicles. You may get a better deal on car rental by going through the **Outback Travel Shop** (✆ **08/8955 5288;** www.outbacktravelshop.com.au) in Alice Springs, a booking agent that negotiates bulk rates with most Alice car-rental companies.

Many rental outfits for motor homes (camper vans) have Alice offices. They include **Apollo Campers,** 40 Stuart Hwy., corner of Smith Street (✆ **1800/777 779** in Australia); **Britz Australia Campervan Hire,** corner of Stuart Highway and Power Street (✆ **08/8952 8814**); and **Kea Campers,** 7 Kidman St. (✆ **08/8955 5525**). Renting a camper van can work out to be significantly cheaper than staying in hotels and going on tours, but it pays to do your sums first. See "Where to Stay," p. 398, for caravan park locations.

The best way to get around town without your own transport is aboard the **Alice Wanderer** bus (see "Organized Tours," below). For a taxi, call **Alice Springs Taxis** (✆ **13 10 08** or 08/8952 1877) or **Territory Taxis** (✆ **08/8953 3322**), or find one at the rank (stand) on the corner of Todd Street and Gregory Terrace. Taxi fares here are high.

CITY LAYOUT **Todd Mall** is the heart of town. Most shops, businesses, and restaurants are here or within a few blocks' walk. Most hotels, the casino, the golf course, and many of the town's attractions are a few kilometers outside of town. The dry Todd River "flows" through the city east of Todd Mall.

Seeing the Sights in Alice

Aboriginal Art & Culture Centre Set up by the Southern Arrernte Aboriginal people, this center houses a small, intriguing museum with exhibits on Aboriginal life. It displays a timeline of the Aboriginal view of history since "contact" (the arrival of Europeans). It also sells artifacts and art. It's worth a visit if you're interested in indigenous cultures; allow up to an hour.

125 Todd St. ✆ **08/8952 3408.** www.aboriginalart.com.au. Free admission. Mon–Fri 9am–5pm.

Alice Springs Desert Park ★★ By means of an easy 1.6km (1-mile) trail through three reconstructed natural habitats, this impressive wildlife and flora park shows you 120 or so of the animal species that live in the desert around Alice but that you won't spot too easily in the wild (including kangaroos you can walk among). Most of the creatures are small mammals (like the rabbit-eared bilby), reptiles (cute thorny devil lizards), and birds. Don't miss the excellent **Birds of Prey ★★** show at 10am and 3:30pm. There's a cafe here, too. The **Alice Wanderer** bus (✆ **1800/722 111** in Australia, or 08/8952 2111; www.alicewanderer.com.au) offers a service to the park as an add-on to its town tour (see "Organized Tours," below). **Desert Tours & Transfers** (✆ **08/8952 1731**) also operates a bus service from accommodations, departing approximately 7:30, 9, and 11:30am, and 2 and 4pm (pickup times vary according to accommodation, so ask when booking). Return buses leave the Desert Park at 9:30am, noon, 2:30, 4:30, and 6pm. The cost is A$40 adults, A$28 children 5 to 15, A$8 to A$115 for families, including return transfers and park entry fee. Allow 2 to 3 hours.

Larapinta Dr., 6km (3¾ miles) west of town. ✆ **08/8951 8788.** www.alicespringsdesertpark.com.au. Admission A$20 adults, A$10 children 5–16, A$55 families of 6. Daily 7:30am–6pm (last suggested entry 4:30pm). Closed Dec 25.

Alice Springs Reptile Centre ☺ Kids love this place, where they can drape a python around their neck or have a bearded dragon (lizard) perch on their shoulders. Rex, the easygoing proprietor, helps you get the best photos and lets kids hand-feed bugs to the animals at feeding time. Some 30 species are on display, including the world's deadliest land snake (the taipan) and big goannas. Also here are brown snakes, death adders, and mulga, otherwise known as king brown snakes. Don't miss the saltwater croc exhibit featuring underwater viewing. The best time to visit is between 11am and 3pm, when the reptiles are at their most active. There are talks at 11am and 1 and 3:30pm. Allow an hour or so.

9 Stuart Terrace (opposite the Royal Flying Doctor Service). ✆ **08/8952 8900.** www.reptilecentre.com.au. Admission A$12 adults, A$6 children 4–16, A$30 families of 4. Daily 9:30am–5pm. Closed Jan 1 and Dec 25.

Alice Springs Telegraph Station Historical Reserve ★ 🎁 This oasis marks the first European settlement of Alice Springs, which takes its name from the water hole nearby. Alice Springs began life here in 1872 as a telegraph repeater station, against a backdrop of red hills and sprawling gum trees. Arm yourself with the free map or join a free 45-minute tour. You can wander around the old stationmaster's residence; the telegraph office, with its Morse-code machine tap-tapping away; the shoeing yard, packed with blacksmithing equipment; and the stables, housing vintage buggies and saddlery. From the on-site computer, you can "telegraph" e-mails to your friends. May through October, "kitchen maids" in period dress serve scones (biscuits) and damper (campfire bread) from the original wood-fired ovens. The park has pet camels and sometimes orphaned kangaroo joeys. Overall, it's a charming and much-underrated place. Allow a good hour—more to walk one of the several hiking trails leading from the extensive grounds—or bring a picnic and stay longer. There is a gift shop, and coffee and snacks are for sale. To get there, take a cab or Alice Wanderer bus (see "Organized Tours," p. 395) or the 4km (2½-mile) riverside pedestrian/bike track that starts near the corner of Wills Terrace and Undoolya Road. Section One of the Larapinta Trail to Simpson's Gap starts here. Walkers are advised to register with the Walker Registration Scheme through the Parks and Wildlife Office or by phoning ✆ **1300/650 730.**

Stuart Hwy., 4km (2½ miles) north of town (beyond the School of the Air turnoff). ✆ **08/8952 3993.** Free admission to picnic grounds and trails; station A$7 adults, A$3.75 children 5–15. Daily 8am–5pm (picnic grounds and trails till 9pm). Station closed Dec 25.

Araluen Cultural Precinct ★ Take several hours to explore the many facets of this interesting grouping of attractions, all within walking distance of one another. The **Museum of Central Australia** mostly shows local fossils, natural history displays, and meteorites. Some impressive Aboriginal and contemporary Aussie art is on display at the **Araluen Arts Centre** (✆ **08/8951 1122**), the town's performing-arts hub, which incorporates the Albert Namatjira Gallery, with works by this famous Aboriginal artist, as well as a display of the Papunya Community School Collection, a group of 14 paintings from the early 1970s. Check out the *Honey Ant Dreaming* stained-glass window in the center's foyer. Aviation nuts may want to browse the old radios, aircraft, and wreckage in the **Central Australian Aviation Museum,** which preserves the territory's aerial history. You can buy stylish crafts, and sometimes catch artists at work, in the **Central Craft** gallery. You may also want to amble among the fabulous outdoor sculptures, including the 15m (49-ft.) *Yeperenye* caterpillar, or among the gravestones in the cemetery, where "Afghani" camel herders (from what is now Pakistan) are buried facing Mecca. To reach the precinct, take a cab, the Alice Wanderer bus, or Desert Park Transfers.

Larapinta Dr., at Memorial Ave., 2km (1¼ miles) west of town. ✆ **08/8951 1120.** Admission (includes Museum of Central Australia, Araluen Arts Centre, Central Australian Aviation Museum, Territory Craft, and Memorial Cemetery) A$10 adults; A$7 seniors, students, and children 5–16; A$30 families of 4. Mon–Fri 10am–4pm; Sat–Sun 11am–4pm. Closed Good Friday and usually for 2 weeks from Dec 25.

Royal Flying Doctor Service Alice is a major base for this airborne medical service that treats people living and traveling in the vast Outback. An interesting 20-minute tour featuring a video and a talk in the communications room runs every half-hour; allow another 30 minutes or so to browse the small museum and listen to some of the recorded conversations between doctors and patients. You can explore a replica fuselage of a Pilatus PC12 or test your hand at the throttle in a flight simulator. There is also a nice garden cafe and a gift shop.

8–10 Stuart Terrace (at end of Hartley St.). ✆ **08/8952 1129.** www.flyingdoctor.org.au. Admission A$7 adults, A$3.50 children 6–15. Mon–Sat 9am–5pm; Sun and public holidays 1–5pm. Closed Jan 1 and Dec 25.

School of the Air Sitting in on school lessons may not be your idea of a vacation, but this school is different—it broadcasts by radio to a 1.3-million-sq.-km (507,000-sq.-mile) "schoolroom" of 140 children on Outback stations. That area's as big as Germany, Great Britain, Ireland, New Zealand, and Japan combined—or twice the size of Texas. Visitors watch and listen in when classes are in session; outside class hours, you may hear taped classes. You can browse the kids' artwork, photos, video, and other displays in the well-organized visitor center. Free 30-minute tours run throughout the day.

80 Head St. (2.5km/1½ miles from town). ✆ **08/8951 6834.** Admission A$6.50 adults; A$4.50 children 5-16; A$18 families of 4; A$22 families of 6. Mon-Sat 8:30am-4:30pm; Sun and public holidays 1:30-4:30pm. Closed Dec 25-Jan 1 and Good Friday. Bus: 3 (costs A$2.20 for 2-hr. ticket) or Alice Wanderer (see "Organized Tours," below).

Organized Tours

AROUND TOWN & OUT IN THE DESERT The **Alice Wanderer** bus (✆ **1800/722 111** in Australia, or 08/8952 2111; www.alicewanderer.com.au) does a running loop of 14 town attractions every 70 minutes, starting at 9am, with the last departure at 4pm. Hop on and off as you please and enjoy the commentary from the driver. The bus departs daily from the south end of Todd Mall. Tickets are sold on board and cost A$42 for adults, and A$28 for kids 4 to 14. Call for free pickup from your hotel. The ticket lasts for 2 days and you can use it on nonconsecutive days. The company also runs full- and half-day tours to outlying areas, including to Palm Valley in the West MacDonnell Ranges, costing A$117 for adults and A$75 for kids (p. 402); to Bond Springs Cattle Station, costing A$95 for adults and A$65 for kids; and to Santa Teresa Aboriginal Community. Here you can meet local Aboriginal artists and view and purchase their work. This half-day tour costs A$130 for adults and A$100 for kids.

The bus calls at most of the attractions above, plus the **Old Ghan Museum & Road Transport Hall of Fame,** housing the original *Ghan* train that plied the Adelaide–Alice Springs line from 1929 to 1980; and **Panorama Guth,** an art gallery housing a 360-degree painting of central Australian landscapes by artist Henk Guth. It's well worth checking out the Alice Wanderer website to help you plan your time before you visit.

Many Alice-based companies offer minicoach or four-wheel-drive day trips and extended tours of Alice and of outlying areas including the East and West Macs, Hermannsburg, and Finke Gorge National Park. Among the well-regarded ones are **Discovery Ecotours** (✆ **08/8953 7800;** www.ecotours.com.au) and **Alice Springs Holidays** (✆ **1800/801 401** in Australia, or 08/8953 1411; www.alicespringsholidays.com.au).

Billy Tea & Damper

Any tour in the Outback isn't complete without the traditional bushman's meal of billy tea and damper. Billy tea is made from tea leaves, and sometimes eucalyptus leaves, put into water (traditionally from a water hole or river) and boiled in an open-topped canister on an open fire. You don't have to stir it; the trick is to pick up the canister by the wire handle and swing the entire thing around, sometimes over your head—centrifugal force keeps the liquid in (don't try this at home, though). Damper is simply flour, water, and salt mixed into dough and thrown in the ashes of the fire to cook into bread. Yummy.

Several companies run tours by motorcycle or four-wheel-drive ATV (all-terrain vehicle). One option is **Central Oz Tours** (✆ **0407/105 899** mobile phone; www.centraloz.biz).

CAMEL SAFARIS The camel's ability to get by without water was key to opening the arid inland parts of Australia to European settlement in the 1800s. With the advent of cars, they were released into the wild, and today more than 200,000 roam Central Australia. Australia even exports them to the Middle East! **Pyndan Camel Tracks** (✆ **0416/170 164;** www.cameltracks.com) runs camel rides daily, with pickup from your hotel. A 1-hour tour, at noon, 2:30pm, or sunset, costs A$45 adults and A$25 for kids 14 and under. Kids under 3 must ride with an adult. A half-day ride, leaving at 9am and returning about noon, costs A$95 per person. Make sure you wear comfortable, casual clothes and sensible shoes—you are likely to get a bit dirty.

HOT-AIR BALLOON FLIGHTS Dawn balloon flights above the desert are popular in central Australia. You have to get up 90 minutes before dawn, though. Several companies offer flights. **Outback Ballooning** (✆ **1800/809 790** in Australia, or 08/8952 8723; www.outbackballooning.com.au) is one of the most upscale. A 1-hour flight followed by champagne breakfast in the bush costs A$385, with a 20% discount for kids 6 to 16. A 30-minute breakfast flight costs A$275. Kids under 6 are discouraged from participating because they cannot see over the basket. Don't make any other morning plans—you probably won't get back to your hotel until close to noon.

Active Pursuits

BIKING A gently undulating 17km (11-mile) **bike trail** weaves from John Flynn's Grave on Larapinta Drive, 7km (4⅓ miles) west of town, through the bushland and desert foothills of the MacDonnell Ranges to Simpson's Gap (p. 403). The **Penny Farthing Bike Shop,** 1 Hearne Place, North Stuart Highway, about 900m (just over a half mile) from the center of town (✆ **08/8952 4551**), rents bikes for A$20 for 24 hours, including helmet, lock, pump, and spare tubes. A tandem bike costs A$40, and they also have other rates for more than a day. The shop is open 8:30am to 5:30pm weekdays, 9am to 2pm Saturdays, and 11am to 2pm Sundays. ***Note:*** Carry water, because the two taps en route are a long way apart. Bike in cooler months only.

BUSHWALKING The 223km (138-mile) **Larapinta Trail** winds west from Alice through the sparse red ranges, picturesque semidesert scenery, and rich bird life of the West MacDonnell National Park (p. 402). This long-distance walking track is divided into 12 sections, each a 1- to 2-day walk. Sections range from easy to hard. The shortest is 8km (5 miles), all the way up to 29km (18 miles). The Larapinta Trail begins at the old Alice Springs Telegraph Station and meanders through many gaps and sheltered gorges and climbs steeply over rugged ranges. Each section is accessible to vehicles (some by high-clearance four-wheel-drive only), so you can join or leave the trail at any of the trail heads. Camping out under a sea of stars in the Outback is a highlight of the experience. Although they vary, most campsites offer picnic tables and hardened tent sites—all trail heads have a water supply and some have free gas barbecues. If you are planning to camp overnight, we strongly recommend that you take advantage of the **Overnight Walker**

Registration Scheme. This is voluntary and requires a refundable deposit of A$50 per person, but ensures that if anything untoward happens, a search party will be sent for you. The **Parks & Wildlife Commission of the Northern Territory** office in Alice Springs (✆ **1300/650 730** in Australia or 08/8951 8211) and the **CATIA Visitor Information Centre** (see "Visitor Information," earlier in this chapter) dispense trail maps and information. Check **www.nt.gov.au/nreta/parks/walks/larapinta** for detailed information on the trail and the walker registration scheme, and for downloadable maps. It also has details of companies that provide transfers to access points along the trail, food drops, camping equipment, or fully guided and supported treks. ***Warning:*** *Always* carry drinking water. The trail may close in extremely hot summer periods.

GOLF The **Alice Springs Golf Club ★**, 1km (just over a half mile) from town on Cromwell Drive (✆ **08/8952 1921;** www.alicespringsgolfclub.com.au), boasts a Thomson-Wolveridge course rated among the world's top desert courses by touring pros. The course is open from sunup to sundown. Nine holes cost A$47; 18 holes, A$80. Club rental costs A$35, and a motorized cart, which many locals don't bother with, goes for A$50 for 18 holes. It's best to book a tee time.

Shopping at the Source for Aboriginal Art

Alice Springs is one of the best places in Australia to buy **Aboriginal art and crafts ★**. You will find no shortage of stuff: linen and canvas paintings, didgeridoos, spears, clapping sticks, *coolamons* (dishes used by women to carry anything from water to babies), animal carvings, baskets, and jewelry, as well as books, CDs, and all kinds of non-Aboriginal merchandise printed with Aboriginal designs. Prices can soar to many thousands for large canvases by world-renowned painters, but you'll also find plenty of smaller, more affordable works. Major artworks sell unmounted for ease of shipment, which most galleries arrange. Store hours can vary with the seasons and the crowds, so it pays to check ahead.

Papunya Tula Artists, 63 Todd Mall (✆ **08/8952 4731;** www.papunyatula.com.au), sells paintings on canvas and linen from Papunya, a settlement 240km (150 miles) northwest of Alice Springs, and work by other artists living in the Western Desert, as far as 700km (434 miles) from Alice Springs.

Gallery Gondwana, 43 Todd Mall (✆ **08/8953 1577;** www.gallerygondwana.com.au), has been selling Aboriginal art in Alice Springs since 1990. It showcases both established and emerging artists, with a changing exhibition program.

The **Aboriginal Australia Art & Culture Centre,** 125 Todd St. (✆ **08/8952 3408;** www.aboriginalaustralia.com), is a community-based, Aboriginal-owned and -operated business that runs painting classes, has a retail gallery, and is a community arts base. It is open 9am to 5pm weekdays; weekends by appointment for serious collectors.

Mbantua Australian Aboriginal Art Gallery and Cultural Museum ★★★ 🎁 Vividly colorful paintings line the walls at this museum-gallery, which is a highly respected and reliable source of authentic Aboriginal art. The selection is dizzying, but prices can be affordable, and chances are good that an artist or two will be around when you visit. The art comes from a harsh desert region called Utopia, 2 hours by car from Alice Springs, which encompasses several Aboriginal communities. Mbantua owner Tim Jennings began supplying locals with paints and canvas during food deliveries to Utopia, first as sheriff, then as the general-store owner. Every 2 weeks, the Mbantua gallery team drops off new materials and pays the artists for finished works. More than 250 Utopia residents paint; the website features artists' portraits and bios in conjunction with their work. Some have garnered international recognition; in 2007, the *New York Times* praised the work of Barbara Weir, Gloria Petyarre, and the late Emily Kame Kngwarreye and Minnie Pwerle. Predictably, as Aboriginal artwork grows in value, forgeries are on the rise. Jennings authenticates every piece of art; he and his team photograph the artist with the work and elicit the Aboriginal dreaming, or traditional meaning, behind it. Works by established artists can range in price from A$850 to tens of thousands of dollars; in early 2007, a painting by Kngwarreye broke a record for Aboriginal art by fetching more than A$1 million. A much smaller investment, however, will fetch you work by lesser known but talented painters.

The museum houses a vast collection of landscape paintings by Aboriginal artists including Albert Namatjira (Australia's first Aboriginal artist and Aboriginal Australian citizen), Gabriella Wallace, and Wenten Rubuntja. A bush tucker display highlights the importance of these plants in traditional medicine, ceremony, diet, and Dreamtime. There is also a large collection of artifacts including spears, bloodstained woomeras, shields, bowls, hair belts, and Kadaitcha shoes (feather boots worn by those who are feared for carrying out punishment). The permanent collection includes the first Emily Kame Kngwarreye painting on canvas purchased by Mbantua Aboriginal Art Gallery in 1987, as well as Gloria Petyarre's first *Leaves* painting. You can watch a 30-minute DVD on the Aboriginal art industry and Mbantua Gallery's relationship with the people of Utopia, and much more. Mbantua Gallery is a member of Art.Trade, an organization that operates to promote the ethical trade of indigenous art. Free half-hour guided tours (excluding the museum) run Monday to Friday at 9:30am.

71 Gregory Terrace, Alice Springs. ✆ **08/8952 5571.** Fax 08/8952 5191. www.mbantua.com.au. Admission (museum only) A$6.60 adults, A$4.40 seniors, A$3.30 children 6–15, A$16 families of 4. Gallery Mon–Fri 9am–6pm; Sat 9:30am–5pm; Sun noon–5pm. Cultural Museum Mon–Fri 9am–6pm; Sat 9:30am–5pm; Sun 1–5pm. Last entry to museum 1 hr. before closing.

Where to Stay

Alice's hotel stock is not grand. Many properties have dated rooms and modest facilities; they're no match for the gleaming **Ayers Rock Resort** (described later in this chapter). You may pay lower rates than those listed in the summer off season (Dec–Mar) and even as late as June. Peak season typically runs from July through October or November. Besides the more upmarket properties below, there are several backpacker resorts offering dorm rooms and doubles. One of the best is **Annie's Place,** 4 Traegar Ave., Alice Springs, NT 0870 (✆ **1800/359 089** in Australia, or 08/8952 1545; www.anniesplace.com.au). Doubles cost between A$55 for a room with shared bathroom and A$65 for one with your own. Dorm rooms (single sex or mixed) sleep four to six and cost A$22 per person. Annie's Place runs **Mulga's Adventures,** which operates a 3-day backpackers' tour of the area, including Uluru, for A$250, with most things included.

If you've rented a camper van, the **Stuart Tourist and Caravan Park,** Larapinta Drive, Alice Springs (✆ **1300/823 404** in Australia or 08/8952 2547; www.stuartcaravanpark.com.au), has powered sites costing A$30 a night. Cabins here cost between A$75 and A$165 per night, depending on the cabin and the season.

EXPENSIVE

Alice Springs Resort ★ This friendly, well-run, low-rise property is a 3-minute walk from town over the Todd River. Standard and superior rooms are quite pleasant, while deluxe rooms are a bit plusher, with such touches as bathrobes, and have a balcony or veranda overlooking the Todd River or the gardens. In summer, it's nice to repair to the pool under a couple of desert palms after a hot day's sightseeing. If you time it right (weather permitting), there's live jazz at the **Barra Poolside Bar.**

34 Stott Terrace, Alice Springs, NT 0870. ✆ **1300/272 132** in Australia or 08/8951 4545 (resort). Fax 08/8953 0995. www.alicespringsresort.com.au. 144 units, 108 with shower only. A$160–A$250 double. Extra person A$40. Children 11 and under stay free in parent's room with existing bedding. Ask about packages with Ayers Rock Resort and Kings Canyon Resort. AE, DC, MC, V. Free parking. **Amenities:** Restaurant; 2 bars; free airport shuttle; babysitting; bikes; concierge; solar-heated outdoor pool; room service. *In room:* A/C, TV w/pay movies, hair dryer, minibar, Wi-Fi (A$10 per hr., A$25 for 24 hr.).

Bond Springs Outback Retreat ★ This working 1,515-sq.-km (591-sq.-mile) cattle ranch is a great place to get a taste of Outback life with a real Aussie family. Hosts Ben and Laura welcome guests to the homestead where Ben grew up, accommodating them in two appealing cottages. The first is Corkwood Cottage, which was originally built for the station's head stockman and his family. The main bedroom features a queen-size bed, and two other bedrooms have twin beds and a single bed. There's a comfortable lounge and dining room, a fully equipped kitchen, and an outdoor barbecue. The second cottage, the "Wurlie," has a main bedroom with a queen-size bed and a second bedroom with twin beds. There's a lounge and dining room, which includes a kitchenette. Gourmet breakfasts are delivered to both cottages, but other meals are not provided, so you'll have to ensure you buy provisions in Alice Springs. No smoking indoors.

Note: All but the last 6km (3¾ miles) of the road to the ranch is paved. Car-rental companies do not allow driving on unpaved roads, but they may permit it here; check with your company. Try to ensure you arrive before dark.

25km (16 miles) north of Alice Springs (P.O. Box 4), Alice Springs, NT 0870. ✆ **08/8952 9888.** Fax 08/8953 0963. www.outbackretreat.com.au. 2 cottages. A$277 Corkwood Cottage; A$231 Wurlie Cottage. Rates include full breakfast. Extra adult A$58; extra child 6–15 A$47. MC, V. Closed Dec 25–Jan. Ask about transfers from Alice Springs. **Amenities:** Swimming pool; tennis court. *In room:* A/C, hair dryer, no phone.

MODERATE

Alice on Todd ★ ☺ This contemporary complex has nice studio, one-bedroom, and two-bedroom apartments. It's a very good option, particularly if you have kids. (If they're under 4, they stay free.) The hotel overlooks the Todd River and is just a short stroll from town. All but the studios have balconies. The two luxury two-bedroom apartments each have an extra sofa bed. There is a washing machine in each unit, and other amenities such as free storage lockers. Another 22 one-bedroom deluxe apartments were being added to the complex at press time and should be ready before you arrive.

Strehlow St. and South Terrace (P.O. Box 8454), Alice Springs, NT 0870. ✆ **08/8953 8033.** www.aliceontodd.com. 56 units. A$120 studio apt; A$147–A$160 1-bedroom apt; A$184–A$198 2-bedroom apt. Additional person A$20. AE, MC, V. Undercover parking. **Amenities:** Babysitting; bikes; children's playground; Jacuzzi; pool. *In room:* A/C, TV, hair dryer, kitchenette, Wi-Fi (A$6 for 1 hr.; A$16 for 24 hr.; A$60 per week).

Aurora Alice Springs This pleasant hotel is smack in the center of town. Rooms in the newer wing are standard motel-style lodgings, all large and nicely decorated. Those in the original wing are small and a little dark; they have a pretty heritage theme, with floral bedcovers and lace curtains. Executive rooms have a king-size bed and private balconies facing the Todd River. Deluxe and standard rooms have one double bed and one single bed. Family rooms have a double bed and two bunk beds. The courtyard has a barbecue. The tiny pool and Jacuzzi are tucked away in a corner, so this is not the place for chilling out poolside; stay here to be within walking distance of shops and restaurants.

11 Leichhardt Terrace (backing onto Todd Mall), Alice Springs, NT 0870. ✆ **1800/089 644** in Australia or 08/8950 6666. Fax 08/8952 7829. www.auroraresorts.com.au. 109 units, all with shower only. A$210 double standard room; A$230 deluxe room; A$299 executive room; A$299 family room. Extra adult A$20. Children 12 and under stay free in parent's room with existing bedding. AE, DC, MC, V. Free parking. **Amenities:** Restaurant (Red Ochre Grill; see review, p. 401); airport shuttle; babysitting; Jacuzzi; small heated outdoor pool; room service. *In room:* A/C, TV/DVD w/pay movies, free Internet (executive rooms only), minibar.

Best Western Elkira Resort Motel The cheapest rooms in the heart of town—decent ones, that is—are at this unpretentious motel, which has been revamped and refurbished. The chandeliers in the lobby may seem a bit incongruous, as the rooms are basic, but you won't get better value. Deluxe rooms have kitchenettes and some have queen-size beds. Deluxe Spa rooms have two-person Jacuzzis. Ask for a room away from the road, because the traffic is noisy during the day.

65 Bath St. (opposite Kmart), Alice Springs, NT 0870. ✆ **131 779** in Australia or 08/8952 1222. Fax 08/8953 1370. http://elkira.bestwestern.com.au. 58 units, some with shower only. A$130 double standard room; A$145 double deluxe room; A$180 double Executive Spa Room. Extra person A$20. AE, DC, MC, V. Free parking. **Amenities:** Restaurant; airport shuttle; nearby golf course; Jacuzzi; outdoor pool; room service. *In room:* A/C, TV, hair dryer, free Wi-Fi.

Desert Palms Resort ★ A large swimming pool with its own palm-studded island is the focal point at this complex of bright cabins. Privacy from your neighbors is ensured by trailing pink bougainvillea and palm trees, making this one of the nicest places to stay in Alice. Don't be deterred by the prefab appearance; inside the cabins are surprisingly large, well kept, and inviting, with pine-pitched ceilings, minikitchens, a sliver of bathroom, and furnished front decks. Four rooms are suitable for travelers with disabilities. The pleasant staff at the front desk sells basic grocery and liquor supplies, and books tours. You are also right next door to Lasseter's Casino (a debatable advantage) and the Alice Springs Golf Club.

74 Barrett Dr. (1km/½ mile from town), Alice Springs, NT 0870. ✆ **1800/678 037** in Australia, or 08/8952 5977. Fax 08/8953 4176. www.desertpalms.com.au. 80 units, all with shower only. A$135 double; A$150 triple; A$165 quad; A$180 family. Free crib. AE, DC, MC, V. Free parking. **Amenities:** Free coach station/train station/airport shuttle twice daily; golf course nearby; access to nearby health club; large pool; half-size tennis court. *In room:* A/C, TV, hair dryer, kitchenette, Wi-Fi (A$6 for 1 hr.; A$25 per day; A$150 per week).

Where to Dine

EXPENSIVE

Barra on Todd ★★ MODERN AUSTRALIAN Ask the locals for the best chow in town, and this is where they'll send you. Part of the Alice Springs Resort, the restaurant usually has two or three barramundi dishes on the menu, as well as lamb shanks, steak, flambéed prawns (in a rum, garlic, and sweet-chili cream sauce, rice, and asparagus), and roasted chicken roulade (with bacon, leek, and sweet-potato filling; parsnip and cream-cheese mash; and oven-roasted tomato salsa). It does a good breakfast menu and has all-day (well, 11:30am–5:30pm) dining by the pool, with dishes costing just A$15.

At the Alice Springs Resort, 34 Stott Terrace. ✆ **08/8951 4545.** Reservations recommended at dinner. Main courses A$18–A$37. AE, DC, MC, V. Daily 6am–9:30pm.

Overlanders Steakhouse ★ STEAK/BUSH TUCKER This landmark on the Alice dining scene is famous for its "Drover's Blowout" menu, which assaults the megahungry with soup and damper, then a platter of crocodile *vol-au-vents,* camel and kangaroo filets, and emu medallions—these are just the *appetizers*—followed by rump steak or barramundi (freshwater fish) and dessert. There's a regular menu with a 700-gram (1½-lb.) steak, plus some lighter fare. The barnlike interior is Outback all through, from the rustic bar to the saddlebags hanging from the roof beams. Vegetarians take heart, there's actually a reasonable menu for you too.

72 Hartley St. ✆ **08/8952 2159.** www.overlanders.com.au. Reservations required in peak season. Main courses A$18–A$43; Drover's Blowout A$45. AE, DC, MC, V. Daily 6–10pm.

Red Ochre Grill ★ GOURMET BUSH TUCKER The chef at this upscale restaurant fuses native Aussie ingredients with dishes from around the world. There are two menus—"Aussie specialties" and "wild foods." If you've never tried kangaroo filet, rubbed with dukkah and served with pumpkin and wattleseed bake, sautéed baby spinach, and a port wine jus, then this is your chance. Maybe start your meal with a gumnut-smoked emu salad. A "game medley" plate combines kangaroo with camel, barramundi, and emu dishes. Although it might seem a touristy formula, the food is delicious. Dine in the contemporary interior fronting Todd Mall, or outside in the attractive courtyard.

Todd Mall. ✆ **08/8952 9614.** www.redochrealice.com.au. Reservations recommended at dinner. Main courses A$25–A$40. "Early Bird" dinner, prebooked before 6pm and ordered before 7pm, gives 20% off your food bill (not available for specials or on Sun or public holidays). AE, DC, MC, V. Daily 6:30am–9:30pm.

MODERATE

Bojangles Saloon and Restaurant ★ BAR FOOD Swing open the saloon doors, confront a life-size replica of Aussie bushranger Ned Kelly, and prepare for a fun night. Old guns, motorbikes, cars, pioneering artifacts, and photos line the walls. Reggie, a wedge-tailed eagle, is suspended over the bar, and an 8-foot carpet python called Jangles is a permanent live attraction. Park yourself on a cowhide seat at a thick wooden Jarrah table, made from old *Ghan* railway sleepers, and order a beer. The front bar is friendly and serves good beers by the bottle or schooner and food such as burgers, nachos, and steak sandwiches. The restaurant has more gourmet offerings, but either way it's a great atmosphere. Aussie country and folk singers strum away in the evenings, and the bar staff is terrific.

80 Todd St. ✆ **08/8952 2873.** www.bossaloon.com.au. Main courses A$15–A$39. AE, DC, MC, V. Daily 11:30am–late.

Casa Nostra ★★ ITALIAN The only difference between this cheery homespun family eatery and every other Italian restaurant in the world is that this one has autographed photos of Tom Selleck pinned to the wall. Judging by his scrawled praise, Tom loved eating here (when on location in Alice filming *Quigley Down Under*) as much as the locals do. You've seen the red-checked tablecloths and the basket-clad Chianti bottles before, but the food is surprisingly good. A long list of pastas (including masterful carbonara), pizzas, and chicken and veal dishes are the main offerings. All meals are available to take out. It's BYO.

Corner of Undoolya Rd. and Stuart Terrace. ✆ **08/8952 6749.** Reservations recommended. Main courses A$13–A$22. MC, V. Mon–Sat 5–10pm. Closed Dec 25–Jan.

INEXPENSIVE

Bar Doppio ★ CAFE If you're in need of a dose of cool—style, as well as air-conditioning—this bohemian cafe is the place to chill over good coffee and feast on cheap, wholesome food. Sacks of coffee beans are stacked all over, Gypsy music plays, no tables and chairs match, and the staff doesn't care if you sit here all day. Sit inside or in the narrow laneway outside. It's largely vegetarian, but fish and meat figure on the blackboard menu. Try lamb chermoula cutlets on Gabriella potatoes with rocket, red onion, and tomato salad; chickpea curry; warm Turkish flatbread with dips; or spuds with hot toppings. Hot and cold breakfast choices stay on the menu until 11am. Takeout is available. It's BYO.

Fan Arcade (off the southern end of Todd Mall). ✆ **08/8952 6525.** Main courses A$7–A$16; sandwiches average A$6. No credit cards. Mon–Thurs 7:30am–5pm; Fri–Sat 7:30am–9pm; Sun 10am–4:30pm. Closed public holidays and Dec 25–Jan 1.

ROAD TRIPS FROM ALICE SPRINGS

The key attraction of a day trip to the MacDonnell Ranges is unspoiled natural scenery and few crowds. Many companies run coach or four-wheel-drive tours—half- or full-day, sometimes overnight—to the West and East Macs. Some options appear in "Organized Tours" in the "Alice Springs" section, earlier in this chapter. Expect to pay about A$100 for a full-day trip. Families and backpackers alike love getting around with **Wayward Bus** ★ (✆ **1300/653 510** in Australia, or 08/8132 8230; www.waywardbus.com.au). The company runs buses from Alice Springs on a 2-night camping trip stopping off at Kings Canyon and Uluru. You can sleep in a tent or outside in a "swag"—a heavy waterproof sleeping bag—so you can see the stars as you drop off. Tours cost A$375 Alice Springs to Alice Springs, or Alice Springs to Uluru, with the option to fly out of Ayers Rock, plus park fees of A$25 and a A$10 fuel levy.

The West MacDonnell Ranges ★

WEST MACDONNELL NATIONAL PARK The 300km (186-mile) round-trip drive west from Alice Springs into West MacDonnell National Park is a stark but picturesque expedition to a series of red gorges, semidesert country, and the occasional peaceful swimming hole. The 12-stage, 223km (138-mile) **Larapinta Walking Trail** takes you along the backbone of the West MacDonnell Ranges through some of the most unique and isolated country in the world. The hills, colors, birds, water holes, gorges, and the never-ending diversity of this trail will leave you spellbound by the beauty of Central Australia. The track stretches from the Telegraph Station in Alice Springs to Mount Sonder, past Glen Helen Gorge. Detailed track notes are on the website of the **Parks & Wildlife Commission** (www.nt.gov.au/nreta/parks/walks/larapinta) and at the visitor information center in Alice Springs. Don't attempt the walk in the height of summer unless you are very well prepared. For great tips, and other information, look up the **Alice Wanderer** website (www.alicewanderer.com.au).

From Alice, take Larapinta Drive west for 18km (11 miles) to the 8km (5-mile) turnoff to **Simpson's Gap,** a water hole lined with ghost gums. Black-footed rock wallabies hop out on the cliffs in the late afternoon (so you may want to time a visit here on your way back to Alice). There are a couple of short trails here, including a .5km (.3-mile) Ghost Gum circuit and a 17km (11-mile) round-trip trail to Bond Gap. Swimming is not permitted. The place has an information center/ranger station and free use of barbecues.

Twenty-three kilometers (14 miles) farther down Larapinta Road, 9km (5½ miles) down a turnoff, is **Standley Chasm** (**✆ 08/8956 7440**). This rock cleft is only a few meters wide but 80m (262 ft.) high, reached by a 10-minute creek-side trail. Aim to be here at midday, when the walls glow orange in the overhead sun. A kiosk sells snacks and drinks. Admission is A$6.50 for adults and A$5.50 for seniors and children 5 to 14. The chasm is open daily from 8am to 6pm (last entry at 5pm; closed Dec 25).

Six kilometers (3¾ miles) past Standley Chasm, you can branch right onto Namatjira Drive or continue to Hermannsburg Historical Precinct (see below). If you take Namatjira Drive, you'll go 42km (26 miles) to picturesque **Ellery Creek Big Hole.** The spring-fed water is so chilly that the tourism authority warns swimmers to take a flotation device in case of cramping. A 3km (2-mile) walking trail explains the area's geological history.

Eleven kilometers (7 miles) farther along Namatjira Drive is **Serpentine Gorge,** where a trail leads up to a lookout for a lovely view of the ranges through the gorge walls. Another 12km (7½ miles) on are **ocher pits,** which Aboriginal people quarried for body paint and for decorating objects used in ceremonial performances. Twenty-six kilometers (16 miles) farther west, 8km (5 miles) from the main road, is **Ormiston Gorge and Pound** (**✆ 08/8956 7799** for the ranger station/visitor center). This is a good spot to picnic, swim in the wide deep pool below red cliffs, and walk a choice of trails, such as the 30-minute Ghost Gum Lookout trail or the easy 7km (4⅓-mile) scenic loop (allow 3–4 hr.). The water is warm enough for swimming in the summer. You can camp here for A$6.60 per adult, A$3.30 per child 5 to 15, or A$15 for a family of six. The campground has no powered sites but does have hot showers, toilets, and free barbecues.

Farther on is **Glen Helen Gorge,** where the Finke River cuts through the ranges, with more gorge swimming, a walking trail, guided hikes, and helicopter flights. Modest **Glen Helen Resort** (**✆ 08/8956 7489;** www.glenhelen.com.au) has 25 air-conditioned motel rooms. Rates are A$150 for a double from December to March and A$160 from April to November; extra guests (over 12 years) in the same room pay A$25, extra children aged 5 to 11 pay A$13. Bunkhouses, each with their own bathroom, sleep four; beds are A$30 per person. Campgrounds are A$12 per person for a tent site or A$30 double for a powered campsite (extra adult A$12, extra child aged 5–11 A$6). There's a restaurant serving three meals a day, a bar, a swimming pool, and barbecues for which the resort sells meat packs. It also offers 2-day trips of the area, including Palm Valley, that cost A$720 adults and A$360 for kids 5 to 12 (no children under 5).

ROAD trips TO THE EAST & WEST MACS

Facilities are scarce outside Alice, so bring food (perhaps a picnic, or meat to barbecue), drinking water, and a full gas tank. Leaded, unleaded, and diesel fuel are for sale at Glen Helen Resort and Hermannsburg. Wear walking shoes.

Many of the water holes dry up too much to be good for swimming—those at Ellery Creek, Ormiston Gorge, and Glen Helen are the most permanent. Being spring-fed, they can be intensely cold, so take only short dips to avoid cramping and hypothermia, don't swim alone, and be careful of underwater snags. Don't wear sunscreen, because it pollutes drinking water for native animals.

Two-wheel-drive rental cars will not be insured on unsealed (unpaved) roads—that means the last few miles into Trephina Gorge Nature Park, and the 11km (7-mile) road into N'Dhala Gorge Nature Park, both in the East Macs. If you are prepared to risk it, you will probably get into Trephina in a two-wheel-drive car, but you will need a four-wheel-drive for N'Dhala and Arltunga. The West MacDonnell road is paved to Glen Helen Gorge; a few points of interest may require driving for short lengths on unpaved road. Before setting off, drop into the **CATIA Visitor Information Centre** (see "Visitor Information," earlier in this chapter) for tips on road conditions and for details on the free ranger talks, walks, and slideshows that take place in the West and East Macs from April through October. Entry to all sights, parks, and reserves (except Standley Chasm) is free.

GETTING THERE You can arrange to be dropped off by the **Alice Wanderer** (✆ **08/8952 2111;** www.alicewanderer.com.au) at several stops in the Ranges. It costs around A$100 for two people for the return trip to Simpson's Gap; A$120 to Standley Chasm; A$215 to Serpentine Gorge; and A$250 to Ormiston Gorge or Glen Helen Gorge. If you plan to camp out, call ✆ **1300 650 730** to register your intentions (it's voluntary but worth it if you get lost—a rescue team will try to find you). You must pay a A$50 refundable deposit by credit card. Take plenty of water. The Alice Wanderer also does group tours to the area.

HERMANNSBURG HISTORICAL PRECINCT An alternative to visiting the West Mac gorges is to stay on Larapinta Drive all 128km (79 miles) from Alice Springs to the old **Lutheran Mission** at the **Hermannsburg Historical Precinct** (✆ **08/8956 7402;** www.hermannsburg.com.au). Some maps show this route as an unpaved road, but it is paved. Settled by German missionaries in the 1870s, this is a cluster of 16 National Trust–listed farmhouse-style mission buildings and a historic cemetery. There is a museum, a gallery housing landscapes by Aussie artist Albert Namatjira, and tearooms serving light snacks and apple strudel from an old German recipe. The mission is open daily from 9am to 4pm. Admission to the precinct is A$10 for adults, A$5 for school-age kids, or A$25 for families of four. The precinct is closed for 5 weeks in December and January.

FINKE GORGE NATIONAL PARK Just west of Hermannsburg is the turnoff to the 46,000-hectare (113,620-acre) **Finke Gorge National Park,** 16km (10 miles) to the south on an unpaved road (or about a 2-hr. drive west of Alice Springs). Turn south off Larapinta Drive just west of Hermannsburg. Access along the last

16km (10 miles) of road, which follows the sandy bed of the Finke River, is limited to four-wheel-drive vehicles only. Heavy rains may cause this section of the road to be impassable. The park is most famous for **Palm Valley,** where groves of rare Livistona mariae cabbage palms have survived since Central Australia was a jungle millions of years ago. You will need to have a four-wheel-drive vehicle or take a tour to explore this park. Four walking trails between 1.5km (1 mile) and 5km (3 miles) take you among the palms or up to a lookout over cliffs; one is a signposted trail exploring Aboriginal culture. There is a campsite about 4km (2½ miles) from the palms; it has showers, toilets, and free barbecues. Collect your firewood outside the park. Camping is A$6.60 for adults, A$3.30 for kids 5 to 15, or A$15 for families of six. For information, call the CATIA Visitor Information Centre in Alice Springs before you leave, because there is no visitor center in the park. The ranger station (✆ **08/8956 7401**) is for emergencies only.

The East MacDonnell Ranges

Not as many tourists tread the path on the Ross Highway into the East Macs, but if you do, you'll be rewarded with lush walking trails, fewer crowds, traces of Aboriginal history, and possibly even the sight of wild camels.

The first points of interest are **Emily Gap,** 10km (6 miles) from Alice, and **Jessie Gap,** an additional 7km (4⅓ miles), a pretty picnic spot. You can cool off in the Emily Gap swimming hole if there is any water. Don't miss the *Caterpillar Dreaming* Aboriginal art on the wall, on your right as you walk through.

At **Corroboree Rock,** 37km (23 miles) farther, you can make a short climb up the outcrop, which was important to local Aborigines. The polished rock "seat" high up in the hole means Aboriginal people must have used this rock for eons.

Twenty-two kilometers (14 miles) farther is the turnoff to **Trephina Gorge Nature Park,** an 18-sq.-km (7-sq.-mile) beauty spot with peaceful walking trails that can take from 45 minutes to 4½ hours. The last 5km (3 miles) of the 9km (5½-mile) road into the park are unpaved, but you can make it in a two-wheel-drive car.

N'Dhala Gorge Nature Park, 10km (6 miles) past Trephina Gorge Nature Park, houses an "open-air art gallery" of rock carvings, or petroglyphs, left by the Eastern Arrernte Aboriginal people. An interesting 1.5km (1-mile) signposted trail explains the Dreamtime meanings of a few of the 6,000 rock carvings, hundreds or thousands of years old, that are thought to be in this eerily quiet gorge. A four-wheel-drive vehicle is a must to traverse the 11km (7-mile) access road.

The Ross Highway is paved all the way to Ross River Resort, 86km (53 miles) from Alice Springs.

KINGS CANYON ★

Anyone who saw the movie *The Adventures of Priscilla, Queen of the Desert* will remember the stony plateau the transvestites climb to gaze over the plain below. You can stand on that same spot (wearing sequined underpants is optional) at **Kings Canyon ★** in **Watarrka National Park** (✆ **08/8956 7460** for park headquarters). As the crow flies, it is 320km (198 miles) southwest of Alice Springs. The sandstone walls of the canyon drop about 100m (330 ft.) to rock pools and centuries-old gum trees. There is little to do except walk the dramatic canyon rim for a sense of the peaceful emptiness of the Australian Outback.

GETTING THERE The best way is to drive. There's no regular air service to Kings Canyon.

Numerous **four-wheel-drive** tours head to Kings Canyon from Alice Springs or Uluru, with time allowed for the rim walk. See "Exploring the Red Centre," earlier in this chapter, for recommended companies.

With a four-wheel-drive, you can get to Kings Canyon from Alice Springs on the unpaved Mereenie Loop Road. The regular route is the 480km (298-mile) trip from Alice Springs south on the Stuart Highway, then west onto the Lasseter Highway, and then north and west on the Luritja Road. All three roads are paved. Uluru is 306km (190 miles) to the south on a paved road; from Yulara, take the Lasseter Highway east for 125km (78 miles), turn left onto Luritja Road and go 168km (104 miles) to Kings Canyon Resort. The resort sells leaded and unleaded gasoline and diesel.

GETTING AROUND **AAT Kings** (✆ **1300/556 100** in Australia, or 08/8956 2171; www.aatkings.com) provides a number of tours, including a 12-hour day tour to Kings Canyon from the Ayers Rock Resort for A$198 per person. You can book through AAT Kings or the resort. Be warned, you will have to start out at 4 or 5am, depending on the time of year.

Exploring the Park

The way to explore the canyon is on the 6km (3¾-mile) **walk** up the side (short but steep!) and around the rim. Even if you're in good shape, it's a strenuous 3- to 4-hour hike. It leads through a maze of rounded sandstone formations, called the Lost City; across a bridge to a fern-fringed pocket of water holes, called the Garden of Eden; and back along the other side through more sandstone rocks. There are lookout points en route. If you visit after the odd rainfall, the walls teem with waterfalls. In winter, don't set off too early, because sunlight doesn't light up the canyon walls to good effect until midmorning.

If you're not up to making the rim walk, take the shady 2.6km (1.6-mile) round-trip trail along the mostly dry **Kings Creek bed** on the canyon floor. It takes about an hour. Wear sturdy boots, because the ground can be rocky. This walk is all right for young kids and travelers in wheelchairs for the first kilometer (.6 miles).

Both walks are signposted. Avoid the rim walk in the middle of the day between September and May, when it's too hot.

An exhilarating option is a guided tour of Kings Creek Station on your own four-wheel **quad bike.** You journey through the rugged Outback, taking in spectacular scenery, including red sand dunes, on the search for wildlife. Your adventure takes you through the cattle country, where you will often see santa/shorthorn cattle and occasionally surprise camels, kangaroos, and dingoes. Kings Creek Station is approximately 20 minutes drive south of Kings Canyon Resort (see below), and the tours are booked though the resort. It costs A$67 for 30 minutes, A$78 for an hour, and A$176 for 2½ hours. The minimum age is 16.

Professional Helicopter Services (✆ **08/8956 2003;** www.phs.com.au) makes 8-minute flights over the canyon for A$80 per person, 15-minute flights for A$130 or 30-minute flights also taking in George Gill Range for A$240 per person.

Where to Stay & Dine

Apart from campgrounds, the only place to stay in Watarrka National Park is at Kings Canyon Resort.

Kings Canyon Resort ★ This attractive, low-slung complex 7km (4⅓ miles) from Kings Canyon blends into its surroundings. The 32 deluxe rooms have Jacuzzis beside large windows giving desert views (and ensuring privacy). Each Deluxe Spa Room also has a balcony looking out onto a magnificent rocky escarpment that is lit at night. The other rooms are typical hotel accommodations, comfortable enough, with range views. The double/twin, shared quad, and family lodge rooms are adequate low-budget choices, with a communal kitchen and shared bathroom facilities. Children are not permitted in lodge (dorm-style) rooms unless you book the entire room. The resort has a well-stocked minimart, where you can buy meat for barbecuing. Live entertainment plays some nights (June–Nov), and you can do a 1-hour sunrise or sunset camel ride for A$55 per adult, A$44 children 5 to 14.

Luritja Rd., Watarrka National Park, NT 0872. ✆ **1300/233 432** in Australia, or 03/9413 6288 (reservations office) or 08/8956 7442 (resort). www.kingscanyonresort.com.au. 164 units, 128 with bathroom; 72 powered campsites and tent sites. A$260 double standard room; A$355 double Deluxe Room. Extra person A$44. Children 11 and under stay free in parent's room with existing bedding. Lodge A$115 double; A$172 quad; A$90 per person in shared quad room. Tent site A$17 per person; powered site A$19 per person; children 6–15 A$7; children 5 and under free. Children 11 and under dine free at restaurant buffet or with kids' menu (1 child per adult). AE, DC, MC, V. **Amenities:** 2 restaurants; cafe; 2 bars; bikes (from nearby gas station); Internet (A$2 for 15 min.); 2 outdoor pools; outdoor lit tennis court. *In room:* A/C, TV, fridge. Hotel only: TV w/pay movies, hair dryer, minibar.

ULURU–KATA TJUTA NATIONAL PARK ★★★

462km (286 miles) SW of Alice Springs; 1,934km (1,199 miles) S of Darwin; 1,571km (974 miles) N of Adelaide; 2,841km (1,761 miles) NW of Sydney

Why travel so far to look at a large red rock? Because it will send a shiver up your spine. Because it may move you to tears. Because there is something indefinable and indescribable but definitely spiritual about this place. Up close, Uluru is more magnificent than you can imagine. It is immense and overwhelming and mysterious. Photographs never do it justice. There is what is described as a "spirit of place" here. It is unforgettable and irresistible (and you may well want to come back again, just for another look). It will not disappoint you. On my first visit—yes, I am one who will keep coming back—a stranger whispered to me: "Even when you are not looking at it, it is always just *there,* waiting to tap you on the shoulder." A rock with a presence.

"The Rock" has a circumference of 9.4km (6 miles), and two-thirds of it is thought to be underground. In photos, it looks smooth and even, but the reality is much more interesting—dappled with holes and overhangs, with curtains of stone draping its sides, creating little coves hiding water holes and Aboriginal rock art. It also changes color from pink to a deep wine red depending on the angle and intensity of the sun. And if you are lucky enough to be visiting when it rains, you will see a sight like no other. Here, rain brings everyone outside to see the spectacle of the waterfalls created off the massive rock formed by sediments laid down 600 to 700 million years ago in an inland sea and thrust up aboveground 348m (1,141 ft.) by geological forces.

In 1985, the **Uluru–Kata Tjuta National Park ★★★** was returned to its Aboriginal owners, the Pitjantjatjara and Yankunytjatjara people, known as the Anangu, who manage the property jointly with the Australian government. Don't think a visit to Uluru is just about snapping a few photos and going home. There are many ways of exploring it and one of the best is to join Aboriginal people on guided walks. You can walk around the Rock, climb it (we'll talk about *that* later), fly over it, ride a camel to it, circle it on a Harley-Davidson, trek through the nearby Olgas, and dine under the stars while you learn about them.

Just do yourself one favor: Plan to spend at least 2 days here, if not 3.

Isolation (and a lack of competition) makes such things as accommodations, meals, and transfers relatively expensive. A coach tour or four-wheel-drive camping safari is often the cheapest way to see the place. See "Exploring the Red Centre," at the beginning of this chapter, for recommended tour companies.

Essentials

GETTING THERE **By Plane** **Qantas** (✆ **13 13 13** in Australia) flies to Ayers Rock (Connellan) Airport direct from Sydney, Melbourne, Alice Springs, Perth, and Cairns. Flights from other airports go via Alice Springs. **Virgin Blue** (✆ **13 67 89** in Australia) flies direct from Sydney daily. The airport is 6km (3¾ miles) from Ayers Rock Resort. A free shuttle ferries all resort guests, including campers, to their door.

By Car Take the Stuart Highway south from Alice Springs 199km (123 miles), turn right onto the Lasseter Highway, and go 244km (151 miles) to Ayers Rock Resort. The Rock is 18km (11 miles) farther on.

If you are renting a car in Alice Springs and want to drop it at Uluru and fly out from there, be prepared for a one-way penalty. Only Avis, Hertz, and Thrifty have Uluru depots.

VISITOR INFORMATION The **Central Australian Tourism Industry Association (CATIA)** has a **Visitor Information Centre** at 60 Gregory Terrace, Alice Springs (✆ **1800/645 199** in Australia or 08/8952 5800; www.centralaustraliantourism.com). Another good source of online information is Ayers Rock Resort's site, **www.voyages.com.au**.

The **Ayers Rock Resort Visitor Centre,** next to the Desert Gardens Hotel (✆ **08/8957 7377**), has displays on the area's geology, wildlife, and Aboriginal heritage, plus a souvenir store. It's open daily from 8:30am to 7:30pm. You can book tours at the **tour desk** in every hotel at Ayers Rock Resort, or visit the **Ayers Rock Resort Tour & Information Centre** (✆ **08/8957 7324**) at the shopping center in the resort complex. It dispenses information and books tours as far afield as Kings Canyon and Alice Springs. It's open daily from 7:30am to 8:30pm.

The Rock in a Day?

It's a *loooong* day to visit Uluru in a day from Alice by road. Many organized coach tours pack a lot—perhaps a Rock-base walk or climb, Kata Tjuta (the Olgas), the Uluru–Kata Tjuta Cultural Centre, and a champagne sunset at the Rock—into a busy trip that leaves Alice around 5:30 or 6am and gets you back late at night. You should consider a day trip only between May and September. At other times, it's too hot to do much from early morning to late afternoon. At press time, there were no companies offering day scenic flights from Alice to Uluru.

One kilometer (a half mile) from the base of the Rock is the **Uluru–Kata Tjuta Cultural Centre ★★** (✆ **08/8956 1128**), owned and run by the Anangu, the Aboriginal owners of Uluru. It uses eye-catching wall displays, frescoes, interactive recordings, and videos to tell about Aboriginal Dreamtime myths and laws. It's worth spending some time here to understand a little about Aboriginal culture. A National Park desk has information on ranger-guided activities and animal, plant, and bird-watching checklists. The center also has a cafe, a souvenir shop, and two Aboriginal arts and crafts galleries. It's open daily from early in the morning to after sundown; exact hours vary from month to month.

PARK ENTRANCE FEES Entry to the Uluru–Kata Tjuta National Park is A$25 per adult, free for children under 16, valid for 3 days. The cost of many organized tours includes the entry fee.

ETIQUETTE The Anangu ask you not to photograph sacred sites or Aboriginal people without permission and to approach quietly and respectfully. For more information on climbing Uluru, see p. 411.

Getting Around

Ayers Rock Resort runs a **free shuttle** every 20 minutes or so around the resort complex from 10:30am to after midnight, but to get to the Rock or Kata Tjuta (the Olgas), you will need to take transfers, join a tour, or have your own wheels. The shuttle also meets all flights. There are no taxis at Yulara.

BY SHUTTLE **Uluru Express** (✆ **08/8956 2152;** www.uluruexpress.com.au) provides a minibus shuttle from Ayers Rock Resort to and from the Rock about every 50 minutes from before sunrise to sundown, and four times a day to Kata Tjuta. The basic shuttle costs A$43 for adults and A$30 for kids 1 to 14. To Kata Tjuta, it costs A$75 for adults and A$40 for children. A 2-day pass that enables you to explore Uluru and Kata Tjuta as many times as you wish costs A$155 adults and A$80 children; a 3-day pass costs A$170 for adults and A$80 for kids. All fares are round-trip. A National Park entry pass, if you don't already have one, is A$25 extra.

BY CAR If there are two of you, the easiest and cheapest way to get around is likely to be a rental car. All roads in the area are paved, so a four-wheel-drive is unnecessary. Expect to pay around A$120 to A$140 per day for a medium-size car. Rates drop a little in low season. Most car-rental companies give you the first 100 or 200km (63–126 miles) free and charge between A17¢ and A25¢ per kilometer after that. Take this into account, because the round-trip from the resort to the Olgas is just over 100km (63 miles), and that's without driving about 20km (13 miles) to the Rock and back. Hire periods of under 3 days incur a one-way fee based on kilometers travelled, up to about A$330. **Avis** (✆ **08/8956 2266**), **Hertz** (✆ **08/8956 2244**), and **Thrifty** (✆ **08/8956 2030**) all rent regular cars and four-wheel-drives.

The **Outback Travel Shop** (✆ **08/8955 5288;** www.outbacktravelshop.com.au), a booking agent in Alice Springs, often has better deals on car-rental rates than you'll get by booking direct.

BY ORGANIZED TOUR Several tour companies run a range of daily sunrise and sunset viewings, circumnavigations of the Rock by coach or on foot, guided walks at the Rock or the Olgas, camel rides, observatory evenings, visits to the Uluru–Kata Tjuta Cultural Centre, and innumerable permutations and combinations of all of

> **Water, Water . . .**
>
> **Water taps are scarce and kiosks nonexistent in Uluru–Kata Tjuta National Park. Always carry plenty of your own drinking water when sightseeing.**

these. Some offer "passes" containing the most popular activities. Virtually every company picks you up at your hotel. Among the most reputable are **Discovery Ecotours, AAT Kings,** and **Tailormade Tours** (see "Exploring the Red Centre" at the start of this chapter for details).

ABORIGINAL TOURS Because **Anangu Tours ★★** (**© 08/8950 3030;** www.ananguwaai.com.au) is owned and run by the Rock's Aboriginal owners, its excellent tours give you firsthand insight into Aboriginal culture. Tours are in the Anangu language and translated by an interpreter. If you are going to spend money on just one tour, this group is a good choice.

The company does a 3½-hour **Kuniya** walk, during which you visit the Uluru–Kata Tjuta Cultural Centre and the Mutitjulu water hole at the base of the Rock, learn about bush foods, and see rock paintings before watching the sun set. It departs daily at 2:30pm March through October, 3:30pm November through February. With hotel pickup, the tour costs A$116 for adults and A$75 for children 5 to 15. There's also a 4½-hour breakfast tour costing A$139 for adults and A$93 for children. It includes a base tour and demonstrations of bush skills and spear-throwing. A standard tour during the day costs A$87 for adults and A$58 for kids. Dot-painting workshops at the Uluru Cultural Centre cost A$87 for adults and A$61 for kids. There are various other combinations of tours to choose from.

Discovering Uluru

AT SUNRISE & SUNSET The peak time to catch the Rock's beauty is sunset, when oranges, peaches, pinks, reds, and then indigo and deep violet creep across its face. Some days it's fiery, other days the colors are muted. A sunset-viewing car park is on the Rock's western side. Plenty of sunset and sunrise tours operate from the resort. A typical sunset tour is offered by **AAT Kings** (**© 08/8956 2171;** www.aatkings.com). It departs 75 minutes before sunset, includes a free glass of wine with which to watch the "show," and returns 20 minutes after sundown; the cost is A$50 for adults, half-price for children 4 to 14. AAT Kings offers several other tours around the area, so if large-group touring is what you want, check out their website before leaving home.

At sunrise, the colors are less dramatic, but many folks enjoy the spectacle of the Rock unveiled by the dawn to birdsong. You'll need an early start—most tours leave about 75 minutes before sunup. A new sunrise viewing area was opened in late 2009, about 3km (1.8 miles) from the Rock, designed to allow visitors to take in the southeastern face of Uluru without revealing any sacred sites.

WALKING, DRIVING, OR BUSING AROUND IT A paved road runs around the Rock. The easy 9.4km (6-mile) **Base Walk** circumnavigating Uluru takes about 2 hours, but allow time to linger around the water holes, caves, folds, and overhangs that make up its walls. A shorter walk is the easy 1km (.6-mile) round-trip trail from the **Mutitjulu** parking lot to the pretty water hole near the Rock's base, where there is some rock art. The **Liru Track** is another easy trail; it runs 2km (1.2 miles) from the Cultural Centre to Uluru, where it links with the Base Walk.

TO climb OR NOT TO CLIMB?

The Pitjantjatjara people refer to tourists as *minga*—little ants—because that's what they look like crawling up Uluru. Climbing this sacred rock is a fraught subject, and one which Australians fall into two camps over. Those who have or want to and those who never will. I fall into the latter category. Climbing Uluru is against the wishes of the traditional owners, the Anangu ("the people," a term used by Aboriginal people from the Western Desert to refer to themselves), because of its deep spiritual significance to them. The climb follows the trail the ancestral Dreamtime *Mala* (rufous hare-wallaby) men took when they first came to Uluru, something you will hear about when you visit. While tourists are still allowed to climb, the traditional owners strongly prefer that they don't, and you will see signs and information to this effect.

Apart from respecting Uluru as a sacred place, there are several good practical reasons for resisting the temptation to become one of the more than 200,000 people each year who complete the 348m (1,142-ft.) hike. "The Rock" is dangerously steep and rutted with ravines about 2.5m (8¼ ft.) deep; and 35 people have died while climbing—either from heart attacks or falls—in the past 4 decades. Anangu feel a duty to safeguard visitors to their land, and feel great sorrow and responsibility when visitors are killed or injured. The climb, by all accounts, is tough. There are sometimes strong winds, the walls are almost vertical in places (you have to hold onto a chain), and it can be freezing cold or maddeningly hot. Heat stress is a real danger. If you're unfit, have breathing difficulties, heart trouble, high or low blood pressure, or are scared of heights, don't do it. The climb takes at least 1 hour up for the fit, and 1 hour down. The less sure-footed should allow 3 to 4 hours. The Rock is closed to climbers during bad weather; when temperatures exceed 97°F (36°C), which they often do from November to March; and when wind speed exceeds 25 knots. It is closed at 8am daily in January and February because of the extreme heat.

The Australian government recognized the existence of the traditional Aboriginal owners in 1979 and created a national park to protect Uluru and Kata Tjuta. In 1983, the traditional owners were granted ownership of the land and the park was leased to the Australian National Parks and Wildlife Service for 99 years, with the agreement that the public could continue to climb it. The issue of climbing was again the subject of heated debate under a new Labour government in 2009; the government's new 10-year management plan states that the climb will close if climber numbers drop to below 20% of all visitors to Uluru. In any case, visitors will be given 18 months' warning of any planned closure.

Before setting off on any walk, it's a good idea to arm yourself with the self-guided walking notes available from the Cultural Centre (see "Visitor Information," above).

Most companies offer base tours. As an example, **Discovery Ecotours** (**© 08/8956 2563;** www.discoveryecotours.com.au) conducts a 6-hour guided base tour that gives you insight into natural history, rock art, and Dreamtime beliefs. It's scheduled to coincide with sunrise. The tour costs A$125 for adults and A$99 for children 6 to 15, but it's not suitable for kids under 10. The company also runs a 4-hour sunset trip to the Olgas for A$99 for adults and A$79 for kids.

FLYING OVER IT Several companies do scenic flights by light aircraft or helicopter over Uluru, Kata Tjuta (the Olgas), nearby Mount Conner, the vast white saltpan of Lake Amadeus, and as far as Kings Canyon. **Professional Helicopter Services** (✆ **08/8956 2003;** www.phs.com.au), for example, does a 12- to 15-minute flight over Uluru for A$130 per person, and a 30-minute flight, which includes Kata Tjuta, for A$240. Helicopters don't land on top of the Rock, however.

MOTORCYCLING AROUND IT Harley-Davidson tours are available as sunrise or sunset rides, laps of the Rock, and various other Rock and Kata Tjuta tours with time for the Olgas walks. A blast out to the Rock at sunset with **Uluru Motorcycle Tours** (✆ **08/8956 2019**) will set you back A$160, which includes a glass of champagne. The guide drives the bike; you sit behind and hang on. If you have an open class motorcycle license and are over 25 years old, you can hire a Harley for a few hours, a half-day, or a full day, at a hefty price. Rates start at A$275 for 2 hours, plus a A$2,500 insurance deposit.

Timing Your Trip

Most tourists visit Uluru in the mornings and Kata Tjuta (the Olgas) in the afternoon. Reverse the order (do the Valley of the Winds walk in the morning and Uluru in the afternoon), and you'll find both spots a little more silent and spiritual.

VIEWING IT ON CAMELBACK Legend has it that a soul travels at the same pace as a camel; it's certainly a peaceful way to see the Rock. **Uluru Camel Tours** (✆ **08/8950 3030;** www.ananguwaai.com.au) makes daily forays aboard "ships of the desert" to view Uluru. Amble through red-sand dunes with great views of the Rock, dismount to watch the sun rise or sink over it, and ride back to the depot for billy tea and beer bread in the morning, or champagne in the evening. The 1-hour rides depart Ayers Rock Resort 1 hour before sunrise or 1½ hours before sunset and cost A$99 per person, including transfers from your hotel. All tours leave from the Camel Depot at the Ayers Rock Resort. Shorter rides are also available.

Exploring Kata Tjuta

While it would be worth coming all the way to Central Australia just to see Uluru, there is a second unique natural wonder to see, just a 50km (31-mile) drive away. Kata Tjuta, or the Olgas, consists of 36 immense ochre rock domes rising from the desert, rivaling Uluru for spectacular beauty. Some visitors find it lovelier and more mysterious than Uluru. Known to the Aborigines as Kata Tjuta, or "many heads," the tallest dome is 200m (656 ft.) higher than Uluru, and Kata Tjuta figures more prominently in Aboriginal legend than Uluru.

This part of Australia's red heart was first discovered in the 1870s by English explorers. Ernest Giles named part of Kata Tjuta "Mount Olga" after the reigning Queen Olga of Wurttemberg, while William Gosse gave Uluru the name "Ayers Rock" after Sir Henry Ayers, the Chief Secretary of South Australia.

Two walking trails take you in among the domes: the 7.4km (4.6-mile) **Valley of the Winds ★★** walk, which is fairly challenging and takes 3 to 5 hours, and the easy 2.6km (1.6-mile) **Gorge** walk, which takes about an hour. The Valley of the Winds trail is the more rewarding in terms of scenery. Both have lookout points and

DINNER IN THE desert

Why sit in a restaurant when you can eat outside and soak up the desert air? **Ayers Rock Resort's Sounds of Silence ★** dinner is not just a meal, it's an event. In an outdoor clearing, you sip champagne and nibble canapés as the sun sets over the Rock to the strains of a didgeridoo. Zero in on people you want to sit with, and then head to communal white-clothed, candlelit tables and a serve-yourself meal that will include kangaroo, emu, crocodile, and barramundi (a large freshwater fish). The food is not exceptional, but you're really here for the atmosphere. After dinner, the lanterns fade and you're left with stillness. For some city folk, it's the first time they have ever heard complete silence. Look up into the usually clear skies and an astronomer will point out the constellations of the Southern Hemisphere. You can also look at the stars through telescopes. Sounds of Silence is held nightly, weather permitting, and costs A$155 for adults and A$79 for children 10 to 12, including transfers from Ayers Rock Resort. Surcharges apply for Christmas Day and New Year's Eve. It's mighty popular, so book as far ahead as you can, even up to 3 months ahead in peak season. Book through the **Ayers Rock Resort** office in Sydney (✆ **1300/134 044** in Australia, or 02/8296 8010) or online (www.ayersrockresort.com.au).

shady stretches. The Valley of the Winds trail closes when temperatures rise above 97°F (36°C).

Where to Stay & Dine

Ayers Rock Resort is not only in the township of Yulara—it *is* the township. Located about 30km (19 miles) from the Rock, outside the national park boundary, it is the only place to stay. It is an impressive contemporary complex, built to a high standard, efficiently run, and attractive—all things you can end up paying an arm and a leg for. Because everyone either is a tourist or lives and works here, it has a village atmosphere—with a supermarket; a bank; a post office; a newsdealer; babysitting services; a medical center; a beauty salon; several gift, clothing, and souvenir shops; a place to buy beer; and a gas station.

You have a choice of seven places to stay within the complex, from hotel rooms and apartments to luxury and basic campsites. In keeping with this village feel, no matter where you stay, even in the campground, you are free to use all the pools, restaurants, and other facilities of every hostelry, except the exclusive Sails in the Desert pool, which is reserved for Sails guests.

Voyages Hotels & Resorts manages Ayers Rock Resort, and you can book any of the seven accommodations options through the central reservations office in Sydney (✆ **1300/134 044** in Australia, or 02/8296 8010, or 0800/700 715 in New Zealand; fax 02/9299 2103; www.voyages.com.au). High season is July through November. Book well ahead, and shop around for special deals on the Internet and with travel agencies. All properties offer special packages for 2- or 3-night stays, which reduce the nightly rate and throw in some extras.

A tour desk, same-day dry-cleaning and laundry service, and babysitting are all available at each hostelry and campground.

In addition to the dining options, the resort's small shopping center has the pleasant **Gecko's Café,** which offers wood-fired pizzas, pastas, and sandwiches; a bakery; an ice cream shop; and takeout. Sails in the Desert, Desert Gardens, and the Outback Pioneer Hotel & Lodge can provide picnic hampers and breakfast backpacks. Kids under 15 dine free at any of the hotels' buffets in the company of an adult. It's a good idea to bring some wine with you, because the place really has things sewn up, including prices.

VERY EXPENSIVE

Longitude 131° ★★★ When you wake in your luxury "tent" here, you can reach out from your king-size bed and press a button to raise the blinds on your window for a view unmatched anywhere in the world: Uluru as dawn strikes its ochre walls. Your bed, under a softly draped romantic white canopy, is in one of 15 five-star ecosensitive "tents" set among isolated sand dunes a mile or two from the main resort complex. Each room is decorated in tribute to the European explorers and pioneers of this region. There's a CD player but no TV (and who needs one?). The central area, the **Dune House,** has a restaurant with superb food, a bar, and a library. Settle in for some after-dinner chess or chat. For a special dining experience, book your place at **Table 131,** where dinner is set up in style under the stars among gently rolling sand dunes. No children under 12.

Yulara Dr., Yulara, NT 0872. ✆ **08/8957 7888.** Fax 08/8957 7474. www.longitude131.com.au. 15 units. A$2,020 double. Rates include walking and bus tours, meals, selected drinks. 2-night minimum. AE, DC, MC, V. **Amenities:** Restaurant; bar; free airport shuttle; outdoor pool. *In room:* A/C, CD player, hair dryer, minibar.

Sails in the Desert ★★ This top-of-the-range hotel offers expensive, contemporary-style rooms with private balconies, many overlooking the pool, some with Jacuzzis. You can't see the Rock from your room, but most guests are too busy sipping cocktails by the pool to care. The pool area is shaded by white shade "sails" and surrounded by sun lounges. The lobby art gallery has artists in residence. The **Kuniya** restaurant serves elegant a la carte fine-dining fare with bush tucker ingredients, **Winkiku** is a smart a la carte and buffet venue, and **Rockpool** offers a tapas-style platter menu with Mediterranean and Asian influences. The hotel's new **Red Ochre Spa** is the only day spa at Yulara. It has four therapy rooms offering a range of treatments and therapies, with two rooms offering "dry" massage therapies and two "wet" rooms, which have tubs on the veranda to soak in.

Yulara Dr., Yulara, NT 0872. ✆ **08/8957 7888.** Fax 08/8957 7474. 232 units. A$480–A$580 double standard room; A$568–A$690 double spa room; A$900–A$950 double deluxe suite. Extra person A$40. Children 12 and under stay free using existing bedding and eat free when dining with a paying adult at the buffet or from children's menu. AE, DC, MC, V. **Amenities:** 3 restaurants, bar; free airport shuttle; large outdoor pool; room service; 2 outdoor lit tennis courts, Wi-Fi (A$10 per hour; A$25 for 3 days). *In room:* A/C, TV w/pay movies, minibar, hair dryer.

EXPENSIVE

Desert Gardens Hotel ★ This is the only hotel with views of the Rock (albeit rather distant ones), from some of the rooms. It is set amid wonderful ghost gum trees and the flowering native shrubs that give it its name. The accommodations are not as lavish as Sails in the Desert, but they're equally comfortable and have elegant

Seeing the Southern Cross for the First Time

Light pollution is extremely low in the Red Centre, so the night sky is a dazzler. At the Ayers Rock Observatory, you can check out your zodiac constellation and take a 1-hour tour of the Southern Hemisphere heavens (they're different from the Northern Hemisphere stars).

To visit the observatory, you must join a tour with **Discovery Ecotours** (✆ **1800/803 174** in Australia, or 08/8956 2563; www.discoveryecotours.com.au), which provides hotel pickup and a tour. Tours depart twice a night; times vary. They cost A$33 for adults, A$25 for children 6 to 15. Family rates are available on request.

furnishings. The **White Gums** restaurant serves a la carte flame grill and buffet meals.

Yulara Dr., Yulara, NT 0872. ✆ **08/8957 7888.** Fax 08/8957 7716. 218 units, 100 with shower only. A$390–A$490 double standard room; A$450–A$550 double deluxe room; A$490–A$590 double deluxe Rock-view room. Extra person A$40. Children 12 years and under stay free in parent's room using existing bedding, and eat free when dining with a paying adult at the buffet or from the children's menu. AE, DC, MC, V. **Amenities:** 2 restaurants, bar; free airport shuttle; outdoor pool; room service. *In room:* A/C, TV w/pay movies, hair dryer, minibar.

Emu Walk Apartments ★ These bright, contemporary apartments have full kitchens, separate bedrooms, and roomy living areas. They have daily maid service, and sleep up to six people, so they're great for families or groups of friends. There's no restaurant or pool, but Gecko's Café and the market are close, and you can cool off in the Desert Gardens Hotel pool next door.

Yulara Dr., Yulara, NT 0872. ✆ **08/8957 7888.** Fax 08/8957 7742. 59 apts, all with shower only. A$398–A$499 double 1-bedroom apt; A$480–A$580 double 2-bedroom apt. Extra person A$40. AE, DC, MC, V. **Amenities:** Free airport shuttle; room service. *In room:* A/C, TV w/pay movies, hair dryer, kitchen, minibar.

The Lost Camel ★ This AAA-rated three-and-a-half-star hotel is aimed at young urbanites and is as bright, crisp, and modern as something you might find in Sydney, with just a touch of an Aboriginal theme about it. If you want to forget that you're in the Outback (but why would you?), head to the lobby bar and lounge, where a plasma screen plays news channels and music videos. The Lost Camel has lush courtyards and a generous swimming pool.

Yulara Dr., Yulara, NT 0872. ✆ **08/8957 7888.** Fax 08/8957 7474. 99 units. A$330–A$430 double. AE, DC, MC, V. **Amenities:** Bar; free airport shuttle; outdoor pool. *In room:* A/C, TV, CD player, hair dryer, minibar.

Outback Pioneer Hotel and Lodge A happy all-ages crowd congregates at this midrange collection of hotel rooms, budget rooms, shared bunkrooms, and dorms. Standard hotel rooms offer clean, simple accommodations with private bathrooms, a queen-size bed, and a single; these have TVs with pay movies, a fridge, a minibar, and a phone. Budget rooms have access to a common room with a TV and Internet access, as well as a communal kitchen and laundry. Each quad bunkroom holds two sets of bunk beds; these are coed and share bathrooms. The single-sex dorms sleep 20. Plenty of lounge chairs sit by the pool. The **Bough House Restaurant** offers buffets, and a kiosk sells burger-style fare. What seems like the entire resort gathers nightly at the great-value **Outback Barbeque.** This barn with big tables, lots of beer, and live music is the place to join the throngs throwing a steak or sausage on the cook-it-yourself barbie.

Yulara Dr., Yulara, NT 0872. ✆ **08/8957 7888.** Fax 08/8957 7615. 125 units, all with private bathroom; 12 budget rooms without bathroom; 30 budget rooms with bathroom; 32 quad bunkrooms; 20-bed male-only dorm without bathroom, 20-bed female-only dorm without bathroom. A$330–A$430 double standard room; A$225–A$235 budget room with bathroom; A$194–A$204 budget room without bathroom; A$44 quad share bed; A$36 dorm bed; A$176 budget quad room per room. AE, DC, MC, V. **Amenities:** 2 restaurants; bar; free airport shuttle; Internet (A$2 for 10 min.); outdoor pool. *In room:* A/C, TV/w pay movies (standard room only), minibar (standard room only).

INEXPENSIVE

Moderately priced cabins and inexpensive bunkhouse and dorm beds are available at the Outback Pioneer Hotel and Lodge, above.

Ayers Rock Campground Instead of red dust, you get green lawns at this campground, which has barbecues, a playground, swimming pool, a small general store, and clean communal bathrooms and kitchen. If you don't want to camp but want to travel cheap, consider the modern two-bedroom cabins. They're a great value; each has air-conditioning, a TV, a kitchenette with a fridge, dining furniture, a double bed, and four bunks. They book up quickly in winter.

Yulara Dr., Yulara, NT 0872. ✆ **08/8957 7001.** Fax 08/8957 7004. 220 tent sites, 198 powered sites, 14 cabins, none with bathroom. A$150 cabin for up to 6; A$33 double tent site or A$42 family of 4; A$38 double powered motor-home site or A$47 family of 4; A$95 double village tents. Extra adult A$16, extra child 6–15 A$9. AE, DC, MC, V. **Amenities:** Free airport shuttle; children's playground; outdoor pool. *In room:* No phone.

THE TOP END

by Lee Mylne

The "Top End" is a last frontier, a vast sweep of barely inhabited country from Broome on the west coast to Arnhemland in the Northern Territory and eastern Queensland. Most of it is in the Northern Territory, and the term also differentiates the northern part of the Territory from the Red Centre. It is a place of wild, rugged beauty and, sometimes, hardship.

10

The Northern Territory's capital, Darwin, is a small city, modern, wealthy, tropical, and rapidly growing. To the east of Darwin is Kakadu National Park, home to wetlands teeming with crocs and birds; a third of the country's bird species are here. Farther east is Arnhemland, a stretch of rocky escarpments and rivers owned by Aborigines and seen by few others. The town of Katherine is famous for its river gorge. You'll find a wealth of experiences: Visit an Aboriginal community, canoe along lonely rivers, and soak in thermal pools.

Life in the Top End is different from life elsewhere in Australia. Its slightly lawless image is one the locals enjoy, but in Darwin you'll also get a sense of a city on the move. And it seems unlikely that development will change its essence. Isolation, the summer Wet season, monsoons, predatory crocodiles, and other dangers make 'em tough up here, but you don't have to do without the comforts you're used to.

EXPLORING THE TOP END

Read "Exploring the Red Centre," in chapter 9, p. 388; it contains information on traveling the entire Northern Territory.

VISITOR INFORMATION **Tourism NT,** Tourism House, 43 Mitchell St., Darwin, NT 0800 (✆ **13 67 68** in Australia or 08/8951 8471; www.travelnt.com), can supply information on Darwin, Litchfield National Park, Kakadu National Park, Katherine, and other destinations in the territory. The website can help you find a travel agent who specializes in the Northern Territory; details many hotels, tour operators, rental-car companies, and attractions; and features a special fishing guide. The Commission's Territory Discoveries division (www.holidaysnt.com) offers package deals.

The **Tourism Top End** information center in Darwin and **Katherine Visitor Information Centre** (listed in the "Katherine" section, later in this chapter) can supply information about the Top End in addition to their local regions.

WHEN TO GO Most folks visit the Top End in the winter **Dry season** ("the Dry"). It's more than likely that not a cloud will grace the sky, and temperatures will be comfortable, even hot in the middle of the day. The Dry runs from late April to late October or early November. It is high season, so book every hotel or tour in advance.

The **Wet season** ("the Wet") runs from November through March or April, sometimes starting as early as October and sometimes lasting a few weeks longer in the Kimberley. While rain does not fall 24 hours a day, it comes down in buckets for an hour or two each day, mainly in the late afternoon or at night. The land floods as far as the eye can see, the humidity is murderous, and the temperatures hit nearly 104°F (40°C). The floods cut off many attractions, and some tour companies close for the season. Cyclones may hit the coast during the Wet, with the same savagery and frequency as hurricanes hit Florida. Some find the "buildup" to the Wet, in October and November, when clouds gather but do not break, to be the toughest time.

Despite that, traveling in the Wet has its own special appeal and you'll see things you'd never encounter at other times of year. Waterfalls become massive torrents, lightning storms crackle across the afternoon sky, the land turns emerald green, cloud cover keeps the worst of the sun off you, crowds vanish, and there is an eerie beauty to it all. Keep your plans flexible to account for floods, take it slowly in the heat, and carry lots of drinking water. Even if you normally camp, sleep in air-conditioned accommodations now. Book tours ahead, because most operate on a reduced schedule. See the tips about traveling in the Wet, below.

GETTING AROUND The **Automobile Association of the Northern Territory (AANT),** 79–81 Smith St., Darwin, NT 0800 (© **08/8925 5901;** www.aant.com.au), is a good source of maps and road advice. See also the Northern Territory Tourist Commission's site, www.travelnt.com, which has sections designed specifically for those setting out on a driving holiday.

Normal restricted speed limits apply in all urban areas, but speed limits on Northern Territory highways (introduced only in 2006) are considerably higher than in other states. The speed limit is set at 130kmph (81 mph) on the Stuart, Arnhem, Barkly, and Victoria highways, while rural roads are designated 110kmph (68 mph) speed limits unless otherwise signposted. However, drivers should be careful to keep to a reasonable speed and leave enough distance to stop safely. The road fatality toll in the Northern Territory is high: 27 fatalities per 100,000 people each year, compared with the Australian average of 8 per 100,000.

Most Aboriginal land is open to visitors, but in some cases you must obtain a permit first. If you are taking a tour, this will be taken care of, but independent travelers should apply to the relevant Aboriginal Land Council (see www.nlc.org.au for more information) for permission. Most permits are free, but some entry fees may apply.

Always carry 4 liters (1 gal.) of **drinking water** per person a day when walking (increase to 1 liter/¼ gal. per person per hour in summer). Wear a broad-brimmed hat, high-factor sunscreen, and insect repellent containing DEET (such as Aerogard

The Northern Territory

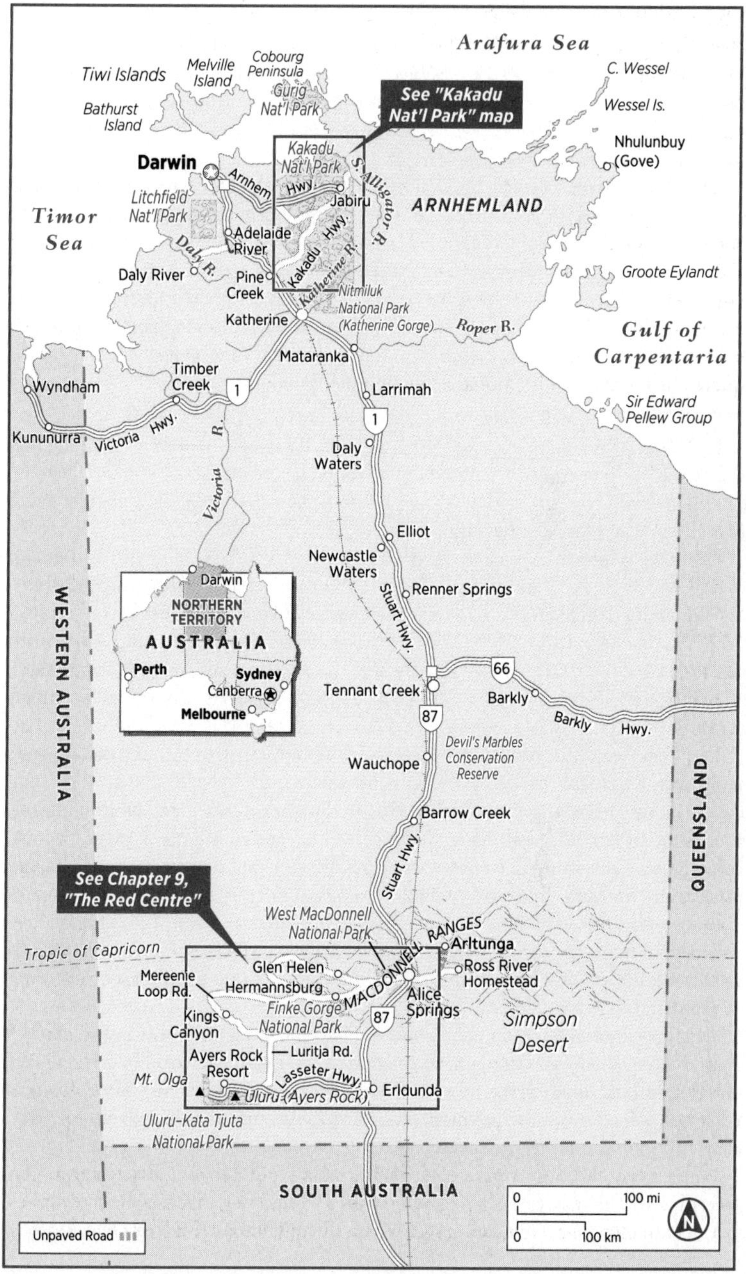

and RID brands) to protect against the dangerous Ross River Fever virus carried by mosquitoes in these parts.

Deadly **marine stingers** (see p. 57) put a stop to ocean swimming in the Top End from roughly October to April or May.

TRAVELING IN THE WET Some roads will be under water throughout the Wet, while others can flood unexpectedly, leaving you cut off for hours, days, or even months. Flash floods pose dangers to unwary motorists. Don't cross a flooded road unless you know the water is shallow, the current gentle, and the road intact. Never wade into the water, because crocodiles may be present. If you're cut off, the only thing to do is wait, so it's smart to travel with food and drinking water in remote parts. Check road conditions every day by calling the Northern Territory Department of Infrastructure, Planning & Environment's 24-hour recorded **report on road conditions** (**✆ 1800/246 199;** www.roadreport.nt.gov.au); dropping into or calling the AANT (see "Getting Around," above) in Darwin during office hours; or tuning in to local radio stations. Tour companies, tourist bureaus, and police stations should also be able to help.

TOUR OPERATORS Organized tours can bust the hassles posed by distance, isolation, and Wet floods in the Top End, and the guides will show and tell you things you almost certainly would not discover on your own. A loop through Darwin, Litchfield National Park, Kakadu National Park, and Katherine is a popular route that shows you a lot in a short time.

Reputable companies include **AAT Kings** (**✆ 1300/556 100** in Australia, or 08/8923 6555; www.aatkings.com); **Odyssey Tours & Safaris** (**✆ 1800/891 190** in Australia, or 08/8952 6811; www.odysaf.com.au); **Intrepid Connections** (**✆ 1300/442 183** in Australia, or 03/9277 8444; www.connections.travel); and **Adventure Tours** (**✆ 1300/654 604** in Australia, or 08/8132 8230; www.adventuretours.com.au).

VIP Touring Australia (**✆ 08/8947 1211;** www.viptouring.com.au) offers luxury organized and tailor-made tours.

Far Out Adventures ★ (**✆ 0427/152 288** mobile; www.farout.com.au) runs award-winning tailor-made four-wheel-drive safaris into Kakadu, Darwin, Arnhemland, Litchfield National Park, Katherine, the Kimberley, and more Top End regions. Proprietor-guide Mike Keighley, who has been operating in the Top End for 15 years, will create an adventure to suit your interests, budget, and time restrictions. Accommodations can range from luxury hotels to "under the stars" in Aussie bush swags. Touring with Mike can involve hiking, fishing, meeting or camping with his Aboriginal mates, canoeing, seeing Aboriginal rock art, extras such as scenic flights, and swimming under (croc-free) waterfalls. Mike is one of a select group of operators with Australia's Advanced Eco Tour Accreditation and Savannah Guide status, and has a great knowledge of the Top End's geography, Aboriginal culture, and ecology. Fun and personal, his trips are accompanied by good wine (sometimes in such places as a bird-filled lagoon at sunset) and "bush gourmet" meals. Mike also runs what he calls—for want of a better name—"Out of the Blue" trips, where solo travelers can join him on trips to relatively unchartered areas. Costs vary, but a private 3-day tour to Kakadu for two people would cost around A$3,000, depending on the time of year and inclusions. You can travel with Mike in his four-wheel-drive vehicle or you can "tag along" for a lower cost in your own. Check the website for details of upcoming trips and costs.

Lord's Kakadu & Arnhemland Safaris (© **08/8948 2200;** www.lords-safaris.com) is based in Jabiru and operates charter tours throughout Kakadu and Arnhemland. Owner Sab Lord was born on a buffalo station in Kakadu before it was a national park and has a strong rapport with local Aborigines. His small-group four-wheel-drive tours, which can be tailor-made, visit the Injalak Hill rock-painting sites in Arnhemland and the Injalak Arts Centre at Oenpelli and have exclusive access to the Minkinj Valley. Day tours to Arnhemland cost A$195 for adults and A$155 for children under 14 from Jabiru, or A$230 adults and A$185 for kids from Darwin. They operate May to October. The company also runs tours to Jim Jim and Twin Falls.

Peregrine Adventures (© **1300/791 485;** www.peregrineadventures.com) runs a range of environmentally and culturally sensitive small-group holidays led by local experts. In the Top End, these include the 8-day Katherine River Adventure, which includes 3 days of hiking, a three-gorges river cruise, and 3 days of canoeing in Nitmiluk (Katherine) Gorge with a local Aboriginal leader. The trek costs A$2,090 per person (carrying your own pack) and includes a tour leader, local guide, transport, canoe hire, park entrance fees, most meals, and camping gear.

DARWIN

1,489km (923 miles) N of Alice Springs

Australia's proximity to Asia is never more apparent than when you are in Darwin. The northernmost capital, named after Charles Darwin, is an exotic blend of frontier town, Asian village, and modern life. With a population of about 90,000, Darwin has had a turbulent history—and it shows. This city has battled just about everything that man and nature could throw at it. Most of its buildings date from the mid-1970s; Cyclone Tracy wiped out the city on Christmas Eve 1974. Despite all this destruction, some of Darwin's historic buildings—or at least parts of them—have survived, and you can see them around the city center.

The Darwin waterfront underwent a major redevelopment in 2009, with a new shopping and recreation precinct springing up near Stokes Wharf, looking out to the Arafura Sea. A large lagoon, wave pool, new hotels, high-rise residential apartments, restaurants, and shops are linked to the city center by a covered, elevated walkway through a corridor of bushland. Some locals think the advent of high-rise buildings—also springing up within the city itself—will alter the face of Darwin forever. Whether it will change the city's character as well, only time will tell. For the moment, it's still relaxed and very casual. Don't bother bringing a jacket and tie; shorts and sandals will be acceptable most places—even the swankiest invitations stipulate "Territory Rig" dress, meaning long pants and a short-sleeved open-neck shirt for men.

Darwin is most commonly used as a gateway to Kakadu National Park, Katherine Gorge, and the Kimberley, and many Australians have never bothered to visit it—or at least not for long. And that's a shame, because it is an attractive and interesting place. Give yourself a day or two to wander the pleasant streets and parklands, see the wildlife attractions, and discover some of the city's rich history. Then take time for some wetlands fishing, or shop for Aboriginal art and the Top End's South Sea pearls. An easy day trip is **Litchfield National Park ★★**, one of the Territory's best-kept secrets, boasting waterfalls that you'd usually only see in vacation brochures to swim under.

Essentials

GETTING THERE **Qantas** (✆ **13 13 13** in Australia; www.qantas.com) serves Darwin daily from Alice Springs, Adelaide, Brisbane, and Canberra, either direct or connecting through Alice Springs. **Virgin Blue** (✆ **13 67 89** in Australia; www.virginblue.com) flies direct to Darwin from Brisbane, Melbourne, and Perth with connections from other cities and regional centers. **Jetstar** (✆ **13 15 38** in Australia; www.jetstar.com.au) flies from Melbourne, Cairns, Brisbane, Sydney, and Adelaide. **Airnorth** (✆ **1800/627 474** in Australia, or 08/8920 4000; www.airnorth.com.au) and **Skywest Airlines** (✆ **1300/660 088** in Australia or 08/9477 8301; www.skywest.com.au) both fly from Perth, Broome, and Kununurra in Western Australia. Airnorth also flies from Mount Isa in Queensland.

Darwin Airport Shuttle Services (✆ **08/8981 5066;** www.darwinairportshuttle.com.au) meets every flight and delivers to any hotel between the airport and city for A$12 one-way or A$22 round-trip adults, or A$8 one-way, A$15 round-trip for children aged 5 to 12. Bookings are only necessary for city–airport transfers. A cab to the city is around A$35. **Avis, Budget, Europcar, Hertz,** and **Thrifty** have airport desks (see "Getting Around," below, for phone numbers).

Greyhound Australia (✆ **1300/473 946** in Australia; www.greyhound.com.au) makes a daily coach run from Alice Springs. The trip takes around 22 hours, and the fare is A$349. Greyhound also has a daily service from Broome via Kununurra and Katherine; this trip takes around 27 hours and costs A$358.

The Adelaide–Alice Springs–Darwin railway line is the Top End's only rail link. Great Southern Railway's ***Ghan*** (✆ **13 21 47** in Australia; www.trainways.com.au) runs a twice-weekly round-trip, leaving Adelaide on Sundays and Wednesdays at 12:20pm and Alice Springs on Mondays and Thursdays at 6pm. The return trip leaves Darwin on Wednesday and Saturday mornings. The adult one-way fare is A$358 for a "day-nighter" seat, A$656 for a sleeper, A$1,019 for a first-class sleeper, more for Platinum Class, which has cabins around twice the size of standard Gold Twin Cabins, each with a double bed, en-suite bathroom, and 24-hour room service.

Darwin is at the end of the Stuart Highway. Allow at least 2 long days, 3 to be comfortable, to drive from Alice. The nearest road from the east is the long and dull Barkly Highway, which connects with the Stuart Highway at Tennant Creek, 922km (572 miles) south. The nearest road from the west is Victoria Highway, which joins the Stuart Highway at Katherine, 314km (195 miles) to the south.

VISITOR INFORMATION **Tourism Top End** runs the official visitor center, 6 Bennett St. (at Smith St.), Darwin, NT 0800 (✆ **1300/138 886** in Australia or **08/8980 6000;** www.tourismtopend.com.au). There is also a visitor center at Darwin Airport (✆ **08/8927 7071**). They can make bookings and provide you with maps, national park notes, and information on Darwin and other regions throughout the Northern Territory, including Arnhemland, Katherine, and Kakadu and Litchfield national parks.

CITY LAYOUT The city heart is the **Smith Street pedestrian mall.** One street over is the **Mitchell Street Tourist Precinct,** with backpacker lodges, cheap eateries, and souvenir stores. Two streets away is the harborfront **Esplanade.** The

Darwin

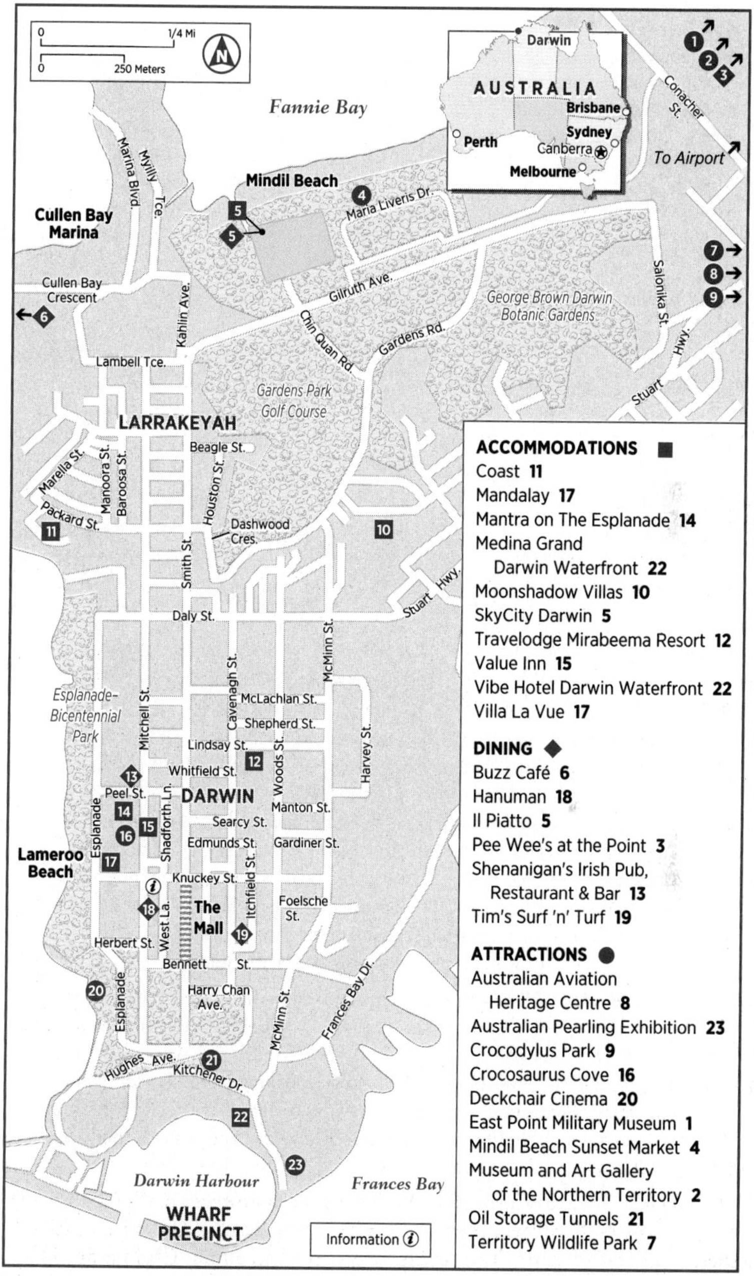

ACCOMMODATIONS ■

Coast **11**
Mandalay **17**
Mantra on The Esplanade **14**
Medina Grand Darwin Waterfront **22**
Moonshadow Villas **10**
SkyCity Darwin **5**
Travelodge Mirabeema Resort **12**
Value Inn **15**
Vibe Hotel Darwin Waterfront **22**
Villa La Vue **17**

DINING ◆

Buzz Café **6**
Hanuman **18**
Il Piatto **5**
Pee Wee's at the Point **3**
Shenanigan's Irish Pub, Restaurant & Bar **13**
Tim's Surf 'n' Turf **19**

ATTRACTIONS ●

Australian Aviation Heritage Centre **8**
Australian Pearling Exhibition **23**
Crocodylus Park **9**
Crocosaurus Cove **16**
Deckchair Cinema **20**
East Point Military Museum **1**
Mindil Beach Sunset Market **4**
Museum and Art Gallery of the Northern Territory **2**
Oil Storage Tunnels **21**
Territory Wildlife Park **7**

Tours of Darwin

The Tour Tub bus (© 08/8985 6322; www.tourtub.com.au) does a loop of major city attractions and hotels between 9am and 4pm daily. Hop on and off all day for A$35 for adults, A$15 for children 4 to 7, or A$90 for a family of four (which includes entry fee to the World War II oil storage tunnels). A 2-day pass is A$55 adults. Your ticket will also get you discounts to some attractions. The bus departs the Knuckey Street end of Smith Street Mall every 70 minutes. Buy your tickets on board (cash only). The bus does not run in December or on Good Friday and New Year's Day.

Wharf Precinct underwent a massive redevelopment in 2009, with a new swimming lagoon with a wave pool and artificial beaches, new apartment and retail blocks, a convention center, and two new hotels. The **Medina Grand Darwin Waterfront** and its neighboring sister property, **Vibe Darwin Waterfront,** are linked by a covered walkway right into the heart of the city, just minutes away (see "Where to Stay" below). The precinct, which also encompasses a couple of preexisting tourist attractions, a jetty popular with fishermen, and a working dock, is now linked to the city center by an elevated walkway from the top of one of the hotels. **Cullen Bay Marina** is a hub for restaurants, cafes, and expensive boats; it's about a 25-minute walk northwest of town. Northwest of town is **Fannie Bay,** where you'll find the Botanic Gardens, the sailing club, a golf course, a museum and art gallery, and the casino.

GETTING AROUND **By Car** For car and four-wheel-drive rentals, call **Avis** (© 08/8945 0662), **Budget** (© 08/8981 9800), **Europcar** (© 08/8941 0300), **Hertz** (© 08/8941 0944), or **Thrifty** (© 08/8924 0000).

BY BUS **Darwinbus** (**© 08/8924 7666**) is the local bus company. A A$2 adult or A50¢ child bus fare gives unlimited travel for 3 hours. A Show&Go ticket gives unlimited bus travel for 1 day for A$5 or for a week (valid Mon–Sun) for A$15. The city terminus is on Harry Chan Avenue (off Smith St., near Civic Sq.). Get timetables there, or from the Tourism Top End visitor center (see "Visitor Information," above).

Darwin Day Tours (**© 1300/721 365** in Australia, or 08/8923 6523; www.darwin daytours.com.au) also has a range of sightseeing tours.

BY TAXI **Darwin Radio Taxis** (**© 13 10 08**) is the main cab company. Taxi stands are at the Knuckey Street and Bennett Street ends of Smith Street Mall.

Exploring Darwin

Darwin's parks, harbor, and tropical clime make it lovely for strolling during the Dry. The tourist office distributes a free map showing a Historical Stroll of 17 points of interest around town. The **Esplanade** makes a pleasantly short and shady saunter, and the 42-hectare (104-acre) **George Brown Darwin Botanic Gardens** (**© 08/8981 1958**), on Gardens Road 2km (1¼ miles) from town, has paths through palms, orchids, every species of baobab in the world, and mangroves. Entry is free. Take bus no. 4 or 6; the buses drop you at the Gardens Road entrance, but you might want to walk straight to the visitor center (daily 8:30am–4pm), near the Geranium

Street entrance (24 hr.), to pick up self-guiding maps to the Aboriginal plant-use trails.

The pleasant 5km (3-mile) trail along **Fannie Bay** from the Skycity Darwin hotel and casino to the East Point Military Museum is also worth doing. Keep a lookout for some of the 2,000 wild wallabies on the east side of the road near the museum.

Darwin has two wildlife parks worth visiting. At the **Territory Wildlife Park** (**© 08/8988 7200;** www.territorywildlifepark.com.au), 61km (38 miles) south of Darwin at Berry Springs, you can take a free shuttle or walk 6km (3¾ miles) of bush trails to see native Northern Territory wildlife in re-created natural habitats, including monsoon rainforest boardwalks, lagoons with hides (shelters for watching birds), a walk-through aviary, a walk-through aquarium housing sting rays and sawfish, and a nocturnal house with marsupials such as the bilby. Bats, birds, spiders, crocs, frill-neck lizards, kangaroos, and other creatures also make their homes here (but not koalas, because they don't live in the Territory). A program of animal talks runs throughout the day. The best is the birds of prey show, at 11am and 2:30pm. Go first thing to see the animals at their liveliest, and allow 4 hours to see everything, plus 45 minutes traveling time. It's open daily from 8:30am to 6pm (last entry at 4pm), and closed December 25. Admission is A$26 for adults, A$13 for children 5 to 16, A$46 for a family of one adult and two children, or A$72 for families of six. Take the Stuart Highway for 50km (31 miles) and turn right onto the Cox Peninsula Road for about another 11km (7 miles).

In addition to housing a small crocodile museum, **Crocodylus Park & Zoo** (**© 08/8922 4500;** www.crocodyluspark.com), a 15-minute drive from town at 815 McMillan's Rd., Berrimah (opposite the police station), holds croc-feeding sessions and free hour-long guided tours at 10am, noon, 2pm, and 3:30pm. It doubles as Darwin's zoo, with exotic species including lions, Bengal tigers, leopards, and monkeys on display. It's open daily from 9am to 5pm (closed Dec 25). Admission is A$30 for adults, A$22 for seniors, A$15 for children 3 to 15, and A$80 for families. Bus no. 5 (Mon–Fri only), from Darwin, will drop you about a 5-minute walk from the park entrance.

The **Museum and Art Gallery of the Northern Territory,** Conacher Street, Bullocky Point (**© 08/8999 8264**), also holds an attraction for crocodile fans—the preserved body of **Sweetheart,** a 5m (16-ft.) man-eating saltwater croc captured in Kakadu National Park. The museum and gallery is a great place to learn about Darwin's place in Australia's modern history. It has sections on Aboriginal, Southeast Asian, and Pacific art and culture, and a maritime gallery with a pearling lugger and other boats that have sailed into Darwin from Indonesia and other northern parts. A highlight is the Cyclone Tracy gallery, where you can stand in a small, dark room as the sound of the cyclone rages around you. The gallery and museum are open from 9am to 5pm Monday through Friday, and 10am to 5pm weekends and public holidays; closed January 1, Good Friday, and December 25 and 26. The cafe has lovely bay views. Admission is free to the permanent exhibits. Take bus no. 4 or 6.

Darwin was bombed 64 times during World War II, and 12 ships were sunk in the harbor. It was an Allied supply base, and many American airmen were based here. The **Darwin Military Museum,** Alec Fong Lim Drive, East Point (**© 08/8981 9702;** www.darwinmilitarymuseum.com.au), housed in a World War II gun command post, plays a video of the 1942 and 1943 Japanese bombings. It has small but fine displays of photos, memorabilia, artillery, armored vehicles, weaponry old and new, and gun emplacements outside. It's open daily from 9:30am to 5pm (closed Good Friday and Dec 25). Admission is A$12 adults, A$10 seniors, A$5 children 5 to 15, and A$30 families.

Empty **World War II oil storage tunnels** (✆ **08/8985 6322**), on Kitchener Drive, in the Wharf Precinct, house a collection of black-and-white photographs of the war in Darwin, each lit up in the dark. The simple but haunting attraction is worth a visit. Admission is A$5 adults and A$3 children. The tunnels are closed in December. They open daily from 9am to 4pm May through September and 9am to 1pm October through April.

Even if you are not a military or aircraft buff, you may enjoy the excellent **Australian Aviation Heritage Centre** ★, 557 Stuart Hwy., Winnellie (✆ **08/8947 2145;** www.darwinsairwar.com.au). A B-52 bomber on loan from the United States is the prized exhibit, but the center also boasts a B-25 Mitchell bomber; Mirage and Sabre jet fighters; rare Japanese Zero fighter wreckage; and funny, sad, and heart-warming (and heart-wrenching) displays on World War II and Vietnam. Hours are daily from 9am to 5pm (closed Good Friday and Dec 25). Admission is A$12 for adults, A$9 for seniors, A$7.50 for students, A$7 for children 5 to 12, and A$30 for families. Guided tours are at 10am and 2 and 4pm. The Heritage Centre is 10 minutes from town; take the no. 5 or 8 bus.

For an insight into Darwin's pearling industry, visit the **Australian Pearling Exhibition** (✆ **08/8999 6573**), on Kitchener Drive near the Wharf Precinct. It has displays following the industry from the days of the lugger and hard-hat diving to modern farming and culture techniques. It's open from 10am to 3pm daily, except January 1, Good Friday, and December 25 and 26. Tickets cost A$6.60 for adults, A$3.30 for children, and A$17 for families of five.

If you have an evening free, get out on the harbor. **Australian Harbour Cruises** (✆ **0428/414 000** mobile phone; www.australianharbourcruises.com.au) offers 3-hour sunset cruises aboard the restored lugger *Anniki*. They leave Cullen Bay Marina daily at 4:45pm and cost A$70 for adults and A$50 for kids 15 and under. The price includes a glass of bubbly and some nibbles. **Darwin Harbour Cruises** (✆ **08/8942 3131;** www.darwinharbourcruises.com.au) operates a sunset champagne cruise aboard the sailing schooner *Tumlaren,* which costs A$66 per adult and A$43 for children 4 to 14, or a barbecue lunch cruise for A$75 adults and A$46 children 4 to 12. A sit-down three-course dinner cruise aboard the *Alfred Nobel* costs A$105 adults and A$65 children 2 to 12. Cruises leave from Cullen Bay Marina.

The Top End's wetlands and warm oceans are **fishing** ★ heaven. The big prey is barramundi, or "barra." Loads of charter boats conduct jaunts of up to 10 days in the river and wetland systems around Darwin, Kakadu National Park, and into remote Arnhemland.

The same company that runs Darwin's Tour Tub bus runs the **Northern Territory Fishing Office** (✆ **1800/632 225** in Australia, or 08/8985 6333; www.ntfishingoffice.com.au), a booking agent for a number of fishing charter boats offering barramundi day trips and extended wetland safaris, reef fishing, light tackle sportfishing, fly-fishing, and estuary fishing. A day's barra fishing on wetlands near Darwin will cost around A$320 per person; for an extended barra safari, budget between A$550 and A$825 per person per day, depending on the size of your group (up to five people). If you simply want to cast a line in Darwin Harbour for trevally,

The Cage of Death

Strong men have known to pale in the face of an attack by Chopper, a 790kg (1,742-lb.) crocodile with no front feet. At Darwin's latest attraction, Crocosaurus Cove, the very brave can get into a Perspex "cage" and be lowered into Chopper's enclosure, which also houses several huge crocs who have survived into their 70s and 80s, as well as large numbers of juveniles. These most territorial of monsters aren't usually happy with the intrusion—and the scratch marks on the 145mm (6-in.) thick walls of the cage tell the rest of the story. I confess: I have not done this and will not—not even in the interests of research! Less scary is the chance to swim in a pool next door to the younger crocs, with just a Perspex wall between you and them. Crocosaurus Cove also has Australia's largest collection of reptiles, about 70 species, all from the Top End. Crocosaurus Cove is at 58 Mitchell St. (✆ 08/8981 7522; www.crocosauruscove.com). It's open daily 9am to 7pm (last admission at 6pm). Admission is A$28 adults, A$16 children 4 to 15, or A$57 to A$99 for families. The Cage of Death experience costs A$120 for one person or A$160 for two in the cage together. You spend about 15 minutes in the water.

queenfish, and barra, the company will take you out for A$110 per person (or A$95 for kids under 12) for a half-day. It also rents skipper-yourself fishing boats and tackle. Also check out the fishing section on www.travelnt.com for detailed information on fishing tours, guides, and everything you need to know to make your arms ache from reeling 'em in!

The Darwin Shopping Scene

Darwin's best buys are Aboriginal art and crafts, pearls, opals, and diamonds.

You will find many shops and galleries selling authentic Aboriginal artworks and artifacts at reasonable prices. To make a heavyweight investment in works by internationally sought-after artists, visit the Aboriginal-owned **Aboriginal Fine Arts Gallery,** on the second floor at the corner of Knuckey and Mitchell streets (✆ **08/8981 1315;** www.aaia.com.au). Its website is a useful guide to art and artists.

The world's best South Sea pearls are farmed in the Top End seas. Buy, or just drool in the window at **Paspaley Pearls,** at the Bennet Street end of the Smith Street Mall (✆ **1300/888 080** in Australia or 08/8982 5515; www.paspaleypearls.com). **The World of Opal,** 52 Mitchell St. (✆ **08/8981 8981**), has a re-creation of an opal mine in the showroom. If you fancy a pink diamond (the world's rarest) from the Argyle Diamond Mine in Kununurra (see "Kununurra," in chapter 11), you can get them at **Creative Jewellers,** 27 Smith St. Mall (✆ **08/8941 1233**), an Argyle-appointed supplier that buys direct from the mine. It also stocks the champagne diamonds, for which Argyle is renowned, and other Argyle diamond colors, as well as South Sea pearls and opals. The jewelers try to fashion pieces for overseas visitors in a short time to match your traveling schedule.

Jokes about "snapping handbags" abound in croc country. For your own croc-skin fashion statement, head to **di Croco,** in the Paspaley Pearls building in Smith Street Mall (✆ **08/8941 4470;** www.dicroco.com). You'll find bags, purses, wallets, card holders, belts, pens, and other accessories, all made from saltwater croc skins farmed locally.

Where to Stay

April through October is the peak Dry season; hotels usually drop their rates from November through March (the Wet).

EXPENSIVE

Mantra on the Esplanade ★★ This eight-floor apartment hotel right on the Esplanade overlooking Darwin Harbour and the Arafura Sea and just a block from Smith Street Mall, is one of Darwin's most comfortable, elegant lodgings. Rich, dark cane lobby armchairs and sofas are welcoming, and there are 64 hotel rooms as well as 140 spacious contemporary-style one-, two-, and three-bedroom apartments that boast their own private balconies with great views. Apartment kitchens feature new modern granite bench tops and stainless-steel appliances, including dishwashers, and all have laundry facilities. The two penthouses include 104-centimeter (40-in.) plasma screens with digital surround sound. All rooms and apartments have city or harbor views. All rooms are nonsmoking.

88 The Esplanade (at Peel St.), Darwin, NT 0800. ✆ **1300/987 604** in Australia, or 08/8943 4333. Fax 08/8943 4388. www.mantracityhotels.com.au. 204 units. A$259–A$284 double hotel room; A$368–A$393 1-bedroom apt; A$479–A$504 2-bedroom apt; A$624 3-bedroom apt; A$641 penthouse. Children 14 and under stay free in parent's room with existing bedding. AE, DC, MC, V. Parking A$10. Bus: 4. **Amenities:** Restaurant; bar; concierge; executive-level rooms; access to nearby golf course and health club; Internet in business center; Jacuzzi; outdoor pool; room service. *In room:* A/C, TV w/pay movies, CD player (premium apts only), hair dryer, minibar, Wi-Fi (55¢ per min. to A$28 for 24 hr.).

Medina Grand Darwin Waterfront ★★ I had a sneak preview of Darwin's newest hotel a week before it opened in March 2009, just before press time. Along with its neighboring sister property, Vibe Darwin Waterfront, this apartment hotel has a prime location overlooking the city's new development, which includes a swimming lagoon and wave pool at Stokes Wharf. From the top floor of the hotel, you can take a covered walkway right into the heart of the city, just minutes away. All one-bedroom apartments have balconies (studios do not), while all rooms have full kitchens with microwaves, and laundry facilities. Most apartments connect with a studio to make a two-bedroom apartment, if needed. There are two two-bedroom apartments, which with a studio combine to make a very spacious three-bedroom.

7 Kitchener Drive, Darwin, NT 0800. ✆ **1300/MEDINA** [633 462] in Australia, 0800/101 100 in New Zealand, 02/9356 5061 (Sydney reservations center) or 08/8982 999. Fax 08/8982 9700. www.medina.com.au. 121 units. A$195–A$420 studio double; A$245–A$470 1-bedroom apt; A$600 2-bedroom apt. Extra person A$50. Crib A$5. AE, DC, MC, V. Free undercover parking. **Amenities:** Restaurant; bar; babysitting; exercise room; outdoor pool; room service; spa. *In room:* A/C, TV w/pay movies, CD player, hair dryer, Internet (A$13 per hr. to A$25 for 24 hr.), kitchen, minibar.

Skycity Darwin ★ A A$30-million refurbishment has given this five-star complex a new outdoor restaurant and bar to further increase the many facilities on offer. Attached to Darwin's casino on Fannie Bay, the hotel is owned by the Skycity Entertainment Group. The complex resembles a tropical palace, with white blocky architecture, an infinity-edge pool, and 7 hectares (18 acres) of gardens on Mindil Beach, next to the Botanic Gardens. The rooms are a cocktail of European-style contemporary Spanish furniture and tropical elegance. All have balconies. It's worth paying a

Where Can I Swim?

Crocodiles and stingers render Darwin's beaches a no-swim zone year-round. The new man-made lagoon at Stokes Wharf has solved the problem for most people. The lagoon has two parts, one a wave pool. Locals also sunbathe on Casuarina Beach and swim within view of the sea in Lake Alexander in East Point Reserve. About an hour's drive from the city, on the way to the Territory Wildlife Park, Berry Springs Nature Park has swimming holes along Berry Creek, with steps for easy access, and small waterfalls that create natural whirlpool action. They may be closed in the Wet season.

little extra for an ocean-facing room so you can watch Darwin's great Dry season sunsets and spectacular monsoon-season lightning storms. Superior rooms feature luxurious spa tubs and cool marble in the bathrooms. Full-length glass windows provide views over a private balcony terrace to lush tropical gardens and Mindil beach. A free shuttle runs four times a day to and from the city. There are also 10 rooms for families and travelers with disabilities.

Gilruth Ave., Mindil Beach, Darwin, NT 0801. ✆ **1800/891 118** in Australia, or 08/8943 8888. Fax 08/8943 8999. www.skycitydarwin.com.au. 117 units. A$260–A$340 double; A$390–A$860 suite. Extra person A$50. Children 13 and under stay free in parent's room with existing bedding. AE, DC, MC, V. Free valet and self-parking. Bus: 4 or 6. **Amenities:** 3 restaurants; 5 bars; babysitting; concierge; executive suites; free access to nearby 9-hole golf course; exercise room; Jacuzzi; heated outdoor pool; room service; sauna; access to 20 nearby tennis courts; free Wi-Fi. *In room:* A/C, TV/DVD w/pay movies, hair dryer, free Internet, minibar.

MODERATE

Moonshadow Villas ★★ This private villa complex is a little bit of Bali, transplanted into Darwin. The villas center around a small but tranquil pool area, complete with stone Buddhas and turtles, shaded by towering palms and surrounded by orchids and lilies. The interiors are equally lush and exotic, and there's a small patio area to sit out in. The villas have two double bedrooms and two bathrooms (one with an enclosed semi-outdoor rainwater shower). There's a gas barbecue for you to use too. The fridge is stocked with chilled champagne and beer for your arrival.

6 Gardens Hill Crescent, The Gardens, NT 0800. ✆ **08/8981 8850** or mobile phone 0412/890 662. www.moonshadowvillas.com. 5 units. Rates from A$249 per night; A$1,999–A$4,893 per week. Min 3-night stay. AE, DC, MC, V. Free off-street parking. **Amenities:** Outdoor pool. *In room:* A/C, TV, VCR, hair dryer, kitchen, free Wi-Fi.

Travelodge Mirambeena Resort You're just a stone's throw from the city center at this modern hotel complex, where the tempting swimming pools and the Treetops restaurant, all shaded by the leaves of a sprawling strangler fig, have a castaway-island feel. Each room is a decent size and has a garden or pool view. As well as a range of hotel rooms, the complex has 32 self-contained one-bedroom town houses, which sleep up to six and are a good option for families. Budget and standard rooms sleep up to four.

64 Cavenagh St., Darwin, NT 0800. ✆ **1300/886 886** in Australia, or 08/8946 0111. Fax 08/8981 5116. www.travelodge.com.au. 256 units, all with shower only. A$325–A$485 double; A$520 town house (sleeps 6). Extra person A$40. Crib A$5 per night. AE, DC, MC, V. Free off-street parking. Bus: 4, 5, 6,

More Than a Room

If you're looking for a bit more space and privacy than a hotel room gives you, or perhaps are traveling as a family, a "home away from home" option is provided by **More Than a Room Holiday Accommodation** (✆ **08/8942 3012** or 0418/616 888 mobile phone; www.morethanaroom.com.au). The company has five properties. The luxurious and stylish **Mandalay,** built in 1988 by Lord McAlpine, is on the Esplanade, close to the city center. It has three bedrooms, free Internet, a pool, barbecue area, off-street parking, and bikes for your use. Breakfast provisions are in the fridge on your arrival, along with a bottle of wine. Next door is **Villa La Vue,** which is equally spacious but has a different style. There's a minimum 2-night stay and the rates are from A$395 in the Wet (Oct–Apr) for one bedroom and A$120 per night for each extra room. In the Dry (May–Sept), you must rent the whole house, for A$695 per night. For a "typical Darwin" style of accommodation, there's **Coast,** a 1970s elevated coastal beach house just outside the city center with four double/twin bedrooms, polished floors, TVs and DVD players in the bedrooms, bikes, a small pool in the yard, and water views. There's a minimum 5-night stay, with rates from A$295 per night in the Wet to A$395 in the Dry for up to six people (A$455 per night during school holidays). Extra person rate is A$25 per person per night. Other properties are available at Cullen Bay and on The Esplanade, near the Darwin Convention Centre.

8, or 10. **Amenities:** Restaurant; poolside cafe; 2 bars; babysitting; bikes; exercise room; 2 Jacuzzis; 2 outdoor pools; children's pool; room service. *In room:* A/C, TV w/pay movies, hair dryer, Internet ($11 per hr. or A$22 for 24 hr.), minibar.

Vibe Hotel Darwin Waterfront Along with its sister property, the adjacent Medina Grand Darwin (see above), this is one of Darwin's newest properties. Less grand than the Medina, it's a casual place to stay and relax. The rooms are spacious and fresh, with a cheery white-and-aqua color scheme, but no balconies. Reception, the pool, and the restaurant are shared with the Medina Grand (see above).

7 Kitchener Dr., Darwin, NT 0800. ✆ **13 VIBE** [84 23] in Australia, 0800/101 100 in New Zealand, 02/9356 5063 (Sydney reservations center) or 08/8982 9998. Fax 08/8982 9700. www.vibehotels.com.au. 120 units. A$199–A$400 double. Extra person A$50. AE, DC, MC, V. Free undercover parking. **Amenities:** Restaurant; bar; babysitting; exercise room; outdoor pool; room service; spa. *In room:* A/C, TV w/pay movies, hair dryer, Internet ($13 per hr. to A$25 for 24 hr.), minibar.

INEXPENSIVE

Value Inn The cheerful rooms at this neat little hotel in the Mitchell Street Tourist Precinct are compact but tidy, with colorful modern fittings. Each room is just big enough to hold a queen-size and a single bed and a small writing table. The views aren't much, but you'll probably spend your time in the nearby cafes. Smith Street Mall and the Esplanade walking path are 2 blocks away. There is a pay phone, cold drink and coffee vending machines, an iron on each floor, microwave ovens on the first and second floors, and a very small garden swimming pool off the parking lot.

50 Mitchell St., Darwin, NT 0800. ✆ **08/8981 4733.** Fax 08/8981 4730. www.valueinn.com.au. 93 units, all with shower only. A$160 double for 1 night; rates reduce with each night you stay. AE, MC, V. Limited

free parking. Bus: 4. **Amenities:** Bikes; access to nearby golf course and health club; outdoor pool; tennis courts. *In room:* A/C, TV, no phone.

Where to Dine

Cullen Bay Marina, a 25-minute walk or a short cab ride from town, is packed with trendy restaurants and cafes. If it's Thursday, don't even think about eating anywhere other than the **Mindil Beach Sunset Market ★★**. And on Saturday, head to the suburban Parap markets for Asian goodies (see the box, "Cheap Eats & More!" below).

EXPENSIVE

Buzz Café CONTEMPORARY This smart, busy waterfront cafe is as well known for its "loo with a view" as it is for its relaxed atmosphere. The men's bathroom just nudges out the women's for interest value. Ladies, get a man to take you in there to see what I mean—everybody does! The food is East-meets-West fare, such as jungle curry of chicken with snake beans and green peppercorns, or pan-fried barramundi on potato mash in lemon-butter sauce. Service can be slow, but the cocktails and views almost make up for it.

Marina Blvd., Cullen Bay. ✆ **08/8941 1141.** Reservations recommended in the Dry (May–Oct). Main courses A$17–A$30. AE, DC, MC, V. Mon–Fri noon–2am; Sat–Sun 10:30am–2am (brunch until 11:30am). Bus: 4 or 6.

Hanuman ★ CONTEMPORARY ASIAN A move to large new premises in the new Holiday Inn Esplanade complex has given this popular Darwin institution an alfresco dining area and stylish cocktail bar—and room for many more diners. With seating for 90 people outside and about the same number inside, this is still one of the most exotic places in Darwin to eat. Its "Nonya"-style cuisine is a fusion of Chinese- and Malaysian-style cooking. You can rely on dishes such as red duck curry with coconut, litchis, kaffir lime, Thai basil, and fresh pineapple; or wok-tossed prawns in a coconut, wild ginger, and curry sauce. There is also a tandoori menu. Service is prompt and friendly.

93 Mitchell St. ✆ **08/8941 3500.** www.hanuman.com.au. Reservations recommended. Main courses A$24–A$33. AE, DC, MC, V. Mon–Fri noon–3pm; daily 6–11pm.

Il Piatto ★ ITALIAN Would you pay A$140—or even A$70—for a pizza? I wouldn't, but plenty of diners at this smart restaurant inside the Skycity Darwin Casino complex have made that grandiose gesture. These "operas from the oven" are laced with Wagyu beef, foie gras, fresh truffles, lobster, and other high-priced delicacies, so perhaps if you have had a big win at the casino, it might be worth splashing out—but this seems largely aimed at people with more money than sense. Less extravagant pizzas cost A$20 to A$28, and there are also three- and four-course set menus for A$60 and A$75, respectively. And even without the gimmicks, the food is very good.

Skycity Darwin, Gilruth Ave., Mindil Beach. ✆ **08/8943 8940.** Reservations recommended. Main courses A$20–A$45. AE, DC, MC, V. Daily noon–3pm and 6:30pm–late.

Pee Wee's at The Point ★★ CONTEMPORARY Surrounded on three sides by forest, this steel-and-glass venue affords views of Fannie Bay from just about every table, inside, out on the deck, or down on the lawn. The owners—two chefs and a sommelier—offer an extensive wine list that includes some older and hard-to-find

Cheap Eats & More!

If it's Thursday, join the entire city and hundreds of other visitors at the **Mindil Beach Sunset Market ★★** to feast at the 60 terrific (and cheap—most dishes are less than A$10 a serving) Asian, Greek, Italian, African, Mexican, and Aussie food stalls; listen to live music; wander among almost 200 arts-and-crafts stalls; and mix and mingle with masseurs, tarot-card readers, and street performers as the sun sets into the sea. The action runs from 5 to 10pm in the Dry (approximately May–Oct). A smaller market of about 50 stalls runs Sunday from 4 to 9pm. The market's season changes from year to year, so if you're visiting on the seasonal cusp, in April or September, check whether it's on by calling the organizers (✆ **08/8981 3454**) or visiting **www.mindil.com.au**. The beach is about a A$10 cab ride from town, or take bus no. 4. The Tour Tub's last run of the day, at 4pm (see "Getting Around," earlier in this chapter), goes by the markets.

On Saturdays (7:30am–1:30pm), head to suburban **Parap Markets ★**, which transform a small street into a corner of Asia. The focus is on food, with a sprinkling of arts and crafts, and it's a favorite place for locals to have breakfast or brunch, choosing from the Southeast Asian soups, noodle dishes, and satays, washed down with fresh-squeezed tropical fruit drinks. The market stalls cover only about a block, on Parap Road in Parap (✆ **08/8942 0805** or 0438/882 373 mobile phone).

Australian wines. The food emphasizes fresh local produce and employs some dishes that have an Asian twist. An example: grilled kangaroo tenderloin filet, marinated in yogurt and tandoori spices, served with mashed sweet potato and a black sesame, mustard seed, and mango mint salsa. Get there in time to watch the sunset.

Alec Fong Lim Dr., East Point Reserve (4km/2½ miles from town). ✆ **08/8981 6868.** www.peewees.com.au. Reservations recommended, especially in the Dry (May–Oct). Main courses A$29–A$46. AE, DC, MC, V. Daily 6pm–late. Closed Dec 26. Free parking. Cab fare from the city about A$15.

MODERATE

Shenannigan's ★ IRISH PUB FARE Hearty Irish stews and slow-cooked beef-and-Guinness (plus the odd pint of Guinness itself) get everyone in the mood for eating, talking, and dancing at this convivial bar and restaurant. A friendly mix of solo travelers, families, seniors, and backpackers eat and drink in atmospheric wooden booths, standing up at bar tables, or by the fire. Besides hearty meat dishes, there is lighter stuff, including vegetarian dishes and a good smattering of local produce. Try the Territory Mixed Grill—crocodile sausage, kangaroo fillet, and barramundi with house dried tomatoes, field mushrooms, and roast garlic butter. There are also daily chef's specials. There's entertainment every night—live bands, a quiz game, or karaoke.

69 Mitchell St. (at Peel St.). ✆ **08/8981 2100.** www.shenannigans.com.au. Reservations recommended. Main courses A$15–A$28. AE, DC, MC, V. Daily 10:30am–2am.

INEXPENSIVE

The Roma Bar ★ CAFE The cool crowd hangs out here. You'll see media types rubbing shoulders with politicians, musicians, artists, and lobbyists. The coffee's good and the food is tasty and well priced. It's a great spot for breakfast (they make their own muesli) and at lunch—if you want something more than a sandwich—there's pasta and Asian-influenced dishes, such as an asparagus-and-shiitake-mushroom omelette with black bean and ginger broth, or maybe a fish curry. BYO wine.

9 Cavenagh St. ✆ **08/8981 6729.** www.romabar.com.au. Main courses A$12–A$15. AE, DC, MC, V. Mon–Fri 7am–4pm; Sat–Sun 8am–2pm.

Tim's Surf 'n' Turf ★ ☺ STEAK/SEAFOOD This Darwin favorite is housed in a classic elevated Darwin home that has been transformed into a modern restaurant. Diners can choose between the air-conditioned open-plan dining and bar area, its walls hung with Top End Aboriginal artworks, or head outside to sit under the shady trees and palms. The lunch menu offers a range of A$10 specials including salads, baguettes, and rolls, or hot dishes such as crocodile schnitzels, Malay curries, crumbed barramundi, and salmon fettuccine. At dinner, the menu includes steaks, seafood platters, oysters, and vegetarian dishes, along with a range of salads, chicken, and pasta dishes. The wine list features mostly Australian wines, with around half offered by the glass.

10 Litchfield St. ✆ **08/8981 1024.** Main courses A$14–A$21. AE, DC, MC, V. Mon–Fri noon–2pm; daily for dinner.

Darwin After Dark

The gaming tables at the **Skycity Darwin Casino,** Gilruth Avenue, Mindil Beach (✆ **08/8943 8888**), are in play from noon until 4am Sunday to Thursday, until 6am Friday and Saturday. Slot machines operate 24 hours. The dress code allows neat jeans, shorts, and sneakers, but men's shirts must have a collar.

A good spot to catch Darwin's Technicolor sunsets is the supercasual **Darwin Sailing Club,** Atkins Drive on Fannie Bay (✆ **08/8981 1700**). Ask a staff member to sign you in. Dine on affordable meals outdoors while a family of goannas (monitor

Movie Stars Under the Stars

Lie back in a canvas deck chair under the stars at the Deckchair Cinema (✆ 08/8981 0700; www.deckchaircinema.com) to watch Aussie hits, foreign films, and cult classics. Located on the edge of Darwin Harbour (at the end of Jervois Rd., opposite Parliament House on the Esplanade), this Darwin institution is run by the Darwin Film Society. Take a picnic dinner and get there early to soak up the scene: the twinkling lights from boats anchored in the Arafura Sea and the fabulous sunsets. A kiosk sells wine, beer, soft drinks, and snacks. There are 250 deck chairs as well as about 100 straight-backed seats, and staffers can supply cushions and even insect repellent if you need it. Entry is by a walkway from the Esplanade, or by car off Kitchener Drive (there's a parking lot). The box office and kiosk open at 6:30pm and movies start at 7:30pm daily in the Dry (Apr–Nov), with double features on Friday and Saturday. Tickets are A$13 adults, A$6 children, and A$30 for families of four, or A$20 adults, A$9 children, and A$45 families for double features. (In the Wet, the movies screen indoors, so call for details of the current venue.)

lizards) swirls around your feet looking for meaty scraps. The bar is open Monday to Friday from 11:30am to midnight and until 2am on Saturdays and Sundays (Dec–Mar), and Monday to Friday from 10am to midnight and on Saturday to Sunday 10:30am to 2am (Apr–Nov). The club is closed on Good Friday and Christmas Day.

The cafes and restaurants of **Cullen Bay Marina** are a good place to be day or night, but especially for Dry season sunsets.

If it's Thursday, you are mad to be anywhere except the **Mindil Beach Sunset Market ★★** (see "Cheap Eats & More!" above).

A Side Trip to Litchfield Park

120km (74 miles) S of Darwin

An easy 90-minute drive south of Darwin is a miniature Garden of Eden full of forests, waterfalls, rocky sandstone escarpments, glorious swimming holes, and prehistoric cycads that look as if they belong on the set of *Jurassic Park.* Litchfield National Park is much smaller (a mere 146,000 hectares/360,620 acres) and much less famous than its big sister, Kakadu, but it is no less stunning.

The park's main attractions are the spring-fed swimming holes, like the magical plunge pool at **Florence Falls ★★★**, 29km (18 miles) from the forest. It's a 15-minute hike down stairs to the water, so the easily accessible pool at **Wangi Falls ★**, 49km (30 miles) from the eastern entrance, gets more crowds. (It's also a beautiful spot, surrounded by cliffs and forests with a lookout from the top.) More idyllic grottoes are 4km (2½ miles) from Florence Falls at **Buley Rockhole,** a series of tiered rock pools and waterfalls. You can't swim at **Tolmer Falls,** but during the Wet when they're flowing, take the boardwalk about 400m (1,312 ft.) to the lookout and see the cascade against a backdrop of red cliffs.

There are a number of short **walking trails** through the park, such as the half-hour Shady Creek Circuit from Florence Falls up to the parking lot.

Parts of the park are also home to thousands of 2m-high (6½-ft.) **"magnetic" termite mounds,** so called because they run north-south to escape the fierce mid-day heat. A display hut and a viewing point are 17km (11 miles) from the park's eastern entrance.

Warning: Most of the park's swimming holes are regarded as crocodile-free; the same is *not* true of the Finniss and Reynolds rivers in the park, so no leaping into those!

To get there from Darwin, head south for 86km (53 miles) on the Stuart Highway and follow the park turnoff on the right through the town of Batchelor for 34km (21 miles). A number of minicoach and four-wheel-drive day trips run from Darwin. Katherine-based tour operator **Travel North** (✆ **1800/089 103** in Australia, or 08/8971 9999; www.travelnorth.com.au) runs a day tour to Litchfield that starts in Darwin and ends in Katherine, a convenient way to combine sightseeing and transport if you plan to visit both. It costs A$199 adults and A$179 children 5 to 15. Crowds of locals can shatter the peace in Litchfield on weekends, especially in the Dry season, but the park is worth visiting, crowds or no crowds. Entry to the park is free.

Roads to most swimming holes are paved, although a few are accessible only by four-wheel-drive. In the Wet (approximately Nov–Apr), some roads—usually the four-wheel-drive ones—may be closed, and the Wangi water hole may be off-limits due to turbulence and strong currents. Check with the **Parks & Wildlife Commission** (✆ **08/8999 4555**) before you leave Darwin during this time.

A number of locations in the park have basic campsites. The camping fee per night is A$6.60 for adults, A$3.30 for kids under 16, or A$15 for families of two adults and four kids. A kiosk at Wangi Falls sells some supplies, but stock up on fuel and alcohol in Batchelor.

KAKADU NATIONAL PARK ★★★

257km (159 miles) E of Darwin

Kakadu National Park, a World Heritage area, is Australia's largest national park, covering a massive 1.7 million hectares (4.2 million acres).

Cruising the lily-clad wetlands to spot crocodiles, plunging into exquisite natural swimming holes, hiking through spear grass and cycads, fishing for prized barramundi, soaring in a light aircraft over torrential waterfalls during the Wet season, photographing thousands of birds flying over the eerie red sandstone escarpment that juts 200m (650 ft.) above the flood plain, and admiring some of Australia's most superb Aboriginal rock-art sites—these are the activities that draw people to Kakadu. Some 275 species of birds and 75 species of reptiles inhabit the park, making it one of the richest wildlife habitats in the country.

Kakadu is an ecological jewel. But be aware that the vast distances between points of interest in the park and the sameness that infects so much Australian landscape can detract from Kakadu's appeal for some people. Wildlife here is not the breathtaking equivalent of an African game park, where herds roam the plains—which is why even Australians get so excited when they spot a kangaroo in the wild. It is best in the late Dry, around September and October, when crocs and birds gather around shrinking water holes. Wildlife viewing is not particularly good in the Wet season, when birds disperse widely and you may not see a single croc.

The name *Kakadu* comes from *Gagudju,* the group of languages spoken by Aborigines in the northern part of the park, where they and their ancestors are believed to have lived for 50,000 years. Today, Aborigines manage the park as its owners, in conjunction with the Australian government. This is one of the few places in Australia where some Aborigines stick to a traditional lifestyle of hunting and living off the land. You won't see them, because they keep away from prying eyes, but their culture is on display at a cultural center and at rock-art sites. Kakadu and the wilds of Arnhemland to the east are the birthplace of the "X-ray" style of art for which Aboriginal artists are famous.

Essentials

VISITOR INFORMATION Both the park entrances—the northern station on the Arnhem Highway used by visitors from Darwin and the southern station on the Kakadu Highway for visitors from Katherine—hand out free visitor guides with maps. In the Dry they also issue a timetable of free ranger-guided bushwalks, art-site talks, and slide shows taking place that week. An A$25 park entry fee was reintroduced in 2010, for all visitors over 16. Park permits can be purchased at Tourism Top End in Darwin (see p. 422) or at the **Bowali Visitor Centre** (✆ **08/8938 1120**), on the Kakadu Highway, 5km (3 miles) from Jabiru, 100km (62 miles) from the northern entry station, and 131km (81 miles) from the southern entry station.

Permits are also available through other outlets; check the website, **www.environment.gov.au/parks/kakadu**, for more information. An online ticketing system was being developed as this book went to print.

The Bowali Visitor Centre is an attractive, environmentally friendly Outback-style building, which shows a program of 1-hour videos on the park's natural history and Aboriginal culture, stocks maps and park notes, has a library and displays, and includes a gift shop and a cafe. Information officers are on hand to help you plan your visit. (They provide tour times, costs, and telephone numbers, but do not make bookings.) You may want to spend a good hour or so here, more to see a video. It is open daily from 8am to 5pm.

You can also book tours and get information at **Kakadu Tours and Travel,** Shop 6, Tasman Plaza, Jabiru, NT 0886 (✆ **08/8979 2548;** www.kakadutours.com.au).

Before you arrive, you can find information on Kakadu, and book tours at the Tourism Top End information center in Darwin. You can also contact the rangers at the park directly (✆ **08/8938 1120**).

WHEN TO GO Kakadu has two distinct seasons: Wet and Dry. The Dry (May–Oct) is overwhelmingly the best time to go, with temperatures around 86°F (30°C) and sunny days. Many tours, hotels, and even campsites are booked a year in advance, so make sure you have reservations.

In the Wet season, November through April, floodwaters cover much of the park, some attractions are cut off, and the heat and humidity are extreme. Some tour companies do not operate during the Wet, and ranger talks, walks, and slide shows are not offered. The upside is that the crowds vanish, the brownish vegetation bursts into green, waterfalls swell from a trickle to a roar, and lightning storms are spectacular, especially in the hot "buildup" to the season in October and November. The landscape can change dramatically from one day to the next as floodwaters rise and fall, so be prepared for surprises—nice ones (such as giant flocks of geese) and unwelcome ones (such as blocked roads). Although it can pour down all day, it's more common for the rain to fall in late-afternoon storms and at night. Take it easy in the humidity, and don't even think about camping in this heat—stay in air-conditioned accommodations.

GETTING THERE Follow the Stuart Highway 34km (21 miles) south of Darwin, and turn left onto the Arnhem Highway to the park's northern entrance station. The trip takes 2½ to 3 hours. If you're coming from the south, turn off the Stuart Highway at Pine Creek onto the Kakadu Highway, and follow the Kakadu Highway for 79km (49 miles) to the park's southern entrance.

A big range of coach, minibus, and four-wheel-drive tours and camping safaris, usually lasting 1, 2, or 3 days, depart from Darwin daily. These are a good idea, because many of Kakadu's geological, ecological, and Aboriginal attractions come to life only with a guide. The best water holes, lookouts, and wildlife-viewing spots change dramatically from month to month, even from day to day.

TIPS ON GETTING AROUND Kakadu is a big place—about 200km (124 miles) long by 100km (62 miles) wide—so plan to spend at least a night. Day trips are available from Darwin, but it's too far and too big to see much in a day.

Most major attractions are accessible in a two-wheel-drive vehicle on sealed (paved) roads, but a four-wheel-drive vehicle allows you to get to more falls, water holes, and campsites. Car-rental companies will not permit you to take two-wheel-drive vehicles

Kakadu National Park

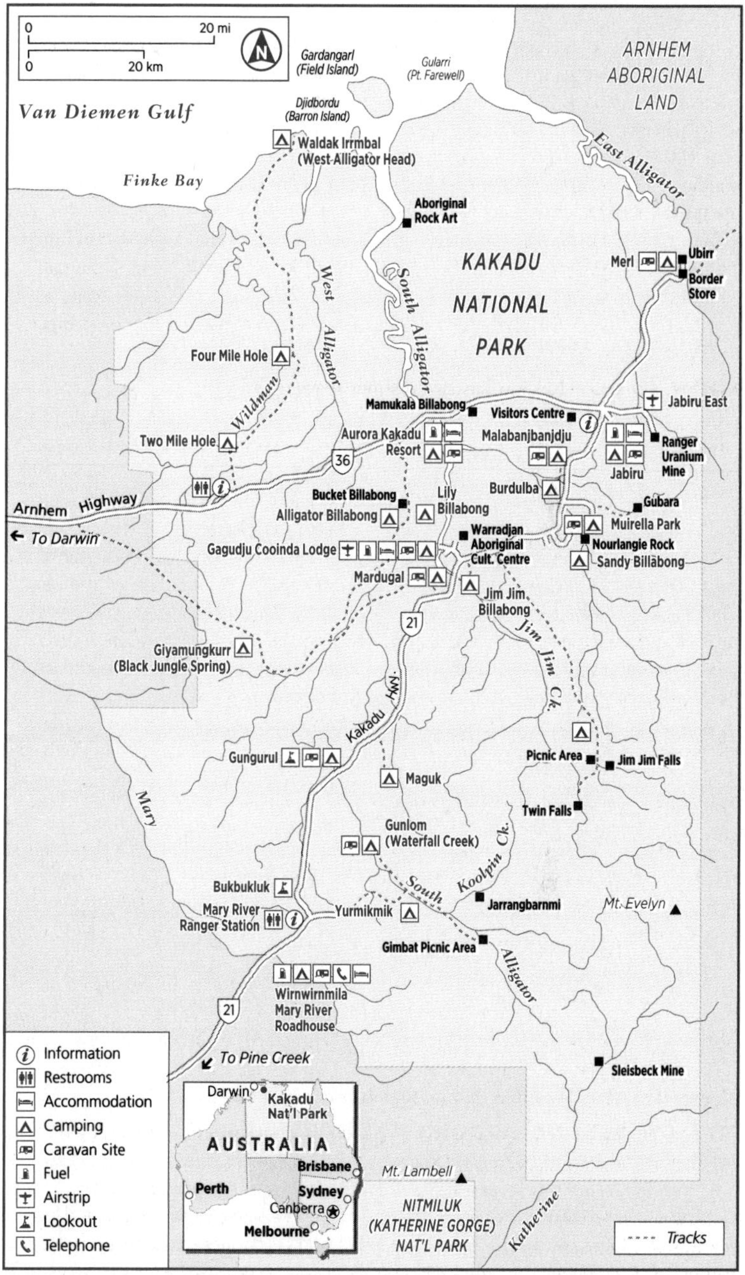
0
20 mi
0
20 km
N
Van Diemen Gulf
Finke Bay
Gardangarl
(Field Island)
Gularri
(Pt. Farewell)
Djidbordu
(Barron Island)
ARNHEM
ABORIGINAL
LAND
Waldak Irrmbal
(West Alligator Head)
Aboriginal
Rock Art
East Alligator
KAKADU
NATIONAL
PARK
Merl
Ubirr
Border
Store
West Alligator
South Alligator
Four Mile Hole
Wildman
Mamukala Billabong
Visitors Centre
Jabiru East
Two Mile Hole
Aurora Kakadu
Resort
Malabanjbanjdju
Ranger
Uranium
Mine
Jabiru
36
Arnhem Highway
Bucket Billabong
Lily
Billabong
Burdulba
Gubara
Alligator Billabong
Muirella Park
To Darwin
Warradjan
Aboriginal
Cult. Centre
Nourlangie Rock
Gagudju Cooinda Lodge
Sandy Billabong
Mardugal
Jim Jim
Billabong
21
Jim Jim Ck.
Giyamungkurr
(Black Jungle Spring)
Kakadu Hwy.
Gungurul
Picnic Area
Jim Jim Falls
Maguk
Mary
Twin Falls
Gunlom
(Waterfall Creek)
Koolpin Ck.
South
Bukbukluk
Jarrangbarnmi
Mary River
Ranger Station
Yurmikmik
Mt. Evelyn
Gimbat Picnic Area
Alligator
Wirnwirnmila
Mary River
Roadhouse
21
To Pine Creek
Sleisbeck Mine
Information
Restrooms
Accommodation
Camping
Caravan Site
Fuel
Airstrip
Lookout
Telephone
Darwin
Kakadu
Nat'l Park
AUSTRALIA
Brisbane
Perth
Sydney
Canberra
Melbourne
Mt. Lambell
NITMILUK
(KATHERINE GORGE)
NAT'L PARK
Katherine
Tracks

NEVER smile AT A YOU-KNOW-WHAT!

The Aboriginal Gagudju people of the Top End have long worshiped a giant crocodile called Ginga, but the way white Australians go on about these reptilian relics of a primeval age, you'd think they worshiped them, too. There is scarcely a soul in the Northern Territory who will not regale you with his or her personal croc story, and each one will be more outrageous than the last.

Aussies may be good at pulling your leg with tall tales, but when they warn you not to swim in crocodile country, they're deadly serious. After all, crocodiles are good at pulling your leg, too—literally. Here are some tips:

* There are two kinds of crocodile in Australia: the highly dangerous and enormously powerful saltwater or "estuarine" croc; and the "harmless" freshwater croc, which will attack only if threatened or accidentally stood on. Saltwater crocs can and do swim in the ocean, but they live in fresh water.
* Don't swim in *any* waterway, swimming hole, or waterfall unless you have been specifically told it is safe. Take advice only from someone such as a recognized tour operator or a park ranger. You can never be sure where crocodiles lurk from year to year, because during every Wet season crocs head upriver to breed, and they spread out over a wide flooded area. As the floodwaters subside, they are trapped in whatever water they happen to be in at the time—so what was a safe swimming hole last Dry season might not be croc-free this year.
* Never stand on or walk along a riverbank, and stand well back when fishing. A 6m (20-ft.) croc can be 2½ centimeters (1 in.) beneath the surface of that muddy water yet remain invisible. It moves fast, so you won't see it until you're in its jaws.
* Plant your campsite and clean your fish at least 25m (82 ft.) from the bank.

And if you do come face to face with a crocodile? There is little you can do. Just don't get into this situation in the first place!

on unpaved roads. **Thrifty** (© **1300/367 227** in Australia or 08/8979 2552) rents cars at the Gagudju Crocodile Holiday Inn, Flinders Street, Jabiru; otherwise, rent a car in Darwin. If you rent a four-wheel-drive in the Wet season (Nov–Apr), always check floodwater levels on all roads at the **Bowali Visitor Centre** (© **08/8938 1120**). The Bowali Visitor Centre, many attractions such as Nourlangie and Yellow Water Billabong, and the towns of Jabiru and Cooinda usually stay above the floodwaters year-round.

Facilities are limited. The only town of any size is **Jabiru** (pop. 1,500), a mining community where you can find banking facilities and a few shops. The only other real settlements are the park's four accommodations houses.

Highlights En Route to Kakadu

En route to the park, stop in at the **Fogg Dam Conservation Reserve** (© **08/8988 8009** is the ranger station), 25km (16 miles) down the Arnhem Highway and 7km (4⅓ miles) off the highway. You'll get a close-up look at geese, finches, ibis, brolgas, and other wetland birds from lookouts over ponds of giant lilies, or by walking through monsoon forests to viewing blinds. There are two lookouts on the road and three walks, two that are 2.2km (1.5 miles) round-trip and one that is 3.6km (2.3 miles) round-trip. Entry is free. Crocs live here, so don't swim, and keep away from the water's edge. To take a ranger-guided walk, reserve by calling ✆ **08/8999 4555.**

Four kilometers (2½ miles) down the Arnhem Highway at Beatrice Hill, you can stop at the **Window on the Wetlands Visitor Centre** (✆ **08/8988 8188**), which offers views across the Adelaide River flood plain, as well as displays and touch-screen information on the wetlands' ecology. It's free and open daily from 8am to 7pm.

Just past Beatrice Hill on the highway at the Adelaide River Bridge (look out for the statue of a grinning croc), **Adelaide River Queen Cruises** (✆ **1800/888 542** in Australia, or 08/8988 8144) runs the **jumping crocodiles cruise.** From the relative safety of a restored paddle steamer (or a smaller boat in the Wet), you can watch wild crocodiles leap out of the water for hunks of meat dangled over the edge by the boat crew—but don't lean out too far! It's an unabashed tourist trap, with a souvenir shop that sells all things croc, including crocodile toilet-seat covers. It may not be to my, or your, taste, but because crocs typically move fast only when they attack, it may be your only chance to witness their immense power and speed. The cruises depart at 9 and 11am and 1 and 3pm daily year-round (except on Dec 24–25 and Sundays from Nov–Feb). The cost is A$35 adults and A$20 for children 5 to 15 for all cruises. If you need transport, **Darwin Day Tours** (✆ **08/8924 1111**) and **Goanna Eco Tours** (✆ **1800/003 880** in Australia) both run tours from Darwin that include the cruise.

Top Park Attractions

WETLANDS CRUISES One of Kakadu's biggest attractions is **Yellow Water Billabong,** a lake 50km (31 miles) south of the Bowali Visitor Centre at Cooinda (pop. about 20). It's rich with freshwater mangroves, Paperbarks, pandanus palms, water lilies, and masses of birds gathering to drink—sea eagles, honking magpie geese, kites, china-blue kingfishers, and jaçanas (called "Jesus birds" because they seem to walk on water as they step across the lily pads). This is one of the best places in the park to spot saltwater crocs. Cruises in canopied boats with running commentary depart near Gagudju Lodge six times a day starting at 6:45am in the Dry (Apr–Oct) and four times a day starting at 8:30am in the Wet (Nov–Mar). A 90-minute cruise is A$56 for adults and A$41 for children 4 to 15. A 2-hour cruise (available in the Dry only) is A$93 for adults, A$69 for children. Book through **Gagudju Lodge Cooinda** (✆ **1800/500 401** in Australia or 08/8979 0145; www.gagudju-dreaming.com).

Fair warning: In the Wet, when the Billabong floods and joins up with Jim Jim Creek and the South Alligator River, the bird life spreads far and wide over the park and the crocs head upriver to breed, so don't expect wildlife viewing to be spectacular.

Another good cruise is the Aboriginal-owned and -operated **Guluyambi Cultural Cruise** on the East Alligator (✆ **1800/089 113** in Australia, or 08/8979 2411; www.guluyambi.com.au). The East Alligator River forms the border between Kakadu and isolated Arnhemland. Unlike the Yellow Water cruise, which focuses on crocs, birds, and plants, this excursion teaches you about Aboriginal myths, bush tucker, and hunting techniques. The cruise lasts about 1 hour and 45 minutes, starting at 9 and 11am and 1 and 3pm daily May through October (tours sometimes operate in the Wet too, so check the website or call for details). A free shuttle will take you from the Border Store, at Manbiyarra just before the river, to the boat ramp. It costs A$45 for adults and A$25 for children 4 to 14. It takes only 25 people.

ABORIGINAL ART & CULTURE There are as many as 5,000 art sites throughout the park, though for cultural reasons the Aboriginal owners make only a few accessible to visitors. Dating the rock art is controversial, but some paintings may be 50,000 years old. The best are **Nourlangie Rock** and **Ubirr Rock.** Nourlangie, 31km (19 miles) southeast of the Bowali Visitor Centre, features "X-ray"-style paintings of animals; a vivid, energetic striped Dreamtime figure of **Namarrgon ★**, the "Lightning Man"; and modern depictions of a white man in boots, a rifle, and a sailing ship. You'll also find rock paintings at **Nanguluwur,** on the other side of Nourlangie Rock, and a variety of excellent sites at Ubirr Rock, which is worth the 250m (820-ft.) climb for the additional sites higher up, and for views of the flood plain.

Ubirr Rock can be cut off in the Wet, but the views of afternoon lightning storms from the top at that time are breathtaking.

Unlike most sites in Kakadu, Ubirr is not open 24 hours—it opens at 8:30am April through November and at 2pm December through March, and closes at sunset year-round. There is a 1.5km (1-mile) signposted trail past Nourlangie's paintings (short trails to the art sites shoot off it), an easy 1.7km (1-mile) trail from the parking lot into Nanguluwur, and a 1km (.5-mile) circuit at Ubirr. Access to the sites is free (once you have your park permit, available from Tourism Top End or the Bowali Visitor Centre; see p. 435).

Displays and videos about bush tucker, Dreamtime creation myths, and lifestyles of the Bininj Aborigines can be found at the **Warradjan Aboriginal Cultural Centre ★** at Cooinda (**✆ 08/8979 0145**). This building was built in the shape of a pig-nose turtle at the direction of the Aboriginal owners. It has a quality gift shop selling such items as didgeridoos, bark paintings by local artists, and baskets woven from pandanus fronds. The center is open daily from 9am to 5pm, and admission is free. A 1km-long (.5-mile) trail connects it to Gagudju Lodge Cooinda and the Yellow Water Billabong.

If you are taking a tour to Arnhemland, check if it goes to **Injalak Arts and Crafts** (**✆ 08/8979 0190;** www.injalak.com) at Gunbalanya (Oenpelli). This small Aboriginal township, about 300km (186 miles) east of Darwin, draws its inspiration from Injalak Hill, a site rich in rock paintings. Since it opened in 1989, the center has gained a reputation for producing fine indigenous contemporary art, carvings, and weavings. This is the place to buy them at their source and to meet the artists, some of whom are likely to be working on the veranda when you visit. Injalak is a nonprofit, community enterprise, and you can be sure that all artists are paid in full, upfront for their work. Injalak is open weekdays from 8am to 5pm. From June to October, it may also be open on Saturdays from 8:30am to 2pm, but it is advisable to check first. It is only possible to drive in the Dry, May to November. Unless you have a 4WD, ensure you check road conditions before setting out. You will need to drive across a flooded causeway on the East Alligator River, so check tide times and seek advice from the **Northern Land Council** (**✆ 08/8920 5100** in Darwin, or 08/8938 3000 in Jabiru). You will also need to buy a permit (A$13 adults, children free) from the NLC. Between December and April, in the Wet, it is not possible to cross the East Alligator River at all and access is by air only. Permits are required whether driving or flying. The permit is to visit Injalak only. Once you cross the East Alligator River you may not stop

A Side Trip to a Tiwi Island

Separated from the northern mainland by a narrow strait are the Tiwi Islands, Bathurst and Melville. The Tiwi culture is distinct from that of the Aborigines, and one of the main reasons for visiting is to see their distinctive art style first-hand. Tiwi Tours (© 1300/721 365 in Australia, or 08/8923 6523; www.aussie adventure.com.au) takes small groups on day tours to Bathurst Island. (Melville Island is closed to the public.) The trip includes visits to two art centers, where you can watch artists at work and buy their paintings, carvings, silk-screen printing, and basketwork at "island prices"—usually up to a third cheaper than buying the same item in Darwin. You will learn the history of the islands, have tea with some Tiwi women and see them making baskets, and visit a mock burial site. The tour, which runs Monday to Friday (except public holidays) from March to November, costs A$465 adults and A$418 children aged 3 to 15, including the round-trip light-plane airfare from Darwin (which takes about 30 min.) and lunch.

anywhere until you arrive at Injalak. It may sound difficult, but if you are fascinated by Aboriginal art and culture you will find it very rewarding.

SCENIC FLIGHTS Scenic flights over the flood plains and the rainforest-filled ravines of the escarpment are worth taking if the strain is not too great on your wallet. They're much more interesting in the Wet than in the Dry, because the flood plains spread and Jim Jim Falls and Twin Falls swell from their Dry season trickle to a flood. Viewing it from the air is also the best way to appreciate the clever crocodile shape of the Gagudju Crocodile Holiday Inn. **North Australian Helicopters** (**© 1800/898 977** in Australia, or 08/8979 2444; www.northaustralianhelicopters.com.au) operates flights from Jabiru from A$190 per person, but to see Jim Jim and Twin Falls, you must take the flight costing A$450 per person. **Kakadu Air Services** (**© 1800/089 113** in Australia, or 08/8941 9611; www.kakaduair.com.au) runs 30-minute fixed-wing flights from Jabiru and Cooinda for A$130 adults and A$103 children, as well as heli-flights from A$195 per person for 20 minutes. **Airborne Solutions ★★** (**© 08/8972 2345,** or 0437/254 121 mobile; www.airborne solutions.com.au) runs a Kakadu helicopter day trip from Darwin for A$1,995 per person (minimum two people), in which you will cover nearly 700km (435 miles) and see places inaccessible to most people. The tour includes a stop at the Injalak Art Centre at Gunbalanya (Oenpelli) in Arnhemland (see above) and isolated rock painting sites. It's expensive, but worth every cent in my book!

FISHING, BUSHWALKING & SWIMMING

Gagudju Adventure Tours ★ (book through Gagudju Lodge Cooinda; **© 1800/500 401** in Australia or 08/8979 0145; www.gagudju-dreaming.com) runs an excellent small-group day trip for active people. You take a 4WD through savannah woodland to the edge of the Arnhemland escarpment; then bushwalk through the monsoon forest along the river gorge to the base of Jim Jim Falls. Another short 4WD trip, then a cruise with an Indigenous guide, and a walk along the gorge cliff-face brings you to the sandy beach at Twin Falls. Tours depart daily from Jabiru and Cooinda from May through November and cost A$168 adults and A$128 children

A Swim in the Falls

Remember the idyllic pool that Paul Hogan and Linda Koslowski plunged into in *Crocodile Dundee*? That was Gunlom Falls, 170km (105 miles) south of the Bowali Visitor Centre. A climb to the top rewards you with great views of southern Kakadu. It is generally regarded as croc-free and safe for swimming. Access is by four-wheel-drive; it is cut off in the Wet.

(no children under 4). Book in advance for July, the busiest month. A less predictable tour program runs during the Wet season; check the website for details.

Kakadu's wetlands are brimful of barramundi, and Territorians like nothing more than to hop in a tin dinghy barely big enough to resist a croc attack and go looking for them. **Kakadu Fishing Tours** (**✆ 08/8979 2025** or book through Gagudju Lodge Cooinda) takes you fishing in a 5.7m (19-ft.) sportfishing boat. Tours depart from Jabiru, 5km (3 miles) east of the Bowali Visitor Centre, and cost A$200 per person for 5½ hours and A$320 per person for a full day (10½ hours).

Wide-ranging **bush and wetlands walking trails,** including many short walks and six half- to full-day treks, lead throughout the park. Typical trails include a less than 1km (less than .5-mile) amble through the Manngarre Monsoon Forest near Ubirr Rock; an easy 3.8km (2.5-mile) circular walk at the Iligadjar Wetlands near the Bowali Visitor Centre; and a tough 12km (7.5-mile) round-trip trek through rugged sandstone country at Nourlangie Rock.

One of the best wetlands walks is at **Mamukala wetlands,** 29km (18 miles) from Jabiru. Thousands of magpie geese feed here, especially in the late Dry season around October. An observation platform gives you a good view, and a sign explains the dramatic seasonal changes the wetlands undergo. Choose from a 1km (.5-mile) or 3km (1.8-mile) round-trip meander. The Bowali Visitor Centre sells hiking-trail maps. There are also some challenging unmarked trails along creeks and gorges, for which you will need good navigational skills.

WHERE CAN I SWIM? In the eastern section of the park rises a massive red-sandstone escarpment that sets the stage for two waterfalls, **Jim Jim Falls** and **Twin Falls.** In the Dry, the volume of water may not be all that impressive, but the settings are magical. Both are accessible by four-wheel-drive only, and neither is open in the Wet. At Twin Falls, you must swim or float the last 500m (1,640 ft.) to the base of the falls—and be warned that saltwater crocodiles have been found in this area.

Some people swim at spots that are generally regarded as croc-free, such as Jim Jim Falls and water holes such as Gubara (it's a long walk, but it can be lovely in the Wet), Maguk, and Koolpin Gorge. However, you do so at your own risk. Although rangers survey the swimming holes at the start of the season, and crocodiles are territorial creatures that stick to one spot, no one can guarantee that a saltwater crocodile has not moved into a swimming hole.

A good indication that a hole is croc-free is the presence of other people swimming. Crocs tend to eat whatever's moving, so if people are swimming happily, the pool is almost certainly croc-free! Macabre it may be, but it's a tool many people use to gauge a pool's safety. Ask at the Bowali Visitor Centre which pools are croc-free that year (it can change from year to year) before setting off into the park. If you are unsure about a water hole's safety, the only place rangers recommend you swim is your hotel pool. Water hole depths change dramatically with the season. Check with the Bowali Visitor Centre for the swimming spots that are best at the time you visit.

A 1km (.5-mile) walk over rocks and through rainforest leads to a **deep green plunge pool** ★ at Jim Jim Falls, 103km (64 miles) from the Bowali Visitor Centre. An almost perfectly circular 150m (492-ft.) cliff surrounds the water. Allow 2 hours to drive the final unpaved 60km (37 miles) off the highway. Due to floodwaters, Jim Jim Falls may not open until as late as June. At Twin Falls, the waterfalls descend into a natural pool edged by a sandy beach, surrounded by bush and high cliffs.

Where to Stay & Dine

A campground near Jim Jim Falls and Twin Falls has sites for 200 people. **Garnamarr Campground** (named for the red-tailed black cockatoo commonly found in Kakadu) doesn't accept reservations, so check at the Bowali Visitor Centre (✆ **08/8938 1121**) before driving there, to see whether it is full. The campground manager collects the fee of A$10 per adult per night (cash only; free for children under 16). A gate at the campground controls access to Jim Jim and Twin Falls and is locked between 8:30pm and 6:30am. High season is usually from April 1 to late October or early November. For information on other campgrounds, check **www.environment.gov.au/parks/kakadu/visitor-activities/camping.html**.

Aurora Kakadu This property is near the northern entrance to the park. The downside is that it is the farthest accommodation from such major attractions as Yellow Waters and Nourlangie, although many tour operators pick up here. The upside is that the resort's green lawns and tropical gardens adorned with wandering peacocks and goannas and chattering native birds are a wonderfully restful haven from the harsh surroundings of Kakadu outside. Don't yield to the temptation to dive into the lily-filled lagoon down the back—like every other waterway in Kakadu, it is home to saltwater crocs! A 3.6km (2-mile) nature trail winds from the hotel through monsoon forest and past a billabong. All rooms have restful views from a balcony or patio. There are also 60 unpowered campsites.

Arnhem Hwy., South Alligator (41km/25 miles west of Bowali Visitor Centre), Kakadu National Park, NT 0886. ✆ **1800/818 845** in Australia, or 08/8979 0166. Fax 08/8979 0147. www.auroraresorts.com.au. 138 units. A$200–A$237 double. Extra person A$45. Free crib. Family rooms (sleep 4) double rate plus extra person rate. AE, DC, MC, V. Free parking. **Amenities:** Restaurant; cafe; bar; Jacuzzi; shaded outdoor pool; day/night tennis court. *In room:* A/C, TV.

Bamurru Plains ★★★ There can be few experiences to beat waking up to the sight of buffalo roaming the green, lush floodplains of Kakadu in the Wet. This stylish luxury lodge on the edge of the Mary River flood plains, between the coast and the western boundary of Kakadu National Park, offers a rich array of wildlife encounters and an eco-friendly environment in which to base yourself. Your luxury tent has a timber floor, fine linens on the bed, and a high-pressure shower in the bathroom but no phone, TV, or other distractions. On three sides, the walls are one-way screens which give stupendous views and total privacy. I have only visited in the Wet, but other guests were repeat visitors, determined to see both seasons . . . a sure indication their first visit—in the Dry—was memorable. Meals are served at the main lodge building around a communal table. Activities include guided walks, river cruises, fishing, four-wheel-drive safaris to view wildlife (*Bamurru* is the Aboriginal name for the magpie geese you will see in the thousands), and day trips to Kakadu and Arnhemland by light plane to see Aboriginal rock art. The best way to get to Bamurru Plains is by light plane, a 20-minute flight from Darwin. If you drive to this working buffalo station, you will have to leave your car at the gate, and a staff member will pick you up for the 20-minute drive to your accommodations. It is about a 3-hour drive from Darwin and 2½ hours from Jabiru.

Swim Creek Station, Harold Knowles Rd. (P.O. Box 1020), Humpty Doo, NT 0836. ✆ **1300/790 561** in Australia, or 02/9571 6399. www.bamurruplains.com. 9 units. A$1,860 double; A$470 children ages 8–15 sharing with adults; A$837 children ages 8–15 sharing a separate room. Extra adult A$699. Minimum 2-night stay. Rates include all meals, drinks, and activities and an A$10 levy donated to the Australian Wildlife Conservancy. AE, DC, MC, V. Closed Nov 1–Jan 31. No children 8 and under. **Amenities:** Restaurant; bar; swimming pool. *In room:* A/C (at a price: to discourage the use of generator power, Bamurru Plains has a A$100 surcharge for the use of the air-conditioning in the 3 guest rooms that have it; A/C must be requested when booking), no phone.

Gagudju Crocodile Holiday Inn ★ Some people think this hotel is kitsch; others declare it an architectural masterpiece. I like it. It was built to the specifications of its owners, the Gagudju Aborigines, in the form of their spirit ancestor, a giant crocodile called Ginga. The building's entrance is the "jaws," the two floors of rooms are in the "belly," the circular parking lot clusters are "eggs," and so on. From the ground, it's hard to see, but from the air, the shape is quite distinct. Love it or hate it, it is the most luxurious place to stay in Kakadu, a stylish modern hotel with basic but comfortable rooms. Guests can use the town's 9-hole golf course, tennis courts, and Olympic-size swimming pool a few blocks away. The lobby doubles as an art gallery selling the works of local Aborigines, and a trail leads to the Bowali Visitor Centre.

1 Flinders St. (5km/3 miles east of Bowali Visitor Centre), Jabiru, NT 0886. ✆ **1800/007 697** in Australia, 800/465-4329 in the U.S. and Canada, 0800/405060 in the U.K., 1800/553 155 in Ireland, 0800/322 222 in New Zealand, or 08/8979 9000. Fax 08/8979 9098. www.holidayinn.com.au. 110 units. A$170–A$275 double. Discounts often available in the Wet. Children 19 and under stay free in parent's room with existing bedding. Free crib. AE, DC, MC, V. **Amenities:** Restaurant; 2 bars; babysitting; concierge; free access to nearby gymnasium; Internet ($2 for 15 min.); small outdoor pool; room service. *In room:* A/C, TV w/free movies, hair dryer, Internet (at standard phone charges for dial-up).

Gagudju Lodge Cooinda These modest but pleasant accommodations are set among tropical gardens at the departure point for Yellow Water Billabong cruises. The simply furnished tile-floor bungalows are big and comfortable, and there are four family rooms that sleep up to four. Budget rooms are twin or triple share (four have double beds) in an air-conditioned corrugated iron demountable, or portable cabin, with shared bathrooms. The lodge is something of a town center, with a general store, gift shop, currency exchange, post office, fuel, and other facilities. Eat at the rustic and ultracasual **Barra Bistro and Bar,** which serves an all-day snack menu, with live entertainment in the Dry season. Dining options can be limited between November and March in the Wet. Scenic flights take off from the lodge's airstrip, and the Warradjan Aboriginal Cultural Centre is a 15-minute walk.

Kakadu Hwy. (50km/31 miles south of Bowali Visitor Centre), Jim Jim, NT 0886. ✆ **1800/500 401** in Australia, or 08/8979 0145. Fax 08/8979 0148. www.gagudjulodgecooinda.com.au. 48 bungalows, all with shower only; 24 budget rooms, none with bathroom; 80 powered and 300 unpowered campsites. Lodge A$169–A$400 double. Budget rooms A$70–A$85 double; A$35 per person for twin or triple share. Campsites A$35–A$50 powered sites; A$15–A$27 unpowered sites. Children 13 and under stay free in campsites. Bungalow and budget room discounts often available in Wet season. AE, DC, MC, V. **Amenities:** Restaurant; babysitting; small outdoor pool. *In room (lodge only):* A/C, TV, hair dryer (on request).

KATHERINE

314km (195 miles) S of Darwin; 512km (317 miles) E of Kununurra; 1,177km (730 miles) N of Alice Springs

The key draw to the farming town of Katherine (pop. 11,000) is Katherine (Nitmiluk) Gorge. It's small by the standards of, say, the Grand Canyon, but its dramatic sheer ochre walls dropping to a blue-green river make it an unexpected delight in the middle of the dry Arnhemland plateau that stretches to the horizon.

The gorge and its surrounding river ecosystem run through the 292,008-hectare (721,260-acre) **Nitmiluk National Park.** In the Dry, the gorge is a haven not just for cruisers but for canoeists, who must dodge the odd "friendly" freshwater crocodiles as they paddle between the walls. In the Wet, the gorge can become a torrent, and jet boating is sometimes the only way to tackle it. Hikers will find trails any time of year throughout the park. Farther afield are hot springs, water holes, uncrowded rivers to canoe, and Aboriginal communities where visitors can make dot paintings and find bush tucker.

Essentials

GETTING THERE **Greyhound Australia** (✆ **1300/473 946** in Australia) buses stop in Katherine on their Darwin–Alice Springs routes. From Darwin, it's about a 4-hour trip costing A$84. From Alice, with departures once a day, it's about a 16-hour journey, for which the fare is A$281. Greyhound also runs to Katherine daily from Broome via Kununurra, a journey of about 22½ hours costing A$307.

Visitors to Katherine can hop aboard the ***Ghan*** (see "Getting There & Getting Around," in chapter 3) in Adelaide or Alice Springs and hop off in Katherine. The train leaves Adelaide on Sundays and Wednesdays at 12:20pm and Alice Springs on Mondays and Thursdays at 6pm. The trip from Alice takes about 15 hours. One-way fares are A$358 for a "day-nighter" seat or A$656 to A$1,019 for a sleeper from Alice. Contact **Great Southern Railways** (✆ **13 21 47** in Australia; www.trainways.com.au) for details on connections from Sydney and Melbourne.

At press time, there were currently no airlines operating flights into Katherine.

Katherine is on the Stuart Highway, which links Darwin and Alice Springs. From Alice Springs, allow a good 2 days to make the drive. The Victoria Highway links Katherine with Kununurra to the west. There is no direct route from the east; from, say, Cairns, you need to go via Townsville, Mount Isa, and Tennant Creek, a long, dull journey.

VISITOR INFORMATION The **Katherine Visitor Information Centre,** Lindsay Street at Katherine Terrace, Katherine, NT 0850 (✆ **1800/653 142** or 08/8972 2650; www.visitkatherine.com.au), has information on things to see—not only all around Katherine, but as far afield as Kakadu National Park and the Kimberley. It's open daily from 8:30am to 5pm in the Dry season (Mar–Oct); in the Wet (Nov–Feb) it's open Monday through Friday from 8:30am to 5pm and on weekends and public holidays 10am to 2pm. Closed Christmas Day and Good Friday.

The **Nitmiluk Visitor Centre,** on the Gorge Road, 32km (20 miles) from town (✆ **08/8972 1886**), dispenses information on the Nitmiluk National Park and sells tickets for gorge cruises, which depart outside. The center has maps; displays on the park's plant life, birds, geology, and Aboriginal history; a gift shop; and a cafe. It's open daily from 7am to 6pm, sometimes closing a little earlier in the Wet. Entry to the park is free.

GETTING AROUND **Hertz** (✆ **08/8971 1111**) and **Thrifty** (✆ **1800/626 515**) have outlets in Katherine.

Nitmiluk Tours (✆ **1300/146 743** in Australia or 08/8971 0877; www.nitmiluktours.com.au) makes transfers from Katherine hotels to the cruise, canoe, and helicopter departure points at the Nitmiluk Visitor Centre every day at 8am, 12:15pm, and 4pm. Return services leave the gorge at 9am, 1pm, and 5:15pm. Round-trip fares are A$24 for adults and A$12 for children.

Most Katherine activities and attractions can be booked through **Travel North** (✆ **1800/089 103** in Australia, or 08/8971 9999; www.travelnorth.com.au) or Nitmuluk Tours (see above). Both companies run a wide range of tours and activities, including horseback cattle musters, visits to an old homestead, half-day trips to Mataranka Thermal Pools (see below), and tours of up to 5 days taking in Katherine, Darwin, Litchfield and Kakadu national parks and outlying Aboriginal communities.

For personalized tours off the beaten path and around town, contact **Far Out Adventures** ★ (✆ **0427/152 288** mobile), described below.

Exploring Katherine Gorge (Nitmiluk National Park)

Cruising the gorge in an **open-sided boat** is the most popular way to appreciate its beauty. Katherine Gorge is actually a series of 13 gorges, but most cruises ply only the first two, because the second gorge is the most photogenic.

Nitmiluk Tours (✆ **1300/146 743** in Australia or 08/8971 0877; www.nitmiluktours.com.au) operates all cruises. Most people take a 2-hour cultural cruise, available four times a day at 9 and 11am and 1 and 3pm. The cost is A$58 for adults and A$35 for children 5 to 15. There is also a 4-hour cruise at least once daily, although you will probably be satisfied with 2 hours. They also run breakfast and lunch cruises. Wear sturdy shoes; because each gorge is cut off from the next by rapids, all the cruises involve some walking along the bank.

Cruising is nice, but in a **canoe** ★ you can discover sandy banks and waterfalls and get up close to the gorge walls, the birds, and those crocs. (Don't worry—they're the freshwater kind and not typically regarded as dangerous to humans.) Rocks separate the gorges, so be prepared to carry your canoe quite often. You may even want to camp out on the banks overnight. A half-day canoe rental is A$44 for a single and A$66 double, with a A$20 cash deposit. Canoeing the gorge is popular, so book canoes ahead, especially in the Dry season. Canoe hire doesn't operate from December to March.

Guided paddles are a good idea, because you will learn and see more. The most knowledgeable company is **Gecko Canoeing** ★ (✆ **1800/634 319** in Australia, or 08/8972 2224; www.geckocanoeing.com.au), whose tours are known for their ecotourism content. Gecko's guides have Australia's elite Savannah Guide status. They offer 3- to 6-day canoeing-camping safaris on the Katherine River. The 3-day trip costs A$750 per person and leaves on Wednesdays and Sundays. The company also runs canoeing and camping safaris (with any other activities you like, such as mountain biking, rock climbing, wildlife photography, hiking, or fishing) of up to 10 days in little-explored wildernesses and river systems across the Top End. Tours run between April and November, with departures on request, and can be tailored to your needs.

Some 100km (62 miles) of **hiking trails** crisscross Nitmiluk National Park, ranging in duration from 1 hour to the lookout to 5 days to Leliyn (Edith Falls; see below). Trails—through rocky terrain and forests, past water holes, and along the gorge—depart the Nitmiluk National Park ranger station, in the Nitmiluk Visitor Centre, where you can pick up trail maps. Overnight walks require a deposit of A$20 to A$50 per person, and a A$3.30 per-person camping permit, payable at the Nitmiluk Visitor Centre.

One of the nicest spots in the park is 42km (26 miles) north of Katherine, 20km (13 miles) off the Stuart Highway: **Leliyn** (also known as Edith Falls) ★ is an Eden of natural (croc-free) swimming holes bordered by red cliffs, monsoonal forest, and pandanus palms. Among the bushwalks leading from Edith Falls is a 2.6km (1.5-mile) round-trip trail, which takes about 2 hours and incorporates a dip at the upper pool en route.

More than the gorge itself, the aerial views of the ravine-ridden Arnhem Plateau, which stretches uninhabited to the horizon, are arresting. **North Australian Helicopters** (✆ **1800/621 717** in Australia, or 08/8972 1666) offers daily flights over the gorges, starting at A$220 per person for 35 minutes. To see all 13 gorges will cost you A$280 per person and takes 45 minutes. **Airborne Solutions** (✆ **08/8972 2345** or 0437/254 121 mobile phone; www.airbornesolutions.com.au) has a helipad near the Nitmiluk Gorge Visitor Centre and runs a range of scenic flights, starting from A$75 per person for an 8-minute flight over the first three gorges.

Aboriginal Culture Tours, Hot Springs & More

On a 1-day visit to the **Manyallaluk Aboriginal community** ★, a 90-minute drive southeast from Katherine, you chat with Aborigines about how they balance traditional ways with modern living; take a short bushwalk to look for native medicines and bush tucker such as green ants; and try lighting a fire with two sticks, weaving baskets, throwing spears, painting on bark, and playing a didgeridoo. You can buy locally made Aboriginal art and artifacts at better prices than you may find elsewhere. Lunch is a barbecue featuring kangaroo tail cooked on hot coals. Don't expect this to be some kind of Aboriginal theme park; it's an unstructured experience (this is the community's home), and taking part, rather than just watching, will make it a better one.

A 1-day tour costs A$165 for adults and A$90 for children 5 to 15, A$60 per adult extra if you need transfers from Katherine. The last 35km (22 miles) of road is unsealed (unpaved), and rental cars will be insured only if they are four-wheel-drive. The tour runs Monday through Saturday from April to November, but hours may be reduced, or the place may close, in the Wet. The Manyallaluk community also has a basic camping ground with powered and unpowered sites if you want to stay longer. The cost is A$12 for adults and A$6 for children 5 to 15. Bookings are essential no matter what the time of year, because sometimes the community may be closed for cultural reasons. You can book through Nitmiluk Tours (see "Getting Around," p. 43).

Mike Keighley of **Far Out Adventures** ★ (✆ **0427/152 288;** www.farout.com.au) runs upmarket tailor-made tours that include Manyallaluk and areas around Katherine. Meet children of the Mangarrayi Aborigines, sample bush tucker, learn a little bush medicine, and swim in a vine-clad natural "spa-pool" in the Roper River. Mike has been accepted as an honorary family member of the Mangarrayi people and is a mine of information about Aboriginal culture and the bush.

About 110km (68 miles) south of Katherine, you can soak your aches away at the **Mataranka Thermal Pools.** The man-made pools are fed by 93°F (34°C) spring water, which bubbles up from the earth at a rate of 16,495 liters (4,124 gal.) per minute! It's a little paradise, surrounded by palms, pandanus, and a colony of flying foxes. The pools are open 24 hours and admission is free. They are 7km (4⅓ miles) along Homestead Road, off the Stuart Highway 1.5km (1 mile) south of Mataranka township. They make a welcome stop on the long drive from Alice Springs.

If you can't be bothered to drive to Mataranka, you can soak in the pleasantly warm **Katherine Hot Springs,** under shady trees 3km (2 miles) from town on Riverbank Drive. Entry is free.

At the **School of the Air,** Giles Street (✆ **08/8972 1833**), you can sit in on an 800,000-sq.-km (312,000-sq.-mile) "classroom" as children from the Outback do their lessons by radio. Forty-five-minute tours begin on the hour at 9, 10, and 11am from mid-March to mid-November. Tours also run during school holidays and public holidays, minus the on-air classes. Admission is A$5 for adults and A$2 for school-age kids.

Where to Stay

The ranger station in the Nitmiluk Visitor Centre has maps of available "bush campsites" throughout the park. These are very basic sites—no showers, no soaps or shampoos allowed (they pollute the river system), and simple pit toilets or none at all. Most are beside natural swimming holes. You must buy a camping permit at the ranger station; the fee is A$3.30 per person per night.

There are caravan and camping sites at **Springvale Homestead** (✆ **08/8972 1355** or book through Travel North), 7km (4⅓ miles) from Katherine township on the banks of the Katherine River. Sites are in a shady park, and there's a licensed bistro and kiosk, swimming pool, and children's water slide. Wallabies roam freely. Fees are A$10 per adult, A$6 per child for a tent site, and A$27 double for a powered site (A$10 for each extra person).

Knotts Crossing Resort At this low-key resort, you have a choice of huge, well-furnished motel rooms, some with kitchenettes, minibars, and in-room dataports and fax machines; cabins with a kitchenette inside and a private bathroom just outside the door (but no phone); or caravan sites, all located amid the tropical landscaping. The "village" rooms are a good budget choice, built in 1998 and smartly furnished with a double bed and bunks, a kitchenette, and a joint veranda facing a small private pool with a barbecue. Locals meet at the casual bar beside the pool, and **Katie's Bistro** is one of the smartest places to eat in town.

Corner of Giles and Cameron sts., Katherine, NT 0850. ✆ **1800/222 511** in Australia, or 08/8972 2511. Fax 08/8972 2628. www.knottscrossing.com.au. 123 units, some with shower only, 75 powered caravan sites. A$98 double cabin; A$20 double "village" room; A$145 double motel room; A$155 deluxe rooms; A$175 family rooms; A$185 executive rooms. Powered site A$35 per night single or double. AE, DC, MC, V. **Amenities:** Restaurant; bar; free airport transfers; Jacuzzi; 2 outdoor pools (1 large, 1 small); room service. *In room:* A/C, TV w/pay movies, kitchenette (except motel rooms), minibar (executive rooms only).

11

PERTH & WESTERN AUSTRALIA

by Ron Crittall

Western Australia (WA or "The West") is huge; it's bigger than the Congo and more than three and a half times the size of Texas. It's also largely empty, with only 2.2 million people in its 2.5 million sq. km (1 million sq. mi.)—almost 75% (1.6 million) of whom live in Perth. And Perth is the most remote large city on earth—with Adelaide 2,700km (1,700 miles) away to the east.

One advantage is that if you want a glorious golden beach to yourself, a spectacular gorge, or a carpet of wildflowers, then you've got a great chance here. Solitude, peace, and far horizons are freely available.

WA has reverted to "Boom State" status with gigantic projects underway to develop or expand the extraction of iron ore, natural gas, nickel, aluminum, and gold across the Outback and offshore. One downside is that the hospitality industry can't compete with the wages being offered, so you may find hotels and restaurants short-staffed.

WA may be enormous, but there are several jewels to entice and entertain. It's worth the trip for great wine regions, some of Australia's best snorkeling and diving, historic towns, magnificent if scattered natural scenery, untouched wilderness, and a chance to really go "Outback." Every spring (Aug–Oct), wildflowers carpet the land.

The capital, **Perth ★★**, one of the world's most livable cities, has a fabulous outdoor lifestyle with parks, rivers and beaches, great walking and biking trails, excellent food, and a beautiful historic port, **Fremantle ★★**.

The **Southwest ★★★** corner of the state, below Perth, is the prettiest part. Vineyards and pastures sit between stands of hardwood forest, the surf is world-class, and there are sparkling limestone caverns. The Margaret River region has some of Australia's most acclaimed wines, and many top-notch eateries. The nearby **South Coast ★★** has some of the tallest trees on earth, superb coastal scenery, more vineyards, and WA's oldest town, Albany, sitting beside a wonderful natural harbor.

Head east 596km (372 miles) inland from Perth and you strike what, in the 1890s, was the richest square mile of gold-bearing earth the world has seen. The mining town of **Kalgoorlie ★** is a repository of ornate 19th-century architecture, and still Australia's biggest gold producer. If Australia has an answer to the Wild West, Kalgoorlie is it.

Going north from Perth you reach the Outback. Red sand, scrubby trees, and spinifex grass are all you'll see for hundreds of miles. About 855km (534 miles) north of Perth, **wild dolphins ★★** make daily visits to the shores of Monkey Mia. Even farther north is Exmouth, entry point to one of Australia's best-kept secrets, the 300km (187-mile) fringing **Ningaloo ★★** coral reef, where you can swim with enormous whale sharks.

The rugged northern portion of Western Australia is known as **The Kimberley ★★★**. It's Australia's last frontier, a vast area of cattle ranches, Aboriginal settlements, and the exotic coastal town of Broome. This is a rugged rocky region of red cliffs, strange bulbous boab trees, waterfalls, and billabongs. You can experience real remoteness, visit a cattle station (ranch), see ancient Aboriginal rock art, ride a camel on the beach, and shop for the world's biggest South Sea pearls.

Exploring the State

VISITOR INFORMATION **Tourism Western Australia** is the official source of information on the state. Its website, **www.westernaustralia.com**, provides a good overview, and you may find the **Australian Tourist Commission**'s website (www.australia.com) useful, or the web pages of local tourism boards (see "Visitor Information" in each regional section of this chapter). A private company, **Visit WA** (www.visitwa.com.au), offers an online tour-planning service.

Also contact the **Western Australian Visitor Centre** in Perth, which dispenses information about the state and makes bookings. See p. 457 for information. The **Department of Environment & Conservation** website (www.dec.wa.gov.au) has information on the numerous national and marine parks.

WHEN TO GO Perth, South Australia, and the southwest are blessed with long, dry summers and mild, wet winters. You'll want some warm gear in winter, but temperatures rarely hit freezing point. In the north, summer is seriously hot; temperatures soar to between 104°F and 120°F (40°C–49°C). The cooler months of May through September (for the Kimberley) or April through October (for the Outback Coast) are the times to go north.

GETTING AROUND Before you plan a driving tour of this state, consider the distances and the mostly flat monotonous countryside. The forests, coastal scenery, and vineyards of the South and Southwest make for pleasant driving; otherwise you should fly, especially if time is a factor.

If you do hit the road, remember that gas stations and emergency help are often far apart. (Keep the gas tank full!) Road trains (convoys up to 53m/174 ft. long) and wildlife pose more of a threat than in any other state. Try to avoid driving at night, dusk, and dawn—all prime animal-hopping and feeding times. Read "Road Conditions & Safety," in "Getting There & Getting Around," in chapter 3, before setting off.

The **Royal Automobile Club of Western Australia,** 832 Wellington St., Perth, WA 6000 (✆ **13 17 03;** www.rac.com.au), is a good source of maps and motoring advice. For a recorded road-condition report, call **Main Roads Western Australia** (✆ **1800/013 314** in Australia).

Western Australia

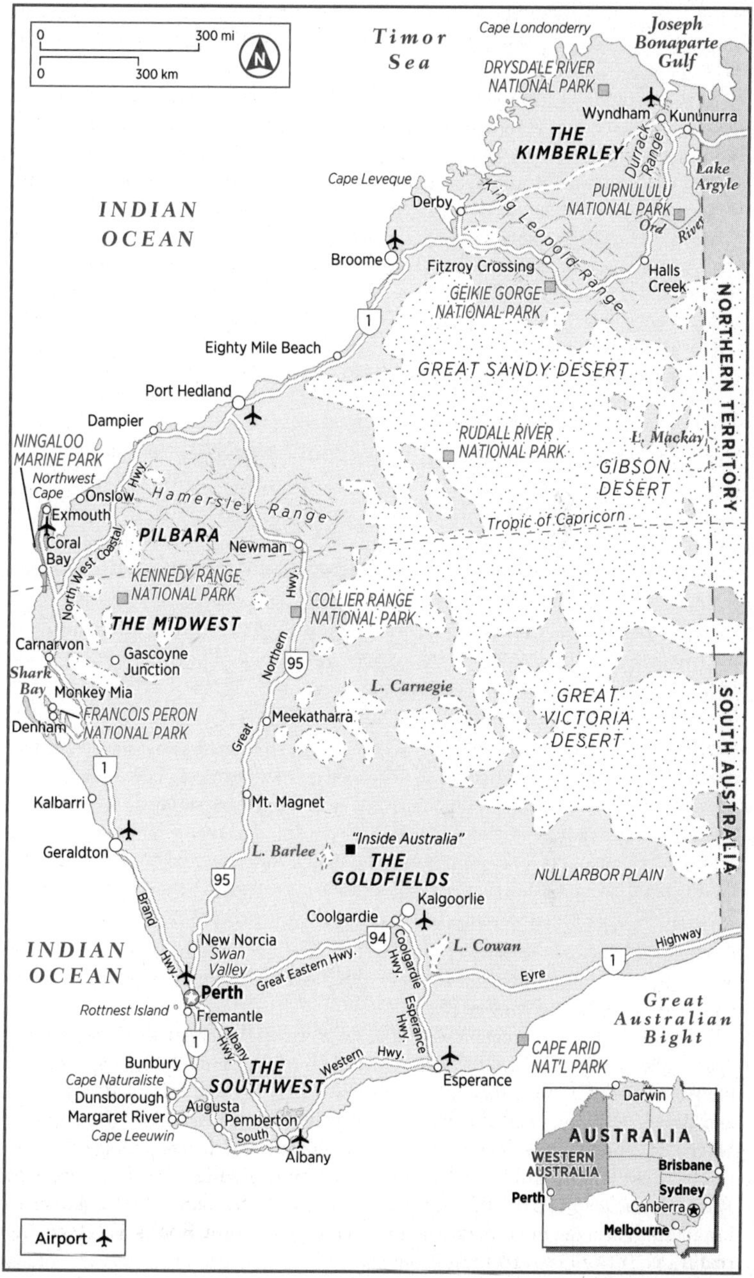

TIPTOEING THROUGH THE wildflowers

Every year from August to mid-November, the southern half of Western Australia is blessed with a magnificent range of **wildflowers** ★★. The drier, more northerly areas produce great carpets of white, yellow, pink, and red daisy-like everlastings, while the southern reaches have an incredible variety of individual flowering plants.

Wildflower shows and festivals in country towns throughout the state accompany the annual blossoming, and coach- and rail-tour companies carry enthusiasts from all around the globe on wildflower tours. You can check out the wildflowers on day trips from Perth or on longer jaunts of up to 5 days or so.

If time is short, you can go to Perth's **Kings Park & Botanic Garden** ★★★ (p. 472), which has a month-long Wildflower Festival every September.

The display of everlastings is not constant, but varies from year to year depending on winter rains. The Western Australian Visitor Centre (see "Visitor Information," below) can keep you up to speed on whatever spot is blooming brightest that week, and the staff can book you on one of the wildflower tours. Tourism WA produces a 40-page **Wildflower Holiday Guide** brochure that describes self-drive wildflower routes, accommodations and events en route, and wildflower tour operators. Download it from the dedicated wildflower website, **www.wildflowerswa.com**.

Interstate buses and trains, and the few local accommodations fill up fast in wildflower season, so book ahead.

Skywest (✆ **1300/660 088** in Australia; www.skywest.com.au) is the state's major regional airline. **Qantas** (✆ **13 13 13** in Australia; www.qantas.com.au) also provides service from Perth to some smaller centers.

One of the great train journeys of the world provides a passenger service from the eastern states. The ***Indian Pacific*** ★ runs once or twice weekly on a continent-covering 66-hour trip from Sydney via Adelaide and Kalgoorlie to Perth (see "Getting There & Getting Around," in chapter 3). **Greyhound Australia** (✆ **13 14 99** in Australia) has one interstate coach service, from Darwin through Broome to Perth.

Inside the state, passenger trains run only in the southwest. They are managed by the **Public Transport Authority (PTA),** which operates as **Transwa** (✆ **1300/662 205** in WA; www.transwa.wa.gov.au) in the country areas of Western Australia (from Perth to Bunbury, 2½ hr. south of Perth; to Northam, an hour or so east in the Avon Valley; and to Kalgoorlie). Transwa also runs coach services throughout the southwest of WA, north to Kalbarri, Geraldton, and Meekatharra; to the wine and forest regions of Margaret River, Augusta, and Pemberton; south to Albany; and southeast to Esperance. The railways in the northern part of WA are there only to cart vast tonnages of iron ore, not passengers.

All major car- and motor-home-rental companies have offices in Perth.

TOUR OPERATORS Western Australia's biggest coach tour company, **Australian Pinnacle Tours** (✆ **1300/551 687** in Australia, or 08/9417 5555; www.pinnacletours.com.au) serves Perth, the Southwest, Monkey Mia, the Northwest Cape, the Kimberley, and attractions about a day's drive away, such as New Norcia and the Pinnacles (see the box "Dragon's Teeth in the Dunes" below). Australian

Dragon's Teeth in the Dunes

The Pinnacles ★★, a 3-hour drive north of Perth, attract thousands of visitors each year. Masses of limestone pillars, from a few inches to over 3m (10 ft.) high, simply rise up out of golden sand dunes. Some are just a small fragile tracery, some are tall, solid mushroom-headed giants, while some of the sharp jagged versions could well be taken for fossilized dragon's teeth. From a distance, the Pinnacles can look like the remnants of a deserted city, and they are best seen around dawn or dusk. See "Tour Operators" above for details on two companies that visit here. A faster driving route to the Pinnacles, using the completed Indian Ocean Drive, will be available mid-2011.

Pinnacle Tours also does four-wheel-drive tours. **Western Xposure** (**✆ 1800/621 200** in Australia; www.westernxposure.com.au) specializes in soft adventure and promotes its tours as "eco-based," covering much of the state. **Global Gypsies** (**✆ 08/9341 6727;** www.globalgypsies.com.au) runs four-wheel-drive tag-along safaris into the Outback, including the Kimberley. The tours are fully escorted and catered, and there is limited passenger seating for nondrivers (three seats per tour). Global Gypsies can help with the hire of four-wheel-drive vehicles and all equipment.

Aerial tours make sense in Western Australia. Look into the personalized or set tours offered by **Kookaburra Air** (**✆ 08/9417 2258;** www.kookaburra.iinet.net.au). Tours from Perth can take you throughout Western Australia, including Ningaloo and Margaret River, as well as to the Red Centre.

If you're looking for background information on indigenous (Aboriginal) issues and more particularly indigenous tours, check the website for the **WA Indigenous Tourism Operators Collective** (www.waitoc.com).

PERTH ★★

4,405km (2,731 miles) W of Sydney; 2,389km (1,481 miles) S of Broome

Perth is probably the most outdoorsy of all Aussie cities. The climate, Perth's brilliant setting along the Swan River and the Indian Ocean, and the abundance of parkland mean that it's almost obligatory to get outside and enjoy the sun and fresh air. One of Perth's great advantages is that virtually the entire river and seafront is public land; everyone can stroll, cycle, or picnic along the waterfront—and they do.

Perth has a wonderful Mediterranean climate that gives it more hours of sun than any other major city in Australia, from October right through to April. This sunshine capital is also home to a thousand mining and exploration companies, which bring a casual, but can-do, Outback feel to the city.

All these elements give Perth a youthful, energetic vibrancy. It's friendly too, partly because of the outdoor openness and partly from the Outback influence. Perth is on the cusp of major change—with significant developments and much intense discussion about how best to plan for the future—as it struggles with the transition from what has really been a big country town into an international city.

There's much to do and see, though the city center tends to be rather dead once the shops close. Wander through the restored historic warehouses, museums, and working docks of bustling **Fremantle ★★**; stroll through the 400-hectare (1,000-acre) Kings Park in the middle of the city; visit art galleries and museums; eat at some of the country's best restaurants; enjoy the riverside parks and gardens; catch a few waves at one of the beaches; stock up at the Aboriginal art and souvenir stores; and pedal your bike around **Rottnest Island ★★**, a small reef resort 19km (12 miles) offshore, to find a great snorkeling spot.

More than most other Aussie capitals, Perth gives you good choices of side trips: Drop in on the Benedictine monks in the Spanish Renaissance monastery town of **New Norcia ★**, nip out to the **Swan Valley ★** vineyards, or spend a few days in **Margaret River ★★★** country, one of Australia's top wine regions.

Perth's climate is fabulous for almost the entire year. Most visitors focus on the brilliant summer months of December through March, with lots of sun, sea, and sand, though the sea breeze can get (annoyingly) strong. The winter months of June to August can be cold and rainy but still average 6 hours of sun a day, while the in-between times of April to May and September to November are often superb with mild, fine, still days.

Orientation

ARRIVING **By Plane** **Qantas,** or its subsidiary **Qantaslink** (✆ **13 13 13** in Australia; www.qantas.com.au), flies at least once a day from all mainland capitals as well as Broome, Kalgoorlie, and Alice Springs. It also services several mining towns in Western Australia. **Virgin Blue** (✆ **13 67 89** in Australia; www.virginblue.com.au) flies direct from Sydney, Melbourne, Adelaide, Brisbane, Darwin, and Broome, with connections from other cities. **Jetstar** (✆ **13 15 38** in Australia; www.jetstar.com) has daily flights from Sydney, Melbourne, Cairns, and Adelaide, with connections from other eastern states cities. **Skywest** (✆ **1300/660 088** in WA; www.skywest.com.au) connects Perth to all significant towns in WA, and to Darwin and Melbourne (weekly). **Tiger Airways** (✆ **03/9335 3033** in Australia; www.tigerairways.com) has daily flights from Melbourne, with connections to other mainland cities.

Perth Airport is 12km (7½ miles) northeast of the city. Be aware that the domestic terminal tends to be overcrowded, and delays and long waits for taxis are common. Luggage trolley hire is an expensive exercise, costing A$4 (have coins with you) curbside at the domestic and international terminals and in the domestic arrivals area. They are free for international arrivals, and there are usually some available in either car park (if you can find them). Allow a minimum of 20 minutes to transfer between the international and domestic terminals. Both terminals have ATMs, showers, baby-changing rooms, a mailbox (newsdealers sell stamps), and limited tourist information. Internet kiosks and currency-exchange bureaus are in the international and Qantas domestic terminals. The international terminal has cellphones for rent. At the international terminal, look out for volunteer Customer Service Officers called "Gold Coats," who can provide assistance and information; domestic terminals have WOWs (West Oz Welcomers) wearing Akubra hats.

Avis (✆ 08/9277 1177 domestic terminal, 08/9477 1302 international terminal), **Budget** (✆ 08/9277 9277), **Europcar** (✆ 08/9237 4325 domestic, 08/9237 6870 international), **Hertz** (✆ 08/9479 4788), and **Thrifty** (✆ 08/9277 1854) have desks at both terminals.

The **Perth Airport CONNECT** shuttle (✆ **1300/666 806** in Australia, www.perthairportconnect.com.au) aims to meet all flights within 30 to 45 minutes of

Perth

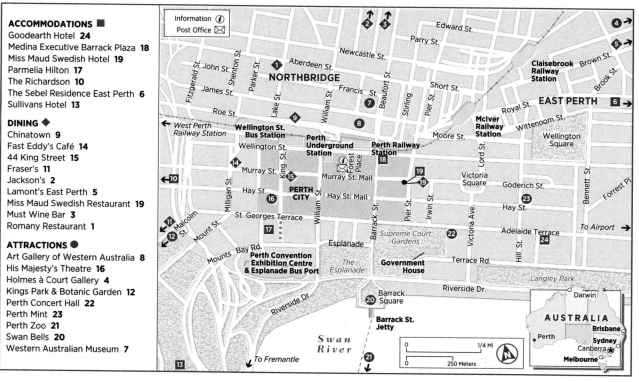

ACCOMMODATIONS ■
Goodearth Hotel **24**
Medina Executive Barrack Plaza **18**
Miss Maud Swedish Hotel **19**
Parmelia Hilton **17**
The Richardson **10**
The Sebel Residence East Perth **6**
Sullivans Hotel **13**

DINING ◆
Chinatown **9**
Fast Eddy's Café **14**
44 King Street **15**
Fraser's **11**
Jackson's **2**
Lamont's East Perth **5**
Miss Maud Swedish Restaurant **19**
Must Wine Bar **3**
Romany Restaurant **1**

ATTRACTIONS ●
Art Gallery of Western Australia **8**
His Majesty's Theatre **16**
Holmes à Court Gallery **4**
Kings Park & Botanic Garden **12**
Perth Concert Hall **22**
Perth Mint **23**
Perth Zoo **21**
Swan Bells **20**
Western Australian Museum **7**

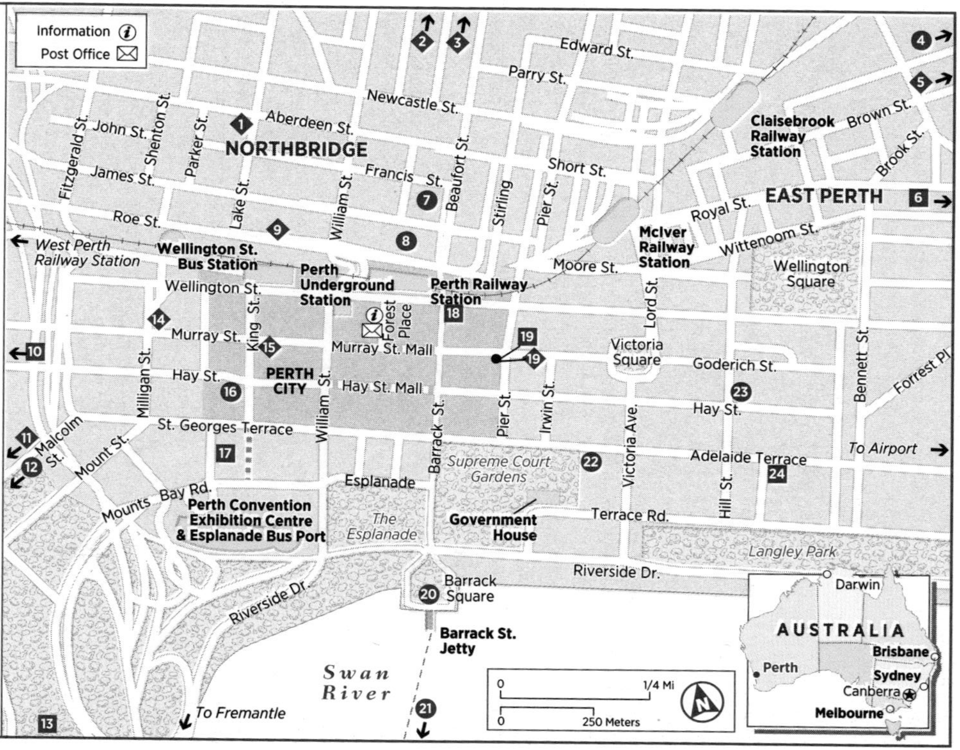

Customs clearance, or luggage collection for domestic flights. The shuttle services hotels, motels, and hostels in the city and Northbridge. There is no need to book. Prices are on a sliding scale depending on numbers in a group. Transfers to/from the international terminal cost A$18 one-way and A$30 return for one passenger, and up to A$48 one-way and A$89 return for four passengers, or A$35 for families; from the domestic terminal, they cost from A$15 one-way and A$25 return for one passenger, up to A$36 one-way and A$67 return for four passengers, and A$28 for families. Transfers can also be booked to or from the northern suburbs, Fremantle and Mandurah.

The **Fremantle Airport Shuttle** (**© 08/9457 7150;** www.fremantleairport shuttle.com.au) transfers from and to both airport terminals to anywhere in Fremantle and nearby suburbs. Bookings, especially to the airport, are essential. The fare is A$25 for one passenger, A$35 for two passengers, A$50 for three, A$55 for four, and A$45 for families, for transfers between 6am and 8pm; hand luggage is free, otherwise luggage is A$2.50 per item.

CONNECT also operates a transfer service between the domestic and international terminals, for bona fide passengers only, from 3am to 2am daily. Qantas/One World interflight passengers are given transfer vouchers, otherwise it costs A$8 per passenger; taxis between the terminals are about A$24.

Public **bus** no. 37 runs to the city from the domestic terminal, but no buses run from the international terminal. A **taxi** to the city is about A$40 from the international terminal and A$32 from the domestic terminal, including a A$2 fee for picking up a taxi at the airport.

BY TRAIN The 3-day journey to Perth from Sydney via Broken Hill, Adelaide, and Kalgoorlie aboard the ***Indian Pacific*** ★, operated by Great Southern Rail (**© 13 21 47** in Australia; www.gsr.com.au), is a great experience. It has the world's longest straight stretch of rail (over 483km/300 miles) along the Nullarbor Plain. The train runs twice a week (Sept 1–Dec 6 and Jan 5–March 31, otherwise once a week) in each direction, and can carry your vehicle. The one-way fare ranges from A$3,450 in the spacious Platinum Service (only certain times of year) to A$2,008 in Gold Service with meals and an en-suite bathroom to A$1,362 in comfy but cramped (if you're large or tall) Red Sleeper Service (meals cost extra, and bathrooms are shared), down to A$716 for sit-up-all-the-way Daynighter Seats (for the young budget traveler). Rail passes are available. There are connections from Melbourne on the ***Overland*** train, and to Alice Springs and Darwin from Adelaide with the ***Ghan.*** See "Getting There & Getting Around," in chapter 3, for contact details in Australia and abroad. The ***Prospector*** train makes the 6¾-hour trip to and from Kalgoorlie daily; call the **Public Transport Authority** (**© 1300/662 205** in Western Australia; www.transwa.wa.gov.au).

All long-distance trains pull into the East Perth Terminal, Summers Street off Lord Street, East Perth. A taxi to the city center costs about A$18.

BY BUS **Greyhound Australia** (**© 13 14 99** in Australia) has no service from the eastern states; there's only a 5-days-a-week service from Darwin via Broome (about 62 hr.), and the full fare is about A$718. The Western Explorer Pass gives greater flexibility; it is valid for 183 days and costs A$849.

BY CAR There are only two interstate routes—the 4,310km (2,694-mile) route from Darwin via Broome in the north, and the 2,708km (1,679-mile) odyssey from Adelaide, which has some of the world's straightest and most featureless roads on the trek across the Nullarbor Plain. Arm yourself with up-to-date details on sightseeing (including whale-watching and the Nullarbor Golf Links) and the limited accommodations before setting off. The South Australian or Western Australian state auto clubs (listed under "Getting There & Getting Around," in chapter 3) can provide advice and information. Both routes are pretty boring, with very few towns along the way, but they certainly bring home just how big and empty much of Australia is.

VISITOR INFORMATION The **Western Australian Visitor Centre,** Albert Facey House, Forrest Place, Perth (✆ **1800/812 808** in Australia; www.wavisitor centre.com), in the city center, is the official visitor information source for Perth and the state. It's open Monday through Thursday from 8:30am to 6pm (to 5:30pm May–Aug), Friday from 8:30am to 7pm (to 6pm in winter), Saturday from 9:30am to 4:30pm, and Sunday from 11am to 4:30pm year-round. The City of Perth's **i-City Information Kiosk,** in the Murray Street Mall, near Forrest Place, is open Monday to Thursday and Saturday 9:30am to 4:30pm, Friday 9:30am to 8pm, and Sunday 11am to 3:30pm (closed public holidays).

Volunteers provide free 90-minute guided tours around the city from the Kiosk, Monday to Friday at 11am and 2pm, Saturday at 11am, and Sunday at 2pm. The morning and Sunday sessions are general city orientation tours, while the other afternoon tours are more heritage-oriented. There's no need to book. You can do the walking tours yourself, using the comprehensive guides available at the Kiosk.

For an untouristy lowdown on the city's restaurants, cultural life, shops, bars, nightlife, concerts, and the like, buy the excellent glossy quarterly magazine ***Scoop*** (www.scoop.com.au; A$11.95), available at bigger newsdealer stands.

CITY LAYOUT The city center is 19km (12 miles) upriver from the Indian Ocean, on the north bank of a broad reach of the Swan River. Four long avenues run east–west between riverside parkland and the railway reserve. **St. Georges Terrace** (it becomes Adelaide Terrace at Victoria Ave.), known colloquially as "The Terrace," is the main thoroughfare and commercial and banking address, while **Hay Street** and **Murray Street** are the major retail avenues with pedestrian malls in the central blocks. All three, plus Wellington Street (which has Perth's suburban railway station on its northern side), are linked by the main north–south streets of Barrack and William, plus several shop-lined arcades.

MAPS Of the many free pocket guides to Perth available at tour desks and in hotel lobbies, ***Your Guide to Perth & Fremantle*** has the best street map. It shows one-way streets, public toilets and telephones, taxi stands, post offices, police stations, and street numbers, as well as most attractions and hotels. The **Royal Automobile Club of Western Australia** (see "Exploring the State," earlier in this chapter) is a good source of maps of the state, as is **Mapworld,** 900 Hay St. (✆ **08/9322 5733**). You will find tourist maps at the Western Australian Visitor Centre and the Perth Tourist Lounge (see "Visitor Information," above). Google Transit (www.google.com/transit) is available in Perth and can help you plan your trip using public transportation in the metro area.

Neighborhoods in Brief

City Center The central business district (CBD) is home to offices, shops, and department stores. It has a modest collection of 19th-century heritage buildings, especially the convict-built Government House and Town Hall. A good introduction to Perth's charms is to take in the views from the pathway that skirts the river along Riverside Drive. Within walking distance is **Kings Park & Botanic Garden ★★**.

Northbridge Most of Perth's nightclubs, and a good many of its cool restaurants, bars, and cafes, are in this 5-block precinct north of the railway line. It's within easy walking distance of the city center, or take the free Blue CAT buses. The Cultural Centre is here too, with the Western Australian Museum, Art Gallery of Western Australia, State Library, new State Theatre Centre (scheduled to open late 2010), and Perth Institute of Contemporary Arts.

Subiaco This well-heeled inner suburb is on the other side of Kings Park. Take a stroll through "Subi's" villagelike concoction of restaurants, cafes, markets, boutiques, antique shops, pubs, and galleries. Most of the action is near the intersection of Hay Street and Rokeby (pronounced *Rock*-er-bee) Road, with the Subiaco Hotel and Art Deco Regal Theatre on opposing corners. Take the train to Subiaco station.

Fremantle Not only is "Freo" a working port, it's also Perth's second city heart, and a favorite weekend spot to eat, drink, shop, and sail. A 1980s restoration of Victorian warehouses and hotels turned Freo into a marvelous example of a 19th-century seaport, although a takeover of many buildings by Notre Dame University has taken away some of the old vibrancy. Take the train 19km (12 miles) to Fremantle, at the mouth of the Swan River.

Scarborough Beach This is one of Perth's prize beaches, 12km (7½ miles) northwest of the city center. The district is a little tatty, with an oversupply of cheap takeout-food outlets, but if you like sun, sand, and surf, this is the place to be. You will find bars, restaurants, and surf-gear rental stores here. Allow 20 to 30 minutes to get here by car, 50 minutes by public transport.

Cottesloe Beach This is another great beach, quieter, safer, and less frenetic than Scarborough, with a protective rocky groyne (jetty) to one side. The surrounding area is very pleasant with grassy slopes, good hotels, and cafes, and the entire suburb is defined by towering Norfolk pines. Allow 20 minutes to get here by car, 30 minutes by bus or train.

Burswood/East Perth These two areas are on opposite sides of the Swan River just upstream of Perth city. Both are on land reclaimed from earlier industrial use, and show enlightened development with parkland, pathways, and artworks. Burswood has major entertainment complexes, a public golf course, and superb gardens. East Perth is mostly modern housing, parks, galleries, and restaurants, based around a river inlet with walkways.

Getting Around

BY PUBLIC TRANSPORTATION **Transperth** (www.transperth.wa.gov.au) runs Perth's buses, trains, and ferries. For route, bus stop, and timetable information, call ✆ **13 62 13** in Western Australia, or drop into the Transperth InfoCentres at the Perth Train Station, the Wellington Street Bus Station, or the Perth Esplanade Busport on Mounts Bay Road. You can transfer between bus, ferry, and train services for up to 2 hours (Zones 1–4) or 3 hours (Zones 5–9). Travel costs A$2.40 in one zone (to Subiaco, for instance), and A$3.60 in two, which gets you most places, including Fremantle, with discounts for kids ages 5 to 14.

Take a Free Ride

A welcome freebie in Perth is the availability of free public transport within the city center and some nearby areas. It's a great facility. There are the free CAT (Central Area Transit) buses (see below for details), and there is the Free Transit Zone (FTZ). You can travel free on all buses within this zone any hour, day or night. For free train travel in the FTZ, a SmartRider (see above) must be used, but it's not practical for most visitors. The FTZ allows free travel to Kings Park, Northbridge, east to major sporting grounds, and anywhere within the city center. Signs mark the FTZ boundaries; just ask the driver if you're unsure.

SmartRider is an electronic ticketing system, which can save up to 25% off the cash fare, but it involves a basic A$10 cost plus a minimum A$10 travel component, so it's of doubtful value to most tourists unless you plan to stay several days. Check the website or an InfoCentre for more information. To use SmartRider, you need to validate in the machines on the bus, train platform, or ferry wharf by tagging on and off as you travel.

A **DayRider** ticket can be purchased to allow 1 day of unlimited travel after 9am on weekdays and all day on weekends and public holidays for A$8.80. A **Family-Rider** pass is valid for unlimited all-day travel to any destination and back, for a group of up to seven people, including two full fares, but only on weekends and public holidays, or from 9am during school holidays, also for A$8.80.

BY BUS The Wellington Street Bus Station (close to Perth Train Station) and the Perth Esplanade Busport on Mounts Bay Road are the two main arrival and departure points. The vast majority of buses travel along St. Georges Terrace. You must hail the bus to ensure that it stops. Buy tickets from the driver. Buses run from about 5:30am until about 10:30 or 11:30pm, depending on the route.

The best way to get around town is on the free **CAT buses** ★ that run a continual loop of the city and Northbridge. The Red CAT runs east-west every 5 minutes, Monday through Friday from 6:50am to 6:20pm, and every 25 minutes from 10am to 6:15pm weekends. The Blue CAT runs north-south, between Northbridge and Barrack Street Jetty every 7 minutes from 6:50am. The last Blue CAT service is at 6:20pm Monday through Thursday, but on Friday it then runs every 15 minutes from 6:20pm until 1am Saturday. Saturday it runs from 8:30am to 1am the next day every 15 minutes, and Sunday every 15 minutes from 10am to 6:20pm. The Yellow CAT runs between East Perth and West Perth every 10 minutes from 6:50am to 6:20pm weekdays, and every 30 minutes 10am to 6:10pm weekends. There are no CAT services on public holidays. Look for the silver CAT bus stops with the black cat on them. Transperth InfoCentres (see above) dispense free route maps. For beach services, check the website.

Perth Tram Co. tours (see "Whale-Watching Cruises, Tram Trips & Other Tours," later in this chapter) are a good way to get around, too.

BY TRAIN Trains are fast, clean, and safe. They start at about 5:30am and run every 15 minutes or more often during the day, and every half-hour at night until midnight. All trains depart from Perth Station or the adjacent Perth Underground

Bring Your Bike, Too!

You are allowed, even encouraged, to take your bicycle on Perth's suburban trains and ferries—free. The limitations are to avoid the Monday to Friday peak services—toward the city between 7 and 9am, and away from the city between 4 and 6:30pm—and to not have your bike at Perth Station during these times.

Station. Buy your ticket before you board, at the vending machines on the platform. There are five lines: north to Clarkson (called the Joondalup Line); northeast to Midland; southeast to Armadale; southwest to Fremantle; and south to the resort town of Mandurah.

BY FERRY You will use ferries to visit South Perth and Perth Zoo. They run every half-hour or so, more often in peak hours, every day from 6:50am weekdays and 7:50am weekends and public holidays, until 7:36pm (or until 9:30pm Fri–Sat in summer, Sept–Apr) from the Barrack Street Jetty to Mends Street in South Perth. Buy tickets before you board from the vending machine on the wharf. The trip takes approximately 7 minutes.

BY TAXI Perth's two biggest taxi companies are **Swan Taxis** (✆ **13 13 30**) and **Black & White Taxis** (✆ **13 10 08**). Ranks (stands) are at Perth Railway Station and at the Barrack Street end of Hay Street Mall.

BY CAR Perth's signposting is reasonably good for helping drivers find their way around. The major car-rental companies are **Avis** (✆ 08/9325 7677), **Budget** (✆ 08/9480 3111), **Europcar** (✆ 08/9226 0026), **Hertz** (✆ 08/9321 7777), and **Thrifty** (✆ 08/9225 4466). All except Hertz also have outlets in Fremantle.

[FastFACTS] PERTH

American Express The foreign exchange office at 645 Hay St. Mall (✆ **1300/139 060**) is open Monday through Friday 9am to 5pm and Saturday 9am to noon.

Business Hours Banks are open Monday through Thursday from 9:30am to 4pm and until 5pm Friday, though some branches open Saturday mornings. Standard suburban shopping hours are 8am to 6pm Monday through Friday (until 9pm on Thurs), and from 8am to 5pm on Saturday. The so-called tourism precincts (including the CBD, Northbridge, Fremantle, and Subiaco) have extended trading until 9pm Monday to Friday and 5pm Saturday and Sunday. Note that not all stores open from 6pm onward.

Currency Exchange Go to the American Express office (see above) or **Interforex,** Shop 24, London Court, off Hay Street Mall (✆ **08/9325 7418;** Mon–Fri 8am–7pm, Sat 9am–5pm, Sun 11am–5pm). Interforex has a Fremantle bureau at the corner of William and Adelaide streets (✆ **08/9431 7022;** Mon–Sat 9am–6pm, Sun 10am–3pm).

Dentists **LifeCare Dental** (✆ **08/9221 2777,** or 0411/960 492 after-hours) is on the Upper Walkway Level, Forrest Chase shopping complex, 419 Wellington St., opposite Perth Railway Station. Open daily 8am to 8pm.

Doctors **Central City Medical Centre** is on the Perth Railway Station concourse, 378 Wellington St. (✆ **08/9221 4747**). Open daily 8am to 6pm.

Embassies & Consulates The **United States Consulate-General** is at 16 St. Georges Terrace (✆ **08/9202 1224**). The **Canadian Consulate** is at 267 St. Georges Terrace (✆ **08/9322 7930**). The **British Consular Agency** is at Level 26, 77 St. Georges Terrace (✆ **08/9224 4700**).

Emergencies Dial ✆ **000** for fire, ambulance, or police for emergencies only. This is a free call; no coins are needed from a public phone.

Hospitals **Royal Perth Hospital,** in the city center, has a public emergency/casualty ward (✆ **08/9224 2244**). Enter from Victoria Square, which is off the eastern end of Murray Street.

Luggage Storage & Lockers The **Perth YHA Backpackers Hostel,** 300 Wellington St. (✆ **08/9287 3333**) stores luggage, and there are baggage lockers at both international and domestic terminals at the airport.

Pharmacies **Forrest Chase Pharmacy** (✆ **08/9221 1691**), on the upper level of the Forrest Chase shopping center, 425 Wellington St. (near the dentist's office listed above), is open Monday through Thursday 8am to 7pm (until 9pm Fri), Saturday 8:30am to 6pm, and Sunday 10am to 6pm. Most pharmacies will make local deliveries—try either Friendlies or Amcal Chemist branches, listed in the telephone directory.

Police Dial ✆ **000** in a life-threatening emergency. Otherwise call ✆ **13 14 44** to be connected to the nearest station. **Perth Police Station,** 60 Beaufort St. (✆ **08/9223 3715**), and **Fremantle Police Station,** 45 Henderson St. (✆ **08/9430 1222**), are open 24 hours.

Safety Perth is safe, but steer clear of the back streets of Northbridge and the city center malls late at night—where groups of teenagers tend to congregate—even if you are not alone.

Time Zone Western Australian time (WS) is Greenwich Mean Time plus 8 hours. Standard time is 2 hours behind Sydney and Melbourne, but 3 hours behind from October to March. Call ✆ **1194** for the exact local time.

Weather Call ✆ **1196** for a recorded local weather forecast, or check **www.bom.gov.au/weather/wa/forecasts/perth.shtml**.

Where to Stay

The city center has loads of hotels, but occupancy levels tend to be high. Friday through Sunday nights, when the business travelers go home, can be quiet, so ask about lower rates on weekends. You may strike a deal on a week night if business is slow. Many hotels throw breakfast or some other feature into weekend packages. Most hotels have rooms for travelers with disabilities. If you can't find a hotel that suits you, there are several B&Bs to choose from in and near the city; check **www.babs.com.au/02_wa/perth.htm** for details.

IN OR NEAR THE CITY CENTER

Very Expensive

The Richardson ★★★ This is style. Opened in late 2006, this quiet, contemporary, elegant, and discreet five-star hotel is tucked away in leafy West Perth, within easy reach of the city center. It is only 2 blocks from Kings Park. There's 24-hour room service, a day spa offering the ESPA range of treatments and products, security-card access, and original artwork throughout. The business center includes meeting rooms and serviced offices. The entire first floor is dedicated to the spa, a good-size gym, and a pool and outdoor area. You can choose your own pillow type, and dine in style at the **Opus Restaurant.** The standard rooms are all spacious and classified (and priced) by size. It received an award for "Favorite Overseas Hotel Spa" in 2009 from *Condé Nast Traveller* magazine.

32 Richardson St., West Perth, WA 6005. ✆ **08/9217 8888.** Fax 08/9214 3931 www.therichardson.com.au. 74 units, including 18 suites, some with shower only. A$450–A$550 standard rooms; A$695 2-bedroom rooms; A$615–A$745 suites; A$850–A$2,500 penthouse suites. Room only prices. Extra person (where possible) A$50. Children 11 and under stay free in parent's room using existing bedding. Ask about packages. AE, DC, MC, V. Valet parking A$25. Bus: Red CAT Stop 23 nearby. **Amenities:** Restaurant; bar; concierge; gym and sauna; indoor heated pool; 24-hr. room service; day spa. *In room:* A/C, TV/DVD w/free movies, fridge, hair dryer, high-speed Internet access (free 2 hr. per day), minibar, MP3 docking station (in suites).

Expensive

Medina Executive Barrack Plaza ★ ☺ This is a modern apartment hotel with contemporary styling in central Perth, within easy walking distance of the pedestrian malls, railway station, Cultural Centre, and Northbridge eateries. It opened in July 2006 and appeals to the corporate market but is also geared toward families. Most units are one-bedroom apartments of a good size, especially the living area. There are studio rooms and two-bedroom apartments, with an option to link these for secure family use. All units have small balconies, with the north-facing units best in the cooler months, getting the most sun. Apartments have full kitchen facilities, while studios have kitchenettes with microwave but no stove or washing machine. You'll get much better rates if you book online, so head for the website if this is your choice. Rates tend to be higher October to March, with a quiet period mid-December to mid-January (not New Year).

138 Barrack St. (btw. Murray and Wellington sts.), Perth, WA 6000. ✆ **1300/633 462** Medina in Australia, or 08/9267 0000. Fax 08/9267 0199. www.medina.com.au. 99 units. A$255–A$335 studio; A$245–A$360 1-bedroom apt; A$350–A$510 2-bedroom apt. Extra person/rollaway A$50, crib A$5. AE, DC, MC, V. Parking A$25. Train: Perth. Bus: All Cats nearby. **Amenities:** Cafe next door with room service and charge-back available; small gym and sauna; 12m (39-ft.) lap pool. *In room:* A/C, TV w/pay movies, CD, hair dryer, Internet (A$13 per hr., A$25 per day), kitchenette (in studios), kitchen (in apts).

Parmelia Hilton Hotel ★★ Perth's first five-star hotel and still one of the best. If you want a city-center hotel with style, this is it. It's only a few steps to the Perth Convention Centre, with the Swan River foreshore not far away. The elegant marble foyer has a brass plaque commemorating the SS *Parmelia,* which brought 150 of the first settlers to these shores. The hotel has subtly striped wallpaper throughout, the spacious standard rooms and deluxe rooms are decorated in cool relaxing shades, while the suites boast separate living, working, and dining areas. In 2009, it won an award as having WA's Best Environmental Initiative for a hotel. Soft furnishings have been replaced since the last refurbishment in 1999. There is key-card elevator access. The **Globe Restaurant** has one of Perth's most innovative menus, and hosts regular fashion and winemaker events.

14 Mill St. (just off St. Georges Terrace), Perth, WA 6000. ✆ **1300/445 866** Hilton in Australia, or 08/9215 2000. Fax 08/9215 2001. www.hilton.com. 284 units. A$210–A$375 double; A$450–A$605 suite. Ask about packages and specials, especially on weekends. AE, DC, MC, V. Valet parking A$39 per 24 hr. Bus: Blue CAT Stop 1 (St. Georges Terrace). **Amenities:** 2 restaurants, 3 bars; babysitting service; concierge; gym; outdoor pool; room service. *In room:* A/C, LCD TV w/pay movies, hair dryer, minibar, Wi-Fi.

The Sebel Residence East Perth ★★ This 7-year-old hotel is in a great location in East Perth, a contemporary redevelopment area just minutes from the city. It's quiet and has good views across Claisebrook Cove, lined with artwork and upmarket housing. Galleries, restaurants, parks, and riverside walkways are a few steps away. A barbecue area and 25m (82-ft.) lap pool overlook the Cove. There is no restaurant, but the corner cafe will deliver breakfast, and it and other local restaurants, including **Lamont's** (p. 467) and a wine shop, offer charge-back facilities to the hotel. Each one-bedroom apartment has a full kitchen with microwave, washer and dryer, and balcony. Studios have kitchenette and shower only. You can combine a studio and a one-bedroom apartment to make a private two-bedroom apartment. The best rooms overlook Claisebrook Cove and involve a premium. Internet access is also available in the lobby, and the staff is friendly and helpful. The prices may have significant seasonal variations. A soft refurbishment program is scheduled for mid-2010.

60 Royal St. (at Plain St.), East Perth, WA 6004. ✆ **1800/010 559.** Mirvac in Australia, or 08/9223 2500. Fax 08/9223 2590. www.mirvachotels.com. 57 units. Prices start from A$235–A$325 city-view studio; others available on application. AE, DC, MC, V. Covered parking A$20 per day. Train: Claisebrook. Bus: Yellow CAT stops 5 and 32. **Amenities:** Small, well-equipped gym; heated outdoor lap pool. *In room:* A/C, TV/DVD w/in-house movies, fridge, hair dryer, kitchenette.

Moderate

Goodearth Hotel Just a 5-minute walk from the CBD is this low-key but comfortable three-and-a-half-star apartment-style hotel. It won the state award the last 3 years for standard accommodations. A casual restaurant offers breakfasts and dinners, while the lobby shop has meals available (prepared daily). Reception operates 24/7. Ask for rooms on the top three floors, which have balconies and views. All have queen beds or two singles. A soft refurbishment is confirmed for 2010.

195 Adelaide Terrace Perth, WA 6004. ✆ **08/9492 7777.** Fax 08/9221 1956. www.goodearthhotel.com.au. 181 units, most with shower only. A$130–A$145 studio; A$150–A$165 executive apt; A$165–A$180 1-bedroom apt; A$190–A$210 2-bedroom apt. AE, DC, MC, V. Limited on-site parking. Bus: stop right outside, in Free Transit Zone. **Amenities:** Restaurant; bar; Internet kiosk; day spa. *In room:* A/C, TV w/free movies, hair dryer, kitchenette, Wi-Fi (A$20 per day).

Miss Maud Swedish Hotel ★ This hotel offers a fresh European *pension*-style presence in the heart of the city, 1 block from the Murray Street Mall. It's a 1911 building so it's a bit of a rabbit warren. The entire place has been refurbished over recent years, but still retains its Swedish ambience, and it has a comfortable "feel." Miss Maud is real: Maud Edmiston started the hotel and restaurant 35 years ago. Many staff have been with her for years, and there's a loyal customer base. Single women find it a safe and comfortable place to stay. Sixty percent of visitors are corporate, and there's a strong European market. There are six single rooms. Two principal aims are to provide sleeping comfort and a good breakfast, so large beds are provided, and there's a fabulous buffet next door at **Miss Maud Swedish Restaurant** (p. 467). All windows are double-glazed to eliminate traffic noise.

97 Murray St. (at Pier St.), Perth, WA 6000. ✆ **1800/998 022** in Australia, or 08/9325 3900. Fax 08/9221 3225. www.missmaud.com.au. 52 units, 35 with shower only. From A$179 double; from A$159 single. Rates include smorgasbord breakfast. Treat for Two package includes smorgasbord dinner from A$23. AE, DC, MC, V. Public parking 1 block away. Bus: Red CAT Stop 1 (Pier St.); Blue CAT Stop 5 (Murray St. Mall E.). **Amenities:** Restaurant, takeout pastry shop; babysitting; discounted access to nearby health club; Internet cafe (A$2 for 15 min.); room service. *In room:* A/C, flatscreen TV/VCR w/free cable, hair dryer, minibar, Wi-Fi.

Sullivans Hotel ★ ☺ This small, intimate, family-owned hotel about 1.5km (1 mile) from town is immediately below Kings Park and close to the Swan River. It's popular with British and other Europeans for its small-scale ambience and friendly service. The rooms are simply furnished, not glamorous but roomy. Larger Deluxe rooms come with balconies and views over parkland and the freeway to the river. There is one two-bedroom apartment with kitchenette. Out back is a pleasant little pool with sun deck. Use of bikes is free, the restaurant is affordable, and free Wi-Fi is available. The city, Swan River, and Kings Park are just a stroll away.

166 Mounts Bay Rd., Perth, WA 6000. ✆ **08/9321 8022.** Fax 08/9481 6762. www.sullivans.com.au. 71 units, 69 with shower only, 5 family rooms. A$155–A$175 standard double; A$175–A$195 Deluxe double; A$170 1-bedroom apt; A$210 2-bedroom apt. Winter package (pay for 3 days, stay 4) available. B&B and weekly rates available. AE, DC, MC, V. Free parking. Bus: Blue Cat by front door, otherwise hotel is within Free Transit Zone. **Amenities:** Restaurant/bar; free bikes; free Internet access; small outdoor pool. *In room:* A/C, TV w/free movies, hair dryer.

IN BURSWOOD

InterContinental Burswood Hotel ★★★ It's the location of this hotel that first grabs your attention: The distinctively tiered building is set within parkland right next to the Swan River, overlooking the city. Then you walk into the full-height, glass-ceiling atrium, all set about with high-flying triangular sails. Glass-sided elevators ascend one wall. The foyer and public facilities have all been upgraded since 2003, with ongoing guest-room refurbishment. The hotel is part of an entertainment complex that includes Perth's only casino, a large theater, and another hotel (Holiday Inn Perth Burswood), with a public 18-hole golf course nearby; the entire complex won a major 2008 award for water savings. The surrounding parks and gardens include lakes and fountains, free barbecue facilities, a heritage walk, an outdoor summer cinema, a tourist helipad, and a children's playground. Being outside the city center, the clientele is a mix of tourists and corporate travelers. The real stars are the spacious suites with large balconies facing straight downriver; otherwise, ask for river-view rooms. The fitness center is staffed from 6am to 9pm.

Great Eastern Hwy. (by the Causeway), Burswood, WA 6100. ✆ **1800/221 335** (reservations) in Australia, or 08/9362 8888. www.perth.intercontinental.com. 402 units. A$275–A$495 Classic room, room only; A$380–A$620 Club Intercontinental room (includes breakfast, valet parking, and club access); A$888–A$1,120 suite. Max usage 3 adults in twin, or with 2 children using existing bedding. AE, DC, MC, V. Valet parking A$30 per day to max A$75 per stay; some free parking available. Bus: Numerous along Great Eastern Hwy. Starting point for Perth Tram. Train: Burswood station. **Amenities:** 8 restaurants; 8 bars (including casino); bikes for hire; concierge; well-equipped fitness center and sauna; enormous free-form pool; heated indoor pool; 24-hr. room service; day/beauty spa; tennis courts. *In room:* A/C, TV w/pay movies, hair dryer, Internet (up to A$29 per 24 hr.), minibar with freezer.

ON THE BEACH

Hotel Rendezvous Observation City Perth ★ ☺ If you're looking for absolute beach frontage, this is it. The only high-rise along Perth's Indian Ocean coast, the Rendezvous has superb views up and down Scarborough's long sandy beach. It's known for its surf lifesaving club and beach amphitheater. There's also a children's playground, and part of the coastal bike/walking track is right here. Surfing lessons and bike hire are available, and the hotel's no-fuss ambience makes it popular with vacationers from around the world, and families. Most of the rooms, refurbished in 2004, have private balconies with ocean views; some are interconnected. Bed configurations are king-size, queen-size plus single, or two doubles. The suites have prime position on the top floors with spacious balconies. It has the largest hotel gym in Perth (refitted 2006), and a large pool area with palm trees and a waterfall—sheltered from the sea breeze.

The Esplanade, Scarborough Beach, WA 6019. ✆ **1800/067 680** in Australia, or 08/9245 1000. Fax 08/9245 1345. www.rendezvoushotels.com. 327 rooms, 6 suites. A$175–A$275 standard room (limited views/balconies); A$215–A$315 deluxe; from A$540 suite. Prices for rooms as configured. Ask about packages. AE, DC, MC, V. Valet parking A$20; self-parking A$7. Bus: 400. **Amenities:** Restaurant; cafe; 2 bars; babysitting; bike rental; concierge; executive-level rooms top 3 floors; fitness center and steam rooms; Jacuzzi; heated outdoor pool; children's wading pool; room service; spa; 2 outdoor day/night tennis courts; limited watersports equipment rentals. *In room:* A/C, TV w/pay movies, hair dryer, Internet (most rooms; A$25 per day), minibar.

IN FREMANTLE

There's something of a perpetual holiday atmosphere in this picturesque port city. Public transport for the 19km (12-mile) journey to Perth's city center is good, especially the train, so you can happily explore all of Perth from here—but many top attractions are in Freo as well. There are good restaurants and a happening nightlife, too.

Esplanade Hotel Fremantle ★★ Freo's best hotel is this low-rise 1897 colonial building wrapped by two verandas, now modernized and extended, and centered on the original glass and iron four-story atrium. It's opposite a leafy park close to the Fishing Harbour and within walking distance of all Freo's cafes, shops, and attractions. A major expansion in 2003 added 41 rooms and a 1,000-seat convention center. Room refurbishment was completed in 2007. The rooms are all of reasonable size, with the suites especially spacious and having large balconies. Some studio units have Jacuzzis. Eleven rooms are designed for wheelchair access. The larger pool in the courtyard is a good sheltered place to chill out without getting buffeted by the pesky sea breeze. The Esplanade claims to be WA's only carbon-neutral hotel and won a national hotel "Environmental Initiative Award" in 2008.

Marine Terrace at Essex St., Fremantle, WA 6160. ✆ **1800/998 201** in Australia, or 08/9432 4000. Fax 08/9430 4539. www.esplanadehotelfremantle.com.au. 300 units, some with shower only. A$415–A$472 double; A$504–A$546 studio; A$578–A$788 suite. Extra person A$50. Children 11 and under stay free in parent's room with existing bedding. Cribs free. Check for impressive Internet discounts and several 1- and 2-night packages. AE, DC, MC, V. Valet parking A$25; paid street parking nearby. Train: Fremantle. **Amenities:** 2 restaurants; cafe; 2 bars; babysitting; bike rental; concierge; small gym; 2 heated outdoor pools; room service; sauna; 3 outdoor spas. *In room:* A/C, TV w/pay movies, hair dryer, minibar, Wi-Fi.

Fothergills of Fremantle ★★ 🎁 One of Perth's best bed-and-breakfast establishments, Fothergills is located in two lovely old restored 1890s limestone mansions. Fremantle, with all its charms, is a 10-minute walk, and Fremantle Prison (see "Seeing the Sights in Fremantle," later in this chapter) is a block away. The houses have been extensively and tastefully modernized; and owner David Cooke has spread his extensive art collection throughout, bringing color, light, and life. The upstairs balconies have views over the roofs of Fremantle to the Indian Ocean, ideal for evening sundowners. Most rooms have queen-size beds, while the O'Connor Suite has a king-size and double fold-out bed. There's no lounge, but the courtyards are quiet, restful havens, and an option for alfresco breakfasts.

18–22 Ord St., Fremantle, WA 6160. ✆ **08/9335 6784.** www.fothergills.net.au. 6 units, most with shower only. A$170–A$235 double. Extra adult A$45. Children 4 and under stay free in parent's room. Minimum stay 2 nights; extra A$10 if 1 night. Week-stay package. Full breakfast included. MC, V. Street parking. Bus: Fremantle Cat bus, stop 4 (High St.), 2 blocks away. **Amenities:** Breakfast conservatory. *In room:* A/C, TV/DVD, CD, fridge, hair dryer, Wi-Fi (free).

Where to Dine

An array of upscale choices plus terrific cheap ethnic spots make Perth's restaurant scene as sophisticated as Sydney's and Melbourne's—which is to say, excellent. You'll find a great range in "restaurant city," Northbridge. Friday and Saturday nights tend to be very busy, so service can suffer. Midweek is less busy, quieter, and generally more pleasant. In addition to the eateries listed below, many hotels have excellent restaurants, including the **Globe** at the **Parmelia Hilton** (p. 462) and **Opus** at the **Richardson** (p. 461).

Many outlets emphasize the use of fresh local produce. Western Australia is blessed with several climate zones plus pristine ocean waters, so look out for seasonal berry, stone, citrus, and tropical fruit; lamb, beef, veal, and goat; seafood such as rock lobster, abalone, and prawns; freshwater crustaceans, such as marron and yabbies; and superb fish, including dhufish, snapper, red emperor, and cobbler.

For inexpensive pasta, a Turkish bread sandwich, or excellent coffee and cake, you can't beat Perth's homegrown **DOME** chain of cafes. Look for the dark green logo at Trinity Arcade between Hay Street Mall and St. Georges Terrace (**© 08/9226 0210**); 149 James St., Northbridge (**© 08/9328 8094**); 13 South Terrace, Fremantle (**© 08/9336 3040**); and 26 Rokeby Rd., Subiaco (**© 08/9381 5664**)—to name a few.

There's been major growth in both the cafe culture and the availability of small bars (often with tapas-style menus). Two adjacent and casual cafes, **Tiger Tiger** (**© 08/9322 8055**) and **Secret Garden** (**© 08/9322 5885**), are in Murray Mews, 329 Murray St., while the sophisticated **Andaluz Bar & Tapas** (**© 08/9481 0093**) is at 29 Howard St., just off St. Georges Terrace.

Western Australian law bans smoking in enclosed public spaces, including bars and restaurants. Some licensed premises are allowed smoking zones in their outdoor areas.

IN OR NEAR THE CITY CENTER

Expensive

Fraser's ★★ MODERN AUSTRALIAN What a sensational view! You look past spiky grass trees and towering lemon-scented gums to Perth's panoply of skyscrapers and the Swan River. Even better, the victuals match the vista. Executive chef Chris Taylor changes the menu daily to focus on the very latest fresh produce, with seafood and fish especially prominent. This place was awarded a national title for "Best Informal Dining in Australia" in 2006. Seared scallops with green leek puree are a great starter, while crisp fried soft-shell crabs with cumin salt or pan-fried goat-cheese gnocchi both come as starters or entrees. For the best view, ask for a seat on the terrace.

Fraser Ave. (near the Information Kiosk), Kings Park. © **08/9481 7100.** www.frasersrestaurant.com.au. Reservations required. Main courses A$35–A$50. AE, DC, MC, V (all with 1.75% surcharge). Breakfast Sun and Dec daily from 8am. Daily noon–late. Closed Good Friday. Bus: 37 and 39 stop behind the information kiosk. Red CAT Stop 26 (Havelock St.) is 2 blocks from the gates.

Jackson's ★★★ MODERN AUSTRALIAN/INTERNATIONAL Understated contemporary design and ambience only help to emphasize the quality of the food here. Chef Neal Jackson has a loyal clientele and a host of awards for his ability to bring out the best in local produce, with some quirky touches based partly on his English background. This place is a short distance out of town but well worth the trip. The menu changes seasonally but with a reputation for duck dishes and soufflés, both sweet and savory, and several vegetarian choices. His degustation menu, called "the Dego," offers nine courses, with suggested matching wines. Friday and Saturday are booked out weeks ahead, and diners are warned, "This food may contain traces of nuts, love, quality produce, and passion!"

483 Beaufort St., Highgate. ✆ **08/9328 1177.** www.jacksonsrestaurant.com.au. Reservations essential. Main courses A$44; "Dego" A$120 or A$175 with wines (A$235 premium wines). AE, DC, MC, V. Mon–Sat 7pm–late. Closed Good Friday. Bus: 21 or 67 (limited night services) by Queen's Tavern.

Lamont's East Perth ★★★ MODERN AUSTRALIAN Kate Lamont has a well-deserved reputation for the flavor-driven food she produces at her three restaurants in Margaret River, Swan Valley, and here. The menu changes regularly depending on the availability of seasonal produce. Marron (a local crustacean) is a specialty, presented in various manners, especially a poached version with pea risotto. The modern glass-fronted restaurant faces directly on to Claisebrook Inlet, with the Swan River 50m (164 ft.) away, and regular food and wine events are held here—check the website for details. There's an extensive wine list, with the option to take away the Lamont family wines at cellar-door prices.

11 Brown St., East Perth. ✆ **08/9202 1566.** www.lamonts.com.au. Reservations essential. Main courses A$36–A$39. AE, DC, MC, V. Wed–Sun noon–late. Closed public holidays. Bus: Yellow Cat Stop 5 (Trafalgar Rd.); then cross Claisebrook Bridge.

Must Winebar ★ FRENCH BISRO This place has one of Australia's finest wine lists, and there's some pretty good food too. Check out the cool contemporary design, with a suspended wine rack separating the bar from the restaurant. It's a trendy hangout especially on Friday and Saturday nights. There are 500 wines in stock, with some 40 available by the glass. Food is contemporary French; the charcuterie plate (shared appetizer) and the pan-fried potato gnocchi with braised rabbit ragout are specialties.

519 Beaufort St., Highgate (close to Jackson's). ✆ **08/9328 8255.** www.must.com.au. Reservations recommended. Main courses A$35–A$40. AE, DC, MC, V. Daily noon–midnight. Closed public holidays. Bus: 21 or 67 (limited night services) by Queen's Tavern.

Moderate

44 King Street BISTRO Socialites, hip corporate types, and plain casuals adorn this bustling hangout—for a meal, a snack, or just good coffee, roasted on-site. The interior is a mix of industrial chic and European cafe, with high ceilings, dark timber tables, exposed air ducts, and windows onto the street. The open kitchen produces all its own bread and pastries and has a menu that changes monthly depending on what's available. (Try the King Street Tasting Plate.) The menu helpfully lists wine suggestions for each dish and offers over 70 wines by the glass in either 150ml or 60ml size. There's also a good beer selection.

44 King St. ✆ **08/9321 4476.** Reservations not accepted. Breakfast A$10–A$18, lunch and dinner A$20–A$50. AE, DC, MC, V. Daily 7am–late. Closed Dec 25 and Good Friday. Bus: Red CAT Stop 29 (King St.); Blue CAT Stop 1 (Cloisters).

Miss Maud Swedish Restaurant ★ INTERNATIONAL "Good food and plenty of it" is the motto at Miss Maud's homey establishment, and the crowds packing

Looking for a Late-Night Bite

Eating after midnight in Perth can be a problem. Fast Eddy's (see above) is an option; otherwise, try Chung Wah Lane in Northbridge. It's more "China Alley" than Chinatown, with several Chinese restaurants, including Uncle Billy's (✆ 08/9228 9388; http://unclebillys.blogspot.com), tucked behind a red-gilt Chinese gateway at 60 Roe St. (behind the Bus Station, btw. William and Lake sts.). The restaurants on this strip mostly open daily between 5 and 6pm and close at 4am.

the place prove it works. Most diners skip the a la carte menu and go straight for the smorgasbord. At breakfast, that means 50 dishes, including pancakes cooked before your eyes. At lunch and dinner you can tuck into soup, salads, a big range of seafood (including oysters at dinner), cold meats, roasts, hot vegetables, pasta, cheeses, European-style breads, half a dozen tortes, fruit, and ice cream—65 dishes in all. Service is fast and polite.

97 Murray St. (at Pier St.), below the Miss Maud Swedish Hotel. ✆ **08/9325 3900.** www.missmaud.com.au. Reservations recommended. Smorgasbord breakfast A$24 Mon–Fri, A$26 Sat, A$28 Sun and holidays; lunch A$31 Mon–Fri, A$32 Sat, A$36 Sun and holidays; dinner A$41 Sun–Fri, A$48 Sat and holidays. Higher prices in December for Christmas Smorgasbord. Significant discounts for children 4–13. A la carte main courses, sandwiches, and light meals A$8–A$30. AE, DC, MC, V. Daily smorgasbord times 6:45–10am (10:30am on Sun and holidays), noon–2:30pm (3pm on Sun and holidays), and 5–9:30pm (10pm Sat and holidays). A la carte, coffee, and cake served all day. Bus: Red CAT Stop 1 (Pier St.); Blue CAT Stop 5 (Murray St. Mall E.).

Inexpensive

Fast Eddy's Café FAST FOOD A hefty menu of steaks, burgers, sandwiches, salads, pancakes, sundaes, shakes, and all-day brekkies (breakfasts) are served at this popular chain—and it's open 24/7. The interior sports 1930s soap-powder posters and Coca-Cola advertisements. One side is table service; the same food minus the side orders will cost you about half of the already-low prices at the Victorian-Era-meets-1950s-counter-service diner and takeout section on the other side. It's licensed.

454 Murray St. (at Milligan St.). ✆ **08/9321 2552.** www.fasteddyscafes.com. Main courses A$16–A$35. MC, V. Daily 24 hr. Bus: Red CAT Stop 28 (Milligan St.).

IN NORTHBRIDGE

The area is jam-packed with cafes and restaurants, many reflecting the waves of migration that have made this part of Perth a staging point in their assimilation. Italian, Greek, Chinese, and Vietnamese have all lived here and now cook here.

Romany Restaurant ★ ITALIAN In new premises since 2006, this long-lasting traditional (and popular, even on weeknights) Italian restaurant has a new life. It has a classy but comfortable appearance with (subtle) maroon chairs and walls, in and out, which show up the brilliant white tablecloths. The effect is to make you feel that you could happily spend several hours here and the staff wouldn't mind. The mains are mainstream Italian, featuring dishes such as *osso buco* and *capretto* (baby goat). It has a good but inexpensive wine list. A lot of regulars appear at lunch and weekends.

105 Aberdeen St., Northbridge. ✆ **08/9328 8042.** Reservations recommended for dinner. Main courses A$22–A$34. 10% surcharge public holidays. AE, DC, MC, V. Mon–Fri noon–2:30pm; Mon–Sat 5:30–9.30pm (last orders). Closed Good Friday, Apr 25, and for 3 weeks from Dec 24. Bus: Blue CAT Stop 11.

IN SUBIACO

Star Anise ★★★ 🎁 ASIAN-INFLUENCED AUSTRALIAN In 12 years, chef-owner David Coomer has propelled this small restaurant on a quiet suburban street to become perhaps the best rated in Perth. The converted house features several dining areas, including a small open courtyard, and the decor is clean and subtle with Asian influences and contemporary artworks. The innovative menu is done daily and features a "Signature Menu" of six fixed courses (with suggested wines). The a la carte section is kept simple with five dishes listed in each of the appetizer, main, and dessert sections. Among David's noted creations are crispy aromatic duck, seared scallops, and licorice ice cream. Tuesday is an optional BYO (bring your own alcohol) night.

225 Onslow Rd., Shenton Park (next to Subiaco). ✆ **08/9381 9811.** www.staraniserestaurant.com.au. Reservations essential. Main courses A$40–A$55; Signature Menu A$110 food only, A$165 with wine (A$195 premium wines). AE, DC, MC, V. Tues–Sat 6:30–10:30pm. Closed Good Friday, Apr 25, Christmas, and Dec 31. Taxi necessary.

Witch's Cauldron ★★ MODERN AUSTRALIAN Australia's best garlic prawns arrive preceded by a wafting cloud of aroma. The Cauldron has twice been voted as Perth's favorite restaurant. Started in a single room in 1971, its owners, Geoff and Tanis Gosling, have expanded it into a large double-story establishment without compromising style or standards. They have even bought some street-side parking bays, effectively extending the restaurant right across the sidewalk. Numerous witches, including political cartoons, adorn the walls and ceilings without being kitsch. One feature is a series of circular banquettes for cozy dining for groups of four to six. Service is brisk, friendly, and efficient. Besides the garlic prawns, there's an emphasis on simple cooking of quality fish and steak. Try *tournedos chasseur* (beef rolled with mushrooms and bacon) or *dhufish meunière* (dhufish grilled in a light lemon-butter sauce). It's also open for breakfast (but without the garlic prawns).

89 Rokeby Rd. (near Hay St.), Subiaco. ✆ **08/9381 2508.** www.witchs.com.au. Reservations essential on weekends. Main courses A$31–A$51; lunch includes set menus, A$39 2 courses, A$55 3 courses. AE, DC, MC, V. Daily 7:30–11am, noon–5pm, and 6pm–late. Closed Good Friday, Apr 25, Dec 25 and 31. Train: Subiaco.

AT THE BEACH

The Blue Duck ☺ INTERNATIONAL/PIZZA For ocean views and a lively atmosphere, it's hard to beat this casual restaurant perched right above the beach. The balcony has pride of place and is always booked out, but the interior isn't bad either, with full-length picture windows. It's popular throughout the day and especially appealing at sunset, but standards can slip when the place is busy. North Cottesloe Beach is a favorite spot for early morning bathers, so breakfast is served from 7am (coffee from 6:30am), with the full menu available from noon. The menu offers a variety of salads, while the seafood tasting plate is always popular.

151 Marine Parade, North Cottesloe. ✆ **08/9385 2499.** www.blueduck.com.au. Reservations recommended. Breakfast A$12–A$20; main courses A$26–A$40, pizzas and salads A$18–A$29. 10% surcharge public holidays. AE, MC, V. Daily 6:30–11:30am and noon–late. Bus: 102 or 381.

IN FREMANTLE

The Capri ITALIAN A Fremantle institution, this place has been owned and run by the Pizzale family for 57 years. This is dining as it once was—no fussy furnishings, just good honest Italian grub, at good honest prices. Free bread and water are served immediately, and complimentary soup is served with main courses. It's unlicensed, so BYO. Here you'll find standard Italian fare, such as spaghetti marinara and scaloppine, available in small or large servings. It's right in the middle of the Cappuccino Strip.

21 South Terrace, Fremantle. ✆ **08/9335 1399.** Main courses A$26–A$31. MC, V. Daily noon–2pm and 5–9:30pm. Train: Fremantle.

Cicerello's SEAFOOD Right on Fremantle's Fishing Boat Harbour, this is one of several places offering freshly cooked, tasty fish and chips—and other seafood. It's a functional, informal, volume restaurant but still has character. Large fish tanks (for show) are the decorative feature, and floor-to-ceiling glass doors lead out to the broad timber balcony, also with seating, directly above the water. Fishing boats are moored next door. The food comes battered and fried, or grilled, but the essential meal is fish and chips. There's a kid's menu.

44 Mews Rd. (Fisherman's Wharf), Fremantle. ✆ **08/9335 1911.** www.cicerellos.com.au. Main courses A$15–A$35. AE, DC, MC, V. Daily 10am–8:30pm. Closed Dec 25. Train: Fremantle.

The Essex ★★ MODERN AUSTRALIAN For a quiet, elegant, romantic night out, the Essex is hard to beat. Located just off Fremantle's Cappuccino Strip, and up the road from the Esplanade Hotel, it's in a restored 120-year-old limestone cottage, with the dining areas spread among several rooms. The service is discreet but can leave you lonely at times. Try the Balmain bugs (a curiously flattened, but tasty, crustacean) and ravioli, or the beef Gabrielle filled with scallops.

20 Essex St., Fremantle. ✆ **08/9335 5725.** www.essexrestaurant.com.au. Reservations recommended. Main courses A$38–A$59; lunch A$38 2 courses, A$45 3 courses. AE, DC, MC, V. Daily 6pm–late; lunches Wed–Fri and Sun from noon. Train: Fremantle. Bus: Fremantle Cat (South or Marine Terrace)—does not run at night.

Little Creatures PUB/PIZZA This place is hard to categorize but is essentially a noshery serving good, cheap food to showcase the beers made onsite. Half the huge tin shed—which was formerly a boatshed, then a croc farm—is the award-winning microbrewery, also called Little Creatures; the stainless-steel tanks are in full view of the bar and eating area. It's all rather barnlike, with ultrasimple furnishings. But there's an open kitchen, an alfresco section by the harbor, and a lively atmosphere. The wood-fired pizzas, tapas-type dishes, and freshly cut frites are best known. The staff, known as "creatures," are young but provide fast, friendly service.

The Cappuccino Strip

Don't leave Freo without a "short black" (that's an espresso) or a "flat white" (coffee with milk) at one of the many alfresco cafes along South Terrace. On weekends, the street bursts at the seams with locals flocking to Italian-style eateries that serve good coffee and excellent focaccia, pasta, and pizza. DOME, The Merchant, and Gino's are three to look for.

40 Mews Rd., Fremantle. ✆ **08/9430 5155.** www.littlecreatures.com.au. Mains A$16–A$32. MC, V. Mon–Fri 10am–midnight; Sat–Sun brunch from 9am–midnight. Closed Dec 25. Train: Fremantle.

IN THE HILLS

The Loose Box ★★★ FRENCH One of the true stars of the Australian dining scene, chef Alain Fabregues gives diners at the Loose Box a chance to experience traditional French cuisine, adapted to reflect fresh local produce. The restaurant has been named "Australia's Best" by both American Express and *Gourmet Traveller* magazine. Alain provides seasonal set degustation menus—either standard or vegetarian (Loose Box has its own vegetable and herb garden). WA has recently become a major source of black truffles (see "The South Coast" later in this chapter), and there's a truffle-based menu in season (June–Aug). It's a 40-minute drive to get here, in the hills at Mundaring, but well worthwhile, and you can stay the night in well-appointed cottages at the bottom of the garden.

6825 Gt. Eastern Hwy., Mundaring. ✆ **08/9295 1787.** www.loosebox.com.au. Degustation menu A$150 food only. AE, DC, MC, V. Wed–Sat from 7pm; Sun lunch from noon. Closed Dec 25.

What to See & Do in Perth

AQWA (Aquarium of Western Australia) ★ ☺ There's plenty to see here, including Australia's largest walk-through aquarium, where you are surrounded by 4m (13-ft.) sharks, stingrays, turtles, and hundreds of colorful fish. You can also come face to fin with pretty leafy sea dragons, and observe some of the ocean's deadliest creatures, such as blue-ringed octopus and stone-like stonefish. AQWA specializes in the various ocean ecosystems around WA, and you can experience each of them during your visit. It has a touch pool, a great attraction for small (and bigger) kids, a lagoon full of stingrays, and exhibits on coral reefs. Ocean Guides provide talks on marine creatures throughout the day. For A$159 plus A$20 for snorkel gear or A$40 for dive gear (diving qualifications required), you can **swim with the sharks** (daily 1 and 3pm). Advance bookings essential. Allow half a day here.

Hillarys Boat Harbour, 91 Southside Dr., Hillarys. ✆ **08/9447 7500.** www.aqwa.com.au. Admission A$28 adults, A$20 seniors and students, A$16 children 4–15, free for children 3 and under, A$75 families of 4. Daily 10am–5pm; sometimes later in Jan. Closed Dec 25. Train: Joondalup line to Warwick, transfer to bus no. 423. By car, take Mitchell Fwy. 23km (14 miles) north, turn left onto Hepburn Ave. and proceed to roundabout at entrance to Hillarys Boat Harbour; AQWA is at the south western end of the harbor.

Art Gallery of Western Australia ★ This is a well laid out and attractive gallery that houses the State Art Collection. Outstanding among the international and Australian sections is the Aboriginal art collection, regarded as the finest in Australia. There are regular visiting exhibitions, with occasional blockbusters. Free 1-hour tours of a particular collection run Mondays, Wednesdays, Thursdays, and Sundays at 11am and 1pm; Friday tours are at 12:30 and 2pm; Saturdays at 1pm.

Cultural Centre, Roe St. and Beaufort St. (enter off the elevated walkway opposite Perth Railway Station), Northbridge. ✆ **08/9492 6600** administration, or 08/9492 6622 recorded info line. www.artgallery.wa.gov.au. Free admission. Entry fee may apply to special exhibitions. Daily 10am–5pm. Closed Good Friday, Dec 25, and Apr 25 (Anzac Day). Train: Perth. Bus: Blue CAT Stop 7 (Museum).

Cohunu Koala Park ☺ WA allows you to actually hold a koala, and this large park set in bushland is the only place to do so. You can also hand-feed kangaroos, wallabies, and emus wandering in natural enclosures, see wombats and dingoes, walk through an aviary housing Aussie native birds, and see wild water birds on the ponds. The Caversham Wildlife Park in the Swan Valley (see "Side Trips from Perth," later in this chapter) has a bigger, more intriguing range of native species, but does not allow koala cuddling. It's hard to get here without a car.

Lot 103, Nettleton Rd., Byford (500m off the South West Hwy.). ✆ **08/9526 2966.** www.cohunu.com.au. Admission A$15 adults, A$5 children 4–13. Koala holding A$25 (take your own photo/video). Daily 10am–5pm; koala photo sessions 10am–4pm. Closed Dec 25. Train: Armadale line to Armadale; then bus no. 251/2, followed by 1km (½-mile) walk. By car, take Riverside Dr. across Swan River onto Albany Hwy. to Armadale, then South West Hwy. for 5km (3 miles); turn left onto Nettleton Rd. for 500m (1,640 ft.)—about a 45-min. drive from city.

His Majesty's Theatre and King Street ★★ A lovely old wedding cake of an Edwardian theater, "The Maj" was rescued from demolition in 1979. It's Perth's major venue for the WA Ballet and Opera companies, cabaret performances (downstairs), and visiting theater productions, including those for the Perth International Arts Festival. Friends (volunteers) of His Majesty's are on hand Monday to Friday 10am to 4pm to provide information and tours of the auditorium (unless it's in use) and public areas for a donation. There's a magnificent "Lyre Bird" curtain backstage which can sometimes be viewed on group tours (minimum of 10 people), which take in this area. Downstairs houses the Museum of Performing Arts, with an engrossing collection of costumes and other memorabilia. A modern cafe, **Barre,** occupies part of the ground floor. King Street, just north of the theater, is a charming little thoroughfare with numerous restored buildings housing upmarket bistros, galleries, and fashion stores.

Theater on corner of Hay St. and King St., Perth. ✆ **08/9265 0900** administration. www.hismajestystheatre.com.au. Check daily newspaper or Web for current productions. Performing Arts Museum Mon–Fri 10am–4pm with gold coin donation. King St. outlets include 44 King St. (see "Where to Dine," earlier in this chapter) and Creative Native (see "The Shopping Scene," later in this chapter).

Kings Park & Botanic Garden ★★★ In prime position, overlooking both the city and Swan River, is this 406-hectare (1,000-acre) hilltop jewel of parkland, a botanical garden, war memorials (including the State War Memorial, which sits imposingly on a steep bluff above the river), and native bush. The main entry, along Fraser Avenue, is lined with magnificent lemon-scented gums, while each tree on the other roads is dedicated to a fallen soldier. You can inspect Western Australian flora; experience the solitude of the bush; and bike, stroll, or drive an extensive network of roads and trails. A walk through the Botanic Garden showcases many of the state's plant species, including banksias and boabs, and leads to the Federation Walkway, a glass arched bridge that soars through the treetops. Visiting the spring **wildflower displays** (which peak Aug–Oct) is a highlight for many, with an excellent Wildflower Festival running through September. A range of excellent maps can be downloaded from the website, showing the locations of barbecue and picnic facilities, playgrounds, tearooms, an information center manned by volunteer guides, the stylish **Aspects of Kings Park** craft shop (p. 482), **Fraser's** restaurant (p. 466), and the **Zamia Café.**

Pick up self-guiding maps from the Visitor Information Centre (✆ **08/9480 3634**), or join one of the free guided walks leaving from opposite the Centre. Walks depart daily at 10am and 2pm and take 1½ hours, or 2½ hours for bushwalks from May to October only. For an Aboriginal take on the park and the entire Perth region, don't miss the **Kings Park Indigenous Heritage Tour ★** (✆ **08/9483 1111**). Greg Nannup provides an excellent 1½-hour tale of his people and their use of the area

Anzac Day Dawn Service

Anzac Day (Apr 25), which commemorates the Australian landings at Gallipoli in 1915 that helped to define the nation, is the most poignant public holiday in Australia. The Perth Dawn Service is held by the War Memorial in Kings Park. You arrive in the dark and ease your way into the throng. The muffled tapping of a drum marks the official procession to the memorial, and then the service starts as the predawn light reveals a hushed crowd of up to 40,000, young and old. The sun rises behind the memorial silhouetted against the Swan River, and the Last Post sounds.

and its resources, including a riveting description of the local Creation story. Bookings are essential; the tour costs A$25 adults, or A$15 children 4 to 16.

The **Perth Tram Co.** (✆ **08/9322 2006**) runs hop-on-and-off tours of the park in replica wooden trams, as part of their standard circuit. Trams depart from the main car park off Fraser Avenue, and it's possible to just ride through the park for A$8. Buy tickets on board.

Fraser Ave. off Kings Park Rd. ✆ **08/9480 3634** Visitor Information Centre, or 08/9480 3600 administration. www.bgpa.wa.gov.au. Free admission. Information Centre daily 9:30am–4pm (closed Dec 25). Bus: 37 stops by the Information Centre; Red CAT Stop 25 (Havelock St.) is 1 block from the entrance.

Perth Mint ★ This lovely historic building—built in the 1890s to refine gold and mint currency from the Kalgoorlie goldfields—is one of the world's oldest mints operating from its original premises. It now produces legal-tender precious metal bullion and commemorative coins for investors and collectors around the world, and bullion is still traded here. Hourly guided tours allow visitors to see Australia's largest collection of nuggets, watch gold coins being minted, handle a 400-ounce gold bar, and engrave their own medallion. Tours start with a guided heritage walk on the half-hour and lead on to the molten-gold pouring demonstration (on the hour 10am–4pm weekdays, and 10am–noon on weekends and public holidays). The shop sells gold coins and jewelry made from West Australian gold, diamonds, and pearls.

310 Hay St. (at Hill St.), East Perth. ✆ **08/9421 7223.** www.perthmint.com.au. Admission to the Gold Exhibition A$15 adults, A$13 seniors and students, A$5 school-age children. Shop admission free. Mon–Fri 9am–5pm; Sat–Sun and holidays 9am–1pm. Closed Jan 1, Good Friday, Apr 25 (Anzac Day), and Dec 25–26. Bus: Red CAT Stop 10 (Perth Mint).

Perth Zoo ☺ This is an excellent modern zoo—with re-created natural habitats including the African savanna, Australian wetlands and Asian rainforest. It has several successful breeding programs, including its world-leading orangutan one; others cover a selection of West Australian fauna, including the numbat, which is WA's animal emblem. This is a good place to see a wide range of Australian wildlife such as the kangaroo, koala, wombat, dingo, emu, echidna (the Aussie answer to the porcupine), and penguin, and there's a walk-through aviary. Exotic animals include other primates, Rothschild's giraffes, lions, African painted dogs, tigers, meerkats, and elephants. Feeding demonstrations and keeper talks run throughout the day. Volunteer guides, called docents, are around 10am to 3pm to provide information, and conduct free daily walking tours at 11am (Oct–Apr) and 1:30pm. Guided 1-hour tours are available on environmentally friendly Zebra cars, while Close Encounter

Catch the Fireworks

Australia Day (Jan 26) commemorates the arrival of the First Fleet in Australia. The main celebrations in Perth are around Perth Water, climaxing with a massive fireworks display set off from moored barges. It's free and draws over 300,000 people, so you need to stake out a vantage point early or, if you're staying in a hotel with river views, make sure you're at the window!

Tours (check website for details; at minimum 3 weeks' notice) offer a real behind-the-scenes adventure.

20 Labouchere Rd., South Perth. ✆ **08/9474 3551** for recorded information, or 08/9474 0444 administration. www.perthzoo.wa.gov.au. Admission A$19 adults, A$9.50 children 4–15, A$50 family of 4. Zebra car tour A$3.50 adults, A$2.50 student/senior rate, with minimum cost of A$10. Daily 9am–5pm. Ferry: Barrack St. Jetty to Mends St. Jetty, South Perth. Bus: 30 or 31.

Swan Bells A needlelike tower, wrapped in copper sails, was specially built to house a complete "ring" of 18 bells, including 12 historic, centuries-old bells from London's St. Martin-in-the-Fields (given to Perth for Australia's bicentenary) and others that were specially cast. The tower stands out above Barrack Street Jetty on the Swan River, immediately below the city. It had to be soundproofed to minimize disturbing people working nearby but, as a result, can hardly be heard away from the jetty, which is sad. Try to visit when ringing is in progress.

Barrack Square, Perth. ✆ **08/6210 0444.** www.swanbells.com.au. Admission A$11 adults, A$8 students/seniors, children 4 and under free. Family discount available. Daily from 10am. Closed Good Friday and Dec 25. Demonstration bell ringing Sat–Tues and Thurs noon–1pm. Bus: Blue CAT to Barrack Square.

Swan River ★★ The river is a great natural and free asset to the city. Perth Water, the section of the Swan immediately below the CBD, is a superb foreground and mirror to the city—best seen from South Perth, and stunning at and just after sunset. The South Perth ferry (see "Getting Around," earlier in this section) is the easiest way of getting there. Perth Water is shallow, ideal for "messing about in boats," and small catamarans can be hired on the South Perth foreshore. Once past the Narrow Bridge, the river widens out and becomes home to several yacht clubs. Biking along the riverside pathways is also a great way to enjoy the city, the river, and the climate. You can rent bikes near the Causeway bridges. See "Active Pursuits" (p. 480).

Surfcat hire: South Perth foreshore. ✆ **0408/926 003** in Australia. www.funcats.com.au. Bike rental: Point Fraser Reserve (Causeway Carpark). ✆ **08/9221 2665.** www.aboutbikehire.com.au.

Western Australian Museum ☺ Kids will like the dinosaur gallery, the drawers full of insects, and assorted other examples of Australia's weird natural creatures. The main attraction for grown-ups is one of Australia's best displays of Aboriginal culture and heritage, and the rare photographs, many housed in the 1856 Old Gaol (jail). Allow 90 minutes to see most highlights.

Off James St. Mall, Cultural Centre, Northbridge. ✆ **08/9212 3700.** www.museum.wa.gov.au. Enter by gold coin donation. Fee may apply for temporary exhibitions. Thurs–Tues 9:30am–5pm. Closed Good Friday, Easter Monday, Dec 25–26 and Jan 1. Train: Perth. Bus: Blue CAT Stop 8 (Museum).

Yanchep National Park ★ ☺ This is the best place in Perth to see some traditional Aboriginal culture, with presentations three times a day on Saturdays and Sundays, and the local wildlife. The park is 51km (32 miles) north of the city, set in glorious natural woodland around a reed-fringed lake. You can follow a boardwalk through the koala enclosure, hire a rowboat (depending on water levels), take a limestone cavern tour, and have a coffee and snack (or beer) at the tearooms or the historic Tudor-style Yanchep Inn. Kangaroos abound, and there are noisy Carnaby's black cockatoos; other birds include swans, pelicans, wrens, parrots, and kookaburras.

Off Wanneroo Rd., Yanchep. ✆ **08/9405 0759.** Entry fee A$11 per vehicle. Tours, including the Aboriginal Experience, A$10 adults, A$5 children, A$25 families (2 adults, 2 children). Daily 9:15am–4:30pm. Aboriginal Experience Sat and holidays 1 and 3pm, Sun 2 and 4pm; didgeridoo and dance tours Sat and holidays 2pm, Sun 3pm. By car, take Wellington St. west and turn into Thomas St., which feeds into Wanneroo Rd. Follow this for about 45km (28 miles) to the park turnoff.

Hitting the Beaches

Perth shares Sydney's good luck in having beaches in the metropolitan area—in an almost continuous line from Fremantle's Port Beach in the south to Quinns Rocks in the north, including a section called the Sunset Coast. Mornings are usually best, because the sea breeze can make the afternoons unpleasant in summer. Evenings and sunsets are lovely on quiet days (remember, Perth faces west over the Indian Ocean). Always swim between the red and yellow flags, which denote a safe swimming zone.

Bus no. 400 runs to Scarborough Beach every 15 minutes weekdays, half-hourly on Saturdays and hourly on Sundays, while 102 goes to Cottesloe every 30 minutes. Bus no. 458 operates a summer timetable along the northern beaches from Scarborough to Hillarys, half-hourly on weekends and public holidays and hourly on weekdays, in both directions. Surfboards of 2m (6 ft. 7 in.) can be carried on the 400 and 458 provided they do not affect safety. Bus no. 381 operates a weekday service between Fremantle and Warwick, with stops at Scarborough.

The three most popular beaches are Cottesloe, Scarborough, and Trigg.

COTTESLOE This pretty crescent, graced by the Edwardian-style Indiana Tea House, is Perth's most fashionable beach. It has grassed slopes overlooking the beach, safe swimming, and a small surf break. Some good cafes and hotels are nearby. Every March the beach is taken over by an eye-popping exhibition of **Sculpture by the Sea** (www.sculpturebythesea.com). Train: Cottesloe, and then walk several hundred meters (btw. a quarter and a half mile). Bus: 102.

SCARBOROUGH Scarborough's white sands stretch for miles from the base of the **Hotel Rendezvous Observation City** (p. 464). Swimming is generally safe,

Find Me a Swan

The black swan is the state emblem, and the Swan River was named after it, but sadly has very few, because most of the swans' preferred habitat, the shallows, has been destroyed. Lake Monger, 3.5km (2 miles) northwest of the city, usually has hundreds by its shores, plus cormorants, native ducks, herons, coots, and swamphens. Taxi is the easiest way to get here; ask for Lake Monger Drive.

A Pesky Sea Breeze

In the summer, Perth gets an easterly offshore breeze in the morning; then, as the land heats up, it switches to a southwesterly on-shore wind. This is called the "Fremantle Doctor," because it blows up the river from Fremantle and provides relief on hot summer days. The timing and strength of the breeze varies and it can be almost gale force, whipping up the sand on exposed beaches. Check the daily weather forecast for likely wind strength.

and surfers are always guaranteed a wave, although inexperienced swimmers should take a rain check when the surf is rough. The busy shopping precinct across the road means there's always somewhere to buy lunch and drinks. Bus: 400.

TRIGG Surfers like Trigg best for its consistent swells, but it can have dangerous rips. Stay within the flags. Bus: 400 to Scarborough, and then walk, or bus no. 458 (summer only).

A Day Out in Fremantle ★★

The heritage port precinct of **Fremantle,** 19km (12 miles) from downtown Perth at the mouth of the Swan River, is probably best known outside Australia as the site of the 1987 America's Cup challenge. In the lead-up to that event, the city embarked on a major restoration of its gracious warehouses and Victorian buildings. Today, "Freo" is a bustling district of 150 National Trust heritage buildings, alfresco cafes, museums, galleries, pubs, markets, and shops in a masterfully preserved historical atmosphere. European influences are strong, thanks to the migrant fishermen, especially Italians, who made Fremantle their new home. It's still a working port, so you can see fishing boats unloading in the Fishing Harbour on one side, and yachts and container ships gliding in and out of the main commercial river-mouth harbor on the other. However, some of the buzz has gone from the historic heart since many buildings were taken over by the local Notre Dame University. Weekends are best, with a wonderful hub-bub of shoppers, merchants, coffee drinkers, locals, tourists, and fishermen. Allow a full day to take in even half the sights, and don't forget to knock back a beer or two on the veranda of one of the gorgeous old pubs, or sip an espresso on the Cappuccino Strip (see p. 470).

ESSENTIALS

GETTING THERE Parking is plentiful, but driving is frustrating in the maze of one-way streets. Most attractions are within walking distance (or accessible on the free CAT bus), so take the train to Fremantle and explore on foot.

A nice way to get to Freo and see Perth's river suburbs is on the cruises that run a few times a day from Barrack Street Jetty. See "Whale-Watching Cruises, Tram Trips & Other Tours," below, for cruise operators.

GETTING AROUND The orange Fremantle CAT bus makes a comprehensive running loop of local attractions every 10 minutes Monday through Friday 7:30am to 6:30pm, and on weekends and holidays from 10am to 6:30pm, except Good Friday and December 25 and 26. It is free and departs from the train station.

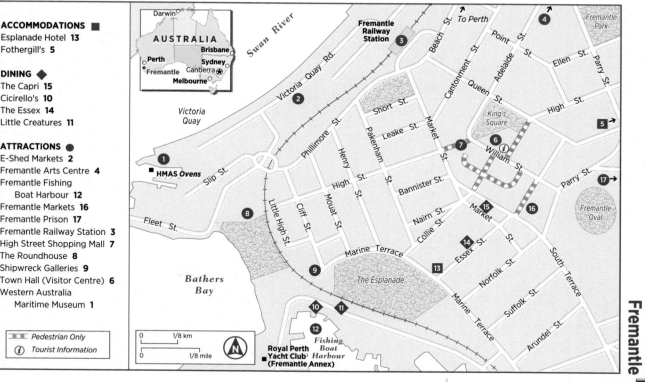

Fremantle

ACCOMMODATIONS ■
Esplanade Hotel **13**
Fothergill's **5**

DINING ◆
The Capri **15**
Cicirello's **10**
The Essex **14**
Little Creatures **11**

ATTRACTIONS ●
E-Shed Markets **2**
Fremantle Arts Centre **4**
Fremantle Fishing Boat Harbour **12**
Fremantle Markets **16**
Fremantle Prison **17**
Fremantle Railway Station **3**
High Street Shopping Mall **7**
The Roundhouse **8**
Shipwreck Galleries **9**
Town Hall (Visitor Centre) **6**
Western Australia Maritime Museum **1**

Pedestrian Only
Tourist Information

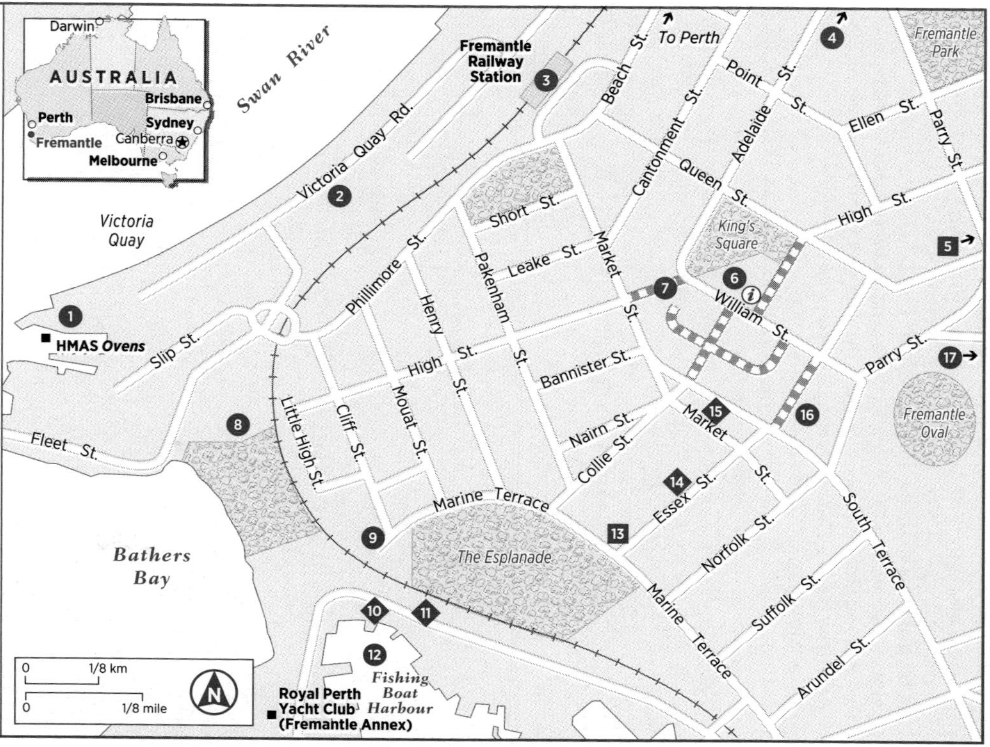

VISITOR INFORMATION The **Fremantle Visitors Centre** is in Town Hall, Kings Square (at High St.), Fremantle, WA 6160 (✆ **08/9431 7878;** www.fremantlewa.com.au). It's open Monday through Friday from 9am to 5pm, Saturday 10am to 3pm, Sunday 11:30am to 2:30pm, closed public holidays.

SEEING THE SIGHTS IN FREMANTLE

You'll want to explore some of Freo's excellent museums and other attractions, but don't forget to stroll the streets and admire the 19th-century offices and warehouses, many painted in rich, historically accurate colors. Take time to wander down to the docks—either Victoria Quay in the main shipping harbor, where sailing and pleasure craft dodge between tugs and container ships, or Fishing Boat Harbour, off Mews Road, where the catches are brought in—and get a breath of salt air.

Fremantle Trams (✆ **08/9433 6674;** www.fremantletrams.com)—an old tram carriage on wheels—conducts hop-on/hop-off commentated tours around the main sights. The tours depart from Fremantle Town Hall eight times a day starting at 9:45am, with the last tour leaving at 3:05pm. Tickets cost A$22 adults, A$18 students, A$5 children, and A$48 for families of four, and include discount entry to the prison. The popular Friday-night Ghostly Tour includes a fish-and-chips dinner and admission to a range of attractions, including a walking tour of Fremantle Prison. It runs from 6:45pm to 10:30pm and costs A$60 adults and A$45 children under 15. You must book for this. On Sundays, the Highway to Hell Tour covers the local story of AC/DC lead singer Bon Scott (A$25 adults, A$10 children; check for times).

Freo's best **shopping** is for arts and crafts, from hand-blown glass to Aboriginal art to alpaca-wool clothing. Worth a look are the assorted art, crafts, and souvenir stores on **High Street** west of the mall; the **E Shed markets** on Victoria Quay ✆ **08/9430 6393** (Fri–Sun and Mon holidays 9am–5pm, Food Court to 8pm); and the **Fremantle Arts Centre** (see below). The **Fremantle Markets,** 74 South Terrace at Henderson Street (✆ **08/9335 2515;** www.fremantlemarkets.com.au), are the oldest and best markets in Perth. Over 150 stalls sell local as well as cheap imported handicrafts, jewelry, housewares, clothing, and inexpensive food. They're open Friday 9am to 8pm; Saturday, Sunday, and Monday 9am to 5pm in winter and 6pm in summer.

The most popular watering holes are the **Sail & Anchor,** 64 South Terrace (✆ **08/9431 1666**); the **Norfolk,** 47 South Terrace at Norfolk Street (✆ **08/9335 5405**); and **Little Creatures** brewery bar and restaurant, 40 Mews Rd., in Fishing Boat Harbour (✆ **1300/722 850;** see "Where to Dine," p. 490). The happening "Cappuccino Strip" (see p. 470) on South Terrace is good for people-watching—oh, and coffee, too.

Fremantle Arts Centre Housed in a striking neo-Gothic 1860s building built by convicts as a lunatic asylum, this center contains some of Western Australia's best contemporary arts-and-crafts galleries, with a constantly changing array of works and exhibitions. A newly renovated shop sells crafts from Western Australia, a bookstore stocks Australian art books and literature, and the leafy courtyard cafe is the perfect place for a quiet break from sightseeing. There's free "Courtyard Music" October to April every Sunday from 2 to 4pm, with numerous other concerts during summer (check website). You can even visit an original asylum cell.

1 Finnerty St. at Ord St. ✆ **08/9432 9555.** www.fac.org.au. Free admission. Daily 10am–5pm. Closed Jan 1 and Dec 25–26. Bus: Fremantle CAT.

Fremantle Prison ★★ Even jails boasted attractive architecture in the 1850s. This limestone jail, built to house 1,000 inmates by convicts who no doubt ended up inside it, was Perth's maximum-security prison until 1991. Take the 75-minute Day Tours "Doing Time" and "Great Escapes" to see cells re-created in the style of past periods of the jail's history, bushranger (highwayman) Moondyne Joe's "escape-proof" cell, the gallows, chapel, jailers' houses, and cell walls featuring artwork by the former inmates. You must book ahead for the spooky 90-minute **Torchlight Tour ★** on Wednesday and Friday nights only, and the 2½ hour **Tunnels Tour ★★**, which takes you by foot and boat through a labyrinth of limestone tunnels 20m (66 ft.) down.

1 The Terrace. ✆ **08/9336 9200.** www.fremantleprison.com.au Free admission to the Gatehouse, which includes an exhibition, cafe, gift shop, and visitor center. Day Tours A$19 adults, A$16 seniors and students, A$10 children 4–15 and people with disabilities, A$52 families (maximum 3 children). Torchlight Tour A$25 adults, A$21 seniors and students, A$15 children and people with disabilities, A$72 families. Tunnel Tour A$59 adults, A$49 seniors and students, A$39 children 12–15. Daily 10am–5pm. Torchlight tours Wed and Fri every 15 min. from sunset. Closed Good Friday and Dec 25.

The Roundhouse This 12-sided jail is the oldest public building in the state (built in 1831). It's worth a visit for history's sake, and for the one o'clock gun. The time cannon (a replica of a gun salvaged from an 1878 wreck) is fired and a **time ball** dropped at 1pm daily from a deck overlooking the ocean, just as it was in the early 1900s. You might be that day's honorary gunner chosen from the crowd! Volunteer guides are on hand to explain it all.

10 Arthur Head (enter over the railway line from High St.). ✆ **08/9336 6897.** Admission by gold coin donation. Daily 10:30am–3:30pm. Closed Good Friday and Dec 25.

Shipwreck Galleries ★★ 🎁 The massive, and magnificent, remnant hulk of the Dutch ship ***Batavia,*** wrecked north of Perth in 1629, will stop you in your tracks as you enter one of the first displays in this fascinating museum, located in a lovely old 1850s limestone building. The *Batavia*'s story is of survival and betrayal; most of the survivors of the wreck were massacred by a handful of mutineers. The mutiny and massacre have been the subject of films and an opera. You will love the tales of old wrecks and displays of pieces of eight, glassware, cannon, and other deep-sea treasure recovered off the Western Australian coast. Displays date from the 1600s, when Dutch explorers became the first Europeans to encounter Australia. The museum is world-renowned for its work in maritime archaeology and preservation.

Cliff St. at Marine Terrace. ✆ **08/9431 8444.** www.museum.wa.gov.au/oursites/shipwreckgalleries. Admission by gold coin donation. Daily except Wed 9:30am–5pm. Free tours daily 10:30am, 11am, and 2:30pm (subject to availability). Closed Good Friday, Easter Monday, Dec 25–26, Jan 1, and Apr 25.

Western Australian Maritime Museum ★ This fascinating museum at the western end of Fremantle's main harbor faces straight out through tall glass panels to the Indian Ocean—and focuses on WA's links to that ocean. The museum also looks at Fremantle's history and operations as a port, shipping in both the Indian Ocean and Swan River, signaling and piloting, current sailing technology, naval defense, and Aboriginal maritime heritage. It features historic boats, including *Australia II* (the Aussie yacht that won the America's Cup back in 1983). You can tour the HMAS *Ovens,* an Oberon-class submarine, every half-hour from 10am to 3:30pm, but bookings are recommended. You can buy a ticket just for the sub, or a joint one for the museum and sub at a discount.

Victoria Quay, Fremantle. ✆ **08/9431 8444.** www.museum.wa.gov.au/maritime. Admission A$10 adults, A$5 seniors and students, A$3 children 5-15, A$22 families (up to 6). Special gold coin admission 2nd Tues of each month. Admission to submarine only A$8 adults, A$5 seniors and students, A$3 children 5-15, A$22 family. Daily except Wed 9:30am–5pm. Closed Good Friday, Easter Monday, Dec 25–26, Jan 1, and Apr 25.

Whale-Watching Cruises, Tram Trips & Other Tours

Captain Cook Cruises (✆ **08/9325 3341;** www.captaincookcruises.com.au) runs a wide assortment of cruises on the Swan River. There are regular departures downstream to Fremantle, with options to spend time in the harbor city and/or to take lunch before cruising back to Perth. Full-day and half-day cruises, with lunch, go upstream to historic homes and vineyards in the Swan Valley, operating daily from 9:45am to 4:45pm (A$146 adults, A$103 children 4–14) or at 1:15pm (A$92 adults, A$71 children). A dinner vineyard cruise on the Swan operates Wednesday to Sunday, leaving at 6:30pm, for A$115.

From September through November, Perth's ocean waters are alive with humpback **whales** returning from the north with their calves. To join a 2- or 3-hour jaunt to watch them, contact **Rottnest Express** (✆ **1300/467 688** in Australia). Departure days and times vary from year to year, so check ahead. Prices are about A$55 adults, A$45 children 13 to 16, A$25 children 4 to 12 from Fremantle, or A$70 adults, A$60 children 13 to 16, A$35 children 4 to 12 from Perth.

The **Perth Tram Co.** (✆ **08/9322 2006;** www.perthtram.com.au) offers frequent daily City Explorer Tours of loops of the city, the casino, and Kings Park in replica 1899 wooden trams with live commentary. You can hop on and off as often as you wish. The full journey takes about 2 hours. Tickets, which you buy on board and are valid for 2 days, cost A$30 for adults, A$12 for children 4 to 14, and A$60 for families (up to four children), and are also valid for the associated Double Decker Tour. Join anywhere; the tram starts at 565 Hay St. at 8:30am and operates on an hourly basis.

Heli West (✆ **08/9499 7700;** www.heliwest.com.au) offers three helicopter trips: around the city for A$75; down the Swan River to Fremantle and return for A$180; and along the northern beaches and back up the Swan for A$300. Prices are subject to change and availability. Takeoff and landing are at Burswood Park by the river, 7 days a week, between 10am and 4pm.

Active Pursuits

BIKING ★★ Perth's superb bike-track network stretches for miles along the Swan River, through Kings Park, around Fremantle, and all the way along the beaches. A great 9.5km (6-mile) track enables a complete loop around Perth Water, the broad expanse of river in front of the central business district. The state Department of Transport's cycling division, Bikewest, publishes a range of useful bike-route maps to the city. They are available in bike shops, from most newsdealers, and at **Perth Map Centre,** 900 Hay St. (✆ **08/9322 5733**).

Rental from **About Bike Hire** by the Swan River at Point Fraser Reserve (Causeway Carpark; ✆ **08/9221 2665;** www.aboutbikehire.com.au), about 2km (1¼ miles) from the city center, is A$10 for an hour, or A$36 for a 24-hour day for adults, and A$7 or A$22 for children under 12. The day rate, which reduces the longer you have the bike, includes a complimentary helmet (required by law in Australia), lock, and pump. Road racers, tandems, kayaks, and other specialized bikes can also be hired. It's open daily 9am to 5pm (8am–6pm in summer).

GOLF Most convenient to the city is **Burswood Park Public Golf Course,** adjacent to (but not part of) the Burswood International Resort Casino, across the river on the Great Eastern Highway, Burswood (✆ **08/9362 7576** for bookings; www.burswoodparkgolfcourse.com). A 9-hole round is just A$18 weekdays and A$25 weekends and public holidays; 18 holes are A$26 or A$35. A cart is A$25 and club rental A$20 for 9 holes.

Even more scenic are the 27 championship fairways designed by Robert Trent Jones, Jr., at **Joondalup Resort ★★**, Country Club Boulevard, Connolly, a 25km (16-mile) drive north of Perth (✆ **08/9400 8811** pro shop; www.joondalupresort.com.au); and the **Vines** in the Swan Valley (✆ **08/9297 3000** resort, or 08/9297 0777 pro shop; www.vines.com.au), which has two 18-hole championship bushland courses. Joondalup has three times been ranked the number-one resort golf course in Australia by *Golf Australia* magazine. Kangaroos are seen regularly on both courses. At Joondalup you'll pay A$65 for 9 holes, A$129 for 18 holes Monday to Thursday, or A$139 for 18 holes Friday to Sunday and holidays (all prices include use of a cart); ask about specials. At the Vines, fees are A$59 for 9 holes Monday to Friday, A$79 weekends; 18 holes cost A$89 Monday to Friday, A$99 weekends and holidays, including use of buggy. Bookings are essential at both courses, and dress standards apply at all courses (that is, in general, shirts with collars, closed footwear, socks, no jeans or running suits; dress shorts are acceptable).

SAILING The tallest Tall Ship in Australia, the barquentine (three-masted) ***SS Leeuwin II*** **★** (✆ **08/9430 4105;** www.sailleeuwin.com), sails from B Shed at Victoria Quay, Fremantle, when it is not on voyages around Western Australia. You get the chance to try your hand at sailing the way it used to be, even clambering up the rigging. The ship takes 3-hour daytime, twilight, or brunch trips at A$95 adults or A$60 children 3 to 13. Check the website for longer, live-on-board ocean voyages.

Experienced sailors can sometimes find a spot in Thursdays' summer twilight events with members of the **Royal Perth Yacht Club,** Australia II Drive, Crawley (✆ **08/9389 1555,** ask for the sailing administrator), if there is a place available. It's not spinnaker sailing, so the action is at an easy pace. Dress standards apply.

Funcats Catamaran Hire & Sailing Centre (✆ **04/0892 6003;** www.funcats.com.au) rents simple, small catamarans from the South Perth Foreshore.

SCUBA DIVING & SNORKELING Just 19km (12 miles) off Perth, Rottnest Island's corals, reef fish, wrecks, and limestone caverns, in 18-to-35m (59–115-ft.) visibility, are a gift from heaven to Perth divers and snorkelers. Contact **Perth Diving Academy** (✆ **08/9344 7844;** www.perthdiving.com.au; see "Rottnest Island" in "Side Trips from Perth," p. 485), to rent gear and/or join a dive trip.

SURFING You will find good surfing at many city beaches, Scarborough and Trigg in particular. See the "Hitting the Beaches" section, earlier in this chapter. Rottnest Island (see "Side Trips from Perth," below) also has a few breaks. **Vision Surf Centre,** Shop 3, Observation City, The Esplanade, Scarborough (✆ **08/9245 3227**), rents surf boards for A$30 for 2 hours or A$50 for the day, body boards for A$15 for 2 hours or A$25 per day, and wetsuits for A$10 per day. **Surfing WA** (✆ **08/9448 0004;** www.surfingwa.com.au) runs surfing classes at Trigg Beach, from A$55 per person for a 2-hour course (minimum two people), to A$120 for four 90-minute classes (maximum eight people). Boards, wet suits, and sunscreen are provided.

The Shopping Scene

Most major shops are downtown on the parallel **Hay Street** and **Murray Street malls,** and in the network of arcades running off them, such as the Plaza, City, Carillon, and Tudor-style **London Court** arcades. Off Murray Street Mall on Forrest Place is the **Forrest Chase shopping complex,** housing the Myer department store and boutiques on two levels. The other major department store, David Jones, opens on to both malls. Add to your collection of international designer brands on posh **King Street,** in the west end. **Harbourtown,** at the western edge of the city, is a large complex housing "factory outlets" of numerous retail chains.

If you want to avoid the chains, spend half a day in **Subiaco ★** or "Subi," where Hay Street and Rokeby Road are lined with smart boutiques, galleries, cafes, antiques shops, and markets. The Colonnade shopping center at 388 Hay St. showcases some groovy young Aussie fashion designers.

Fremantle's shopping is mostly limited to a good selection of crafts, markets, and Aboriginal souvenirs, with several galleries in High Street.

Most shops are open until 9pm on weeknights in the city, Subiaco, and Fremantle.

LOCAL ARTS & CRAFTS Two shops showcase contemporary ceramic, textile, glass, and jewelry products: **Form,** at 357 Murray St. just round the corner from King Street (✆ **08/9226 2161**); and **Aspects of Kings Park,** behind the Visitor Centre in Kings Park (✆ **08/9480 3900**).

ABORIGINAL ARTS & CRAFTS **Creative Native,** Shop 58, Forrest Chase, opposite the Visitor Centre (✆ **08/9221 5800;** www.creativenative.com.au), stocks Perth's widest range of Aboriginal arts and crafts, and includes a gallery that sells original works by some renowned Aboriginal artists. There's another branch at 73 High St., Fremantle (✆ **08/9335 6995**).

Indigenart (incorporating the Mossenson Gallery), 115 Hay St., Subiaco (✆ **08/9388 2899,** www.indigenart.com.au), stocks works on canvas, paper, and bark, as well as artifacts, textiles, pottery, didgeridoos, boomerangs, and sculpture, by Aboriginal artists from all over Australia.

JEWELRY Western Australia is renowned for farming the world's best **South Sea pearls** off Broome, for Argyle **diamonds** mined in the Kimberley, and for being one of the world's biggest **gold** producers.

Kailis Jewellery, 29 King St. (✆ **08/9422 3888;** www.kailisjewellery.com.au), sells elegant South Sea pearls and gold jewelry. Another branch is located at the corner of Marine Terrace and Collie Street, Fremantle (✆ **08/9239 9330**).

Some of Perth's other leading jewelers, where you can buy Argyle diamonds, Broome pearls, and opals set within locally designed WA gold jewelry, are **Linneys,** 37 Rokeby Rd., Subiaco (✆ **08/9382 4077;** www.linneys.com.au), and **Costello's,** Shop 5–6, London Court (✆ **08/9325 8588**). Linneys also has locations at 39 King St. and Burswood Resort.

For opals to suit all budgets, head to the Perth outlet of **Quilpie Opals,** Shop 6, Piccadilly Arcade off Hay Street Mall (✆ **08/9321 8687**).

Aboriginal Fine Art

Japingka Gallery, 47 High St., Fremantle (✆ 08/9335 8265; www.japingka.com.au), is dedicated to encouraging and exhibiting Aboriginal art from around Australia. It has a large stock of certificated art, covering a broad cross section of areas and styles. There's an ongoing exhibition program, which usually involves having the artist present for discussion and explanation. The gallery is based over two floors in a historic building in central High Street.

Perth After Dark

Scoop (see "Visitor Information," earlier in this chapter) is a good source of information on festivals and concerts, theater, classical music, exhibitions, and the like. Your best guide to dance clubs, rock concerts, gig listings, and art-house cinemas is the free weekly ***X-press*** magazine, available at pubs, cafes, and music venues every Thursday. The ***West Australian*** (especially the Sat. edition) and ***Sunday Times*** newspapers publish entertainment information, including cinema guides.

Three ticket agencies handle most of the city's major performing arts, entertainment, and sporting events: the performing arts–oriented **BOCS** (**✆ 1800/193 300** in Australia, or 08/9484 1133; www.bocsticketing.com.au), the sports-and-family-entertainment-oriented **Ticketmaster** (**✆ 13 61 00;** www.ticketmaster.com.au), and **Ticketek** (**✆ 13 28 49;** www.ticketek.com.au). Book opera, ballet, and the various theater companies (see below) through BOCS. The orchestra handles its own bookings.

THE PERFORMING ARTS The **West Australian Opera** (**✆ 08/9278 8999** administration; www.waopera.asn.au) and **West Australian Ballet** (**✆ 08/9214 0707** administration; www.waballet.com.au) usually perform at **His Majesty's Theatre,** 825 Hay St. (see earlier in "What to See & Do in Perth"). Perth's leading theater company, the **Black Swan State Theatre Company** (**✆ 08/6389 0311** administration; www.bsstc.com.au), plays at theaters around town, but is planning to move into the new State Theatre Centre, corner of William and Roe streets, Northbridge, in late 2010, together with the **Perth Theatre Company** (**✆ 08/9323 3433;** www.perththeatre.com.au). The **West Australian Symphony Orchestra ★★** (**✆ 08/9326 0000;** www.waso.com.au) usually performs at the **Perth Concert Hall,** 5 St. Georges Terrace, but with other performances (for example, the open-air summer series) in **Kings Park.** Perth Concert Hall has the best acoustics of any such venue in Australia and features a wide range of other artists.

Perth is an outdoors kind of place. In summer, look for outdoor concerts or jazz at **Perth Zoo** (**✆ 08/9474 3551** for recorded information, or 08/9474 0444 administration); movies at Perth's several outdoor cinemas; and open-air concerts, plays, and movies in **Kings Park** (**✆ 08/9480 3600** administration; **08/9480 3666** 24-hr. events information).

The **Perth International Arts Festival ★★** (**✆ 08/6488 2000** administration; www.perthfestival.com.au; bookings through BOCS) is the oldest arts festival in the Southern Hemisphere, producing 3½ weeks of local and international theater, dance, music, and a wide variety of free performances every February. It makes great

Movies & Stars

Catch an art house movie in the superb tree-lined Somerville Auditorium in the grounds of the University of WA. Picnic on the grass beforehand (you can buy food and drinks there) while the sun sets; then watch the film from rows of deck chairs, with the stars visible overhead. The season runs nightly at 8pm from December through mid-February, or at 7:30pm from March 1 to mid-April, as part of the Perth International Arts Festival.

use of Perth's summer weather and outdoor venues, especially with its 4-month film festival (see "Movies & Stars," below), and Beck's Music Box (see under "Pubs, Bars & Nightclubs," below).

One of Australia's premier arts training colleges, the **West Australian Academy of Performing Arts (WAAPA)** is based in Perth, at 2 Bradford St., Mt Lawley. The students, as part of their training, regularly put on some of Perth's best performances of drama, musical theater, dance, jazz, classical music and song, and percussion. Check ✆ **08/9370 6636** (box office) or **www.waapa.ecu.edu.au** for current productions.

PUBS, BARS & NIGHTCLUBS Northbridge houses most of the city's lively pubs and dance clubs, but don't forget that Freo has good pubs, too (see "A Day Out in Fremantle," p. 476).

For a take on the traditional pub, head to the **Brass Monkey,** 209 William St., at James Street, Northbridge (✆ **08/9227 9596;** www.thebrassmonkey.com.au). Downstairs are several bars, including the Grapeskin Wine and Tapas Bar, and there's a refurbished grill room upstairs. The Laugh Resort comedy club performs upstairs in the Glass House at 8pm on Wednesdays for an A$12 cover.

The **Subiaco Hotel,** also known as the "Subi," 465 Hay St. at Rokeby Road, Subiaco (✆ **08/9381 3069;** www.subiacohotel.com.au), is a popular historic pub with great cocktails, live music on Wednesday and Saturday nights, and an eatery rated as WA's Best Hotel/Tavern Restaurant in 2009.

The Perth International Arts Festival (see above) has a vibrant, jumping music scene, nightly, for the entire 3½ weeks, at **Beck's Music Box,** a specially created and licensed open-air venue on Perth's Esplanade. There are ticketed headline acts at 8:30pm, followed by varied performers from 10:30pm until late with free entry, but numbers limited by capacity—check **www.perthfestival.com.au**.

The biggest place on the nightclub scene is **Metro City,** 146 Roe St., Northbridge (✆ **08/9228 0500**), with 10 bars over three levels. It opens every Saturday night from 10pm with its "Empire" party, featuring R&B, house, and commercial music. The cover of A$10 increases to A$15 after 11pm. It opens frequently on other weekend nights, with varying cover charge, for special events with visiting bands and artists; check **www.metroconcertclub.com** for details.

In Fremantle, the **Metropolis,** 58 S. Terrace (✆ **08/9336 1880**), is a complex of two dance floors and eight bars on several levels. It has disco nights Fridays from 9:30pm to 4am, and Saturday 9pm to 5am; the cover varies depending on the entertainment, but is usually in the A$15 range. It may open other nights for visiting bands and artists; see **www.metropolisfremantle.com.au** for details.

Jazz is alive and well with a strong local following. There are several jazz clubs run on a not-for-profit basis, including the **Perth Jazz Society,** with modern contemporary music played every Monday night at the Charles Hotel, 509 Charles St., North Perth (www.perthjazzsociety.com), and **Jazz Fremantle,** with "crossover" music played most Sundays from 4 to 7pm at the Navy Club, 64 High St., Fremantle (www.mediahighway.com.au/jazzfremantle). But Perth's jazz scene took a considerable leap with the opening of its first dedicated commercial jazz establishment in 2009, the **Ellington Jazz Club,** at 191 Beaufort St., Northbridge, Perth (✆ **04/0806 9867;** www.ellingtonjazz.com.au). It has a performance/cabaret area and upstairs bar, open Tuesday to Sunday and some Mondays.

GAMING **Burswood International Resort Casino** complex, on the Great Eastern Highway just over the river from the city (✆ **08/9362 7777;** www.burswood.com.au), is WA's only legal casino, with 137 tables and 1,500 gaming machines, and the premium gaming Pearl Room. Some of the casino's most popular games include roulette, keno, blackjack, and two-up. The casino operates 24 hours every day except Good Friday and December 25 (closed 3am–10pm), and April 25 (Anzac Day; closed 3am–noon), and is open to everyone over the age of 18. Dress code is "neat and tidy," with smarter standards after 7pm. There are multiple restaurants and bars, a 900-seat nightclub, and a 2,300-seat theater which features numerous major international acts. Live bands, disco, cabaret performers, or karaoke play nightly. It's an A$15 to A$20 cab ride from the city, or take a train to Burswood station.

SIDE TRIPS FROM PERTH

Rottnest Island ★★

19km (12 miles) W of Perth

The delightful wildlife reserve of Rottnest Island, off the Perth coast, has been WA's favorite holiday island for a hundred years. It's surrounded by sheltering reefs, which ensure safe swimming and snorkeling in glorious, protected bays. Its jewel-bright waters, warmed by a south-flowing current, harbor **coral outcrops** and 400 kinds of fish. The island is also home to 10,000 **quokkas,** cute little marsupials that reach up to your knees when they sit up and beg for a piece of lettuce (though you're not supposed to feed them). The island and the water have a wonderful Mediterranean feel. Rottnest is publicly owned and accessible to all. It's the sort of place where you feel your cares fall away as soon as you arrive, and it's almost decadent in the way that everything is so laid back and casual. Try to spend a night here; the experience tends to be so much better than just taking a day trip.

The island is only 11km (7 miles) long and 4.5km (3 miles) across at its widest point with two main areas of settlement, where self-catering cottages and villas can be rented from the **Rottnest Island Authority.** Getting about is restricted to walking and cycling, with a few buses taking visitors around the island or linking the settlements. There are strong historical links: Following mainland clashes between settlers and Aborigines, Rottnest was a "native prison" from 1839 until 1931. The main settlement now has WA's oldest and most intact precinct of heritage buildings and an Aboriginal cemetery. The island was then a major military base during World War II.

ESSENTIALS

GETTING THERE **Rottnest Express** (© **1300/GO ROTTO** [467 688] in Western Australia; www.rottnestexpress.com.au) operates trips from Perth (trip time: about 1 hr. 45 min.) and, more frequently, from Fremantle (about 30 min.). Round-trip same-day adult fares average about A$75 from Perth, or about A$60 from Fremantle, with varying children's prices depending on age. There's free pickup from most Perth and Fremantle hotels. You may pay about A$8 extra if you return on a later day. Bike hire and various day trips (including Rottnest Express's Eco Adventure, cruising around the island bays and coves) are available, and accommodations packages. There's an online booking service.

Rottnest Air Taxi (© **1800/500 006** in Western Australia, or 08/9292 5027; www.rottnest.de) provides aerial transfers in four- or six-seater aircraft (allow one seat for the pilot!), about 15 minutes each way. A same-day round-trip in a four-seater costs about A$300 for up to three passengers, and a six-seater A$400 for up to five. **Kookaburra Air** (© **08/9417 2258;** www.kookaburra.iinet.net.au) also operates a range of tours to Rottnest. Both operate from Jandakot Airport, 18km (11 miles) or 20 minutes south of Perth.

VISITOR INFORMATION The **Rottnest Island Visitor & Information Centre** (© **08/9372 9732**) is right at the end of the jetty on the island. The center is run by the **Rottnest Island Authority** (© **08/9432 9111;** www.rottnestisland.com), as is the entire island. The Western Australian Visitor Centre (see "Visitor Information" in the Perth section, earlier in this chapter) also has information.

GETTING AROUND Ferries pull into the jetty in Thomson Bay (it's often just called "The Settlement"), which has most of the facilities and accommodations lining its shores. **Rottnest Island Bike Hire** (© **08/9292 5105**), next to the Rottnest Hotel near the jetty, rents 1,300 bikes of every size, speed, and type, as well as trailers or carriers for everything from surfboards to babies. A multispeed bike is A$26 for 24 hours (plus a A$25 refundable deposit), including a helmet (compulsory in Australia) and lock. The price reduces for subsequent days.

The air-conditioned **Bayseeker** ★ bus does half-hourly circumnavigations in summer (hourly in winter), calling at 18 stops, including all the best bays. You can get on and off as often as you like, with an all-day ticket costing A$13 for adults, A$6 for children 4 to 12, and A$26 for families of four. Buy tickets for this and the tours below at the Visitor & Information Centre, gift shop, main ticket booth, or on board.

A free shuttle bus runs regularly between the airport and Thomson Bay, and the secondary settlement at Geordie, Fay's, and Longreach Bays on the northern shore. It does not run to the Basin, which is a 15-minute walk from the Settlement.

ISLAND ORIENTATION TOURS

Many first-time visitors take the 1½-hour **Discovery Tour,** a good introduction to the bays and the island's cultural and natural history, which includes a stop to see the quokkas. It costs A$33 for adults, A$16 for kids 4 to 12, and A$70 for families of four. Standard departure times are 11:30am and 1:30pm daily.

SNORKELING, DIVING, FISHING & SURFING

Most people come to Rottnest to snorkel, swim, surf, dive, or fish. As soon as you arrive, rent a bike and your preferred aquatic gear, and pedal around the coast until you come to a beach that suits you. (Don't forget to carry drinking water and food, because the only shops are at the Settlement and Geordie Bay.) The Basin, Little Parakeet Bay, Little Armstrong Bay, Little Salmon Bay, and Parker Point are good **snorkel** spots. There are two snorkel trails, with underwater information points, at Little Salmon and Parker Point. **Surfers** should try Cathedral Rocks or Strickland Bay. **Fishermen** will catch squid, herring, and tailor, as well as all kinds of reef fish, but several areas are now off-limits to fishing. The **Rottnest Adventure Centre** (**© 08/9292 5292**), behind the DOME Café, rents snorkel gear, kayaks, fishing rods, beach shelters, and umbrellas. It operates a semisubmersible boat, the ***Underwater Explorer,*** for the warmer months of September through April. It's used for 45-minute wreck-and-reef viewing tours from the main jetty (A$29 adults, A$15 children 4–12, A$75 families of four) at 10:45am, 2pm, and 3pm, and for guided 90-minute snorkeling tours (A$39 adults, A$30 children 4–12, more if gear is hired) on Friday to Monday at 11:45am. Both tours are dependant on numbers.

Several companies conduct boat trips to some of the 100-plus dive sites around Rottnest, which feature reefs, limestone caverns, and the island's 14 shipwrecks. **Perth Diving Academy** (**© 08/9225 7555;** www.perthdiving.com.au) has round-trip boat trips to Rottnest from Fremantle that include two dives and lunch for A$150. From December to February tours operate daily; from June to August they operate only Thursday to Sunday. Single-dive trips are also available on Saturdays and Sundays only: The dives take place at night or in the early morning; the boat departs at 6:30am and returns at 9am the following day. Bookings are essential, and hire of equipment is extra. Trips are always subject to the weather.

FOR HISTORY BUFFS

Rottnest has a lot to offer for history buffs. There are numerous heritage buildings, especially along the Thomson Bay foreshore, which make up WA's oldest and best preserved heritage precinct. The Salt Store, Pilot's Boatshed, and numerous accommodation cottages date from the mid–19th century when the island was a prison and convict labor was employed.

The island became a major base during World War II, protecting the sea lane to Fremantle, and the Oliver Hill 9¼-inch guns are still there. Guided 1-hour tours (gold coin fee) take visitors around them as well as the battery tunnels housing an engine room, a plotting room, and observation posts. You can make your own way there, or take a train. The tours start at 9:30am or on the hour 11am to 2pm. The train, the *Captain Hussey,* departs from the station near the Visitor & Information Centre hourly from 10:30am to 2:30pm (the last trip is a train ride only—no tour). The return train ride plus the gun tour costs A$26 for adults, A$21 students, A$16 for children 4 to 12, and A$52 for families. Lower prices apply if you take only the train ride or the gun tour.

Volunteer guides run several free 1-hour walking tours. One is a historical tour around Thomson Bay, including the governor's residence, chapel, octagonal prison, small **museum** (**© 08/9372 9752;** open daily 10:45am–3:30pm), and the former boys' reformatory. Another heritage trail takes you to the memorial commemorating de Vlamingh, the Dutch explorer who named the island *Rottenest* ("Rat's Nest") in 1696 when he mistook quokkas for (very large) rats. There are also quokka walks, and the "Reefs, Wrecks, and Daring Sailors" tour, which includes a walk to Bathurst lighthouse.

WHERE TO STAY & DINE

Call the **Rottnest Island Authority's accommodations booking service** (**© 08/9432 9111**) to book one of the island's 300-plus holiday homes, villas, or historic cottages, or the campground. Don't expect anything grand, and there is no air-conditioning. Book well in advance all through summer and autumn; accommodations during the WA school vacation times are allocated through a ballot system, for which you must submit an online application. Reduced pricing applies May through September.

The Authority's units are all furnished and self-catering, with gas stoves and barbecues. Both hotels (listed below) have good restaurants; otherwise, dining is available at the licensed **Aristos Waterfront Rottnest,** the **Geordie Bay Café** (Thurs–Sat evenings, summer only), the **DOME Café** (rebuilt in 2008), and a couple of lackluster takeout joints.

Hotel Rottnest Known to generations as the Quokka Arms, this 1864 building near the jetty began life as the state governor's summer residence and has undergone a major renovation and upgrade. It's been brought into the 21st century, and even the lovely old timber balcony is back in service.

Bedford Ave., Rottnest Island, WA 6161. ✆ **08/9292 5011.** Fax 08/9292 5188. www.hotelrottnest.com.au. 18 units. A$320–A$350 Bayside doubles; A$270–A$290 Courtyard doubles. Twin rooms available. Ask about packages. AE, DC, MC, V. **Amenities:** Restaurant; 2 bars. *In room:* A/C, ceiling fans, TV w/pay movies, fridge, hair dryer.

Rottnest Lodge This former colonial barracks has been heavily modified to provide attractive, comfortable visitor accommodations, with newer units added at the rear, facing across salt lakes to the main Rottnest Lighthouse. The Premium Lakeside rooms, updated in 2005, are the island's most luxurious accommodations. They have king-size beds, flagstone floors, private balconies, and a spacious living area. The standard Lakeside rooms, upgraded in 2009, are set up with both queen-size and single beds and also have balconies, but with limited views. The remaining rooms are in the historic quarters. The Deluxe rooms are bright and cheery, with courtyard entry and French windows opening on to a colonial veranda. The two-bedroom family rooms have the advantage of a kitchen and laundry. The area known as the Quod has budget accommodations. The lodge is just a short stroll from the jetty and Visitor & Information Centre.

Kitson St., Rottnest Island, WA 6161. ✆ **08/9292 5161.** Fax 08/9292 5158. www.rottnestlodge.com.au. 80 units, all with shower only. A$260–A$330 Deluxe double; A$215–A$285 standard double; A$270–A$340 Lakeside double; A$310–A$385 Premium Lakeside double; A$455–A$550 family apt. Extra person A$75. Rates include continental breakfast and are seasonal. Ask about packages. AE, DC, MC, V. **Amenities:** Restaurant; 2 bars; Internet; small lagoon-style pool. *In room:* Ceiling fan, TV w/pay movies, fridge, hair dryer, Internet (maximum A$25 per day).

In Pursuit of the Grape in the Swan Valley ★

20km (13 miles) NE of Perth

You don't have to go all the way to Margaret River to find rolling vineyards, local produce, good food and wine, and some of WA's early heritage. The Swan Valley is only 25 minutes from the Perth city center, but has 30 or so wineries, a wildlife park, antiques shops, galleries, several restaurants, and one of Australia's best golf resorts. Some outlets are closed Monday to Wednesday. Good times to visit are during two annual festivals, "Spring in the Valley" (second weekend in Oct), and "Taste of the Valley" (during Feb).

Lord Street from the Perth city center becomes Guildford Road and takes you to the historic town of Guildford at the start of the Swan Valley. The **Swan Valley**

Visitor Centre is in the historic old courthouse at the corner of Meadow and Swan streets, Guildford (✆ **08/9379 9400;** www.swanvalley.com.au). It's open daily, except Christmas, from 9am to 4pm. It provides helpful information, advice, maps—including an excellent Food & Wine Trail map—and separate sheets listing the venues that are open during the quiet times of Mondays, Tuesdays, and Wednesdays. Several companies (see "Whale-Watching Cruises, Tram Trips & Other Tours," earlier in this chapter) run day tours or cruises from Perth, and local companies run tours by black cab or Rolls-Royce.

The **Swan Valley Shuttle Service** (✆ **08/9274 6569**) is a hop-on-hop-off service to and from the Visitor Centre and Guildford Train Station, calling at Houghton Wines, Chesters, and the Novotel Vines Resort (see below), and a few other wineries and breweries. It runs hourly 8:30am to 4:30pm, Wednesday to Sunday, A$30 round-trip.

TOURING THE WINERIES & OTHER THINGS TO DO

Most Swan wineries are small, family-run affairs, many with links to early Italian or Yugoslav origins. An exception is **Houghton Wines ★**, Dale Road, Middle Swan (✆ **08/9274 9540;** www.houghton-wines.com.au), Western Australia's oldest, biggest, and most venerable winery. The tasting room is light, airy, and appealing. and there are lovely picnic grounds, where jacaranda trees blossom gloriously in November. There's a pleasant cafe, and an art gallery housed in old beamed timber cellars lined with barrels (still in use). Hours are 10am to 5pm (cafe 10am–4pm) daily except Good Friday and December 25.

The other big-name winery, and winner of the "Best Tourism Winery" award in 2008 and 2009, is **Sandalford Wines,** 3210 W. Swan Rd., Caversham (✆ **08/9374 9374;** www.sandalford.com). It has twice-daily 90-minute winery tours (minimum five people), which take you along walkways over the high-tech production areas. The A$22 fee includes a tasting of premium wine and a wine-education kit. A very popular tour is "Become a Winemaker for a Day," Saturdays at 11am. Besides the winery tour, you get a chance to blend your own wine, which you can then drink over a three-course lunch, all for A$125. The winery also has a good gift shop and a pleasant restaurant (lunch noon–3pm) with a pretty vine-covered alfresco area. It's open 10am to 5pm daily except Good Friday and December 25.

In general, the tastings at the Swan wineries are free, with some wineries charging a small fee for their premium offerings.

The popular **Margaret River Chocolate Company** has an outlet at 5123 W. Swan Rd. (near the Reid Hwy.), West Swan (✆ **08/9250 1588**). It offers tastings, and you can watch chocolate-making through the viewing window. It's open daily from 9am to 4:30pm, except December 25. A more recent addition to the sweet scene is **Mondo Nougat,** 640 Great Northern Hwy., Herne Hill (✆ **1300/997 875** in Australia, or 08/9296 0111; www.mondonougat.com.au), run by a migrant family following their southern Italian traditions. The cafe opens daily except Monday.

Caversham Wildlife Park (✆ **08/9248 1984;** www.cavershamwildlife.com.au) is a large reserve of 4,300 hectares (10,621 acres) with a collection of 200 species of mostly Western Australian wildlife, the majority kept in natural surroundings. You can stroke koalas (but not hold them), feed kangaroos, pet farm animals, take a camel ride, and sometimes cuddle joeys and wombats. There are barbecue and picnic sites, train and tram rides, and a cafe. It's at Whiteman Park, West Swan, and open daily from 9am to 5:30pm (last entry 4:30pm), closed December 25. Admission is A$22 for adults, A$8 for children 3 to 14.

Antiques lovers should browse the strip of shops on James Street, Guildford (most shops are open daily), or visit **Woodbridge House,** a beautifully restored 1883 manor house on Ford Street, West Midland (✆ **08/9274 2432**). The house is open Thursday to Sunday from 1 to 4pm; closed December 24 to February 6. Admission is A$5 adults, A$3 seniors and children under 16, and A$12 families of four. The Riverside at Woodbridge cafe opens 9am to 5pm daily (except Wednesday) for breakfast, lunch, and tea.

Drop into **Guildford Village Potters,** 22 Meadow St., next to the Visitors Centre (✆ **08/9279 9859;** www.guildfordpotters.webs.com), to check out work by about two dozen local potters. You may find it hard to resist the raku (open-fired) glazes. It's open 9:30am to 3pm weekdays, 10am to 4:30pm weekends and holidays. One of Perth's finest galleries is half-hidden within woodland just off the Roe Highway: The **Gomboc Gallery and Sculpture Park ★**, at 50 James Rd., Middle Swan (✆ **08/9274 3996;** www.gomboc-gallery.com.au), has been in operation for 25 years. The grounds feature an eclectic array of sculptures, while the gallery houses regular exhibitions of major WA artists. Open 10am to 5pm Wednesday to Sunday.

WHERE TO STAY

Grandis Cottages ★ Two excellently furnished two-bedroom cottages sit in a rural setting, looking over rolling lawns, a small dam, and a large bed of roses. Birds include kookaburras, cockatoos, and blue wrens, while kangaroos roam the back lawn. A breakfast hamper is supplied, otherwise the cabins are self-catering, with full kitchens and comfortable lounges featuring gas stoves and two recliners. The large veranda has a seating area with gas barbecue. The water supply is 100% rainwater, and all wastewater is recycled.

45 Casuarina Place (off West Swan Rd.), Henley Brook, WA 6055. ✆ **08/9296 3400.** Fax 08/9296 3500. www.grandiscottages.com.au. 2 self-contained cottages, 1 with facilities for people with disabilities. Sun–Thurs A$300 double; Fri–Sat A$320 double. Extra adult A$50; extra child (to 12 years) A$30. Ask about packages. AE, DC, MC, V. Take West Swan Rd. to Henley Brook, turn left onto Woolcott St. and right into Casuarina Place. *In room:* A/C, TV/DVD, CD player, hair dryer.

Novotel Vines Resort This rural retreat has one of the best resort golf courses in Australia and is the most upmarket place in the Swan Valley. Most rooms or apartments in the low-rise accommodations have balconies looking onto the 36-hole championship golf course or over the pool or vineyard. Kangaroos are a regular sight along the bush-fringed fairways. The rooms are of a high standard, if a bit stiff and citified. A suite consists of a room with a living area and some feature spas.

Verdelho Dr., The Vines (Swan Valley), WA 6069. ✆ **1300/656 565** Accor in Australia, 800/221 4542 in the U.S. and Canada, or 08/9297 3000. Fax 08/9297 3333. www.vines.com.au. 103 hotel rooms, 54 apts. From A$255 double; A$285 suite; A$310 2-bedroom apt; A$365 3-bedroom apt. Children 14 and under stay free in parent's room with existing bedding. Ask about packages. AE, DC, MC, V. Take West Swan Rd. to Upper Swan and turn left on to Millhouse Rd. The resort entrance is about 1.5km (1 mile) on the right. **Amenities:** Restaurant; 2 cafes; 2 bars; golf course (guest discounts available); exercise room; outdoor heated Jacuzzi; large outdoor pool; room service; 4 tennis courts (2 floodlit). *In room:* A/C, TV w/pay movies, hair dryer, minibar.

WHERE TO DINE

Chesters MODERN AUSTRALIAN This simple, casual setting with a semiopen kitchen provides a good venue for easy dining. Originally a fruit shed, it has views

A Side of Art with Your Meal

Taylor's art and coffee house, 510 Great Northern Hwy., Middle Swan (✆ 08/ 9250 8838; www.taylorstudio.com.au), is a quirky, even eccentric, cafe that is simple yet appealing. The Taylor family has converted the old family home, with corrugated iron walls and polished floorboards, into an intriguing venue—part cafe (run by daughter Caroline), part gallery (by matriarch Jude). The outside has a shady courtyard with a mix of tables, chairs, and sculptures, many made by son Michael. "The Shed" is an old workshop, which is the venue for quarterly professional theater productions (seating for 150). The cafe is open for "brekky" and lunch Wednesday to Sunday. The food is tasty and cheap.

past gum trees to open paddocks. Chesters is part of the Heafod Glen Winery, and the food is excellent; try the mushroom galette.

8691 West Swan Rd., Henley Brook. ✆ **08/9296 3444.** www.heafodglenwine.com.au. Reservations recommended on weekends. Main courses A$35–A$50. AE, DC, MC, V. Wed–Sat 11am–3pm; Sun and public holidays noon–3pm; Fri–Sat 6–11pm. Closed Good Friday.

Lamont Winery Cellar Door ★ TAPAS The cellar-door kitchen serves food Friday to Monday from a "small tastes" bar menu that features fresh seasonal produce for eating indoors or outside at the farm tables. Lamont's wines are also available for sale.

85 Bisdee Rd. (off Moore Rd.), Millendon, near Upper Swan. ✆ **08/9296 4485.** www.lamonts.com.au. Reservations recommended. Platters A$12–A$18. AE, DC, MC, V. Sat–Sun and holidays noon–4pm (cellar door 11am–5pm). Closed weekdays, Dec 25–26, Jan 1, and Good Friday. Take the Great Northern Hwy. to Baskerville, near Upper Swan, take a right onto Haddrill Rd. for 1.6km (1 mile), turn right onto Moore Rd. for 1km (just over ½ mile), and make a right onto Bisdee Rd.

New Norcia: A Touch of Spain in Australia ★

132km (82 miles) N of Perth

It's the last thing you expect to see in the Australian bush—a Benedictine monastery town, with elegant European architecture, a fine museum, and a collection of Renaissance art—but New Norcia is no mirage. Australia's only monastic town (and still a working community) retains an aura of peace and quiet and calming spirituality. The pretty town and the surrounding 8,000-hectare (19,760-acre) farm were established in 1847 by Spanish Benedictine missionaries. Visitors can tour beautifully frescoed chapels, marvel at one of the finest religious art collections in Australia, attend prayers with the monks who live here, and stock up on Abbey Wines, Abbey Ale, or famous New Norcia nut cake or bread from the monastery's 120-year-old wood-fired oven.

Ten kilometers (6¼ miles) south of the town is the New Norcia Deep Space Ground Station, run by the European Space Agency. It's not open to the public, but visitors can learn about it at the town's Education Centre.

New Norcia is an easy 2-hour drive from Perth. From downtown, take Lord Street, which becomes Guildford Road, to Midland, and follow the Great Northern Highway to New Norcia. The **Public Transport Authority** (PTA; ✆ **1300/662 205** in Western Australia, or 08/9326 2000; www.transwa.wa.gov.au) runs a coach from Perth on Tuesday and Thursday at 9:30am, returning at 2:50pm from the roadhouse, at A$20 one-way. Day tours from Perth are available (check with Perth's WA Visitor Centre, under "Visitor Information" earlier in the chapter).

You can get information and book guided town tours at the **New Norcia Tourist Information Centre,** New Norcia, WA 6509 (✆ **08/9654 8056;** www.newnorcia.wa.edu.au), in the Museum and Art Gallery, off the highway behind St. Joseph's. It keeps the same hours as the museum (see below). Reserve accommodations in advance, especially in the wildflower season of August through October.

EXPLORING THE TOWN & MONASTERY

The intriguing 2-hour walking tours are a must. Tickets cost A$23 for adults and A$14 for children 12 to 17, free for younger children, and include entrance to the Museum and Art Gallery, and tastes of local produce. Tours depart daily at 11am and 1:30pm, except December 25, and they allow time for you to attend prayers with the monks (see below) if you wish. The guide leads you around some of the town's 27 National Trust–classified buildings and gives insight into the monks' lifestyle. You will also see the frescoes in the old monastery chapel and in St. Ildephonsus's and St. Gertrude's colleges.

The Museum and Art Gallery ★ is full of relics from the monks' past—old mechanical and musical instruments, artifacts from the days when New Norcia was an Aboriginal mission, gifts from the queen of Spain, and an astounding collection of paintings by Spanish and Italian artists, dating from the 1400s. Give yourself at least an hour here. The Museum and Art Gallery are open daily from 9am to 4:30pm (closed Dec 25). Admission is A$10 for adults, A$6 for children 12 to 17, free for younger children. Don't leave the gift shop without some of the famous New Norcia Nut Cake.

Apart from joining the monks for 15-minute prayers in the monastery chapel five times a day (noon and 2:30pm are the most convenient for day visitors), you can join them for Mass in the Holy Trinity Abbey Church Monday to Saturday at 7:30am, Sunday at 9am, or 6:30pm for vespers.

WHERE TO STAY & DINE

St. Benedict's rules of hospitality are paramount, which means that part of the monastery is open to guests, but it's really for those who are looking for a quiet, reflective place to stay and don't mind abiding by a few rules. The accommodation is spartan, and the cost is a donation, with A$75 suggested. Contact the guesthouse (✆ 08/9654 8002; guesthouse@newnorcia.wa.edu.au) to book. For other visitors, the hotel (see below) is the best bet.

New Norcia Hotel When they thought a Spanish royal visit to New Norcia was imminent in 1926, the monks built this grandiose hotel fit for, well, a king. Sadly, the story is a myth, and the building was used for parents visiting children boarding at the town's colleges. In 1955, it became a hotel. The grand central staircase, soaring pressed-metal ceilings, and imposing Iberian facade hint at its former splendor. The rooms are simple but comfortable, and there are only shared facilities. It's nice to eat a meal at the bar or the charmingly faded dining room and to wander out of your room to sit on the massive veranda upstairs. The bar gets jumping (everything is relative) on Friday and Saturday nights when local farmers come to town. An exclusive beer, Abbey Ale, is available on tap and for takeaway. No smoking.

Great Northern Hwy., New Norcia, WA 6509. ✆ **08/9654 8034.** Fax 08/9654 8011. hotel@newnorcia.wa.edu.au. 15 units. A$95 double/twin with shared facilities. Extra person A$22. Continental breakfast included. AE, MC, V. **Amenities:** Restaurant; bar; smoke-free rooms. *In room:* Fridge, no phone.

MARGARET RIVER & THE SOUTHWEST ★★★

Margaret River: 277km (173 miles) S of Perth

For most Australians, the name "Margaret River" is synonymous with great wine. This is an area where every prospect pleases; no wonder U.S.-based *Wine Market Report* gave it the award for "Wine Tourism Region of the World" in 2006. It's a mere 3½ hours' drive from Perth.

Forty years ago, this was a quiet backwater, a simple countryside of dairy farms and forest, with a few insiders aware of some great surfing spots. A survey then found that the climate was remarkably similar to that of Bordeaux, and the first vineyards were planted. The area now has about 100 wineries and, while they produce only about 1% of Australia's wine output, they turn out around 15% of the country's "premium" wines. There's a growing selection of quality lodges and B&Bs, galleries, gourmet food outlets, and superb restaurants. Many craftspeople have set up here, together with producers of venison, cheese, chocolate, and olive oil. Statuesque forests, including tall but graceful karri trees (the world's third-tallest plant species), create beautiful dappled drives; the west coast has curving sandy beaches, spectacular surf breaks, and cliffs perfect for abseiling (rappelling) and rock climbing; the northern coast has wonderfully peaceful safe beaches; and there's a honeycomb of limestone caves filled with stalagmites, stalactites, and superb reflecting pools. Whales pass by June through December, wildflowers line the roads August through October, and wild birds, kangaroos, and shingle-backed lizards are everywhere. And the climate is kind to humans as well as vines.

The Margaret River region isn't very large, so is easy to get around. It reaches 120km (75 miles) from Cape Naturaliste in the north to Cape Leeuwin on the southwest tip of Australia, both with attendant lighthouses. If you like hiking, pack your boots, because there are plenty of trails, from a 15-minute stroll around Margaret River township or an hour's stroll along the Dunsborough beaches to a 6-day Cape-to-Cape trek along the western shore.

The main settlements are Dunsborough in the north, Margaret River Township in the center, and Augusta in the south. Busselton is the gateway to the region, though not really part of it.

Essentials

GETTING THERE It's a 3½-hour drive to Margaret River from Perth; take the Kwinana Freeway, which becomes the Forrest Highway, to Bunbury and pick up the Bussell Highway to Busselton. Beyond Busselton you turn left for Margaret River town and Augusta, or go straight on for Dunsborough and Caves Road.

Air Australia (✆ **08/9332 5011;** www.airaustralia.net) operates charter flights from Perth's Jandakot airport, from about A$660 same day return for up to three passengers. **Leeuwin Estate** winery (✆ **08/9759 0000;** www.leeuwinestate.com.au) arranges charter flights from Perth for A$550 per person (minimum two

TAKING A dip WITH FLIPPER

The wild dolphins that come to Monkey Mia's shore (see "The Coral Coast," p. 522) are justly famous. But you can **swim** with these creatures on the way to Margaret River, at Rockingham, 45 minutes south of Perth, and Bunbury 2 hours away.

Rockingham Wild Encounters ★ offers a "Swim with Wild Dolphins" adventure cruise from the Val Street Jetty, Rockingham (✆ **08/9591 1333;** www.dolphins.com.au). You are taken out into Cockburn Sound, where guides use aqua scooters to tow snorkelers into the action. The dolphins certainly seem to enjoy the encounter and a 99% success rate is claimed. Tours are daily September to May and include a light lunch, at A$205 per person, A$20 more with pickup from your Perth hotel. An alternative is the 2-hour "Dolphin Watch Eco Adventure" at A$65 adults, A$50 kids 3 to 12, and A$205 families of two adults and two children, more with Perth pickup. This leaves from the Penguin Island Jetty in nearby Shoalwater, as does the more extensive "Dolphins, Penguins, and Sea Lions" tour, which includes time on Penguin Island and a light lunch. Costs are A$108 adults, and A$84 children 3 to 12; more with Perth pickup.

At the Bunbury **Dolphin Discovery Centre,** Koombana Drive, Bunbury (✆ **08/9791 3088;** www.dolphindiscovery.com.au), bottlenose dolphins come into shore in Koombana Bay. You can stand with them free in the waist-deep "interaction zone" on the beach. The dolphins show up about 90% of the time in summer, but less so in winter; the best chance to see them is between 8am and noon. However, the water rarely has the same clarity as at Monkey Mia. Reservations are not necessary. From November to April (weather dependent), 3-hour **"Dolphin Swim Encounter"** tours enable you to snorkel, accompanied by a marine biologist, with some of the bay's 200-plus dolphins, for A$185 including equipment; you must be over 6 years old. **Dolphin Eco Cruises** run twice daily (except Dec 25 or in bad weather) from the center at 11am and 3:15pm (2pm in winter); they cost A$53 adults, A$35 kids 4 to 14, or A$161 families of two adults and two kids. The center has showers, a cafe, and a good little eco-display on the dolphin life cycle; admission is A$8 adults; A$5 seniors, students, and children; A$21 families. Tour costs include center entry. The center opens daily 8am to 4pm October to May, and 9am to 2pm June to September; closed December 25. For information about the ethics of swimming with dolphins, visit the **Whale and Dolphin Conservation Society** site (www.wdcs.org).

passengers), including return flights, tea, winery tour and tastings, and full a la carte lunch (excluding drinks) in the restaurant.

Southwest Coachlines (✆ **08/9324 2333;** www.southwestcoachlines.com.au) runs a daily service to Margaret River from Perth for about A$34. **Transwa** (✆ **1300/602 205** in Western Australia, or 08/9326 2600; www.transwa.wa.gov.au) also runs a coach service from Perth. The services take between 4½ and 5½ hours, so are not recommended. There is no train service to Margaret River, though the twice-daily *Australind* train does run from Perth to Bunbury, with coach connections onward.

Margaret River & the Southwest

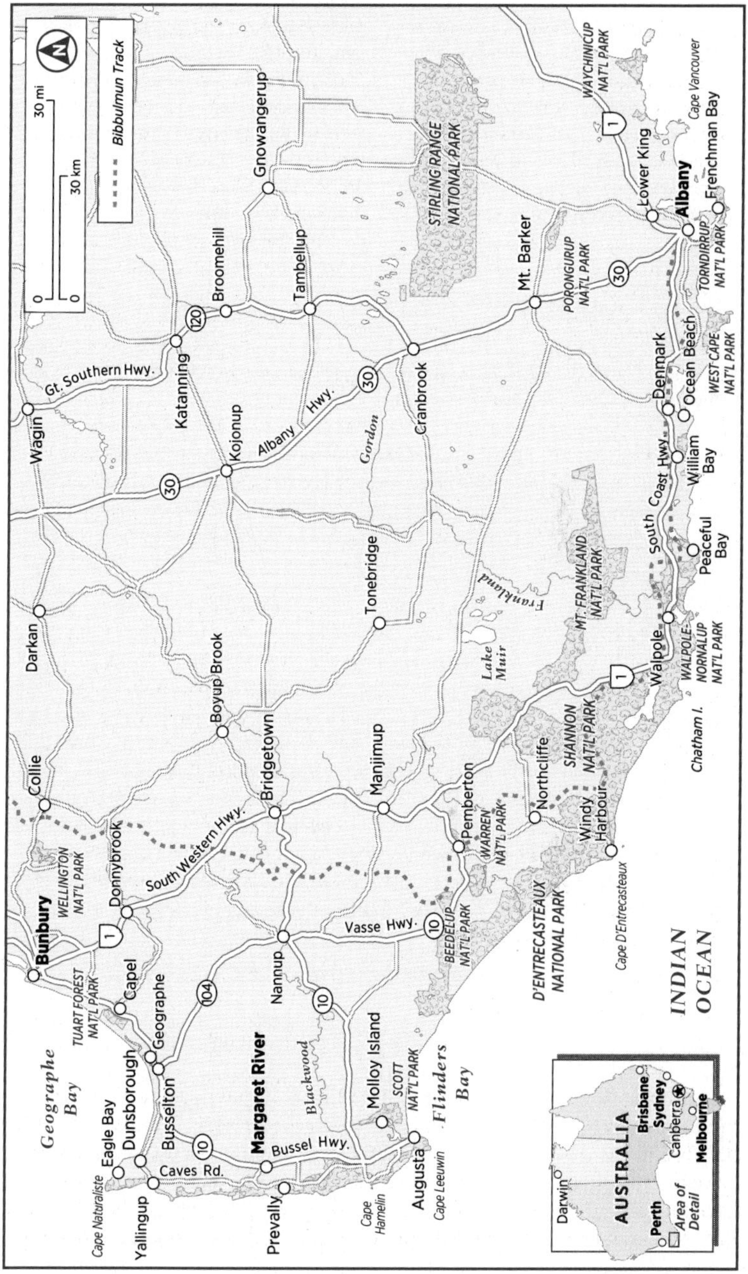

Concerts & Kookaburras

Every summer, Leeuwin Estate Winery (✆ 08/9759 0000; www.leeuwin estate.com.au) stages its Leeuwin Concert Series ★★★ starring leading showbiz lights (past performers have included Sting, k.d. lang, Dame Kiri Te Kanawa, Julio Iglesias, and Diana Ross) and usually a major orchestra, attended by 6,000 picnicking guests. Tickets are about A$130. There may be three of these events in a season, and they sell out months ahead. The concerts are held in the open air, below the winery, just as the sun is setting, accompanied by kookaburras cackling in the surrounding karri trees.

Driving yourself is the best way to get to Margaret River, and it gives you the necessary freedom to get around the region.

VISITOR INFORMATION The award-winning **Margaret River Visitor Centre** is one of the best and most helpful in the country. It's at 100 Bussell Hwy., Margaret River, WA 6285 (✆ **08/9780 5911;** www.margaretriverwa.com). You can book accommodations and pick up a winery guide, one listing the artisans of the region, and maps. The **Dunsborough Visitor Centre,** Shop 14, Dunsborough Park Shopping Centre, Dunsborough, WA 6281 (✆ **08/9755 3299;** www.geographebay.com), provides similar information. Both are open daily from 9am to 5pm; closed December 25.

GETTING AROUND Two north–south roads service the area, Bussell Highway and the slower, winding Caves Road. Numerous smaller roads connect the two, or loop down to bayside settlements renowned for their surfing opportunities. The Bussell Highway turns south 9km (5½ miles) past Busselton and runs down the middle of the region, through Margaret River town to Augusta and windswept Cape Leeuwin. Caves Road runs past Dunsborough, and then swirls southward, closer to the coast, past limestone caves and through karri forests toward Augusta.

A car is essential. **Hertz** (✆ **13 30 39** in Australia) has an office in Bunbury, or call **Avis** (✆ **13 63 33** in Australia) for reservations in the Southwest. For a taxi, call **Margaret River Taxi Service** (✆ **08/9757 3444**).

Several companies run sightseeing and winery tours from Margaret River or Perth, including **Margaret River with Neil McLeod** (see below, "Beyond the Wineries: Caves, Bush Tucker & More").

Touring the Wineries

Fans of premium wines will have a field day. Cabernet sauvignon and merlot are the star red varieties, with most wineries making a straight cabernet and/or a cabernet-merlot blend. Shiraz is also popular and Cape Mentelle makes a powerful zinfandel. Chardonnay is the standard single variety white wine, while fresh vibrant semillon–sauvignon blanc blends have become synonymous with the region. A few wineries make (Australian-style) Rieslings. Most wineries offer free tastings from 10am to 4:30pm daily, and several have restaurants serving lunch. There are two main clusters of vineyards; the biggest grouping is in the northern half in the Willyabrup area, with a smaller number, including several big names, around Margaret River Township.

A Pretty Jetty

Busselton Jetty (✆ 08/9754 0900; www.busseltonjetty.com.au) is the longest timber pile jetty in the Southern Hemisphere, stretching 1,841m (over 1 mile) out into shallow Geographe Bay. An underwater observatory has been built at the end, allowing visitors to go 8m (26 ft.) down and look out at the marine life that congregates around the massive 145-year-old timber supports. A major refurbishment to be completed in 2010 has restored damaged supports and facilities, widened the jetty, and allowed the jetty train to operate once more. The observatory is open daily except December 25, weather permitting, with tours operating hourly from 9:25am to 4:25pm October to April, and 10:25am to 3:25pm May to September. Jetty entry is A$2.50 adults over 14 years; the return train journey is A$10 adults and A$5 children 3 to 14; the train and observatory tour is A$28 adults, A$14 children, and A$75 families (two adults and two kids).

The region's best known winery is **Leeuwin Estate ★★**, Stevens Road, Margaret River (✆ **08/9759 0000;** www.leeuwinestate.com.au), set within magnificent grounds. It has a towering reputation with its Art Series chardonnay often rated Australia's finest. Winery tours run three times a day (see "Concerts & Kookaburras," p. 496). Its next-door neighbor, **Voyager Estate ★★**, Stevens Road, Margaret River (✆ **08/9757 6354;** http://voyagerestate.com.au), has exquisite rose gardens and a South African Cape Dutch–style cellar and top-notch restaurant (see p. 504).

The three pioneer vineyards from the late 1960s all still rate very highly. **Moss Wood ★★**, 926 Metricup Rd., Willyabrup (✆ **08/9755 6266;** www.mosswood.com.au), accepts visitors for really comprehensive tours Monday to Friday by appointment, while both **Vasse Felix ★**, Corner Caves Road and Harmans South Road, Cowaramup (✆ **08/9756 5000;** www.vassefelix.com.au), and **Cullen Wines ★★**, Caves Road, just north of Harmans South Road, Cowaramup (✆ **08/9755 5277;** www.cullenwines.com.au), have tasting rooms and restaurants. Other labels to look for are Cape Mentelle, Devil's Lair, Madfish (Howard Park Wines), Lenton Brae, Pierro, Woodlands, and Cape Grace Wines. **Ashbrook ★**, 379 Harman's Rd. South, Willyabrup (✆ **08/9755 6262;** www.ashbrookwines.com.au), takes a very serious approach to style and quality, and makes one of the best WA Rieslings. Some wineries make excellent "quaffers"—Aussie slang for easy-drinking, inexpensive wines. Vasse Felix makes Theatre Red and Theatre White, while Cape Mentelle sells 1.5-liter bottles of its red and white CMV wines.

Beyond the Wineries: Caves, Bush Tucker & More

Two lighthouses still operate (automatically) and are open to the public. **Cape Naturaliste Lighthouse** (✆ **08/9755 3955;** www.geographebay.com) is 13km (8 miles) outside Dunsborough set among wildflower-rich bushland, and surrounded by a variety of walk trails. It's a great spot for whale-watching in season. The entry fee, A$12 adults, A$6 children 5 to 16, and A$29 families of two adults and two kids, includes a guided tour. It's open 9am to 4:30pm (tours from 9:30am–4pm), closed

A Wine-Buying Tip

Most wineries don't deliver internationally, and the wine you like might not be exported to your country of residence, so use the services of the Margaret River Regional Wine Centre, 9 Bussell Hwy., Cowaramup (© 08/9755 5501; www.mrwines.com). It stocks most local wines, does daily tastings, and sells maps and guides. The expert staff will help you make your choices and even tailor your day's foray. It's open Monday to Saturday 10am to 8pm, and Sunday noon to 6pm (closed Good Friday and Dec 25). You can also order through the website.

December 25. **Cape Leeuwin Lighthouse** (© **08/9758 1920**), just south of Augusta, stands proudly where two oceans meet. It's the tallest lighthouse on mainland Australia. Guided tours run throughout the day, and the price includes the precinct entry fee—A$15 adults, A$7 children 4 to 16 (children under 4 not allowed up the tower). Precinct entry is A$5 adults and A$3 children. It's open daily, except December 25, from 8:45am to 5pm.

Six of the Southwest's 100 or so limestone caves are open to the public. Some contain elaborate formations and have lighting, stairs, and boardwalks to help you along the way. Stop at **CaveWorks**'s eco-interpretive center, Lake Cave, Caves Road (© **08/9757 7411;** www.margaretriver.com), before or after you visit the caves. It's open daily, except December 25, from 9am to 5pm. Entry is free if you tour Lake, Jewel, or Mammoth caves, otherwise it's A$2 per person.

Lake Cave, outside CaveWorks and 300 steps down an ancient sinkhole, contains a tranquil pond that reflects the exquisite formations. Four kilometers (2½ miles) north along Caves Road is **Mammoth Cave,** where you can see the fossilized jaw of an extinct giant wombat. **Jewel Cave ★**, 8km (5 miles) north of Augusta on Caves Road, is the prettiest. Tours of Lake and Jewel, and self-guided tours of Mammoth (using an MP3 system), each cost A$20 adults, A$10 children 4 to 16, A$50 for families of four. A Grand Tour Pass to all three costs A$48 adults, A$22 children 4 to 16, A$135 families, and is valid for 7 days. Mammoth is open from 9am to 5pm (last tour at 4pm); tours of Lake and Jewel run hourly from 9:30am to 3:30pm, daily except December 25. Booking is not required.

Calgardup and Giants Caves, run by the Department of Environment and Conservation, are more challenging. Both are unlit and self-guided but there are elevated boardwalks and marked paths. Visitors receive helmets, lamps, and information, and may spend as long as they like exploring (wear old clothes and sturdy footwear). Calgardup Cave on Caves Road, about 12 minutes' drive south of Margaret River, has seats throughout the cave and a stream that trickles through, all year. It opens daily (except on Dec 25 and 26) 9am to 4:15pm, and is suitable for all ages. Giants Cave, 20 minutes south of Margaret River on Caves Road, is one of the largest and deepest caves on the Leeuwin-Naturaliste Ridge, and provides a more adventurous experience. The infrastructure is minimal, and you clamber down 86m (282 ft.) utilizing ladders and tunnels. Entry times vary seasonally so check with **National Park Information Centre** (© **08/9757 7422**). Children under 6 are not allowed in Giants Cave. Tickets are available at either cave for A$15 adults, A$8

Scenic Forest Drives

Boranup Drive ★ is a magical detour off Caves Road through towering karris. It leaves Caves Road 6km (3¾ miles) south of Mammoth Cave and meanders through the forest on gravel roads on a glorious 14km (8¾-mile) drive. Boranup Forest, despite its impressive height, is regrowth, the entire area having been logged in the early 20th century. Make sure to check that your hire car can be driven on gravel roads.

children 6 to 15, and A$40 families (two parents and two kids), all including helmets and lamps. The center, at Calgardup Cave, also has walking maps and information on camping sites and activities in the Leeuwin-Naturaliste National Park.

Ngilgi Cave, Caves Road, Yallingup (✆ **08/9755 2152;** www.geographebay.com), farther north (closer to Dunsborough), has beautiful translucent stalactite "shawls" in its main chamber. Semiguided tours (guides are available to answer questions) run half-hourly from 10am to 3:30pm for A$19 adults, A$9.25 children 5 to 15, or A$47 for families of four. Ngilgi offers excellent guided adventure tours, where you go "backstage," crawling and even sliding through the farther reaches of the cave, in protective clothing. The tours usually run at 9:30am with a minimum of two people. The Ancient River Bed Tour takes 2 hours (A$42 adults and A$21 children); the Crystal Crawl Tour is 3 hours (A$93); the Ultimate Ngilgi Adventure takes 4 hours and costs A$135. The last two tours have a minimum age of 16 years. Book all tours at least 48 hours ahead. The cave is open every day except December 25. Guided walking tours around Ngilgi and Cape Naturaliste can also be booked here.

Food-based attractions are opening up in the area all the time. The **Berry Farm,** 43 Bessell Rd., outside Margaret River (✆ **08/9757 5054;** www.berryfarm.com.au), has attractively packaged, fruit-based preserves, wines, jams, and vinegars. The Cottage Café offers seasonal produce, open daily 10am to 4pm, except December 24, 25, and 26, Good Friday, and January 1. At the **Margaret River Chocolate Company ★**, Harman's Mill Road (at Harman's Rd. S.), Metricup (✆ **08/9755 6555**), you can participate in free tastings, watch the candy-making through a window, buy coffee and cakes at the cafe, and, of course, buy some mouth-watering chocolate. It's open daily 9am to 5pm, closed December 25. **Olio Bello ★★**, 1 Armstrong Rd., off Cowaramup Bay Road, Cowaramup (✆ **1800/982 170** in Australia or 08/9755 9771; www.oliobello.com), was the 2006 Australian Olive Grower of the Year. You can buy a range of organic olive oils, soaps, and body creams, dips, and tapenades, and there's a cafe. Olio Bello also has macadamias, fruit trees, and native shrubs, so the place is full of birds. It's open daily 10am to 4:30pm, closed Good Friday, December 25 and 26, and January 1.

Margaret River Venison, Caves Road, Margaret River, just south of Olio Bello (✆ **08/9755 5028;** www.mrvenison.com), is a family-run enterprise, selling products derived from deer raised on the property. It's open daily 9am to 5pm, closed December 25. The **Margaret River Dairy Company,** Bussell Highway, Cowaramup, just north of the village (✆ **08/9755 7588;** www.mrdc.com.au), uses local milk to make a range of award-winning cheeses and yogurts and is open 9:30am to 5pm; it's closed Good Friday, December 25 and 26, and January 1. Some of WA's

galleries GALORE

The natural beauty of the Margaret River region and its associated lifestyle have inspired many artists to make their homes here. You can watch them work and perhaps buy a unique souvenir from around 35 studios and galleries, mostly found close to Dunsborough or Margaret River town. Follow the **Artisans Map,** available from tourist information centers, hotels, and galleries, or check **www.margaretriverartisans.com.au**.

Near Dunsborough, **John Miller Design ★**, 51 Marrinup Dr. (off Caves Rd.), Yallingup (✆ **08/9756 6336**), showcases the creative handcrafted jewelry of John Miller. Others in the "don't miss" category here are **Gunyulgup Galleries,** Gunyulgup Valley Drive (off Caves Rd.) near Yallingup (✆ **08/9755 2177**), and **Yallingup Galleries** on Caves Road (✆ **08/9755 2372**), where you can see the work of many fine Australian artists, jewelers, and craftspeople. Not far away is **Happs Vineyard and Pottery,** Commonage Road, Dunsborough (✆ **08/9755 3479**). Miles Happ runs the pottery side while his father is in charge of the winery.

Just outside Margaret River, stop off to see potters Rod Dilkes and Tova Hoffman creating their lustrous "phoenix" bowls with iridescent glazes. **Dilkes-Hoffman Ceramics** is on Caves Road, 4km (2½ miles) north of Walcliffe Road (✆ **08/9757 2998**).

Serious lovers of glass art should head to **Fox Galleries,** Brockman Highway, Karridale, south of Margaret River (✆ **08/9758 6712**), which master glassmaker Alan Fox only opens by appointment. His superb creations are in numerous collections, including Buckingham Palace.

Beautiful furniture is made at several places, using the magnificent local jarrah timber. The best is at **Boranup Gallery ★★**, Caves Road, close to the Boranup Road turnoff (✆ **08/9757 7585**), featuring stunning jarrah burl inlays, as well as art, glass, and ceramic works.

An unusual gallery celebrates the life and work of one the world's greatest cartoonists, Paul Rigby. Rigby worked in Australia, London, and New York, including 25 years with the *New York Post* and the *New York Daily News.* He was also a prolific artist and illustrator, but sadly died in 2006. His widow and son now run the **Rigby Gallery & Studio,** featuring his work, at 282A Caves Rd., 2km (1¼ miles) south of Wallcliffe Road (✆ **08/9757 3713**), open Wednesday, Saturday, and Sunday 11am to 4pm or by appointment.

finest ice cream is made at **Simmo's Ice Creamery ★**, southeast of town at 161 Commonage Rd., Dunsborough (✆ **08/9755 3745;** www.simmos.com.au), which is open 10:30am to 5pm but closed December 25.

If you want to learn more about this region and see kangaroos in the wild, make time for an excellent value **Margaret River with Neil McLeod tour ★** (✆ **08/9757 2747;** www.margaretriver-mcleodtours.com). Neil was raised in the area on his parents' dairy farm and now runs illuminating tours covering the karri forest, vineyards and wildflowers; aspects of the region's early history; visits to Surfer's Point and Redgate Beach; and even his own bush property bounding with kangaroos. Billy tea and "Mum's orange cake" are served as part of the Sunset Kangaroo Safari, which costs A$45 adults and A$20 children 4 to 14. The full day winery, gallery, and brewery tour costs A$90 adults and A$65 children, including lunch. Tours depart daily, from the Margaret River Visitor Centre, or free from accommodations within 10km (6¼ miles) of the town. Neil also offers a comprehensive 3-day "Escape Package" out of Perth, including 2 nights of bed and breakfast and three lunches, for A$650 per person; it leaves on Tuesdays with a two-passenger minimum.

Surfing lessons from four-time Western Australian professional surfing champion **Josh Palmateer** (© **08/9757 3850,** or 0418/958 264 mobile; www.mrsurf.com.au) are a must! Two-hour lessons at Margaret River mouth (they will collect you from Margaret River town) cost A$130 for an individual lesson, and A$50 per person if you join a group (daily at 11am), including use of wet suits and boards. You can also have a private group, and discounts for 3-day attendance. Lessons run November to July. He also rents boards and wet suits and offers surf-guiding tours, if you are already a master of the surf universe and want to try any of the legendary breaks along the coast. Canoes and kayaks are available for hire, for paddling up the river.

From June through December, **whales** play just offshore all along the coast. There is a whale lookout near the Cape Naturaliste lighthouse. Daily 3-hour whale-watching cruises with **Naturaliste Charters ★★** (© **08/9725 8511;** www.whales-australia.com) depart June to August from Augusta and cruise around Flinders Bay, where you'll usually see both humpback and southern right whales, often in large numbers, and dolphins. September to December, the cruise departures switch to Dunsborough, where the migrating humpbacks rest their calves in sheltered Geographe Bay. Cruises cost A$75 adults, A$45 students 13 to 17, A$35 children 4 to 12, and A$200 for families of four.

For an intelligent and comprehensive take on the local indigenous history and culture, visit the **Wardan Aboriginal Cultural Centre ★**, 55 Injidup Spring Rd., Yallingup (© **08/9756 6566;** www.wardan.com.au).

Where to Stay

There's an amazing selection of places to stay in **Margaret River** town and **Dunsborough,** and around the vineyards. A couple of medium-size hotels can be found near Dunsborough on the edge of Geographe Bay; otherwise there are B&B establishments, self-catering villas and cottages, and many excellent lodges. Some places may require a minimum 2-night stay on weekends. The **Margaret River Visitor Centre** is a good place to get advice and suggestions. Nowhere here is far away, so the best idea is just to find a place that really suits your style and wallet, and use it as a base to tour the region.

Cape Lodge ★★★ A lovely secluded lodge in Cape Dutch style, it has been voted in the world's top 100 hotels and was rated Australia's best boutique hotel in 2008 and 2009. A member of the Small Luxury Hotels of the World group, it's set within 16 hectares (40 acres) of vineyards and natural forest, with lakes, rolling lawns, and rose beds. The immediate impression is of space and tranquillity—accompanied by birdsong. A number of small blocks or wings are strategically located so there are uninterrupted views, and you're never really aware of other people. The rooms are large and elegantly furnished with king-size beds and balconies or small courtyards. The Lodge Suite, in the original homestead, has an extremely comfortable lounge and two en-suite bathrooms. The restaurant, incorporating a guest lounge, has a glass wall and decking on the edge of the main lake. It has won several awards and opens for breakfast and dinner, with limited evening space for nonguests. About 50% of guests are international, mostly from the United Kingdom. There is no smoking indoors. The pool, the garden wing, and the Superior Spa Suites were refurbished in 2008.

Caves Rd. (btw. Abbey Farm and Johnson roads), Yallingup, WA 6282. ✆ **08/9755 6311.** Fax 08/9755 6322. www.capelodge.com.au. 22 units, with tub or spa and shower; unit for those with disabilities has shower only. A$475 garden suite; A$575–A$675 superior and forest suite; A$695 lodge suite. Rates include gourmet breakfast. 2-night stay required Sat–Sun. Inclusive packages at Christmas, Easter, and for special events. Ask about special offers. AE, DC, MC, V. Free parking. Children not recommended. **Amenities:** Licensed restaurant (14,000-bottle cellar); golf nearby; outdoor pool; tennis court; Wi-Fi main lodge (free). *In room:* A/C, LCD TV/DVD, CD player, hair dryer, minibar, MP3 docking station available.

Heritage Trail Lodge ★ Although it's on the highway in Margaret River town (within walking distance of restaurants), this row of cabin-style rooms, built in 1997 and renovated in 2007, sits in a serene karri forest, out of sight. Each spacious unit (including one for travelers with disabilities) has a veranda, a king-size double or king-size twin beds, and a double Jacuzzi, from which you can see the forest. Go for the rooms that overlook the bushwalk trails. No smoking indoors.

31 Bussell Hwy. (almost .5km/¼ mile north of town), Margaret River, WA 6285. ✆ **08/9757 9595.** Fax 08/9757 9596. www.heritage-trail-lodge.com.au. 10 units, all with shower and spa tub. A$259–A$370 double Dec–Apr, slightly less in low season. Extra person A$75. Rates include continental breakfast. Ask about midweek and romantic packages. Minimum 2-night stay weekends and holidays. AE, DC, MC, V. Free parking. Not suitable for children. **Amenities:** Wi-Fi in conservatory (free). *In room:* A/C, TV/DVD, CD player, hair dryer, minibar.

Redgate Beach Escape ★★ Four comfortable contemporary cottages sit on a hill, looking out across native bush to an expanse of ocean. There is no noise, just the breeze, birdsong, and the distant sound of the sea, with an occasional eagle floating past. The nearest traffic lights are 30 minutes away! The fully furnished cottages have a Balinese theme, feature full-height doors and windows facing the ocean, and are self-catering. Hosts Roger and Mim Budd built with a philosophy of clean uncluttered lines and sustainability. All utilities are underground, including a 250-kiloliter (66,000-gallon) rainwater tank that supplies the cottages. The Margaret River supermarket and several gourmet-produce outlets are nearby. No smoking indoors.

Lot 14 Redgate Rd., off Caves Rd. (12km/7½ miles southwest of) Margaret River, WA 6285. ✆ **08/9757 6677** or 0407/049 044 mobile. www.redgatebeachescape.com.au. 4 2-bedroom cottages, with indoor and outdoor showers. A$230–A$290 double. A$20 per extra person. Minimum 2-night stay. Long stay discounts. Ask about packages. AE, DC, MC, V. *In room:* A/C, TV/DVD, fridge, hair dryer, full kitchen, no phone.

Seashells Resort Yallingup ★ The restored Art Deco gem of Caves House (built 1938) is the heart of this resort, just a short walk up the slope from Yallingup Beach. The house, gardens, and croquet lawn (yes indeed milord) are all heritage-listed. Refurbishment completed in January 2006 retained the essential character of the place while introducing modern facilities, such as marble en-suite bathrooms with double spa baths. The property was further enhanced with the opening of the Garden Wing, featuring spa studios and self-contained apartments, in December 2007.

Yallingup Beach Rd., Yallingup, WA 6282. ✆ **1800/800 850** in Australia or 08/9750 1500. Fax 08/9750 1533. www.seashells.com.au. 22 units. A$185–A$215 Heritage rooms (shower only); A$255–A$315 Spa rooms and suites; A$385–A$425 Indijup (Caves House) suite; A$260–A$355 1-bedroom apt; A$375–A$555 2-bedroom apt. Ask about packages. AE, DC, MC, V. Free parking. **Amenities:** Restaurant; bar, guest lounge. *In room:* A/C, TV w/in-house movies, CD player, hair dryer, broadband Internet (A$10 per hr., A$35 per day), kitchen (in apts), minibar, MP3 docking station.

Where to Dine

Some of WA's finest dining is to be found in Margaret River, with quality chefs attracted by the opportunities, the produce, and the lifestyle. Many of the better wineries have restaurants, several of them superb, but most are open only for lunch. Besides the wineries listed below, you should consider Driftwood Estate, Brookland Valley Vineyard (Flutes Restaurant), Amberley Estate, Wise Vineyard, Lamont's Margaret River, and Rivendell Wines. **Leeuwin Estate's restaurant ★★**, Stevens Road, Margaret River (✆ **08/9430 4099**), also has terrific food. It's cozy in winter, and in summer its deck overlooking lawns is just the spot for lunch; it is open Saturday night.

Cullen Wines ★ MODERN AUSTRALIAN/ORGANIC Both the vineyard and the kitchen garden here are certified biodynamic. The granite-and-timber restaurant is unpretentious but comfortable, with a shady outdoor option, and offers casual, relaxed dining using totally fresh local produce. All dishes are defined as organic, biodynamic, gluten-free, vegetarian, and/or free-range. (Ask for the Organic Platter.) Cullen's produces an excellent semillon–sauvignon blanc blend, and its Diane Madeleine cabernet-merlot is perhaps the best in Margaret River.

Caves Rd., just north of Harmans South Rd., Cowaramup. ✆ **08/9755 5656.** www.cullenwines.com.au. Reservations recommended, especially on weekends. Main courses A$28–A$42 lunch only. AE, DC, MC, V. Daily 10am–4:30pm.

Must Margaret River ★ MODERN AUSTRALIAN Russell Blaikie, part-owner and chef of Must Winebar in Perth, has extended his winning wine bar/French bistro recipe to the heart of WA's wine country. Must Margaret River has added a new dimension to the region's dining and drinking options; the slick, smart, city-type place, which is slightly at odds with the usual laid-back style of the region, is attractive and appealing. Numerous wines are available by the glass or the taste, and there's also a snack-style menu. Dry-aged beef is a specialty.

107 Bussell Hwy., Margaret River. ✆ **08/9758 8877.** www.must.com.au. Reservations recommended. Main courses A$29–A$42. AE, DC, MC, V. Daily noon–midnight.

Newtown House ★★ MODERN FRENCH/AUSTRALIAN Folks come from far and wide to savor owner-chef Stephen Reagan's dishes, such as rare local venison with roast pears or quince. Desserts are no letdown—caramel soufflé with lavender ice cream is typical. The menu changes seasonally. Located in a historic 1851 homestead, the restaurant consists of two simple, intimate rooms with log fires in winter, and it's BYO. It was voted "Best Country Restaurant in WA" five times.

737 Bussell Hwy. (9km/5½ miles past Busselton), Vasse. ✆ **08/9755 4485.** www.newtownhouse.com.au. Reservations recommended, especially for dinner. Main courses about A$34. AE, DC, MC, V. Tues–Sat lunch from 10am, dinner from 6:30pm.

Vasse Felix ★★ MODERN AUSTRALIAN One of Margaret River's original wineries, the restaurant and cellar door are set within forest and vineyards 2km (1¼ miles) from Caves Road. They occupy an attractive modern two-story building, with the upstairs dining area presenting fresh regional cuisine. Some of the extensive Holmes à Court family art collection is displayed downstairs. The restaurant is frequently rated as the best in the area, and the menu varies seasonally.

If Wine Is Not Your Tipple

If you need a "cleansing ale" after your wine-tasting, head for Bootleg Brewery, Pusey Road, Wilyabrup (✆ 08/9755 6300), for a range of amber fluids, all brewed on the premises. There's a tasty golden pils and a real snorter—a prizewinning porter called Raging Bull. Complementing the beers is a menu of tasty dishes, such as Bootleg Stockman's Pie and a Brewers Platter, as well as the usual pub-style food. Main courses cost around A$20 to A$30, and the lakefront setting—with a playground—is a relaxing spot for lunch after a tough morning on the tourist trail. It's open daily 11am to 6pm, with lunch served from noon. Make a reservation on weekends and holidays.

Corner Caves Rd. and Harmans South Rd., Cowaramup. ✆ **08/9756 5000.** www.vassefelix.com.au. Reservations recommended, especially on weekends. Main courses A$30–A$40; set menu A$45 for 2 courses, A$55 for 3 courses (lunch only). AE, DC, MC, V. Daily from noon. Closed Dec 25–26, and Good Friday.

Voyager Estate ★★★ 🎁 MODERN AUSTRALIAN Nothing has been spared in attention to style and detail at WA's finest winery and restaurant. Palatial white gates lead into spotless grounds lined with rose gardens and what surely is the tallest flagpole in WA. In one corner, tucked behind a formal Cape-style garden, is the elegant white Cape Dutch cellar and restaurant (based on the mansions and wineries in South Africa's Cape region). The restaurant is in a long timber-vaulted room strung with chandeliers; it won WA's award for "Best Winery Restaurant" for 3 successive years. The menu is imaginative, varies seasonally, and comes with recommended wines (available by the glass). Try the taste plate or seafood *assiette,* and leave room for the specially selected range of cheeses. There are alternative vegetarian and gluten-free menus.

Stevens Rd. (just south of) Margaret River. ✆ **08/9757 6354.** www.voyagerestate.com.au. Reservations recommended, especially on weekends. Main courses A$29–A$44; degustation menu with wine for A$145 (lunch only). AE, DC, MC, V. Daily 10am–5pm. Winery tours at A$25 Tues, Thurs, and Sun at 11am, or with set lunch for A$65. Closed Good Friday and Dec 25–26.

Watershed Wines ★ ☺ MODERN AUSTRALIAN Most restaurants here have beautiful settings, but Watershed tops the lot. You sit on the balcony, looking out over serried vineyards with a stunningly blue lake sitting in the middle distance. It's enough to make you forget your lunch—almost. Once again, quality food is married with wine by the glass, with the restaurant winning an award for "Best Family Dining" 2 years in a row. There's also a cafe, which caters to kids and provides more casual dining. Try the beef fillet with the savoury fig baklava.

Corner Bussell Hwy. and Darch Rd., Margaret River. ✆ **08/9758 8633.** www.watershedwines.com.au. Reservations recommended, especially on weekends. Main courses A$32–A$40 lunch only. AE, DC, MC, V. Daily noon–3pm; cafe 10am–4:30pm.

THE SOUTH COAST ★★

The coastal region from Albany westwards to Margaret River has suffered—and gained—from the proximity of its famous neighbor. Like Margaret River it is a rich region of forests and pastures, vineyards and craft outlets, coastal scenery, and appealing accommodation options, but without the crowds and sophistication, and there's more wilderness. It's a simpler existence here, closer to nature and without the need to instantly impress. You're encouraged to linger, to savor the countryside and its bounty, based upon a mild climate tempered by the nearby ocean.

Albany ★★ is WA's oldest settlement, set alongside a superb natural harbor. It has been involved with some of Australia's most significant historical events, but has retained an essential simplicity. West from here are the two adjacent but very different towns of **Denmark ★** and **Walpole.** Denmark is a bustling town, part seaside resort, part retirement/lifestyle retreat, and part tourist center, while Walpole is much smaller and more basic. They are "tied" together by the magnificent forest that sits midway between the two, and the magical **Treetop Walk ★★★** that soars through the upper reaches of giant tingle and karri trees. The karri is one of the world's tallest trees, growing up to 90m (295 ft.) high; it's also one of the most graceful, growing true and straight with no branches in its lower half, and with a beautiful smooth bark that shades from pale grey to creamy-gold.

Another 120km (75 miles) northwest of Walpole is the timber town of **Pemberton ★**. The timber industry is slowly dying, with most "old growth" forests now preserved for posterity, but vineyards and truffle farms are taking over. There are superb tree-lined drives and, for the adventurous, the chance to climb towering old fire-lookout trees.

Sweeping through the region is Australia's greatest bushwalk, the **Bibbulmun Track ★**, which takes in the best of the wilderness areas. That's the real focus of this region—the wilderness—and why many of the listed accommodation options are outside the towns; they are by streams, forests, or vineyards, surrounded by the sights and sounds of nature.

Albany ★★

409km (256 miles) SE of Perth

First settled in 1826, Albany (pop. 25,000) is now the largest town and port along the south coast. It's set among wooded granite hills on the shores of an enormous double-bay natural harbor. The outer portion is the broad King George Sound, while the inner part is Princess Royal Harbour, where the port stands. Albany has several strong links to the Anzac story, and the first great Anzac Convoy assembled here, but these days the harbor plays host only to grain carriers, fishing boats, dolphins, and pelicans.

History of a different sort can be found on the opposite side of the Sound, on the site of Australia's last whaling station at Cheynes Beach, now converted to the **Whale World Museum ★★**. The whaling only stopped in 1978, and the whales have since become a tourist attraction, with increasing numbers cruising past and into King George Sound. The untamed Southern Ocean is very close to here, with various natural features carved into the granite as testament to the power of the sea.

Modern developments and high-rises have passed Albany by, so it remains a quietly bustling and attractive town, with numerous buildings reflecting its early days. It's the centre of a rich agricultural region, historically important for sheep and wheat but now with numerous vineyards producing high class wines. The local national parks are ablaze with wildflowers every spring, with WA's only "mountain" range, the Stirlings, 80km (50 miles) north of town, a major center.

Albany's heritage and business activities are based along York Street, which slopes down to the harbor. Several 19th-century buildings, and many of the town's cafes and restaurants, line the street, which is wide enough to have center parking. There are numerous scenic drives and walkways.

ESSENTIALS

GETTING THERE **Skywest Airlines** (✆ **1300/660 088** in Australia; www.skywest.com.au) has approximately 1¼-hour flights up to three times daily from Perth. Airfares start at approximately A$140 one-way. The airport is 11km (7 miles) north of town.

Transwa (✆ **1300/662 205** in Australia) operates a daily coach service between Perth and Albany. The journey takes about 6 hours and costs A$56 adults and A$28 children 5 to 15.

If driving yourself, beware of wildlife at dusk and nighttime. A good spot to stop on the journey is Kojonup with its excellent Kodja Place which tells the graphic story of a country community.

Several tour companies, including **Australian Pinnacle Tours** (✆ **1300/551 687** in Australia, or 08/9417 5555; www.pinnacletours.com.au) and **Western Xposure** (✆ **1800/621 200** in Australia; www.westernxposure.com.au), offer package trips to Albany and the surrounding regions.

VISITOR INFORMATION The **Albany Visitor Centre** (✆ **08/9841 9290;** www.albanytourist.com.au) is in the old railway station, Proudlove Parade, Albany WA 6330, on the foreshore. It is open daily from 9am to 5pm except December 25.

GETTING AROUND **Avis** (✆ **08/9842 2833**) and **Budget** (✆ **08/9841 7799**) have offices in Albany. You may want to drive on gravel roads in the forest areas to the west, so check for restrictions for driving on such roads before hiring.

What to See & Do

Stroll the streets of downtown, taking in historic buildings such as the Town Hall, St. John's Church, and those along Stirling Terrace—especially the wonderful brick confection of the Old Post Office. Walk or cycle along the bush-lined Marine Drive Scenic Path, which loops around the Mt. Adelaide headland between Albany Port and Middleton Beach, passing the Ataturk statue.

You must visit **Whale World ★★**, Frenchman Bay Road, 22km (14 miles) south of Albany (✆ **08/9844 4021;** www.whaleworld.org), to see how Australia's last whaling station operated. The entire process is there for you to see or rather, imagine, with all the original decks and boilers, vats and cranes still in place. Several whale skeletons provide an impressive reminder of the size to which whales can grow. The site opens daily from 9am to 5pm, except December 25. Admission is A$25 adults, A$10 children 6 to 12, A$15 students 13 to 18, and A$55 families (up to three children). This includes free guided tours which leave on the hour from 10am to 3pm. There's a cafe with views across the sound. Allow 2 to 3 hours.

A short distance across the headland is the Southern Ocean with all its uncertainties: brilliant sparkling blue sea when fine, and wind-swept storm-laden fury when roused. Sheer granite cliffs plunge into the water, with dramatic sea-eroded features such as the Gap, the Blowholes, and the Natural Bridge.

The road back into town passes an unusual venture, the **Great Southern Distilling Company ★**, 252 Frenchman Bay Rd., Albany (✆ **08/9842 5363;**

The Anzac Trail

The **Princess Royal Fortress** was built in the late 19th century overlooking King George Sound, to counter a perceived Russian threat. It is now a museum that commemorates, among other things, the start of the Anzac legend. The Anzac Convoy that assembled here in October 1914 had 20,000 men on 36 troop-carrying ships, and six accompanying warships. Albany later saw the start of the Anzac Day dawn service tradition when Padre Arthur White, who had been a chaplain with the forces, returned to Albany and decided there should be a commemoration, here where the troops last saw Australia.

A statue of Turkish leader Kemal Ataturk was erected between King George Sound and Princess Royal Harbour, in recognition of the bond that later developed between Australia and Turkey. The Desert Mounted Corps Memorial on nearby Mt. Clarence was originally built at Port Said after World War I, but blown up during the 1956 Suez conflict. The remnants came back to Australia and this is a replica, but using the stones of the original base.

www.distillery.com.au). This boutique distillery uses mostly local produce to generate small quantities of gin, brandy, grappe, and WA's first single-malt whisky. There are plans to create a peated whisky as well. The stylish tasting room and coffee lounge is open daily 10am to 5pm. A nearby turnoff leads to the **Albany Wind Farm ★**, located in prime position high above the ocean some 12km (7½ miles) southwest of the town. Twelve giant turbines spin endlessly, generating about 75% of Albany's power needs. It's a surprisingly attractive and feel-good installation, open to the public.

Several wineries provide cellar doors and tastings, in and near Albany. One of the more unusual is **Oranje Tractor ★**, 198 Link Rd., off South Coast Highway, 12km (7½ miles) from town, Albany (✆ **08/9842 5175;** www.oranjetractor.com), named after its still-working 1964 Fiat tractor. The grapes are organically grown and hand-picked, and their Riesling won a trophy at the 2008 National Wine Show. A cellar door tasting plate is offered, based on "food miles" to support local producers.

If natural fragrances or oils are your thing, make your way to **Mount Romance ★**, on the corner of Down Road and Albany Highway, 15km (9½ miles) north of Albany (✆ **08/9845 6888;** www.mtromance.com.au), open daily 9am to 5pm. The wafting soothing scent of sandalwood is almost palpable. A distillery and factory produce a wide range of sandalwood (and emu) oils and other body-care products, and there are free daily tours of the facility. Sandalwood oil is a major element of the on-site Santal Signature Spa treatments, and of "The Cone, the Gong, and the Bowl" experience, which is available in 1-hour sessions for A$18. Bookings are essential.

Try to be in town on a Saturday morning, to experience the **Albany Farmers Market ★**, on Collie Street, when the local farmers and orchardists bring their produce to town, or follow the **Taste Albany Trail,** which takes you to the individual farm gates.

For a gentle relaxing time, take a half-day scenic cruise around King George Sound, with **Silver Star Cruises** (✆ **04/2842 9876;** www.whales.com.au). You'll have the company of passing dolphins and optimistic pelicans and the chance to see whales from June to October. The 2½-hour cruises leave at 9:30am and 1pm (subject to weather conditions) and cost A$75 adults, A$40 children, and A$200 families of four.

The **Albany Waterfront** is being extensively redeveloped, with plans for a marina, an entertainment center, a hotel, a promenade, shops, cafes, and restaurants. They're all scheduled to open late 2010.

WHERE TO STAY

The **Albany Visitor Centre** offers a free accommodation booking center (✆ **08/9841 9290;** www.albanytourist.com.au).

Dog Rock Motel Albany has numerous motels and this is probably the best of them. Close to the center, it's named after a nearby granite boulder that looks like a dog's head. Go for the front rooms which have been renovated and have something of a view. The motel's Lime 303 Restaurant has won a WA award for best casual licensed restaurant.

303 Middleton Rd., Albany, WA 6330. ✆ **1800/035 265** in Australia, or 08/9841 4422. Fax 08/9842 1027. www.dogrockmotel.com.au. 81 units, 66 with shower only. A$125–A$189 double; A$229 family room. Extra person A$20. Children 2 and under stay free in parent's room. AE, DC, MC, V. **Amenities:** Restaurant. *In room:* A/C, TV, fridge, hair dryer, Internet.

Norman House Half-hidden behind an enormous magnolia tree, this house was built in 1852 but has been extensively modified. It's something of a rabbit warren and rather cluttered but with an idiosyncratic charm. This is a friendly, quirky, home-style bed and breakfast place. The house, magnolia, and oak tree out the back are all heritage-listed, and the town center is just steps away.

28 Stirling Terrace, Albany, WA 6330. ✆ **08/9841 5995.** Fax 08/9841 5995. http://members.westnet.com.au/normanhouse. 6 units, 3 with en-suite bathroom, 3 with private bathroom, all with showers only. A$130–A$140 double including breakfast. Extra adult A$35, extra child (3–12) A$25. MC, V. **Amenities:** Breakfast room, TV lounge; Internet. *In room:* Fridge, hair dryer.

The Rocks Albany ★★★ This is the best accommodation on the south coast. It has style, location, comfort, and an impeccable pedigree. Once a vice-regal summer residence, it has been lovingly restored to provide that same level of luxury. The elegant, two-storied, balconied stone mansion sits on 0.8 hectares (2 acres) of tended gardens and rolling lawns, with a secure parking area and sloping brick pathways to allow full wheelchair access. Inside are a library, billiard and music rooms, lounges, and six superbly furnished bedrooms, some with four-poster beds and most with views across Princess Royal Harbour. A genuine gourmet breakfast is provided.

182–188 Grey St. West (500m/⅓ mile from town center), Albany, WA 6330. ✆ **08/9842 5969.** Fax 08/9842 5972. www.therocksalbany.com.au. 6 units, 2 with shower only. A$355–A$455 double. Rates include gourmet breakfast. Minimum 2 nights on long weekends, 3 nights Christmas and Easter. Ask about packages. AE (3.5% extra), MC, V. Not suitable for children 11 and under. **Amenities:** Dining room; lounge; tennis court. *In room:* A/C, TV/DVD, fridge, hair dryer, Wi-Fi (free).

WHERE TO DINE

Albany has numerous, mostly casual eating places, which largely promote the use of fresh local produce.

Calamari's at Beachside SEAFOOD The setting is great, right on Middleton Beach, gazing out to King George Sound. The service is friendly, but the cooking of fish dishes can be uneven. The wine list has local wines at excellent prices, by the glass or bottle.

2 Flinders Parade, Middleton Beach, Albany. ✆**08/9841 7733.** Mains A$29–A$45. MC, V. Daily from 6pm.

Lavender Cottage ★ FRENCH This is a delightful place, with friendly service and good food in a charming old cottage. It's open for tea and cakes or lunches through the week, with fresh salads and French-inspired blackboard menu. The *pièce de résistance* is the Friday night gourmet dinner, with a set menu based on whatever is fresh at the time.

55 Peels Place (close to York St.), Albany. ✆**08/9842 2073.** Fri evening gourmet dinner A$60; bookings essential. MC, V. Mon–Fri 9am–3:30pm; Fri from 6:30pm.

Tanglehead Brewing Company PUB FOOD Based in a revamped and refurbished old hotel, Tanglehead (the name is based on an old Scottish myth) is a microbrewery clearly seen behind glass panels, with adjacent eating area. The large modern kitchen dishes up good-size appetizing meals from an adventurous menu. The "hand-crafted" pilsner goes very well with the 'roo filet.

72 Stirling Terrace, Albany. ✆**08/9841 1733.** Main courses A$19–A$35. MC, V. Daily from 11am.

Venice Pizza Bar & Restaurant ITALIAN This is a popular, bustling place slap bang in the center of town. Open all day, it provides an excellent spot for coffee or a casual meal, with friendly service. A few tables on the pavement allow you to become part of the York Street ambience. Pizzas are popular, as well as the standard Italian and seafood dishes, and it's BYO.

179 York St., Albany. ✆ **08/9841 3978.** Mains A$19–A$33. MC, V. Mon–Sat 9:30am–10:30pm; Sun 4:30–10:30pm.

Wild Duck MODERN AUSTRALIAN This restaurant has been reported as the best in Albany and one of the best in WA. The menu is limited but imaginative, with unusual combinations and contrasts. The focus is apparently very much on the food, with duck a feature, and the place is BYO.

112 Lower York St., Albany. ✆**08/9842 2554.** www.wildduckrestaurant.com. Reservations essential. Mains A$28–A$40. MC, V. Wed–Sun from 6pm.

Denmark & Walpole

Denmark: 54km (34 miles) W of Albany; Walpole: 120km (75 miles) W of Albany

These two towns, strung out along the South Coast Highway, both lay claim to the magnificent **Valley of the Giants** ★★★, which stands between them. The rolling forested countryside has green paddocks and vineyards where cleared, with a number of rivers slicing down to coastal inlets. The area is made for slow touring, with winding roads, frequent vistas, and a succession of wineries, craft outlets, cafes, and restaurants—and friendly open people.

Denmark sits on the Denmark River, just above where the paperbark-tree-lined river runs into the broad Wilson Inlet. It's a compact, busy little place with all the essential services. The inlet is an ideal spot for quiet fishing, sailing, and canoeing. Two significant tourist drives loop away into the hills north and west of the town. Mt. Shadforth Drive is the shorter, while Scotsdale Road has a greater variety of interesting places to visit.

Walpole is a much smaller and quieter place, hemmed in by national parks on all sides, with the finest areas designated as the Walpole Wilderness. It's a pleasant little spot, with a few accommodation and eating options. The adjacent waterways are one of the highlights of this area.

The jewel in the crown, however, is the Valley of the Giants, some 15km (9 miles) east of Walpole. This area has never been logged and the trees are simply magnificent, mostly a mix of towering karri and red tingle. Looping through the upper branches is the elevated walkway of the **Treetop Walk ★★★**, while a boardwalk at ground level leads through the **Ancient Empire.**

There are several roads that lead down to bays and beaches along the coast, such as rightly named Peaceful Bay and the granite-boulder-decorated beaches of Greens Pool and Elephant Rocks. Like everywhere in this region, they are quiet, uncrowded places, except during the Christmas holidays and summer long weekends.

The **Bibbulmun Track ★** weaves its slow and scenic way through the entire area. If you really want to get away from it all, this is the way to do it.

ESSENTIALS

GETTING THERE There are tours that take in the area, but otherwise you're best driving yourself and going at your own pace. If so, be aware of the potential wildlife and gravel road problems. A normal car is fine for this area, unless you want to take some of the four-wheel-drive tracks that lead down to remote coastal bays.

Several tour companies, including **Australian Pinnacle Tours** and **Western Xposure** (see "Albany" earlier) offer package trips that traverse this region.

VISITOR INFORMATION The **Denmark Visitor Centre,** 73 South Coast Hwy. at Ocean Beach Road, Denmark, WA 6333 (✆ **08/9848 2055;** www.denmark.com.au), provides information on the area and an accommodation booking service. The center was designed especially to house the Bert Bolle Barometer (see below) and is open daily 9am to 5pm except December 25.

WHAT TO SEE & DO

When you arrive in Denmark call into the Visitor Centre, to look at the world's largest barometer, as recognized by *Guinness World Records*. The **Bert Bolle Barometer** is a giant water-based working instrument 12m (47 ft.) high housed in its own tower.

Take a day's leisurely driving to follow the **Scotsdale** and/or **Mount Shadforth tourist drives** that wind through the countryside north and west of Denmark. On the Scotsdale route, call in on modern, sophisticated **Howard Park Winery,** 2km (1¼ miles) from town (✆ **08/9848 2345;** www.howardparkwines.com.au), one of the highly regarded producers in this area. Try their Riesling and shiraz wines. It's open 10am to 4pm daily, except on December 25, Good Friday, and until noon on April 25. Take a short diversion on to Lantzke Road to visit the Denmark Berry Farm and the **Jonathan Hook Studio** (✆ **08/9848 1436;** www.jonathanhook.com) to see some striking ceramic work. The studio opens 10am to 5pm Monday to Friday and holiday weekends noon to 4pm. Farther on, at the junction with McLeod Road, make sure you stop at the **Pentland Alpaca Tourist Farm** (✆ **08/9840 9262;** http://pentlandalpacafarm.com.au), which has an amazing collection of animals—not just alpacas—for you to get really close and intimate with. There are koalas, dingoes, baby kangaroos, emus (with inquisitive habits), and Tyson the Bison. There's also a cafe and craft gallery. The farm is open daily 10am to 4pm, with koala

Swaying Through the Treetops

The Treetop Walk ★★★ (✆ 08/9840 8263; www.dec.wa.gov.au/content/view/355/1045) is something really special. A 600m (2,000-ft.) see-through steel-mesh walkway some 40m (131 ft.) above the ground reaches out across a forested valley. The walkway, ensconced within the tops of the trees, is built upon tall anchored pylons at the end of each walkway section, which allows the structure to sway with the wind or as a reaction to people walking along it. It can be a spooky feeling to realize that the steel structure you're standing on is moving, and not necessarily in concert with the branches all around you. But it's exciting and wonderful, too. Each anchor point has a platform where you can catch your breath and let others overtake you. It's impossible to take everything in on your first walk, so there's provision to go round again at no extra charge.

feeding at 10am and bottle feeding of the "babies" at 3pm; it's closed December 24 and 25. Entry is A$12 adults, A$6 children 3 to 15, and A$35 families with up to three children. The Mount Shadforth Drive has some great views, as well as the charming rural retreat of the **Lake House ★**, Turner Road off Mount Shadforth (**✆ 08/9848 2444;** www.lakehousedenmark.com.au), with its wine tasting area and restaurant (serving fresh lunches and coffee) overlooking a tranquil lake and terraced gardens. It's open 11am to 5pm daily except December 25.

Other attractions worth visiting in the Denmark area include the **South Coast Wood Works Gallery,** South Coast Highway, 17km (10 miles) east of Denmark (**✆ 08/9845 2028;** www.wn.com.au/dmalcolm/ww), which showcases the work of some 40 local craftspeople. It's open 10am to 5pm Wednesday to Sunday and daily during school holidays, except May to August, when it's open by appointment. The sweetest place of all around Denmark is **Bartholomew's Meadery,** South Coast Highway, 16km (10 miles) west of Denmark (**✆ 08/9840 9349;** www.honeywine.com.au), which sells a wide range of honey-based products, including ice cream and mead (honey wine). It's open daily 9:30am to 4:30pm, 9am to 5pm during school holidays, and is closed on December 25.

The **Valley of the Giants ★★★** is the must-see attraction around here. In addition to the Treetop Walk (see "Swaying Through the Treetops," below), there's the **Ancient Empire,** at ground level, where a boardwalk takes you round and even through the gnarled and buttressed trunks of the venerable red tingles. One ticket covers both. Both are open 9am to 5pm daily, and 8am to 6pm December 26 to January 26 (closed Dec 25). The cost is A$10 adults, A$6 children 6 to 15, and A$25 families. There's a shop and interpretive center.

In Walpole, the **WOW Wilderness Ecocruise ★★** (**✆ 08/9840 1036;** www.wowwilderness.com.au) sails through the shallow Walpole and Nornalup Inlets to the coastal wilderness. Guide Gary Muir provides one of the most informative, entertaining, and thought-provoking tours you will find, and has fittingly won the state's top guiding award. The tours run daily from 10am to 12:30pm, except in August and on December 25, and cost A$40 adults and A$15 children 5 to 15.

WHERE TO STAY

The **Denmark Visitor Centre** offers a free tour and accommodation booking service (✆ **08/9848 2055;** www.denmark.com.au). It's open daily 9am to 5pm except on December 25.

Bayside Villas Walpole has limited facilities, and these self-catering villas, built in late 2000, on the edge of town provide simple but comfortable accommodation. One villa has three bedrooms, while two others have two stories (with spas). They're close to the WOW cruises jetty.

2 Boronia Ave., Walpole, WA 6398. ✆ **08/9840 1888.** www.baysidevillas.com.au. 6 units, most with shower only. High season (long weekends and Christmas holidays) A$160–A$180 double; low season A$135–A$155 double. Extra person A$20 (high) or A$15 (low). MC, V. Free parking. *In room:* A/C, TV/DVD, hair dryer, kitchen.

Karma Chalets Ten well-appointed cedar chalets, each with private balcony, stand on the edge of eucalypt woodland, with views over forests, vineyards, and paddocks to Wilson Inlet. It's all very peaceful, with ample birdlife, semitame possums, and wandering kangaroos. Two chalets are designed for a couple while the others have additional upstairs accommodations. Most have two-person spa baths.

1572 South Coast Hwy., 5km (3 miles) west of Denmark (next to Forest Hill Winery), WA 6333 ✆ **08/9848 1568.** www.karmachalets.com.au. 10 units. From A$155–A$255 double, extra adult A$25–A$30, extra child A$15–A$25. Ask about specials. MC, V. *In room:* A/C, TV/DVD, fridge, hair dryer, kitchen, BBQ.

Tree-Elle Retreat ★★ ☺ 🎁 Four beautifully furnished double-story houses with stocked pantries stand among landscaped gardens looking across natural bush to Irwin Inlet. A large communal organic veggie and herb garden—and chicken coop—are there for guest consumption, while the numerous pets on the grounds will entertain the youngsters. Fresh food (including marron) and wine can be provided if ordered ahead.

Bow Bridge, Denmark, WA 6333 (38km/24 miles west of Denmark on South Coast Hwy.). ✆ **08/9840 8471.** www.treeelle.com. 4 units. A$290–A$310 2 guests in 3-bedroom house, extra person A$40; A$310–A$330 2 guests in 4-bedroom house, extra person A$45. Minimum 2-night stay; A$50 extra for less than 2-night stay. Breakfast included. Ask about packages. AE, DC, MC, V. **Amenities:** Spa studio. *In room:* A/C, TV/DVD w/free movies, CD, hair dryer, kitchen.

WHERE TO DINE

A few of the wineries have lunchtime restaurants, including Lake House (see above) and Forest Hill (see Greenpool below), and there are several cafes in both towns. Below are some of the best restaurants in the area.

Denmark Bakery 🎁 BAKERY This is no ordinary pie shop; it makes award-winning gourmet varieties, including "Garlic Tiger Prawn" and "Vinda-Roo." The pies are a good size with plenty of filling, and you can eat at veranda tables or take away. Because it's a bakery, you can also buy cakes, rolls, and sandwiches.

27 Strickland St., Denmark. ✆ **08/9848 2143.** Gourmet pies A$5–A$7. MC, V. Daily 7am–5pm.

Greenpool Restaurant ★ MODERN AUSTRALIAN This stylish, modern eatery is part of the Forest Hill winery complex, 4km (2½ miles) west of Denmark. The menu is short and reflects the chef's focus on fresh local produce. Try the Regional Tasting Plate.

South Coast Hwy., Denmark. ✆ **08/9848 0091.** www.foresthillwines.com.au. Reservations recommended. Main courses A$30–A$40. AE, DC, MC, V. Mid-Feb to mid-Dec Fri–Sun noon–4pm and 6–9pm (Fri only); mid-Dec to mid-Feb daily noon–4pm and 6–9pm (Fri only).

Nornalup Teahouse Restaurant ★★ AUSTRALIAN This was a real surprise. Nornalup is not even big enough to be called a village, but we'd asked for suggestions on where to eat, and this was the first to come up. The enterprising chef at the Nornalup Teahouse is producing some top-notch food, with a good locally based wine list. Try the marron with scallops and fennel.

6684 South Coast Hwy., Nornalup. ✆ **08/9840 1422.** www.nornalupteahouse.com.au. Main courses A$24–A$38. MC, V. Wed–Sun, Mon, and school holidays 11:30am–9pm.

Pemberton

335km (209 miles) S of Perth; 122km (76 miles) NW of Walpole.

Pemberton and nearby Manjimup have been major timber towns and still have operating mills—though at much reduced capacity. The surrounding countryside is a mosaic of forest (mostly karri), pasture, orchards and vineyards, crisscrossed by numerous flowing rivers, many with wild trout. Pemberton has been slowly changing its focus, and now has appealing hideaways, modern wineries producing high-quality wines, olive and cherry orchards, tours to the nearby South Coast, glorious forest drives, and a rattling good ride along an old timber railway. And truffles are the new black gold—after years of trial and error, the quantity and quality of truffles coming out of Pemberton are repaying the investment.

ESSENTIALS

GETTING THERE This area is best accessed and enjoyed with your own vehicle.

VISITOR INFORMATION The **Pemberton Visitor Centre,** Brockman Street, Pemberton, WA 6260 (✆ **1800/671 133** in Western Australia, or 08/9776 1133; www.pembertontourist.com.au), offers a free tour and accommodation booking service. It's open daily from 9am to 5pm, except on December 25 and 26.

GETTING AROUND Be aware that some of the roads are unsealed and can be narrow, slippery, and steep in forest areas. Check your car hire restrictions. Sandy areas are found near the coast and require four-wheel-drive.

WHAT TO SEE & DO

Most of the activities and attractions around Pemberton are related to the forest, the karri trees in particular. The **Karri Forest Explorer Drive** provides a comprehensive tour of the main highlights. You can pick up a map from the Visitor Centre and/or follow the signposted roads. One magical route that's part of the drive is the **Heartbreak Trail** ★, off the Old Vasse Road, south of Pemberton. This one-way gravel track winds through magnificent old-growth forest, at times just above the Warren River, and with a few steep sections. You have to get out of your car to really appreciate the grandeur. There are some tranquil stopping places.

Anther special adventure, not for the faint of heart or those with no head for heights, is climbing the **Gloucester Tree** ★★, just 3km (2 miles) east of the town. Some of the forest's tallest trees were converted to be fire lookouts in the 1940s; series of wooden stakes have been hammered into their trunks in spiral fashion, leading up to a sort of tree house where the rangers could watch out for smoke or fire. Visitors today are the ones who clamber the 60m (200 ft.) to the top—and it's the climb rather than the view that excites. Wire netting surrounds the spiraling stakes as a nod to safety. Passing people going the other way can be interesting.

Taking a **Pemberton Discovery Tour,** 48 Brockman St. (✆ **08/9776 0484;** www.pembertondiscoverytours.com.au), is an informed and entertaining way of seeing the countryside. The half-day "Beach and Forest Eco Adventure" takes you through remote old-growth forest and on to the enormous Yeagarup Dunes, before driving along an empty beach by the Southern Ocean. The tour operates all year at 9am and 2pm, including lunch or tea, for A$90 adults, A$50 children under 14, or A$270 families, with a minimum of two passengers. Booking is essential.

Then there's the **Pemberton Tram,** which leaves from the railway station (✆ **08/9776 1322;** www.pemtram.com.au). The diesel-powered tram rattles its way along a narrow-gauge line over several wooden trestle bridges. There's an informative commentary, and opportunities to stroll into the forest. The tram runs daily, except December 25, at 10:45am and 2pm. Fares are A$18 adults, A$9 children 4 to 15, A$2.50 under 4.

Trout fishing is an option, and most local rivers are stocked, but you need to be aware of seasonal and licensing requirements. Several accommodations have their own lakes where guests can cast a line; **King Trout Restaurant & Marron Farm,** Northcliffe Road and Old Vasse Road (✆ **08/9776 1352;** see "Where to Dine," below), also provides for fishing and/or dining.

Pemberton is yet another quality wine-producing region boasting cool conditions, and it's becoming particularly known for its Burgundy-style wines, including WA's best pinot noir. **Salitage ★★**, Vasse Highway near Pemberton (✆ **08/9776 1195;** www.salitage.com.au), is the top winery (with two wines classified in Australia's Top 100), established and owned by Margaret River pioneer John Horgan. The sleek modern winery is set in carefully tended gardens and vineyards, open 9am to 5pm daily, closed December 25 and 26.

The newest attraction around Pemberton is that amazing delicacy the truffle. The **Wine & Truffle Company ★★** (see "Where to Dine," below) has established its trufferie (13,000 trees, mostly hazelnut), refined its harvesting techniques, and is now producing commercial quantities of the famed black truffle. Guided truffle hunts are available at A$95 adults and A$58 children 16 and under, available throughout the year but best during the in season. The company also produces quality wines, which can be tasted at the cellar door, together with a range of truffle-based products. The restaurant serves excellent lunches, with a gourmet truffle menu in season May to August. Both are open daily.

WHERE TO STAY

Big Brook Retreat A quiet, peaceful, relaxing place to stay, set in farmland and overlooking Big Brook Forest, 6km (4 miles) outside Pemberton. There are two well-laid-out rooms available for bed-and-breakfast stays in the main house, plus four stand-alone, self-catering chalets on the grounds.

Stirling Rd., Pemberton, WA 6260. ✆ **08/9776 0279.** www.bigbrookcottages.com.au. 6 units: 2 B&B rooms, 1 with spa; 4 chalets, 2 with spa. A$130–A$150 double B&B; A$190 1-bedroom spa chalet; A$160 2-bedroom chalet. A$10 extra for chalets on weekends and school holidays. Surcharges on Christmas and long weekends. Extra person A$25. Ask about packages and weekly rates. AE, DC, MC, V. **Amenities:** Dining area. *In room:* A/C, TV/DVD w/free movies, CD player (in chalets), fridge, hair dryer, kitchen (in chalets).

Salitage Suites ★★ This adult retreat is really a set of beautifully furnished, self-contained two-bedroom chalets, carefully laid out in a grove of soaring stringybark and karri trees. It's a stunning and tranquil setting. Each suite has its own large balcony and private outlook to the surrounding vineyards, with the background sound of bird calls and a small reticulated stream. The spacious interiors have all you could need, with the furniture made locally from marri timber. The premium Salitage winery is just next door, and guests receive a free winery tour.

Vasse Hwy., Pemberton, WA 6260. ✆ **08/9776 1195.** Fax 08/9776 1504. www.salitagesuites.citysearch.com.au. 6 units, showers only. A$250 1 couple; A$350 2 couples. Minimum 2 nights, more on peak weekends. MC, V. No pets. Not suitable for children. *In room:* A/C, flatscreen TV w/DVD, CD player, hair dryer, kitchen.

Stonebarn ★★★ This adults-only luxury retreat opened in late 2008, built from local stone and timber. It's a real hideaway, tucked deep within the forest. The whole place has been created with love, attention to detail, and the feel of a top African safari lodge. The six large elegantly furnished bedrooms are upstairs, most with four-poster kings, other locally made bespoke furniture, and small but well designed balconies. Downstairs has the dining room and lounge, which opens onto a broad patio above a lake stocked with trout and marron. This is a very superior B&B (with gourmet breakfasts), but the resident chef will produce an excellent dinner on request.

Langley Rd., Pemberton (take Southwest Hwy. south from Manjimup for 23km/14 miles, turn left 600m/⅓ mile after Roonies Bridge, and follow Stonebarn signs), WA 6258. ✆ **08/9773 1002.** www.stonebarn.com.au. 6 units. A$345–A$375 double, more over Easter and Christmas period. Minimum 2-night stay. Ask about packages. AE, DC, MC, V. Not suitable for children. **Amenities:** Dining room. *In room:* A/C, ceiling fans, TV w/free movies, hair dryer, kitchenette, MP3 docking station, Wi-Fi (free).

WHERE TO DINE

With a few exceptions, the area is still finding its feet as far as dining is concerned. There are several cafes making the transition from country town to tourist venue, and some of the vineyards offer lunches. **King Trout Restaurant & Marron Farm,** Northcliffe Road and Old Vasse Road (✆ **08/9776 1352**), offers fresh home-grown trout and marron. Main courses are A$20 to A$35. It's open Friday to Wednesday 9:30am to 5pm daily, except on December 25 and Good Friday.

Shamrock Restaurant ★ AUSTRALIAN An old-fashioned cafe in appearance and style, it generates a certain nostalgia with its values and friendly service. Helen Lowe has been running the place for 19 years with the philosophy "value for money." Her home farm grows avocados and has 25 hectares (62 acres) of potatoes, as well as cattle and marron in a large dam, and she serves everything in the restaurant. You have to try the marron—large, sweet, and succulent. Wagyu beef is another specialty.

18 Brockman St., Pemberton. ✆ **08/9776 1186.** www.shamrockdining.com.au. Main courses A$35. MC, V. Tues–Sun from 6:30pm.

The Wine & Truffle Company ★ MODERN AUSTRALIAN WA's truffle industry has come of age, with a regular commercial crop of the black gold being produced at the Wine & Truffle Company just outside Manjimup in WA's South Coast region. The in-house restaurant produces good-quality lunches; the menu changes every 3 months, and always includes some truffle-flavored dishes, using preserved truffle or truffle oil out of season (although that cannot compare with the fresh product). They may start evening meals in conjunction with an abbreviated truffle hunt in 2010, so check the website.

Seven Day Rd., Manjimup. ✆ **08/9777 2474.** www.wineandtruffle.com.au. Reservations recommended on weekends and truffle season (May–Aug). Main courses A$20–A$40. Daily 10am–4:30pm; lunch served noon–3pm. Closed Dec 25, 26, and Good Friday.

THE GOLDFIELDS ★

595km (369 miles) E of Perth

The adjoining towns of Kalgoorlie and Boulder were at the heart of an incredible Gold Rush in the late 19th century, which has left a wonderful repository of gloriously extravagant architecture, which sits cheek by jowl with the scale and innovation of 21st-century mining. After Paddy Hannan struck gold here in 1893 in WA's vast Outback, one area soon became known as the "Golden Mile," the richest square mile of gold-bearing earth in the world, and the entire state was transformed.

Today, the **City of Kalgoorlie-Boulder ★** (pop. 32,000) has lost none of its zing; nickel mining is important here, and gold still holds great appeal. The city has retained most of its original gold-fueled architectural extravagances, such as towers and turrets, and wrought-iron lace verandas and balconies. It's like stumbling onto a Western movie set: The broad streets are wide enough to turn a camel train, and countless bars (some with skimpily dressed barmaids) enjoy a roaring trade as they did in the 1890s, serving young miners with often more money than sense.

THE O'connor LEGACY

Charles Yelverton (C. Y.) O'Connor is one of WA's heroes. He was appointed Engineer-in-Chief for Western Australia in 1891, a position he held until his death in 1902. His first significant success was the creation of Fremantle Harbour at the mouth of the Swan River. This was against all current advice, including that of one of England's top marine engineers, who recommended the building of an offshore jetty. O'Connor knew this would be subject to damaging storms, and instead took the option of blasting the rock bar at the river mouth, opening up what has remained WA's main port for over 100 years.

The project for which he is justly most famous is the **Goldfields Water Supply Scheme.** Gold had been discovered in the 1890s in the arid hinterland of WA around Kalgoorlie, where the lack of water was a major problem—whisky was said to be cheaper than fresh water. C. Y. devised a daring and challenging scheme to build a reservoir near the coast and then pipe the water some 560km (350 miles) inland. It would be one of the world's greatest engineering schemes of the era, and required new techniques for the construction and laying of the pipes, as well as the building of eight pumping stations in mostly remote, uninhabited locations.

The scheme, and C. Y., were subjected to massive criticism and doubt, which finally wore him down: He committed suicide a year before water finally flowed into Kalgoorlie. The Goldfields Pipeline has celebrated its centenary and has been expanded so that it now feeds some 8,000km (4,970 miles) of pipe throughout the interior.

Streets Paved with . . . Gold?

In Kalgoorlie's early days, its streets were paved with a blackish spoil from the mining process called "tellurides." When someone realized tellurides contain up to 40% gold and 10% silver, those streets were ripped up in a big hurry. The city fathers had paved the streets with gold and didn't know it!

Kalgoorlie is semidesert (260 mm/10 in. annual rainfall), though you wouldn't know it, given the vast and unique woodland (including salmon gums up to 25m/82 ft. high) that surrounds the town. But the lack of water was a serious problem, both for the population and the mining processes, until one of the world's great engineering projects pumped water from the hills outside Perth some 600km (372 miles) to Kalgoorlie (see "The O'Connor Legacy," below).

Just outside town, where dozens of head frames and chimneys were once starkly silhouetted against the skyline earlier in the 20th century, there is now an enormous, terraced hole: the **Super Pit ★★**. Australia's biggest open-cut gold mine, it is unbelievably massive: 3.5km (2 miles) long, 1.5km (almost 1 mile) wide, and 360m (1,181 ft.) deep. The Empire State Building would almost disappear inside it.

Not all the old mining centers around here are still vibrant, and ghost towns abound. Just 39km (24 miles) down the road is **Coolgardie** (pop. 1,100), another 1890s boomtown whose semi-abandoned air is a sad foil to Kalgoorlie's energy. Some of the lovely architecture remains, and you can wander the gracious streets and a few museums for a pleasant nostalgic buzz.

Don't miss the sensational installation called **"Inside Australia" ★★★**, which was created by renowned British sculptor Antony Gormley in the Outback north of Kalgoorlie. A series of metal figures is scattered across a salt lake, forging an unforgettable image of endeavor, vulnerability, and loneliness.

Essentials

GETTING THERE **Qantas** (✆ **13 13 13** in Australia; www.qantas.com.au) has several flights a day between Kalgoorlie and Perth. **Skywest** (✆ **1300/660 088** in Australia; www.skywest.com.au) also flies from Perth daily. Fares range from about A$170 one-way.

Kalgoorlie is a stop on the 3-day ***Indian Pacific*** **★** train service, which runs between Sydney and Perth once or twice a week in both directions. See the "Getting There & Getting Around" section in chapter 3 for contact details. The ***Prospector*** train makes nine trips a week from Perth to Kalgoorlie (and back) in just over 6½ hours, for A$82 adults, A$41 children under 16. Contact **Transwa** (✆ **1300/662 205** in Western Australia, or 08/9326 2600; www.transwa.wa.gov.au).

Driving from Perth, take the Great Eastern Highway, through the Perth Hills and the Wheatbelt on to Coolgardie and Kalgoorlie. The otherwise boring trip can be livened up by following the **Golden Pipeline Heritage Trail ★** (map and booklet available from the National Trust: ✆ **08/9321 6088;** www.ntwa.com.au), which celebrates the Goldfields' Pipeline, with its old pumping stations, reservoirs, and isolation. Both the pipeline and highway follow much the same track and, at times, both they and the railway loop together in parallel lines across the countryside.

If you want to make the long 2,182km (1,353-mile) journey on the Eyre Highway from Adelaide, contact the South Australian or Western Australian state auto clubs listed under "Getting There & Getting Around," in chapter 3, for advice.

VISITOR INFORMATION The **Kalgoorlie Goldfields Visitor Centre,** in the Town Hall, 250 Hannan St., Kalgoorlie, WA 6430 (✆ **1800/004 653** in Australia, or 08/9021 1966; www.kalgoorlietourism.com), dispenses information on Kalgoorlie, Coolgardie, and outlying regions. The center's inexpensive walking trail map (A$3.50) to the town's heritage is worth buying. The center is open Monday to Friday 8:30am to 5pm, and Saturday, Sunday, and public holidays 9am to 5pm. The **Coolgardie Visitor Centre,** 62 Bayley St., Coolgardie, WA 6429 (✆ **08/9026 6090**), is open Monday to Friday 8:30am to 4:30pm, and Saturday, Sunday, and public holidays 9am to 4pm.

GETTING AROUND **Avis** (✆ **08/9021 1722**), **Budget** (✆ **08/9093 2300**), **Hertz** (✆ **08/9093 2211**), and **Thrifty** (✆ **13 61 39**) have offices in Kalgoorlie. Bear in mind that each company has different rules and restrictions for driving on unsealed roads, so check before hiring.

Goldrush Tours (✆ **1800/620 440** in Australia; www.goldrushtours.com.au) has several coach tours around the Goldfields, ranging from a half-day town tour at A$50 adults and A$25 children. **Kalgoorlie Tours & Charters** (✆ **08/9021 2211;** www.kalgoorlietours.com) has a 2-hour tour Monday to Friday at 1:30pm for A$30 adults and A$20 children. **Finders Keepers Tours** (✆ **08/9093 2222;** www.finderskeepersgold.com) has gold prospecting and Super Pit tours (see below).

What to See & Do

As you might guess, gold is a common thread running through many of the town's attractions. One of the best is the **Australian Prospectors & Miners Hall of Fame ★**, Broad Arrow Road, 3km (2 miles) north of the Tourist Centre on the Goldfields Highway (✆ **08/9026 2700;** www.mininghall.com). Opened in late 2001, it has five interactive galleries focusing on modern high-tech mining, plus a number of historic mining and processing facilities, including several derricklike head frames. There's a statue of Paddy Hannan (the prospector who started the region's gold rush), and you can find out how prospecting was done in the past and is done now, learn how the business of mining is conducted, and then revisit the old days. The underground tour goes 36m (118 ft.) underground in a mining cage and explores the tunnels where "real" miners once worked. You can pan for gold, watch a gold pour, see a video in a re-created miner's tent, and pore over an extensive collection of mining memorabilia in a miners' village. The site is open daily 9am to 4:30pm March to October, and 10am to 4pm November to February; it's closed January 1 and December 25 and 26. Admission, which includes a level-1 underground tour, is A$30 adults, A$20 children, and A$80 families. The Pitch Black Tour (level 2 underground) costs A$60 adults, A$40 children (over 10 years), and A$180 families. Allow half a day to see everything.

The **WA Museum Kalgoorlie–Boulder,** 17 Hannan St. (✆ **08/9021 8533;** www.museum.wa.gov.au), is worth a look. You'll find it easily, with its enormous red head frame dominating upper Hannan Street and making a grand entrance statement. A glass elevator within it takes you to a great view over the city. You'll see the first 400-ounce gold bar minted in town, nuggets and jewelry, mementoes of the

Time for the Gee-Gees

The Kalgoorlie Race Round is the high point in the local social calendar, with a week of horse (*gee-gees* in Aussie-speak) races, the World Two Up Championship, and a variety of events around Kalgoorlie, including a bush picnic. The Round has been running since 1896, and finishes with over half of the town partying at the Kalgoorlie Cup. It's held in the second week of September. Check www.kbrc.com.au.

Goldfields Pipeline, a wooden bicycle, and other historical displays. It is open daily (except Wednesday) 9:30am to 4:30pm; it's closed Good Friday, Easter Monday, January 1, April 25, and December 25 and 26. Admission is by donation. Tours are at 11am and 2:30pm. Allow an hour.

Don't leave town without goggling at the **Super Pit ★★** open-cut mine (www.superpit.com.au)—it makes giant dump trucks (which carry 225 tons of ore apiece) look like ants. The lookout is off the Goldfields Highway in Boulder. It's open daily from about 8am to about 9:30pm, but check with the visitor center when the daily blast will take place (the lookout may be closed then for safety reasons). Entry is free. KCGM, the mining company, operates the **Super Pit Shop** (**© 08/9093 3488**), where you can find out all about the mine and buy memorabilia; open Monday to Friday 9am to 4pm and Boulder Market Days (every third Sun). KCGM also provides free Super Pit tours on Market Days at 10, 10:30, 11, and 11:30am, departing from the Shop, or with a small charge if prebooked.

Finders Keepers Super Pit Tours (**© 08/9093 2222;** www.superpittour.com) provide a more comprehensive firsthand look at the mining and milling operations. The 2½-hour tours run Monday to Saturday at 9am all year, and at 1pm March to December; tours cost A$60 adults and A$40 children under 17 (not recommended for children under 10). Advance bookings are essential. A shorter family-oriented tour operates at 9am during school holidays for A$40 adults, A$25 children.

The **Royal Flying Doctor Service** (**© 08/9093 7500**) base at Kalgoorlie–Boulder Airport is open for visitors to browse memorabilia, see a video, and look over an aircraft (if one is in). It is open Monday to Friday 10am to 3pm. Admission is by A$2 donation. Tours run on the hour, the last one at 2pm, and take 45 minutes.

Kalgoorlie's—and maybe Australia's—most unusual attraction must be **Langtrees 181 ★**, 181 Hay St. (**© 08/9026 2181**), a working brothel presented as a sort of sex-industry museum, in the heart of Kal's infamous red-light district. Despite laws to the contrary, brothels flourished in red and pink corrugated-iron sheds festooned with colored lights, known as "starting stalls," and became a popular drive-by spot for gawping tourists. Langtrees is a swish modern establishment offering 90-minute tours, which are fun rather than sleazy, showing some of the 12 themed (only if unoccupied) rooms, at a cost of A$35 (A$25 for seniors!). Tours depart at 1, 3, and 6pm daily.

The two town halls are both worth a visit. **Kalgoorlie Town Hall** houses the Visitor Centre and has a replica statue of Paddy Hannan (complete with drinking fountain) outside, while the **Boulder Town Hall** has the magnificent 100-year-old Goatcher Theatre Curtain, depicting the Bay of Naples, inside. It's lowered for viewing

Play the World's Longest Golf Course

Opened in October 2009, the **Nullarbor Links** bring a new and unique attraction to the long, lonely crossing of the Nullarbor Plain along the Eyre Highway. Billed as the "World's Longest Golf Course," the 18 holes are spread along 1,365km (853 miles) between Ceduna in South Australia and Western Australia's gold-mining center of Kalgoorlie. Most of the intermediate holes are sited in glorious isolation at each of the remote roadhouses that punctuate the Outback highway. This is one golf course where you won't be walking between the holes; they're up to 180km (113 miles) apart. Life memberships are available and include some memorabilia; check **www.nullarborlinks.com** for information and membership.

Tuesday to Thursday 10am to 3pm, and on Boulder Market Days (every third Sun of the month) 9:30am to 1pm.

Take a step, and a taste, back to your childhood with a visit to the **Little Boulder Sweet Shop,** 41 Burt St., Boulder (✆ **08/9093 0011**). It's a visual delight, stocking all the old style sweets and chocolates.

Wandering **Coolgardie**'s quiet streets, which are graced with historic facades, is a stroll back in time. More than 100 signboards throughout the town, many with photos, detail what each site was like at the turn of the 20th century. The **Goldfields Exhibition Museum,** 62 Bayley St. (✆ **08/9021 1966**), tells the town's story in a lovely 1898 building once used as the mining warden's courthouse. (The Tourist Bureau is also here.) Admission is free, and it's open 9am to 5pm Monday to Friday, 10am to 3pm weekends and holidays (except Dec 25).

"Inside Australia" ★★★ is a series of sculptures scattered across a salt lake 187km (116 miles) north of Kalgoorlie. Fifty-one metal figures, derived from computer scans of the residents of nearby Menzies, were created by the renowned British sculptor Antony Gormley in 2003. They are spread in lonely splendor across the brilliant white salt surface of Lake Ballard, creating an eerily beautiful effect. Sunset can be particularly evocative. You can drive here, getting supplies and meals at Menzies, or Goldrush Tours offers trips with a minimum of 10 passengers.

The **Golden Quest Discovery Trail** is a 965km (598-mile) self-drive tour through old and new mining areas to the north of Kalgoorlie, including ghost towns and the "Inside Australia" statues. A comprehensive guidebook, with associated CDs, adds immeasurably to the drive and can be bought at all local visitor centers.

If you fancy trying your hand at a bit of prospecting, grab a half-day tour with **Finders Keepers Prospecting Adventures,** 20 Burt St., Boulder (✆ **08/9093 2222;** www.finderskeepersgold.com). The tours, on Wednesdays, Fridays, and Saturdays at 8:30am, provide an introduction to the local bush and a chance to use a metal detector; you keep any gold that you find. The tour costs A$95 adults, A$50 children under 13. Advance bookings are recommended.

Where to Stay

The **Kalgoorlie Goldfields Visitor Centre** offers a free accommodation booking service (✆ **08/9021 1966;** fax 08/9021 2180; www.kalgoorlietourism.com).

Palace Hotel The "Grand Old Lady of Kalgoorlie" was built 110 years ago at the height of the gold rush, on the town's principal intersection. It was the most luxurious hotel outside Perth and has been restored to its original grandeur, and maintains a more genteel atmosphere than most of the other, rowdier pubs. An elegant two-story building, it's graced with a splendid balcony, part of which is now the Balcony Restaurant (see below) and the rest of which provides private settings for the Superior rooms. The hotel has a magnificent carved mirror donated by mining engineer (and later U.S. president) Herbert Hoover. He apparently fell in love with a Palace barmaid while working on the Goldfields. All rooms reflect their era and are somewhat cramped, but there's a spacious suite in the next-door building.

137 Hannan St., corner Boulder Rd., Kalgoorlie, WA 6430. ✆ **08/9021 2788.** Fax 08/9021 1813. www.palacehotel.com.au. 50 units, some with shared facilities, all with showers only. A$130 Balcony double; A$110 Balcony single; A$90 standard double; A$120 standard family; A$160 1-bedroom suite; A$260 2-bedroom suite (sleeps 5); A$500 apt (5 bedrooms). AE, DC, MC, V. Free parking. **Amenities:** Restaurant; cafe; 3 bars. *In room:* A/C, TV w/in-house movies, fridge, Wi-Fi most rooms (free).

Rydges Kalgoorlie ★★ Kalgoorlie's only AAA-rated five-star hotel opened in 2003, bringing much-needed luxury accommodations to this major mining center and has already won awards for both its accommodations and dining. The studios are comfortable and spacious, and there are 10 one-bedroom and two two-bedroom apartments—all with spa tubs. It's about 2km (1¼ miles) from the town center and has a free shuttle service to Hannan Street. The low-profile blocks of units are expertly screened by banks of native plants (using gray water) and set around the outdoor pool. The rooms are modern and well-appointed, the staff are helpful, and the security includes pass-controlled parking. There's an excellent restaurant, **Larcombe's Grill,** renovated in 2009.

21 Davidson St., Kalgoorlie, WA 6430. ✆ **1300/857 922** in Australia, or 08/9080 0800. Fax 08/9080 0900. www.rydges.com. 92 units. A$290 deluxe studio; A$365 1-bedroom apt; A$500 2-bedroom apt (sleeps 4). Ask about packages. AE, DC, MC, V. Free parking. **Amenities:** Restaurant; bar; free airport transfers; bike hire; outdoor and indoor pool; outdoor spa. *In room:* A/C, TV/VCR w/in-house movies, fridge, hair dryer, Internet.

Where to Dine

Kalgoorlie's dining has come of age, with quality produce and innovative cooking served in a casual but friendly atmosphere.

Balcony Restaurant MODERN AUSTRALIAN The restaurant, on the balcony of the Palace Hotel (or indoors), overlooks some of the Goldfields' finest buildings. The food is almost as good as the setting, ideal for a sunset drink followed by dinner as the evening air and the sounds of the passing parade come wafting in.

137 Hannan St. (inside Palace Hotel), Kalgoorlie. ✆ **08/9021 2788.** www.palacehotel.com.au/Balcony.html. Reservations recommended. Main courses A$30–A$50. AE, DC, MC, V. Mon–Sat 6pm–late.

Blue Monkey Restaurant ★ MODERN AUSTRALIAN One of Kalgoorlie's mainstays, the lunches stand out, with tasty salads and Turkish bread offerings. It's also open for breakfast and dinner.

418 Hannan St., Kalgoorlie. ✆ **08/9091 3833.** www.bluemonkeyrestaurant.com.au. Reservations recommended. Main courses A$24–A$40. 15% surcharge public holidays. AE, DC, MC, V. Mon–Fri 6am–2pm and 6pm–late; Sat–Sun 7am–2pm and 6pm–late.

Danny's Restaurant ★★ MODERN AUSTRALIAN Danny's is housed in a lovely refurbished high-ceilinged 1897 building and has a clean modern appearance. The excellent food is based on fresh WA produce enhanced by Asian herbs and spices, served from the semiopen kitchen.

14 Wilson St. (2 blocks from Town Hall), Kalgoorlie. ✆ **08/9022 7614.** Reservations recommended. Mains A$28–A$45. AE, DC, MC, V. Mon–Sat 6:30pm–late.

Larcombe's Bar & Grill ★★ MODERN AUSTRALIAN This modern setting in the Rydges Kalgoorlie Hotel has full glass windows giving sunset views. The open kitchen here produces food of imagination and flair, including wild mushroom risotto with truffle oil and *grana padano.*

21 Davidson St., Kalgoorlie. ✆ **08/9080 0800.** Reservations recommended. Main courses A$25–A$45. AE, DC, MC, V. Mon–Sat 5am–midnight; Sun 6am–10pm.

Saltimbocca Restaurant ★ ITALIAN This is one of Kal's favorite eateries, with good crowds—even on Monday nights. Its central location helps, with modern decor, friendly service, and a nice candlelit atmosphere. Opened in 2003, it serves up modern takes on the standard Italian fare, with the veal saltimbocca a standout.

90 Egan St. (1 block from Hannan St.), Kalgoorlie. ✆ **08/9022 8028.** Reservations recommended. Main courses A$23–A$30. AE, DC, MC, V. Mon–Sat 6–10pm.

THE CORAL COAST ★★

There is magic in the waters of the Indian Ocean where it brushes the shores of the northern portions of Western Australia's west coast. Brilliant coral reefs just offshore, whale sharks, dolphins, turtles, and manta rays make this one of the world's most marvelous (and accessible) marine environments. Much of this is paradoxically due to the fact that inland is largely treeless semidesert, occupied by vast sheep stations and a mere handful of people. This is real Outback, with soaring summer temperatures and little rain, but this also means there are no rivers—or towns—to introduce sediments and pollutants to the sea. The ocean is untainted and has been able to develop some glorious natural attractions.

Since the 1960s, a pod of **bottlenose dolphins** has been coming into shallow water at **Monkey Mia ★★**, in the World Heritage–listed Shark Bay Marine Park, to greet shore-bound humans. The dolphins' magical presence has drawn people from every corner of the globe.

Another 730km (453 miles) by road north on the Northwest Cape, adventure seekers from around the world come to **swim with whale sharks ★★★**—measuring up to 18m (59 ft.) long—from March to June. The Cape's parched shore and green waters hide another dazzling secret—a fringing coral reef 300km (186 miles) long called **Ningaloo ★★**, protected by a Marine Park. It contains 250 species of coral and 450 kinds of fish, dolphins, manta rays, whales, turtles, and dugongs. Even the Great Barrier Reef can't beat Ningaloo Reef's proximity to shore—just a step or two off the beach delivers you into a wondrous underwater garden. What is amazing is that so few people seem to know about it. That and the remoteness means beaches you'll pretty much have to yourself, seas teeming with life because humans haven't scared (or fished) it away, pristine surrounds, and a genuine sense of the frontier. There are also carpets of everlastings (daisy-like wildflowers) stretching across vast areas in August and September in good years.

This coast, called both Coral and Outback, is lonely and remote—and often too hot and too windy to enjoy between November and March. The best time to visit is April through October, when it is warm enough to swim and the weather is balmy, though snorkelers might want a wet suit June and July. Humidity is always low. Facilities, gas, and fresh water are scarce, and distances are immense, so be prepared.

Shark Bay (Monkey Mia) ★★

857km (535 miles) N of Perth; 1,867km (1,157 miles) SW of Broome

Monkey Mia's celebrity dolphins may not show on time—but they rarely pass up a visit. Apart from these delightful sea mammals, Shark Bay's waters heave with fish, turtles, the world's biggest population of dugongs (11,000 at last count), manta rays, sea snakes, and, June through October, humpback whales.

Shark Bay is an enormous body of clean clear shallow water, sheltered by a line of islands and protected by its status as a Marine Park and World Heritage Site. The Peron Peninsula, a strangely shaped prong of land, juts far out into the bay and features some of the cleanest most brilliant beaches you will find anywhere, other beaches composed entirely of shells, and "living fossils"—rocklike structures by the shore (called **stromatolites**) that are earth's first life. On the northern tip of the peninsula, **Francois Peron National Park ★** is home to many endangered species, thanks to a fence built across the narrowest point to keep out feral cats and foxes.

The bay's only municipality is the one-time pearling town of **Denham** (pop. 500), 129km (80 miles) from the main coastal highway. It has a couple of hotels, a bakery, a newsdealer, some fishing-charter and tour operators, and the World Heritage Discovery Centre. Monkey Mia, 25km (16 miles) away on the opposite side of the peninsula, exists purely because of the dolphins. It has a dolphin information center and the pleasant but basic Monkey Mia Dolphin Resort (p. 526).

ESSENTIALS

GETTING THERE **Skywest Airlines** (© **1300/660 088** in Australia; www.skywest.com.au) has approximately 2-hour flights from Perth, Friday to Sunday and Tuesdays. Skywest also links Monkey Mia to the other Coral Coast destination of Exmouth. Airfares start at approximately A$260 one-way. The **Monkey Mia Dolphin Resort** (© **08/9948 1320**) bus meets every Skywest flight and transfers you to the resort for A$13 per person one-way.

Greyhound Australia (© **13 14 99** in Australia) travels 5 days a week between Perth and Broome. A separate service runs three times a week between Monkey Mia and the Overlander Roadhouse at the Shark Bay turnoff on the North West Coastal Highway. It connects with the services between Perth and Broome (and Exmouth). From Broome, it's about 25 hours through featureless landscape—not recommended.

If driving yourself, beware of wildlife on the lonely 10-hour trip from Perth, and keep the gas tank full. From Perth, take the Brand Highway 424km (263 miles) north to Geraldton, then the North West Coastal Highway for 278km (172 miles) to the Overlander Roadhouse. Turn left onto the Denham–Hamelin Road, and follow it for 154km (96 miles) to Monkey Mia. If you want to break the journey, the **Ocean Centre Hotel,** at Foreshore Drive and Cathedral Avenue, Geraldton, WA 6530 (© **08/9921 7777;** www.oceancentrehotel.com.au), has the best rooms and location in Geraldton, overlooking the bay and the spanking new foreshore redevelopment. Doubles range from A$130; ask about specials. It also has a relaxing breakfast

The Lost Battleship

It was November 1941, at the height of World War II, when the pride of the Australian Navy, the battle cruiser HMAS *Sydney,* disappeared off the West Australian coast somewhere near Geraldton. Survivors from the German raider *Kormoran* told of a battle at sea with the Sydney, and how it was seen ablaze shortly before their own ship sunk, but there were no survivors from the Sydney's crew. The mystery was only solved in March 2008, when the wreckage was finally located offshore.

Geraldton is home to an evocative memorial to the *Sydney* and its crew. Located on a hill with sweeping views across the Indian Ocean, it features a woman looking out to sea anxiously waiting for a sighting, as well as a superb silver dome of 645 seagulls in flight—one for each lost sailor.

cafe and bar, in-house movies, secure parking, and Wi-Fi. While in Geraldton, do not miss the brilliantly inspirational **HMAS *Sydney* Memorial ★★**, Gummer Avenue, Mount Scott, Geraldton. The *Sydney* (see "The Lost Battleship," below) was an Australian cruiser that sank with all hands in 1941. Free half-hour tours run daily at 10:30am.

Numerous tour companies, including **Australian Pinnacle Tours** (✆ **1800/999 069** in Australia, or 08/9417 5555; www.pinnacletours.com.au) and **Western Xposure** (✆ **1800/621 200** in Australia; www.westernxposure.com.au), offer package trips to Monkey Mia.

VISITOR INFORMATION Wide-ranging ecological information on Shark Bay Marine Park, Francois Peron National Park, and Hamelin Pool Marine Nature Reserve, as well as details on local tours, is available at the **Monkey Mia Visitor Centre** (✆ **08/9948 1366**) in the Monkey Mia Reserve; videos run throughout the day, and researchers give free talks and slide shows most nights. It's run by the WA Department of Environment and Conservation, which has an excellent local website: **www.sharkbay.org**. The regional information outlet is the **Shark Bay World Heritage Discovery Centre,** 53 Knight Terrace, Denham, WA 6537 (✆ **08/9948 1590;** www.sharkbayinterpretivecentre.com.au), open daily 8am to 6pm and closed December 25, April 25 (Anzac Day), and Good Friday.

GETTING AROUND **Shark Bay Car Hire** (✆ **08/9948 3032**) delivers cars and four-wheel-drives to the airport and the resort from its Denham office. Several local companies run tours to the various attractions.

FAST FACTS Daily admission to the **Monkey Mia Reserve,** in which Monkey Mia Dolphin Resort is located, is A$8 per adult, A$3 per child under 16, and A$15 per family. A 4-week pass can be worthwhile at A$30 for families. Resort guests as well as day-trippers pay this fee.

There are ATMs at the **Heritage Resort,** 73 Knight Terrace (at Durlacher St.), Denham (✆ **08/9948 1133**), and at the local supermarket, but there are no banks. A banking agency is in the post office in Denham.

MEETING THE DOLPHINS ★★

At 7am, guests at Monkey Mia Dolphin Resort are already gathering on the beach (as are the resident pelicans) in anticipation of the dolphins' arrival. By 8am, three

Where Can I See the Dolphins?

The main advantages to making the trek to Monkey Mia ★★ are that dolphin sightings are virtually guaranteed every day; they swim into the shallows and lie in the ultraclear water, and you can watch them being fed and interacting with the rangers. But it can be crowded, and rangers strictly monitor behavior with the dolphins—not the interactive frolic you might have imagined. The first sightings, generally around 8am, are the most popular and crowded, after which the tour groups all disappear. If you stay around, the dolphins will often return, and you can have a much more satisfying encounter. At Rockingham ★ and Bunbury, south of Perth, you can *swim* with wild dolphins (see "Taking a Dip with Flipper," earlier in this chapter), but the dolphins there don't show up as reliably.

or more dolphins usually show, and they come and go until the early afternoon. Because of the crowds the dolphins attract (about 40 people a session in low season, busloads in high season), park rangers instruct everyone to line up knee-deep in the water as the playful swimmers cruise by your legs. You may not approach them or reach out to pat them, but they sometimes come up to touch people of their own accord, and you may be chosen to help feed them. Feeding times are different each day, and the quantities are strictly limited, so the dolphins won't become dependent on the food. Apart from the Monkey Mia Reserve entry fee, there is no charge to see the creatures.

THE SEA-LIFE CRUISE, "LIVING FOSSILS" & MORE

Don't do what so many visitors do—see the dolphins, and then shoot off to your next sight. Stay to see Shark Bay's other fascinating attractions.

Observe the incredible marine life from the sailing maxi-catamaran ***Shotover*** ★ (© **1800/241 481** in Australia, or 08/9948 1481; www.monkeymiawildsights.com.au). During a 3-hour dugong (sea-cow) cruise, you may see sharks, sea snakes, turtles, dolphins, and, of course, dugongs—and possibly have a swim in the bay. Every passenger is given polarized sunglasses, which help you spot animals underwater. The cruise departs from Monkey Mia Dolphin Resort at 1pm daily and costs A$84 adults, half-price for children 7 to 16, and includes a free sunset cruise as well. The *Shotover* also runs a fascinating 2½-hour dolphin cruise at 9am—worth doing even if you've already seen the dolphins on the shore. It costs A$69 adults, free for children under 17. Sundown cruises are a daily option, at A$54 adults, half-price children 7 to 16. Package prices are available.

On your way in or out of Monkey Mia, stop by the **Hamelin Pool Historic Telegraph Station,** 29km (18 miles) from the highway turnoff (© **08/9942 5905**). A small museum houses old equipment, farming tools, and historical odds and ends from the 19th-century days when this was a telegraph repeater station. The A$5 admission fee to the museum includes an explanation of the **stromatolites,** rocky formations about a foot high that were created by the planet's first oxygen-breathing cells—in other words, earth's first life. You might want to skip the museum, but do wander down to the shoreline and stroll out along a boardwalk to see them close up. (***Warning:*** They look, and act, just like rocks!)

Save on Park Passes

Entry to most national parks in Western Australia, including Cape Range and Francois Peron, costs A$10 per car (maximum eight people) per day. If you are planning to visit several, a **Holiday Park Pass** at A$35 per vehicle is worth the money and is valid for 4 weeks in all WA national parks. Obtain passes from the **Department of Environment and Conservation** (www.dec.wa.gov.au). The passes are not valid for Monkey Mia Dolphin Reserve.

Nearby **Shell Beach ★**, 43km (27 miles) from the highway, is amazing. The beach is said to be 110km (68 miles) long and over 10m (33 ft.) deep, made up of billions of tiny snow-white shells; the numbers are incalculable. They crunch beneath your feet as you walk along and stretch beneath the rich, clear blue water. Solidified blocks of the shells were quarried nearby to build many local buildings. There is a café and gift store.

The conservation plan "Project Eden" is reintroducing and protecting various endangered small marsupials, such as bilbies, woylies, and wallabies, to the isthmus. An electronic fence has been built across the peninsula at its narrowest point, to keep out cats and foxes; there's even an electronic "barking dog" to deter the predators. Dirk Hartog Island has recently been purchased by the WA Government and will add a new dimension to Project Eden.

The northern part of the peninsula, beyond Denham and Monkey Mia, is the 52,500-hectare (130,000-acre) **Francois Peron National Park ★**. You can explore its salt pans, dunes, coastal cliffs, beaches, and old homesteads, either alone (you will need a four-wheel-drive, but stay on the marked road—the clay pans, known as *birridas,* are seriously boggy) or on a full-day tour with **Monkey Mia Wildsights** (**© 1800/241 481;** www.monkeymiawildsights.com.au). The scenery is harsh, but there is great coastal beauty where the red cliffs meet beaches fringed with vivid turquoise water. You should spot kangaroos, birds, and emus, and you may see turtles, dolphins, rays, dugongs, and sharks from the cliffs. Other activities include game- and deep-sea-fishing trips from Denham, scuba diving, excursions to the deserted beaches and 180m (590-ft.) cliffs of nearby Dirk Hartog Island, and a couple of pearl-farm tours.

WHERE TO STAY & DINE

Monkey Mia Dolphin Resort Set right on the beach the dolphins visit, this oasis of green lawns and palms doubles as a town settlement, and is the only place to stay at Monkey Mia. (All other accommodations are 25km/16 miles away, in Denham.) The beachside Dolphin Lodge (and backpacker lodge) opened in 2004, offering 24 motel-style units. Each has a king-size bed and private bathroom. Ground-floor units open right onto the dolphin beach, and first-floor units have balconies with views across the bay. The backpacker lodge, with its own Monkey Bar and large communal kitchen, is behind the lodge. It holds four- and seven-bed dormitories as well as shared and family rooms with bathrooms. The new accommodations complement the existing villas (which sleep three to five people), and the trailer and camping sites. The pleasant open-sided all-day restaurant overlooks the sea; the resort has a minimarket, an Internet cafe, and a dive shop, and you can hire a kayak or boat. Most tours in the area depart from here. A 1.5km (1-mile) nature trail leads from the resort.

Monkey Mia Rd., Shark Bay (P.O. Box 119), Denham, WA 6537. ✆ **1800/653 611** in Australia, or 08/9948 1320. Fax 08/9948 1034. www.monkeymia.com.au. 57 powered trailer sites, 20 tent sites; 60 villas; 24 motel units, all with shower only. A$14 per person tent site; from A$27 per person in backpacker dorm; A$229 double or triple Garden Villa; A$308 double or triple Beachfront Villa; A$229 Beachside Dolphin Unit. Extra person A$25. Children under 6 free with existing bedding. Weekly rates available. AE, DC, MC, V. Free parking. **Amenities:** Restaurant; bar; takeout cafe; Jacuzzi (fed by naturally warm underground water); outdoor pool; outdoor tennis court; use of snorkel gear. *In room:* A/C, TV w/in-house movies, small fridge, hair dryer.

The North West Cape & Ningaloo

Exmouth: 1,260km (781 miles) N of Perth; 1,567km (972 miles) SW of Broome

Driving along the only road on the Exmouth Peninsula toward North West Cape is surreal. Hundreds of anthills march through the scrub and away to the horizon, clumps of spinifex dot the red earth, occasional sheep and 'roos threaten to get under the wheels, and the sun shines down from a cloudless blue sky. On the western shore is the tiny reef resort settlement of **Coral Bay** (pop. 120), a cluster of dive shops, backpacker lodges, a low-key resort, and charter boats nestled on sand so white, water so blue, and ocher dust so orange you'd think the townsfolk had computer-enhanced the colors. Another 141km (88 miles) farther north is **Exmouth** (pop. 2,400), built in 1967 as a support town to the Harold E. Holt Naval Communications Station, a joint Australian–United States base. It has since become the principal center for trips and tours to Ningaloo and has a new marina.

Apart from **swimming with the whale sharks,** the reason you come here is to scuba dive and snorkel in the **Ningaloo Marine Park ★★**, which hugs the peninsula's western shores. You can also take four-wheel-drive trips into the **Cape Range National Park,** which forms the spine of the peninsula, and the adjacent sheep stations.

Exmouth is on the eastern shore, facing Exmouth Gulf, and tends to be several degrees warmer than the west (Ningaloo-facing) coast. Coral Bay, on the west coast, is one of Australia's most casual resorts, but it has divine diving, swimming, and snorkeling. Exmouth has more facilities, including a supermarket, an outdoor cinema, rental cars, and smarter accommodations and dining options. Most tours pick up or leave from Exmouth. Both places have plenty of dive, snorkel, fishing, and whale-watch

'Roos & Wedgies

Driving between Shark Bay and Exmouth, you need to be aware not just of live kangaroos on the road (mostly at dusk, dawn, and at night), but also of the ones that didn't make it. You do not want to hit one of the carcasses, but you should also be aware of scavengers, mostly crows and wedge-tailed eagles. The crows are not a problem, but wedgies are large and ponderous when trying to get out of your way. Getting one of these in your windshield is not recommended, so slow down and beep your horn if you see a large bird on the road ahead.

companies. Wherever you stay, book ahead in whale-shark season (from late Mar to June) and school holidays. Carry drinking water everywhere you go.

ESSENTIALS

GETTING THERE **Skywest** (✆ **1300/660 088** in Australia; www.skywest.com.au) flies from Perth daily. A shuttle bus meets every flight and takes you to your Exmouth hotel for A$20 one-way. Reservations can be made with **Exmouth Bus Charter** (✆ **08/9949 4623;** www.exmouthwa.com.au). Have cash on you; there's no ATM at the airport. **Coral Bay Adventures** (✆ **08/9942 5955;** http://coralbayadventures.com) makes transfers, on demand, from the airport to Coral Bay, approximately 120km (74 miles) away, for A$80 adults, A$40 children under 13, one-way (minimum charge A$160).

Greyhound Australia (✆ **13 14 99** in Australia) has a service to Coral Bay and Exmouth from Minilya on the Great Northern Highway. It connects with both the Perth-Broome and Broome-Perth services, in the wee hours of the morning. The trip time from Perth is 19 hours, and the full fare is A$264.

If driving from Perth, the 14-hour journey (plus rest stops) is through lonely country on a two-lane highway. Check that your contract allows you to drive your rental car this far north and includes unlimited mileage. Wildlife can be a problem, and gas stations are few. From Perth, take the Brand Highway or Indian Ocean Drive (the last portion of which won't open until mid-2011) north to Geraldton, 424km (263 miles) away, then the North West Coastal Highway for 618km (386 miles) to Minilya gas station; the Exmouth turnoff is 7km (4⅓ miles) north of Minilya. The Coral Bay turnoff is 79km (49 miles) farther north, and Exmouth another 145km (90 miles). Overnight at the **Ocean Centre Hotel,** Geraldton (see "Shark Bay," p. 523), or **Best Western Kalbarri Palm Resort,** 8 Porter St., Kalbarri, WA 6536 (✆ 13 17 79 in Australia or 08/9937 2333; http://kalbarri.bestwestern.com.au). Rooms are from A$150 double. Kalbarri, 166km (104 miles) north of Geraldton, is one of WA's favorite resorts, located where the Murchison River has broken through the coastal cliffs to reach the Indian Ocean. Kalbarri has dramatic scenery and, with its parrot and seahorse breeding centers, is well worth a couple of days. Everything else that looks like a town on your map is just a roadhouse (a gas station with shop, cafe, and perhaps some limited accommodations), other than Carnarvon. Keep in mind that the roadhouses can be 200km (124 miles) apart.

VISITOR INFORMATION The **Exmouth Visitor Centre,** Murat Road, Exmouth, WA 6707 (✆ **1800/287 328** in Western Australia, or 08/9949 1176; www.exmouthwa.com.au), is open daily 9am to 4:30pm, 9am to 1pm on public holidays; it's closed on Saturday and Sunday October through March and Good Friday, December 25 and 26, and January 1. The **Milyering Visitors Centre,** on the west coast, 52km (32 miles) from Exmouth, is the Cape Range and Ningaloo National Parks' information center (✆ **08/9949 2808**), run by the Department of Environment and Conservation (DEC). It is open daily 9am to 3:45pm (closed Dec 25). You can also pick up information, including a hiking-trail map of the Cape Range park from DEC's office on Nimitz Street, Exmouth. **Coastal Adventure Tours** runs an information and booking center, and Internet cafe, in Coral Bay Shopping Arcade, Coral Bay, WA 6701 (✆ **08/9948 5190;** www.coralbaytours.com.au).

GETTING AROUND Tour and dive operators pick up from either Exmouth or Coral Bay accommodations. The roads to Exmouth and Coral Bay are paved, as is much of the only road that runs from Exmouth along the west (Ningaloo) coast. Two-wheel drive is possible as far south as Yardie Creek, thereafter it's four-wheel drive. **Avis** (✆ 08/9949 2492), **Europcar** (✆ 08/9949 2940), **Hertz** (✆ 08/9949 4610), **Budget** (✆ 08/9949 1534), and local operator **Allens Car Hire** (✆ 08/9949 2403) have offices in Exmouth; there is no car rental in Coral Bay.

SWIMMING WITH WHALE SHARKS ★★★

Whale sharks are sharks, not whales, and are the world's biggest fish, reaching a railway engine size of 12 to 18m (39–58 ft.) in length. Terrified? Don't be. Their gigantic size belies their gentle nature and swimming speed and, despite having mouths big enough to swallow a boatload of snorkelers, they eat plankton. Several boat operators, using spotter planes, take people out to swim alongside the whale sharks when they appear from late March to June and possibly into July. You simply float in the water wearing mask and snorkel and watch this magnificent speckled fish moving effortlessly past you; it's mind-blowing that you can be so close to such a huge, beautiful, and harmless creature. The images stay with you forever. A day trip with one of the longest established whale-shark companies, **Exmouth Diving Centre** (✆ **08/9949 1201;** www.exmouthdiving.com.au), or its Coral Bay alternative, **Ningaloo Reef Diving Centre** (✆ **08/9942 5824;** www.ningalooreefdive.com), costs about A$385 for snorkeling or A$415 including a subsequent scuba dive on the reef, including all gear.

DIVING, SNORKELING, FISHING & FOUR-WHEEL-DRIVE TOURS

Dive and snorkel ★★ Ningaloo's unspoiled waters at a dozen or more sites and you will see marvelous reef formations, groper, manta rays, octopus, moray eels, small reef sharks, potato cod (which you can hand-feed), and other marvels. Divers often spot humpback and false killer whales and large sharks, while snorkelers may see dolphins, dugongs, manta rays, and turtles. Loads of dive companies in Exmouth and Coral Bay (including the two listed in "Swimming with Whale Sharks," above) rent gear and run daily dive or snorkel trips and learn-to-dive courses. A two-dive day trip costs from A$200 with all gear supplied (snorkelers A$150).

Three great accessible snorkeling spots are: right off the shore at Coral Bay, where you can stroll up the beach, put on your mask and snorkel, drift with the current past corals and limitless fish, and then climb out and do it all over again; Pilgramunna Ledges, 72km (45 miles) from Exmouth, where you're rarely more than 10m (33 ft.) from the beach; and sheltered **Turquoise Bay ★★**, a 60km (37-mile) drive from Exmouth, which also has a drift option, but you need to be a reasonable swimmer. In deeper waters off Coral Bay, you can **snorkel with manta rays ★** with a "wingspan" of up to 7m (23 ft.). If you're lucky, the rays may encounter a good feeding patch, and they will perform a series of backward somersaults to keep themselves within the same area. Companies in both towns run manta and reef-snorkel trips and rent gear. The Ningaloo shores have loads of swimming beaches, but, for safety's sake, never swim alone.

Reef fish, tuna, and Spanish mackerel are common catches in these waters, and black, blue, and striped marlin run outside the reef September through January. Up to a dozen boats operate reef and **game-fishing day trips ★** out of Exmouth and Coral Bay, and tackle and fishing dinghies are easy to rent in either town. Note that several fishing sanctuary zones have been established, so check with DEC or visitor centers for their locations.

Green and loggerhead **turtles** ★ lay eggs at night November to February or March on the Cape's beaches. You can join one of several turtle-watch tours from either town. Cruises run from either town to spot **humpback whales** August to October.

You can take an off-road 240km (149-mile) four-wheel-drive escapade with **Ningaloo Safari Tours** (✆ **08/9949 1550;** www.ningaloosafari.com). Their "Top of the Range" tour will allow you to cross the arid limestone ridges of 50,581-hectare (124,935-acre) Cape Range National Park, snorkel Turquoise Bay, climb a lighthouse, and cruise orange-walled Yardie Creek Gorge to spot rock wallabies. This full-day trip departs your Exmouth hotel at 7:30am and returns at 6pm, at A$195 adults and A$140 children under 13. A full day snorkeling tour is also available depending on numbers.

Coral Bay's **Coastal Adventure Tours** (✆ **08/9948 5190;** www.coralbaytours.com.au) has quad bike tours which head off to quiet deserted beaches via bush tracks and over sand dunes. A 3-hour snorkel trek is A$105 and a 2-hour sunset trek is A$90. Passengers are A$45 adults and A$30 children.

WHERE TO STAY & DINE

In or Near Exmouth

Novotel Ningaloo Resort ★★ This four-star resort has brought a new standard and style to Exmouth—and it's brought recognition of the quality of the local attractions. Opened in December 2006, it sits just outside town, where a new marina is being developed. It has a superb position looking east across Exmouth Gulf. The low-rise buildings have an Outback theme (rammed earth and corrugated iron) and all face the sea and/or pools. There's a mix of hotel rooms and apartments, all spacious with king-size beds and balconies, and spa tubs in Superior rooms, bungalows, and two-bedroom apartments. Apartments have kitchens. High season is April to October and December 19 to January 12. The in-house restaurant, **Mantaray's,** has become Exmouth's top eating spot, garnering a major award in 2008.

Madaffari Dr. (Exmouth Matina), Exmouth, WA 6707. ✆ **08/9949 0000.** Fax 08/9949 0001. www.novotelningaloo.com.au. 68 units, all with showers, and most with spa tubs. High season A$275 double; A$325–A$400 Superior room, 1-bedroom apt, 1-bedroom bungalow; A$425–A$495 2-bedroom apt, 2-bedroom bungalow. AE, DC, MC, V. Free parking. No bus; taxis available. **Amenities:** Restaurant; bar; exercise room; large pool and kid's pool. *In room:* A/C, TV/DVD w/movies on demand, fridge, hair dryer, kitchen (in apt and 2-bedroom bungalow).

Sal Salis ★★ If you want a quiet, remote, and luxurious—but environmentally sensitive—place to stay, this is it. Set in Cape Range National Park, within sight and smell of the Indian Ocean, you stay in spacious new "wilderness" tents connected by boardwalks and gravel paths to the "Retreat," which contains a lounge, dining area, kitchen, sun deck, and small reference library. This small exclusive eco-camp provides "Wild Bush Luxury": All meals; guided snorkeling, walking, and kayaking tours; park fees; transfers; and most drinks are included. The kayak and snorkel trip to "Blue Lagoon," the best snorkel site in Ningaloo, is not to be missed. Fresh food is delivered daily from Exmouth and cooked by the resident chef. Evenings are special, with the sun setting over a quiet sea and, almost invariably, kangaroos in the foreground. All power is solar-generated.

Yardie Creek Rd., Cape Range National Park, 66km (41 miles) from Exmouth, WA 6707. ✆ **02/9571 6677.** www.salsalis.com.au. 9 tents, with solar shower and private facilities. A$730 (min 2 nights) based on twin share, inclusive of all meals, select open bar, airport transfers, and guided local activities. Extra adult A$514, extra child 16 and under A$365 (using swags). Inquire about whale-shark packages Apr–July. DC, MC, V. No smoking in covered areas. No children 4 and under. **Amenities:** Dining tent; lounge; bar. *In room:* No phone.

In Coral Bay

Ningaloo Reef Resort ☺ This low-rise complex of motel rooms, studios, and apartments stands out as the best place to stay among Coral Bay's selection of camp grounds and backpacker hostels. Located on a blissfully green lawn with a swimming pool overlooking the bay, the rooms are nothing fancy, but they're clean, with views toward the bay and the pool. The place has a nice communal air, thanks to the bar doubling as the local pub. The entire place is being progressively refurbished over the next few years, with a new bar and restaurant and to make all rooms self-catering. **Fins Restaurant** farther up Robinson Street is worth checking out.

1 Robinson St., Coral Bay, WA 6701. ✆ **08/9942 5934.** Fax 08/9942 5953. www.ningalooreefresort.com.au. 34 units, all with shower only. A$196–A$218 double; A$250–A$370 apt, penthouse. Extra person A$18. Weekly rates available. MC, V. **Amenities:** Restaurant; bar; outdoor pool. *In room:* A/C, TV w/ in-house movies, hair dryer, no phone.

THE KIMBERLEY ★★★

The Kimberley has been called Australia's last frontier. This is true wilderness, a vast, empty, rugged chunk in the far north of Western Australia that pushes out into the Timor Sea like a giant fist. Dry in winter and impassable in summer after one of the regular cyclones passes through, it is a region of endless bush punctuated with enormous bulbous boab trees, rough rocky ridges, a lonely but beautiful island-strewn and croc-infested coastline, and a surprising number of running rivers with long, life-giving waterholes. The dry lightly wooded savanna scenery calls to mind parts of Africa or India.

It's the rivers and gorges that make the Kimberley special even at the end of the dry season. It often seems like a miracle, after a long dusty drive, to find a broad sparkling pool fringed by paperbark trees and pandanus palms. Where the rivers have carved their way through the ranges there are spectacular gorges and plunging waterfalls. Two massive river systems define the Kimberley's outer reaches: the Ord and Fitzroy. The Fitzroy loops around the south and southwestern flanks and runs into the sea near Derby, while the Ord in the east has been dammed to provide irrigation for a major scheme below Kununurra.

Few people live here, other than on the vast cattle stations or remote Aboriginal reserves. It's over three times the area of England, but with only two roads traversing it. One is the sealed, sanitized Great Northern Highway, skirting around the south of the region, along which the Kimberley's few settlements are found. The other, the **Gibb River Road ★★**, cuts through the heart of the Kimberley. Most of it is unsealed—a rough, dusty, corrugated route. If you haven't been along this road, you haven't experienced the real Kimberley. One other rough, unsealed road heads north half way along the Gibb River Road: the Kalumburu Road that leads to the Aboriginal community of the same name. **Mitchell Falls ★★**, one of the major if hard-to-get-to attractions of the Kimberley, is accessible from the Kalumburu Road.

Starry, Starry Nights

It can be hard for people who've lived their entire lives in the Northern Hemisphere—especially city folk—to appreciate the glory of the southern skies, with the Milky Way curving majestically through the heavens. The Kimberley is one place where there is no pollution, or city lights, to diminish the evening show. Find time to go away from your camp or lodge, lie on the ground, and try to take in the immensity of what's up there. You'll probably see a satellite and maybe a shooting star.

The Kimberley is a land of extremes, with incredible light and vibrant colors—of sea, sky, and terrain—including the fiery red fine soil called pindan. The region is famous for ***Wandjina*** ★★★ Aboriginal rock art depicting people with circular hairdos that look more than a little like beings from outer space. It is also known for the "Bradshaw figures" rock paintings, sticklike representations of human forms that may be the oldest art on earth.

The unofficial capital of the East Kimberley is **Kununurra.** The small agricultural town serves as the base for wildlife cruises on the Ord; tours to the **Bungle Bungle** ★★★, a massive labyrinth of beehive-shaped rock formations; and **El Questro** ★★, a cattle station where you can hike, fish, and cruise palm-filled gorges by day and sleep in comfy permanent safari tents or glamorous homestead rooms by night.

The largest town, **Broome** ★★, is the gateway to the West Kimberley and starting point for most tours. It's not really part of the Kimberley but rather an exotic resort which started life as a 19th-century pearling port. Its waters now produce the world's biggest and best South Sea pearls, and it has become a major winter holiday destination. There are only four other small towns, all on the fringes of the region.

The **Kimberley coast** ★★★ between Broome and Kununurra is littered with islands, gulfs, and long inlets, almost all uninhabited and with no trace of human activity. Everything is affected by massive tides of up to 10m (33 ft.), which create impressive effects when funneled through narrow passages. Cruises to this remote and dramatic coastline have become progressively more popular.

Essentials

VISITOR INFORMATION **Australia's North West Tourism** (✆ **08/9193 6660;** www.australiasnorthwest.com) supplies information on the entire region. The **Kununurra Visitor Centre** (p. 535) and the **Broome Visitor Centre** (p. 541) also handle inquiries and bookings about things to see and do, and places to stay, across the Kimberley, and you can drop into their offices once you arrive.

Best of the Kimberley (✆ **1800/450 850** in Australia, or 08/9192 6070; www.kimberleytravel.net) is a Broome-based one-stop agency marketing a large range of tours and experiences, and it specializes in personalized vacations.

GETTING AROUND Enormous distances, high gasoline costs (A$1.50 per liter or more), and very limited roads and facilities can make traveling the Kimberley difficult and time-consuming. The region is effectively closed during the cyclone season from November to April, other than along the sealed highway. Most attractions

The Kimberley Region

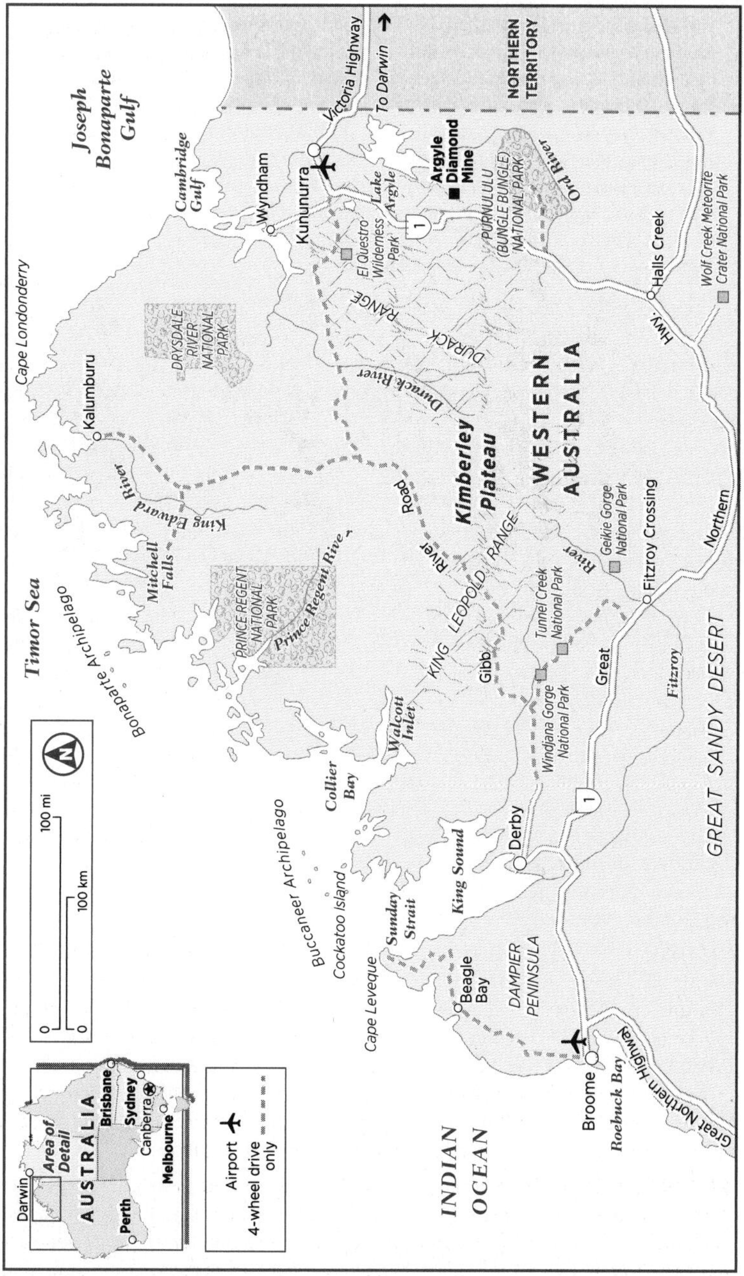
Joseph Bonaparte Gulf
Timor Sea
INDIAN OCEAN
NORTHERN TERRITORY
WESTERN AUSTRALIA
GREAT SANDY DESERT
Victoria Highway
To Darwin
Cambridge Gulf
Wyndham
Kununurra
Lake Argyle
Argyle Diamond Mine
El Questro Wilderness Park
PURNULULU (BUNGLE BUNGLE) NATIONAL PARK
Ord River
Halls Creek
Hwy.
Wolf Creek Meteorite Crater National Park
DURACK RANGE
Durack River
Cape Londonderry
Kalumburu
DRYSDALE RIVER NATIONAL PARK
King Edward River
Mitchell Falls
Bonaparte Archipelago
PRINCE REGENT NATIONAL PARK
Prince Regent River
Kimberley Plateau
Gibb River Road
KING LEOPOLD RANGE
Walcott Inlet
Collier Bay
Geikie Gorge National Park
Fitzroy Crossing
Fitzroy River
Tunnel Creek National Park
Windjana Gorge National Park
Great Northern Highway
Buccaneer Archipelago
Cockatoo Island
Cape Leveque
Sunday Strait
King Sound
Derby
Beagle Bay
DAMPIER PENINSULA
Broome
Roebuck Bay
Great Northern Highway
1
100 mi
100 km
0
Darwin
Area of Detail
AUSTRALIA
Brisbane
Sydney
Canberra
Melbourne
Perth
Airport
4-wheel drive only

Aboriginal Culture

The Kimberley is one area where Aboriginal culture, to a larger extent than elsewhere, has remained intact. Try to get involved with some aspects. Find a gallery that encourages and stocks the work of local artists, such as those of the Warmun (Turkey Creek) school, which owes much to the superb interpretations of Rover Thomas. An Aboriginal commentary on the Kimberley landscape and/or the Wandjina rock art can add immeasurably to one's understanding. You have a good chance of getting some Aboriginal contact and input when staying at Kooljaman Resort or traveling on an APT Kimberley Wilderness Adventure—both are at least part-owned by local Aboriginal communities.

are only accessible along unsealed roads, for which a two-wheel-drive rental car is totally unsuitable, while others can only be reached by aerial tours or charter boats. If you don't want to rely on tours, rent a four-wheel-drive (available in Broome and Kununurra), but check on restrictions (Hertz and Thrifty have fewest). Allow for an average speed of 80kmph (50 mph) or less on the area's rough unsealed roads, and be prepared for soft patches where the road surface has collapsed. Most outfits will allow one-way rentals between Broome and Kununurra, at a surcharge of approximately A$500 to A$750. Review "Road Conditions & Safety," "What If Your Vehicle Breaks Down?" and "Tips for Four-Wheel Drivers," in the "Getting There & Getting Around" section of chapter 3, before starting.

Kimberley Camping & Outback Supplies, 65 Frederick St., Broome (✆ **08/9193 5909;** fax 08/9193 6878; www.kimberleycamping.com.au), sells and rents every piece of camping equipment you might need, from tents and "mozzie" (mosquito) nets to cooking utensils and outdoor clothing.

Taking a guided four-wheel-drive camping or accommodated safari is usually the best way to travel the Kimberley. Safaris depart Broome, Kununurra, or Darwin, and last between 2 days and 2 weeks. Popular tours make the cross-Kimberley journey between Broome and Kununurra, especially along the **Gibb River Road,** and into the **Bungle Bungle.**

Most safaris run only in the Dry season, April or May through October or November. Respected operators include **APT Kimberley Wilderness Adventures** (✆ **1800/889 389** in Australia or 03/9277 8444; www.kimberleywilderness.com.au) for the most comprehensive selection including cruises; **East Kimberley Tours** (✆ **1800/682 213** in Australia, or 08/9168 2213; www.eastkimberleytours.com.au) concentrating on the Bungle Bungle; **Australian Adventure Travel** (✆ **1800/621 625** in Australia, or 08/9248 2355; www.safaris.net.au); and **Kimberley Wild** (✆ **1300/738 870** in Australia, or 08/9193 7778; www.kimberleywild.com), dealing mostly with West Kimberley. Kimberly Wild was named WA's "Best Tour Operator" in 2009.

Both APT Kimberley Wilderness and East Kimberley (in the Bungles only) operate semipermanent, catered, and environmentally sensitive camps in remote scenic spots. While primarily for people on their tours, they may be available to independent travelers, from A$195 per person twin share, including dinner, bed, and breakfast. The APT Bungles and Ungolan (Mitchell Plateau) camps boast en-suite facilities and cost A$225 to A$255 twin share for dinner, bed, and breakfast. You should book well ahead; go to **www.kimberleywilderness.com.au** for more information.

Broome Aviation (✆ **08/9192 1369;** www.broomeaviation.com) and **King Leopold Air** (✆ **08/9193 7155;** www.kingleopoldair.com.au), based in Broome, and **Alligator Airways** (✆ **1800 632 533** in Australia, or 08/9168 1333; www.alligatorairways.com.au) and **Slingair Heliwork** (✆ **1800/095 500** in Australia, or 08/9169 1300; www.slingair.com.au), based in Kununurra, run a range of flightseeing tours all over the Kimberley, lasting from a couple of hours to several days. Some also involve sightseeing on the ground, hiking, four-wheel-drive trips, overnights at fishing camps, or stops at cattle stations.

Kununurra

827km (513 miles) SW of Darwin; 1,032km (640 miles) E of Broome

Given the generally arid and rocky conditions in the Kimberley, it's quite a surprise to swoop over broad green fields as you come in to land at Kununurra. This relatively new town (pop. 6,000) was developed as an agricultural center based on major irrigation works created by the damming of the mighty Ord River. There are two dams: **Lake Argyle,** Australia's largest, and the smaller, downstream, Lake Kununurra that actually feeds the irrigation areas.

Kununurra (the name is Aboriginal for "meeting of big waters") has become the base for visiting several outstanding attractions and is now a significant tourist center. A cruise or canoe trip down the **Ord River ★★** to see real wilderness, dramatic cliffs, birds, and crocs is a must. So is a flight over, or a trip into, the **Bungle Bungle ★★★**, monumental striped domes of rock that look like giant beehives. The world's biggest diamond mine is not in South Africa but out in the rugged Kimberley wilds near Kununurra, and it can be visited by air. The town is a gateway to the Kimberley proper via the **Gibb River Road ★★**. There's also **El Questro Wilderness Park ★★**, a 405,000-hectare (million-acre) cattle station (ranch) where you can hike magnificent gorges, fish, cruise rivers, and ride horses. The port of **Wyndham,** terminus for some Kimberley cruises and with a superb lookout over Cambridge Gulf, is 101km (63 miles) away on a sealed road.

ESSENTIALS

GETTING THERE **Air North** (✆ **1800/627 474** in Australia, or 08/8920 4000; www.airnorth.com.au) flies from Broome and Darwin most days. **Skywest** (✆ **1300/660 088** in Australia; www.skywest.com.au) flies to and from Perth most days, from A$320. **Greyhound Australia** (✆ **13 14 99** in Australia) serves the town five times a week from Perth via Broome and from Darwin via Katherine. From Perth, the trip takes about 48 hours, from Broome about 14 hours. The one-way fare from Perth is A$640. From Darwin, the trip time is around 9 hours, and the fare is A$186.

Kununurra is 512km (317 miles) west of Katherine on the Victoria Highway. The Great Northern Highway from Broome connects with the Victoria Highway 45km (28 miles) west of Kununurra. The Gibb River Road connects with the Great Northern Highway a few miles further north, 53km (33 miles) west of Kununurra.

VISITOR INFORMATION The **Kununurra Visitor Centre** is at 75 Coolibah Dr., Kununurra, WA 6743 (✆ **1800/586 868** in Australia, or 08/9168 1177; www.kununurratourism.com). Hours change with the season (May–Sept daily 8am–5pm weekdays, 9am–4pm weekends; Oct–Mar daily 8am–4pm weekdays, closed weekends; Apr 8am–5pm weekdays, 8am–4pm Sat, 9am–1pm Sun).

GETTING AROUND **Avis** (✆ 08/9169 1258), **Budget** (✆ 08/9168 2033), **Europcar** (✆ 08/9168 3385), **Hertz** (✆ 08/9169 1424), and **Thrifty** (✆ 08/9169 1911) all rent four-wheel-drive vehicles. All have restrictions on where you can take these vehicles (especially Budget) so check before you commit. Hertz also rents camping gear.

WHAT TO SEE & DO

ON THE ORD RIVER & AROUND KUNUNURRA Several operators offer tours on the Ord River and/or Lake Argyle, a man-made inland sea bigger than 19 Sydney Harbours and ringed by red hills. Both options are good, but do not miss the Ord trip. The Ord is one of the most picturesque waterways in Australia, lined with raw scenery and teeming with all kinds of wetland birds and freshwater crocodiles. **Triple J Tours ★★** (✆ **1800/242 682** in Australia, or 08/9168 2682; www.triplejtours.net.au) runs excellent cruises, with several itineraries which vary from Dry season to Wet. The most popular starts with a 70km (43-mile) narrated coach ride to Lake Argyle, including a visit to the historic Durack homestead, and ends with a 55km (34-mile) cruise down the Ord back to Kununurra. The boat travels through rock-lined gorges and along still satiny reaches, and pulls in at numerous tranquil spots. This costs A$155 adults and A$115 for children 15 and under, including pickup from your hotel and afternoon tea. You usually catch the sunset with flocks of birds going home over the river as the cruise is finishing. The same tour, plus a 2-hour cruise on Lake Argyle, costs A$210 and A$155.

If you have a vehicle, Kununurra has a few sights worth visiting, including the **Mirima (Hidden Valley) National Park,** the **Ivanhoe Crossing** over the Ord River, and the **Hoochery,** Lot 300 Weaber Plains Rd. (✆ **08/9168 2122**), a small distillery producing very acceptable rum in the middle of the irrigation area. The **Lovell Gallery,** 144 Konkerberry Dr. (✆ **08/9168 1781**), has some excellent local artworks. Wyndham, 101km (63 miles) northwest of Kununurra, has the magnificent **Five Rivers Lookout ★**, with immense views taking in the five major rivers which flow into the mangrove-fringed Cambridge Gulf. On the way, take a short diversion to the bird sanctuary of **Parry Lagoons Nature Reserve.**

A full day on the river to fish for barramundi with Greg Harman's **Ultimate Adventures** (✆ **08/9168 2310;** www.ultimateadventures.citysearch.com.au) costs around A$320 per person, based on a minimum of two people. Greg also offers half-days, and trips of 2 to 7 days at his Hairy Dog's Fishing Camp.

Triangle Tours (✆ **08/9168 1272;** triangletours@bigpond.net) has half-day tours to the Ord River irrigation area at A$75 adults, A$45 children (under 16); and full-day tours (on weekends) to the historic port of Wyndham at A$175 adults, A$110 children. Ask about packages.

DIAMONDS IN THE ROUGH Turning out an impressive 38 million carats a year is the world's biggest diamond mine, the **Argyle Diamond Mine,** 176km (109 miles) south from Kununurra. It is the only mine in the world that produces pink diamonds in commercial quantities; champagne, cognac, yellow, green, and white ones are also found. **Slingair Heliwork** (✆ **1800/095 500** in Australia, or 08/9169 1300; www.slingair.com.au) can take visitors to the mine. The visits include the process plant and diamond display room (closed shoes must be worn for security reasons!), and are part of two all-day tours. The flights also go over nearby Purnululu (Bungle Bungle) National Park and Lake Argyle, while one includes a helicopter trip around the Bungles. Costs are A$575, or A$875 with the helicopter flight. Children under 12 are not permitted on the mine tours.

A FARAWAY ADVENTURE ★ This is about as far from everything as you can get. Nestled right in the middle of nowhere on the pristine Kimberley coast, a 70-minute flight from Kununurra, **Faraway Bay** (✆ **08/9169 1214;** www.farawaybay.com.au) is an ecofriendly bush camp offering comfort, luxury, and tranquillity on the edge of the Timor Sea. It has won the Australian Tourism Award for Unique Accommodation in 2003, 2007, and 2008.

SPENDING A DAY OR MORE AT EL QUESTRO WILDERNESS PARK ★★ You do not have to stay at El Questro (see "Where to Stay," below), in the eastern Kimberley, to enjoy the facilities. The 405,000-hectare (million-acre) cattle ranch has been turned into a kind of Outback resort, which provides a good introduction to the nature and attractions of the Kimberley without the distances and discomfort, but also without the real wilderness impact and isolation. It's still a working cattle station with 5,000 head of Brahman cattle, but you're unlikely to see any of this.

You can go barramundi fishing and heli-fishing in pristine wetlands and rivers; soak under palm trees in the thermal waters of Zebedee Springs; hike gorges with pockets of rainforest; take four-wheel-drive fishing safaris; cruise tranquil Chamberlain Gorge; horseback ride across stony plains; or join rangers on bird-watching or "bush tucker" tours. If you're short on time, the station's 10-hour ranger-guided **day tour** from Kununurra is a good option, for A$230 per person.

El Questro is open April 1 to October 31 (closed during the Wet) and offers a variety of accommodations options (see below). All visitors must purchase a **Wilderness Park Permit,** valid for 7 days, for A$18; children under 12 go free.

Four-wheel-drive transfers for guests operate from Kununurra; a ranger drives and gives a commentary en route. The costs for daily scheduled transfers is A$82 per person one-way to Emma Gorge, A$98 to Station Township, or A$120 to Homestead. If you are driving yourself, take the Great Northern Highway 58km (36 miles) from Kununurra toward Wyndham, then the (unsealed) Gibb River Road 25km (16 miles) to Emma Gorge Resort at the foot of the Cockburn Range. A separate turnoff 11km (7 miles) farther on leads to Station Township (16km/10 miles) and the Homestead (another 9km/5½ miles). A light aircraft from Kununurra will cost from A$570.

Station Township has the main facilities (bungalows, restaurant, store, airstrip, camping areas, stables, and so forth), and most tours and activities depart from here. Hiring a four-wheel-drive in Kununurra (check limitations) is recommended, to allow you to explore at your leisure and avoid the cost of transfers to and within the resort.

WHERE TO STAY

At El Questro

All of the accommodations place a 1% surcharge on credit card payments, and all have public pay phones but no in-room phones or TVs. In addition to the listings below, there are two camping areas with a total of 73 campsites at **Station Township Riverside Camping** (see El Questro Homestead below for contact information). All campsites are A$16 per person per night; free for children under 12.

Campers share shower facilities and a laundry, and use the **Steakhouse** restaurant.

El Questro Homestead ★★★ Perched over the Chamberlain River on the edge of a gorge, this homestead is one of the world's most luxurious yet simple and private getaways. Visitors (make that *wealthy* visitors) come for the seclusion and the comfort-within-wilderness experience. You stay in airy rooms furnished with modern designer pieces blended with Aussie country style, with a view of the gardens and the river from your veranda. Rooms were refurbished in 2008.

Mailing address: P.O. Box 909, Kununurra, WA 6743. ✆ **08/9169 1777.** Fax 08/9169 1383. www.elquestro.com.au. 6 units, 3 with shower only and 3 with bathtub on the veranda. From A$945 per person per night double or twin. Rates include all meals, open bar, and most tours and activities excluding helicopter flights. 2-night minimum. 15% off for 3 or more nights. AE, DC, MC, V. Children 12 and under not catered for. **Amenities:** Internet (free); Jacuzzi; small outdoor pool; tennis court. *In room:* A/C, CD, hair dryer, complimentary minibar, MP3 docking stations, no phone.

Emma Gorge Resort ★ The neatly kept oasis of permanent tent cabins set among pandanus palms and boab trees sits at the foot of the stunningly red Cockburn Range. The "tents" are very comfortable, with en-suite facilities. The rustic restaurant serves excellent gourmet bush-tucker meals and has a retractable roof for stargazing.

See contact details for El Questro Homestead, above. 60 tented cabins, all with shower only. A$270 deluxe tented cabins twin share. Extra adult A$40. 15% off 3 or more nights. AE, MC, V. **Amenities:** Restaurant; bar; outdoor pool. *In room:* No phone.

Station Township Bungalows These basic but comfortable bungalow-style rooms are good for anyone without their own transportation—tours depart from right outside—and for families. The nicest units are the eight newish ones with balconies overlooking the Pentecost River. Two of the four original stone bungalows sleep six. The **Steakhouse** restaurant and bar serves three meals a day of the steak and barramundi kind, and there is often live entertainment at the Swinging Arm Bar.

See contact details for El Questro Homestead, above. 12 bungalows, all with shower only. A$312 bungalow twin share. Extra adult A$40. Transfers A$950 per person. AE, MC, V. **Amenities:** Restaurant; bar. *In room:* A/C, fridge, no phone.

In Kununurra

Kimberley Grande ★ The best offering in Kununurra, the Grande is appropriately defined by an avenue of boab trees. It has a quiet secluded feel; the decor has muted tones and all the rooms are well back from the road, many set around the large 25m (82-ft.) pool. Spaciousness is the key, especially with the spa suites.

20 Victoria Hwy., Kununurra, WA 6743. ✆ **1800/746 282** in Australia; 08/9166 5600. Fax 08/9169 1172. www.thekimberleygrande.com.au. 72 units, all with showers except spa suites. Dry season (Apr–Oct) A$395 spa suites, A$260 Premier King, A$220 Deluxe Queen; Wet season (Nov–Mar) rates 25% less but include breakfast. Children 11 and under stay free in parent's room with existing bedding. Extra person A$50. AE, DC, MC, V. **Amenities:** Bistro; 2 bars; outdoor pool with lap lanes. *In room:* A/C, fan, TV, fridge, hair dryer, Internet (A$12/day).

Kununurra Country Club Resort Just down the road from the tourist bureau, this low-rise hotel is set in tropical gardens. It has a lovely shaded pool with sun lounges and a bar, and a couple of simple dining and bar venues. The rooms have recently been refurbished and have plenty of space.

47 Coolibah Dr., Kununurra, WA 6743. ✆ **1800/808 999** in Australia, or 08/9168 1024. Fax 08/9168 1189. www.kununurracountryclub.com.au. 88 units, 80 with shower only. Dry season (Apr–Oct) A$216 Club room, A$247 triple, A$283 2-bedroom apt; Wet season (Nov–Mar) rates are about 10% less. Extra person A$30. AE, DC, MC, V. **Amenities:** Restaurant; 3 bars; airport transfers; outdoor pool. *In room:* A/C, TV w/in-house movies, fridge, hair dryer.

Purnululu (Bungle Bungle) National Park ★★★

250km (155 miles) S of Kununurra

Rising precipitously out of the landscape 250km (155 miles) south of Kununurra are thousands of enormous striped sandstone domes 200 to 300m (656–984 ft.) high, called the Bungle Bungle, and often simply the Bungles. The Bungle Bungle get their distinctive orange-and-gray stripes from algae found in the permeable layers and mineral staining in nonpermeable layers. The domes look spectacular from the air, which is the only way to see them in the Wet, when the roads are closed. They are even better from close up, with sheer cliffs and narrow gorges slicing deep into the massif. Several of the gorges end in enormous precipitous amphitheaters, where giant boulders squat like king-size dollops of cake mix. High up, straight up, watercourses come to an abrupt end where the runoff just drops into the gorge.

Highlights are the beehive-shaped walls of Cathedral Gorge, the rock pool at Frog Hole Gorge, and palm-filled Echidna Chasm. Keep an eye peeled for rainbow bee-eaters, flocks of budgerigars, and rare nail-tailed wallabies. The Bungles aren't intimidating, but this is one place where you feel incredibly small and insignificant. It's quiet, contemplative, and seriously dramatic.

VISITOR INFORMATION For information, call the **Department of Environment and Conservation** (✆ **08/9168 4221**) in Kununurra. There's also a **visitor center/ranger station** (✆ **08/9168 7300**) in the park.

GETTING THERE & GETTING AROUND One road leads into the Bungles, a 52km (32-mile) bone-shaker four-wheel drive; no caravans are allowed. The access road is closed to ground traffic January 1 to March 31. Scenic flights over the park from Kununurra are available with **Slingair Heliwork** (✆ **1800/095 500** in Australia, or 08/9169 1300) or **Alligator Airways** (✆ **1800/632 533** in Australia, or 08/9168 1333). The flight takes about 2 hours, incorporates a flight over Lake Argyle and Argyle Diamond Mine, and costs about A$295 adults and A$245 children 3 to 12. Slingair also has 45-minute scenic heli-flights from Turkey Creek on the Great Northern Highway for A$225. Both companies have day trips that combine the flight with ground tours, though they're pricey, starting at A$640 adults and A$590 kids. Heliwork has a helicopter option over the Bungles from the local airstrip, the 30-minute award-winning flight costing A$295 adults and A$245 kids. **APT Kimberley Wilderness Adventures** and **East Kimberley Tours** (see "Getting Around," in the Kimberley section, earlier in this chapter) run an array of four-wheel-drive and fly-drive camping (using semipermanent camps) tours, with some 1-day "express" versions.

Broome ★★

2,389km (1,481 miles) N of Perth; 1,859km (1,152 miles) SW of Darwin

Part rough Outback town, part glam seaside resort, the pearling port of **Broome** (pop. 15,000) is a hybrid of Australia, Asia, and some exotic tropical island that you

Midday & Sunset

Try to be in Echidna Chasm at midday. This incredibly narrow gorge runs straight back into the rock. The walls rise to impossible heights, curving and slipping out of sight somewhere high above. At midday, the dark impenetrable shadows give way to roseate glows and sudden, blinding, glaring flashes of direct sunlight. A great sunset spot is on a small ridge near the Kurrajong Campsite, where you watch the rock face turn orange and fiery red in the fading light. If you're lucky, you may then get a great big fat full moon rising over the Bungles.

won't see anywhere else. Chinese and Japanese pearl divers worked the pearling luggers (for the pearl shell, to make buttons) in the old days, and brought some of their distinctive architecture. The result is **Chinatown,** with neat rows of corrugated iron buildings wrapped by verandas and trimmed with Chinese peaked roofs. Many Japanese divers also died here—cyclones and the "bends" took their toll—and their legacy is the **Japanese pearl divers' cemetery ★★**, with ornate inscriptions on 900 rough-hewn headstones.

The wonderfully casual free-and-easy Broome is a marine oasis, mere kilometers from the Great Sandy Desert, with dramatic colors, swaying palm trees, and masses of blooming bougainvillea and frangipani. It's situated on a small peninsula that partially defines the broad **Roebuck Bay** to the east of the town. The mangrove-fringed bay is shallow and changes dramatically between high and low tide. At low tide, masses of mudflats are exposed, which at full moon create the impression of a **Staircase to the Moon ★** (see p. 542), while at high tide the water has a vivid milky turquoise color. It's stunning. (The old pearling luggers used to tie up here, and so this was where Chinatown developed.) On the western side, broad, gleaming **Cable Beach ★★★** faces straight out on to the Indian Ocean, and many of the modern developments have taken place here.

For such a small and remote place, Broome can be surprisingly sophisticated. Walk the streets of Chinatown and you'll rub shoulders with Aussie tourists, itinerant workers, Asian food-store proprietors, tough-as-nails cattle hands, and well-heeled visitors from Europe and America who down good coffee in Broome's few trendy cafes. Broome's South Sea pearls are its bread and butter (together with tourism), but the old timber pearling luggers have been replaced with gleaming high-tech vessels.

To be honest, it's kind of hard to explain Broome's appeal. There is not much to do, but it's like nowhere else in Australia and it's such a pleasant, relaxing place to be. It has generated its own laid-back style, epitomized by the expression "Broome Time," where nothing is ever urgent. Most people simply come to laze by the jade-green Indian Ocean on Cable Beach, ride camels along the sand as the sun plops into the sea, fish the pristine seas, mosey around the art galleries and jewelry stores, and soak up the atmosphere. One experience not matched anywhere is an evening sitting in the deck chairs watching a film at **Sun Pictures ★**.

Broome is the main departure point for tours into the Kimberley, whether by boat or by four-wheel-drive along the **Gibb River Road ★★**.

ESSENTIALS

GETTING THERE **Qantas/Qantaslink** (✆ **13 13 13** in Australia) flies direct from Perth daily, and Sydney and Melbourne in peak season. **Virgin Blue** (✆ **13 67 89** in Australia) flies direct to Broome from Perth and Adelaide, with connections from other cities. **Skywest** (✆ **1300/660 088** in Australia; www.skywest.com.au) flies from Perth daily. Landing at Broome is surreal, either sweeping low across Cable Beach or roaring in at rooftop height over the town. Never mind inner-city suburbs; this is an inner-city airport—literally within walking distance.

Greyhound Australia (✆ **13 14 99** in Australia) has five services a week from Perth, taking around 33 hours. The fare is A$432. Greyhound's daily service from Darwin via Katherine and Kununurra takes around 27 hours; the one-way fare is A$396.

Broome is 34km (21 miles) off the Great Northern Highway, which leads from Perth in the south and Kununurra to the east.

VISITOR INFORMATION The **Broome Visitor Centre** on the Broome Highway at Bagot Street, Broome, WA 6725 (✆ **1800/883 777** in Australia, or 08/9192 2222; www.broomevisitorcentre.com.au), provides information and a booking service. It's open Monday to Friday 8am to 4pm, and Saturday and Sunday 8:30am to 4pm. It's closed Good Friday, December 25, and open with restricted hours on other public holidays.

Book hotels and tours well in advance of the peak June to August season.

GETTING AROUND **Avis** (✆ 08/9193 5980), **Budget** (✆ 08/9193 5355), **Europcar** (✆ 08/9193 7788), **Hertz** (✆ 08/9192 1428), and **Thrifty** (✆ 08/9193 7712) all rent conventional cars and four-wheel-drives. Check the rules on where you're allowed to take your vehicle. Hertz also rents camping-gear kits and car-top tents that affix to larger four-wheel-drives. Among the motor-home companies are **Britz** (✆ 1800/331 454 in Australia, or 08/9192 2647) and **Australian Pinnacle Tours** (✆ 08/9192 8080).

The **Town Bus Service** (✆ **08/9193 6585;** www.broomebus.com.au) does an hourly loop of most attractions, including Chinatown and Cable Beach, 7:10am to 7:10pm daily. During May to October, it also runs every half-hour 8:40am to 6:40pm. On public holidays the service starts at 10:23am. A single adult fare is A$3.50, a day-pass is A$10, and a five-trip multirider is A$16. Children under 16 travel free with a parent; otherwise the fare is A$1.50.

There are several taxi companies, including **Broome Taxis** (✆ **13 10 08**) and **Roebuck Taxis** (✆ **1800/880 330**).

Many companies (including those listed under "Essentials" in the Kimberley section, earlier in this chapter) run a variety of day tours of the town, plus trips to natural attractions farther afield, like Windjana and Geikie Gorges, Tunnel Creek, and the Dampier Peninsula, or four-wheel-drive camping safaris along the Gibb River Road (both described in "Beyond Broome & the Gibb River Road," below).

WHAT TO SEE & DO

When you arrive, head to **Chinatown,** in the town center on Carnarvon Street and Dampier Terrace, to get a feel for the town. The wide streets, the tropical-style buildings with their broad verandas and Chinese influences, the corrugated iron frontages, and the **Sun Pictures** ★ outdoor cinema (see below) are typical Broome.

Staircase to the Moon ★

On the happy coincidence of a full moon and low tide (which happens on about 3 consecutive nights a month Mar–Oct), nature treats the town to a show. The light of the rising moon falls on the remnant channels between the exposed mudflats in Roebuck Bay, with the reflections creating a "staircase to the moon." The best places to see it are from the cliff-top gardens at the Mangrove Resort Hotel (see "Where to Stay & Dine," below) or the food and crafts markets at Town Beach. Live music plays at the Mangrove most staircase nights, including a didgeridoo player to accompany the rising moon.

The main shops and cafes are here, with every corner featuring a pearl shop, which reflects the growth of both the pearling and the tourist industries.

Probably the most popular pastime is lazing on the 22km (14 miles) of glorious, white sandy **Cable Beach ★★★**. The beach is 6km (3¾ miles) out of town; the bus runs there regularly. In the Wet, about November through April or May, the water is off-limits due to nasty marine stingers. Crocodiles, on the other hand, seem not to like surf, so you should be safe swimming here. Go to the beach for at least one of the magnificent sunsets, when the sun sinks into the sea behind the romantic outlines of a pearling lugger, while strings of camels sway along the edge of the water. The sand is very firm so don't be surprised to find you're sharing the beach and sunset with dozens of four-wheel-drives parked facing out to sea—and their owners, who have set up tables and chairs for drinks. (This is Broome after all.)

A novel way to experience the beach is on a **camel ride.** Several outfits offer rides, with sunset the most popular time. A 1-hour sunset ride with **Red Sun Camels** (**✆ 08/9193 7423;** www.redsuncamels.com.au) costs A$60 adults (maximum 100kg/220 lbs.), A$40 children 6 to16, and A$10 kids under 6 (they must sit in an adult's lap).

Four-time state surf champ **Josh Palmateer ★** (**✆ 0418/958 264** mobile; www.mrsurf.com.au) gives 2-hour surf lessons on the beach August to October for A$130 for individual lessons, or A$50 per person in group lessons. Discounts are available for 3-day attendees, and he supplies the boards and the wet suits.

Don't miss the **Pearl Luggers ★★** exhibition at 31 Dampier Terrace (**✆ 08/9192 2059;** www.pearlluggers.com.au). A 1-hour tour includes a look over two beautifully restored Broome pearling luggers, a browse through a small pearling museum, and a riveting and hilarious talk about pearl diving and its history. You also get a taste of pearl shell meat. Admission is A$20 adults, A$17 students, A$10 children under 16. Tours run daily. Closed December 25 and Good Friday.

A **dinosaur footprint** 120 million years old is on show at very low tide on the cliff at Gantheaume Point, 6km (3¾ miles) from town. The town authorities have set a plaster cast of it higher up on the rocks, so you can see it anytime. Bring your camera to snap the point's breathtaking palette of glowing scarlet cliffs, white beach, and jade-turquoise water.

You should also take a walk through the haunting **Japanese pearl divers' cemetery ★★** on Port Drive. Entry is free.

During a tour of the **Willie Creek Pearl Farm ★★**, 38km (24 miles) north of town (✆ **08/9192 0000;** www.williecreekpearls.com.au), you will see the delicate process of an oyster getting "seeded" with a nucleus to form a pearl, learn about pearl farming, and discover what to look for when buying a pearl. The tour includes a cruise along Willie Creek and morning or afternoon tea. You can also buy pearls in the showroom. You must book the tour whether you drive yourself or not. Tides can limit access to the farm (four-wheel-drive vehicles are recommended), so it could be wise to take a coach tour, which costs A$90 adults, A$45 children 6 to 16, and A$225 families of four, including pickup and drop-off at your hotel. Self-drive prices are A$50 adults, A$25 children 6 to 16, and A$125 for families. Willie Creek has won WA tourism awards in 2006, 2007, 2008, and 2009.

If you want to see crocs up close and mean, even if you have seen them in the wild during your travels, take a 1-hour tour at the **Broome Crocodile Park,** next to Cable Beach Club Resort Broome, Cable Beach Road (✆ **08/9192 1489**). It's open April to November Monday to Friday 10am to 5pm, and Saturday and Sunday 2pm to 5pm; from December to March it's open from 3:30 to 5:50pm daily. Admission is A$30 adults; A$25 seniors, backpackers, and students; A$20 kids 5 to 15; and A$75 for families. Ring for tour times, and ask about combined passes for here and Malcolm Douglas Park (see below).

The superb **Malcolm Douglas Wilderness Wildlife Park ★★**, about 16km (10 miles) out of town on the Highway (✆ **08/9193 6580;** www.malcolmdouglas.com.au), has 30 hectares (74 acres) of bush, billabongs, and enclosures featuring an array of Australia's wildlife. Two huge billabongs hold about 200 crocs, there are beautiful dingoes, and the most "macho" big red 'roo you're ever likely to see lives there. It's open daily from 3:30pm to 5:50pm December to March, with crocodile feeding tours at 4pm; from April to November, it's open 10am to 5pm Monday to Friday, with alligator feedings at 11am and crocs at 3pm, and 2pm to 5pm Saturday and Sunday with tours at 3pm. Prices are A$35 adults, A$20 children 5 to 15, or A$90 families.

Several art galleries sell vivid oil and watercolor Kimberley landscapes and a range of Aboriginal art. **Monsoon Gallery** (✆ **08/9193 5379**), in a historic pearling master's house at 48 Carnarvon St., stocks a large range of European and Aboriginal paintings, sculpture, pottery, carvings, and books, and has regular exhibitions by noted artists. **Matso's,** next door, has a lovely veranda cafe and a boutique brewery that turns out unusual recipes, such as alcoholic ginger beer. The brewery displays many of the Monsoon pictures. The gallery is open daily 10am to 5pm May to October (shorter hours out of season), while the cafe is open 7am to late.

On Saturdays from 8am to 1pm, browse the **town markets** in the gardens of the colonial courthouse at the corner of Frederick and Hamersley streets. It used to be the official station for the telegraph cable from Broome to Java (thus Cable Beach).

A number of boats, including a restored pearling lugger, run **sunset cruises** off Cable Beach. **Fishing** for trevally, barracuda, barramundi, queenfish, tuna, shark, sailfish, marlin, salmon (in the May–Aug run), and reef fish is excellent around Broome; fly- and sport-fishing are also worth a go. Rent tackle and try your luck from the deepwater jetty beyond Town Beach 2km (1¼ miles) south of town, or join one of several charter boats, such as **Sentosa Charters** (✆ **08/9192 8163;** www.sentosacharters.com), for a day, or longer, trip. **Pearl Sea Coastal Cruises** (see "Boating the Kimberley Coast," below) runs live-aboard fishing safaris up the coast.

Cyclones, rain, and strong tides restrict fishing from December to April. **Whale-watching** has recently become a major attraction, with dozens of migrating humpbacks passing through from May to October. Sentosa Charters runs 3-hour cruises.

More than a third of Australia's bird species live in the Kimberley, and Roebuck Bay has the greatest diversity of shorebird species anywhere, with over 800,000 birds visiting every year. The **Broome Bird Observatory** research station ★★, 25km (16 miles) out of town on Roebuck Bay (✆ **08/9193 5600;** www.broomebirdobservatory.com), monitors the thousands of migratory wetlands birds that gather here from Siberia. Entry is by donation (A$5 suggested), while a 2-hour tour costs A$70 if you drive yourself or A$115 with pick up from Broome. Tour timings depend on the tides; check the excellent website. The all-day Lakes Tour is A$150 per person, or A$190 from Broome. Children 8 to 12 are half-price, and under 8 go free (except on the Lakes Tour). There are basic accommodations and camping facilities at the observatory.

Australia's "first family of pearling," the Paspaleys, sell their wonderfully elegant jewelry at **Paspaley Pearls,** Carnarvon Street at Short Street (✆ **08/9192 2203**). **Linneys** (✆ **08/9192 2430**) is another reputable jeweler nearby.

Don't leave without taking in a movie at the Heritage-listed **Sun Pictures** ★ outdoor cinema, 8 Carnarvon St. (✆ **08/9192 1077;** www.sunpictures.com.au). Built in 1916, these are the oldest "picture gardens" in the world. The occasionally vocal audience sits in canvas deck chairs, and the show may be interrupted by the evening flight roaring just overhead. Tickets are A$16 adults, A$11 children, A$50 families (two adults and two kids). It's open nightly except December 25—even through the Wet.

WHERE TO STAY & DINE

Broome has developed enormously over the last 5 years, leading to a large increase in the number of places offering accommodations, with many superior offerings close to Cable Beach—including Pinctada Cable Beach and The Frangipani. Many places are self-catering. The **Broome Visitor Centre** (✆ **1800/883 777** in Australia) can provide expert advice and bookings. As far as dining is concerned, both hotels listed below and Pinctada have good restaurants, and there are numerous other cafes and restaurants, including **Matso's** (see p. 543).

Originally the entrance to a zoo that no longer exists, the very pleasant, quiet, and casual **Old Zoo Cafe** ★, 2 Challenor Dr. (✆ **08/9193 6200**), is half enclosed and half alfresco, in a tropical garden setting. It has a good ambience and is close to Cable Beach.

The Aarli ★, on the corner of Fredrick and Hamersley streets (✆ **08/9192 5529**), is a small and casual eatery centrally situated on the edge of Chinatown, and serves breakfast, wood-fired meals, and tapas plates. Try the whole fresh fish, but beware, it may be big enough for two or three.

Cable Beach Club Resort & Spa Broome ★★★ For some Aussies, a visit to Broome is just an excuse to stay at this chic Asia-meets-Outback resort. Its corrugated-iron walls (inside as well as out), verandas, and Aboriginal artworks are blended with red-and-green latticework, pagoda roofs, and polished timber floors. The entire place is laid out within mature gardens, giving a gracious colonial atmosphere. Electric buggies carry guests and luggage to their rooms. A major refurbishment was completed in 2008. Bungalows (some sleep up to seven) have kitchens and central bedrooms wrapped on three sides by a veranda. The luxurious villas have private courtyards with plunge pools and butler service. Pool Terrace studios have direct access to the adults-only pool. For sheer indulgence, the Colonial Pearling Master suites are lavishly decked out with eye-popping Asiatic antiques and valuable Australian art. These are truly to die for, so ask about suite packages. The resort has a guest-activities program, including art and history tours, and a pearl boutique.

Cable Beach Rd., Broome, WA 6725. ✆ **1800/199 099** in Australia, or 08/9192 0400. Fax 08/9192 2249. www.cablebeachclub.com. 263 units, some with shower only. June–Oct 10 A$423, Apr–May A$349, Oct 11–Mar A$313 Garden View Studio; 5% less for 4-night stay; check website for other room prices. Extra person A$50. Children 12 and under stay free in parent's room with existing bedding. Ask about packages. AE, DC, MC, V. Free on-site parking. **Amenities:** 4 restaurants (2 seasonal); cafe; bar; airport shuttle; babysitting; concierge; golf course nearby; gymnasium; 2 outdoor pools (family pool and adults-only saltwater pool); room service; Chahoya Spa; 2 flood-lit tennis courts; Wi-Fi (free). *In room:* A/C, TV w/free movies, hair dryer, minibar.

Mangrove Resort Hotel ★ The best views in Broome across Roebuck Bay—especially for the "staircase to the moon" (see above)—are from this recently refurbished, modest-but-appealing cliff-top hotel, a 5-minute walk from town. The executive rooms are of a good size and contain a queen and single beds. The four Premier suites are spacious, with spa baths. Soft furnishings are being refurbished in 2010. The **Tides ★** is a lovely outdoor restaurant set under the palms and along the cliff edge. Inside, **Charters** restaurant is one of Broome's best.

47 Carnarvon St., Broome, WA 6725. ✆ **1800/094 818** in Australia, or 08/9192 1303. Fax 08/9193 5169. www.mangrovehotel.com.au. 70 units, most with shower only; suites have spa baths. Apr–Oct A$195–A$225 double, A$299 standard suite, A$375 Premier suite; Nov–Mar 5%–10% lower. Extra person A$35. Children 2 and under stay free in parent's room. Ask about packages. AE, DC, MC, V. **Amenities:** 2 restaurants; 2 bars; free airport transfers; 2 outdoor pools with spa; room service. *In room:* A/C, TV w/free movies, fridge, hair dryer.

McAlpine House ★★ This is the place to stay for a genuine touch of the style and charm of old Broome. Built in 1910 for a pearling master, the house has been extended and converted into an intimate boutique hotel with all the comforts and facilities of the 21st century, though it retains its essential colonial features of corrugated iron and latticed verandas. It's set within a luxuriant tropical garden.

84 Herbert St., Broome, WA 6725. ✆ **1800/746 282** in Australia; 08/9192 3886. Fax 08/9192 3887. www.mcalpinehouse.com. 8 units, all with en-suite bathroom. Apr–Oct A$500–A$550 Veranda and Library rooms, A$675 Garden suites, A$800 McAlpine Suite; low season (Nov–Mar) rates up to 50% lower. Minimum 2-night stay, or A$50 surcharge. Includes gourmet breakfast. AE, DC, MC, V. Secured parking. No children 15 and under. **Amenities:** Alfresco dining 5 nights per week Apr–Sept; 24-hr. bar; free airport transfers; small outdoor pool. *In room:* A/C, fans, TV w/free movies, fridge, hair dryer, Internet (free).

Seashells Resort ★ ☺ This is one of the best self-catering resorts, situated among tropical gardens and palm trees a short distance back from Cable Beach. The attractive colonial-style two-story blocks of units surround the large freeform pool and children's paddling pool. The units are spacious, with full kitchens and laundries, queen beds (and singles), and a surprising degree of privacy. Everything has been refurbished since January 2007.

4–6 Challenor Dr., Cable Beach, Broome, WA 6725. ✆ **1800/800 850** in Australia, or 08/9192 6111. Fax 08/9192 6166. www.seashells.com.au. 49 units. Nov–Mar (low season) A$210 1-bedroom apt, A$245 2-bedroom apt (4 people), A$300 3-bedroom bungalow (6 people); high-season A$295 1-bedroom apt, A$345 2-bedroom apt, A$425 3-bedroom apt. Children 13 and under stay free in parent's room with existing bedding. Ask about packages. AE, DC, MC, V. **Amenities:** Babysitting on request; outdoor pool and paddling pool. *In room:* A/C, fans, TV w/free movies, fridge, hair dryer, Internet (A$9.95 for 1 hr.; A$30 per day).

Beyond Broome & the Gibb River Road ★★

North and east of Broome is wilderness at its best, suited to those who love nature at its most raw and isolated. Swimming in the ocean and river mouths, however, is off-limits due to crocodiles, although many of the inland rivers and pools are free of saltwater crocodiles and can provide welcome relief from heat and dust.

Stretching 220km (136 miles) north of Broome, the **Dampier Peninsula** is home to several Aboriginal communities and a small resort at the northern tip of Cape Leveque. The four-wheel-drive Cape Leveque Road runs through the fine red pindan dust, past **Beagle Bay**'s wonderful pearl-shell church built by missionaries, and up to the remote red-cliffed cape. The Aboriginal community-run **Kooljaman Resort** here has cabins and deluxe safari tents gazing out over an empty azure sea.

Traveling the **Gibb River Road ★★** is not for everyone, being rough, dusty, and lacking the world's little luxuries; it's for those who love wilderness and adventure in a primal land. Facilities really are few and far between. Both this road and the Kalumburu Road are classified as four-wheel-drive, but you must check whether your rented vehicle can travel them. The roads are often closed during the Wet from December to April; call ✆ **13 81 38** for up-to-date road conditions.

The western part of the Kimberley is the most accessible and can be explored on a long day trip (or two) from Broome. The **Mowanjum Aboriginal Community,** 12km (7½ miles) beyond Derby, has an excellent art gallery worth visiting. The 350-million-year-old **Windjana Gorge,** 240km (149 miles) east of Broome, has tall gray limestone cliffs enclosing long, silent pools separated by enormous sand banks—basking places for freshwater crocodiles. Another unsealed road leads south, past **Tunnel Creek,** a limestone cavern which you can walk through, to the Great Northern Highway. Some 100km (62 miles) farther east (or 418km/259 miles east of Broome) is **Geikie Gorge** (pronounced *Geek*-ee). Its 30m-high (98-ft.) walls are part of the same ancient coral-reef system as Windjana; you explore Geikie Gorge on walking trails or on small cruise boats.

Traveling farther along the Gibb River Road, you wind through rough rocky ranges, with detours to take in the delights of stunning pools and waterfalls such as those at Bell and Manning Gorges. Facilities exist only at isolated homesteads and Aboriginal communities, and there are a few designated camping areas. At night the stars are absolutely magnificent, with the Milky Way a silvery blaze across the sky.

Up the Kalumburu Road 130km (81 miles) is the turnoff to **Mitchell Plateau.** The plateau is heavily dissected and marked by tall mop-headed livistona palms. This is the home of magnificent **rock art ★★★**. Some rock outcrops contain superb painted images, particularly the Wandjina, showing vivid haloed figures, sometimes with a body, or simply a head, but never with a mouth. The Bradshaw figures, or *Gwion,* are also found here; these are stylized human figures, often stick-like in appearance, of unknown but certainly great age.

There's a scenic 3.5km (2.3-mile) walk to the **Mitchell Falls ★★**, although you can take a helicopter transfer. The falls drop down in three tiers, with deep pools enclosed by sheer rock walls. The best chopper trip goes from the falls way out to Admiralty Gulf, a milky turquoise sea with sharks and crocs visible in the shallows, and back along the lower Mitchell River gorge. The flight shows the immensity and

One Big River

The Fitzroy River is Australia's largest wild river. It has no dams, it's totally unfettered, and its flow after the summer cyclones has been rated among the highest in the world. This makes its waters highly desirable to Australia's drying cities well to the south—there are regular (and perhaps not totally farfetched) plans to harness it and carry the precious water thousands of kilometers away. The Greens and local Aborigines do not agree! Most visitors only see the Fitzroy in the Dry, either at Geikie Gorge or the long Willare Bridge east of Broome, when it is but a quiet and unremarkable stream.

emptiness of the Kimberley, bringing a superb vista of rocky terraces, islands, mangroves, bays, and creeks extending in all directions—with absolutely nothing else to be seen.

Several operators offer tours along the Gibb River Road. **APT Kimberley Wilderness Adventures** (see "Getting Around," at the beginning of the Kimberley section) has an excellent 13-day tour from Broome to Broome that takes in Mitchell Falls, Kununurra, Ord River, Bungle Bungle, and Geikie Gorge at A$6,395 per person twin share.

BOATING THE KIMBERLEY COAST ★★★

Boating this vast, unspoiled Kimberley coastline is a true adventure. There are no towns, marinas, or service facilities. You take everything with you. But it allows some unforgettable experiences: magnificent if stark scenery, utter isolation, showering under pristine waterfalls, experiencing the size and power of the tides, including the so-called "Horizontal Falls," and the brilliant night skies.

Several boat operators run fishing and adventure trips from Broome, Derby (221km/137 miles northeast of Broome), or Wyndham. Otherwise, there are cruises that can only be described as luxurious. North Star Cruises even travels with its own helicopter for sightseeing and heli-fishing. Some boats take scuba divers and snorkelers to Rowley Shoals, a marvelous outcrop of coral reef and giant clams 260km (161 miles) west of Broome. Find a trip and vessel that suits you—some provide comfortable en-suite private cabins, while others are camp-on-the-beach jobs.

Some of the most established operators are **North Star Cruises** (**© 08/9192 1829;** www.northstarcruises.com.au), **Pearl Sea Coastal Cruises** (**© 1300/156 035** in Australia or 08/9193 6131; www.kimberleyquest.com.au), and **Coral Princess Cruises** (**© 931/924 5253** in North America, or 07/4040 9999; www.coralprincesscruises.com), all operating from Broome; **Buccaneer Sea Safaris** (**© 08/9191 1991;** www.buccaneerseasafaris.com) operates out of Derby. The cruises run only in the Dry, generally between April and October, and tend to book up well in advance, with many 2011 trips already sold out at press time.

The 34m (112-ft.) ***North Star*** can carry 36 passengers on 13-day cruises between Broome and Wyndham at A$16,495 to A$24,995 per person. It also offers some 6- or 7-day intermediate options, and September trips to Rowley Shoals. Pearl Sea carries 18 passengers onboard the 25m (82-ft.) Kimberley Quest II, with its

13-day Broome-Wyndham prices ranging from A$12,095 to A$19,355, but most of its cruises are 7 days, from A$8,345 to A$12,085. Coral Princess has the largest vessels: the 35m (115-ft.) ***Coral Princess*** and the 63m (207-ft.) ***Oceanic Discoverer,*** with 10-night cruises between Broome and Darwin for A$6,850 to A$9,750. All the above prices are based on twin share. Buccaneer has beach camping with swags and tents, and trips of between 5 and 10 days from Derby. You need to check what is supplied with the cruises in the way of excursions or transfers, such as seaplane and/or helicopter flights.

ADELAIDE & SOUTH AUSTRALIA

12

by Lee Atkinson

South Australia is a state of extremes: It's the country's driest state with some of the most inhospitable deserts on the continent, and at the same time, it's also one of the country's most fertile—the lush green valleys and hills produce some of the best wines in Australia, if not the world. With its red, rocky gibber plains and wild windswept coastlines, pristine beaches, ancient mountain ranges, wide sweeping rivers, soft forested hills, and sea-scrapped islands, South Australia is Australia in microcosm.

Despite all this variety, it's the one state that often gets left off travelers' itineraries in favor of other states, with their reefs, rainforests, tropical beaches, big bustling cities, and monolith rocks. I reckon it's not such a bad thing really, because it means that those who do make the effort to get here don't have to share it with hordes of others.

The capital, **Adelaide,** is an elegantly laid out city, the only metropolis in the country other than Canberra that was actually planned, and it's big enough to offer lots of variety and excitement without losing its country-town vibe. On its doorstep are the vineyards of the Adelaide Hills, McLaren Vale, Clare, and Barossa valleys, but wherever you venture in the countryside, you're almost always guaranteed to find some of the freshest and best food and wine in the country.

Australia's longest river, the Murray, spills into the sea in the east of the state; to the west, the spectacular cliffs of the **Great Australian Bight** follow the path of the longest, straightest road in the world across the **Nullarbor Plain.** Along the Indian Ocean, peninsulas and islands provide a rugged and beautiful coastline.

Offshore, **Kangaroo Island** is the place to be bowled over by the wildlife—spend a couple of days here and you'll see more wild kangaroos, wallabies, koalas, penguins, and sea lions than you thought possible in one place.

You don't have to travel very far north of the capital city to find yourself in the midst of some of the meanest, harshest, and most ethereally beautiful desert landscapes in the world; 70% of the South Australia is "Outback." Out here you'll find bizarre opal-mining towns, such as **Coober Pedy,** where summer temperatures can reach 122°F (50°C), where most people live underground to escape the heat. The beautiful **Flinders Ranges,** the eroded stumps of mountains that were once higher than the Himalayas and are some of the oldest in the world, are another "must see."

If you prefer your landscape with more moisture, head to the **Coorong,** a waterbird sanctuary rivaled only by Kakadu National Park in the Northern Territory (see chapter 10).

Exploring the State

VISITOR INFORMATION **The South Australia Visitor & Travel Centre,** 18 King William St., Adelaide, SA 5000 (© **1300/655 276** in Australia, or 08/8463 4547; www.southaustralia.com), is the best place to find information on Adelaide and South Australia. It's open weekdays from 8:30am to 5pm and weekends from 9am to 2pm. There's also an information booth at the Adelaide airport.

GETTING AROUND The best way to see South Australia is by car. Limited rail service connects Adelaide with some areas. The Stuart Highway bisects the state from south to north; it runs from Adelaide through the industrial center of Port Augusta (gateway to the Flinders Ranges) and through Coober Pedy to Alice Springs in the Red Centre. The Eyre Highway travels westward along the coastline and into Western Australia, and the Barrier Highway enters New South Wales just before the city of Broken Hill (see chapter 6). The Princes Highway takes you east to Melbourne. If you plan to drive into the Outback regions, contact the **Royal Automobile Association of South Australia (RAA),** 55 Hindmarsh Sq., Adelaide, SA 5000 (© **13 11 11** in South Australia, or 08/8202 4600; www.raa.net). The RAA provides route maps and emergency breakdown service.

Greyhound Australia (© **1300/473 946** in Australia; www.greyhound.com.au) operates bus services to and around South Australia. Within the state, **Premier Stateliner** (© **08/8415 5555;** www.premierstateliner.com.au) runs daily services to most regional centers. There are also a number of private sightseeing companies that run full and half-day tours of the city, the Barossa Valley, and Adelaide Hills. Visit or call the South Australia Visitor & Travel Centre (see above) for details and recommendations.

ADELAIDE

Adelaide (pop. 1,180,000) has always been a free-spirited, free-thinking type of place—the first to outlaw sexual and racial discrimination, the first to do away with capital punishment, the first to recognize Aboriginal land rights and legalize nude swimming, and the first state to give women the vote. Perhaps that's because Adelaide was the only capital to have been settled by free settlers, rather than convicts, and was totally self-sufficient, receiving no financial backing from the British government. The fledgling colony promised settlers civil and religious liberty, a 19th-century vision of utopia that attracted thousands of European immigrants escaping religious persecution.

South Australia

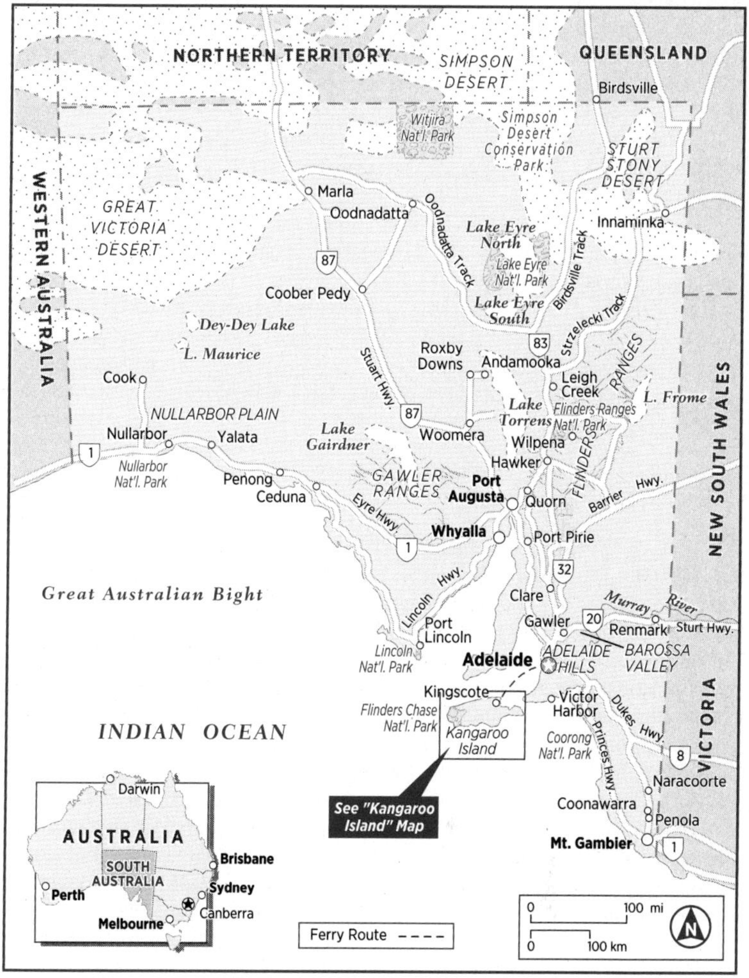

Australians who have never visited Adelaide tend to dismiss the city as little more than a large country town, but that is the city's greatest charm. Meticulously planned by surveyor-general Colonel William Light in 1837, the city is an elegant grid of broad streets surrounded by a green belt of parkland set beside the River Torrens, between the Adelaide Hills and the waters of Gulf St. Vincent. Light's grand plan has produced an easily navigable city with next to no traffic jams and, best of all, a city center where everything is within easy walking distance of everything else.

Any season is a good time to visit Adelaide, though May through August can be chilly and January and February hot.

Essentials

GETTING THERE **By Plane** **Qantas** (✆ **13 13 13** in Australia; www.qantas.com.au), **Virgin Blue** (✆ **13 67 89** in Australia; www.virginblue.com.au), and **Jetstar** (✆ **13 15 38** in Australia; www.jetstar.com) all fly to Adelaide from the other major state capitals. Check their websites for cheap deals. **Tiger Airways** (✆ **03/9335 3033;** www.tigerairways.com) also has daily flights from most capital cities apart from Perth and Darwin. Within South Australia, Regional Express (**REX airlines;** ✆ **13 17 13** in Australia; www.rex.com.au) offers daily services to some regional centers.

Adelaide International Airport is 8km (5 miles) west of the city center. Major car-rental companies (Avis, Budget, Hertz, and Thrifty) have desks in both the international and domestic terminals.

The **Skylink** (✆ **1300/383 783** in Australia; www.skylinkadelaide.com) connects the airport with major hotels and the rail and bus stations. On weekdays, buses leave the terminals at 30-minute intervals from 5:30am to 9:30pm, and on weekends and public holidays hourly (on the half-hour). Adult tickets are A$8.50 one-way, kids A$3.50. A cheaper alternative is the **JetBus** (✆ **08/8210 1000;** www.adelaidemetro.com.au), which links the airport to Glenelg, West Beach, and the North Eastern suburbs and costs A$1.80 from 9am to 3pm on weekdays and A$2.60 at most other times one way. It operates daily, 4:30am to 11:35pm.

BY TAXI A taxi to the city from the airport will cost around A$20.

BY TRAIN The **Keswick Interstate Rail Passenger Terminal,** 2km (1¼ miles) west of the city center, is Adelaide's main railway station. The terminal has a small snack bar and a cafe.

Contact **Great Southern Railways** (✆ **13 21 47** in Australia; www.gsr.com.au) for information, timetables, fares, and bookings for all trains described below.

One of the great trains of Australia, the ***Indian Pacific*** ★★ transports passengers from Sydney to Adelaide (trip time: 28 hr.) every Saturday and Wednesday at 2:55pm and from Perth to Adelaide (trip time: 36 hr.) on Wednesday and Sunday at 11:55am. One-way tickets from Sydney to Adelaide are around A$694 for adults and A$527 for children in first class; A$501 for adults and A$365 for children in an economy sleeper; and A$308 for adults and A$130 for children in coach. From Perth to Adelaide, the one-way fare is A$1,514 for adults and A$1,022 for children in first class; A$1,036 for adults and A$628 for children in an economy sleeper; and A$458 for adults and A$211 for children in coach. Prices keep going up, so check before you leave home, but take it from me, you'd be crazy to consider anything less than a sleeper.

The other legendary Australian train is the ***Ghan,*** which runs from Adelaide to Alice Springs and on to Darwin twice a week on Sunday and Wednesday at 12:20pm. Trip time from Alice Springs to Adelaide is 20 hours. From Alice Springs to Adelaide and vice versa, the one-way fare is A$1,019 for adults and A$701 for children in first class; A$656 for adults and A$400 for children in an economy sleeper; and A$358 for adults and A$166 for children for an economy seat. From Adelaide to Darwin, which is a 2-night trip, it costs A$1,973 for adults and A$1,357 for kids in first class; A$1,312 for adults and A$800 for kids in an economy sleeper; and A$716 for adults and A$331 for kids in an economy seat. If you can't afford a sleeper though, you'd be better off flying, and you'd save yourself a whole lot of time,

Adelaide

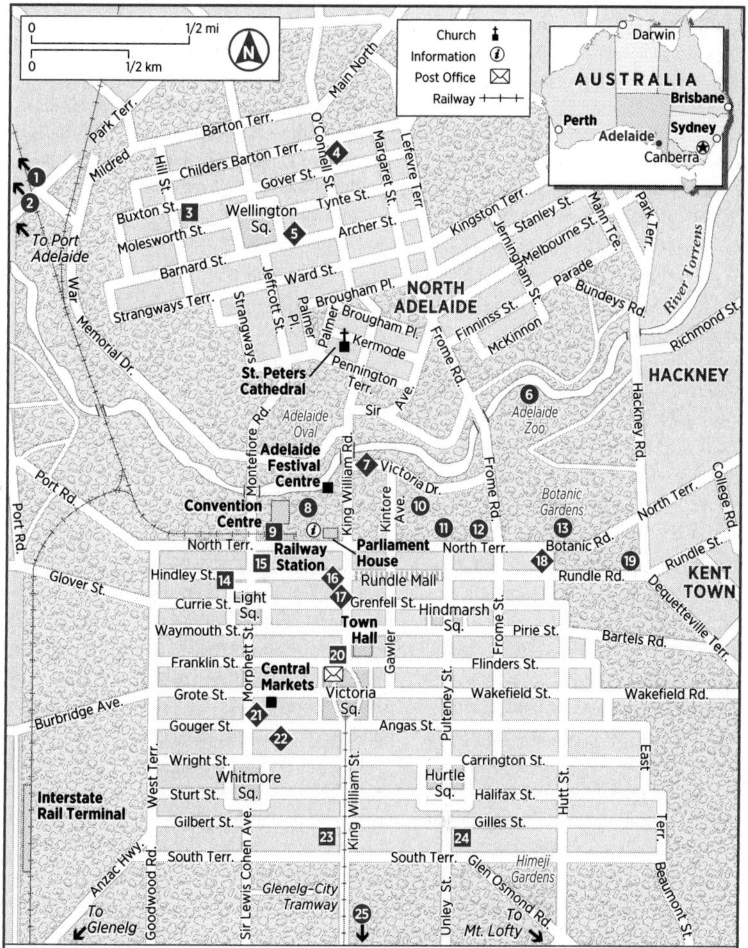

ATTRACTIONS ●

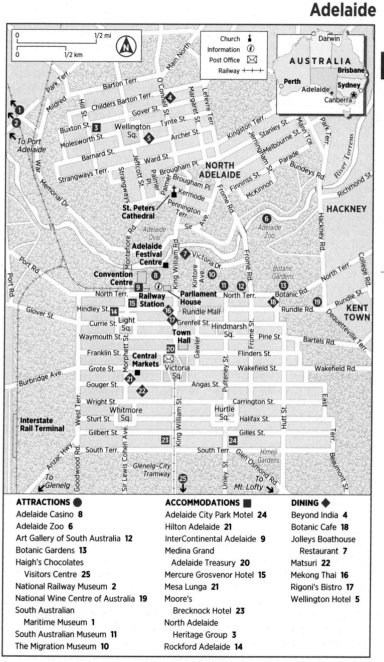

Adelaide Casino **8**
Adelaide Zoo **6**
Art Gallery of South Australia **12**
Botanic Gardens **13**
Haigh's Chocolates Visitors Centre **25**
National Railway Museum **2**
National Wine Centre of Australia **19**
South Australian Maritime Museum **1**
South Australian Museum **11**
The Migration Museum **10**

ACCOMMODATIONS ■

Adelaide City Park Motel **24**
Hilton Adelaide **21**
InterContinental Adelaide **9**
Medina Grand Adelaide Treasury **20**
Mercure Grosvenor Hotel **15**
Mesa Lunga **21**
Moore's Brecknock Hotel **23**
North Adelaide Heritage Group **3**
Rockford Adelaide **14**

DINING ◆

Beyond India **4**
Botanic Cafe **18**
Jolleys Boathouse Restaurant **7**
Matsuri **22**
Mekong Thai **16**
Rigoni's Bistro **17**
Wellington Hotel **5**

World-Class Festivals in Adelaide

Adelaide is home to Australia's largest performing arts festival, the Adelaide Festival ★, which takes place over 3 weeks in March in even-numbered years. The festival includes literary and visual arts as well as dance, opera, classical music, jazz, cabaret, and comedy. The festival includes a Writers' Week and the Adelaide Fringe Festival. Visit www.adelaidefestival.com.au.

In February or March, the 3-day WOMADelaide Festival of world music takes place. Crowds of 60,000 or more turn up to watch Australian and international artists. Visit www.womadelaide.com.au.

money, and back pain. If you really want to splurge, the Platinum Service offers luxury cabins twice the size of standard first class cabins, with double beds and full en-suite and lots of extras thrown in. It only operates on the Adelaide to Darwin service and costs A$2,987 per adult. No kids' fares are available.

The ***Overland*** operates three weekly trips from Adelaide to Melbourne (Mon, Wed, and Fri at 7:40am) and Melbourne to Adelaide (Tues and Thurs at 8:05am and Sat at 8:40am). Trip time is 12 hours. From Melbourne to Adelaide, one-way ticket prices are A$134 for adults and A$95 for children in first class, and A$90 for adults and A$45 for children in an economy seat.

BY BUS Intercity coaches serve the central bus station, 101 Franklin St. (✆ **08/8415 5533**), near Morphett Street in the city center. **Greyhound Australia** (✆ **1300/473 946** in Australia; www.greyhound.com.au) runs buses between Adelaide and all other major cities. The trip from Melbourne takes 10 hours and costs A$70; from Sydney, 23 hours and A$190; and from Alice Springs, 21 hours and A$280. Check the website for discounts before you book.

Adventurous types should consider traveling to Adelaide from Melbourne (or vice versa) on the **Wayward Bus,** operated by the Wayward Bus Touring Company (✆ **1300/654 604** in Australia, or 08/8132 8230; www.waywardbus.com.au). The fare is A$445 with backpacker's accommodations and around A$510 with twin motel accommodations. You spend about 3 hours a day on the bus, and the driver acts as your guide. The fare includes a picnic or cafe lunch each day and entry to national parks. You can leave the trip and rejoin another later. Reservations are essential. Wayward Bus also runs 8-day overland trips traveling between Adelaide and Alice (or vice versa), via Uluru, Kata Tjuta (the Olgas), Kings Canyon, Coober Pedy, Lake Eyre, William Creek, Wilpena Pound, the Flinders Ranges, and the Clare Valley wineries. Accommodations are a mix of camping, swags (thick sleeping bags), dugout caves, and hostels. It costs A$1,095. Check the website for more tours, including to Outback South Australia and Kangaroo Island.

Another bus company, the **Nullarbor Traveller** (✆ **08/8687 0455;** www.thetraveller.net.au), takes adventurous travelers from Adelaide to Perth in 10 days across the Nullarbor Plain. The tour includes a mixture of camping and farmstay accommodations and most meals. It costs A$1,450. A good area website is **www.nullarbornet.com.au**.

BY CAR To drive from Sydney to Adelaide on the Hume and Sturt highways takes roughly 20 hours; from Melbourne it takes around 10 hours on the Great Ocean

Road and Princes Highway; from Perth it takes 32 hours on the Great Eastern and Princes highways; and from Alice Springs it takes 15 hours on the remote Stuart Highway. For more information on driving distances, consult the website **www.auinfo.com/distancecalc_process.asp**.

VISITOR INFORMATION Go to the **South Australia Visitor & Travel Centre,** 18 King William St. (✆ **1300/655 276** in Australia, or 08/8463 4547; fax 08/8303 2249), for maps, travel advice, and hotel and tour bookings. It's open weekdays from 8:30am to 5pm, weekends from 9am to 2pm.

CITY LAYOUT Victoria Square is the geographical heart of the city, surrounded by grand government buildings, some of which have been reborn into elegant hotels. This is also where you'll find the historic tram that takes 20 minutes to trundle to the seaside suburb of Glenleg, with its famous long pier and white sandy beaches. On the western side of the square is the Central Market, Australia's oldest continuously operating produce market (it's been going since 1869), which is today home to the best range of international foods in Australia.

Bisecting the city from south to north is the main thoroughfare, **King William Street.** Streets running perpendicular to King William Street change their names on either side; Franklin Street, for example, changes into Flinders Street. Of these cross streets, the most interesting are the restaurant strips of **Gouger** and **Rundle streets,** the latter running into the pedestrian-only shopping precinct of Rundle Mall. Another is **Hindley Street,** with inexpensive restaurants and nightlife. On the banks of the River Torrens just north of the city center, you'll find the Riverbank Precinct, the home of the Festival Centre, the Convention Centre, and the SkyCity Adelaide Casino.

North Terrace is one of the four boundary streets that mark the edge of the city center and the beginning of the parkland belt that slopes down toward the River Torrens, where you'll find almost all of the city's major attractions and museums, most of which are free.

Follow King William Street north and it crosses the River Torrens and flows into sophisticated **North Adelaide,** an area crammed with Victorian and Edwardian architecture. The main avenues in North Adelaide, **O'Connell** and **Melbourne streets,** are lined with restaurants, cafes, and bistros that offer the tastes of a multicultural city.

Northwest of the city center is **Port Adelaide,** a seaport and the historic maritime heart of South Australia. It's home to some of the finest colonial buildings in the state, as well as good pubs and restaurants.

GETTING AROUND **By Bus** Adelaide's public bus network covers three zones, and fares are calculated according to the number of zones traveled. The city

A Money-Saving Transit Pass

If you plan to get around the city on public transportation, it's a good idea to purchase a Daytrip ticket, which covers unlimited travel on buses, trams, and city trains within the metropolitan area for 1 day. The pass costs A$8.30 for adults and A$4.20 for children 5 to 15 and is available at most train stations, newsagents, and the Adelaide Metro InfoCentre (✆ 1300/311 108 in Australia).

center is in Zone 1. The fare in Zone 1 is A$1.80 from 9am to 3pm on weekdays and A$2.60 at most other times. Kids travel for around half-price. You can buy tickets on board or at larger newsdealers around the city. You can get timetable and destination information over the phone or in person from the **Adelaide Metro InfoCentre** (✆ **08/8210 1000;** www.adelaidemetro.com.au), on the corner of Currie and King William streets. It's open Monday to Friday from 8am to 6pm, Saturday 9am to 5pm, and Sunday from 11am to 4pm.

The free **CityLoop bus** (no. 99C) operates every 15 minutes (Mon–Thurs 8am–6pm; Fri 8am–9pm; Sat 8am–5pm) around the city center, along North Terrace, East Terrace, Grenfell Street, Pulteney Street, Wakefield Street, Grote Street, Morphett Street, Light Square, Hindley Street, and West Terrace. There is also a free tram that runs between South Terrace and North Terrace approximately every 7 minutes.

Bus nos. 181 and 182 run from the city to North Adelaide.

BY TRAM The **Glenelg Tram** runs between Victoria Square and the beachside suburb of Glenelg. Tickets cost A$2.70 for adults and A$1.20 for children 5 to 14 from 9am to 3pm, A$4.40 for adults and A$2.10 for children at other times. The journey takes 29 minutes.

BY TAXI & CAR The major cab companies are **Yellow Cabs** (✆ **13 19 24** in South Australia), **Suburban** (✆ **13 10 08** in South Australia), and **Adelaide Independent Taxi Service** (✆ **13 22 11** in South Australia). **Access Cabs** (✆ **1300/360 940** in South Australia) offers wheelchair taxis.

Major car-rental companies are **Avis,** 136 North Terrace (✆ **08/8410 5727**); **Budget,** 274 North Terrace (✆ **08/8418 7300**); **Hertz,** 233 Morphett St. (✆ **08/8231 2856**); and **Thrifty,** 23 Hindley St. (✆ **08/8410 8977**).

The **Royal Automobile Association of South Australia (RAA),** 55 Hindmarsh Sq. (✆ **13 11 11** in South Australia, or 08/8202 4600; www.raa.net), has route maps and provides emergency breakdown services.

[FastFACTS] ADELAIDE

American Express The office, at Shop 32 in Rundle Mall (✆ **1300/139 060**), is open Monday to Friday 9am to 5pm, and Saturday 9am to noon.

Business Hours Generally, banks are open Monday through Thursday from 9:30am to 4pm and Friday from 9:30am to 5pm. Stores are generally open Monday through Thursday from 9am to 5:30pm, Friday from 9am to 9pm, Saturday from 9am to 5pm, and Sunday from 11am to 5pm.

Currency Exchange Banks and hotels, the casino, and the Myer department store in Rundle Mall cash traveler's checks. The **Travelex** office is at Shop 4, Rundle Mall (✆ **08/8231 6977**). It's open Monday to Saturday 9am to 5:30pm (7pm on Fri).

Dentists Contact the **Australian Dental Association Emergency Information Service** (✆ **08/8272 8111**), open weeknights from 5 to 9pm, and Saturday and Sunday from 9am to 9pm. It will put you in touch with a dentist.

Doctors In an emergency, go to the casualty department of the **Royal Adelaide Hospital,** North Terrace (✆ **08/8222 4000**). **The Travellers' Medical & Vaccination Centre,** 29 Gilbert Place (✆ **08/8212 7522**), offers vaccinations and travel-related medicines.

Emergencies Dial ✆ **000** to call an ambulance, the fire department, or the police in an emergency.

Hospitals The **Royal Adelaide Hospital** (✆ **08/8222 4000**), is on North Terrace in the city center.

Hot Lines Call the **Crisis Care Centre** (✆ **13 16 11** in Australia); the **Royal Automobile Association of South Australia,** or RAA (✆ **08/8202 4600**); the **Disability Information and Resource Centre** (✆ **08/8236 0555**) for information on those respective services.

Internet Access The **State Library of South Australia,** at the corner of North Terrace and Kintore Avenue (✆ **08/8207 7250**), has e-mail facilities available Monday through Wednesday 10am to 8pm, Thursday and Friday 10am to 6pm and Saturday and Sunday 10am to 5pm. Internet access is readily available around town at other libraries and in Internet cafes. For free Wi-Fi hot spots see **https://hotspot.internode.on.net**.

Lost Property If you've lost something on the street, contact the nearest police station. For items left on public transport, contact the **Lost Property Office,** on the main concourse of the Adelaide Railway Station on North Terrace (✆ **08/8218 2552**); it's open Monday through Friday from 9am to 5pm.

Luggage Storage & Lockers There are luggage lockers at **Adelaide Airport** in the domestic terminal as well as the **Central Bus Station** on Franklin Street.

Pharmacies (Chemist Shops) **Burden Chemists,** Shop 11, Southern Cross Arcade, King William Street (✆ **08/8231 4701**), is open Monday through Thursday from 8am to 6pm, Friday from 8am to 8pm, and Saturday from 9am to 1pm.

Post Office The **General Post Office (GPO),** 141 King William St., Adelaide, SA 5000 (✆ **13 13 18** in Australia), is open Monday through Friday from 8:30am to 5:30pm. General delivery mail *(poste restante)* can be collected Monday through Friday during opening hours.

Restrooms Public restrooms are at the Central Market Arcade, between Grote and Gouger streets, in both Hindmarsh and Victoria squares, and at James Place (off Rundle Mall).

Safety Adelaide is a safe city, though it's wise to avoid walking along the River Torrens and through side streets near Hindley Street after dark.

Where to Stay

The **South Australia Visitor & Travel Centre** (see "Visitor Information," above) can supply information on B&Bs and home stays around the state. The rates given below are rack rates, or what the hotels hope they'll get on a good day—you can often get a room for much less, especially by booking directly through the hotel's website.

IN THE CITY CENTER

Expensive

Hilton Adelaide ★★ The Hilton is a great business hotel in the very heart of the city center and just around the corner from a host of restaurants on Gouger Street. Guest rooms are quite spacious and pleasant, with all you might expect from a five-star establishment, and the service has always been spot on every time I've stayed. Some rooms have great views of the city and Adelaide Hills. There are 11 rooms equipped for travelers with disabilities.

233 Victoria Sq., Adelaide, SA 5000. ✆ **08/8217 2000.** Fax 08/8217 2001. www.hilton.com. 374 units. A$210–A$320 standard double; suites from A$410 and up. Children 11 and under stay free in parent's

room. AE, DC, MC, V. Valet parking A$28. Tram stops in front of hotel. **Amenities:** Restaurant; bar; babysitting; concierge; health club; Jacuzzi; heated outdoor pool; room service; sauna; tennis court. *In room:* A/C, TV w/pay movies, fridge, hair dryer, minibar, Wi-Fi (A55¢ per minute up to A$29 for 24 hr.).

InterContinental Adelaide ★★ The 20-story InterContinental is in the heart of the city and part of the complex that includes the Adelaide Festival Centre, the Casino, the Exhibition Hall, and the Convention Centre. The property overlooks the River Torrens and nearby parklands, and there are some wonderful views from the higher floors. Guests staying in club-level rooms get a good complimentary breakfast and free evening drinks and canapés.

North Terrace, Adelaide, SA 5000. ✆ **08/8238 2400.** Fax 08/8231 1120. www.ichotelsgroup.com. 367 units. A$225–A$350 double; suites from A$500 and up. Extra person A$50. Children 11 and under stay free in parent's room. Executive Club Level rates include breakfast and access to the Club InterContinental, which includes complimentary canapés and drinks 5:30–7:30pm each day. Ask about packages and weekend discounts. AE, DC, MC, V. Parking A$27. Bus/tram: CityLoop. **Amenities:** 2 restaurants; bar; lounge; nightclub; babysitting; concierge; health club; Jacuzzi; heated outdoor pool; room service. *In room:* A/C, TV w/pay movies, fridge, hair dryer, minibar, Wi-Fi (A$5.50 for 5 min. up to A$29 for 24 hr.).

Medina Grand Adelaide Treasury ★★★ My favorite place to stay in Adelaide, the Medina is part of a very clever makeover of the former treasury building—it has managed to combine stylish modern design without sacrificing the heritage of this beautiful sandstone building right on Victoria Square, in the heart of the city. Apartments are so big you can get lost in them, with the highest ceilings I've ever seen in a hotel room. There is a gorgeous garden courtyard with fountain. The only downside is that there is no parking, but the State Centre car park is just 3 minutes away. You can almost always get a good deal on the hotel's website, so check before booking.

2 Flinders St., Adelaide, SA 5000. ✆ **08/8112 0000.** Fax 08/8112 0199. www.medina.com.au. 80 units. A$185–A$395 studio room; A$220–A$420 1-bedroom apt; A$350–A$425 2-bedroom apt. Extra person A$50. Check the website for good deals. AE, DC, MC, V. Parking nearby. Bus: CityLoop/tram. **Amenities:** Restaurant; bar; fitness center; Jacuzzi; indoor swimming pool; sauna. *In room:* A/C, TV w/pay movies, hair dryer, Internet (A$13 for 1 hr. up to A$25 for 24 hr.), kitchen, minibar.

Moderate

The Mercure Grosvenor Hotel This pleasant hotel is conveniently located in the center of Adelaide, opposite SkyCity Casino and the Convention and Exhibition Centre. It's modern and the rooms are light filled. The economy and standard rooms are small with a tiny en-suite bathroom, but are great value. If you want more space, opt for a deluxe room and try to get one with a balcony.

125 North Terrace, Adelaide, SA 5000. ✆ **08/8407 8888.** Fax 08/8407 8866. www.mercuregrosvenorhotel.com.au. 243 units. A$105–A$220 double. Check website for good deals, especially on weekends. Children 14 and under stay for free in parent's room. AE, DC, MC, V. Parking A$16. Bus: CityLoop. **Amenities:** Restaurant; bar; concierge; fitness center; room service; sauna. *In room:* A/C, TV w/pay movies, fridge, hair dryer, Internet (A50¢ per minute up to A$28 for 24 hr.), minibar.

Rockford Adelaide This contemporary boutique hotel is a 10- to 15-minute walk from the center of town, 5 minutes from the casino, and near the nightclub and red-light district. There are nice spa rooms, each with a large LCD TV. All rooms are spacious and comfortable, and modern and riverside rooms have balconies. The hotel has a lovely heated rooftop pool with great views.

164 Hindley St., Adelaide, SA 5000. ✆ **1800/788 155** in Australia, or 08/8211 8255. Fax 08/8231 1179. www.rockfordhotels.com.au. 68 units. A$159–A$249 standard double. Children 11 and under stay free in

Plan Ahead

If you plan to be in town during the Adelaide Festival, make sure you book accommodations *well* in advance. The town can be packed during Christmas and New Year's, so it's wise to book well in advance then, too.

parent's room. Off-season and weekend discounts available. Check for Internet specials and ask about package deals. AE, DC, MC, V. Parking A$15, must be prebooked. **Amenities:** Restaurant; bar; concierge; golf course nearby; access to nearby health club; heated outdoor pool; limited room service; sauna. *In room:* A/C, TV/DVD w/free movies, fridge, hair dryer, minibar, Wi-Fi (free in club rooms, other rooms A$3 for 15 min. up to A$25 for 24 hr.).

Inexpensive

Adelaide City Park Motel ★ The spacious rooms in this high-end boutique motel have modern furnishings and nice bathrooms with showers. Some rooms have private balconies overlooking parkland. Family rooms sleep from four to six people: The largest has a double bed and two sets of bunks. The best double room is no. 45, which has two double beds and a large balcony.

471 Pulteney St., Adelaide, SA 5000. ✆ **1800/231 444** in Australia, or 08/8223 1444. Fax 08/8223 1133. www.citypark.com.au. 18 units. A$99 budget double with shared bathroom; A$120 standard double with en-suite; A$150 double with balcony. Extra person A$20. AE, DC, MC, V. Limited parking by arrangement. The tram to Glenelg is a 5-min. walk away; 4 streets up is a bus stop for the free City Loop Bus. **Amenities:** Restaurant; bar. *In room:* A/C, TV, fridge.

Moore's Brecknock Hotel Adelaide's original Irish pub, built in 1851, still attracts a lot of Irish patrons who come here for the great selection of beer and reasonably priced home-style cooking—it reputedly serves Adelaide's best hamburgers. Live bands play downstairs on Friday, Saturday, and Sunday, but the music finishes at 1am on Friday and Saturday and at 10pm on Sunday, so you shouldn't have too much trouble sleeping. Rooms are large, if a little spartan, and decorated in your granny's old-world style. Some rooms have a single bed as well as a double. Each has a sink, with the bathrooms down the hall.

401 King William St., Adelaide, SA 5000. ✆ **08/8231 5467.** Fax 08/8410 1968. www.brecknockhotel.com.au. 10 units, none with bathroom. A$110 double; A$145 triple. Rates include continental breakfast. AE, DC, MC, V. Free parking. Tram: Glenelg route. **Amenities:** Restaurant; 3 bars; bike rental. *In room:* A/C, fridge.

IN NORTH ADELAIDE

This leafy and attractive suburb across the river is an interesting place with nice architecture and a great restaurant strip. It's about a 10-minute bus ride from the city center.

North Adelaide Heritage Group ★★★ It's worth coming all the way to Adelaide just for the experience of staying in one of these apartments, cottages, or suites. Each of the 20 properties in North Adelaide and Eastwood are good but I particularly recommend the very elegant Bishop's Garden on Molesworth Street. Originally the house and gardens of Bishop Nutter Thomas, the fourth Anglican Bishop of Adelaide, it's full of gorgeous antiques and artwork collected by the current owners, Rodney and Regina Twiss, who have added little touches that make you feel at home, from magazines liberally piled everywhere to bacon and eggs in the fridge. The company also offers a suite in the old North Adelaide Fire Station which comes complete with a full-size, bright red, very old fire engine and the original fireman's pole. All properties are within easy walking distance of the main attractions in the area.

Office: 109 Glen Osmond Rd., Eastwood, SA 5063. ✆ **08/8272 1355.** Fax 08/8272 1355. www.adelaideheritage.com. 20 units. A$240–A$445 double. Extra person A$60–A$85. Child 11 and under A$30. AE, DC, MC, V. Free parking. **Amenities:** Concierge; golf course nearby; Jacuzzi; limited room service; tennis courts nearby. *In room:* A/C, TV, hair dryer, kitchenette.

Where to Dine

With more than 600 restaurants, pubs, and cafes, Adelaide boasts more dining spots per capita than anywhere else in Australia. Many cluster in areas such as Rundle Street, Gouger Street, and North Adelaide—where you'll find almost every style of cuisine you can imagine. For cheap noodles, laksas, sushi, and cakes, head to Adelaide's popular **Central Markets** (✆ **08/8203 7494**), behind the Hilton Adelaide between Gouger and Grote streets.

Glenelg has a host of nice cafes, including **Zest Café Gallery,** 2A Sussex St. (✆ **08/8295 3599**), which serves baguettes and bagels; and **Café Blu,** Oaks Plaza Pier Hotel, 16 Holdfast Promenade (✆ **08/8350 3108**), which has good pizzas.

Because of South Australia's healthy wine industry, you'll find that many of the more expensive restaurants have extensive wine lists—though with spicier foods, it's probably wiser to stick with beer. Many Adelaide restaurants allow diners to bring their own wine (BYO), but most charge a steep corkage fee to open the bottle—A$6 or so is not uncommon.

IN THE CITY CENTER

Expensive

Botanic Café ITALIAN New York meets Tuscany in this buzzy bistro overlooking the Botanic Gardens. If it's a sunny day or balmy evening, try to secure an outside table. The menu features Italian classics with a stylish twist. The fried local squid with fresh rocket and chili garlic aioli is some of the best I've had in a long time.

4 East Terrace. ✆ **08/8232 0626.** Reservations recommended. Main courses A$28–A$38. AE, DC, MC, V. Mon–Fri noon–3pm; Mon–Sat 6:30–10pm.

Jolleys Boathouse Restaurant ★★ MODERN AUSTRALIAN Jolleys, housed in an 1880s boathouse on the banks of the River Torrens with views of boats, ducks, and black swans, is best suited for long lunches, as it closes very early at night (8:30pm). There are a handful of outside tables, but if you miss out, the bright and airy interior, with its cream-colored tablecloths and directors' chairs, isn't too much of a letdown. You might start with miso-crusted venison with grilled mushroom, mizuna salad, and Japanese mustard sauce. Moving on, you could tuck into the crisp-fried tea-smoked duck, with Chinese spinach, and blood plum and tamarind sauce. (Ignore the peaceful quacking out on the river if you can.)

Jolleys Lane. ✆ **08/8223 2891.** www.jolleysboathouse.com. Reservations recommended. Main courses A$26–A$40. AE, DC, MC, V. Sun–Fri noon–2pm; Mon–Sat 6–8:30pm.

Moderate

Matsuri JAPANESE There's a great atmosphere at this popular but authentic restaurant that serves ups some fantastic sushi and sashimi dishes. Try the *"funamori"*—a brilliant array of delicate sushi and sashimi artfully presented on a decorative boat.

Something Different: Market Tours

Adelaide's Top Food and Wine Tours (✆ 08/8263 0265; www.topfoodandwinetours.com.au) offers a range of food-based tours, including both dawn and midmorning tours of the Central Market. Dawn Tours cost A$48 for adults and A$25 for kids, and start at 7:15am on Tuesday and Thursday through Saturday; midmorning tours depart at 9:30am and cost A$35 for adults and A$19 for kids.

Other popular dishes include vegetarian and seafood tempura, *yose nobe* (a hot pot of vegetables, seafood, and chicken), and *chawan mushi* (a steamed custard dish). The service is friendly and considerate. Make sure you wear your best socks though—no shoes allowed!

167 Gouger St. (upstairs). ✆ **08/8231 3494.** Reservations recommended. Main courses A$20–A$28. AE, DC, MC, V. Fri noon–2pm; Wed–Mon 5:30–10pm.

Mesa Lunga ★★ SPANISH/ITALIAN I love this wine bar and restaurant—it's housed in an old shop that's been transformed into a very groovy bar with quirky decorating touches (think antler chandeliers, Moorish mosaics, and dark timbers). Most of the eating's done at the long communal table, and the menu is a clever mix of Spanish and Italian. One half of the space is the **Sangria Bar,** with a great wine and cocktail list and a handful of bar snacks and *pintxos* (tiny tapas)—try the miniature hamburgers. The other half, **Mesa Lunga,** serves up more substantial plates of tapas to share, gourmet pizzas, traditional pastas, and other main courses. The outside tables on the street make for fascinating people-watching.

140 Gouger St. ✆ **08/8410 7617.** www.mesalunga.com. Tapas A$7–A$14; pizzas A$15–A$24; main courses A$19–A$36. AE, DC, MC, V. Wed–Sun noon–3pm; Tues–Sun 6pm till late.

Rigoni's Bistro ITALIAN On a narrow lane west of King William Street, this traditional Italian trattoria is often packed at lunch and less frantic in the evening. It's big and bright, with high ceilings and russet quarry tiles. A long bar runs through the middle of the dining room; brass plates mark the stools of regular diners. The food is very traditional and quite good. The chalkboard menu often changes, but you're likely to find lasagna, veal in white wine, marinated fish, and various pasta dishes. It's a good place for a nice pasta lunch.

27 Leigh St. ✆ **08/8231 5160.** Reservations recommended. Main courses A$25–A$35; pastas A$19–A$34. AE, DC, MC, V. Mon–Fri 7am till late.

Inexpensive

Mekong Thai ★★ ASIAN/HALAL Though this place is not much to look at—with simple tables and chairs, some outside in a portico—it has a fiery reputation for good food among in-the-know locals. The food is spicy and authentic, and the portions are filling. It's also a vegetarian's paradise, with at least 16 meat-free mains on the ethnically varied menu. It's Adelaide's only fully halal (suitable for Muslims) restaurant. Be warned: The laksa is addictive.

68 Hindley St. ✆ **08/8231 2914.** Main courses A$12–A$18. AE, MC, V. Mon–Fri 11:30am–3pm and 5:15–10:45pm.

IN NORTH ADELAIDE

Beyond India ★★ INDIAN This busy eatery, Adelaide's favorite Indian diner, serves up a range of really, really good southern and northern Indian dishes with a modern twist. My vegetarian friends can't get enough of the house-made paneer (fresh cheese) with puréed spinach, but I can never get past the famous *lucknawi* lamb shanks—slowly simmered in a double-glazed onion masala, they are simply the best. Service is warm, friendly, and fast, and the menu includes lots of great wine suggestions to go with each dish.

170 O'Connell St. ✆ **08/8267 3820.** www.beyondindia.net.au. Main courses A$12–A$23. AE, DC, MC, V. Daily noon–3pm and 5–11pm.

Wellington Hotel ★ PUB/STEAK The garden atrium restaurant at the back of this historic two-storied, verandaed pub on Wellington Square has some of the best steaks in Adelaide. Take your pick from the pile of huge (500g, or just over 1 lb.) Coroong and Wagyu beef and it's whisked away to be cooked just how you like it. There's also plenty of fresh seafood and Coffin Bay oysters (from South Australia's Eyre Peninsula—in my opinion, the best oysters on the planet). The wine list's predominately South Australian, and there are 32 Aussie beers on tap. The atmosphere is cheerful and friendly.

36 Wellington Sq. ✆ **08/8267 1322.** Main courses A$14–A$19; steaks priced by weight but average A$20–A$40. AE, DC, MC, V. Daily noon–3pm and 6–9pm.

Seeing the Sights

Adelaide is a laid-back city. It's not jam-packed with tourist-oriented attractions like some of the larger state capitals, though the Migration Museum (see below) is easily one of the best museums in Australia. The best way to enjoy this pleasant city is to take things nice and easy. Walk beside the River Torrens, ride the tram to the beachside suburb of Glenelg, and spend the evenings sipping wine and sampling some of the country's best alfresco dining.

THE TOP ATTRACTIONS

Art Gallery of South Australia ★ Adelaide's premier public art gallery has a good range of local and overseas works and a fine Asian ceramics collection. Of particular interest are Charles Hall's *Proclamation of South Australia 1836;* Nicholas Chevalier's painting of the departure of explorers Burke and Wills from Melbourne; several works by Australian painters Sidney Nolan, Albert Tucker, and Arthur Boyd; and some excellent contemporary art. For an introduction, take a free guided tour. The bookshop has an extensive collection of art publications. Allow 1 to 2 hours.

North Terrace. ✆ **08/8207 7000.** Free admission. Daily 10am–5pm. Guided tours daily 11am and 2pm. Closed Dec 25. Bus: City Loop.

Botanic Gardens A green haven in the heart of the city. First opened in 1857, the gardens are European in style, the original garden plans being influenced by Kew Gardens in England and Versailles in France. Highlights include several grand avenues and arched walkways crowned in wisteria, the ornate 1868 glass house, and the new Bicentennial Conservatory, the largest single span conservatory in the Southern Hemisphere, which houses tropical rainforest plants and looks like a huge beetle from the air. The newly restored **Museum of Economic Botany,** the last purpose-built colonial museum in the world, is also onsite. The museum is open Wednesday to Sunday from 10am to 4pm and every day during exhibitions.

North Terrace. ✆ **08/8222 9311.** www.environment.sa.gov.au/botanicgardens. Free admission. Mon-Fri 8am-sundown; Sat-Sun 9am-sundown.

Haigh's Chocolates Visitors Centre ☺ If you have a sweet tooth, head to Haigh's Chocolates Visitors Centre (a 5 min. drive from the city center) for free tastings, displays, and a peek into the chocolate production process. Established in 1915, Haigh's is Australia's oldest chocolate manufacturer, and Adelaide locals swear it is the best-tasting chocolate anywhere. Free guided tours are run Monday to Saturday at 11am, 1, and 2pm (the factory is not fully operational on Sat, so go midweek if you can), and bookings are essential. Wheelchair and pram access is limited.

154 Greenhill Rd., Parkside. ✆ **08/8372 7077.** www.haighschocolates.com.au. Free admission. Mon-Fri 8:30am-5:30pm; Sat 9am-5pm. Closed public holidays. Bus: 197 from Victoria Sq.

The Migration Museum ★★★ This tiny museum dedicated to immigration and multiculturalism is one of the most important and fascinating in Australia. With touching personal displays, it tells the story of the waves of immigrants who have helped shape this amalgamated society, from the boatloads of convicts who came in 1788 to the ethnic groups who have trickled in over the past 2 centuries. Allow 1 hour.

82 Kintore Ave. ✆ **08/8207 7580.** Admission by donation. Mon-Fri 10am-5pm; Sat-Sun and public holidays 1-5pm. Closed Good Friday and Dec 25. Bus: any to North Terrace.

National Railway Museum This former Port Adelaide railway yard houses Australia's largest collection of locomotive engines and rolling stock. The 104 or so items on display include some 30 engines. Among the most impressive trains are the gigantic "Mountain" class engines, and "Tea and Sugar" trains that once ran between railway camps in remote parts of the desert. Entrance includes a train ride. You need to be a train buff to really enjoy this place.

Lipson St., North Adelaide. ✆ **08/8341 1690.** Admission A$12 adults, A$5 children, A$29 families. Daily 10am-5pm. Bus: 151 or 153 from North Terrace, opposite Parliament House, to stop 40 (approximately 30 min.).

The National Wine Centre of Australia ★★ This architectural masterpiece concentrates on Australia's 53 wine regions. Interactive exhibits and displays allow you to blend your own virtual wine. It's not as simple as you think; sadly, my Riesling turned out to be "the perfect accompaniment to an appalling meal, better suited as a niche cleaning agent for exterior surfaces." The Tasting Gallery displays an extensive range of Australian wines and wine-tasting packages allow you to sample some of the rarest vintages. A restaurant and bar overlook the Wine Centre, which has its own vineyard. You can fit in a trip here with a visit to the nearby Botanic Gardens.

Hackney Rd. (eastern end of North Terrace). ✆ **08/8303 3355.** www.wineaustralia.com.au. Free admission. Wine-tasting packages A$5-A$30. Mon-Fri 9am-5pm; Sat-Sun 10am-5pm. Closed Good Friday and Dec 25. Limited parking. Bus: CityLoop to Botanic Gardens.

South Australian Maritime Museum This Port Adelaide museum commemorates more than 150 years of maritime history. Most of the exhibits are in the 1850s Bond Store, but the museum also incorporates an 1863 lighthouse and three vessels moored alongside Wharf No. 1, a short walk away. The fully rigged replica of the 16m (52-ft.) ketch *Active II* is very impressive. Allow 1½ hours. Port Adelaide is approximately 30 minutes from the city center by bus.

126 Lipson St., Port Adelaide. ✆ **08/8207 6255.** Admission A$8.50 adults, A$3.50 children, A$22 families. Daily 10am–5pm. Closed Dec 25. Bus: 151 or 153 from North Terrace opposite Parliament House to stop 40 (Port Adelaide). Train: Port Adelaide.

South Australian Museum ★★ The star attraction of this interesting museum is the Australian Aboriginal Cultures Gallery. On display is an extensive collection of utensils, spears, tools, bush medicine, food samples, photographs, and the like. Also in the museum is a sorry-looking collection of stuffed native animals (sadly including a few extinct marsupials, such as the Tasmanian tiger); a good collection of Papua New Guinea artifacts; and a fascinating gallery devoted to South Australia's most famous explorer, Antarctic expedition leader Douglas Mawson (the man on the Australian A$100 note). There are free guided museum tours Monday to Friday at 11am and weekends and public holidays at 2 and 3pm.

North Terrace, btw. State Library and Art Gallery of South Australia. ✆ **08/8207 7500.** www.samuseum.sa.gov.au. Free admission. Daily 10am–5pm. Closed Good Friday and Dec 25.

ORGANIZED TOURS

Grayline Day Tours (✆ **1300/858 687** in Australia; www.grayline.com.au) operates a city sightseeing tour for A$59 for adults and A$30 for children. It operates from 9:30am to 12:45pm daily and departs from the Sightseeing Travel Centre, 211 Victoria Square. Other Grayline tours take in central Adelaide, with either Hahndorf or Cleland Wildlife Park included; the Flinders Ranges; and Kangaroo Island.

ENJOYING THE GREAT OUTDOORS

BIKING Adelaide's parks and riverbanks are very popular with cyclists. The city bikes scheme allows you free bike hire for use anywhere within the city limits. All you need is either your driver's license, proof of identity card, or passport. Your ID will be held as a deposit for the duration of the hire and will be returned to you when you return your city bike. You can get bikes from the Rundle Street Market on Sundays; Bicycle SA at 111 Franklin St. (✆ **08/8168 9999**). For other locations around the city, check **www.bikesa.asn.au** or call the Bicycle SA number above. **Recreation SA** (✆ **08/8226 7301**) publishes a brochure showing Adelaide's bike routes. Pick one up at the South Australia Visitor & Travel Centre (see "Visitor Information," earlier in this chapter). In January, Adelaide is host to the **Tour Down Under** (✆ **08/8463 4701;** www.tourdownunder.com.au), which attracts some of the biggest names in world cycling. Keen cyclists can take part in special legs of the race and there are routes open to children and families too.

GOLF The **Adelaide Golf Links** (✆ **08/8267 2171**) in North Adelaide have great views of the city. Greens fees for the full-size championship course are A$24 weekdays and A$29 weekends. To play the par-3 course (great for families) costs A$14 for adults and A$11 for kids. Club rental is available.

HIKING & JOGGING The banks of the River Torrens are a good place for a jog. The fit and adventurous might want to tackle the **Heysen Trail,** a spectacular 1,600km (992-mile) walk through bush, farmland, and rugged hill country that starts 80km (50 miles) south of Adelaide and goes to the Flinders Ranges by way of the Adelaide Hills and the Barossa Valley. For more information on the trail, visit the South Australia Visitor & Travel Centre (see "Visitor Information," earlier in this chapter).

SPECTATOR SPORTS

CRICKET The **Adelaide Oval** (✆ **08/8300 3800**), on the corner of War Memorial Drive and King William Street, is the venue for international matches during the summer season and is widely regarded as the most picturesque Test cricket ground in the world. Take a guided behind-the-scenes tour of the oval to find out all you ever wanted to know about Australia's national game, and national hero, cricketing legend Sir Donald Bradman (who lived in Adelaide for most of his adult life). Tours depart Monday to Friday, nonmatch days, at 10am (no tours on public holidays). You'll need to book by calling ✆ **08/8300 3800,** and tickets are A$10 for adults, A$5 for kids. If you're a real cricket tragic, you'll also love the **Bradman Collection Museum** here, which has all sorts of memorabilia on show and charts the cricketer's rise to national hero status. It's open weekdays 9:30am to 4:30pm. Entry is free.

FOOTBALL Unlike New South Wales, where Rugby League is the most popular winter sport, in Adelaide you'll find plenty of Australian Rules fanatics. Games are usually played on Saturday at the **Adelaide Oval** (see above) or at **AAMI Stadium** (formerly known as Football Park), Turner Drive, West Lakes. The home teams are the Adelaide Crows and the Port Adelaide Power. Games are played February through October, with the finals in September and October. Tickets must be purchased well in advance from **Ticketmaster** (✆ **13 60 00** in South Australia; www.ticketmaster.com.au).

The Shopping Scene

Rundle Mall (btw. King William and Pulteney sts.) is Adelaide's main shopping street. This pedestrian-only thoroughfare is home to the big names in fashion, but you'll also find stores along King William Road at Hyde Park; Glen Osmond Road at Eastwood is the place to go for designer seconds and clearance shops.

Adelaide's **Central Markets** (✆ **08/8203 7203**), behind the Adelaide Hilton Hotel between Gouger and Grote streets, make up the largest produce market in the Southern Hemisphere. They're a good place to shop for vegetables, fruit, meat, fish, and the like, although the markets are worth popping into even if you're not looking for picnic fixings. The markets, held in a warehouselike structure, are open Tuesday from 7am to 5:30pm, Thursday from 9am to 5:30pm, Friday from 7am to 9pm, and Saturday from 7am to 3pm. Some stalls are open on Wednesdays.

The six-story **Myer Centre,** next door to the Myer department store, 22–38 Rundle Mall, has more than 100 specialty stores and is open Monday to Thursday 9am to 5:30pm, Friday until 9pm, Saturday 9am to 5pm, and Sunday 11am to 5pm.

Shopping for Opals

South Australia is home to the world's largest sources of white opals. (The more expensive black opals generally come from Lightning Ridge in New South Wales.) There are plenty of places to buy around town, but **Opal Field Gems,** 33 King William St. (✆ **08/8212 5300**), has a re-created opal mine downstairs. It's a bit touristy, and as a rule you're not going to find any bargains, so just buy what you like (and can afford—good opals cost many thousands of dollars).

The renowned **Jam Factory Craft and Design Centre,** 19 Morphett St. (✆ **08/8410 0727**), sells an excellent range of locally made ceramics, jewelry, glass, furniture, and metal items. You can also watch the craftspeople at work here.

Head to the **R. M. Williams** shop at 5 Gawler Place (✆ **08/8232 3611**) for the best hand-crafted elastic-sided boots you're likely to find (although they are expensive), as well as other Aussie fashion icons, including Akubra hats, moleskin pants, and Driza-bone coats.

Adelaide After Dark

The ***Adelaide Advertiser*** lists all performances and exhibitions in its entertainment pages. Tickets for theater and other entertainment events in Adelaide can be purchased from **BASS ticket outlets** (✆ **13 12 46** in South Australia, or 08/8400 2205) at the following locations: Festival Theatre, Adelaide Festival Centre, King William Road; Adelaide Symphony Orchestra, 91 Hindley St.; City Cross Lotteries, City Cross Arcade, Rundle Mall; Chemist Warehouse, Level 1, Adelaide Central Plaza (David Jones), 100 Rundle Mall; SA Travel & Visitor Centre, Ground Floor, 18 King William St.

THE PERFORMING ARTS

The major concert hall is the **Adelaide Festival Centre,** King William Road (✆ **08/8216 8600** for general inquiries, or 08/8400 2205 for box office). The Festival Centre encompasses four auditoriums: the 1,978-seat Festival Theatre, the 612-seat Playhouse, the 1,000-seat Her Majesty's Theatre, and the 350-seat Space Centre. This is the place in Adelaide to see opera, ballet, drama, orchestral concerts, the Adelaide Symphony Orchestra, plays, and experimental drama.

The complex also includes an outdoor amphitheater used for jazz, rock 'n' roll, and country-music concerts; an art gallery; a bistro; a piano bar; and the Silver Jubilee Organ, the world's largest transportable concert-hall organ (built in Austria to commemorate Queen Elizabeth II's Silver Jubilee).

The Adelaide Repertory Festival presents 13 productions a year, ranging from drama to comedy, at the **Arts Theatre,** 53 Angus St. (✆ **08/8221 5644**). For more information visit **www.theatreguide.com.au**.

THE BAR & CLUB SCENE

The popular **Universal Wine Bar,** 285 Rundle St. (✆ **08/8232 5000**), is the perfect place to start an evening, with great atmosphere and good wines by the glass.

Most pubs are open from 11am to midnight. For all-age pubs, locals will point you toward the **Austral,** 205 Rundle St. (✆ **08/8223 4660**), which has good stand-up comedy; the **Exeter,** 246 Rundle St. (✆ **08/8223 2623**); the **Lion,** at the corner of Melbourne and Jerningham streets (✆ **08/8367 0222**), with live entertainment every night; and the atmospheric **British Hotel,** 58 Finniss St. (✆ **08/8267 2188**), in North Adelaide, where you can cook your own steak on the courtyard barbecue. Also popular with visitors and locals alike is the **Earl of Aberdeen** (also known as **Coopers Alehouse**), 316 Pulteney St., at Carrington Street (✆ **08/8223 6433**), a colonial-style pub popular for after-work drinks and the official home of South Australia's Coopers beer. The **Port Dock,** 10 Todd St., Port Adelaide (✆ **08/8240 0187**), was licensed as a pub in 1864 and brews its own beers.

You'll find most of the dance clubs on **Hindley Street,** and there are also a few on **Gouger Street,** but the biggest club—with 10 bars across three floors—is **HQ,** at 1 North Terrace (✆ **08/7221 1245;** open Wed–Sat 9pm until late). For adult entertainment (clubs with the word *strip* in the name) also head to Hindley Street. Adelaide's most famous gay & lesbian night spot is the **Mars Bar,** 120 Gouger St. (✆ **08/8231 9639**). For information on gay and lesbian options, pick up a copy of ***Blaze,*** South Australia's only newspaper specifically for the gay and lesbian community or check out the online version at **http://blaze.e-p.net.au**.

TRYING YOUR LUCK AT THE CASINO

Right next to the Adelaide Hyatt, and dwarfed by the old railway station containing it, is the **Adelaide Casino** (officially called "SkyCity"), on North Terrace (✆ **08/8212 2811**). The casino has two floors of gaming tables and slot machines, as well as four bars and several dining options. The casino is open Sunday through Thursday from 10am to 4am and Friday and Saturday from 10am to 6am.

THE ADELAIDE HILLS

Just a 25-minute drive from Adelaide are the tree-lined slopes and pretty valleys, orchards, vineyards, winding roads, and historic townships of the **Adelaide Hills.** You might want to walk part of the Heysen Trail (see "Enjoying the Great Outdoors" in the Adelaide section, above), browse through the shops in Hahndorf, stop in Melba's Chocolate Factory in Woodside, or visit Cleland Wildlife Park. Otherwise, it's a nice outing just to hit the road and drive. Should you decide to stay overnight, the area offers lots of cozy B&Bs.

Essentials

GETTING THERE The Adelaide Hills are 25 minutes from Adelaide by car on the South Eastern Freeway. **Adelaide Sightseeing** (✆ **1300/769 762** in Australia; www.adelaidesightseeing.com.au) runs outings to the quaint but somewhat touristy town of Hahndorf (see below). An afternoon excursion to Hahndorf costs A$59 for adults and A$30 for children. The company also offers a range of trips to Kangaroo Island, the Flinders Ranges, the Coorong, Cleland Wildlife Park, and the Great Ocean Road.

VISITOR INFORMATION Visitor information and bookings are available through the **Adelaide Hills Tourist Information Centre,** 41 Main St., Hahndorf (✆ **1800/353 323** in Australia). It's open Monday through Friday from 9am to 5pm, weekends 10am to 4pm. Check out **www.visitadelaidehills.com.au**. Maps are also available at the **South Australia Travel Centre** in Adelaide.

Where to Stay

Cladich Pavilions ★★ Perfect for couples looking for a luxurious romantic getaway. Gaze out over the surrounding bushland from your own private balcony in these gorgeous timber, glass, and steel villas. If you're lucky, you'll spot wallabies from the comfort of your deck chair or sofa. If it's all too hard to leave when it comes time to eat, owners Andrew and Helen McArthur can arrange to have your meal prepared by a local chef. Or you can cook it yourself with all the goodies you've bought from local farm gate stalls throughout the hills, or pop into nearby Aldgate for a hearty pub meal. This is not the type of place you'd want to take kids.

27-29 Wilpena Terrace, Aldgate, SA 5154. ✆ **08/8339 8248.** Fax 08/8339 8248. www.cladichpavilions.com. 3 units. A$180–A$220. MC, V. Free parking. **Amenities:** Outdoor pool; limited room service; tennis court. *In room:* A/C, TV/DVD, CD and DVD player, hair dryer, kitchen, no phone.

The Manna of Hahndorf These new motel-style rooms lie in the heart of Hahndorf. Some rooms have spas (Jacuzzis) and balconies, and guests have free use of the heated pool at the nearby Hahndorf Inn Motor Lodge. A good choice if you want to be within walking distance of the town's pubs, restaurants, and shops.

25 Main St., Hahndorf, SA 5245. ✆ **08/8388 1000.** Fax 08/8388 1092. www.themanna.com.au. 50 units. A$145–A$225. Extra adult A$20; extra child 3–18 years A$5. AE, DC, MC, V. Free Parking. **Amenities:** Restaurant. *In room:* A/C, TV, hair dryer, kitchenette, Wi-Fi (A$5 1 hr.; A$10 24 hr.).

Where to Dine

If you want a treat, head to the **Bridgewater Mill,** Mt. Barker Road, Bridgewater (✆ **08/8339 9200;** www.bridgewatermill.com.au). In an impressive 1860s stone building that was the first water-powered flour mill to operate in South Australia, this place serves some of the best-regarded food in the country. It's also the cellar door for Petaluma Wines and the cellars where the company's sparkling wines are made. A fixed-price three-course menu, served Sunday only, is A$90, otherwise mains are A$32 to A$39. It's open for lunch Thursday to Monday but you'll need to book well in advance.

For a more casual lunch, try the **Organic Market** (✆ **08/8339 7131**) in Stirling, where the cafe in front of the market store serves delicious light lunches, organic beer and wine, and good coffee. There's a great range of gluten and diary-free foods, and the antipasto plates with dolmades, goat's curd, eggplant, capsicum (pepper), olives, and gourmet bread make a perfect midmorning snack for two. It's at 5 Druids Ave., behind the State and National Banks, and is open daily 8:30am to 5pm. Mains are A$13.

What to See & Do in the Adelaide Hills

WOODSIDE: CHOCOHOLICS REJOICE

Visitors come to Woodside for **Melba's Chocolate Factory**, 22 Henry St. (✆ **08/8389 7868**), where chocoholics will find a huge range of handmade chocolates—and you can watch them being made on historic machinery. Most likely though, you'll just want to gobble as much as you can. Melba's is part of **Woodside Heritage Village,** a complex that includes a fantastic cheese maker **(Woodside Cheesewrights)** and the **Mill Shop** which sells a range of crafts and fabrics. It's open daily from 10am to 4pm.

BIRDWOOD: REV IT UP

At first glance, it seems a little strange that this tiny village would be home to one of Adelaide best museums, but who says that all the top shelf attractions need to be in the city? Even if you don't like cars, plan to spend a couple of hours in the **National Motor Museum ★★★** (✆ **08/8568 4000**) here. Not just for rev heads, this museum examines the social influence of the motor car in Australia and has some great fun interactive family exhibits, as well as one of the largest collections of cars, motorcycles, and commercial vehicles in the world, with more than 300 vehicles dating from the turn of the century to the present day. You'll find it on Shannon Street and it's open daily (except Christmas Day) 10am to 5pm. Admission is A$9 adults, A$4 children, A$24 families.

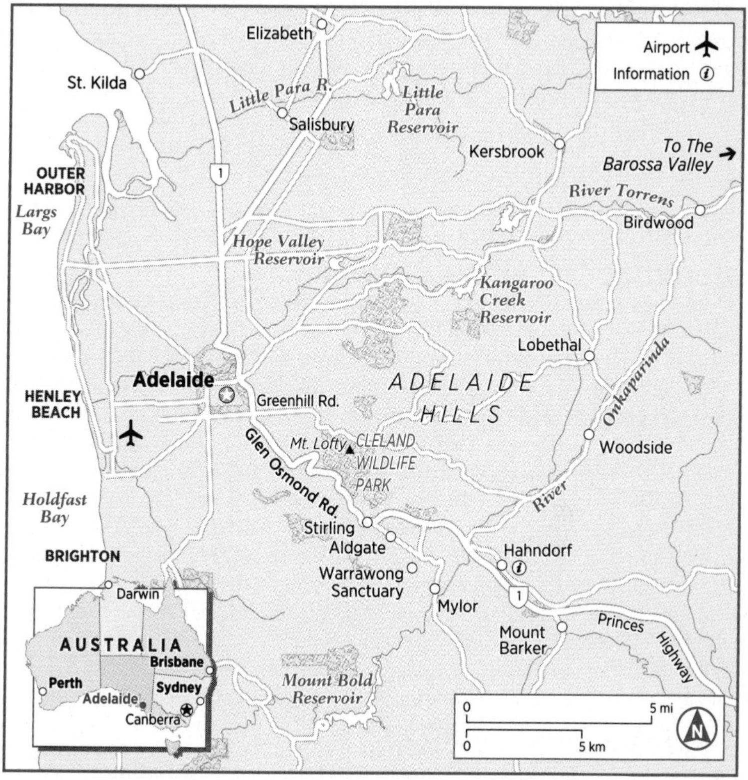

HAHNDORF: GERMAN HERITAGE, CRAFTS & MORE ★

This historic German-style village (pop. 1,850) is one of South Australia's most popular tourist destinations. Lutherans fleeing religious persecution in eastern Prussia founded the town, which is 29km (18 miles) southeast of Adelaide, in 1839. They brought their winemaking skills, foods, and architectural inheritance, and put it all together here. Hahndorf still resembles a small German town in appearance and atmosphere, and is included on the State Heritage List as a Historical German Settlement. The main street is packed with a range of craft shops, art galleries, and specialty shops, and can become quite crowded on weekends.

Beerenberg Strawberry Farm ☺ You probably have come across the cute little pots of delicious Beerenberg jams (jelly) by now; they are favorites at hotel breakfast tables across Australia. Here you can taste (and buy) some of the extensive range of other jams, jellies, sauces, and pickles. During the strawberry season (Oct–May) you can get a bucket from the shop and pick your own strawberries. You can't get much fresher than that!

Mount Barker Rd., Hahndorf. ✆ **08/8388 7272.** Admission to strawberry patch A$3 adults, children 13 and under free. Daily (except Christmas Day) 9am–5pm.

The Cedars ★★★ Make time to visit the Cedars, on the outskirts of town. Home to famous Australian landscape painter Hans Heysen, it is full of family treasures and paintings by Heysen, including many portraits and still lifes. His studio is just as he left it, and inside the house is the studio of his daughter, Nora, a renowned artist in her own right. The homestead has virtually remained unchanged since the 1930s and is furnished with original artifacts. You can follow a walking trail around the 60-hectare (148-acre) property to favorite painting sites used by the artist. Guided tours of the house and studio daily at 11am and 1 and 3pm, from September to May, and 11am and 2pm, from June to August.

Heysen Rd., Hahndorf. ✆ **08/8388 7277.** Admission A$10 adults, children 13 and under free. Tues–Sun and public holidays 10am–4:30pm. Guided tours at 11am, 1pm, and 3pm Sept–May and 11am and 2pm June–Aug.

MOUNT LOFTY: VIEWS & 'ROOS

Visitors make the pilgrimage to the top of 690m (2,263-ft.) **Mount Lofty,** 16km (10 miles) southeast of Adelaide, for the panoramic views over Adelaide, the Adelaide plains, and the Mount Lofty Ranges. There are several nice bushwalks from the top.

Almost at the top of Mount Lofty, off Summit Road, is the **Cleland Wildlife Park** (✆ **08/8339 2444;** www.parks.sa.gov.au). Here you'll find all the usual Australian animals, including the largest male red kangaroo I've ever seen. Though the park is not as good as similar wildlife parks elsewhere in Australia, it does have a very good wetlands aviary. One of the drawbacks of Cleland is that it has some unimaginative enclosures, notably the one for the Tasmanian devils. The park is open daily from 9:30am to 5pm. Visitors can meet at the Tasmanian devil enclosure at 2pm and join the animal feed run by following a tractor around the park as it drops off food.

Admission to Cleland is A$16 for adults, A$9.50 for children 3 to 14, and A$43.50 for families. Koala holding is allowed during photo sessions from 2 to 4pm daily (but not on very hot summer days); on Sunday and public holidays there's an additional session from 11am to noon. The privilege will cost you A$15 per photo. A kiosk and restaurant are on the premises.

Public transport to either place is a bit of a hassle, so this is one trip that is best done with your own wheels.

Where to Dine

While you're atop Mount Lofty, have lunch (or a special occasion dinner) at the **Summit** restaurant (✆ **08/8339 2600;** www.mtloftysummit.com). Look out for the kangaroo filet with chili, lemon grass, and coconut sauce; and venison on rosemary polenta. Main courses cost A$30 to A$36. It's open for lunch daily, and for dinner Wednesday to Sunday. The **Summit Café** here also sells good sandwiches and cakes, fish and chips, Thai curry, and Devonshire tea.

THE BAROSSA ★★

More than a quarter of Australia's wines, and a disproportionate number of top labels, originate in the Barossa and Eden valleys—collectively known as the **Barossa,** 70km (43 miles) northeast of Adelaide. While its reputation in the wine world may be larger than life, in the real world the Barossa Valley is a snug collection of country towns surrounded by vineyards that is very easy to explore on a day trip from Adelaide. Distances between towns are small, and wineries sit next door to one another, so you can visit a few in a very short time—just make sure you have a designated driver!

The Barossa

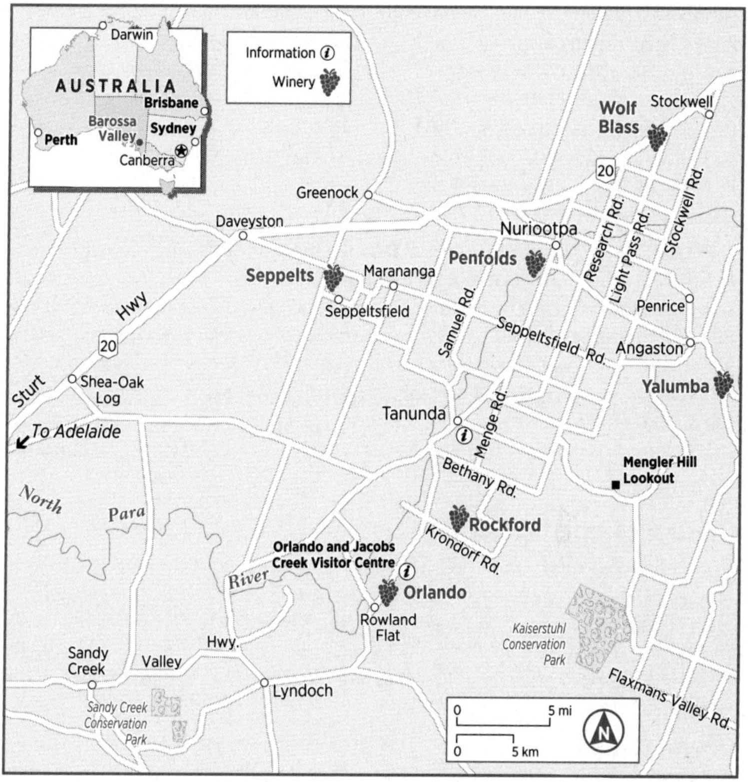

The Barossa has been famous for its rich, big-bodied Shiraz (Syrah) for many years, but the region's heritage of growing, curing, preserving, and cooking its own unique foods is less well known. The largely Lutheran settlers who came here 160 years ago have left not only a legacy of beautiful churches but a bounty of wonderful small meats, sausages, preserved fruits, cheeses, and delicious breads, all unique to the valley. Most restaurants and cafes pride themselves on serving as much local produce as possible—look for the distinctive "cork on a fork" FOOD BAROSSA logo. Tasting plates with a range of local specialties are served at many cellar doors.

The focal points of the area are **Angaston,** farthest from Adelaide; **Nuriootpa,** the center of the rural services industry; and **Tanunda,** the nearest town to the city. Each has interesting architecture, crafts and antiques shops, and specialty food outlets.

Essentials

WHEN TO GO The best times to visit the Barossa and other South Australian wine regions are in the spring (Sept–Oct), when it's not too hot and there are plenty of flowering trees and shrubs, and in the fall (Apr–May), when the leaves turn red.

The main wine harvest is in late summer and early autumn (Feb–Apr). The least crowded time is winter (June–Aug). Hotel prices can be more expensive on the weekend and many insist on a minimum 2-night stay.

GETTING THERE If you have a car (by far the most flexible way to visit the Barossa), I recommend taking the scenic route from Adelaide. (The route doesn't have a specific name, but it's obvious on a map.) It takes about half an hour longer than the Main North Road through Gawler, but the trip is well worth it. Follow signs to Birdwood, Springton, Mount Pleasant, and Angaston.

Public buses run infrequently to the major centers from Adelaide. There are no buses between wineries.

ORGANIZED TOURS FROM ADELAIDE Various companies run limited sightseeing tours. **Adelaide Sightseeing** (✆ **08/8413 6199;** www.adelaidesightseeing.com.au) offers a day trip from Adelaide, stopping off at four wineries. It costs A$124 for adults and A$60 for children (although they'll probably be bored), including lunch.

VISITOR INFORMATION The **Barossa Wine and Visitor Information Centre,** 66–68 Murray St., Tanunda, SA 5352 (✆ **08/8563 0600;** www.barossa.com.), is open Monday through Friday from 9am to 5pm, and Saturday and Sunday from 10am to 4pm.

Touring the Wineries

With some 75 wineries offering free cellar-door tastings, daily tours charting the winemaking process, or both, you won't be stuck for places to visit. All wineries are well signposted and most are open every day. Below are just a few of my favorite places, but don't be shy about stopping whenever you come across a winery that takes your fancy. ***A tip:*** Try a sparkling red; it's the perfect red to drink in the hot Australian summer.

Jacobs Creek Visitor Centre This large winery was established in 1847 and is the home of many award-winning brands. Its big seller is the Jacobs Creek brand, now sold worldwide. Take a vineyard tour to learn about the wine-making process. Tours depart at 11:15am daily and cost A$13, but you'll need to book in advance. There's also a restaurant and a picnic area with barbecues, open daily 10am to 5pm. Barossa Valley Way, Rowland Flat. ✆ **08/8521 3000.**

Penfolds *Wine Spectator* magazine named Penfolds' iconic 1990 vintage Grange the "Best Red Wine in the World"—not bad considering Penfolds started when Dr. Christopher Rawson planted a few vines in 1844 to make wine for his patients. The winery now houses the largest oak barrel maturation cellars in the Southern Hemisphere. (Penfolds also owns other wineries all over the country.) For A$150 you can take a tour of Penfolds (daily at 2pm) that includes a taste of the legendary Grange. The tour includes an A$100 voucher you can use to help pay off your own bottle of Grange if you decide to buy. Bookings are essential, 24 hours prior. Open daily, including public holidays, 10am to 5pm; closed New Year's Day, Christmas Day, and Good Friday. Tanunda Rd., Nuriootpa. ✆ **08/8568 9408.**

Seppeltsfield ★ This National Trust–listed property was founded in 1857 by Joseph Seppelt, an immigrant from Silesia. The wine tour around the gardens and bluestone buildings is well worth doing. On a nearby slope, check out the family's

Fresh from the Farm

If you're here on a Saturday morning, drop into the Barossa Farmers Markets ★★★ in the Vintners Sheds at Angaston. A "food only" market, the warehouse is packed with stalls laden with all the fresh produce associated with the heritage and traditions of the region, with everything from fresh fruit and vegetables to meats, preserves, and breads. It's open each Saturday morning from 7:30 to 11:30am. Get there early rather than later though, as food sells out fast. It's a great place to breakfast, as coffee carts sell fresh espresso, and the fresh breads and pastries are to die for.

Romanesque mausoleum, skirted by planted roadside palms, built during the 1930s recession to keep winery workers employed. Open daily 10:30am to 5pm. The Daily Heritage Tour runs every day at 11:30am, 1:30 and 3:30pm and costs A$15 (including tastings); other tours cover everything from rare wines to barrel-making but must be scheduled in advance. Seppeltsfield. ✆ **08/8568 6200.** www.seppeltsfield.com.au. Tastings: A$5; tours: A$8–A$79 (including tastings).

Wolf Blass This winery's Germanic-style black-label vintages have an excellent international reputation, while its cheaper yellow-label vintages are the toast of many a Sydney dinner party. The Wolf Blass **museum** is worth a look. Open Monday to Friday 9:15am to 5pm and Saturday to Sunday 10am to 5pm. 97 Sturt Hwy., Nuriootpa. ✆ **08/8568 7311.**

Yalumba This winery was built in 1849, making it the oldest family-owned winemaking business in Australia. It's also huge. The winery's **Signature Red Cabernet-Shiraz ★** is among the best you'll ever taste. Open daily 10am to 5pm. Eden Valley Rd., Angaston. ✆ **08/8561 3200.** www.yalumba.com.au.

Where to Stay

There are plenty of standard motels and lots of interesting B&Bs throughout the Barossa, but weekends can often find lodgings sold out and prices higher than on weekdays. The **Barossa Wine and Visitor Information Centre** (see "Visitor Information," above) can provide information on additional accommodations choices and off-season deals.

Collingrove Homestead ★★★ Built in 1856, this homestead was originally the home of John Howard Angas, one of those involved in the initial settlement of South Australia. English oak paneling and creaky floorboards add atmosphere, and the cedar kitchen, library, glorious dining room, and various other places burst with antiques and knickknacks. What the quaint, individually decorated guest rooms lack in modern amenities (phones and TVs) they make up for in charm. The modern communal Jacuzzi is in the old stables, with flagstone floors and old horse harnesses; there's also a flagstone-floored tennis court.

Eden Valley Rd., Angaston, SA 5353. ✆ **08/8564 2061.** Fax 08/8564 3600. www.collingrovehomestead.com.au. 6 units, 4 with bathroom. A$220 luxury double; A$250 deluxe double. Rates include full breakfast. AE, DC, MC, V. **Amenities:** Restaurant; babysitting; Jacuzzi; tennis court. *In room:* Hair dryer, no phone.

The Louise ★★★ If you're looking for somewhere special to stay in the Barossa, this luxurious all-suite hotel is the place. All of the large, gorgeous rooms have great views over the valley and surrounding vineyards, best enjoyed from your own spacious gated courtyard and secluded rear terrace with a bottle of local wine. It's also home to one of Barossa's best restaurants, **Appellation** (✆ **08/8562 4144**), which is worth dining at even if you aren't staying here, although you may have to book up to a month in advance to get a table. It's open for dinner daily and three courses cost A$105.

Seppeltsfield and Stonewell roads, Marananga, SA 5355. ✆ **08/8562 2722.** www.thelouise.com.au. 15 units. A$395–A$765. Rates include full breakfast. AE, DC, MC, V. **Amenities:** Restaurant; bar; free bicycle hire; Jacuzzi; pool; room service; sauna. *In room:* A/C, TV, DVD player, fridge, hair dryer, minibar, Wi-Fi (free).

Where to Dine

The Barossa prides itself on its cuisine as well as its wine, so you'll find plenty of places of note to eat, many of them serving traditional German food. A hot spot for lunch or dinner is **Vintners Bar & Grill,** Nuriootpa Road, Angaston (✆ **08/8564 2488**); the wine list is six pages long! Try the slow-cooked veal shank with Shiraz glaze. Main courses cost A$28 to A$35. It's open for lunch daily and Monday through Saturday for dinner. Another choice is **Salters,** Saltram Winery, Nuriootpa Road, Angaston (✆ **08/8561 0200**); local produce is the specialty, with main courses such as slow-roasted baby pork, milk-fed lamb, and crisp-based pizzas. Main courses are A$21 to A$28. It's open daily for lunch.

Perhaps the best German-style bakery in the valley is the **Lyndoch Bakery,** on the Barossa Highway, Lyndoch (✆ **08/8524 4422**). One place to not miss is celebrity foodie and chef **Maggie Beer's Farm Shop** on Pheasant Farm Road, Tanunda (✆ **08/8562 4477**), where you can sample some of the extensive range of Maggie Beer Foods, Barossa Farm Produce, and both Pheasant Farm and Beer Bros wines. It's a great place to stock up on picnic fare, although you can eat there as well. It's open daily (except Good Friday, Christmas Day, Boxing Day, and New Year's Day) 10:30am to 5pm.

The Riesling Trail

An hour's drive to the north of Angaston is the **Clare Valley,** another of Australia's great wine-producing areas. But whereas the Barossa is famous for its reds, the Clare is best known for its whites, in particular, Riesling. The best way to explore the area is along the **Riesling Trail,** a 27km (16.5-mile) walking and cycling track that follows an unused railway line between Clare and Auburn that passes several cellar doors and historic attractions. There are three loop trails along the way for those that want to park and ride. Parking is available at Clare, Sevenhill, Watervale, and Auburn. Bike hire is available from **Clare Valley Cycle Hire** (✆ **08/8842 2782**) and costs A$17 for 4 hours and A$25 for all day (9am–5pm); baby seats are available for A$6. Free trail maps are available from tourist information centers, or visit **www.southaustraliantrails.com.**

THE FLEURIEU PENINSULA ★★★

Practically on the outskirts of Adelaide, the Fleurieu Peninsula is one of South Australia's most popular holiday destinations, famous for its wine, gourmet produce, breathtakingly scenic coastline, and wildlife—expect to see plenty of kangaroos, sea lions, seals, dolphins, whales (whale-watching season is June–Oct), and Little Penguins, the world's smallest penguin species.

The heart of the wine-growing area is **McLaren Vale,** where olives and almond groves are scattered amongst the 50-plus vineyards, although you'll also find some very good wineries in and around **Currency Creek** and **Langhorne Creek** on the southeastern side of the peninsula. On Saturday mornings, the tiny village of **Willunga,** just a few minutes' drive from McLaren Vale, comes alive with the weekly farmers' markets, where local growers and producers sell whatever they've picked or baked that morning. There are lots of fresh organic vegetables, boutique cheeses, homemade preserves, freshly baked sourdough breads, and delicious pies and pastries, as well as the olive oil and almonds that the area is also famous for. On the second Saturday of the month, the stalls spill over into the Quarry markets across the road, where you can browse the stalls piled high with bric-a-brac, secondhand books, and handmade jewelry and clothes.

Pretty **Stathalbyn** was settled by Scottish immigrants in the 1830s, a heritage town with 30 or so historic buildings and popular place to shop for antiques and crafts, as is the equally quaint township of **Port Elliot. Victor Harbor** on the southern ocean side is the most popular seaside resort, with lots of family attractions, and is a great place to go bushwalking (hiking), whale watching, and surfing. The historic river port of **Goolwa** is at the mouth of the Murray River, Australia's longest river.

Essentials

GETTING THERE McLaren Vale is a 45-minute drive from Adelaide via the one-way Southern expressway. It changes direction according to peak hour, so in the morning it heads north to Adelaide, in the afternoons and early evening, south to McLaren Vale. If it's not going in the direction you want it to, you can take the Main South Road.

Adelaide Metro operates a public bus service from Adelaide and a public train service to Noarlunga (see www.adelaidemetro.com.au for details). **Premier Stateliner Coaches** (**© 08/8415 5555**) runs daily services to McLaren Vale for A$8.40 adults or A$4.20 children; and to Victor Harbor, Port Elliot, and Goolwa, all of which cost A$20 for adults and A$9.75 for children.

VISITOR INFORMATION Visitor information and bookings are available through the **Victor Harbor Visitor Information Centre,** The Causeway, Victor Harbor, SA 5211 (**© 08/8552 5738**), and the **McLaren Vale and Fleurieu Visitor Centre,** Main Road, McLaren Vale, SA 5171 (**© 08/8323 9944**). Both centers are open daily. See also **www.southaustralia.com/FleurieuPeninsula.aspx**.

Peninsula Highlights

The Cockle Train ☺ Take a ride along the oldest public railway line in Australia between the towns of Victor Harbor, Port Elliot, and Goolwa aboard the historic, iconic Cockle Train. Built in 1887 to ferry goods from the last navigable port on the Murray River (Goolwa) to the seaports of Port Elliot and Victor Harbor, the 30-minute steam-train trip quickly became a popular trip for tourists as well, earning its rather quaint name from the large cockles that the sandy surf beaches of Goolwa are famous for. The train only runs on Wednesdays and Sundays (daily during school holidays), so a good alternative if you've got bicycles with you is the 30km (19-mile) **Encounter Bikeway,** a dedicated bike path between the Bluff and Signal Point at Goolwa Wharf. The sealed path is suitable for escorted toddlers on tricycles through to those wanting a gentle, seaside cycle. (You can also walk a section of it.) Between June and October, you may be able to spot southern right whales as you ride.

✆ **1300/655 991** in Australia. Victor Harbor Station: ✆ **08/8552 2782.** Goolwa Station: ✆ **08/8555 2691.** Return fares cost A$26 adults, A$15 children, A$64 families. Runs most Sun and Wed but with varying timetables; to confirm train running times on the day, call either station.

Encounter Coast Discovery Centre and Old Customs and Station Masters House Victor Harbor is on the shores of Encounter Bay, where in 1802, Englishman Matthew Flinders met the French explorer Nicholas Baudin, while they were both circumnavigating Australia. England and France were at war at the time, but despite this, the meeting between the two scientists was friendly and Flinders named the bay after the encounter. You can learn all about the meeting between English and French naval captains in this great museum, as well as plenty of local history. A great rainy day activity.

2 Flinders Parade, Victor Harbor. ✆ **08/8552 5388.** Admission A$4 adults, A$2 children, A$10 families. Daily 1–4pm. Closed Dec 25 and Good Friday.

Granite Island Nature Park ☺ Take the country's only horse-drawn tram out to Granite Island, once a whaling station but now a lovely park linked to the township of Victor Harbor by a wooden causeway. It's home to a colony of 700 or so Little Penguins. The tramway is open daily, 10am to 4pm, and a return trip costs A$7 for adults and A$5 for children. There is a cafe and kiosk on the island, and even if you don't catch the tram, it's a nice walk out along the causeway, as you'll often see fur seals lazily drifting underneath the piers. If you want to see the penguins, you'll need to join one of the evening guided tours run by the national parks and Wildlife Service. Just remember, penguins have right of way!

Granite Island, Victor Harbor. ✆ **08/8552 7555.** www.graniteisland.com.au. Penguin tours cost A$13 adults, A$7.50 children, A$36 families. Tours run daily but departure times vary as sunset times and daylight saving times change. Telephone or check website for details.

South Australian Whale Centre ☺ Victor Harbor is one of the easiest places in South Australia to see southern right whales, who swim into the sheltered waters of Encounter Bay each winter to breed. They often come very close to shore along the coastline of the peninsula, and there are a number of good vantage points in and around town. The South Australian Whale Centre keeps records of whale sightings, so call in to see where they are. They have an extensive collection of displays, murals, and videos, with lots of hands-on fun activities for the kids.

2 Railway Terrace, Victor Harbor. ✆ **08/8551 0750.** www.sawhalecentre.com. A$8 adults, A$4 children 14 and under, A$20 families. Daily 9:30am–5pm. Closed Dec 25.

The Fleurieu Peninsula

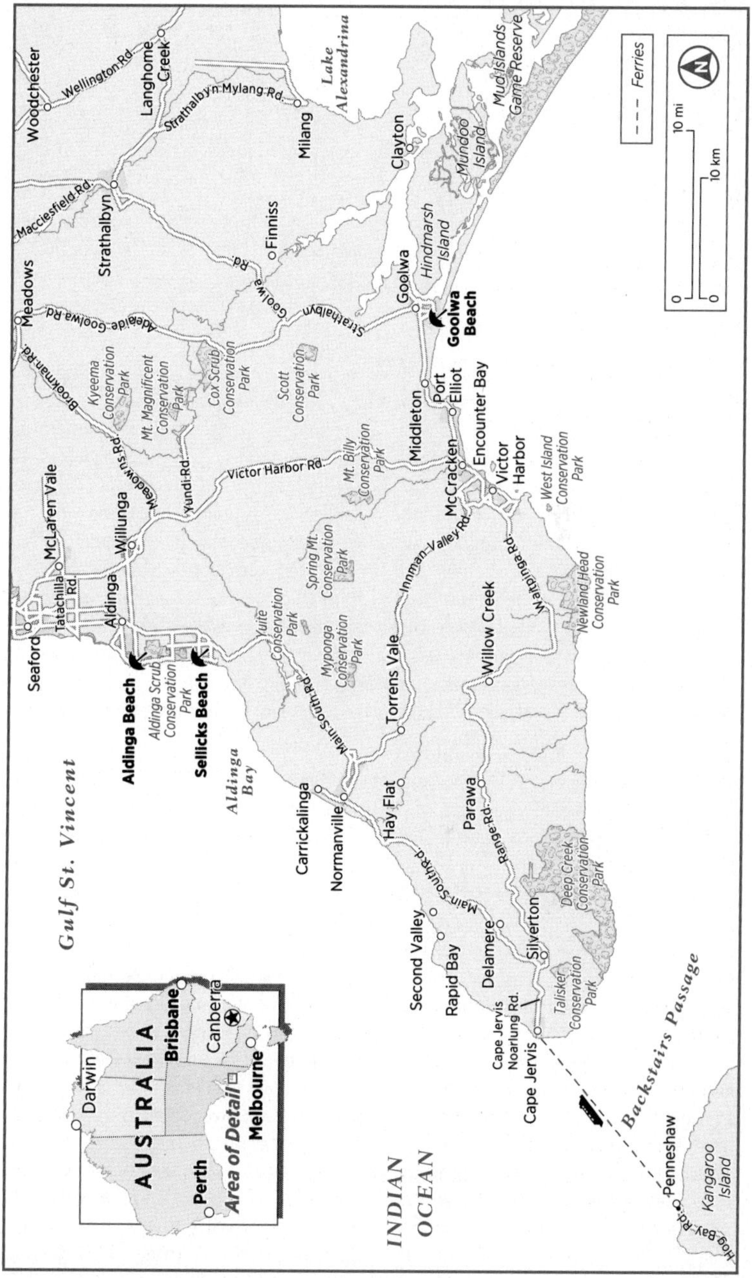
Ferries
0
10 mi
0
10 km
Gulf St. Vincent
Seaford
Tatachilla Rd.
McLaren Vale
Aldinga
Aldinga Beach
Aldinga Scrub Conservation Park
Sellicks Beach
Aldinga Bay
Willunga
Meadows Rd.
Yundi Rd.
Brookman Rd.
Meadows
Woodchester
Wellington Rd.
Macclesfield Rd.
Strathalbyn
Langhorne Creek
Strathalbyn Mylang Rd.
Milang
Lake Alexandrina
Finniss
Goolwa Rd.
Adelaide-Goolwa Rd.
Kyeema Conservation Park
Mt. Magnificent Conservation Park
Cox Scrub Conservation Park
Scott Conservation Park
Strathalbyn
Victor Harbor Rd.
Mt. Billy Conservation Park
Spring Mt. Conservation Park
Yuite Conservation Park
Myponga Conservation Park
Main South Rd.
Carrickalinga
Normanville
Torrens Vale
Hay Flat
Inman Valley Rd.
Middleton
Port Elliot
Goolwa
Goolwa Beach
Hindmarsh Island
Clayton
Mundoo Island
Mud Islands Game Reserve
Encounter Bay
McCracken
Victor Harbor
West Island Conservation Park
Waitpinga Rd.
Newland Head Conservation Park
Willow Creek
Parawa
Range Rd.
Second Valley
Rapid Bay
Delamere
Silverton
Deep Creek Conservation Park
Talisker Conservation Park
Cape Jervis Noarlung Rd.
Cape Jervis
Backstairs Passage
Penneshaw
Hog Bay Rd.
Kangaroo Island
INDIAN OCEAN
AUSTRALIA
Darwin
Brisbane
Canberra
Perth
Area of Detail
Melbourne

Where to Stay

The Boathouse at Birks Harbour ★★★ It's almost impossible to tear yourself away from the view at Birks Harbour, a beautifully restored boathouse and marina on the edge of the Murray River in the historic river port of Goolwa. Inside the renovated single-accommodation boatshed, there is, as you would expect, a maritime theme—a wooden oar here, a couple of intricately carved beautiful wooden model boats there, and some local paper prints of, you guessed it, wooden boats, plus a dash of red and blue. It's got floor-to-ceiling windows, a big pot-bellied fireplace in the corner and a bookcase stacked with gorgeous picture books. A big claw-foot tub, a stack of luxury bath products, and big fluffy robes greet you in the bathroom. But if you're anything like me, you'll spend most of your time on the deck watching life on the river float by.

138B Liverpool Rd., Goolwa, SA 5214. ✆ **08/8555 0338.** www.birksharbour.com.au. 1 unit. A$250 per double including breakfast provisions; extra person A$45. Packages available. MC, V. *In room:* A/C, TV/DVD, CD player, hair dryer, kitchen, no phone.

Dee's Villa ★★ This great self-contained two-bedroom cottage is a good place to base yourself if you are planning on spending a few days exploring the peninsula. It's a 10-minute drive from the beaches of Myponga and Carrickalinga and some of the most spectacular coastal scenery to be found in Australia. And the views from the villa across rolling hills are pretty good, too. It features a fully equipped kitchen (provisions for cooked and continental breakfast are supplied, but bring your own dinner ingredients), open fireplace, and huge Jacuzzi in the courtyard. It can be hard to find, so call first for directions, and there are no neighbors within earshot, so if being in the middle of the countryside with no one else around makes you nervous, it might not be the place for you. But if you like your privacy and plenty of peace and quiet, I heartily recommend it.

Carrickalinga, SA 5172. ✆ **08/8558 3616** or 0409/124 324. www.dees.com.au. 1 unit. A$200 per double; extra person A$50. MC, V. **Amenities:** Jacuzzi. *In room:* Ceiling fans, TV, CD player, kitchen, no phone.

Willunga House Bed & Breakfast ★ This Georgian stone residence built in 1850 originally served as the first general store and post office for the village of Willunga, in the heart of the main wine producing area. It has now been lovingly restored and remade into a gorgeous B&B full of beautiful period furniture, including huge brass beds. Most rooms have their own en-suite bathrooms, but two have private bathrooms just across the hall. There's a big sitting room with an open fire, a lovely garden with a pool, and it's right in the heart of the village, great for an early morning visit to the Saturday farmers' market. Hosts Kingsley and Rosie Knott can provide massages on request, and the breakfasts feature homemade jams, organic eggs, and fruit straight from the garden. Kingsley also makes a killer cappuccino.

1 St. Peter's Terrace, Willunga, SA 5172. ✆ **08/8556 2467.** Fax 08/8556 2465. www.willungahouse.com.au. 5 units. A$190–A$250 including breakfast. MC, V. **Amenities:** Outdoor pool. *In room:* A/C, TV, hair dryer, Wi-Fi (free).

Where to Dine

There's no shortage of great places to eat in the Fleurieu. For restaurants with million-dollar views, you can't go past the cliff-top **Star of Greece Cafe ★★★** on the Esplanade, Port Willunga (✆ **08/8557 7420**), or the **Flying Fish Cafe ★★★** on the water's edge of Horseshoe Bay, Port Elliot (✆ **08/8554 3504**). Both serve up

Sea & Vines

Not your typical food and wine festival, which tend to be more refined sip-and-taste affairs, the annual **Sea and Vines Festival** in McLaren Vale is a rollicking celebration of food and wine that's more like a giant progressive party. Held over 2 days in June, it has become one of the biggest of its type in South Australia: It attracts upwards of 40,000 people each year to the more than 26 wineries in the valley that put up marquees, set out tables, bring in their favorite bands, and serve their wines matched up with local seafood cooked by local restaurants. Wine and food prices are set: A$5 for a glass of wine and A$15 for an appetizer-size plate of seafood, plus a variety of other dishes should you want something other than the signature plate. To get the best out of the festival, get a copy of the program before you go and plan your day, because you'll need to book in advance. Tickets are available at **www.mclarenvale.info.**

fantastic fresh seafood, but quite frankly, with views this good, it's hard to concentrate on what's on your plate. The Star of Greece is open Wednesday to Sunday noon to 3pm (also open for dinner in summer on those same days), and mains cost A$25 to A$35. The Flying Fish Cafe is open daily noon to 3pm, and 6pm to 8:30pm Friday to Sunday; mains cost A$30 to A$49. Or try the restaurants below, which have more of an emphasis on food than view.

Fino ★★ MEDITERRANEAN A bit more casual that the Salopian Inn (see below), the Mediterranean-styled food here is made to share, which means the atmosphere is more boisterous. The food is very regional: What you get depends on what is fresh that day and in season, but it is always very, very good.

8 Hill St., Willunga. ✆ **08/8556 4488.** Mains A$25–A$35. AE, MC, V. Tues–Sat for lunch; Fri–Sat 6:30–9pm.

Russell's ★ PIZZA Almost next door to Fino is a quirky pizzeria housed in an eclectically decorated 1800 stone cottage. Don't expect your average pizza though: Toppings include such delights as Turkish-style slow-cooked lamb with tomato, yogurt, and pickled lime. It's only open on Friday and Saturday nights, so competition for tables can be fierce.

13 High St., Willunga. ✆ **08/8556 2571.** 2 courses A$30; 3 courses A$35. MC, V. Fri–Sat nights only.

Salopian Inn ★★★ MODERN AUSTRALIAN This award-winning dining institution is housed in an 1850s slate-floored stone building. It offers superb seasonal, regional food in a relaxed country setting among the vines. If it's on the menu, try the blue swimmer crab tortellini with truffle cream sauce and Coorong cockles.

Corner of McMurtrie and McLaren Vale Main roads, McLaren Vale. ✆ **08/8323 8769.** Reservations recommended. Mains A$32. AE, MC, V. Lunch daily except Wed; dinner Fri–Sat.

KANGAROO ISLAND ★★★

110km (68 miles) S of Adelaide

Kangaroo Island is one of Australia's best-kept secrets. While lots of people overseas sing its praises—it was ranked the Best Island in the Asia Pacific region in the U.S.

Kangaroo Island

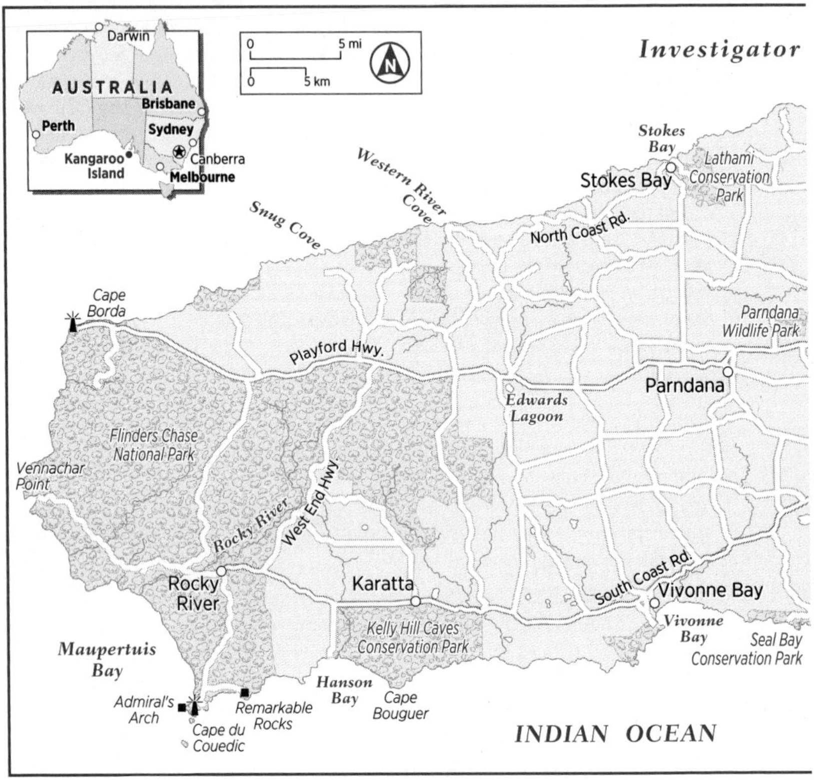

magazine *National Geographic Traveler* in late 2007 and was also voted Best Australian Experience by 8,500 North American travel agents at the industry's 2007 Opal Awards—it's a place that seems to have slipped under the radar of many Australians. (When they consider an island holiday, they tend to automatically think tropical sun, sand, and sea and head to the Northern Queensland islands.) Which is a shame, because KI, as the locals call their island home, is the best place Down Under to see Australian marsupials in the wild.

Close to half of the island is either natural bushland or national park; and according to the boffins, who count these type of things, it is home to 4,000 penguins, 6,000 fur seals, 600 rare Australian sea lions, 5,000 koalas, 15,000 kangaroos, 254 species of birdlife, and somewhere between 500,000 and 1 million tammar wallabies, thanks largely to an environment free of introduced foxes or rabbits, who prey on the native inhabitants or their environment. While the animals are what most people come to see, the scenery is also spectacular. Think rugged coastal cliffs with startling rock formations, rolling pasture-clad hills, dense eucalypt forests, gorgeous beaches, caves, lagoons, and black-water swamps.

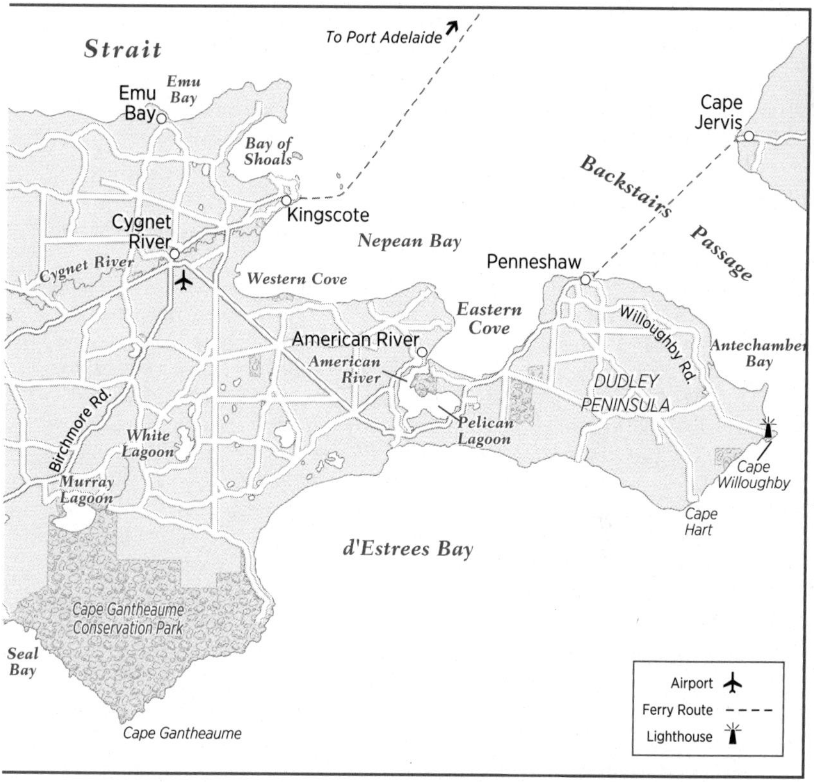

The island's history is a harsh one. Aborigines inhabited KI as early as 10,000 years ago but abandoned it for unexplained reasons. In the 19th century, pirates, mutineers, deserters from English, French, and American ships, and escaped convicts from the eastern colonies settled here. Sealers also arrived and devastated the seal and sea lion population: In just 1 year, from 1803 to 1804, they killed more than 20,000 animals. Between 1802 and 1836, Aboriginal women from both the mainland and Tasmania were kidnapped, brought to Kangaroo Island, and forced to work catching and skinning seals, kangaroos, and wallabies, and lugging salt from the salt mines.

In 1836, Kangaroo Island became the first place in South Australia to be officially settled. The state's capital was Kingscote (which was abandoned a couple of years later in favor of Adelaide). In spite of its early settlement, Kangaroo Island had very few residents until after World War II, when returning soldiers set up farms here. Today, more than a million sheep are raised on the island. The island also acts as an official bee sanctuary to protect the genetic purity of the Ligurian bee, introduced in 1881; it is believed to be the only place in the world where this strain of bee survives.

Island Essentials

WHEN TO GO The best time to visit Kangaroo Island is between November and March (though you'll have difficulty finding accommodations over the Christmas school-holiday period). July and August tend to be rainy, and winter can be cold (though often milder than on the mainland around Adelaide). Many companies offer 1-day trips to Kangaroo Island from Adelaide, but I would advise you to tailor your holiday to spend at least 2 days here—3 or even 5 days would be even better. There really is a lot to see, and you won't regret spending the extra time.

GETTING THERE **Regional Express (REX; ✆ 13 17 13** in Australia, or 08/8553 2938; www.regionalexpress.com.au) flies to Kangaroo Island from Adelaide. The flight usually takes about 30 minutes.

If you prefer to go by sea, **Kangaroo Island SeaLink** (**✆ 13 13 01** in Australia, or 08/8202 8688; www.sealink.com.au) operates two vehicle and passenger ferries twice daily at 9am and 6pm (more frequently in peak periods) from Cape Jervis on the tip of the Fleurieu Peninsula on the mainland to Penneshaw on Kangaroo Island. The trip takes 40 minutes and costs A$86 round-trip for adults, A$48 for children 3 to 14, and A$168 for cars. Connecting bus service from Adelaide to Cape Jervis costs an extra A$44 for adults, and A$22 for children round-trip. Off-peak prices may be cheaper; check when booking. Count on 3 hours for the entire trip from Adelaide if you take the connecting bus. Bookings are essential.

SeaLink also runs a range of island tours, including the 2-day, 1-night "KI Coast to Coast," which costs from A$434 per person sharing a double room. SeaLink also offers a wide range of accommodations, day tours, and adventure activities and offers Adelaide hotel pickups for selected tours.

VISITOR INFORMATION **Tourism Kangaroo Island,** Gateway Information Centre, Howard Drive (P.O. Box 336), Penneshaw, Kangaroo Island, SA 5222 (**✆ 08/8553 1185;** fax 08/8553 1255; www.tourkangarooisland.com.au), has plenty of maps and information and can help visitors with accommodations and tour information. In addition, hotel and motel staff members generally can provide tourist brochures and sightseeing advice.

ISLAND LAYOUT Kangaroo Island is Australia's third-largest island, 156km (97 miles) long and 57km (35 miles) wide at its widest point. The distance across the narrowest point is only 2km (1¼ miles). Approximately 3,900 people live on the island. More than half live on the northeast coast in the three main towns: Kingscote (pop. 1,800), Penneshaw (pop. 250), and American River (pop. 200). The island's major attractions are farther from the mainland: Flinders Chase National Park is in the far west, Lathami Conservation Park is on the north coast, and Seal Bay and Kelly's Caves are on the south coast.

GETTING AROUND Kangaroo Island is a big place, and apart from twice-daily SeaLink bus service, which connects Kingscote, Penneshaw, and American River, there is no public transport on the island. While you can get a lot out of the tours, I would heartily recommend you hire a car and spend at least 3 days here. **Airport Shuttle Service** (**✆ 0427/887 575**) meets all flights to Kangaroo Island and will take passengers to Kingscote, Emu Bay, and American River. Book the return trip from your accommodations to the airport in advance.

An Island Bargain

I'd advise buying a national parks **Kangaroo Island Pass** if you're going to explore the island on your own for 3 days or more and visit the national park and attractions more than once. It costs A$59 for adults, A$36 for children, and A$160 for families, and includes guided tours of Seal Bay, Kelly Hill Caves, Cape Borda, and Cape Willoughby. The pass also includes access to Flinders Chase National Park. The pass doesn't cover penguin tours or camping fees. It's available at Tourism Kangaroo Island in Penneshaw and at the national parks office at 37 Dauncey St. in Kingscote (✆ 08/8553 2381).

Major roads between Penneshaw, American River, Kingscote, and Parndana are paved, as is the road to Seal Bay and all major roads within Flinders Chase National Park. Most other roads are made of ironstone gravel and can be very slippery if the driver approaches corners too quickly. All roads are accessible by two-wheel-drive vehicles; if you're in a rental car from the mainland, make sure your policy allows you to drive on Kangaroo Island's roads. Avoid driving at night—animals rarely fare best in a car collision.

Car-rental agencies on the island include **Budget** (✆ **08/8553 3133**), FCBS 4WD Hire (✆ **08/8553 7278**), and **Hertz** (✆ **13 30 39** in Australia). You can pick up cars at the airport or ferry terminals.

ORGANIZED TOURS If you want to keep expenses down, you can't go wrong with one of the tours organized by **Kangaroo Island Ferry Connections** (✆ **08/8202 8688;** www.sealink.com.au). The most popular includes early morning pickup from the main bus station in Adelaide, coach and ferry to the island, and a full day of touring, taking in most of the main attractions. That evening you return to Adelaide. It's a very long day. The tour costs A$238 for adults, A$152 for children.

More expensive options include **Kangaroo Island Wilderness Tours** (✆ **08/8559 5033;** www.wildernesstours.com.au), which operates from the island with several small four-wheel-drive vehicles (maximum six people). The 1-day trips cost A$392 to A$412 per person, including an excellent lunch with wine and park entry fees. Two- and 3-day trips, including all meals and accommodations, start at A$970 and A$1,548 per person, respectively, but vary according to the type of accommodation you choose. Packages are also available that include flights.

Another excellent operator on the island is **Exceptional Kangaroo Island,** Playford Highway, Cygnet River, SA 5223 (✆ **08/8553 9119;** www.exceptionalkangarooisland.com), with the knowledgeable Craig Wickham at the helm. Day trips cost A$377 a day with a big lunch, or A$733 for a 1-day safari including flights from and to Adelaide. A 2-day and 1-night safari including accommodations and flights costs A$1,382, per person, twin share.

Another option is **Wayward Bus** (✆ **08/8132 8230;** www.waywardbus.com.au) from Adelaide. Two-day trips depart daily between December and March, with fewer departures at other times. They cost A$409 in a hostel bunk and A$432 per person in a twin/double shared room.

Exploring the Island

At seven times the size of Singapore, Kangaroo Island is bigger than you might think, and you can spend a fair bit of time getting from one place of interest to the next. Of the many places to see on the island, **Flinders Chase National Park ★★★** is one of the most important. Your first stop should be the Flinders Chase Visitors Centre, where you can purchase park entry, view the interpretive display, dine at the licensed cafe, buy souvenirs, and obtain parks information. After 30 years of lobbying, reluctant politicians finally agreed to preserve this region of the island in 1919. Today it makes up around 17% of the island and is home to true wilderness, some beautiful coastal scenery, two old lighthouses, and plenty of animals. Birders have recorded at least 243 species here. Koalas are so common that they're almost falling out of the trees. Platypuses have been seen, but you'll probably need to make a special effort and sit next to a stream in the dark for a few hours for any chance of spotting one. The Platypus Waterholes walk is a 2-hour walk that's great for all ages. It begins at the Flinders Chase Visitors Centre and has a shorter option that's suitable for wheelchairs. This walk offers the best opportunity to see the elusive platypus. Kangaroos, wallabies, and brush-tailed possums, on the other hand, are so tame and numerous that the authorities were forced to erect a barrier around the Rocky River Campground to stop them from carrying away picnickers' sandwiches!

Don't Feed the Animals, Please

Don't feed *any* native animals. Kangaroos and wallabies might beg, but they are lactose intolerant and can go blind or fall ill from being fed human food.

The most impressive coastal scenery is at **Cape du Couedic ★★★**, at the southern tip of the park. Millions of years of crashing ocean have created curious structures, such as the hollowed-out limestone promontory called Admiral's Arch and the aptly named Remarkable Rocks, where you'll see huge boulders balancing on top of a massive granite dome. Admiral's Arch is home to a colony of some 4,000 New Zealand fur seals that play in the rock pools and rest on the rocks. During rough weather, this place can be spectacular. A paved road leads from Rocky River Park Headquarters to Admiral's Arch and Remarkable Rocks, where there is a parking lot and a loop trail. There's a road, parking lot, and trail system around the Cape du Couedic heritage lighthouse district as well.

You shouldn't miss out on the unforgettable experience of walking through a colony of Australian sea lions at Seal Bay. The **Seal Bay Conservation Park ★★★** (**✆ 08/8559 4207**) was created in 1972, and some 100,000 people visit it each year. Boardwalks through the dunes to the beach reduce the impact of so many feet. The colony consists of about 500 animals, but at any one time you might see up to 100 basking with their pups. The rangers who supervise the area lead guided trips throughout the day, every 15 to 30 minutes from 9am to 4:15pm. If you come here without a coach group, you must join a tour. Beach tours that take you on to the sand and up close to the sea lions cost A$28 for adults and A$17 for children. A cheaper option is a boardwalk tour (A$13 for adults and A$8 for children), but you will not get nearly as close to the animals. Do the beach tour, it's worth it!

CULLING koalas—A NATIONAL DILEMMA

Koalas are cute. They also eat an awful lot. In the early 1920s, 18 koalas were introduced to Kangaroo Island. Over the years, without predators and disease, and with an abundant supply of eucalyptus trees, they have prospered. By 2001, there were an estimated 27,000 koalas, and their favorite trees were looking ragged. Some of the koalas were already suffering; some people even claimed the animals were starving to death.

The state government decided that the only option was to shoot Australia's ambassador to the world. The public outcry was enormous; Japan even threatened to advise its citizens to boycott Australia. But what could be done? Some scientists maintained that the koalas could not be relocated to the mainland because there were few places left to put them. Conservationists blamed Kangaroo Island's farmers for depleting the island of more than 50% of its vegetation. The koala is endangered; the smaller northern variety is threatened with extinction in New South Wales; the larger subspecies in Victoria, which includes the Kangaroo Island koalas, is also under threat. A compromise was reached: The koalas are to be trapped and neutered, a few thousand per year, until their numbers stabilize. A few conscientious farmers will plant more trees. Other farmers will, no doubt, continue to see the koalas as pests.

Lathami Conservation Park, just east of Stokes Bay, is a wonderful place to see wallabies in the wild. Just dip under the low canopy of casuarina pines and walk silently, keeping your eyes peeled. You're almost certain to spot them. If you're fortunate, you may even come across a rare glossy cockatoo—it's big and black and feeds mainly on casuarina nuts.

Another interesting spot, especially for birders, is **Murray Lagoon,** on the northern edge of Cape Gantheaume Conservation Park. It's the largest lagoon on the island and a habitat for thousands of water birds. Contact the DEH for information on a ranger-guided Wetland Wade.

If you want to see **Little Penguins**—tiny animals that stand just 33 centimeters (13 in.) tall—forget the touristy show at Phillip Island near Melbourne. On Kangaroo Island, you can see them in a natural environment at both Kingscote and Penneshaw. Call ahead to confirm times, which are subject to change. Twice-nightly tours depart from **Kangaroo Island Penguin Centre** at Kingscote Wharf (✆ **08/8553 3112**) and cost A$16 for adults, A$6 for children. The **Penneshaw Penguin Centre** (✆ **08/8553 1103**), adjacent to the beach and Lloyd Collins Reserve, has the largest penguin colony on the island. Tours cost A$10 for adults, A$8.50 for kids, free for children under 12. Reservations are not required, but note that there are no tours at either Penguin Centre during most of February (Feb 1–21), when the penguins head out to sea to feed.

Finally, Kangaroo Island is renowned for its fresh food, and across the island you'll see signs beckoning to you to have a taste of cheese, honey, wine, or the like. One place worth a stop is **Clifford's Honey Farm ★** on Elsegood Road (✆ **08/8553 8295**), which is open daily from 9am to 5pm. The farm is the home of the only pure strain of Ligurian bee in the world. The honey ice cream is divine. **Island Pure Sheep Dairy** on Gum Creek Road (✆ **08/8553 9110**) is another worthwhile stop. Tours and tastings are conducted at milking time (3–5pm). It's a great chance to sample delicious sheep's milk, yogurts, and mouthwatering halloumi cheese. Tours cost A$5.50 for adults and A$4.50 for kids and include tastings of all the cheeses. It's open daily, 1 to 5pm. Ask at the tourist office for directions to both.

Where to Stay

The island has a wide variety of places to choose from, from B&Bs to campgrounds. The most popular accommodations, however, are self-contained cottages, many of which have spectacular coastal views. Visit the accommodation section of **www.tourkangarooisland.com.au** for a wide range of options; you can also book online.

The DEH (Department for Environment and Heritage) also rents basic but comfortable lodgings, including relatively isolated **lighthouse cottages ★★** (✆ **08/8559 7235;** kiparksaccom@saugov.sa.gov.au) at Cape Willoughby, Cape Borda, Rocky River, and Cape du Couedic. The price is A$155 per night in the lighthouse cottages.

If money is no object, book a suite at **Southern Ocean Lodge** (✆ **02/9918 4355** in Sydney [the lodge does not handle reservations or inquiries]; www.southernoceanlodge.com.au), a new superluxury wilderness lodge that sits high on the cliff tops above Hanson Bay on the southwest coast. Facilities include the Southern Spa Retreat, which features the Australian-made Li'Tya range of spa products. Super luxury, of course, means super expensive, but for those that can afford it, it's a great way to see the best of the island's attractions in exclusive style. Rates are A$900 to A$1,800 per person per night and there's a minimum 2-night stay; that includes all meals, drinks, transfers, and a range of guided activities.

If you're on a supertight budget, head to the **Kangaroo Island YHA** hostel, 33 Middle Terrace, Penneshaw, Kangaroo Island, SA 5222 (✆ **08/8553 1344;** fax 08/8553 1278). Dorm beds are A$30 and doubles with private bathrooms are A$100. It costs a few dollars less for YHA members.

Camp It Up

Go bush in style at the privately owned Flour Cask Bay Sanctuary. You can bush camp beside the salt lake or stay in one of the two "Eco Camps." Each Eco Camp annex provides Kimberley Kamper portable camper trailers as accommodation, which are set up with a queen-size bed, a private en-suite bathroom with hot-water shower and toilet, solar-powered lights, and a fully equipped camp kitchen that slides away when not in use. The beach is just minutes away, and the entire 600-hectare (1,483-acre) nature reserve is yours to explore by four-wheel-drive, canoe, or bicycle. Owned by a former National Park ranger, the remote Eco Camps have a zero-footprint policy, and the entire sanctuary has been set up as a conservation and land rehabilitation trust. A 1-night stay in the Eco Camp costs A$139 for up to four people. The sanctuary is off Flour Cask Bay Road, Flour Cask Bay (✆ 08/8553 7278; www.eco-sanctuaries.com).

Camping is allowed at designated sites around the island and in national parks for a minimal fee. There are many beach, river, and bush camping spots, including the Rocky River site in the Flinders Chase National Park. Call ✆ **08/8559 7235** to book. Camping costs A$10 per car and A$5 per person if traveling without a car (in addition to the park entry fee of A$8.50 per adult and A$5 per child).

IN KINGSCOTE

Aurora Ozone Hotel ★★ The best known of Kangaroo Island's lodgings, the Ozone gets its name from the aroma of the sea—which virtually laps at its door. It's a nice, centrally located choice offering comfortable rooms with plenty of space; the majority of the more expensive ones have views of Nepean Bay. You can choose from motel style rooms or the new apartments across the road.

The Foreshore (P.O. Box 171), Kingscote, SA 5223. ✆ **08/8553 2011.** Fax 08/8553 2249. www.ozonehotel.com. 63 units. A$165–A$225 double, extra person A$23; A$225–A$449 penthouse-style apartments, extra person A$30. AE, DC, MC, V. **Amenities:** 2 restaurants; 3 bars; babysitting; golf course nearby; Jacuzzi; heated outdoor pool; limited room service; sauna. *In room:* A/C, TV, fridge, hair dryer, Wi-Fi (hotel rooms only; A$3 45 min., A$15 12 hr.).

Where to Dine

Most accommodations on Kangaroo Island provide meals for guests (usually at an additional cost). In addition, most day tours around the island include lunch. You'll find a few cheap takeout booths scattered about the island at the most popular tourist spots. For lunch, you can get sandwiches at **Roger's Deli** on Dauncey Street, behind the Ozone Hotel, in Kingscote. **Bella Restaurant,** also on Dauncey Street (✆ **08/8553 0400**), offers a range of tasty pizzas, grilled snacks, and salads during the day and contemporary Mediterranean and Asian cuisine at night. The **Vivonne Bay General Store,** on South Coast Road not far from Seal Bay (✆ **08/8559 4285**), is famous for its fresh whiting burgers and does a good coffee.

THE EYRE PENINSULA ★★

Wild, beautiful, uncrowded, and undeveloped, the Eyre Peninsula—the triangle of land jutting into the sea between Adelaide and the Great Australian Bight—seems to be the place that tourism has overlooked, at least for now. But with one of the country's most dramatic coastlines, fantastic wildlife-watching opportunities and incredibly good seafood, it won't stay forgotten for long. In fact, it seems set to become the new holiday hot spot, thanks to several new hotel developments. Not the place to go if you like to cram your days full of museums and attractions, the Eyre Peninsula is all about taking it slowly, getting out into the countryside, meeting the wildlife (swimming with sea lions is a must-do activity while you're here; see p. 592), wandering along the historic jetties, and eating as much of the local seafood as you possibly can.

First settled in the 1840s, almost every town on the peninsula has a long wooden jetty, usually lined with people fishing—most were originally built to service the ships that would visit the small coastal towns to load up the annual wheat crop. Wheat is the region's main industry, apart from fishing and aquaculture, and the Eyre Peninsula produces more than 45% of SA's wheat crop. You'll see the massive white silos long before you'll see the townships.

In the northeast, the industrial town of **Whyalla** is famous for its giant cuttlefish, which arrive in the tens of thousands each year between May and August for their annual ritual of mating and spawning. This phenomenon is the greatest mass gathering of the animal anywhere and attracts divers from all over the world to see it.

To the south, **Cowell** is famous for its oysters, and for one of the oldest and largest deposits of nephrite jade in the world. Farther on is a string of fabulously deserted beaches and the pretty coastal town of **Tumby Bay.**

At the tip of the peninsula is the regional center of **Port Lincoln,** the biggest town on the peninsula. It's home to the largest commercial fishing fleet in the Southern Hemisphere, so take a walk around the marina in the early morning or evening and check out the trawlers as they come and go.

The western coast has the most must-see sights, including beautiful **Coffin Bay** (also famous for its oysters), a sea-lion colony, sea caves, stunning coastal cliffs, and the attractive towns of **Streaky Bay** and **Ceduna.** Continue west and you'll end up on the **Nullarbor.** At **Head of Bight,** a dip in the coastline 20km (12 miles) east of Nullarbor Roadhouse, there is a whale-viewing platform where, during the whale season between June and October, you can see up to 100 southern right whales and their calves lolling in the waters at the foot of the cliffs.

Across the north of the peninsula, the **Gawler Ranges** are a line of volcanic rock hills more than 1.5 billion years old (twice as old as the Flinders Ranges). Most of the area is protected by national park and it's a great place to see kangaroos, emus, and other wildlife.

Essentials

GETTING THERE Port Lincoln is 650km (400 miles) from Adelaide, around an 8-hour drive. A new ferry service, **SeaSA ferries** (✆ **08/8823 0777;** www.seasa.com.au), from Wallaroo on the Yorke Peninsula to Lucky Bay near Cowell will cut a couple of driving hours off the trip and is expected to be operating by the end of 2010 with twice-daily crossings in each direction. Check the website for latest timetables and fares.

Regional Express (**REX;** ✆ **13 17 13** in Australia; www.regionalexpress.com.au) has daily flights in and out of Whyalla, Port Lincoln, and Ceduna.

Premier Stateliner Coaches (✆ **08/8415 5555**) runs daily services down the east coast to Port Lincoln (a one-way fare from Adelaide costs A$97 adults or A$48 children), as well as to Ceduna (one-way fare from Adelaide costs A$113 adults or A$57 children) and Streaky Bay (one-way fare from Adelaide costs A$101 adults or A$51 children) on the west coast.

GETTING AROUND Apart from the bus service along the east and west coasts, there is no public transport available on the peninsula, so you either need to have your own wheels (car hire is available in Port Lincoln) or join an organized tour. **Nullarbor Traveller** (✆ **08/8687 0455;** www.thetraveller.net.au) offers a 6-day adventure tour of the peninsula that includes a camel trek, swimming with sea lions, swimming in a tuna farm, an optional great-white-shark cage dive, surfing lessons, sand-dune 4WD trips, and swimming with the giant cuttlefish (in season). The tour includes a mixture of camping and farmstay accommodations and most meals. It costs A$840, but you'll have to pay extra if you want to swim with the sea lions or get into the shark cage. **XploreEyre** (✆ **08/8687 0455;** www.xploreeyre.com.au)

The Eyre Peninsula

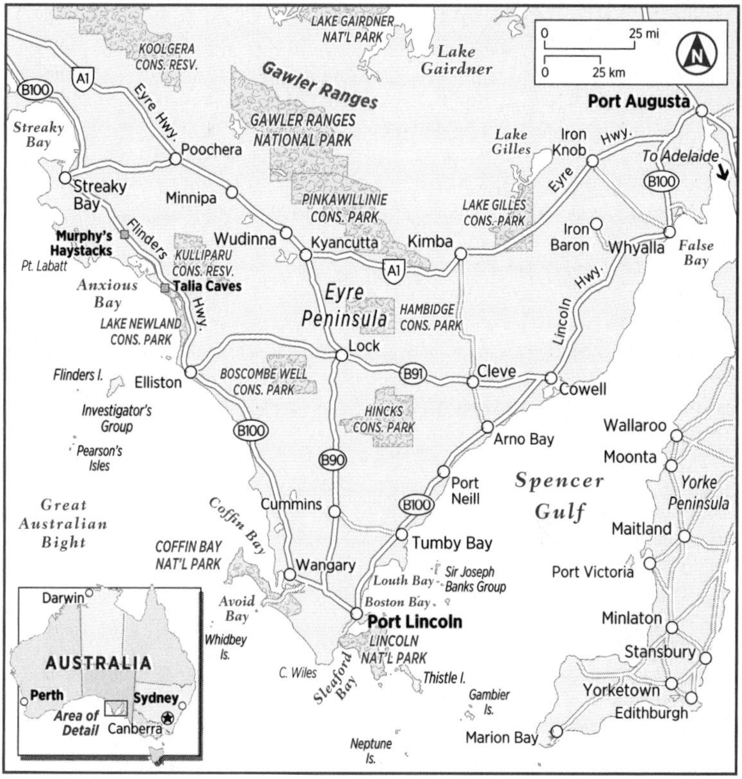

has a range of 2-, 3-, and 4-day tours in 4WD vehicles for up to six people; they cost A$1,325 to A$2,950 per person, including meals, accommodation, and activities.

VISITOR INFORMATION Visitor information and bookings are available through the **Port Lincoln Visitor Information Centre,** 3 Adelaide Place, Port Lincoln (✆ **1300/788 378** in Australia or 08/8683 3544); the **Whyalla Visitor Information Centre,** Lincoln Highway at the northern entrance to Whyalla (✆ **1800/088 589** in Australia or 08/8645 7900); and **Ceduna Visitor Information Centre,** 58 Poynton St., Ceduna (✆ **1800/639 413** in Australia or 08/8625 2780). All three centers are open daily. See also **www.southaustralia.com/EyrePeninsula.aspx**.

Peninsula Highlights

Coffin Bay Explorer You'll learn everything you've ever wanted to know about the oyster-growing business and more than likely see dolphins as well on this 3-hour cruise around the waters of Coffin Bay. It passes oyster beds (yes, you'll get to try some!) and the national park.

Departs from the Coffin Bay boat ramp. ✆ **0428/880 621.** www.coffinbayexplorer.com. Reservations essential. A$75 adults, A$40 kids. Daily at 9:30am.

Coffin Bay National Park ★★ You'll need a four-wheel drive to explore the best bits, but it's well worth spending a day or two in this gorgeous coastal park if you have one. You'll also need an air compressor to reinflate your tires, as most of the tracks are sandy and require a low tire pressure to avoid getting bogged. Features of the park include a diverse coastal landscape with several good beaches and cliff-top lookouts. Keep an eye out for the resident mob of wild Coffin Bay brumbies (wild horses). Highlights include four-wheel driving on the beach, beach camping, fishing and swimming. At the very least, take the drive (fine for a two-wheel drive) out to Point Avoid for some stunning coastal scenery.

50km (31 miles) west of Port Lincoln. ✆ **08/8688 3111.** A$8 per vehicle.

Cowell Jade Cowell is home to Australia's only commercial jade mine. You can see and buy jade, including the rare black jade, at the Cowell Jade Motel. There's a showroom beside the reception area with a reasonable range of jewelry and sculptures.

Lincoln Hwy., Cowell. ✆ **08/8629 2002.** Free admission. Daily 8am–6pm.

Elliston's Great Ocean Drive ★★★ This 12km (7½-mile) cliff-top drive just north of Elliston is, in a word, stunning. Every 2 years (the next year is 2011), the Sculpture on the Cliffs festival transforms the coastline into a huge outdoor sculpture gallery between March and June. Some of the sculptures remain on permanent exhibition.

Elliston. Free admission.

Gawler Ranges Wilderness Safaris ★★★ The Gawler Ranges is one of South Australia's best-kept secrets, one that even most Aussies don't know about. Rough, rugged, and remote, the weathered ranges were formed more than 1.5 billion years ago by a massive volcanic eruption, leaving behind a dramatic landscape of rock formations. It's almost all protected by national park, and local bushman Geoff Scholz, who knows the ranges and dry salt lakes like the back of his hand, will take you to all the best spots that you just can't get to any other way. Expect long days bouncing around the back of a four-wheel drive, but also expect to see more kangaroos and emus than you can count and some jaw-dropping scenery. Tours include transport to and from Port Lincoln (or from Wudinna if you are self-driving), all meals (wine and beer included), and accommodation in luxury safari tents, complete with en-suite bathrooms—nothing beats a hot shower after a day in the dust. The best time to go is during the cooler months, when temperatures are less extreme and animals are more active during the day. Summer tours include swimming with sea lions at Baird Bay (p. 592).

P.O. Box 76, Wudinna SA 5652. ✆ **1800/243 343** in Australia or 08/8680 2045. www.gawlerrangessafaris.com. 3-day tour A$1,546 per person, twin share; 4-day tour A$1,906 per person, twin share. Tours depart Port Lincoln every Mon.

Koppio Smithy Museum It's worth visiting this National Trust museum just for the Bob Dobbins barbed wire collection. The focus is on farming in the old days (prior to the late 1940s), and the complex includes a pine-log thatched-roof shepherd's hut, the Koppio school house, a blacksmith's shop, lots of old rural machinery and tractors, and a woman pioneers room.

Koppio Rd., Koppio. ✆ **08/8684 4243.** Admission A$5 adults, A$2 children. Tues–Sun 10am–5pm.

Lincoln National Park ★★ This is another national park that really needs a 4WD to explore the best of it. Highlights include the massive wind-sculpted sand dunes, pounding surf, and limestone cliffs of Memory Cove, a pretty beach protected by two headlands that was named by explorer Matthew Flinders as a reminder of a tragic accident that took the lives of his eight crewmen in 1802. Take a walk up Stamford Hill for spectacular views of Boston Bay, Port Lincoln, and the park. A monument commemorating Matthew Flinders is at the top. There is also a good 2-hour walk around the tip of the Donington Peninsula (one of the few places in the park you can get to in a conventional two-wheel-drive vehicle; you can stay at historic **Donington Cottage; ✆ 08/8683 3544**), with great views of offshore islands, granite outcrops, and sandy beaches. You can often see Australian sea lions and New Zealand fur seals on Donington Island near the lighthouse.

15km (9 miles) south of Port Lincoln. ✆ **08/8688 3111.** Admission A$8 per vehicle.

Murphy's Haystacks The "haystacks" are actually a hilltop outcrop of large granite boulders with walkways between them. Local legend has it that an Irish agricultural expert advocated that to produce good hay, farmers should harrow their land. While traveling past in a coach, he noticed the rocks (technically called inselbergs) and told his fellow passengers that the famer had obviously harrowed his land to produce such good haystacks. The farmer in question was Murphy. It's a nice spot for a picnic.

40km (25 miles) SE of Streaky Bay, just off the Flinders Hwy. Admission A$2 adults, A$5 family. Open daily.

Point Labatt Sea Lion Colony The Australian sea lion is one of the world's rarest seals; less than 12,000 survive in the wild today. The sea-lion colony at Point Labatt is the only permanent breeding colony on mainland Australia (all other colonies occur on offshore islands) and it's one of the few places where you can watch seal pups learning to swim and play. The cliff-top viewing platform overlooks the colony, but you'll need binoculars and a zoom lens for a close-up view.

40km (25 miles) south of Streaky Bay. Free admission.

Talia Sea Caves ★ Granite and limestone cliffs here were hollowed out by the sea to form caves. "The Woolshed" is a large cavern carved into the cliff, and there are steps down to the cliff base. Or check out "The Tub," a large, craterlike hole in the cliff around 30m (98 ft.) deep and 50m (164 ft.) wide. Look out for the tree-trunk ladder and climb down into the crater to walk into the mouth of the cave. Don't get too close to the edge, however; a slip into the swirling surf would be fatal.

60km (37 miles) north of Elliston. Free admission.

Triple Bay Cruises ★ Watch the sunset while sipping local wine and sampling local seafood (tuna sashimi, Coffin Bay oysters, and other local delights) on a 2-hour **Twilight Cruise** of Boston Bay. Skipper Peter Dennis knows just about everything there is to know about the local seafood and fishing industries, and lots of local gossip as well. Or, if you really want to find out about the tuna business, take the **Tuna Farm & Sightseeing Cruise** to visit working tuna farms.

Departs daily from the pontoon outside the Marina Hotel, Port Lincoln. ✆ **08/8682 4119.** www.triplebaycharters.net.au. Tuna Farm & Sightseeing Cruise A$55 for adults, A$35 for kids. Twilight Cruise A$75 adults. Bookings essential.

SWIMMING WITH sea creatures

The Eyre Peninsula offers plenty of ways to get up close and personal to the wildlife, but nothing beats **swimming with wild sea lions ★★★**. The puppy dogs of the sea, these endangered marine mammals are insatiably curious, and love to play. The sea lions are never fed, and all interaction is initiated by the animals. They come to you. But the more you interact with them, the more they like it—after all, no one likes a boring playmate who just stares! The more you splash and duck dive, the more they respond, often mimicking your actions, circling when you do, diving and surfacing with you. Believe me, making eye contact with a wild animal in its own habitat, on its own terms, is an experience you'll not soon forget.

Ocean Eco Tours, between Streaky Bay and Port Lincoln (✆ **08/8626 5017;** www.bairdbay.com), offers half-day trips swimming with sea lions at Baird Bay, and depending on weather, swimming with the resident pod of bottlenose dolphins. You must be able to swim and parents or guardians must accompany children under 12. The best season is from September through to May. It costs A$120 for adults or A$60 for kids, and wet suits are included.

The Port Lincoln–based **Adventure Bay Charters** (✆ **0488/428 862;** www.adventurebaycharters.com.au) runs trips to the colony at Hopkins Island, around a 90-minute cruise from Port Lincoln; the half-day tour includes a **swim in a tuna farm** afterward. It costs A$195 for adults, kids A$145. Wet suit hire is an extra A$20. (A separate 2-hr. tuna-farm tour is available for A$65 adults, A$45 kids.)

Both sea lion tours are excellent, but the Baird Bay tour is a little more personal, has a stronger conservation ethic, and you'll learn a lot more about the animals than you do on the more commercialized Adventure Bay trip.

Whatever you do, don't visit the **replica of the biggest white pointer shark ever caught** by rod and reel (a very scary 5m/16 ft. long and 1,520kg/3,344 lb. heavy) before you take the plunge. The shark, which was caught in the waters off Streaky Bay in 1990, is on show at the Shell Roadhouse in Streaky Bay. If you are interested in getting a closer look at a real, live great white shark, you can go **shark cage diving** with **Calypso Star Charters** (✆ **08/8682 3939;** www.sharkcagediving.com.au), based in Port Lincoln. It's a full-day trip and costs A$495, and you don't have to be a certified diver to do it. You may have to be certifiably crazy however, and I must admit I haven't quite worked up the courage yet to do it.

Where to Stay

Port Lincoln Hotel ★★ An unbeatable location in the heart of town opposite Boston Bay makes this a great place to stay—as long as you pay the extra A$60 and opt for an ocean-view room with a balcony. Don't bother if all you can get is the town-view room, which just looks out over the car park. Rooms are bright, modern, and spacious, and I could spend days lounging beside the pool looking out to sea while snacking on the local oysters.

1 Lincoln Hwy., Port Lincoln, SA 5606. ✆ **1300/766 100** in Australia or 08/8621 2000. www.portlincolnhotel.com.au. 111 units. A$220–A$280 double; A$340–A$600 suite. Extra person A$35. MC, V. **Amenities:**

Restaurant; bar; gymnasium; Jacuzzi (suites only); outdoor pool. *In room:* A/C, TV, hair dryer, Internet (A55¢ per minute; A$28 per 24 hr.), minibar, MP3 docking station.

Streaky Bay Hotel Motel This classic stone double-story pub, built in 1866, looks very atmospheric from the outside (it has a veranda), but slightly shabby motel-style units are all you'll get here. The hotel's location, smack bang in the middle of town opposite the bay and jetty, make up for the basic (but comfortable) rooms.

3 Alfred Terrace, Streaky Bay, SA 5680. ✆ **08/8626 1008.** www.streakybayhotel.com.au. 37 units. A$90–A$130 double, including breakfast; A$50 budget room with shared bathroom. Extra person A$15. MC, V. **Amenities:** Restaurant; bar. *In room:* A/C, TV, fridge, hair dryer.

Tanonga Luxury Eco-Lodges ★★★ Lots of places pretend they are eco-friendly, but these new lodges on a 200-hectare (494-acre) property about a 35-minute drive from Port Lincoln "walk the walk": They use solar energy, harvested rainwater, and a very smart architectural design to really live up to the sustainable claim. "Green" doesn't mean going without though—the lodges prove that you don't have to rough it to be kind to the environment, and they have all modern conveniences, including air-conditioning, plasma TVs, and dishwashers. The real reason to come here, however, is for the knockout views, particularly from the ridge-top lodge, where you can stargaze from your seriously comfy bed. I also loved the chin-deep Japanese bath. The owners are oyster farmers, so order a cook-your-own seafood hamper and pour yourself a glass of local wine as you watch the sun set and kangaroos nibble the grass at your doorstep. A close to perfect retreat in a gorgeous spot.

Charlton Gully, near Port Lincoln, SA 5606. ✆ **08/8684 5066.** www.tanonga.com.au. 2 units. A$320–A$350 double, including breakfast provisions. Extra person A$50. MC, V. *In room:* A/C, TV/DVD, CD player, hair dryer, kitchen, minibar, MP3 docking station.

Tumby Bay Hotel Seafront Apartments ☺ These two-bedroom seafront apartments each have large rooms, private balconies overlooking the water, and fully equipped kitchens and laundry, which make them a good choice for families or those looking to stay more than just 1 or 2 nights.

1 North Terrace, Tumby Bay, SA 5605. ✆ **08/8688 2005.** www.tumbybayhotel.com.au. 4 units. A$140 double. Extra person A$30. AE, DC, MC, V. Undercover parking (free). *In room:* A/C, TV/DVD, hair dryer, kitchen.

Where to Dine

Eating on the Eyre Peninsula is all about fresh seafood, and there is plenty of choice, from stylish waterfront restaurants to simple takeaway fish and chips by the sea. Look for King George whiting, usually served battered and fried with chips, and Port Lincoln tuna, served rare or even raw as great sashimi. Of course, nothing beats slurping a just-shucked oyster straight from the shell. Every local you meet on the peninsula will have an opinion on which bay or inlet produces the best oysters, be it Cowell, Streaky Bay, Smoky Bay, Coffin Bay, or Ceduna. They're all magnificent, but I reckon those from Coffin Bay are the best, although those on offer at the **Ceduna Oyster Bar,** Eyre Highway (✆ **08/8626 9086**), where you can snack on freshly shucked oysters and sip white wine while sitting in the sun on the roof of the shed overlooking the bay, are a pretty close second. You can buy direct from many of the seafood farmers, and many also offer tours of their processing plants.

Mocean Café ★★★ 🎁 MODERN AUSTRALIAN/SEAFOOD This fabulous cafe-cum-restaurant is a great place to try some of the peninsula's best seafood. Overlooking the historic jetty at Streaky Bay, the airy eatery has a sun-soaked deck and an extensive menu featuring local delicacies such as local greenlip abalone, Venus Bay prawns, King George whiting, and of course, Streaky Bay oysters, done four ways. The seafood antipasto plate (A$25) with local bush spices is a great way to try most of it.

34b Alfred Terrace, Streaky Bay. ✆ **08/8626 1775.** www.moceancafe.com.au. Reservations recommended. Main courses A$21–A$34. AE, MC, V. Tues–Sat 10am–late; Sun 10am–5pm.

The Oysterbeds ★★ 🎁 MODERN AUSTRALIAN/SEAFOOD "Everything but the chicken is local," was the proud boast of the owner on the day I visited this great spot. The menu changes daily according to what's fresh and best, but you can expect lots of local seafood, including the delectable Coffin Bay oysters. The kangaroo with haloumi cheese was superb. The waterfront views are pretty good too. This one is well worth going out of your way for.

61 Esplanade, Coffin Bay. ✆ **08/8685 4000.** Main courses A$17–A$32. AE, DC, MC, V. Wed–Sat 10:30am–9pm, Sun 11am–5pm. Closed June–Aug.

Pier Hotel ☺ BISTRO The servings are huge and the view is just as big at this friendly bayside pub in the center of town. There's a great choice of local seafood (try the local kingfish or the tuna skewers) as well as traditional pub fare such as plate-size schnitzels and steaks. There's a playroom to keep the kids entertained while you eat.

33 Tasman Terrace, Port Lincoln. ✆ **08/8682 1322.** Main courses A$14–A$30. MC, V. Sun–Wed noon–2pm and 6–8.30pm, Thurs–Sat noon–2pm and 6–9pm.

Sarin's ★★ MODERN AUSTRALIAN/SEAFOOD Spilling out of the ground floor of the Port Lincoln Hotel, this great restaurant has two sections: a casual bar with alfresco dining and the smarter a la carte area. Both areas overlook the beautiful curve of Boston Bay, but the real reason to eat here, especially in the posher section, is the seafood, most of it local. The Port Lincoln tuna is superb, whether you have it as an appetizer-size sashimi with wakami salad (a type of seaweed) or crusted with sesame seeds on a crispy noodle base for mains. The local King George whiting is pretty good too. The wine list includes most of the local wines.

1 Lincoln Hwy., Port Lincoln. ✆ **1300/766 100** in Australia. Main courses A$25–A$30. MC, V. Lunch and dinner daily.

OUTBACK SOUTH AUSTRALIA ★★

South Australia is the driest state in Australia. This becomes quite apparent once you leave behind the parklands of Adelaide and head into the interior. The Outback is as harsh as it is beautiful. Much of it consists of stony desert, salt pans, and sand hills, roamed by kangaroos, emus, dingoes, and wild goats. After spring rains, though, the area can burst alive with wildflowers.

It was always difficult to travel through these parts, and even today only four main routes traverse it. One of them, the **Birdsville Track,** is famed in Outback history as the trail along which stockmen once drove their herds of cattle south from Queensland. Another, the **Strzelecki Track,** runs through remote sand-dune country

> **An Outback Travel Warning**
>
> **If you intend to drive through the Outback, take care. Distances between points of interest can be vast; water, gas, food, and accommodations are far apart; and fuel and supply outlets in remote areas are not often open after hours or on weekends. Properties are often unfenced in the Outback—watch for cattle and wildlife on roads and avoid driving at night. Always travel with a good map and get local advice on road conditions before you set out. If you plan to travel off-road, a four-wheel-drive vehicle is a must. If you do get into trouble in the Outback, never, ever leave your vehicle. Most people who have perished in the Outback have died while trying to walk to help. Wait until help comes to you.**

to Innaminka and on to Coopers Creek. Both of these tracks cut through the "dog fence"—a 5,600km-long (3,472-mile) barrier designed to keep dingoes out of the pastoral lands to the south.

If you follow the **Stuart Highway** or the **Oodnadatta Track,** you'll pass the mining towns of Coober Pedy, Andamooka, and Mintabie, where people from all over the world have been turned loose in the elusive search for opal. Out here, too, are national parks, such as the daunting Simpson Desert Conservation Park, with its seemingly endless blood-red sand dunes and spinifex plains; and Lake Eyre National Park, with its dried-up salt pan that, during rare floods, is a temporary home to thousands of water birds.

The Flinders Ranges ★★★

460km (285 miles) N of Adelaide

The dramatic craggy peaks and ridges that make up the Flinders Ranges rise out of the South Australian desert. The ragged mountaintops are actually the eroded stumps of a range that was once higher than the Himalayas. And, as well as being one of the oldest landscapes on the planet, the Flinders are also some of the richest geological areas in the country—even those who have no interest in geology soon become fascinated by the rich, primeval colors of the ranges, which vary from deep red to orange, blue, and purple, depending on the light, and the sedimentary lines that are clearly visible running down the sides of cliffs.

The heart of the Flinders is Wilpena Pound, inside Flinders Ranges National Park, a massive 83-sq.-km (32-sq.-mile) craterlike circular ridge accessible through a gorge. There are several good lookouts giving great views of the Elder Range and the outer ramparts of Wilpena Pound, but it's really best seen from the air, which you can arrange at Wilpena Pound Resort. It's a remote and rugged place; most of the main roads are unsealed and some of the side tracks are four-wheel-drive only. The best time to visit is in spring, when the hills and valley floors are carpeted in wildflowers.

ESSENTIALS

GETTING THERE By car, take Highway 1 out of Adelaide to Port Augusta (3½ hr.), and then head east on Route 47 via Quorn and Hawker (45 min.). It's another hour to Wilpena Pound, next to the tiny settlement of Wilpena. Alternatively, take the scenic route, which doesn't have a specific name, through the Clare Valley (around 5 hr.): From Adelaide, head to Gawler and then through the Clare Valley; follow signs to Gladstone, Melrose, Wilmington, and Quorn.

Premier Stateliner (© **08/8415 5500;** www.premierstateliner.com.au) runs several buses every day from Adelaide to Port Augusta for A$49 one-way (half-price for kids), but if you want to explore further (and you will, the best bits are north of Port Augusta) you'll need you own vehicle, or take a tour. **Heading Bush Adventures** (© **08/8356 5501;** www.headingbush.com) has great trips, including a 10-day tour to the Flinders Ranges, the Oodnadatta Track, Coober Pedy, the Simpson Desert, Uluru, the Olgas, Kings Canyon, and Aboriginal communities. This remarkable four-wheel-drive trip, which focuses on Aboriginal culture, costs A$1,595—or A$1,540 with a student or YHA card—and includes meals and bush camping. It departs Adelaide every Monday and alternate Thursdays and has a maximum of 10 passengers.

Another good operator is **Banksia Adventures** (© **08/8431 9311;** www.banksia-adventures.com.au), which has 1- to 4-day trips to the Flinders, either in hotels or camping. The 2-day trip, including a hotel, costs A$836 for adults and A$495 for kids.

Most operators will also make up personalized tours on request if you have a small group.

VISITOR INFORMATION Before setting off, visit the **Wadlata Outback Centre,** 41 Flinders Terrace, Port Augusta, SA 5700 (© **08/8641 9194**), an award-winning interactive museum and information center. The museum costs A$12 for adults and A$8 for children and is open Monday through Friday from 9am to 5:30pm, Saturday and Sunday from 10am to 4pm.

In Hawker, the information center is on the corner of Wilpena and Cradock roads, Hawker (© **1800/777 880** in Australia), and there is an information center at the Wilpena Pound Resort (© **08/8648 0048**).

GETTING AROUND If you decide to explore on your own using a rental car, I recommend renting one in Adelaide (see "Getting Around," in the "Adelaide" section earlier in this chapter, for details) but try and avoid driving at dawn, dusk, or nighttime as wildlife is prolific and a collision with a kangaroo can be very expensive, not to mention very dangerous. While you don't need a 4WD, many of the roads are unsealed, so consider renting an SUV—and check your contract, as many car-hire companies will not allow their vehicles to be driven on dirt roads.

WHERE TO STAY

Arkaba Station ★★★ Arkaba Station, a 24,000-hectare (60,000-acre) working sheep station located on the edge of Wilpena Pound, is one of the oldest properties in the Flinders. The homestead, built in 1856, is a classic bush building, with thick stone walls, deep shady verandas, and a corrugated iron roof. It has been transformed into a stylish lodge with five en-suite bedrooms—four in the main homestead, one in the coachman's cottage. Understated and elegant, with quirky decorating touches such as glass-topped wool bales for bedside tables, bed posts fashioned from old Myall fence posts, and sheepskin rugs on the floor, it's the type of place where you feel instantly at home, rather like visiting a wealthy uncle in the country. Rates are all inclusive, and meals prepared by a resident chef are eaten around a convivial and relaxed shared table and accompanied by a selection of South Australian wines. Still, it's the range of activities on offer, such as four-wheel-drive safaris and guided bushwalks, that make this place worth flying halfway across the country for. Overnight walks in particular—which provide the opportunity to camp out under the stars in a swag on a specially constructed sleeping platform—are a magical, unforgettable experience.

Arkaba Station, via Hawker, SA 5434. ✆ **1300/790 561** in Australia. Fax 02/9571 6655. www.arkabastation.com. 5 units. A$1,580 double including meals, transfers, beverages, and activities; 2-night stay minimum. Extra person A$592. AE, DC, MC, V. **Amenities:** Dining room; bar; library; guest lounge; pool. *In room:* A/C.

Arkaroola Wilderness Sanctuary ★★ Arkaroola is a privately owned and operated 610-sq.-km (235-sq.-mile) wilderness sanctuary at the far northern tip of the Flinders. The accommodations here are in comfortable motel-style units, and there is also a caravan park and campsites. Even more stunning visually than the southern Flinders and Wilpena Pound, Arkaroola features rugged mountains, soaring granite peaks, deep gorges and waterholes. It is also home to more than 160 species of birds and the rare yellow-footed rock wallaby. The 4-hour four-wheel-drive ridge-top tour, run by the sanctuary, that travels along the spine of the mountains to a stunning lookout is a must (A$99 adult; A$66 children), but you can also follow one of the many self-drive four-wheel-drive tracks. With no light pollution, it is also one of the best places to view the night sky, and there are two observatories on the property. A "Tour the Universe" observatory tour costs A$40 per person. Scenic flights are also available.

Arkaroola, SA 5434. ✆ **1800/676 042** in Australia, or 08/8648 4848. Fax 08/8648 4846. www.arkaroola.com.au. 52 units. A$65–A$175 motel double; A$130–A$175 self-contained cottages. 2-night stay minimum. Campsite A$15; powered site A$20. AE, DC, MC, V. **Amenities:** Restaurant; bar; bistro. *In room:* A/C, TV, fridge.

Prairie Hotel ★★★ 🎁 If you are going to stay anywhere near the Flinders Ranges, stay here. The tiny, tin-roofed, stonewalled pub offers a memorable Outback experience. A new addition to the pub contains nice rooms, each with a queen-size bed and a shower. The older-style rooms are smaller and quaint. The bar out front is a great place to meet the locals and other travelers. Meals, prepared in a style the hotel likes to call "Flinders Feral Food," are very nearly the best of this kind I've had in Australia. Among the specialties are kangaroo-tail soup to start and a mixed grill of emu sausages, camel steak, and kangaroo as a main course. The owner's brother runs scenic flights over Wilpena Pound and out to the salt lakes.

Corner of High St. and West Terrace, Parachilna, SA 5730. ✆ **08/8648 4844.** Fax 08/8648 4606. www.prairiehotel.com.au. 12 units. A$160–A$225 double; A$320 double with Jacuzzi. Extra person A$35–A$45. AE, DC, MC, V. **Amenities:** Restaurant; bar. *In room:* A/C, fridge, hair dryer, minibar.

Wilpena Pound Resort The nearest place to the Wilpena Pound, this newly refurbished resort has a range of accommodation options from camping sites and permanent hard-floored tents through to motel-style rooms and self contained units. There are some excellent walks around the area. Twenty-minute scenic flights over the Pound and ranges cost A$145 per adult, A$100 per child for a minimum of two people. If you can afford it, it's definitely worth doing, as the only way to really appreciate the size and shape of the Pound is by air. The resort also offers four-wheel-drive tours.

Wilpena Pound, SA 5434. ✆ **08/8648 0004.** Fax 08/8648 0028. www.wilpenapound.com.au. 60 units. A$195–A$240 motel double; A$220–A$275 self-contained unit. Extra adult A$25. Permanent tent

A$68 without linen; A$90 with linen. Campsite A$20; powered site A$30. AE, DC, MC, V. **Amenities:** Restaurant; bar; bistro; bike hire; outdoor pool. *In room:* A/C, TV, fridge, hair dryer.

WHERE TO DINE

The **Wild Lime Cafe,** Mine Road, Blinman (✆ **08/8648 4679**), does a great quandong pie. (It's a sweet native tree fruit and it's delicious.) The cafe, which is housed in an old schoolhouse and also has a small gallery attached, is open Tuesday to Sunday 9am to 5pm and every day during school and public holidays. The best food in the Flinders, though, is undoubtedly at the **Prairie Hotel** (see above).

Coober Pedy ★

854km (529 miles) NW of Adelaide; 689km (427 miles) S of Alice Springs

People come to this Outback town for one thing: opal. If you're not in Coober Pedy looking for opal, then you're probably here to buy some. And there's lots of it. Coober Pedy is the largest opal-mining town in the world.

No matter how you get to Coober Pedy, it always feels as if you are in the middle of nowhere—and you pretty much are. Hours of remote driving, much of it on dirt tracks, are required to get anywhere else—Oodnadatta is 195km (121 miles) away, and William Creek (pop. 12) is 166km (103 miles).

Even when you get here, on first glance, there doesn't seem to be much here—but that's because most people live underground. In summer, temperatures can and often do climb to a searing 125°F (50°C), so the locals, well used to digging underground tunnels in their day-to-day work as opal miners, have created a subterranean town—the biggest in Australia. Underground homes remain at a constantly pleasant 71° to 78°F (22°–26°C) and renovations are simple: Simply dig yourself a new cupboard, bookshelf, or room—and who knows, you may even find some opal in the process!

The first opal was found here in 1915, but it wasn't until 1917, when the Trans Continental Railway was completed, that people began seriously digging for the stones. The town got its name from the Aboriginal words *kupa piti,* commonly thought to mean "white man's burrow." Remnants of the holes left by early miners are everywhere, mostly in the form of bleached-white hills of waste called "mullock heaps." You can look for opals (called "noodling") on the public noodling reserve in the center of town—it's free, and occasionally visitors do find good-size opals. Noodling on the mine sites around town is discouraged, however, as visitors have been known to come to grief after falling down the mine shafts.

ESSENTIALS

GETTING THERE **Regional Express** (**REX;** ✆ **13 17 13** in Australia; www.regionalexpress.com.au) flies to Coober Pedy from Adelaide. Check the website for discounted fares and specials. **Greyhound Australia** (✆ **13 14 99** in Australia, or 07/4690 9950; www.greyhound.com.au) runs buses from Adelaide to Coober Pedy for A$167 for adults and A$147 for children one-way. The trip takes about 12 hours. The bus from Alice Springs to Coober Pedy also costs A$165 for adults and A$144 for children. Passengers bound for Uluru transfer at Erldunda.

If you drive from Adelaide, it takes 9 hours to reach Coober Pedy along the Stuart Highway. It takes 7 hours to drive the 700km (434 miles) to Alice Springs.

VISITOR INFORMATION The **Coober Pedy Tourist Information Centre,** Hutchison Street, Coober Pedy (✆ **1800/637 076** in Australia, or 08/8672 5298), is open Monday through Friday from 8:30am to 5pm (closed holidays). A good website, **www.opalcapitaloftheworld.com.au**, gives a rundown of adventure operators in the area.

SEEING THE TOWN

You can visit one of the five **underground churches** in town, as well as **dugout cafes,** bookshops, galleries, and plenty of **underground opal showrooms.** Most are located along the main street, or you can find details at the visitor's information center.

Worth seeing is **Umoona Opal Mine and Museum,** on Lot 14, Hutchison Street, one of a couple of opal-mines-cum-museums in town. There are four tours daily at 10am, noon, and 2 and 4pm (A$10 for adults and A$5 for kids), which each include a good 20-minute documentary on how opal was first found in Coober Pedy (in 1915, by 14-year-old William Hutchison while searching for water). Inside the museum is also an Aboriginal interpretive center, a gallery, an old opal mine, and of course the ubiquitous opal showroom and shop. Entry to the museum is free.

About 30km (18 miles) from town are the Breakaways, a series of flat-topped hills or "jump-ups." Head out here at sunset, when it's not only cooler but the sandstone pillars, pinnacles, and gully edges glow pink, red, brown, purple, yellow, and white in the fading light. Just a bit farther down the road, you'll find the famous dog fence and the Moon Plains—the local nickname for the moonlike desert landscape along the fence. The 2m-high (6⅓-ft.) dog fence stretches across three states for more than 5,300km (3,293 miles) in an effort to keep northern dingoes away from southern sheep; it's the longest fence in the world.

If you want to see parts of Australia that most Australians never see, join an honest-to-goodness **Mail Run** ★ (**© 1800/069 911** in Australia), with a postal carrier, for a 12-hour journey out into the bush. Tours leave Monday and Thursday from Coober Pedy's **Underground Books** (**© 08/8672 5558**) and travel along 600km (372 miles) of dirt roads to Oodnadatta and the William Creek cattle station, stopping at five stations along the route. It's relatively comfortable inside the air-conditioned four-wheel-drive, and you'll have the chance to see such wildlife as eagles, emus, and the ever-present kangaroos. Bring your own lunch or buy it along the way at Oodnadatta or William Creek. Tours cost around A$190 for adults (I wouldn't really recommend it for kids under 12, as they find the long trip difficult). This up-close-and-personal look at life in the bush could easily be one of the most memorable experiences you have in Australia.

WHERE TO STAY

The Backpacker's Inn at Radeka's Downunder Motel ★ The other "underground" dwellings in Coober Pedy are built into the side of a hill, but the centrally located hostel here is *actually* underground—some 6.5m (21 ft.) directly below the topside building. (The rooms in the attached motel are dug out of the side of a hill.) This makes for nice temperatures year-round. Odd-looking dorms have no doors and are scooped out of the rock. Most contain just four beds; two large dorms sleep up to 20 people. The twin rooms are simply furnished but pleasant. The motel rooms are quite comfortable and come with TVs, coffeemakers, and attached bathrooms with shower. Some have a kitchenette. Room no. 9 is huge, with a double and two sets of bunk beds. Radeka's also runs a good opal tour.

Golf Without Grass

Coober Pedy's golf course has to rank as one of the world's top-10 most unusual golf courses. The 18-hole course has "mod grass" (green plastic woven "grass"), crushed-rock fairways, and no water hazards—although the dry creek beds make great sand traps. A special club rule is "rock relief": You are allowed a little grace if your ball lands on a rock. In summer, when it's too hot to play during the day, night golf is the way to go. Using luminous balls, you simply aim for the illuminated flag stick! *Tip:* Take your oldest clubs. It's around A$10 for a game, and you'll need to organize access through the folks at the Old Timers Mine (✆ 08/8672 5555) on Crowders Gully Road.

1 Oliver St., Coober Pedy, SA 5723. ✆ **08/8672 5223.** Fax 08/8672 5821. www.radekadownunder.com.au. 150 units, 10 motel rooms. A$25 dorm bed; A$65 double with shared bathroom; A$110 motel double; A$150 motel family suite. Extra person A$25. AE, MC, V. Free parking. **Amenities:** Dining room; bar. *In room:* (Motel rooms only) TV, fridge.

The Desert Cave Hotel Though it's not the only underground hotel in the world (there's also one in White Cliffs, New South Wales; see the Underground Motel, p. 233), this is the only one with a pool and Jacuzzi. Nineteen units are underground. Rooms lead off tunnels, and while each room is well ventilated and airy, there are no windows or natural light, so think twice if you suffer from claustrophobia. The hotel can arrange transfers from the airport (A$10). The tours from here go off to the Painted Desert (A$210), and you can also join the Mail Run from here.

Hutchison St. (P.O. Box 223), Coober Pedy, SA 5723. ✆ **1800/088 521** in Australia, or 08/8672 5688. Fax 08/8672 5198. www.desertcave.com.au. 50 units. A$225 double; A$260 family room. Extra person A$35. Ask about packages. AE, DC, MC, V. Free parking. **Amenities:** Restaurant; bar; babysitting; golf nearby; health club w/Jacuzzi; outdoor pool; limited room service; sauna; Wi-Fi (A$4 1 hr.; A$12 24 hr.). *In room:* TV, fridge, hair dryer, minibar.

WHERE TO DINE

The **Opal Inn** (✆ **08/8672 5054**) offers good-value counter meals of the typical pub-grub variety. Head to **Tom & Mary's Greek Taverna** on Hutchison Street (✆ **08/8672 5622**) for some surprisingly good Greek food. Despite being so far from the sea, the two signature dishes are the garlic prawns and Saganaki prawns, and they are both delicious. It's open daily from 5pm.

THE COORONG

Few places in the world attract as much wildfowl as the **Coorong,** one of Australia's most precious sanctuaries. The Coorong area includes the mouth of the Murray River, huge Lake Alexandrina, smaller Lake Albert, and a long, thin sand spit called the Younghusband Peninsula. The **Coorong National Park** encompasses a small but by far the most scenic part of this area and supports large colonies of native and visiting birds, such as the Australian pelican, black swan, royal spoonbill, greenshank, and extremely rare hooded plover.

If it were possible to count all the birds here, you'd probably run out of steam after some 45,000 ducks, 5,000 black swans, 2,000 Cape Barren geese, and 122,000 waders. This last figure is even more significant when you consider the total South Australian population of waders (200,000) and the overall Australian population (some 403,000).

Add to these figures the thousands of pelicans—with around 3,000 birds nesting here, it's the largest permanent breeding colony in Australia—and gulls, terns, and cormorants, and you'll realize why the Coorong and Lower Murray Lakes form one of the most important water-bird habitats in Australia.

The national park, which stands out starkly against the degraded farmland surrounding it, is also home to several species of marsupials, including wombats.

The best time to visit the Coorong is in December and January, when the lakes are full of migratory birds from overseas. However, plenty of birds can be spotted year-round. ***Note:*** Binoculars and patience are highly recommended.

Essentials

GETTING THERE The best way to visit the Coorong is by car. I highly recommend a guided tour of the area once you arrive at the main settlement of Goolwa, on the western fringe of the waterways, or at Meningie, on the eastern boundary. From Adelaide, follow the Princes Highway along the coast.

VISITOR INFORMATION The **Goolwa Tourist Information Centre,** BF Lawrie Lane, Goolwa (✆ **08/8555 1144**), has information on the area and can book accommodations. It's open from 9am to 5pm daily.

GETTING AROUND You can either sightsee by car, with a tour operator from Adelaide, or by boat. **Coorong Cruises** (✆ **08/8555 2203;** www.coorongcruises.com.au) offers both a half-day and a day trip exploring the waterway. The day trip costs A$82 for adults and A$63 for children, including lunch. The half-day cruise costs A$78 for adults and A$58 for kids and leaves at noon from the main wharf at Goolwa. Add A$107 for return coach pick up from Adelaide. Trips do not leave every day, so call ahead to check the schedule.

Where to Stay

Meningie, on Lake Albert, is the main town in the Coorong. You could stay at **Coorong Wilderness Lodge,** at Point Hack (✆ **08/8234 8324**), a stunning site on the sand dunes about 25km (16 miles) south of Meningie. Waterfront cabin accommodations cost A$200 a night; bunkhouse dorm bed A$40. It's Aboriginal owned and you can try bush foods, or take a kayak out onto the lake.

Poltalloch On the eastern edge of the Coorong, Poltalloch is a working farm property. The whole place is classified as a heritage building by the National Trust of South Australia, and history is evident everywhere, from the cottages once used by farmhands to the giant wooden shearing shed and other outbuildings crammed with relics from the past. You have a choice of five cottages on the property. All of the units are modern and comfortable inside and have their own kitchen facilities and barbecues. There's a private beach if you want to swim in the lake, and guests have the use of a dinghy, a canoe, and a Ping-Pong table.

Poltalloch, P.M.B. 3, Narrung via Tailem Bend, SA 5260. ✆ **08/8574 0043.** Fax 08/8574 0065. www.poltalloch.com.au. 5 units. A$140–A$190 cottage. Extra person A$40. MC, V. **Amenities:** Tennis court; use of watersports equipment. *In room:* A/C, TV, kitchen.

13

MELBOURNE

by Lee Mylne

It's rare to find anyone who lives in Melbourne who doesn't adore it. I'm biased, of course, because I've chosen it for my home, and here are just a few of the reasons why: Victoria's capital, Melbourne (pronounced *Mel*-bun), is a cultural melting pot. For a start, more people of Greek descent live here than in any other city except Athens. Chinese, Italian, Vietnamese, and Lebanese immigrants have all left their mark. Almost a third of Melbournians were born overseas or have parents who were born overseas. With such a diverse population, and with trams rattling through the streets and stately European architecture surrounding you, you could forget you're in Australia.

Melbourne, which has a population of more than three million, is at the head of the pack when it comes to shopping, restaurants, fashion, music, nightlife, and cafe culture. It frequently beats other state capitals in bids for major concerts, plays, exhibitions, and sporting events.

Melbourne's roots go back to the 1850s, when gold was found in the surrounding hills. British settlers took up residence and prided themselves on coming freely to their city, rather than having been forced here in convict chains. The city grew wealthy and remained a conservative bastion until World War II, when another wave of immigration, mainly from southern Europe, made it a more relaxed place.

ORIENTATION

Arriving

BY PLANE **Qantas** (✆ **13 13 13** in Australia; www.qantas.com.au) and discount airline **Virgin Blue** (✆ **13 67 89** in Australia; www.virgin blue.com.au) both fly to Melbourne from all state capitals and some regional centers. Qantas's discount arm, **Jetstar** (✆ **13 15 38** in Australia, or 03/8341 4901; www.jetstar.com.au) flies to and from Darwin, Perth, Cairns, Townsville, Hamilton Island, the Sunshine Coast and Gold Coast, and Hobart and Launceston. Jetstar also flies between **Avalon Airport,** about a 50-minute drive outside Melbourne's city center,

Greater Melbourne

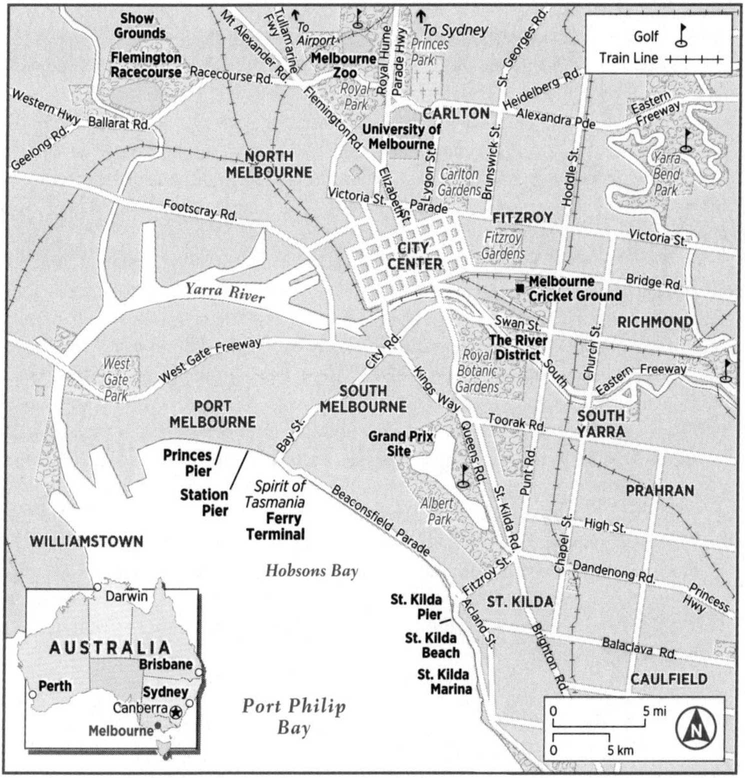

and Sydney and Brisbane. Low-cost carrier **Tiger Airways** (✆ **03/9335 3033;** www.tigerairways.com.au) has its hub in Melbourne, and from there flies to Brisbane, Adelaide, Alice Springs, Canberra, Perth, Hobart and Launceston in Tasmania, Mackay, Rockhampton, and the Gold and Sunshine Coasts in Queensland. The skies are highly competitive, and, with rapidly expanding networks, more flights are likely to have been added by both Jetstar and Tiger before you arrive in Australia.

Melbourne Airport's international and domestic terminals (www.melair.com.au) are all under one roof at Tullamarine, 22km (14 miles) northwest of the city center (often referred to as Tullamarine Airport). Tiger Airways has a separate terminal next door, distinguished by the tiger-striped water-tower landmark outside it. A travelers' information desk is on the ground floor of the international terminal and is open from 6am until the last flight. The international terminal has snack bars, a restaurant, currency-exchange facilities, and duty-free shops. ATMs are available at both terminals. Showers are on the first floor of the international area. Baggage carts are free in the international baggage claim hall but cost A$4 in the parking lot, departure lounge, or domestic terminal. Baggage storage is available in the international terminal and costs from A$10 to A$20 per day, depending on size. The storage desk is open from 5am to 12:30am daily, and you need photo ID. The **Hilton Melbourne Airport** (✆ **03/8336 2000**) and **Holiday Inn Melbourne Airport** (✆ **1300/724 944** in Australia, or 03/9933 5111) are both within 5 minutes' walk of the terminals.

Avis (✆ **13 63 33** in Australia, or 03/9338 1800), **Budget** (✆ **1300/362 848** in Australia, or 03/9353 9399), **Europcar** (✆ **1300/131 390** in Australia, or 03/9241 6800), **Hertz** (✆ **13 30 39** in Australia, or 03/9338 4044), and **Thrifty** (✆ **1300/367 227** in Australia, or 03/9241 6100) have airport rental desks. The Tullamarine freeway to and from the airport joins with the CityLink, an electronic toll-way system. Drivers need a CityLink pass. A 24-hour pass costs A$11. Check with your car-rental company.

The distinctive red **Skybus** (✆ **03/9335 3066** for recorded information; www.skybus.com.au) runs between the airport and Melbourne's Southern Cross station in Spencer Street every 10 to 15 minutes throughout the day and every 30 to 60 minutes overnight, 24 hours a day, every day. Buy tickets from Skybus desks outside the baggage claim areas or at the information desk in the international terminal. A free Skybus hotel shuttle will pick you up at your hotel to connect with the larger airport-bound bus at Southern Cross, but you must book this. It operates from 6am to 10pm weekdays and 7:30am to 5:30pm weekends. One-way tickets cost A$16 for adults, and A$26 gets you a two-way journey. Kids aged 4 to 14 cost A$6 each way. A family ticket for up to six people costs A$36 one-way or A$56 round-trip. The trip takes about 20 minutes from the airport to Southern Cross station, but allow longer for your return journey.

Sita Coaches (✆ **03/9689 7999;** www.sitacoaches.com.au) operates a transfer service to Avalon Airport for Jetstar flights. One-way fares from Avalon Airport are A$20 adults and half-price for children 4 to 14 to Southern Cross station, more to other CBD locations and other suburbs.

A **taxi** to the city center takes about 30 minutes and costs around A$45.

BY TRAIN Interstate trains arrive at **Southern Cross Railway Station,** Spencer and Little Collins streets (5 blocks from Swanston St., in the city center). After a multimillion-dollar face-lift completed in 2006, the station was renamed Southern Cross, but you will still hear locals refer to it as Spencer Street Station. Taxis and buses connect with the city.

The **Sydney–Melbourne *XPT*** travels between Australia's two largest cities daily; trip time is 11 hours. The adult fare is A$91 for economy class or A$128 first class. A first-class sleeper costs A$216. For more information, contact **Countrylink** (✆ **13 22 32** in Australia; www.countrylink.info).

The ***Overland*** train provides daylight service between Melbourne and Adelaide (trip time: just under 11 hr.) three times a week. The adult one-way fare is A$134 in first class and A$90 in economy. For more information, contact **Great Southern Railways** (✆ **13 21 47** in Australia; www.gsr.com.au).

V/Line services also connect Melbourne with Adelaide. This trip is by train from Melbourne to either Ballarat or Bendigo and by bus for the rest of the trip to Adelaide. Total trip time is around 10 to 12 hours, and the fare is A$45 for adults (children under 16 travel free with parents on off-peak times). The **Canberra Link** connects to Melbourne; it's a 1-hour train journey from Melbourne to Seymour, and then a 7-hour bus trip to Canberra. The journey costs A$45 for adults, free for an accompanied child under 16 off-peak. For reservations, contact **V/Line** (✆ **13 61 96** in Australia or 03/9697 2076; www.vline.com.au).

BY BUS Several bus companies connect Melbourne with other capitals and regional areas of Victoria. Among the biggest are **Greyhound Australia** (✆ **1300/473 946** in Australia, or 07/3868 0937; www.greyhound.com.au). Coaches serve Melbourne's **Transit Centre,** 58 Franklin St., 2 blocks north of the Southern Cross Railway station on Spencer Street. Trams and taxis serve the station; **V/Line buses** (✆ **13 61 96** in Australia; www.vline.com.au), which travel all over Victoria, depart from the Spencer Street Coach Terminal.

BY CAR You can drive from Sydney to Melbourne along the Hume Highway (a straight trip of about 9½ hr.), via Goulburn in NSW (good for supplies), and Wangaratta in Victoria (where you can detour into the Victorian Alps if you wish). Another route is along the coastal Princes Highway, for which you will need a minimum of 2 days, with stops. For information on all aspects of road travel in Victoria, contact the **Royal Automotive Club of Victoria** (✆ **13 13 29** in Australia, or 03/9790 2211; www.racv.com.au).

Visitor Information

The first stop on any visitor's itinerary should be the **Melbourne Visitor Centre,** Federation Square, Swanston and Flinders streets (✆ **03/9658 9658;** www.thatsmelbourne.com.au). The center serves as a one-stop shop for tourism information, accommodations and tour bookings, event ticketing, public transport information, and ticket sales. Also here are an ATM, Internet terminals, and interactive multimedia providing information on Melbourne and Victoria. The center is open daily from 9am to 6pm (except Christmas and Good Friday). The **Melbourne Greeter Service** also operates from the Melbourne Visitor Centre. This service connects visitors to enthusiastic local volunteers, who offer free one-on-one, half-day orientation tours of the city at 9:30am daily. Book at least 2 days in advance (✆ **03/9658 9658**). The Melbourne Visitor Centre also operates a staffed information booth in Bourke Street Mall, between Swanston and Elizabeth streets. You'll find some information services at **Information Victoria,** 505 Little Collins St. (✆ **1300/366 356** in Australia or 07/9603 9900). It's open 8:30am to 5pm weekdays. In the central city area, also look for **Melbourne's City Ambassadors**—people, usually volunteers, who give tourist information and directions. They'll be wearing bright red shirts and caps.

Good websites about the city include **CitySearch Melbourne, http://melbourne.citysearch.com.au**; as well as the official City of Melbourne site, **www.melbourne.vic.gov.au**; and the official tourism site for the city, **www.visitmelbourne.com**. Also worth a look is the locally run site **www.onlymelbourne.com.au**.

City Layout

Melbourne is on the Yarra River and stretches inland from Port Philip Bay, which lies to its south. On a map, you'll see a distinct central oblong area surrounded by Flinders Street to the south, Latrobe Street to the north, Spring Street to the east, and Spencer Street to the west. Cutting north-to-south through its center are the two main shopping thoroughfares, Swanston Street and Elizabeth Street. Cross streets between these major thoroughfares include Bourke Street Mall, a pedestrian-only shopping promenade. If you continue south along Swanston Street and over the river, it turns into St. Kilda Road, which runs to the coast. Melbourne's various urban "villages," including South Yarra, Richmond, Carlton, and Fitzroy, surround the city center. The seaside suburb of St. Kilda is known for its diverse restaurants. If you've visited Sydney, you'll find Melbourne's city center smaller and far less congested with people and cars.

Neighborhoods in Brief

At more than 6,110 sq. km (2,383 sq. miles), Melbourne is one of the biggest cities in the world by area. Below are the neighborhoods of most interest to visitors.

City Center Made up of a grid of streets north of the Yarra River, the city center is bordered by Flinders, Latrobe, Spring, and Spencer streets. There's good shopping and charming cafes, and in recent years an active nightlife has sprung up with the opening of a swath of funky bars and restaurants playing live and recorded music to suit all ages. The gateway to the city is the Flinders Street Station, with its dome and clock tower, flanked by the Federation Square precinct.

Chinatown This colorful section centers on Little Bourke Street between Swanston and Exhibition streets. The area marks Australia's oldest permanent Chinese settlement, dating from the 1850s, when a few boardinghouses catered to Chinese prospectors lured by gold rushes. Plenty of cheap restaurants crowd its alleyways. Tram: Any to the city.

Carlton North of the center, Carlton is a rambling suburb famous for Italian restaurants along Lygon Street with outdoor seating—though the quality of the food varies. It's the home of the University, so there's a healthy student scene. From Bourke Street Mall, it's a 15-minute walk to the restaurants. Tram: 1 or 22 from Swanston Street.

Fitzroy A ruggedly bohemian place 2km (1¼ miles) north of the city center, Fitzroy is raw and funky, filled with students and artists and popular for people-watching. Fitzroy revolves around Brunswick Street, with its cheap restaurants, busy cafes, late-night bookshops, art galleries, and pubs. Around the corner, on Johnston Street, is a growing Spanish quarter with tapas bars, flamenco restaurants, and Spanish clubs. Tram: 11 from Collins Street.

Richmond One of Melbourne's earliest settlements is a multicultural quarter noted for its historic streets and back lanes. Victoria Street is reminiscent of Ho Chi Minh City, with Vietnamese sights, sounds, aromas, and restaurants everywhere. Bridge Road is a discount-fashion precinct. Tram: 48 or 75 from Flinders Street to Bridge Road; 70 from Batman Avenue at Princes Bridge to Swan Street; 109 from Bourke Street to Victoria Street.

Southgate & Southbank This flashy entertainment district on the banks of the Yarra River opposite Flinders Street station (linked by pedestrian bridges) is home to the Crown Casino, Australia's largest gaming venue. Southbank has a myriad of restaurants, bars, cafes, nightclubs, cinemas, and designer shops. On the city side of the river is the Melbourne Aquarium. All are a 10-minute stroll from Flinders Street Station. Tram: 8 from Swanston Street.

Docklands Near the city center, at the rear of the Spencer Street station, this industrial area has become the biggest development in Melbourne. NewQuay on the waterfront has a diverse range of restaurants, shops, and cinemas. This is also where you'll find Melbourne's celebration of the dominance of Australian Rules football, the 52,000-seat stadium, currently called Etihad Stadium (but also known as "the Dome"). Docklands is accessible by the free City Circle Tram or by river cruise boats.

St. Kilda Hip and bohemian in a shabby-chic sort of way, this bayside suburb (6km/3¾ miles south of the city center) has Melbourne's highest concentration of restaurants, ranging from glitzy to cheap, as well as some superb cake shops and delis. Historically it was Melbourne's red-light district. The Esplanade hugs a beach with a historic pier and is the scene of a lively arts-and-crafts market on Sundays. Acland Street houses many restaurants. Check out Luna Park, one of the world's oldest fun parks, built in 1912, and ride the wooden roller coaster. Tram: 10 or 12 from Collins Street; 15 or 16 from Swanston Street; 96 from Bourke Street.

South Yarra/Prahan This posh part of town abounds with boutiques, cinemas, nightclubs, and galleries. Chapel Street is famous for its upscale eateries and designer-fashion houses, while Commercial Road is popular with the gay and lesbian community. Off Chapel Street in Prahan is Greville Street, a bohemian enclave of retro boutiques and music outlets. Every Sunday from noon to 5pm, the Greville Street Market offers arts, crafts, old clothes, and jewelry. Tram: 8 or 72 from Swanston Street.

South Melbourne One of the city's oldest working-class districts, South Melbourne is known for its historic buildings, old-fashioned pubs and hotels, and markets. Tram: 12 from Collins Street; 1 from Swanston Street.

The River District The muddy-looking Yarra River runs southeast past the Royal Botanic Gardens and near other attractions such as the Arts Centre, the National Gallery of Victoria, the Sidney Myer Music Bowl, and the Melbourne Cricket Ground, all described later in this chapter. Birrarung Marr is the first new major parkland in Melbourne in over 100 years. It is accessible by the free City Circle Tram.

Williamstown A lack of extensive development has left this outer waterfront suburb with a rich architectural heritage. It centers on Ferguson Street and Nelson Place—both reminiscent of old England. On the Strand overlooking the sea is a line of bistros and restaurants, and a World War II warship museum. Ferry: From Southgate, the World Trade Center, or St. Kilda Pier.

GETTING AROUND

By Public Transportation

Trams, trains, and buses are operated by several private companies, including the National Bus Company, Yarra Trams, and Connex, to name a few. Generally, both tourists and locals travel around the city and inner suburbs by tram.

BY TRAM ★ Melbourne has the oldest tram network in the world. Trams are an essential part of the city, a major cultural icon, and a great non-smoggy way of getting around. Several hundred trams run over 325km (202 miles) of track.

Melbourne is progressively moving to a new ticketing system called **myki** (a fraught process which has been slow in happening). However, while it is, there are two types of ticketing on trains, trams, and buses, and you will be able to use either a myki or a **Metcard** if you are travelling in Zones 1 and 2. At press time for this book, myki tickets were in use on trains but not yet on all buses or any trams.

The cheapest tram travel within the city center is with a **City Saver** ticket, which costs A$2.80 for adults, A$1.60 for children for a single journey. Or you can buy a **2-hour Metcard,** good for unlimited transport on buses or trams for up to 2 hours to all the attractions and suburbs listed in this book, for A$3.70 for adults and A$2.30 for children. If you plan to pack in the sightseeing, try the **Zone 1 Metcard Daily ticket,** which allows travel on all transport (trams and trains) within the city and close surrounding suburbs mentioned in this chapter from 5:30am to midnight (when transportation stops). It costs A$6.80 for adults and A$3.70 for children.

Buy single-trip and 2-hour tram tickets at ticket machines on trams, special ticket offices, at most newsdealers, and at Metcard vending machines at many railway stations. A Metcard needs to be validated by the Metcard validation machine on the tram, on the station platform, or on the bus before each journey; the only exception to this is the Metcard purchased from a vending machine on a tram, which is automatically validated for that journey only. Vending machines on trams only accept coins—but give change—whereas larger vending machines at train stations accept coins and paper money and give change up to A$10.

You can pick up a free route map from the Melbourne Visitor Centre, Federation Square, or the **MetShop,** Melbourne Town Hall building, corner of Swanston Street and Little Collins Street (✆ **13 16 38** in Australia; www.metlinkmelbourne.com.au), which is open Monday through Friday from 9am to 5:30pm, and Saturday from 9am to 1pm.

Trams stop at numbered tram-stop signs, sometimes in the middle of the road (so beware of oncoming traffic!). To get off the tram, press the button near the handrails or pull the cord above your head.

The **City Circle Tram** is the best way to get around the center of Melbourne—and it's free. The burgundy-and-cream trams travel a circular route between all the major central attractions, and past shopping malls and arcades. The trams run, in both directions, every 12 minutes between 10am and 6pm (and until 9pm Thurs–Sat), except on Good Friday and December 25. The trams run along all the major thoroughfares including Flinders and Spencer streets. Burgundy signs mark City Circle Tram stops.

BY BUS The free **Melbourne City Tourist Shuttle** operates buses that pick up and drop off at 13 stops around the city, including the Melbourne Museum, Queen Victoria Market, Immigration Museum, Southbank Arts Precinct, the Shrine of Remembrance and Botanic Gardens, Chinatown, and Flinders Lane, and many other attractions. You can hop on and off during the day. The entire loop takes about 90 minutes nonstop, and there's a commentary. The bus runs every 30 minutes from 9:30am until 4:30pm daily (except Christmas and some public holidays).

By Boat

Melbourne River Cruises (✆ **03/8610 2600;** www.melbcruises.com.au) offers a range of boat trips up and down the Yarra River, taking about 1 hour and 15 minutes. It's a really interesting way to get a feel for the city, and the tours include commentaries. Tours cost A$23 adults, A$11 for kids, or A$50 for a family of four. Or you can combine both up- and downriver tours for A$29 adults, A$16 kids, or A$75 families. Call ahead to confirm cruise departure times, as they change, and pick up tickets from the blue Melbourne River Cruises kiosks at the Federation Square riverfront (opposite Flinders St. Station).

By Taxi

Cabs are plentiful in the city, but it may be difficult to hail one in the city center late on Friday and Saturday night. From 10pm to 5am, anywhere in Victoria, you must pre-pay your fare. The driver will estimate the fare at the start of the journey, give you a receipt and then adjust it according to the meter reading plus any fees such as road tolls, at the end of your trip. Taxi companies include **Silver Top** (✆ **13 10 08** in Australia), **Embassy** (✆ **13 17 55** in Australia), and **Yellow Cabs** (✆ **13 22 27** in Australia). A large, illuminated rooftop light indicates that a cab is available for hire.

By Car

Driving in Melbourne can be challenging. Roads can be confusing, there are trams everywhere, and there is a rule about turning right from the left lane at major intersections in the downtown center and in South Melbourne (which leaves the left-hand lane free for trams and through traffic). Here, you must wait for the lights to turn amber before turning. Also, you must always stop behind a tram if it stops, because passengers usually step directly into the road. Add to this the general lack of parking and expensive hotel valet parking, and you'll know why it's better to get on a tram instead. For road rules, pick up a copy of the Victorian Road Traffic handbook from bookshops or from a **Vic Roads** office (✆ **13 11 71** in Australia for the nearest office).

Major car-rental companies, all with offices at Tullamarine Airport, include **Avis,** Shop 2, 8 Franklin St. (✆ **03/9663 6366**); **Budget,** Shop 3, 8 Franklin St. (✆ **03/9203 4844**); **Hertz,** 10 Dorcas St., South Melbourne (✆ **13 30 39** in Australia, or 03/9698 2444); and **Thrifty,** 390 Elizabeth St. (✆ **1300/367 227** in Australia or 03/8661 6000).

[FastFACTS] MELBOURNE

American Express The main office is at 233 Collins St. (✆ **1300/139 060** in Australia, or 03/9633 6333). It's open Monday through Friday from 9am to 5pm, and Saturday from 10am to 1pm.

Business Hours In general, stores are open Monday through Wednesday and Saturday from 9am to 5:30pm, Thursday from 9am to 6pm, Friday from 9am to 9pm, and Sunday from 10am to 5pm. The larger department stores stay open on Thursday until 6pm and Friday until 9pm. Banks are open Monday through Thursday from 9:30am to 4pm, and Friday from 9:30am to 5pm.

Camera Repair **Vintech Camera Service Centre,** Fifth Floor, 358 Lonsdale St. (✆ **03/9602 1820**), is well regarded.

Consulates The following English-speaking countries have consulates in Melbourne: United States, Level 6, 553 St. Kilda Rd. (✆ **03/9526 5900**); United Kingdom, Level 17, 90 Collins St. (✆ **03/9652 1600**); New Zealand, Level 10, 454 Collins St. (✆ **03/9642 1279**); and Canada, Level 27, 101 Collins St. (✆ **03/9653 9674**).

Dentists Call the **Dental Emergency Service** (✆ **03/9341 1040**) for emergency referral to a local dentist.

Doctors The "casualty" department at the **Royal Melbourne Hospital,** Grattan Street, Parkville (✆ **03/9342 7000**), responds to emergencies. The **Traveller's Medical & Vaccination Centre,** Second Floor, 393 Little Bourke St. (✆ **03/9935 8100**), offers full vaccination and travel medical services.

Emergencies In an emergency, call ✆ **000** for police, ambulance, or the fire department.

Internet Access There are many Internet cafes along Elizabeth Street, between Flinders and Latrobe streets, and around Flinders Lane and Little Bourke Street in Chinatown. Most are open from early until well into the night.

Lost Property Contact the nearest police station or visit the Melbourne Town Hall, Swanston Street (✆ **03/9658 9779**). If you lose something on a tram, call ✆ **1800/800 166**

between 6am and 10pm. If you lose something on a train, call ✆ **03/9610 7512** between 9am and 5pm weekdays (including public holidays).

Pharmacies (Chemist Shops) The **Mulqueeny Pharmacy** is on the corner of Swanston and Collins streets (✆ **03/9654 8569**). It's open Monday through Friday from 8am to 8pm, Saturday from 9am to 6pm, and Sunday 11am to 6pm.

Post Office The General Post Office (GPO) at 250 Elizabeth St. (✆ **13 13 18** in Australia) is open Monday through Friday 8:30am to 5:30pm, and on Saturday 9am to 5pm.

Safety St. Kilda might be coming up in the world, but walking there alone at night still isn't wise. Parks and gardens can also be risky at night, as can the area around the King Street nightclubs.

Taxes Sales tax, where it exists, is included in the price, as is the 10% Goods and Services Tax (GST). There is no hotel tax in Melbourne.

Telephones For directory assistance, call ✆ **1223;** for international directory assistance, call ✆ **1225.**

Weather Call ✆ **1196** for recorded weather information.

WHERE TO STAY

Getting a room is easy enough on weekends, when business travelers are back home. You need to book well in advance, however, during the city's hallmark events (say, the weekend before the Melbourne Cup, and during the Grand Prix and the Australian Open). Hostels in the St. Kilda area tend to fill up quickly in December and January.

You'll feel right in the heart of the action if you stay in the city center, which seems to buzz all day (and night). The city center has been rejuvenated in recent years, and you'll be certain to find plenty to do. Otherwise, the inner city suburbs are all exciting satellites, with good street life, restaurants, and pubs—and just a quick tram ride from the city center. Transportation from the airport to the suburbs is a little more expensive and complicated than to the city center, however.

The **Best of Victoria** booking service, Federation Square (✆ **1300/780 045** in Australia, or 03/9928 0000; www.bestof.com.au), open daily 9am to 6pm, can help you book accommodations after you arrive in the city.

In the City Center

VERY EXPENSIVE

Adelphi Hotel It may be worth staying in this designer boutique hotel, a minute's walk from the city center, just for the experience of taking a dip in its top-floor 25m (82-ft.) lap pool, which juts out from the end of the building and overhangs the streets below. The pool has a glass bottom, so you can watch pedestrians below as you float. One of the sexiest bars in Melbourne is adorned with the owner's eclectic private art collection, as is the whole hotel. The rooms are similarly modern, with colorful leather seating and lots of burnished metal but have no views. Deluxe rooms differ from the Premier rooms in that they come with a bathtub. I liked small touches like the wind-proof umbrella (essential sometimes in Melbourne!) and the clock that reflects the time on your bedroom ceiling. There are robes, slippers, and coffee in the rooms.

187 Flinders Lane, Melbourne, VIC 3000. ✆ **03/8080 8888.** Fax 03/8080 8800. www.adelphi.com.au. 34 units, most with shower only. A$500 Premier king room; A$600 deluxe double; A$1,200 executive

Where to Stay in Central Melbourne

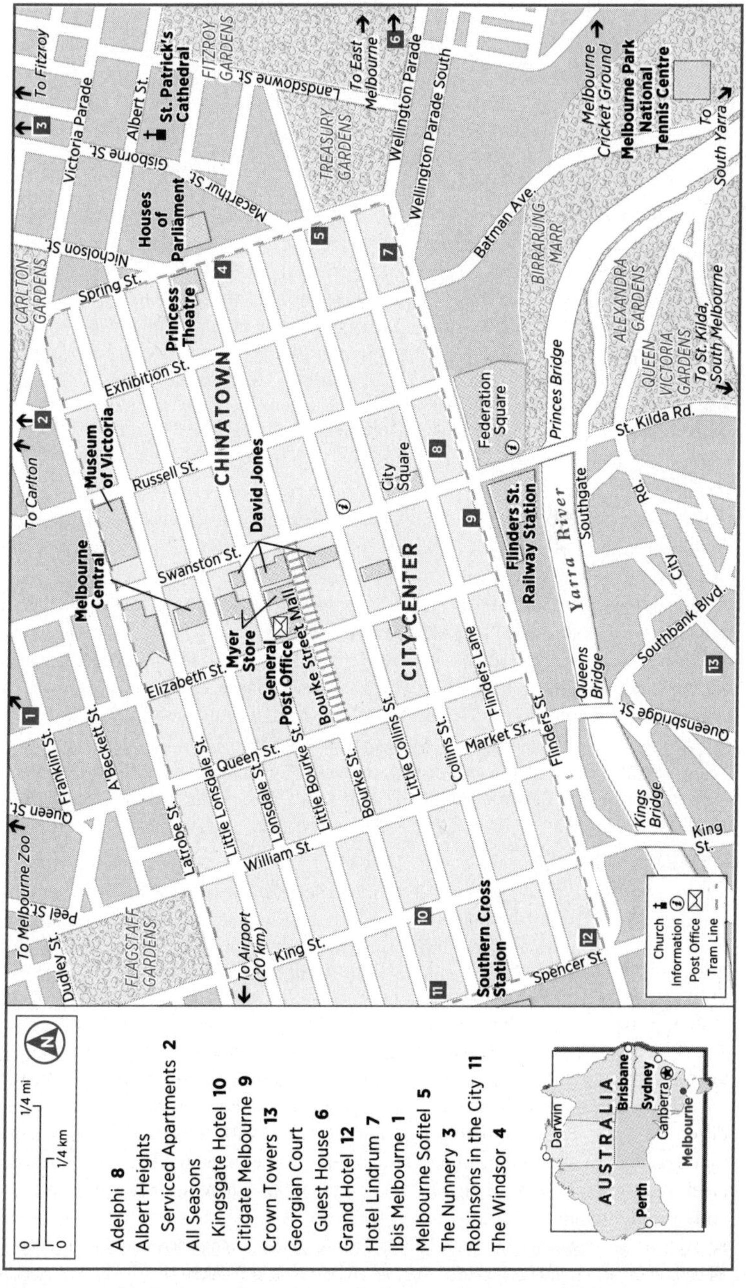

suite. Rates include breakfast. AE, DC, MC, V. Parking A$16. **Amenities:** 2 restaurants; bar; babysitting; bikes; concierge; executive rooms; health club; heated outdoor pool; sauna; spa. *In room:* A/C, TV, DVD, CD player, hair dryer, Internet (A$15 for 24 hr.; A$20 unlimited), minibar.

Crown Towers ★★ One of Melbourne's grandest and most impressive hotels, Crown Towers is part of the Crown Casino complex, on the banks of the Yarra River. Entry to the hotel is through a glittering lobby paved in black marble. The complex has an enormous collection of gambling machines (called "pokies" in Australia), as well as gaming tables. Upstairs in the hotel, standard guest rooms are cozy and all have been recently refurbished. Superior guest rooms occupy floors 5 to 15, and those above the 10th floor have spectacular city views. Deluxe rooms, which run up to the 28th floor, are similar, and all have great views. Rooms above the 28th floor are part of Crown's Crystal Club, which offers club lounge services. From the 32nd floor upward are the luxury villas. The hotel is a 10-minute walk from the main shopping streets; trams stop right outside. **Crown Casino** offers 24-hour gambling.

8 Whiteman St., Southbank, Melbourne, VIC 3006. ✆ **1800/811 653** in Australia, or 03/9292 6868. Fax 03/9292 6299. www.crowntowers.com.au. 482 units. A$355–A$465 double; A$530–A$665 double suite; A$1,380 2-bedroom suite; from A$900 villas. Extra person A$60. Children 12 and under stay free in parent's room. AE, DC, MC, V. Parking A$27. **Amenities:** 3 restaurants; babysitting; concierge; executive rooms; health club; Olympic-size indoor pool; room service; spa. *In room:* A/C, TV w/pay movies, hair dryer, minibar, Wi-Fi (A$25 for 24 hr.).

Hotel Lindrum ★★ If you like your hotels stylish and contemporary, then the Hotel Lindrum is for you. It's quite typical of the new wave of modern hotels that emphasize trendy interior design. Standard rooms, if you can call them that, have queen-size beds or two singles, lots of hardwood, soft lighting, and forest-green tones. Superior rooms have king-size beds and lovely polished wood floorboards, and deluxe rooms have wonderful views across to the Botanic Gardens through large bay windows. The hotel boasts a smart restaurant, a billiard room, and a bar with an open fire.

26 Flinders St., Melbourne, VIC 3000. ✆ **03/9668 1111.** Fax: 03/9668 1199. www.hotellindrum.com.au. 59 units. A$245 standard double; A$275 superior room; A$315 deluxe room; A$340 suite. AE, DC, MC, V. Parking off-site A$15. **Amenities:** Restaurant; bar. *In room:* A/C, TV w/free movies, DVD player w/movie library, CD player w/CD library, free Internet.

EXPENSIVE

Grand Hotel Melbourne ★★ This majestic heritage-listed building, which was originally home to the Victorian railway administration, is striking for its remarkable scale and imposing Italianate facade. Building started on the six-story site in 1887, and additions were still being made in 1958. It became a hotel in 1997. Suites have plush red Pullman carpets and full kitchens with dishwashers; one-bedroom loft suites have European-style espresso machines, a second TV in the bedroom, and great views over the new Docklands area beyond—though rooms are whisper quiet. All rooms are similar but vary in size; some have balconies. Many of the suites are split-level, with bedrooms on the second floor.

33 Spencer St., Melbourne, VIC 3000. ✆ **1300/361 455** in Australia, or 03/9611 4567. Fax 03/9611 4655. www.mgallery.com. 103 units. A$229–A$259 studio suite; A$265–A$518 1-bedroom suite; A$355–A$638 2-bedroom suite; A$800 3-bedroom suite. Extra person A$75. Children 11 and under stay free in parent's room. Ask about weekend and seasonal packages. AE, DC, MC, V. Parking A$15. Tram: 48 or 75 from Flinders St. **Amenities:** Restaurant; bar; babysitting; concierge; golf course nearby; exercise room; Jacuzzi; heated indoor swimming pool (with retractable roof); room service; sauna. *In room:* A/C, TV/

Melbourne's Art Hotels

Melbourne's Deague family has combined a passion for the arts and a desire to join the global boutique hotel trend by dedicating a series of new hotels—six in all—to well-known Australian artists. The flagship of the Art Series Hotel Group is The Olsen, at Chapel Street and Toorak Road, South Yarra (✆ 03/9040 1222), with 229 rooms. The A$60-million hotel is named for the man regarded as Australia's greatest living painter, John Olsen, and claims to have the world's largest glass bottomed swimming pool, hanging over the street. Rates start from A$239 double per night for a studio suite. The Cullen, an A$30-million 115-room boutique hotel and entertainment precinct at 164 Commercial Rd., Prahran (✆ 03/9098 1555) is named after controversial artist Adam Cullen, and has a rooftop cocktail bar and two restaurants. Each hotel features a major artwork commissioned especially for the hotel foyer by the naming artist, including one from Adam Cullen's Ned Kelly series and Olsen's 6m (19-ft.) mural, *The Yellow Sun and Yarra,* set in the spectacular glass lobby of The Olsen. Prints and a photographic history of the artist's life adorn walls of rooms and public spaces of the hotel while the architecture, interior design, linen, and stationery also reflect each artist's style. Still to open at press time for this book were The Blackman, named for Sydney artist John Blackman and housed within the heritage-listed Airlie House (backed by a modern high-rise annex) on St. Kilda Road, as well as The Larwill, The Knight, and The Whitely. For updates, visit www.artserieshotels.com.au.

DVD w/pay movies, CD player, hair dryer, Internet (on 4th and 5th floors; A$27 for 24 hr.), kitchen, minibar, Wi-Fi (on 6th floor; A$27 for 24 hr.).

The Windsor ★★ The Windsor opened in 1883 (as "The Grand") and since then this upper-crust establishment has oozed sophistication. It holds a special place in Australia's history as the setting for the drafting of the country's Constitution in 1898. But controversy has dogged plans for an A$260 million redevelopment plan for Australia's only surviving authentic "grand" hotel for several years now. At press time for this book, the issues surrounding the plans seemed no closer to a resolution—though by the time you visit, restoration *may* be underway. The plans for the extensive face-lift and the possible addition of a modern town behind the existing building would add an extra 152 rooms, bringing total accommodation to 332 rooms. But some things won't change: The renowned "high tea" will continue to be served each afternoon, as it has been for more than 100 years. And the staff remains friendly and efficient. The current standard rooms are comfortable, with high ceilings and good-size bathrooms. Deluxe rooms are twice as big, and many have striking views of Parliament House and the Melbourne Cathedral. Rates may also change after the refurbishment is completed.

103 Spring St., Melbourne, VIC 3000. ✆ **1800/033 100** in Australia, or 03/9633 6000. Fax 03/9633 6001. www.thewindsor.com.au. 332 units. A$190–A$280 double; A$330–A$520 double suite. Extra person from A$55. AE, DC, MC, V. Valet parking A$35 per night. **Amenities:** Restaurant; 2 bars; babysitting; concierge; health club; room service. *In room:* A/C, TV w/pay movies, hair dryer, Internet (A$25 for 24 hr.), minibar.

MODERATE

Hotel Ibis Melbourne ★ A good deal, the Ibis is next door to the bus station and a short walk from the central shopping areas. Rooms in the AAA-rated three-star hotel are spacious, immaculate, and bright, and have attached showers. Apartments have kitchenettes and tubs. Guests can make use of the swimming pool, sauna, and Jacuzzi up the road at the historic Melbourne City Baths.

15–21 Therry St., Melbourne, VIC 3000. ✆ **1300/656 565** in Australia, 800/221-4542 in the U.S. and Canada, 0800/444 422 in New Zealand, or 03/9666 0000. Fax 03/9666 0052. www.ibishotels.com.au. 250 units, some with shower only. A$119–A$139 double; A$149 1-bedroom apt; A$239 2-bedroom apt. Extra person A$36. Children 11 and under stay free in parent's room. Ask about packages. AE, DC, MC, V. Parking A$11. **Amenities:** Restaurant; bar. *In room:* A/C, TV, hair dryer, Internet (all floors; A55¢ per minute or A$27 for 24 hr.), Wi-Fi (on 9th and 11th floors; A55¢ per minute or A$27 for 24 hr.).

Robinsons in the City ★ Artfully created in what was once Melbourne's first commercial bakery, this lovely boutique hotel is tastefully elegant as well as being casual and comfortable, with lots of personal touches. Built around 1850, the building retains some original features, including the brick ovens that are now a feature of the breakfast room. All rooms have either queen- or king-size beds and each guest room has its own private bathroom just across the hallway. There's a guest lounge with an extensive library, and a "butler's pantry" with a bar that operates on an honor system. Owner Paul Humphreys is passionate about Melbourne and happy to help you with your travel plans.

405 Spencer St. (at Batman St.), Melbourne, VIC 3003. ✆ 03/9329 2552. Fax 03/9329 3747. www.robinsonsinthecity.com.au. 6 units, some with shower only. A$258–A$342 double. Rates include full "farmhouse" breakfast. Ask about discount rates. AE, DC, MC, V. Limited free off-street parking, which must be prebooked. In room: A/C, TV, hair dryer, minibar, free Wi-Fi.

INEXPENSIVE

All Seasons Kingsgate Hotel A 10-minute walk from the city, this interesting hotel resembles a terrace building from the outside, but inside it's a maze of corridors and rooms. It has a real B&B feel to it, and the staff is very friendly. The least expensive economy rooms have two single beds, a wardrobe, and a hand basin; there's barely enough room to swing a backpack, and the bathroom is down the hallway. Standard rooms are light and spacious, with double or twin beds as well as en-suite bathrooms. The 15 or so family rooms have double beds and two singles. There is a 24-hour reception desk, free luggage-storage facilities, and free use of the safety deposit boxes. Check the hotel's website for really good deals.

131 King St., Melbourne, VIC 3000. ✆ **1300/734 171** in Australia, or 03/9629 4171. Fax 03/9629 7110. www.kingsgatehotel.com.au. 225 units, 104 with bathroom. A$99–A$209 double; A$245–A$265 quad. AE, DC, MC, V. Parking at Crown Casino, a 7-min. walk away. **Amenities:** 2 restaurants; bar. *In room:* A/C, TV.

In East Melbourne

Albert Heights Serviced Apartments ★ For good, moderately priced accommodations with cooking facilities (so you can cut down on meal costs), try the Albert Heights. It's in a nice area of Melbourne, about a 10-minute walk from the city center. There are parks at each end of the street. Each self-contained unit in the brick building is large and attractive. If you want your own space or are traveling with your family, you can use the sofa bed in the living room. Superior apartments come with a double bed; deluxe one-bedroom apartments with a queen-size bed; and deluxe two-bedroom apartments with a queen-size and two large singles. Premier apartments have a queen-size bed in the master bedroom, with a separate lounge room with a single divan and single trundle bed. Each unit comes with a full kitchen with a microwave (no conventional oven), dining area, and large bathroom. Check the website for major discounts.

83 Albert St., East Melbourne, VIC 3002. ✆ **1800/800 117** in Australia, or 03/9419 0955. Fax 03/9419 9517. www.albertheights.com.au. 34 units. A$245 superior apt; A$260 premier apt; A$275 deluxe 1-bedroom apt; A$310 deluxe 2-bedroom apt. Extra adult A$25; extra child A$20. Ask about special deals. AE, DC, MC, V. Free parking. Tram: 42 or 109. **Amenities:** Babysitting; Jacuzzi. *In room:* A/C, TV, hair dryer, kitchen, free Wi-Fi.

Georgian Court Guest House The appearance of the comfortable Georgian Court, set on a beautiful tree-lined street, hasn't changed much since it was built in 1910. The sitting and dining rooms have high ceilings and offer old-world atmosphere. The guest rooms are simply furnished, and some are in need of a refurbishment; others have already had one. Some have en-suite bathrooms; others have private bathrooms in the hallway. One room comes with a queen-size bed and a Jacuzzi. The Georgian Court is a 15-minute stroll through the Fitzroy and Treasury Gardens from the city center and is also close to the fashion shops of Bridge Road.

21 George St., East Melbourne, VIC 3002. ✆ **03/9419 6353.** Fax 03/9416 0895. www.georgiancourt.com.au. 31 units, 21 with bathroom. A$139 double without bathroom; A$159 double with bathroom; A$179 family room with bathroom; A$170 queen spa room. Extra adult A$20, extra child A$12. Rates include buffet breakfast. AE, DC, MC, V. Free parking. Tram: 75 from Flinders St., or 48 from Spencer St. **Amenities:** Access to nearby health club. *In room:* A/C, TV, hair dryer, Wi-Fi (A$8 for 1 hr.; A$20 for 24 hr.).

In Fitzroy

The Nunnery ★★ This former convent offers smart budget accommodations—and something a little more upmarket—a short tram ride from the city center, close to the restaurant and nightlife of Brunswick and Lygon streets in nearby Carlton. The informal, friendly 1860s main building has high ceilings, handmade light fittings, polished floorboards, marble fireplaces, and a hand-turned staircase. There's also a clever and rather irreverent play on its past in the decor. It's well suited to couples and families. The Guesthouse next door, built in the early 1900s, is also comfy, stylish, and decorated with tasteful furnishings and artwork. All rooms share bathrooms. The Nunnery, former home of the Daughters of Charity, also houses dorm rooms that have four, eight, or twelve beds. ***Warning:*** There are no elevators.

112–120 Nicholson St., Fitzroy, Melbourne, VIC 3065. ✆ **1800/032 635** in Australia, or 03/9419 8637. Fax 03/9417 7736. www.nunnery.com.au. 30 units, none with bathroom. Guesthouse A$130 double, A$145 double family room, plus A$30 per extra adult or A$15 per extra child 5–12 years; Budget section A$30–A$34 per person bunk rooms, A$90–A$115 double, A$75 single private rooms. MC, V. Free parking (reservation required). Tram: 96. **Amenities:** Kitchen. *In room:* TV, Wi-Fi (A$4 per hr.; A$15 per day).

In St. Kilda

Fountain Terrace ★★ Built in 1880, Fountain Terrace has been lovingly restored to its former glory by Penny and Heikki Minkkinen. This boutique guesthouse has real character and is a wonderful alternative to traditional city hotels. It's on a tree-lined street just a few minutes' walk from the sea and to the many restaurants on Fitzroy and Acland streets. It's very classy inside, with comfortable communal areas that include a sunny drawing room where breakfast is served at an antique refectory table. The rooms, which are named after famous Australian writers, artists, and pioneers, have all those classic old-fashioned hallmarks of a historic house, including nice prints on the walls and old fireplaces. Each one is a real individual, so it's well worth while checking out the pictures on the website. Guests also have free access to the St. Kilda Sea Baths and the gymnasium, a 5-minute walk away. If you want a little bit more space and privacy, the owners also have two smart apartments around the corner on Fitzroy Street.

28 Mary St. (parallel to Fitzroy St.), St. Kilda West, Melbourne, VIC 3182. ✆ **03/9593 8123.** Fax 03/9593 8696. www.fountainterrace.com.au. 7 units. A$175–A$245 double. Rates include breakfast. AE, DC, MC, V. Free parking. Tram: 96, 16, or 112. **Amenities:** Access to St. Kilda Sea Baths pool and gym. *In room:* A/C, TV, hair dryer.

Hotel Tolarno ★ The quirky Hotel Tolarno is in the middle of St. Kilda's cafe and restaurant strip, and a short stroll from the beach. Rich red carpets bedeck the corridors throughout the 1950s and 1960s retro-style building. In an earlier life, the building was owned by Melbourne artist Mirka Mora (after whom the hotel's new restaurant has been named), and the tradition continues today, with the walls hung with work by Melbourne artists. Rooms vary, but all are modern and colorful. The most popular, the deluxe doubles, are in the front of the building and have balconies overlooking the main street. They are larger than the standard rooms. Superior doubles come with a microwave and two have Japanese baths. Suites come with a separate kitchen and lounge. Suites don't have balconies, though some have Jacuzzis.

42 Fitzroy St., St. Kilda, Melbourne, VIC 3182. ✆ **1800/620 363** in Australia, or 03/9537 0200. Fax 03/9534 7800. www.hoteltolarno.com.au. 36 units. A$145–A$180 double; A$200–A$275 suite; A$385 2-bedroom suite (sleeps 4). AE, DC, MC, V. Free on-street parking. Tram: 16 from Swanston St. or 96 from Flinders St. **Amenities:** Restaurant; bar; babysitting; bikes; concierge; room service; 4 lit tennis courts. *In room:* A/C, TV, hair dryer, kitchenette, Wi-Fi (A$10 per hr.).

Olembia Guesthouse This sprawling Edwardian house, built in 1922, is set back from a busy street behind a leafy courtyard. It's popular with backpackers, tourists, business travelers, and young families. The rooms are simply furnished, with little more than a double bed or two singles, a desk, a hand basin, and a wardrobe. Dorm rooms have between three and six beds (there are mixed and girls-only dorms). Guests share six bathrooms. There's a comfortable sitting room, a communal kitchen and a coin-operated laundry. The Olembia is near St. Kilda beach and the restaurants lining Acland Street.

96 Barkly St., St. Kilda, Melbourne, VIC 3182. ✆ **03/9537 1412.** Fax 03/9537 1600. www.olembia.com.au. 23 units, none with bathroom. A$85 double; A$100 triple; A$30 dorm room; A$60 single room. AE, MC, V. Free parking. Tram: 96 from Bourke St. or 16 from Swanston St. **Amenities:** Bikes; kitchen. *In room:* No phone.

In South Yarra & Toorak

The Como Melbourne ★★★ The Como deservedly basks in its reputation for excellent service and terrific accommodations, which include studio rooms (some with shower only), open-plan suites (all with spa tubs, some with private offices and/or wet bars), one- or two-bedroom suites (all with kitchen, some with an office), and luxurious penthouse and executive suites (split-level, with oversize spa tubs). Most rooms are at least 40 sq. m (431 sq. ft.), and the bathrooms have a bathing menu (and a rubber duck for you to take home). Some suites have a private Japanese

Where to Stay & Dine in St. Kilda

ACCOMMODATIONS ■
Fountain Terrace **1**
Hotel Tolarno **2**
Olembia
Guesthouse **3**

DINING ◆
Chinta Blues **6**
Donovans **5**
Cicciolina **4**
Lentil as Anything **7**

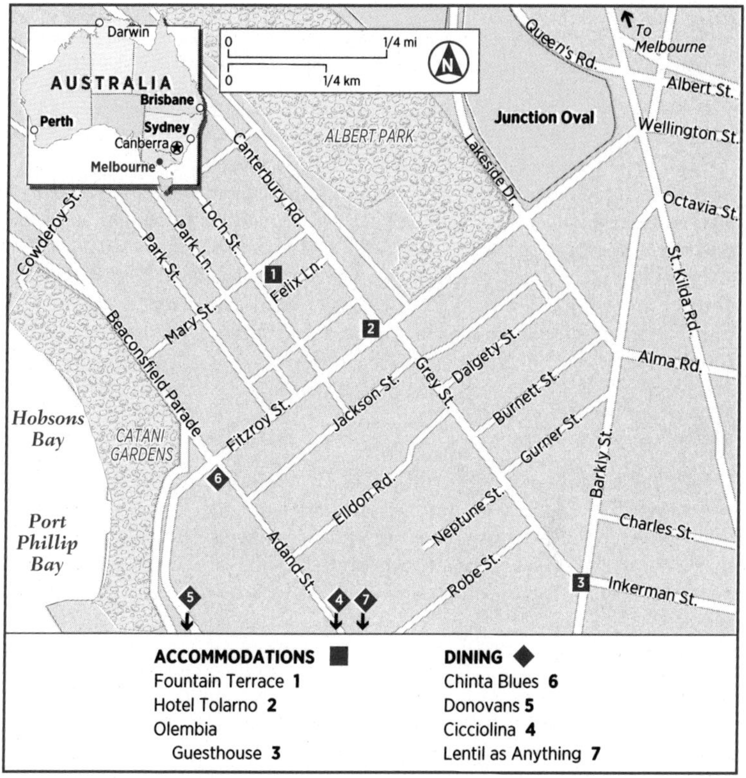

garden, and the Como Suite has a grand piano. The hotel is right in the heart of South Yarra, Melbourne's renowned restaurant, shopping, and cafe district, and is popular with the fashion and entertainment set. The health club is painted in vibrant energizing colors and the pool has a wonderful retractable roof.

630 Chapel St., South Yarra, VIC 3141. (©) **1800/033 400** in Australia or 03/9825 2222. Fax 03/9824 1263. www.mirvachotels.com.au. 107 units. A$255 studio; A$295 open-plan suite; A$335 1-bedroom suite; A$590 2-bedroom suite; A$950 penthouse suite; A$1,150 Como suite. Extra person A$40. Ask about weekend packages. AE, DC, MC, V. Parking A$28. **Amenities:** Restaurant; bar; airport limousine transfers (A$85); babysitting; bikes; concierge; health club; Jacuzzi; indoor pool; room service; sauna; spa. *In room:* A/C, TV w/pay movies, DVD player (on request), CD player w/CD library, hair dryer, Internet (A$10 per hr.; A$29 for 24 hr.), kitchen, minibar.

Cotterville ★ You will love the courtyard gardens as much as the art and music that surround you in this beautifully restored terrace house and will likely go home fast friends with your hosts and their two schnauzers. Owners Howard Neil and Jeremy Vincent are extremely knowledgeable about the city's arts scene—Jeremy works at the Arts Centre and Howard is a former theater and television director. You can join them for "happy hour" drinks at 5pm, and, for an extra A$50 per person (and advance notice), Howard will whip up a three-course gourmet dinner.

204 Williams Rd., Toorak, Melbourne, VIC 3142. ✆ **03/9826 9105** or 0409/900 807 mobile. www.cotterville.com. 2 units with shared bathroom. A$130 single; A$160 double. Weekly rates available. Rates include breakfast. MC, V. Free on-street parking. Train: Hawkesburn. *In room:* TV/DVD.

The Hatton ★ This striking Italianate mansion was built as a hotel in 1902. Its latest incarnation came 5 years ago, when it was meticulously restored and stylishly updated to become a sophisticated and contemporary boutique hotel. Many of the original features—rosettes, cornices, stained-glass windows, wide verandas, and high ceilings—have been retained, and the guest rooms have been fashioned from the original structure, making each an individual space. Clever combinations of old and new—antiques alongside specially commissioned modern art pieces—give it an unusual but welcoming atmosphere. A massive kauri pine counter dominates the front lounge, where you can read the papers or use the guest computer.

65 Park St., South Yarra, VIC 3141. ✆ **03/9868 4800.** Fax 03/9868 4899. www.hatton.com.au. 20 units. A$215–A$240 double; A$350 suite. Extra person A$50. Crib A$30. Rates include continental breakfast. AE, DC, MC, V. Free off-street parking. Tram: No. 8 from Swanston St. *In room:* A/C, TV, CD player, hair dryer, kitchenette, minibar, free Wi-Fi.

Hotel Claremont The high ceilings and the mosaic tiles in the lobby welcome visitors into this old-world hotel. It's an attractive place, though sparsely furnished. The AAA-rated three-star rooms are comfortable enough; each comes with a single, double, or queen-sized bed. Some rooms have a double bed and a single. There is no elevator in this three-story building with 72 stairs, so it could be a bad choice for travelers with disabilities.

189 Toorak Rd., South Yarra, Melbourne, VIC 3141. ✆ **1300/301 630** in Australia, or 03/9826 8000. Fax 03/9827 8652. www.hotelclaremont.com. 77 units, none with bathroom. A$79 twin bunk room; A$89–A$125 double; A$119 triple; A$159 family room; A$42 dorm (6 beds). Extra person A$30. Rates include continental breakfast. AE, DC, MC, V. Off-street parking A$14 per day. Tram: 8 from Swanston St. *In room:* TV, hair dryer, Wi-Fi (A$8 for 1 hr.; A$20 for 24 hr.).

WHERE TO DINE

Melbourne's ethnically diverse population ensures a healthy selection of international cuisines. Chinatown, in the city center, is a fabulous hunting ground for Chinese, Malaysian, Thai, Indonesian, Japanese, and Vietnamese fare, often at bargain prices. Carlton has plenty of Italian cuisine, but the outdoor restaurants on Lygon Street aim at unsuspecting tourists and can be overpriced and disappointing; avoid them. Richmond is crammed with Greek and Vietnamese restaurants, and Fitzroy has cheap Asian, Turkish, Mediterranean, and vegetarian food. To see and be seen, head to Chapel Street or Toorak Road in South Yarra, or to St. Kilda, where you can join the throng of Melbournians dining out along Fitzroy and Acland streets. Most of the cheaper places in Melbourne are strictly BYO (bring your own wine or beer). Smoking is banned by law in cafes and restaurants, so don't even think about lighting up.

In the City Center

EXPENSIVE

Flower Drum ★★★ CANTONESE Praise pours in from all quarters for this upscale restaurant just off Little Bourke Street, Chinatown's main drag. Take a slow

Where to Dine in Central Melbourne

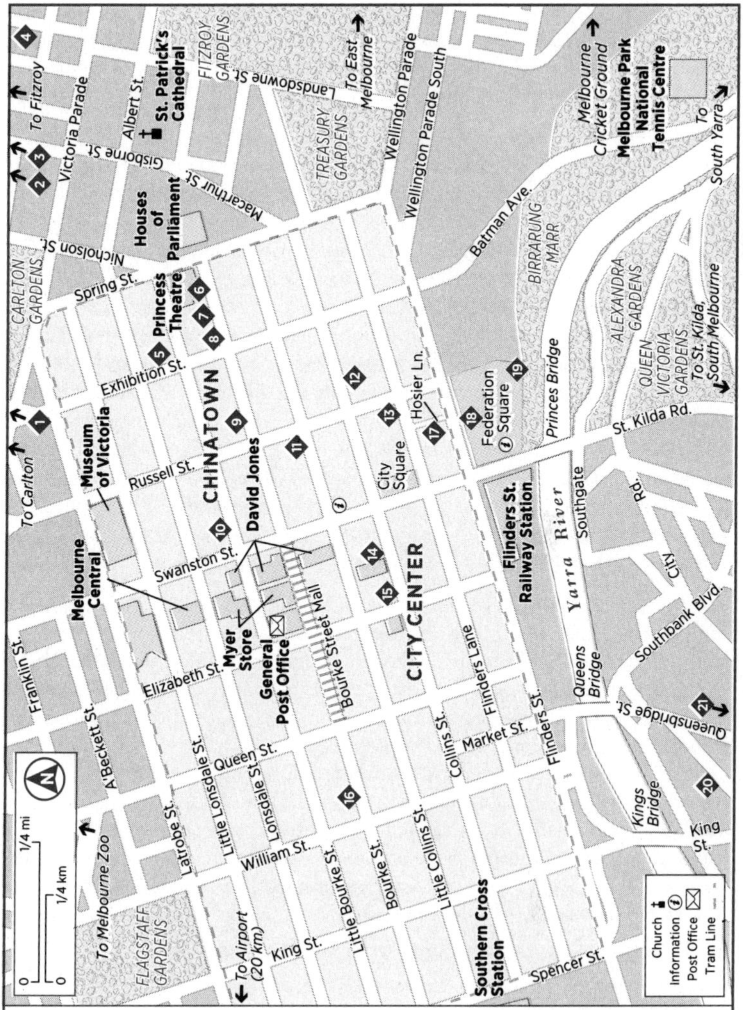

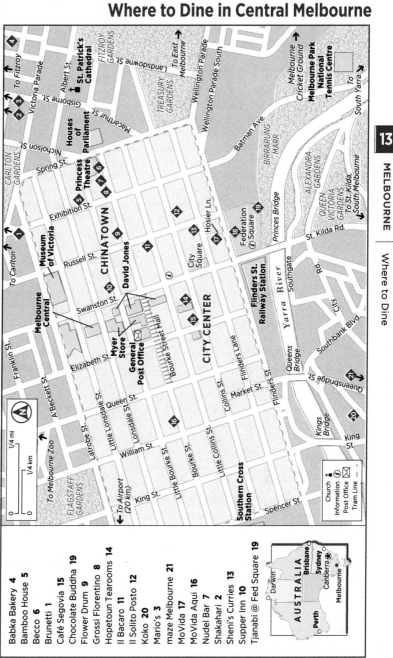

Babka Bakery **4**
Bamboo House **5**
Becco **6**
Brunetti **1**
Café Segovia **15**
Chocolate Buddha **19**
Flower Drum **9**
Grossi Florentino **8**
Hopetoun Tearooms **14**
Il Bacaro **11**
Il Solito Posto **12**
Koko **20**
Mario's **3**
maze Melbourne **21**
MoVida **17**
MoVida Aqui **16**
Nudel Bar **7**
Shakahari **2**
Sheni's Curries **13**
Supper Inn **10**
Tjanabi @ Fed Square **19**

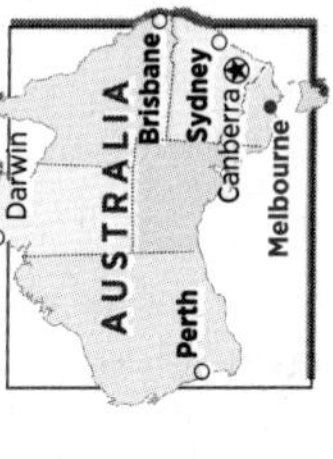

elevator up to the restaurant, which has widely spaced tables (perfect for politicians and businesspeople to clinch their deals). Take note of the specials—the chefs are extremely creative and use the best ingredients they find in the markets each day. The best idea is to put your menu selections into the hands of the waiter. The signature dish is Peking duck. King crab dumplings in soup is a great starter, and you can also order more unusual dishes, such as abalone (at a price: A$135 per 100 grams). The atmosphere is clubby and a bit old-fashioned, but the service is beyond reproach. But be prepared to pay for the privilege.

17 Market Lane. ✆ **03/9662 3655.** www.flower-drum.com. Reservations required. Main courses A$37–A$50. AE, DC, MC, V. Mon–Sat noon–3pm and 6–11pm; Sun 6–10:30pm.

Grossi Florentino ★ ITALIAN Under the management of the Grossi family, this is probably the best Italian restaurant in Melbourne. It has a casual bistro downstairs, next to the Cellar Bar (where you can pick up a bowl of pasta for less than A$20); upstairs is the fine-dining restaurant, with its chandeliers and murals reflecting the Florentine way of life. The food is traditional Italian, with such dishes as rabbit "in porchetta" (boned and rolled, with spices, fennel, and orange and black cabbage); or grass-fed veal filet, with a herb crust, lentils, porcini, and bone marrow. On the menu, too, are risotto, seafood, and steak dishes. Save room for dessert: perhaps the chocolate soufflé with malt ice cream and chocolate syrup? Or you could try the eight-course tasting menu, for A$195 per person, or A$265 per person with matching wines.

80 Bourke St. ✆ **03/9662 1811.** Fax 03/9662 2518. www.grossiflorentino.com. Reservations recommended. Main courses A$39–A$55. AE, DC, MC, V. Mon–Fri noon–3pm; Mon–Sat 6–11pm.

Koko ★★ JAPANESE Though you'll find plenty of Japanese sushi and noodle bars around Chinatown, there's nothing quite like raw fish with a bit of panache. A visit to Crown Casino Entertainment Complex can be a memorable experience in itself, but stop off here and you'll wish you could remember these tastes forever. The restaurant has contemporary-traditional decor, with a goldfish pond in the center of the main dining room and wonderful views over the city. There are separate teppanyaki grills and screened tatami rooms where you sit on the matted floor. There's a vast and changing seasonal menu that includes lots of seafood dishes, including pan-fried Patagonian tooth-fish and tempura baby lobster, or you can opt for a set menu to take the agony out of choosing. A large selection of different sakes helps digestion.

Level 3, Crown Towers, Southbank. ✆ **03/9292 6886.** www.kokoatcrown.com.au. Reservations required. Main courses A$36–A$49. AE, DC, MC, V. Daily noon–2:30pm and 6–10:30pm.

maze Melbourne ★★ FRENCH/AUSTRALIAN There was much hype surrounding the opening of British celebrity chef Gordon Ramsay's first Melbourne restaurant in mid-2010—and much discussion about whether it lived up to the hype. The opening was just weeks before press time for this book; on my one visit, I found the service impeccable, the food delicious and well-priced. The menu has quite a few dishes not often found in Australian restaurants, including a seared leg of rabbit and slow-cooked pigeon breast, but there are plenty of more mainstream options, such as barramundi, salmon, and steaks. A chef's menu offers seven courses for A$95 per person. At night, the restaurant is candlelit, and if you want a more casual option, there's maze Grill.

Level 1, Crown Metropole, Whiteman St. (at Clarendon St.), Southbank. ✆ **03/9292 8300.** www.gordonramsay.com/mazemelbourne. Reservations recommended. Main courses A$19–A$33. AE, MC, V. Daily 6:.30–10:30am, noon–2:30pm, and 6–11pm.

MODERATE

Bamboo House ★ CHINESE/CANTONESE If Flower Drum (see above) is full or breaks your budget, try this place, esteemed by both the Chinese community and local business big shots. The service is a pleasure, and the food is worth writing home about. The waiters will help you construct a feast from the myriad Cantonese and northern Chinese dishes. It's worth ordering ahead to get a taste of the signature dish, Szechuan crispy fragrant duck. Other popular dishes include pan-fried beef dumplings and spring onion pancakes. The set menus for two to four people start at A$48 per person, for which you'll get eight or nine dishes.

47 Little Bourke St. ✆ **03/9662 1565.** www.bamboohouse.com.au. Reservations recommended. Main courses A$25–A$32. AE, DC, MC, V. Mon–Fri noon–3pm; Mon–Sat 5:30–11pm; Sun 5:30–10pm.

Becco ★ MODERN ITALIAN Tucked away on a quiet lane, this favorite of Melbournians has not disappointed in 7 years of winning awards and accolades. Here you find stylish service and stylish customers, all without pretension. The cuisine mixes Italian favors with Australian flair. Try the roast duck with muscatel and grappa sauce, one of the tasty pasta dishes, or the specials, which your waiter will fill you in on. If you prefer something lighter, there's a bar menu of equally tempting dishes from A$6.50 to A$22. On the upstairs level is the ultracool late-night bar, **Bellavista Social Club** (p. 639).

11–25 Crossley St., near Bourke St. ✆ **03/9663 3000.** www.becco.com.au. Main courses A$38–A$49. AE, DC, MC, V. Mon–Sat noon–3pm and 6–11pm; Sun 5:30–10pm.

Chocolate Buddha 🎁 NOODLES This place offers mostly organic produce, including some organic wines. Based generally on Japanese-inspired noodle, ramen, and soba dishes to which the kitchen adds meat, chicken, or seafood, it's casual yet particularly satisfying dining. The food is creative, and the view across the square to the Yarra River and Southbank is a delight at dusk.

Federation Sq., corner of Flinders and Swanson sts. ✆ **03/9654 5688.** www.chocolatebuddha.com.au. Main courses A$20–A$32. AE, MC, V. Daily noon–10:30pm.

Il Bacaro ★ ITALIAN Walk into Il Bacaro and you'll feel as if you've been transported to Venice. Dominated by a horseshoe-shaped bar, it's jam-packed with small tables and weaving waiters carrying such dishes as organic baby chicken filled with pumpkin and ricotta and wrapped in prosciutto, served on an oyster mushroom ragout. The pasta dishes and the risotto of the day always go down well, as do the salad side dishes. It's often crowded at lunch with businesspeople digging into the excellent wine list.

168–170 Little Collins St. ✆ **03/9654 6778.** www.ilbacaro.com.au. Reservations recommended. Main courses A$26–A$42. AE, DC, MC, V. Mon–Sat noon–3pm and 6–11pm.

Il Solito Posto NORTHERN ITALIAN This below-ground restaurant consists of two parts. The casual bistro has a blackboard menu offering good pastas, soups, and salads. Then there's the sharper and more upmarket trattoria, with its a la carte menu offering the likes of steak, fish, and veal dishes such as *osso buco* or twice-cooked duck breast filet, served on polenta, with baby vegetables and a blood orange and blueberry jus. The coffee is excellent, too.

113 Collins St., basement (enter through George Parade). ✆ **03/9654 4466.** www.ilsolitoposto.com.au. Reservations recommended. Main courses A$25–A$33 in bistro, A$22–A$44 in trattoria. AE, DC, MC, V. Mon–Fri 7:30am–1am; Sat 9am–1am. Closed late Dec to early Jan.

MoVida ★★ SPANISH MoVida chef and co-owner Frank Camorra was born in Barcelona and spent his first 5 years in his parents' hometown of Córdoba in Andalucía before coming to Australia. His restaurant reflects the spirit of Spain, relaxed and fun, with seriously good food and good wine. Melbournians flock here, and it's truly one of those places I was tempted to keep a secret (if that's possible due to the fact that everyone talks about how great it is). MoVida offers a choice of tapas (small individual dishes) or *raciones* (plates to share among two or more people, or a larger dish for one). Specials are available every night to keep the regulars happy. And if you have a large group, or want to dine outdoors, there is now **MoVida Aqui,** at level 1, 500 Bourke St. (entry off Little Bourke St.), which has a huge casual dining area and a terrace, and serves the same great food.

1 Hosier Lane. ✆ **03/9663 3038** (for all restaurants). www.movida.com.au. Reservations recommended (maximum group is 6). Tapa A$3.50–A$8; racion (main courses) A$9–A$20. AE, DC, MC, V. Daily noon–late.

Nudel Bar NOODLES A favorite with city slickers, the Nudel Bar serves a variety of noodle dishes to diners at the crowded tables and bar. Examples include cold, spicy green-tea noodles and *mie goreng* (a noodle dish with peanuts and, here, often chicken). The signature dish is macaroni and cheese; and sticky rice pudding is a favorite for dessert.

76 Bourke St. ✆ **03/9662 9100.** Reservations recommended Fri–Sat night. Main courses A$13–A$24. AE, DC, MC, V. Mon–Sat 11am–10pm (closes at 3pm Mon in winter).

Tjanabi @ Fed Square INDIGENOUS AUSTRALIAN If you want to get a taste of what indigenous Australians have been eating for thousands of years, stop in at Aboriginal elder Carolyn Briggs' Tjanabi (it means "to celebrate") restaurant at Federation Square. Native produce, including plants, fruits, and berries (such as native pepper, lemon myrtle, roasted wattleseed, and saltbush leaves), matched with quality Australian game (kangaroo, emu, barramundi) and fresh steaks from regional Victoria are on the menu. Service can be slow, even when they are not busy—but the food is very good. A good option, especially at lunch, is a "taster plate" offering a selection of four, six, or eight dishes from a special menu. The walls are adorned with contemporary Aboriginal artworks.

Federation Sq. ✆ **03/9662 2155.** www.tjanabi.com.au. Reservations recommended. Taster plates A$20, A$28, or A$35. Main courses A$24–A$38. AE, DC, MC, V. Daily 11am–11pm.

INEXPENSIVE

Café Segovia ★★ 🎁 CAFE This is one of my favorites. Café Segovia is always friendly, always busy, and in an atmospheric laneway. It has an intimate interior, and there's also seating outside in the arcade, but you'll have to come early at lunchtime to nab a chair. It serves typical cafe food, such as focaccias, cakes, and light meals (but the servings are generous). There's live music Thursday and Friday.

33 Block Place. ✆ **03/9650 2373.** Main courses A$16–A$27. AE, DC, MC, V. Mon–Sat 8am–11pm; Sun 9am–5pm.

Hopetoun Tearooms ★ CAFE The first cup of coffee served in this Melbourne institution left the pot in 1892. It's very civilized, with green-and-white Regency wallpaper and marble tables, but fine china has gone by the wayside in favor of rather chunky railway-style cups, and the sugar is in paper packets. The cakes are very good. Scones, croissants, and grilled food are also available. The clientele is a mix of old ladies and students, with the odd tourist or businessman. A minimum charge of A$5 per person applies from noon to 2pm.

Shops 1 and 2, Block Arcade, 280–282 Collins St. ✆/fax **03/9650 2777.** Main courses A$12–A$15; sandwiches A$6.50–A$9.50. AE, DC, MC, V. Mon–Thurs 8:30am–5pm; Fri 8:30am–6pm; Sat 10am–3:30pm.

Sheni's Curries SRI LANKAN This tiny (it seats 30), basic, very busy place offers a range of excellent-value authentic Sri Lankan curries. You can dine here or take your lunch special to go. Choose from three vegetable dishes and a selection of meat and seafood options. All meals come with rice, three types of chutney, and a pappadum. You can also buy extra items such as samosas and roti.

Shop 16, 161 Collins St. (corner of Flinders Lane and Russell St., opposite the entrance to the Grand Hyatt). ✆ **03/9654 3535.** Main courses A$5.50–A$15. No credit cards. Mon–Fri 8am–9pm.

Supper Inn CANTONESE Head here if you get the Chinese-food munchies late at night. It's a friendly place with a mixed crowd of locals and tourists chowing down on such dishes as steaming bowls of *congee* (rice-based porridge), barbecued suckling pig, mud crab, or stuffed scallops. Everything here is the real thing.

15 Celestial Ave. ✆/fax **03/9663 4759.** Reservations recommended. Main courses A$14–A$25. AE, DC, MC, V. Daily 5:30pm–2:30am.

In Carlton

Brunetti ★ ITALIAN Don't be daunted by the crowds around the cake counters—and there will be crowds. This is a real Italian experience. If you can get past the mouthwatering array of excellent cakes, have lunch in the a la carte restaurant section for authentic Italian cuisine, done very well. Or pop in for breakfast, coffee and cake, or a gelato. If you can't get to Carlton, there's the cafe-style **Brunetti City Square** at Swanston Street and Flinders Lane in the city.

194–204 Faraday St., Carlton. ✆ **03/9347 2801.** www.brunetti.com.au. Main courses A$14–A$19. AE, DC, MC, V. Sun–Thurs 6am–11pm, Fri–Sat 6am–midnight. Tram: 1, 15, 21, or 22 traveling north on Swanston St.

Shakahari VEGETARIAN Good vegetarian food isn't just a meal without meat; it's a creation in its own right. Shakahari assures you of a creative meal that's not at all bland. The large restaurant is quite low-key, but the service can be a bit inconsistent. The "Satay Legend"—skewered, lightly fried vegetables and tofu pieces with a mild but spicy peanut sauce—is a perennial favorite. Also available are curries, croquettes, tempura avocado, and a fragrant laksa. Wine is available by the glass.

201–203 Faraday St., Carlton. ✆ **03/9347 3848.** www.shakahari.com.au. Main courses A$20–A$21. AE, DC, MC, V. Mon–Sat noon–3pm; Sun–Thurs 6–9:30pm; Fri–Sat 6–10pm. Tram: 1, 15, 21, or 22 traveling north along Swanston St.

In Fitzroy

Mario's ITALIAN This place has ambience, groovy '60s decor, great coffee, and impeccable service. Offerings include a range of pastas and cakes. Breakfast is served all day. The art on the wall of the cafe, all by local artists, is always interesting—and for sale.

303 Brunswick St., Fitzroy. ✆ **03/9417 3343.** Reservations not accepted. Main courses A$11–A$21. No credit cards. Daily 7am–11pm.

The Staff of Life

The aroma of fresh bread will attract you to Babka Bakery, a Russian-style cafe-bakery that is nearly always packed. Come for breakfast or a light lunch of eggs on fresh sourdough, or any of the quiches, tarts, and brioches. Or perhaps try the homemade borscht. It's at 358 Brunswick St., in Fitzroy (✆ 03/9416 0091), and is open Tuesday to Sunday 7am to 7pm.

Seaside Dining in St. Kilda

Chinta Blues MALAYSIAN Head to this very popular eatery if you're looking for simple, satisfying food with a healthy touch of spice. The big sellers are laksa, *mie goreng,* chicken curry, *sambal* spinach, and a chicken dish called "*Ayam* Blues." Lots of noodles, too. It's very busy, but usually there's not more than a 30-minute wait for a table. They do takeout as well.

6 Acland St., St. Kilda. ✆ **03/9534 9233.** www.chintablues.com.au. Reservations not accepted at dinner. Main courses A$13–A$25. AE, MC, V. Daily noon–2:30pm (4:30pm on Sun); Mon–Thurs 6–10:15pm; Fri–Sat 6–11pm; Sun 5:30–10pm. Tram: 16 from Swanston St. or 96 from Bourke St.

Cicciolina ★★ CONTEMPORARY It's difficult enough to get a table at this wonderful place, which doesn't take bookings, without encouraging more people to line up. But I'd be depriving you of a terrific night out if I kept quiet. So let's just say that if you're looking for somewhere that's intimate, crowded, well-run, and has superb but simple food, you should look no further. You may have to wait for an hour or so for your seat (have a drink in the back bar, and they'll call you), but it will be worth it for delights such as yellowfin tuna carpaccio soused in lime-infused olive oil, beef carpaccio crusted with mustard and coriander seeds, or—my favorite—spaghettini tossed with spinach, chili, and oil.

130 Acland St., St. Kilda. ✆ **03/9525 3333.** www.cicciolinastkilda.com.au. Main courses A$19–A$40. AE, DC, MC, V. Daily noon–11pm (10pm on Sun). Tram: 16 from Swanston St., or 94 or 96 from Bourke St.

Donovans ★★ CONTEMPORARY A glass in hand while the sun goes down over St. Kilda beach, watched from the veranda at Donovans, is a perfect way to end the day. Gail and Kevin Donovan have transformed a 1920s bathing pavilion into a welcoming restaurant that's designed so you feel you're in their home (or at least their beach house). Lots of cushions, a log fire, coffee-table books, and the sound of jazz and breakers on the beach complete the picture. If that's not enough, the menu includes a mind-boggling array of dishes, many big enough for two, and a children's menu. Chef Robert Castellani's trademarks include steamed mussels, linguine with seafood, and stuffed squid.

40 Jacka Blvd., St. Kilda. ✆ **03/9534 8221.** www.donovanshouse.com.au. Reservations recommended. Main courses A$25–A$48. AE, DC, MC, V. Daily noon–10:30pm. Tram: 12 from Collins St., 16 from Swanston St., or 94 or 96 from Bourke St.

In Docklands

Mecca Bah ★★ 🎁 ☺ MIDDLE EASTERN Overlooking the Yarra River in the up-and-coming waterside precinct of Docklands, and a short trip from the city

Pay What You Think

With a novel approach that's not surprisingly become a hit, vegetarian restaurant Lentil as Anything has a menu without prices. Here, you eat—then pay whatever you feel the meal and service was worth. The food is organic, with lots of noodles and vegetables and such things as tofu, curries, and stir-fries. Before you leave, you put your money in a box. There are two restaurants. The original is at 41 Blessington St., St. Kilda (✆ 03/9534 5833), open noon to 9pm daily, and you can BYO liquor here. A second outlet is at the Abbotsford Convent, 1 Saint Heliers St., Abbotsford (✆ 03/9419 6444), open daily from 9am to 9pm (but not serving breakfast on Mondays, just drinks). They take cash only. Check the website www.lentilasanything.com.

center, is this highly recommended and excellent Middle Eastern restaurant. You could go for a main course, such as a lamb or chicken tagine, but the best way to eat is to order several of the *meze* plates—little dishes of delicacies. Expect the likes of pastry filled with Middle Eastern cheeses; chickpea battered mussels; or spicy lamb and pine nut *boureks* (meat-filled pastries)—whatever you choose, you'll be really impressed. There's also an interesting range of Turkish pizzas, too. The wine list is good and not too expensive. You could cruise up the river to get here with Melbourne River Cruises (see "Getting Around," earlier in this chapter).

55 Newquay Promenade, Docklands. ✆ **03/9642 1300.** www.meccabah.com. Reservations not accepted. Main courses A$19–A$23; *meze* plates A$6–A$14. AE, DC, MC, V. Daily 11am–11pm. Tram: 30 or 48 from Latrobe or Swanston sts.

SEEING THE SIGHTS

Melbourne's attractions may not have quite the fame as some of Sydney's, but visitors come here to experience the contrasts of old-world architecture and the exciting feel of a truly multicultural city.

The Top Attractions

Eureka Skydeck 88 The vertigo-challenging Eureka Skydeck 88 is the highest public vantage point in the Southern Hemisphere. On the 88th floor of the Eureka Tower, a viewing deck gives a 360-degree panorama of the city from 285m (935 ft.) above the ground. But there's more adrenaline-pumping action than just the view: A huge glass cube called the Edge is actually a 6-ton horizontal elevator, which emerges from inside the walls of Skydeck 88 carrying 12 passengers out over the tower's east side. As the opaque glass cube reaches its full extension, the reinforced, 45-millimeter-thick (1¾-in.) glass becomes clear, giving passengers uninterrupted views below, above, and to three sides. All this accompanied by recorded sounds of creaking chains and breaking glass—just to scare you more! Actually, it's not as scary as it sounds and the ride is only 4 minutes long.

Eureka Tower, Riverside Quay, South Bank. ✆ **03/9693 8888.** www.eurekaskydeck.com.au. Admission A$17 adults, A$9 children 4–16, A$39 family of 4; A$12 adults, A$8 children, A$29 families extra for the Edge. Daily 10am–10pm (last entry 9:30pm). Closed Dec 25–26 and Good Friday.

Federation Square ★★ You have to get into Federation Square, physically, to appreciate it. The controversial design—Melbournians either love it or hate it (I fall into the former category)—has given the city a gathering place, and you only have to visit on the weekends to see that it works. A conglomerate of attractions are centered on a large open piazza-style area cobbled with misshapen paving. Here you'll find the **Ian Potter Centre** (see below), **Champions—The Australian Racing Museum & Hall of Fame,** and the **Australian Centre for the Moving Image (ACMI),** which has two state-of-the-art cinemas and large areas where visitors can view movies, videos, and digital media. A one-stop visitor center (see "Visitor Information," earlier in this chapter) operates, and there are many cafes and coffee shops throughout the precinct. It's worth visiting "Fed Square" just to see the architecture, made up of strange geometrical designs, and the glassed atrium. Lots of events happen in the square's 450-seat amphitheater, including theatrical performances and free concerts. Other events take place on the plaza and along the banks of the Yarra River. Every Saturday from 11am to 5pm in the Atrium, you'll find Melbourne's biggest **book market,** with 5,000 titles, new and second-hand.

Flinders St. (at St. Kilda Rd.). www.fedsquare.com. Free admission; charges for some special events and exhibitions. Outdoor spaces open 24 hr. Tram: City Circle.

The Ian Potter Centre ★★ This fascinating gallery, featuring 20 rooms dedicated to Australian art, opened in 2002 in the heart of Federation Square. Part of the National Gallery of Victoria (NGV), it contains the largest collection of Australian art in the country, including works by Sidney Nolan, Russell Drysdale, and Tom Roberts, as well as Aboriginal and Torres Strait Islanders. Some 20,000 objects are stored here, but only about 800 are on display at any one time. Aboriginal art and colonial art collections are the centerpieces of the gallery, but you will find modern paintings here, too. Temporary exhibitions include anything from ceramics to shoes.

Federation Sq. (corner of Flinders St. and St. Kilda Rd.). ✆ **03/8660 2222**. www.ngv.vic.gov.au. Free admission. Tues–Sun 10am–5pm. Closed Mon (except public holidays), Good Friday, Dec 25, and until 1pm on Apr 25. Tram: City Circle. Bus: City Explorer.

IMAX Theatre ☺ This eight-story movie screen rivals the world's largest screen, at Sydney's Darling Harbour. Recent subjects have been surfing in Tahiti, dinosaurs, the deep oceans, and African safaris. As part of the Melbourne Museum precinct, your movie ticket also gets you free admission to the museum.

Melbourne Museum Complex, Rathdowne St., Carlton. ✆ **03/9663 5454.** www.imaxmelbourne.com.au. Admission from A$18 adults, A$13 children 3–15, A$50 family of 4. Daily 10am–10pm. Closed Dec 25. Tram: City Circle.

Melbourne Aquarium ★★ ☺ The Melbourne Aquarium has undergone a A$28-million expansion, opening its prize exhibit in late 2008—an Antarctica display featuring King and Gentoo penguins playing in the pool (with underwater viewing) and sliding across the snow-covered ice. The 18 beguiling birds are Australia's only collection of sub-Antarctic penguins. The aquarium also features a reef exhibit, some interesting jellyfish displays, and a 2.2-million-liter (581,000-gallon) Oceanarium walk-through tank with larger fish, sharks, and rays. There are dive-feeding demonstrations at 10:30am and 2pm. You can also take a glass-bottom-boat ride over the Oceanarium and a "behind the scenes" tour with divers and marine biologists. The 45-minute tour costs A$14 adults and A$7.50 children 4 to 15, and leaves daily

Melbourne Attractions

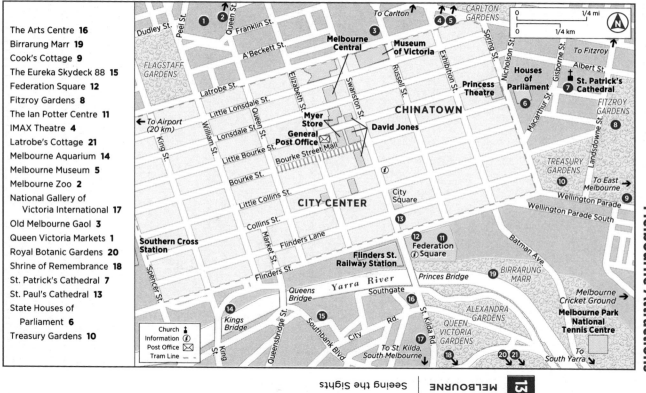

The Arts Centre **16**
Birrarung Marr **19**
Cook's Cottage **9**
The Eureka Skydeck 88 **15**
Federation Square **12**
Fitzroy Gardens **8**
The Ian Potter Centre **11**
IMAX Theatre **4**
Latrobe's Cottage **21**
Melbourne Aquarium **14**
Melbourne Museum **5**
Melbourne Zoo **2**
National Gallery of Victoria International **17**
Old Melbourne Gaol **3**
Queen Victoria Markets **1**
Royal Botanic Gardens **20**
Shrine of Remembrance **18**
St. Patrick's Cathedral **7**
St. Paul's Cathedral **13**
State Houses of Parliament **6**
Treasury Gardens **10**

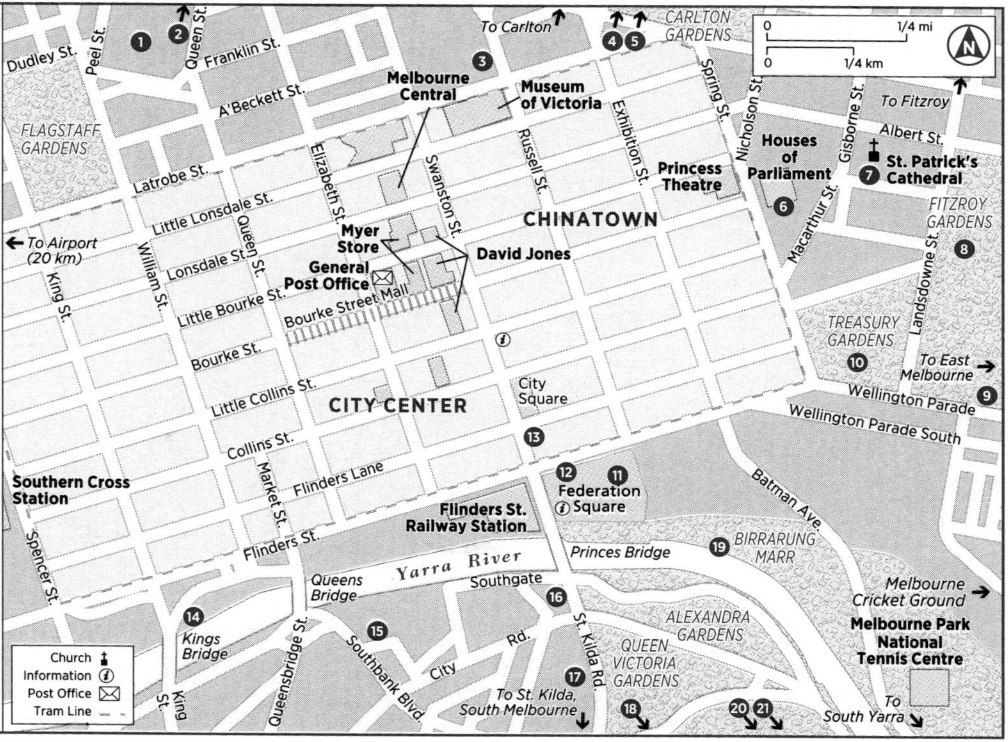

at 10:45am, 12:15pm, 1:15pm, and 2:15pm. You can also arrange to dive with the sharks for A$242 for qualified divers or A$349 for nondivers. Booking are essential for this; call ✆ **03/9510 9081.**

Corner of Flinders and Kings St. ✆ **03/9923 5999** info line or 03/9923 5925. www.melbourneaquarium.com.au. Admission A$33 adults, A$19 children 3–15, A$62–A$88 families, extra child A$14. Daily 9:30am–6pm (until 9pm Jan 1–26). Tram: City Circle.

Melbourne Museum ★ ☺ This museum opposite the 19th-century Royal Exhibition Buildings is Australia's largest and one of the most interesting. For me, the highlight is Bunjikata, the award-winning Aboriginal and Torres Strait Islander Centre. Others include a real blue whale skeleton, an indoor rainforest, and a truly brilliant insect and butterfly collection with lots of real-life exhibits, including cockroaches, ant colonies, and huge spiders. Apart from that, there are interactive exhibits and science displays, and bits and pieces of social history, including a stuffed racehorse called Phar Lap. Check out the brightly colored Children's Museum, which will bring hours of enjoyment to the little ones. Allow 2 hours.

Melbourne Museum, 11 Nicholson St., Carlton. ✆ **13 11 02** in Victoria, 1300/130 152 in Australia or 03/8341 7777. http://museumvictoria.com.au. Admission A$8 adults, free for children 15 and under. Daily 10am–5pm. Closed Good Friday and Dec 25. Tram: 86 or 96 to the Museum and Royal Exhibition Building tram stop at the corner of Nicholson and Gertrude sts., or the free City Circle Tram to Carlton Gardens.

Melbourne Zoo ★★ ☺ Built in 1862, this is the oldest zoo in the world and makes a great day out with kids. There are some 3,000 animals here, including kangaroos, wallabies, echidnas, koalas, wombats, and platypuses. Rather than being locked in cages, most animals are in almost natural surroundings or well-tended gardens. Don't miss the butterfly house, with its thousands of colorful occupants flying around; the free-flight aviary; the lowland gorilla exhibit; and the treetop orangutan exhibit. Allow at least 90 minutes if you just want to see the Australian natives, and around 4 hours for the entire zoo.

Elliott Ave., Parkville. ✆ **03/9285 9300.** www.zoo.org.au. Admission A$24 adults, A$12 children 4–15, A$55–A$77 families. Daily 9am–5pm. Free parking. Tram: 55 going north on William St. to stop 25; 19 from Elizabeth St. to stop 16 (then a short walk to your left, following signposts). Train: Royal Park Station.

National Gallery of Victoria International The NGV International is a showcase for Australia's finest collections of international art. There are four Gainsboroughs and four Constables here, as well as paintings by the likes of Bonnard, Delacroix, Van Dyck, El Greco, Monet, Manet, Magritte, and Rembrandt. Architecturally, the building is a masterpiece, with high ceilings, fabulous lighting, and great open spaces.

180 St. Kilda Rd. ✆ **03/8620 2222.** www.ngv.vic.gov.au. Free admission to general collection; fees for some temporary exhibitions. Wed–Mon 10am–5pm. Closed Good Friday, Dec 25, and until 1pm on Apr 25 (Anzac Day). Tram: 1, 3, 5, 6, 8, 16, 22, 25, 64, 67, or 72 from Swanston St. to Victorian Arts Centre stop (ask driver).

National Sports Museum In a nation of sporting enthusiasts, it seems fitting finally to have a National Sports Museum. This outstanding museum, opened in March 2008 within the Melbourne Cricket Ground (p. 633), tells Australia's sporting story from its early beginnings to the present, celebrating Australian sporting heroes, memorable moments, and achievements. It covers a range of sports, including Australian football, basketball, boxing, cricket (it includes the Australian Cricket Hall of Fame), cycling, golf, hockey, netball, Olympic and Paralympic Games, rugby union, rugby league, soccer, and tennis. It also tells the Melbourne Cricket Ground (MCG) story, features the Sport Australia Hall of Fame, and includes a large interactive area. The extensive collection includes Australia's first ever Olympic gold medal, Ian Thorpe's swimsuit, and the Malvern Star bicycle that Hubert Opperman rode in his record-breaking 24-hour cycling marathon in Sydney in 1940. Allow 1 hour (more if you are a real sports fan).

During MCG major event days, including the AFL Grand Final, Day 1 of the Boxing Day Test, and Anzac Day football, access to the National Sports Museum (at half-price) is restricted to patrons holding an event day ticket. Opening hours on weekends when events are being held within the MCG arena will vary. Check the website for details.

Melbourne Cricket Ground, Brunton Ave., Richmond. ✆ **03/9657 8879.** www.nsm.org.au. Admission A$15 adults, A$8 children 5–15, or A$50 families of 6 for museum only; A$30 adults, A$12 children, or A$60 families for museum and MCG tour. Daily 10am–5pm (last admission 4:30pm). Closed Good Friday and Christmas Day. Bus: Melbourne City Tourist Shuttle. Tram: 75 or 70 from the city center. Train: Jolimont. Entry is through Gate 3 at the MCG.

Old Melbourne Gaol ★★★ This is one of my favorite Melbourne attractions. Maybe I'm mad to enjoy being locked up in a cell, but the Old Melbourne Gaol's **Crime & Justice Experience** is an interesting way to spend a few hours. Start off at the historic old prison, with its tiny cells and spooky collection of death masks and artifacts of 19th-century prison life. Some 135 hangings took place here, including that of notorious bushranger (and Australian folk hero) Ned Kelly, in 1880. The scaffold where he was hanged still stands, and his gun, as well as a suit of armor used by a member of his gang, is on display. The jail closed in 1929. Profiles of former prisoners give a fascinating perspective of what it was like to be locked up here. Each Saturday, free performances of "The Real Ned Kelly Story—Such a Life" are held at 12:30 and 2pm. (***Be warned:*** When we attended, a small girl burst into tears.) Then move next door for a guided tour of the former City Watch House to find out first-hand what it might have been like to spend time here. The lockup, which operated from 1908 to 1994, is just across the road from the scene of one of Melbourne's most notorious crimes, the 1986 bombing of the Russell Street police station. There's role-playing involved for everyone, and it can be quite confronting for children. During holiday times, you can also visit the adjacent former Magistrate's Court and take part in a reenactment of a real life court case, the trial of Elizabeth Scott, the first woman hanged in Victoria. Chilling night tours run every Monday, Wednesday, Friday, and Saturday, where you can experience the jail by candlelight with a "hangman," who will recount stories of the jail, its inmates, and his infamous art—not for the fainthearted or children under 12. Tickets, available from Ticketek (✆ **13 28 49** or www.ticketek.com.au), cost A$30 for adults, A$23 for children under 15.

Russell St. ✆ **03/9663 7228.** www.oldmelbournegaol.com.au. Admission A$21 adults, A$11 children, A$49 families of 6. Daily 9:30am–5pm. Closed Good Friday and Dec 25. Tram: City Circle to corner of Russell and Latrobe sts.

Parliament House Victoria Now the home of the Victorian Parliament, this monument to Victorian (as in Queen Victoria) architecture at the top of a run of sandstone steps was built in 1856. During the Australian Federation (1900–27), it was used as the national parliament. When the state government is in session—generally on Tuesday afternoon and all day Wednesday and Thursday between March and July, and again between August and November (there's a break btw. sessions)—you can view the proceedings from the public gallery. However, you should ring ahead or check the website, as sitting times do vary. During nonsitting times, both the opulent Upper House and the less ornate Lower House chambers are open to the public. Allow 30 minutes.

Spring St. ✆ **03/9651 8568.** www.parliament.vic.gov.au. Mon–Fri 9am–5pm. Free guided tours Mon–Fri at 9:30, 10:30, 11:30am, 1:30, 2:30, and 3:45pm when Parliament is not in session. Bookings are not necessary.

Queen Victoria Market This Melbourne institution covers several blocks. Ignore the hundreds of stalls selling everything from live rabbits to bargain clothes. There's a lot of junk here and the crowds can be awful. The best part of the markets are the indoor food section, particularly the interesting delicatessen section. The 2-hour **Foodies Dream Tour** ★ of the market explores its food and heritage and is well worth doing. It departs Tuesday, Thursday, Friday, and Saturday at 10am and costs A$35 per person, including generous tastings. Bookings (✆ **03/9320 5822**) are essential. **Night markets** are held every Wednesday from 5:30 to 10pm in summer (from late Nov to late Mar, except the last week of Dec).

Btw. Peel, Victoria, Elizabeth, and Therry sts. on the northern edge of the city center. ✆ **03/9320 5822.** www.qvm.com.au. Tues and Thurs 6am–2pm; Fri 6am–5pm; Sat 6am–3pm; Sun 9am–4pm. Closed public holidays. Tram: Any tram traveling north along William St. or Elizabeth St.

Rippon Lea Estate This grand Victorian house, 8km (5 miles) from the city center, is worth a visit to get a feel for old-money Melbourne. Socialite Sir Frederick Thomas Sargood built Rippon Lea House between 1868 and 1903; a pool and ballroom were added in the 1930s. Though the Romanesque architecture is interesting (note the stained glass and polychrome brickwork), the downside is that entry to the house is by guided tour only. (I prefer to wander at my own pace.) The real attraction is the 5.3 hectares (13 acres) of landscaped gardens, which include a conservatory, lake, and lookout tower. The tearoom is open on weekends, public holidays, and during school vacations, from 11am to 4pm. Allow 2 hours.

192 Hotham St., Elsternwick. ✆ **03/9523 6095.** Admission A$12 adults, A$6.50 children under 16, A$30 families of 6; garden only A$7 adults, A$3 children, A$17 families. Daily 10am–5pm (last entry at 4:30pm). Daily guided tours of house every half-hour 10:30am–3:30pm. Closed Good Friday and Dec 25. Tram: 67 to stop 42; then walk up Hotham St. Bus: 216/219 from Bourke and Queen sts. in the city to stop 4. Train: Sandringham line from Flinders St. station to Rippon Lea station.

St. Patrick's Cathedral Though lacking the intricacy of design of St. Paul's (see below), Roman Catholic St. Patrick's is another interesting Gothic Revival construction with exceptional stained-glass windows. Built between 1858 and 1940 (consecrated in 1897), St. Patrick's was closely associated with immigrants from Ireland escaping the mid-19th-century potato famine. In the courtyard out front is a statue of the Irish patriot Daniel O'Connell.

Corner Gisborne St. and Cathedral Place, East Melbourne. ✆ **03/9662 2233.** www.stpatrickscathedral.org.au. Free admission. Mon–Fri 6:30am–6pm; Sat–Sun 7:30am–7:30pm; public holidays 9am–noon.

St. Paul's Cathedral Built from 1880 to 1892 from the designs of William Butterfield, a famous English Gothic Revival architect, St. Paul's Cathedral is noteworthy for its decorative interior and the English organ built by T. S. Lewis. Step in to see mosaics on the walls, Victorian tessellated tiles on the floors, woodcarvings, and stained-glass windows. The cathedral sports the second-highest spire (98m/321 ft.) in the Anglican Communion. A boys' choir sings at 5:10pm Tuesday through Friday during school times, and at Sunday services. Outside is a statue of Matthew Flinders, the first sailor to navigate the Australian mainland between 1801 and 1803.

Flinders and Swanston sts. ✆ **03/9650 3791.** www.stpaulscathedral.org.au. Sun–Fri 8am–6pm; Sat 9am–5pm. Services Sun 8, 9, and 10:30am; Evensong 6pm. Eucharist Mon–Fri 7:45am, 12:15pm, 5:10pm; Sat 12:15pm. Cathedral shop daily 9:45am–3:45pm.

Parks & Gardens

Birrarung Marr, along the Yarra River east of Federation Square on Batman Avenue (✆ **03/9658 9658;** www.melbourne.vic.gov.au/parks), is Melbourne's first new major parkland in more than 100 years. *Birrarung* means "river of mists" in the Woiwurrung language of the Wurundjeri people who originally inhabited the area; *marr* equates with the side of the river. Wide-open spaces and large, sculptured terraces were designed to host some of Melbourne's best events and festivals throughout the year, and the terraces give way to spectacular views of the city, Southbank, King's Domain, and the Yarra River.

The **Royal Botanic Gardens ★★**, 2km (1¼ miles) south of the city on Birdwood Avenue, off St. Kilda Road (✆ **03/9252 2429;** www.rbg.vic.gov.au), are the best gardens in Australia and well worth a few hours of wandering. More than 40 hectares (99 acres) are lush and blooming with more than 12,000 plant species from all over the world. Don't miss a visit to the oldest part of the garden, the Tennyson Lawn, with its 120-year-old English elm trees. Other special corners include a fern gully, camellia gardens, an herb garden, rainforests packed with fruit bats, and ponds full of ducks and black swans. Take time to do a guided **Aboriginal Heritage Walk** through the ancestral lands of the Boonerwrung and Woiwurrung people. The 90-minute walk costs A$25 adults, A$10 children 6 to 17. It will make you look at the gardens in a different light. Bookings essential on ✆ **03/9252 2429.** The gardens are open daily from 7:30am to sunset. Admission is free. To get there, catch the no. 8 tram traveling south and get off at stop 21. Allow 2 to 4 hours.

Nearby, in King's Domain, take a look at Victoria's first Government House, **Latrobe's Cottage** (✆ **03/9656 9800**). It was built in England and transported to Australia brick by brick in 1836. The cottage is open as part of the Government House tours (bookings essential: ✆ **03/9656 9800**) on Mondays and Wednesdays. On the other side of Birdwood Avenue is the **Shrine of Remembrance,** a memorial to the servicemen lost in Australia's wars. It's designed so that at 11am on Remembrance Day (Nov 11), a beam of sunlight hits the Stone of Remembrance in the Inner Shrine. Note the eternal flame in the forecourt. King's Domain is stop 12 on the no. 15 tram traveling south along St. Kilda Road.

In **Fitzroy Gardens,** off Wellington Parade, is **Cooks' Cottage** (✆ **03/9419 4677**), which was moved to Melbourne from Great Ayton, in Yorkshire, England, in 1934 to mark Victoria's centenary. The cottage was built by the parents of Captain Cook, and today it provides the opportunity to learn about his voyages of discovery around the world. Inside, it's spartan and cramped, not unlike a ship's cabin. Admission is A$4.50 for adults, A$2.20 for children 5 to 15, and A$12 for families. It's open daily from 9am to 5pm (except Dec 25). Also east of the central business district are the **Treasury Gardens.** Look for the memorial to John F. Kennedy near the lake. To reach Treasury Gardens and Fitzroy Gardens, take tram no. 48 or 75 (or the City Circle) traveling east along Flinders Street. Get off at stop 14 for Treasury Gardens, stop 14A for Fitzroy Gardens.

ENJOYING THE GREAT OUTDOORS

Outdoor Activities

BALLOONING **Balloon Sunrise** (✆ **1800/468 247** in Australia, or 03/9730 2422; fax 03/9730 2433; www.hotairballooning.com.au), offers flights over the city plus a champagne breakfast at the Langham Hotel afterward. Dawn flights cost A$345 for adults, and A$240 for children ages 6 to 12. Hotel pickup (but not drop-off) is included. Reservations are essential.

BIKING Extensive bicycle paths wind through the city and suburbs. For details on popular routes, pick up a copy of *Bike Rides Around Melbourne,* by Julia Blunden (Open Spaces Publishing), which has 37 great rides with good directions and clear maps. *Bike Paths Victoria* also has some good maps of rides around Melbourne and Victoria. You can also buy books and maps from **Bicycle Victoria,** Level 10, 446 Collins St., Melbourne (✆ **1800/639 634** in Australia, or 03/9636 8888; www.bv.com.au); it is also worth checking out their website, which is a font of information. Bicycle Victoria runs several major cycling tours throughout the state every year.

Real Melbourne Bike Tours (✆ **0417/339 203** mobile phone; www.rentabike.net.au/biketours) can help you find your bearings and discover some of hidden Melbourne . . . the back streets and bluestone lanes, markets, cafes, arcades, and bike paths. Run by journalist Murray Johnson, the tours are fun and interesting. The cost is A$99 adults and A$79 children ages 12 to 18, including bike hire, helmet, guided tour, and coffee and cake and lunch along the way. There's even an option to ride an electric bike if you don't want to work up a sweat! Tours leave at 10am (or other times by arrangement) from Rentabike at Federation Square and return around 2pm. Tours can be customized to suit your needs. Bookings are essential.

GOLF One of the best public golf courses in Australia is **Yarra Bend,** Yarra Bend Road, Fairfield (✆ **03/9481 3729**). Greens fees A$24 Monday to Friday, A$25 Saturday and Sunday; juniors pay A$11. Club rental is an extra A$25 for a full set and A$15 for a half set.

The exclusive **Royal Melbourne Golf Club** (✆ **03/9598 6755;** www.royalmelbourne.com.au), in the suburb of Black Rock, 24km (15 miles) from the city center, is rated as one of the world's 10 best golf courses. If you have a letter of introduction from your golf club at home, a handicap of under 26 for men and 45 for women, and don't mind the greens fees—A$200 for Australian visitors, A$300 for overseas visitors—you might be able to get a round. Club hire is A$55. For more information on golf in Victoria, contact the **Victorian Golf Association,** 15 Bardolph St., Burwood (✆ **03/9889 6731;** www.golfvic.org.au).

TENNIS The venue for the Australian Open, the **Melbourne Park National Tennis Centre,** on Batman Avenue (✆ **1300/836 647** in Australia, or 03/9286 1244; www.mopt.com.au), is a great place to play. When tournaments are not scheduled, its 22 outdoor courts (including the show courts) and seven indoor courts are open to the public. You can rent courts Monday through Friday from 7am to 11pm,

Saturday and Sunday from 9am to 6pm. Charges range from A$26 to A$40 per hour, depending on the court and time (outdoor courts are cheapest). Show courts 1, 2, and 3 are for rent at the same prices. Rackets are available for hire.

Spectator Sports

CAR RACING The annual **Australian Formula One Grand Prix** takes place in March at Albert Park, about 3km (2 miles) from central Melbourne. Call **Ticketek** (✆ **13 28 49** in Australia) or check out the Grand Prix's website at **www.grandprix.com.au** for information on tickets, accommodations, and airfares.

CRICKET From October through March, cricket's the name of the game in Melbourne. The **Melbourne Cricket Ground (MCG),** Brunton Avenue, Yarra Park, Jolimont, is perhaps Australia's most hallowed cricket field. The facility (the main stadium for the 1956 Melbourne Olympic games) can accommodate 97,500 people. For the uninitiated, "one-day" games are the ones to look out for; "Test" games take several days to complete. Buy tickets at the gate or in advance from **Ticketmaster** (✆ **13 61 00** in Australia; www.ticketmaster.com).

Tours of the MCG (✆ **03/9657 8864;** www.mcg.org.au) start every half-hour daily from 10am to 3pm. Tours take about an hour and cost A$30 for adults, A$15 for children 5 to 15, or A$60 for a family of six, including admission to the new National Sports Museum, which is also at the MCG (see p. 628). Tours leave from Gate 3 in the Olympic Stand on nonevent days only.

FOOTBALL Melbourne's number-one sport is **Australian Rules football**—or simply "the footy"—a skillful, fast, and sometimes violent game the likes of which you've never seen (unless you have ESPN). Melbourne is home to 10 of the 16 Australian Football League (AFL) teams, with the others coming from Adelaide, Perth, Sydney, and Brisbane. The season starts on the third weekend in March and ends with the Grand Final on the last Saturday in September. The most accessible fields are at the Melbourne Cricket Ground (take tram no. 75 along Wellington Parade), Etihad Stadium (behind Southern Cross station on Spencer St.), and the Optus Oval at Carlton (take tram no. 19 from Elizabeth St.). The cheapest tickets cost around A$25 per person, or A$60 for families of four. For game information, call **AFL Headquarters** (✆ **03/8663 3000;** www.afl.com.au). Buy tickets through **Ticketmaster** (✆ **1300/136 122** in Australia; www.ticketmaster.com.au).

Melbourne's newest stadium, with capacity for 30,000 spectators, opened in May 2010 as the home of three other forms of football—**soccer, rugby league, and rugby union.** The "Rectangular Stadium" is officially known as **AAMI Park** (an insurance company holds naming rights). It is located on Olympic Boulevard, in the Melbourne and Olympic Parks complex (www.mopt.com.au).

HORSE RACING The **Melbourne Cup,** on the first Tuesday in November, has been contested by the best of Australia's thoroughbreds (and a few from overseas) since 1861. Melbourne society puts on a show, dressing up for the occasion, and the entire nation stops in its tracks to at least tune in on TV.

The city has four racetracks: **Flemington** (which holds the Melbourne Cup), 400 Epsom Rd., Flemington (✆ **1300/727 575** in Australia, or 03/8378 0888; www.vrc.net.au); **Moonee Valley,** McPherson Street, Mooney Ponds (✆ **03/9373 2222;** www.mvrc.net.au); **Caulfield,** Station Street, Caulfield (✆ **03/9257 7200;** www.melbourneracingclub.net.au); and **Sandown,** Racecourse Drive, Springvale

(✆ **03/9518 1300**). If you're staying in the city center, Flemington and Moonee Valley are the easiest to get to. Take tram no. 57 from Flinders Street to reach the Flemington racetrack, and catch tram no. 59 from Elizabeth Street to Moonee Valley.

TENNIS The **Australian Open ★**, one of the four Grand Slam events, is played during the last 2 weeks of January every year at the **Melbourne Park National Tennis Centre,** Batman Avenue (✆ **03/9286 1244**). Tickets go on sale in mid-October and are available through **Ticketek** (✆ **13 28 49;** www.ticketek.com.au) and on the Open's website, **www.australianopen.com**. To get there, take a train from the Flinders Street station at the bottom of Swanston Street to Richmond Station, and catch the special Tennis Centre tram from there.

SHOPPING

Ask almost any Melbournian to help you plan your time in the city, and he or she will advise you to shop until you drop. All Australia regards Melbourne as a shopping capital—it has everything from fashion houses to major department stores and unusual souvenir shops. So even if you're also visiting Sydney, save your money until you get to Melbourne, and then indulge!

Start at the magnificent city arcades, such as the **Block Arcade** (btw. Collins and Little Collins sts.), which has more than 30 shops, including the historic **Hopetoun Tearooms** (p. 622), and the **Royal Arcade** (stretching from Little Collins St. to the Bourke St. Mall). Then hit the courts and lanes around **Swanston Street** and the huge **Melbourne Central shopping complex** between Latrobe and Lonsdale streets.

Next, fan out across the city, taking in **Chapel Street** in South Yarra, for its Australian fashions, and the **Jam Factory,** 500 Chapel St., South Yarra, which is a series of buildings with a range of shops and food outlets, including a large branch of Borders bookshop, as well as 16 cinema screens. Get there on tram no. 8 or 72 from Swanston Street.

There's also **Toorak Road** in Toorak, for Gucci and other high-priced, high-fashion names; **Bridge Road** in Richmond, for budget fashions; **Lygon Street** in Carlton, for Italian fashion, footwear, and accessories; and **Brunswick Street** in Fitzroy, for a more alternative scene.

Serious shoppers might like to contact **Shopping Spree Tours** (✆ **03/9596 6600;** www.shoppingspree.com.au), a company that takes you on a day tour of 8 to 10 factories and warehouses for bargains you might not find by yourself. Tours depart Monday through Saturday (except public holidays) at 8:20am and cost A$110 for adults and A$55 for children under 11, including lunch. They will pick you up at one of six hotel locations in the city center.

Melbourne Shopping From A to Z

ABORIGINAL ART & CRAFTWORK

Aboriginal Galleries of Australia This private gallery stocks an extensive range of paintings by some of Australia's most famous indigenous artists, including Emily Kame Kngwarreye, Minnie Pwerle, Clifford Possum, and Kathleen Petyarre. 35 Spring St. ✆ **03/9654 2516.** www.agamelbourne.com.

Gallery Gabrielle Pizzi One of Melbourne's most respected dealers in Aboriginal art. You will find paintings by artists from the communities of Papunya, Utopia,

Haasts Bluff, and the Tiwi Islands, among others. This gallery also showcases urban indigenous artists working in contemporary media. Closed Saturday mornings, Sundays, and Mondays. Level 3, 75-77 Flinders Lane. ✆ **03/9654 2944.** www.gabriellepizzi.com.au.

Original & Authentic Aboriginal Art Stop here for original artworks and traditional bark paintings from the Central Western Desert, the Kimberley, and Arnhemland. They also sell boomerangs, didgeridoos, clap sticks, and Aboriginal glass art. 90 Bourke St. ✆ **03/9663 5133.** www.authaboriginalart.com.au.

CRAFTS

A good **arts-and-crafts market** is held on the Esplanade in St. Kilda on Sundays from 9am to 4pm. Take tram no. 16 from Swanston Street or no. 96 from Bourke Street. Another is at the Arts Centre on St. Kilda Road, near Princes Bridge.

The Australian Geographic Shop Head here for high-quality Australiana, including crafts, books, and various gadgets. Shop 253, Melbourne Central, La Trobe St. and Elizabeth St. ✆ **03/8616 6726;** and Galleria Shopping Plaza, Elizabeth St. at Little Collins St. ✆ **03/8616 6735.**

Counter Run by Craft Victoria, this basement shop and gallery features handmade pieces—including lovely scarves and shoes—by local craftsmen. This is the place to find one-off originals. 31 Flinders Lane. ✆ **03/9650 7775.** www.craftvic.asn.au.

DEPARTMENT STORES

David Jones Like Myer (see below), its direct competition, David Jones—or DJ's, as it's affectionately known—spans 2 blocks, separated into men's and women's stores, and offers similar goods. Don't miss the food hall. 310 Bourke St. Mall. ✆ **03/9643 2222.** www.davidjones.com.au.

Myer This is the grand dame of Melbourne's department stores and is in hot competition with David Jones. It has household goods, perfume, jewelry, and fashions, as well as a food section. The clothes here are usually more modern and stylish than those at David Jones. 295 Lonsdale St. Mall. ✆ **03/9661 1111.** www.myer.com.au.

FASHION

High-fashion boutiques line the eastern stretch of **Collins Street,** between the Grand Hyatt and the Hotel Sofitel, and **Chapel Street** in South Yarra. In addition, thousands of retail shops and factory outlets are around the city, many of them on **Bridge Road** near Punt Road and **Swan Street** near Church Street in Richmond. You'll find designer clothes, many just last season's fashions, at a fraction of the original price.

In the city, the hottest new fashion center is the QV building, which takes up a whole block, bordered by Swanston, Russell, Lonsdale, and Little Lonsdale streets. Despite its size, it has a nice feel to it. This is where you will find, tucked into QV's laneways, top Australian and international designers. The premium fashion alley is Albert Coates Lane, where you'll find the likes of Christensen Copenhagen, Cactus Jam, and Wayne Cooper.

Collins Street features most international labels, as well as shoe heaven **Miss Louise,** 205 Collins St. (✆ 03/9654 7730). Nearby Flinders Lane has earned style status with the likes of **Christine,** 181 Flinders Lane (✆ 03/9654 2011), where women are reputed to sometimes faint over the accessories. Down the road is **Little Collins Street,** another fashion-rat run. Look for local labels **Bettina Liano** (✆ 03/9654 1912), **Scanlan & Theodore** (✆ 03/9650 6195), and **Verve** (✆ 03/9639 5886).

Alice Euphemia, in Cathedral Arcade, 37 Swanston St. (✆ 03/9650 4300), also stocks upcoming Australian and New Zealand designers.

Country Road Country Road is one of Australia's best-known names for men's and women's fashion. The cool, classic looks don't come cheap, but the quality is worth it. County Road also sells designer cooking equipment and housewares. 260 Collins St. and Melbourne Central on Lonsdale St., and other locations, including Toorak Rd., South Yarra. ✆ **1800/801 911** in Australia, or 03/9650 5288. www.countryroad.com.au.

Ozmosis In addition to surfboards, boogie boards, and sunglasses, this store stocks a wide range of hip and happening beachwear at reasonable prices. All the big names in Australian surf wear are here, including Ripcurl, Quicksilver, and Billabong. 2 Melbourne Central, Lonsdale St. ✆ **03/9662 3815.** www.ozmosis.com.au.

Saba Australian designer Joseph Saba has several in-vogue, very expensive boutiques for men and women in Melbourne, including one in the Melbourne Central complex. 234 Collins St. ✆ **03/9654 3524.** www.saba.com.au.

Sam Bear Sam Bear is a good bet for Outback-style fashions: Driza-bone coats, Akubra bush hats, R. M. Williams boots and clothing, and Blundstone boots. It also sells a solid range of camping equipment. 225 Russell St. ✆ **03/9663 2191.** www.sambear.com.au.

Vegan Wares Instead of leather, Vegan Wares uses microfiber to create tough, stylish shoes, bags, and belts. It's not just for vegetarians; carnivores enjoy it, too! 78 Smith St., Collingwood. ✆ **03/9417 0230.** www.veganwares.com.

FOOD

Haigh's Chocolates Indulge in some 50 types of Australia's best chocolate, from milk to dark to fruit-flavored. Try the Sparkling Shiraz truffle if you need a serious treat. 26 Collins St. ✆ **03/9650 2114;** Shop 6, 191 Swanston Walk ✆ **03/9662 2262;** and Shop 7–8, Block Arcade, 282 Collins St. ✆ **03/9654 7673.** www.haighschocolates.com.

JEWELRY

Altmann & Cherny Even if you're not in the market to buy, it's worth coming here to check out "Olympic Australis," the largest precious-gem opal in the world. It was found in Coober Pedy in South Australia in 1956 and is valued at A$2.5 million. The store offers tax-free shopping for tourists armed with both a passport and an international airline ticket. 128 Exhibition St. ✆ **03/9650 9685.** www.almanncherny.com.au.

Dinosaur Designs Dinosaur Designs is taking the jewelry design world by storm with its range of artistic pieces made out of resin. The shop has modern housewares as well. None of it's cheap, but the odd item won't break the bank. 562 Chapel St., South Yarra. ✆ **03/9827 2600.** www.dinosaurdesigns.com.au.

e.g.etal Shop here for fresh, innovative jewelry by 50 or so of Australia's leading and emerging designers. Basement, 167 Flinders Lane. ✆ **03/9639 5111.** www.egetal.com.au.

MELBOURNE AFTER DARK

Melbourne can be an exciting place once the sun has set. The pubs and bars are far better than those in Sydney. Friday and Saturday nights will see most pubs (of both the trendy and the down-to-earth variety) packed to the rafters, and at lunchtime those that serve food are popular, too. To find out what's happening, check the Friday entertainment guide in *The Age,* Melbourne's daily broadsheet.

The Performing Arts

Melbourne is the most dynamic performing-arts city in Australia. Its theaters offer the gamut, from offbeat independent productions to large-scale Broadway-style musicals. The city is also the home of the most prestigious festivals, with the annual **Melbourne Fringe Festival** (3 weeks in late Sept/early Oct; www.melbournefringe.com.au) and the annual **Melbourne International Comedy Festival** (Mar 30–Apr 24, 2011; www.comedyfestival.com.au), attracting top Australian and international talent.

Venues all over the city participate in the Melbourne International Comedy Festival, and the Fringe Festival sees the streets, pubs, theaters, and restaurants playing host to everyone from jugglers and fire-eaters to musicians and independent productions covering all art forms. Try to get tickets if you're in town during either festival, but keep in mind that hotels fill up fast at these times. Another good time to plan your visit is during the annual **Melbourne International Film Festival** (late July through early Aug; www.melbournefilmfestival.com.au), when new releases, shorts, and avant-garde movies play at venues around the city. In 2011, the festival will celebrate 60 years.

The official government entertainment information site, **www.thatsmelbourne.com.au/whatson**, shows "What's On" in the theater world for up to a month in advance, as well as what's happening in dance, film, comedy, music, exhibitions, sports, and tours.

The best place to buy tickets for everything from theater to major sporting events, and to obtain details on schedules, is **Ticketmaster** (© **13 61 00** in Australia; www.ticketmaster.com.au).

The Heart of Melbourne's Cultural Life

The Arts Centre ★★ The spire atop the Theatres Building of the Arts Centre, on the banks of the Yarra River, crowns the city's leading performing arts complex. Beneath it, the State Theatre, the Playhouse, and the Fairfax Studio present performances that are the focal point of culture in Melbourne.

The **State Theatre,** seating 2,085 on three levels, can accommodate elaborate stagings of opera, ballet, musicals, and more. The **Playhouse** is a smaller venue that often books the Melbourne Theatre Company. The **Fairfax** is more intimate still and is often used for experimental theater or cabaret. Adjacent to the Theatres Building is **Hamer Hall,** home of the Melbourne Symphony Orchestra and often host to visiting orchestras. Many international stars have graced this stage, which is known for its excellent acoustics. Hamer Hall is currently undergoing a major revamp as part of an a$128.5 million redevelopment of the Southbank Cultural Precinct, expected to be completed sometime in 2012. Until it reopens, the Melbourne Symphony Orchestra will hold most of its concerts in the Melbourne Town Hall.

Guided tours of the Arts Centre are run at 11am Monday to Saturday, and backstage tours on Sundays at 12:15pm. Tours cost A$15 adults and A$30 for a family of two adults and two or more children. On Sundays, they cost A$20 per person (no children under 12). Buy tickets from the concierge in the foyer of the Theatres Building.

Half-Price Tickets

Buy tickets for entertainment events, including opera, dance, and drama, on the day of the performance from the Half-Tix Desk (www.halftixmelbourne.com) in the Melbourne Town Hall on Swanston Street. The booth is open Monday from 10am to 2pm, Tuesday through Thursday 11am to 6pm, Friday 11am to 6:30pm, and Saturday 10am to 4pm (also selling for Sun shows). Tickets must be purchased in person and in cash. Available shows are displayed on the booth door and on the website.

100 St. Kilda Rd. ✆ **1300/136 166** for tickets (plus a A$7.15 booking fee), or 03/9281 8000. Fax 03/9281 8282. www.theartscentre.net.au. Ticket prices vary depending on the event. Box office 9am–9pm Mon–Sat in the Theatres Building.

Additional Venues & Theaters

Check *The Age* to see what productions are scheduled during your visit. Odds are that the leading shows will take place in one of the following venues.

The Comedy Club The Comedy Club is a Melbourne institution. Come here to see local and international comedy acts, musicals, and special shows. It offers a dinner and show Friday and Saturday for A$48 and A$52. Discount ticket offers can bring the show-only prices down to as low as A$8 sometimes, so ask what's on offer. Athenaeum Theatre, 188 Collins St. ✆ **03/9650 6668.** www.thecomedyclub.com.au.

The Comedy Theatre The Comedy Theatre, with its ornate Spanish rococo interior, feels intimate even though it seats more than 1,000 people. Plays and musicals usually fill the bill, but dance companies and comedians also appear. 240 Exhibition St. (at Lonsdale St.). ✆ **03/9299 4950.** www.marrinertheatres.com.au.

The Forum Theatre The Forum books well-known bands and international comedians. Tables and chairs are in cabaret-style booths, from which you can order drinks and meals. 154 Flinders St. ✆ **03/9299 9700.** www.marrinertheatres.com.au.

Her Majesty's Theatre A fire destroyed the original theater here, but the current structure, revamped in 2002, retains the original facade and the Art Deco interior added during a 1936 renovation. Musicals, such as *Mamma Mia!, Billy Elliot,* and *Mary Poppins,* frequent the boards. 219 Exhibition St. All bookings through Ticketek. ✆ **1300/792 012.** www.hmt.com.au.

The Princess Theatre This huge facility hosts extravaganza productions such as *The Producers* and *Jersey Boys*. The theater opened its doors in 1886, and it still has a dramatic marble staircase and ornate plaster ceilings. 163 Spring St. ✆ **03/9299 9800.** www.marrinertheatres.com.au.

The Regent Theatre Built in 1929, the Regent fell into disrepair, and its stage was dark for 25 years. Now, after a A$35-million renovation, it's been restored to its former glory. The theater offers a range of dining packages and has recently been home to the production of *West Side Story*. 191 Collins St. ✆ **03/9299 9500.** www.marrinertheatres.com.au.

Sidney Myer Music Bowl This huge outdoor entertainment center, run under the auspices of the Arts Centre, is the venue for major concerts, opera, jazz, and ballet in the warmer months. It is the venue for Carols by Candlelight and the Melbourne Symphony Orchestra's free summer concert series. It seats 2,000 people, with room for another 11,000 on the lawns. King's Domain, Linlithgow Ave. Bookings through Ticketmaster. ✆ **1300/136 166.**

Cinemas

Most of the city cinemas are within 2 blocks of the intersection of Bourke and Russell streets. Tickets usually cost around A$15 for adults. Among the independent cinemas, the one that stands out is the **Astor,** 1 Chapel St. (at Dandenong Rd.), East St. Kilda (✆ **03/9510 1414**). Housed in a superb Art Nouveau building, the Astor shows a mix of classic movies and interesting recent releases.

The Bar & Music Scene

Melbourne's nightclub scene used to center on King Street, and while that area is still popular with large disco-style venues, the city is now awash in unique, hidden bars and clubs. It's best just to follow the crowds—or in some cases, that couple slipping down a side lane and disappearing into a dimly lit entrance. Otherwise, the options below are more enduring in their appeal.

Bellavista Social Club Owned by the team at Becco (see "Where to Dine," earlier in this chapter), BVSC is upstairs from the popular restaurant, in a converted diamond-cutting workshop. Ultramodern in a microsuede way, this place jumps with a late-night crowd of many splendid hues—arty young things mingling with the suits, all watching the goings-on in the laneway below on a large-screen hookup. Open Wednesday to Saturday 6pm to 3am. 11–25 Crossley St. ✆ **03/9663 3000.** www.becco.com.au.

Bennetts Lane Jazz Club ★ Often exceptional and always varied, this venue has a reputation as the best jazz club in Australia and is sought out by the best international players. The back-lane location may be a little hard to find, but that doesn't stop it being packed out most nights. Get there early if you want a table, otherwise it's standing room only or a perch on the steps at the back. Open every night from 8:30pm (music starts at 9:30pm). 25 Bennetts Lane. ✆ **03/9663 2856.** www.bennettslane.com. Entry prices vary depending on the performer, but start at around A$20.

Chaise Lounge Any semblance of barroom normality breaks down at this chic boudoir-style place featuring lipstick-colored walls, a bust of a Roman god, diamante-strung curtains, lounges, and glitter balls. It's open from 4:30pm to 3am Friday and 9pm to 3am Saturday. Basement, 105 Queen St. ✆ **03/9670 6120.** www.chaiselounge.com.au.

Cicciolina Back Bar This softly lit, alluring hideaway offers plush leather booths and a fine range of cocktails. Add an attentive staff, and you've got one of the best little bars in the greater St. Kilda region. Open Monday to Saturday 4:30pm to 1am, Sunday 3:30 to 11pm. 130 Acland St. (enter from arcade), St. Kilda. ✆ **03/9525 3333.** www.cicciolinastkilda.com.au.

Cookie This unlikely combination of good-value Thai eatery, beer hall, and smart cocktail bar, complete with plastic doilies and murals gets packed after work is done for the day. It's open from noon to 3am daily. 252 Swanston St. ✆ **03/9663 7660.** www.cookie.net.au.

The Croft Institute This laneway (at the end of an alley) bar is a small, lurid, bottle-green establishment, which is notably famous for its powerful cocktails and the city's largest private collection of laboratory apparatus. For the young only. Open Monday to Thursday 5pm to 1am, Friday 5pm to 3am, and Saturday 8pm to 3am. 21–25 Croft Alley. ✆ **03/9671 4399.** www.thecroftinstitute.net.

Double Happiness This tiny but hugely atmospheric bar is detail at its best. The retro-Asian theme would make Chairman Mao proud. Mix with the hip crowd from the business world, and try the "Gang of Four" cocktail (mango, vodka, Cointreau, and lemon). Open Monday to Wednesday 5pm to 1am, Thursday 5pm to 3am, Friday 4:30pm to 3am, Saturday 6pm to 3am, Sunday 6pm to 1am. 21 Liverpool St. (off Bourke St.). ✆ **03/9650 4488.** www.double-happiness.org.

1806 Did you know this was the year the word cocktail was first used in print? Neither did I, until I slipped inside the discreet red door of this seductive bar, sank into a leather wing chair, and opened up the drinks menu. One of Melbourne's best bars, this is a sophisticated, comfortable, and smooth place to hang out. The staff are attentive and smart, the crowd mixed, and the cocktails range from inventive to classic. It's open Monday to Thursday 5pm to 3am, Friday 4pm to 5am, Saturday 6pm to 5am, and Sunday 7pm to 3am. 169 Exhibition St. ✆ **03/9663 7722.** www.1806.com.au.

Hi-Fi Bar & Ballroom Featuring lots of live music—mostly of the hard rock and contemporary persuasion—and patronized by the younger set, this cavernous underground venue features many visiting acts. Ticket prices vary but can be anywhere between A$15 and A$75. 125 Swanson St. (opposite Melbourne Town Hall). ✆ **1300/843 4434.** www.thehifi.com.au.

Jimmy Watson's Wine Bar Jimmy's is something of an institution. One of Melbourne's oldest wine bars, it's a cozy affair where all types of people chat while sampling a vast range of wines. In the attached dining area, excellent food is expertly teamed with the perfect wine. Come to talk or simply read the paper. Open daily noon to 3pm, Tuesday to Saturday 6pm till late. 333 Lygon St., Carlton. ✆ **03/9347 3985.**

KingPin Why not combine your love for bowling and drinking? Experience the purple lounge, which really mixes it up, with cool DJs and great cocktails. This venue in the Crown Casino complex is open until 2am, so happy days really are here again. Bowling costs A$14 for the first game and A$10 for extra games until 6pm every day; A$18 for the first game and A$16 after 6pm on Friday and Saturday; or A$16 and A$12 after 6pm Sunday to Thursday. Shoe hire is included. 8 Whiteman St., Southbank. ✆ **13 26 95** in Australia, or 03/8646 4100. www.kingpinbowling.com.au.

Melbourne Supper Club Upstairs from an ever-popular European cafe/restaurant, the Melbourne Supper Club is a perfect post-theater venue. Deep leather lounges and a giant circular window that looks onto the beautifully lit Parliament House buildings make this bar a place to idle, smoke a cigar, or dwell over a bottle of your favorite wine. It's open Sunday and Monday 7pm to 4am, Tuesday to Thursday 5pm to 4am, Friday 5pm to 6am, and Saturday 8pm to 6am. 161 Spring St. ✆ **03/9654 6300.**

Misty Funk meets Barbarella in this ultrahip and arty venue, one of the quintessential Melbourne bars. Here, down a cobbled lane (and then upstairs), smooth cocktails mix with live combos or soulful DJs. Open Tuesday to Thursday 5pm to 1am, Friday 5pm to 3am, and Saturday 6pm to 3am. 3–5 Hosier Lane. ✆ **03/9663 9202.**

Paris Cat This is an intimate jazz bar that doesn't take itself too seriously. Head down the stairs into an inviting space with warm brick walls, cozy tables, lounges, bar stools, and jazz-themed art on the walls. You might hear local musicians with original music, or top international acts. A very cool place, with a great atmosphere. Open Tuesday to Saturday from 8pm. The cover varies from free to around A$20. 6 Goldie Place. ✆ **03/9642 4711.** www.pariscat.com.au.

Tony Starr's Kitten Club Don't be put off by the name—this is one great place. A restaurant-bar on the lower level serves an array of excellent tapas and more exotic fare. But the action is at the upstairs Galaxy Space, where most nights you'll find entertainment ranging from the peculiar to the animated to the just plain bizarre. Don't forget to visit the Love Lounge, with its floor-to-ceiling red fabric, heart-shaped lounges, and secluded booths. Opens at 4pm daily until 1am Monday to Thursday, 3am Friday and Saturday, and midnight on Sundays. Cover is usually A$5. 267 Little Collins St. ✆ **03/9650 2448.** www.kittenclub.com.au.

Troika Here you'll find industrial chic with heart. Behind a heavy metal sliding door, with a cool concrete-floor interior livened with spots of color, this stylish bar is frequented by the arts and design crowd. The drink prices are great value for an inner-city bar, and there's a covered courtyard out the back for smokers. Open Tuesday and Wednesday 4pm to midnight, Thursday and Friday 4pm to 2am, Saturday 5pm to 3am. 106 Little Lonsdale St. ✆ **03/9663 0221.**

Where to Share a Pint

Pubs generally stay open from midmorning until at least midnight most nights. Many remain open until 2 or 3am on Friday and Saturday nights, and you can always find a few open 24 hours.

Belgian Beer Café Bluestone Pretend that you're in Brussels in this atmospheric cafe featuring Belgian beer culture in all its forms. Full-bodied Belgian brews dominate. While downing your pint, try the traditional steamed mussels. In warmer weather, sitting in the parklike garden is a delight. There's live music on Sundays from 4 to 7pm. It's open daily 11am till late. 557 St. Kilda Rd. ✆ **03/9529 2899.** www.belgianbeercafemelbourne.com.

Prince of Wales Hotel This pub is a legend among the locals. Though the accommodation at the back has been gentrified in a big way, the pub itself retains its original rough-at-the-edges appearance. A huge blackboard at the front lets you know which bands, some of them big names, will be playing, and you can buy tickets for the gigs at the bar. Open every day except New Year's Day until 2 or 3am. 29 Fitzroy St. (at Acland St.), St. Kilda. ✆ **03/9536 1111.** www.princebars.com.au.

Windsor Castle Do elephants fly? They do at the Windsor Castle—and they're pink! Head up Chapel Street and through Prahran to Windsor and its best-kept secret, the Windsor Castle Hotel, a perfect weekend meeting place for good pub food, which you can enjoy in the sunny courtyard or in the plush interior. You'll find DJs and barbecue on weekends. Look for the giant pink elephants on the roof. 89 Albert St. (at Upton St.), Windsor. ✆ **03/9525 0239.**

Pick a Card . . . for a Unique Pub-Crawl

All the rage in Melbourne (and developed by clever Melbourne girl Michelle Matthews) is a pack of 52 playing cards called **Bar Secrets Melbourne.** The cards have pictures of and information (including maps) on the hippest and most unusual pubs and cocktail bars in town. Locals pick out a few at random, and the night's planned. The cards cost A$9.95 at bookshops and newsdealers, or you can buy them online at **www.bar-secrets.com.** They are well worth seeking out. You will find yourself weaving up dark alleyways, climbing into lofts and down into basements, and always faced with something unique.

Young & Jackson Melbourne's oldest and most famous pub is a great place to stop in for a drink, or a meal in the stylish upstairs restaurant or bistro areas. Head upstairs to see the nude *Chloe,* a famous painting brought to Melbourne for the Great Exhibition in 1880. The pub, which was built in 1853 and started selling beer in 1861, has a few years on *Chloe,* which was painted in Paris in 1875. The painting has a special place in the hearts of customers and Melbournians. The pub opens at 10am daily (9am on weekends) and closes at midnight every day except Friday and Saturday, when it is open until 3am. At the corner of Flinders and Swanston sts. ✆ **03/9650 3884.** www.youngandjacksons.com.au.

The Casino

Crown Casino Australia's largest casino is a plush affair that's open 24 hours. You'll find all the usual roulette and blackjack tables and so on, as well as an array of gaming machines. This is also a major venue for international headline acts, and there are around 25 restaurants and 11 bars on the premises, with more in the extended Southgate complex. See p. 612 for a review of the casino's attached hotel, the Crown Towers. Clarendon St., Southbank. ✆ **03/9292 6868.** www.crowncasino.com.au.

SIDE TRIPS FROM MELBOURNE

Dandenong Ranges

40km (25 miles) E of Melbourne

Melbournians traditionally do a "day in the Dandenongs" from time to time, topping off their getaway with Devonshire tea, scones, and jam at one of the many cafes en route. Up in the cool, high country, you'll find native bush, famous gardens, the Dandenong Ranges National Park, historic attractions such as the Puffing Billy—a vintage steam train—and plenty of restaurants and cozy B&Bs. The Dandenong Ranges National Park is one of the state's oldest, set aside in 1882 to protect its mountain ash forests and lush tree-fern gullies. Parts of the Dandenongs were affected by the 2009 summer bushfires, but by the time you visit the process of regeneration will be well underway.

ESSENTIALS

GETTING THERE To get to the area, take the Burwood Highway from Melbourne, and then the Mount Dandenong Tourist Road, which starts at Upper Ferntree

Side Trips from Melbourne

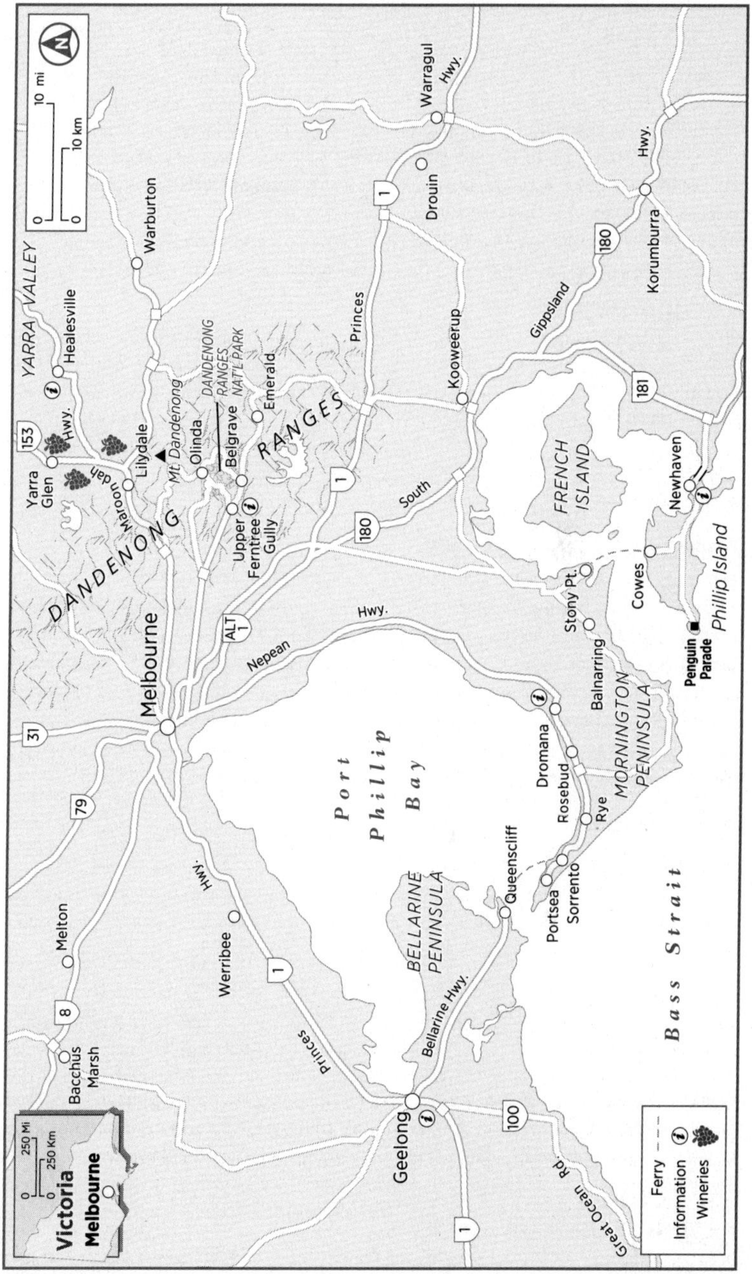

Gully and winds through the villages of Sassafras, Olinda, Mount Dandenong, and Kalorama to Montrose. If you take a turnoff to Sherbrook, or extend your journey into a loop taking in Seville, Woori Yallock, Emerald, and Belgrave, you'll see a fair slice of the local scenery. A really good tour operator is **A Tour with a Difference** (✆ **1300/36 27 36** in Australia, or 03/9754 1699; www.atwad.com.au). They pick up from Melbourne hotels in a 10-person bus and do lots of great things in the Dandenongs, including a ride on the Puffing Billy. The tour costs A$165 and includes morning tea, lunch, and all entry fees.

VISITOR INFORMATION The **Dandenong Ranges & Knox Visitor Information Centre,** 1211 Burwood Hwy., Upper Ferntree Gully, VIC 3156 (✆ **1800/645 505** in Australia, or 03/9758 7522; fax 03/9758 7533; www.dandenongrangestourism.com.au), is open daily (except Good Friday and Dec 25) from 9am to 5pm.

NATURE WALKS

Most people come here to get out of the city for a pleasant bushwalk, and in that way it's the equivalent of Sydney's Blue Mountains. Some of the better walks include the easy 2.5km (1.5-mile) stroll from the **Sherbrook Picnic Ground** through the forest, and the **Thousand Steps** and the **Kokoda Track Memorial Walk,** a challenging rainforest track from the Fern Tree Gully Picnic Ground up to One Tree Hill. Along the way are plaques commemorating Australian troops who fought and died in Papua New Guinea in World War II.

FOR GARDENING BUFFS

National Rhododendron Gardens From September through November, thousands of rhododendrons and azaleas burst into bloom in these magnificent gardens. There are 42 hectares (104 acres) in all, with a 3km (1.8-mile) walking path leading past flowering exotics and native trees as well as vistas over the Yarra Valley. In spring, the Garden Explorer people-mover helps get you around. Visitors flock here in summer for the walks, and in autumn when the leaves are turning.

The Georgian Rd., Olinda. ✆ **13 19 63** or 03/8627 4699. www.parkweb.vic.gov.au. Admission Sept–Nov A$11 adults, A$5.60 children 15–17, A$28 families; Dec–Aug A$7.10 adults, A$3.20 children, A$17 families. Children 14 and under free. Daily 10am–5pm. Closed Dec 25. Train to Croydon; then bus no. 688 to the gardens, or train to Belgrave and bus no. 694.

Tesselaar's Bulbs and Flowers Tens of thousands of flowers are on display at this gardening center, putting on a flamboyantly colorful show in the spring (mid-Sept to mid-Oct). Expect to see a dazzling variety of tulips, daffodils, rhododendrons, azaleas, fuchsias, and ranunculi. Bulbs are on sale at discount prices at other times.

357 Monbulk Rd., Silvan. ✆ **1300/428 527** in Australia or 03/9737 7701. www.tesselaar.net.au. Admission during Tulip Festival (mid-Sept to mid-Oct) A$16 adults, free for children 15 and under accompanied by an adult; free for everyone rest of the year. During tulip festival daily 10am–5pm; rest of year Mon–Fri 8:30am–4:30pm, Sat–Sun 1–5pm. Free parking. Train: Lilydale; then bus no. 679.

William Ricketts Sanctuary This interesting garden, in a forest of mountain ash, features almost 100 clay figures representing the Aboriginal Dreamtime. The sculptures were created over the lifetime of sculptor William Ricketts, who died in 1993 at the age of 94. The garden encompasses fern gullies and waterfalls spread out over 13 hectares (32 acres), with the sculptures occupying a little less than a hectare (2 acres).

Mt. Dandenong Tourist Rd., Mt. Dandenong. ✆ **13 19 63** or 03/9751 1300. www.parkweb.vic.gov.au. Admission A$7.10 adults, A$3.20 children 15–17, A$17 families of 5. Children 14 and under free. Daily 10am–4:30pm. Closed Dec 25 and days of total fire ban. Train to Croydon; then bus no. 688.

FOR TRAIN BUFFS

Puffing Billy Railway ☺ For almost a century, Puffing Billy steam railway has chugged over a 13km (8-mile) track from Belgrave to Emerald and Lakeside. Passengers ride on open carriages—often dangling their legs from the "windows"—and enjoy lovely views as the train passes through forests and fern gullies and over a National Trust–classified wooden trestle bridge. Trips take around an hour each way, and there's time to walk around the lake before the return journey. Timetables can be complicated and change, so check the website to ensure you have the right information. Special "Steam and Cuisine" fares (A$95 adults; A$86 children) including a three-course lunch in a "first class" enclosed carriage with white tablecloths and wine, are also available daily, and on Friday and Saturday nights you can take the train to dinner at a historic packing shed for A$84. Trains do not run on days of total fire ban.

Belgrave Station, Belgrave. ✆ **03/9757 0700** or 1900/937 069 (recorded information). www.puffingbilly.com.au. Round-trip fares A$21–A$35 adults, A$11–A$24 children 4–16, A$71–A$97 families of 6. Closed Dec 25. Train from Flinders St. station in Melbourne to Belgrave; Puffing Billy station is a short walk away.

WHERE TO DINE

Wild Oak CONTEMPORARY Chef Ben Higgs has turned this former cafe into the best restaurant in the Dandenongs. The food includes the likes of lemon-myrtle roasted baby barramundi fillet served with root vegetables and lime aioli; red curry of roasted pumpkin, chickpeas, and baby spinach with coconut rice; or the signature slow-cooked confit duck leg, served with carrot and pinenut gratin, minted pea puree, and red currant jus. There are daily specials, steaks, and imaginative vegetarian selections. They open for breakfast on Sundays, and there's live jazz on the last Friday night of each month. In winter, there's a log fire.

232 Ridge Rd., Olinda. ✆ **03/9751 2033.** www.wildoak.com.au. Main courses A$24–A$39. AE, DC, MC, V. Wed–Sat noon–4pm and 6–11pm; Sun 9am–11pm.

Yarra Valley ★

61km (38 miles) E of Melbourne

Large tracts of the Yarra Valley, one of Melbourne's best wine-growing regions, have been affected by bushfires during the past two summers, and you will still see evidence of this when you visit. But the main attractions remain untouched and visitors are welcomed warmly in the villages, historic houses, gardens, crafts shops, antiques centers, and restaurants that dot the region.

ESSENTIALS

GETTING THERE **McKenzie's Bus Lines** (✆ **03/5962 5088;** www.mckenzies.com.au) operates bus service from Lilydale Railway Station to Healesville. (Catch a train from Melbourne's Spencer St. station to Lilydale; the trip takes about an hour.) Buses connect with trains frequently throughout the day (less often on weekends); check exact connection times.

If you're driving, pick up a map of the area from the Royal Automotive Club of Victoria (✆ **13 72 28** in Australia) in Melbourne. Maps are free if you're a member of an auto club in your home country, but remember to bring your membership card. Alternatively, you can pick up a map at the tourist office. Take the Maroondah Highway from Melbourne to Lilydale and on to Healesville. The trip takes around 1 hour and 15 minutes.

VISITOR INFORMATION Pick up details on attractions and lodging at the **Yarra Valley Visitor Information Centre,** Old Court House, Harker Street, Healesville (✆ **03/5962 2600;** fax 03/5962 2040; www.visityarravalley.com.au). It's open daily (except Dec 25) from 9am to 5pm.

EXPLORING THE VALLEY

There are three principal roads in the valley: Melba Highway, Maroondah Highway, and Myers Creek Road, which form a triangle. Within the triangle are three smaller roads, Healesville–Yarra Glen Road, Old Healesville Road, and Chum Creek Road, which all lead to wineries. Most people start their tour of the Yarra Valley from Lilydale and take in several cellar-door tastings at vineyards along the route.

Healesville Sanctuary This sanctuary played a major role in saving and rehabilitating the hundreds of animals injured or displaced by the 2009 bushfires. You can visit the Wildlife Health Centre (an animal rescue hospital) to see veterinarians caring for (and operating on) injured or orphaned wildlife. This sanctuary is a great place to spot native animals in almost-natural surroundings. You can see wedge-tailed eagles, dingoes, koalas, wombats, reptiles, and more, all while strolling through the peppermint-scented gum forest, which rings with the chiming of bellbirds. Sir Colin McKenzie started the sanctuary in 1921 as a center to preserve endangered species and educate the public. There's a gift shop, a cafe serving light meals, and picnic grounds.

Badger Creek Rd., Healesville. ✆ **03/5957 2800.** Fax 03/5957 2870. www.zoo.org.au. Admission A$24 adults, A$12 children ages 4–15, A$56–A$77 families. Daily 9am–5pm. Train from Flinders St. station to Lilydale; then bus no. 685 to Healesville and bus no. 686 toward Badger Creek, which will stop at the sanctuary.

WHERE TO STAY & DINE

Healesville Hotel ★★ This lovely old hotel is great for either a leisurely lunch in the beer garden or an elegant dinner and an overnight stay. There are only seven rooms, with three bathrooms down the hallway. Each has a queen-size bed, high pressed-metal ceilings, and small personal touches like handmade soaps. The old-world dining room is candlelit, with a log fire in winter; in summer you can dine in the lamp-lit courtyard.

256 Maroondah Hwy., Healesville, VIC 3777. ✆ **03/5962 4002.** Fax 03/5962 1037. www.healesvillehotel.com.au. 7 units, none with bathroom. Mon–Thurs A$100 double; Fri and Sun A$130 double; Sat A$315 double, including 3-course dinner; long weekends or public holidays A$160 double. AE, DC, MC, V. **Amenities:** Restaurant; bar. *In room:* TV.

Melba Lodge ★ These modern accommodations are in Yarra Glen, in the heart of the Yarra Valley wine region. Of the luxurious guest rooms, four have queen-size beds, and two have king-size beds and a Jacuzzi; all have private bathrooms. There's a comfortable lounge with an open fire, and a billiard room. If you prefer, there's also a self-contained cottage. The lodge is only a few minutes' walk from historic Yarra Glen, which has antiques shops and a crafts market. There are plenty of restaurants and wineries around, too. It's a short drive to Healesville Sanctuary.

939 Melba Hwy., Yarra Glen, VIC 3775. ✆ **03/9730 1511.** Fax 03/9730 1566. www.melbalodge.com.au. 8 units. A$140–A$175 queen room; A$170–A$205 king room, penthouse, or cottage. Extra person A$20. Ask about weekend, golf, or dinner packages. Rates include cooked breakfast. AE, DC, MC, V. **Amenities:** Bar; Jacuzzi. *In room:* A/C, TV.

Sanctuary House Resort Motel This place is very handy for visiting Healesville Sanctuary, as it is just 400m (1,312 ft.) away (and guests here get discounted entry). Set in some 4 hectares (10 acres) of gardens, it is also a good choice if you just want to relax and sample some good Yarra Valley wine. The rooms are typical motel-style. Also available are two units with kitchens and amenities to assist travelers with disabilities. A cedar cottage has two suites, each with a queen-size bed. There is a giant adventure playground for kids.

Badger Creek Rd. (P.O. Box 162), Healesville, VIC 3777. ✆ **03/5962 5148.** Fax 03/5962 5392. www.sanctuaryhouse.com.au. 22 units, all with shower. A$99–A$190 double; A$120–A$150 family room (sleeps 5); A$120–A$165 self-contained units (sleep 4–6); A$110–A$120 cottage (sleeps 4). MC, V. Train from Flinders St. station to Lilydale; then bus no. 685 or 686. **Amenities:** Restaurant; 2 bars; babysitting; exercise room; Jacuzzi; small outdoor solar-heated pool; sauna. *In room:* A/C, TV, hair dryer, kitchenette (self-contained units only).

Phillip Island: Penguins on Parade ★

139km (86 miles) S of Melbourne

Phillip Island's **penguin parade,** which happens every evening at dusk, is one of Australia's most popular animal attractions. There are other, less crowded places in Australia where watching homecoming penguins feels less staged (such as Kangaroo Island in South Australia), but at least the guides and boardwalks protect the little ones and their nesting holes from the throngs. Nevertheless, the commercialism of the penguin parade puts a lot of people off—busloads of tourists squashed into a sort of amphitheater hardly feels like being one with nature. Phillip Island also offers nice beaches, good bushwalking, fishing, and Seal Rocks. If you have the time, you could spend at least 2 days here.

ESSENTIALS

GETTING THERE Most visitors come to Phillip Island on a day trip from Melbourne and arrive in time for the penguin parade and dinner. Several tour companies run day trips. Among them are **Gray Line** (✆ **1300/858 687** in Australia or 03/9663 4455; www.grayline.com or www.grayline.com.au), which operates a number of different tours, including the daily "penguin express" trips for those who are short of time. The express tour departs Melbourne at 3pm and returns at around 9pm. Tours cost A$120 for adults and A$60 for children, and can be booked online in U.S. dollars before arrival. Upgrades to premium seating at the penguin parade and various other options are available.

If you're driving yourself, Phillip Island is an easy 2-hour trip from Melbourne along the South Gippsland Highway and then the Bass Highway. A bridge connects the island to the mainland.

V/Line (✆ **13 61 96** in Australia) runs a bus from Melbourne to Cowes, but does not take you to any of the attractions on Phillip Island. Once on the island, you need to hire a car, take a tour, or hire a push bike to get around. The parade is 15km (9½ miles) from the center of Cowes.

VISITOR INFORMATION There are two information centers on the island. The **Phillip Island Information Centre** (✆ **03/5956 7447**) is at 895 Phillip

EXPLORING werribee

This small country town, 32km (20 miles) southwest of Melbourne—just a 30-minute drive along the Princes Freeway—has a cluster of great attractions that combine for a great day (or two) out. **The Mansion at Werribee Park ★★**, K Road, Werribee (✆ **03/8734 5100;** www.werribeepark.com.au), is always on my list of places to take visitors. The 60-room Italianate mansion, dubbed "the palace in the paddock," was built in 1877 and is surrounded by 132 hectares (326 acres) of magnificent formal gardens and bushland. You can tour the house, which has wonderful antique furniture, and there is also an interesting contemporary sculpture garden to wander in. There's a cafe, too. Admission is free to the park and picnic grounds; admission to the mansion is A$14 adults, A$8 children 4 to 15, and A$33 families of four. It's open daily 10am to 5pm, until 4pm on weekdays from May through Oct, and closed December 25. A guided tour of the tower is run at 1:30pm daily and costs A$4 per person.

Adjacent to the mansion is **Werribee Open Range Zoo** (✆ **03/9731 9600;** www.zoo.org.au). Getting around the open range part of the zoo, where you will see giraffes, hippos, rhinoceros, zebras, and more, is strictly by guided tour on a safari bus. The tour takes about an hour. On busy days, it might pay to spend the extra to take a small group tour in an open-sided jeep, as you'll get a better view and better photo opportunities. The zoo also has a walk-through section featuring African cats, including cheetahs, and monkeys. If you've been to Africa, you may find little to excite you, but kids love it and it's crowded with families. Admission is A$24 adults, A$12 children ages 4 to 15, and A$56 to A$77 families. It's open daily 9am to 5pm (entrance gate closes at 3:30pm). Safari tours run hourly from 10:30am to 3:40pm. Trains run from Melbourne to Werribee station; a taxi from the station to the zoo costs around A$5. A joint ticket to the mansion and the zoo costs A$35 adults, A$18 children ages 4 to 15, or A$80 to A$99 for families. It can be purchased at either attraction.

On the other side of the mansion is the **Victoria State Rose Garden,** which has 5,000 bushes in themed gardens. Entry is free, and the best time to view the roses in bloom is November to April.

If you want to stay longer in Werribee, the magnificently modern **Sofitel Werribee Park Mansion Hotel & Spa** (✆ **03/9731 4000;** www.mansionhotel.com.au) is attached to the back of the original mansion. Room rates start at A$249 double per night. Also on the property is the boutique winery **Shadowfax** (✆ **03/9731 4420;** www.shadowfax.com.au), open daily from 11am-5pm. Stay for lunch; they have delicious antipasto platters and wood-fired pizzas.

Island Tourist Rd., Newhaven, just a few kilometers onto the island, and the **Cowes Visitor Information Centre** is at Thompson Avenue, Cowes (✆ **03/5951 3396**). Both are open daily from 9am to 5pm (except Christmas Day), and share the toll-free number ✆ **1300/366 422** in Australia and the website **www.visitphillipisland.com**.

EXPLORING THE AREA

Visitors approach the island from the east, passing through the town of **Newhaven.** The main town on the island, **Cowes** (pop. 2,400), is on the north coast. A stroll along its Esplanade is worthwhile. The penguin parade is on the far southwest coast.

The trip to the west coast of Phillip Island's Summerland Peninsula ends in an interesting rock formation called the **Nobbies.** This strange-looking outcropping can be reached at low tide by a basalt causeway. You'll get some spectacular views of the coastline and two offshore islands from here. On the farthest of these islands is a population of up to **12,000 Australian fur seals,** the largest colony in Australia. (Bring your binoculars.) This area is also home to thousands of nesting silver gulls. The **Nobbies Centre** (✆ **03/5951 2883;** www.penguins.org.au) is a marine interpretive center with information about the wildlife, binoculars for better viewing, and a cafe. Entry is free from 10am daily (11am in winter) until sunset, when the area is closed to the public to protect the wildlife.

On the north coast of the island, you can explore **Rhyll Inlet,** an intertidal mangrove wetland inhabited by wading birds such as spoonbills, oystercatchers, herons, egrets, cormorants, and the rare bar-tailed godwit and whimbrel. Birders will also love **Swan Lake,** another breeding habitat for wetland birds.

Elsewhere, walking trails lead through heath and pink granite to **Cape Woolamai,** the island's highest point, where there are fabulous coastal views. From September through April, the cape is home to thousands of short-tailed shearwaters (also known as mutton birds).

A **ThreeParks Pass** gives discounted entry to the Koala Conservation Centre, the penguin parade, and the island's other major attraction, **Churchill Island Heritage Farm** (✆ **03/5956 7214;** www.churchillisland.org.au). The pass costs A$36 adults, A$18 children ages 4 to 15, and A$90 for families of four; it can be purchased online (www.penguins.org.au) or at any of the attractions.

PHILLIP ISLAND ATTRACTIONS

Koala Conservation Centre Koalas were introduced to Phillip Island in the 1880s, and at first they thrived in the predator-free environment. However, overpopulation, the introduction of foxes and dogs, and the clearing of land for farmland and roads have taken their toll. Though you can still see a few koalas in the wild, the best place to find them is at this sanctuary, set up for research and breeding purposes. Visitors can get quite close to them, especially on the elevated boardwalk, which lets you peek into their treetop homes. At around 4pm, the ordinarily sleepy koalas are on the move—but this is also the time when a lot of tour buses converge on the place, so it can get crowded.

Fiveways, Phillip Island Tourist Rd., Cowes. ✆ **03/5952 1610.** www.penguins.org.au. Admission A$10 adults, A$5 children 4–15, A$26 families of 4. Daily 10am–5pm.

National Vietnam Veterans Museum This might seem an oddly out-of-the-way place for a national museum, but it's first-class. The collection includes about 6,000 artifacts, including the marbles used in Australia's conscription lottery, uniforms, vehicles, and weapons. The big-ticket item is a Bell AH-IG HueyCobra helicopter gunship, one of only three in Australia. A moving audio-visual exhibit and dioramas on aspects of Australia's involvement in the war from 1962 to 1972 are complemented by a photo gallery and a display about the Australian-Vietnamese community. The museum is also restoring a Canberra bomber, the only surviving example of its kind in the world. You can have a coffee in the Nui Dat Café, and there's a shop selling books and memorabilia.

25 Veterans Dr., Newhaven. ✆ **03/5956 6400.** www.vietnamvetsmuseum.org. Admission A$9 adults, A$4 children 14 and under, A$20 families of 4. Daily 10am–5pm. Closed Good Friday and Christmas Day.

Phillip Island Penguin Reserve ★ ☺ The penguin parade takes place every night at dusk, when hundreds of Little Penguins appear at the water's edge, gather in the shallows, and waddle up the beach toward their burrows in the dunes. They're the smallest of the world's 17 species of penguins, standing just 33 centimeters (13 in.) high, and they're the only penguins that breed on the Australian mainland. **Photography is banned,** because it scares the penguins, as are smoking and touching the penguins. Wear a sweater or jacket, because it gets chilly after the sun goes down. A kiosk selling food opens an hour before the penguins turn up. Reservations for the parade are essential during busy holiday periods such as Easter and in summer.

For a better experience, there are more exclusive small group tours which allow you a better view of the penguins. **Penguins Plus** allows you to watch the parade from an exclusive boardwalk in the company of rangers, while the **Penguin Sky Box** is an adults-only elevated viewing tower staffed by a ranger. The **Ultimate Penguin Tour** for groups of only 10 people (no children under 16) takes you to a secluded beach away from the main viewing area to see penguins coming ashore. Another option is a ranger-guided tour, a few hours before the penguins appear, to see behind-the-scenes research.

Summerland Beach, Phillip Island Tourist Rd., Cowes. ✆ **03/5951 2820.** www.penguins.org.au. Admission A$21 adults, A$11 children 4–15, A$53 families of 4. Penguins Plus A$40 adult, A$20 child, A$100 families; Penguin Sky Box A$60; Private Penguin Parade Experience (no children 11 and under) A$69; Ultimate Penguin Tour A$75; ranger guided tour A$10 adult, A$5 child, A$25 family, in addition to visitor center entry. Visitor center summer daily 9am–6pm; winter daily 9am–5pm.

WHERE TO STAY

Abaleigh on Lovers Walk ★ The beach is right on the doorstep of these gorgeous town-house suites. The studios are designed for couples, and a beachfront apartment sleeps up to six. All come with log fires, double showers, and water views. The kitchen is stocked with breakfast items for your arrival, and the best place to enjoy it is either in the private courtyard or on the veranda. You also get free fishing gear, beach chairs and umbrellas, magazines and books, and fresh flowers. Lovers Walk, a romantic floodlit path along the foreshore, is a 5-minute walk from the center of Cowes, with its cafes, restaurants, and shops.

6 Roy Court, Cowes, Phillip Island, VIC 3922. ✆ **03/5952 5649.** Fax 03/5952 2549. www.abaleigh.com. 3 units. A$175–A$200 double. Extra person A$50. Rates include breakfast. AE, MC, V. Children not accepted. **Amenities:** Golf course nearby. *In room:* A/C, TV/VCR, CD player, hair dryer, Jacuzzi, kitchen.

Glen Isla House ★★ This is one of the best places to stay in Phillip Island. Set in lovely heritage gardens, the house was built around 1870 and is one of the oldest homes on the island, offering old-world charm and elegance. It's beachside location is perfect for visiting the penguins. There are five guest rooms in the house, as well as the Anderson Suite Cottage, which features a king-size four-poster bed and a Jacuzzi, and the Gate Cottage, which has two bedrooms. No children under 12.

230 Church St., Cowes, Phillip Island, VIC 3922. ✆ **03/5952 1882.** Fax 03/5952 5028. www.glenisla.com. 7 units. A$285 double; A$425 double Anderson Suite Cottage; A$325 double Gate Cottage, extra person A$35. Rates include breakfast. AE, DC, MC, V. Secure off-street parking. No children 11 and under. **Amenities:** Restaurant; bar. *In room:* A/C, TV/DVD (cottages only), hair dryer, free Wi-Fi.

Holmwood Guesthouse ★ This charming 1934 guesthouse is set in lovely cottage gardens, just a short walk from the beach and the center of Cowes. You can choose between three rooms, all with private bathrooms, in the main house, two stylish cottages built alongside, or a three-bedroom budget studio apartment, each with their own courtyard garden. Guesthouse rooms have a slightly old-fashioned feel (one is called the Jane Austen Room), but the cottages are modern—one's theme is seaside or nautical, the other Asian. The studio has one double and two single bedrooms and is self-catering. Breakfasts are hearty, and you can stay in for dinner if you choose. The guest lounge has a fireplace.

37 Chapel St., Cowes, Phillip Island, VIC 3922. ✆ **03/5952 3082** or 0421/444 810 mobile phone. Fax 03/5952 3083. www.holmwoodguesthouse.com.au. 6 units. A$195–A$220 double B&B; A$215–A$250 double cottage; A$150 double studio, extra person A$20. Rates include breakfast. Ask about packages. 2-night minimum or longer on Sat–Sun or holiday periods. AE, DC, MC, V. Free off-street parking. **Amenities:** Restaurant; bar; bikes; room service. *In room:* A/C, TV, CD player, hair dryer, free Internet.

The Bellarine Peninsula

75km (47 miles) SW of Melbourne

The seaside villages of the Bellarine Peninsula are a gentle reminder of how the pace of life can still be. With lots of attractions and increasingly good options for dining and accommodation, these villages nevertheless remain slow-moving and unspoiled. In summer, crowds of holiday-makers flock to the beaches along the peninsula coast, but outside the hectic high season, there's a serenity about this region that's hard to beat. The region starts at Geelong, Victoria's second largest city, and takes in the seaside hamlets of Queenscliff, Port Arlington, Point Lonsdale, Barwon Heads, and Ocean Grove.

ESSENTIALS

GETTING THERE The city of Geelong, at the start of the Bellarine Peninsula, is about an hour's drive from Melbourne on the Princes Highway. From there, take the Bellarine Highway to Queenscliff, Portarlington, Point Lonsdale, Barwon Heads, and Ocean Grove. **V Line** (✆ **13 61 96** in Australia) runs a train service from Melbourne's Southern Cross Station to Geelong. A vehicle and passenger ferry operates between Queenscliff and Sorrento on the Mornington Peninsula (p. 654).

VISITOR INFORMATION The **Geelong Visitor Information Centre,** 26 Moorabool St., Geelong, VIC 3220 (✆ **1800/620 888** in Australia or 03/5222 2900; www.visitgreatoceanroad.org.au) is open daily (except Christmas Day) from 9am to 5pm. The **Queenscliff Visitor Information Centre,** 55 Hesse St., Queenscliff, VIC 3225 (✆ **1300/884 843** in Australia or 03/5258 4843; fax 03/5258 3726; www.queenscliff.org) is open daily 9am to 5pm (except Christmas Day) and until 6pm from December 26 to January 31.

EXPLORING THE AREA

Geelong is a waterfront city, set on a north-facing bay with lots of restaurants, cafes, landscaped gardens, and walking paths set against the backdrop of **Corio Bay.** The foreshore is dotted with colorful sculptured bollards representing characters from the city's past and present—1930s lifesavers, fishermen, a town band, young ladies in neck-to-knee bathing costumes, and of course, a Geelong footballer. Nearby **Eastern Beach** has an Art Deco–style pool and a restored bathing pavilion that is now a cafe. The city also has about 100 heritage-listed colonial buildings.

Queenscliff started as a fishing village, then became a fashionable holiday destination for Melbourne's elite. It has remained trendy in recent years, and there's a plethora of art galleries, shops, and restaurants, but you can get away from it all on the beach or the tree-lined foreshore. **Fort Queenscliff,** on King Street

(✆ **03/5258 0730**), is Australia's largest and best-preserved military fortress. You can tour the complex on weekends and public holidays (call for times), with its historic buildings, including gun positions and ammunition vaults. There is a large collection of war memorabilia in the museum, as well as World War I and World War II guns.

From **Barwon Heads,** cross Victoria's longest wooden bridge, built in 1927, to reach **Ocean Grove.** From the heads at nearby **Point Lonsdale,** unbroken sands stretch to the mouth of the Barwon River, providing one of Victoria's most popular ocean beaches.

BELLARINE ATTRACTIONS

The Blues Train Sway to the rhythm of the steam train and the music aboard this locomotive as it makes its way from Queenscliff to Drysdale and back again, with the scenery of the Bellarine passing by outside. This is dinner and a show, with different acts in four carriages, each seating 50 people. Drinks to take on the journey are available on the platforms at each of the four stops along the way. At each stop, passengers swap carriages to find a new band tuning up for them. One carriage only has seating running along each wall, leaving room for a bit of a dance floor! The train runs from August to May.

Queenscliff Railway Station. ✆ **03/5258 4829.** www.bluestrain.com.au. Tickets A$80. Book through Ticketek: ✆ **13 28 49.** Sat Aug–May 6:30–11pm.

National Wool Museum For much of its colonial history, Australia was said to "ride on the sheep's back," so important was the wool industry to the nation. Times have changed, but this interesting museum, housed in a restored 1872 bluestone wool store, tells the story of wool from the birth of the industry in the 1840s to the present day. The museum has two permanent galleries. "The Wool Harvest" looks at sheep farming and wool production and follows the path of a fleece through shearing, classing, wool pressing, and dispatch. There's a re-created shearing shed and a film about shearing, and if you visit during school holiday times, you may see a shearing demonstration. Another area of the museum looks at the processing of wool into fabric, and you can see a 1910 carpet loom in operation, producing the museum's own "Manor House Rug."

26 Moorabool St., Geelong, VIC 3220. ✆ **03/5272 4701.** www.nwm.vic.gov.au. Admission A$7.30 adults, A$3.65 children, A$20 family of 6. Mon–Fri 9:30am–5pm; Sat–Sun 1–5pm. Closed Good Friday and Dec 25–26.

WHERE TO STAY

Athelstane House ★★ Built in 1860, Athelstane House is Queenscliff's oldest operating guesthouse. A renovation in 1999 added modern conveniences and luxury touches to its rooms. As well as guest rooms, four of which have verandas, there is a self-contained ground floor apartment. Choose the King balcony room, which has a fireplace for cozy winter nights, or the apartment if you want a bit of space. There's a communal sitting room downstairs, with a fireplace, dining table, and library. A day spa is next door.

4 Hobson St., Queenscliff. ✆ **03/5258 1024.** www.athelstane.com.au. 9 units. A$170–A$200 double standard room midweek, A$195–A$235 weekends; A$200–A$230 double balcony room midweek, A$235–A$260 weekends; A$230 double apartment midweek, A$260 weekends. 2 night minimum stay on weekends. Ask about dinner, golf, and spa packages. Rates include breakfast. AE, V. **Amenities:** Restaurant; bar; access to nearby golf course. *In room:* A/C, TV, Jacuzzi.

WHERE TO DINE

Athelstane House ★★ CONTEMPORARY Relaxed and unpretentious, but still with plenty to say for itself, this is a popular venue with locals, so make sure you book ahead. The menu is innovative: Try the free-range lamb rump, or the yellowtail kingfish with a scallop omelette, peas, rice noodles, and dashi broth. Vegetarians won't get past the cumin potato roesti, roasted beetroot, and chargrilled zucchini and asparagus, with hazlenut cream and hung yogurt. At lunch, there are set-price menus—two courses for A$35 or three for A$45, with a glass of wine and tea or coffee.

4 Hobson St., Queenscliff. ✆ **03/5258 1024.** www.athelstane.com.au. Reservations recommended. Main courses A$32–A$41. AE, V. Daily for breakfast and dinner; Sat–Sun for lunch.

At the Heads CONTEMPORARY This open, casual restaurant, with huge windows overlooking the water and a view of the old wooden bridge, juts out over the water on the southern side of the Barwon River mouth. It's a great spot for lunch on a sunny day. The menu includes fish and chips, as well as a range of pastas, seafood dishes, and steaks. You find things like whole baby snapper roasted with leeks and lemongrass; or perhaps a King Island eye fillet with hash browns, baby fennel, mushrooms, and green peppercorn jus—and it's all consistently good. A seafood platter comes in two sizes, for A$50 or A$90. The wine list is almost exclusively Australian, with a good selection of local wines.

Jetty Rd., Barwon Heads. ✆ **03/5254 1277.** www.attheheads.com.au. Main courses A$21–A$36. AE, DC, MC, V. Mon–Fri 10am–late; Sat–Sun 8am–late.

The Mornington Peninsula

80km (50 miles) S of Melbourne

The Mornington Peninsula, a scenic 40km (25-mile) stretch of windswept coastline and hinterland, is one of Melbourne's favorite day-trip and weekend-getaway destinations. The coast is lined with good beaches and thick bush. The **Cape Shanck Coastal Park** stretches along the peninsula's Bass Strait foreshore from Portsea to Cape Shanck. It's home to gray kangaroos, southern brown bandicoots, echidnas, native rats, mice, reptiles, bats, and many forest and ocean birds. The park has numerous interconnecting walking tracks providing access to some remote beaches. You can get more information on this and all the other Victorian National Parks by calling ✆ **13 19 63.**

The Mornington Peninsula is a popular wine-producing region. The peninsula's fertile soil, temperate climate, and rolling hills produce excellent wine, particularly pinot noir, Shiraz, and chardonnay. Many wineries offer cellar-door tastings, others have excellent restaurants.

Along the route to the south, stop at the **Mornington Peninsula Regional Gallery,** Dunns Road, Mornington (✆ **03/5975 4395;** http://mprg.mornpen.vic.gov.au), to check out the work of well-known Australian artists (Tues–Sun 10am–5pm), or visit the summit at **Arthurs Seat State Park** for glorious views of the coastline. At Sorrento, take time out to spot pelicans on the jetty or visit the town's many galleries.

If you are traveling with kids, stop in at Australia's oldest maze, **Ashcombe Maze & Water Gardens,** Red Hill Road, Shoreham (✆ **03/5989 8387;** www.ashcombemaze.com.au). Mine loved it. As well as the big maze, there are extensive water and woodland gardens, and even a rose maze made out of 1,300 rose bushes. There's also a pleasant cafe with indoor and outdoor dining. The park is open daily from 10am to 5pm, except Christmas Day; admission is A$16 for adults, A$9 for children 4 to 16, and A$40 for families of four.

For fabulous wildlife viewing, take a night tour of **Moonlit Sanctuary ★**, 550 Tyabb Tooradin Rd., Pearcedale (✆ **03/5978 7935;** www.moonlit-sanctuary.com), at the northern end of the peninsula. The sanctuary is open daily from 11am but the best way to see Australia's nocturnal animals is on a guided evening tour, from 8:30pm October to March (8pm Apr–Sept). The bushland tour will enable you to see animals such as the eastern quoll, the red-bellied pademelon, and the southern bettong, all of which are extinct in the wild on Australia's mainland. Day admission is A$12 adults, A$7.50 children, and A$36 families. Night-time admission and guided tour is A$25 adults, A$14 children, or A$85 for a family of five. With transfers from Melbourne city hotels, the cost is A$109 adults or A$99 children.

ESSENTIALS

GETTING THERE From Melbourne, take the Mornington Peninsula Freeway to Rosebud, and then the Point Nepean Road. If you want to cross Port Phillip Bay from Sorrento to Queenscliff, take the **Sea Road Ferry** (✆ **03/5258 3244;** www.searoad.com.au), which operates daily every hour on the hour between 7am and 6pm in both directions. The one-way fare is around A$56 for a car and driver, and about A$7 per extra passenger, but changes slightly depending on the season. Foot-passenger fares (one-way) are A$10 for adults, A$9 for students 16 and over, A$8 for children 5 to 15, and A$1 for children under 5. The crossing takes 35 to 40 minutes.

VISITOR INFORMATION The **Peninsula Visitor Information Centre,** Point Nepean Road, Dromana (✆ **1800/804 009** in Australia, or 03/5987 3078; www.visitmorningtonpeninsula.org), has plenty of maps and information on the area and can also help book accommodations. It's open daily from 9am to 5pm, except December 25 and Good Friday.

WHERE TO STAY & DINE

The Portsea Hotel The motel-style rooms in this Tudor-style pub motel on the seafront are smartly done up, and the recently refurbished Executive Suite has a romantic look without being chintzy, as well as a fireplace, sofas, and a big-screen TV. The standard twin rooms are basic; all share bathrooms. Doubles have double beds and attached bathrooms with showers. Units with bathrooms also have TVs and refrigerators. The large **restaurant** is very popular and the outdoor **beer garden** overlooking the sea is hard to beat on a sunny day.

3746 Point Nepean Rd., Portsea, VIC 3944. ✆ **03/5984 2213.** www.portseahotel.com.au. 26 units, 6 with bathroom. A$110–A$155 double without bathroom; A$160–A$190 double with bathroom; A$190–A$225 bayview suite; A$275 executive suite (minimum 2-night stay, no children allowed). Extra adult A$45 or A$75 in the executive suite, extra child ages 5–12 A$30. More expensive prices are for Sat–Sun. AE, DC, MC, V. **Amenities:** Restaurant; 3 bars; golf course nearby. *In room:* A/C, TV (except standard rooms).

The Macedon Ranges

Some of Victoria's finest gardens dot the hills and valleys of the Macedon Ranges, just an hour from Melbourne. In bygone times, the wealthy swapped the city's summer heat for the cooler climes of Macedon. Their legacy of "hill station" private gardens and impressive mansions, along with the region's 40 cool-climate wineries and gourmet foods, are enough reason to visit. The best times to visit the Macedon Ranges for the gardens are April (autumn) and November (spring). These are **Open**

Garden months (www.opengarden.org.au), when private gardens can be viewed by the public. Some homestead gardens are open year-round, including **Duneira** (**© 03/5426 1490;** www.duneira.com.au) and **Tieve Tara** (**© 0418/337 813** mobile phone; www.gardensoftievetara.com) at Mount Macedon; **Bringalbit,** near Kyneton (**© 03/5423 7223;** www.bringalbit.com.au); and the Edna Walling garden at **Campaspe Country House,** Woodend (**© 03/5427 2273;** www.campese house.com.au). It pays to call ahead to check times and access. Entry fees apply.

At **Hanging Rock Reserve ★★**, South Rock Road, Woodend (**© 1800/244 711;** www.hangingrock.info), the ghost of Miranda, the fictional schoolgirl who vanished at Hanging Rock in author Joan Lindsay's 1967 novel *Picnic at Hanging Rock,* is never far away. Peter Weir's 1975 film of the novel cemented its fame, but the natural beauty of the area overshadows its slightly spooky reputation. You can climb the rock, walk the tracks, and explore caves like the Black Hole of Calcutta and the Cathedral. The Hanging Rock Discovery Centre explains the geology and history of the area, and revisits the book and movie. There are guided tours, including night tours during summer, and lots of wildlife including koalas, kangaroos, sugar gliders, echidnas, and wallabies. Picnic races have been run every Australia Day (Jan 26), New Year's Day, and Labour Day for the past 80-plus years and are hugely popular. The reserve is open daily 8am to 6pm. Admission is A$10 per car or A$4 per pedestrian.

After the gold rush of the 1850s, Woodend became a resort town with guesthouses, private gardens, a racecourse, a golf club, and hotels. Reminders of those days can be found in the historical buildings and clock tower on High Street. Cafes, provedores, boutiques, and galleries abound. For example, stop in for a beer at the family-run **Holgate Brewhouse,** in the historic Keatings Hotel on High Street (**© 03/5427 2510;** www.holgatebrewhouse.com). The brewery produces a range of draught beers and you can buy "tastings" until you decide on your favorite. The beer is brewed using just four ingredients—malt, hops, yeast, and pure Macedon Ranges water. It's open daily noon till late (from 2pm on Mon).

The hamlet of **Malmsbury** has two main things worth stopping for on the Calder Highway. First, the **Malmsbury Botanic Gardens,** next to the Town Hall, were designed to take advantage of the Coliban River valley and a billabong that was transformed into a group of ornamental lakes. The 5-hectare (12-acre) gardens have a superb collection of mature trees; it's also a popular spot for barbecues, and at Apple Hole you'll find kids leaping into the river from a rope swing. At quiet times, you may even spot a platypus. But Malmsbury's most famous landmark may be the bluestone railway viaduct built by 4,000 men in 1859. At 25m (82 ft.) high, with five 18m (59-ft.) spans, it is one of Australia's longest stone bridges and is best viewed from the gardens. I also like to pop in to **Tin Shed Arts** (**© 03/5423 2144**), a spacious gallery on the highway that always has something interesting and unexpected. It hangs contemporary and traditional art from both local artists and well-known names from around Australia. You'll find paintings, mixed media, sculpture, and craftwork. Open Thursday to Monday 10am to 5pm.

In **Kyneton,** turn down **Piper Street ★** for antiques, homewares, cafes, a heritage pub, and much more. The **Kyneton Farmers' Market** is held at Saint Paul's Park in Piper Street on the second Saturday of the month from 8am to 1pm.

With more than 40 vineyards and 20 cellar doors in the region, wine buffs who want to sample the product should consider a tour. **Victoria Winery Tours** (**© 1300/946 386;** www.winetours.com.au) runs small-group (minimum of two people) day tours from Melbourne, visiting four or five wineries. Pick up in Melbourne is at 9am, returning by about 5:30pm. The cost is A$150 per person, including morning tea and lunch.

ESSENTIALS

GETTING THERE & GETTING AROUND The Macedon Ranges are less than an hour's drive from Melbourne along the Calder Freeway, which is a continuation of the Tullamarine Freeway. Follow the signs towards Bendigo until you reach Gisborne, and then move off the freeway. **V/Line** (© **13 61 96** in Australia) trains from Melbourne to Bendigo pass through the Macedon Ranges, stopping at stations including Macedon, Woodend, Kyneton, and Malmsbury. Fares range from A$15 round-trip to Macedon to A$25 round-trip to Malmsbury.

Plan your own discovery of the region with personalized tours in a Jaguar with local Lyn Currie. **Jag Tours Kyneton** (© **03/5422 6738** or 0428 312 798 mobile phone; www.jagtourskyneton.com) will customize a tour for up to four people and take you anywhere for as long as you want, for about A$70 an hour.

VISITOR INFORMATION There are two visitor information centers in the region: the **Woodend Visitor Centre,** 711 High St., Woodend, and the **Kyneton Visitor Information Centre,** 127 High St., Kyneton. Both share the same telephone information line (© **1800/244 711**) and are open daily 9am to 5pm. The website **www.visitmacedonranges.com** is also a good source of information.

WHERE TO STAY

Apartment 61A This self-contained apartment on two levels has a lounge room upstairs overlooking Piper Street, and two fresh, modern bedrooms. Downstairs is a kitchen and all supplies are provided for breakfast, including organic juice, bacon and eggs, cereal, organic muesli, and yogurt. The real drawback, especially at night, is that the bathroom is also downstairs. Take a flashlight for negotiating the staircase in the dark.

61A Piper St., Kyneton, VIC 3444. © **03/5422-1211.** www.macedonrangesinteriors.com.au. 2 units. A$180 double. A$30 per extra person. *In room:* TV, hair dryer.

Campaspe Country House ★★ If playing lord and lady of the manor is your thing, this 1920s English-style country house with Art Deco touches will be just the place to stay. There are two guest rooms upstairs in the grand old manor house (with private bathrooms down the hall), as well as a more modern extension across the lawn with 16 rooms, and a private two-bedroom cottage. Campaspe House also boasts one of the Macedon Ranges' best **restaurants,** and if you overindulge (and you may well), you can walk it off in the lovely gardens.

29 Goldies Lane, Woodend. © **03/5427 2273.** Fax 03/5427 1049. www.campaspehouse.com.au. 19 units. A$280 double for all room types. Rates include breakfast. Ask about packages. AE, V. **Amenities:** Restaurant; bar; pool; tennis court; croquet courts. *In room:* TV, DVD, CD player, free Wi-Fi.

WHERE TO DINE

Pizza Verde ★★ PIZZA If you like your pizza thin and crisp, made from organic or gluten-free flour and adorned with tasty organic toppings, then this 1950s-style diner is the place for you. Owner-chef Damien Sandercock succeeds with such unlikely combinations as the "green" pizza—topped with zucchini, ricotta, mint, garlic, and lemon (with optional chili)—or the potato-topped pizza with caramelized onions. Some have the traditional tomato base, others an olive oil base. There's also meatballs or a vegetable pasta for those who don't want pizza. BYO wine (corkage A$5 per bottle), or you can try the house wine made by Damien's brother-in-law, Luke. There's beer too.

62 Piper St., Kyneton. © **03/5422 7400.** www.pizzaverde.com. Main courses A$15–A$18. V. Thurs–Mon 5pm–late; Sun noon–late.

Star Anise Bistro ★★ CONTEMPORARY The tiny dining room in this cottage on Kyneton's trendy Piper Street is proof that you don't have to be in a city to get seriously good food. Chef Emma Chapple, with husband Chris at the front of house, serves up some sensational and innovative dishes. Start with a few of the tasting plates, move on to main courses—the signature dish is spiced duck with pickled cherries, roasted baby beetroot, and braised red cabbage—but make sure you leave room for dessert. Desserts are color-coded—"Mr. Pink" is Turkish delight, fairy floss, raspberry semifredo, and rose and strawberry jelly. There's also Mr. Brown, Mr. White, and Mr. Yellow, and their friend Carmen Miranda. I'll leave you to ponder what each might be.

29 Piper St., Kyneton. © **03/5422 2777.** www.staranisebistro.com. Reservations recommended. Main courses A$25–A$34. AE, V. Thurs–Sun noon–3pm; Thurs–Sat 6:30–9:30pm.

Daylesford

108km (67 miles) NW of Melbourne

Daylesford can be a terrific day trip from Melbourne, or can also easily be combined with a trip to the Macedon Ranges (see above). Part of "spa country," this village is a bit of a trendy getaway for Melbournians. Along the main street, you'll find small galleries, homewares shops, and some smart foodie outlets.

Australians have been heading to Hepburn Springs, neighboring Daylesford, to "take the waters" since 1895, and there are now about a dozen or so day spas in the region. The original, and most famous, is **Hepburn Bathhouse & Spa** (© **03/5321 6000;** www.hepburnbathhouse.com). Not everyone likes the slick, modern, and rather cold new extension that has replaced the elegant old wooden building, but sink into the hot pools and it's easy to forget what the exterior looks like. There's traditional communal bathing in the Bathhouse and the Sanctuary, or you can book in to the Spa (in the original bathhouse building; reservations essential) for the usual range of therapies and treatments. The complex includes an aroma steam room, salt therapy pool, relaxation pool, and "spa couches" submerged in mineral water (which I didn't find very comfortable). The complex is on Mineral Springs Reserve Road and is open daily 9am to 6:30pm. Entry to the Bathhouse costs A$23 per person or A$73 for a family of four Tuesday to Friday, A$30 per person or A$98 families Saturday to Monday and on public holidays (towel hire is A$3.50). Entry to the Sanctuary is A$55 Tuesday to Friday, A$75 Saturday to Monday and public holidays (including towel and robe). Both are for a 2-hour period. A 30-minute private mineral bath at The Spa costs A$65.

On the hill behind Daylesford's main street is the **Convent** (© **03/5348 3211;** www.theconvent.com.au), a three-level historic 19th-century mansion, complete with twisting staircases. It is comprised of a restaurant, a gallery, gardens, a chapel, and shops, as well as a small museum that speaks to its origins as a private home, which later became the Holy Cross Convent and Boarding School for Girls. After years of dereliction, it reopened as a gallery in 1991, but the nuns' infirmary and one of the "cells," or bedrooms, were left unrestored. You'll find it on the corner of Hill and Daly streets. It's open daily 10am to 4pm, and admission is A$5 per person. A self-contained luxury "penthouse" on the second level can be yours from A$295 per night, with breakfast. Take time to wander through the lovely gardens, with their sculptures and bench seats.

Just outside Daylesford is **Lavandula** (✆ **03/5476 4393;** www.lavandula.com.au), a Swiss-Italian lavender farm that features a rustic trattoria-style cafe and a cobblestone courtyard with a cluster of farmhouse buildings. Swiss immigrants ran a dairy farm here in the 1860s, but today you can see the process of lavender farming and buy all manner of lavender products. The restored stone farmhouse is a picturesque backdrop to gardens where you can picnic, play boules (like bocce), or just relax and admire the scenery. The lavender is in full bloom in December, with harvesting in January. Lavandula is at 350 Hepburn-Newstead Rd., Shepherds Flat, about 10 minutes' drive north of Daylesford. It is open daily from 10:30am to 5:30pm September to May (except Dec 24 and 25), and on weekends, public holidays, and school holidays only in June, July, and August. The cafe is closed during August. Admission is A$3.50 adults, A$1 school-age children. There's also a modern three-bedroom house on the property which can be rented, starting from A$280 for one room for 1 night.

ESSENTIALS

GETTING THERE From Melbourne, take the Citylink toll-road (the M2) north towards Melbourne Airport. Take the Calder Highway turnoff towards Bendigo (M79), and continue until you see the turnoff to Daylesford (C792); then follow the signs. The road will take you through Woodend, Tylden, and Trentham. At Trentham take the C317 to Daylesford. When you arrive in Daylesford, turn right at the roundabout as signposted to get to Hepburn Springs.

VISITOR INFORMATION The **Daylesford Regional Visitor Information Centre,** 98 Vincent St. (✆ **03/5321 6123;** www.visitdaylesford.com), features an interpretive display about the area's mineral waters. It's open daily from 9am to 5pm, except December 25.

WHERE TO STAY & DINE

The Lake House ★★★ The Lake House is set on the edge Lake Daylesford, on 2.4 hectares (6 acres) of beautiful gardens. Walking tracks circle the lake and also lead into Wombat State Forest. Lodge rooms have private courtyards and are clustered around a common lounge room, which has a roaring log fire in winter. Waterfront rooms have balconies and king-size beds, and the suites have double Jacuzzis. Throughout the property, the walls are adorned with vibrant art works. The Lake House **restaurant** is renowned for its commitment to local and seasonal produce and is widely regarded as one of the best restaurants in Australia.

King St., Daylesford, VIC 3460. ✆ **03/5348 3329.** www.lakehouse.com.au. 33 units. A$500 double lodge room; A$600 double waterfront room; A$740 double waterfront suite. Rates include breakfast. AE, DC, MC, V. **Amenities:** Restaurant; bar; spa; tennis court. *In room:* A/C, TV, hair dryer, free Wi-Fi.

VICTORIA

by Lee Mylne

Most visitors to Victoria start out exploring Melbourne's cosmopolitan streets before taking a few day trips to the wineries or the gold fields around the historic city of Ballarat. But that's only a fraction of what Victoria has to offer—this wonderfully diverse area is worth a closer look.

14

The Murray River, which separates Victoria from New South Wales, has been the lifeblood of the region, providing irrigation for vast tracts of semidesert land. In recent years, as Australia's drought has worsened, the state of the once-mighty Murray has been a focus of environmental concerns; you're likely to still hear talk of this when you visit.

While devastating bushfires ravaged parts of Victoria in early 2009, making headlines around the world, most of Victoria's major tourist destinations escaped the worst of the disaster. Parts of the High Country and Gippsland may still be recovering when you visit, and this will give you a first-hand look at the wonder of the Australian bush regenerating. And the bush here is vast: Australia's southernmost mainland state has 35 national parks, encompassing every possible terrain, from rainforest and mountain ranges to sun-baked Outback desert and a coast where waves crash dramatically onto rugged sandstone outcroppings.

This chapter covers the bulk of Victoria, but for more information on the Dandenong Ranges, Yarra Valley, Phillip Island, Macedon Ranges, Daylesford, and the Mornington Peninsula, see "Side Trips from Melbourne," in chapter 13.

BALLARAT: GOLD-RUSH CITY ★★

113km (70 miles) W of Melbourne

History buffs will love Ballarat. Victoria's largest inland city (pop. 90,000) is synonymous with two major events of Australia's past: the gold rush of the 1850s and the birth of Australian democracy in the early 20th century. It all started with gold; in 1851 two prospectors found gold nuggets scattered on the ground at a place known as, ironically, Poverty Point. Within a year, 20,000 people had drifted into the area, and Australia's El Dorado gold rush had begun.

In 1858, the second-largest chunk of gold discovered in Australia (the Welcome Nugget) was found, but by the early 1860s, most of the easily obtainable yellow metal was gone. Larger operators continued digging until 1918, and by then Ballarat had developed enough industry to survive without mining. Today, you can still see the gold rush's effects in the impressive buildings, built from the miners' fortunes, lining Ballarat's streets.

Essentials

GETTING THERE From Melbourne, Ballarat is a 1½-hour drive on the Great Western Highway. **V/Line** (✆ **13 61 96** in Victoria, or 03/8608 5011; www.vline.com.au) runs trains between the cities every day; the trip takes about 90 minutes. The return fare is A$30 for adults and A$15 for children. Ask about off-peak and family-saver fares.

Several companies offer day trips from Melbourne. They include **AAT Kings** (✆ **1300/556 100** in Australia, or 03/9663 3377; www.aatkings.com). A full-day tour costs A$146 for adults and A$73 for children.

VISITOR INFORMATION The **Ballarat Visitor Information Centre** is located near the Prisoner-of-War Memorial at the Ballarat Botanic Gardens, near Lake Wendoree (✆ **1800/446 633** in Australia, or 03/5320 5758; www.visitballarat.com.au). There is also an information center at the Ballarat Fine Art Gallery, 40 Lydiard St. N. Both are open daily from 9am to 5pm except Christmas Day.

Seeing the Sights

Art Gallery of Ballarat The highlight of a visit to this gallery—especially after you've learned the story of the Eureka Uprising (see "A Eureka Moment," p. 662) is the sight of the original Eureka flag, made from petticoat fabric by the women of the uprising and now enshrined here. This excellent gallery, founded in 1884, is Australia's oldest regional gallery and houses a fine collection of Australian art, including paintings from the Heidelberg School and a stunning collection of 20th-century modernists. It also hosts interesting contemporary exhibitions on popular themes.

40 Lydiard St. N. ✆ **03/5320 5858.** www.balgal.com. Free admission. Daily 9am–5pm. Closed Dec 25. Guided tours at 2pm Wed–Sun.

Ballarat Botanical Gardens These delightful gardens are suffering in Australia's drought conditions but still well worthwhile visiting. The gold-rich citizens of Ballarat bestowed magnificent gifts on the gardens from its early days, including the collection of 12 marble statues that now stand in the conservatory, the elegant Statuary Pavilion and its contents—including the wonderful *Flight from Pompeii*—and a statue of William Wallace near the gardens' entrance. Other highlights include Prime Ministers Avenue, lined with bronze busts of Australia's 25 PMs, and the striking Australian Ex-Prisoners of War Memorial at the southwestern end of the gardens. One of the greatest attractions is an avenue of 70 giant redwoods, planted about 130 years ago. The gardens' cafe overlooks Lake Wendouree.

Wendouree Parade. ✆ **03/5320 5135.** www.ballarat.vic.gov.au. Free admission. Conservatory daily 9am–5pm. Bus: 16.

Blood on the Southern Cross ★ This breathtaking sound-and-light show re-creates the Eureka Uprising, one of the most important events in Australia's history.

Victoria

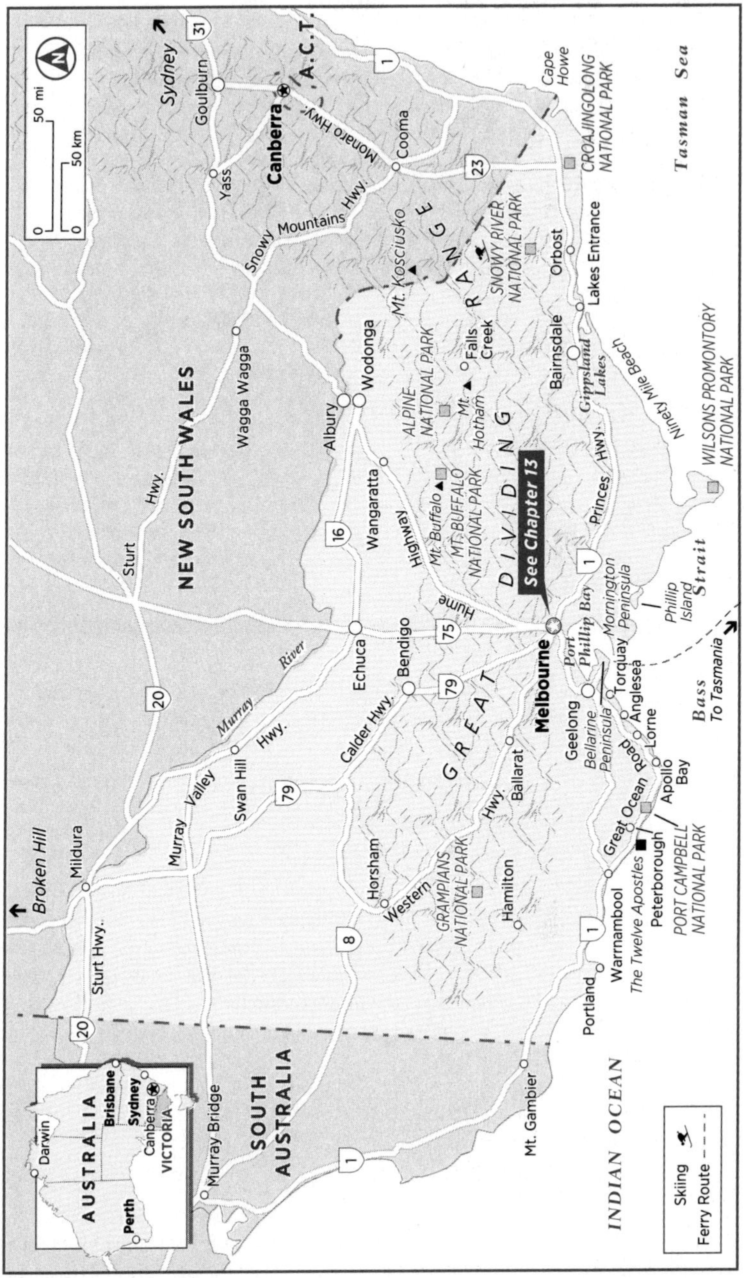
0 50 mi
0 50 km
N
Sydney
Goulburn
Yass
Canberra
A.C.T.
Monaro Hwy.
Cooma
Snowy Mountains Hwy.
Wagga Wagga
NEW SOUTH WALES
Sturt Hwy.
Broken Hill
Mildura
Murray Valley Hwy.
Swan Hill
Murray River
Echuca
Albury
Wodonga
Wangaratta
Hume Highway
Bendigo
Calder Hwy.
Mt. Kosciusko
GREAT DIVIDING RANGE
ALPINE NATIONAL PARK
Mt. Hotham
Falls Creek
Mt. Buffalo
MT. BUFFALO NATIONAL PARK
SNOWY RIVER NATIONAL PARK
Cape Howe
CROAJINGOLONG NATIONAL PARK
Tasman Sea
Orbost
Lakes Entrance
Bairnsdale
Gippsland Lakes
Ninety Mile Beach
Princes Hwy.
WILSONS PROMONTORY NATIONAL PARK
See Chapter 13
Melbourne
Port Phillip Bay
Mornington Peninsula
Phillip Island
Bass Strait
To Tasmania
Geelong
Bellarine Peninsula
Torquay
Anglesea
Lorne
Apollo Bay
Great Ocean Road
Ballarat
Western Hwy.
Horsham
GRAMPIANS NATIONAL PARK
Hamilton
Warrnambool
The Twelve Apostles
Peterborough
PORT CAMPBELL NATIONAL PARK
Portland
Mt. Gambier
INDIAN OCEAN
SOUTH AUSTRALIA
Murray Bridge
AUSTRALIA
Darwin
Brisbane
Sydney
Canberra
VICTORIA
Perth
Skiing
Ferry Route

A eureka MOMENT

The story that is central to Ballarat's history, and many of its attractions, is that of the **Eureka Uprising** in 1854. The story goes like this: After gold was discovered, the government introduced gold licenses, charging miners even if they came up empty-handed. The miners had to buy a license every month, and corrupt gold-field police (many of whom were former convicts) instituted a vicious campaign to extract the money. When license checks intensified in 1854, resentment flared. Prospectors began demanding political reforms, such as the right to vote, parliamentary elections, and secret ballots. The situation exploded when the Eureka Hotel's owner murdered a miner but was set free by the government. The hotel was burned down in revenge, and more than 20,000 prospectors joined together, burned their licenses in a huge bonfire, and built a stockade over which they raised a flag. Troops arrived at the "Eureka Stockade" the next month, but only 150 miners remained. The stockade was attacked at dawn, with 24 miners killed and 30 wounded. The uprising forced the government to act: The licenses were replaced with "miners' rights" and cheaper fees, and the vote was introduced to Victoria. It was a definitive moment in Australia's history and the Eureka flag is still a potent (and often controversial) symbol of nationalism. The original flag is on display at the Art Gallery of Ballarat (see below). The Eureka Centre, a major attraction commemorating the event, is closed for an A$11-million redevelopment during 2011, but visitors can still visit the original site of the uprising on Eureka Street—though there's not much to see there.

You will be outdoors, so bring something warm to wear, because it can get chilly at night. It's stirring stuff, and the reenactment does the story justice. The show runs 90 minutes and is full of surprises.

Sovereign Hill, Bradshaw St. ✆ **03/5337 1199.** www.sovereignhill.com.au. Reservations required. Admission A$50 adults, A$27 children 5–15, A$134 families of 4. Package with daytime entry to Sovereign Hill (see below) A$90 adults, A$45 children, A$238 families. Package with buffet dinner and stay at Sovereign Hill Lodge (see below) A$190 adults, A$80 children, A$499 families. Call ahead for information about other packages. 2 shows nightly (times vary seasonally).

The Gold Museum This surprisingly interesting museum houses a large collection of gold nuggets found at Ballarat, as well as alluvial deposits, gold ornaments, and coins. It also holds gallery displays relating to the history of gold mining in the area. One hour should be enough to take in the museum.

Bradshaw St. (opposite Sovereign Hill). ✆ **03/5337 1107.** Admission A$10 adults, A$5.20 children. See Gold Pass (below). Daily 9:30am–5:20pm.

Sovereign Hill ★★ ☺ Ballarat's history all comes to life in the Colonial-era re-creation on Sovereign Hill. Australia's best outdoor museum transports you back to the 1850s and the heady days of the gold rush. More than 40 stone-and-wood reproduction buildings, including shops and businesses on Main Street, sit on the 25-hectare (62-acre) former gold-mining site. There are also tent camps around the diggings on the lowest part of the site, which would have been the outskirts of town. There is a lot to see and do, so expect to spend at least 4 hours. The township bustles with actors in period costumes going about their daily business. In addition to seeing how miners and their families lived, visitors can pan for real gold, ride in horse-drawn carriages, and watch potters, blacksmiths, and tanners make their wares. Don't miss the gold pour at the smelting works, or the redcoats as they parade through the streets. On top of Sovereign Hill are the mine shafts and pithead equipment. The guided tour of a typical underground gold mine takes around 45 minutes. The **Voyage to Discovery** museum has artifacts from the gold rush, dioramas of mining scenes, and interactive computer displays. A restaurant and several cafes, coffee shops, and souvenir stores are around the site.

Bradshaw St. ✆ **03/5331 1944.** www.sovereignhill.com.au. Admission (including mine tour and Gold Museum) A$41 adults, A$19 children 5–15, A$75–A$104 families. Daily 10am–5pm. Closed Dec 25. Bus: 9 from Curtis St. or the railway station. A free bus meets the daily 9:08am (9:28am on Sun) train (the "Goldrush Special" from Melbourne's Southern Cross railway station) when it arrives at Ballarat Station, and takes visitors direct to Sovereign Hill. Return service connects with the 4pm (4:10pm on Sat) train back to Melbourne.

Where to Stay

Abena's 🎁 This stylish cottage has three bedrooms, one with a romantic queen-size four-poster bed. The other rooms have a double bed and two singles respectively. There's a small garden at the back and plenty of space for a family. Gregarious owner Sandy Guy provides the makings for a gourmet breakfast and is a font of information about the city. If you don't feel like cooking dinner, cross the road to the Grapes Hotel, one of Ballarat's great old pubs. If you do, there's a full kitchen with dishwasher, fridge, and microwave.

210 Grant St., Ballarat, VIC 3350. ✆ **03/5338 7397** or 0412/308 390 mobile phone. www.ballarat.com/abenas. 3 units. A$160 double. A$20 extra person, A$15 children 2–12. Minimum 2-night stay. AE, DC, MC, V. Free secure parking. *In room:* A/C, TV/DVD, CD player, hair dryer, kitchen.

Craig's Royal Hotel Built in 1853, this lovely old landmark has been slowly restored over the past 6 years or so. Each room is different in size and shape and has been given an individual look of its own—ranging from the utterly romantic to the fabulously ornate. Among the most special are the Anglo-Japanese suite and the bedroom furnished with an antique Chinese wedding bed. While still a pub at heart, the hotel offers some of Ballarat's finest accommodation, with wonderful attention to detail and a true sense of history.

10 Lydiard St. S, Ballarat, VIC 3350. ✆ **03/5331 1377.** Fax 03/5331 7103. www.craigsroyal.com.au. 41 units. A$230–A$500 double. Ask about packages. Rates include breakfast. AE, DC, MC, V. Free parking. **Amenities:** 2 restaurants; 2 bars. *In room:* A/C, TV, hair dryer, free Internet.

Kingsley Place ★ 🎁 If you'd enjoy staying in a historic house, you might want to try this grand gentleman's residence built in the gold-rush days. The house has three bedrooms and two bathrooms (one with a Jacuzzi). Two rooms have queen-size beds and the third has a double. The house also has an open fireplace (don't worry, there's central heating, too, if you prefer), and full laundry facilities. A continental breakfast is provided for your first morning. The owners also have a similar heritage cottage available in Creswick, about 15km (9 miles) outside Ballarat.

85 Victoria St., Ballarat, VIC 3350. ✆ **03/5332 8296.** Fax 03/5331 3358. www.heritagehomestay.com. A$350 double weekdays, A$450 double weekends. 2-night minimum. Extra adult A$30; extra child 17 and under A$15. AE, DC, MC, V. **Amenities:** Kitchen, TV lounge. *In room:* TV/VCR, CD player, hair dryer.

Sovereign Hill Lodge The colonial-style wooden buildings adjacent to Sovereign Hill were built to resemble an 1850s government camp that was used to control (and tax) the minefields. The Residence building has rooms with queen-size beds and a set of single bunks, and the Offices building has heritage rooms with four-poster beds and Baltic pine furnishings, some with Jacuzzis. There are eight double rooms in the Superintendent's house; the Barracks houses dorm rooms that sleep up to 10 people, with shared bathroom facilities. There's a bar, 24-hour reception, and a game room. Guests get a 10% discount off entry to Sovereign Hill. **Steinfeld's** is a new accommodation complex at the top of Sovereign Hill's Main Street, so visitors can stay in the heart of the recreated goldfields town. The building, formerly a furniture warehouse, has been transformed to create four guest rooms across the front of the building; the large lounge room has views down Main Street. Steinfeld's is booked through Sovereign Hill Lodge.

Magpie St., Ballarat, VIC 3350. ✆ **03/5333 3409.** Fax 03/5333 5861. www.sovereignhill.com.au. 37 units. A$135–A$175 double; A$68 double for Barracks. Ask about the many packages. AE, DC, MC, V. Free parking. **Amenities:** Restaurant; bar; babysitting. *In room:* A/C, TV, hair dryer.

Where to Dine

Eclectic Tastes CAFE You might find it hard to concentrate on your breakfast, lunch, or coffee and snack, as your eyes will be on the surroundings, which live up to the cafe's name—it's five rooms packed to the rafters with colorful trash and treasure! Your menu is pasted inside the cardboard covers of a Little Golden Book (think *The Shy Little Kitten* and other titles from your childhood) and might include a great Thai chicken curry, a seafood laksa, or something more simple, like a sandwich. You'll find it opposite the Ballarat Cemetery (also worth a wander through) near the shores of Lake Wendouree.

2 Burbank St., Ballarat. ✆ **03/5339 9252.** Main courses A$7–A$18. MC, V. Daily 9am–4pm; Wed–Sun 6–9pm.

Oscar's CONTEMPORARY This cafe and bar inside one of Ballarat's historic old pubs is in the heart of the town, walking distance from shopping, the art gallery, and many other attractions. The former gold rush–era hotel was redeveloped in 2003, and now has an appealing open-plan restaurant, with a courtyard and bar. It's open for breakfast, lunch, and dinner and you can get snacks all day. Meals include Asian, pizzas, pasta, steaks, and gluten-free dishes.

18 Doveton St. S., Ballarat. ✆ **03/5331 1451.** Reservations recommended. Main courses A$19–A$32. AE, DC, MC, V. Daily 7am–10pm.

THE GREAT OCEAN ROAD ★★

Geelong: 75km (47 miles) SW of Melbourne; Torquay: 94km (58 miles) SW of Melbourne; Port Campbell National Park: 285km (177 miles) SW of Melbourne; Peterborough: 200km (124 miles) SW of Melbourne; Warrnambool: 263km (163 miles) SW of Melbourne

The Great Ocean Road—which hugs the coast from Torquay through Anglesea, Lorne, Apollo Bay, Port Campbell, and Peterborough, until it ends at Warrnambool—is one of Australia's most spectacular drives. The scenery along the 106km (66-mile) route includes huge cliffs, ocean vistas, beaches, rainforests, and some incredible rock formations. The most spectacular section is the 27km (17-mile) stretch between Princeton (the start of Port Campbell National Park) and

Peterborough. The settlements along the highway are small, but they offer a number of accommodations.

The main attractions are in the coastal Port Campbell National Park, so don't be surprised if you're not overly impressed until you get there. If you are traveling on to Adelaide, you could stop off for a night along the Great Ocean Road and spend another night in the Coorong in South Australia (see p. 600).

Essentials

ORGANIZED TOURS Even on an organized tour, when you are not doing the driving, I'd be reluctant to try this in 1 day unless absolutely pressed for time. All the tours which operate to the Great Ocean Road take around 12 hours (sometimes more), which makes for a big day out. The large coach operator **AAT Kings** (✆ **03/9663 3377;** www.aatkings.com) runs daily trips which cost A$159 for adults, and A$90 for children. **Gray Line Sightseeing Tours** (✆ **1300/858 687** in Australia, or 03/9663 4455; www.grayline.com) also has day trips for a similar price and duration. A better option would be Gray Line's 2-day Great Ocean Road tour, which overnights in Lorne. It costs A$373 adults double (single rate is A$455) and A$142 for children.

Wild-Life Tours (✆ **1300/661 730** in Australia, or 03/9396 1938; www.wildlifetours.com.au) offers several well-priced multiday backpacker-style tours that take in the Great Ocean Road tour from Melbourne. A 1-day tour costs A$95, and a 2-day tour which overnights at Hall's Gap and also takes in the Grampians (p. 680) costs A$169. Hostel-style accommodations are extra: A$23 for a dorm bed or A$60 for a twin or double room.

Autopia Tours (✆ **1800/000 507** in Australia, or 03/9419 8878; www.autopiatours.com.au) offers a 1-day tour from Melbourne that takes in all the sights and includes lunch and a bushwalk in the fabulous Otway National Park. It costs A$125. The company also does a more relaxed 3-day tour, including the Grampians (see p. 680). This costs upwards from A$445, with dorm accommodations both nights, but you can upgrade to double or single rooms.

VISITOR INFORMATION Most places along the route have their own information centers. If you're coming from Melbourne, stop at the **Geelong & Great Ocean Road Visitors Centre,** Princess Highway, Little River, VIC 3214 (✆ **1800/620 888** in Australia, or 03/5283 1735; www.visitgreatoceanroad.org.au). You can book accommodations here, which you should do in advance, especially in summer. The website gives you plenty of tour options. There's also a visitor center at the **National Wool Museum,** 26 Moorabool St. (at Brougham St.), Geelong (✆ **1800/620 888** in Australia, or 03/5222 2900).

Along the route, the **Twelve Apostles Visitor Information Centre,** 26 Morris St., Port Campbell (✆ **1300/137 255** in Australia or 03/5598 6089; www.visit12apostles.com.au), is a good place to pick up brochures. It has some interesting displays and an audiovisual show, and also acts as a hotel-booking service for the area. All these information centers are open from 9am to 5pm daily, except Christmas Day.

Exploring the Coastal Road

Along the route you might want to stop off at **Torquay,** a township dedicated to surfing. The main surf beach is much nicer than the one farther down the coast in

Lorne. Check out **Surfworld Museum,** Surfcity Plaza, Beach Road, West Torquay (© **03/5261 4606;** www.surfworld.org.au), which has exhibits dealing with surfboard design and surfing history, and video of the world's best surfers. Admission is A$10 for adults, A$6 for children, and A$20 for families of five. It's open 9am to 5pm daily, except December 25. **Bells Beach,** just down the road, is world famous in surfing circles for its perfect waves.

Lorne has some nice boutiques and is a good place to stop for lunch or stay the night. The stretch from Lorne to Apollo Bay is one of the most spectacular sections of the route; the road narrows and twists and turns along a cliff edge with the ocean on the other side. **Apollo Bay** is a pleasant town that was once a whaling station. It has good sandy beaches and is more low-key than Lorne.

Next you come to the **Angahook-Lorne State Park,** which protects most of the coastal section of the Otway Ranges from Aireys Inlet, south of Anglesea, to Kennett River. It has many well-marked rainforest walks and picnic areas at Shelly Beach, Elliot River, and Blanket Bay. There's plenty of wildlife around.

About 13km (8 miles) past Apollo Bay, just off the main road, you can stroll on the **Maits Rest Rainforest Boardwalk.** A little farther along the main road, an unpaved road leads north past Hopetoun Falls and Beauchamp Falls to the settlement of **Beech Forest.** Seven kilometers (4⅓ miles) farther along the main road, another unpaved road heads south for 15km (9⅓ miles) to a windswept headland and the **Cape Otway Lightstation** (© **03/5237 9240;** www.lightstation.com), one of several along the coast. Built by convicts in 1848, the 100m-tall (328-ft.) lighthouse is open to tourists. Admission is A$17 for adults, A$7.50 for children under 18, and A$42 for families of 6, including a guided tour of the lighthouse. It's open daily from 9am to 5pm. The lighthouse is manned by a guide, who will greet you at the top of the tower to recount stories of the Cape's traditional owners, shipwrecks, the colorful lighthouse keepers, and much more, including one of Australia's most famous UFO mysteries. The Lightkeeper's Shipwreck Discovery Tour, which runs twice a day from 10am to noon or 2 to 4pm, takes you away from the Lightstation to nearby related sites including Parker River inlet and Blanket Bay, and you will see the remains of shipwrecks lost in the treacherous Bass Strait and Southern Ocean. Morning or afternoon tea is included at the Lightkeeper's Café and the tour continues in the Lightstation grounds. The cost is A$36 adults and A$21 children.

Back on the main road, your route heads inland through an area known as **Horden Vale** before running to the sea at Glenaire—there's good surfing and camping at **Johanna,** 6km (3¾ miles) north of here. Then the Great Ocean Road heads north again to **Lavers Hill,** a former timber town. Five kilometers (3 miles) southwest of Lavers Hill is small **Melba Gully State Park,** where you can spot glowworms at night and walk along routes of rainforest ferns. Keep an eye out for one of the last giant gum trees that escaped the loggers—it's some 27m (88 ft.) in circumference and is estimated to be more than 300 years old.

The next place of note is Moonlight Head, which marks the start of the **Shipwreck Coast**—a 120km (74-mile) stretch running to Port Fairy that claimed more than 80 ships in only 40 years at the end of the 19th century and the beginning of the 20th.

Just past Princetown starts the biggest attraction of the trip, **Port Campbell National Park ★★**. With its sheer cliffs and coastal rock sculptures, it's one of the most immediately recognizable images of natural Australia. You can't miss the

The Great Ocean Walk

Getting out of your car and walking at least a part of Victoria's spectacular west coast is well worth the effort. The Great Ocean Walk stretches 91km (56 miles) from Apollo Bay to Glenample Homestead (near the Twelve Apostles), passing through National Parks and overlooking the Marine National Park and Sanctuary. The trail has been designed so walkers can "step on" or "step off" at a number of places, completing short walks of around 2 hours, up to day or overnight hikes. If you are planning to stay overnight, you must register with Parks Victoria (© 13 19 63; www.greatoceanwalk.com.au) at least 2 weeks ahead. Camping fees are A$22 per tent site per night. The walk winds through beautiful and remote areas such as Station Beach and Moonlight Head, which were previously difficult to access. It also reveals wet fern and rainforest gullies, which have huge specimens of the world's tallest flowering tree, the mountain ash; crosses coastal heathlands; and goes in and out of the sheltered coastal estuaries of the Aire and Gellibrand rivers. Check the website for detailed information on all aspects of the walk, including guided walks, assisted overnight walks with tour operators, camping and walking equipment hire, and food provision.

Twelve Apostles, a series of rock pillars (actually, there are eight left standing) in the foam just offshore. Other attractions are the **Blowhole,** which throws up huge sprays of water; the **Grotto,** a rock formation intricately carved by the waves; **London Bridge,** which looked quite like the real thing until the center crashed into the sea in 1990 (leaving a bunch of tourists stranded on the wrong end); and the **Loch Ard Gorge. Port Fairy,** a lovely fishing town once called Belfast by Irish immigrants who settled here to escape the potato famine, is also on the Shipwreck Coast.

Not far past the town of Peterborough, the Great Ocean Road heads inland to Warrnambool. It eventually joins the Princes Highway heading toward Adelaide.

Where to Stay Along the Way

The **Great Ocean Road Accommodation Centre,** 136 Mountjoy Parade, Lorne, VIC 3232 (© **03/5289 4233;** www.gorac.com.au), rents cottages and units along the route.

IN LORNE

Lorne is a good option for a night's rest. The beach is nothing special, but it's a great place to learn to surf. There are plenty of restaurants and lots of boutiques.

Cumberland Lorne Conference & Leisure Resort ★ This large resort sticks out conspicuously between the sea and the foothills of the Otway Ranges. Still, I highly recommend it—it's a good deal, and quite luxurious. Every apartment has a queen-size bed and a sofa bed, a kitchen, a laundry, a Jacuzzi, a balcony, Internet access, free in-house movies, and a CD player. All units have large bathrooms with tub/shower combinations. More than half of the rooms have panoramic ocean views; the rest overlook gardens. Two-bedroom apartments have two extra single beds, and split-level penthouses have two Jacuzzis and two balconies.

150–178 Mountjoy Parade, Lorne, VIC 3232. ✆ **1800/037 010** in Australia, or 03/5289 2400. Fax 03/5289 2256. www.cumberland.com.au. 99 units. A$270–A$330 1-bedroom apt, A$355–A$415 2-bedroom apt, A$480–A$510 penthouse. Rates are higher in peak season (Easter and summer), when 2- and 3-night minimum stays apply. Stays must include a Fri and Sat night on weekends. Ask about packages. AE, DC, MC, V. Free covered parking. **Amenities:** Restaurant; babysitting; bikes; children's center; concierge; exercise room; Jacuzzi; heated indoor pool and toddlers' pool; room service; sauna; spa; 2 lit tennis courts. *In room:* A/C, TV w/pay movies, hair dryer, kitchenette, Wi-Fi (A$13 for 2 hr.).

Great Ocean Road Cottages ☺ This complex has it all, although with so many people (and quite a few children) around, it can be a little noisy in summer. The self-contained cottages, set away from one another in a quiet patch of bushland, lie about a 5-minute walk from the town center. Each cottage is a two-story wooden hut with a double bed, two twin beds, and a pullout mattress. There's also a bathroom and a full kitchen and free laundry facilities. Also on the property is **Great Ocean Road Backpackers** (✆ **03/5289 1809;** www.yha.com.au), which offers dorm-style accommodations. It has 30 dorm beds, three double rooms and one twin room, and two family rooms (each with a queen-size bed and two singles). Dorms for YHA members are A$20 and A$24 for nonmembers; doubles and twin rooms are A$55 and A$65; family rooms are A$75 to A$90.

10 Erskine Ave. (P.O. Box 60), Lorne, VIC 3232. ✆ **03/5289 1070.** Fax 03/5289 2508. www.greatoceanroadcottages.com. 10 cottages. A$150 double weekdays; A$170 double Sat–Sun. Extra adult A$25, extra child A$10. Minimum 7-night stay in high season (Dec 26–Jan 26). AE, DC, MC, V. **Amenities:** Bikes; Jacuzzi. *In room:* A/C, TV/VCR, hair dryer, kitchenette.

IN APOLLO BAY

Chris's Beacon Point Villas Perched high in the Otways, above the Great Ocean Road, these villas have wonderful views of the coast. Host Chris Talihmanidis is well known as a local restaurateur, with a passion for the food of southern Europe. There are two studios and six self-contained, stylishly furnished two-bedroom villas, all with the same panoramic views. Villas have a queen-size bed and a double or two singles, while studios sleep two in a king-size bed. Don't miss the chance to eat at Chris's award-winning **restaurant.**

280 Skenes Creek Rd., Apollo Bay, VIC 3233. ✆ **03/5237 6411.** Fax 03/5237 6930. www.chriss.com.au. 8 units. A$290–A$320 double studio; A$265–A$320 villa (sleeps 4). Rates include breakfast. AE, DC, MC, V. **Amenities:** Restaurant; bar; babysitting. *In room:* TV/VCR w/pay movies, kitchen, free Wi-Fi.

IN PORT CAMPBELL

Macka's Farm Lodge ★ 🎁 ☺ If you have kids, this working farm inland from the Twelve Apostles may be just the place for a break from touring. The units all have kitchens, so you can cook your own feast. Otherwise, you can order meals by prior arrangement outside peak season, or visit one of the nearby restaurants. There are four self-contained lodges and a farmhouse. The lodges form the "homestead" complex and have wonderful views across the farm, bush, and to the ocean. Two of them sleep three people. The third lodge has three bedrooms, with a queen-size bed, a king-size bed (interchangeable to two singles), and a bedroom with singles and bunks. The fourth lodge has two bedrooms, each with a queen-size bed. The farmhouse has four bedrooms, three with queen-size beds, one with four singles. All have a TV, DVD, and CD player—but you may not even turn them on, when there are lots of piglets, calves, ducks, and chickens running around to entertain the kids. Overall, it's a great farm experience.

RSD 2305 Princetown Rd., Princetown, VIC 3269. ✆ **03/5598 8261.** Fax 03/5598 8201. www.mackasfarm.com.au. 5 units. A$150–A$320, depending on the house, the number in your group, and the season (check the website because there are dozens of different price categories). MC, V. From the Twelve Apostles, go 2km (1¼ miles), turn at the sign for Macka's Farm, and go 4km (2½ miles) inland. *In room:* TV, DVD, CD player, hair dryer, kitchen.

Where to Dine

Marks Restaurant ★ CONTEMPORARY Seaside chic, friendly staff, and great food are a winning recipe for this favorite with locals and travelers. Marks is a stylish, simple, and smart bistro, with an emphasis on seafood and local produce. The menu changes every day, depending on what's freshly available, but some things are constants: oysters, mussels, local whitebait, Atlantic salmon, usually some game such as duck or kangaroo, and there's also—a relative rarity in restaurants—always an offal dish. Vegetarians are also well catered for. The signature dessert is chocolate mousse. There's a good wine list, or you can BYO (corkage charge A$7 per bottle).

124 Mount Joy Parade, Lorne. ✆ **03/5289 2787.** www.marksrestaurant.com.au. Main courses A$17–A$16. AE, MC, V. Daily 6–10pm. Closed Aug and Sept. Check first, because opening days do change.

The Victoria Hotel ★ CONTEMPORARY Built in 1874, this historic bluestone pub in Port Fairy is a great place to recharge your batteries while driving the Great Ocean Road. By day, you can eat in the casual cafe overlooking the courtyard; by night it is transformed into an a la carte restaurant. As well as traditional pub favorites like fish and chips, you're likely to find the menu includes dishes such as lamb curry, Scotch fillet, fresh fish—changing daily—and delicious pasta. There's often live music in the courtyard on Friday or Saturday nights.

42 Bank St., Port Fairy. ✆ **03/5568 2891.** www.thevichotelportfairy.com.au. Main courses A$11–A$18 at lunch, A$16–A$28 at dinner. AE, DC, MC, V. Tues–Sun noon–2pm and 6pm–late.

THE MURRAY RIVER ★

Mildura: 544km (337 miles) NW of Melbourne; Albury-Wodonga: 305km (189 miles) NE of Melbourne; Echuca: 210km (130 miles) N of Melbourne

Though it's a rushing torrent of white water at its source in the Snowy Mountains, the Murray River becomes slow and muddy brown by the time it forms the meandering border between Victoria and New South Wales. The Darling River, which starts in Queensland, feeds the Murray; together they make Australia's longest river. Drought has made the fate of the Murray one of Australia's greatest environmental concerns in recent years, and by the time you get here, it may well be a trickle of its former self. That said, its importance is unlikely to diminish, one way or another—it is a river close to Australians' hearts.

Aborigines once used the Murray as a source of food and transportation, and later the water carried paddle steamers, laden with wool and crops from the land it helped irrigate. In 1842, the Murray was "discovered" by explorers Hamilton Hume and William Howell on the first overland trek from Sydney to Port Phillip, near Melbourne. You can still see Hume's carved initials on a tree standing by the riverbank in Albury, on the border between the two states.

Essentials

GETTING THERE Most visitors cross the river during an overland drive between cities. There are two ways to the Murray from Melbourne: the 2½-hour route down the Midland Highway to Echuca, and the Calder Highway to Mildura, a 6-hour drive. Traveling from Melbourne to Mildura is practical only if you're continuing to Broken Hill, which is 297km (184 miles) north of Mildura. Those in a hurry to get to and from Sydney can travel via the river-straddling twin towns of Albury-Wodonga on the Hume Highway (about a 12-hr. trip with short stops).

Virgin Blue (✆ **13 67 89** in Australia; www.virginblue.com.au) and **Qantas** (✆ **13 13 13** in Australia; www.qantas.com.au) both operate daily flights to Mildura from Melbourne.

V/Line (✆ **13 61 96;** www.vline.com.au) runs regular train service to Mildura, Echuca, and Albury–Wodonga.

VISITOR INFORMATION The **Echuca-Moama Visitor Information Centre,** 2 Heygarth St., Echuca, VIC 3564 (✆ **1800/804 446** in Australia, or 03/5480 7555; fax 03/5482 6413; www.echucamoama.com), has plenty of maps and information about accommodations and river cruises. It's open daily from 9am to 5pm (closed Dec 25). The **Mildura Visitor Information & Booking Centre,** 180–190 Deakin Ave., Mildura, VIC 3502 (✆ **1800/039 043** in Australia or 03/5018 8380; fax 03/5021 1836; www.visitmildura.com.au), offers similar services. It's open Monday through Friday from 9am to 5:30pm and weekends and public holidays from 9am to 5pm (closed Dec 25). If you're passing through Albury–Wodonga, contact the **Gateway Visitor Information Centre,** Lincoln Causeway, Wodonga, VIC 3690 (✆ **1300/796 222** or 02/6051 3750; www.destinationalburywodonga.com.au). It's open daily from 9am to 5pm (closed Dec 25).

River Cruises

IN MILDURA Mildura is one of Australia's most important fruit-growing areas, but it also has the reputation as a hot spot for food and wine and the arts. There was a time, however, when this was semi-arid red-dust country. The area bloomed because of a little ingenuity and, of course, the Murray. The original irrigation system consisted of two English water pumps and the manual labor of hundreds of immigrants, who worked clearing scrub and digging channels through the new fields. Today, the hungry land soaks up water and everyone prays for rain.

Several paddle steamers leave from Mildura wharf to cruise the Murray. One of the nicest boats is the PS ***Melbourne*** (✆ **03/5023 2200** or mobile phone 0409/502 322; www.murrayriver.com.au), which was built in 1912 and is still powered by steam. It offers 2-hour trips leaving at 10:50am and 1:50pm daily (check times in advance as they do change). The fare is A$25 for adults and A$15 for children 14 to 17 or A$10 for children 5 to 13, free for children under 5.

The *Melbourne*'s sister ship, the ***Rothbury,*** was built in 1881; a conventional engine has replaced its steam engine. It offers a winery cruise every Thursday from 10:30am to 3:30pm, stopping at a winery for tastings and a barbecue lunch. The trip costs A$60 for adults, A$48 for children 14 to 17, and A$28 for children 5 to 13. The *Rothbury* has evening dinner cruises Thursday from 7 to 10pm for A$58 for adults, A$46 children 14 to 17, and A$26 for children 5 to 13. From September to April (excluding February and public holidays), it runs a Tuesday lunch cruise which costs A$26 adults, A$16 children 14 to 17, and A$10 children 5 to 13. It leaves at 11:30am and returns at 3pm. You buy your own lunch at the historic Gol Gol Hotel, with special rates for *Rothbury* passengers.

IN ECHUCA The paddle steamer ***Emmylou*** (✆ **03/5480 2237;** fax 03/5480 2927; www.emmylou.com.au) operates out of Echuca. The *Emmylou* offers short trips costing A$25 for adults and A$11 for kids ages 1 to 15, or A$65 for a family of four for 1 hour, leaving at 10am and 3pm; and 90-minute lunch cruises costing A$29 for adults, A$14 for kids, or A$75 for families, leaving at 11:15am and 1pm. Three-hour dinner cruises cost A$98 adults and A$50 children. *Emmylou* also has an overnight cruise, leaving at 6pm and returning at 9:30am the next day (check sailings beforehand). It costs A$195 to A$250 per person, including breakfast and dinner. A 2-day, 2-night cruise leaves Wednesday at 6pm and returns at noon on Friday. The cruise includes (depending on river levels) a visit to the Barmah, an area famous for its wetlands and the largest red gum trees in the world, or a stop at Perricoota Station. The trip costs A$400 to A$500 per person, including meals. Three-night cruises are also available.

The **Port of Echuca** (✆ **03/5482 4248;** www.portofechuca.org.au) is definitely worth a look. The three-level red-gum wharf was built in 1865 and is still in use by paddle steamers. The Port owns the PS *Adelaide,* the oldest operating wooden-hulled paddle steamer in the world (1866), the PS *Pevensey* (1911), and the PS *Alexander Arbuthnot* (1923). One-hour cruises, including a port tour, run daily at 10:15 and 11:30am, and 1:15 and 2:30pm, with an extra tour at 3:45pm on weekends and public and school holidays. They cost A$20 for adults, A$9 for children 4 to 14, and A$52 for families. You can look around the wharf on a guided tour, priced at A$12 for adults and A$8 for children, and A$35 for a family. A combined cruise/tour ticket makes it cheaper. Outside the Port, the Echuca Port Precinct offers various things to do, including carriage rides and old penny arcade machines in Sharpes Magic Movies, in an old riverboat warehouse.

A TRIP INTO THE OUTBACK **Mungo National Park ★★** is a unique arid region 110km (68 miles) northeast of Mildura, off the Sturt Highway, in New South Wales. The park is famous for its red dunes and shifting sands (so it's best to have a four-wheel-drive vehicle to get around it). The most famous feature of the park is the Walls of China, a moonscape of weathered red sand. The walls edge Lake Mungo, once a huge freshwater lake during the last Ice Age, now dry. A 60km (37-mile) driving tour starting at the visitor center at the park's entrance takes you across the lake bed to the Walls of China. You must pay an A$7 per car entry fee at the visitors center at the park entrance. Several short walks also begin here. Just outside the park, the newly renovated **Mungo Lodge** (✆ **03/5029 7297;** fax 03/5029 7296; www.mungolodge.com.au) offers 17 air-conditioned, contemporary cabins with luxury touches such as bathrobes and slippers. Each has a small deck to sit out on. Rates are A$500 double, A$630 double family cabin (sleeps four), or A$780 double for a self-contained cabin (sleeps four). Extra person A$65. The lodge has a good restaurant and a smart lounge area with a bar and two fireplaces. For visitors on a budget, the **Shearers Quarters** (✆ **03/5021 8900** for bookings), near the visitors center, has five rooms with combinations of double, twin, and bunk beds, sleeping up to 26 people, but you will need your own bedding (sleeping bags and so on). Only four rooms have air-conditioning. There is a fully equipped communal kitchen/dining room, and barbecues, as well as a toilet block and hot showers. Rates are A$30

ned kelly COUNTRY

The bushranger Ned Kelly is an Australian icon. His story is a legend, and Kelly is a folk hero to many people. Opinion can be divided, but there's no question that his tale still resonates 125 years after the events that made him famous. Now, the area of Victoria in which he lived is called "Kelly Country," and in 2005, to mark the anniversary of his death, the government created the **Ned Kelly Touring Route** (www.nedkellytouringroute.com.au), linking important sites in the story.

Ned Kelly was the eldest of eight children born to Irish parents in Victoria in 1854. When Ned was 12, his father died and the family moved to be near relatives at Greta, 240km (150 miles) northeast of Melbourne. Like many poor families, the Kellys took up the government's offer of cheap land and battled to clear the bushland, build a house, and plant crops. More often than not, the land parcels were too small and the soil too poor for them to make a living.

At 16, Ned was convicted of horse-rustling and sentenced to 3 years in jail. A few years later, his mother was imprisoned for attacking a police officer named Fitzpatrick, who was accused of attacking Ned's sister first. During the scuffle, Ned shot Fitzpatrick through the wrist. Ned escaped—with a bounty on his head.

On October 26, 1878, together with friends Joe Byrne and Steve Hart, Ned and his brother Dan came across police camped at Stringy Bark Creek. Ned believed the police intended to kill him, so he called on them to surrender. Three officers resisted, and in the fight that followed Ned Kelly shot them dead.

In the years that followed, the Kelly Gang avoided capture with the help of sympathetic locals. They robbed two banks, and during each robbery Ned gave his hostages a letter, explaining to the government how he'd been persecuted by police.

In June 1880, police surrounded the Kelly Gang at the Glenrowan Hotel. Prepared for the fight, the four bushrangers put on homemade suits of armor. It was no use—Ned's body took 28 bullets, and

per adult per night (16 years and over), A$10 per child per night (5–15 years); children under 5 years free. Minimum charge of A$50 per night. Contact the **National Parks & Wildlife Service NSW** (✆ **1300/361 967** in Australia; www.nationalparks.nsw.gov.au) for more information.

Where to Stay

IN MILDURA

Quality Hotel Mildura Grand ★★★ This 19th-century hotel is right in the center of Mildura, overlooking the Murray River. Double rooms are comfortable, and many have been refurbished. Suites are bigger, and some have balconies and garden views. State suites are plush and come with a king-size bed. The Presidential Suite (the most expensive) is Art Deco inspired, with a large marble bathroom and Jacuzzi. This place is famous for the multi-award-winning **Stefano's ★★**, one of several dining spots run by celeb chef Stefano de Pieri. There is no menu, just a fixed price of A$95 for a five-course Italian meal.

Seventh St., Mildura, VIC 3500. ✆ **1800/034 228** in Australia, or 03/5023 0511. Fax 03/5022 1801. www.qualityhotelmilduragrand.com.au. 102 units. A$100–A$200 double; A$230–A$400 suite. Rates include the others were all killed. Ned was hanged in Old Melbourne Gaol (see p. 629 in chapter 13) on November 11, 1880. He was 25 years old.

Historic **Beechworth,** one of Victoria's best-preserved gold-rush towns, is a good base for exploring this region. There are more than 30 buildings listed by the National Trust here, from pubs, churches, and government offices to miners' cottages and the jail where Ned Kelly was imprisoned. For stylish self-contained accommodations, the charming **Stone Cottage,** 6 Taswell St. (✆ **03/57 282857** or 0411/324 797 mobile phone; fax 03/5728 2857), is ideal for two people. The cottage has a roomy attic bedroom with a queen-size bed and windows overlooking the garden. Downstairs is a cozy sitting room (with a roaring log fire on those chilly nights), a dining area, and a kitchen. It costs A$160 double. For a little pampering, check out the **Spa at Beechworth** (✆ **03/5728 3033;** www.thespaatbeechworth.com.au), a day spa located in the gorgeous Birches Building on Albert Road, which was once a lunatic asylum. (They don't mince words in these parts.)

You can also visit **Glenrowan,** a quiet little town surrounded by wineries and orchards. Here you'll find a 6m-high (20-ft.) outdoor statue of Ned Kelly clad in his homemade armor and helmet, with rifle in hand, as well as a couple of small museums full of Kelly memorabilia—and much more besides.

Other towns on the route include Avenel, Benalla, Mansfield, and Jerilderie in southern New South Wales. You can pick up a touring route brochure from the **Old Melbourne Gaol** before setting out, or from the **Beechworth Visitor Information Centre,** in the town hall, Ford Street (✆ **1300/366 321** in Australia, or 03/5728 8065; www.beechworthonline.com.au). Other information centers will also have them.

breakfast. Extra person A$30. Children 11 and under stay free in parent's room. Ask about packages. AE, DC, MC, V. Limited undercover parking. **Amenities:** 5 restaurants; 4 bars; babysitting; concierge; executive rooms; golf course nearby; gymnasium; Jacuzzi; large heated outdoor pool; room service; sauna. *In room:* A/C, TV w/free movies, hair dryer, minibar, Wi-Fi (A$3.30 for 30 min. to A$28 for 24 hr.).

IN ECHUCA

Echuca Gardens B&B and YHA Accommodations here are all self-contained, but you have a choice of style. There are the reproduction gypsy wagons, suitable for couples, the guesthouse for up to four people (in part of the owner's home, but with its own entrance), or the restored 140-year-old cottage which sleeps up to 10. All are set in landscaped water gardens and just a short walk from the river or a state forest. The cottage has three bedrooms—two with bunk beds—and is a good option for families or groups. It has a full kitchen and two bathrooms, and a private backyard with a barbecue.

103 Mitchell St., Echuca, VIC 3564. ✆ **03/5480 6522** or 0419 881 054 mobile. Fax 03/5482 6951. www.echucagardens.com. A$80–A$160 gypsy wagon; A$110–A$220 guesthouse; A$140–A$280 cottage, depending on the season. Minimum 2-night stay, 3 nights in peak seasons. No children in the gypsy wagons. MC, V. **Amenities:** Bikes; Jacuzzi; sauna. *In room:* A/C, TV, hair dryer.

Bright

310km (193 miles) NE of Melbourne; 700km (435 miles) SW of Sydney; 74km (46 miles) E of Wangaratta

Set in a valley and surrounded by pine forests, Bright offers good access to the surrounding High Country and ski fields. The town is famous for the colors of its European trees in fall. There are nice walks around here, especially along the pretty Ovens River, while another option is to hire bicycles and take off through the countryside down a former railway track. Cycling at least part of the **Rail Trail ★** (www.railtrail.com.au) will give you a nice feel for the area, with its surrounding mountains, farms, and river. The track stretches 94km (58 miles) from Bright to Wangaratta. Rent bikes (and skis, if you're off to the snowfields) in Bright.

ESSENTIALS

GETTING THERE **V/Line** trains (www.vline.com.au) run between Melbourne and Bright, via Wangaratta or Seymour, daily. Return fares cost A$54 and the trip takes about 4½ hours, with a bus between Wangaratta or Seymour and Bright. However, it's difficult to get around the area without your own transport.

VISITOR INFORMATION Stop by the **Alpine Visitors Centre,** 119 Gavan St., Bright (✆ **1800/111 885** in Australia or 03/5750 1233; www.brightvictoria.com.au), open 9am to 5pm daily (except Christmas Day and Good Friday). Another useful website is **www.visitalpinevictoria.com.au**.

WHERE TO STAY & DINE

The website **www.alpinelink.com.au** offers a comprehensive list of places to stay in Bright. The best place to eat is **Simone's of Bright,** 98 Gavan St. (✆ **03/5755 2266;** www.simonesrestaurant.com.au). It serves great Italian food in a refined atmosphere, with main courses around A$35. It is open Tuesday to Saturday for dinner only. Otherwise, Bright has plenty of family-friendly cafes, restaurants, and pizza joints.

Alinga-Longa Holiday Units The large two-bedroom units here are spacious, clean, and comfortable. They are nothing special, but fine for a couple of days, especially if you're traveling with kids. The full kitchen means you never have to eat out, and there's also a barbecue area.

12 Gavan St. (Great Alpine Rd.), Bright, VIC 3741. ✆ **03/5755 1073.** www.alingalongaholidays.com.au. 6 units. A$100–A$180 double. AE, DC, MC, V. **Amenities:** Bikes; small outdoor pool. *In room:* A/C, TV/VCR, kitchen, free Wi-Fi.

Villa Gusto This luxury Italian-style villa caters to only 18 guests. Built at the foot of Mount Buffalo, with dramatic views, it is furnished with antiques and leather sofas, and is set on a little less than a hectare (2 acres) of Tuscan gardens. The central focus is the Great Room, with a log fire, and there is also an in-house cinema. The Grande Suite and three deluxe suites have Jacuzzis, and all have private terraces. There are also such luxury touches as bathrobes, Bulgari toiletries, and fine linens. A five-course Italian degustation menu is available from the restaurant for A$70 per person, but bookings are essential. The villa is about 6km (3¾ miles) from Bright.

630 Buckland Valley Rd., Buckland, VIC 3740. ✆ **03/5756 2000.** www.villagusto.com.au. 9 units. A$245 double standard room; A$285–A$325 suite. Rates include breakfast. MC, V. No children 9 and under. **Amenities:** Restaurant (Wed–Sun nights only). *In room:* A/C, TV, minibar.

THE HIGH COUNTRY

Victoria's High Country consists of the hills and mountains of the Great Dividing Range, which runs from Queensland, through New South Wales, to just before Ballarat, where it drops away and reappears in the mountains of the Grampians, in the western part of Victoria. The range separates inland Australia from the greener coastal belt. The main attractions of the High Country are its natural features, which include moorland and mountainous alpine scenery. It's also popular for outdoor activities, including hiking, canoeing, white-water rafting, mountain-bike riding, and rock climbing. The High Country is also the home of the Victorian ski fields, based around Mount Buller, Mount Stirling, Falls Creek, Mount Buffalo, and Mount Hotham. If you plan to go walking here, make sure you have plenty of water and sunscreen, as well as a tent and a good-quality sleeping bag. As in any alpine region, temperatures can plummet dramatically. In summer, days can be very hot and nights very cold.

Snowy River National Park ★

390km (242 miles) NE of Melbourne

The Snowy River National Park, with its lovely river scenery and magnificent gorges, protects Victoria's largest forest wilderness areas. The Snowy River was once a torrent worthy of Banjo Paterson's famous poem, but since Snowy Mountain Hydro-Electric erected a series of dams, it's become a mere trickle of its former self.

GETTING THERE & GETTING AROUND There is no public transit in this area. The two main access roads are the Gelantipy Road from Buchan and the Bonang Freeway from the logging township of Orbost. MacKillop's Road (also known as Deddick River Rd.) runs across the park's northern border from Bonang to a little south of Wulgulmerang. The area around MacKillop's Bridge, along MacKillop's Road, has spectacular scenery and the park's best campgrounds, set beside some nice swimming holes and sandy river beaches. The Barry Way leads through the main township of Buchan, where you'll find some of Australia's best caves.

VISITOR INFORMATION The main place to get information on the Snowy River National Park and Alpine National Park is the **Buchan Caves Information Centre,** in the Buchan Caves complex. It's open daily from 9am to 4pm (closed Dec 25). Or call **Parks Victoria** (✆ **13 19 63** in Australia).

EXPLORING THE BUCHAN CAVES

The **Buchan Caves ★** (✆ **13 19 63**) are in a scenic valley that is particularly beautiful in autumn, when all the European trees are losing their leaves. Tourists can visit the Royal and Fairy caves (which are quite similar), with their fabulous stalactites and stalagmites. There are several tours daily; from the end of Easter to September they're at 11am and 1 and 3pm, and from October to Easter they're at 10 and 11:15am and 1, 2:15, and 3:30pm. Entry to one cave costs A$14 for adults, A$8 for children 5 to 16, and A$39 for families of four.

To reach the caves from the Princes Highway, turn off at Nowa Nowa. (It's well signposted.) If you're coming south from Jindabyne in New South Wales (see chapter 6), follow the Barry Way, which runs alongside the Snowy River.

The Great Alpine Road

This 308km (191-mile) drive, one of Australia's great touring routes, winds through stunning landscapes and character-filled small towns between Wangaratta in Victoria's northeast and Bairnsdale, near the coast. You could do it without stopping in about 4½ hours, but that would be a shame. The joy of the journey is in the stops. Break it up with stops at Bright (p. 674) and Omeo or anywhere else that takes your fancy. Stay at the Art Deco Golden Age Hotel Motel (✆ 03/5159 1344; www.goldenageomeo.com.au), which is a great country pub, or for a touch of luxury, stay at Payne's Hut (✆ 03/5159 7255; www.payneshut.com) in Shannon Vale.

Alpine National Park ★★

333km (206 miles) NE of Melbourne; 670km (415 miles) SW of Sydney

Victoria's largest national park, at 646,000 hectares (1.6 million acres), the Alpine National Park connects the High Country areas of New South Wales and the Australian Capital Territory. The park's scenery is spectacular, encompassing most of the state's highest mountains, wild rivers, impressive escarpments, forests, and high plains. Some parts of the park have been devastated by horrific bushfires, but it is slowly recovering. It's green, but evidence of the fire lingers; you'll still see swathes of blackened tree trunks. The flora is diverse; in all, some 1,100 plant species have been recorded within the park's boundaries, including 12 not found anywhere else. Walking here is particularly good in spring and summer, when a carpet of wildflowers covers the Bogong High Plains. The best known of the numerous walking trails is the Alpine Walking Track, which bisects the park for 400km (248 miles) from Walhalla to the township of Tom Groggin, on the New South Wales border. There are plenty of access roads into the park, some of which close in winter.

Horseback-riding treks are another option for seeing the area. **Watson's Mountain Country Trail Rides** (✆ **03/5777 3552;** www.watsonstrailrides.com.au) are just outside Mansfield and offer short rides daily year-round. Rides run for between 1 hour and all day (A$35 to A$150 per person, depending on the length of ride and if lunch or dinner is included). **McCormack's Mountain Valley Trail Rides** (✆ **03/5775 2886**) offers a day ride to Craig's Hut, the set for the movie *The Man from Snowy River,* for A$180 per person including lunch; an extension of this ride over 2 days, with camping in the lovely King Valley, costs around A$400. Longer rides are also available, generally including camping, food, and just about everything else, though you should check whether you'll need a sleeping bag. It's a little out of the way, but worth the detour, to go riding with **Packer High Country Horse Riding** (✆ **03/5159 7241;** www.horsetreks.com), whose trail rides start near Anglers Rest. Other horseback-riding operators include **Falls Creek Trail Rides** (✆ **0419/244 773** mobile phone), **Bogong Horseback Adventures** (✆ **03/5754 4849;** www.bogonghorse.com.au), and **Lovick Country Adventure** (✆ **03/5777 5715**).

Angling Expeditions (✆ **03/5754 1466** or 0409/241 762 mobile phone; www.anglingvic.com.au) is the best option for fly-fishing for trout in the alpine area during spring, summer, and fall. Trips last from 3 hours to all day and are suitable for everyone from beginners to experts. Overnight trips are also available.

Walhalla: The Valley of the Gods

Tucked in a lush valley in the Victorian Alps, the village of Walhalla ★★ is home to only 11 people. A century ago, it was one of the world's richest gold-mining towns, and what remains of it is faithfully preserved, but without a suggestion of theme-park fakery. The gold ran out in 1914 and Walhalla was simply abandoned; today it has the fabulous Star Hotel (✆ 03/5165 6262; fax 03/5165 6261; www.starhotel.com.au), rebuilt in 1999 just after electricity was connected to the town, and a surprising number of things to do. You can take an interesting guided tour of the old gold mine, ride a steam train through lovely bushland, explore the historic cemetery, potter in the small shops and museums, or take a walk along some of the many tracks. Star Hotel owner Michael Leaney will point you in all the right directions. Or you can just hole up in his comfortable, stylish hotel for the weekend. Walhalla is at the end of the Australian Alps Walking Track (which runs 650km/403 miles from Canberra), but the best option for visitors is the 2-day guided 40km (25-mile) walk developed last year by the Star Hotel and nearby Mt. Baw Baw Alpine Resort (www.greatwalhallaalpinetrail.com). Walhalla is also a good stopover point to break the Sydney-Melbourne coastal drive. It is about 180km (112 miles) from Melbourne and is a popular day trip and weekend destination. Walhalla's Star Hotel has 12 air-conditioned guest rooms, all of a good size, some with verandas overlooking the street. There is also a restaurant and bar with wood fires for those chilly nights, a cozy guest lounge with tea- and coffee-making facilities, a small library (with books and CDs), and a guest computer. Next door, the GreyHorse Café sells snacks and drinks. Rates are A$219 double, including breakfast. No children under 12.

GETTING THERE Routes from Melbourne include the Great Alpine Road (B500), the Kiewa Valley Highway (C531), and the Lincoln Road from Heyfield. The Bluff is accessible from Mansfield along the Maroondah Highway.

Hitting the Slopes: The High Country Ski Resorts

Most of Victoria's ski areas are in, or on the edge of, the Alpine National Park (see above). Victoria's main snowfields are **Mount Buller, Mount Hotham,** and **Falls Creek,** all of which have a wide range of on-mountain accommodations. Closer to Melbourne, **Mount Baw Baw** offers gentle slopes for beginners, while **Lake Mountain** and **Mount Stirling** are for cross-country skiing. The ski season in the Victorian High Country is June through October, with July and August the most popular months.

MOUNT HOTHAM

373km (231 miles) NE of Melbourne

Hotham Snow Resort (1,750m/5,740 ft.) is the only resort in Australia with its own airport and summit-top village. Just 10km (6¼ miles) from the ski slopes of Mount Hotham lies the alpine hamlet of Dinner Plain. There are 14 lifts (including those at Dinner Plain) servicing 320 hectares (791 acres) of terrain ranging from beginner to advanced. A shuttle bus service runs between Dinner Plain and Hotham Village. Ski lift tickets are available from **Hotham Skiing Company** (✆ **1800/468 426** in Australia, or 03/5759 4444; www.hotham.com.au). Full-day lift tickets cost A$102 for adults and A$51 for children ages 6 to 14, or A$166 adults and A$95 children with gear hire. The resort also offers some good cross-country skiing, including a route across the Bogong High Plains to Falls Creek. Resort entry costs A$35 per car for a day, payable at the entry gates or at the Mount Hotham Alpine Resort Management office (see "Visitor Information," below). If you are traveling by bus the entry fee is A$12 adults, half price for kids.

GETTING THERE From Melbourne, take the Hume Highway via Harrietville, or the Princes Highway via Omeo. The trip takes around 5½ hours. (The Hume Hwy. is slightly quicker.) **Qantaslink** (✆ **13 13 13** in Australia) flies to Mount Hotham Airport from Sydney during the snow season.

Snowball Express (✆ **1300/656 546;** www.snowballexpress.com.au) runs buses to Hotham daily from mid-June to mid-September. They depart Melbourne's Southern Cross Station on Spencer Street at 9am. The trip takes 6 hours and costs A$105 one-way or A$160 return for adults, and A$72 one-way and A$105 return for children under 15, or A$425 return for a family of four. There are also coaches from Bright to Hotham. Bookings are essential.

VISITOR INFORMATION **Mount Hotham Alpine Resort Management,** Great Alpine Road, Mount Hotham (✆ **03/5759 3550**), is as close as you'll come to an information office. It has plenty of brochures. It's open daily from 8am to 5pm during ski season, and Monday through Friday from 9am to 5pm at other times. The general Mount Hotham website is **www.mthotham.com.au**.

WHERE TO STAY **Hotham Holidays** (✆ **1800/468 426** in Australia; www.hotham.com.au) has more than 180 properties for you to choose from, ranging from motel-style rooms to luxury chalets. They can book rooms and advise you on special deals, including flights. Another option is the **Mount Hotham Accommodation Service** (✆ **1800/032 061** in Australia, or 03/5759 3636; www.mthothamaccommodation.com.au). During the ski season, most places will want you to book for a week. Prices are significantly lower outside the ski season.

FALLS CREEK ★

375km (233 miles) NE of Melbourne

One of Victoria's best ski resorts, Falls Creek is on the edge of the Bogong High Plains overlooking the Kiewa Valley. This compact alpine village is the only one in Australia where you can ski from your lodge to the lifts and back again from the ski slopes. The nightlife is also very good in the ski season, with plenty of party options as well as a range of walk-in lodge restaurants.

The ski slopes are in two parts, the Village Bowl and Sun Valley, with 17 lifts covering more than 90 trails. There are plenty of intermediate and advanced runs, as well as a sprinkling for beginners. You'll also find some of Australia's best cross-country skiing; Australia's major cross-country skiing event, the Kangaroo Hoppet, takes place here on the last Saturday in August every year. Entry to the resort costs A$32 per car per day. If you are arriving by bus, the fee is A$11 per adult and A$5.25 per child, per day. Full-day lift tickets cost A$102 for adults, A$69 for teens 15 to 18, and A$41 for children 6 to 14. For a combined lift and ski-rental ticket, the cost is A$162 per adult, A$147 per teen, and A$96 per child. Call **Falls Creek Ski Lifts** (✆ **03/5758 1000**) for details.

GETTING THERE **Falls Creek Coach Service** (✆ **03/5754 4024;** www.fallscreekcoachservice.com.au) runs buses to the ski resort from Melbourne every day during the ski season (mid-June to late Sept), departing Melbourne at 9am and arriving at Falls Creek at 3pm. The round-trip fare is A$161 for adults and A$121 for school-age children and includes the resort entrance fee. The company also runs shuttle buses to and from Albury (A$90 round-trip for adults and A$76 for kids), just over the border in New South Wales and accessible by train or air from Sydney, and between Mount Beauty and Falls Creek. Reservations are essential.

If you're driving from Melbourne, take the Hume Highway to Wangaratta, and then through Myrtleford and Mount Beauty to Falls Creek. The trip takes around 4½ hours. From Sydney, take the Hume Highway to Albury-Wodonga and follow the signs to Mount Beauty and the snowfields (about 8 hr.). If you're driving yourself to Falls Creek, you are legally obliged to carry a pair of snow chains. These can be hired for a small charge from either of Mount Beauty's service stations and several ski rental stores. There is no petrol at Falls Creek, so make sure you fill up before setting out. If you arrive in the ski season, a resort worker will direct you to a car park and bring you back in a little buggy to the resort entrance, where you can take a caterpillar-tracked Oversnow taxi to your hotel. It costs A$19 one-way and A$34 round-trip for adults; A$13 one-way and A$23 round-trip for children 5 to 15. Or you could attempt the short but (probably) slippery walk yourself.

VISITOR INFORMATION The **Mount Beauty Visitor Information Centre,** 31 Bogong High Plains Rd., Mount Beauty (✆ **1800/111 885** in Australia, or 03/5754 1962; www.visitalpinevictoria.com.au), has all the information you need about activities and also an accommodations service. It is open daily 9am to 5pm (except Good Friday and Dec 25–26). The **Falls Creek Resort Management** office, Slalom Street (at Bogong High Plains Rd.), Falls Creek (✆ **03/5758 1200;** www.fallscreek.com.au), also offers loads of information and is open daily 8am to 5pm during the ski season, weekdays 9am to 5pm other times.

Where to Stay & Dine

Falls Creek is a year-round resort with a good range of accommodations. It tends to fill up fast during the ski season. As you might expect, room rates are much higher during the ski season. **Falls Creek Central Reservations** (✆ **1800/033 079** in Australia, or 03/5758 3733; www.fallscreek.com.au) or **Falls Creek Reservations Centre** (✆ **1800/453 525** in Australia or 03/5758 1050) can tell you what deals are available.

If you fancy a self-contained apartment or free-standing chalet, try the **Frueauf Village** complex (✆ **1300/300 709** in Australia; www.fvfalls.com.au). These 28 properties were built in 2002. The smallest unit, basically a nice studio, costs A$528 per couple for a 2-night stay in the earliest and latest part of the ski season and jumps to A$1,154 for 2 nights at peak times.

Summit Ridge Alpine Lodge ★ Summit Ridge is an AAA-rated four-and-a-half-star property made from local rock and timber. All rooms are quite nice, if a little stark. Standard rooms come with a set of bunk beds and a couple of useless little desks. Queen suites have a queen-size bed and a couch, plus beautiful mountain views. The mezzanine suites are split-level with the bedroom upstairs; they have king-size beds and an attached bathroom with tub. There's a lounge and dining room on the ground floor and a library on the second. If the mist holds off, there are some fine valley views. The hosts pay a lot of attention to detail, and the homemade bread is worth waking early for. The owner can also take you on early morning ski runs. The most expensive rates in the ranges below apply in August.

8 Schuss St., Falls Creek, VIC 3699. ✆ **03/5758 3800.** Fax 03/5758 3833. www.summitridge.com.au. A$155–A$240 per person standard bunk room; A$330–A$520 queen double; A$370–A$580 mezzanine suite. Children 5–14 pay 25% off adult rate. Rates include breakfast and dinner. AE, DC, MC, V. Closed Oct to mid-June. Children 4 and under not accepted. **Amenities:** Restaurant; bar; babysitting; exercise room; Jacuzzi; sauna. *In room:* TV, hair dryer, minibar.

THE NORTHWEST: GRAMPIANS NATIONAL PARK

260km (161 miles) NW of Melbourne

One of Victoria's most popular attractions, the rugged **Grampians National Park** rises some 1,000m (3,280 ft.) from the plains, appearing from the distance like some kind of monumental island. The park, which is an ecological meeting place of Victoria's western volcanic plains and the forested Great Dividing Range, contains a third of all the wildflowers native to Victoria and most of the surviving Aboriginal rock art in southeastern Australia. The wildlife is rich and varied, and kangaroos, koalas, emus, gliders, and echidnas are easy to spot.

In early 2009, parts of the Grampians were ravaged by bushfires, and you will still see some of the effects on the landscape when you visit, including the fabulous process of nature regenerating the bush.

The main town is **Halls Gap,** in a valley between the southern tip of the Mount Difficult Range and the northern tip of the Mount William Range. It's a good place to stock up on supplies. The Wonderland Range, with its stunning scenery, is close to Halls Gap, too. There are plenty of short strolls, and longer bushwalks are available.

A must-do stop is the **Brambuk Aboriginal Cultural Centre ★** (✆ **03/5361 4000;** www.brambuk.com.au), adjacent to the National Park and Cultural Centre (see below). It offers an excellent introduction to the area's Aboriginal history and seven accessible rock-art sites. The Gariwerd Dreaming Theatre there shows two short movies depicting the creation story of the Grampians and an account of the area's Aboriginal and European history, geology, flora, and fauna; presentations are hourly. Entrance to the center is free, and it's open daily from 9am to 5pm. Guided tours, which include rock painting sites, run on weekdays at 9:30am and cost from A$20 adults and A$15 children for a 2-hour tour, including entry to the Gariwerd Dreaming Theatre. Allow 2 to 3 hours.

Essentials

GETTING THERE By car, the park is accessible from the Western Highway at Ararat, Stawell (pronounced *Storl*), and Horsham. Alternatively, you can reach the southern entrance from the Glenelg Highway at Dunkeld. The western areas of the park are off the Henty Highway (A200).

V/Line (✆ **13 61 96** in Victoria; www.vline.com.au) has daily train and bus service to Halls Gap from Melbourne. (The train goes to Ballarat, and a bus continues to Halls Gap via Ararat and Stawell.) The trip takes around 4½ hours, and there is a half-hour wait at Ballarat.

GETTING AROUND Paved roads include the **Grampians Tourist Road,** which cuts through the park from Dunkeld to Halls Gap; the **Mount Victory Road,** from Halls Gap to Wartook; and the **Roses Gap Road,** which runs from Wartook across to Dadswells Bridge on the Western Highway. Many other roads in the park are unpaved, but most are passable with a two-wheel-drive car.

Autopia Tours (✆ **1800/000 507** in Australia, or 03/9419 8878; www.autopiatours.com.au) offers all-day tours of the park and surroundings from Melbourne on Mondays, Wednesdays, and Saturdays (call for departure times and pickup points). The tour includes a stop at Brambuk, as well as Aboriginal rock-painting sites, waterfalls, and lookouts. There's a bit of walking involved, so you need to be reasonably fit, but you're almost certain to see native wildlife. The tour includes morning tea and National Park entry fees and costs A$120.

VISITOR INFORMATION The **Bambruk National Park and Cultural Centre** (✆ **03/5361 4000**), 2.5km (1½ miles) south of Halls Gap, is open daily from 9am to 5pm. It has plenty of maps and brochures, and the rangers can advise you on walking trails and camping spots. Check out **www.bambruk.com.au**. Other good websites are **www.visitgrampians.com.au** and **www.visithallsgap.com.au**.

Where to Stay

Boroka Downs ★★★ Sleep in five-star luxury and then wake up to breaking light over rolling farmland and kangaroos outside your floor-length windows. Boroka Downs has five private contemporary Australian style self-contained residences, about 7km (4⅓ miles) from Hall's Gap. Each has stunning views from your choice of the circular spa, the king-size bed, or the fireside. You'll be dazzled by the quality of the place, from the state-of-the-art sound system to the espresso coffee machine (fresh beans and grinder provided) and gourmet kitchen. Service here is "on demand," to ensure guests have their own desired level of privacy. There are lots of extras provided, such as backpacks and binoculars for walking, and bathrobes for lounging around. Breakfast and supper packs can be provided for A$30 to A$50 extra. It's private, elegant, and you probably won't want to leave. It's not suitable for children. Check out time is wonderfully late, at 6pm.

51 Birdswing Rd., Hall's Gap, VIC 3381. ✆ **03/5356 6243.** Fax 03/5356 6343. www.borokadowns.com.au. 5 units. A$595 double midweek; A$645 double Sat–Sun. Rates include breakfast hamper and are reduced the more nights you stay. Ask about packages. AE, MC, V. *In room:* A/C, TV/VCR/DVD, hair dryer, free Internet, kitchen, MP3 docking station.

Royal Mail Hotel & Bluestone Cottages ★ You have a choice of lodgings at this renovated historic hotel located between the Great Ocean Road and the Grampians National Park. There are motel-style rooms with either garden or mountain views, or eight private one- and two-bedroom bluestone cottages on a working sheep farm at Mount Sturgeon, about 5km (3 miles) from the hotel, and these are my pick. Built by Chinese workers in the 1870s, they are a peaceful retreat, with huge comfortably worn brown-leather armchairs, an open fireplace, a CD player, and patchwork quilts on the beds. Equally appealing are the rustic table and chairs outside, where you can watch the changing light on Mount Sturgeon. The water tank against the back wall cunningly conceals your bathroom. There's a kitchen with a microwave and a gas barbecue outside. A continental breakfast for your first morning is included and can be picked up when you check in (at the Royal Mail). There's no television, no phone, and no mobile phone reception.

98 Parker St., Dunkeld, VIC 3294. ✆ **03/5577 2241.** Fax 03/5577 2577. www.royalmail.com.au. 33 units. A$160–A$240 double motel room with breakfast; A$310–A$350 double 1-bedroom apt including breakfast; A$290–A$320 2-bedroom apt (sleeps 4) including breakfast; A$200–A$320 bluestone cottages. Extra person A$45. AE, DC, MC, V. **Amenities:** 2 restaurants; bar; pool; room service (hotel only). *In room:* A/C, TV (except cottages), CD player, kitchen (cottages and apts only).

GIPPSLAND & WILSONS PROMONTORY

200km (124 miles) SE of Melbourne

Victoria's major touring routes will take you through Gippsland, taking in some wonderful coastal and alpine scenery. The Great Alpine Road tours through forests and national parks that are popular destinations for skiing in winter and bushwalking, fishing, and cycling in the warmer months. The Sydney to Melbourne Coastal Drive is a great way to tour the coastline and countryside. This drive will take you to—or near enough to divert for a visit—some of Victoria's best-loved holiday spots, including several of the state's most beautiful national parks. It's worth the time to explore these places, even briefly.

Beyond Phillip Island (see "Side Trips from Melbourne," p. 647), the Bass Coast Highway follows the coast to the towns of **Wonthaggi** and **Inverloch.** Inverloch has inviting sandy beaches (patrolled in summer), as well as plenty of small galleries, markets, and antiques stores. The road to Wilson's Promontory will take you through many small villages; one of the cutest is **Fish Creek,** where everything "fishy" will greet you, from the giant mullet atop the Fishy Pub (Promontory Gate Hotel) to the fish-shaped seats and the roof of the local church. Take time to stop off at the **Celia Rosser Gallery** (✆ **03/5683 2628;** www.celiarossergallery.com.au), home to one of Australia's foremost botanical artists famed for her banksia drawings, which are even owned by the Queen.

Wilsons Promontory is affectionately known as "the Prom" by Victorians who have flocked here for generations for holidays. The southernmost point of the Australian mainland, the Prom is famous for abundant flora and fauna, wild beaches, rugged landscapes, and coastal beauty. The 50,000-hectare (123,000-acre) national park has a 30km (19-mile) coastline and features a host of winding walking tracks and plenty to do. The park contains the largest coastal wilderness area in Victoria. From the entrance at Yanakie, it is 30km (19 miles) to the Tidal River settlement, which has car parking, camping, caravan sites and cabins to rent (bookings essential), a café, and a lovely sandy beach at Norman Bay. Other major attractions are Squeaky Beach (yes, it does), and Mount Oberon for one of Victoria's best views. A guide to good walks—short and long—is *Discovering the Prom,* available from the park's information center at Tidal River. Wilsons Promontory is a 3-hour drive from Melbourne on the South Gippsland Highway via Meeniyan or Foster.

Other highlights along the coast include Cape Conran Coastal Park, Point Hicks, and Croajingolong National Park. **Cape Conran Coastal Park** is located near Marlo, 396km (246 miles) from Melbourne. The park covers 11,700 hectares (29,000 acres) and has 60km (38 miles) of beach facing south over Bass Strait. The park also has banksia woodlands brimming with birdlife.

One of Australia's most spectacular parks, **Croajingolong** is so extraordinary that UNESCO made it a World Biosphere Reserve. From white sandy beaches to rocky coastal headlands and granite peaks, to rambling heaths, rainforests, and towering eucalypt forests, it supports more than 1,000 native plant species and 300 bird species. If that all sounds too fragile, don't worry—it is a great spot for hiking, surfing, swimming, diving, snorkelling and sea kayaking, and touring by four-wheel drive or mountain bike. Take the short walk to West Beach via Sledge Track or try the longer Dunes Walk, starting from Thurra Campground.

Within Croajingolong National Park, you will find mainland Australia's tallest lighthouse, **Point Hicks** Light Station. Unless you are staying at the lighthouse cottages, you will have to walk the 2km (1.2 miles) or so from the padlocked entry gate—but it's worth the hike! Built in 1890, the lighthouse marks Captain Cook's first sighting of Australia's east coast in 1770. Point Hicks was named for Lieutenant Zachary Hicks, who first sighted the headland from aboard *Endeavour.* Wander out to the monument to Cook and Hicks on the headland beyond the light station and then tackle the 162 steps of the spiral staircase to the top of the lighthouse—easier than it sounds—for great views of the coastline. Lighthouse tours cost A$20 per cottage or A$7 adults and A$4 children and run at 1pm Friday to Sunday and daily during Easter and Christmas school holidays (except Christmas Day and New Year's Day). Point Hicks lighthouse **cottages** (✆ **03/5158 4268** [10am–3pm weekdays only]; www.pointhicks.com.au) cost A$330 per night and sleep up to six.

Back on the Princes, the road leads to Mallacoota, an unspoiled seaside village with the distinction of recording Victoria's warmest winter temperatures.

Essentials

GETTING THERE The best way to get to Gippsland from Melbourne is by car. Take the Monash Freeway southeast and then take the M1 (Princes Freeway) through many of central Gippsland's cities and townships, including Warragul, Traralgon, and Sale, and on to Bairnsdale, Lakes Entrance, Orbost, and Cann River. An alternate route is the South Gippsland Highway, which runs closer to the coast through Korumburra, Leongatha, and Foster before joining the Princes Highway at Sale.

V/Line (✆ **13 61 96** in Victoria; www.vline.com.au) has daily train service to Bairnsdale from Melbourne. There is a connection bus service to Lakes Entrance. A round-trip adult fare to Bairnsdale costs A$52.

VISITOR INFORMATION The **Bairnsdale Visitor Information Centre** (✆ **1800/637 060** in Australia or 03/5151 3444; www.discovereastgippsland.com.au) is at 240 Main St., Bairnsdale. The **Lakes Entrance Visitor Information Centre** (✆ **1800/637 060** in Australia or 03/5155 1966; www.discovereastgippsland.com.au) is on the corner of Marine Parade and Princes Highway. **Prom Country Visitor Information Centre** (✆ **1800/630 704** in Australia or 03/5655 2233; www.visitpromcountry.com.au) is on the South Gippsland Highway at Korumburra. The **Wonthaggi Visitor Information Centre** (✆ **1300/854 334** in Australia, or 03/5671 2444; www.visitbasscoast.com) is at 37 Watt St., Wonthaggi. All are open 9am to 5pm daily (except Christmas Day).

Where to Stay & Dine

Karbeethong Lodge ★★ This charming, historic guesthouse has views over Mallacoota Inlet and Croajingolong National Park, especially lovely from the wide verandah at sunset. Built in 1903, the lodge is comfortable, unpretentious, and stylish.

Some rooms open out onto the front verandah, the lawns, and the rose gardens running down to the water's edge. Others have bush views or open onto an internal courtyard. All are individually decorated in a relaxed seaside or country style, and guests share the lodge's large well-equipped kitchen and comfortable living and dining rooms. The lodge is self-catering, with a big communal table and barbecues outside.

16 Schnapper Point Dr., Mallacoota, VIC 3892. ✆ **03/5158 0411.** Fax 03/5158 0081. www.karbeethonglodge.com.au. 11 units. A$75–A$220 double. Rates include breakfast. Ask about packages. MC, V. *In room:* A/C, hair dryer.

RACV Inverloch Resort ★★ All budgets will find somewhere to stay here, from those seeking luxury style to caravanners. Owned and operated by Victoria's state motoring association, the Royal Automobile Club of Victoria, this resort opened in November 2007. Perched on 32 hectares (79 acres) on a hillside above the rugged sweep of the Bass Coast, it has 26 rooms in the main lodge with ocean views and private decks, 20 private villas, and 32 caravan sites (12 with private en-suite bathrooms). Some villas have no sea view but are spacious and light-filled, smart and functional, if a bit bland. Top of the range are the eight premium ocean-view rooms with 180-degree uninterrupted views of the coastline. The resort is 5km (3 miles) from Inverloch. Midweek, you'll find it filled with mostly retired couples or small-group conference delegates, but at weekends and on holidays, families and caravanners move in. Friendly staff, log fires in the bar, and electric blankets on the beds for those chilly Victorian winter nights give a level of warmth to staying here.

70 Cape Paterson-Inverloch Rd., Inverloch, VIC 3996. ✆ **03/5674 0000.** Fax 03/5571 1000. www.racv.com.au. 46 units, 32 caravan sites. A$210–A$300 ocean-view rooms; A$255–A$415 2-bedroom villas (sleep 4); A$295–A$440 double 3-bedroom villas (sleep 5); A$40–A$60 double caravan sites ($10 extra for en-suite bathroom). Lower rates apply for RACV members. MC, V. **Amenities:** Restaurant; bar; exercise room; golf course nearby; Jacuzzi; heated indoor pool; sauna; 2 outdoor lit tennis courts. *In room:* A/C, TV, CD player, hair dryer, kitchen, Wi-Fi (A$10 for 1 hr.).

Wilderness Retreats ★ Parks Victoria offers a camping experience with all creature comforts—this is really "glamping." There are four Wilderness Retreats at Tidal River in Wilsons Promontory National Park and five at Cape Conran National Park. In each retreat, you stay in large permanent tents with hardwood floors, raised from the ground and furnished with local handmade mahogany furniture—a queen-sized bed, two roll-out single beds, a table, and chairs. They are comfortable, weatherproof, and have a lockable canvas door. At Wilsons Prom, the tents have their own built-in (and plumbed) bathrooms; at Cape Conran you are a short walk from the showers and toilets. Communal kitchens are well equipped, but you need to take all food and supplies with you. The locations are superb. If you want to get back to nature in style, this is the way to go. There are also Wilderness Retreats at Buchan Caves (see p. 675).

32nd Ave., Tidal River, VIC 3960, or Cape Conran Road (19km/12 miles E of Marlo). ✆ **13 19 63.** www.parkweb.vic.gov.au or www.conran.net.au. 9 units. A$250 double at Wilsons Prom, extra person A$20; A$150 double at Cape Conran and Buchan Caves, extra person A$18. Minimum 2-night stay. Bookings essential. AE, DC, MC, V. **Amenities:** Kitchen. *In room:* Fridge.

CANBERRA

by Lee Atkinson

Lovers of symmetry, symbolism, and architecture will love Canberra (pronounced *Can*-bra, with the accent on the "Can," not Can-*behr*-a). Unlike most other Australian cities that grew up organically around pioneer settlements, there is nothing haphazard about the nation's capital. Not only is it Australia's only completely planned city, even its location, rising unexpectedly from the surrounding high grass plains, shimmering and heat-parched in summer and often dusted with snow in winter, was by careful design. It is a city surrounded by bush and farmland, earning it the nickname the "Bush Capital," although that may hint more at its relative remoteness (every other major city in the country is on the coast) than at the wild and rugged peaks of the snowy mountain wilderness on its doorstep.

Prior to Federation in 1901, Canberra was just a large sheep station called Canberry. Post-Federation debates on possible locations for the new seat of government raged for a number of years—both Sydney and Melbourne believed they were the natural seat of power—so in a magnificent compromise, the new Commonwealth Parliament decided to put an end to the bitter rivalry in 1908 by simply choosing a point between the two cities, declaring the sheep station they found there to be the new national capital. Thankfully, they decided to call it Canberra (from the local Aboriginal word for "meeting place") rather than "Sydmelperadbrisho" or the equally silly "Meladneyperbane," both dreadful amalgamations of the names of each of the other capital cities.

In 1911, an international competition to design the new city was held. More than 130 entries were received from around the world, and the winning entry was submitted by Chicago architect Walter Burley Griffin and his partner, Marion Mahony Griffin, a design based on a series of geometrically precise circles and axes. The Australian Capital Territory (ACT) was declared on January 1, 1911. It became a self-governing territory in 1989.

Fast-forward almost 100 years and the city remains true to the Griffin's original "garden city" vision, with streets lined with large trees and buildings set in expanses of grassed parkland. The streets radiate out in a wheel-and-spoke design from Capital Hill, rather than following the grid design of most other cities. Trouble is, unless you live there, the endless circular roads can be confusing, and almost every Australian you meet that has been to Canberra will tell you how easy it is to get lost there.

Most of the 340,000 people who live here are civil servants of some type. And most visitors come simply to see Canberra's amazing range of museums, including the National Museum of Australia, the Questacon science museum, and the National Gallery of Australia. But dig a little deeper and you'll find many more aspects to Canberra, such as a thriving festival and arts scene and an emerging food and wine culture, with 30 of the country's best cool-climate wineries less than 30 minutes drive from the center of the city.

ORIENTATION

Getting There

BY PLANE **Qantas** (✆ **13 13 13** in Australia; www.qantas.com.au) runs frequent daily service to Canberra from all state capitals. **Virgin Blue** (✆ **13 67 89** in Australia; www.virginblue.com.au) offers discount daily flights to Canberra from Melbourne, Brisbane, the Gold Coast, Adelaide, Hobart, Townsville, and Sydney. **Tiger Airways** (✆ **03/9335 3033;** www.tigerairways.com) also has daily flights from Melbourne and Adelaide and **Brindabella Airlines** (✆ 1300/668 824**;** www.brindabella airlines.com.au) has weekday flights from the regional centers of Newcastle and Albury. The Canberra Airport is about 10 minutes from the city center. It has car-rental desks, a currency exchange, a bar, a bistro, and a mailbox for cards and letters (but no post office). The newsdealer sells stamps. There are no lockers or showers.

The **Airliner Bus** (✆ **02/6299 3722;** www.airliner.com.au) operates a 20-minute shuttle between the central business district and the airport Monday to Friday, leaving every half-hour on weekdays and hourly on weekends. The one-way fare is A$9 and a round-trip costs A$15.

BY TRAIN **Countrylink** (✆ **13 22 32** in Australia; www.countrylink.info) runs two Canberra Xplorer trains daily between Sydney and Canberra. The 4¼-hour trip costs around A$80 in first class and A$57 in economy during peak season (school and public holidays), but seasonal discounts apply so check when booking; children pay half-price, and a round-trip costs double. Many people book Countrylink transport-hotel packages (call **Countrylink Holidays,** ✆ **13 28 29**), which can save you quite a bit. Countrylink has an office at Central Railway station in Sydney.

From Melbourne, the **Canberra Link,** run by **V/Line** (✆ **13 61 96** in Australia; www.vlinepassenger.com.au), involves a 3½-hour train trip and a 4-hour bus trip. It costs A$45 for adults and A$35 for children and students.

Canberra Railway Station (✆ **02/6239 6707**) is on Wentworth Avenue, Kingston, about 5km (3 miles) southeast of the city center. Coaches connect the railway station to the center.

BY BUS **Greyhound** (✆ **1300/473 946** in Australia; www.greyhound.com.au) does nine runs a day from Sydney to Canberra; the trip takes around 4 hours. Tickets cost around A$37 for adults, A$34 for students with an ISAC (International

Canberra

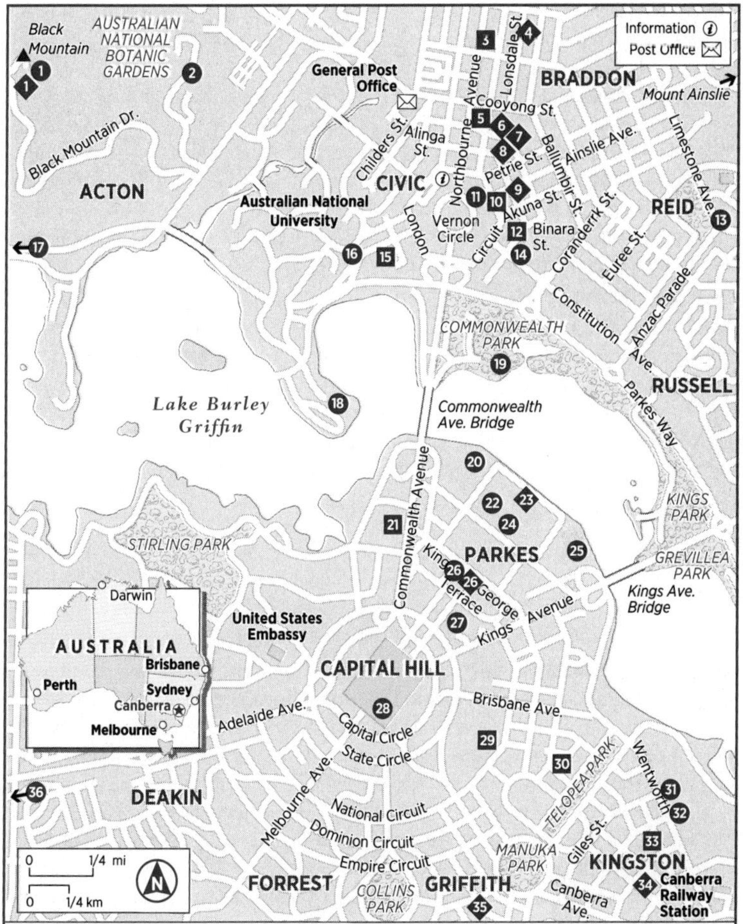

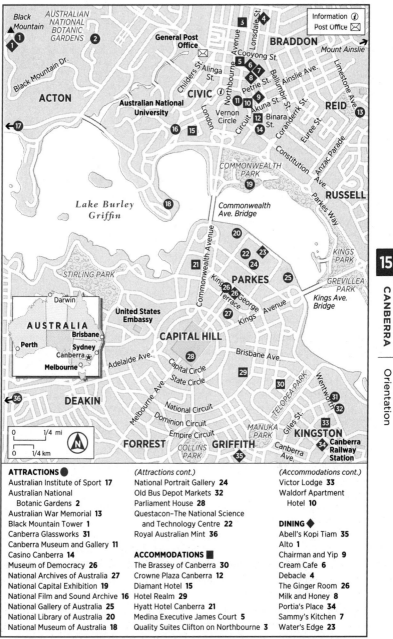

ATTRACTIONS ●
Australian Institute of Sport **17**
Australian National Botanic Gardens **2**
Australian War Memorial **13**
Black Mountain Tower **1**
Canberra Glassworks **31**
Canberra Museum and Gallery **11**
Casino Canberra **14**
Museum of Democracy **26**
National Archives of Australia **27**
National Capital Exhibition **19**
National Film and Sound Archive **16**
National Gallery of Australia **25**
National Library of Australia **20**
National Museum of Australia **18**

(Attractions cont.)
National Portrait Gallery **24**
Old Bus Depot Markets **32**
Parliament House **28**
Questacon–The National Science and Technology Centre **22**
Royal Australian Mint **36**

ACCOMMODATIONS ■
The Brassey of Canberra **30**
Crowne Plaza Canberra **12**
Diamant Hotel **15**
Hotel Realm **29**
Hyatt Hotel Canberra **21**
Medina Executive James Court **5**
Quality Suites Clifton on Northbourne **3**

(Accommodations cont.)
Victor Lodge **33**
Waldorf Apartment Hotel **10**

DINING ◆
Abell's Kopi Tiam **35**
Alto **1**
Chairman and Yip **9**
Cream Cafe **6**
Debacle **4**
The Ginger Room **26**
Milk and Honey **8**
Portia's Place **34**
Sammy's Kitchen **7**
Water's Edge **23**

Student Activity Card), and A$32 for children 3 to 14, although you can often pick up fares for as low as A$20 online.

From Melbourne, tickets to Canberra cost A$75 for adults, A$66 for students, and A$65 for children, although once again, check for specials online before you book.

Murrays Australia (✆ **13 22 51** in Australia; www.murrays.com.au) runs from Sydney to Canberra six times a day for A$36 for adults and A$30 for students and children. Book over the Internet for discounts of up to half price. Sydney-based sightseeing company **Australian Pacific Touring** (✆ **1300/655 965** in Australia; www.aptouring.com.au) offers day trips to Canberra.

Interstate buses arrive at **Jolimont Tourist Centre,** at the corner of Northbourne Avenue and Alinga Street, Canberra City.

BY CAR The ACT is surrounded by New South Wales. Sydney is 280km (174 miles) northeast, and Melbourne is 651km (404 miles) southwest of Canberra. From Sydney, you can use an extension to the M5 motorway that links with the Eastern Distributor highway near Sydney Airport. Veer left before you reach the airport, follow signs heading toward Canberra, and veer left onto the M5. The drive takes between 3 and 3½ hours. From Melbourne, take the Hume Highway to Yass and switch to the Barton Highway; the trip will take about 8 hours.

Visitor Information

The **Canberra Visitors' Centre,** 330 Northbourne Ave., Dickson (✆ **1300/554 114**), dispenses information and books accommodations. The office is open Monday through Friday from 9am to 5pm, and Saturday and Sunday from 9am to 4pm. The official government website, **www.visitcanberra.com.au**, is worth checking out.

SPECIAL EVENTS A host of free events—from concerts to competitions—is part of the annual **Canberra National Multicultural Festival** held over 10 days each February. The city also celebrates its founding with more free events on Canberra Day, which is a local public holiday, on the second Monday in March. There are many other major events scattered throughout the year, the biggest of which is the annual free spring flower show **Floriade,** when Commonwealth Park erupts in a blaze of color with more than 1.5 million bulbs and annuals in bloom. The **Summernats** street machine car festival in January, the Easter **National Folk Festival,** and the **Australian Science Festival** in August also draw big crowds. Check dates at **www.visitcanberra.com.au**.

City Layout

Canberra's focal point is the pondlike **Lake Burley Griffin,** an artificial lake with the **Captain Cook Memorial Jet** (a spire of water that reaches 147m/482 ft. into the air) at its center. Most of the country's more culturally and politically significant buildings—Australia's most expensive building, **Parliament House,** the much smaller (in comparison) **Old Parliament House,** the **National Archives,** the **National Library,** the **National Gallery** and **National Portrait Gallery,** the **High Court of Australia,** and **Questacon,** the National Science and Technology Centre—are clustered around it, making it easy for visitors to go from one attraction to the next. Officially, the area is called Parkes (after Sir Henry Parkes, the "father of Federation"), but it is more commonly referred to as the Parliamentary Triangle, which is bounded by Commonwealth, Kings, and Constitution avenues. Capital Hill is at the apex of the triangle, while City Hall, in the city center, and the headquarters of the Australian Defense Force, in the suburb of Russell, are at the other two points.

Most of the embassies and consulates are in the suburb of **Yarralumla,** east of Capital Hill; Canberra's main shopping district, Civic, is on the other side of the lake, centered on Northbourne Avenue, one of the city's main thoroughfares. Compared to other capital cities, the Central Business District (CBD) there is quite small. The inner suburbs of **Manuka** and **Kingston** are the places to go for boutique shopping and the best restaurants and cafes. On the outskirts of the city you'll find the **National Zoo and Aquarium,** and just a few minutes drive away is Black Mountain, crowned with its 195m-high (640-ft.) communications tower with a viewing platform, revolving restaurant, and exhibition hall.

Getting Around

BY CAR **Avis** (✆ 13 63 33), **Budget** (✆ 1300/362 848), **Europcar** (✆ 1300/131 390), **Hertz** (✆ 13 30 39), and **Thrifty** (✆ 1300/367 227) all have desks at the airport.

If you rent your own wheels, you might follow one or more of the six tourist drives marked with signs; pick up details from the Canberra Visitors' Centre.

BY TAXI Canberra has three taxi companies that can be accessed by phone bookings or from designated ranks (stands) that are clearly signposted throughout the city. For taxi bookings call **Canberra Cabs** (**✆ 13 22 27**), **Cabxpress** (**✆ 02/6260 6011**), or **Silver Service** (**✆ 13 31 00**), which has seven-seater vans as well as sedans. An average taxi fare to the city center is around A$25.

BY BUS **ACTION** (**✆ 13 17 10** in Australia, or 02/6207 7611; www.action.act.gov.au) coordinates Canberra's bus system. The central bus terminal is on Alinga Street, in Civic. Single tickets cost A$3.80 for adults and A$1.90 for children 5 to 15. Daily tickets cost A$7.40 for adults and A$3.70 for kids, and weekly tickets cost A$27 for adults and A$14 for kids. Purchase single tickets on the bus and daily and weekly tickets from most newsdealers and ACTION interchanges (transfer points).

For schedules, check its website, or you can pick up bus route maps at bus interchanges, newsdealers, and the Canberra Visitors' Centre.

Canberra Day Tours (**✆ 0418/455 099;** www.canberradaytours.com.au) offers a hop-on and hop-off day tour by bus, including stops at Old Parliament House, the Australian War Memorial, Parliament House, the Embassy region, Telstra Tower, and Lake Burley Griffin. It costs A$35 for adults and A$15 for kids under 16. The first bus leaves at 9:30am from the Canberra Visitors' Centre.

BY BICYCLE Canberra is unique in Australia for its extensive system of cycle tracks—some 120km (74 miles) of them—which makes sightseeing on two wheels a pleasure. See "Outdoor Pursuits," later in this chapter, for details on bike rental.

[FastFACTS] CANBERRA

American Express The office at 185 City Walk (at the corner of Petrie Plaza, inside the Westpac Bank), Civic, is open during normal business hours (see below). In an emergency, dial ✆ **1300/132 639** in Australia.

Business Hours Banks are generally open Monday through Thursday from 9:30am to 4pm and Friday from 9:30am to 5pm. Stores and offices are open Monday through Friday from 9am to 5:30pm. Many shops, particularly in the large malls, are open on weekends and until 9pm Fridays.

Climate The best time to visit Canberra is in spring (Sept–Nov) or autumn (Mar–May). Summers are hot and winters are cool and crisp.

Currency Exchange Cash traveler's checks at banks; at **American Express** (see above); or at **Travelex,** in the **Harvey World Travel** office at the Petrie Plaza entrance of the Canberra Centre (✆ **02/6247 9984**), open Monday through Friday from 9am to 5pm and Saturday from 9am to 1pm.

Doctors **Canberra after hours locum medical service** (CALMS; ✆ **1300/422 567,** appointment necessary) is in Building 2 at the Canberra Hospital (enter through the Emergency Department entrance). The **Travellers' Medical & Vaccination Centre,** Level 5, 8–10 Hobart Place (at the corner of Marcus Clarke St.), Civic (✆ **02/6222 2300**), offers vaccinations and travel medicines. Standard 20-minute consultations cost A$80 and up.

Embassies & Consulates The **British High Commission** (consular section) is on Commonwealth Avenue, Yarralumla (✆ **02/6270 6666**); the **Canadian High Commission** is also on Commonwealth Avenue, Yarralumla (✆ **02/6270 4000**); the **U.S. Embassy** is at Moonah Place, Yarralumla (✆ **02/6214 5600**); and the **New Zealand High Commission** is at Commonwealth Avenue, Yarralumla (✆ **02/6270 4211**).

Emergencies Call ✆ **000** for an ambulance, the police, or the fire department.

Eyeglasses For repairs, glasses, and contact lenses, try **OPSM Express,** on the Lower Ground Floor, Canberra Centre, Civic (✆ **02/6249 7344**). It's open 9am to 5:30pm Monday through Thursday, 9am to 9pm Friday, and 9am to 4pm Saturday.

Hospitals For medical attention, go to the **Canberra Hospital,** Yamba Drive, Garran (✆ **02/6244 2222**), or call the **Accident & Emergency Department** (✆ **02/6244 2324**).

Hot Lines For information and counseling, call the **Rape Crisis Centre** (✆ 02/6247 2525; 24 hr.); the **Drug/Alcohol Crisis Line** (✆ 02/6207 9977; 24 hr.); **Lifeline Crisis Counselling** (✆ 13 11 14; www.lifeline.org.au); the **Salvation Army Counselling Service** (✆ 1300/363 622); the **Poison Information Centre** (✆ 13 11 26); and the **National Roads & Motorists Association** (✆ 13 11 11).

Internet Access The **National Library,** Parkes Place, Parkes (✆ **02/6262 1111**), has e-mail facilities available Monday through Thursday 9am to 9pm, Friday and Saturday 9am to 5pm, Sunday 1:30pm to 5pm. Internet access is readily available around town at other libraries and in Internet cafes. The Canberra Visitors' Centre can provide you with a full list.

Pharmacies (Chemist Shops) There are three pharmacies in the **Canberra Centre,** Civic, open during general shopping hours. A number of after-hours pharmacies are listed in the Canberra Yellow Pages.

Photographic Needs **Ted's Camera House** has stores at 9 Petrie Plaza (✆ **02/6247 8711**) and in the Canberra Centre (✆ **02/6249 7364**), and both are good places to buy camera gear and film and to have photos printed.

Post Office The **Canberra GPO,** 53-73 Alinga St., Civic (✆ **02/6209 1680**), is open Monday through Friday from 8:30am to 5:30pm. The general delivery *(poste restante)* address is c/o Canberra GPO, ACT 2601.

Restrooms Public restrooms can be found near the city bus exchange, City Hall, and London Circuit.

WHERE TO STAY

Generally, accommodations are much cheaper in Canberra than in most other state capitals. Many people travel to Canberra during the week, so many hotels offer cheaper weekend rates and you should always ask about special deals. The **Canberra Visitors' Centre** (✆ **1300/554 114**) can provide information about other accommodation options.

Very Expensive

Hyatt Hotel Canberra ★ For a very long time, the Hyatt Hotel was the only five-star hotel in the city, which made it a favorite with visiting heads of state and celebrities and the Art Deco masterpiece is still the place to see and been seen in the capital. It has a great location—a 2-minute drive from the city center—in the shadow of Parliament House and between Lake Burley Griffin and the Parliamentary Triangle. Standard rooms have a king-size bed and marble bathrooms. Children under 12 stay free in parent's room and you'll get 50% discount if you book a second room for children under 12.

Commonwealth Ave., Yarralumla, ACT 2600. ✆ **800/633-7313** in the U.S. and Canada, or 02/6270 1234. Fax 02/6281 5998. http://canberra.park.hyatt.com. 248 units. A$365-A$475 standard double; suites from A$600 and up. Extra person A$80. Ask about weekend packages and special rates. AE, DC, MC, V. Free parking. Bus: 2, 3, 6, 934, or 935. **Amenities:** Restaurant; cafe; bike rental; concierge; health club and spa; indoor pool; room service; lit tennis court. *In room:* A/C, TV w/pay movies, fridge, hair dryer, minibar, MP3 docking station (in deluxe rooms and suites), Wi-Fi (A$1.65 for 3 min. up to A$29 for 24 hr.).

Expensive

Crowne Plaza Canberra ★ This hotel is next door to the National Convention Centre and Casino Canberra. Its car-oriented approach makes it a little inconvenient for pedestrians, but the gardens (Glebe Park) at the back are good for early morning strolls. Rooms face onto internal balconies that look down to the restaurants below. Standard rooms are user friendly and comfortable; most come with one queen-size bed or two doubles. Parkview doubles overlook the gardens. Weekend rates drop dramatically, so it's worth checking the website.

1 Binara St., Canberra, ACT 2601. ✆ **1800/007 697** in Australia, or 02/6247 8999. Fax 02/6257 4903. www.crowneplaza.com. 295 units. A$162-A$414 standard double. Extra person A$65. Weekend discounts available. Children 18 and under stay free in parent's room. AE, DC, MC, V. Parking A$15; A$25 for valet parking. Bus: 4, 5, 30, or 80. **Amenities:** Restaurant; bar; concierge; medium-size indoor pool; room service; day spa; Wi-Fi (free in lobby). *In room:* A/C, TV, fridge, hair dryer, minibar.

Diamant Hotel ★★ This new luxury boutique hotel, with its eclectic art collection and dark moody color schemes, has more personality than most of Canberra's businesslike hotels. The rooms are a bit on the small side (so opt for a deluxe or premier room rather than the standard), but it's in a good location close to Lake Burley Griffin and a 5-minute walk from the city center.

15 Edinburgh Ave., Canberra, ACT 2601. ✆ **02/6175 2222.** Fax 02/6175 2233. www.diamant.com.au. 80 units. A$185–A$320 double; A$300 and up suite. AE, DC, MC, V. Parking A$25. Bus: 3, 81, 981, or 984. **Amenities:** 2 restaurants; 2 bars; health club; room service; Wi-Fi (free in lobby). *In room:* A/C, TV, DVD/CD player, fridge, hair dryer, Internet (A$7 for 1 hr.; A$20 for 24 hr.), minibar, MP3 docking station.

Hotel Realm ★★★ Canberra's other five-star hotel (there are only two) is not nearly as stuffy as the Hyatt (see above) and is another good choice for those that like a bit of design rather than pure function in their hotel rooms. Located a stone's throw away from Parliament House and within walking distances of the restaurants and bars of Manuka and Kingston, all rooms are light, bright, and airy. Suites have spacious balconies and kitchens. The **Mudd Spa** has a range of (expensive) pampering treatments.

18 National Circuit, Barton, ACT 2600. ✆ **02/6163 1800.** Fax 02/6163 1801. www.hotelrealm.com.au. 158 units. A$225–A$340 double; A$285 and up for suite. AE, DC, MC, V. Parking A$10; A$15 for valet parking. Bus: 6, 28, or 935. **Amenities:** Restaurant; bar; gymnasium (fee); health club and spa; heated pool. *In room:* A/C, TV, fridge, hair dryer, Internet (A$9.95 1 hr.; A$30 24 hr.), minibar, Wi-Fi (suites only, A$9.95 1 hr.; A$30 24 hr.).

Medina Executive James Court ★★ Medina hotel apartments always offer great value. As with others scattered around the country, the Medina Executive James Court is modern, spankingly clean, centrally located, and has a fully equipped kitchen and laundry. The one- and two-bedroom apartments have a TV in the living room and another in the bedroom, and all apartments come with a balcony and corner spa in the en-suite bathroom. A sister property, the **Medina Classic,** at 11 Giles St., Kingston (✆ **02/6239 8100;** fax 02/6239 7226), is just 4km (2½ miles) from the city center in fashionable Kingston. It has both an indoor and outdoor pool and also offers one- and two-bedroom apartments. Rates for this property are A$200 for a one-bedroom apartment and A$246 for a two-bedroom apartment.

74 Northbourne Ave., Canberra, ACT 2601. ✆ **1300/300 232** in Australia, or 02/6240 1234. Fax 02/6240 1235. www.medinaapartments.com.au. 150 units. A$235 1-bedroom apt; A$290 2-bedroom apt. A$50 extra person. AE, MC, V. Parking A$8. Bus: 30, 31, 58, 56, 958, 956, 980, or 982. **Amenities:** Restaurant; bar; concierge; health club/sauna; outdoor pool; room service. *In room:* A/C, TV, hair dryer, Internet (A$11 1 hr.; A$22 24 hr.), kitchen, laundry, minibar.

Waldorf Apartment Hotel ★ An easy walk to the Canberra Convention Centre and many government and corporate offices, this is a great option for business travelers. There's a range of bright and cheerful rooms, from functional studios to one-bedroom (some with a separate office) and two-bedroom serviced apartments. All come with a fully equipped kitchen and laundry and private in-room fax. The rooftop barbecue area is popular with families. Ask about weekly rates.

2 Akuna St., Canberra, ACT 2601. ✆ **1800/188 388** in Australia, or 02/6229 1234. Fax 02/6229 1235. www.waldorfcanberra.com.au. 80 units. A$155–A$235 studio apt; A$175–A$255 1-bedroom apt; A$255–A$335 2-bedroom apt. A$15 extra person. AE, DC, MC, V. Undercover parking A$15. Bus: 4, 5, 30, or 80. **Amenities:** Restaurant; bar; gymnasium; indoor heated lap pool; sauna; half-size tennis court. *In room:* A/C, TV, fax, hair dryer, kitchen, minibar, Wi-Fi (A$5 1 hr.; A$15 24 hr.).

Moderate

The Brassey of Canberra Rooms in this 1927 heritage-listed building, formerly a boarding house for visiting government officials, are large, quiet, and somewhat plush. The garden bar and piano lounge are popular. Other good points include its proximity to Parliament House and other major attractions, and the hearty breakfasts. The hotel underwent extensive renovations a few years ago, which included the remodeling of many of the doubles into larger heritage rooms.

Belmore Gardens, Barton, ACT 2600. ✆ **1800/659 191** in Australia, or 02/6273 3766. Fax 02/6273 2791. www.brassey.net.au. 81 units. A$177 double; A$197 heritage double; A$240 heritage family room. Rates include buffet breakfast. Check for specials. AE, DC, MC, V. Free parking. Bus: 4, 5, 80, 938, or 980. **Amenities:** Restaurant; bar. *In room:* A/C, TV, fridge, hair dryer, minibar.

Quality Suites Clifton on Northbourne Canberra's newest government-rated four-and-a-half-star apartment hotel is just minutes from the heart of the shopping, dining, and entertainment district. The apartments can be a little soulless, but if you are after lots of room to move, you'll appreciate their generous size. All of the one- and two-bedroom apartments have private balconies, fully equipped kitchens, cable TV, and laundry facilities. A complimentary airport shuttle is available on request Monday to Friday. It's primarily a business hotel, which means you can often get a great weekend rate.

100 Northbourne Ave., Canberra City, ACT 2601. ✆ **02/6262 6266.** Fax 02/6203 8444. www.cliftonsuites.com.au. 153 units. A$170–A$390 1-bedroom apt; A$245–A$490 2-bedroom apt. A$45 extra person. AE, DC, MC, V. Free parking. Bus: 30, 31, 58, 56, 958, 956, 980, or 982. **Amenities:** Restaurant; gymnasium; 25m (82-ft.) pool. *In room:* A/C, TV, hair dryer, kitchen, Wi-Fi (A$4 per hr.).

Inexpensive

Victor Lodge Backpackers and budget travelers frequent this friendly place, next to Kingston's shops and about a 10-minute drive from the city center and a short walk from the train station. Rooms vary, from dorms with four or five beds to modern, simple doubles. Each has a wash basin. There are communal showers and toilets and a courtyard.

Next door is the reasonable **Best Western Motel Monaro,** at 27 Dawes St. (✆ **02/6295 2111;** http://motelmonaro.bestwestern.com.au). It charges A$145 for a double. Apparently, parents often park their teenage kids at the lodge and live it up at the motel.

29 Dawes St., Kingston, ACT 2604. ✆ **02/6295 7777.** Fax 02/6295 2466. www.victorlodge.com.au. 29 units, none with bathroom. A$96 double; A$38 dorm bed. Rates include continental breakfast. MC, V. Free parking. Bus: 4, 5, 80, 938, or 980. **Amenities:** Dining room; bike rental. *In room:* A/C, Wi-Fi (A$10 24 hr.).

WHERE TO DINE

Expensive

Alto ★★ MODERN AUSTRALIAN At the top of Black Mountain Tower, Alto has a revolving floor that does a full circuit in just under 90 minutes. The decor is modern and bright, but it's pretty hard to drag your eyes away from the view, and unlike most revolving restaurants atop tourist attractions, the food here (modern Australian with a European twist and lots of fresh seasonal produce) is actually quite good. Try the Wagyu carpaccio with shaved black Perigold truffle, white asparagus, and a fine leaf salad (in season), followed by crispy skinned red snapper with a white bean purée and zucchini ribbons.

Black Mountain Dr., Acton. ✆ **02/6247 5518.** www.altotower.com.au. Reservations required. Main courses A$36–A$41. AE, MC, V. Daily 6–11pm; Thurs–Fri and Sun noon–3pm.

The Poachers Way

The Poachers Way, a recommended self-drive route through the ACT's wine country, is a great way to explore Canberra's surrounding regions of Hall, Murrumbateman, Gundaroo, and Yass while indulging in some of the area's best wine and food along the way. The cool climate wines of the Canberra district are coming of age, with more than 140 vineyards and 30 cellar doors open to the public, and eateries such as the Poachers Pantry are redefining the capital's culinary landscape. Try some gourmet smoked meats and taste the wines at the Pantry's Smokehouse Café, 431 Nanima Rd., Hall (✆ 02/6230 2487; daily 10am–5pm), and enjoy a long lunch at the Royal Hotel's Grazing restaurant in Gundaroo, at the corner of Cork and Harp streets (✆ 02/6236 8777; Fri–Sun and most public holidays for lunch, Thurs–Sat for dinner). The menu at the Royal is uniquely focused on the Canberra district, showcasing the best local fresh farm produce and probably the world's largest Canberra district wine list. Download a map of the trail and cellar-door opening times at www.thepoachersway.com.au.

The Chairman and Yip ★★★ ASIAN/AUSTRALIAN One of Canberra's best restaurants: Upbeat and popular with political bigwigs, it has a reputation of being the place to see and be seen. Chinese classics are given an East-meets-West twist, and the result is delicious. I love the decor, especially the Mao-style pop art decorating the walls. The signature dishes are the roasted duck and shiitake pancakes, and the peppered beef and scallop hot pot, but everything on the menu is good.

108 Bunda St., Civic. ✆ **02/6248 7109.** www.thechairmanandyip.com. Reservations required. Main courses A$28–A$34. AE, DC, MC, V. Tues–Fri noon–2:30pm; Mon–Sat 6–10:30pm.

The Ginger Room ★★★ 🎁 FRENCH/VIETNAMESE/AUSTRALIAN If only the walls could talk, what secrets they could tell. The private members' dining room in Old Parliament House has been transformed into a fine dining experience. Chef Janet Jeffs serves up a mouthwatering array of very clever Indochine meals with quirky Australian overtones: Rare roasted kangaroo rice paper rolls with beetroot and watercress salad are just one of the delights on offer when we last visited. All menus have set prices, and you can choose two, three, four, or five courses; each is really quite a good value. Whatever you do, don't leave without trying the chef's signature dish, the eastern king prawn egg net with *nu cham* dressing. Sublime.

Old Parliament House (back entrance, upper level), Queen Victoria Terrace, Parkes. ✆ **02/6270 8262.** www.gingercatering.com.au. Reservations required. Fixed-course menus: 2 courses A$59; 3 courses A$69; 4 courses A$79; 7 courses A$89. AE, DC, MC, V. Tues–Sat 6–11pm.

Waters Edge ★★★ EUROPEAN This restaurant, with sweeping views across Lake Burley Griffin to the Australian War Memorial, is the perfect place for a long, languid lunch. Dinner's just as good, but of course the views are hard to see in the dark. It's an eclectic European menu that changes with the seasons, but the dishes from southern France are what the chef seems to excel at, and the duck, however it is prepared, has never been disappointing. Leave room for dessert.

40 Parkes Place, Parkes. ✆ 02/6273 5066. www.courgette.com.au/watersedge. Reservations required. Main courses A$36. AE, DC, MC, V. Wed–Sun noon–3pm; Tues–Sun 6:30–10pm.

Moderate

Cream Café ★ CAFE/MODERN AUSTRALIAN You'll find a mixed crowd in this little corner eatery at the heart of the Canberra center restaurant and bar strip, whatever the time of day or night. There's a range of eating areas, with a bar, a dining room, and outside space, and dishes have a fair amount of Asian, European, and Mediterranean influences. It's open all day serving coffees, breakfast, and light lunches; after dinner, the space morphs into a nice cocktail bar with tapas-style snacks.

Bunda and Genge sts., Canberra City. ✆ **02/6162 1448.** www.creamcafebar.com.au. Main courses A$21–A$33. AE, MC, V. Mon 11:30am–late; Tues–Fri 7:30am–late; Sat 9am–late; Sun 9am–4pm.

Milk and Honey CAFE/MODERN AUSTRALIAN There's a happy buzz in this bright retro-styled cafe that offers everything from light snacks, smoothies, and milkshakes to full meals. There's also a great choice of alcoholic drinks from the bar, including cocktails, and freshly squeezed fruit juices. Milk and Honey also does pasta well, and its generous risotto stacked with seafood is recommended. It can get crowded though and seating is cramped.

Centre Cinema Building, 29 Garema Place, Civic. ✆ **02/6247 7722.** www.milkandhoney.net.au. Reservations recommended. Main courses A$18–A$28. AE, MC, V. Mon–Fri 7:30am–late; Sat 8am–late; Sun 9am–6pm.

Podfood ★★ FRESH/AUSTRALIAN It's not the cheapest cafe in town, but it's pretty hard to beat this place if you're looking for somewhere to linger over a lazy late-morning breakfast (although they also serve lunch here). Set on the grounds of Pialligo Plant Farm just near the airport, Podfood serves sophisticated, contemporary food in a renovated 1930s cottage, and seating spills out onto a lovely outdoor area. The field mushrooms with Persian feta mousse are sublime. The chef also runs regular cooking classes.

Pialligo Plant Farm, 12 Beltana Rd., Pialligo. ✆ **02/6257 3388.** www.podfood.com.au. Breakfast A$17–A$19; main lunch courses A$25–A$32. AE, DC, MC, V. Tues–Sat 10am–4pm.

Portia's Place ASIAN A small restaurant serving excellent home-style cookery, Portia's Place often fills up early and does a roaring lunchtime trade. The best things on the menu are lamb ribs in *shang tung* sauce, King Island steak in pepper sauce, flaming pork (brought to your table wrapped in foil and, yes, flaming), and Queensland trout stir-fried with snow peas, although the steamed dumplings—home-style *gow-tse* filled with pork and freshly chopped chives served in a bamboo basket—are hard to pass up.

11 Kennedy St., Kingston. ✆ **02/6239 7970.** Reservations recommended. Main courses A$20–A$33. AE, DC, MC, V. Sun–Fri 11:30am–2:30pm; daily 5–10:30pm.

Inexpensive

Abell's Kopi Tiam INDONESIAN/MALAYSIAN Bright, cheap, and cheerful—what this little place lacks in decor it makes up for in flavor. The menu is a mix of southeast Asian cooking, with a strong Nonya (fusion of Malay and Chinese) influence. It gets busy, but service is brisk and the food is always good.

7 Furneaux St., Manuka. ✆ **02/6239 4199.** Main courses A$14–A$25. AE, MC, V. Tues–Sun 11:30am–2:30pm; Tues–Sat 5:30–10pm; Sun 5:30–9pm.

Market Mania

Every Sunday, the old bus depot in Kingston is home to the Old Bus Depot Markets, 21 Wentworth Ave. (✆ 02/6292 8391; www.obdm.com.au; Sun 10am–4pm), where you can pick up some great handmade souvenirs—arts, crafts, clothes, soaps, jewelry, just about anything really. The quality is generally excellent, and it's also a great place to stock up on fresh fruit, cheeses, and produce if planning a picnic. There's a range of food stalls serving inexpensive lunches and good coffee and always a mix of buskers to entertain the crowd.

Debacle MODERN AUSTRALIAN/TAPAS It's hard to say whether you'd call this place a pub or a restaurant, but really, who cares? Casual and always busy, there are more than 120 beers to choose from, almost as many wines, and a great menu of tapas-size dishes as well as hearty fare like risotto, pasta, some killer gourmet burgers, and really good pizzas. The food's fresh—the management likes to boast that they don't even own a freezer! There's two-for-one pizza on Mondays and Tuesdays.

30 Lonsdale St., Braddon. ✆ **02/6247 1314.** Reservations recommended. Main courses A$12–A$20. AE, MC, V. Daily 8:30am–midnight.

Sammy's Kitchen CHINESE/MALAYSIAN Sammy's is a bit of Canberra institution, with a perennially buzzing atmosphere. It's always busy, even though it has room for 100 diners. Food is great, but the brisk service can be a bit hit and miss at times. It's the place to go for the best *laksa* in Canberra.

North Quarter, Canberra Centre, Bunda St., Canberra City. ✆ **02/6247 1464.** Main courses A$12–A$20. AE, MC, V. Daily 11:30am–2:30pm; Mon–Thurs 5–10:30pm; Fri–Sat 5–11:30pm; Sun 5:30–10pm.

SEEING THE SIGHTS

Australian Institute of Sport (AIS) ☺ Sports nuts and champions in the making love the AIS, where Australian sporting superstars are made. Go behind the scenes on a guided tour and learn the secrets of what it takes win a gold medal, watch gymnasts in action or the country's top swimmers doing their laps.

Leverrier Cres, Bruce (about 7km/4 miles from the city center). ✆ **02/6214 1010.** www.ausport.gov.au. Guided tours A$16 adults, A$9 children, A$44 family (2 adults and up to 3 children). Tours depart daily at 10, 11:30am, 1, and 2:30pm. Bus: 7 or 980.

Australian War Memorial ★★★ ☺ More than just a monument to Australian troops who gave their lives for their country, the relics, artifacts, and displays tell the story of Australia's conflicts abroad, but unlike many military museums, the displays do not glorify war. The main focus of the memorial is the Hall of Memory, where the body of an unknown soldier brought back from a World War I battlefield lies entombed among beautiful mosaics and stained-glass windows. I love coming here for the art collection alone. Kids will gravitate toward the Discovery Zone where you can dodge sniper fire in a WWI trench, take control of an Iroquois helicopter, and peer through the periscope of a Cold War submarine. New is the "Conflicts 1945 to Today" gallery, which looks at Asian conflicts and peacekeeping operations since 1947.

At the head of Anzac Parade on Limestone Ave. ✆ **02/6243 4211.** www.awm.gov.au. Free admission. Daily 10am–5pm (when the Last Post is played). Closed Dec 25. Free guided 90-min. tours every half-hour 10–11am and 1–2pm. Bus: 10, 930, or 931.

Black Mountain Tower The 195m (640-ft.) tower on the summit of Black Mountain is both landmark and must-see attraction for every first time visitor to Canberra. From the top, the open-air and enclosed viewing galleries provide magnificent 360-degree views over the city and the surrounding countryside. The tower also provides telecommunications facilities for the city and most people still refer to it by its former name, Telstra Tower.

Black Mountain Dr. ✆ **02/6219 6111.** Admission A$7.50 adults, A$3 children. Daily 9am–10pm. Bus 81 or 981.

Canberra Deep Space Communication Complex ★★ ☺ This information center, which stands beside huge tracking dishes, is a must for anyone interested in space. There are plenty of models, audiovisual recordings, and displays, including a space suit, space food, and archival film footage of the Apollo moon landings. The complex is still active, tracking and recording results from the Mars Pathfinder, *Voyager 1* and 2, and the Cassini, Soho, Galileo, and Ulysses space exploration projects, as well as providing a link with NASA spacecraft. This is a great stop on the way back from the **Tidbinbilla Nature Reserve** (p. 700). There's no public bus service, but several tour companies offer programs that include the complex.

421 Discovery Dr., Tidbinbilla, 39km (24 miles) southwest of Civic. ✆ **02/6201 7880.** www.cdscc.nasa.gov. Free admission. Daily 9am–5pm.

Canberra Museum and Gallery A small museum and art gallery focusing just on the Canberra district, the highlight here is the Nolan collection, which includes some of the famous Ned Kelly series. It's a good gallery to visit on a rainy day, but not at the expense of the National Gallery, Portrait Gallery, or National Museum of Australia.

Corner London Circuit and Civic Square, Canberra City. ✆ **02/6207 3968.** Admission free. Tues–Fri 10am–5pm (4pm in winter), Sat–Sun noon–5pm (4pm in winter).

Museum of Australian Democracy at Old Parliament House ★★ It was only ever meant to be temporary until the "proper" house was built on Capital Hill, but the Old Parliament House was the seat of government from 1927 to 1988—despite the objections of city architect Walter Burley Griffin (who likened the placement of the Old Parliament to "filling the front yard with outhouses"). If you need a refresher course as to precisely how democracy is meant to work (as opposed to how it really works), you'll find the Museum of Australian Democracy inside. Exhibitions focus on the history of democracy and some of the key Australian figures in the political past. It's interesting but primarily aimed at school kids, although political junkies will love walking through the old rooms, including the Prime Minister's office, that have been pretty much left exactly as they were when the politicians moved out to the new Parliament House on the hill. The free guided tours (there are 12 throughout the day focusing on various aspects of the house) bring the history of the house alive and are highly recommended. Outside on the lawn is the Aboriginal Tent Embassy, which was set up in 1972 in a bid to persuade the authorities to recognize the land ownership claims of Aboriginal and Torres Strait Islander people.

It was the first place the red, black, and yellow Aboriginal flag was flown. The Australian Heritage Commission now recognizes the campsite as a place of special cultural significance.

On King George Terrace, midway btw. the new Parliament House (see below) and the lake. ✆ **02/6270 8222.** www.moadoph.gov.au. Admission A$2 adults, A$1 children, A$5 families. Daily 9am–5pm. Bus: 3, 934, or 935.

National Archives of Australia ★ The National Archives holds the records of all Australian Government activities since Federation in 1901, as well as a huge amount of documents from the 19th century. Sounds boring, but they put together some great exhibitions that are anything but—most are well worth seeing. Expect to see letters, photos, books, bowls, guns, clothes, and suitcases, among other things.

Queen Victoria Terrace, Parkes. ✆ **02/6212 3600.** www.naa.gov.au. Free admission. Daily 9am–5pm. Bus: 2, 3, 6.

National Capital Exhibition ★ This little information center beside the lake is a great way to come to grips with the original vision of Walter Burley Griffin and Marion Mahony Griffin, the architects behind the city's unique design.

On the lakeshore at Regatta Point in Commonwealth Park. ✆ **02/6257 1068.** Free admission. Mon–Fri 9am–5pm; Sat–Sun 10am–4pm. Closed public holidays except Australia Day (Jan 26) and Canberra Day (second Mon in Mar).

National Film and Sound Archive ★★★ The National Film and Sound Archive holds 100 years of Australian film, radio, and television history in a gorgeous Art Deco building that used to be the Institute of Anatomy (and is reputedly the most haunted building in Canberra). There are a range of changing exhibitions, but the best reason to come here is for one of the regular movie screenings, where you can catch some of the Australia's best classics and international cult films on the big screen. Check out the website for programs.

McCoy Circuit, Acton. ✆ **02/6248 2000.** www.nfsa.afc.gov.au. Free admission (movies extra). Free shows weekends 11am and 3pm. Mon–Fri 9am–5pm; Sat–Sun and public holidays 10am–5pm. Bus: 3 or 934.

National Gallery of Australia ★★★ Home to more than 100,000 works of art, the National Gallery showcases Australian and international art in 11 galleries, including a permanent one and traveling blockbuster exhibitions from international collections. The free 1-hour guided tours are brilliant and depart daily at 11:30am and 2:30pm; an Australian art tour departs daily at 11am and 2pm. On Tuesdays, Thursdays, and Sundays, a free tour focuses on Aboriginal art at 12:30pm. A sculpture garden surrounding the gallery is always open to the public.

Parkes Place. ✆ **02/6240 6501.** www.nga.gov.au. Free admission (except for major touring exhibitions). Daily 10am–5pm. Closed Dec 25. Bus: 2, 3, 6, 934, or 935.

National Museum of Australia ★★★ ☺ If you visit only one museum in Australia, make it this one. Using state-of-the-art technology and hands-on exhibits that rely more on images, soundscapes, and personal stories than dusty old objects, the museum profiles 50,000 years of indigenous heritage, settlement since 1788, and key events including Federation and the 2000 Sydney Olympics. The collection has everything from a carcass of the extinct Tasmanian tiger to Australia's largest collection of bark paintings, racehorse Phar Lap's heart, and the No. 1 Holden Prototype car. A new gallery called "Australian Journeys" features more than 750 objects

Glass Act

Canberra Glassworks, 11 Wentworth Ave., Kingston (✆ 02/6260 7005; www.canberraglassworks.com), one of the city's best contemporary glass art galleries and studio spaces, offers "off the street" glass-making classes on weekends. Blow your own paperweight, make a fused glass tile, or create some beautiful glass beads. Each class is 20 minutes and no experience is necessary, although bookings are. Your finished artwork is mailed home to you after it has been fired or cooled. Admission is free; classes are A$30 to A$70. It's open Wednesday to Sunday 10am to 4pm; classes on weekends only.

related to trade, exploration, travel, and migration. Highlights include a rich collection of Captain Cook artifacts and convict tokens. I love this museum, but it is designed with an Australian audience in mind and overseas visitors may find locals' affection for some of the displays baffling. Guided tours (daily 9:30am, noon, 1:30pm, and 3pm; First Australian tour focusing on Aboriginal and Torres Strait Islander history and culture daily at 11am) may help make things a little more clear.

Acton Peninsula (about 5km/3 miles from the city center). ✆ **1800/026 132** in Australia or 02/6208 5000. www.nma.gov.au. Free admission (fees for special exhibitions). Guided tours A$7.50 adults, A$5 children, A$20 family (2 adults and up to 3 children). Daily 9am–5pm. Bus: 3, 934, or 981.

National Portrait Gallery ★★★ Don't come to this gallery expecting to see lots of gold-framed figures in suits and robes because you'll be disappointed, although there are a few if you look really hard. The National Portrait Gallery tends to focus instead on more modern faces. It's all about the people who have shaped Australia and portrays them in a range of styles, from digital media and sculpture, textiles and photography, even cartoons. It's well worth a look.

King Edward Terrace, Parkes. ✆ **02/6102 7000.** www.portrait.gov.au. Free admission (fees for special exhibitions). Daily 10am–5pm. Bus: 2, 3, or 934.

National Zoo and Aquarium ★ ☺ Private zoos tend to be rundown, dinky affairs that seldom offer good value for money or humane animal enclosures. This one, though, looks after 28 endangered species in a nice bushland setting and has Australia's largest collection of big cats, including even a couple of ligers—or are they tigons? It's not cheap (A$95 on weekdays and A$125 on weekends and public holidays), but the 2-hour ZooVenture Tour is a great way to get up close and personal to tigers, lions, and bears. There's a safety fence between you and the big cats, but that doesn't feel like much protection when you're looking a 110-kilogram (243-lb.) Sumatran tiger in the eye as he takes a piece of meat from your hand. There is also a "Meet a Cheetah" program that takes you inside the cheetah's enclosure.

Scrivener Dam, Lady Denman Dr., Yarralumla. ✆ **02/6287 8400.** www.nationalzoo.com.au. Admission A$30 adults, A$19 kids 4–15, A$90 families. Daily 10am–5pm. Bus: 81 or 981.

Parliament House ★★ Conceived by American architect Walter Burley Griffin in 1912, but not built until 1988, Canberra's focal point was designed to blend organically into its setting at the top of Capital Hill; only a national flag supported by a giant four-footed flagpole rises above the peak of the hill. Inside are more than

INTO THE bush CAPITAL

The **Australian National Botanic Gardens,** Clunies Ross Street, Acton (✆ **02/6250 9540**), are a must-see for anyone with a passing interest in Australian native plants. The 51-hectare (126-acre) gardens on the lower slopes of Black Mountain contain more than 600 species of eucalyptus, a rainforest, a Tasmanian alpine garden, and walking trails. Free guided tours depart from the visitor center at 11am and 2pm each day. The gardens are open daily from 8:30am to 5pm (extended in Jan to 6pm weekdays and 8pm weekends). The visitor center is open daily from 9am to 4:30pm.

Namadgi is the Aboriginal word for the rugged mountains southwest of Canberra, and **Namadgi National Park,** at 105,900 hectares (261,684 acres), makes up more than half of the Australian Capital Territory. **Bimberi Peak** (1,911m/6,270 ft.) is the park's highest feature and is only 318m (1,043 ft.) lower than Mount Kosciuszko, Australia's highest mountain. There is a network of public roads within the park that pass through the majestic mountain country, but the unsealed roads are narrow and can be slippery when wet or frosty. (Watch out for kangaroos, too.) Much of Namadgi's beauty, however, lies beyond its main roads and picnic areas. There are 170km (106 miles) of marked walking trails in the park, but you will need to be well prepared if you are going to walk into the more remote areas. Before you depart, make sure you sign one of the bushwalking registers located at the visitor center and elsewhere in the park. The **Namadgi Visitors Centre,** on the Nass/Boboyan Road, 3km (1¾ miles) south of the township of Tharwa (✆ **02/6207 2900**), has maps and information on walking trails.

Another great place to see some Australian wildlife is at the **Tidbinbilla Nature Reserve,** a 40-minute drive from the city center along Tourist Drive 5. There are walking trails, ranger-guided activities, great picnic facilities, and prolific wildlife, including koalas and the endangered brush-tailed rock wallaby. The surrounding mountains are of huge cultural significance to Aboriginal people; Tidbinbilla is derived from the Aboriginal word *jedbinbilla,* a place where "boys were made men." There are lots of Aboriginal sites in the reserve, including the 21,000-year-old **Birrigai Rock Shelter.** The new elevated boardwalk across the wetlands is well worth taking, especially if you like bird-watching. Bush-bird feeding time is 2:30pm daily.

Go Bush Tours (✆ **02/6231 3023**) runs tours to the reserve as well as the neighboring Canberra Deep Space Communication Complex from A$130, including morning tea and lunch. Or, for the same price, you can go on a tour of Namadgi National Park.

3,000 works of Australian arts and crafts, and extensive areas of the building are open to the general public. Just outside the main entrance, look for a mosaic by Michael Tjakamarra Nelson, *Meeting Place,* which represents a gathering of Aboriginal tribes. There's also a 20m-long (66-ft.) tapestry of an Arthur Boyd painting in the Great Hall on the first floor and one of the four known versions of the Magna Carta in the Great Hall beneath the flagpole. Parliament is usually in session Monday through Thursday between mid-February and late June and from mid-August to mid-December (check www.aph.gov.au for scheduled sittings). Both the Lower

House (the House of Representatives, where the prime minister sits) and the Upper House (the Senate) have public viewing galleries. The best time to see the action is during Question Time, which starts at 2pm in the Lower House. Make reservations for gallery tickets through the **sergeant-at-arms** (© **02/6277 4889**) at least a day in advance. Free 45-minute tours of the building start every 30 minutes beginning at 9am.

Capital Hill. © **02/6277 2727.** Free admission. Daily 9am–5pm. Closed Dec 25. Bus: 3 or 934.

Questacon—The National Science and Technology Centre ★★★ ☺ Finally, a museum that makes science fun. Questacon has more than 200 hands-on exhibits that can keep you (and your kids) entertained for hours. Exhibits cluster in seven galleries, each representing a different aspect of science. The full-motion roller-coaster simulator and artificial earthquake are usually big hits.

King Edward Terrace, Parkes. © **02/6270 2800.** www.questacon.edu.au Admission A$18 adults, A$12 children, A$49 families. Daily 9am–5pm. Closed Dec 25. Bus: 3, 934, or 935.

Royal Australian Mint ☺ If you're interested in making money, you'll love the Mint. The cascading coins being made on the factory floor are mesmerizing, and you can learn about the history of Australian currency, view rare coins, and watch the big robots at work. Or hand over A$3 to mint your very own A$1 coin—at those prices, you'd think they have a license to print money. But then again, I guess they do!

Denison St, Deakin. © **02/6202 6853.** www.ramint.gov.au Admission free. Mon–Fri 9am–4pm; weekends and public holidays 10am–4pm. Closed Good Friday and Dec 25. Bus: 2 or 932.

OUTDOOR PURSUITS

BIKING With 120km (74 miles) of bike paths, Canberra is made for exploring on two wheels. Rent a bike from **Mr. Spoke's Bike Hire,** Barrine Drive, near the boat hire on the Acton side of the lake (© **02/6257 1188**). Bikes for adults cost A$15 for an hour, A$25 for a half-day, and A$35 for a day.

BOATING **Burley Griffin Boat Hire,** Barrine Drive, Acton (© **02/6249 6861**), rents paddle boats for A$28 per hour, kayaks for A$15, and two-person canoes for A$20 per hour. It's open daily from September until May.

SWIMMING Swim in the wake of Ian Thorpe and other famous Australian superswimmers. The indoor heated pool at the **Australian Institute of Sport** (© **02/6214 1281;** see p. 696) is open to the public at certain times during the day (call ahead to check schedules). Adults pay A$4.70 to swim, children A$3.20.

TENNIS The **National Sports Club,** Mouat St, Lyneham (© **02/6248 0929**), has tennis, squash, and indoor sports facilities. Call for court bookings and prices.

CANBERRA AFTER DARK

Most of Canberra's best cocktail bars, clubs, and pubs can be found around Garema Place and nearby City Walk, and in the Sydney and Melbourne Buildings, or head farther afield to Kingston and Manuka.

For grown-up drinks, the **Julep Lounge,** 8 Franklin St. in Manuka (© **02/6239 5060**), has a sophisticated 1920s Parisian style and a huge cocktail list. In the city, the **Muddle Bar** on West Row (© **02/6262 7898**) also does great cocktails.

Weird Canberra

If you're looking for something different to do on a Friday night, try the **Weird Canberra Ghost and History Tour.** Led by "cryptonaturalist" Tim the Yowie Man (yes, that's his real name; he changed it after spotting an unidentified big black hairy creature in Canberra's Brindabella Mountains in 1994), the 3-hour tour visits around 20 weird and/or spooky sites, including a funeral parlor that was once a hot bed of espionage activity, a haunted pioneer's house, the hotel room where one of Australia's prime ministers died, and a very spooky air-disaster memorial that had us all shrieking in terror when weird orbs appeared in our photographs. Tours depart on selected Friday evenings at 8pm and cost A$69. Tours are very popular, so book in advance. To check dates, visit **www.destinytours.com.au/canberra.htm** or call ✆ **02/9487 2895.**

Of the pubs in town, the best in the city center are the British-style **Wig & Pen,** on the corner of Limestone and Alinga streets (✆ **02/6248 0171**), which brews its own beers; the popular **Moosehead's Pub,** 105 London Circuit, in the south of the city (✆ **02/6257 6496**); the **Phoenix,** 21 East Row (✆ **02/6247 1606**); and **P. J. O'Reileys,** on the corner of Moore and Alinga streets (✆ **02/6230 4752**). **King O'Malleys,** 131 City Walk (✆ **02/6257 0111**), is another popular Irish pub in the city, despite (or perhaps because of) being named after the man responsible for ensuring that alcohol was illegal in the ACT from 1910 until 1928. When Federal Parliament moved to Canberra in 1927, one of the first pieces of legislation passed in the new Parliament House was the repeal of O'Malley's prohibition laws.

If you're looking to roll some dice, the **Casino Canberra,** 21 Binara St., Civic, in Glebe Park (✆ **02/6257 7074**), is a small, older-style casino offering all the usual casino games daily from noon to 6am. Dress regulations prohibit leisurewear, running shoes, and denim, but overall it's a good place to lose some money.

For details on what's happening on the Canberra party scene check out **www.outincanberra.com.au**.

TASMANIA

by Lee Mylne

Tasmania is a place of wild beauty colored by a tragic past. Separated from the rest of Australia by Bass Strait, this island state has forged its own, not always smooth, path. Its isolation has preserved much of its wilderness, despite the worst efforts of man to spoil it at times.

Some of the environmental issues Tasmanians (and the rest of Australia) are grappling with right now include the possible extinction of Tasmanian devils due to a spreading facial-tumor disease, reports of introduced foxes, and a proposed pulp mill that will pump vast quantities of effluent into Bass Strait. You will also not, despite local legend, run into any Tasmanian tigers here.

Tasmania's history is rocky as well. Tasmania made its mark as a dumping ground for British convicts, who were often transported for petty crimes. The brutal system of control, still evident in the ruins at Port Arthur and elsewhere, spilled over into persecution of the native population. The last full-blooded Tasmanian Aborigine died in 1876, 15 years after the last convict transportation.

Despite its history, Tasmania is a tranquil and largely unspoiled place to visit—more than 20% of it has been declared a World Heritage area, and nearly a third of the island is protected by national parks. The locals are friendly and hospitable—and they have a reputation for producing some of Australia's best food. Remains of the Aboriginal people who lived here for thousands of years are evident in rock paintings, engravings, stories, and the aura of spirituality that still holds in places that modern civilization has not yet reached.

EXPLORING TASMANIA

VISITOR INFORMATION **Tourism Tasmania** (**© 1300/827 743** in Australia, or 03/6230 8235; www.discovertasmania.com.au) is the official tourism body and operates visitor centers in more than 20 towns throughout the state. The **Tasmanian Travel and Information Centre,** 20 Davey St. (at Elizabeth St.), Hobart (**© 1800/990 440** in Australia, or 03/6230 8233; www.hobarttravelcentre.com.au) can arrange travel passes, ferry and bus tickets, car rentals, cruises, and accommodations. It is open weekdays 8:30am to 5:30pm, and 9am to 5pm weekends and public holidays (closed Christmas Day).

WHEN TO GO The best time to visit Tasmania is between October and April, when the weather is at its best. By May, nights are getting cold, days are getting shorter, and the deciduous trees are starting to turn golden. Winters (June–Aug), especially in the high country, can be quite harsh—though that's the best time to curl up in front of a blazing fire. The east coast is generally milder than the west coast, which is buffeted by the "Roaring 40s"—the winds that blow across the ocean and the 40-degree meridian from as far away as Argentina.

The busy season for tourism runs December through February, as well as during public- and school-holiday periods. Unlike the rest of Australia, Tasmanian schools have three terms. Term dates are from the second week in February to the last week in May, the third week in June to the first week in September, and the fourth week in September to the first or second week in December.

GETTING THERE The quickest way to get to Tasmania is by air. **Qantas** (**© 13 13 13** in Australia; www.qantas.com) flies from Sydney and Melbourne to Hobart and Launceston. **Virgin Blue** (**© 13 67 89** in Australia; www.virginblue.com.au) flies from Sydney, Melbourne, Brisbane, Canberra and Adelaide to Hobart and from Melbourne, Brisbane, and Sydney to Launceston. **Jetstar** (**© 13 15 38** in Australia; www.jetstar.com.au) flies to Hobart from Sydney and Melbourne, and to Launceston from Brisbane, Melbourne and Sydney. **Tiger Airways** (**© 03/9335 3033;** www.tigerairways.com.au) flies to Launceston and Hobart from Melbourne and to Hobart from Adelaide. **Regional Express** (**© 13 17 13** in Australia or 02/6393 5550; www.regionalexpress.com.au) flies from Melbourne to Burnie in the state's north.

Two high-speed ferry services connect Melbourne and Tasmania. The ***Spirit of Tasmania I*** and ***II*** can each carry 1,400 passengers as well as cars. They make the crossing from Melbourne's Station Pier to Tasmania's Devonport (on the north coast) in around 10 hours. The ferries leave both Melbourne and Devonport at 7:30pm and arrive at around 6am. During peak times, there's also day service leaving both ports at 9am and arriving at 6pm. Prices are based on "off-peak" and "peak" times: Off-peak season is from mid-April to mid-December and again from around January 24 to mid-April; peak season is roughly mid-December to around January 23, and from mid-April to mid-May (seasons change slightly each year). A one-way day seat costs A$95 to A$175 for adults and A$38 to A$105 for children aged 3 to 18. Reclining seats for the overnight crossing cost A$110 to A$194 adults and A$44 to A$116 for kids. Twin cabins cost A$179 to A$299 for adults and A$71 to A$179 for children. Deluxe cabins cost A$280 to A$440 for adults and kids. Four-berth cabins cost from A$148 to A$249 for adults and A$59 to A$155 for kids depending

Tasmania's Tricky Roads

Driving in Tasmania can be dangerous; there are more accidents involving tourists on Tasmania's roads than anywhere else in Australia. Many roads are narrow, and bends can be tight, especially in the mountainous inland regions, where you may also come across black ice early in the morning or at anytime in winter. Marsupials are also common around dusk, and swerving to avoid them has caused countless crashes. In fact, you may be shocked by the amount of roadkill you will see here.

Tasmania

Bonorong Wildlife Park **4**
Cataract Gorge **1**
Freycinet National Park **3**
Royal Tasmanian Botanical Gardens **5**
Tasmanian Devil Conservation Park **6**
Trowunna Wildlife Park **2**

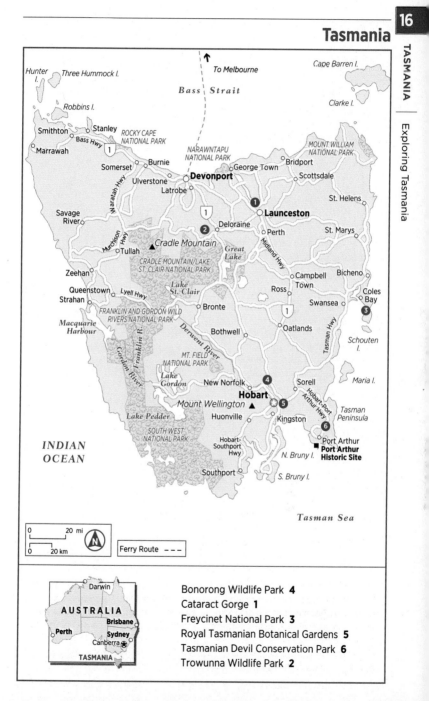

National Park Entry Fees

A Tassie Holiday Pass costs A$60 and allows entry for a car and up to 8 passengers to Tasmania's national parks for 8 weeks. Pedestrians, cyclists, motorcyclists, and coach passengers pay A$30 for 8 weeks. Occasional users can buy a 24-hour pass for A$24 per car; walkers, cyclists, motorcyclists, and coach passengers pay A$12 per day. Passes are available at all major parks and Tasmanian visitor centers. For more information, contact the Parks and Wildlife Service (© 03/6233 2621; www.parks.tas.gov.au).

on the season and whether you have a porthole. Transporting a standard car costs A$79 to A$89, depending on size, year-round.

Make reservations for any of the ferries through **TT-Line** (**© 1800/634 906** in Australia, or 03/6421 7209; www.spiritoftasmania.com.au). Special offers are regularly available. **Tasmanian Redline Coaches** (see below) connect with each ferry and transfer passengers to Launceston and Hobart.

GETTING AROUND The regional airline **Tasair** (**© 03/6427 9777;** www.tasair.com.au) flies between Hobart and Devonport and Burnie (Wynyard Airport) and operates services to King Island from Burnie and Devonport. It also operates a range of aerial sightseeing tours, as does **Par Avion** (**© 1800/144 460** in Australia or 03/6248 5390; www.paravion.com.au), which concentrates on the southwest World Heritage areas of the state.

Tasmanian Redline Coaches (**© 1300/360 000** in Australia, or 03/6336 1446; www.redlinecoaches.com.au) and **Tassielink** (**© 1300/300 520** in Australia, or 03/6230 8900; www.tigerline.com.au) operate coach service statewide and offer a series of coach tours to major places of interest. **Metro Tas** (**© 13 22 01** in Australia or 03/6233 4232; www.metrotas.com.au) runs bus services in and around Hobart, Launceston, and Burnie.

The cheapest way to get around by coach is to buy a travel pass. The **Tassielink Explorer Pass,** which covers all Tassielink routes, comes in four categories: A 7-day pass good for travel within 10 days is A$208; a 10-day pass for travel in 15 days is A$248; a 14-day pass for travel in 20 days is A$286; a 21-day pass for travel in 30 days is A$329. Kids' passes are half-price. Redline Coaches has a **Tassie Pass** which allows unlimited travel on main route services for A$135 for 7 days, A$160 for 10 days, A$185 for 14 days or A$219 for 21 days.

Driving a car from Devonport on the north coast to Hobart on the south coast takes less than 4 hours. From Hobart to Strahan on the west coast also takes around 4 hours, while the journey from Launceston to Hobart takes about 2 hours. The **Royal Automobile Club of Tasmania,** Murray and Patrick streets, Hobart (**© 13 27 22** in Australia or 03/6232 6300), can supply maps.

TOUR OPERATORS Dozens of operators run organized hiking, horse-trekking, sailing, caving, fishing, bushwalking, diving, cycling, rafting, climbing, kayaking, and canoeing trips.

One of the best operators is **Tasmania Adventure Tours** (**© 1300/654 604** in Australia, or 08/8132 8230; www.adventuretours.com.au). It offers a 3-day East Coast Explorer tour from Devonport, taking in Launceston, Freycinet National Park, and Port Arthur, before finishing in Hobart. The tour costs A$470 to A$770 depending on accommodations. Other tours are available.

Peregrine Adventures (✆ **1300/791 485** in Australia; www.peregrine adventures.com) runs several trips in Tasmania, including a 5-day Franklin River rafting adventure and others that include kayaking and hiking. Another good operator is the **Roaring 40s Wilderness Tours** (✆ **03/6267 5000;** www.roaring40s-kayaking.com.au), which offers kayaking expeditions for 3 or 7 days, as well as other tours. **Tasmanian Expeditions,** in Launceston (✆ **1300/666 856** in Australia, or 03/6339 3999; www.tasmanianexpeditions.com.au), runs a range of cycling, trekking, rafting, rock-climbing, and sea-kayaking trips around the island, departing from either Hobart or Launceston.

HOBART

198km (123 miles) S of Launceston

Tasmania's capital (pop. 120,000), set on the Derwent River, is worth visiting for a couple of days. Hobart's main features are its wonderful harbor (the city's focal point) and the colonial cottages that line the narrow lanes of Battery Point. At the waterfront, picturesque Salamanca Place bursts with galleries, pubs, cafes, and an excellent market on Saturdays. Europeans settled in Hobart in 1804, a year after Tasmania's first colony was set up at Risdon (10km/6¼ miles up the Derwent River), making it Australia's second oldest city after Sydney. Hobart is the southernmost Australian state capital and is closer to the Antarctic coast than it is to Perth in Western Australia; navigators, whalers, and explorers have long regarded it as the gateway to the south.

Essentials

GETTING THERE The trip from the airport to the city center takes about 20 minutes and costs about A$40 by taxi. The **Airporter Shuttle Bus** (✆ **1300/385 511** in Australia) meets planes and delivers passengers to hotels in the city and farther afield for A$15 one-way or A$25 round-trip to the city center for adults and A$7.50 each way for kids. Bookings are essential, and if you are departing Hobart on an early flight (6, 6:30, or 7:25am), you need to make a booking by 8pm the previous evening.

> **Staying Connected**
>
> **It's relatively hard to find public Web access in Hobart. One of the few Internet cafes is Drifters Internet Café, in Salamanca Galleria, Shop 9/33, Salamanca Place (✆ 03/6224 6286). They charge A$1 for 10 minutes or A$5 per half-hour.**

Car- and camper-rental offices at the airport include **Avis** (✆ **03/6248 5424**), **Budget** (✆ **1300/362 848** in Australia, or 03/6248 5333), **Europcar** (✆ **1800/030 118** in Australia or 03/6248 5849), and **Thrifty** (✆ **1300/367 227** in Australia or 03/6248 5678). Cars cost around A$55 for 1 day, A$50 per day for 2 days, A$45 per day for 4 days, and A$40 per day for a week or more. You might find even better bargains in town, with lower-priced rental companies such as **Lo-Cost Auto Rent** (✆ **03/6231 0550**) and **Rent-a-Bug** (✆ **03/6231 0300**).

Hello, Sailor!

The **Sydney-to-Hobart Yacht Race,** starting in Sydney on December 26, fills the Constitution Dock Marina and harbor area close to overflowing with spectators and partygoers when the yachts turn up in Tasmania. The race takes anywhere from 2 to 4 days, and the sailors and fans stay on to celebrate New Year's Eve. Food and wine lovers indulge themselves after the race during the **Hobart Summer Festival,** which starts on December 28.

VISITOR INFORMATION Information is available from the **Tasmanian Travel and Information Centre,** 20 Davey St. at Elizabeth Street (✆ **03/6230 8233;** www.hobarttravelcentre.com.au). It's open Monday through Friday from 8:30am to 5:30pm, weekends and public holidays from 9am to 5pm (closed Christmas Day). You can pick up information on the state's national parks at the **Parks & Wildlife Service,** 134 Macquarie St. (✆ **1300/135 513**).

CITY LAYOUT Hobart straddles the Derwent River on the south coast of Tasmania. **Salamanca Place** and nearby **Battery Point** abut Sullivan's Cove, home to hundreds of yachts. The row of sandstone warehouses that dominate Salamanca Place date to the city's heyday as a whaling base in the 1830s. Behind Princes Wharf, Battery Point is the city's historic district, which in colonial times was the home of sailors, fishermen, whalers, coopers, merchants, shipwrights, and master mariners. The open ocean is about 50km (31 miles) down the river, though the Derwent empties into Storm Bay, just 20km (12 miles) downstream. The central business district is on the west side of the water, with the main thoroughfares—**Campbell, Argyle, Elizabeth, Murray,** and **Harrington streets**—sloping down to the busy harbor. The Tasman Bridge and regular passenger ferries cross the Derwent River. Set back from and overlooking the city is 1,270m-tall (4,166-ft.) **Mount Wellington.**

GETTING AROUND Central Hobart is very small, and most of the attractions are in easy walking distance. **Metro Tasmania** (✆ **03/6233 4232** or 13 22 01; www.metrotas.com.au) operates public buses throughout the city and suburban areas. The buses operate on an electronic Green Card system, or you can just buy a ticket on board. Single tickets cost from A$2.40. **Day Rover** tickets are good after 9am daily and cost A$4.50.

Exploring the City & Environs

Simply strolling around the harbor and popping into the shops at Salamanca Place can keep you nicely occupied, but don't miss the lovely colonial stone cottages of Battery Point. This area got its name from a battery of guns set up on the promontory in 1818 to defend the town against potential invaders (particularly the French). Today, there are tearooms, antiques shops, restaurants, and atmospheric pubs interspersed between grand dwellings. One of the houses worth looking into is **Narryna Heritage Museum,** 103 Hampden Rd. (✆ **03/6234 2791**), which depicts the life of upper-class pioneers. It's open Tuesday through Friday from 10:30am to 5pm and Saturday and Sunday from 2 to 5pm (closed Anzac Day, Good Friday, Christmas Day, and all of July). Admission is A$6 for adults and A$3 for children, or A$12 for a family. Also in this area is the **Maritime Museum of Tasmania ★,** 16 Argyle St. at Davey

The Female Factory Historic Site Unless you are really into convict history, you may wish to save yourself for Port Arthur. All that is left here are the stone walls of this prison, a memorial garden, and little in the way of interpretation for those not on a tour, despite its important history. The "factory" prison, where women worked at spinning, washing, and sewing, operated from 1828 to 1856, housing up to 1,200 women and children. After it ceased operation as a female factory, the institution continued as a jail until 1877. Again, make sure you time your visit to take a guided tour or you won't get much from your visit. Another option besides a tour is "Morning Tea with the Matron," which you must book 24 hours in advance, on Monday, Wednesday, and Friday at 10:30am for A$12 per person.

16 Degraves St., South Hobart. ✆ **03/6223 1559.** Fax 03/6223 1556. www.femalefactory.com.au. Tours A$12 adults, A$5 children, A$28 families of 4. Mon–Fri 9am–5pm. Tours Dec–Apr Mon–Fri 9:30am and 2pm; May–Nov Mon–Fri 9:30am only. Closed public holidays. Bookings essential. Bus: 44, 46, 47, or 49 from Franklin Square in the city to South Hobart and Cascade Rd. (stop 14 or 16).

MONA at Moorilla ★★ It's hard to put a label on MONA, which consists of a winery, a microbrewery, a restaurant (The Source; see p. 717), and stunning accommodations (the MONA Pavilions; see p. 714). But the best part of MONA at Moorilla may be the opening (scheduled for January 2011) of its namesake: the Museum of Old and New Art, Australia's largest privately owned art gallery. Owner David Walsh promises to "shock and offend," so daring and provocative will it be. But the museum also aims to challenge, inform, and entertain with a collection that ranges from antiquities from Egypt, Greece, Italy, Africa, and Mesoamerica to contemporary art, including Australian modernism and contemporary Australian, British, European, and American art.

Moorilla Estate, 655 Main Rd., Berriedale. ✆ **03/6277 9900.** Fax 03/6275 0588. www.mona.net.au. Free entry to the permanent collection.

Royal Tasmanian Botanical Gardens ★ Established in 1818, these gardens are known for English-style plant and tree layouts—including a great conifer collection—a superb Japanese garden, and seasonal blooming plants. A busy road nearby can disturb the peaceful atmosphere. One-hour guided tours by volunteers are run regularly and cost A$5. A restaurant provides lunch and teas. To walk here from the city center, partly along a pleasant country lane known as Soldier's Walk, takes around 40 minutes, or you can use the cycle track or arrive by ferry. There are maps of the gardens at each entrance, or visitor guides and self-guided tour brochures are available at the Visitor Centre, which is near the entrance on Lower Domain Road.

Queens Domain, near Government House. ✆ **03/6236 3076.** www.rtbg.tas.gov.au. Free admission. Oct–Mar daily 8am–6:30pm; May–Aug daily 8am–5pm; Apr and Sept daily 8am–5:30pm. Bus: 17 from the GPO.

Tahune Airwalk A 2-hour drive from Hobart, the Airwalk is a lofted treetop walkway situated in the Tahune Forest Reserve, overlooking the Huon and Picton rivers. You can take the stairs to the start of the walk, or wait for a shuttle bus that runs by every hour. Once on the elevated cantilevered steel walkway—which extends 500m (1,640 ft.) out over the forest—you are 48m (158 ft.) above the river. The whole thing allows a close-up view of rare species, some found only in Tasmania, such as King Billy and Celery Top pines, myrtle, beech, blackwood, and sassafras. Other attractions in the forest include the Huon Pine Walk and a couple of swinging bridges over the Picton River. As the forest and facilities are run by Forestry Tasmania (a private enterprise), your tour is likely to involve some subtle propaganda. There's a good cafe here before you head off again.

Arve Rd. Geeveston (29km/18 miles west of the town). ✆ **03/6295 7177.** www.forestrytas.com.au. Admission A$26. Daily 10am–5pm.

Tasmanian Museum and Art Gallery ★ Come here to find out more about Tasmania's Aboriginal heritage, its history since settlement, and the island's wildlife. Traveling exhibitions are mounted from time to time, but always on display are colonial-era paintings, including an impressive collection of works by Tom Roberts and several convict artists. The pride of the collection is the historically significant *The Conciliation,* by Benjamin Duttereau. You can also find out about the fate of the Tasmanian tiger and see archival film of this lost treasure. Free 50-minute guided tours are run Wednesday to Sunday at 2:30pm (for bookings, call ✆ **03/6211 4189**).

40 Macquarie St. ✆ **03/6211 4177** or 03/6211 4114 for recorded information. www.tmag.tas.gov.au. Free admission. Daily 10am–5pm. Closed Good Friday, Anzac Day, and Christmas Day.

CRUISES

Navigators, Murray Street Pier (✆ **03/6223 1914;** www.navigators.net.au), offers cruises of the Upper Harbour and River Derwent daily for visitors wanting to take the scenic route to the MONA and Moorilla estate (see p. 711). Check the website for up-to-date details. The company also runs cruises to Port Arthur.

The **Bruny Wildlife Adventure** cruise (✆ **1300/137 919** in Australia; www.brunywildlifeadventure.com.au) leaves Brooke Street Pier at 8:30am, returning at 4:30pm. A 45-minute cruise takes you to Bruny Island, where you then take a bus to Adventure Bay and transfer to a smaller, faster expedition boat for 48 people. Then the "adventure" part of the day starts, with a 3-hour spin along the coastline to a seal colony and a memorable (but sometimes wet; warm shower-proof coats are provided) foray into the wild Southern Ocean. On returning to the bus, you are delivered to a scenic setting for an elegantly boxed lunch (with Tassie wine), before being picked up by the cruise boat to return to Hobart. It's a pleasant day out, but for the hours spent, serious wildlife fans might be disappointed. The trip costs A$185 adults, A$110 children 4 to 14. It runs daily from December to March; Fridays, Sundays, and Mondays only in May and Oct; Mondays, Wednesdays, Fridays, Saturdays, and Sundays only in April and November; and Sundays only from June to September.

HE SHOPPING SCENE

you are in Hobart on a Saturday, don't miss the **Salamanca Market ★★**, in Salamanca Place—it's one of the best markets in Australia. Some 200 stalls offer everyng from fruit and vegetables to crafts made from pottery, glass, and native woods. T e market is open from 8:30am to 3pm.

Salamanca Place has plenty of crafts shops that are worth exploring, though the es sometimes reflect the fashionable area. Pop into the **Tasmania Shop & Gal-**, 65 Salamanca Place (✆ **03/6223 5022;** www.tasmaniashopgallery.com.au). is a cut above your normal souvenir shop, offering innovative and interesting entos and artworks by Tasmanian artists and designers, including glassware, s, jewelry, and sculptures.

Book Ends

The best bookshop in town is a beauty; it sells a large range of new and secondhand books, many relating to Tasmania. Find the Hobart Bookshop at 22 Salamanca Sq. (© 03/6223 1803). For some good reading on Tasmania, among my favorites is *In Tasmania,* by Nicholas Shakespeare, a blend of Tasmania's history and future and the author's discovery of his own convict heritage. For a different take on convict history, *Closing Hell's Gates: The Death of a Convict Station,* by Tasmanian writer Hamish Maxwell-Stewart gives an insight into life on the notorious Sarah Island in Macquarie Harbour. *Ronnie, Tasmanian Songman,* by Aboriginal elder Ronnie Summers, tells the story of growing up on Cape Barren Island and a life sharing the traditions of Cape Barren music (it comes with a music CD). For those interested in nature, *Where to See Wildlife in Tasmania* by Dave Watts and Cathie Plowman is an easy to use full-color guide to spotting Tasmania's unique fauna.

There are plenty of other interesting shops and small galleries here and in the surrounding streets. On Hunter Street, on the other side of the marina from Salamanca Place and next to the Henry Jones Art Hotel, you will find **Art Mob** (**© 03/6236 9200;** www.artmob.com.au), where you can buy Aboriginal fine art at reasonable prices. Director Euan Hills will happily give advice on what you are looking at, without pressure to buy, and will also impart other tips for your stay in Hobart. The gallery specializes in works by Tasmanian Aboriginal artists, including paintings, prints, jewelry, and baskets.

Hours for most stores are Monday through Thursday from 9am to 6pm, Friday from 9am to 9pm, and Saturday from 9am to noon (though some are open all day).

Where to Stay

VERY EXPENSIVE

The Henry Jones Art Hotel ★★ One of Australia's most unique and interesting hotels, the Henry Jones takes its name from one of Hobart's most successful pioneering entrepreneurs. Henry Jones's name, and that of his IXL brand of jam, is still on the factory building that became Australia's first dedicated art hotel. The walls of this five-star hotel are hung with more than 250 works, in changing exhibitions, often by young emerging Tasmanian artists, many from the Tasmanian School of Arts (next door). Guest rooms are also works of art in themselves, reflecting Australia's early trade with China and India in an eclectic mix of modern and historic. Sandstone walls abut ultramodern glass and stainless steel bathrooms. (All but standard rooms have double spa tubs.) Every room has a view, either of the harbor or the hotel's magnificent glass atrium. I've stayed here several times, and so far my favorite is the spacious Art Installation Suite, which has a small balcony.

22 Hunter St., Hobart, TAS 7000. © **1300/665 581** in Australia or 03/6210 7700. Fax 03/6331 6393. www.thehenryjones.com. 50 units. A$240–A$385 double; A$330–A$405 double deluxe spa room; A$510–A$950 double suites. Extra person or crib A$55. AE, DC, MC, V. Free parking. **Amenities:** Restaurant; bar; concierge; access to nearby health club; room service. *In room:* A/C, TV/DVD, CD player, hair dryer, Internet (A$7.50 per 30 min. to A$17 per day), kitchen (some suites only), minibar.

The Islington ★★★ This luxury boutique hotel, just 10 minutes' walk from the city center, may make you feel as if you are staying in someone's home. Someone wealthy. The Islington is lavishly but tastefully decorated with fine artworks and antiques, its contemporary extension (with soaring glass walls and ceilings, and views of Mount Wellington) blending beautifully with the original 1847 Regency-style building (one of the first in Hobart's "dress circle" area). At the end of a busy day's sightseeing there's nothing better than a long soak in the generous bathtub, and sinking into an "Islington Angel," a king-size bed custom-made in Tasmania, for a fabulous night's sleep.

321 Davey St., Hobart, TAS 7000. ✆ **1800/703 006** in Australia, or 03/6220 2123. Fax 03/6220 2124. www.islingtonhotel.com. 11 units. A$300–A$550 double including breakfast. AE, DC, MC, V. Free parking. No children 15 and under. **Amenities:** Restaurant (dining on request); bar (honor system); airport transfers; Wi-Fi (free). *In room:* A/C, TV/DVD w/pay movies and movie library, CD player w/CD library, hair dryer, Internet (free), minibar.

The MONA Pavilions ★★ Four new pavilions opened here in late 2009, each with state-of-the-art electronics (wireless touch panels control temperature, audiovisual components, lighting, blinds, and more) and interesting artworks. The new pavilions are named for noted architects, with the four original pavilions named after Australian modernist painters. All sit high above the banks of the Derwent Estuary, with large balconies overlooking the water. Antiquities and artworks from owner David Walsh's private collection are included in the decor of each pavilion. Each of the one- or two-bedroom pavilions has a private cellar stocked with Moorilla wines and Moo Brew beer from the estate. You can arrive by private boat or on the fast catamaran from Hobart. MONA is about 15 minutes' drive from the city center, but the river is a more appealing way to travel.

655 Main Rd., Berriedale. ✆ **03/6277 9900.** Fax 03/6275 0588. www.mona.net.au. 8 units. A$490–A$950 double including breakfast. AE, DC, MC, V. Free parking. **Amenities:** Restaurant; bar; gym; pool; room service; sauna. *In room:* A/C, TV, CD player, hair dryer, kitchen, Wi-Fi (free).

EXPENSIVE

Macquarie Manor ★★ As soon as you walk into this classic colonial-style manor, you'll know you want to stay. Macquarie Manor was built in 1875 as a surgeon's operating office and residence. Extra rooms were added in 1950. Thick carpets and double-glazed windows keep the place very quiet, even though it's on the main road, 2 blocks from the central bus terminal. Rooms, which vary enormously and include single rooms, are comfortable and elegantly furnished. One room is suitable for people with disabilities. Check out the delightful dining room and the drawing room complete with old couches and a grand piano. Smoking is not permitted.

172 Macquarie St., Hobart, TAS 7000. ✆ **03/6224 4999.** Fax 03/6224 4333. www.macmanor.com.au. 18 units, most with shower only. A$160 single; A$200 double; A$275 Heritage Suite; A$300 Macquarie Suite. Extra person A$50. Rates include full breakfast. Sat–Sun room-only rate of A$170 available. AE, DC, MC, V. Free parking. *In room:* A/C, TV, hair dryer, Internet (free), minibar.

Salamanca Inn Conveniently located on the edge of the central business district and toward the waterfront near Battery Point, Salamanca Inn features modern and pleasant suites and apartments. They have queen- or king-size beds, leather couches, Tasmanian oak furniture, galley-style kitchens, and spacious living areas. The more expensive suites are a bit plusher. There's a rooftop indoor pool.

10 Gladstone St., Hobart, TAS 7000. ✆ **1800/030 944** in Australia or 03/6223 3300. Fax 03/6223 7167. www.salamancainn.com.au. 68 units. A$185–A$280 double. Ask about packages. AE, DC, MC, V. Free parking. Bus: 54B. **Amenities:** Restaurant; bar; babysitting; Jacuzzi; indoor pool; room service. *In room:* TV w/free in-house movies, hair dryer, kitchenette, minibar, Wi-Fi (A$5.50 per hr.).

Wrest Point ★ This Hobart icon, built in 1973, launched Australia's annual A$2-billion casino industry. Beside the Derwent River, 3km (almost 2 miles) from the city center, the casino-hotel complex looks out across the harbor and the city and up to Mount Wellington. All rooms feature Tasmanian oak furniture and plush carpets, and more expensive units have exceptional views. While it may be a little out of the city center (though it's certainly walkable), the views make it a worthwhile choice. The hotel's signature restaurant, the **Point Revolving Restaurant,** is another icon. It's open for dinner from 6:30pm every night, and for lunch on Fridays from noon.

410 Sandy Bay Rd., Sandy Bay, TAS 7005. ✆ **1800/420 155** in Australia, or 03/6225 7016. www.puretasmania.com.au. 197 units. A$105–A$204 double; A$220–A$264 suite. Extra adult A$35. Children 4 and under stay free in parent's room using existing bedding. Free crib. AE, DC, MC, V. Free valet parking. Bus: Busy Bee route 54 or 55 from Franklin Sq., Macquarie St., to stop 15. **Amenities:** 4 restaurants; 7 bars; free airport transfers; babysitting; concierge; 9-hole putting course; health club; large indoor pool; room service; 2 lit tennis courts; Wi-Fi (in lobby, A$10 per hr.). *In room:* A/C, TV w/free movies, hair dryer, Internet (free), minibar.

Zero Davey ★ Opened in 2004, Zero Davey has gone for a time-warp decor (think Austin Powers) that will appeal to some but not to others—if the word *funkadelic* puts you off, don't book the penthouse! (You could perhaps cope with one of the studio, two-, or three-bedroom serviced apartments, but definitely not the penthouse.) The three-bedroom Zero Penthouse, with its psychedelic pink, orange, and red decor, will fulfill those rock-star fantasies; the Hunter Penthouse is a bit more restrained and has harbor views, a grand piano, and a 12-seat theater. However, you can't fault the hotel's waterfront location, and the apartments are fresh, contemporary, and functional. Some studios have balconies and Jacuzzis. It's all fun and, yes, funky.

15 Hunter St., Hobart, TAS 7000. ✆ **1300/733 422** in Australia, or 03/6270 1444. Fax 03/6270 1400. www.escapesresorts.com.au. 34 units. A$280–A$340 studio double; A$450–A$600 apt. MC, V. Free parking. **Amenities:** Exercise room; sauna. *In room:* A/C, TV/VCR, hair dryer, kitchen, minibar, Wi-Fi (A10¢ per min. or A$12 per day).

MODERATE

Customs House Hotel ★ You won't find a better value than the rooms above this historic sandstone pub overlooking the waterfront. Built in 1846, the property offers large, colonial-style rooms, seven of which look across at the water. Some of the other rooms look across Parliament House and its gardens, and the rest are toward the back of the hotel with no views to speak of. Downstairs, the restaurant and public bar overlook the water. Live music is on hand downstairs between Wednesday and Saturday nights and during the summer period, when the Sydney–Hobart Yacht Race comes to town, it can be noisy but is central to all the action.

1 Murray St., Hobart, TAS 7000. ✆ **03/6234 6645.** Fax 03/6223 8750. www.customshousehotel.com. 22 units. A$135–A$155 double; A$240 family room (sleeps 5). Extra person A$40. Rates include hot breakfast. AE, DC, MC, V. Free parking about 5 min. walk away. **Amenities:** Restaurant; bar. *In room:* A/C (some rooms only), TV, Internet (free).

The Lodge on Elizabeth ★ The convict-built Lodge on Elizabeth is among the oldest buildings in Tasmania, completed in 1829 and now listed by the National Trust. Originally a gentleman's residence (including, at one time, a Tasmanian premier),

Budget Sleeps

There are seven YHA hostels in Tasmania. In Hobart, the best is Montgomery's Private Hotel & YHA Backpackers, 9 Argyle St. (✆ 03/6231 2660), right in the heart of the city, which has bunk rooms for A$29 to A$32 and double rooms from A$106 to A$118. Adelphi Court YHA (✆ 03/6228 4829) is in North Hobart. The state YHA office is at 9 Argyle St., Hobart (✆ 03/6234 9617; www.yha.com.au).

it later became the first private boys' school in Tasmania. It's well situated just a 12-minute walk from Salamanca Place and is surrounded by restaurants. All rooms are decorated with antiques; many are quite romantic, with four-poster beds and some with Jacuzzis. Complimentary drinks are served in the communal living room in the evening. The Convict's Cottage is a cute self-contained spa cottage, just for two, on the grounds.

249 Elizabeth St., Hobart, TAS 7000. ✆ **03/6231 3830.** Fax 03/6234 2566. www.thelodge.com.au. 13 units, some with shower only. A$120–A$170 double; A$160–A$195 convict cottage (minimum 2-night stay). Extra person A$30. Rates include breakfast. AE, DC, MC, V. Free parking. No children 13 and under. *In room:* TV, hair dryer.

INEXPENSIVE

Central City Backpackers Fresh paintwork, new computers, and new beds and mattresses have raised standards at this typical backpacker accommodation. It's cheap and cheerful, right in the heart of Hobart, in a classic 1870s building that started life as the Imperial Hotel and became a backpacker hostel in 1992. You can use your own sleeping bag or hire linen and towels for A$2 per stay. The central shopping district is outside the door; it's only a short walk to the harbor and a 2-minute walk to the central bus terminal.

138 Collins St., Hobart, TAS 7000. ✆ **1800/811 507** in Australia, or 03/6224 2404. Fax 03/6224 2316. www.centralcityhobart.com. 80 units (none with private bathroom). A$55 single room; A$69 double; A$23–A$27 dorm bed. MC, V. **Amenities:** Bar (summer only); Internet (A$3 for 15 min. to A$12 for 2 hr.). *In room:* No phone.

Where to Dine

Tasmania is known for its fresh seafood, including oysters, crab, crayfish, salmon, and trout. Once cheap, in recent years prices have crept up to match or even surpass those on the mainland. Generally, the food is of very good quality.

EXPENSIVE

Smolt ★★ CONTEMPORARY This chic new addition to Hobart's dining scene is a great spot for people watching, with windows opening onto busy Salamanca Square. Great for breakfast, a caffeine hit, lunch, or dinner, it offers modern cuisine with Italian (pizza, risotto) and Spanish (tapas) influences. The food is simple but imaginative, delicious and presented with flair. There's also a good wine list featuring selections from around Australia (heavily weighted toward Tassie) and a couple of options from New Zealand, Spain, and Italy.

2 Salamanca Square, Hobart. ✆ **03/6224 2554.** www.smolt.com.au. Reservations recommended. Main courses A$25–A$35. AE, MC, V. Daily 9am–10pm.

The Source ★★ TASMANIAN/AUSTRALIAN As you climb the stairs to this amazing restaurant, your eyes will be drawn to the painting from which it takes its name: *The Source,* by Australian artist John Olsen, is a stunning 6m (20-ft.) work set into the ceiling directly above the central staircase. It will take your breath away. So too will the entire experience of dining here, which promises to be delivered "with a MONA twist" (the restaurant is part of the Museum of Old and New Art; see p. 711). And you will be assured that seasonal and local produce (with an eye to "food miles") is very important here. Huge windows allow stunning views of the Derwent River.

Moorilla Estate, 655 Main Rd., Berriedale. ✆ **03/6277 9900.** www.moorilla.com.au. Reservations recommended. Main courses A$26–A$38. AE, DC, MC, V. Daily noon–2:30pm; Fri–Sat 6:30pm–late.

MODERATE

Drunken Admiral Restaurant ★ SEAFOOD The Drunken Admiral, on the waterfront, is an extremely popular spot with tourists and can get raucous on busy evenings. The main attraction to start the meal is the famous seafood chowder, swimming with anything that was on sale at the docks that morning. The large Seafood Platter for two (A$106) is a full plate of squid, oysters, fish, mussels, and prawns, but there are plenty of simpler dishes on the menu, too. Try the crunchy fried prawns or the salt-and-pepper squid.

17–19 Hunter St. ✆ **03/6234 1903.** www.drunkenadmiral.com.au. Reservations required. Main courses A$17–A$35. AE, DC, MC, V. Daily 6–10:30pm.

Flathead Fish Café ★ SEAFOOD This small, unpretentious cafe is just a short walk from the grand Islington Hotel in South Hobart. The fish is fresh (you can buy it to cook yourself if you wish) and the staple is fish and chips, but they also do a range of chargrilled and pan-fried fish dishes as well as vegetarian, and gluten-free dishes. Start with Thai fish cakes; they're delicious. Flathead is licensed and has a great wine list featuring Tasmanian wines and local beers (including a gluten-free beer). If you choose, you can BYO (wine only) as well.

4 Cascade Rd., South Hobart. ✆ **03/6224 3194.** Reservations recommended. Main courses A$16–A$26. AE, DC, MC, V. Tues–Sat 10am–10:30pm; Mon 4–10:30pm. Closed Sun.

Peppermint Bay ★ CONTEMPORARY You'd be hard pressed to find a more lovely setting for lunch, even in Tasmania. From Peppermint Bay's **Dining Room** restaurant, soaring cathedral ceilings and full-length windows frame water's-edge views of Bruny Island and the D'Entrecasteaux Channel. The menu includes fresh Tasmanian crayfish, Bruny Island oysters, Huon ocean trout, locally grazed beef, and more. You won't be disappointed. The relaxed **Terrace Bar** (with the same views) is another option with a more casual menu. The **Providore** sells fine Tasmanian fare (think olive oil, smoked salmon, or ripe cheeses) and housewares, or you can browse the art and craft gallery next door. Outside, a 150-year-old oak tree dominates the gardens. **Hobart Cruises** (✆ **1300/137 919** in Australia) runs 90-minute scenic cruises to Peppermint Bay.

Channel Hwy., Woodbridge (35km from Hobart). ✆ **03/6267 4088.** www.peppermintbay.com.au. Reservations recommended. Main courses A$16–A$30 in the Terrace Bar; A$33–A$35 in the Dining Room. MC, V. Terrace Bar daily from noon to 3pm; Thu–Sat 5:30–8:30pm; Dining Room daily noon–3pm.

INEXPENSIVE

Cumquat on Criterion ★ ASIAN/AUSTRALIAN Well-known for its great coffee, this cafe is also an excellent breakfast venue, offering everything from egg on

DISCOVERING bothwell ★

Bothwell is a charming little town an hour's drive north of Hobart, with several claims to fame. Set on the picturesque Clyde River at the foothills of the central Tasmanian highlands, the town was settled by Scottish colonists in 1822, with convict labour building many of the sandstone establishments still lining the streets today. Bothwell's major claim to fame is as the home of **Ratho,** Australia's oldest golf course, established the same year (✆ **0409/595 702** mobile phone; www.rathogolf.com). Ratho is a public course and green fees are only A$15.

After a round, drop into the **Australasian Golf Museum** (✆ **03/6259 4033**) and the local information center on Market Place. While you're there, pick up a brochure that gives you a self-guided tour of Bothwell's many historic buildings.

And then there's the lure of a whisky distillery at nearby **Nant Estate** (✆ **03/6259 5790;** www.nantdistillery.com.au), built in 1821. Today, it offers whisky tours, tastings, dinners, and the option to buy a 100-liter barrel of whisky with bespoke bottling and labeling. Tours (A$20) run daily between 10am and 4pm.

For accommodations befitting such an historic town, head straight for **The Priory Country Lodge,** 2 Wentworth St. (✆ **03/6259 4012;** www.thepriorycountry lodge.com.au) on the edge of town. Owner Greg Peacock has transformed this lovely stone Tudor-style country house (circa 1848) into a manor that's both stylish and comfortable. It has only four guest rooms, but plenty of living spaces to choose from, including a library, hunting room, parlor, and drawing room. Bedrooms are up a narrow staircase opening into a wide central sitting area, and are of similar decor, with marble bathrooms, underfloor heating—and a teddy bear. For those who prefer more privacy, there are two contemporary timber pavilions (one with a private sauna) overlooking the lake. The Priory is priced from A$400 to A$500 per room, including breakfast and dinner.

toast to porridge with brown sugar. On the menu for lunch and dinner you could find Thai beef curry, laksa, a daily risotto, and chermoula-marinated fish. The desserts can be great. Vegetarians, vegans, and those on a gluten-free diet are very well catered to, as are carnivores.

10 Criterion St. ✆ **03/6234 5858.** Reservations recommended. Main courses A$8–A$15. No credit cards. Mon–Fri 8am–6pm.

Hobart After Dark

Built in 1837, the 747-seat **Theatre Royal,** 29 Campbell St. (✆ **03/6233 2299;** www.theatreroyal.com.au), is the oldest live theater in the country. It's known for its excellent acoustics and its classical Victorian decor. It is Hobart's major stage venue. Ticket prices vary depending on the performance.

Opened in 1829 as a tavern and a brothel frequented by whalers, **Knopwood's Retreat,** 39 Salamanca Place (✆ **03/6223 5808**), is still a raucous place to be on Friday and Saturday evenings, when crowds cram the historic interior and spill out onto the streets. Light lunches are popular throughout the week, and occasionally you'll find jazz or blues on the menu.

A popular drinking hole in Hobart is **Irish Murphy's,** 21 Salamanca Place (✆ **03/6223 1119**), an atmospheric pub with stone walls and lots of dark wood. Local bands play Sunday to Thursday nights.

If you want to tempt Lady Luck, head to the **Wrest Point Casino,** in the Wrest Point Hotel, 410 Sandy Bay Rd. (✆ **03/6225 0112**), Australia's first legal gambling club. Smart, casual attire is required (collared shirts for men).

A Day Trip to Mount Field National Park

80km (50 miles) NW of Hobart

Mount Field National Park is one of the prettiest in Tasmania. It was proclaimed a national park in 1916 to protect a plateau dominated by dolerite-capped mountains (**Mount Field West** is the highest point at 1,417m/4,647 ft.) and dramatic glaciated valleys (some of the lakes and tarns were formed 30,000 years ago). The most mountainous regions support alpine moorlands of cushion plants, pineapple and sword grass, waratahs, and giant pandani. You can get a look at these changing environments on a 16km (10-mile) drive from the park entrance to Lake Dobson along an unpaved and often badly rutted road, which is not suitable for conventional vehicles in winter or after heavy rains. Wallabies, wombats, bandicoots, Tasmanian devils, and quolls are prolific, as is the birdlife. You may see black cockatoos, green rosellas, honeyeaters, currawongs, wedge-tailed eagles, and lyrebirds. There are many walking trails, including one to the spectacular 45m (148-ft.) **Russell Falls,** near the park's entrance. The walk to the falls along a paved, wheelchair-accessible track takes 15 minutes and passes ferns and forests, with some of Tasmania's tallest trees, swamp gums up to 85m (279 ft.) high.

GETTING THERE Mount Field National Park is just over an hour's drive from Hobart via New Norfolk. From Hobart, take the Brooker Highway (A10) northwest to New Norfolk. After New Norfolk you can follow the road on either side of the Derwent River (the A10 or B62) until you reach Westerway. From there, it is a short drive to the clearly marked entrance to Mount Field National Park. There is an entrance fee of A$12 per person or A$24 per car (up to eight people). **Grayline** (✆ **1300/858 687** in Australia; www.grayline.com.au) offers a day tour from Hobart on Sundays and Wednesdays, costing A$106 for adults and A$55 for kids ages 4 to 14, including entrance fees to the national park and a local salmon farm.

VISITOR INFORMATION The park's visitor center (✆ **03/6288 1149;** www.parks.tas.gov.au) on Lake Dobson Road has a cafe and information on walks. It's open daily from 8:30am to 5pm between November and April and 9am to 4pm in winter.

PORT ARTHUR ★★★

102km (63 miles) SE of Hobart

Port Arthur, on the Tasman Peninsula, is an incredibly picturesque yet haunting place. Set on one of Australia's prettiest harbors, it shelters the remains of Tasmania's largest penal colony. It's the state's number-one tourist destination, and you really should plan to spend at least a day here.

From 1830 to 1877, Port Arthur was one of the harshest institutions of its type anywhere in the world. It was built to house the most notorious prisoners, many of whom had escaped from lesser institutions. Nearly 13,000 convicts found their way

WALKING maria island ★★

Within minutes of arriving on Maria Island, you'll be charmed by the local wildlife. Wombats, to be precise. When they waddle into view, you'll let out a chorus of *wows*—a word that you will surely overwork if you choose to visit this lovely spot. Maria Island is about 50 minutes by ferry across Mercury Passage from Triabunna on Tasmania's east coast, north of Hobart. You can take a day trip to **Darlington,** the island's only settlement, or stay overnight in bunkhouse accommodations in former penitentiary cells. I recommend you take the time to do a 4-day guided Maria Island Walk, which takes you beyond Darlington, to discover the true beauty of this place.

Once home to the Tyreddeme Aboriginal people of the Oyster Bay area, Maria Island was also a penal settlement for up to 150 convicts from 1825 to 1832, until it was abandoned in favor of Port Arthur. More than 600 convicts were returned to the island from 1842 to 1850. The Darlington precinct, one of Tasmania's most significant historic sites, is listed on the National Heritage Register. The **commissariat store** is now an information center.

The rest of the island is **Maria Island National Park**—11,550 hectares (28,540 acres), including 1,878 hectares (4,640 acres) of marine reserve and the 7.4-hectare (18-acre) Ile des Phoques island. The entire place is largely untouched sandy beaches, forests, mountains, and rugged coastline, including the Painted Cliffs and the Fossil Cliffs near Darlington. Wildlife is abundant—you are almost guaranteed to see kangaroos, wallabies, wombats, echidnas, and rare Cape Barren Geese at close quarters. There are no shops, private vehicles, or houses, and the only vehicles are used by two park rangers. Those who venture farther afield can climb the 709m (2,326-ft.) summit of **Mount Maria** or the more achievable—if you have a head for

here, and nearly 2,000 died while incarcerated. A strip of land called Eaglehawk Neck connects Port Arthur to the rest of Tasmania. Guards and dogs kept watch over this narrow path, while the authorities circulated rumors that the waters around the peninsula were shark-infested. Only a few convicts ever managed to escape, and most of them either perished in the bush or were tracked down and hanged. Look out for the blowhole and other coastal formations, including Tasman's Arch, Devil's Kitchen, and the Tessellated Pavement, as you pass through Eaglehawk Neck.

Essentials

GETTING THERE Port Arthur is a 1½-hour drive from Hobart on the Lyell and Arthur highways. This scenic drive forms part of the **Convict Trail Touring Route** and takes in breathtaking seascapes, rolling farmlands and villages, vineyards, and artists' studios. On the way to Port Arthur, you might want to stop off at the historic village of Richmond and at the Tasmanian Devil Conservation Park (see p. 722). **Richmond** is 26km (16 miles) northeast of Hobart and is the site of the country's oldest bridge (1823), the best-preserved convict jail in Australia (1825), and several old churches, including St. John's Church (1836), the oldest Catholic church in the country.

Grayline (✆ **1300/858 687** in Australia; www.grayline.com.au) offers day tours to Port Arthur from Hobart daily (except Saturdays). The tours cost A$145 for adults heights—**Bishop and Clerk,** with its coastline views north to the Freycinet Peninsula, from 599m (1,965 ft.) up.

The guided **Maria Island Walk** (✆ **03/6234 2999;** www.mariaisland walk.com.au), leaves Hobart three times a week from October to April. You carry your own 7- to 10-kilogram (15–22-lb.) pack, but other supplies are carried by your two guides, who then whip up amazing food and wine at the end of the day. You will walk an easy 10 to 12km (6.25–7.5 miles) per day. Accommodation is in comfortable beachfront camps (tents with beds and wooden floors), except for the final night, which is spent in the luxury of the colonial home of pioneer Diego Bernacchi. Dinner there is served around the 1850s dining table, and the house is warmed by roaring fires. Walks cost A$2,100 per person including all gear and meals.

To book the penitentiary, contact the **Parks and Wildlife Service** on Maria Island (✆ **03/6257 1420;** www.parks.tas.gov.au). Bookings are not necessary to camp, but you must pay a fee of about A$13 per double. The ferry to Maria Island leaves Triabunna (about 90 min. drive from Hobart) at 9:30am and 4pm October to mid-April, and 10:30am and 3pm mid-April to September. The ferry departs Maria Island at 10:30am and 5pm for the return trip (11:30am and 4pm Apr–Sept). You should arrive at the jetty 20 minutes prior to departure. The ferry runs daily from mid-December to mid-April, and on Monday, Wednesday, Friday, and Sunday the rest of the year. The ferry service is provided by **Maria Island Ferry & Eco Cruises** (✆ **0419/746 668** mobile phone; www.mariaislandferry.com.au). The fare is A$50 adults, A$37 children 6 to 16, and A$25 children ages 2 to 5 round-trip. You can take a bike on the ferry for A$10. You must also pay a park entry fee of A$12 per person.

and A$73 for kids ages 4 to 14 and include admission fees, guided tours of Port Arthur and the Isle of the Dead, lunch, an audio guide and a harbor cruise.

Take a cruise with **Navigators** (✆ **03/6223 1914;** www.navigators.net.au), and you will follow the sea route of convicts transported from Hobart to Port Arthur. The all-day journey includes a 2½-hour cruise along the coastline to Port Arthur, entrance to the historic site, and a return by bus to Hobart. In 2010, it cost A$229 for adults, A$183 for kids, and A$700 for a family of four. The cruise runs on Sundays, departing at 8am.

Exploring the Site

The **Port Arthur Historic Site ★★** (✆ **1800/659 101** in Australia or 03/6251 2310; www.portarthur.org.au) is large and scattered, with around 30 19th-century buildings. (Most of the main ones were damaged during bushfires in 1877, shortly after the property ceased to be a penal institution.) You can tour the remains of the church, the guard tower, a prison, and several other buildings. Don't miss the fascinating museum in the old lunatic asylum, which has a scale model of the prison complex, as well as leg irons and chains.

Port Arthur's tragic history did not finish at the end of the convict era. In 1996, the Port Arthur Historic Site became the scene of one of Australia's worst mass murders, when a lone gunman killed 35 people and injured dozens more, including tourists and staff. The devastating events of that day led to new gun-control laws for

Australia that are among the strictest in the world. The gunman was sentenced to life imprisonment with no eligibility for parole. Many of the staff at Port Arthur lost friends, colleagues, and family members, and still find it difficult and painful to talk about. Visitors are requested not to question their guide about these events, but to instead read the plaque at the Memorial Garden.

The site is open daily from 8:30am to dusk; admission is A$28 for adults, A$14 for children 4 to 17, and A$62 for families of two adults and up to six children. The admission price includes a guided walking tour and a boat cruise around the harbor, which leaves eight times daily in summer. Passes for overnight or 2 full days are also available. Twice a day, you can get off the harbor cruise for a 45-minute guided walk on the **Isle of the Dead,** where 1,769 convicts and 180 free settlers were buried, mostly in mass graves with no headstones. The tour costs an extra A$12 for adults, A$8 for kids, and A$34 for families. Lantern-lit **Historic Ghost Tours** of Port Arthur leave nightly at 9pm (8:30pm during winter months) and cost A$20 for adults and A$12 for children. Reservations are essential; call ✆ **1800/659 101** in Australia or 03/6251 2310. Tours run for about 90 minutes.

The main feature of the visitor center is an interesting **Interpretive Gallery,** which takes visitors through the process of sentencing in England to transportation to Van Diemen's Land. The gallery contains a courtroom, a section of a transport ship's hull, a blacksmith's shop, a lunatic asylum, and more.

Where to Stay & Dine

Stewarts Bay Lodge ★ 🎁 Just 1km (⅔ mile) from the Port Arthur Historic Site, this collection of 20-year-old log cabins and 2-year-old deluxe "spa" cabins makes a great place to stay for those who want to self-cater or have a bit more space. There are one-, two-, or three-bedroom cabins to choose from. All have private decks overlooking

Tasmanian Devil Disaster

Tasmania's unique carnivorous mammal, the handsomely sleek Tasmanian Devil, is in real trouble. Since 1996, the Devils have been afflicted by a cancer known as Devil Facial Tumour Disease (DFTD). It has decimated the wild population—in some areas by an estimated 90%—and the disease is spreading rapidly. It's believed that around half the state's 150,000 Tasmanian devils have died, and some scientists fear it may wipe out the wild population entirely. Healthy specimens are being captured and relocated to try and preserve the species from extinction. There are several places where you can see captive Devils and learn more. About 80km (50 miles) from Hobart, on the Port Arthur Highway, Taranna, is the **Tasmanian Devil Conservation Park** (✆ **03/6250 3230;** www.tasmaniandevilpark.com), which is breeding devils with genes that could make them resistant to the disease. The park is open daily from 9am to 5pm. Another great place to see Devils near Hobart is **Bonorong Park Wildlife Centre** (see p. 710). In the north, **Trowunna Wildlife Park** at Mole Creek, near Deloraine (✆ **03/6363 6162;** www.trowunna.com.au), is a rehabilitation and conservation center with a population of 40 Devils, as well as other native wildlife. For more information on Devil conservation efforts, visit **www.tassiedevil.com.au.**

the water, and there is a lovely 20-minute walk along a bush track beside the water to the Port Arthur Historic Site (see above). You are quite likely to spot wildlife (take the supplied flashlight when you go out at night). The restaurant isn't open for breakfast, but if you don't want to make your own there are a couple of good cafes nearby.

6955 Arthur Hwy., Port Arthur, TAS 7182. ✆ **03/6250 2888.** Fax 03/6250 2999. www.stewartsbaylodge.com.au. 40 units. A$232–A$340 1-bedroom cabin; A288–A$390 2-bedroom cabin; A$427 3-bedroom cabin. Crib A$6.60. AE, DC, MC, V. Free parking. **Amenities:** Restaurant; bar; Internet kiosk (A$5 for 30 min.); tennis court. *In room:* A/C (deluxe cabins only), TV w/free in-house movies, DVD, CD player, hair dryer, kitchen, no phone.

FREYCINET NATIONAL PARK ★★

206km (128 miles) NE of Hobart; 214km (133 miles) SW of Launceston

The Freycinet Peninsula hangs down off the eastern coast of Tasmania. It's a place of craggy pink-granite peaks, spectacular white beaches, wetlands, heathland, coastal dunes, and dry eucalyptus forests. You may spot sea eagles, wallabies, seals, pods of dolphins, and humpback and southern right whales during their migration to and from the warmer waters of northern New South Wales from May through August. The town of **Coles Bay** is the main staging post, and there are many **bushwalks** in the area. The Moulting Lagoon Game Reserve—an important breeding ground for black swans and wild ducks—is signposted along the highway into Coles Bay from Bicheno. Some 10,000 black swans inhabit the lake. Six kilometers (3¾ miles) outside town, and inside the national park, is the Cape Tourville Lighthouse, which allows extensive views along the coast and across the Tasman Sea. **Wineglass Bay ★★** is simply spectacular and has made it onto lists of the world's top beaches.

Essentials

GETTING THERE **Tassielink** (✆ **1300/300 520** in Australia or 03/6230 8900; www.tigerline.com.au) runs a bus from Hobart to Bicheno on Wednesdays and Fridays at 8:50am and on Sundays at 11am. The trip takes nearly 3 hours. **Bicheno Coaches** (✆ **0419/570 923** mobile phone) provides the 15-minute transfer from Bicheno to the National Park. The fare is A$36 one-way.

VISITOR INFORMATION The **Visitor Information Centre** (✆ **03/6375 1333;** fax 03/6375 1533) on the Tasman Highway at Bicheno can arrange tour bookings. Otherwise, the **Tasmanian Travel and Information Centre** in Hobart (✆ **03/6230 8383**) can supply you with maps and details. Daily entry to the park costs A$24 per vehicle. The National Parks office (✆ **03/6256 7000**) can also provide information.

Exploring the Park

Head out from Freycinet Lodge on a 30-minute uphill hike past beautiful pink-granite outcrops to **Wineglass Bay Lookout** for breathtaking views. You can then head down to Wineglass Bay itself and back up again. The walk takes around 2½ hours. A longer route takes you along the length of **Hazards Beach,** where you'll find plenty of shell middens—seashell refuse heaps—left behind by the Aborigines who once lived here. This walk takes 6 hours.

Tasmanian Expeditions (✆ **1300/666 856** in Australia, or 03/6339 3999; www.tas-ex.com) offers a 3-day trip from Launceston and back that includes 2

THE heritage HIGHWAY

By the 1820s, several garrison towns had been built between Launceston and Hobart, and by the middle of the 19th century, convict labor had produced what was considered to be the finest highway of its time in Australia. Today, many of the towns along the **Heritage Highway** harbor magnificent examples of Georgian and Victorian architecture. It takes about 2 hours to drive between Launceston and Hobart on this route (also known as the A1, or the Midland Hwy.), but you could easily spend a couple of days exploring. Picturesque **Ross** (121km/75 miles north of Hobart or 78km/48 miles south of Launceston) is one of Tasmania's best-preserved historic villages. Ross was established as a garrison town in 1812 on a strategically important crossing point on the Macquarie River. **Ross Bridge,** the third oldest in Australia, was built in 1836. The bridge is decorated with Celtic symbols, animals, and faces of notable people of the time. It is lit up at night, and there are good views of it from the river's north bank.

The town's **main crossroads** is the site of four historic buildings, humorously known as "Temptation" (the Man-o'-Ross Hotel), "Salvation" (the Catholic church), "Recreation" (the town hall), and "Damnation" (the old jail). The **Tasmanian Wool Centre,** 48 Church St., details the growth of the region and the wool industry since settlement. It also houses the **Ross Visitor Information Centre** (**✆ 03/6381 5466;** www.visitross.com.au), and both are open daily from 9am to 5pm. If you are so charmed you want to stay overnight, try the historic **Colonial Cottages of Ross** (**✆ 03/6381 5354;** www.cottagesofthecolony.com.au) or the **Ross Bakery Inn** (**✆ 03/6381 5246;** www.rossbakery.com.au), an 1832 convict-built coaching inn. Both are on Church Street.

nights in cabins at Coles Bay. The trip includes walks to Wineglass Bay and Mount Amor. It costs A$850 and departs on Wednesdays from October to June.

Not to be missed is a trip aboard Freycinet Sea Charter's vessel ***Schouten Passage*** (**✆ 03/6257 0355;** www.freycinetseacruises.com), which offers whale-watching between June and September, bay and game fishing, dolphin-watching, diving, scenic and marine wildlife cruises, and sunset cruises. Half-day cruises to Wineglass Bay cost A$120 per person.

Where to Stay & Dine

Camping is available in the park for A$13 for two people or A$16 family of five. Bookings are necessary for most sites and a ballot system applies from December 18 to February 10 and for Easter. For inquiries, call the **Parks and Wildlife Service** (**✆ 03/6256 7000;** www.parks.tas.gov.au).

Freycinet Lodge ★★ This ecofriendly lodge offers comfortable one- and two-room cabins spread unobtrusively through the bush, connected by raised walking tracks. Each has a balcony, and the more expensive ones have huge Jacuzzis. The deluxe cabins were refurbished in 2008, and some have water views. Twenty cabins have their own kitchens. The main part of the lodge houses a lounge room and an excellent restaurant that sweeps out onto a veranda overlooking the green waters of

Great Oyster Bay. The lodge is right next to the white sands of Hazards Beach, and from here it's an easy stroll to the start of the Wineglass Bay walk.

Freycinet National Park, Coles Bay, TAS 7215. © **1800/420 155** or 03/6225 7000. www.puretasmania.com.au. 60 units. A$228–A$312 double. Extra person A$59. Children 4 and under stay free in parent's room. Free crib. Rates include breakfast. Ask about packages. AE, DC, MC, V. **Amenities:** 2 restaurants; bar; bikes; tennis court; Wi-Fi (A$2 for 15 min.). *In room:* A/C, CD player, hair dryer, minibar, no phone.

LAUNCESTON ★

198km (123 miles) N of Hobart

Tasmania's second-largest city is Australia's third oldest, after Sydney and Hobart. Situated at the head of the Tamar River, 50km (31 miles) inland from the state's north coast, and surrounded by delightful undulating farmland, Launceston is crammed with elegant Victorian and Georgian architecture and plenty of remnants of convict days. Launceston (pop. 104,000) is one of Australia's most beautiful cities and has delightful parks and churches. It's also the gateway to the wineries of the Tamar Valley, the highlands and alpine lakes of the north, and the stunning beaches to the east.

Essentials

GETTING THERE **Qantas** (© **13 13 13** in Australia; www.qantas.com) and discount carrier **Tiger Airways** (© **03/9335 3033;** www.tigerairways.com.au) both fly to Launceston from Melbourne. **Virgin Blue** (© **13 67 89** in Australia; www.virginblue.com.au) and **Jetstar** (© **13 15 38** in Australia; www.jetstar.com.au) both fly from Melbourne, Brisbane, and Sydney. The **Airporter Shuttle** (© **03/6343 6677**) runs between city hotels and the airport from 8:45am to 5pm daily for A$14 one-way or A$24 round-trip.

Tasmania's Redline Coaches (© **1300/360 000** in Australia; www.redlinecoaches.com.au) departs Hobart for Launceston several times daily (trip time: around 2½ hr.). The one-way fare is A$39. If you plan to take a ferry from Melbourne to Devonport, Launceston is 1½ hours from Devonport and the bus ride will cost A$24. Driving from Hobart to Launceston takes just over 2 hours on Highway 1.

VISITOR INFORMATION The **Launceston Visitor Information Centre,** Cornwall Square, 12-16 St. John St. (© **03/6336 3133;** fax 03/6336 3118), is open Monday through Friday from 9am to 5pm, Saturday from 9am to 3pm, and Sunday and holidays from 9am to noon.

CITY LAYOUT The main pedestrian shopping mall, **Brisbane Street,** along with St. John and Charles streets on either side, forms the heart of the central area. The Victorian-Italianate Town Hall is 2 blocks north on **Civic Square,** opposite the red-brick post-office building dating from 1889. The **Tamar River** slips quietly past the city's northern edge and is crossed at two points by **Charles Bridge** and **Tamar Street. City Park,** to the northeast of the central business district, is a nice place for a stroll.

Exploring the City & Environs

Launceston is easy to explore on foot. A must for any visitor is a stroll with **Launceston Historic Walks ★** (© **03/6331 2213**), which leaves from the "1842" building on the corner of St. John and Cimitiere streets at 4pm on Mondays and 10am Tuesday to Saturday. The 1-hour walk gives a fascinating insight into Launceston's history and costs A$15. **Grayline** (✆ **1300/858 687** in Australia; www.grayline.com.au) operates a 2½ hr. coach tour of the city. It costs A$40 for adults and A$20 for children.

A must-see is **Cataract Gorge ★**, the result of violent earthquakes that rattled Tasmania some 40 million years ago. It's a wonderfully scenic area, and you can walk there along the river bank from the city in about 15 minutes. The South Esk River flows through the gorge and collects in a small lake called the Basin, traversed by a striking suspension bridge and the longest single-span chairlift in the world (308m/1,010 ft.). The **chairlift** (✆ **03/6331 5915;** www.launcestoncataractgorge.com.au) is open daily from 9am to 4:30pm and costs A$15 for adults and A$10 for children under 16, round-trip. The hike to the **Duck Reach Power Station,** now an interpretive center, takes about 45 minutes. Other walks in the area are shorter and easier. The **Gorge Restaurant** (✆ **03/6331 3330;** closed Mon) and the kiosk next door serve meals with glorious views from the outdoor tables.

Tamar River Cruises (✆ **03/6334 9900;** www.tamarrivercruises.com.au) offers regular 50-minute cruises to Cataract Gorge up the Tamar River from Home Point Wharf in Launceston. The cost is A$22 adults, A$12 children 5 to 17, and A$56 for families of four.

OTHER ATTRACTIONS

Design Centre Tasmania ★ Inspiring and innovative contemporary design is the focus here, from the building itself—a light-filled structure added on to a heritage-listed church hall—to its contents. The permanent display is the Tasmanian Wood Design Collection, but you will also find changing exhibitions of ceramics, textiles, works on paper, and mixed media. There is a new exhibition every month, from the industrial to the aesthetic. There's a shop as well.

City Park, Brisbane St. (at Tamar St.). ✆ **03/6331 5506.** www.designcentre.com.au. Free admission. Mon–Sat 9:30am–5:30pm; Sun 10am–4pm.

The Old Umbrella Shop Built in the 1860s, this unique shop is the last genuine period store in Tasmania and has been operated by the same family since the turn of the 20th century. Umbrellas spanning the last 100 years are on display, and modern "brollies" and souvenirs are for sale. The shop is listed by the National Trust.

60 George St. ✆ **03/6331 9248.** Free admission. Mon–Fri 9am–5pm; Sat 9am–noon.

The Queen Victoria Museum & Art Gallery This museum, opened in honor of Queen Victoria's Golden Jubilee in 1891, is in two parts: one on Wellington Street, Royal Park, in the heart of Launceston, and the other in the inner suburb of Inveresk. The Inveresk complex, a smart redevelopment of old railyards, is home to the Launceston Planetarium and focuses on science, which kids will find fun. The Royal Park museum, devoted largely to fine and decorative arts, was scheduled to reopen in late 2010 after a major redevelopment.

2 Invermay Rd., Inveresk, and 2 Wellington St., Royal Park. ✆ **03/6323 3777.** www.qvmag.tas.gov.au. Free admission. Daily 10am–5pm. Closed Good Friday and Dec 25.

Woolmers Estate ★ 🎁 The pioneering Archer family, once the most powerful family in Tasmania's north, settled at this homestead near Longford, about 25km (16 miles) from Launceston, in 1817. The six generations who lived here until 1994 have left an unrivaled legacy in the almost-untouched Woolmers Estate. There are 20 buildings, from the grand mansion to the servants' quarters, shearing sheds, a blacksmith's

Launceston

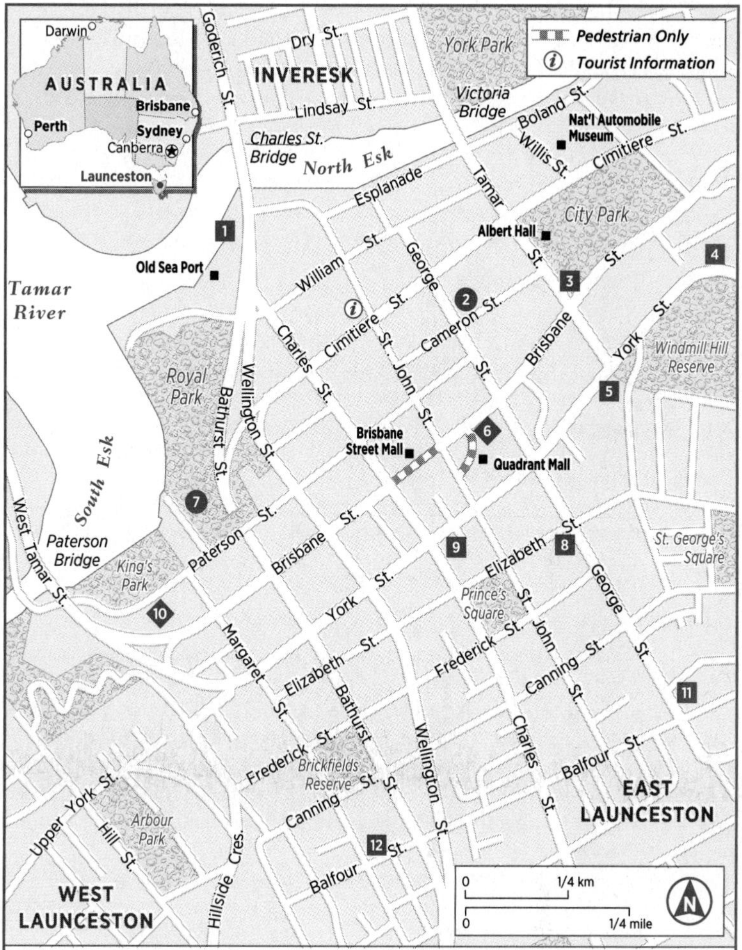

ACCOMMODATIONS ■

Alice's Cottages & Spa Hideaways **12**
Colonial Launceston **8**
Hillview House **11**
Hotel Tasmania **9**
Peppers Seaport Hotel **1**
Waratah on York **4**
York Mansions **5**

DINING ◆

Croplines Coffee Bar **6**
Stillwater River Café **10**

ATTRACTIONS ●

Design Centre Tasmania **3**
The Old Umbrella Shop **2**
The Queen Victoria Museum & Art Gallery **7**

shop, and seven free settler's cottages. (You can stay in them.) Entry to the homestead is by guided tour only, or you can take a self-guided tour of the gardens and outbuildings. There's also a restaurant serving Devonshire teas, lunches, and snacks. Take time to smell the roses next door at the **National Rose Garden of Australia** (free entry), where more than 2 hectares (5 acres) are planted with around 4,000 bushes.

Woolmers Lane, Longford. ✆ **03/6391 2230.** www.woolmers.com.au. A$18 adults, A$5 children 15 and under. Daily 10am–4:30pm. Closed Christmas Day. Guided house tours 10 and 11am, and 12:30, 2, and 3:30pm. Cottages A$178 double, A$35 extra adult, A$30 extra child 15 and under, including breakfast and free house tour.

Where to Stay

EXPENSIVE

Peppers Seaport Hotel ★★ Built in 2004 on the site of an old dry dock and designed in the shape of a ship, this hotel is part of a major redevelopment of the Seaport Dock area—just 5 minutes by car from downtown—which also includes new restaurants, entertainment venues, and shopping facilities. The decor is smart contemporary nautical in style, using soft, light colors, natural timbers, and chromes. Rooms are spacious, and most have balconies either looking out over the Tamar River and marina or over the town center to the mountains beyond. Each has a good kitchenette and an extra fold-out sofa bed.

28 Seaport Blvd., Launceston, TAS 7250. ✆ **03/6345 3333.** Fax 03/6345 3300. www.peppers.com.au. 60 units. A$210–A$271 double; A$282–A$393 suite. Extra person 13 and over A$66. AE, DC, MC, V. Amenities: Restaurant; bar; babysitting; concierge; room service; spa. In room: A/C, TV, DVD (suites only), hair dryer, kitchenette, minibar, Wi-Fi (from A$5.25 for 30 min.).

Quamby Estate ★★ This historic house, built in 1848, is about a 20-minute drive from Launceston and is the starting point for those undertaking walks of the Overland Track given by Cradle Mountain Huts (see p. 731). Rooms are large, with massive bathtubs (just the thing for when you return from the track!), and beautifully appointed. Each room is different from the others; room 12 is all forest greens and creams, while room 1 has a sleeker feel, with doors opening onto the wraparound verandah. Some of the layout is a little odd, but that adds to the historic feel. The kitchen is open to guests to help themselves to tea or coffee (or the bar, run on an honesty system).

1145 Westwood Rd., Hagley, TAS 7292. ✆ **03/6392 2211.** Fax 03/6392 2277. www.quambyestate.com. 9 units. A$300–A$590 double; A$60–A$80 children 12 and under sharing room with parents. Rates include breakfast. AE, DC, MC, V. Free parking. Amenities: Restaurant; babysitting; CD, DVD, and book library; golf course; tennis court. In room: A/C, TV, DVD player, docking station, hair dryer, minibar.

Waratah on York ★ This carefully renovated Victorian mansion was built in 1862 for Alexander Webster, an ironmonger who was mayor of Launceston in the 1860s and 1870s. Some original features—pressed brass ceiling roses and a staircase with a cast-iron balustrade—remain, while others have been faithfully re-created. Six rooms come with a Jacuzzi, one with a balcony, and another with a sunroom. All have high ceilings and ornate (but nonfunctional) fireplaces. The executive rooms have four-poster beds and sweeping views of the Tamar River. A three-bedroom apartment, in what was once the ballroom, is also available.

12 York St., Launceston, TAS 7250. ✆ **03/6331 2081.** Fax 03/6331 9200. www.waratahonyork.com.au. 10 units. A$202–A$288 double; A$300 apt. Rates include breakfast. AE, DC, MC, V. Free parking. No children 7 and under. **Amenities:** Bar. *In room:* TV, hair dryer, minibar, Wi-Fi (A$5 per day).

York Mansions ★★★ Within the walls of the National Trust–classified York Mansions, built in 1840, are five spacious two-bedroom apartments, each with a distinct character. The Lodge apartment is fashioned after a gentleman's drawing room, complete with rich leather sofa, antiques, and an extensive collection of historical books. The light and airy Duchess of York and Countess apartments are more feminine. Each apartment has its own kitchen, dining room, living room, bedrooms, bathroom, and laundry. There's also a delightful cottage garden with a massive heritage-listed Oak tree—just the spot for sundowners.

9-11 York St., Launceston, TAS 7250. ✆ **03/6334 2933.** Fax 03/6334 2870. www.yorkmansions.com.au. 5 units. A$220–A$248 double. Extra person A$47. Breakfast provisions A$12. AE, DC, MC, V. Free parking. *In room:* TV/VCR, CD player w/CD library, hair dryer, kitchen, minibar, free Wi-Fi.

MODERATE

Alice's Cottages & Spa Hideaways ★★ Tucked down a romantic lane and known collectively as the Shambles, these themed cottages are designed to bring out the romantic in you. Four of the six cottages, which sleep only two, are named for the places the "colonials" came from: England, Wales, Ireland, and Scotland. The other two are the Camelot and Boudoir "spa hideaways." Four-poster beds, soft drapes, roaring log fires . . . you get the picture.

129 Balfour St., Launceston, TAS 7250. ✆ **03/6334 2231.** Fax 03/6334 2696. www.alicescottages.com.au. 6 units. A$170–A$206 double including breakfast. AE, DC, MC, V. Free parking. *In room:* A/C, TV, kitchen.

Colonial Launceston ★ Those who desire tried-and-true above-standard motel lodging will feel at home at the recently refurbished Colonial, a place that combines old-world ambience with modern facilities. The large rooms have attractive furnishings. They're fairly standard and attract a large corporate clientele. Beautiful gardens surround this property.

31 Elizabeth St., Launceston, TAS 7250. ✆ **1800/060 955** in Australia, or 03/6331 6588. Fax 03/6334 2765. www.colonialinn.com.au. 66 units. A$150–A$300 double. Children 2 and under stay free in parent's room. AE, DC, MC, V. Free parking. **Amenities:** Restaurant; exercise room; room service. *In room:* A/C, TV, hair dryer, minibar, Wi-Fi (A$10 per day).

Country Club Resort & Villas ★ Wallabies grazed outside my window when I stayed at this resort-style hotel located between Launceston city and the airport. This is a place that will appeal to those who want space, entertainment, and activities. There is an 18-hole golf course, a small casino, and lots of things to do, from fly-fishing on the private lake to horse riding and more. All rooms have everything you'd expect—as well as a toaster—and Manor suites have a separate bedroom, lounge, private balcony, and spa tub. There are also one-, two-, and three-bedroom villas with full kitchens and car parking right outside. Villas are set apart from the main complex, but there is a free shuttle bus to take you there.

Country Club Ave., Prospect Vale, TAS 7250. ✆ **1800/030 211** in Australia, or 03/6225 7092. Fax 03/6331 7347. www.countryclubtasmania.com.au. 182 units. A$169–A$179 double; A$198–A$333 suite; A$133–A$186 villa. Extra person A$35. AE, DC, MC, V. Free parking. **Amenities:** 5 restaurants, 4 bars; babysitting; concierge; golf course; exercise room; Jacuzzi; indoor heated pool; room service; sauna; 2 lit tennis courts. *In room:* A/C, TV w/pay movies, hair dryer, minibar, Wi-Fi (A$15 per day).

INEXPENSIVE

Hillview House The rooms at this restored farmhouse are cozy and quite comfortable. Each comes with a double bed and a shower. The family room has an extra single bed; it's the nicest unit and has the best views. The hotel overlooks the city, and the large veranda and colonial dining room have extensive views over the city and the Tamar River.

193 George St., Launceston, TAS 7250. ✆ **03/6331 7388.** Fax 03/6331 7388. www.hillviewhouse.net.au. 9 units. A$105–A$120 double; A$120–A$130 family room for 3. Rates include full breakfast. MC, V. Free parking. *In room:* TV.

Where to Dine

EXPENSIVE

Stillwater River Café ★★ MODERN AUSTRALIAN This fabulous eatery is located inside an old mill beside the Tamar River. Come here for a good breakfast, a casual lunch at one of the tables outside overlooking the river, or an atmospheric dinner. The dinner menu is fascinating, with all sorts of delicacies on the menu. Try the seared scallops or the crispy twice-cooked duck with caramelized rhubarb. The wine cellar brings up a good selection of Tasmanian wines. It's a good idea to go for the six-course tasting menu, which comes in at a respectable A$105, or A$144 including matching wines. A vegetarian menu is available on request.

Ritchies Mill (bottom of Paterson St.). ✆ **03/6331 4153.** www.stillwater.net.au. Reservations recommended. Lunch A$20–A$30; dinner A$70 2 courses, A$85 3 courses. AE, DC, MC, V. Daily 8am–10pm.

INEXPENSIVE

Croplines Coffee Bar ★ CAFE If you crave good coffee, bypass every other place in Launceston and head here. It's a bit hard to find, and you may have to ask for directions, but basically it's behind the old Brisbane Arcade. The owners are dedicated to coffee, grinding their beans on the premises daily. If coffee's not your cup of tea, then try the excellent hot chocolate.

Brisbane Court, off Brisbane St. ✆ **03/6331 4023.** Coffees and teas A$1.80–A$2.60. Cakes under A$4. AE, MC, V. Mon–Fri 7:30am–5:30pm; Sat 8:30am–12:30pm.

CRADLE MOUNTAIN & LAKE ST. CLAIR ★★

85km (53 miles) S of Devonport; 175km (109 miles) NW of Hobart

The national park and World Heritage area that encompasses both Cradle Mountain and Lake St. Clair is one of the most spectacular regions in Australia and, after Hobart and Port Arthur, the most visited place in Tasmania. The 1,545m (5,068-ft.) mountain dominates the north part of the island, and the long, deep lake is to its south. Between them lie steep slopes, button grass plains, majestic alpine forests, dozens of lakes filled with trout, and several rivers. **Mount Ossa,** in the center of the park, is Tasmania's highest point at 1,617m (5,304 ft.). The **Overland Track** (see "Hiking the Overland Track," below), links Cradle Mountain with Lake St. Clair and is the best known of Australia's walking trails.

Essentials

GETTING THERE **Tassielink** (✆ **1300/300 520** in Australia, or 03/6230 8900; www.tigerline.com.au) runs buses to Cradle Mountain from Hobart, Launceston, and Devonport. Its summer Overland Track service drops off passengers at the beginning of the walk (Cradle Mountain) and picks them up at Lake St. Clair. It costs A$99 starting from Launceston and returning to Hobart; A$131 starting at and

HIKING THE overland track ★★★

The best-known hiking trail in Australia is the **Overland Track,** a 65km (40-mile) route between Cradle Mountain and Lake St. Clair. The trek takes 6 to 10 days and can be tough going in some parts, but is an excellent way to see the beauty of Tasmania's pristine wilderness. You will pass through high alpine plateaus, button grass plains, heathland, and rainforests, all studded with glacial lakes, ice-carved crags, and waterfalls. There are many rewarding side trips, including the ascent (weather permitting) of **Mount Ossa** (1,617m/5,304 ft.), Tasmania's highest peak.

During the peak season (Nov 1–Apr 30), you must pay a National Parks fee of A$160 adults or A$128 children 5 to 17, as well as the normal park entry fee. Only 60 people per day are allowed on the track (34 bookings are reserved for independent walkers), and you must book at **www.overlandtrack.com.au**. Simple public huts (first-come, first-served) and camping areas are available along the track for independent walkers. You may only walk in one direction: Cradle Mountain to Lake St. Clair.

Cradle Mountain Huts (**© 03/6331 2006;** www.cradlehuts.com.au) runs 3-, 4-, and 6-day guided walks. The full 6-day hike costs between A$2,550 and A$2,750, depending on the season; rates are all-inclusive and include transfers to and from Launceston. You stay in a fully equipped and heated private hut with twin-share bunkrooms, showers, a lounge, a full kitchen, and a drying room. A three-course meal is prepared each night by your guides. Groups are limited to 10, with no children under 12. You must carry your own backpack (about 10kg/22 lbs.)—but if the weather is good and you have chosen one of the shorter treks, you may soon be wishing you'd gone for the full 6 days! **Tasmanian Expeditions** (**© 1300/666 856** in Australia, or 03/6339 3999; www.tas-ex.com) offers a 7-day trek departing from Launceston.

returning to Hobart; A$129 starting at and returning to Launceston; and A$133 Devonport to Devonport.

Maxwells Cradle Mountain–Lake St. Clair Charter Bus and Taxi Service (**© 03/6492 1431**) runs buses from Devonport and Launceston to Cradle Mountain. The fare starts at A$35. The buses also travel to other areas nearby, such as Lake St. Clair. Buses also run from the Cradle Mountain campground to the start of the Overland Track.

VISITOR INFORMATION The park headquarters, the **Cradle Mountain Visitor Centre** (**© 03/6492 1100;** www.parks.tas.gov.au), on the northern edge of the park outside Cradle Mountain Lodge, offers the best information on walks and treks. It's open daily 8am to 5pm (6pm in summer).

Exploring the Park

Cradle Mountain Lodge (see "Where to Stay & Dine," below) runs a daily program of guided walks, abseiling (rappelling), rock-climbing, and trout-fishing for lodge guests. The park has plenty of trails that can be attempted by people equipped with directions from the staff at the park headquarters (see "Visitor Information," above). Be warned, though, that the weather changes quickly in the high country; go prepared with wet-weather gear and always tell someone where you are headed. Of the shorter walks, the stroll to Pencil Pines and the 5km (3-mile) walk to Dove Lake are the most pleasant.

Where to Stay & Dine

Cradle Mountain Lodge ★★ If you like luxury with your rainforests, then this award-winning lodge is the place for you. Just minutes from your bed are giant buttresses of 1,500-year-old trees, moss forests, mountain ridges, limpid pools and lakes, and scampering marsupials. The cabins are comfortable, the food excellent, the staff friendly, and the open fireplaces well worth cuddling up in front of for a couple of days. Each modern wood cabin has either a fire or gas heater for chilly evenings. There are no TVs in the rooms—but there is a TV lounge in the casual, comfortable main lodge. For a bit of pampering after all your outdoor activity, head to the **Waldheim Alpine Spa** for massage and other treatments.

4038 Cradle Mountain Rd., Cradle Mountain, TAS 7306. ✆ **1300/806 192** in Australia, or 03/6492 2103. www.cradlemountainlodge.com.au. 86 units. A$310 Pencil Pine cabin double; A$386 spa cabin double; A$474–A$760 suite. Children 11 and under stay free in parent's room. Rates include breakfast. Ask about packages. AE, DC, MC, V. Free parking. **Amenities:** 2 restaurants; 2 bars; Internet kiosk (A$2 for 15 min.); spa. *In room:* CD player (except Pencil Pine cabins), hair dryer, minibar.

Waldheim Cabins For a real wilderness experience, head to these cabins run by the Parks and Wildlife Service, located 5km (3 miles) from Cradle Mountain Lodge. Nestled between button grass plains and temperate rainforest, they are simple and affordable and offer good access to plenty of walking tracks. Each heated cabin has single bunk beds, basic cooking utensils, crockery, cutlery, and a gas stove. Each accommodates four or eight people, but if your party is smaller you have exclusive use. Two outbuildings with composting toilets and showers serve all the cabins. Generated power is provided for lighting between 6 and 11pm only. Stores and fuel can be bought at Cradle Mountain Lodge. Bring your own bed linen or hire it. Guests can pick up keys from the National Park Visitor Centre between 8:30am and 4:30pm daily.

Cradle Mountain Visitor Centre, P.O. Box 20, Sheffield, TAS 7306. ✆ **03/6492 1110.** Fax 03/6492 1120. www.parks.tas.gov.au. 8 cabins. Cabins A$95–A$185. Linen A$7.50 per person. MC, V. *In room:* No phone.

THE WEST COAST

296km (184 miles) NW of Hobart; 245km (152 miles) SW of Devonport

Tasmania's west coast is wild and mountainous, with a scattering of mining and logging towns and plenty of wilderness. The pristine Franklin and Gordon rivers tumble through World Heritage areas once contested by loggers, politicians, and environmentalists, whereas the bare, poisoned hills that make up the eerily beautiful "moonscape" of Queenstown show the results of mining and industrial activity. **Strahan** (pronounced *Strawn*), the only town of any size in the area, is the starting point for cruises up the Gordon River and tours into the rainforest. You need at least 3 days here to do and see everything.

Essentials

GETTING THERE **Tassielink** (✆ **1300/300 520** in Australia, or 03/6230 8900; www.tigerline.com.au) runs coaches between Strahan and Launceston, Devonport, and Cradle Mountain and to Hobart. The trip from Launceston takes more than 8 hours. The drive from Hobart to Strahan takes about 4½ hours without stops. From Devonport, allow 3½ hours. Although the roads are good, they twist and turn and are particularly hazardous at night, when nocturnal animals come out to feed. The cheapest way to travel between these places is by bus with a **Tassielink Explorer Pass.**

VISITOR INFORMATION The **West Coast Visitor Information Centre,** on the Esplanade at Strahan (✆ **03/6472 6800;** www.tasmaniaswestcoast.com.au), is open daily from 10am to 6pm in autumn and winter and to 7pm in spring and summer. Closed Christmas Day and Good Friday.

Cruising the Rivers

Gordon River Cruises (✆ **1800/084 620** in Australia, or 03/6225 7075; www.puretasmania.com.au) offers a 6-hour trip daily at 8:30am, returning at 2:15pm. In peak season, a second cruise leaves at 2:45pm and returns at 8:30pm. Cruises take passengers across Macquarie Harbour and up the Gordon River past historic **Sarah Island,** where convicts—working in horrendous conditions—once logged valuable Huon pine. The trip includes an entertaining guided tour through the ruins on Sarah Island with actor/historian Richard Davey. Cruises depart from the Main Wharf on the Esplanade, in the town center. The fare, including lunch, is A$85 adults and A$40 children 3 to 14 for internal seats; A$110 adults and A$60 kids for window seats; and A$189 for all seats upstairs with the captain.

World Heritage Cruises (✆ **1800/611 796** in Australia or 03/6471 7174; www.worldheritagecruises.com.au) offers morning and afternoon cruises, leaving Strahan Wharf at 9am and returning at 2:45pm and again at 3pm and returning at 8:30pm. The company's 35m (115-ft.) catamaran *Eagle* stops at Sarah Island, Heritage Landing, and at a salmon farm. The cruises cost A$90 to A$115 for adults, A$48 to A$63 for children 5 to 16 (free for children under 5), and A$247 to A$310 for families of five, including a buffet lunch or dinner.

West Coast Yacht Charters (✆ **03/6471 7422** or mobile phone 0419/300 994) runs overnight sailing cruises (including Sarah Island) for A$320 per person, all-inclusive. The company also offers other cruises.

Other Adventures

Bonnet Island Experience ★★ Little Penguins come ashore on this tiny island at the mouth of Macquarie Harbour each night during summer to burrow and breed. Join an evening cruise from Strahan to view them and learn about the history of this islet and its lighthouse. After a twilight dawdle—the island can be walked in just a few minutes—it's back to the boat for wine and cheese, and then another shore visit after dark, using infrared torches to see the penguins. When you step ashore, mind your feet—the penguins are unafraid and may almost trip you up! Tour time is 90 minutes. Cruise departs from Strahan harbor. ✆**1800/084 620.** www.puretasmania.com.au. A$85 adults, A$40 children (minimum age 5 years), A$200 family of 4. Daily at twilight.

Piners & Miners ★★ This day tour will tell you everything you need to know about the history of the West Coast—and bring alive some of the fascinating characters who shaped it. Start off in a unique four-wheel-drive vehicle that runs on the old rail tracks while you listen to the story of the miners who sought riches here (and who also poisoned the King and Queen Rivers, today considered "dead" rivers). Then you'll take a 2-hour walk through lush rainforest to a rendezvous with a gourmet barbecue lunch whipped up by a waiting chef in the shadow of the ghost town of East Pillinger. From there, it's a boat ride back to Strahan. A big day out, but highly recommended.

Departs The Esplanade, Strahan. ✆ **1800/084 620.** www.puretasmania.com.au. A$365 per person (not suitable for children under 10). Daily 7:30am–4:30pm.

West Coast Wilderness Railway You can take this historic train ride in either of two directions, from Queenstown to Strahan (my preferred option) or vice versa. A bus provides the return trip. Choose from the all-inclusive Premier Carriage, with a personal valet serving gourmet goodies (almost constantly!), or "tourist" class, which looks perfectly comfortable. Along the way there is an extensive commentary and the chance to get off the train at each stop for a look around. Those who have already done the Piners & Miners tour (see above) will find themselves covering the same ground. The whole trip takes around 6 hours.

Driffield Street, Queenstown. ✆ **1800/628 288** in Australia or 03/6225 7075. www.puretasmania.com.au. Premier Carriage A$210 per person; tourist carriage A$111 adults, A$20 children 3–14, A$262 family of 4, plus A$18 adults and A$10 children for bus transfer. Daily (except Christmas Day); times change seasonally so check when booking.

Where to Stay & Dine

Gordon Gateway Chalets These modern self-contained units are on a hill with good views of the harbor and Strahan township, and range from studio units to luxury penthouses. Each has cooking facilities, so you can save on meal costs. The two-bedroom suites have bathtubs, the studios just showers. Breakfast is provided on request. Guests have the use of a barbecue area. One unit has facilities for travelers with disabilities.

Grining St., Strahan, TAS 7468. ✆ **1300/134 425** in Australia, or 03/6471 7165. Fax 03/6471 7588. www.gordongateway.com.au. 19 units. A$55–A$350 double. Winter discounts available. MC, V. **Amenities:** Babysitting. *In room:* TV, CD player (executive suites only), hair dryer, kitchenette, minibar.

Ormiston House ★★ Ormiston House is a gem. Built in 1899 for the family that gave it its name, under the present owners it has become a sort of shrine to their predecessors. Each room is styled to represent one of the original family members. They are all intricately furnished, wallpapered in busy designs, and come with a good-size bathroom. There's a morning room and a restaurant serving good food. The owners are friendly and have plenty of time for their guests. No children under 12.

1 The Esplanade, Strahan, TAS 7468. ✆ **03/6471 7077.** www.ormistonhouse.com.au. 5 units, 1 with shower only. A$210–A$260 double. Rates include breakfast. AE, DC, MC, V. No children 11 and under. **Amenities:** Restaurant; bar; concierge. *In room:* A/C, TV, hair dryer, Wi-Fi (free).

Strahan Village This complex is mostly based on the hill overlooking the harbor and town. The rooms in the hilltop accommodation are large, many of them with fantastic views, but are otherwise fairly standard. More luxurious are the Waterfront Executive rooms, and there are also rooms in terrace houses opposite the harbor. The 11 reproduction "colonial" cottages along the main street that are available for rent look cute, but their white picket fences and manicured gardens might make you feel you've stepped onto the set of *The Truman Show.*

The Esplanade, Strahan, TAS 7468. ✆ **1300/134 425** in Australia, or 03/6471 4200. Fax 03/6471 43989. www.puretasmania.com.au. 141 units. A$100–A$165 double (higher in peak times). MC, V. **Amenities:** Restaurant; bar; Wi-Fi (A$10 per hr.). *In room:* TV, DVD player (some units only), hair dryer, minibar.

FAST FACTS

17

FAST FACTS: AUSTRALIA

Area Codes Each state has a different area code: **02** for New South Wales and the ACT; **07** for Queensland; **03** for Victoria and Tasmania; and **08** for South Australia, the Northern Territory, and Western Australia. You must dial the appropriate code if calling outside the state you are in; however, you also need to use the code if you are calling outside the city you are in. For example if you are in Sydney, where the code is 02 and you want to call another New South Wales town, you still dial 02 before the number. See "Staying Connected," p. 72.

Business Hours Banks are open Monday through Thursday from 9:30am to 4pm, Friday 9:30am to 5pm. General business hours are Monday through Friday from 8:30am to 5:30pm. Shopping hours are usually 8:30am to 5:30pm weekdays and 9am to 4pm or 5pm on Saturday. Many shops close on Sunday, although major department stores and shops in tourist precincts are open 7 days.

Cellphones (Mobile Phones) See "Staying Connected," p. 71.

Drinking Laws Hours vary from pub to pub, but most are open daily from around 10am or noon to 10pm or midnight. The minimum drinking age is 18. Random breath tests to catch drunk drivers are common, and drunk-driving laws are strictly enforced. Getting caught drunk behind the wheel will mean a court appearance, not just a fine. The maximum permitted blood-alcohol level is .05%. Alcohol is sold in liquor stores, in the "bottle shops" attached to every pub, and in some states in supermarkets.

Driving Rules See "Getting There and Getting Around," p. 49.

Electricity The current is 240 volts AC, 50 hertz. Sockets take two or three flat, not rounded, prongs. Bring a **connection kit** of the right power and phone adapters, a spare phone cord, and a spare Ethernet network cable—or find out whether your hotel supplies them to guests. North Americans and Europeans will need to buy a converter before they leave home. (Don't wait until you get to Australia, because Australian stores are likely to stock only converters for Aussie appliances to fit American and European outlets.) Some large hotels have 110V outlets for electric shavers (or dual voltage), and some will lend converters, but don't count on it in smaller, less expensive hotels, motels, or B&Bs. Power does not start automatically when you plug in an appliance; you need to flick the switch beside the socket to the "on" position.

Embassies & Consulates Embassies or consulates with posts in state capitals are listed in "Fast Facts" in the relevant state chapters of this book. But most diplomatic posts are in Canberra:

Canada: High Commission of Canada, Commonwealth Avenue, Yarralumla, ACT 2600 (✆ 02/6270 4000).

Ireland: Embassy of Ireland, 20 Arkana St., Yarralumla, ACT 2600 (✆ 02/6273 3022).

New Zealand: New Zealand High Commission, Commonwealth Avenue, Canberra, ACT 2601 (✆ 02/6270 4211).

The United Kingdom: British High Commission, Commonwealth Avenue, Canberra, ACT 2601 (✆ 02/6270 6666).

The United States: United States Embassy, 21 Moonah Place, Yarralumla, ACT 2600 (✆ 02/6214 5600).

Emergencies Dial ✆ **000** anywhere in Australia for police, ambulance, or the fire department. This is a free call from public and private telephones and needs no coins. The TTY emergency number is ✆ **106.**

Gasoline (Petrol) Gasoline (petrol) prices tend to fluctuate, but at press time were around A$1.32 a liter for unleaded petrol in Sydney, and A$1.47 a liter or more in the Outback. One U.S. gallon equals 3.78 liters or .85 imperial gallons. Most rental cars take unleaded gas, and motor homes run on diesel, which at press time was averaging around the same price as unleaded gas. Taxes are already included in the printed price. Fill-up locations are known as petrol or service stations.

Holidays Major public holidays—where almost everything shuts down—are New Year's Day, Good Friday, Easter Sunday and Easter Monday, Christmas Day, and Boxing Day (Dec 26). If December 26 falls on a weekend, the following Monday is a holiday. On Anzac Day (Apr 25), a war veterans' commemorative day, most shops and all government departments are closed, but some tourist attractions reopen at around 1pm. Australia Day is a national public holiday on January 26.

In addition to the period from late December to the end of January, when Aussies take their summer vacations, the 4 days at Easter (from Good Friday to Easter Monday) and all school holidays are very busy, so book ahead. The school year in Australia is broken into four semesters, with 2-week holidays around Easter, the last week of June and the first week of July (or first 2 weeks of July), and the last week of September and the first week of October. Some states break at slightly different dates. There's a 6-week summer (Christmas) vacation from mid-December to the end of January.

Other major state public holidays are: Labour Day (second Mon in Mar, WA and VIC; first Mon in May, QLD; first Mon in Oct, NSW and SA); Eight Hours Day (first Mon in Mar, TAS); Canberra Day (third Mon in Mar, ACT); May Day (first Mon in May, NT); Adelaide Cup (third Mon in May, SA); Foundation Day (first Mon in June, WA); Queen's Birthday (Mon in late Sept/early Oct, WA; second Mon in June, all except WA); Royal National Show Day (second or third Wed in Aug, QLD); and Melbourne Cup Day (first Tues in Nov, in Melbourne only). For more information on holidays, see "Australia Calendar of Events," on p. 39.

Insurance Standard medical and travel insurance is advisable for travel to Australia, especially if you are planning to travel to remote areas in the Outback. Divers should also ensure they have the appropriate insurance. For information on traveler's insurance, trip cancelation insurance, and medical insurance while traveling, please visit www.frommers.com/tips.

Internet Access See "Staying Connected," p. 72.

Legal Aid If you find yourself in trouble with the long arm of the law while visiting Australia, the first thing you should do is contact your country's embassy or nearest consulate in Australia. See contact details for Canberra diplomatic posts under "Embassies & Consulates" above. Embassies or consulates with posts in state capitals are listed in "Fast Facts," in the relevant state chapters of this book. The U.S. Embassy considers an "emergency" to be either your arrest or the loss of your passport. If arrested in Australia, you will have to go through the Australian legal process for being charged, prosecuted, possibly convicted and sentenced, and for any appeals process. However, U.S. consular officers (and those of other countries) provide a wide variety of services to their citizens arrested abroad and their families. These may include providing a list of local attorneys to help you get legal representation, providing information about judicial procedures, and notifying your family and/or friends, if you wish. However, they cannot demand your release, represent you at your trial, give you legal advice, or pay your fees or fines.

Mail A postcard costs A$1.40 to send anywhere in the world. A card will take 4-6 working days to reach the U.S.

Newspapers & Magazines See "Staying Connected," p. 72.

Passports See "Embassies & Consulates," above, for whom to contact if you lose your passport while traveling in Australia. For other information, contact the following agencies:

For Residents of Australia Contact the **Australian Passport Information Service** at ✆ **131-232,** or visit www.passports.gov.au.

For Residents of Canada Contact the central **Passport Office,** Department of Foreign Affairs and International Trade, Ottawa, ON K1A 0G3 (✆ **800/567-6868;** www.ppt.gc.ca).

For Residents of Ireland Contact the **Passport Office,** Setanta Centre, Molesworth Street, Dublin 2 (✆ **01/671-1633;** www.foreignaffairs.gov.ie).

For Residents of New Zealand Contact the **Passports Office,** Department of Internal Affairs, 47 Boulcott Street, Wellington, 6011 (✆ **0800/225-050** in New Zealand or 04/474-8100; www.passports.govt.nz).

For Residents of the United Kingdom Visit your nearest passport office, major post office, or travel agency or contact the **Identity and Passport Service (IPS),** 89 Eccleston Square, London, SW1V 1PN (✆ **0300/222-0000;** www.ips.gov.uk).

For Residents of the **United States** To find your regional passport office, check the U.S. State Department website (travel.state.gov/passport) or call the **National Passport Information Center** (✆ **877/487-2778**) for automated information.

Police Dial ✆ **000** anywhere in Australia. This is a free call from public and private telephones and requires no coins.

Smoking Smoking in most public areas, such as museums, cinemas, and theaters, is restricted or banned. Smoking in restaurants may be limited—Western Australia and New South Wales ban it altogether, and in many other states, restaurants have smoking and nonsmoking sections. Pubs and clubs, for a long time the last bastion for smokers, now have total bans across the country. Australian aircraft on all routes are completely nonsmoking, as are all airport buildings.

Taxes Australia applies a 10% **Goods and Services Tax** (GST) on most products and services. Your international airline tickets to Australia are not taxed, nor are domestic airline tickets for travel within Australia *if you bought them outside Australia.* If you buy Australian airline tickets once you arrive in Australia, you will pay GST on them.

Through the **Tourist Refund Scheme** (TRS), Australians and international visitors can claim a refund of the GST (and of a 14.5% wine tax called the Wine Equalisation Tax, or WET) paid on a purchase of more than A$300 from a single outlet, within the last 30 days before you leave. More than one item may be included in that A$300. For example, you can claim the GST you paid on 10 T-shirts, each worth A$30, as long as they were bought from a single store. Do this as you leave by presenting your receipt or "tax invoice" to the Australian Customs Service's TRS booths, in the International Terminal departure areas at most airports. If you buy several things on different days from one store that together add up to A$300 or more, you must ask the store to total all purchases on one tax invoice (or receipt)—now there's a nice piece of bureaucracy to remember Australia by! Pack the items in your carry-on baggage, because you must show them to Customs. You can use the goods before you leave Australia and still claim the refund, but you cannot claim a refund on things you have consumed (film you use, say, or food). You cannot claim a refund on alcohol other than wine. Allow an extra 15 minutes to stand in line at the airport and get your refund.

You can also claim a refund if you leave Australia as a cruise passenger from Circular Quay or Darling Harbour in Sydney, Brisbane, Cairns, Darwin, Hobart, or Fremantle (Perth). If your cruise departs from elsewhere in Australia, or if you are flying out from an airport other than Sydney, Melbourne, Brisbane, Adelaide, Cairns, Perth, Darwin, or the Gold Coast, telephone the **Australian Customs Service** (✆ **1300/363 263** in Australia, or 02/6275 6666) to see if you can still claim the refund.

Items bought in duty-free stores will not be charged GST. Nor will items you export—such as an Aboriginal painting that you buy in a gallery in Alice Springs and have shipped straight to your home outside Australia.

Basic groceries are not GST-taxed, but restaurant meals are.

Other taxes include a **departure tax** of A$38 for every passenger 12 years and over, included in the price of your airline ticket when you buy it in your home country; landing and departure taxes at some airports, also included in the price of your ticket; and a "reef tax," officially dubbed the **Environmental Management Charge,** of A$5 for every person over the age of 4 every time he or she enters the Great Barrier Reef Marine Park. (This charge goes toward park upkeep.)

Most airlines and an increasing number of tour operators, such as cruise companies and long distance trains also impose a "fuel surcharge" to help them combat rising fuel costs. This is usually added to the price of your ticket.

Telephones See "Staying Connected," p. 72.

Time Australian Eastern Standard Time (EST, sometimes also written as AEST) covers Queensland, New South Wales, the Australian Capital Territory, Victoria, and Tasmania. Central Standard Time (CST) is used in the Northern Territory and South Australia, and Western Standard Time (WST) is the standard in Western Australia. When it's noon in New South Wales, the ACT, Victoria, Queensland, and Tasmania, it's 11:30am in South Australia and the Northern Territory, and 10am in Western Australia. All states except Queensland, the Northern Territory, and Western Australia observe daylight saving time, usually from the first Sunday in October to the first Sunday in April. However, not all states switch over to daylight saving on the same day or in the same week. The east coast of Australia is GMT (Greenwich Mean Time) plus 10 hours. When it is noon on the east coast, it is 2am in London that morning, and 6pm in Los Angeles and 9pm in New York the previous night. These times are based on standard time, so allow for daylight saving in the Australian summer, or in the country you are calling. New Zealand is 2 hours ahead of the east coast of Australia, except during daylight saving, when it is 3 hours ahead of Queensland.

Tipping Tipping is not expected in Australia. It is usual to tip around 10% or round up to the nearest A$10 for a substantial meal in a family restaurant. Some passengers round up to the nearest dollar in a cab, but it's okay to insist on every bit of change back. Tipping bellboys and porters is sometimes done, but no one tips bar staff, barbers, or hairdressers.

Toilets Public toilets are easy to find—and free—in most Australian cities and towns. If you are driving, most towns have "restrooms" on the main street (although the cleanliness may vary wildly). In some remote areas, toilets are "composting," meaning there is no flush, just a drop into a pit beneath you.

Visas Along with a current passport valid for the duration of your stay, the Australian government requires a visa from visitors of every nation, except New Zealand, to be issued before you arrive. See p. 41 for more information on obtaining a visa.

Visitor Information **Tourism Australia** is the best source of information on traveling Down Under. Its website, **www.australia.com**, has more than 10,000 pages of listings of tour operators, hotels, car-rental companies, special travel outfitters, holidays, maps, distance charts, suggested itineraries, and much more. The site provides information tailored to travelers from your country of origin, including packages and deals. By signing up for the free e-newsletter, you will receive updates on hot deals, events, and the like on a regular basis. You can also order brochures online. Tourism Australia operates a website only, no telephone lines. Other good sources are the websites of Australia's state tourism marketing offices. They are:

- **Australian Capital Tourism:** www.visitcanberra.com.au.
- **Northern Territory Tourist Commission:** www.travelnt.com.
- **South Australian Tourism Commission:** www.southaustralia.com.
- **Tourism New South Wales:** www.visitnsw.com.au or www.sydneyaustralia.com.
- **Tourism Queensland:** www.queenslandholidays.com.au.
- **Tourism Tasmania:** www.discovertasmania.com.
- **Tourism Victoria:** www.visitvictoria.com.
- **Western Australian Tourism Commission:** www.westernaustralia.com.

Water Water is fine to drink everywhere. In the Outback, the taps may carry warm brackish water from underground, called "bore water," for showers and laundry, while drinking water is collected in rainwater tanks.

Wi-Fi See "Staying Connected," p. 72.

Index

See also Accommodations and Restaurant indexes, below.

General Index

A

D

L

M

N

Y

Z

Accommodations

Restaurants